Lecture Notes in Compute 4810

Commenced Publication in 1973
Founding and Former Series Editors:
Gerhard Goos, Juris Hartmanis, and Jan va

Horace H.-S. Ip Oscar C. Au
Howard Leung Ming-Ting Sun Wei-Ying Ma
Shi-Min Hu (Eds.)

Advances in Multimedia Information Processing – PCM 2007

8th Pacific Rim Conference on Multimedia
Hong Kong, China, December 11-14, 2007
Proceedings

Springer

Horace H.-S. Ip
Howard Leung
City University of Hong Kong
Department of Computer Science
83, Tat Chee Avenue, Kowloon Tong, Hong Kong
E-mail: {cship, howard}@cityu.edu.hk

Oscar C. Au
Hong Kong University of Science and Technology
Department of Electronic and Computer Engineering
Clear Water Bay, Hong Kong
E-mail: eeau@ust.hk

Ming-Ting Sun
University of Washington
M418 EE/CSE, Box 352500, Seattle, WA 98195, USA
E-mail: sun@ee.washington.edu

Wei-Ying Ma
Microsoft Research Asia
5F, Sigma Building, No 49, Zhichun Road, Beijing, 100080, China
E-mail: wyma@microsoft.com

Shi-Min Hu
Tsinghua University, Department of Computer Science and Technology,
Beijing 10084, China
E-mail: shimin@tsinghua.edu.cn

Library of Congress Control Number: 2007940868

CR Subject Classification (1998): H.5.1, H.3, H.5, C.2, H.4, I.3, K.6.5, I.7, I.4

LNCS Sublibrary: SL 3 – Information Systems and Application, incl. Internet/Web and HCI

ISSN 0302-9743
ISBN-10 3-540-77254-5 Springer Berlin Heidelberg New York
ISBN-13 978-3-540-77254-5 Springer Berlin Heidelberg New York

Springer is a part of Springer Science+Business Media

springer.com

Printed in Germany

Typesetting: Camera-ready by author, data conversion by Scientific Publishing Services, Chennai, India
Printed on acid-free paper SPIN: 12197866 06/3180 5 4 3 2 1 0

Preface

The Pacific-Rim Conference on Multimedia (PCM) was held in Hong Kong, at the City University of Hong Kong, during December 11–14, 2007. Started in 2000, PCM has been held in various places around the Pacific Rim, including Sydney, Beijing, Hsinchu, Singapore, Tokyo, Jeju, and Zhejiang in chronological order. PCM is a major annual international conference organized as a forum for the dissemination of state-of-the-art technological advances and research results in the fields of theoretical, experimental, and applied multimedia analysis and processing.

PCM 2007 was organized into 5 different tracks with a total of 247 submissions from 26 countries and regions including Australia, Belgium, Canada, China, Japan, Korea, New Zealand, Singapore, Spain, Taiwan, the UK and the USA. Among the five tracks, "multimedia analysis and retrieval" received the most number of submissions (34% of the submissions). After a rigorous review process, 73 papers were accepted for oral presentations, giving an acceptance rate of under 29% for PCM 2007. In addition, 21 papers were accepted for poster presentations. We would like to thank all the Track Chairs and the reviewers for their timely handling of the paper reviews. We are particularly grateful to Chong-Wah Ngo and his team for their support of the Web-based review system throughout the process. We are also indebted to the Special Sessions Chairs, Qi Tian and Timothy Shih, for the organization of the two special sessions on "The AVS China National Standard" and "Multimedia Information System for Biomedical Research," respectively. Papers in this volume cover a range of pertinent topics in the field including, content-based and semantic analysis of images, audio and video data as well as 3D models; video multicasts over wireless ad hoc networks; and image and video watermarking and authentication, etc.. We also thank our keynote speakers, Edward Chang and Alan Hanjalic for their enlightening speeches.

The local organization of PCM 2007 would not have been possible without the concerted effort and support of researchers from Hong Kong and the region who work in the multimedia field. Their contributions are duly acknowledged in the following pages. Last but not least, we thank the K.C. Wong Foundation for their generous sponsorship to PCM 2007.

December 2007

Horace H.S. Ip
Oscar C. Au
Howard Leung
Ming-Ting Sun
Wei-Ying Ma
Shi-Min Hu

Organization

Organizing Committee

Conference Chairs	Horace H. S. Ip (City University of Hong Kong)
	Oscar C. Au (Hong Kong University of Science and Technology)
Program Chairs	Ming-Ting Sun (University of Washington, USA)
	Wei-Ying Ma (Microsoft Research Asia, China)
	Shi-Min Hu (Tsinghua University, China)
Special Session Chairs	Qi Tian (University of Texas San Antonio, USA)
	Timothy K. Shih (Tamkang University, Taiwan)
Tutorial Chairs	Kiyo Aizawa (University of Tokyo, Japan)
	Weichuan Yu (Hong Kong University of Science and Technology)
Special Issue Chairs	Qing Li (City University of Hong Kong)
	Borko Furht (Florida Atlantic University, USA)
Local Arrangements Chair	Jiying Wang (City University of Hong Kong)
Financial Chair	Howard Leung (City University of Hong Kong)
Secretary	Raymond H. S. Wong (City University of Hong Kong)
Registration Chairs	Yan Liu (Hong Kong Polytechnic University)
	Wu Fei (Zhejiang University, China)
Publication Chairs	Wenyin Liu (City University of Hong Kong)
	Qing Li (City University of Hong Kong)
Publicity Chairs	Peter Hon Wah Wong (Hong Kong University of Science and Technology)
	Phoebe Y. P. Chen (Deakin University, Australia)
	Yo-Sung Ho (Gwangju Institute of Science and Technology, Korea)
Web Chair	Chong-Wah Ngo (City University of Hong Kong)

Advisory Committee

Ramesh Jain (University of California, Irvine, USA)
Thomas S. Huang (University of Illinois at Urbana Champaign, USA)
Sun-Yuan Kung (Princeton University, USA)
Yong Rui (Mircrosoft China Research and Development Group)
Hongjiang Zhang (Microsoft China Research and Development Group)

Technical Committee

Track: Multimedia Analysis and Retrieval
Track Chairs: Alan Hanjalic (Delft University of Technology, Netherlands)
Chong-Wah Ngo (City University of Hong Kong)

Track: Multimedia Security Rights and Management
Track Chairs: Qibin Sun (I2R Singapore)
Oscar C. Au (Hong Kong University of Science and Technology)

Track: Multimedia Compression and Optimization
Track Chairs: Lap-Pui Chau (Nanyang Technological University, Singapore)
Man Wai Mak (Hong Kong Polytechnic University)

Track: Multimedia Communication and Networking
Track Chairs: Pascal Frossard (EPFL, Switzerland)
Irwin King (Chinese University of Hong Kong)

Track: Multimedia Systems and Applications
Track Chairs: Pong Chi Yuen (Hong Kong Baptist University)
Shing-Chow Chan (University of Hong Kong)

Technical Program Committee

Ishfaq Ahmad (University. of Texas at Arlington)
Kiyoharu Aizawa (University of Tokyo)
Selim Aksoy (Bilkent University)
Antonios Argyriou (Philips Research)
Luigi Atzori (University of Cagliari)
Noboru Babaguchi (Osaka University)
Ivan Bajic (Simon Fraser University)
Ali Begen (Cisco Systems)
Oliver Brdiczka (INRIA Rhône-Alpes)
Jianfei Cai (Nanyang Technological University)
Wai-Kuen Cham (Chinese University of Hong Kong)
C.F. Chan (City University of Hong Kong)
H.W. Chan (The University of Hong Kong)
Yui-Lam Chan (The Hong Kong Polytechnic University)
Yuk Hee Chan (The Hong Kong Polytechnic University)
Rocky Chang (The Hong Kong Polytechnic University)
Jing Chen (National ICT Australia)
Lei Chen (Hong Kong University of Science and Technology)
Liang-Gee Chen (National Taiwan University)
Yixin Chen (The University of Mississippi)
Wen-Sheng Chen (Shenzhen University)

Liang-Tien Chia (Nanyang Technological University)
Tihao Chiang (National Chiao Tung University)
Cheng-Fu Chou (National Taiwan University)
Michael Christel (Carnegie Mellon University)
Tat-Seng Chua (National University of Singapore)
Cristina Costa (Create-Net)
Pedro Cuenca (Universidad Castilla La Mancha)
Aloknath De (STMicroelectronics)
Juan Carlos De Martin (Politecnico di Torino)
Alberto Del Bimbo (University of Florence)
Jana Dittman (Otto von Guericke University)
Ajay Divakaran (Mitsubishi Electric Research Laboratories)
Chitra Dorai (IBM T.J. Watson Research Center)
Abdulmotaleb El Saddik (University of Ottawa)
Sabu Emmanuel (Nanyang Technological University)
Guoliang Fan (Oklahoma State University)
Jianping Fan (University of North Carolina)
G.C. Feng (SYS UNIV)
Xiaodong Gu (Thomson, Inc.)
Ling Guan (Ryerson University)
Jing-Ming Guo (National Taiwan University of Science and Technology)
Hsueh-Ming Hang (National Chiao Tung University)
Frank Hartung (Ericsson)
Alexander Hauptmann (Carnegie Mellon University)
Dajun He (Zhangjiang Industry Park)
Tai-Chiu Hsung (The Hong Kong Polytechnic University)
Yongjian Hu (South China University of Technology)
Xian-Sheng Hua (Microsoft Research Asia)
Byeungwoo Jeon (Sung Kyun Kwan University)
Qiang Ji (Rensselaer Polytechnic Institute)
Weijia Jia (City University of Hong Kong)
Xing Jin (Hong Kong University of Science and Technology)
Antonius Kalker (Hewlett-Packard)
Markus Kampmann (Ericsson Research)
Mohan Kankanhalli (National University of Singapore)
John Kender (Columbia University)
Johg Won Kim (Gwangju Institute of Science and Technology)
Markus Koskela (Helsinki University of Technology)
Ragip Kurceren (Nokia Research, USA)
Kenneth Lam (The Hong Kong Polytechnic University)
Bertrand Le Saux (Ecole Normale Supérieure de Cachan France)
Gwo-Giun Lee (National Cheng Kung University)
Jack Y.B. Lee (Chinese University of Hong Kong)
Clement Leung (University of Victoria)
Michael Lew (Leiden University)
Bo Li (Hong Kong University of Science and Technology)
Dongge Li (Motorola Labs)
Hongliang Li (The Chinese University of Hong Kong)
Richard Y.M. Li (The Hong Kong University of Science and Technology)
Shipeng Li (Microsoft Research Asia)
Ze-Nian Li (Simon Fraser University)
Zhengguo Li (Institute for Infocomm Research)
Zhu Li (Hong Kong University of Science and Technology)

Mark Liao (Academia Sinica)
Rainer Lienhart (University of Augsberg)
Chia-Wen Lin (National Tsing Hua University)
Chih-Jen Lin (National Taiwan University)
Weisi Lin (Nanyang Technological University)
Nam Ling (Santa Clara University)
Jiangchuan Liu (Simon Fraser University)
Chun-Shien Lu (Institute of Information Science, Academia Sinica)
Guojun Lu (Monash University)
Lie Lu (Microsoft Research Asia)
Jiebo Luo (Eastman Kodak Company)
Maode Ma (Nanyang Technological University)
Enrico Magli (Politecnico di Torino)
Manuel Malumbres (Miguel Hernández University)
Shiwen Mao (Auburn University)
Stephane Marchand-Maillet (University of Geneva)
Jean Martinet (National Institute of Informatics)
Mitsuji Matsumoto (Waseda University)
Tao Mei (Microsoft Research Asia)
Bernard Merialdo (Institut Eurecom)
Dalibor Mitrovic (Vienna University of Technology Austria)
Apostol Natsev (IBM T. J. Watson Research Center)
Noel O'Connor (Dublin City University)
Fernando Pereira (IST-TUL)
Manuela Pereira (University of Beira Interior)
Lai Man Po (City University of Hong Kong)
Tony Pridmore (Nottingham University)
Guoping Qiu (University of Nottingham)
Regunathan Radhakrishnan (Dolby Laboratories, Inc.)
Shin'ichi Satoh (National Institute of Informatics)
Andreas Savakis (Rochester Institute of Technology)
Gerald Schaefer (Aston University, Birmingham, UK)
Raimondo Schettini (Milano-Bicocca University)
Nicu Sebe (University of Amsterdam)
Linlin Shen (Shenzhen University)
Timothy Shih (Tamkang University)
Ronggong Song (National Research Council Canada)
Huifang Sun (Mitsubishi Electric Research Laboratories)
Hari Sundaram (Arizona State University)
Ashwin Swaminathan (University of Maryland, College Park)
Jun Tian (Thomson Corporate Research)
Qi Tian (University of Texas at San Antonio)
C.S. Tong (Hong Kong Baptist University)
Duc Tran (University of Dayton)
Nuno Vasconcelos (University of California, San Diego)
Remco C. Veltkamp (Utrecht University)
Anthony Vetro (Mitsubishi Electric Research Laboratories)
Giuliana Vitiello (University of Salerno)
Demin Wang (Communications Research Center)
Feng Wang (Hong Kong University of Science and Technology)
Haohong Wang (Marvell Semiconductors)
Jhing-Fa Wang (National Cheng Kung University)
Xin Wang (ContentGuard, Inc.)
Yang Wang (National ICT Australia)
Yunhong Wang (Beihang University)
Lynn Wilcox (FXPAL)
Youjip Won (Hanyang University)
Raymond Wong (National ICT Australia)
Marcel Worring (University of Amsterdam)
Min Wu (University of Maryland, College Park)
Xiao Wu (City University of Hong Kong)
Xiaoxin Wu (Intel)

Yi Wu (Intel Corporation)
Yihong Wu (Chinese Academy of Sciences)
Lexing Xie (IBM Research)
Xing Xie (Microsoft Research Asia)
Zixiang Xiong (Texas A&M University)
Changsheng Xu (Institute for Infocomm Research)
Jar-Ferr Yang (National Cheng Kung University)
Suki Yip (VP Dynamics)
Heather Yu (Huawei Technologies, USA)
Cha Zhang (Microsoft Research)
Lei Zhang (Microsoft Research Asia)
Zhishou Zhang (Institute for Infocomm Research)
Zhongfei Zhang (State University of New York at Binghamton)
Lei Zhang (The Hong Kong Polytechnic University)
Jiying Zhao (University of Ottawa)
Jiantao Zhou (Hong Kong University of Science and Technology)
Bin Zhu (Microsoft Research China)

Additional Reviewers

Tomasz Adamek (Dublin City University)
Lamberto Ballan (University of Florence)
Marco Bertini (University of Florence)
Michael Blighe (Dublin City University)
Jian Cheng (Chinese Academy of Sciences)
Ling-Yu Duan (Institute for Infocomm Research)
Hongmei Gou (University of Maryland, College Park)
Alexander Haubold (Columbia University)
Shan He (University of Maryland, College Park)
Shuqiang Jiang (Institute of Computing Technology, Chinese Academy of Sciences)
Yu-Gang Jiang (City University of Hong Kong)
Jing Liu (Institute of Automation, Chinese Academy of Sciences)
Michael McHugh (Dublin City University)
Naoko Nitta (Osaka University)
Yuxin Peng (Peking University)
Sorin Sav (Dublin City University)
Giuseppe Serra (University of Florence)
Evan Tan (National ICT Australia)
Avinash Varna (University of Maryland, College Park)
Jinqiao Wang (Institute of Automation, Chinese Academy of Sciences)
Qiang Wang (Microsoft Research Asia)
Xiao-Yong Wei (City University of Hong Kong)
Hau San Wong (City University of Hong Kong)
Zhuan Ye (Motorola Labs)
Xiaoyi Yu (Osaka University)
Guangtao Zhai (Shanghai Jiaotong University)
Yan-Tao Zheng (National University of Singapore)
Xiangdong Zhou (Fudan University)
Ce Zhu (Nanyang Technological University)
Guangyu Zhu (Harbin Institute of Technology)

Table of Contents

Session-1: Image Classification and Retrieval

Special Session-1: The AVS China National Standard - Technology, Applications and Products

Session-2: Human Face and Action Recognition

Session-3: H.264 Video Coding

Session-4: Video Analysis and Retrieval

Session-5: Media Security and DRM

Best Paper Session

Session-6: Audio, Speech and Sound Processing

Session-7: Digital Watermarking

Poster Session

Special Session-2: Multimedia Information Systems for Biomedical Research

Session-8: Media Delivery

Session-9: Video Communication and Systems

Session-10: Video Compression and Processing

Session-11: Face and 3D Model Analysis

Session-12: Multimedia Applications

Session-13: Image Indexing, Identification and Processing

Session-14: Multimedia Processing

FADA: An Efficient Dimension Reduction Scheme for Image Classification

Yijuan Lu[1], Jingsheng Ma[2], and Qi Tian[1]

[1] Department of Computer Science, University of Texas at San Antonio, TX, USA
{lyijuan, qitian}@cs.utsa.edu
[2] Institute of Petroleum Engineering, Heriot-Watt University, Edinburgh, UK,
{Jingsheng.ma}@pet.hw.ac.uk

Abstract. This paper develops a novel and efficient dimension reduction scheme--Fast Adaptive Discriminant Analysis (FADA). FADA can find a good projection with adaptation to different sample distributions and discover the classification in the subspace with naïve Bayes classifier. FADA overcomes the high computational cost problem of current Adaptive Discriminant Analysis (ADA) and also alleviates the overfitting problem implicitly caused by ADA. FADA is tested and evaluated using synthetic dataset, COREL dataset and three different face datasets. The experimental results show FADA is more effective and computationally more efficient than ADA for image classification.

Keywords: Adaptive Discriminant Analysis, Image Classification.

1 Introduction

Linear discriminant analysis (LDA) [1] and Biased Discriminant Analysis (BDA) [2] are both effective techniques for feature dimension reduction. LDA assumes that positive and negative samples are from the same sources (distributions) and makes the equivalent (unbiased) effort to cluster negative and positive samples.

Compared to LDA, BDA assumes that positive samples must be similar while negative samples may be from different categories. Hence, BDA is biased towards the positive examples. It tries to find an optimal mapping that all positive examples are clustered and all negative examples are scattered away from the centroid of the positive examples. Studies have shown that BDA works very well in image retrieval especially when the size of the training sample set is small [2].

Obviously, both LDA and BDA have their own pros and cons. In addition, many applications do not fit exactly into either of the two assumptions. Hence, an Adaptive Discriminant Analysis (ADA) [3] was proposed, which merges LDA and BDA in a unified framework and offers more flexibility and a richer set of alternatives to LDA and BDA in the parametric space.

However, ADA is a parametric method. How to find good parameters is still a difficult problem for ADA. In ADA, it needs searching the whole parameter space to find the optimal one. Hence, the computational cost is very expensive and the method becomes less efficient. In addition, excessively searching also causes overfitting problem.

H.H.S. Ip et al. (Eds.): PCM 2007, LNCS 4810, pp. 1–9, 2007.

In this paper, we propose an efficient dimension reduction scheme for image classification, namely FADA, which stands for Fast Adaptive Discriminant Analysis. FADA overcomes the difficulties of ADA, while achieving effectiveness. The key difference between FADA and ADA lies in the adaptation method. Instead of searching parameters, FADA can directly calculate the close-to-optimal prediction very fast based on different sample distributions.

Extensive experiments on synthetic dataset, COREL and three well-known face datasets are performed to evaluate the effectiveness of FADA and compare it with ADA. Our experiments show that: (1) FADA implicitly avoids the problem encountered in ADA; (2) FADA has distinctly lower costs in time than ADA, and achieves classification accuracy that is comparable to ADA.

2 Fast Adaptive Discriminant Analysis

2.1 Adaptive Discrimiant Analysis

In 2006, Adaptive Discriminant Analysis (ADA) [3] was proposed, which merges LDA and BDA in a unified framework and offers more flexibility and a richer set of alternatives to LDA and BDA in the parametric space. ADA can find a good projection with adaptation to different sample distributions and discover the classification in the subspace with naïve Bayes classifier.

To provide a better model fitting the complex distributions for positive and negative samples, ADA finds an optimal projection.

$$W_{\text{opt}} = \arg\max_{W} \frac{|W^T[(1-\lambda)\cdot S_{N\to P} + \lambda\cdot S_{P\to N}]W|}{|W^T[(1-\eta)\cdot S_P + \eta\cdot S_N]W|} \tag{1}$$

in which

$$S_{N->P} = \sum_{i\in Negative}(\boldsymbol{x}_i - \boldsymbol{m}_P)(\boldsymbol{x}_i - \boldsymbol{m}_P)^T \tag{2}$$

$$S_{P->N} = \sum_{i\in Positive}(\boldsymbol{x}_i - \boldsymbol{m}_N)(\boldsymbol{x}_i - \boldsymbol{m}_N)^T \tag{3}$$

$$S_P = \sum_{i\in Positive}(\boldsymbol{x}_i - \boldsymbol{m}_P)(\boldsymbol{x}_i - \boldsymbol{m}_P)^T \tag{4}$$

$$S_N = \sum_{i\in Negative}(\boldsymbol{x}_i - \boldsymbol{m}_N)(\boldsymbol{x}_i - \boldsymbol{m}_N)^T \tag{5}$$

The $\boldsymbol{m}_P$ and $\boldsymbol{m}_N$ are the means of positive and negative samples, respectively. S_P (or S_N) is the within-class scatter matrix for the positive (or negative) examples. $S_{N\to P}$ (or $S_{P\to N}$) is the between-class scatter matrix from the negative (or positive) examples to the centroid of the positive (or negative) examples. The two parameters λ and η control the bias between positive and negative samples and range from $(0,0)$ to $(1,1)$. When λ and η are set to be 0 and 0, ADA recovers BDA and when λ and η are set to 0.5 and 0.5, ADA corresponds to a LDA-like projection. Alternatives to LDA and BDA can be obtained by setting parameters λ and η.

ADA has been demonstrated that it outperforms many state-of-the-art linear and nonlinear dimension reduction methods including PCA, LDA, DEM, kernel DEM (KDEM), BDA, kernel BDA (KBDA) etc. in many various applications [3].

2.2 Fast Adaptive Discriminant Analysis

Since ADA is a parametric method, parameter optimization and selection are important but difficult. i) It needs searching the whole parametric space to find the optimal projection. Its computational cost is very expensive. ii) It is hard to decide a trade-off between computational cost and accuracy. When the step-searching size is large, it will miss the global optimal value and when the size is small, it always causes overfitting problem.

In order to solve these problems, in this paper, we propose a Fast Adaptive Discriminant Analysis (FADA). Instead of searching the parametric space, FADA provides a novel and stable solution to find close-to-optimal ADA projection very fast. It saves a lot of computational cost and alleviates the overfitting problem.

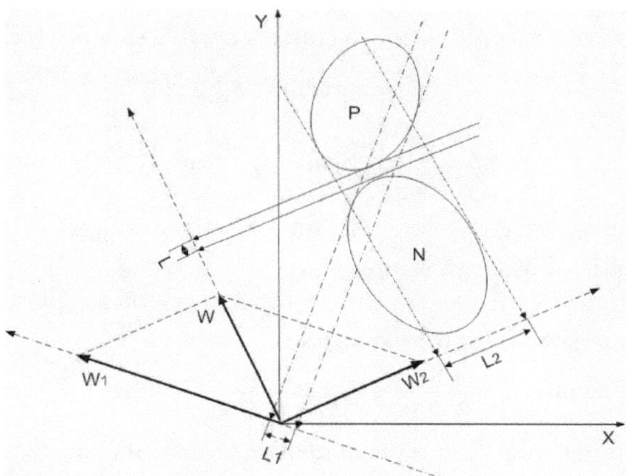

Fig. 1. Illustration of FADA algorithm

The basic idea of FADA is to find projections to cluster positive samples and negative samples respectively. Then adjust these projections to separate two classes as far as possible. Figure 1 gives an illustration of the basic idea of the FADA in two dimensional space.

The scenario can be described in the following steps (Fig. 1):

1. Firstly, find a projection W_1 that all positive samples (**P**) are clustered in the low dimensional space.
   The problem of finding the optimal W_1 can be mathematically represented as the following minimization problem:

$$W_1 = \arg\min_{W} \left| W^T S_W^P W \right| \tag{6}$$

$$S_W^P = \sum_{i=1}^{N_P} \left(\mathbf{x}_i^{(P)} - \mathbf{m}_P\right)\left(\mathbf{x}_i^{(P)} - \mathbf{m}_P\right) \tag{7}$$

Here, the within-class scatter matrix S_W^P measures the within-class variance of positive samples. $\{x_i^{(P)}, i = 1, \ldots, N_P\}$ denote the feature vectors of positive training samples. N_P is the number of the samples of the positive class, $\boldsymbol{m}_P$ is mean vector of the positive class. Obviously, W_1 is the eigenvector(s) corresponding to the smallest eigenvalue(s) of within-class scatter matrix of positive samples.

2. Project all positive and negative data to W_1, calculate the number of samples R_1 within the overlapping range L_1 of these two classes after projection. The smaller R_1, the more separated of these two classes. If $R_1 = 0$, the positive samples and negative samples can be completely separated by the projection W_1.
3. Similarly, find a projection W_2 to cluster negative samples (**N**).

$$W_2 = \arg\min_W \left| W^T S_W^N W \right| \tag{8}$$

$$S_W^N = \sum_{i=1}^{N_n} \left(\mathbf{x}_i^{(N)} - \mathbf{m}_N\right)\left(\mathbf{x}_i^{(N)} - \mathbf{m}_N\right) \tag{9}$$

   W_2 is the eigenvector(s) with the smallest eigenvalue(s) of S_W^N, within-class scatter matrix of negative samples.
4. Project all data to W_2 and calculate the number of samples R_2 belong to the overlapping range L_2 of the two classes.
5. Calculate the ratio $\lambda = \frac{R_2}{R_1 + R_2}$, $1 - \lambda = \frac{R_1}{R_1 + R_2}$
6. The final projection W is a linear combination of W_1 and W_2:

$$W = \lambda W_1 + (1 - \lambda) W_2 \tag{10}$$

Obviously, final W depends on the value of R_1 and R_2 (separability of two classes after projected by W_1 and W_2). If W_1 can better separate two classes than W_2 ($R_2 > R_1$), W will approach W_1 (W_1 has more weight). Shown in Fig. 1, after projection by the calculated W, there is no overlapping between positive samples and negative samples. Hence, in the low dimensional space, these two classes can be separated well.

3 Experiments and Analysis

3.1 FADA on Synthetic Datasets

In order to validate the effectiveness of FADA, we first use synthetic data to simulate different sample distributions as shown in Fig 2. Original data are simulated in 2-D feature space, and positive examples are marked with "+" s and negative examples are marked with "o" s in the figure. In each case, we apply BDA, LDA and FADA to find the best projection direction by their criterion functions. The resulting projection lines are drawn in dotted, dash-dotted and solid lines, respectively. In addition, the distributions of the examples along these projections are also drawn like bell-shaped curves along projection line, assuming Gaussian distribution for each class. The thicker curves represent the distribution of projected positive examples and the thinner curves denote the distribution of projected negative examples.

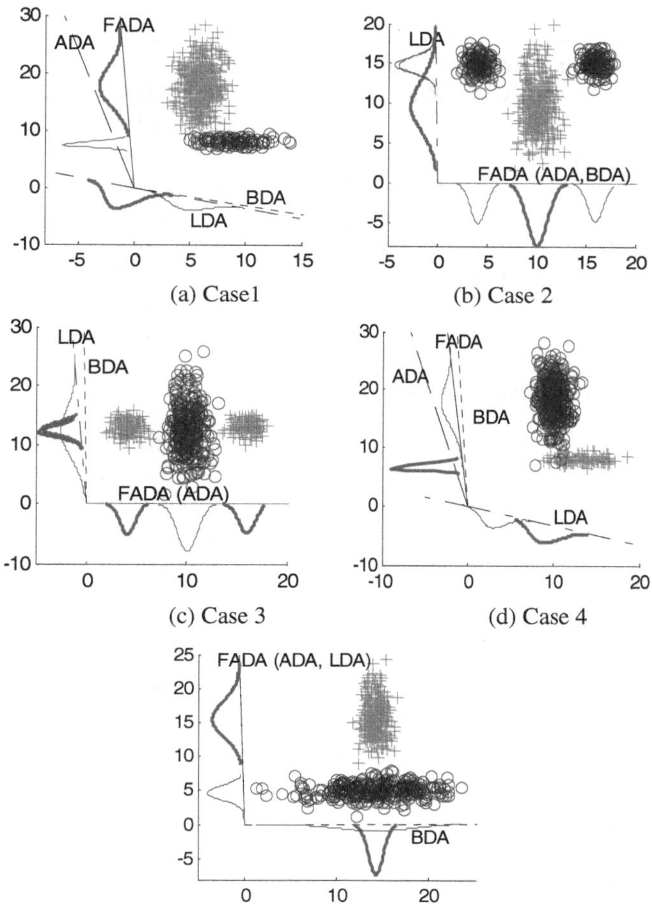

(a) Case1 (b) Case 2 (c) Case 3 (d) Case 4 (e) Case 5

Fig. 2. Comparison of optimal projections founded by LDA, BDA, ADA and FADA on synthetic data

Shown in Fig.2, we can see these five cases actually represent several typical data distribution scenarios. Case 1 and Case 4 best represent the imbalanced data set, where the size of positive (negative) sample set is much larger than that of negative (positive) samples (*Fig 2. (a) and (d)*). Case 2 and Case 3 best fit the distribution that the positive (negative) samples all look alike while negative (positive) ones may be irrelevant to each other and from different distributions (*Fig 2. (b) and (c)*). Case 5 is the scenario where the major descriptive directions of positive samples and negative samples are upright (*Fig 2. (e)*).

From the simulation results, we can see LDA treats positive and negative samples equally, *i.e.*, it tries to cluster the positive samples and decrease the scatter of the negative samples, even some from different sub-classes. This makes it a bad choice in Case 2 and Case 3. Similarly, since BDA assumes all positive samples are projected together, it fails in Case 3 and Case 5. In Case 1 and Case 4, BDA and LDA are found not applicable for imbalanced data sets. The reason for this is that LDA or BDA tends to severely bias to the dominating samples.

In all five cases, FADA yields as good projection as ADA with positive samples and negative samples well separated. The difference is that FADA directly computes a close-to-optimal projection easily, while ADA finds the good projection by complex and expensive parameter searching. FADA outperforms BDA and LDA as well. Note in Case 3, both BDA and LDA totally fail while FADA still produces a good projection. It clearly demonstrates that no matter if it is an imbalanced data set or samples are from different sub-classes, FADA can adaptively fit different distributions of samples fast and find a balance between clustering and separating, which are embedded in the criterion function.

3.2 FADA for Image Classification

In section 3.2 and 3.3, we experimentally evaluate the performance of FADA on real image datasets: COREL image data set and three popular face image data sets, which cover a wide range of data in computer vision applications. The use of ADA, LDA, BDA and other state of the art methods have been investigated on the same data set [3]. The congruent results are that ADA outperformed the other algorithms with Bayesian as the base classifier. Therefore in our experiments, we focused on comparing ADA with FADA in terms of classification accuracy and efficiency (computational time). In COREL data set, ADA searches 36 parameter combinations (λ, η) sampled from 0 to 1 with step size of 0.2 to find the best one. Bayesian classifier is used on the projected data for all projection-based methods. In all experiments, average classification accuracy of 30 runs is reported. We performed our experiments using Matlab on a Pentium IV 2.26GHz machine with 1GB RAM.

In our experiments, COREL image database contains 1386 color images, which are categorized into 14 classes. Each class contains 99 images. Each image is represented by 37 feature components including color moments [4], wavelet-based texture [5] and water-filling edge-based structure features [6]. For simplicity, we randomly pick up two classes of images for classification.

Figure 3 shows the performance of ADA and FADA as the size of training samples changes from 1/5 to 2/3 of the total samples. For example, 1/5 means one-fifth of the images are used for training while the rest are used for testing. In Fig.3 (a), we find that the accuracy of our proposed FADA and ADA both change with different training sets. No matter the training size is small or large, FADA outperforms ADA in most cases or at least is comparable with ADA. Another key observation from Fig. 3 (b) is that FADA is much faster than ADA. As the size of the training set increases, the speedup of FADA over ADA significantly increases because ADA spends a lot of time in training and searching. It demonstrates that FADA is a more effective and efficient dimension reduction algorithm than ADA, as it is competitive to ADA in classification while it has much lower time costs.

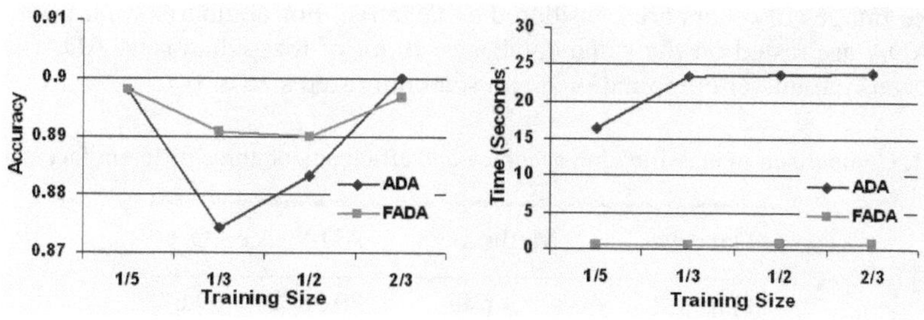

(a) (b)

Fig. 3. Comparison of accuracy and efficiency for ADA and FADA with different sizes of training set

3.3 FADA for Face Classification

To evaluate FADA for face classification, we tested FADA on three well-known face image databases with change in illumination, expression and head pose, respectively. The Harvard Face image database contains images from 10 individuals, each providing 66 images, which are classified into 10 sets based on increasingly changed illumination condition [7]. The AT&T Face Image database [8] consists of grayscale images of 40 persons. Each person has 10 images with different expressions, open or closed eyes, smiling or non-smiling and wearing glasses or no glasses. The UMIST Face Database [9] consists of 564 images of 20 people, which cover a range of poses from profile to frontal views. Figure 4 gives some example images from the

(a) Change of illumination condition, size is 84×96

(b) Change of expressions, size is 92×112

(c) Change of head pose, size is 92×112

Fig. 4. Example Face images from three facial databases

databases. Sixty image features are extracted to represent these images including histogram (32), wavelet-based texture (10) and water-filling edge-based structure features (18).

For each database, we randomly chose one person's face images as positive and the rest face images of others are considered as negative. For comparison purpose, ADA, and FADA are tested on the same databases. In all of these data sets, ADA searches 121 various parameter combinations with searching step size of 0.1.

Table 1. Comparison of classification accuracy and efficiency on three different face databases

Datasets	Method	ADA	FADA
Harvard Subset1	*Accuracy (%)*	89.56	**89.67**
	Time (Second)	78.67	**0.72**
Harvard Subset2	*Accuracy (%)*	88.62	**88.70**
	Time (Second)	114.34	**0.98**
Harvard Subset3	*Accuracy (%)*	88.98	**89.58**
	Time (Second)	155.93	**1.31**
ATT Dataset	*Accuracy (%)*	**97.88**	97.28
	Time (Second)	328.77	**2.89**
UMIST Dataset	*Accuracy (%)*	95.55	**95.76**
	Time (Second)	471.56	**4.31**

Table 1 shows the comparison of ADA and FADA on accuracy and efficiency, with the largest accuracy and the smallest computational time in bold. It can be seen that FADA performs better in 4 out of 5 datasets on classification accuracy and at least two orders of magnitude faster than ADA in all 5 datasets. It is to be noted that the computation requirements of ADA increase cubically with the increase size of datasets (from Harvard to UMIST dataset) and the speed difference between ADA and FADA becomes more significant with the increase of face database scale. It is proved that FADA not only reduces the computational cost, but also increases the accuracy. It is an efficient dimension reduction scheme for image classification on small or large image datasets.

4 Conclusion and Future Work

In this paper, we propose a Fast Adaptive Discriminant Analysis (FADA) to alleviate the expensive computation cost of ADA. The novelty lies in that instead of searching a parametric space, it calculates the close-to-optimal projection automatically according to various sample distributions. FADA has asymptotically lower time complexity than ADA, which is desirable for large image datasets, while it implicitly alleviates the overfitting problem encountered in classical ADA. All experimental results show that FADA achieves competitive classification accuracy with ADA, while being much more efficient. Extensions of FADA to high dimensional application are our future work.

Acknowledgments. This work was supported in part by Army Research Office (ARO) grant under W911NF-05-1-0404, by Department of Homeland Security (DHS) and by the San Antonio Life Science Institute (SALSI).

References

1. Ruda, R., Hart, P., Stork, D.: Pattern classification, 2nd edn. John Wiley & Sons, Inc, Chichester (2001)
2. Zhou, X., Huang, T.S.: Small sample learning during multimedia retrieval using biasMap. IEEE CVPR (2001)
3. Yu, J., Tian, Q.: Adaptive discriminant projection for content-based image retrieval. In: Proc. of Intl. Conf. on Pattern Recognition, Hong Kong (August 2006)
4. Stricker, M., Orengo, M.: Similarity of color images. In: Proceedings of SPIE Storage and Retrieval for Image and Video Databases, San Diego, CA (1995)
5. Smith, J.R., Chang, S.F.: Transform features for texture classification and discrimination in large image database. In: Proceedings of IEEE International Conference on Image Processing, Austin, TX (1994)
6. Zhou, X., Rui, Y., Huang, T.S.: Water-filling algorithm: a novel way for image feature extraction based on edge maps. In: Proceedings of IEEE International Conference on Image Processing, Kobe, Japan (1999)
7. Belhumeur, P., Hespanha, J., Kriegman, D.: Eigenfaces vs. Fisherfaces: recognition using class specific linear projection. IEEE Trans. PAMI 19(7) (1997)
8. Rowley, H.A., Baluja, S., Kanade, T.: Neural network-based face detection. IEEE Trans. PAMI 20 (1998)
9. Samaria, F., Harter, F.: Parameterisation of a stochastic model for human face identification. In: IEEE Workshop on Applications of Computer Vision, Sarasota FL (December 1994)

Using Camera Settings Templates ("Scene Modes") for Image Scene Classification of Photographs Taken on Manual/Expert Settings

William Ku[1], Mohan S. Kankanhalli[1], and Joo-Hwee Lim[2]

[1] National University of Singapore, 3 Science 2, Singapore 117543
[2] Institute of Infocomm Research, 21 Heng Mui Keng Terrace, Singapore 119613
{wku, mohan}@comp.nus.edu.sg, joohwee@i2r.a-star.edu.sg

Abstract. *The automatic point-and-click mode of Digital Still* Cameras (DSCs) may be a boon to most users whom are simply trigger-happy. However, this automatic mode may not generate the best photos possible or be even applicable for certain types of shots, especially those that require technical expertise. To bridge this gap, many DSCs now offer "Scene Modes" that would easily allow the user to effortlessly configure his camera to specifically take certain types of photos, usually resulting in better quality pictures. These "Scene Modes" provide valuable contextual information about these types of photos and in this paper, we examine how we could make use of "Scene Modes" to assist in generic Image Scene Classification for photos taken on expert/manual settings. Our algorithm could be applied to any image classes associated with the "Scene Modes" and we demonstrated this with the classification of fireworks photos in our case study.

Keywords: Image Scene Classification, Scene Modes, EXIF, Contextual Information.

1 Introduction

Digital Still Cameras (DSCs) are getting more powerful by the day but they are still not quite the magical devices that can automatically help users to take good quality pictures for simply any types of photos. The point-and-click automatic mode of the DSC does provide an easy and convenient way for the user to take photos because the DSC would automatically configure itself based on the environmental response (such as the amount of light or subject distance) to its sensors and render a best attempt.

However, this automatic mode is only suitable for a few types of shots such as outdoor types of shots and when there is ample lighting. For example, trying to take photos of a fireworks display using this automatic mode would very likely to result in a disaster (see Figure 2). To take good quality pictures of any type (such as for the firework displays), one must possess certain photographic skills such as knowing how to configure the camera to compensate for motion or lighting, framing and etc. This technical expertise is usually beyond most users whom just want to take photos effortlessly without having to tweak their cameras.

H.H.S. Ip et al. (Eds.): PCM 2007, LNCS 4810, pp. 10–17, 2007.

To bridge this divide, many camera manufacturers now offer DSCs with "Scene Modes". "Scene Modes" are essentially optimized camera settings templates that the user can select for certain specialised types of pictures such as face portrait, scenery, nightshot, fireworks and etc. When a particular "Scene Mode" is selected, the DSC will be automatically configured with approximately similar settings that an expert photographer would have chosen for the same type of shot. Thus, "Scene Modes" empower users to take specialty shots in a point-and click manner.

The user is highly motivated to make full use of "Scene Modes" because firstly it is very easy and secondly usually renders better quality photos or photos that would not be possible if taken using the camera's automatic mode. We think that more and more people will be using "Scene Modes" as they become more familiar with their cameras and as more "Scene Modes" are being better defined and made available.

1.1 The Use of "Scene Modes" for Image Scene Classification

We observe a novel use of this "Scene Modes" feature for image scene classification. When an user selects a "Scene Mode" such as "Fireworks", he has effectively provided a basis for image scene classification. This is because the user already had in mind the type of shot that he was going to make and this would be reflected in his deliberate choice of a "Scene Mode". The user would not have selected a particular "Scene Mode" if he has no intention of taking a certain type of photo. For example, one would not choose a fireworks "Scene Mode" to take a portrait (when there is a portrait "Scene Mode"). It is interesting to note (and we had shown it that) the camera settings associated with the selected "Scene Mode" can be effectively used to determine if other photos could be similar in type (based on the camera settings), particularly those taken in the manual/expert mode.

There might be instances whereby the user accidentally select the wrong "Scene Mode" to take a picture but when that happens, the quality of the photo will usually turn out to be bad or that the desired effect is not captured such that that the photo will then be deleted.

The organization of this paper is as follows. We will next look at some related work and state our contribution. We then provide our methodology on how we make use of the contextual information rendered by the use of "Scene Modes". This is followed by a discussion on our experimental results whereby we demonstrated our technique through a case study of fireworks photo scene classification.

2 Related Work

Image scene classification has its roots established in the use of content-based features such as colour and texture for automatic scene classification. Here, we are concerned with a non-content-based approach that employs contextual information such as the metadata of the image. In this instance, we look at the camera settings behind the "Scene Modes" which would be reported in the form of EXIF [4] metadata.

The use of EXIF metadata for image scene classification is not new. Certain EXIF metadata parameters such as the *Exposure Time, Aperture, Fnumber, Shutter Speed,*

Subject Distance and the use/non-use of *Flash*, could be used independently or fused with content-based features to determine certain image scene classification such as indoor/outdoor and sunset images [1, 2, 7, 8].

2.1 Contribution

Our contribution lies in the novel use of specific "Scene Modes" or camera settings templates to assist in classifying photos that were not taken with such modes but rather with photos taken on manually selected camera settings or those taken in the point-and-click automatic mode. We do not make direct use of EXIF per se as in previous work but in the form of domain (expert) knowledge through the use of the "Scene Modes".

In our previous work [6], we had established that camera settings in the various "Scene Modes" are sufficiently distinct to accurately differentiate photos taken in the "Scene Modes" to be uniquely classified to their respective "Scene Modes". In this paper, we made use of the "Scene Modes" to classify photos taken on manual (expert) settings.

3 Methodology

In this section, we shall outline our approach of how we can make use of the "Scene Modes" for Image Scene Classification. Essentially, "Scene Modes" are camera settings templates that the user can choose to take specific types of pictures such as fireworks or close-ups. These types of shots usually require some technical expertise to set the camera for image capture and that it is usually not possible to use the point-and-click automatic mode of the camera to effectively capture these specialty shots.

In other words, the camera settings behind a specific "Scene Mode" would be very similar to the settings that an expert photographer would have used in order to capture that specific type of picture.

In our previous work [6], we had established that the contextual information given by "Scene Modes" can be used to classify photos taken using "Scene Modes" very accurately. This means that the various "Scene Modes" are distinct from one another.

In this paper, we aim to establish that that specialty shots taken by expert photographers using the camera on manual mode, can be classified into respective categories by virtue of the contextual information provided by the "Scene Modes".

Figure 1 outlines our methodology. From a database of photos taken with specific "Scene Modes" (of a particular camera), we observed the EXIF metadata to extract useful EXIF parameters.

The selected base EXIF parameters were: *Exposure Time, F Number, Exposure Program, Metering Mode, Light Source, Focal Length, White Balance Bias, White Balance, Object Distance, Focus Mode, CCD ISO Sensitivity, Enhancement, Filter, Custom Rendered, Exposure Mode, White Balance, Contrast, Saturation, Sharpness* and *Hyperfocal Distance*.

One point to note is that these parameters were chosen in a data-driven process whereby we examined the EXIF data of the photos to extract the discerning parameters.

Our next step is to pass these selected EXIF parameters into the learning module of SVMLite Version 6.01 [5] to generate learning models for these "Scene Modes" which form the classification module.

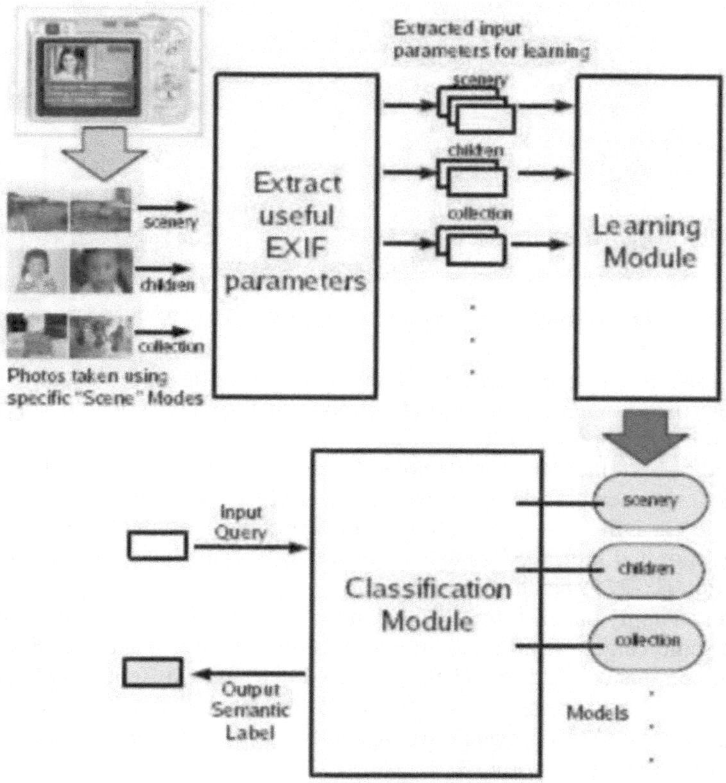

Fig. 1. Our system illustrating the use of "Scene Modes" for image scene classification

To classify a photo taken on manual settings, we pass its EXIF metadata to the classification module in order to extract a semantic label based on the above learning models.

For our experiments, we made use of photos taken with a *Casio Exilim EX-Z750* [3]. This camera comes default with 31 "BestShot modes" ("Scene Modes") with the option for the user to define up to 999 custom modes. This camera also comes with an automatic mode and a manual mode. By making use of the same camera with the above three types of modes, we eliminated the EXIF metadata deviations due to different camera hardware specifications.

In order to demonstrate our hypothesis, we look at one class of specialty photos namely fireworks. The main reason why we had chosen to look at fireworks photos is that fireworks photos cannot be effectively captured using the automatic mode of the camera (see Figure 2 for an example). Instead, the camera has to be set to have a long

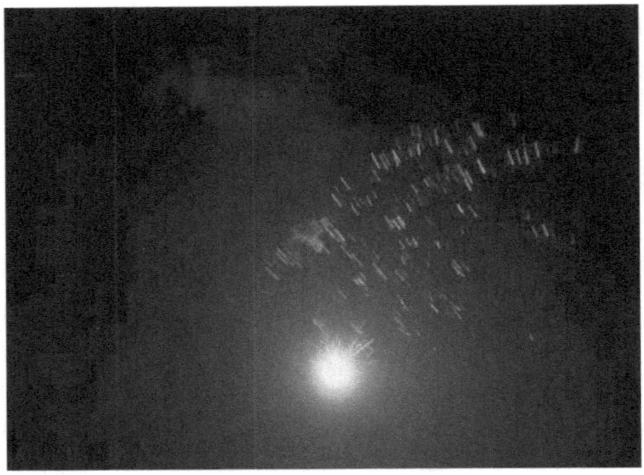

Fig. 2. Example of fireworks photo taken on automatic mode

exposure time, long-range focus and etc in order to have the desired effect. Thus most users using the automatic point-and-click mode of their DSCs would not be able to capture fireworks photos.

It would be extremely frustrating not to be able to capture the magical effects of the fireworks for remembrance given that these users do not know how to manually configure their DSCs as stated above. However, they would be able to take the fireworks photos if their DSCs have a fireworks "Scene Mode" as is the case in the *Casio Exilim EX-Z750* camera.

In order to apply our methodology, we downloaded photos taken by various users, using the same camera from a public photo database, taken using the "Scene Mode" feature and on manual settings. These photos can be easily differentiated via an EXIF attribute. We next processed those "Scene Mode" photos as training examples and used those photos taken on manual settings as the testing examples. We presented our results in the following section.

4 Experimental Results and Discussion

In this section, we showed the results from the application of our methodology to classify fireworks photos. For the purpose of our experiments, we have downloaded photos strictly taken with the *Casio Exilim EX-Z750* camera from Flickr.com [9]. Table 1 tabulates the various types of photos downloaded and deployed for our experiments.

For our training set, we made use of a total of 606 training examples comprising 223 fireworks (positive) photos from 28 unique users. These photos were taken using the fireworks "Scene Mode" feature of the camera. For the remaining training examples, we have 383 non-fireworks (negative) examples (a random selection).

We next queried 401 testing examples obtained from 16 unique users. These photos are taken using the same camera but on manual settings.

Table 1. Photos taken with the *Casio Exilim EX-Z750* camera

Type of photos	**Number of photos**	**Number of unique users**
Fireworks training photos	223	28
Non-fireworks training photos	383	N/A (random)
Total training photos	606	N/A
Fireworks testing photos	401	16
Non-fireworks testing photos	171	N/A (random)

We obtained a classification accuracy of 80.80% (324 correct, 77 incorrect, 401 total). We also queried 171 non-fireworks (a non-subset of the training set and a random selection) for false positives and obtained a classification accuracy of 98.25% (168 correct, 3 incorrect, 171 total).

The above indicated that the training set can be effectively used to differentiate fireworks and non-fireworks photos to a high extent. Table 2 summaries the above results.

Table 2. Classification results

Types of photos	Number of photos correctly classified / misclassified	Classification Accuracy
Fireworks testing photos	324 / 77	80.80%
Non-fireworks testing photos	168 / 3	98.25%

We also investigated the reasons to why some photos are misclassified. Figure 3 shows some examples of the photos not being classified correctly. That is, they should be classified as fireworks photos but were not done so due to some reasons. We found out that for quite a number of those photos that are not being classified correctly, they usually have some additional background or that their EXIF metadata are truncated due to software editing. Removing these types of photos will definitely yield a better classification accuracy. However, we chose not to do so as manual inspection will be required in order to filter out these photos.

In addition, as the testing photos are taken on manual settings, it is expected that the users may have different settings from one another even though it is for the same type of shot. This is particularly so due to the diverse intent and skill of the photographers. This presents another challenge that we need to work on in order to factor this diversity in our methodology.

Fig. 3. Example photos not being classified correctly

5 Conclusion and Future Work

We have presented a novel approach to classify certain types of photos (taken on manual camera settings) by making use of only contextual information given by the "Scene Modes" feature.

In this paper, we have shown that we can make use of the contextual information from the use of a certain fireworks "Scene Mode" to classify fireworks photos to the accuracy of about 80%. Our algorithm is generic and can be easily applied to other specific types of photos or photo classes associated with available "Scene Modes". This approach provides a viable alternative for image scene classification and can be used to complement existing (content-based) methods. We are also currently working on fusing our algorithm with a content-based method to achieve better results.

In addition, we have only made use of one camera in our experiments and we are presently in the process of applying our method to different camera makes. The main issue here is that the different hardware of the cameras made it difficult for our method to be applied in an inter-operable manner.

We have also shown that users taking the same type of shots may apply different manual settings, depending on their intent and skill. This presents another challenging issue that we need to work on.

We are also working on our algorithm to be applicable for photos taken on automatic settings. However, preliminary results are unsatisfactory. The difficulty lies in that the contextual information provided by these photos is not distinctive enough to enable differentiation of various image scenes.

Acknowledgments. We would like to thank Prof Ramesh Jain for his valuable inputs on this work. We also thank the reviewers for their constructive suggestions.

References

1. Boutell, M., Luo, J.: Bayesian Fusion of Camera Metadata Cues in Semantic Scene Classification. Proceedings of CVPR 2004 2, 623–630 (2004)
2. Boutell, M., Luo, J.: Beyond Pixels: Exploiting Camera Metadata for Photo Classification. Pattern Recognition 38(6), 935–946 (2005)
3. Casio Exilim EX-Z750. Product manual, available at http://ftp.casio.co.jp/pub/world_manual/qv/en/EXZ750_e.pdf
4. Exchangeable Image File Format (EXIF), Version 2.2, JEITA (2002), http://www.exif.org/Exif2-2.PDF
5. Joachims, T.: Making large-Scale SVM Learning Practical. In: Schölkopf, B., Burges, C., Smola, A. (eds.) Advances in Kernel Methods - Support Vector Learning, MIT-Press, Cambridge (1999)
6. Ku, W., Kankanhalli, M.S., Lim, J.H.: Using Camera Settings Templates to Classify Photos. In: IIWAIT 2007. Proceedings of International Workshop on Advanced Image Technology, pp. 445–450 (2007)
7. Luo, J., Boutell, M., Brown, C.: Pictures are not taken in a vacuum - an overview of exploiting context for semantic scene content understanding. IEEE Signal Processing Magazine 23(2), 101–114 (2006)
8. O'Hare, N., Gurrin, C., Lee, H., Murphy, N., Smeaton, A.F., Jones, G.J.F.: My digital photos: where and when? In: Proceedings of the 13th Annual ACM International Conference on Multimedia, pp. 261–262 (2005)
9. Photos hosted at Flickr.com and taken with the Casio Exilim EX-Z750, http://www.flickr.com/cameras/casio/ex-z750/

Modeling User Feedback Using a Hierarchical Graphical Model for Interactive Image Retrieval

Jian Guan and Guoping Qiu

School of Computer Science, The University of Nottingham, UK
{jwg, qiu}@cs.nott.ac.uk

Abstract. Relevance feedback is an important mechanism for narrowing the semantic gap in content-based image retrieval and the process involves the user labeling positive and negative images. Very often, it is some specific objects or regions in the positive feedback images that the user is really interested in rather than the entire image. This paper presents a hierarchical graphical model for automatically extracting objects and regions that the user is interested in from the positive images which in turn are used to derive features that better reflect the user's feedback intentions for improving interactive image retrieval. The novel hierarchical graphical model embeds image formation prior, user intention prior and statistical prior in its edges and uses a max-flow/min-cut method to simultaneously segment all positive feedback images into user interested and user uninterested regions. An important innovation of the graphical model is the introduction of a layer of visual appearance prototype nodes to incorporate user intention and form bridges linking similar objects in different images. This architecture not only makes it possible to use all feedback images to obtain more robust user intention prior thus improving the object segmentation results and in turn enhancing the retrieval performance, but also greatly reduces the complexity of the graph and the computational cost. Experimental results are presented to demonstrate the effectiveness of the new method.

Keywords: Image retrieval, image segmentation, graphical model, semi-supervised learning, relevance feedback.

1 Introduction

Reducing the semantic gap is one of the key challenges in image retrieval research. One popular approach is through user interaction where the user provides relevance feedbacks to the retrieval system which will then incorporate the user's intention to refine the retrieval results to better match the user's intention and expectation. Relevance Feedback, first used in document retrieval, was introduced into Content-Based Image Retrieval (CBIR) in early 1990s. A comprehensive review of relevance feedback in image retrieval can be found in [22].

One of the crucial problems in relevance feedback is modelling users' feedback, i.e., building a retrieval model based on user supplied labelled data. There are two aspects to this problem. One is what (low-level) features to use to represent the image

H.H.S. Ip et al. (Eds.): PCM 2007, LNCS 4810, pp. 18–29, 2007.

content and the other is what algorithms to use for building the retrieval model. Early approaches mainly use global features; colour histogram and texture descriptors are the most commonly used. For the retrieval model, machine learning approaches such as Support Vector Machines (SVMs) are popular [8, 15].

In many situations, users are more likely looking for certain objects or parts of the images. Recent works by several authors e.g. [4, 17] have introduced region based approaches and achieve good results. To enable region based image retrieval, image segmentation algorithm is first employed to segment images into regions and then measure the similarity between the images using region-based features. There are two main obstacles to region based image retrieval (RBIR) approaches. Firstly, fully-automatic image segmentation is a hard problem in computer vision and its solutions remains unstable and will remain so for the near future. Secondly, even if the segmentation results are satisfactory, we have no way of knowing which region is the one that the user is most interested in unless the user labels the segmented regions [4]. However, manually labeling the interested regions requires extra user effort. Such extra burden may be unacceptably heavy if the user has to label interested regions on more than one relevant image.

To model the user's intention in the relevance feedback process, specifically, we first want to find in the feedback images the regions that the users are interested in and we then want to use information from these specific regions to drive feedback features to refine image retrieval results. Suppose the user uses the image (a) in Figure 1 as a query image, which has been reasonably well-segmented, what is his/her intention? Is the user looking for images with a cow, or grassland, or lake, or all of them? Even another human user can not give the answer without other priors. Using relevance feedback, if the user supplies some more image samples, e.g. (d) and (e) in Figure 1, as positive feedback, it is very reasonable to assume that the user is actually interested in images with cows. Base on this intuition, some recent work e.g. [8, 9, 17] combine image segmentation and relevance feedback and obtain good results. However, these approaches rely on the performance of automatic image segmentation which is still a hard problem. Actually, we can make better use of relevance feedback. When the user selects some positive image samples, it is reasonable to assume that there is a common object or region across these images. This information can be used to refine the segmentation results and further reveal the user's intention.

(a) (b) (c) (d) (e) (f) (g)

Fig. 1. What is the user's intention? Assuming (a) is the querying image, when (d) and (e) are used as the positive feedback the segmentation result of (a) should be (b); when (f) and (g) are used as positive feedback the segmentation result of (a) should be (c).

This paper presents a novel framework for region based image retrieval using relevance feedback. The new framework is based around a novel hierarchical graphical model for simultaneously segmenting the positive feedback images into figure (user interested) and background (user uninterested) regions via a graph cut algorithm. The new model incorporates user's intentions as priors, which not only can provide good segmentation performance but also will result in the segmented regions reflect user feedback intentions and can be readily exploited to perform image retrieval.

2 Extracting Relevant Objects and Features

One of the drawbacks of the segmentation methods used in traditional region based image retrieval is that these methods usually segment an image into several regions. In some cases, one object could be divided into different regions. In other cases, even though the segmentation result is reasonably correct, e.g. image (a) in Figure 1, the retrieval methods need to figure out the region corresponding to the object which the user is interested in. Although the user can scribble on the interested objects, e.g. the cow or the grassland in Figure1 to indicate his/her intentions, we will address this scenario in future work whilst this paper will only study the use of statistical prior from the feedback images to model the user intention.

In our approach, we do figure-ground segmentation, i.e. an image will be segmented into 2 regions only: the figure, which is the object the user intends to find, and the background. In the presence of relevance feedback as user supplied priors, the segmentation results are context sensitive as shown in Figure 1. In the case when a user uses image (a) as query image and supplies images (d) and (e) as positive samples, the segmentation result of (a) would be (b), where the figure is the cow; whilst using (f) and (g) as positive samples, the result would be (c), where the figure is the grassland. This result is to reflect the assumption that users are interested in the objects that occur most frequently in the positive feedback images.

2.1 CPAM Features

The coloured pattern appearance model (CPAM) is developed to capture both colour and texture information of small patches in natural colour images, which has been successfully used in image coding, image indexing and retrieval [10]. The model built a codebook of common *appearance prototypes* based on tens of thousands of image patches using Vector Quantization. Each prototype encodes certain chromaticity and spatial intensity pattern information of a small image patch.

Given an image, each pixel i can be characterized using a small neighbourhood window surrounding the pixel. This small window can then be approximated (encoded) by a CPAM appearance prototype p that is the most similar to the neighbourhood window. We can also build a CPAM histogram for the image which tabulates the frequencies of the appearance prototypes being used to approximate (encode) a neighbourhood region of the pixels in the image. Another interpretation of the CPAM histogram is that each bin of the histogram corresponds with an appearance prototype, and the count of a bin is the probability that pixels (or more precisely small windows of pixels) in the image having the appearance that can be best approximated by the CPAM appearance prototype of that bin. Such a CPAM histogram captures the appearance statistics of the image and can be used as image content descriptor for content-based image retrieval.

2.2 A Hierarchical Graph Model

A weighted graph $G = \{V, E\}$ consists of a set of nodes V and a set of edges E that connect the nodes, where both the nodes and edges can be weighted. An *st-cut* on a graph divides the nodes into to 2 sets S and T, such that $S \cup T = V$ and $S \cap T = \Phi$. The sum of weights of the edges that connect the 2 sets is called a *cut*, which measures the connection between the 2 sets.

$$cut(S,T) = \sum_{i \in S} \sum_{j \in T} e_{ij} \quad (1)$$

The classical *minimum cut* problem (*min-cut*) in graph theory is to find the division with minimum cut amongst all possible ones [3].

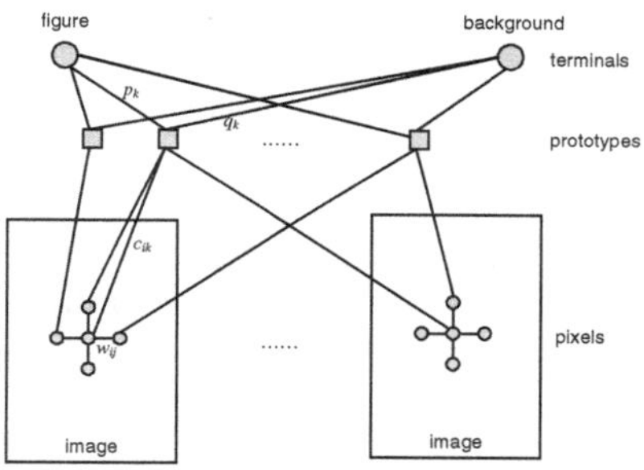

Fig. 2. A hierarchical graphical model jointly modeling pixels, appearance prototypes, figure and background.

If we view the pixels as nodes and the edges measure their similarity, figure-ground segmentation problem can be naturally formulated as a *minimum cut* problem, i.e. dividing the pixels into 2 disjoint sets with minimum association between them. This formulation has been used in, for example [14] for automatic single image segmentation using spectral graph cut, and [2] for semi-automatic single image/video segmentation with user scribbles using max-flow based method.

We construct a hierarchical decision graph, as shown in Figure 2, where there are three types of nodes. At the lowest level are nodes corresponding to pixels in the images; at the intermediate level are nodes corresponding to the CPAM appearance prototypes; and at the highest level are two terminal nodes corresponding to figure and ground. The weighted edges measure the likelihood that two connected nodes fall in the same class, the figure or the background. In this way, we formulate the joint image segmentation problem as finding the minimum cut on the decision graph. Note that we only segment the query image and the positive samples which contain the desired objects to capture the user's intention. Details are explained in the following subsections.

2.2.1 Intra-image Prior

According to the image formation model, neighbouring pixels are highly correlated. When we divide an image into regions, two pixels close to each other are likely to fall into the same region. We measure the connection between two neighbouring pixels i and j in a single image using a widely adopted function [e.g. in 14] as follows.

$$w_{ij} = e^{-d(i,j)^2/\sigma_g^2} e^{-\|f_i - f_j\|^2/\sigma_p^2} \quad (2)$$

where $d(i, j)$ is the spatial distance between the 2 pixels i and j; f_i and f_j are feature vectors computed around the pixels; σ_g and σ_p are the variances of the geometric coordinates and the photometric feature vectors.

2.2.2 Inter-image Prior

From a high level vision perspective, similar objects in different images consist of similar pixels. Reversely, similar pixels in different images are likely to belong to the same object. Hence there should be connections between them in the decision graph. However, searching for similar pixels across the images is computationally intensive. Moreover, establishing edges amongst pixels in different images will make the graph dense and in turn exponentially increase the computational complexity. Instead, we introduce a new type of nodes as intermediate hops.

Using the CPAM scheme described in section 2.1, each pixel can be associated with an appearance prototype, i.e., a small neighbourhood window of the pixel is encoded by an appearance prototype that is the most similar to the window. Without other prior knowledge, a pixel and its associated prototype should be classified similarly. In our graphical model, each prototype is a node; if pixel i is associated with prototype k, we establish an edge between them with a weight c_{ik}. The connection between them can be measure according to their distance. For simplicity, we set all $c_{ik}= 1$. Note that a pixel is connected to both its neighbouring pixels and a prototype, i.e. its status is affected by 2 types of nodes. To control the relative influences between the 2 different types of nodes, we introduce a factor λ_1 and set all $c_{ik} = \lambda_1$. In all the experiments, we find $\lambda_1 = 0.3$ produce satisfactory results.

2.2.3 Statistical Prior

The above two priors have not taken into account the information the user provides through relevance feedback. Decision made according to them would be ambiguous. We further introduce two special nodes, termed *terminals*, one represents the figure and the other represents the background. Furthermore, introducing these terminal nodes will enable us to make use of the max-flow algorithm [5] to cut the graph.

Clearly, it would be difficult to establish links between terminals and pixels whilst it is possible to establish links between terminals and prototypes. We consider the scenario where user provides both positive and negative feedbacks and interpret them in such a way that there is a common (similar) object or region across the positive samples whilst the object does not exist in the negative samples.

For each image m, we build a CPAM histogram h_m as described in section 2.1. A summary histogram h^+, named *positive histogram*, can be computed by adding the histograms of the query image and positive image samples. In the same way, we can compute a *negative histogram* h^- from the negative image samples. To eliminate the influences of the image size and the sample size, all these histograms are normalized. Suppose the bin corresponding to the appearance prototype k counts b_k^+ in the *positive histogram* and counts b_k^- in the *negative histogram*, we could roughly estimate the probability that k belongs to the figure and background as:

$$p(k \in F) \propto b_k^+ \text{ and } p(k \notin F) \propto b_k^- \tag{3}$$

Thus we can further derive the connection between prototype k and terminal *figure* as $p_k=\lambda_2 p(k \in F)$ and that between k and *background* as $q_k=\lambda_2 p(k \notin F)$, where λ_2 is a factor that weight the influences between inter-image prior and statistical prior. In the implementation, we set λ_2 as λ_1 times the total pixel number in the query image and the positive image samples, in order to make the magnitude of edges connecting terminals and pixels approximately equal to each other.

The underlying assumption here is that the desired objects in different images are similar to each other in the sense that they all consist of similar features whilst the background varies. Thus the size of the positive image sample set is large enough to make the features which indicate the desired object adequately significant. For example, in the case of finding human faces from an image database, if we simply use colour as feature, it could be expected that the colour of skin is the most significant in the statistic of positive samples.

2.3 Graph Cut Implementation

Using the graphical model constructed above, we have successfully transformed the problem of finding the desired objects as the classical graph min-cut problem: dividing the pixels and prototypes into two disjoint sets with weakest connections between them, i.e. the two sets that are most unlikely belong to the same class, and each of the two sets connect to one of the terminals, respectively. According to [6], this is equivalent to the problem of finding the *maximum flow* between the two terminals *figure* and *background*.

Note that the hierarchical graphical model proposed here is different from the one in [2] for interactive single image segmentation in two ways. Firstly, we have introduced a new layer consisting of feature prototype nodes whilst [2] only uses pixel nodes. Secondly, in [2], each node represents a pixel connects to both terminals whilst our pixel nodes are connected to prototypes only. Though the graph cut method proposed in [3] and used in [2] is also based on max-flow, it is optimized for the graphs where most nodes are connected to the terminals and more importantly, it does not has a polynomial bound for the computational complexity. Whilst in our case, only prototype nodes which take up less than 1% of the total number of the nodes are connected to the terminals. Instead, we use an improved "push-relabel" method H_PRF proposed in [5] in this implementation. According to [2] and [5], the method is known to be one of the fastest both theoretically and experimentally with a worst case complexity of $O(n^2\sqrt{m})$, where $m = |E|$ and $n = |V|$. Clearly, compared to that in [2], the way we construct the hierarchical graph only slightly increases the number of nodes (by less than 1%) and significantly decreases the number of edges (by the total number of pixels).

A recent work [11] which also uses max-flow method solves the problem of segmenting the common parts of two images, which requires that the histograms of the figures in the two images are almost identical. A novel cost function consisting of two terms was proposed, where the first one leads to spatial coherency within single image and the second one attempt to match the histograms of the two figures. The optimization process starts from finding the largest regions in two images of the same size whose histograms match perfectly via a greedy algorithm that adds one pixel at a time to the first and second foreground regions, and then iteratively optimize the cost function over one image whilst fix the other by turns. The assumption and the optimization process limits its application in image retrieval, where there are usually more than two positive samples and the object histograms might sometimes vary significantly (See Figure 3 for an example where there are both red and yellow buses). It is worth pointing out that our framework and solution is very different from these previous works. Since we emphasis more on capturing user intention than segmentation, we use simple features and weak priors only to illustrate the effectiveness of our hierarchical graph model framework.

2.4 An Iterative Algorithm

The initial statistical prior described in section 2.2.3 is weak, where the positive histogram represents the global statistics of all positive image samples, whilst we actually intend to capture the features of the desired objects. When we obtain the figure-ground segmentation results, we can refine the estimation by computing the positive histogram h^+ on the figures only and the negative histogram using both the negative samples and the background regions extracted from the positive samples. Then we update the weights of the edges connecting the terminals and the prototypes. Using the segmentation results obtained in the previous round to update the graph and cut the new graph, it usually takes no more than 3 iterations to converge and produces satisfactory results in our experiments.

2.5 Relevant Feature Selection

Note that we only segment the query image and the positive samples which contain the desired objects to capture the user's intention. In the retrieval phase, when we need to measure the similarity between two images, one or even both of them may not have been segmented. To measure the similarity of two un-segmented images, we can use global descriptors such as colour histogram, CPAM histogram, and other descriptors; and make use of the knowledge learned in the graphical model and weight the features appropriately.

Given the joint segmentation results, we build a new positive histogram h_w^+ on all the figures, which captures the statistical characteristics of the desired object. We call h_w^+ *weighting vector* and use it to indicate the importance of difference feature prototypes. Note that some prototypes might weight 0 and will not affect the future decision. Let h be the original histogram, after relevant feature selection, the new relevant histogram h^r is computed as $h^r = Wh$, where $W = \text{diag}(h_w^+)$.

3 Interactive Image Retrieval Using Semi-supervised Learning

We use a graph-based semi-supervised method similar to that in [20] to perform interactive image retrieval. The query-by-sample image retrieval problem is tackled using a classification paradigm. Consider a given dataset consists of N images $\{x_1, x_2, \ldots, x_N\}$, we want to divide it into 2 classes where the first one C_1 consists of the desired images and other images fall into the second one C_0. For each image, we assume that there is an associated membership score, $\{(x_1, \alpha_1), (x_2, \alpha_2), \ldots, (x_N, \alpha_N)\}$, where $0 \le \alpha_i \le 1$ is interpreted as follows: the larger α_i is, the more likely x_i belongs to C_1; conversely, the smaller α_i is, the more likely x_i belongs to C_0. Now consider the case where some of the samples are labeled, i.e., $\alpha_i = y_i$, for $i = 1, 2, \ldots L$, where $y_i \in \{0, 1\}$ is the class label of x_i. The rest $\alpha_{L+1}, \alpha_{L+2}, \ldots, \alpha_N$ are unknown. Our task is to assign membership scores to those unlabeled data.

Let α_i defined above be the probability that a certain image x_i belongs to C_1. Let all images that can affect the state of x_i form a set S_i and call it the *neighborhood* of x_i. In a Bayesian Inference framework, we can write:

$$\alpha_i = p(x_i \in C_1) = \sum_{j \in S_i} p(x_i \in C_1 \mid x_j \in C_1)\, p(x_j \in C_1) \tag{4}$$

Define $\delta_{ij} = p(x_i \in C_1 \mid x_j \in C_1)$, then we have

$$\alpha_i = \sum_{j \in S_i} \delta_{ij} \alpha_j \qquad \text{and} \qquad \sum_{j \in S_i} \delta_{ij} = 1 \tag{5}$$

By making a mild assumption that the given data follow the Gibbs distribution, the conditional probabilities can be defined as follows

$$\delta_{ij} = \frac{1}{Z} e^{-\beta d(x_i, x_j)} \qquad \text{where} \qquad Z = \sum_{j \in S_i} e^{-\beta d(x_i, x_j)} \tag{6}$$

where β is a positive constant, $d(x_i, x_j)$ is a metric function, and $\delta_{ij} = 0$ for $j \notin S_j$. In this paper, we use the weighted distance according to Equation (4) as the metric function and the scaling constant β was set as the inverse of the variance of all feature variables in S_i.

These definitions can be interpreted as a Bayesian decision graph where the nodes represent α_i's, and the weighted edge connecting two nodes x_i and x_j represent δ_{ij}. Whilst others have hard classification in mind, e.g. using min-cut-based methods, we want to exploit the continuous membership scores directly and the benefits will become clear later. The task of classifying the data is therefore to compute the states of the nodes, α_i's, of the Bayesian decision graph.

To make the 2nd equality of equation (5) holds, one need to collect all data that will have an influence on a given data point. Since the given dataset cannot be infinite and it is impossible and computationally unacceptable to find all images that will have an influence on a given x_i, we cannot make the equality of (5) hold exactly. The best we can do is to make the quantities on both sides of equation (1) as close as possible. Therefore, the classification problem can be formulated as the following quadratic optimization problem:

$$\alpha = \arg\min \left\{ \sum_i \left(\alpha_i - \sum_{j \in S_i} w_{i,j} \alpha_j \right)^2 \right\} \tag{7}$$

To solve the optimization problem in (7), we use the labeled samples as constraints and solve for the unknown membership scores. For the labeled images, according to the definitions, we have $\alpha_i = y_i$, for $i = 1, 2, \ldots L$, where $y_i \in \{0, 1\}$. Because the cost function is quadratic and the constraints are linear, the optimization problem has a unique global minimum. It is straightforward that the optimization problem yields a large, spares linear system of equations, which can be solved efficiently using a number of standard solvers and we use multi-grid method [7] with linear complexity in the implementation. Therefore, the formulation of the classification problem in an optimization framework has yielded simple and efficient computational solutions.

4 Experiments

We performed experiments on a subset of the popular Corel colour photo collection. The dataset consists of 600 images divided into 6 categories: faces, buses, flowers, elephants, horses and aircrafts, each containing 100 images. Each image is represented by a CPAM histogram [10].

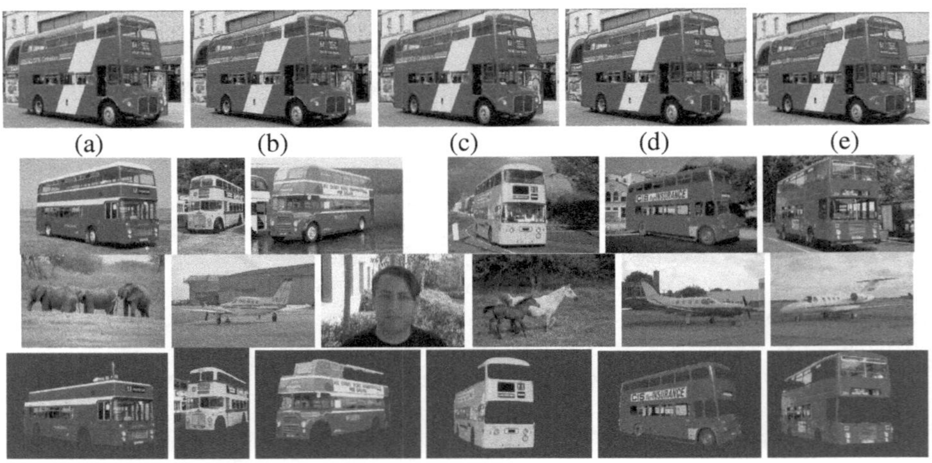

Fig. 3. Segmentation process of a "bus" image. 1st row: (a) the query image; (b) the segmentation result after the 1st round feedback; (c) an intermediate result of the 3rd round feedback; (d) final result of the 3rd round feedback, after applying the iterative algorithm described in Section 2.3; (e) result of Normalized cut [14]. 2nd row: some positive samples, the left 3 image are supplied in the 1st round and the right 3 are supplied in the 3rd round. 3rd row: some negative samples, the left 3 images are supplied in the 1st round and the right 3 are supplied in the 3rd round. 4th row: extracted relevance objects in the positive image samples.

In the experiments, we first choose one image from the dataset as query image and randomly pick 5 images from the same category as positive samples, and 5 images, one from each of the other five categories as negative samples. The query image and positive samples will be segmented and the weighting vector will be obtained using the hierarchical graphical model proposed in section 2 and then fed to the semi-supervised learning interactive image retrieval technique described in Section 3 to produce the first round results. In the subsequent iterations, each time another 5 positive and 5 negative samples are supplied. In the following, we first present relevant object/region extraction/segmentation results, and then we will show the effectiveness of relevance feature selection, and finally report interactive image retrieval results.

Figure 3 shows examples of segmenting out user interested objects from positive relevance feedback images. It is seen that when more and more samples are supplied by the user, the desired object becomes more and more significant whilst the background varies more and more. Hence the segmented figures become more and more homogeneous. In terms of human labour, our approach takes no more input than other Region-Based Image Retrieval methods that use relevance feedback [e.g. 8], where they use third-party automatic segmentation methods to segment the dataset off-line. In Figure 3, we also show the segmentation result of a state-of-the-art automatic segmentation technique [14] as comparison. These results illustrate that learning from relevance feedback can provide context-aware segmentation results that are much better than single image segmentation.

Fig. 4. Two images from the bus category. Left two: original images; Middle two: our results; Right two: results of [11].

We compare the object extraction ability of our method and the cosegmentation method of [11], results are shown in Figure 4. In general, our technique is able to extract object of interest and the accuracy increases as more iterations is used. Note that the results are produced under different conditions, where our results used 16 positive samples and 15 negative samples (see Figure 3) whilst those of [11] used only 2 images.

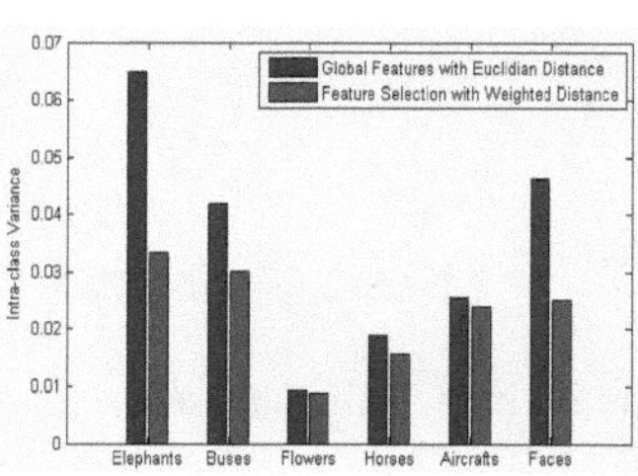

Fig. 5. Intra-class variances based on original features and weighted relevance features.

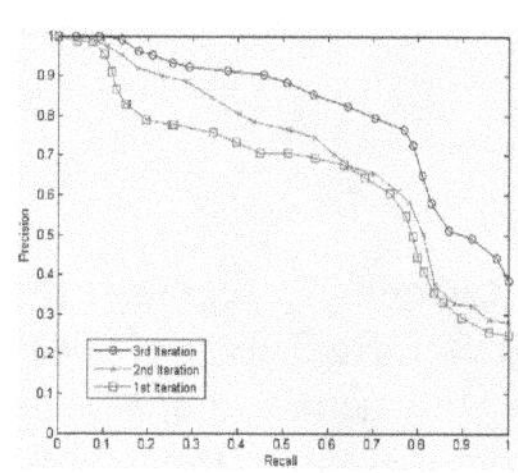

Fig. 6. Precision-Recall Curve of retrieving Bus category of images.

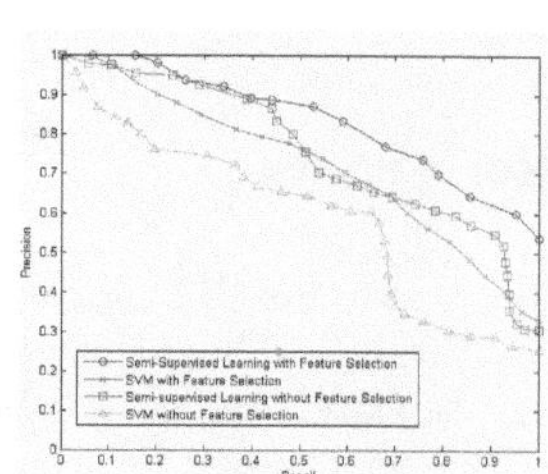

Fig. 7. Average Precision-Recall Curves for all 6 categories after 3 iterations.

As described in Section 2.5, once we have extracted relevant regions, we can weight the features of the image for relevant image retrieval. Figure 5 shows the intra-class variances using the global histograms via standard Euclidian distance and weighted histograms after 3 rounds of interactions. It can be seen that learning the feature weights from relevance feedback generally decreases the variance within each class. The improvement is especially significant for the categories that have large intra-class variances before relevant feature selection.

To show the effectiveness of the method in interactive image retrieval, we plot precision-recall curves. Figure 6 shows an example result of retrieving the Bus category of images using the method detailed in Section 3. It is seen that the retrieval performance improves significantly in 3 rounds of interaction.

SVMs have been extensively used in relevance feedback image retrieval [8, 15]. Figure 7 shows the precision recall performance of using SVM and the method of Section 3 (also see [20]) with both the original features and weighted features. It is seen that for both feedback methods, using our relevant feature selection improves the performances. These results demonstrate that our new framework for relevant region/object segmentation and relevant feature selection can effectively model the user feedback for improving interactive image retrieval.

5 Concluding Remarks

In this paper, we have presented an innovative graphical model for modelling user feedback intentions in interactive image retrieval. The novel method embeds image formation prior, statistical prior and user intention prior in the edges of a hierarchical graphical model and uses graph cut to simultaneously segment all positive feedback images into user interested and user uninterested regions. These segmented user interested regions and objects are then used for the selection of relevant image features. An important feature of the new model is that it contains visual appearance prototype nodes which form bridges linking similar objects in different images which not only makes it possible to use all positive feedback images to obtain more robust user intention priors thus improving the object segmentation results but also greatly reduces the graph and computational complexity. We have presented experimental results which have shown that the new method is effective in modeling user intentions and can improve image retrieval performance.

References

1. Borenstein, E., Ullman, S.: Learning to segment. In: Pajdla, T., Matas, J.G. (eds.) ECCV 2004. LNCS, vol. 3024, Springer, Heidelberg (2004)
2. Boykov, Y., Jolly, M.P.: Interactive graph cuts for optimal boundary & region segmentation of objects in n-d images. In: Pro. ICCV 2001 (2001)
3. Boykov, Y., Kolmogorov, V.: An experimental comparison of min-cut/max-flow algorithms for energy minimization in vision. IEEE TPAMI 26, 1124–1137 (2004)
4. Carson, C., Belongie, S., Greenspan, H., Malik, J.: Blobworld: image segmentation using expectation-maximization and its application to image querying. IEEE TPAMI 24, 1026–1038 (2002)

5. Cherkassky, B.V., Goldberg, A.V.: On implementing push-relabel method for the maximum flow problem. Algorithmica 19(4), 390–410 (1997)
6. Ford, L.R., Fulkerson, D.R.: Flows in Networks. Princeton University Press, Princeton (1962)
7. Hackbusch, W.: Multi-grid Methods and Applications. Springer, Berlin (1985)
8. Jing, F., Li, M., Zhang, H.J., Zhang, B.: Region-based relevance feedback in image retrieval. IEEE Trans. on Circuits and Systems for Video Technology 14(5), 672–681 (2004)
9. Minka, T.P., Picard, R.W.: Interactive Learning Using A Society of Models. Pattern Recognition 30(4), 565–581 (1997)
10. Qiu, G.: Indexing chromatic and achromatic patterns for content-based colour image retrieval. Pattern Recognition 35, 1675–1686 (2002)
11. Rother, C., Kolmogorov, V., Minka, T., Blake, A.: Cosegmentation of Image Pairs by Histogram Matching - Incorporating a Global Constraint into MRFs. In: Proc. CVPR 2006 (2006)
12. Rui, Y., Huang, T.S.: Optimizing Learning in Image Retrieval. In: Proc. CVPR 2000 (2000)
13. Rui, Y., Huang, T.S., Ortega, M., Mehrotra, S.: Relevance feedback: A power tool in interactive content-based image retrieval. IEEE Trans. on Circuits and Systems for Video Technology 8(5), 644–655 (1998)
14. Shi, J., Malik, J.: Normalized cuts and image segmentation. In: Proc. CVPR 1997(1997)
15. Tong, S., Chang, E.Y.: Support vector machine active learning for image retrieval. In: Proc. ACM International Multimedia Conference (2001)
16. Vasconcelos, N., Lippman, A.: Learning from user feedback in image retrieval system. In: Proc. NIPS 1999 (1999)
17. Wang, J., Li, G., Wiederhold, G.: Simplicity: Semantics-sensitive integrated matching for picture libraries. IEEE TPAMI 23, 947–963 (2001)
18. Winn, J., Jojic, N.: LOCUS: Learning Object Classes with Unsupervised Segmentation. In: Proc. ICCV 2005 (2005)
19. Wood, M.E., Campbell, N.W., Thomas, B.T.: Iterative refinement by relevance feedback in content based digital image retrieval. In: Proc. ACM International Multimedia Conference (1998)
20. Yang, M., Guan, J., Qiu, G., Lam, K-M.: Semi-supervised Learning based on Bayesian Networks and Optimization for Interactive Image Retrieval. In: Proc. BMVC 2006
21. Yu, S-X., Shi, J.: Segmentation given partial grouping Constraints. IEEE TPAMI 26(2), 173–183 (2004)
22. Zhou, X.S., Huang, T.S.: Relevance feedback in image retrieval: A comprehensive review. Multimedia Syst. 8(6), 536–544 (2003)

Graph Cuts in Content-Based Image Classification and Retrieval with Relevance Feedback

Ning Zhang and Ling Guan

Department of Electrical and Computer Enineering,
Ryerson Uiversity, Toronto, Canada
ning.zhang@ryerson.ca, lguan@ee.ryerson.ca

Abstract. Content-based image retrieval (CBIR) has suffered from the lack of linkage between low-level features and high-level semantics. Although relevance feedback (RF) CBIR provides a promising solution involving human interaction, certain query images poorly represented by low-level features still have unsatisfactory retrieval results. An innovative method has been proposed to increase the percentage of relevance of target image database by using graph cuts theory with the maximum-flow/minimum-cut algorithm and relevance feedback. As a result, the database is reformed by keeping relevant images while discarding irrelevant images. The relevance is increased and thus during following RF-CBIR process, previously poorly represented relevant images have higher probability to appear for selection. Better performance and retrieval results can thus be achieved.

Keywords: Graph Cuts, Relevance Feedback, Content-based Image Retrieval, Radial Basis Function, Maximum-flow/minimum-cut.

1 Introduction

Image retrieval has been a very active research area with text-base image retrieval well-studied and commercialized. However, text-based image retrieval suffers several limitations, such as long and inconvenient annotation and description of retrieval images, ambiguity of different wording and language barrier from different countries. On the other hand, the idea of content-based image retrieval (CBIR) idea has been raised and investigated world-wide to provide a solution to these shortages. The most significant advantage of CBIR is expressed simply by the old saying: A picture is worth a thousand words. In CBIR, images are represented by their own visual features, [1, 2] such as colour, shape, texture, and motion with which high level semantics of images can be embodied.

Although certain level of achievements have been achieved in CBIR, the gap between low level features and high level semantics is still not filled. Such bottlenecks restrict the performance of CBIR and also limit its application [2].

One of the most successful attempts in filling such semantic gap involves human interaction and guidance with retrieval system, first introduced by Y. Rui and T. S. Huang [2, 3]. Such relevance feedback content-based image retrieval (RF-CBIR) integrates human factor to guarantee the retrieval process so that it is carried on along the right track.

H.H.S. Ip et al. (Eds.): PCM 2007, LNCS 4810, pp. 30–39, 2007.

On the other hand, in the field of image segmentation, similar human involvement ideas have been implemented. Quite a few successful segmentation techniques are based on user interaction. For example, active contour (snake) segmentation requires user feedback for every step. Graph cuts require binary seeded object and background as do random walk segmentations which support multiple seeds [4].

In CBIR, images described using features similar to a query image (e.g. texture, colour, shape) are selected as retrieval results, whilst in segmentation, pixels with similar features (e.g. histogram) are grouped together as one segment. As such an analogy may be drawn between CBIR and image segmentation and represents the inspiration for this work. The motivation of this paper is to improve the RF-CBIR retrieval accuracy and shorten the searching effort, since from time to time, image features do not always successfully represent its semantic content. A given query image in such scenario thus has little chance to lead to a satisfactory retrieval result based on image contents. One typical syndrome for such a weakly represented query image is that the convergence value of retrieval precision rate is too low to bring up enough number of retrieval results. For instance, an RF-CBIR system has the best 20 retrieval images drawn from a target database. Precision rate is defined as the number of relevant images among a total of 20 retrieved images. If only 2 images are retrieved as relevant images the precision rate is merely 10% and this result does not help the retrieval purpose much in practice.

In order to solve above problem and obtain a good precision rate using RF-CBIR for a query image with less representative features, increasing the relevant image percentage in target image database is one possible solution. Ideally, relevant images are kept intact as much as possible, while as many as non-relevant images are disposed of. Consequently, relevant image percentage rate would be elevated. We propose an innovative approach by adopting graph cuts theory with the maximum-flow/minimum-cut algorithm from image segmentation technique. This method calculates the minimum cut and divides the total pool of target image database into two groups, i.e. relevance (source) group and irrelevance (sink) group, with the hope that each result group is as close as possible to the natural classifications of real relevant images and irrelevant images. Source and sink notations are brought in from graph cuts theory [4, 6]. Finally, the result "relevant"-source group is kept while "irrelevant"-sink group is discarded. The new image database, which is consists of relevant-source group only, has a better real relevant image percentage rate than the original database.

In the section 2, background information of RF-CBIR and graph cuts theory used in image segmentation are introduced. In section 3, methodology of graph cuts to the RF-CBIR is presented. Following, experiments setup, results and discussions are give in section 4. Lastly, the paper is finalized by a conclusion and expected future works in section 5.

2 Background

2.1 Relevance Feedback Content Based Image Retrieval (RF-CBIR)

In CBIR, relevance feedback is one of the best solutions to fill the gap between low level features and high level semantics in image retrieval. RF-CBIR provides a powerful tool as its interactive platform allows for users to tailor a search to their own needs and requirements. In addition, RF-CBIR also adapts to same user's different needs at different times [2, 3].

The process of RF-CBIR is achieved by certain level of human computer interaction. The decision on both relevancy and non-relevancy made by the user will be treated as feedback and affect the next retrieval iteration [5]. The iterations are terminated when retrieval precision rate is satisfying.

Relevant images are considered as positive feedback while non-relevant ones are considered as negative feedback, in which both of them are contributed to find a more representative relevant centroid in image feature space. As you can see, the key of RF-CBIR is to convert the concept of relevancy from semantics into a quantified measurement that computer could learn and apply.

2.2 Graph Cuts in Image Segmentation

The *Graph Cuts* technique formulates the segmentation energy over a binary variables labeled by users, in which only two groups of segmentations are achieved. Pixels belonging to the object of interest and those not, are separate into "object" and "background" respectively [4]. It utilizes an optimization process, maximum-flow/minimum-cut from graph theory of flow networks, which states that the maximum amount of flow equals to the capacity of a minimal cut [4, 8]. Such an optimization problem is achieved by minimizing a cost function enlightened by a solution for statistics problems, i.e. maximizing a posterior estimation of a Markov Random Field (MAP-RMF) [4, 6].

The initial and significant stage of graph cuts is to label the seed pixels for both user-interested "object" and non-important background information. A source (s) & sink (t) two-node representation has been used to indicate user verified information of image pixels relating object/background, which is denoted as *s-t graph cut*. This is defined as a hard constraint of such segmentation problems. A soft constraint on the other hand is defined as the cost function, which includes every pixel of the image. [4, 6] A good reason of using Gaussians in the cost function is that this equation emphasizes the similarities between individual and neighboring pixels, meaning the higher the cost function value, the more likelihood a pair of pixels belongs to the same group ("object" or "background"). Higher similarity is represented by closer feature space distance measurement after the Gaussian process. This can also be interpreted that the cost function penalizes discrepancy.

3 RF-CBIR with *Graph Cuts*

As we can see, user interaction has been involved in both RF-CBIR process and graph cuts technique. By combining the above approaches, selected relevant/irrelevant images are used as seeds information with max-flow/min-cut algorithm applied to an ad-hoc cost function. The target image database is classified into two groups, i.e. the "relevant"-source group and the "irrelevant"-sink group. In the following, notations of source-group and sink-group are used to indicate the result group and discarded group respectively. By disregarding the sink-group, the new database consisted of source-group has a better relevant percentage rate and performs better retrieval processes.

The methodology of this experiment is inspired by both graph cuts technique in image segmentation as in reference [4] and relevant feedback content-based image retrieval (RF-CBIR) using a network of radial basis functions (RBFs) [5]. The intention is to resize the original database by removing as many irrelevant images as possible and achieve better relevancy percentage.

The first step is the preprocessing stage of image database. This process can be performed off-line prior to any retrieval actions. In total, four types of image features, colour moment, colour histogram, shape and Gabor texture are used in image index, with a vector size of 131. Secondly, user-interaction is used to indicate seed information by choosing relevant/irrelevant images from an interface consisting of images displayed. In the third step, weighting measurement of each image of the database is computed in terms of both unitary-information with respect to source and sink seeds as terminals, as well as pair-wise boundary information with neighbourhood images. A cost function is obtained for individual images using distance measurement and consequently, a total weights matrix is achieved. Lastly, images are classified by applying the max-flow/min-cut algorithm as [6] describes. As a result, cuts are drawn and the image database is divided into two desired groups: source and sink. The result source image database is then applied by RF-CBIR process. In the following, a block diagram is given to depict such a retrieval process.

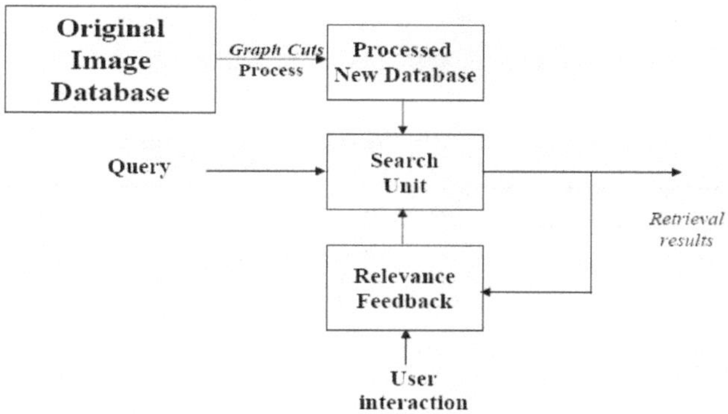

Fig. 1. Relevance feedback block diagram

Cost function plays a key role in this experiment. Two metrics for weighting calculation have been used in this work. One is Euclidian distance as equation (1), in which I is the dimension of feature space (131 for this experiment), f_q is the query feature, f_p is the feature of another image.

The other metric is radial basis functions (RBFs) as equation (2), representing a summation of mixture Gaussian type equations with f_{qi} and f_{pi} as scalar value of a single dimension in query representation and its counterpart of another image. Index i belonging to the total dimension I of the entire space.

$$d = \sqrt{\sum_{i=1}^{I} \left(f_q - f_p\right)^2} \tag{1}$$

$$m = \sum_{i=1}^{I} \exp\left(-\frac{\left(f_{q_i} - f_{p_i}\right)^2}{2\sigma^2}\right) \tag{2}$$

As we have described, the seeds information is measured using Euclidian distance. Weighting scheme, which is related to graph cuts *ad-hoc* cost functions for image segmentation is designed. Two sub-functions need to be specified for both unitary regional weights R and pair-wise boundary weights B. For calculating regional weights (R), distance to the centre (average value) of seed samples clustering is used; for the boundary weights (B), the top N closest images of metrics in feature space are used. N is a parameter chosen by user and an optimal N would be decided prior to the experiment. The total cost function is shown in equation (3). R function is represented in equation (4), which is consisted of two parts as source (S) and sink (T).

$$E(A) = R(A) + B(A) \tag{3}$$

$$R(A) = R_S(A) + R_T(A) \tag{4}$$

For the case of terminal weights, a general expression is presented, similarly as the one used in reference [4], $K = \sum_{a=1}^{A} B(A) + 1$ in which A is the total number of the images. In summary, weights are generalized as in Table 1.

Table 1. Look-up table for weights of each image inside the database

Edge	Weight Function	Condition
$\{q,n\}$	$B_{q,n}$	$\{q,n\} \in N$
	R_S	$q \notin S \hbar T$
$\{q,S\}$	K	$q \in S$
	0	$q \in T$
	R_T	$q \notin S \hbar T$
$\{q,T\}$	0	$q \in S$
	K	$q \in T$

Three *ad-hoc* weighting schemes are proposed, similarly to graph cuts *ad-hoc* cost functions for image segmentation [4]. First weighting scheme uses RBF distance for both regional (R) and boundary (B) weighting functions. Second one uses Euclidian distance for R and B weights. And third one is a hybrid of previous two schemes.

For the first weighting scheme, in which only RBFs are used, the unitary regional weights with two parts and pair-wise boundary weights are given in equation (5) - (7) respectively.

$$R_S = \frac{1}{S}\sum_{s=1}^{S}\sum_{i=1}^{I}\exp\left(-\frac{(f_{qi}-f_{si})^2}{2\sigma^2}\right) \quad (5)$$

$$R_T = \frac{1}{T}\sum_{t=1}^{T}\sum_{i=1}^{I}\exp\left(-\frac{(f_{qi}-f_{ti})^2}{2\sigma^2}\right) \quad (6)$$

$$B \propto \sum_{n=1}^{N}\sum_{i=1}^{I}\exp\left(-\frac{(f_{qi}-f_{ni})^2}{2\sigma^2}\right) \quad (7)$$

In the above, q is the indication of query image, σ is the variance value. In regional case as equation (5) and (6) showed, $s \in S$ is the source image, and $t \in T$ is the sink image. S, T are total number of source and sink seeds respectively. In calculating boundary weights in equation (7), N is the number of edges defined by users as previously mentioned, which varies from 1 to the size of the database. I is the total number of features used (131 in my experiment).

The other two candidate schemes are listed in Table 2. In the case of second weighting scheme, using Euclidian distance for both regional and boundary weights are similar with RBF case but negative sign is necessary to be suitable with max-flow/min-cut algorithm. In the third weighting scheme, the hybrid with Euclidian distance of R and RBF functions of B are listed.

Table 2. List of weighting scheme 2 and 3

Weight Fn	Scheme 2	Scheme 3
R_S	$R_S = -\frac{1}{S}\sum_{s=1}^{S}\sqrt{\sum_{i=1}^{I}(f_{qi}-f_{si})^2}$	$R_S = -\frac{1}{S}\sum_{s=1}^{S}\sqrt{\sum_{i=1}^{I}(f_{qi}-f_{si})^2}$
R_T	$R_T = -\frac{1}{T}\sum_{t=1}^{T}\sqrt{\sum_{i=1}^{I}(f_{qi}-f_{ti})^2}$	$R_T = -\frac{1}{T}\sum_{t=1}^{T}\sqrt{\sum_{i=1}^{I}(f_{qi}-f_{ti})^2}$
$B_{q,n}$	$B \propto \sum_{n=1}^{N}\sqrt{\sum_{i=1}^{I}(f_{qi}-f_{ni})^2}$	$B_{q,n} \propto \sum_{n=1}^{N}\sum_{i=1}^{I}\exp\left(-\frac{(f_{qi}-f_{ni})^2}{2\sigma^2}\right)$

4 Experiments

4.1 Experiment Setup

The experiment was carried out by applying the graph cuts algorithm to various sizes of databases with different images content and themes. Percentage of relevant images of result database was also computed and compared to the original image database. In addition, RF-CBIR process with and without graph cuts pre-processing are compared.

Since the experiment was inspired by both RF-CBIR and graph cuts techniques, two streams of previous works were adopted in conducting this experiment [5, 6], with source code of graph cuts downloaded from [7].

Images used in database design are randomly chosen from Corel image database of size 40,000 without duplications [8]. For each database used in the experiment, both the size of database and percentage of relevant images are specified as ground truth. Therefore, percentage of relevancy as well as actual number of relevant and irrelevant images is given explicitly in database names. For instance, a database named as "(old style) airplane_T1000_15%" means that an image database with a theme of (old style) airplane has total of 1000 images, in which 150 images are relevant to the theme.

To judge the relevancy, a query image is always chosen from the same group as the database and the relevancy calculation is always unique with no ambiguity. However, the query image may or may not be included in the target database.

4.2 Results

After several preliminary try-outs, weighting scheme 1 which uses RBF functions had outperformed the other two. Scheme 2 had no constructive result so far and was abandoned for this experiment. Scheme 3 had achieved some good results but extremely heavy computation. Consequent experiments would be focused on applying cost function of scheme 1. Different sizes of input databases with different relevant percentages would be tested on. Such *graph cuts* process would also be incorporated with RF-CBIR. In Figure 2, a snapshot of seeds selection interface is depicted with first two rows as source seed images and the rest as sink seeds.

Weighting scheme using RBF-based cost function provides promising result. One issue raised at this point is that what number of edge parameter N should be considered. Several example databases are listed in Table 3.

Table 3. Results of different databases

Input Database	Result			
	Best Edge Parameter N	Relevant (R)	Total Image Number (T)	New Percentage R/T (%)
Poker_T90_50%	2	44	51	86.27%
Poker_T70_50%	5	34	34	100%
Old_style_airplane_T250_20%	2	23	46	50%
Old_style_airplane_T400_75%	2	300	395	75.95%
Old_style_airplane_T500_30%	2	146	400	36.5%

As we see from Table 3, most of the cases have their best performance with optimal parameter N=2, meaning only the closest image in feature space were used to calculate boundary cost functions. It is because parameter N includes the central image itself. In the case of Poker_T70_50%, best performance obtained at N=5, but for N=2, a high percentage rate at 90.32% is also obtained with relevant image number of 28 with total of 31. Figure 3 illustrates such selection of N as relevancy percentage respect to different number of N. Different size of databases with various

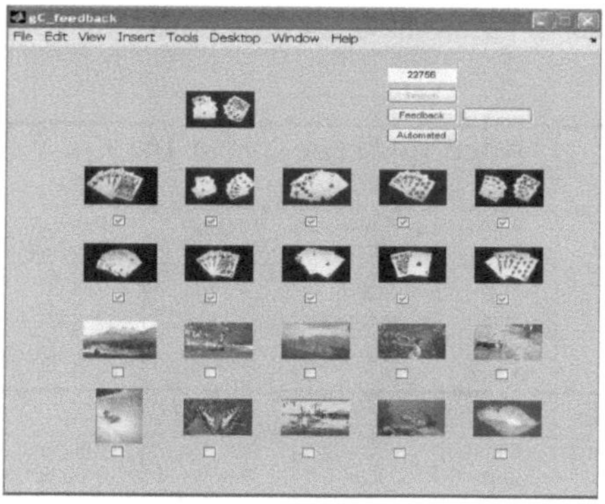

Fig. 2. An interface snapshot of seeds image selection from displayed top and bottom ten results

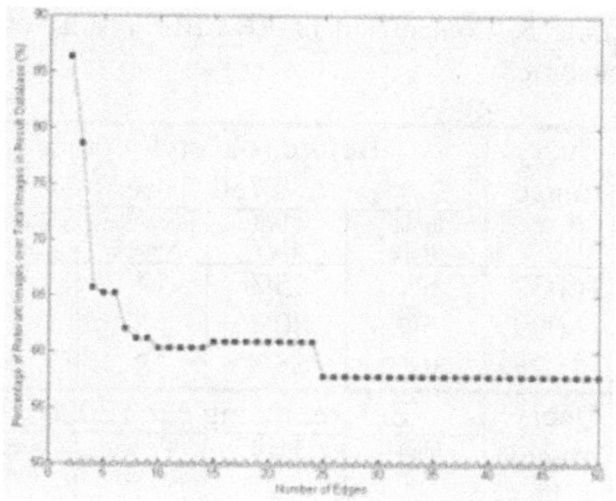

Fig. 3. Relevancy percentage value respect to different selection of edge N

relevance percentages were processed by graph cuts. As the outputs shown in Table 4, after graph cuts, number of relevant (R) and total (T) images are given and the ratio of R/T is calculated as the new percentage rates opposing to old ones as in input databases.

Table 4. Graph cuts on various size of image databases with different relevance percentage

Input Database	Outputs			
Old style airplane T=400_	Relevant (R)/ Total (T)	New Percentage R/T (%)	Seed # S (source)	Seed # T (sink)
20%	78/312	25	5	15
40%	159/332	47.89	7	13
Old style airplane T=750_	Relevant (R)/ Total (T)	New Percentage R/T (%)	Seed # S (source)	Seed # T (sink)
30%	169/425	39.76	7	13
40%	154/317	48.58	11	9
Girl T=1000 _	Relevant (R)/ Total (T)	New Percentage R/T (%)	Seed # S (source)	Seed # T (sink)
5%	36/515	6.99	16	4
10%	85/730	11.64	15	5

As in Table 5, a comparison of RF-CBIR results are given in two situations, which firstly uses the method proposed with no pre-process as [5] and the proposed method with graph cuts pre-process. Two datasets with size 750 and 2000 respectively designed with randomly chosen images from Corel database provide complete knowledge of ground truth. Three and four queries images are used for RF-CBIR process in each database respectively and precision rates, number of relevant images, iteration numbers of human interaction in retrievals are presented and compared in both cases of before and after graph cuts pre-process.

Table 5. Comparison of RF-CBIR results with original database and graph cuts processed database

Query Image ID	Before:(old style) plane T750_10%				After: (old style) plane T619_11%			
	Initial Rate	Final Rate	Iteration Number	Relevant Image #	Initial Rate	Final Rate	Iteration Number	Relevant Image #
16032	5%	55%	4	11	5%	80%	6	16
16099	5%	80%	8	16	5%	90%	9	18
21925	30%	65%	2	13	35%	75%	3	15
Query Image ID	Before: racing car T2000_10%				After: racing car T619_11%			
	Initial Rate	Final Rate	Iteration Number	Relevant Number	Initial Rate	Final Rate	Iteration Number	Relevant Number
37216	5%	70%	4	14	15%	75%	5	15
37217	15%	55%	3	11	15%	70%	4	14
37287	15%	50%	3	10	35%	55%	3	11
37232	20%	60%	3	12	30%	70%	3	14

4.3 Discussion

As the result shows, we saw that a mixture of Gaussian RBFs (scheme 1) provides best performance in terms of a weighting scheme. It is because Euclidian distance is a metric of difference while RBFs on the other hand is a metric of similarity. Due to the property of Gaussian function, the further two feature vectors are apart, the larger the cost function after applying the RBFs. Furthermore, feature difference has been more penalized with the increase of the discrepancy. Another advantage of using weighting scheme 1 is its much faster computation time as compared with the others.

By choosing the best edge parameter N for cost function, as experiment results indicated, N=2 edge parameter provides the most feasible results.

The modified graph cuts method using weight scheme 1 and edge parameter N=2 was demonstrated to be effective in actual RF-CBIR process. In the situation where the query image is difficult to retrieve due to its poor representation in low-level features, as Table 5 indicated, final convergent rate (precision) of RF-CBIR has been increased from 5% to 25%, using graph cuts modified image database. Although the relevancy percentage was not raised as much as smaller databases in Tables 3 and 4 precision rate is still improved from RF-CBIR without graph cuts pre-process. It is because that by getting seeds information, cost function in graph cuts algorithm emphasizes the non-linear RBF (similarity) relations as well as penalizes features discrepancy.

5 Conclusions and Future Works

An original approach was raised to fill the gap between semantic and low level features, based on increasing the probability of relevant image appearance. By incorporating graph cuts theory using max-flow/min-cut algorithm, such a proposal was confirmed and proved by experiments from which a single neighboring image was used as an edge parameter (N=2) in designing RBFs-based cost function. This method was applied to RF-CBIR and better retrieval results were obtained than with the traditional RF-CBIR process.

In future, such a method will be worthy of investigation by incorporating with automatic content-based image retrieval process.

Acknowledgments. Acknowledgements are given to Dr. Boykov and Dr. Kolmogorov for sharing the source code of graph cuts algorithm.

References

1. Rui, Y., Huang, T.S., Chang, S.F.: Image retrieval: current techniques, promising directions and open issues. Journal of visual communication and image representation [1047-3203] 10(4), 39 (1999)
2. Zhou, X.S., Huang, T.S.: Relevance feedback in image retrieval: A comprehensive review. Multimedia systems [0942-4962] Zhou 8(6), 536 (2003)
3. Rui, Y., et al.: Relevance Feedback: A Power Tool for Interactive Content-Based Image Retrieval. IEEE Trans. Circuits and Systems for Video Technology 8(5), 644–655 (1998)
4. Boykov, Y., Funka-Lea, G.: Graph Cuts and Efficient N-D Image Segmentation. International Journal of Computer Vision (IJCV) 70(2), 109–131 (2006)
5. Muneesawang, P., Guan, L.: An interactive approach for CBIR using a network of radial basis functions. IEEE Trans. Multimedia 6(5), 703–716 (2004)
6. Boykov, Y., Kolmogorov, V.: An Experimental Comparison of Min-Cut/Max-Flow Algorithms for Energy Minimization in Vision. IEEE Trans. Pattern Analysis and Machine Intelligence (PAMI) 26(9), 1124–1137 (2004)
7. Source code for graph cuts max-flow/min-cut algorithm. http://www.adastral.ucl.ac.uk/~Vladkolm/software.html 2004
8. Corel Gallery Magic 65000 (1999), http://www.corel.com

A Novel Active Learning Approach for SVM Based Web Image Retrieval

Jin Yuan, Xiangdong Zhou*, Hongtao Xu, Mei Wang, and Wei Wang

Department of Computing and Information Technology
Fudan University, Shanghai, China
{052021159,xdzhou,061021054,051021052,wwang1}@fudan.edu.cn

Abstract. There is a great deal of research conducted on hyperplane based query such as Support Vector Machine (SVM) in Content-based Image Retrieval(CBIR). However, the SVM-based CBIR always suffers from the problem of the imbalance of image data. Specifically, the number of negative samples (irrelevant images) is far more than that of the positive ones. To deal with this problem, we propose a new active learning approach to enhance the positive sample set in SVM-based Web image retrieval. In our method, instead of using complex parsing methods to analyze Web pages, two kinds of "lightweight" image features: the URL of the Web image and its visual features, which can be easily obtained, are applied to estimate the probability of the image being a potential positive sample. The experiments conducted on a test data set with more than 10,000 images from about 50 different Web sites demonstrate that compared with traditional methods, our approach improves the retrieval performance significantly.

1 Introduction

Statistical learning methods based on the optimal classification hyperplane, such as Support Vector Machine, are promising tools for learning complex, subjective query concepts in CBIR. It is widely understood that the major bottleneck of CBIR is the "semantic gap" between low-level visual feature representations and high-level semantic concepts of images. To reduce the gap, relevance feedback(RF) [1] was brought into CBIR to improve the retrieval performance [11,12].

Relevance feedback is a human-computer interaction process, in which users evaluate the search results. According to the evaluation, the retrieval system adjusts the classification function and returns the improved results. This process is repeated until users satisfy or abandon the search.

Traditional relevance feedback is a kind of passive learning, where the feedback samples are acquired randomly. However, randomly chosen samples often contain rare information which will increase the iterative number of relevance

* This work was partially supported by the NSF of China Grant 60403018, 973-Plan Grant 2005CB321905. Corresponding author.

H.H.S. Ip et al. (Eds.): PCM 2007, LNCS 4810, pp. 40–49, 2007.

feedback. Active learning [3,4,5] aims at actively choosing the most informative images in each feedback iteration. For example, a typical active learning method—Angle-Diversity[3], actively selects a candidate sample set which is close to the classification hyperplane as well as maintains the sample's diversity. In active learning, the performance of CBIR is suffered from the following two problems[3]: 1. *The imbalance of the positive and negative samples.* In real applications, for a certain query concept, most of the images of the database are irrelevant. Angle-diversity selects samples near hyperplane (the most uncertain) for users' feedback. However, due to the data imbalance, the probability of those samples being negative ones is higher than that as positive ones, which makes the feedback sample set containing inadequate positive samples. 2. *Visual diversity.* Due to the well-known "semantic gap", the images relevant to a certain query concept usually distribute loosely in a large scale feature space. It is often difficult to find sufficient positive sample images close to the hyperplane.

Compared to the standard image data sets, Web images are more diverse in the feature and concept space. Thus the traditional relevance feedback strategy often fails to provide sufficient positive samples. The context of Web images such as surrounding text, the Web page URLs, etc. have been exploited to improve Web images retrieval in many previous work[13,14]. However, most of the known work need to deal with the problem of "intelligently" parsing Web pages. To improve the performance of relevance feedback in Web images retrieval, we propose a new active learning approach using "lightweight" Web image features: the visual feature and image's URL, which can be obtained easily. The heuristic idea is: images with similar URLs and visual features have higher probability of similar semantics. For example, we have a positive image about concept "car" which is located in the Web set "www.acar.com.cn". Due to the "semantic gap", searching this image in the whole database will bring in a lot of negative samples. However, if we know there are some images in the result set having similar URLs with this positive sample, for instance, having the same domain name and directory path, or a similar domain name such as "www.car.com", we can "guess" such images may have similar semantic with the positive sample. Distance measure can be used to evaluate the similarity of the URLs between images. Therefore, visual features of the image sample, URL and other information can be exploited to estimate the possibility of sample as positive one. Images with the highest probability will be provided as feedback samples for the users, which compensates for the shortage of positive samples in traditional feedback strategy. In addition, in light of the returned results of SVM[2], we also propose a new ranking method. The framework of our Web image retrieval system is given in Fig.1.

2 Related Work

SVM based image retrieval and relevance feedback had been studied for decades. Chen and Huang propose one-class SVM[6] to solving the imbalance of positive and negative samples. They construct a tight hyper-sphere in the feature space to include most positive training samples. However, for some widely distributed

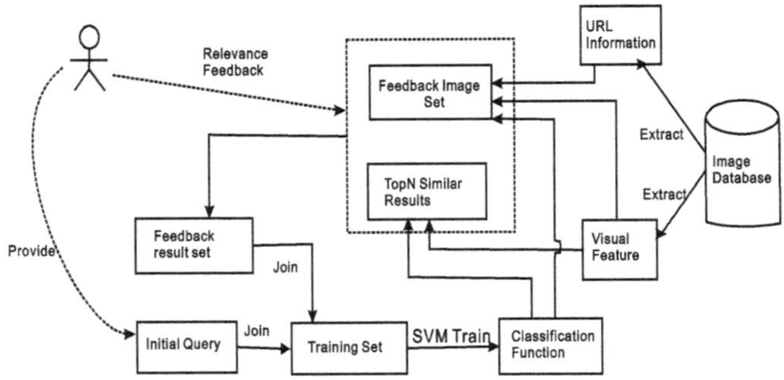

Fig. 1. The Web Image Retrieval System Framework

"concept ", how to select a proper Kernel to map those positive samples in a tight hyper-sphere is still an unsolved problem.

Gosselin and Cord [7] proposed a method to shift the hyperplane dynamically according to the ratio of the number of positive samples to negative samples learned in the last-round feedback. Due to the diversity of images in the visual space, this method results in marginal improvement especially for Web image data. Goh and Chang[9] proposed a new active learning strategy for solving the problem of scarce positive samples in feedback set.

There are a lot of work dealing with content-based Web images retrieval. Cai et al.[8] proposed a retrieval method combining visual feature, text and Web page links. It was shown that their method can improve the performance. Their Web pages preprocessing needs some "intelligent" parsing tools and suffers from parameter tuning. Quack et al.[11] proposed a Web image retrieval system *Cortina*, which combines visual feature and keywords to find relevant images. The correlations between image and keywords are estimated by data mining approach.

3 Positive Enhanced Feedback Strategy

Angle-diversity algorithm is the most commonly used active learning approach, which selects a candidate sample set close to the classification hyperplane as well as maintain the samples' diversity. It is believed that samples close to hyperplane are the most uncertain ones[3], in other words, the possibility of those samples being positive ones is near 0.5. However, compared with standard image data sets, Web image data set has more kinds of categories which means the imbalance of image data is more serious and the isolation[9] is worse. When applying angle-diversity to Web image retrieval, the improvement of retrieval performance is not significant due to lacking positive samples in feedback result set.

To deal with this problem, we propose an active learning approach based on angle-diversity by adding some potential possible positive samples to the feedback set returned to the users.

3.1 Finding High Possible Positive Sample(HPPS)

In this section, we will first give some definitions. Let $X = \{x_1, x_2, \ldots, x_n\}$ denote the set of Web images, $\mid X \mid= n$, where n is the number of instances, $Y = \{y_1, y_2, \ldots, y_n\}$ denote the set of the corresponding labels of X. y_i represents the class label of instance x_i, namely, $y_i = +1$ means x_i being a positive sample, otherwise, $y_i = -1$. $W = \{w_1, w_2, \ldots, w_m\}$ denotes the set of Web sites, $\mid W \mid= m$, where m is the number of Web sites. We assume each $x_i \in X$ is corresponded to only one element of W, and p_k denotes the number of instances in w_k. $P(x_i, +1)$ corresponds to the joint probability of x_i being positive sample. The aim of HPPS is to find the sample x_i with higher $P(x_i, +1)$ and less $P(x_i, -1)$. Let $\hat{y}_i$ denote the estimated class label of x_i, the probability $P(x_i, \hat{y}_i)$ can be given as follows:

$$\begin{aligned}
p(x_i, \hat{y}_i) &= \sum_{k=1}^{m} P(\hat{y}_i|x_i, w_k) \times P(w_k|x_i) \times P(x_i) \\
&= \sum_{k=1}^{m} P(\hat{y}_i|w_k) \times P(w_k|x_i) \times P(x_i) \\
&= \sum_{k=1}^{m} P(\hat{y}_i|w_k) \times P(x_i|w_k) \times P(w_k) \\
&= \sum_{k=1}^{m} (\sum_{j=1}^{p_k} P(\hat{y}_i|x_j) \times P(x_j|w_k)) \times P(x_i|w_k) \times P(w_k) \\
&= \sum_{k=1}^{m} (\sum_{j=1}^{p_k} P(x_i, \hat{y}_i|x_j, \hat{y}_j) \times P(x_i|x_j) \times P(\hat{y}_j|x_j) \times P(x_j|w_k)) \\
&\quad \times P(x_i|w_k) \times P(w_k)
\end{aligned} \tag{1}$$

The followings are the details of the computation of the above formula:

1. The probability $P(w_k)$ is related to two factors: the first is the ratio of the number of samples in Web site w_k to the total sample number n, the second is the confidence of w_k. We define the confidence W_k denoting the ability of the classification of the Web site w_k, and will discuss it in the next section. $P(w_k)$ can be calculated as follow:

$$P(w_k) = W_k \times \frac{\mid w_k \mid}{n} \tag{2}$$

2. For $P(x_i|x_j)$, sample x is drawn from a probability distribution, thus, for a new sample x_i, a non-parametric Gaussian Kernel density estimation is used to estimate the probability density $P(x_i|x_j)$, which is given by:

$$P(x_i|x_j) = (2\pi)^{-d/2}\sigma^{-d} exp^{-\frac{1}{2\sigma^2}\|x_i - x_j\|^2}, \tag{3}$$

where σ is the standard deviation, σ and d are the same for each x_i, so we ignore them in the following calculation.

3. We employ an approximate method to calculate the probability of x_j with estimated label $\hat{y}_j$, $P(\hat{y}_j|x_j)$. Given an training instance x_j, if $\hat{y}_j$ equals to the label y_j of x_j, $P(\hat{y}_j|x_j)=1$, otherwise $P(\hat{y}_j|x_j)=0$. In the following calculation we simply only use those instances in the training set with y_j equaling to $\hat{y}_i$ to calculate $p(x_i,\hat{y}_i)$. In this case, $P(x_j|w_k)$ corresponds to the reciprocal of the number of training data x_j with y_j equaling to $\hat{y}_i$ in w_k, which is $P(x_j|w_k)=\frac{1}{|\{x_j \mid x_j \in trainingset, x_j \in w_k, y_j=\hat{y}_i\}|}$.

4. We employ the factor α_{ij} to represent the value of $P(x_i,\hat{y}_i|x_j,\hat{y}_j)(\hat{y}_j=\hat{y}_i)$. α_{ij} can be calculated by the URLs' similarity between the instance x_i and x_j. In fact, the similarity between instances' URLs is used to measure the probability that these two instances have the same label.

5. The probability $P(x_i|w_k)$ is calculated as follows:

IF $x_i \in w_k$ $\quad P(x_i|w_k)=1/\mid w_k \mid$
ELSE $\quad P(x_i|w_k)=1/\mid n \mid$

Therefore, Eqn.1 can be rewritten as follows:

$$P(x_i,\hat{y}_i)=\sum_{k=1}^{m}(W_k\frac{\mid w_k \mid}{n}P(x_i \mid w_k)\frac{1}{p_k}\sum_{j=1,x_j\in w_k,y_j=\hat{y}_i}^{p_k}\alpha_{ij}e^{-\|x_i-x_j\|^2}) \quad (4)$$

where

$$P(x_i|w_k)=\begin{cases}\frac{1}{|w_k|}, & x_i \in w_k\\ \frac{1}{|n|}, & x_i \notin w_k\end{cases}$$

For each x_i, $f(x_i)=P(x_i,+1)-P(x_i,-1)$ is applied to estimate the probability of x_i being positive sample. Eqn.4 indicates that for a given instance x_i and a positive training data x_j, the possibility of x_i being positive sample depend on the following two factors: 1.The distance between x_i and x_j, the smaller the distance, the more possibility; 2. The URL similarity between x_i and x_j, higher similarity(leading to a large α_{ij}, higher possibility. Finally, $f(x_i)$ implies that the instance which is near positive sample set and far away from negative sample set is more possible to be a positive instance. At next section, we will discuss how to calculate α_{ij} and W_k in Eqn.4.

3.2 Web Site Weight Calculation Based on URL Similar Sample(USS)

Our method calculates W_k based on USS and users' relevance feedback. The system returns some instances which have the same Web site's URL and small distance to a positive training sample(USS), then users are prompt to label these instances. Web site weight W_k is calculated based on the feedback results. Let r_k denote the number of historic positive feedback about Web site w_k, where c_k is the number of historic negative feedback about Web site w_k. If user labels one of USS sample in w_k positive, $r_k=r_k+1$. Otherwise, $c_k=c_k+1$. Thus,

Algorithm 1. URL Similar Sample(USS)

Input: n,r_i,c_i {the number of feedback sample provided by USS,the number of historic positive feedback in w_i,the number of historic negative feedback in w_i}
Output: W_i,r_i,c_i{weight of Web site i}
Initialization: $w_i = r_i/(r_i + c_i)$
BEGIN
$x_p \longleftarrow Random(S_{positivetrainset})${randomly select a sample from positive training set}
$U \longleftarrow SomeURL(x_p, S - S_{trainset})${select all instances with same URL with x_p from non-training set}
$R \longleftarrow min(U, x_p, n)${select n instances from U with smallest distance with x_p}
for $i = 0; i < n; i++$ **do**
  if R_i is positive by users'feedback **then**
    r_i++;
  else
    c_i++
  end if
end for
$W_i = r_i/(r_i + c_i)$
return and save W_i,r_i,c_i
END

we have the formula of Web site weight, $W_k = \frac{r_k}{(r_k+c_k)}$. The process is listed in algorithm 1:

W_i reflects the confidence weight of Web site w_i, the large value of W_i implies that Web site w_i has strong classification ability. In the practical application, some kind of Web set with great classification ability should be assigned a high confidence weight. For example, the instances in Web set "www.acar.com.cn" are almost cars, the confidence weight of this Web site is high. On the contrary, images in "www.image.taobao.com" almost belong to different categories, so this kind of Web sites should be assigned lower weight.

3.3 α_{ij} Calculation

For some Web images, their URLs can be divided into multiply layers. For example, the image "http://sina/data/cartoon/1328.jpg" has 3 layers. The image file name "1328.jpg" is not considered because it is unique in the same sub-directory. If the URLs between two images are more similar, they are more likely to be related with the same concept. We propose a method to calculate α_{ij} as follows.

We assume that $\alpha_{ij} = l_a(0 < l_a < 1)$, when x_i and x_j have not common part in their m-layer URLs, where x_j is a training instance. If the URLs of x_i and x_j are the same from the root layer to the kth-layer, and from $(k+1)^{th}$-layer they are different, then we calculate α_{ij} according to Eqn.5:

$$\alpha_{ij} = l_a + (1 - l_a) * \frac{\sum_{n=0}^{k} n}{\sum_{n=0}^{m} n} \tag{5}$$

where m is the number of directory layers. We can see that when the URL of x_i's and x_j's are completely different, α_{ij} is l_a. The value l_a has important influence on the results. If l_a is too large, α_{ij} will have little effect on $f(x_i)$, thus it is not confident to find positive samples in the same URL. Otherwise, if l_a is too small, the effect on $f(x_i)$ is too great, then the samples are likely to come from the same URL. To deal with it, we propose a method based on statistics to adjust l_a dynamically. The basic idea is to record the number of images provided in HPPS. If the number of instances coming from the same URL excesses a given threshold, l_a increases; otherwise l_a decreases. The algorithm 2 is given in the followings.

Algorithm 2. l_a adjusting algorithm

Input: a,l,h {the initial l_a,the low boundary of the ratio of same URL instances number to total instance number,the high boundary of the ratio of same URL instances number to total instance number}
Output: l_a
Procedures:
maxurlnum(S_{HPPS}){the maximal instance number coming from same URL provided by HPPS in a query}
total(S_{HPPS}){the total number provided by HPPS in a query}
BEGIN
if l_a not exist **then**
  l_a=a
end if
if maxurlnum(S_{HPPS}) $> total(S_{HPPS})$*h **then**
  $l_a = 1 - (1 - (\frac{maxurlnum(S_{HPPS})}{total(S_{HPPS})} - \frac{l+h}{2})) * (1 - l_a)$
end if
if maxurlnum(S_{HPPS}) $< total(S_{HPPS})$*l **then**
  $l_a = (1 - (\frac{l+h}{2} - \frac{maxurlnum(S_{HPPS})}{total(S_{HPPS})})) * l_a$
end if
return l_a
END

4 The New Ranking Method for SVM

According to the theory of SVM, the higher the value returned by SVM classification function, the more possibility the instance is positive. However, in the content-based Web image retrieval, the performance by ranking the score from high to low is not very significative. One reason is that the positive and negative samples are not sufficient in the previous rounds of feedback, so the classification hyperplane is not good enough to describe the characteristics of such "concept". In this case, many negative samples will obtain high SVM scores which would exclude the positive samples from the result set. Second, in content-based image retrieval, an image often contains hundreds of dimensional features, but the user can not label hundreds of instances, so the number of training data is far less than the dimension number. Thus the number of non-support vector in the training result is less than that of support vector, which is especially true for positive support vector due to the imbalance of image data. In our experiments, we found that the number of positive support vector is far more than that of positive non-support vector, which means that it is more reasonable to obtain positive samples in the local area of the positive support vector.

According to the above discussion, this paper presents a re-ranking method for the results returned by SVM. The details are given as follows:

First, we choose the samples whose SVM score value $f(x)$ is between [1-β,1+β]($\beta > 0$) and rank them according to $| f(x) - 1 |$ in ascending order. These samples have higher possibility to be positive support vector. Second, we choose samples with $f(x) > 1 + \beta$, and rank them according to $f(x)$ in increasing order. Finally, we select the sample with $f(x) < 1 - \beta$, and sort them according to $f(x)$ in descending order. In the experiments, we set $\beta = 0.01$.

5 Experimental Results

Our experiment data set is obtained from 57 Web sites. It contains more than 11,000 images. Each image is characterized as a 528-dimension feature vector based on the color and texture features according to MPEG7. We select 23 categories as initial query categories. Because the instances are labeled manually, which is label-intensive, only 47 image queries are provided. Each initial query contains two instance, one positive and one negative. The positive instance is obtained from Google query results which is not contained in image database, while the negative one is selected by the system randomly. Six rounds feedback for each query is performed and 100 images will be returned by the system at each round.

Three experiments are conducted: the first experiment is to compare our feedback method with the traditional method(NFM) and the Angle-diversity. For the traditional method, in each feedback session, five positive images and five negative images on the top100 results are selected and returned to the retrieval system. If the number of positive images is less than 5, we increase the number of negative images until the total feedback number becomes 10. Our method is based on Angle-Diversity and HPPS+USS feedback model. The initial value of l_a is set to 0.6. l and h is set to 0.4, 0.6 respectively. The top 90 result images and 10 images obtained from Angle-Diversity+HPPS+USS are provided for users' feedback, where Angle-Diversity will provide three images, HPPS provides five, and USS provides two, respectively. Finally, five negative and five positive images are selected and return to retrieval system. In the second experiment, we compare the performance of Angle-Diversity+HPPS+USS and NFM in two different SVM

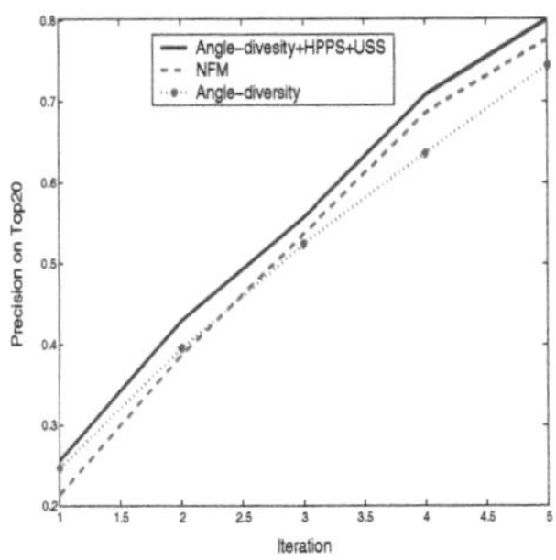

Fig. 2. Precision of three feedback strategies Top20

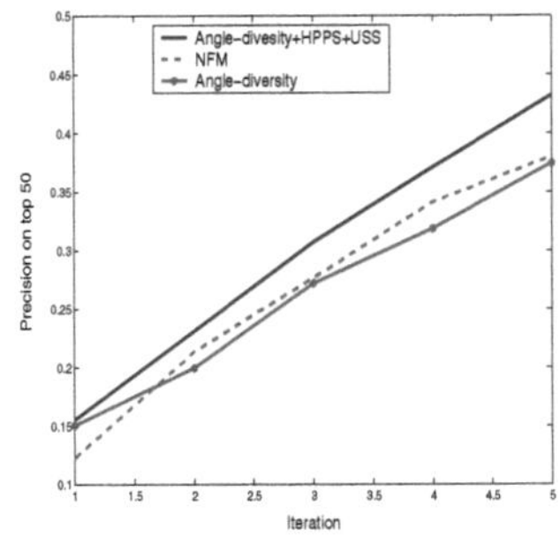

Fig. 3. Precision of three feedback strategies on Top50

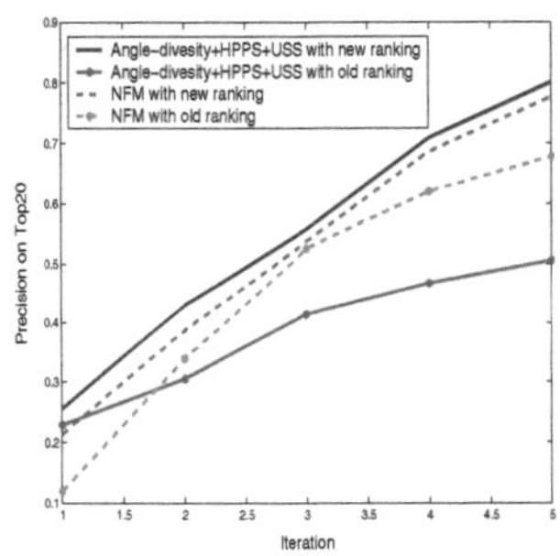

Fig. 4. Precision of Angle-diversity+HPPS+USS and NFM with different ranking methods on Top20

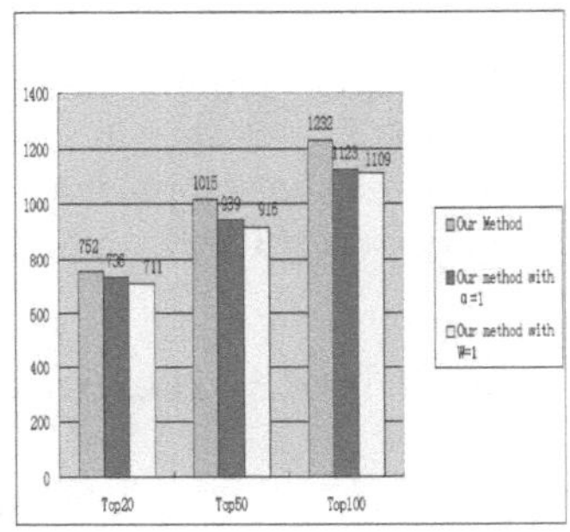

Fig. 5. The Comparison on Our Feedback Strategy with Parameters α and W

ranking methods, feedback methods are the same as the previous experiment. The third experiment evaluates the contributions of α and w to the retrieval performance based on the relevance feedback of Angle-diveristy+HPPS+USS. We compare the retrieval performance of using parameter α, W and setting these parameters as constants, $\alpha = 1$ or $W = 1$. In each of the three experiments, 47 images as provided as initial queries, 6 rounds of relevance feedback are performed. The experimental results are shown in the following figures.

From Fig.2, Fig.3, we can observe that compared with NFM and angle-diversity, our new feedback method with new SVM ranking approach can improve the precision in both top 20 and top 50 search results.

Fig.4 shows that the new ranking method in both of our new feedback method and the NFM can improve the retrieval performance significantly compared with the theory SVM ranking method.

Fig.5 shows that when we set the parameter α and W being constant, the retrieval precision is decreased, which proves that the introducing of the parameter α and W can improve the retrieval performance.

6 Conclusion

This paper presents a new active learning method and a new ranking approach for SVM based image retrieval to deal with the imbalance problem of the Web image retrieval. The experimental results show that the proposed methods improve the image retrieval performance significantly compared with the traditional methods. In the future work, the theory of our new ranking approach for SVM based Web image retrieval will be studied further.

References

1. Rui, Y., Huang, T., Ortega, M., Mehrotra, S.: Relevance feedback:A power tool in interactive content-based image retrieval. IEEE Tran. on Circuits and Systems for Video Technology 8(5) (1998)
2. Burges, C.: A Tutorial On Support Vector Machines For Pattern Recognition. Data mining and Knowledge Discovery (1998)
3. Chang, E.Y., Lai, W.-C.: Active Learning and its Scalability for Image Retrieval. In: IEEE ICME (2004)
4. Brinker, K.: Incorporating diversity in active learning with support vector machines. In: ICML (2003)
5. Tong, S., Chang, E.: Support vector machine active learning for image retrieval. In: ACM MM 2001 (2001)
6. Chen, Y., Zhou, X., Huang, T.: One-class SVM For Learning In Image Retrieval. In: IEEE ICIP 2001, Thessaloniki, Greece (2001)
7. Gosselin, P.H., Cord, M.: Active Learning Techniques for User Interactive Systems: Application to Image Retrieval, Machine Learning Techniques for Processing Multimedia Content, Bonn, Germany (2005)
8. Cai, D., Xiaofei,: Hierarchical Clustering of WWW Image Search Results Using Visual, Textual and Link Information. In: ACM MM 2004 (2004)
9. Goh, K.S., Chang, E., Lai, W.C.: Multimodal Concept-Dependeng Active Learning for Image Retrieval. In: ACM MM 2004 (2004)
10. Quack, T., Monich, U., Thiele, L., Manjunath, B.S.: Cortina: A System for Large-scale, Content-based Web Image Retrieval. In: ACM MM 2004 (2004)
11. Jing, F., Li, M., Zhang, H.J., Zhang, B.: Support Vector Machines for Region-Based Image Retrieval. In: IEEE ICME (2003)
12. Huang, T.S., Zhou, X.S.: Image retrieval by relevance feedback:from heuristic weight adjustment to optimal learning methods. In: IEEE ICIP (2001)
13. He, X., Ma, W.Y., Zhang, H.-J.: ImageSeer:Clustering and Searching WWW Images Using Link and Page Layout Analysis, Micsoft Technical Report (2004)
14. Hua, Z., Wang, X.J., Liu, Q.: Semantic knowledge Extraction and Annotation for Web Images. In: ACM MM 2005 (2005)

An End-to-End Application System of AVS: AVS-IPTV in China

Wen Gao[1], Siwei Ma[2], and Cliff Reader[2]

[1] Institute of Digital Media, Peking University, Beijing, China,
[2] Institute of Computing Technology, Chinese Academy of Sciences, Beijing, China
wgao@jdl.ac.cn, swma@jdl.ac.cn, cliff@reader.com

Abstract. The AVS video coding standard is established by China. However it is not limited to be a national standard but an open standard. In September 2006, AVS was adopted as a candidate for IPTV standards by the ITU. AVS is becoming more and more well known by the world. Many related products and systems have been released in the past years. This paper will introduce an end-to-end application system of AVS in China—AVS-IPTV. The AVS-IPTV system is built by CNC (China Netcom Group), which is a leading broadband communications and fixed-line telecommunications operator in China. The AVS-IPTV system proves AVS can meet the application requirements well.

Keywords: AVS, IPTV, H.264.

1 Introduction

The AVS video coding standard is a standard established by the China Audio Video Coding Standard (AVS) Working Group. Although it is established by a national working group of China instead of an international standard organization, e.g. MPEG, VCEG, it is not limited to be a national standard but is an open international standard. In September 2006, AVS was adopted as a candidate for IPTV standards by the ITU. Compared with other state-of-the-art video coding standards, AVS achieves a good trade-off solution between coding complexity and coding efficiency. The testing results show that AVS can achieve similar performance with H.264 with much lower complexity. Now AVS becomes more and more well known by the world. Many related products and systems have been released in the past few years. This paper will introduce an end-to-end application system of AVS in China—AVS-IPTV. The AVS-IPTV system is built by CNC (China Netcom Group), which is a leading broadband communications and fixed-line telecommunications operator in China. The AVS-IPTV system proves that AVS can meet the application requirements well.

The rest of this paper is organized as follows: section 2 gives an overview and feasibility analysis of the AVS standard; section 3 describes the end-to-end system—AVS-IPTV built by CNC and gives some testing results of the AVS-IPTV system; section 4 concludes the paper.

H.H.S. Ip et al. (Eds.): PCM 2007, LNCS 4810, pp. 50–57, 2007.

2 AVS Video Coding Standard

As with MPEG standards, the AVS standard is also composed of several parts, such as system, video, and audio plus conformance testing, software etc. For video, the AVS video coding standard includes two parts. One part is Part 2, called AVS1-P2, which is targeted to high resolution, high bit rate coding applications, such as broadcasting; the other is Part 7, called AVS1-P7, which is for low resolution, low bit rate coding applications, such as streaming, and wireless multimedia communication. So far, AVS1-P2 has been released as a national standard, and AVS1-P7 is still under revision. As shown in Figure 1, the AVS video encoder has the same architecture as H.264. In the coding process, each input macroblock is predicted with intra prediction or inter prediction. After prediction, the predicted residual is transformed and quantized. Then the quantized coefficients are coded with an entropy coder. At the

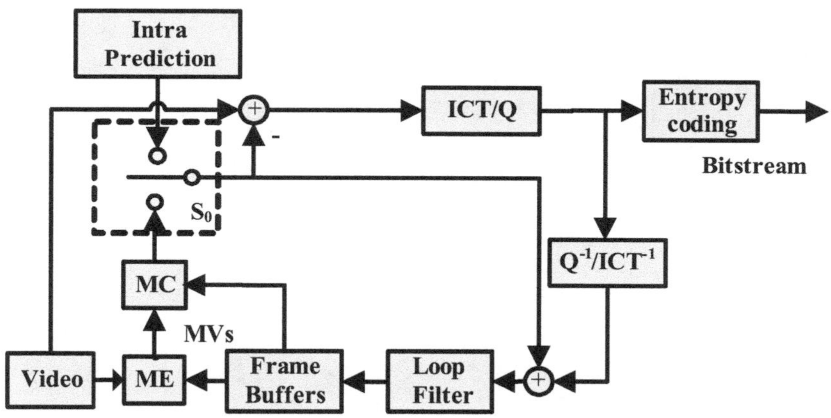

Fig. 1. The block diagram of AVS video encoder

Table 1. Test conditions for comparison between AVS1-P2 and H.264/AVC main Profile

Coding Tools	H.264 Main Profile	AVS1-P2 Jizhun Profile
Intra prediction	Intra 16x16 (4 modes), Intra 4x4 modes (9 modes)	Intra8x8 modes (5 modes)
Multi-reference frames	2 reference frames (3 reference frames for B frame)	2 reference frames
Variable block-size MC	16x16-4x4	16x16-8x8
Entropy coding	CABAC	VLC
RDO	On	On
Loop filter	On	On
Interlace Coding	MBAFF	PAFF
Hierarchical B frames	Off	None

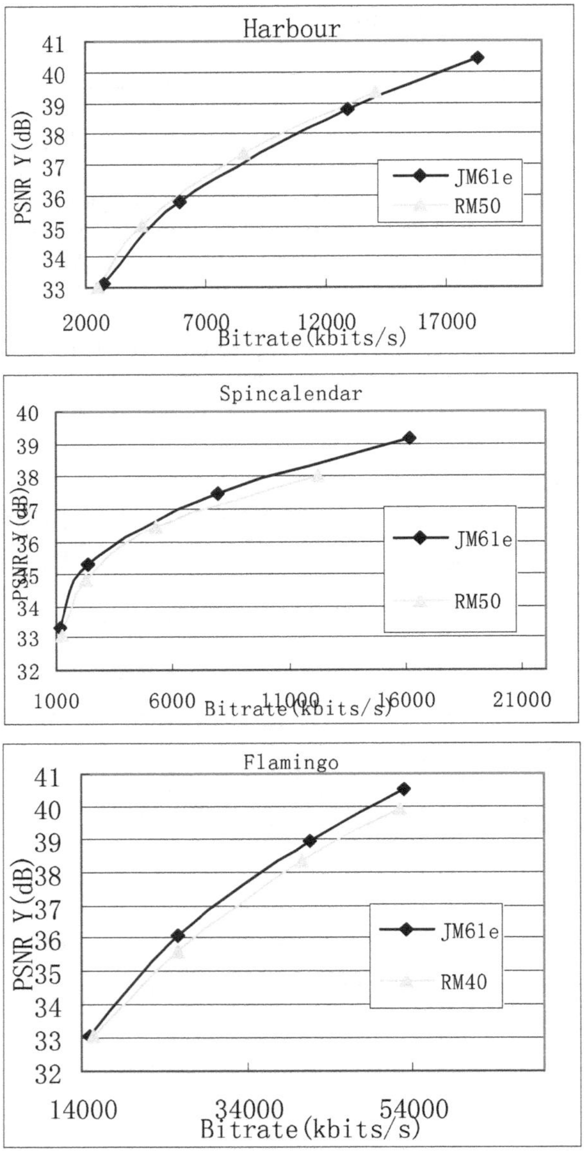

Fig. 2. Experimental results for comparison between H.264/AVC and AVS1-P2 Baseline Profile

same time, the quantized coefficients are processed with inverse quantization and inverse transform to produce reconstructed prediction error, and the reconstructed prediction error and prediction sample are added together to get the reconstructed picture. The reconstructed picture is filtered and sent to the frame buffer.

Although AVS has the same framework as H.264, the complexity of AVS is reduced compared with H.264. So far, several optimized AVS1-P2 software decoders and decoder chips have been released [1][2][3]. In the software and hardware implementation, the coarse complexity estimation for AVS1-P2 is that H.264 main profile encoder/decoder is about 1.5 times more complex than AVS1-P2. The complexity reduction for AVS mainly comes from inter prediction, interpolation, loop-filter and entropy coding.

According to the statistical data in [4][5], the two most complex operations in a decoder are interpolation and loop filtering. For interpolation in AVS1-P2, the spatial complexity and computation complexity comparison with H.264 is analyzed in [6]. Memory bandwidth is reduced nearly 11%, which is very important for high definition coding. For loopfitlering, the most important factor is boundary strength computation and the number of edges to be filtered. In AVS1-P2, the number of edges to be filtered is reduced significantly, as the filter is 8x8 block based while H.264 is 4x4 block based. Except for interpolation and loopfiltering, intra prediction and entropy coding complexity is also reduced significantly in AVS1-P2. For intra prediction, the number of prediction modes is reduced. For entropy coding, 2D VLC coding in AVS is much simpler than CABAC, especially for hardware design. Moreover, the inter prediction complexity of AVS is also reduced significantly. The block size smaller than 8x8 block is not used in AVS.

In AVS1-P2, only one profile is defined now, named Jizhun profile, and an enhancement profile (X-Profile) of AVS1-P2 is still in development. There are five levels in Jizhun profile. Each level specifies upper limits for the picture size, the maximal video bit-rate, the BBV buffer size etc.

The performance of AVS1-P2 and H.264 is tested. The JM6.1e and RM5.0 reference software developed by the standards committees is used as the test platform for H.264, and AVS respectively. Table 1 shows the test conditions for the performance comparison of AVS1-P2 Jizhun Profile and H.264 Main Profile. From the curves in Figure 2, it can be seen that the AVS1-P2 Jizhun Profile shows comparable performance with H.264, but the complexity of AVS is much lower than H.264.

3 An End-to-End Application System: AVS-IPTV

IPTV is a very promising application, which can provide an integration of multimedia services such as television, video, audio, text, graphics, data etc. delivered over IP based networks. From July 2006, an AVS-IPTV group has been founded in CNC to push AVS applications in IPTV. Now CNC has built up an end-to-end system, including an AVS encoder, transport system and set-top box receiver. In the system, the encoder is provided by NSCC. The transport system providers include ZTE, Huawei, Bell, UT and PCCW. The set-top box providers include Chaoge, ZTE, Bell, Huawei, UT and Changhong.

Before building up the application network, the image quality of H.264 and AVS were tested by the AVS-IPTV group. The testing environment is shown in Figure 3. PQR (Picture Quality Rating) is used to measure the performance. The testing results from the AVS-IPTV laboratory of CNC's Research Institute show that the Huawei

AVS set-top box achieves better performance than the Huawei H.264 set-top box. The PQR of H.264 AVS set-top box is 17.17 and that of H.264 set-top box is 18.8. Detail testing results are listed in Table 1 and Table 2. In the RTNet Lab of the Telecommunication Research Institute of Department of Information, both Huawei's set-top box and ZTE's set-top box were tested. The testing results also show that both

Table 2. AVS set-top box testing results under 3 kinds of bitrate

Item	1M	1.5M	2M
Mnimum	13.10	12.79	12.59
Maximum	22.21	22.23	22.21
Average	17.32	17.14	17.04
All average	17.17		

Table 3. H.264 set-top box testing results under 3 kinds of bitrate

Item	1M	1.5M	2M
Minimum	15.24	14.59	14.43
Maximum	23.28	22.91	22.89
Average	19.18	18.67	18.55
Total average	18.80		

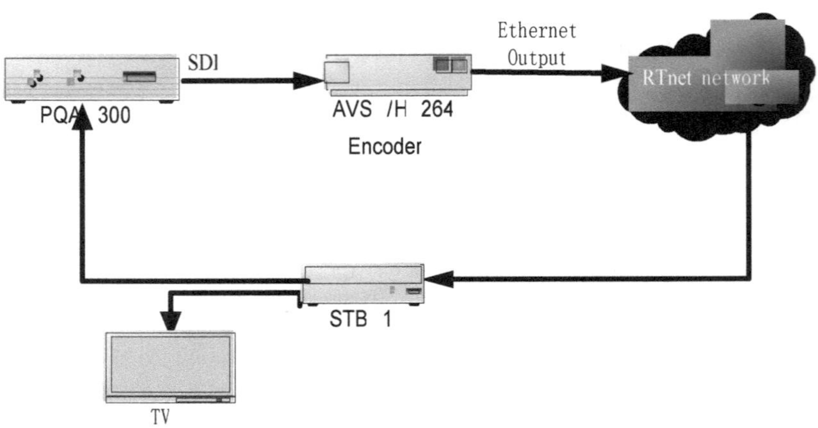

Fig. 3. AVS/H.264 image quality testing environment

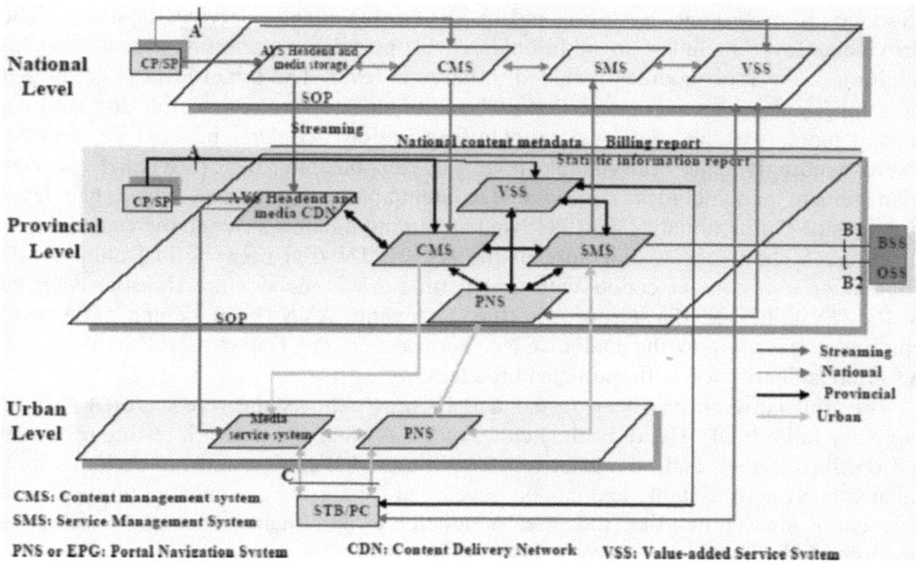

Fig. 4. Three-level AVS-IPTV system

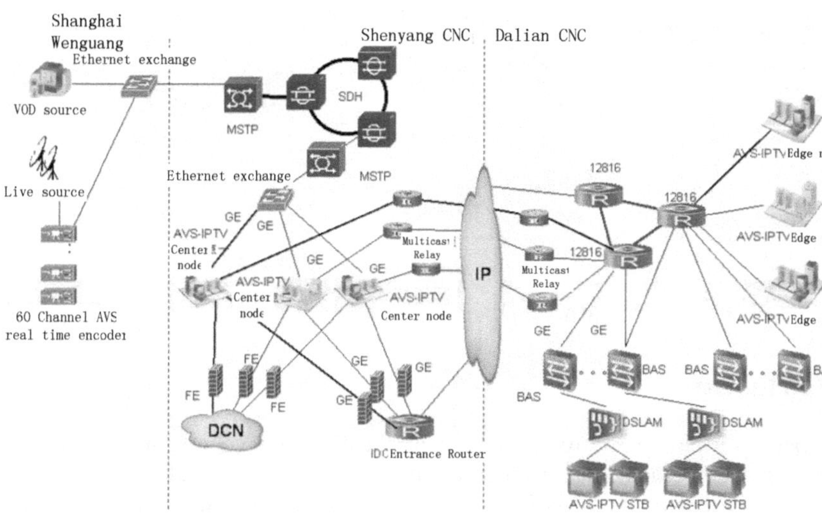

Fig. 5. AVS-IPTV Trial network architecture in Dalian

the Huawei AVS set-top box and the ZTE AVS set-tops have better image quality than H.264 set-top boxes.

Based on the CNC business network, a three-level AVS-IPTV system has been constructed. As shown in Figure 4, the national level is composed of four modules: AVS Headend and media storage, CMS (Content Management System), SMS

(Service Management System) and VSS (Value-added Service System). The provincial level includes an additional service/portal navigation system (PNS), in addition to the four modules included in national level. The urban level is composed of a media service system and PNS. The national level is responsible for national management, which is the content/application center in IPTV service. Correspondingly, the provincial level is responsible for provincial service management and includes a provincial content/application center. The urban level provides EPG functionality with PNS and streaming media service to the customers.

Figure 5 shows the architecture of the AVS-IPTV trial network in Dalian. VOD content or live content coded with a real time AVS encoder are transported from SMG (Shanghai Media Group) to the Shenyang AVS-IPTV center node with continued transport to the Dalian CNC network. In the Dalian CNC network, the program is distributed with multicast broadcasting.

The trial network has been tested and Figure 6 shows the Average MDI (Media Delivery Index): DF (Delay Factor) curve of the AVS-IPTV network testing results at a 1.65Mbps bitrate, and no packet was lost in the 24 hours monitoring period, which means the system is stable and can be developed for further commercial applications. The curve also shows that the jitter parameter is less than 1 second for all three vendors (A, B, C) tested system

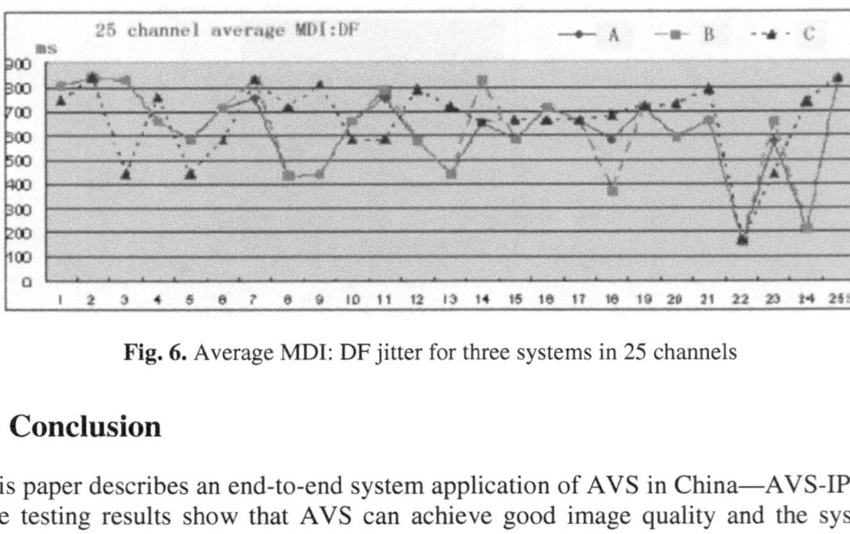

Fig. 6. Average MDI: DF jitter for three systems in 25 channels

4 Conclusion

This paper describes an end-to-end system application of AVS in China—AVS-IPTV. The testing results show that AVS can achieve good image quality and the system status is also robust. The AVS-IPTV system proves AVS can meet the application requirements well.

References

1. Sheng, B., Gao, W., Xie, D., Wu, D.: An Efficient VLSI Architecture of VLD for AVS HDTV Decoder. IEEE Transactions on Consumer Electronics 52(2), 696–701 (2006)
2. Sheng, B., Gao, W., Xie, D.: Algorithmic and Architectural Co-design for Integer Motion Estimation of AVS. IEEE Transactions on Consumer Electronics 52(3), 1092–1098 (2006)

3. Zheng, J.-H., Deng, L., Zhang, P., Xie, D.: An Efficient VLSI Architecture for Motion Compensation of AVS HDTV Decoder. Journal of Computer Science & Technology 21(3), 370–377 (2006)
4. Horowitz, M., Joch, A., Kossentini, F., Hallapuro, A.: H.264/AVC Baseline Profile Decoder Complexity Analysis. IEEE Transactions on Circuits and Systems for Video Technology 13(7), 704–716 (2003)
5. Lappalainen, V., Hallapuro, A., Hämäläinen, T.D.: Complexity of Optimized H.26L Video Decoder Implementation. IEEE Transactions on Circuits and Systems for Video Technology 13(7), 717–725 (2003)
6. Wang, R., Huang, C., Li, J., Shen, Y.: Sub-pixel Motion Compensation Interpolation Filter in AVS. In: ICME 2004. The 2004 IEEE International Conference on Multimedia and Expo, Taibei, Taiwan (June 27-30, 2004)

An AVS Based IPTV System Network Trial*

Zhifeng Jiang, Wen Gao, and Hongqi Liu

China Netcom Group Labs and Broadband Service Application National Engineering Labs
No.21, Financial Street, Xicheng District, Beijing, PRC 100032
{jiangzhifeng, gaowen, liuhongqi}@cnc-labs.com

Abstract. This paper unveils the solution of an AVS1-P2 based IPTV (AVS-IPTV) system network trial, which is architected with the common three levels such as national, provincial and urban level, and each system function of each level is described. In order to verify the solution, the AVS-IPTV testing and verification environment has been setup in the China Netcom Group labs, which promoted STB (Set-top box) to support AVS. An AVS-IPTV system network commercial trial has been successfully deployed to test and verify the performance of the AVS-IPTV system function, EPG (Electronic Program Guide), AVS streaming service, and the quality of experience. The trial makes AVS standard and AVS-IPTV system commercially applicable in the real world.

Keywords: AVS standard, AVS-IPTV, network trial.

1 Introduction

With the continuous broadband network technology development, the broadband application service such as IPTV has been paid extensive attention in industry chain from every aspect, in which the telecom operators, various service providers and content providers hope to gain some new revenue from it. In ITU-T Focus Group IPTV study, IPTV is defined as multimedia services such as television /video /audio /text/ graphics/ data delivered over IP based networks managed to provide the required level of QoS/QoE, security, interactivity and reliability. Sometimes IPTV is also called triple-play or multi-play.

IPTV is a prospective and novel potential service to customers. The video codec is one of the keys for IPTV's future success. Currently, MPEG-2 Video, MPEG-4 Visual and H.264, etc. have been adopted in some IPTV systems worldwide. In comparison with those video codecs, AVS1-P2 (GB/T20090.2-2006) is among a handful of domestic standards that China is promoting in order to lessen its reliance on foreign intellectual property, with low patent fee and implementation complexity, which won the booster of China Netcom for its commercial verification and industrial development.

* This work was supported by National Key Technology R&D Program under contract No. 2006BAH02A10.

H.H.S. Ip et al. (Eds.): PCM 2007, LNCS 4810, pp. 58–64, 2007.

In this paper, we first present a complete system design solution for lab testing and commercial trial. Through the test and the particular trial, the technology and quality of experience results about the AVS-IPTV system have been investigated. Finally the conclusion about AVS-IPTV system trial was given.

2 System Solution Design

Currently many standard organizations such as ITU-T and ATIS are actively working on high level IPTV architecture and requirements standardization [1, 2, 3]. In ITU-T, IPTV architecture and requirements obtain lots of benefits from NGN (Next generation network) study [4]. However, IPTV standards haven't been stable until now, and most of them are in high level from logical and functional meaning, which allows people to implement them by their reasonable reality. Under this situation, we designed and deployed the AVS-IPTV system solution in terms of implementation and trial purpose.

Based on the current China telecom operators' network situation and their provincial and urban network conditions, usually IPTV system may adopt two-level architectures such as national and provincial center platform, also it can take three-level architectures with another new urban center level platform added. How to choose and build the system depends on the requirements. One essential requirement in our design is to meet the current management system for ease service development. Each province can be divided into several areas, and each area may include one or several cities in the IPTV system deployment. In the AVS-IPTV system solution design, China Netcom adopts the three-level architecture with national center platform, provincial center platform and urban level platform, as shown in Figure 1. Note that the urban level platform hasn't been equipped with service management system.

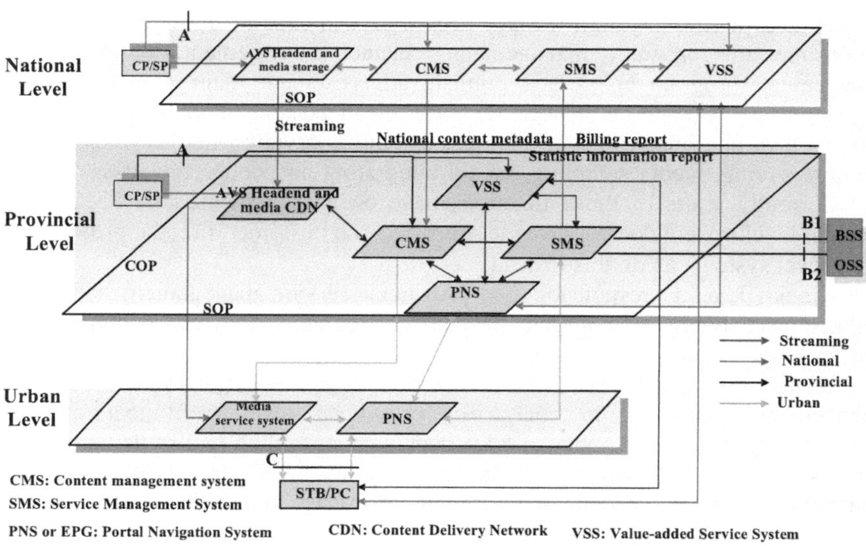

Fig. 1. AVS-IPTV system trial solution

The Content Operation Platform (COP) and the Service Operation Platform (SOP) are two key parts in a complete AVS-IPTV platform system. COP usually consists of content monitoring and control, coding/decoding, content management, and content security functional entities. In the design, AVS headend, media storage and content management system (CMS), etc. play the COP roles. However, for the current China strict media management policy, telecom operator can not handle many COP issues without media owner support such as SMG (Shanghai Media Group) which is in charge of content supply and management. Thus, our design focuses on the SOP with telecom operator key features. The conventional SOP consists of service management system (SMS), service/portal navigation system (PNS), value-added service system (VSS), media delivery system or content delivery network (CDN) functional entities, etc. SMS consists of user management, product management, billing management, system management, statistic analysis, portal management and service provider/ content provider (SP/CP) management functions, etc. PNS consists of service navigation server and WEB server. VSS contains SP gateway and service capability system. CDN system includes media scheduling control, delivery, streaming service and storage, etc. In order to provide service, the Operational Support Systems (OSS) and Business Support systems (BSS) are also necessary. OSS contains an integrated customer management system called 97 system in China telecom operators, prepaid, integrated billing, customer service and access authentication system functions, etc. BSS mainly includes IPTV terminal maintenance and network management system.

In order to understand the solution well, the three-level architecture is described separately in functions.

National level is responsible for national management and content/application center in IPTV service. Its platform contains AVS headend and content broadcast and monitoring system, content management system, service management system and value-added service system. The service management system is in charge of national level fulfillment of SP/CP management, service management, settlement, statistic analysis and platform system management, etc. The content management system is responsible for program management, channel management, program source management, program check and publish, advertisement management, scheduling management and planning arrangement, etc. Headend and monitoring system takes charge of various media source storage, content encryption and key management, media receiving, media sampling, media integrating and code converting functions, etc.. Currently, parts of those functions have been implemented by SMG mainly. National level system doesn't provide service to end customer directly, provincial and urban level system can do this instead.

Provincial level is responsible for provincial service management and content/ application center in the solution. Its platform includes AVS headend and content broadcast and monitoring system, content management system, service management system and value-added service system, service/portal navigation system. The service management system is in charge of provincial level fulfillment of SP/CP management, user management, service management, billing and settlement, statistic analysis, STB management and the platform system management, etc. The content management system, headend, and content broadcast monitoring system have the similar function with national level system. The portal navigation system provides a uniform IPTV service interactive communication portal to STB users, for handling various users' requests and indicating results to users.

Urban level mainly focuses on customers and provides EPG function with PNS and streaming media service to them. The PNS provides an IPTV service interactive communication portal to the local STB users, for handling various users' requests and indicating results to local users. The streaming media service system is responsible for storing various media content for VOD/Broadcast/TSTV(Time-shift TV)/PVR (Personal video recorder) service, etc.

3 AVS-IPTV Commercial Trial

3.1 AVS-IPTV Lab Verification

In order to verify the system solution depicted in Figure 1, a complete AVS-IPTV system testing network and platform environment has been setup in the national engineering labs of CNC group. The environment simulates all level real situation of the system solution, and different AVS-IPTV service system has been placed in different carrier network level. National level platform includes satellite systems, AVS real-time coding system and national service operation platform. Provincial level platform includes AVS real-time coding system and provincial service operation platform. Urban level includes user access authentication system and access equipments such as DSL and PON; and the user access adopts the fixed IP and PPPoE authentication method. User terminals are AVS-IPTV STB and TV. The general platform tests and enhances four independent vendors' IPTV system successfully in labs environment, which makes the first successful step to commercial system trial.

3.2 AVS-IPTV Commercial Trial System

In the commercial trial, the national level role has been played in SMG with 60 channel AVS coding content and storage, etc., which supports real-time broadcast service from satellite. The VoD server provides VOD service. All of the service systems connects to Ethernet switch and have been sent to Shenyang of CNC by optical transport network such as MSTP (Multiple service transport platform) and SDH equipments. The provincial and urban levels are keys to our system solution described in greater detail later.

The provincial level node has been put in Shenyang of CNC, and the urban level node has been settled in Dalian of CNC. The design and construction aim is to set up a complete end-to-end AVS-IPTV service commercial trial platform, which includes streaming visual and listening, video communication and various value-added services. This may bring great experience to the successful AVS-IPTV service operation. In this trial, we used three independent IPTV systems come from Alcatel Shanghai Bell, Huawei and ZTE, respectively, and the real network system is as depicted in Figure 2.

Some features of AVS-IPTV system trial in Shenyang of CNC node are below:

1) There are three independent systems in this node, which are running independently.

2) The AVS-IPTV central node (1, 2, 3) is only responsible for account numbering, user management, CP/SP management, billing, content injection, and content delivery to edge node, etc., which doesn't manage users directly.
3) It outputs bill data to BOSS (Business Operation Supporting System).
4) VOD program is from SMG by transport, which enters into IPTV system platform center node in Shenyang of CNC. Three independent AVS-IPTV system platform center nodes connect to two IDC entrance routers through firewall by using GE (Gigabit Ethernet port or equipment), respectively. It then enters into Dalian metro network by provincial IP network.
5) Broadcast program originates from Shanghai SMG by transport line, which enters into Shenyang of CNC and has been multicast relayed to Dalian metro network of CNC. The uplink adopts POS port to connect to the line from Shanghai, and the downlink has two GEs to connect to three independent AVS-IPTV systems, respectively.
6) The multicast relay routers in three systems obtain the corresponding multicast data from their independent AVS-IPTV system platform, and connect them to Cisco router 12816 by GE in Dalian of CNC.
7) Three independent IPTV service platforms connect to DCN (Data Communication Network) through firewall by FE (Fast Ethernet port or equipment) connection.

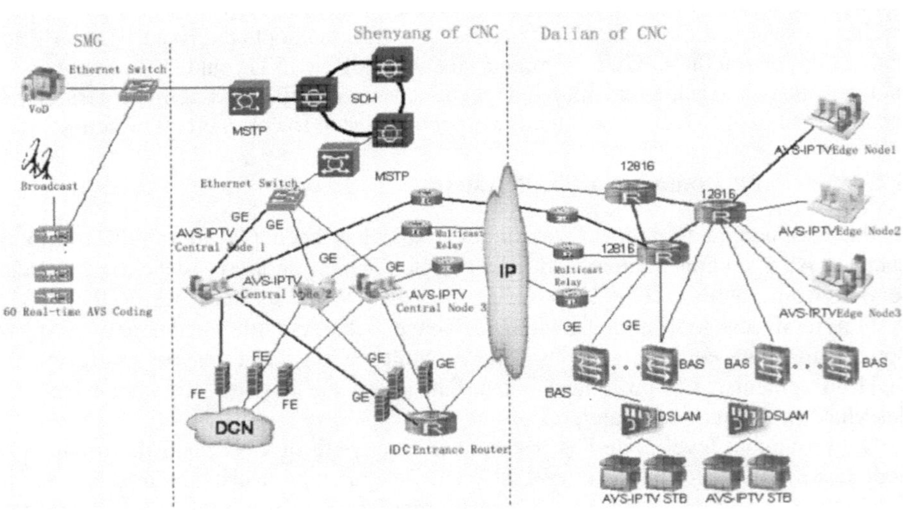

Fig. 2. AVS-IPTV Dalian of CNC commercial trial system

Some features of AVS-IPTV system trial in Dalian of CNC node are below:

1) There are three AVS-IPTV edge nodes (1, 2, 3) in metro core network, which can provide service independently with direct user management, etc.
2) The broadcast program has been multicast relayed into BAS (Broadband Access Server).
3) The user connects to DSLAM and BAS for service by the AVS-IPTV STB.

4 AVS-IPTV Commercial Trial Testing

4.1 AVS-IPTV Commercial Network Technology Test

The commercial network technology test aims to evaluate the maturity of Dalian AVS-IPTV system and provide a complete assessment to vendors system. The test is to verify independent vendor AVS-IPTV system function, to test performance of EPG, streaming service system (VOD) and multicast system, etc. The test adopts IQMediaMonitor video tester, and there are a certain number of real users in the whole test duration.

All tested systems fulfill the essential AVS-IPTV functions in terms of account acceptance, authentication and billing, information inquiry, user service application, system redundancy and load balance, content management, content distribution, network management, system user management, statistic analysis, VCDN, time-shift service and value-added service, etc., which are proved to provide service normally. The EPG system respond time is less than 0.5s in fast forward, backward and pause action switch, less than 2s in broadcast channel switch, and less than 5s in VOD for all tested system. After the burst carrier ability test in N : 1 and N : N model, and 8 hours full load stability test, the VOD system is proved to be stable and meet the service operation requirements. Under 1.65 Mbps reference rate, all three vendors (A, B, C) tested system MDI (Media Delivery Index) : DF (Delay Factor) jitter parameter is within 1s in Figure 3, and no packet loss during a 24 hours real IPTV operation test. In the complete test duration, AVS broadcast and VOD program picture quality is clear and stable. Those test results show that three tested AVS-IPTV systems including system equipments and terminals have the scalable commercial application capability.

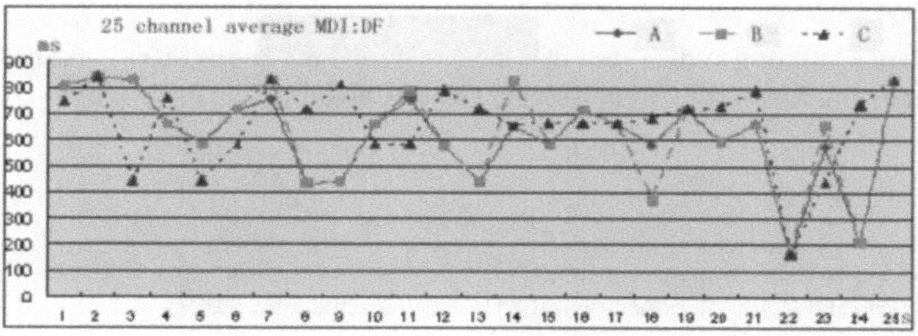

Fig. 3. Average MDI : DF jitter for three systems in 25 channels

4.2 AVS-IPTV Trial Quality of Experience Test

The average quality of experience result is drawn from CNC employee and customers by their subjective experience in terms of broadcast program, VOD, STB applicable, picture quality, etc. Around 120 persons involve the test and score the AVS-IPTV system for the three systems in accordance with ITU-R BT.500-11. The test score average results are showed in Table 1 for three systems (A, B, C).

Table 1. The average quality of experience score

Average quality of experience score			
Items	**A**	**B**	**C**
Broadcast	87.84	86.87	87.69
VOD	87.93	88.96	87.7
STB applicable	89.22	86.41	87.41
Self-service	90	91.22	89.33
Picture quality	79.33	76.22	78.06

From those results, all of the three systems have a good average quality of experience score with satisfied picture quality and all smooth service application processes. Notes the score 100 is full mark.

5 Conclusions and Achievements

By Dalian network trial construction, test and half year of operation, we can extract a conclusion that the three tested AVS-IPTV systems have had the commercial development ability. The trial verifies AVS standard and the AVS based IPTV system includes signal source, carrier network, access network, service process, etc. to reach commercial development level in good performance and quality of experience. The network trial boosts AVS and AVS-IPTV application to a new development stage.

Acknowledgements

Appreciation of the test data provided by Mr. Lunyong Zhang, Mr. Zaixiong Ke and Mrs. Shaohong Ma in the China Netcom Group Labs.

References

1. ITU-T FG IPTV working document [083]: IPTV service requirements (2007)
2. ITU-T FG IPTV working document [084]: IPTV Architecture (2007)
3. ATIS-0800002: IPTV Architecture Requirements (2006)
4. ITU-T Recommendation Y.2012: Architecture and Requirement of the NGN (2006)

Usage of MPEG-2 to AVS Transcoder in IPTV System

GuoZhong Wang, HaiWu Zhao, and Guowei Teng

Central Research Academy SVA Group CO., LTD ShangHai 200233
{wang_gz, zhao_hw, teng_gw}@sva.com.cn

Abstract. AVS Standard is the abbreviation of Advanced Audio Video Coding Standard made by China with the main purpose to efficiently compress digital audio and video data. The standard may be applied in the field of information industry, such as high-resolution digital broadcast, high-density laser-digital storage media, wireless broadband multimedia communication and broadband stream media. MPEG-2 is the most popular international video compression standard, and has existed in different systems and networks for a long time. At present, most of video programs are made in MPEG-2 format. AVS is expected to become popular in the coming decade. There is a requirement to convert the MPEG-2 programs into AVS ones. This paper presents the usage of MPEG-2 to AVS transcoders in IPTV systems.

Keywords: MPEG-2, AVS, Transcode, IPTV.

1 Introduction

At present, the popular source code standard is MPEG-2, which is generally adopted in digital television and other domain broadcast programs, DVD/HD-DVD, IPTV and personal video recorder (PVR), through satellites, cable and terrestrial channel. But MPEG-2 is a standard that was established 10 years ago. Its establishment was based on the compression technology level and the integrated circuit (IC) technology level at that time. Today, a lot of breakthroughs have been achieved in the field of the audio and video compression technology. The compression efficiency has at least been doubled by these technologies.

In recent years, a number of new digital audio and video coding standards have been established, including international standards such as MPEG-4 and AVC/H.264, while China has also independently developed the AVS standard, in which the majority of the intellectual property rights are China's own patents. In addition, since AVS has established One-Stop Licensing and a new Patent Pool Management Strategy, the patent issues of AVS have been better resolved. Furthermore, AVS has obvious performance advantages compared with MPEG-4 and MPEG-2. The compression efficiency of AVS has increased 2-3 times of MPEG-2, and is equivalent to that of H.264, but AVS has lower implementation complexity than H.264.

H.H.S. Ip et al. (Eds.): PCM 2007, LNCS 4810, pp. 65–70, 2007.

The diversification of coding standards makes transcoding more and more important, especially from MPEG-2 to AVS for us. In order to promote the industrialization of AVS standard, we have devoted a lot of effort on the transcoding from MPEG-2 to AVS, and achieved a complete real-time transcoding device at the server platform, which not only realizes transcoding from the MPEG-2 video data to AVS ones, but also the multiplex and de-multiplex of video stream and MPEG Audio stream or AC-3 audio stream as well. The device can be widely used in various broadcasting and streaming media business. This paper introduces that the transcoder from MPEG-2 to AVS is applied in IPTV system.

2 Introduction of MPEG2-to-AVS Transcoding Technologies and Products

Video transcoding technology provides an end-to-end process for video compression, that is, the data flow of input and output in the device are both compressed. The compressed bit stream by transcoding can adapt to the requirements of transmission bandwidth and the receiver. There are two kinds of transcoding: one is for similar standards and the other is for heterogeneous standards. According to the principal of transcoding for similar standards, the decoder and the encoder can be designed together to simplify transcoding, for instance MPEG-2 to MPEG-2, H.263 to H.263, etc.. There are two ways to translate heterogeneous standards: one is the direct mapping of the bit stream, for instance the translation between MPEG-4 and H.263, which requires that the two standards are reasonably similar; the other is to make a grammatical change, for which the process of decoding and re-coding becomes necessary, such as MPEG2-to-AVS. [1]

In response to the different types of conversion, there are two main methods to realize the transcoding. The most straightforward method is to decode the stream fully at first into the pixel domain, then re-encode the picture, which is called Cascade Pixel Domain Transcoding (CPDT). Since this method needs to re-calculate the motion vectors of the code-block data and re-calculate the coding mode in the process of recoding, the quality of the output images can be very high. However, the implementation of CPDT is rather inefficient, which cannot meet the requirements of real-time broadcasting.

Another way is called Compressed Domain Transcoding (CDT), the basic idea of which is to take the advantage of information in the compressed stream from the input code as much as possible, such as the information of video sequence header, macroblock coding mode, motion vectors, quantized DCT coefficient, etc., to generate the translated code stream directly. The method is more intricate, but it can be used to greatly reduce computation of the conversion process, which is now widely used in such fields as non-linear editing, etc. The algorithm at the present condition can be realized by software, and the efficiency of transcoding is very high with low delay. This method of translation can be used only when the video processing algorithms are similar. [2]

This paper will give an enhanced solution, which combines CPDT and CDT to produce an optimum way of transcoding: At first, the input bit stream is decoded completely, and is then re-coded. However, in the encoding process, the input bitstream of the information of the video sequence header, macroblock coding mode and motion vector encoding from the input bitstream is used as much as possible to speed up the coding, which as shown in Figure-1. In this way, the transcoding will be guaranteed to realize by high speed.

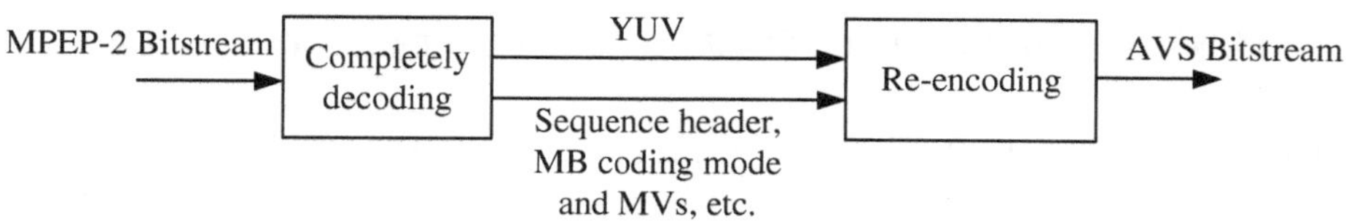

Fig. 1. Enhanced Pixel Domain Transcoding

Currently, SVA is providing an AVS Real-time transcoder for business applications. The main functions and features are shown as in Table1.

Table 1. Features of AVS Real-time Transcoder

Video	Coding Standard for Input Stream	ISO/IEC13818 (MPEG-2) (MPEG-2 Class MP@ML Grade); ISO/IEC11172 (MPEG-1)
	Coding Standard for Output Stream	GB/T 20090.2 JZ profile @ level 4.0
	Video Format	QVGA,CIF,SIF@30fps,SDTV,ITU-R601,ITU-R 656
	Input Interface	ASI(Asynchronous Serial Interface)、RJ-45 Ethernet interfaces, etc..
	Output Interface	ASI(Asynchronous Serial Interface)、RJ-45 Ethernet interfaces, etc..
	Pretreatment	Adaptive de-interlacing filter
	Mode of Bitrate	CBR(Constant BitRate)and VBR(Variable Bitrate)
	Bitrate	200kbps–1.5Mbps(CIF/SIF/ QVGA) , 800kbps-4Mbps(SDTV) (The fluctuation should range from -3% to 3%, at CBR mode.)
	GOP Structure	Adjustable or the same as the input
	Configurability	Configuration for the length of GOP, number of BP、Elementary Stream PID, etc..
Audio	Coding Standard	MPEG-1 Layer Ⅰ、Ⅱand Ⅲ, AC3、AVS Part3
	Coding Bitrate	32Kbps – 384Kbps
	Audio Mode	Stereo or double track
Output format	Encapsulation Format	TS、PS、ISMA and TS over UDP/IP
Delay	Delay Time	Not more than two seconds

It can be seen from the above table that the device can be used to achieve real-time transcoding between MPEG-2 and AVS for SD TV programs, working at a stable bitrate, which supports the mainstream audio standards. The output bit stream can be multiplexed into TS, PS or RTP format and transmitted through ASI and IP ports which can be widely used in digital television broadcasting and streaming media, such as IPTV. The applications of MPEG2-to-AVS transcoder in IPTV system will be introduced in the next section.

3 IPTV System Based on MPEG-2-to-AVS Transcoder

Most of contents of IPTV system are from DVD films, VCD films, and live broadcasting that is telecasted by satellite broadcast or by cable television. The data of these programs are mainly compressed by MPEG-2 standard. Therefore, the transcoding from MPEG-2 to AVS in AVS IPTV system is an efficient way to enrich the supply of AVS programs, which are relatively scarce at present. So it is important to redesign the structure of IPTV system and integrate AVS transcoders with the existing IPTV system, which is shown in Figure-2.

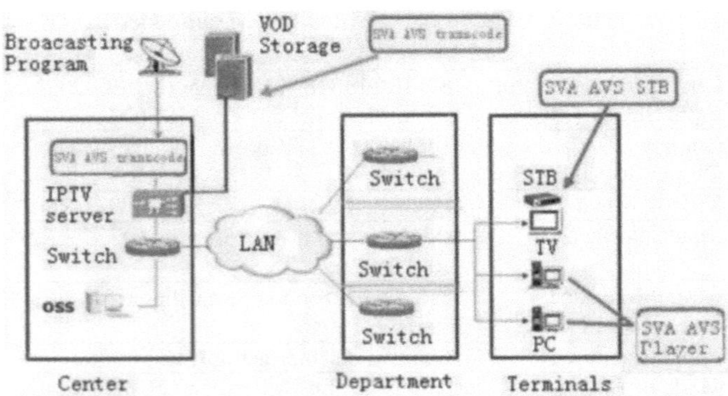

Fig. 2. IPTV System Based on MPEG-to-AVS Transcoder

In Figure-2, the MPEG-to-AVS transcoder plays two roles: one is used as broadcasting server, another is used as the codec for storage server. As broadcast server, the transcoder supports IP outport and can provide multicast. As a codec for the storage server, it can store the converted AVS bit stream into the VOD storage server to be accessed by the streaming media server. In addition, two terminal access modes are provided: IPTV STB and media player, which can meet the requirements of different users.

4 Advantages of the Application of MPEG-to-AVS Transcoder in IPTV System

There are two methods to achieve AVS end-to-end transmission system of the existing television system: encoder and transcoder, as shown in figure 3.

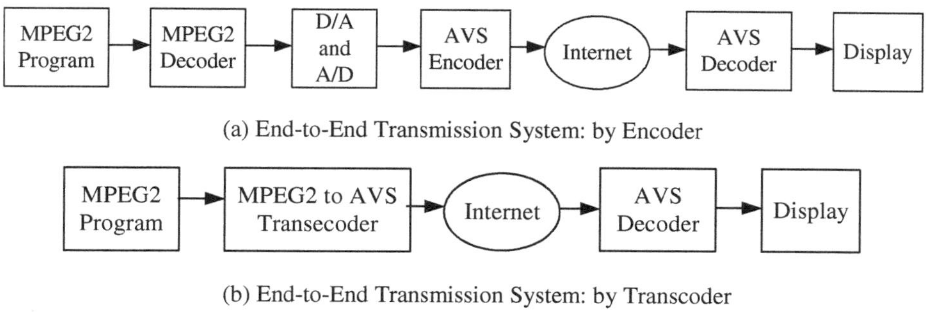

Fig. 3. AVS end-to-end Transmission System

Actually, there are two ways to use an AVS codec as the front-end device: One is direct to upgrade the entire front-end system, by which the former MPEG-2 modules are replaced by AVS modules. Since coding efficiency of AVS is quite high, this AVS system can save a lot of transmission bandwidths. But the shortcoming of the solution is obvious: on the one hand, all the MPEG-2 equipment will be eliminated, which means a waste for the operators; on the other hand, the cost of replacement for AVS programs is rather high, especially the cost of programming is very expensive, which brings the producer a great pressure. Another way is to decode the stream at the first step, and then encode to AVS flows, the structure of which is depicted in Fig-3(a). However, the method involves the conversion of D/A and A/D, which would decrease the quality of image significantly.

To solve these problems, the third method comes, which is designed on the basis of the MPEG-2- to-AVS transcoders, as shown in Figure-3(b). The solution, which can be implemented easily, avoids the loss of conversion of D/A and A/D. In addition, the transcoder will be compatible with the terminal equipment, that is, the former MPEG-2 equipments will still be made use of in this low-delay solution. Compared with the system shown in Figure-3(a) the system of the third method can save 0.5 second delay; which enables the former MPEG-2 equipments to continue to function, for example the MPEG-2 encoder, multiplexer, user management system, charge system and CA system, etc..

From the above, we can conclude that it is wiser to choose MPEG2-to-AVS transcoder to solve the problem of the shortage of AVS programs under current conditions, and this scheme can save the cost for upgrading of MPEG-2 equipments as well, which is more significant.

References

1. Vetro, A., Christopulos, C., Sun, H.: Video Transcoding Architectures and Techniques: An Overview. IEEE Signal Process. Mag. 20(2), 18–29 (2003)
2. Bjork, N., Christopoulos, C.: Transcoder Architecture for Video Coding. IEEE Trans. Consum. Electron. 44(1), 88–98 (1998)

The Audio and Video Synchronization Method Used in AVS System

Zhijie Yang, Xuemin Chen, Jiang Fu, and Brian Heng

Broadcom Corporation
Room 201, Block B, Innovation Building,
Tsinghua Science Park, Tsinghua University,
Haidian District,
Beijing, China 100084
zhyang@broadcom.com, schen@broadcom.com, jfu@broadcom.com,
bheng@broadcom.com

Abstract. Audio and video synchronization is an important technique for many video applications. This paper introduced a new synchronization method used in the emerging AVS system. The decoder system clock is recovered from transport rate info. The audio and video are synchronized according to relative display time info. Some error concealment strategies are also discussed.

1 Introduction

Audio and video synchronization is an important technique for many video applications. The objective of the audio video synchronization mainly includes three folds. The first objective is to synchronize the decoding and display of the audio, video and auxiliary data; the second is to avoid the buffer underflow and overflow; the third is to generate a clock accurate enough to drive the display. The third is optional since in some system design the display uses a separate clock [1].

MPEG-2 Transport Stream (TS) has been widely used in digital video broadcasting. Audio and video synchronization in MPEG-2 TS requires time-stamps, system clock and digital phase-lock loop (D-PLL). Three kinds of timestamps are created by a single, common system clock in the encoder and carried in the transport stream. Presentation Time Stamps (PTS) indicate the correct presentation time of audio and video. Decoding Time Stamps (DTS) indicates the correct decoding time of audio and video. Program Clock References (PCR) indicates the instantaneous value of the system clock itself at the sampled intervals. In the decoder, these time stamps are extracted. PCRs are used to reconstruct the system clock together with D-PLL, DTS and PTS are used to control the timing of decoding and presentation of audio and video [2].

In this paper, a new audio and video synchronization method, which is adopted by the emerging AVS system [3], is introduced. This method can synchronize the audio and video presentation without using PCR/DTS/PTS. Detailedly, section 2 introduces the clock recovery method. Section 3.1 and 3.2 introduce the video and audio synchronization method respectively. Several error concealment strategies are also discussed there. Finally, section 4 concludes the paper.

H.H.S. Ip et al. (Eds.): PCM 2007, LNCS 4810, pp. 71–77, 2007.

2 System Clock Recovery with Transport Rate Reference

A practical clock may have jitter, frequency error, slewing and other non-idealities. For a video sequence sampled at 30 frames per second, if the encoder and decoder use their own clocks, a 60 ppm difference will underflow or overflow the compressed video buffer of 20 frames in just over three hours.

On the other hand, the display may use the decoder system clock to derive the needed synchronization signal. Hence inaccuracy in system clock will impair the picture quality. The most common way to fix this issue is to use a PLL. In the traditional MPEG-2 transport system, a PLL in the decoder side can lock to the encoder clock by using the difference between the PCR timestamp and its current STC. The PCR is required to be sent at least every 100ms to guarantee the clock accuracy.

In our method, three items are carried in the TS stream for system clock recovery, i.e. the relative_display_time, transport_rate and packet_count. Relative_display_time is a 32 bit timestamp to indicate the relative presentation time of the first access unit starting in the current TS packet. Relative_display_time is based on a 90K Hz clock and are required to be sent at least at every random access point. Transport_rate is a 32 bit field to indicate the TS stream transport rate in the unit of bit per second. The duration of the transport_ rate is between the current TS packet and the next TS packet containing the transport_rate field, either forward or backward. In the rest of this paper, forward transport rate is assumed. All discussion can be easily extended to the backward case. Transport_rate is required to be sent at least at every random access point. Packet_count is 32 bit field to indicate the packet number of the current TS packet. The packet number may be accumulated at the decoder side. It is transmitted explicitly here for error resilience.

Detailedly, at the encoder side, the transport rate is calculated as follows:

$$transport\_rate(n) = \frac{((n-m) \bmod 2^{32}) \cdot 188 \cdot 8 \cdot system\_clock\_frequency}{t(n)-t(m)}$$

where m and n are the packet count encoded in the packet_count fields, t(m) and t(n) are the encoding time of the first bit of the carrying packet, which is based on a nominal 27M Hz clock. Here we assume $t(m) < t(n)$. System_clock_frequency is the encoder system clock frequency measured in Hz and shall meet the following constraints:

$$27000000 - 810 \le system\_clock\_frequency \le 27000000 + 810 \tag{1}$$

At the decoder side, when the first random access point arrives, the STC is reset to 0 or any other values. Packet_count m and arrival time of the first bit based on local clock $t(m)$ is kept for decoder side transport rate calculation. When the following transport rate arrives, packet_count n is extracted and $t'(n)$ is sampled. The actual transport rate at the decoder side can be calculated as

$$transport\_rate'(n) = \frac{((n-m) \bmod 2^{32}) \cdot 188 \cdot 8 \cdot system\_clock\_frequency'}{t'(n)-t'(m)}$$

where system_clock_frequency' is the decoder system clock frequency, which also satisfies the constraint (**1**).

Fig. 1 is an example of system clock recovery PLL based on the above method. Transport_rate and packet_count is parsed by data interpreter. Packet_count is buffered in jitter calculator together with a sample of STC. Let total data bit between packet number *m* and packet number *n* be *b*. *R* is transport_rate carried by packet number *m*. *R'* is the transport_rate derived by local counter. Difference between *b/R* and *b/R'* is low pass filtered and used to control VCXO for system clock recovery.

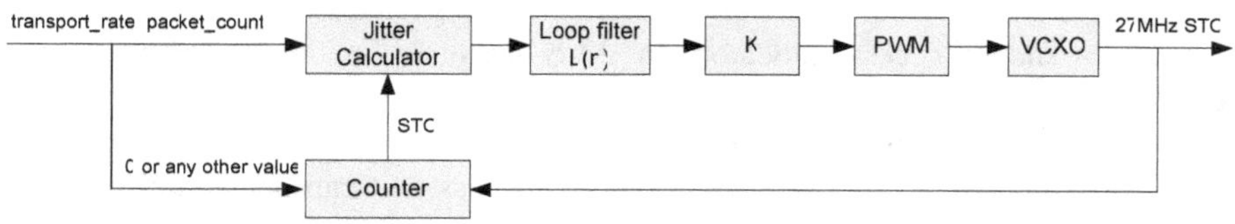

Fig. 1. A diagram of STC recovery using PLL

A tolerance is specified for transport_rate values. The transport_rate tolerance is defined as the maximum relative inaccuracy allowed in received transport_rate. The inaccuracy may be due to the clock drift or to the transport_rate modification during remultiplexing. It does not include errors in packet arrival time due to network jitter or other causes. The relative transport_rate tolerance is 5×10^{-6} according to [3].

In fact, the jitter of transport rate is directly related to the PCR jitter. Consider a transport stream with the nominal transport rate of 12.5Mbps. The PCR value is carried as follows

Table 1. Jitter relation between PCR and transport rate

Packet	PCR	PCR Jitter (ns)	Transport_rate (bps)
113	14695		
430	1044514	-4.421	12499998.54
747	2074333	-4.421	12499998.54
1064	3104152	-4.421	12499998.54
1381	4133971	-4.421	12499998.54
1698	5163790	-4.421	12499998.54
2015	6193608	32.616	12500010.68
2332	7223427	-4.421	12499998.54

In Table 1, the first column contains the packet numbers of packets where pcr_flag = 1. The second column shows the PCR value carried in the corresponding packet. The third column is PCR jitter calculated based on the traditional MPEG-2 algorithm. The fourth column is the calculated transport rate based on packet number and Δt, where Δt equals the difference between two consecutive PCR values. Thus if we transfer *transport_rate(m)* explicitly, the decoder can use transport rate as well as the *packet_count* info to recover the system time clock.

Since the parameters we send are needed for decoder initialization, the above three fields shall be transferred within the packet containing random access unit which is labeled by random_access_indicator. In AVS system, the data is carried in the transport_private_data of the adaptation_field. Refer to [2] for detailed description of random_access_indicator and transport_private_data.

Normally the distance between each random access unit can be as large as one to five seconds depending on infrastructure. However, to guarantee successfully system clock recovery, transport_rate and packet_count have to be sent at least every 100ms. In other words, Time recovery private field might be carried in TS packet even if random_access_indicator equals 0.

If the infrastructure does not use PES packetization, all PIDs shall carry time recovery private field containing *relative_display_time* to synchronize to each other. But only one PID is required to carry *transport_rate* and *packet_count* for system clock recovery.

In case of time base discontinuity, if *discontinuity_indicator* is set, the *packet_count* and sampled STC value in the buffer of jitter calculator should be reset.

3 Audio and Video Synchronization

3.1 Video Presentation

Fig. 2 shows a diagram of the video presentation process. Detailedly, when stream comes, relative_display_time field is extracted. The display_time is calculated based on the relative_display_time as follows:

$$display\_time_n(k) = relative\_display\_time(k) + STC\_base(r) \qquad (2)$$

where r represents the byte that contains the last bit of *relative_display_time(k),* and *STC_base(r)* represents the STC value when r arrives at the decoder.

The derived *display_time* is then buffered together with the picture data; for a picture without *relative_display_time* field, its *display_time* value is extrapolated based on the previous *display_time* and frame rate. A picture is decoded when it arrives and there is available display buffer, which is indicated by signal rdy. The decoded picture is then sent for presentation when the corresponding *display_time* mature.

It is required that the picture at the random access unit should contain the *relative_display_time* field. It is permitted that some pictures contains no

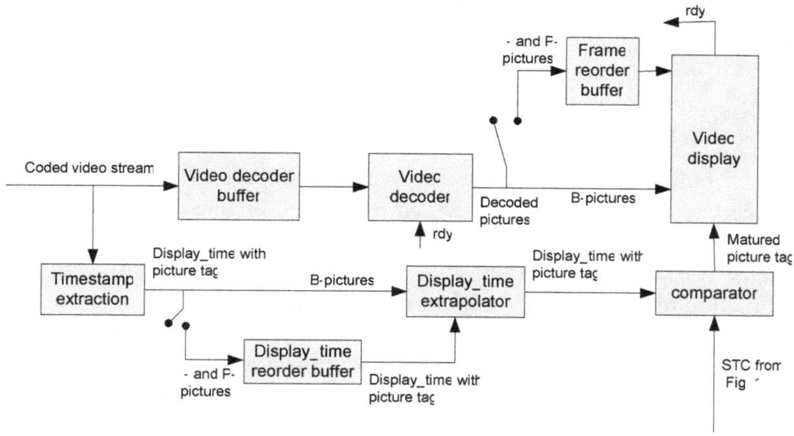

Fig. 2. A diagram of the video presentation process

relative_display_time fields. *The display_time* extrapolator in Fig. 2 is to address this problem. The extrapolation algorithm is described as follows:

For all incoming frames :

$$\textit{if(frame has coded display\_time)}$$

$$\textit{Running display\_time} = \textit{Coded display\_time}$$

else

$$\textit{Running display\_time} = \textit{Extrapolated display\_time}$$

$$\textit{Extrapolated display\_time} = \textit{Running display\_time} + \Delta\textit{display\_time}$$

where

$$\Delta display\_time = \begin{cases} repeat\_count \times \dfrac{90000}{frame\_rate}, \text{for frame picture} \\ \dfrac{45000}{frame\_rate}, \text{for field picture} \end{cases}$$

$$repeat\_count = \begin{cases} 3, & \text{if progressive\_sequence = repeat\_first\_field = top\_field\_first = 1} \\ 2, & \text{if progressive\_sequence = repeat\_first\_field = 1, top\_field\_first = 0} \\ 1.5, & \text{if progressive\_sequence = 0, repeat\_first\_field = top\_field\_first = 1} \\ 1, & \text{otherwise.} \end{cases}$$

When the *display_time* does not match the video STC, five cases are distinguished by three thresholds and addressed separately:

1) If *display_time – STC < threshold2*, the picture is displayed immediately.
2) If *threshold2 < display_time – STC < threshold3, the display_time* for this picture has not matured. The picture is not displayed until the *display_time* and STC match.
3) If *display_time – STC ≥ threshold3*, the display_time for this picture is very far in the future. This picture is not displayed until the *display_time* and STC match. To allow the host to correct this by reloading the STC, a *display_time* error signal is generated to notify the host of this situation.

4) If *STC - display_time* < *threshold4*, the current picture is slightly old. The picture is display immediately.
5) If *STC - display_time* ≥ *threshold4*, the current picture is extremely old. The picture is discarded without being displayed. A *display_time* error signal is generated to notify the host of this situation.

The decoder buffer may be underflow or overflow. In case of underflow, the decoder will wait certain amount of time till the current coded picture completely entering the buffer for decoding. In case of overflow, a simple method is just to drop the incoming data till there is available buffer. This strategy is fast but not efficient, since the dropped picture may be used as the reference for the following pictures, and then the referring pictures will be un-decodable. A more efficient strategy is to drop the pictures according to the frame dependency. In this strategy, it is needed to pre-read the picture type of each picture in the buffer and drop pictures according to the following rules:

1) Drop the last B frame in the buffer. If there is no B frame in the buffer, go to 2).
2) If there is I frames in the buffer, drop the last P frame before the last I frame. Otherwise, drop the last P frame. If there is no P frame in the buffer, go to 3).
3) Drop the last I frame in the buffer.

3.2 Audio Presentation

Fig. 3 shows the diagram of the proposed transport method. When stream comes, *relative_display_time* field is extracted, and *display_time* is derived from *relative_display_time* according to the formula (**2**). For a frame without *relative_display_time* field, its *display_time* value is extrapolated based on the previous *display_time*, *frame_size* and sampling frequency. A frame is decoded when it arrives and there is available display buffer, which is indicated by signal rdy. The decoded audio frame is then sent for presentation when the corresponding *display_time* matures.

It is permitted that some audio frames have no corresponding *relative_display_time* fields. The audio *display_time* extrapolator in Fig. 3 is to address this problem.

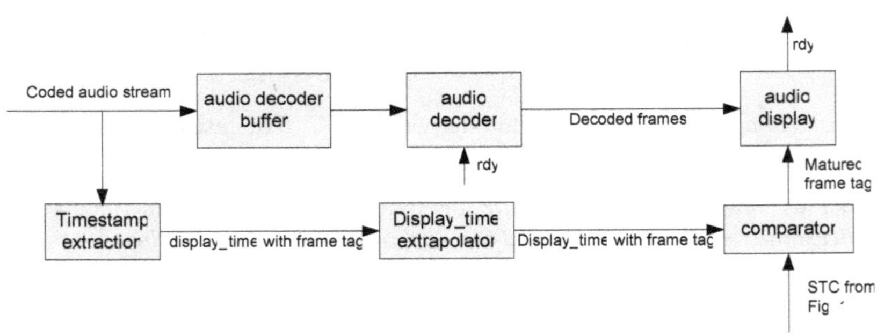

Fig. 3. A diagram of the audio presentation process

Display_time is derived from the previous running *display_time*, *frame_size* and sampling frequency. If the very first frame does not have the *relative_display_time* field, the running *display_time* is initialized to zero. Therefore, the *display_time* extrapolation algorithm can be summarized as follows:

$$1.Initialization : Extrapolated\ display\_time = 0;$$

2.For all incoming frames :

$$if(frame\ has\ coded\ display\_time)$$

$$Running\ display\_time = Coded\ display\_time$$

else

$$Running\ display\_time = Extrapolated\ display\_time$$

$$Extrapolated\ display\_time = Running\ display\_time + \Delta display\_time$$

where

$$\Delta display\_time = \frac{90000 * sampling\ frequency}{frame\_size}$$

In case that *display_time - STC > threshold5*, the *display_time* for this frame has not matured. This frame will not be displayed until the *display_time* and STC match. In case *STC - display_time > threshold6*, the current frame is old and hence is discarded without being played.

When the decoder buffer overflows, the decoder always discard the incoming data. When the decoder buffer underflows, the decoder waits a certain amount of time for the current coded audio frame to completely enter the buffer for decoding.

4 Conclusion

In this paper, a new audio and video synchronization method without using PCR/DTS/PTS is systematically introduced. In this method, transport rate is calculated at the encoder and inserted in the transport private data of the transport packet adaptation field. The transport rate can mathematically closely track the variation of the encoder STC. At the decoder, the transport rate info is extracted together with the *packet_count* to recover the system clock. In addition, audio and video are synchronized according to *relative_display_time*. Several error concealment strategies when there is timing error or buffer underflow and overflow are also given. This method has been adopted by the emerging AVS system.

References

[1] Chen, X.: Transporting Compressed Digital Video. Kluwer Academic Publishers, Boston (2002)

[2] ITU-T Recommendation H.222.0 | ISO/IEC 13818-1: 1996, Information technology – Generic coding of moving pictures and associated audio information: Systems (1995)

[3] N1404, Information technology - Advanced coding of audio and video - Part 1: System (2007)

Expression-Invariant Face Recognition with Accurate Optical Flow

Chao-Kuei Hsieh[1], Shang-Hong Lai[2], and Yung-Chang Chen[1]

[1] Dept. of Electrical Engineering, National Tsing Hua University, Taiwan
[2] Dept. of Computer Science, National Tsing Hua University, Taiwan
d903915@oz.nthu.edu.tw, lai@cs.nthu.edu.tw,
ycchen@ee.nthu.edu.tw

Abstract. Face recognition is one of the most intensively studied topics in computer vision and pattern recognition, but few are focused on how to robustly recognize expressional faces with one single training sample per class. In this paper, we modify the regularization-based optical flow algorithm by imposing constraints on some given point correspondences to obtain precise pixel displacements and intensity variations. By using the optical flow computed for the input expressional face with respect to a referenced neutral face, we remove the expression from the face image by elastic image warping to recognize the subject with facial expression. Numerical validations of the proposed method are given, and experimental results show that the proposed method improves the recognition rate significantly.

Keywords: Face recognition, expression invariant, accurate optical flow.

1 Introduction

Face recognition has been studied for the past few decades. A comprehensive review of the related works can be found in [1]. Pose, illumination, and expression variations are three essential issues to be dealt with in the research of face recognition. In this paper, we focus on the issue of facial expression on face recognition performance.

For expression-invariant face recognition, the algorithms can be roughly divided into three categories: the subspace model based [2], morphable model based, and optical flow based approaches. In the first category, Tsai and Jan [2] applied subspace model analysis to develop a face recognition system that is tolerant to facial deformations. Note that multiple training images in each class were needed for this method.

Some other approaches were proposed to warp images to be the same shape as the ones used for training. Ramachandran et al. [3] presented pre-processing steps for converting a smiling face to a neutral face. Li et al. [4] applied a face mask for face geometry normalization and further calculated the eigenspaces for geometry and texture separately, but not all images can be well warped to a neutral image because of the lack of texture in certain regions, like closed eyes. Moreover, linear warping

H.H.S. Ip et al. (Eds.): PCM 2007, LNCS 4810, pp. 78–87, 2007.

was usually applied, which was not consistent to the non-linear characteristic of human expression movements.

Another approach is to use optical flow to compute the face warping transformation. However, it is difficult to learn the local motion within feature space to determine the expression changes of each face, since different persons have expressions with different ways. Martinez [5] proposed a weighting method that weights independently those local areas which are less sensitive to expressional changes. The intensity variations due to expression may mislead the calculation of optical flow. A more considerable drawback is that the optical flow field to every reference image is calculated, which may require huge computational cost.

Our aim in this paper is to solve the expression-invariant face recognition under the circumstance that there is only one neutral training sample per class. Under such condition, subspace approach is not appropriate for insufficient training data. In order to avoid inconsistent linear warping in model-based algorithm, our previous accurate optical flow algorithm [6] is applied for expression normalization. Not only pixel deformations but also intensity variations are computed in this algorithm. In our proposed system, the recognition accuracy was significantly improved and the optical flow computation for each input face is required only once with reference to a given universal neutral face. We show our experimental results on the Binghamton University 3D Face Expression (BU-3DFE) Database [8].

The remaining parts of this paper are organized as follows. We will introduce our proposed system in section 2, including the constrained optical flow estimation and the expression-invariant face recognition system. Section 3 presents the experimental results on applying the proposed optical flow estimation and the expression-invariant face recognition algorithm. Section 4 concludes this paper.

2 Proposed Face Recognition System

In this section, an expression-invariant face recognition system based on the constrained optical flow estimation is proposed.

2.1 Feature Selection and Face Alignment

The main purpose of this work is to apply expression normalization on frontal faces for face recognition. We labeled 15 feature points manually (as shown in Fig. 1(b) and Fig. 1(c)) to achieve approximate face alignment, though there exist some automatic feature extraction methods [7]. With the labeled points, the distance between the outer corners of both eyes was used as the reference to scale the face images, as shown in Fig. 1(a).

2.2 Accurate Optical Flow Computation

The original formulation of the gradient-based regularization method proposed by Horn and Schunck involved minimizing an energy function of the following form:

$$E(u,v) = \iint_{\Omega} \left[\left(I_x u + I_y v + I_t \right)^2 + \lambda \left(u_x^2 + u_y^2 + v_x^2 + v_y^2 \right) \right] d\mathbf{x}$$

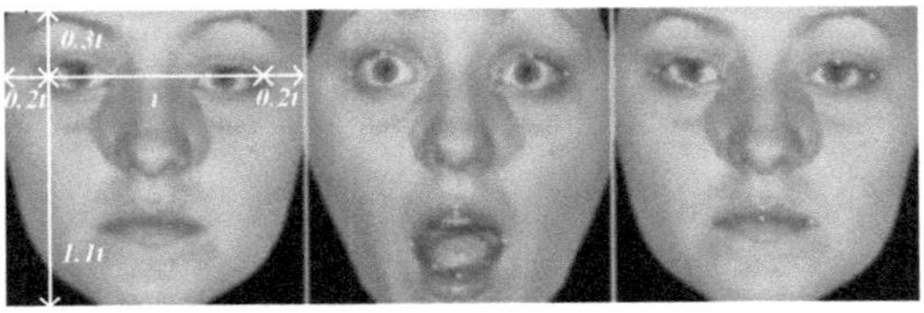

(a) (b) (C)

Fig. 1. (a) Face region selection; (b) 14 feature points on surprising face; (c) 14 feature points on neutral face

where I is the image intensity function, $\left[u(\mathbf{x},t),v(\mathbf{x},t)\right]^T$ is the motion vector to be estimated, subscripts x, y, and t denote the direction in the partial derivatives, Ω represents the image domain and λ is a parameter controlling the degree of smoothness. With the generalized dynamic image model, the optical flow constraint can be extended to [6]:

$$I_x(\mathbf{r})u(\mathbf{r})+I_y(\mathbf{r})v(\mathbf{r})+I_t(\mathbf{r})+m(\mathbf{r})I(\mathbf{r})+c(\mathbf{r})=0 \tag{1}$$

where $m(\mathbf{r})$ and $c(\mathbf{r})$ are the multiplier and offset fields of the scene brightness variation field and $\mathbf{r}=[x,y,t]^T$ is a point in a spatiotemporal domain. Thus, the energy function to be minimized in our algorithm can be written in a discrete form as follows:

$$\begin{aligned} f(\mathbf{u}) = {} & \sum_{i\in D}\left(\frac{I_{x,i}u_i+I_{y,i}v_i+I_{t,i}+m_iI_i+c_i}{\sqrt{I_{x,i}^2+I_{y,i}^2+I_i^2+1}}\right)^2 \\ & +\lambda\sum_{i\in D}\left(u_{x,i}^2+u_{y,i}^2+v_{x,i}^2+v_{y,i}^2\right)+\mu\sum_{i\in D}\left(m_{x,i}^2+m_{y,i}^2+c_{x,i}^2+c_{y,i}^2\right) \end{aligned} \tag{2}$$

where the subscript i denotes the ith location, vector $\boldsymbol{u}$ is the concatenation of all the flow components u_i and v_i and all the brightness variation multiplier and offset fields m_i and c_i, λ and μ are the parameters controlling the degree of smoothness in the motion and brightness fields, and D is the set of all the discretized locations in the image domain.

We further developed a dynamic smoothness adjustment scheme to effectively suppress the smoothness of constraint at motion boundaries and brightness variation boundaries in the multiplier and offset fields, thus yielding the following energy function:

$$\begin{aligned} f(\mathbf{u}) = {} & \sum_{i\in D}w_i\left(\frac{I_{x,i}u_i+I_{y,i}v_i+I_{t,i}+m_iI_i+c_i}{\sqrt{I_{x,i}^2+I_{y,i}^2+I_i^2+1}}\right)^2 \\ & +\lambda\sum_{i\in D}\left(\alpha_{x,i}u_{x,i}^2+\alpha_{y,i}u_{y,i}^2+\beta_{x,i}v_{x,i}^2+\beta_{y,i}v_{y,i}^2\right)+\mu\sum_{i\in D}\left(\gamma_{x,i}m_{x,i}^2+\gamma_{y,i}m_{y,i}^2+\delta_{x,i}c_{x,i}^2+\delta_{y,i}c_{y,i}^2\right) \end{aligned} \tag{3}$$

where $\alpha_{x,i}$, $\alpha_{y,i}$, $\beta_{x,i}$, $\beta_{y,i}$, $\gamma_{x,i}$, $\gamma_{y,i}$, $\delta_{x,i}$, $\delta_{y,i}$, are the weights for the corresponding components of the *i*th smooth constant along *x*- and *y*- directions.

Equation (3) can be rewritten in a matrix-vector form as $f(\mathbf{u}) = \mathbf{u}^T K\mathbf{u} - 2\mathbf{u}^T\mathbf{b} + \mathbf{c}$, thus minimizing this quadratic and convex function is equivalent to solving a large linear system $K\mathbf{u} - \mathbf{b} = 0$, where $\mathbf{b} = \begin{bmatrix} -\mathbf{e}_{xt}^T & -\mathbf{e}_{yt}^T & -\mathbf{e}_{It}^T & -\mathbf{e}_t^T \end{bmatrix}^T \in \hbar^{4wh}$ (*w* and *h* denote image width and height, and $\mathbf{e}_{xt}$, $\mathbf{e}_{yt}$, $\mathbf{e}_{It}$, $\mathbf{e}_t$ are all *wh*-dimensional vectors with entries $w_i I_{x,i} I_{t,i} / N_i$, $w_i I_{y,i} I_{t,i} / N_i$, $w_i I_i I_{t,i} / N_i$, and $w_i I_{t,i} / N_i$, respectively. $N_i = I_{x,i}^2 + I_{y,i}^2 + I_i^2 + 1$ is the normalization term and w_i is the weight.) and

$$K = \begin{bmatrix} \lambda K_{s,\alpha} + E_{xx} & E_{xy} & E_{xI} & E_x \\ E_{xy} & \lambda K_{s,\beta} + E_{yy} & E_{yI} & E_y \\ E_{xI} & E_{yI} & \mu K_{s,\gamma} + E_{II} & E_I \\ E_x & E_y & E_I & \mu K_{s,\delta} + E \end{bmatrix} \in R^{4wh\times 4wh}$$

The matrix $K \in R^{4wh\times 4wh}$ is a symmetric positive-definite matrix, where E_{xx}, E_{xy}, E_{xI}, E_x, E_{yy}, E_{yI}, E_y, E_{II}, E_I, and E arise from the optical flow constraints and they are all $wh\times wh$ diagonal matrices with diagonal entries $w_i I_{x,i}^2 / N_i$, $w_i I_{x,i} I_{y,i} / N_i$, $w_i I_{x,i} I_i / N_i$, $w_i I_{x,i} / N_i$, $w_i I_{y,i}^2 / N_i$, $w_i I_{y,i} I_i / N_i$, $w_i I_{y,i} / N_i$, $w_i I_i^2 / N_i$, $w_i I_i / N_i$, and w_i / N_i, respectively. We approximate the partial derivative of the flow field using forward difference, thus the matrix $K_{s,\alpha}$, which comes from the smoothness constraint, takes the following form:

$$K_{s,\alpha} = \begin{bmatrix} G_1 & H_1 & & \\ H_1 & G_2 & \hbar & \\ & \hbar & \hbar & H_{w-1} \\ & & H_{w-1} & G_w \end{bmatrix} \in R^{wh\times wh}$$

where the submatrices G_i and H_i are all of size $h\times h$. The other matrices $K_{s,\beta}$, $K_{s,\gamma}$, and $K_{s,\delta}$ are obtained with α replaced by β, γ, and δ, respectively. The detailed definitions of these submatrices can be found in [6].

We apply the preconditioned conjugate gradient algorithm to solve this linear system efficiently. To accelerate the convergence speed of the conjugate gradient algorithm, the preconditioner P must be carefully designed. It must be a good approximation to K and a fast numerical method is required to solve the linear system $Pz = r$ in each iteration of the preconditioned conjugate gradient algorithm. The incomplete Cholesky factorization is a good choice with the preconditioner P is given in the following form $P = LL^T \approx K$. The detailed steps of this algorithm (ICPCG) are summarized as follows:

(a) Initialize $\mathbf{u}_0$; compute $\mathbf{r}_0 = b - K\mathbf{u}_0$; $k = 0$.

(b) Solve $P\mathbf{z}_k = \mathbf{r}_k; k = k+1$.

(c) If $k=1, \mathbf{p}_1 = \mathbf{z}_0$; else compute $\beta_k = \mathbf{r}_{k-1}^T \mathbf{z}_{k-1} / \mathbf{r}_{k-2}^T \mathbf{z}_{k-2}$, and update $\mathbf{p}_k = \mathbf{z}_{k-1} + \beta_k \mathbf{p}_{k-1}$

(d) Compute $\alpha_k = \mathbf{r}_{k=1}^T \mathbf{z}_{k-1} / \mathbf{p}_k^T \boldsymbol{K} \mathbf{p}_k$.

(e) Update $\mathbf{r}_k = \mathbf{r}_{k-1} - \alpha_k \boldsymbol{K} \mathbf{p}_k$, $\mathbf{u}_k = \mathbf{u}_{k-1} + \alpha_k \mathbf{p}_k$.

(f) If $\mathbf{r}_k \approx \mathbf{0}$, stop; else go to step (b).

In our application, the initial value of $\mathbf{u}_0$ is calculated using RBF interpolation from all the feature points. This optical flow algorithm has been proven superior to others. However, the proposed ICPCG algorithm cannot guarantee the computed optical flow is consistent to the motion at the corresponding feature points. Therefore, we modify the optimization problem to be

$$\begin{aligned} &\textit{minimize } f(\mathbf{u}) = \mathbf{u}^T K \mathbf{u} - 2\mathbf{u}^T \mathbf{b} + \mathbf{c}, \\ &\textit{subject to } u_{(x_i, y_i)} = \bar{u}_i, \textit{ and } v_{(x_i, y_i)} = \bar{v}_i, \forall (x_i, y_i) \in S \end{aligned} \tag{4}$$

where S is the set of feature points and $(\bar{u}_i, \bar{v}_i)$ is the specified optical flow vector at the i-th feature point. Instead of using the Lagrange multiplier, we modify the original procedure of ICPCG to satisfy these specified data constraints. After initializing the first guess of $\mathbf{u}_0$ in step (a), we reset the motion vectors at the feature points to be the specified flow vectors. After solving z_k in step (b), the z values for the facial feature pixels in S is then set to 0. By doing so, the motion vector value of the feature points will not be changed in the decision step (c) of the next gradient direction.

2.3 Face Recognition Flowchart

Fig. 2 shows the flowchart of our proposed face recognition system (lower part) and the benchmark system using PCA dimension reduction (upper part).

In our proposed system, only the optical flow field for the input face image with respect to the universal neutral face image NE_1 is required to compute for each

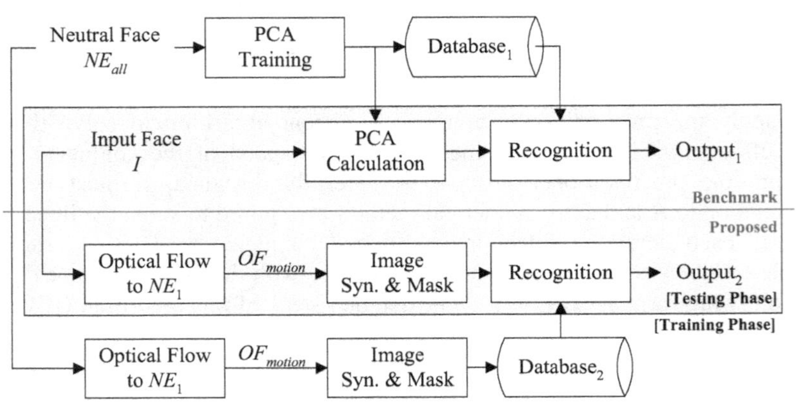

Fig. 2. Flowchart of the proposed face recognition system

training and testing image. In the image synthesis block, we discard the intensity part of optical flow, m_i and c_i, and take the motion part only, u_i and v_i, for neutral face warping. A mask is then put on the synthesized image to remove some border regions. Such procedure is applied on both training phase and testing phase as the pre-processing step. It can unify the geometry coordinate of training neutral images in the training phase and neutralize the input expressional image in the testing phase. A simple direct subtraction and the nearest-neighbor classification was employed in the face recognition.

3 Experimental Results

Our experiments were performed on the Binghamton University 3D Face Expression (BU-3DFE) Database [8].

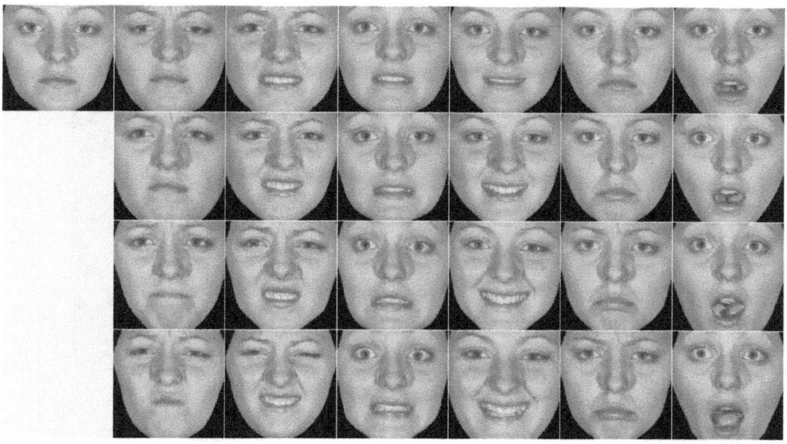

Fig. 3. Sample images in BU-3DFEDB. The left-top most is the neutral face. The others are sad, fear, disgust, happy, sad, and surprise expressions in columns; level1 to level 4 in rows.

The BU-3DFE database contains the face images and 3D face models of 100 subjects (56 females and 44 males) with neutral face and 6 different expressions (happy, disgust, fear, happy, sad, and surprised) at different levels (from level 1-weak to 4-strong), but only 2D face images were used in our experiments. Fig. 3 shows the 25 normalized face images of one subject with the proposed method.

3.1 De-expression with Accurate Optical Flow

We try to verify the effectiveness of expression normalization with accurate optical flow by checking the face recognition rates. In the training phase for original data, we first use PCA to calculate the reduced vector for all the 100 neutral images of each subject. In the testing phase, the input image is projected to the PCA subspace and classified by the nearest neighbor as shown in Fig. 2. The average recognition rate is 56.88%, and the recognition results are shown in Fig. 4 for all expressions and levels separately. The surprising and disgust expressions had the worst results, and the recognition rate is decreased while the degree of facial expression gets stronger.

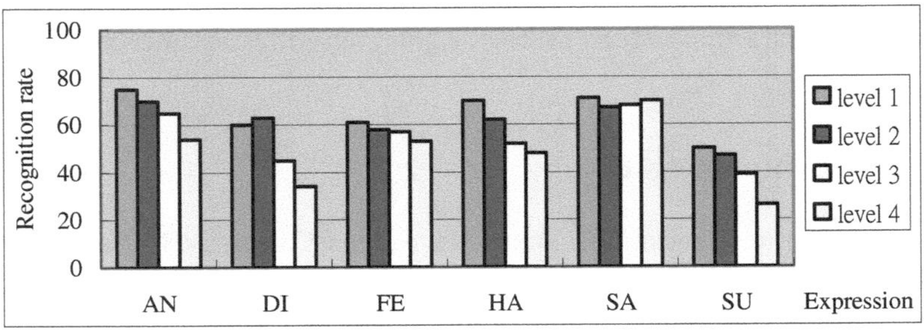

Fig. 4. Recognition rates of original images under different expressions and levels (with average recognition rate 56.88%)

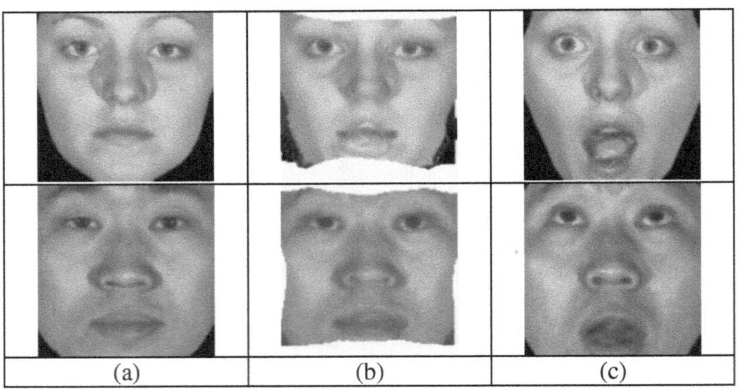

Fig. 5. Illustrations of expression normalization using accurate optical flow, (a) original neutral faces; (b) expression normalized faces from (c) to (a); (c) surprising face at level 4

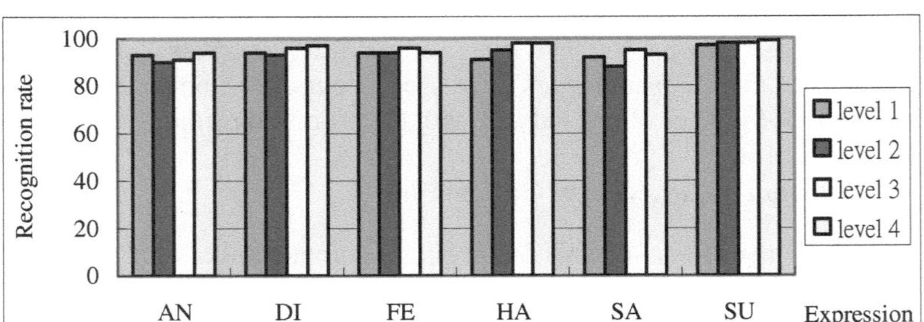

Fig. 6. Recognition rates of reconstructed face with original optical flow to known subject. (average recognition rate: 94.5%)

With the accurate optical flow between the expression and neutral faces of the same subject, we can generate a synthesized neutral face image as shown in Fig. 5. The recognition rates by using the synthesized neutral face images with the optical flow warping are shown in Fig. 6, which can achieve an average value of 94.5%.

The recognizing process is basically same as that in the benchmark test, except that regions in the training neutral faces corresponding to the black and white parts are unified to white. As shown in the result, the constrained optical flow estimation is excellent for removing expression deformation even with exaggerative facial motions. For example, the recognition rate for surprising level 4 is improved from 26% to 99%.

3.2 Face Recognition with Synthesized Neutral Face

In the face recognition experiment, the constrained optical flow estimation algorithm is employed to find the warping transformation for the facial expression image and synthesize the corresponding neutral face image for classification. Since intensity variation is also involved in the optical flow computation, the synthesized image looks just like the person with neutral face even if the reference neutral face belongs to someone else, like Fig. 7. In the experiments, the universal neutral face image NE_1 was arbitrarily selected as the neutral face of #1 subject, and the comparison was based on the average recognition rates.

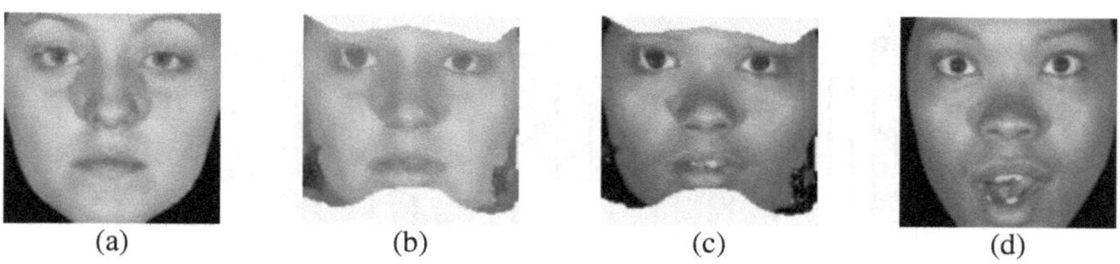

Fig. 7. Illustrations of accurate optical flow from one person to another, (a) referenced neutral face; (b) synthesized face from (d) to (a) with full optical flow; (c) synthesized face from (d) to (a) with motion optical flow only; (d) input image of surprising face at level 4

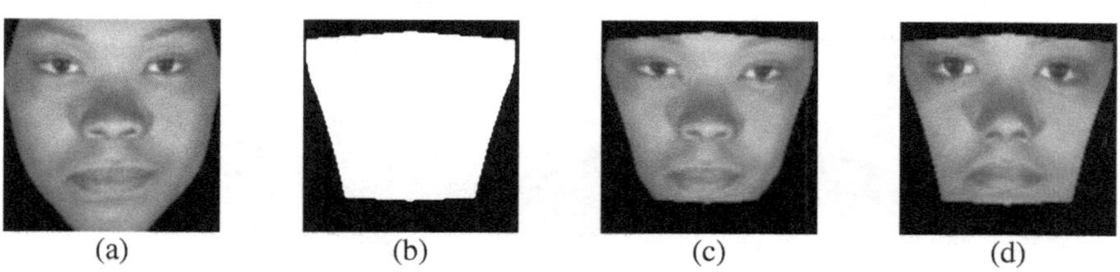

Fig. 8. Illustrations of accurate optical flow from one person to another, (a) referenced neutral face; (b) mask image; (c) bilinear warped face to from (a) NE_1; (d) synthesized face with only motion vector from (a) to NE_1

Therefore, as mentioned in section 2.3, only motion information in the optical flow estimation was used for neutral face image synthesis. As shown in Fig. 7(c), there will be some missing area in the synthesized image due to large motion, and a mask is employed to reduce the area of image comparison.

Fig. 9 and Fig. 10 depict the recognition results with partially masked synthesized image using different methods, PCA and direct subtraction. Obviously, the direct subtract algorithm outperforms the PCA method, which means that the synthesized images are very similar to each other due to the same reference neutral image.

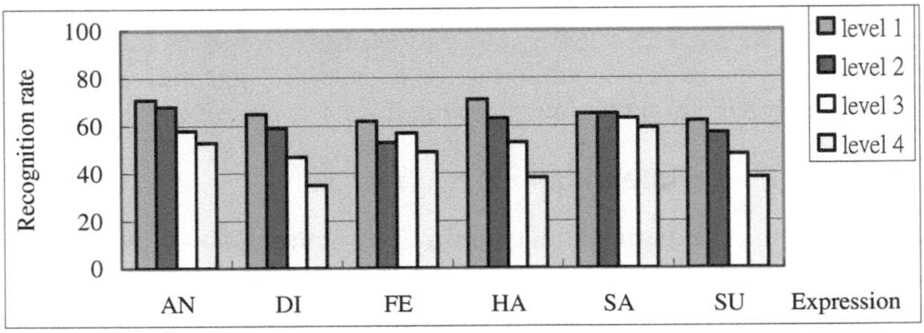

Fig. 9. Recognition rate from the synthesized neural face image by using the estimated optical flow only, compared to synthesized neutral face by using the same method, by using PCA dimensional reduction with 95% energy preservation. The average recognition rate is 57.19%.

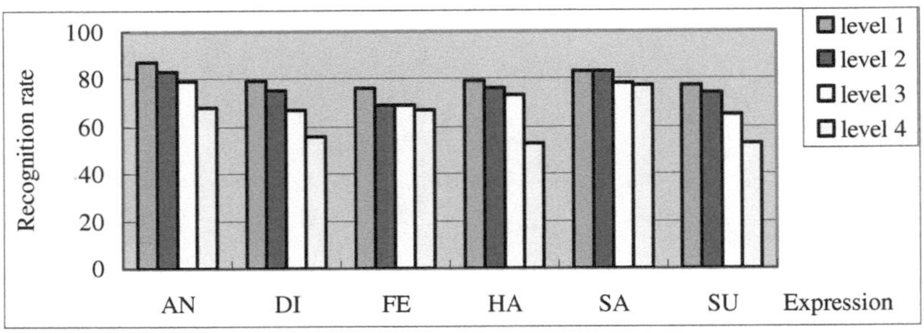

Fig. 10. Recognition rate from the synthesized neural face image by using the estimated optical flow only, compared to synthesized neutral face by using the same method, by using direct difference and nearest neighbor method. The average recognition rate is 73.48%.

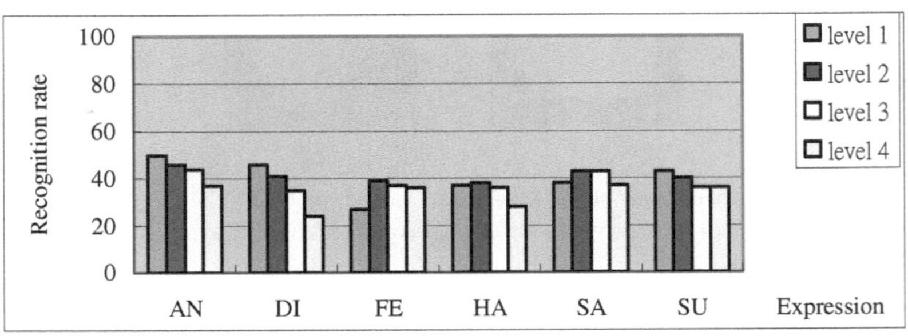

Fig. 11. Recognition rate from the synthesized face image by using the estimated optical flow only, compared to bilinearly warped neutral face, by using direct difference and the nearest neighbor classification. The average recognition rate is 39.02%.

Therefore, direct subtraction is more suitable in this application. Our proposed method (Fig. 10) is better than the benchmark result (Fig. 4) by 17% in average.

Different pre-processing procedures are performed in our experiments for comparison: one is bilinear warping from neutral faces (Fig 8(a)) to the universal neutral image NE_1, like Fig. 8(c); the other is by using the same procedure for the testing image, e.g. Fig. 8(d). The experimental results are shown in Fig. 11 and Fig. 10, respectively. We can see that the second way is better than the first one, since the face geometry is more uniform in the processed testing image.

4 Conclusion and Future Works

In this paper, we apply the constrained optical flow estimation for removing the facial expression for expression-invariant face recognition. With some modification in the optical flow computation, we can guarantee that the motion vector of the feature points to be consistent during the ICPCG iterations. The proposed method can improve the recognition rate about 17% under the circumstance that only one training neutral image of each subject is available, and the optical flow computation is performed only once for each testing image.

The lighting condition is restricted in our experiments. It is apparent that accurate optical flow varies dramatically when the illumination variation is large, which may influence the expression-normalized face image. In the future works, we plan to compensate the global lighting effect by using the spherical harmonics technique. After removing the illumination variations, the optical flow can be subsequently used to estimate the warping transformation due to facial expression.

References

1. Li, S.Z., Jain, A.K.: Handbook of Face Recognition. Springer, NewYork (2005)
2. Tsai, P.-H., Jan, T.: Expression-Invariant Face Recognition System Using Subspace Model Analysis. In: 2005 IEEE Conference on Systems, Man and Cybernetics (October 10-12, 2005) vol. 2, pp. 1712–1717 (2005)
3. Ramachandran, M., Zhou, S.K., Jhalani, D., Chellappa, R.: A Method for Converting a Smiling Face to a Neutral Face with Applications to Face Recognition. In: Proceedings of ICASSP 2005, vol. 2 (March 18-23, 2005)
4. Li, X., Mori, G., Zhang, H.: Expression-Invariant Face Recognition with Expression Classification. In: CRV 2006. The 3rd Canadian Conference on Computer and Robot Vision 2006 (June 07-09, 2006)
5. Martinez, A.M.: Recognizing expression Variant Faces from a Single Sample per Class. In: CVPR 2003. Proceedings of 2003 IEEE Computer Society Conference on Computer Vision and Pattern Recognition (June 18-20, 2003)
6. Teng, C.-H., Lai, S.-H., Chen, Y.-S., Hsu, W.-H.: Accurate optical flow computation under non-uniform brightness variations. Computer Vision and Image Understanding 97, 315–346 (2005)
7. Lin, S.C., Li, M.J., Zhang, H.J., Cheng, Q.S.: Ranking prior Likelihood Distributions for Bayesian Shape Localization Framework. In: Proceedings of ICCV 2003 (2003)
8. Yin, L., Wei, X., Sun, Y., Wang, J., Rosato, M.J.: A 3D Facial Expression Database For Facial Behavior Research. In: FGR 2006. Proceedings of 7th International Conference on Automatic Face and Gesture Recognition, pp. 211–216 (April 10-12, 2006)

Real-Time Facial Feature Point Extraction

Ce Zhan, Wanqing Li, Philip Ogunbona, and Farzad Safaei

University of Wollongong, Wollongong, NSW 2522, Australia
{cz847,wanqing,philipo,farzad}@uow.edu.au

Abstract. Localization of facial feature points is an important step for many subsequent facial image analysis tasks. In this paper, we proposed a new coarse-to-fine method for extracting 20 facial feature points from image sequences. In particular, the Viola-Jones face detection method is extended to detect small-scale facial components with wide shape variations, and linear Kalman filters are used to smoothly track the feature points by handling detection errors and head rotations. The proposed method achieved higher than 90% detection rate when tested on the BioID face database and the FG-NET facial expression database. Moreover, our method shows robust performance against the variation of face resolutions and facial expressions.

1 Introduction

Localization of facial feature points is often a critical step in many multimedia applications including face recognition, face tracking, facial expression recognition, gaze detection and face animation [1,2,3,4]. The fiducial facial feature points needed to be detected are usually the salient points on the face, such as eye corners, mouth corners, eyebrow corners and nostril corners. Various approaches have been proposed in the literature to extract these facial points from images or video sequences of faces. In general, these approaches can be categorized either as appearance-based or geometric-based. Appearance-based methods use feature vectors to model local texture around the facial feature points. To obtain the feature vectors, several methods such as Gabor wavelets [5], principal components analysis (PCA) [6] and Gaussian derivative filters [7] are often used to transform the local textures. The transformed features are then selected and processed by machine learning techniques such as multi-layer perceptrons (MLP) [8] and support vector machines (SVMs) [9]. In geometric-based methods, the prior knowledge of the face structure is used to constrain the facial feature point search, and the search is based on certain rules which can be learned from a set of labeled faces and often involve distance and angles [10,11].

It is interesting to note that most of the existing methods attempt to locate facial feature points from images/video captured in a highly controlled laboratory environment and with high spatial resolution. Furthermore, the face regions are always larger than 160×160 pixels. This resolution is equivalent to a person sitting only 30cm away from a webcam with focal length of 3cm and image capture resolution at 320×240 (see Table 1). It is obvious that many applications require

H.H.S. Ip et al. (Eds.): PCM 2007, LNCS 4810, pp. 88–97, 2007.

a much wider range of working distances than this, especially when wireless input devices and lower resolution cameras are used. In addition, most existing methods extract facial landmarks from expressionless face images which are unsuitable for facial expression recognition, in particular, when the recognition is based on local features. Finally, computational cost of the methods involving multiple classifications cannot be afforded by most real-time applications with limited computing resources.

To overcome the above mentioned problems, this paper proposes a new method for extracting 20 facial feature points. The method employs a number of modifications to the conventional Viola-Jones AdaBoost detection method and is relatively insensitive to the resolution of face images. It performs well within a practical range of working distances. With the goal of reducing the computational load, a coarse-to-fine strategy is adopted.

The rest of this paper is organized as follows: Section 2 describes the proposed method. Section 3 presents the experimental results obtained on a number of face databases. Conclusions are given in Section 4.

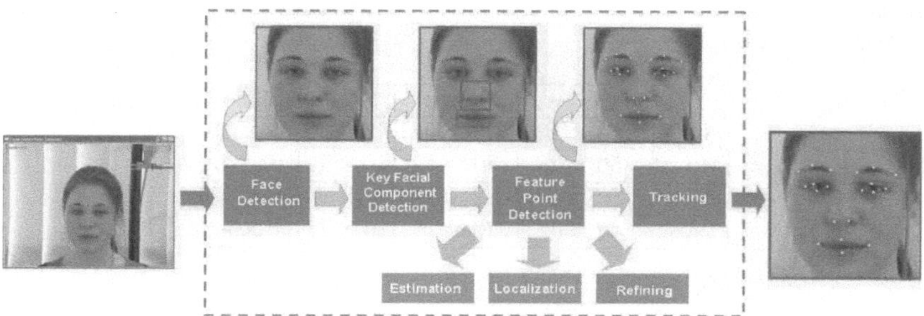

Fig. 1. The coarse-to-fine facial feature point extraction process

2 The Proposed Method

The proposed coarse-to-fine method consists of four stages, as shown in Figure 1: Face Detection, Key Facial Component Detection, Feature Point Detection and Feature Point Tracking.

2.1 Face Detection

The face region is detected and localized by the conventional Viola-Jones AdaBoost method. For details on the method, readers are referred to [12,13].

2.2 Key Facial Component Detection

The second stage of the coarse-to-fine process is to locate key facial components (nose, mouth and eyes) within the detected face area. To take advantage of the low computation overhead associated with Haar-like features and highly efficient cascade structure used in Viola-Jones AdaBoost face detection method, "AdaBoost" detection principle is adopted. However, low detection rate was observed when the conventional Viola-Jones method was trained with the facial components and employed in the detection process. This is probably due to the lack of significant structure information of the facial components (compared to the entire face). In general, the structure of the facial components become less detectable when the detected face is at low resolution. Table 1 shows approximate size of facial components at different distances for a webcam with focal length of 3cm and resolution of 320×240. Another cause of the low detection rate is probably the substantial variations in the shape of the components, especially mouth, among the different expressions conveyed by the same or different people. This is also true for high resolution face images. To solve these problems, we improve the "AdaBoost" detection method by employing: extended Haar-like features, modified training criteria, regional scanning and probabilistic selection of candidate sub-window.

Table 1. The approximate relationship between distance of user to camera and facial component resolution

	30cm	50cm	80cm	130cm
Face	165×165	100×100	65×65	45×45
Mouth	56×28	30×15	20×10	12×6
Eyes	36×18	22×11	14×7	8×4
Nose	42×42	26×26	16×16	9×9

Extended Haar-like Feature Set. An extended feature set with 14 Haar-like features (Figure 2) based on [14] is used in the facial component detection. Besides the basic upright rectangle features employed in face detection, 45° rotated rectangle features and center-surround features are added to the feature pool. The additional features are more representative for different shapes than the original Haar-feature set, and would therefore improve the detection performance.

High Hit Rate Cascade Training. In the conventional Viola-Jones method, the cascade classifier is trained based on the desirable hit rate and false positive rate. Additional stage is added to the cascade classifier if the false positive is higher. However, when the false positive rate decreases, the hit rate also decreases. In the case of facial components detection, hit rate will dramatically fall

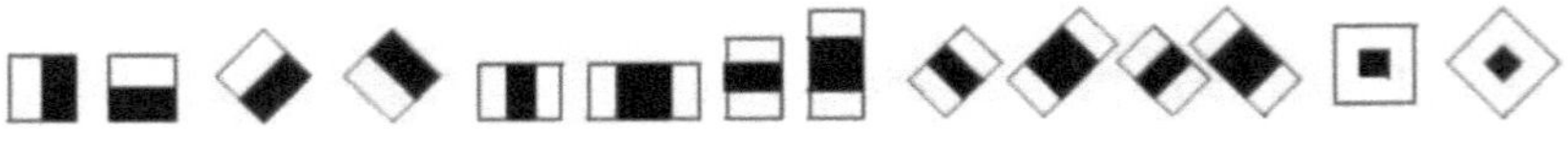

Fig. 2. The extended Haar-like feature set

for low resolution face images if the cascade classifier is training with low false positive rate.

To ensure that low resolution facial components could be detected, a minimum overall hit rate is set before training. For each stage in the training, the training goal is set to achieve a high hit rate and an acceptable false positive rate. The number of features used is then increased until the target hit rate and false positive rate are met for the stage. If the overall hit rate is still greater than the minimum value, another stage is added to the cascade to reduce the overall false positive rate. In this way, the trained detectors will detect the facial components at a guaranteed hit rate though some false positives will occur, which can be reduced or removed by the modifications introduced below.

Regional Scanning With a Fixed Classifier. Rather than rescaling the classifier as proposed by Viola and Jones, to achieve multiscale searching, input face images are resized to a range of predicted sizes and a fixed classifier is used for facial component detection. Due to the structure of face, we predict the face size according to the size of facial component used for training. In this way, the computation of the whole image pyramid is avoided. If the facial component size is bigger than the training size, fewer false positives would be produced due to down sampling; when the component is smaller than the training sample, the input image is scaled up to match the training size.

In addition, prior knowledge of the face structure is used to partition the region of scanning. The top region of the face image is used for eye detection; the central region of the face area is used for nose detection; and mouth is searched in the lower region of the face. The regional scanning not only reduces the false positives, but also lowers the computation.

Candidate sub-window selection. To select the true sub-window which contain the facial component, it is assumed that the central position of the facial components among different persons follows a normal distribution. Thus, the probability that a candidate component at $\mathbf{k} = \left[x\ y\right]^T$ is the true position can be calculated as:

$$P(\mathbf{k}) = \frac{1}{(2\pi)\left|s\mathbf{\Sigma}\right|^{1/2}} \exp\left(-\frac{1}{2}(\mathbf{k} - s\mathbf{m})^T s\mathbf{\Sigma}^{-1}(\mathbf{k} - s\mathbf{m})\right)$$

where the mean vector $\mathbf{m}$ and the covariance matrix $\mathbf{\Sigma}$ is estimated from normalized face image data set. The scale coefficient, s, can be computed as $s = w_d/w_n$, where w_d is the width of detected face and w_n is the width of normalized training faces. The candidate with maximum probability is selected as the true component.

Specialized classifiers. Two cascade classifiers are trained for mouth. One is for detecting closed mouths, and the other is for open mouths. During scanning, if the closed mouth detector failed to find a mouth, the open mouth detector is triggered. In addition, the left and right eye classifiers are trained separately.

2.3 Facial Feature Point Detection

The facial feature point detection process entails estimation, localization and refinement. First, positions of the 20 facial feature points are approximated based on the boundary box of the detected facial components, as shown in Figure 3. It is assumed that the actual landmark is localized within a $D \times D$ neighborhood of the approximated landmark, where D is determined by the size of facial components. For instance, 4 neighbourhoods of the mouth landmarks are indicated in Figure 3.

The localization is achieved by finding the position within the neighbourhood that maximizes eigenvalues of local structure matrix C,

$$C = w_G\left(r;\sigma\right) * \begin{bmatrix} f_x^2 & f_x f_y \\ f_x f_y & f_y^2 \end{bmatrix}$$

where $w_G\left(r;\sigma\right)$ is the Gaussian filter for smoothing the matrix entries and $f(x, y)$ is the intensity function. The classic Harris [15] corner finder is applied to refine the detected landmark positions so as to achieve sub-pixel accuracy.

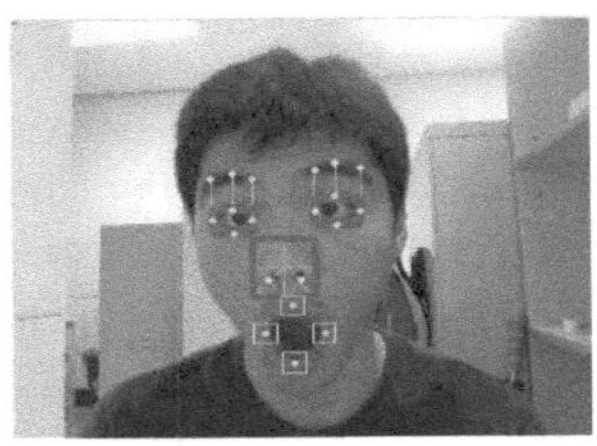

Fig. 3. Facial feature points estimation

2.4 Facial Feature Point Tracking

Occasionally, key facial components may not be reliably detected due to head rotations. There are also cases where the true facial feature points are not located in the $D \times D$ neighborhood of the estimated landmarks. With the goal of obtaining more accurate and smooth feature point positions, linear Kalman filters are employed to track the detected landmarks. In the linear Kalman filter the state vector consists of position, velocity and acceleration.

The Kalman filter predicts facial landmark positions in the next frame and corrects the localization results in the current frame. The prediction makes the feature points extraction process more stable when previous processing stages failed or some error occurred. At the same time, the correction enhances the accuracy.

3 Experimental Results

3.1 Facial Component Detection

As introduced in Section 2.2, five cascade classifiers were trained to detect the key facial components, one each, for left eye, right eye and nose, and two for mouth.

Positive training samples of eyes, mouths, noses and negative samples (non-facial components) were cropped from AR database [16] and AT&T database [17]. To accommodate low resolution facial components, the training samples were rescaled to small sizes: 10×6 for eyes, 16×8 for mouth and 15×15 for nose. For each detector about 1200 positive samples and 5000 negative samples were used for training. The trained detectors were first tested on BioID database [18]. The BioID database consists of 1521 images of frontal faces captured in uncontrolled conditions using a web camera in an office environment. For each image in the database, the ground truth of 20 facial feature points were obtained through manual annotation and supplied with the database. To evaluate the performance on low resolution input, the test images were downsized to different resolutions to simulate low resolution faces which are not included in the database. In this way, 300 images were tested at each face resolution. In the testing phase, a detection was regarded as SUCCESS if and only if the distance between the center of a detected and actual facial component was less than 30% of the width of the actual facial component as well as the width of the detected facial component was within ±50% of the actual width. To show the improvement obtained in comparison with the original detection method proposed by Viola and Jones, mouth detection results at different face resolutions are presented in Figure 4. The average detection rate for nose, left eye, right eye and mouth at different face resolutions is 91.3%, 95.7%, 97.2% and 95.6% respectively. A few detection examples are shown in Figure 5. The detectors were also tested on facial expression database FG-NET [19]. The database contains 399 video sequences of 6 basic emotions and a neutral expression from 18 individuals. The overall detection rate for all the detectors is 93.8%. Figure 6 shows typical detection examples of FG-NET. Figure 7 shows snap shots from a real-time example.

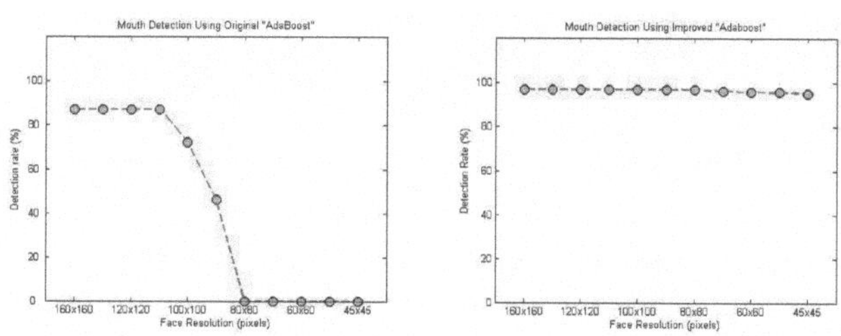

a. Original "AdaBoost" b. Improved "AdaBoost"

Fig. 4. Mouth detection result. Both detectors are trained using same dataset.

3.2 Facial Feature Point Extraction

The feature point extraction method were also tested on BioID database. In the testing phase, images from the same individual were reordered and treated as an image sequence. A detection is regarded as SUCCESS when the distance between the located facial point and the annotated true point was less than 10% of the inter-ocular distance (distance between left and right eye pupils). Unfortunately,

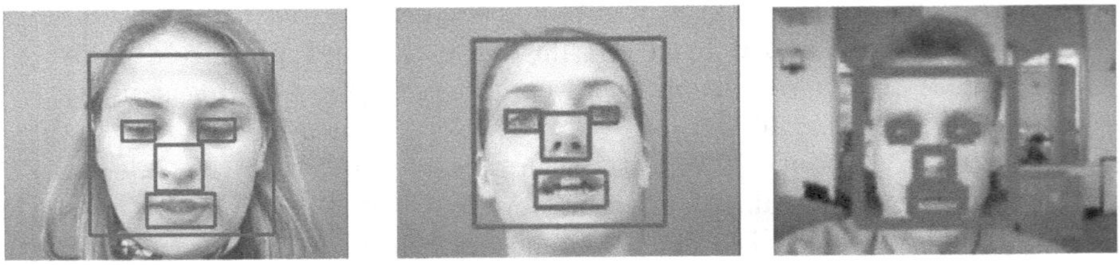

a. Face resolution: 160 × 160 b. Face resolution: 100 × 100 c. Face resolution: 50 × 50

Fig. 5. Facial component detection results from BioID database

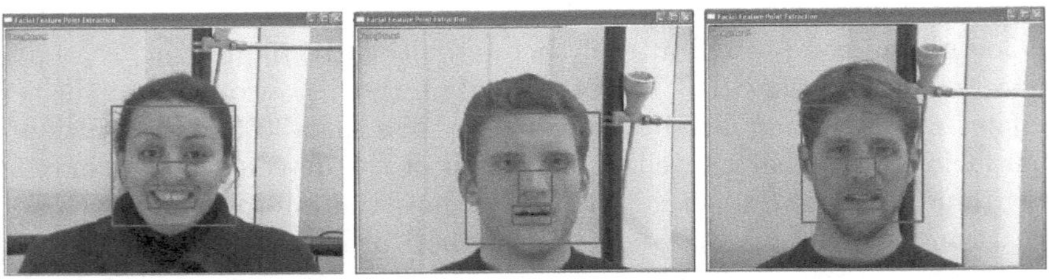

Fig. 6. Facial component detection results from FG-NET database

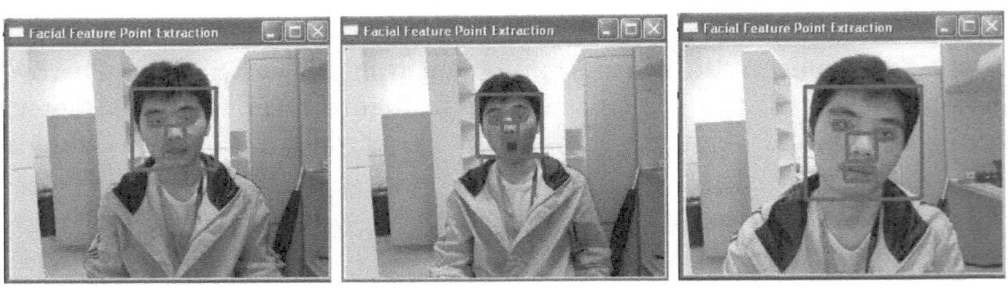

Fig. 7. Real-time facial component detection results

only 14 of the facial points we detected are annotated in the BioID database. The testing result is presented in Table 2; the average detection rate for all of the 14 points is 93%. The same method was used as Section 3.1, to test the feature extraction approach on different resolution faces, the results is shown in Figure 8, and test examples are presented in Figure 9. When testing the proposed method on FG-NET database, each of the 20 automatically detected facial landmarks was compared to manually labeled facial point. The average detection rate for all of the points is 91%, and some examples are shown in Figure 10. During the real-time test, the proposed facial feature points extraction method exhibited robust performances against variations in face resolutions and facial expressions. The tracking module also enabled the proposed method to handle some degree of in-plane and out-of-plane rotations. Figure 11 are a few test examples.

Table 2. Facial feature point extraction results based on BioID database

Feature Point	Rate	Feature Point	Rate
1: Right mouth corner	96%	2: Left mouth corner	91%
3: Outer end of right eye brow	92%	4: Inner end of right eye brow	94%
5: Inner end of left eye brow	97%	6: Outer end of left eye brow	91%
7: Outer corner of right eye	90%	8: Inner corner of right eye	96%
9: Inner corner of left eye	97%	10: Outer corner of left eye	88%
11: Right nostril	95%	12: Left nostril	94%
13: Center point on outer edge of upper lip	87%	14: Center point on outer edge of lower lip	85%

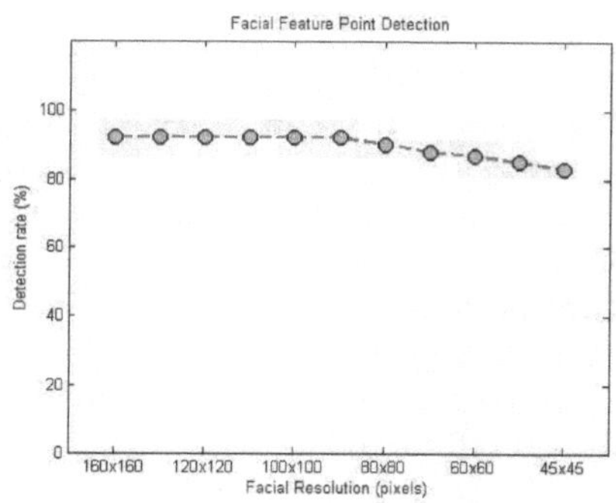

Fig. 8. Average feature point detection rates for different face resolutions

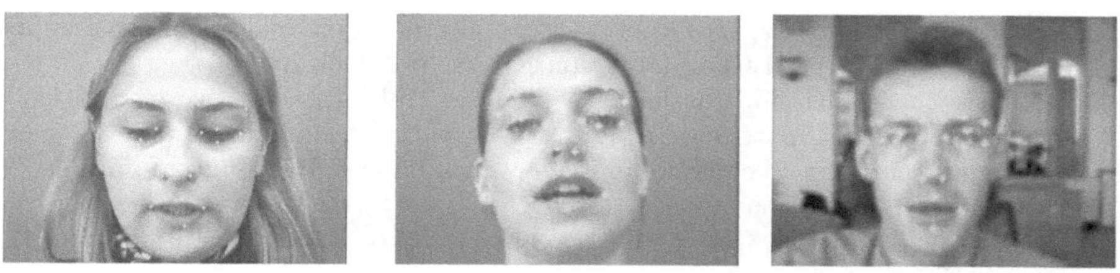

a. Face resolution: 160 × 160 b. Face resolution: 100 × 100 c. Face resolution: 50 × 50

Fig. 9. Facial feature point detection results from BioID database

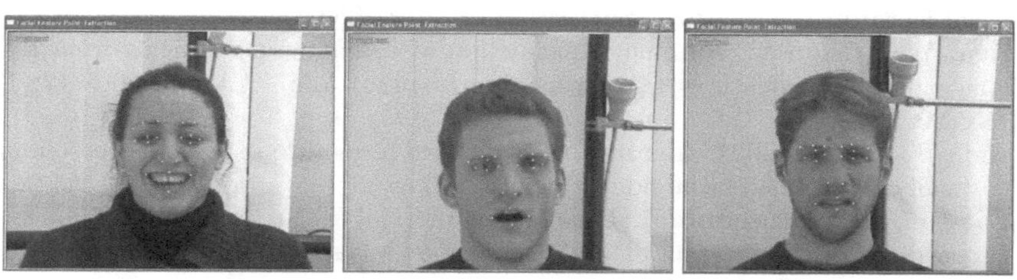

Fig. 10. Feature point extraction results from FG-NET database

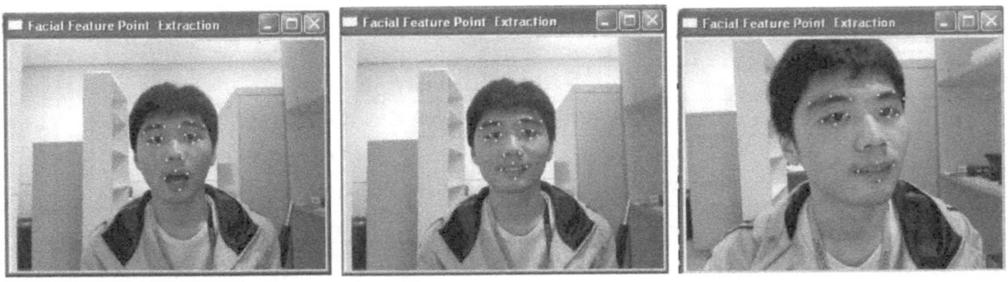

Fig. 11. Real-time facial point extraction results

4 Conclusions

Various approaches have been proposed in the past to extract facial feature points from face images or video sequences. Most of the previous methods attempt to locate facial feature points from data collected in a highly controlled laboratory environment and characterized by high resolution and expressionless faces. This paper proposes a new method, based on previous research, for extracting 20 facial feature points from expressional face images at in varying resolutions. The proposed method can handle a certain degree of head rotations and achieved higher than 90% detection rate when tested on BioID face database and FG-NET facial expression databases.

References

1. Pantic, M., Rothkrantz, L.: Expert system for automatic analysis of facial expression. Image and Vision Computing Journal 18, 881–905 (2000)
2. Wiskott, L., Fellous, J.M., Krüger, N., von der Malsburg, C.: Face recognition by elastic bunch graph matching. In: Jain, L.C., Halici, U., Hayashi, I., Lee, S.B. (eds.) Intelligent Biometric Techniques in Fingerprint and Face Recognition, pp. 355–396. CRC Press, Boca Raton (1999)
3. Dailey, M.N., Cottrell, G.W.: PCA = gabor for expression recognition. Technical Report CS1999-0629 (1999)
4. Turk, M., Pentland, A.: Eigenfaces for recognition. Journal of Cognitive Neuroscience 3, 71–76 (1991)
5. Shih, F.Y., Chuang, C.F.: Automatic extraction of head and face boundaries and facial features. Information Sciences 158, 117–130 (2004)
6. Ryu, Y.S., Oh, S.Y.: Automatic extraction of eye and mouth fields from a face image using eigenfeatures and ensemble networks. Applied Intelligence 17, 171–185 (2002)
7. Arca, S., Campadelli, P., Lanzarotti, R.: A face recognition system based on automatically determined facial fiducial points. Pattern Recognition 39, 432–443 (2006)
8. Campadelli, P., Lanzarotti, R.: Localization of facial features and fiducial points. In: Proceedings of the International Conference on Visualisation, Imaging and image Processing, pp. 491–495 (2002)
9. Liao, C.T., Wu, Y.K., Lai, S.H.: Locating facial feature points using support vector machines. In: Proceedings of the 9th International Workshop on Cellular Neural Networks and Their Applications, pp. 296–299 (2005)

10. Zobel, M., Gebhard, A., Paulus, D., Denzler, J., Niemann, H.: Robust facial feature localization by coupled features. In: Proceedings of the 4th International Conference on Automatic Face and Gesture Recognition, pp. 2–7 (2000)
11. Yan, S., Hou, X., Li, S.Z., Zhang, H., Cheng, Q.: Face alignment using view-based direct appearance models. International Journal of Imaging Systems and Technology 13, 106–112 (2003)
12. Viola, P., Jones, M.: Robust real-time object detection. International Journal of Computer Vision (2002)
13. Freund, Y., Schapire, R.E.: A decision-theoretic generalization of online learning and an application to boosting. In: Vitányi, P.M.B. (ed.) EuroCOLT 1995. LNCS, vol. 904, pp. 23–37. Springer, Heidelberg (1995)
14. Lienhart, R., Maydt, J.: An extended set of haar-like features for rapid object detection. In: Proceedings of the International Conference on Image Processing, vol. 1, pp. I–900–I–903 (2002)
15. Harris, C., Stephens, M.: A combined corner and edge detector. In: Alvey Vision Conference, pp. 147–151 (1998)
16. http://cobweb.ecn.purdue.edu/aleix/aleix_face_DB.html
17. http://www.cl.cam.ac.uk/research/dtg/attarchive/facedatabase.html
18. http://www.bioid.com/
19. http://www.mmk.ei.tum.de/waf/fgnet/feedtum.html

Local Dual Closed Loop Model Based Bayesian Face Tracking

Dan Yao, Hong Lu, Xiangyang Xue, and Zhongyi Zhou

Department of Computer Science and Engineering,
Fudan University, Shanghai, China
{041021075, honglu, xyxue, zhouzy}@fudan.edu.cn

Abstract. This paper presents a new Bayesian face tracking method under particle filter framework. First, two adaptive feature models are proposed to extract face features from image sequences. Then the robustness of face tracking is reinforced via building a local dual closed loop model (LDCLM). Meanwhile, trajectory analysis, which helps to avoid unnecessary restarting of detection module, is introduced to keep tracked faces' identity as consistent as possible. Experimental results demonstrate the efficacy of our method.

1 Introduction

Face tracking has become a hot research topic in recent years when more and more important applications in digital video, surveillance and human-computer interaction appear. Normally, tracking task is meaningful only when being applied within one video shot or continuous surveillance situation, and makes no sense in most cross-shots cases where the targets are often different. The most important two purposes of face tracking are accurate face detection and identity association of faces located at different time instants.

1.1 Related Work

Different tracking methods have been proposed in the literature. As the matching mode considered, these methods can be classified into three categories: template-based methods [1, 2, 3] deal with complex situations; feature-based methods [4, 5, 6, 7, 8] build corresponding relationship between candidates and the targets by extracting features like color, contour, Gabor, etc.; while learning-based methods [9, 10] are based on recognition algorithms or subspace analysis.

However, several problems still need further research.

First, *matching modes have more strength on representation other than discrimination.* Many researchers developed adaptive matching modes which can model appearance variability well but lack of discrimination power. It is hard to distinguish the target and some other similar objects, unless recognition algorithms are applied.

Secondly, *wrong information is accumulated without correction.* In consideration of computation cost, many algorithms select candidates somehow at random

H.H.S. Ip et al. (Eds.): PCM 2007, LNCS 4810, pp. 98–107, 2007.

in spite of obeying some distribution rules or from a limited small area. Thereby, it is very often to lead to a local optimal value. And with such inaccurate tracking results passing to next frames, the wrong information will usually be accumulated without being corrected.

Thirdly, *detection module is restarted unnecessarily.* If the output of matching function keeps decreasing due to temporal occlusion, rotation, noise, etc., conventional tracking systems will simply stop current tracking and restart the detection module to search the following whole frames until a face is detected. Then this face will be treated as a new target to continue tracking, and the identity association with the prior corresponding faces is lost.

1.2 Overview of Our Method

To address the above mentioned problems, a new particle filter based Bayesian face tracking system is proposed. The whole framework is shown in Fig.1.

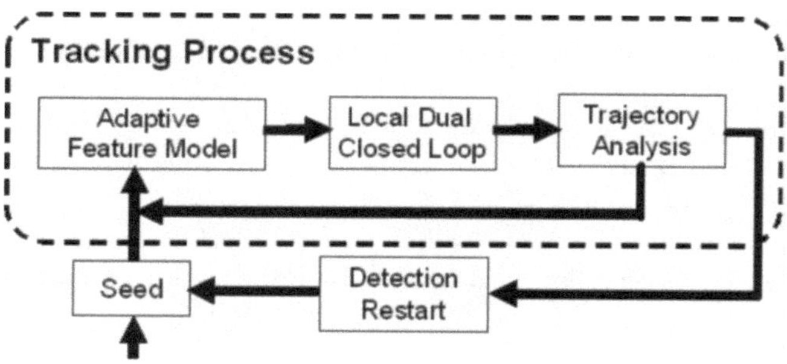

Fig. 1. System framework

The tracking process begins with a *seed* which specifies the target object. The seed is located by the detection algorithm with high confidence in the first frame of the video shot.

To improve the discrimination power of features, the adaptive feature models, which include a special face color model (FC) and a simple color layout distribution model, are built. The FC is adaptive to different tracked objects and used to locate target face area; and the CLD acts as an auxiliary measure to help the extraction of color layout features. The feature information with time stamps will be recorded for trajectory analysis.

After feature extraction, a local dual closed loop model (LDCLM) is constructed by using self feedback technique. In different steps of the model, FC feature or CLD feature is extracted accordingly. The feedback technique, which has been widely used in control theory, is applied to correct possible tracking errors to avoid wrong information being accumulated.

During the tracking process, trajectory analysis is used to determine whether the object has moved out of the image vision and determine the necessity to restarting the detection module. In many cases that the matching confidence of the tracked object keeps decreasing, the object still stays in the current image vision, we do not have to restart detection which will bring a new seed and a new tracking process. We avoid unnecessary restarting of detection though trajectory analysis, which is very simple, however, is very useful, especially in some long shots with the object rotating his/her head or walking behind others very slowly.

This paper is organized as follows. Section 2 introduces the Bayesian face tracking framework, the adaptive feature models, the LDCLM algorithm, and the trajectory analysis; experimental results are given in section 3 and the paper is concluded in section 4.

2 Bayesian Face Tracking

In this method, at time instant t, the state vector is defined as $s_t = (x_t, y_t, w_t, h_t)$, where (x_t, y_t, w_t, h_t) represents the central position, width and height of a face candidate respectively; the observations from the two feature models are denoted as: z_t^{fc} for FC model and z_t^{cld} for CLD model .

Initially, at time instant $t = 0$, a frontal face, which is detected by the AdaBoost face detector [13], is denoted as the seed s_0. Around s_0, a zero-mean multivariate Gaussian model is built to generate N initial candidates with corresponding prior probability $p(s_0^i)_{i=1}^N$. Prior weights are normalized by $\pi_0^i = p(s_0^i)/\sum_{i=1}^N p(s_0^i)$.

During the tracking iterations, we have the prediction-update rule of particle filter based on Bayesian rules used in [11] for propagation of state density over time as Eq.(1):

$$\begin{aligned} p(s_t \mid Z_t) &\propto p(z_t \mid s_t)p(s_t \mid Z_{t-1}) \\ p(s_t \mid Z_{t-1}) &= \int_{s_{t-1}} p(s_t \mid s_{t-1})p(s_{t-1} \mid Z_{t-1}) \end{aligned} \quad (1)$$

where $z_t = z_t^{fc}$ or $z_t = z_t^{cld}$ according to the corresponding steps in LDCLM. $Z_t = (z_1, z_2, ..., z_t)$. With weighted samples $\{s_{t-1}^i, \pi_{t-1}^i\}_{i=1}^N$, the dynamic model $p(s_t \mid s_{t-1})$ is realized by factor sampling [11] and multivariate zero-mean Gaussian random sampling techniques.

After sample selection and prediction, for each candidate s_t^i, the weight is updated as $\pi_t^i = p(z_t^i \mid s_t^i)$ using observation z_t^{fc} from FC model or z_t^{cld} from CLD model, which will be explained later.

2.1 Adaptive Feature Models

The two feature models, FC model and CLD model, are built to extract face color feature z_t^{fc} and color layout distribution feature z_t^{cld}. The final optimal target $s_t^{optimal}$ in time instant t is selected from the candidate set $\{s_t^i\}_{i=1}^N$ by Eq.(2):

$$optimal = \max_i(p(z_t \mid s_t^i))_{i=1}^N \quad (2)$$

Adaptive face color model (FC). Generic skin color model like [12] is not sufficient to effectively distinguish the face color features of persons with different skin color. So we design a three-layer FC model.

The first layer of the model uses a general model by the method in [12], and only detect skin pixels of the seed in the initial phase of tracking process.

The second layer of the model builds a specific Gaussian model using these detected skin pixels from seed s_0 in YUV color space. We only use the U and V components (u, v). The Gaussian face color likelihood of pixel ν is defined as:

$$p(z^{fc} \mid \nu) = \frac{1}{2\pi} \exp\left(-\frac{1}{2}(r-\mu)^T C^{-1}(r-\mu)\right) \tag{3}$$

Where $r = (u, v)$, $\mu = E\{r\}$ and $C = E\{(r-\mu)(r-\mu)^T\}$. For different seeds, we have different Gaussian models. The Gaussian model is then used in the whole tracking process to give the confidence of each pixel in every candidate. An adaptive threshold δ is used to judge if the pixel $\nu = (x, y)$ in a candidate is a skin pixel or not. δ is set as Eq.(4):

$$\delta = p(z^{fc} \mid \nu_{opt}) \tag{4}$$

$$opt = \max_m\left(\frac{\sum_{i=1}^{m} p(z^{fc} \mid \nu_i)}{\sum_{j=1}^{M} p(z^{fc} \mid \nu_j)}\right) < \zeta \tag{5}$$

where $p(z^{fc} \mid \nu)$ is sorted in descending order; M is the pixel number of current candidate; the skin color likelihood of the m_{th} pixel will be taken as optimal threshold δ; ζ denotes the skin color energy proportion which is set based on empirical study. Thereby, δ is changing with the tracking process. In each time instant, δ finds a proper value to segment skin pixels from the background adaptively.

The face color likelihood of candidate s_t^i is set by Eq.(6):

$$p(z_t^{fc} \mid s_t^i) = N_{ps}^2 / (N_{pc} * \kappa) \tag{6}$$

where N_{ps} is the skin pixel number, N_{pc} is the total pixel number in candidate s_t^i, and κ denotes the normalization factor.

The third layer of the model is a post processing to filter small noise properly and finely for the results from the second layer. The filter threshold η_t, which varies with FC likelihood and adaptively adjusts the filter criterion, is set as:

$$\eta_t = \tau * \left(p(z_{t-1}^{fc} \mid s_{t-1}^{optimal}) / p(z_0^{fc} \mid s_0)\right) \tag{7}$$

where τ is a constrained factor.

This Gaussian face color model will be updated in each time instant by those new face skin pixels with very high confidence ξ times larger than δ to alleviate possible pollution by background pixels, and it has more discrimination to distinguish faces with different skin color. An example is shown in Fig.2. Fig.2(b) and Fig.2(c) show the skin color confidence outputs of Fig.2(a) by two different Gaussian skin color models, which are trained respectively by the face skin pixels of the woman and the man. The skin color responses in Fig.2(b) and Fig.2(c) are apparently different in the confidence and the size of skin color area.

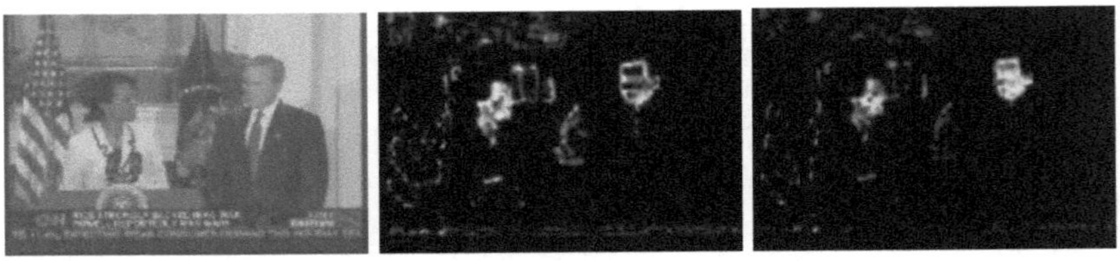

(a) (b) (c)

Fig. 2. Face Color Model. (a) is the raw image. Two different Gaussian skin color models are trained respectively by the face pixels of the woman and the man. (b) uses the Gaussian model of the woman and (c) uses the Gaussian model of the man. The skin color confidence outputs of (b) and (c) is apparently different.

Color layout distribution model(CLD). FC model can help to locate face area fast and easily, however, the FC likelihood drops in the cases of rotation, occlusion, etc. and can't distinguish faces with very similar skin color even when these faces' appearance are very different. Thereby a simpler adaptive color layout distribution model based on [5] is built to find the optimal layout matching result and to compensate the loss of FC model.

In this model, each candidate is divided equally into 16 blocks. Eq.(8) denotes the model likelihood of candidate s_t^i:

$$p(z_t^{cld} \mid s_t^i) = \frac{1}{16}\sum_{k=1}^{16}\left(\sqrt{\frac{|\Sigma_i^k|^{\frac{1}{2}}|\Sigma_{ref}^k|^{\frac{1}{2}}}{|\bar{\Sigma}^k|}}\exp\left(\frac{\hat{\mu^k}^T\,\bar{\Sigma^k}^{-1}\,\hat{\mu^k}}{8}\right)\right) \tag{8}$$

where, μ_i^k, Σ_i^k means the mean vector and covariance matrix of the k_{th} block in candidate s_t^i, $\hat{\mu^k} = \mu_i^k - \mu_{ref}^k$, $\bar{\Sigma^k} = (\Sigma_i^k + \Sigma_{ref}^k)/2$. The reference pair $(\Sigma_{ref}^k, \mu_{ref}^k)$ is updated from the target in time instant $t-1$.

2.2 Local Dual Closed Loop Model (LDCLM)

In the tracking process, FC and CLD models are used in different steps of LDCLM according to their characteristics. FC model locates the rough face areas, and CLD model can help to correct and refine the results of FC. In all the tracking iterations, trajectory analysis is combined into LDCLM.

The instability of observation often leads to inaccurate detection results is corrected by integrating self feedback technique into LDCLM. An illustration in illumination case about self feedback is shown in Fig.3. And the LDCLM is sketched in Fig.4.

1. *First Closed Loop*
   Step 1, Step 2 and Step 3 in Fig.4 construct the first closed loop. The target in time instant $t-1$, noted as $target_{t-1}$, is regarded as reliable. Step1 is carried by FC model as Eq.(9):

$$p(target_t^1) = p(z_t^{fc} \mid s_t^{optimal}) \tag{9}$$

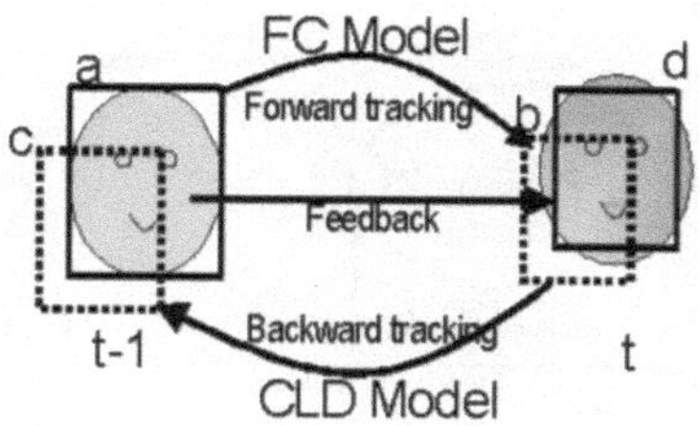

Fig. 3. Self Feedback Illustration. Object on left is regarded as a reliable target in time instant $t-1$, the state of which is described by solid box a, and in time instant t, it is affected by illumination. After forward tracking using face color features from FC model, we get the inaccurate target, the state of which is described by dot box b. Using features from CLD model of this inaccurate target in backward tracking, we get state dot box c. Compare the sizes and center positions of a and c, the state box b in time instant t is corrected to state solid box d.

Since the appearance difference between faces in consecutive frames is limited and can be characterized by CLD, Step2 is:

$$p(target^*_{t-1}) = p(z^{cld}_{t-1} \mid s^{optimal}_{t-1}) \tag{10}$$

Comparing the state vector of $target^1_{t-1}$ and $target^*_{t-1}$, the possible tracking error can be found in Step 1. By feeding back the center coordination and size difference, the result of Step 1 can be corrected into $target^2_t$.

2. *Second Closed Loop*
The Step 4 and Step 5 construct the second closed loop. Using the candidates generated by the results of Step 1, second forward tracking in Step 4 is also carried by FC model as Eq.(11) :

$$p(target_{t+1}) = p(z^{fc}_{t+1} \mid s^{optimal}_{t+1}) \tag{11}$$

In Step 5, second backward tracking takes CLD model as Eq.(12)

$$p(target^3_t) = p(z^{cld}_t \mid s^{optimal}_t) \tag{12}$$

3. *Interpolation*
To avoid sudden big noise due to stochastic sampling and to restrict the tracking error, we take the interpolation result from $target_{t-1}$ and $target_{t+1}$ as $target^4_t$.
4. *Optimal target strategy*
In the whole tracking process, only the seed is highly reliable, and in every time instant, due to the stochastic nature in particle filter, the above four results ($target^i_t, i = 1, .., 4$) in time t may be not accurate enough. Thus we propose an optimal target strategy as Eq.(13) and show one sample in Fig.4.

$$\begin{aligned}(X_t, Y_t, W_t, H_t) &= sort(target^i_t.(x, y, w, h))^4_{i=1},\\ target^{optimal}_t.(x, y, w, h) &= mean(X^i_t, Y^i_t, W^i_t, H^i_t)^3_{i=2},\end{aligned} \tag{13}$$

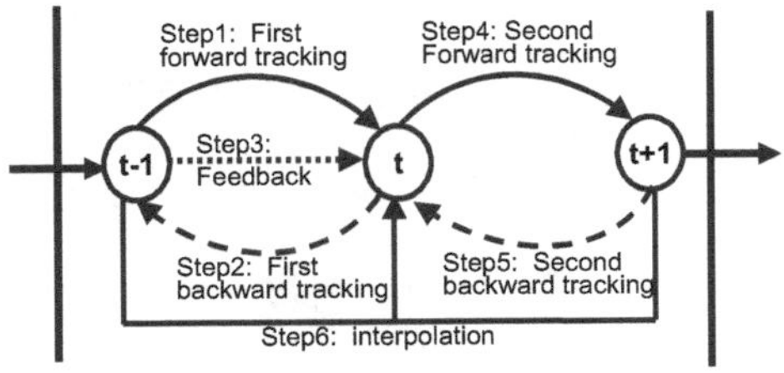

Fig. 4. Local Dual Closed Loop Model

In this model, the closed loop tracking is implemented only in three adjacent time instants. The reasons are given below: a) if involving more time instants, the uncertainty will increase heavily especially in rapid motion; b)such model can be applied in both video clips and real time surveillance by cache techniques.

2.3 Trajectory Analysis

During the whole tracking process, we keep paying attention to the trajectory state of the tracked object. A trajectory container (TC) is built to record the state vector and the FC likelihood of the target in time instant t:

$$TC_t = (s_t^{optimal}, p(z_t^{fc} \mid s_t^{optimal})) \tag{14}$$

As soon as the tracking process begins, taken the seed state as a reference, in each time instant, we compute the movement direction tendency and the movement velocity of the target.

The trajectory container is checked in each time instant. If the FC likelihood drops to below a pre-set threshold γ and keeps decreasing, and meanwhile the state vector analysis shows that the object might have moved out of the image vision, we will restart the detection module, otherwise, keep tracking.

3 Experimental Results

This method is implemented on various video clips from TV programs including out-door (11 clips, 4021 frames) and in-door (14 clips, 6532 frames). For detection ratio, it is compared with frame-based method [13] and tabulated the results in Table 1. For tracking performance, it is compared with two particle framework based tracking algorithms [8] and [10] (source codes are downloaded from the homepages of the authors). [8] is appearance-adaptive model based. [10] is incremental subspace based. We also compare with another version of our method using the same feature models and trajectory analysis but without LDCLM. The results are shown in Table 2. In these comparisons, the criterion of successful tracking in [5] is considered. Specifically, the target center must be in the ground truth rectangle and the size of the bounding rectangle on the target

Table 1. Performance comparison of detection

Method	Detection Rate (%)
Frame-based detector [13]	54.3
Our method	89.5

Table 2. Performance comparison of tracking

Method	In-door (%)	out-door (%)
Appearance-adaptive model [8]	77.11	81.04
Incremental subspace [10]	79.56	80.43
Without LDCLM	64.1	75.05
Our method	89.1	90.4

(a) Appearance-adaptive model based method [8]

(b) Incremental subspace based method [10]

(c) Our feature models and trajectory analysis based, and without LDCLM

(d) our method

Fig. 5. Face tracking results under significant occlusion, zoom and moderate illumination. From left to right are image frames 2587*th*, 2608*th*, 2642*th*, 2707*th*.

Fig. 6. Tracking results using our method. From left to right are frames $3th$, $42th$, $57th$, $109th$.

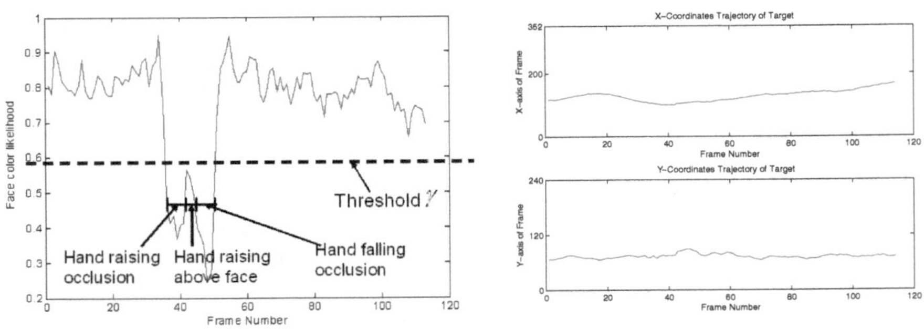

(a) Face color (FC) confidence trajectory. (b) Target state trajectory

Fig. 7. Trajectory analysis. Fig.6 is the raw frame sequence. Although the FC likelihood keeps low confidence for a longer time in (a), we can find that the target stably stays in the image vision from (b). Thereby, it is unnecessary to restart a new detection process during the period of low face color confidence outputs.

should be within [0.5,1.5] times of the size of the bounding rectangle of ground truth. Furthermore, some tracking results are presented in Fig.5.

Our method excels mainly because it can handle occlusion and rotation cases better. [13], [8] and [10] tend to lose faces in many occlusion and drastic rotation cases. For the occlusion case such as Fig.5, [8] and [10] both lose the targets in the frame $2642th$ and $2707th$. In Fig.5(a), [8] updates the appearance model inappropriately. In Fig.5(b), [10] updates the eigenbase by incorrect results during occlusion, consequently it fails to catch up targets finely after occlusion. Especially, both [8] and [10] couldn't recover from tracking errors. Once they lose the target, they will give wrong state information for all the rest frames.

Using the feature models, the recovering from errors is possible and we illustrate in Fig.5(c). FC and CLD models are used to locate face areas, and note that the third frame $2642th$ gives wrong response because the woman's shadow is just projected on the face of the man and affects his face color. In this example, since the Gaussian model is built by the skin pixels of the man, the skin pixels of the woman will usually have lower confidence and won't be use to update the Gaussian model. Once the shadow disappear, the Gaussian feature model will give correct respondence. Thus in the forth frame $2707th$, the target is recovered.

However, Without LDCLM to correct the errors, these outputs are inaccurate. Adding LDCLM into the method, the results shown in Fig.5(d) presents that such errors are corrected by LDCLM and are more accurate.

With the help of trajectory analysis, it is easily to judge the target state and avoid unnecessary restarting of detection module. Specifically, the raw frame sequence in Fig.6 gives the recorded trajectory as in Fig.7. Although the FC likelihood keeps low confidence for a longer time in Fig.7(a), from the trajectory states in Fig.7(b) we can find that the target stably stays in the image vision.

4 Conclusion

We have presented a new Bayesian face tracking system to improve the performance. With adaptive feature models, a LDCLM is constructed to enhance the robustness of tracking. Then, trajectory analysis helps to avoid unnecessary restarting of detection module. Our method can be easily extended to multi-faces tracking, and new feature models can also be integrated conveniently. Future work will focus on further improving the discrimination of feature models and analyzing the motion trajectory.

References

1. Nanda, H., Davis, L.: Probabilistic template based pedestrian detection in infrared videos, IEEE Intelligent Vehicles, Versailles, France, 15–20 (2002)
2. Stauffer, C., et al.: Similarity templates for detection and recognition. In: IEEE Int'l Conf. on CVPR, Kauai, HI, pp. 221–228 (2001)
3. Adam, A., Rivlin, E., Shimshoni, I.: Robust Fragments-based Tracking using the Integral Histogram. In: IEEE Int'l Conf. on CVPR, vol. 1, pp. 798–805 (2006)
4. Perez, R.P., Hue, C., Vermaak, J., et al.: Color-based probabilistic tracking. In: Tistarelli, M., Bigun, J., Jain, A.K. (eds.) ECCV 2002. LNCS, vol. 2359, pp. 661–675. Springer, Heidelberg (2002)
5. Yuan, L.I., Haizhou, A.I., et al.: Robust Head Tracking with Particles Based on Multiple Cues Fusion. In: Leonardis, A., Bischof, H., Pinz, A. (eds.) ECCV 2006. LNCS, vol. 3954, pp. 29–39. Springer, Heidelberg (2006)
6. Zhu, Z., Liao, W., Ji, Q.: Robust Visual Tracking Using Case-Based Reasoning with Confidence. In: IEEE Int'l Conf. on CVPR, vol. 1, pp. 806–816 (2006)
7. Comaniciu, D., Ramesh, V., Meer, P.: Real-time tracking of nonrigid objects using mean shif. In: Proc. IEEE Int'l Conf. on CVPR, vol. 2, pp. 142–149 (2000)
8. Zhou, S.K., Chellappa, R., Moghaddam, B.: Visual Tracking and Recognition Using Appearance-Adaptive Models in Particle Filters. IEEE Trans. on Image Processing 13(11), 1491–1506 (2004)
9. Avidan, S.: Support Vector Tracking. IEEE Trans. on PAMI 26(8), 1064–1072 (2004)
10. Lim, J., Ross, D., Lin, R.S., Yang, M.H.: Incremental Learning for Visual Tracking. In: NIPS, vol. 18, pp. 793–800 (2005)
11. Isard, M., Blake, A.: Condensation-Conditional Density Propagation for Visual Tracking. Int'l J. Computer Vision 29, 5–28 (1998)
12. Hsu, R.L., Abdel-Mottaleb, M., Jain, A.K.: Face detection in color images. IEEE Trans. on PAMI 24(5), 696–706 (2002)
13. Viola, P., Jones, M.: Robust real-time object detection, Technical Report, Compaq CRL (2001)

View-Independent Human Action Recognition by Action Hypersphere in Nonlinear Subspace*

Jian Zhang and Yueting Zhuang

College of Computer Science & Technology, Zhejiang University, Hangzhou 310027, P.R. China
zhangsdust@yahoo.com.cn, yzhuang@cs.zju.edu.cn

Abstract. Though recognizing human action from video is important to applications like visual surveillance, some hurdles still slower the progress of action recognition. One of the main difficulties is view dependency, and this causes the degeneration of many recognition algorithms. In this paper, we propose a template-based view-independent human action recognition approach. The action template comprises a series of "action hyperspheres" in a nonlinear subspace and encodes multi-view information of several typical human actions to facilitate the view-independent recognition. Given an input action from video, we first compute the Motion History Image (MHI) and corresponding polar feature according to the extracted human silhouettes; recognition is achieved by evaluating the distances between the embedding of the polar feature and the virtual centers of the hyperspheres. Experiments show that our approach maintains high recognition accuracy in free viewpoints, and is more computationally efficient compared with classical *k*NN approach.

Keywords: action recognition, action hypersphere, manifold embedding.

1 Introduction

Human action recognition from video is an open issue in computer vision with the important applications in visual surveillance, social security and human-computer-interaction. In recent years, some representative works have been done to recognize human actions from video. Some researchers considered action recognition as a problem of 3D reconstruction [1][2]. The human pose at each time instance was recovered by fitting pre-defined models based on the 2D body silhouette. However, acquiring 3D information from image sequences is currently a complicated process with poor robustness. Ekinci [3] presented a real-time people tracking and posture estimation technique for visual surveillance system. The human motion was segmented by background modeling technique, and then posture estimation was performed based on a skeleton structure of human silhouette. This work considered

* This work is supported by National Natural Science Foundation of China (No.60533090, No.60525108), 973 Program (No.2002CB312101), Science and Technology Project of Zhejiang Province (No.2005C13032, No.2006C13097), and Program for Changjiang Scholars and Innovative Research Team in University (IRT0652).

H.H.S. Ip et al. (Eds.): PCM 2007, LNCS 4810, pp. 108–117, 2007.

only scattered human silhouettes without temporal representation or modeling of human actions. Hidden Markov Model (HMM) has been widely used in human action recognition [4][5][6] which aimed to model the temporal pattern of a moving object. The rationale of these works was to extract a set of features from image frames of a sequence and use those features to train HMMs for recognition. Since HMMs rely on probabilities, they require extensive training to ensure the reliability. Therefore, one needs to have a large number of training sequences for each activity to be recognized, this is sometimes unavailable. Optical flow is an important cue for human motion, in [7], the author combined optical flow with HMMs to perform action recognition, but the computational complexity of optical flow was high, thus this approach was unsuitable for some real-time applications. 2D motion templates proposed by Davis and Bobick [8] was an effective way to describe temporal actions. They introduced Motion Energy Image (MEI) and Motion History Image (MHI) to capture motion information in image sequences. MEI and MHI contain temporal information of an action inherently, thus help to avoid the complex visual tracking problem. In this way, action recognition can be elegantly simplified as an image classification problem. Nevertheless, the representation described in [8] was view dependent, thus the recognition result was fine only in some specific views. In [9], the authors combined MHI and k-Nearest-Neighbor (kNN) algorithm to recognize the motion of facial action units, but the recognition efficiency heavily depended on the amount of sample data. Much time was needed to perform kNN classification on a large dataset. Weinland [10] introduced Motion History Volume (MHV) as an extension of MHI, though MHV is a free-viewpoint representation of human action, it is constructed in the case of multiple strictly calibrated video cameras. Therefore it is incompetent for recognizing actions in monocular video.

In this paper, we propose a view-independent human action recognition approach which is based on template matching. The action template includes multiple human actions, and recognition is performed by evaluating the distances between an input and the actions contained in the template. To achieve view-independent recognition, for each action to be enclosed into the template, we first construct a "hypersphere" in low-dimensional subspace based on the manifold embeddings [11] of polar features of the action's multi-view MHIs. Thus the action template is composed of multiple hyperspheres with known centers and radiuses. The recognition is then performed by computing the distances between the low-dimensional embedding of the input polar feature and the centers of the hyperspheres, and comparing the distances with the known radiuses, when the error is below some threshold, the input can be labeled as the "closest" action in the template. Compared with existing works, the motion template can be conveniently obtained from some uncalibrated camera views; moreover, the proposed action hypersphere encodes multi-view information and contributes to view-independent action recognition. Also, the hypersphere recognition beats kNN classification in terms of time efficiency. Since general human action and behavior recognition is still a difficult task, our approach aims at recognizing several classes of typical human actions, and this is reasonable to specific visual surveillance applications.

The rest part of this paper is organized as follows. In Section 2, we introduce the construction of action hypersphere in detail and the action template is described in

Section 3. We present the action recognition approach in Section 4. Experimental results are given in Section 5 and Section 6 concludes this paper.

2 Action Hypersphere: View-Independent Action Representation

The action hypersphere is constructed based on the low-dimensional embeddings of polar features of the action's multi-view MHIs. To do this, we first perform motion capture using our Mocap system by Motion Analysis Corporation, and then the 3D motion data is rendered in multiple views by the Poser software to get the multi-view 2D human motion silhouettes. Thus, we can compute the multi-view MHI of this action. By further extracting polar features of the multi-view MHIs and computing the low-dimensional embeddings of these polar features, we can construct the action hypersphere. Detailed method will be introduced as below.

2.1 Polar Feature of MHI

Motion History Image (MHI) was firstly introduced by Davis and Bobick [8] to capture motion information in image sequences. Let $I(x,y,t)$ be an image sequence and let $D(x,y,t)$ be a binary image sequence indicating regions of motion which can be easily obtained through background modeling. In an MHI H_τ, pixel intensity is a function of the temporal history of motion at that point which can be defined as formula (1) where τ is the maximum duration an action is stored.

$$H_\tau(x,y,t) = \begin{cases} \tau & \text{if } D(x,y,t)=1 \\ \max(0, H_\tau(x,y,t-1)-1) & \text{otherwise} \end{cases} \quad (1)$$

$$H(x,y,t) = H_{\tau=t_{\max}-t_{\min}}(x,y,t_{\max})/(t_{\max}-t_{\min}) \quad (2)$$

Formula (2) describes the normalized MHI with respect to the duration of an action. The result is a scalar-valued image where more recently moving pixels are brighter. The example MHIs of six actions are presented in Figure 1. Note that for the sake of visualization, the pixel value has been scaled within the range between 0 and 255.

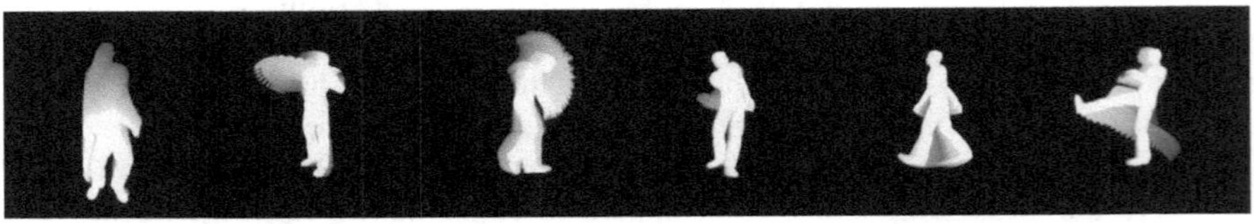

(1) (2) (3) (4) (5) (6)

Fig. 1. MHIs of six actions. (1) Crouch. (2) Punch. (3) Smash. (4) Knock. (5) Walk. (6) Kick.

For action recognition, it is important for a representation of action to be scale invariant, i.e., independent of body size and camera zoom. Consequently, we further extract polar feature from MHI as the action representation. Firstly, the centroid of a MHI C_{MHI} is computed by averaging the nonzero-value pixel locations along x and y

directions, then we make a minimum circle that covers the motion region centered on C_{MHI}. The minimum circle is further partitioned into 36 sectors with an interval of $\pi/18$, and the angle ranges from 0 to 2π. Moreover, each sector is evenly divided into 6 zones along radial direction. In this way, the motion region of MHI is covered by 216 zones distribute in a polar coordinate system. Thus, a MHI can be represented by a 216-dimensional vector, and each entry is assigned the average pixel value of specific zone in the MHI. This vector is the polar feature of the MHI.

The MHI pixels falling between the angle range θ_p and θ_q and having magnitude within the range r_i and r_j can be expressed as:

$$m_p = \left\{ \mathrm{MHI}(m_x, m_y) \mid r_i \le |m_\theta| \le r_j \text{ and } \theta_p \le \angle m_\theta \le \theta_q \right\} (1 \le i < j \le 6,\ 0 \le \theta_p < \theta_q \le 2\pi) \quad (3)$$

where m_θ is the MHI pixel location in polar coordinates with $|m_\theta| = \sqrt{m_x^2 + m_y^2}$ and $\angle m_\theta = \tan^{-1}(m_y / m_x)$.

The extraction of MHI's polar feature can be described by Figure 2.

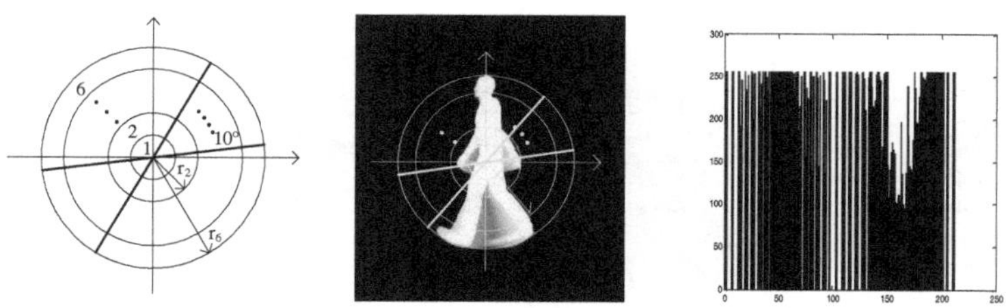

(1) (2) (3)

Fig. 2. (1) The partition of the minimum circle. (2) Sampling the MHI using 216-zone minimum circle. (3) 216-dimensional polar feature of a MHI.

2.2 Action Hypersphere

For view-independent action recognition, the action template should incorporate multi-view information, thus how to find a view-independent action representation is the primary problem to be solved.

Suppose each action is captured simultaneously by multiple cameras distribute on the upper hemisphere centered on the actor with certain rotational angle interval, we can obtain the multi-view MHIs of this action. The distribution of these cameras can be roughly described by Figure 3 where the red dots are surrounding cameras. Since the same action appears differently in different views mainly due to various camera positions on the hemisphere, it is possible to assume that the polar features of these multi-view MHIs also distribute on a "hypersphere" surface. Moreover, we believe that it is a 4-dimensional hypersphere because the view difference is mainly caused by left pan, right pan, up tilt and zoom of the cameras. The 4-DOF (degree-of-freedom) camera pose is indicated by blue arrows in Figure 3. Our assumption stems from the theory of nonlinear dimensionality reduction [12] which interpreted face images with pose and illumination changes as 3-dimensional embeddings.

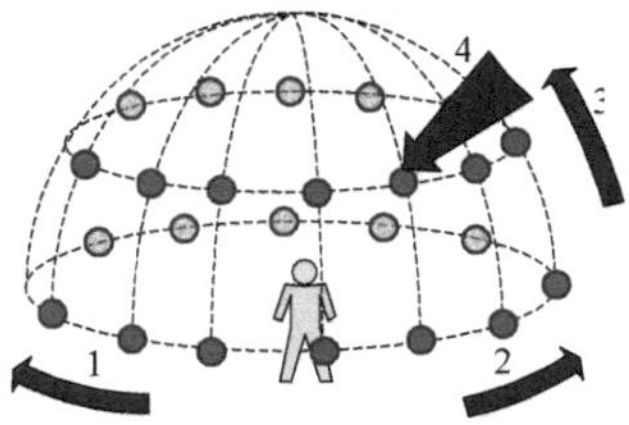

Fig. 3. The distribution of multiple cameras. The blue arrows indicate 4-DOF camera pose.

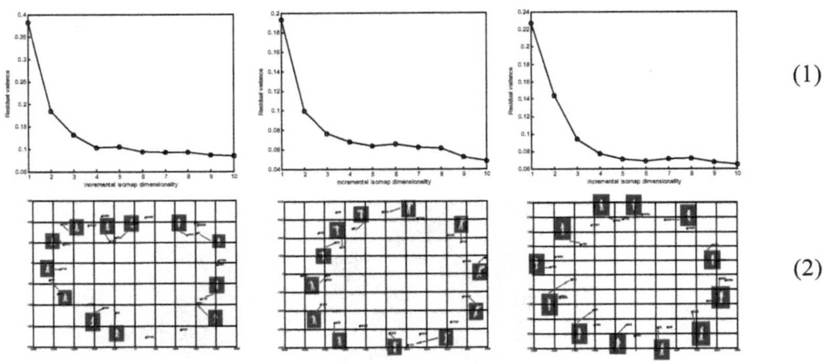

Fig. 4. (1) The residual error against dimensionality variation in manifold projection. (2) The 2D manifold embeddings of 24 polar features.

To testify our assumption, we capture 3D human action and use Poser software to simulate 24 cameras around the actor. Twelve cameras distribute evenly on the horizontal plane with pan angle interval of 30 degree, and the other twelve cameras are on the plane with tilt angle 45 degree. The setup can also be approximately described by Figure 3. Thus, for a specific action, 24 MHI with different views can be obtained. We select three actions (walk, punch, knock), compute the polar features of their MHIs and project the polar features into a nonlinear manifold subspace [11] respectively. The residual error against dimensionality variation is shown as Figure 4 (1). Observe that when the dimensionality surpasses 4, the residual error remains stable at a low level. This indicates that the intrinsic dimensionality of the 24 polar features is 4. Furthermore, we present 2D manifold embeddings of the 24 polar features (for the sake of visualization) as well as part of the MHIs in Figure 4 (2), and the manifold embeddings do form a circle in 2D nonlinear subspace approximately according to the pan angles of the cameras. Therefore we speculate that the multi-view polar features of an action form a hypersphere in 4-dimensional nonlinear subspace. The 4th dimension feature about camera zoom is implicitly hidden behind the scale-invariant action representation.

We name the hypersphere in 4-dimensional subspace as "action hypersphere", whose virtual center represents the intrinsic essence of this action hidden behind the multi-view appearances that distribute on the hypersphere surface with approximately equal distances to the center. Therefore, given a set of multi-view polar features, we can construct the action hypersphere by computing the virtual center and radius based on these features. Suppose we have m polar features x_i ($i = 1,\ldots,m$) of a given action, the virtual center O and radius R of this action hypersphere can be approximately obtained by solving equation (4) via least square method.

We obtain similar hyperspheres by adjusting the camera positions along the hemisphere described in Figure 3, and this indicates that calibration is unnecessary in this stage. The hypersphere can be well constructed when the number of virtual cameras surpasses 20. We will not report relative experiments here for lack of space.

$$\begin{cases} \| x_1 - O \|_2 = R \\ \| x_2 - O \|_2 = R \\ \quad \cdots \\ \| x_m - O \|_2 = R \end{cases} \tag{4}$$

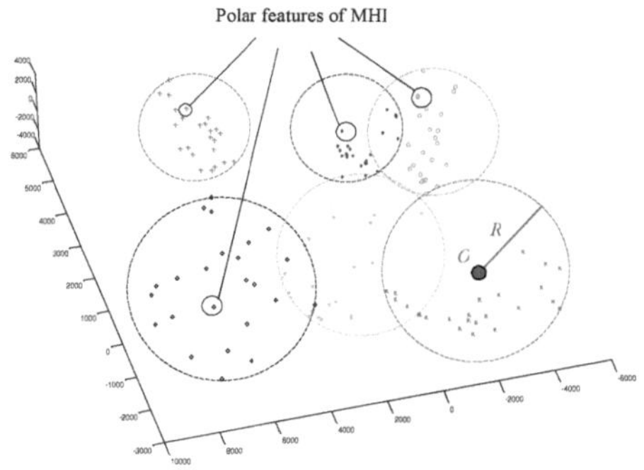

Fig. 5. 3D visualization of action template

3 Action Template

The action template includes several typical human actions. For each action, 24 MHIs as well as the polar features are computed as we did in Section 2. We project the polar features of all the typical actions into a 4-dimensional nonlinear subspace, the 4-dimensional embeddings of same action congregate together and the discrimination between action classes is relatively clear. In this 4-dimensional subspace, we construct action hypersphere and compute the virtual center and radius of the hypersphere for each action using the method introduced in Section 2. Thus, the action template composed of three parts, i.e., multi-view polar features of the sample actions, the virtual centers of the action hyperspheres, and the radiuses of the action hyperspheres. Figure 5 is the visualization of action template, where the multi-view polar features of six actions are projected into a 3D nonlinear subspace, and the dashed circles with different colors denote six action hyperspheres with respective center O and radius R.

4 Action Recognition

Since for each action, the multi-view polar features distribute on the hypersphere surface with approximately equal distances to the center, the recognition can be done by finding the closest hypersphere surface to the input. Given an input action, we first extract a sequence of 2D human silhouettes, and compute the MHI as well as the corresponding polar feature. Then we obtain 4-dimensional embedding of the polar feature by projecting the polar feature into a 4-dimensional subspace covered by the sample actions in the action template. The projection is done based on incremental manifold algorithm [11] efficiently. Then we just need to compute the distance between the 4-dimensional embedding of the input and the centers of the hyperspheres, and compare the distances with the known radiuses, when the error is below some threshold, the input can be labeled as the "closest" action in the template. The threshold is adaptively determined.

Suppose the action template contains n actions, each action is represented by an action hypersphere with the center O_i and radius R_i ($i = 1,\ldots, n$), F is the input polar feature. The detailed action recognition algorithm is listed as below:

Step1: Compute F's 4-dimensional embedding P via the algorithm provided in [11];

Step2: Compute $d_k = \min_{i=1,\ldots,n} |\ \| P - O_i \|_2 - R_i\ |$. This is to find the closest hypersphere surface to P in the action template; the hypersphere is a representation of certain action A_k, with center O_k and radius R_k.

Step3: Let T_j ($j = 1,\ldots, m$) be the 4-dimensional embeddings of action A_k in the action template,

If $d_k \le \max_{j=1,\ldots,m} |\ \| T_j - O_k \|_2 - R_k\ |$

the input action can be recognized as action A_k;

else

return;

The first step aims to select the relatively similar action in the template, and the second step provides a threshold to evaluate the absolute similarity. The threshold is automatically determined as the maximum distance between the embeddings and the hypersphere surface of specific sample action in the action template.

5 Experimental Results

We evaluate our action recognition approach using a 6-class action template. We first capture 6 classes of typical human actions (i.e., a circle of walk, punch, kick, crouch, knock, and smash) using our Mocap system with a frame rate 30fps, each action instance lasts for about 1 second. Then we render these 3D motion data in 24 different views using Poser software. The 24 virtual cameras are set up as introduced in Section 2.2. Thus, 24-view MHIs of each action instance are obtained, and we extract polar features of these MHIs to construct the action template. The 6 actions are performed each 3 times by 6 persons of our lab; therefore there are multiple choices on selecting an action for each class to construct the action template. Fortunately, we find that various combinations of these actions impose little influence on recognition accuracy, and table 1 shows the standard deviation of each action's recognition accuracy under 18 different template combinations. So we freely choose the actions to construct the action template for the following two experiments.

Table 1. Standard deviation of recognition accuracy (STD) under 18 different template combinations

	Crouch(%)	*Walk(%)*	*Punch(%)*	*Kick(%)*	*Knock(%)*	*Smash(%)*
STD	1.58	1.26	1.39	1.42	1.28	1.53

Table 2. Recognition accuracy and execution time of three approaches

Action	*Accuracy (%)*			*Execution time (ms)*		
	*k*NN approach	Bobick's approach	Our approach	*k*NN approach	Bobick's approach	Our approach
Crouch	73	86	85	350	116	107
Walk	72	89	91	420	108	109
Punch	83	87	87	380	110	104
Kick	86	92	90	470	96	92
Knock	78	85	84	320	95	82
Smash	80	83	86	510	120	115

For the synthesized dataset, there are 18 instances for each action. Since one instance has been chosen as template, the rest 17 can be used as test data. Though Weinland reported fine result in their work [10], it heavily depended on 3D reconstruction of input action in volume space, and we cannot expect this approach to be applied on monocular videos, like in visual surveillance. So, we only compare our approach with the other two, i.e., the original temporal template approach proposed by Bobick [8], and the *k*NN approach. In this *k*NN approach, we preserve the multi-view polar feature extraction and manifold projection, and just substitute *k*NN classification for the proposed action hypersphere method. Since the approach proposed by Bobick is view-dependent, for this approach, we construct 24 temporal templates using the same action instances as we have used to construct our action template according to the same 24 virtual camera views. The input is the polar feature of MHI whose viewpoint is within the 24 known camera views, thus the possible case of input is $17 \times 24 = 408$. We repeat the recognition 100 times with different input, and the recognition accuracy as well as execution time of three approaches is shown in Table 2. In this test, our approach performs better than *k*NN approach in either accuracy or efficiency, because *k*NN approach is to classify the input data according to the labels of its *k* nearest neighbors. In *k*NN classification, data from different classes may interlap and searching for *k*NN is a time consuming job. The proposed approach is especially efficient on a relatively large dataset because we just need to compare the distances between the input and the hypersphere centers. The execution time is linear to the number of action classes. So our approach will be competent for some real-time applications, e.g., visual surveillance.

We can see from Table 2 that Bobick's approach has similar performance to our approach, and this is because the viewpoint of input action is carefully selected so as to meet the temporal template. To test the generalization capability of our approach and Bobick's approach, we execute two approaches on the *IXMAS* dataset which is publicly available on the INRIA PERCEPTION research group's website [13]. The dataset contains 13 daily motions, each performed 3 times by 11 actors. The actors freely change their orientations to demonstrate view-independency. Thus, for one motion, 33 action instances can be used as test data. We choose walk, punch, kick and crouch from the dataset, and compute the MHIs as well as corresponding polar features as input of recognition algorithm. The recognition accuracy of these actions from 5 free viewpoints by two approaches is shown in Figure 6.

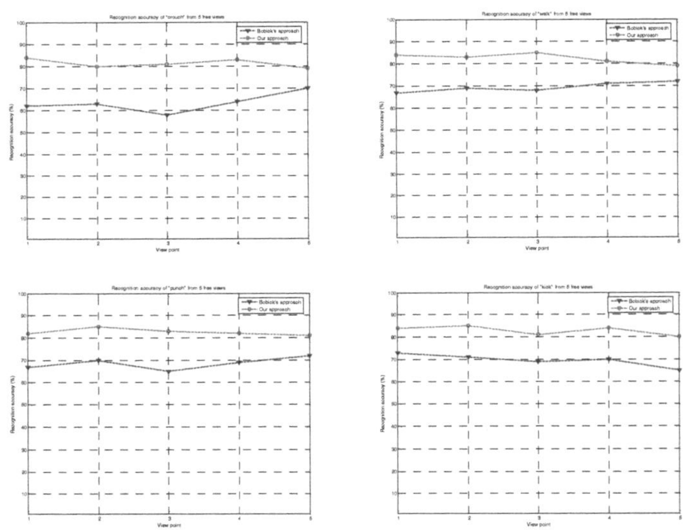

Fig. 6. Recognition accuracy of crouch, walk, punch and kick from 5 free views respectively by two approaches

The accuracy of Bobick's approach drops significantly with freely changing viewpoint, whereas our approach still maintains higher recognition rate. This testifies the view-independency of the proposed approach. For real-time visual surveillance, the silhouettes can be extracted by a standard background subtraction method, and segmented into latent actions in each short time interval. The MHI and polar feature are then computed as input of recognition algorithm. The segmentation can be automatically done by the algorithm proposed by Elgammal [14].

6 Conclusion

A view-independent approach is proposed in this paper to recognize specific human actions from video. The recognition is performed in a way of template matching. We proved that the polar features of an action's multi-view MHIs approximately form a hypersphere in a 4-dimensional nonlinear subspace, thus the action template containing specific actions is composed of multiple hyperspheres with known centers and radiuses. The recognition is achieved by evaluating the distances between the manifold embedding of input action's polar feature and the centers of the hyperspheres. Compared with existing template matching approach, the proposed approach maintains higher recognition rate under various camera viewpoints. Moreover, the hypersphere classification is much faster than classical *k*NN classification. Thus, the proposed approach is suitable for some real-time applications.

References

1. Clement, M., Edmond, B., Bruno, R.: 3D Skeleton-Based Body Pose Recovery. In: Third International Symposium on 3D Data Processing, Visualization, and Transmission, pp. 389–396 (2006)
2. Ronald, P., Mannes, P.: Comparison of Silhouette Shape Descriptors for Example-based Human Pose Recovery. In: FGR 2006. Proceedings of the 7th International Conference on Automatic Face and Gesture Recognition, pp. 541–546 (2006)
3. Murat, E., Eyüp, G.: Background Estimation Based People Detection and Tracking for Video Surveillance. In: Yazıcı, A., Şener, C. (eds.) ISCIS 2003. LNCS, vol. 2869, pp. 421–429. Springer, Heidelberg (2003)
4. Neil, R., Ian, R.: A General Method for Human Activity Recognition in Video. Computer Vision and Image Understanding 104, 232–248 (2006)
5. Venkatesh Babu, R., Anantharaman, B., Ramakrishnan, K.R., Srinivasan, S.H.: Compressed Domain Action Classification Using HMM. Pattern Recognition Letters 23, 1203–1213 (2002)
6. Mohiuddin, A., Seong-Whan, L.: Human Action Recognition Using Multi-view Image Sequences Features. In: FGR 2006. Proceedings of the 7th International Conference on Automatic Face and Gesture Recognition, pp. 523–528 (2006)
7. Ahmad, M., Seong-Whan, L.: HMM-based Human Action Recognition Using Multiview Image Sequences. In: Proceedings of the 18th International Conference on Pattern Recognition, pp. 263–266 (2006)
8. Aaron, F.B., James, W.D.: The Recognition of Human Movement using Temporal Templates. IEEE Transactions ON PAMI 23(3), 257–267 (2001)
9. Michel, V., Ioannis, P., Maja, P.: Facial Action Unit Recognition using Temporal Templates. In: IEEE International Workshop on Human-Robot Interaction, pp. 253–258 (2004)
10. Daniel, W., Remi, R., Edmond, B.: Free Viewpoint Action Recognition using Motion History Volumes. Computer Vision and Image Understanding 104, 249–257 (2006)
11. Anil, K.J., Martin, H.C.L.: Incremental Nonlinear Dimensionality Reduction by Manifold Learning. IEEE Transactions on PAMI 28(3), 377–391 (2006)
12. Tenenbaum, J.B., Silva, V.D., Langford, J.C.: A Global Geometric Framework for Nonlinear Dimensionality Reduction. Science 290, 2319–2323 (2000)
13. http://perception.inrialpes.fr
14. Ahmed, E., Chan-Su, L.: Nonlinear Manifold Learning for Dynamic Shape and Dynamic Appearance. Computer Vision and Image Understanding 106, 31–46 (2007)

Efficient Adaptive Background Subtraction Based on Multi-resolution Background Modelling and Updating

Ruijiang Luo[1], Liyuan Li[1], and Irene Yu-Hua Gu[2]

[1] Institute for Infocomm Research, Singapore
{rjluo,lyli}@i2r.a-star.edu.sg
[2] Dept. of Signals and Systems, Chalmers Univ. of Technology, Sweden
irenegu@chalmers.se

Abstract. Adaptive background subtraction (ABS) is a fundamental step for foreground object detection in many real-time video surveillance systems. In many ABS methods, a pixel-based statistical model is used for the background and each pixel is updated online to adapt to various background changes. As a result, heavy computation and memory consumption are required. In this paper, we propose an efficient methodology for implementation of ABS algorithms based on multi-resolution background modelling and sequential sampling for updating background. Experiments and quantitative evaluation are conducted on two open data sets (PETS2001 and PETS2006) and scenarios captured in some public places, and some results are included. Our results have shown that the proposed method requires a significant reduction in memory and CPU usage, meanwhile maintaining a similar foreground segmentation performance as compared with the corresponding single resolution methods.

Keywords: Adaptive background subtraction, multi-resolution modelling, principal feature representation, statistical modelling.

1 Introduction

Adaptive background subtraction (ABS) is a fundamental step in video surveillance [1,2,3,4]. A video surveillance system often employs a stationary camera directing at the scene of interest. A background model is then generated and dynamically maintained to follow the background changes.

Much work has been done on adaptive background subtraction (ABS) using pixel-based statistical modelling. Wren [3] employed a single Gaussian model to describe the color distribution of each pixel. In [4], a model of mixture of Gaussians (MoG) is proposed to handle more complicated situations, e.g., moving bush under windy conditions. Many enhanced variants of MoG have been proposed. Some integrated the gradients [5], depth [6], or local features [7] into the Gaussians. Others employed the non-parametric models, e.g. kernels, to replace the Gaussians [8,9]. In [10], a model of principal feature representation (PFR)

H.H.S. Ip et al. (Eds.): PCM 2007, LNCS 4810, pp. 118–127, 2007.

was proposed to characterize each background pixel. Using PFR, multiple features from the background, such as color, gradient, and color co-occurrence, can be learned online and used for classification of background and foreground.

By employing various statistical models and multiple features for background modelling, adaptive background subtraction (ABS) methods become robust with respect to a variety of complex backgrounds. The price, however, is the requirement of large memory space and heavy computation [11]. This makes the methods difficult to be applied to real time surveillance on high-resolution images.

It is observed that for images captured by surveillance cameras in public places, most pixels belong to some objects or patches, e.g., road surfaces, vegetation and sky. Such pixels only contain small local feature variations. It indicates that a single statistical model can be employed to monitor a local patch in such smooth image regions. For those small percentage of image pixels that are associated with neighborhoods containing high local visual feature variations, *e.g.* edges between smooth regions, individual statistics is required to accurately characterize each pixel. Motivated by the above, we propose a novel method of multi-resolution adaptive background subtraction (MRABS) for efficient foreground detection. Compared to the region-based method in [12], ours uses gradient statistics to select smooth patches with a fixed memory consumption for background modelling, which is more robust for long-term running and easier for hardware implementation. Meanwhile, a sequential sampling is proposed to improve the efficiency of model updating.

The proposed method is implemented on both PFR-based and MoG-based algorithms. Our analysis shows that using the proposed method, only around 1/8 of memory and 1/6.4 of CPU resource are needed. In real implementation, some extra memory and computations are required. Overall, for a similar background subtraction performance, it is found that the multi-resolution PFR-based algorithm requires about 20.7% memory space and 29.4% CPU consumption as compared with the single-resolution version of the algorithm, while the required memory space and CPU usage for the multi-resolution MoG-based algorithm are reduced to 36.5% and 57.5% as compared with its single-resolution version.

The rest of the paper is organized as follows. Section 2 describes the multi-resolution modelling method, including the analysis of computational efficiency. Section 3 describes the experiments with some results and performance evaluation included. Finally, conclusions are given in Section 4.

2 Multi-resolution Adaptive Background Subtraction

The proposed method contains four parts: Multi-Resolution (MR) Management, MR Background Modelling, MR Background Subtraction, and MR Model Updating, as shown in Fig.1. To make it easy to understand, we use PFR-based algorithm as the example. However, the proposed multi-resolution background maintenance method can also be applied to other algorithms in a similar manner, e.g. we have applied the method to the MoG-based algorithm.

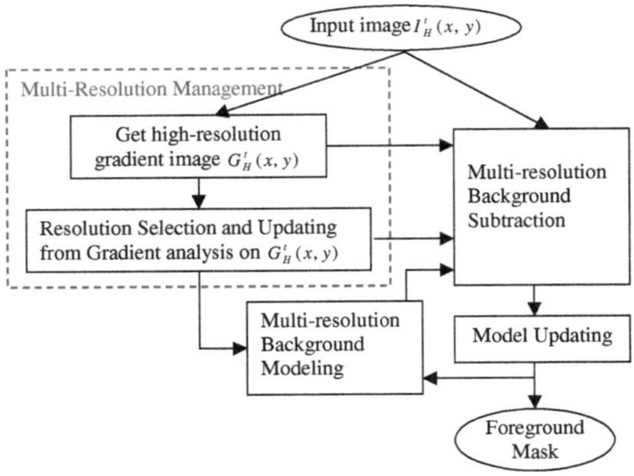

Fig. 1. Block diagram of the multi-resolution adaptive background subtraction method

2.1 Multi-resolution Management

To achieve multi-resolution background modelling, a high resolution image is first divided into small blocks of fixed size ($W_B \times H_B$ pixels). A block is classified as either low or high resolution based on the statistics of local variations.

Since image gradient is a good feature to indicate local variations, we use an accumulated gradient feature, *variance of the gradient power*, for resolution management. Let (g_x,g_y) be the gradient vector generated by a Sobel operator at the pixel $\mathbf{x}$=(x,y) in frame I_t. The power of gradient, $G^t_H(\mathbf{x}) = g_x^2 + g_y^2$, is then accumulated along time using

$$\tilde{G}^t_H(\mathbf{x}) = \alpha \cdot G^t_H(\mathbf{x}) + (1-\alpha)\tilde{G}^{t-1}_H(\mathbf{x}) \tag{1}$$

where α is a constant used as a smooth factor (α=0.01 in our tests). The variance of the gradient power for the i-th block is computed over all pixels in the block,

$$\sigma^2_{t,i} = E(\tilde{G}^t_H - E(\tilde{G}^t_H))^2 \tag{2}$$

where $E(\cdot)$ is the expectation. Since most blocks have smooth local neighborhoods, the corresponding variances $\sigma^2_{t,i}$ are small. From the histogram of $\sigma^2_{t,i}$ over all blocks in the image, a small threshold value *Th* can be found such that the histogram area below this threshold covers γ_m% of image blocks. These blocks are set as the low resolution blocks. The $1-\gamma_m$% blocks that exceed the threshold (i.e., having high local variations) are assigned as high resolution blocks. Examples of multi-resolution block representation on several scenes are shown in Fig.2. With a fixed γ_m, the memory usage is also fixed.

All blocks are initially set as low resolution when the system starts. The resolution of each block is then updated every t_{train} seconds by the resolution management module: For the i-th block, if $\sigma^2_{t,i} \geq Th$ is satisfied at time t and block was in low-resolution at $t-1$, it is changed to a high resolution block. Conversely, if the i-th block was in high resolution and $\sigma^2_{t,i} < Th$ is satisfied at time t, the block is switched to low resolution block.

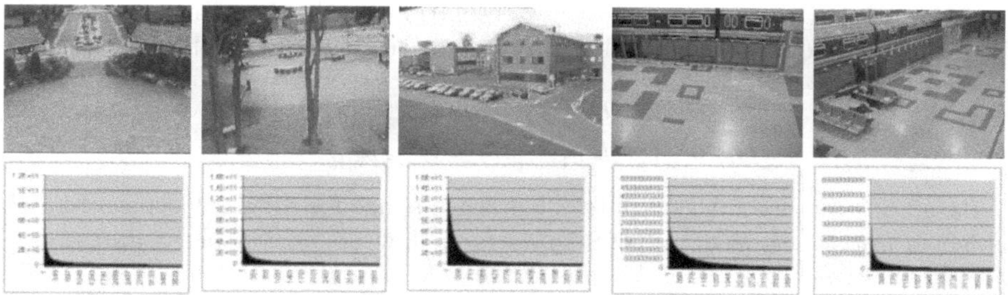

Fig. 2. Images contain high/low resolution blocks and their variance of gradient power values. Row-1: images where small red rectangles denote high-resolution blocks, $\gamma_m = 90$. Row-2: the corresponding sorted histograms of $\sigma_{t,i}^2$ (showing the top 16%)

2.2 Multi-resolution Background Modelling

Since the low-resolution blocks represent areas with low local variations, it implies that pixels within these blocks have similar colors and gradients. For PFR-based method, the features of co-occurrences (M_{cc}), which are employed as the feature for dynamic background, can be deleted. For a high-resolution block, all three types of the principal features (M_c, M_e, M_{cc}) are maintained at each pixel in the block. The number of these principal features is described in Table 1.

Table 1. Values of parameters

Parameter	Value
M_c: number of principle colors	30
M_e: number of principle gradients	30
M_{cc}: number of color co-occurrence	60
(W_B, H_B): width and height of each block	(4, 4)

Let B_i be a high-resolution block, and $N_B = W_B \times H_B$ be the size of the block (4×4 in our tests). The tables for the PFR algorithm can be expressed as

$$T_v(B_i) = \{T_v^i(\mathbf{x}_j)\}_{j=1}^{N_B} \tag{3}$$

for the j-th pixel $\mathbf{x}_j \in B_i$, its feature vector contains 3 component vectors: color, gradient and color co-occurrence ($\mathbf{v} = \mathbf{c}, \mathbf{e}$ and $\mathbf{cc}$). For each component feature vector, the table can be expressed by

$$T_v(\mathbf{x}_i) = \{p_v^{i,t}(b), \{S_v^{i,t}(l) = (p_{v_l}^t, p_{v_l|b}^t, v_l)\}_{l=1}^{M_v}\} \tag{4}$$

All together, $3 \times N_B$ tables are used for each block. We use unsigned char (1 byte) for color vector $\mathbf{c}$ and color co-occurrence vector $\mathbf{cc}$, short integer (2 bytes) for gradient vector $\mathbf{e}$ and floating point (4 bytes) for all the possibilities p. The size of the features are shown in Table 1. We can estimate the memory space required for the three principal features at a pixel in a high resolution block by:

$$\begin{aligned} m_e &= (2S_i + 2S_f) \times M_e + S_f = 364 \; bytes \\ m_c &= (3S_c + 2S_f) \times M_c + S_f = 334 \; bytes \\ m_{cc} &= (6S_c + 2S_f) \times M_c c + S_f = 844 \; bytes \end{aligned} \tag{5}$$

If the block B_i is assigned as a low-resolution block, then there is one table for principal colors and one table for principal gradients in the block:

$$\begin{aligned} T_c(B_i) &= \{p_c^{i,t}(b), \{S_c^{i,t}(l) = (p_{c_l}^t, p_{c_l|b}^t, c_l)\}_{l=1}^{M_c}\} \\ T_e(B_i) &= \{p_e^{i,t}(b), \{S_e^{i,t}(l) = (p_{e_l}^t, p_{e_l|b}^t, e_l)\}_{l=1}^{M_e}\} \end{aligned} \quad (6)$$

Based on this, we can compute the storage space for different types of block, which is $m_{lb} = m_e + m_c = 698$ *bytes* for a low resolution block and $m_{hb} = (W_B \times H_B) \times (m_e + m_c + m_{cc}) = 24672$ *bytes* for a high resolution block.

Let $N_I = M \times N$ be the image size, $\gamma_m\%$ be proportion of the low-resolution blocks, N_{hb} and N_{lb} be the number of high-resolution and low-resolution blocks, respectively, where

$$\begin{aligned} N_{hb} &= \tfrac{N_I}{W_B \times H_B} \times (1 - \gamma_m\%), \\ N_{lb} &= \tfrac{N_I}{W_B \times H_B} \times \gamma_m\% \end{aligned} \quad (7)$$

Set $\gamma_m\% = 90\%$, from Table 1 one can obtain $N_{hb} = 0.00625N_I$ and $N_{lb} = 0.05625N_I$. Hence, the total memory consumption for the background in the multi-resolution PFR-based models is $mem_{MR} = m_{lb} \times N_{lb} + m_{hb} \times N_{hb} \sim 193N_I$. Original single resolution PFR method equivalents to treating all blocks as in high resolution, the required memory space is $mem_{normal} = 1542N_I$. Hence, the required memory space of the multi-resolution PFR-based method is reduced to

$$mem_{MR} \sim \frac{193N_I}{1542N_I} \sim \frac{1}{8} mem_{normal} \quad (8)$$

2.3 Multi-resolution Background Subtraction

Under multi-resolution background modelling, the background model of the block is used for background and foreground classification if a pixel is in a low-resolution block. If a pixel is in a high-resolution block, the background model of that pixel is used. Since the computational in feature matching is high for the PFR-based method, the following coarse to fine process is proposed.

First, *background differencing* (BD) between input frame and the maintained background image, and *temporal differencing* (TD) between two consecutive input frames are performed at a lower resolution. The results are then zoomed-in to the original resolution to yield an initial coarse foreground mask. In most scenarios captured by a surveillance camera, a large portion of the image does not contain foreground objects. As a result, much CPU power can be saved. To keep small objects of interest in scene, a quarter-sized image is used for the BD and TD operations (i.e., $W_L = (1/2)W$, $H_L = (1/2)H$).

Next, Bayesian classification is performed pixel by pixel on the obtained foreground mask to refine the segmentation. For a pixel in a low-resolution block, only color and gradient are used. For a pixel in a high-resolution block, all three features, color, gradient, and color co-occurrence, are taken into consideration.

2.4 Multi-resolution Background Maintenance

Different updating strategies are applied to the blocks of different resolutions. For a high-resolution block, pixel by pixel updating operation is applied. However, for a low-resolution block, the following sequential sampling method is proposed since the visual features from different pixels inside the block are similar and stable through the time: at each time step, the background model of the block is updated by the features from one pixel sequentially sampled from the block, as indicated by Fig.3.

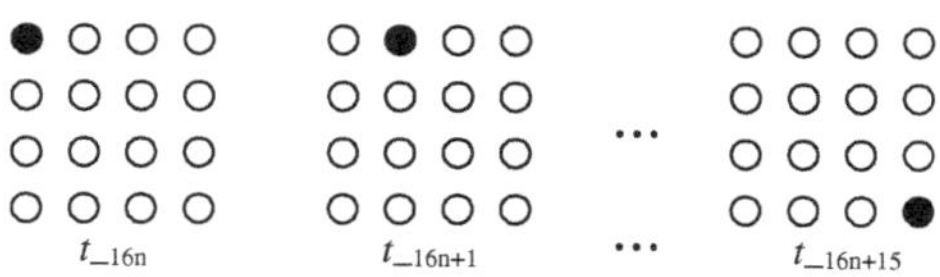

Fig. 3. Updating the background model for a 4×4 block using the sequential sampling

Using 4×4 blocks, a pixel in a low-resolution block is sampled once every 16 frames to update the block background model. Similarly, we can obtain the computational cost for the updating with respective to conventional method,

$$Update_{MR} = \frac{N_{lb}+(W_B \times H_B \times N_{hb})}{N_I} Update_{normal} = \frac{1}{6.4} \times Update_{normal} \quad (9)$$

That implies that only 15.6% of the updating time is needed as compared to conventional single resolution updating routine.

3 Experimental Results

The proposed method has been tested on image sequences from several open data sets, including PETS 2001 and 2006 data sets, and some sequences captured in the public places at Santosa (Singapore). In our tests, 10% of the blocks are set as high resolution (i.e., $\gamma_m\% = 90\%$). Our tests were conducted using both multi-resolution PFR-based method and multi-resolution MoG-based method.

3.1 Evaluation: Computational Cost and Memory Usage

The text results in Table 2 shows the average memory consumption and frame rate of PFR-based and MoG-based background subtraction operations on the PETS data set with the conventional single resolution and the proposed multi-resolution technique. The results were obtained using a 3.0GHz Dell Desktop with 1GB memory. In the real implementation, some extra memories are needed to save temporal results. Therefore, the obtained memory usage is higher than the theoretical analysis.

Table 2. Average memory consumption for the PETS dataset (image size 768×576): the conventional single resolution (SR) technique vs. the proposed multi-resolution (MR) technique

Method	Using SR	Using MR
Principal Feature Representation (PFR)	870MB, 1.62fps	180MB, 5.5fps
Mixture of Gaussians (MoG)	63MB, 6.3fps	23MB, 11.0fps

One can observe that by employing multi-resolution strategy, the processing speed of the PFR-based algorithm is increased by 3.4 times, with only about 20.7% of the memory space consumption as compared with the conventional single resolution method. That is, to reach real-time processing ($\geq 8fps$) using PFR-based algorithm, previously one system can only process one input color stream at a small resolution of 176×144. With the proposed multi-resolution technique, the same system can now process two input color streams of 352×288 resolution at 11fps each without any hardware upgrading. For some cases where a lower frame rate is acceptable, the reduced memory requirement enables one system to process even more inputs at same time.

For the multi-resolution MoG-based method, we achieved less significant improvements, with nearly doubling the processing speed, and requiring only 36.5% of memory as compared with conventional single resolution alternative. It is because the feature matching in MoG algorithm is really simple. It actually takes less time to perform direct feature matching for foreground and background classification on image in original resolution than the coarse to fine operations (image zooming down, "TD", "BD", and zooming back to its original size). But for mass deployment, this 50% resource saving could be rather significant.

Table 3. Detailed processing time for modules: SR technique vs. MR technique

	TD	BD	GD	Classification	Updating	Others
PFR	4.55	7.82	0.54	5.79	37.25	4.36
MR-PFR	1.08	2.07	0.33	3.20	9.19	2.24
MoG	-	-	-	6.87	9.33	-
MR-MoG	-	-	0.39	4.80	2.94	0.94

Table 3 shows some details on how much time each module takes in PFR-based and MoG-based background subtraction operations with and without the proposed multi-resolution technique. Each item is average time consumed (in seconds) for processing 100 input frames of 768×576 resolution. "TD" and "BD" represent temporal differencing and background differencing, respectively. "GD" means gradient detection using Sobel algorithm, "Classification" is foreground and background classification, "Updating" means background model updating, and "Others" is for all other processing, such as memory copying to save temporary results, etc. For original PFR-based method, the "TD" and "BD" operations are performed on the input resolution images, while those in MR-PFR method are performed on quarter-size inputs. It clearly shows the proposed MR technique can well improve the efficiency of both complicated (e.g. PFR) and simple (e.g. MoG) background subtraction algorithms.

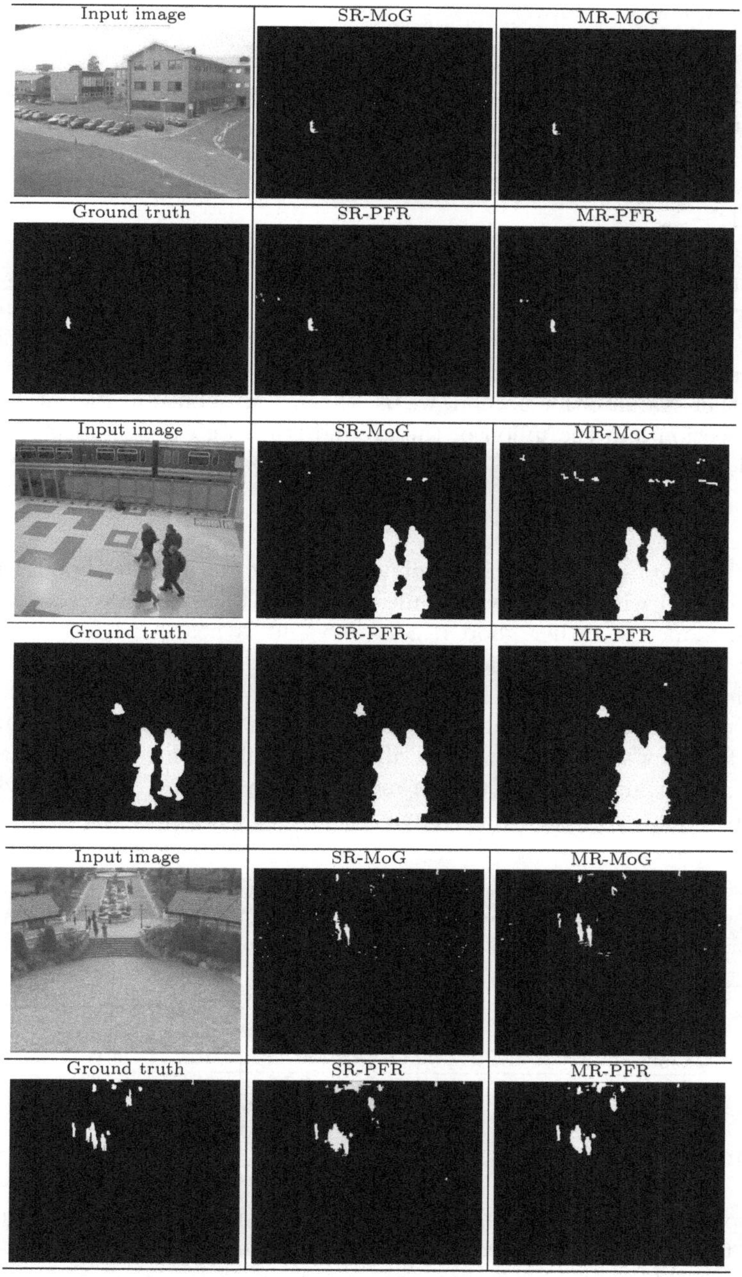

Fig. 4. Background subtraction: conventional single resolution (SR) method vs. the proposed multi-resolution (MR) technique. Rows 1 to 2: PETS2001 Dataset-1 Camera-1; Rows 3 to 4: PETS2006 Scene-3 Clip-1; and Rows 5 to 6: Santosa Dataset-1

3.2 Evaluation: Effectiveness of the Method

The performance of the foreground segmentation by adaptive background subtraction is evaluated and compared for algorithms using the conventional single resolution and the proposed multi-resolution technique . The quantitative evaluation is performed on three blindly picked sequences from the testing data set, they are: PETS2001 Dataset-1 Camera-1, PETS2006 Scene-3 Clip-1 and Santosa Dataset-1.

For each sequence, processing results are sampled on every 100-frame intervals. The segmentation results of these sample frames are then compared with the manually generated "ground truths". The example of the segmented results from the PFR-based and MoG-based methods with single and multi- resolution, and the ground truth are shown in Fig.4.

To further evaluate the method, we use the metric defined as the ratio between the intersection and the union of the ground truth and the segmented regions, as used in [10],

$$S(A, B) = \frac{A \bigcap B}{A \bigcup B} \tag{10}$$

Table 4 includes the resulting metric values for the two methods, PFR and MoG, with and without applying multi-resolution technique. According to [10], the performance is rather good if $S > 0.5$ and is nearly perfect if $S > 0.8$. Since the regional information from all pixels is used to update its background model along the time in the low-resolution blocks, and most blocks belong to low-resolution, from Table 4, it is observed that one can significantly improve the system efficiency with very little sacrifice of the effectiveness by using the proposed multi-resolution technique. For most cases on the PETS dataset, where the images have higher quality, the system performance are even slightly improved.

Table 4. The resulting metric values S (defined in Eq.(10)) for quantitative evaluation and comparison of the effectiveness of adaptive background subtraction methods: single resolution (SR) technique vs. multi-resolut (MR) technique

Name of dataset	SR-PFR	MR-PFR	SR-MoG	MR-MoG
PETS01 Dataset-1 Camera-1	0.7	0.8	0.6	0.65
PETS06 Scene-3 Clip-1	0.74	0.76	0.51	0.6
Santosa	0.75	0.73	0.5	0.47
Average	0.73	0.763	0.537	0.573

4 Conclusion

The proposed multi-resolution background maintenance method, aimed at improving the efficiency on memory usage and computational cost in adaptive background subtraction, has been applied and tested to the principal feature representation (PFR)- and the mixture of Gaussians (MoG)-based methods. By dividing each input image into fix-size high and low resolution blocks using a gradient-based analysis, and using a sequential sampling method for updating the background model, we have achieved 3.4 times faster speed in computation, with only 20.7% memory consumption as compared with the conventional pixel-based PFR algorithm. For MoG-based method, the proposed multi-resolution approach has resulted in 1.74 times faster speed, and requires 36.5% of memory space as compared with its pixel-based correspondence.

References

1. Haritaoglu, I., Harwood, D., Davis, L.: W^4: Real-time surveillance of people and their activities. IEEE Trans. PAMI 22(8), 809–830 (2000)
2. Hu, W., Tan, T., Wang, L., Maybank, S.: A survey on visual surveillance of object motion and behaviors. IEEE Trans. Systems, Man, and Cybernetics, Part C 34(3), 334–352 (2004)
3. Wren, C., Azarbaygaui, A., Darrell, T., Pentland, A.: Pfinder: Real-time tracking of the human body. IEEE Trans. PAMI 19(7), 780–785 (1997)
4. Stauffer, C., Grimson, W.: Learning patterns of activity using real-time tracking. IEEE Trans. PAMI 22(8), 747–757 (2000)
5. Javed, O., Shafique, K., Shah, M.: A hierarchical approach to robust background subtraction using color and gradient information. In: Proc. IEEE Workshop Motion and Video Computing, pp. 22–27 (2002)
6. Harville, M., Gordon, G., Woodfill, J.: Foreground segmentation using adaptive mixture model in color and depth. In: Proc. IEEE Workshop Detection and Recognition of Events in Video, pp. 3–11 (2001)
7. Eng, H., Wang, J., Kam, A., Yau, W.: Novel region-based modeling for human detection within high dynamic aquatic environment. In: Proc. IEEE Conf. CVPR, vol. 2, pp. 390–397 (2004)
8. Elgammal, A., Duraiswami, R., Harwood, D., Davis, L.S.: Background and foreground modeling using nonparametric Kernal density estimation for visual surveillance. In: Proc. of the IEEE, vol. 90(7) (July 2002)
9. Sheikh, Y., Shah, M.: Bayesian modeling of dynamic scenes for object detection. IEEE Trans. PAMI 27, 1778–1792 (2005)
10. Li, L., Huang, W., Gu, I.Y.H., Tian, Q.: Statistical modeling of complex background for foreground object detection. IEEE Trans. IP 13(11), 1459–1472 (2004)
11. Chen, T.P., et al.: Computer Vision Workload Analysis: Case Study of Video Surveillance Systems. Intel Technology Journal 09(02), 109–118 (2005)
12. Beeck, K., Gu, I.Y.H., Li, L., Viberg, M., Moor, B.D.: Region-Based Statistical Background Modelling for Foreground Object Segmentation. In: Proc. IEEE Conf. IP, pp. 3317–3320 (2006)

Towards a Stringent Bit-Rate Conformance for Frame-Layer Rate Control in H.264/AVC

Evan Tan[1] and Jing Chen[2]

[1] School of Computer Science and Engineering,
University of New South Wales, NSW 2052, Australia
evant@cse.unsw.edu.au
[2] National ICT Australia, Neville Roach Laboratory,
223, Anzac Parade, Kensington, NSW 2052, Australia
jing.chen@nicta.com.au

Abstract. This paper presents a novel frame-layer rate control technique that adaptively determines the frame complexity for bit allocation in order to satisfy the target bit-rate constraints without degrading the decoded video significantly. To do this, we first obtain the edge energy of each frame to measure the frame complexity as well as to determine the weighting of a frame for bit allocation. We then present a new bit-rate traffic model for bit allocation to achieve a better conformance to the target bit-rate. Finally, we integrate the edge energy complexity measure into the rate-quantization (R-Q) model. Our results shows robust improvements over the current rate control methods adopted in H.264/AVC in terms of meeting the target bit-rate as well as determining the quality of the decoded video.

Keywords: bit allocation, complexity measure, frame-layer, H.264/AVC, linear R-Q model, rate control.

1 Introduction

The rate control component regulates the coded video bit-stream in order to meet the network bandwidth and buffer constraints as well as to enhance the video quality as much as possible. This makes rate control one of the key components of a video coder especially in video streaming applications. A typical rate controller first allocates a target number of bits for each frame based on a bit budget. Then for each frame a quantization parameter (QP) is selected either for the whole frame (frame-layer) or for each macroblock (MB layer) based on some rate-quantization (R-Q) model in order to meet the specified target bits.

One of the main issue with rate control in H.264/AVC is that the the bit allocation and QP selection are conducted before the selection of INTER and INTRA modes. This means that various vital information about a frame, such as the mean absolute difference (MAD), is not readily available to the rate controller. As a consequence, many current rate control techniques make use of different kinds of estimates to obtain information about the frame.

H.H.S. Ip et al. (Eds.): PCM 2007, LNCS 4810, pp. 128–137, 2007.

The original rate control scheme that was adopted by the H.264/AVC standard and proposed by Li et al [1] solves this issue by performing a linear prediction of a P-frame's MAD value based on the MAD of the previous P-frame. However, this approach has problems handling scene changes within a video [5]. And the rate control algorithm is only performed on P-frames, while I-frames and B-frames have their QPs estimated based on the QPs calculated for P-frames without consideration of the actual characteristics of the I-frames and B-frames [2]. This makes it only ideal for videos with IPPP group-of-pictures (GOP) format.

Recently, Leontaris and Tourapis [2] have attempted to fix this problem by introducing a complexity measure for P-frames and made use of complexity ratio parameters to determine the complexity of I-frames and B-frames. This technique made the adopted rate control algorithm much more compliant to the bit-rate constraints. However, sudden complexity changes such as scene changes are not handled implicitly. Furthermore, the performance of the improved algorithm is strongly correlated to the fixed parameters introduced, which has to be tuned for various videos. Their approach also assumed the total size of the sequence is available at the start, which may not always be the case (e.g. for real-time video communication).

Liu et al [5] and Yu et al [9] proposed a technique that uses preanalyzed information from the video. This approach is ideal for the transmission of stored videos like video-on-demand, but is normally not suitable for applications such video-conferencing. Other approaches made use of complexity measures that are predicted [8,10] or by using some image processing techniques [4,6] or histogram difference techniques [7]. All these approaches have shown that scene change can be detected reasonably well, however, none of them account for the differences between I-frames, P-frames and B-frames in their complexity measures. Normally, I-frames uses more bits than P-frames which in turn uses more bits than B-frames, but this relationship might change in a high motion video sequence due to the increased intra-coded macroblocks (MB) being introduced into the frame. A proper complexity measurement scheme should take into account of *all* these.

Additionally, current approaches made use of the fluid flow traffic model with each frame assumed to take up R_B/R_F bits, where R_B is the channel bit-rate and R_F is the frame rate. Some approaches set a fixed upper bound on target bits [7,8], this is not a proper approach as the bit-rates may vary dramatically in high-motion videos. Other approaches [1,2,6,9,12] made use of the number of remaining bits in a GOP as an upper bound. The problem with making use remaining GOP bits is that it may cause the allocated bits to exceed the target bit-rate.

To illustrate this problem, we define a *bit-rate period* to be the amount of bits available for the bit allocation of R_F frames in one second (time needed for encoding is assumed to be negligible here for simplification), in this case it would be R_B bits. Let us assume the GOP structure is defined as a I-B-P-B format, Fig. 1 then illustrates this setup.

Suppose a scene change occurs on 6th frame of the second GOP (unshaded section) resulting in a high complexity value for that frame. Since the second GOP only has an I-frame (5th frame) coded, the 6th frame could potentially use up a large fraction of the remaining GOP bits. This will cause the rate controller to allocate more bits than allowed within a bit-rate period, thus exceeding the bit-rate constraint.

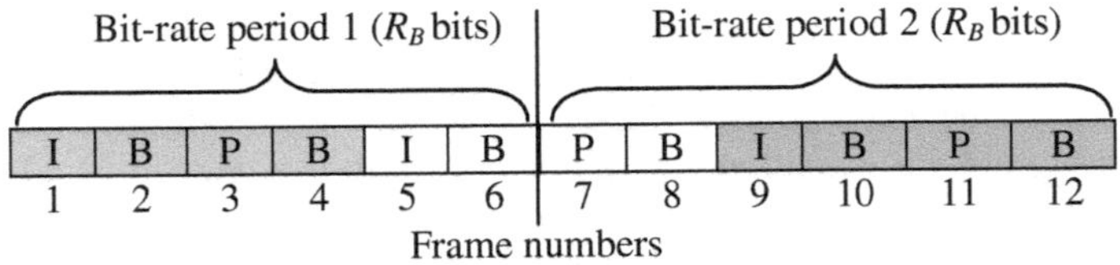

Fig. 1. An illustration of a bit-rate period imposed on the IBPB GOP structure

In this paper, we address these issues by firstly, calculating the edge energy of each frame as a form of perceptual complexity measure and make use of this to handle bit-rate variations due to scene change as well as to allocate bits to a frame with respect to the complexities of other frames within a bit period. Then, we define a bit-rate traffic model based on a bit-rate period to ensure that the bit allocations by the rate controller meet the target bit-rate. Finally, we modify the linear quadratic R-Q model [3] to account for the different bit allocations for different frames.

The rest of this paper is organized as follows. Section 2 describes how the complexity measure of a frame is calculated and weighted with other frames. Section 3 introduces the bit-rate traffic model and shows how frame bit allocation is performed. Section 4 describes our modification to the R-Q model to account for the different frame complexity. Section 5 discusses the experiments we performed. Finally, Section 6 concludes this paper.

2 Frame Complexity Measure

2.1 Edge Energy

In our proposed method, we made use of the edge energy extracted from a frame to calculate the frame complexity. This is because the AC coefficients represent edge information, so a frame with higher edge energy would tend to imply containing more AC coefficients which typically means that the I-frame would end up using more bits. Furthermore, motion information can be represented by the localized differences of edge energy between frames, as edge energy tends to change more when there is high motion.

To calculate the edge energy of a frame, we made use of the edge filters by Won et al [11]. Our modified algorithm starts by linearly quantizing the Y component of the frame into 128 levels as a way of noise removal. We then set an image block to be of size 8x8. Given $m_v(i,j,k)$, $m_h(i,j,k)$, $m_{d\text{-}45}(i,j,k)$, $m_{d\text{-}135}(i,j,k)$ and $m_{nd}(i,j,k)$ represents the vertical, horizontal, 45° diagonal and 135° diagonal edge magnitudes respectively for the *(i,j)*th image block on frame *k*. The edge energy can be calculated by:

$$B_E(i,j,k) = \sum m_x(i,j,k) \quad x \in \{v, h, d\text{–}45, d\text{–}135, nd\} \ , \tag{1}$$

Given a frame with *MxN* image blocks, the edge energy of an I-frame is:

$$E_I(k) = \sum_{j=0}^{M} \sum_{i=0}^{N} B_E(i,j,k) \ , \tag{2}$$

Let ρ be the previous anchor frame, then the edge energy of a P-frame is:

$$E_P(k) = \sum_{j=0}^{M}\sum_{i=0}^{N}\left|B_E(i,j,k) - B_E(i,j,\rho)\right| , \tag{3}$$

Let η be the next anchor frame, then the edge energy of a B-frame is:

$$E_B(k) = \sum_{j=0}^{M}\sum_{i=0}^{N}\frac{\left|B_E(i,j,k) - B_E(i,j,\rho)\right| + \left|B_E(i,j,k) - B_E(i,j,\eta)\right|}{2} , \tag{4}$$

Finally, the complexity measure of frame K is calculated by:

$$C(k) = \frac{E_x(k)}{\left(\frac{1}{k-1}\right)\sum_{l=0}^{k-1}E_x(l)} \quad x \in \{I,P,B\} . \tag{5}$$

3 Bit Allocation

3.1 Bit-Rate Traffic Model

We proposed a traffic model based on the actual bit-rate of the system as illustrated in Fig. 2.

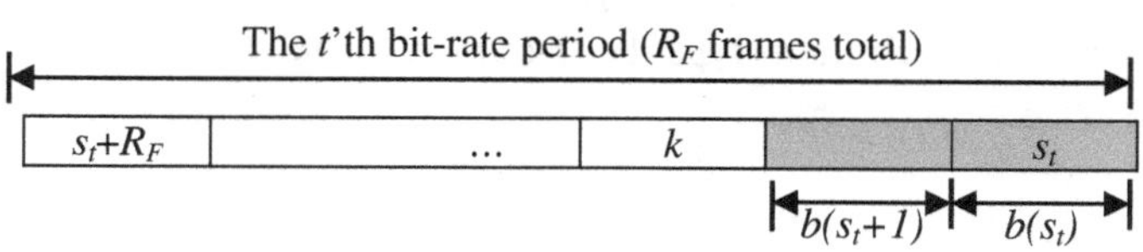

Fig. 2. Illustration of the bit-rate traffic model for one bit-rate period

Given a frame rate R_F, frame s_t as the frame at the start of the t'th bit-rate period and the instant available bit-rate $R_B(k)$ for the current frame k where $k \geq 0$. The available bits for frame s_0 in the first bit-rate period are:

$$A_0(s_0) = R_B(s_0) , \tag{6}$$

If the actual bits used by an encoded frame k is $b(k)$ then the bits left for frame allocation for frame k in the t'th bit-rate period are:

$$A_t(k) = A_t(k-1) - b(k-1) + (R_B(k) - R_B(k-1)) , \tag{7}$$

Subsequently, frame s_{t+1} on the $t+1$'th bit-rate period has its bit allocation updated as:

$$A_{t+1}(s_{t+1}) = R_B(s_{t+1}) + A_t(s_t + R_F) - b(s_t + R_F) . \tag{8}$$

3.2 Frame-Layer Bit Allocation

To determine the bits allocated to a frame, we first calculate the frame complexity value as described in section 2. As the complexity of the remaining frames to be encoded in the bit period is not known beforehand, we estimate it by using the mean complexity value of each I/P/B-frame.

To do this, a complexity value sliding window for *each* I/P/B-frame is maintained. The mean complexity value for each I/P/B frame is then calculated by averaging the values in the sliding windows. In our experiments, the sliding window sizes were set to 2 for I-frame complexity and 3 for both P and B frame complexity. This sliding window technique is used to make the system more responsive to bit allocation changes due to scene change.

The target bits for frame k on the t'th bit-rate period is then calculated by:

$$T(k) = \frac{C(k)}{NR_I \cdot AvgC_I + NR_P \cdot AvgC_P + NR_B \cdot AvgC_B} \times A_t(k) \times \frac{T(k-1)}{b(k-1)} \cdot \quad (9)$$

Where $AvgC_{I/P/B}$ is the mean complexity for I/P/B-frame and $NR_{I/P/B}$ are the remaining number of I/P/B-frames left to code in the bit-rate period.

4 QP Selection

QP selection is conducted using the quadratic R-Q model [3]. Three quadratic models are used for each I-frame, P-frame and B-frame respectively as the linear prediction model is different for each frame type. For I-frames, the model is:

$$\frac{T(k)-h(k)}{C(k)} = \frac{a_1}{QP(k)} + \frac{a_2}{QP^2(k)} , \quad (10)$$

While the model for P-frames as well as the model for B-frames is:

$$\frac{T(k)-h(k)}{\alpha \cdot PMAD(k) + (1-\alpha) \cdot C(k)} = \frac{a_1}{QP(k)} + \frac{a_2}{QP^2(k)} \cdot \quad (11)$$

Where $h(k)$ is the header bits, a_1 and a_2 are the first and second order coefficients respectively, $QP(k)$ is the quantization level for frame k, $PMAD(k)$ is the linearly predicted mean absolute value (MAD) for frame k as defined in [1] and α is a weighting factor (set to 0.5 in our experiments).

5 Experimental Results

5.1 Setup

We tested our proposed method on seven different video sequences of CIF size, comprising of both high and low motion contents. The H.264/AVC reference software JM12.2 was used to conduct our simulations. RD optimizations were turned off in the software and the GOP structure was specified as I-B-B-P-B-B-P-B-B (GOP size of 9).

We ran our simulations with a frame rate of 15Hz with no frame skipping and at a constant bit-rate. We then compared our proposed method, named here as RC4, with the original adopted H.264/AVC rate control scheme [1], called RC0 here, as well as the modified H.264/AVC rate control scheme by Leontaris and Tourapis [2], called RC3 here. The frame-layer rate control was enabled for RC0 and RC3. The parameters for RC3 were fixed with RCISliceBitRatio set to 1, RCBSliceBitRatio0 set to 0.5, RCBoverPRatio set to 0.45 and RCIoverPRatio set to 3.8. Hierarchial coding was disabled.

5.2 Satisfying the Bit-Rate Constraint

To check if the method meets the bit-rate constraint at the given frame rate, we summed up all the actual bits used by the frames in a bit-rate period (the actual bits used by every set of 15 frames in this experiment). Note that the assumption made here is that the coding time is negligible. This assumption is made purely for an easier comparison between the different methods. The actual mean bit-rate is computed along with the bit-rate deviation (error) for each method as shown in Table 1. The breakdown of the actual bits used for each bit-rate period for Foreman is shown in Fig. 3.

Discussion. RC0 shows a large deviation (almost 4 times) from the target bit-rate, this highlights the inability of RC0 to do a proper rate control on I-frames and B-frames. In contrast, RC3 shows a much better conformance to the bit-rate and frame rate constraints compared to RC0. However, RC4 still outperforms RC3 by a fair amount. The main reason for this is the problem of using the number of remaining bits in a GOP as an upper bound as discussed previously. Also the larger bit-rate variation of RC3 due to frequent scene changes is evident in the results for high motion sequences (i.e. Football and Stefan), while our proposed method shows a much smaller bit-rate variation in the same high-motion sequences.

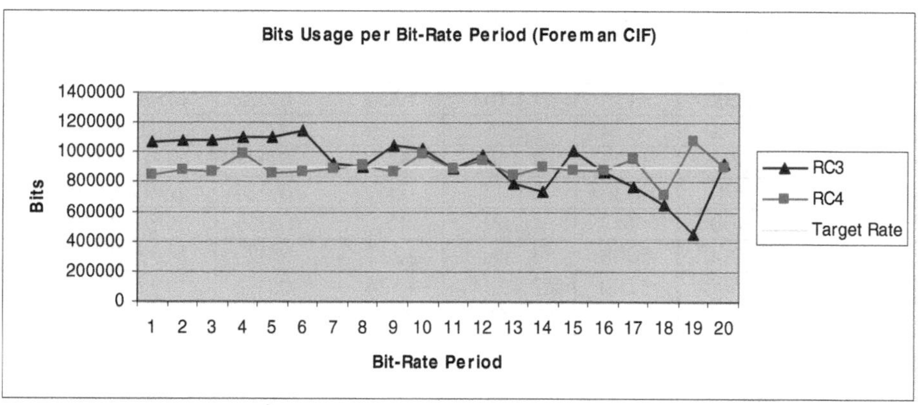

Fig. 3. The actual bits used for each bit-rate period for Foreman. RC0 is not shown here as the excessive bit-rates it generates skew the graph.

Table 1. Results showing the actual mean bit-rates and error of the proposed method (*RC4*), the original H.264/AVC method (*RC0*) and the modified H.264/AVC method (*RC3*)

Sequence	Target Rate (kbps)	RC0		RC3		RC4	
		Actual Rate (kbps)	Error	Actual Rate (kbps)	Error	Actual Rate (kbps)	Error
Container	500	3460	5.920	513	0.026	497	0.006
	700	3987	4.696	704	0.006	696	0.006
	900	4149	3.610	903	0.003	897	0.003
	1200	4682	2.902	1208	0.007	1193	0.006
	1500	4823	2.215	1524	0.016	1493	0.005
Football	500	1122	1.244	528	0.056	493	0.014
	700	1122	0.603	730	0.043	693	0.010
	900	1122	0.247	947	0.052	891	0.010
	1200	1963	0.636	1284	0.070	1195	0.004
	1500	1963	0.309	1603	0.069	1497	0.002
Foreman	500	4551	8.102	515	0.030	501	0.002
	700	4771	5.816	722	0.031	700	0.000
	900	5182	4.758	928	0.031	900	0.000
	1200	5618	3.682	1238	0.032	1198	0.002
	1500	5998	2.999	1545	0.030	1498	0.001
Mobile	500	7249	13.498	515	0.030	499	0.002
	700	7249	9.356	718	0.026	700	0.000
	900	7249	7.054	927	0.030	900	0.000
	1200	8945	6.454	1234	0.028	1198	0.002
	1500	8945	4.963	1538	0.025	1499	0.001
News	500	2720	4.440	508	0.016	497	0.006
	700	2925	3.179	711	0.016	697	0.004
	900	3015	2.350	914	0.016	896	0.004
	1200	3415	1.846	1226	0.022	1193	0.006
	1500	3474	1.316	1536	0.024	1491	0.006
Salesman	500	4178	7.356	512	0.024	500	0.000
	700	4636	5.623	717	0.024	699	0.001
	900	4742	4.269	917	0.019	899	0.001
	1200	5088	3.240	1227	0.023	1197	0.002
	1500	5180	2.453	1524	0.016	1497	0.002
Stefan	500	1834	2.668	547	0.094	503	0.006
	700	1834	1.620	764	0.091	696	0.006
	900	1834	1.038	980	0.089	895	0.006
	1200	2922	1.435	1304	0.087	1195	0.004
	1500	2922	0.948	1584	0.056	1491	0.006
Mean Overall Error:			3.795		0.036		0.004

Table 2. Results showing the mean Y PSNR of the proposed method (*RC4*) and the modified H.264/AVC method (*RC3*)

Sequence	Target Rate (kbps)	RC3 Mean Y PSNR (dB)	RC4 Mean Y PSNR (dB)	PSNR Gain (dB)
Container	500	38.84	38.38	-0.46
	700	40.27	40.98	0.71
	900	41.36	42.29	0.93
	1200	43.04	43.99	0.95
	1500	44.38	45.21	0.83
Football	500	35.59	35.67	0.08
	700	37.15	37.33	0.18
	900	38.43	38.77	0.34
	1200	39.89	40.34	0.45
	1500	41.25	41.68	0.43
Foreman	500	35.41	36.5	1.09
	700	36.74	37.78	1.04
	900	37.82	39.17	1.35
	1200	39.2	40.7	1.5
	1500	40.5	41.92	1.42
Mobile	500	25.39	26.44	1.05
	700	26.8	27.75	0.95
	900	28.25	29.35	1.1
	1200	30.1	31.68	1.58
	1500	31.69	33.08	1.39
News	500	41.34	42.13	0.79
	700	43.16	44.1	0.94
	900	44.59	45.56	0.97
	1200	46.11	47.77	1.66
	1500	47.89	49.28	1.39
Salesman	500	38.78	39.22	0.44
	700	40.09	41.3	1.21
	900	41.36	42.76	1.4
	1200	42.87	44.96	2.09
	1500	43.82	46.15	2.33
Stefan	500	29.32	29.7	0.38
	700	31.02	32	0.98
	900	32.44	33.37	0.93
	1200	34.41	35.23	0.82
	1500	36.19	37.28	1.09
			Mean Overall Gain:	0.98

5.3 Video Quality Test

We did a comparison on the decoded video quality output to show that our proposed method do not compromise heavily on the quality in order to meet the bit-rate and frame rate. We chose not to include RC0 in this test due to the fact that it deviates far too much from the target bit rate to make a fair comparison on the decoded video quality. We calculate the mean output PSNR of the Y-component of the frames and the PSNR gain of our proposed method compared to RC3 as shown in Table 2. The breakdown of the Y PSNR for each frame for Foreman is shown in Fig. 4.

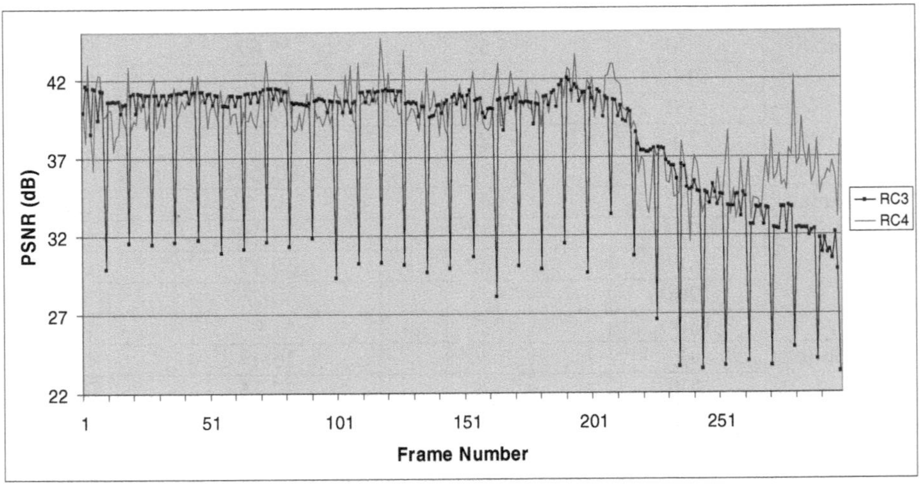

Fig. 4. The Y PSNR of each frame for Foreman

Discussion. The results show that our proposed method not only did not perform worse than RC3, but in general performed better by a fair amount in almost all cases with a mean PSNR gain of 0.98dB. RC3 requires its parameters to be tuned for each sequence and this is difficult to do in general. Using fixed parameter values causes RC3 to perform badly as shown in the results. Moreover, RC3 tends to allocate a smaller amount of bits for the I-frames, doing this may sometimes degrade the quality on subsequent P-frames and B-frames. Our proposed method, on the other hand, allocates bits purely based on the derived complexity measure of the frame, avoiding the issue of choosing parameters by providing an accurate estimated weighting to I-frames, P-frames and B-frames.

6 Conclusion

In this paper, we proposed a novel rate control scheme by using the edge energy of a frame to estimate the frame complexity and integrated it into the R-Q model. We also proposed a new bit-rate traffic model to replace the fluid flow traffic model. Results showed that our proposed method has a more stringent adherence to the target bit-rates without significantly sacrificing the quality of the video output. Additionally, our proposed method does not assume that any information on the whole video sequence is available, making it suitable for real-time video applications.

Acknowledgment. National ICT Australia (NICTA) is funded by the Australian Government's *Backing Australia's Ability* initiative, in part through the Australian Research Council.

References

1. Li, Z.G., Pan, F., Lim, K.P., Feng, G.N., Lin, X., Rahardja, S.: Adaptive Basic Unit Layer Rate Control for JVT. JVT-G012, 7th JVT Meeting, Pattaya, Thailand (March 2003)
2. Leontaris, A., Tourapis, A.M.: Rate Control Reorganization in the Joint Model (JM) Reference Software. JVT-W042, 23rd JVT Meeting, San Jose, California, USA (April 2007)
3. Lee, H.J., Chiang, T., Zhang, Y.Q.: Scalable rate control for MPEG-4 video. IEEE TCSVT 10(6), 878–894 (2000)
4. Jing, X., Chau, L.P.: A novel intra-rate estimation method for H.264 rate control. In: IEEE ISCAS 2006, pp. 21–24 (May 2006)
5. Liu, Y., Li, Z.G., Soh, Y.C.: A Novel Rate Control Scheme for Low Delay Video Communication of H.264/AVC Standard. IEEE TCSVT 17(1), 68–78 (2007)
6. Yu, H., Pan, F., Lin, Z., Sun, Y.: A perceptual bit allocation scheme for H.264. In: IEEE ICME 2005 (July 2005)
7. Lee, J.H., Shin, I.H, Park, H.W.: Adaptive Intra-Frame Assignment and Bit-Rate Estimation for Variable GOP Length in H.264. IEEE TCSVT 16(10), 1271–1279 (2006)
8. Jiang, M.Q., Ling, N.: An improved frame and macroblock layer bit allocation scheme for H.264 rate control. In: IEEE ISCAS 2005, vol. 2, pp. 1501–1504 (May 2005)
9. Yu, H.T., Lin, Z.P., Pan, F.: An improved rate control algorithm for H.264. In: IEEE ISCAS 2005, vol. 1, pp. 312–315 (May 2005)
10. Lee, C.Y., Lee, S.J., Oh, Y.J., Kim, J.S.: Cost-Effective Frame-Layer H.264 Rate Control for Low Bit Rate Video. In: IEEE ICME 2006, pp. 697–700 (July 2006)
11. Won, C.S., Park, D.K., Park, S.J.: Efficient use of MPEG-7 edge histogram descriptor. ETRI Journal 24(1) (February 2002)
12. Li, Z.G., Zhu, C., Ling, N., Yang, X.K., Feng, G.N., Wu, S., Pan, F.: A Unified Architecture for Real Time Video Coding Systems. IEEE TCSVT 13(6), 472–487 (2003)

A Quantized Transform-Domain Motion Estimation Technique for H.264 Secondary SP-Frames

Ki-Kit Lai, Yui-Lam Chan, and Wan-Chi Siu

Centre for Signal Processing
Department of Electronic and Information Engineering
The Hong Kong Polytechnic University
Hung Hom, Kowloon, Hong Kong
{kikit.lai, enylchan, enwcsiu}@polyu.edu.hk

Abstract. The brand-new SP-frame in H.264 facilitates drift-free bitstream switching. Notwithstanding the guarantee of seamless switching, the cost is the bulky size of secondary SP-frames. This induces a significant amount of additional space or bandwidth for storage or transmission. For this reason, a new motion estimation and compensation technique, which is operated in the quantized transform (QDCT) domain, is designed for coding secondary SP-frames in this paper. So far, much investigation has been conducted to evaluate the trade off between the relative sizes of primary and secondary SP-frames by adjusting the quantization parameters. But, our proposed work aims at keeping the secondary SP-frames as small as possible without affecting the size of primary SP-frames by incorporating QDCT-domain motion estimation and compensation in the secondary SP-frame coding. Simulation results demonstrate that the size of secondary SP-frames can be reduced remarkably.

Keywords: Video coding, SP-frame, H.264, QDCT-domain, motion estimation, motion compensation.

1 Introduction

H.264 is the latest video coding standard [1], which was jointly developed by the ISO Moving Picture Experts Group (MPEG) and the ITU Video Coding Experts Group (VCEG). It is shown to achieve gains in coding efficiency of up to 50% over a wide range of bit rates as compared with previous video coding standards [2]. In addition to achieving superior coding efficiency, this new standard includes a number of new features to provide more flexibility for applications to a wide variety of network environments.

The new SP-frame is one of these features. The motivation of introducing SP-frames is to facilitate error resilience, bitstream switching, splicing, random access, fast forward, and fast backward [1]. It is now part of the Extended Profile in the H.264 standard. This special SP-frame is composed of primary and secondary SP-frames. They both exploit temporal redundancy with predictive coding, but use different reference frames. Although different reference frames are used, it still allows identical reconstruction.

H.H.S. Ip et al. (Eds.): PCM 2007, LNCS 4810, pp. 138–147, 2007.

This property can be applied to drift-free switching between compressed bitstreams of different bit rates to accommodate the bandwidth variation, as illustrated in Figure 1. This figure depicts a video sequence encoded into two bitstreams (B1 and B2) with different bit rates. B1 is a sequence encoded in high bitrate while B2 is a low bitrate bitstream. Within each bitstream, two primary SP-frames –$SP_{1,t}$ and $SP_{2,t}$ are placed at frame *t* (switching point). To allow seamless switching, a secondary SP-frame($SP_{12,t}$) is produced, which has the same reconstructed values as $SP_{2,t}$ even different reference frames are used. When switching from B1 to B2 is needed at frame *t*, $SP_{12,t}$ instead of $SP_{2,t}$ is transmitted. After decoding $SP_{12,t}$, the decoder can obtain exactly the same reconstructed values as normally $SP_{2,t}$ decoded at frame *t*. Therefore it can continually decode B2 at frame *t+1* seamlessly.

Nevertheless, there is a trade-off between the coding performance of primary SP-frames and the storage cost for secondary SP-frames [3]. For example, a primary SP-frame with high quality results in a significantly high storage requirement for the secondary SP-frame. It is unfeasible to store such huge size of the secondary SP-frame. In this paper, we propose a novel coding arrangement to reduce the size of secondary SP-frames.

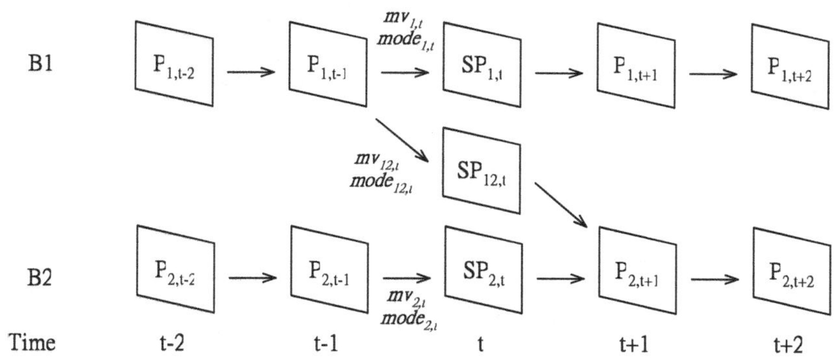

Fig. 1. Switching bitstream from B1 to B2 using SP-frames

The rest of this paper is organized as follows. In Section 2, a brief introduction of H.264 SP/SI-frame coding is given. Section 3 presents an in-depth study of the problem on applying the traditional pixel-domain motion estimation technique into the secondary SP-frame encoder. Analysis of using QDCT-domain motion estimation is also covered here. After the detailed analysis, a novel secondary SP-frame encoded is proposed. In Section 4, we present some experimental results to show the performance of the proposed scheme. We also compare its performance with the conventional secondary SP-frame encoder. Concluding remarks are provided in Section 5.

2 Background of Coding SP-Frames

The way of encoding primary SP-frames is similar to that of encoding P-frames except additional quantization/dequantization steps with the quantization level *Qs* are applied to the transform coefficients of the primary SP-frame ($SP_{2,t}$ in Figure 1), as shown in Figure 2. Interested readers are encouraged to read the references [4-6]. These extra steps ensure that the quantized transform coefficients of $SP_{2,t}$ (denoted as $SP_{2,t}^{Q_s}$) can be quantized and de-quantized without loss at Qs, which is used in the encoding process of the secondary SP-frame, $SP_{12,t}$.

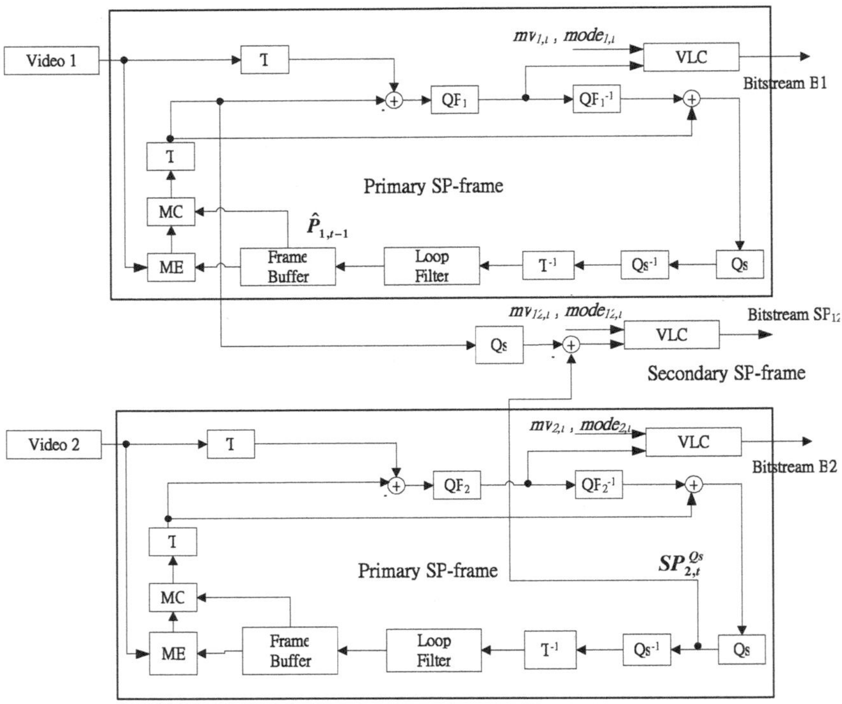

Fig. 2. Simplified encoding block diagram of primary and secondary SP-frames [5]

For coding $SP_{12,t}$, the reconstructed $P_{1,t-1}$($\hat{P}_{1,t-1}$) acts as the reference and its target is to reconstruct $SP_{2,t}^{Q_s}$ perfectly. By using the reference frame $\hat{P}_{1,t-1}$, its prediction is first transformed and quantized using Qs before generating the residue with $SP_{2,t}^{Q_s}$. Both the prediction and $SP_{2,t}^{Q_s}$ are thus synchronized to Qs and there is no further quantization from this point, meaning that the decoder, with $\hat{P}_{1,t-1}$, Qs, and the residue available, can perfectly reconstruct $SP_{2,t}^{Q_s}$.

3 Size Reduction of Secondary SP-Frames in QDCT Domain

3.1 Motion-Compensated Prediction in Secondary SP-Frames

Producing secondary SP-frames involves the processes of motion estimation and motion compensation. In H.264, it supports motion estimation using different block sizes such as 16×16, 16×8, 8×16, 8×8, 8×4, 4×8, and 4×4 [7]. To compute the coding modes and motion vectors for the secondary SP-frame, motion estimation is firstly performed for all modes and submodes independently by minimizing the Lagrangian cost function J_{motion}.

$$J_{motion}(mv_{12}, \lambda_{motion}) = SAD(s,r) + \lambda_{motion} \cdot R_{motion}(mv_{12} - pmv_{12}) \quad (1)$$

where mv_{12} is the motion vector used for prediction, λ_{motion} is the Lagrangian multiplier for motion estimation, $R_{motion}(mv_{12} - pv_{12})$ is the estimated number of bits for coding mv_{12}, and SAD is sum of absolute differences between the original block s and its reference block r [7].

After motion estimation for each mode, a rate-distortion (RD) optimization technique is used to get the best mode and its general equation is given by

$$J_{mode}(s,c,mode_{12}, \lambda_{mode}) = SSD(s,c,mode_{12}) + \lambda_{mode} \cdot R_{mode}(s,c,mode_{12}) \quad (2)$$

where λ_{mode} is the Lagrangian multiplier for mode decision, $mode_{12}$ is one of the candidate modes during motion estimation, SSD is sum of the squared differences between s and its reconstruction block c, and $R_{mode}(s,c,mode_{12})$ represents the number of coding bits associated with the chosen mode. To compute J_{mode}, forward and inverse integer transforms, and variable length coding are performed. In the implementation of H.264 codec such as JM11.0[8], the motion estimation of the secondary SP-frame uses $\hat{P}_{1,t-1}$ and the original $SP_{1,t}$ as the reference and current frames respectively. This arrangement allows the reuse of coding modes ($mode_{1,t}$ in Figure 1) and motion vectors ($mv_{1,t}$ in Figure 1) during secondary SP-frame encoding. It means that

$$mv_{12,t} = mv_{1,t} \quad (3)$$

and

$$mode_{12,t} = mode_{1,t} \quad (4)$$

However, the reuse of coding modes and motion vectors reduces the coding efficiency of a secondary SP-frame since the purpose of the secondary SP-frame is to reconstruct $SP_{2,t}$ instead of $SP_{1,t}$. In [9], a secondary SP-frame is encoded to match the exact target frame (reconstructed $SP_{2,t}$, $\hat{SP}_{2,t}$) based on the exact reference ($\hat{P}_{1,t-1}$), as depicted in Figure 3. By using the correct target and reference frames, better compression performance of secondary SP-frames can be achieved. Note that the computational complexity evidently increases without reusing coding modes and motion vectors. Nevertheless, secondary SP-frames are always generated in off-line for bitstream switching applications. Thus, complexity is not the major concern for coding secondary SP-frames.

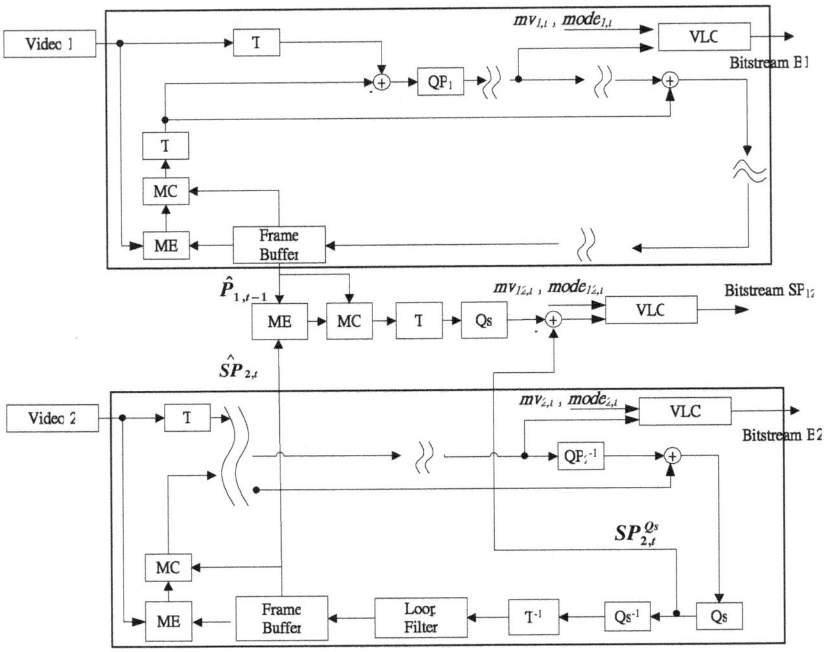

Fig. 3. Motion estimation and compensation of a secondary SP-frame encoder [9]

3.2 Motivation of Using QDCT-Domain Motion-Compensation Prediction

Nevertheless, the improvement in [9] is not so significant. In this section, we explain the deficiency in using the conventional motion estimation and compensation processes, which are operated in the pixel domain, for secondary SP-frames. Figure 4 illustrates the step of encoding a block in a P-frame using pixel-domain motion estimation. In this case, most of the transform coefficients become zero after transformation and quantization. This property benefits entropy coding. However, in Figure 3, the encoding of a secondary SP-frame involves carrying out transformation and quantization of original $SP_{2,t}$ and $\hat{P}_{1,t-1}$ first. Then, quantized coefficients of the secondary SP-frame at t, $Qs[T(SP_{12,t})]$, can be obtained as,

$$Qs[T[SP_{12,t}]] = Qs[T[SP_{2,t}]] - Qs[T[MC(\hat{P}_{1,t-1})]] \quad (5)$$

where MC() is the motion-compensation operator. Figure 5 uses the same example in Figure 4 again to show the residue of a secondary SP-frame in which a block is transformed and quantized before calculating the residue. In this case, their quantized coefficients are only near, but not equal, resulting in generating many non-zero residue, especially for a small Qs. Since there is no further quantization from this point, these coefficients should be encoded completely. In entropy coding, even only one high-frequency coefficient exists, significant demanding of bits is required. Therefore, size of secondary SP-frames becomes large, and this also explains why the pixel-domain motion estimation is not suitable for coding secondary SP-frames. In this paper, we propose performing motion estimation and compensation in the quantized transform (QDCT) domain rather than the pixel domain to improve the coding efficiency of secondary SP-frames.

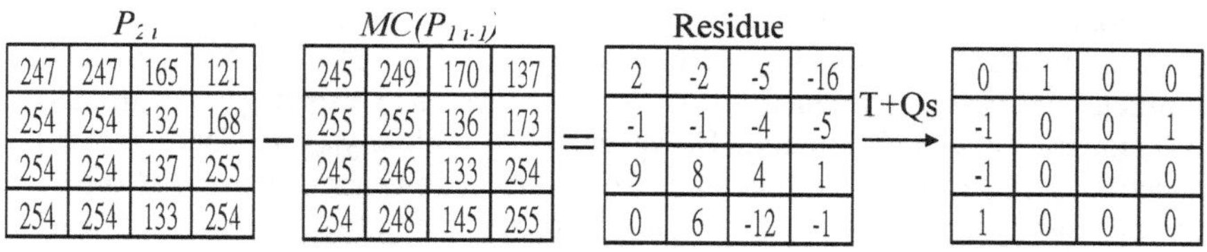

Fig. 4. Motion-compensated prediction using pixel-domain motion estimation in encoding a P-frame

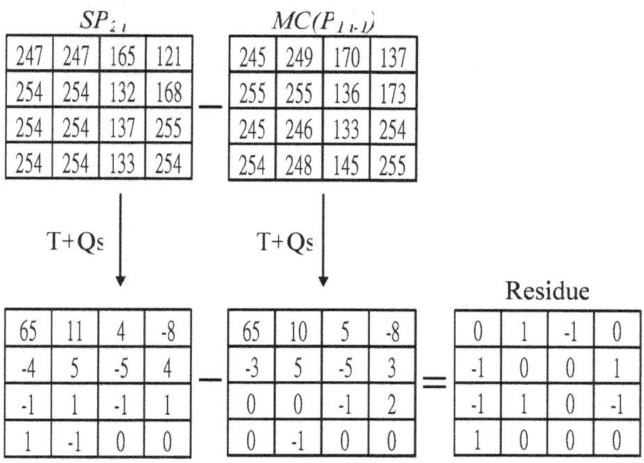

Fig. 5. Motion-compensated prediction using pixel-domain motion estimation in encoding a secondary SP-frame

3.3 The Proposed Scheme for Secondary SP-Frame Encoding

In this section, we propose a quantized transform-domain motion estimation (TME) technique that minimizes $Qs[T[SP_{2,t}]] - Qs[T[MC(P_{1,t-1})]]$ (quantized transform domain) instead of $SP_{2,t} - MC(P_{1,t-1})$ (pixel domain). From (1), SAD between pixels of the original block s and its reference block r is used to compute the distortion of J_{motion}. The aforementioned investigation reveals that pixel-domain distortion measure is not appropriate for coding secondary SP-frames. In the proposed TME, the Lagrangian cost function J_{motion} in (1) needs to be rewritten as

$$J'_{motion}(mv_{12}, \lambda_{motion}) = SATD(s,r) + \lambda_{motion} \cdot R_{motion}(mv_{12} - pmv_{12}) \qquad (6)$$

where *SATD(s,r)* is now the sum of absolute differences between the quantized transform coefficients of the original block *s* and the quantized transform coefficients of its reference block *r*, and it can be defined as

$$SATD(s,r) = \sum \left| Qs[T(s)] - Qs[T(r)] \right| \quad (7)$$

For coding a secondary SP-frame, this distortion measure can find a better motion vector and mode for minimizing the residue, $Qs[T[SP_{12,t}]]$, in (5). Note that SATD is computationally intensive since all the pixel blocks are necessary to be transformed and quantized to QDCT domain. However, the complexity is not the major concern for secondary SP-frame encoding since this frame type is always encoded off-line for bitstream switching applications. On the other hand, the accuracy of distortion measure increases the coding efficiency of secondary SP-frames which results in the significant reduction of the storage requirement in the video server.

Figure 6 shows the block diagram of applying our new QDCT-domain motion estimation technique in the secondary SP-frame encoder. The reference and target frames in the QDCT domain are the inputs of TME. After the motion vectors for each block are obtained, a corresponding QDCT-domain motion compensation (TMC) is used to compute the motion-compensated frame, $Qs[T[MC(\hat{P}_{1,t-1})]]$. With $Qs[T[MC(\hat{P}_{1,t-1})]]$ and $Qs[T[SP_{2,t}]]$, as depicted in Figure 6, the residue $Qs[T[SP_{12,t}]]$ can then be calculated.

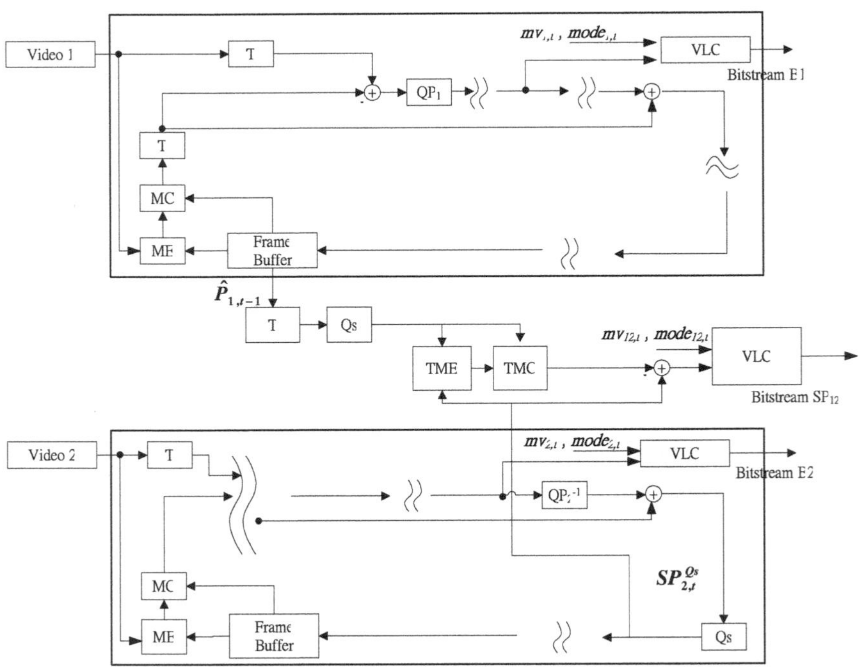

Fig. 6. The proposed secondary SP-frame encoder in the QDCT domain

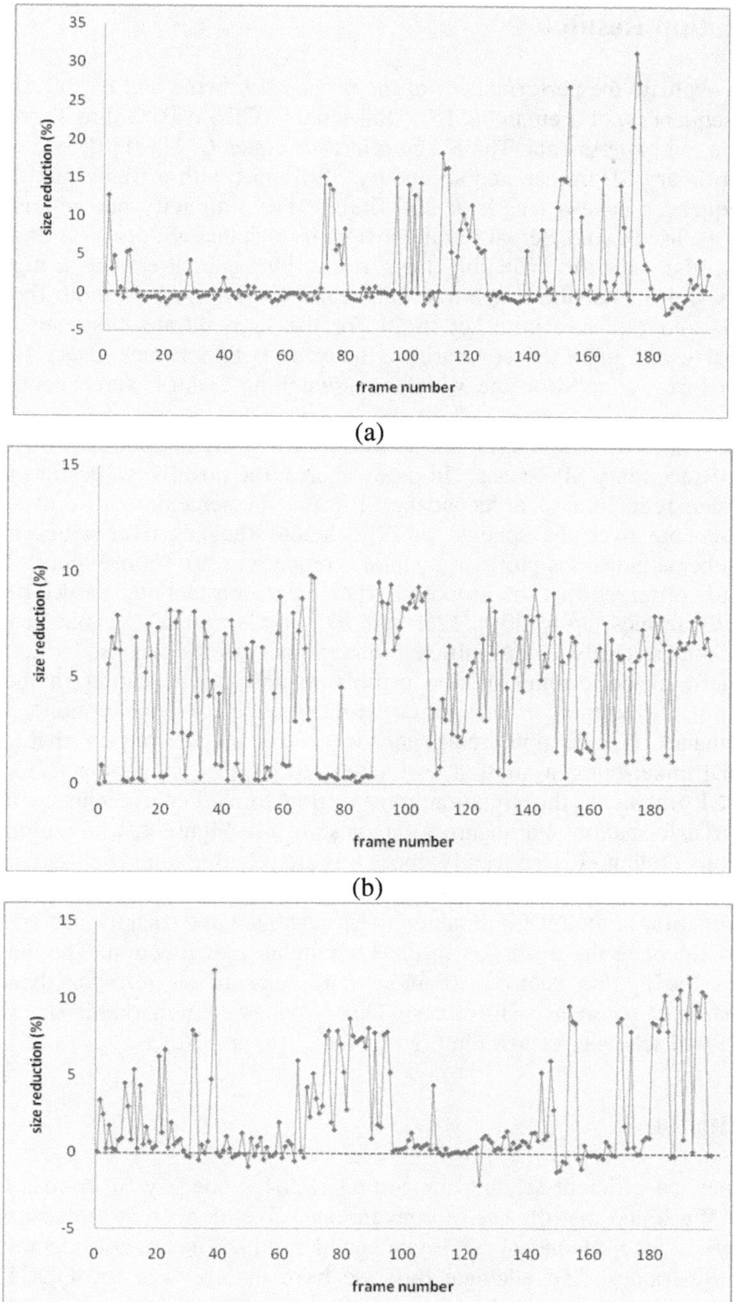

(a)

(b)

(c)

Fig. 7. Size reduction of secondary SP-frames in percentage difference achieved by the proposed scheme over the scheme in [9], (a) Foreman, (b) Salesman, and (c) Table Tennis

4 Simulation Results

In order to evaluate the performances of the proposed scheme and the scheme in [9], three test sequences, "Foreman" (CIF), "Salesman" (CIF) and "Table Tennis" (SIF) were used in our experiments. The H.264 reference codec (JM11.0 [8]) was employed to encode primary SP-frames and secondary SP-frames with a frame rate of 30 fps. All test sequences have a length of 200 frames. For simplicity but without loss of generality, we used two different bitrate bitstreams encoded with two different sets of Q_P and Q_S, and only the switching from a low bitrate bitstream to a high bitrate bitstream is shown. For the low bitrate bitstream, Q_P and Q_S were both fixed to 41, whereas Q_P and Q_S were both set to 21 for the high bitrate bitstream. To have comprehensive and impartial comparisons between both schemes, every frame was encoded in turn as an SP-frame while non-switching frames were encoded as P-frames.

Figures 7(a), 7(b) and 7(c) show the frame-by-frame comparisons of size reduction of secondary SP-frames. In these figures, the positive values of the Y-axis mean the size reduction of a secondary SP-frame in percentage difference of our proposed scheme over the scheme in [9] whereas the negative values mean the proposed scheme generates more bit-count as compare to [9]. From Figures 7(a), 7(b) and 7(c), it is observed that the proposed scheme can substantially reduce the size of secondary SP-frames, up to 30%, 12% and 10% in "Foreman", "Table Tennis" and "Salesman", respectively. The significant improvement of the proposed scheme is due to the benefit of performing motion estimation and compensation in the QDCT domain. In [9], even though a proper target frame is selected for motion estimation, the performance is still not significant. It is due to the reason that only the conventional pixel-domain motion estimation technique is employed for coding secondary SP-frames. In this situation, most of transformed coefficients become non-zero after transformation and quantization, as shown in Figure 4, which unfavour the use of entropy coding. Consequently, more bits are required to encode secondary SP-frames. On the other hand, our proposed scheme produces secondary SP-frames using motion estimation in the QDCT domain. The quantized and transformed coefficients are used to calculate the distortion in the Lagrangian cost function. The new SATD really finds the motion vector with more cofficients to be zero that benefits the entropy coding of secondary SP-frames. This provides the remarkable size reduction of our proposed scheme as shown in Figures 7(a), 7(b) and 7(c).

5 Conclusion

In this paper, an efficient scheme for coding H.264 secondary SP-frames has been proposed. We found that the use of conventional pixel-domain motion estimation is not appropriate for a secondary SP-frame encoder, which incurs considerable size of secondary SP-frames. To alleviate this, we have incorporated the QDCT-domain motion estimation technique in the encoding process of secondary SP-frames. Experimental results show that the proposed scheme can significantly reduce the size of H.264 secondary SP-frames. Besides, the proposed technique does not affect the coding efficiency of primary SP-frames.

Acknowledgments. The work described in this paper is partially supported by the Centre for Signal Processing (1-BB9A), Department of Electronic and Information Engineering, The Hong Kong Polytechnic University and a grant from the Research Grants Council of the Hong Kong Special Administrative Region, China (PolyU 5125/06E). Ki-Kit Lai acknowledges the research studentships provided by the University.

References

1. Joint Video Team of ISO/IEC MPEG and ITU-T VCEG: ITU-T Recommendation H.264 Advanced video coding for generic audiovisual services (2005)
2. ITU-T Recommendation H.263: Video coding for low bitrate communication(1998)
3. Chang, C.P., Lin, C.W.: R-D optimized quantization of H.264 SP-frames for bitstream switching under storage constraints: In: IEEE International Symposium on Circuits and Systems, vol. 2, pp. 1242–1235 (2005)
4. Karczewicz, M., Kurceren, R.: The SP- and SI-frames design for H.264/AVC. Transations on Circuits and Systems for video technology 13(7), 637–644 (2003)
5. Sun, X., Li, S., Wu, F., Shen, K., Gao, W.: The improved SP frame coding technique for the JVT standard. IEEE International Conference on Image Processing 2, 297–300 (2003)
6. Kurceren, R., Karczewicz, M.: Synchronization-Predictive coding for video compression: The SP frames design for JVT/H.26L. In: IEEE International Conference on Image Processing, vol. 2, pp. 497–500 (2002)
7. Schafer, R., Wiegand, T., Schwarz, H.: The emerging H.264/AVC standard. EBU Technical Review (2003)
8. Suhring, K.: H.264 Reference Software JM11.0. (2006), http://iphome.hhi.de/suehring/tml/
9. Tan, W.T., Shen, B.: Methods to improve coding efficiency of SP frames. In: IEEE International Conference on Image Processing, Atlanta, USA (2006)

Efficient Intra Mode Decision Via Statistical Learning

Chiuan Hwang and Shang-Hong Lai

Department of Computer Science, National Tsing Hua University, Hsinchu, Taiwan
g946319@oz.nthu.edu.tw, lai@cs.nthu.edu.tw

Abstract. Intra mode selection and motion estimation for spatial and temporal prediction play important roles for achieving high video compression ratio in the latest video coding standards, such as H.264/AVC. However, both components take most of the computational cost in the video encoding process. In this paper, we propose an efficient intra mode prediction algorithm based on using the mode conditional probability learned from a large amount of training video sequences with the ground truth modes of each block to be encoded and its neighboring block modes as well as its associated image content features. By applying the proposed intra-mode selection algorithm into the H.264 reference code, we show significant reduction of the computation time with negligible video quality degradation for H.264 video encoding.

Keywords: Image coding, image analysis, video coding, video compression, intra prediction, video codec.

1 Introduction

To improve the computational efficiency of the intra-mode decision in H.264 video coding [1], there have been many different algorithms proposed recently. The traditional method is to run all intra modes, as listed in Table 1, for Luma and Chroma blocks, but it takes too much encoding time. Later, Cheng and Chang [2] used the block content characteristics, such as the block RD-cost correlation between the mode and its neighboring modes, to reduce the search of nine Luma 4x4 modes to no more than six modes. In addition, the block gradient information in the local block was used to determine a rough edge direction in some previous works [3-5]. Based on this direction, they used the corresponding directional mode and its two neighboring modes plus the DC mode to determine the mode with the lowest cost. In addition, Pan et al. [4] proposed a different way to predict the direction in a block. They collected statistics by computing the gradient of every pixel in a block and then chose the most possible direction from the statistics as their primary prediction mode. Sim and Kim [6] presented an efficient mode decision algorithm based on the conditional probability of the best mode with respect to the best modes of the adjacent blocks. Furthermore, Huang et al. [7] developed a fast intra frame coding system by combining several improved components, including context-based decimation of unlikely candidates, subsampling of matching operations, bit-width truncation, and interleaved full-search/partial-search strategy.

H.H.S. Ip et al. (Eds.): PCM 2007, LNCS 4810, pp. 148–157, 2007.

In this paper, we propose a new and efficient intra mode decision algorithm based on the mode conditional probability with respect to its neighboring encoded modes and its image features. This mode conditional probability is learned from a collection of video sequences with the ground truth modes determined by the H.264 reference program. We demonstrate the superior performance of the proposed algorithm over previous mode decision methods through experiments.

2 Intra Prediction in H.264/AVC

The H.264/AVC standard [1] provides variable block size on motion estimation and more different directional modes for intra prediction than previous MPEG standards. For the Luma 16x16 component and Chroma 8x8 component, they support four modes, including three directional modes and one DC mode. These different modes are listed in Table.1.

Table 1. (a) Luma 16x16 prediction modes and (b) Chroma 8x8 prediction modes

(a)

Mode	Mode description
0	Vertical
1	Horizontal
2	DC
3	Plane

(b)

Mode	Mode description
0	DC
1	Vertical
2	Horizontal
3	Plane

The modes for Luma 16x16 and Chroma 8x8 are different only with their orders. For Luma 4x4 sub-blocks, there are nine modes, including eight directional modes and one DC mode. The Luma 4x4 modes are listed in Figure 1.

Mode	Mode description
0	Vertical
1	Horizontal
2	DC
3	Diagonal_Down_Left
4	Diagonal_Down_Right
5	Vertical_Right
6	Horizontal_Down
7	Vertical_Left
8	Horizontal_Up

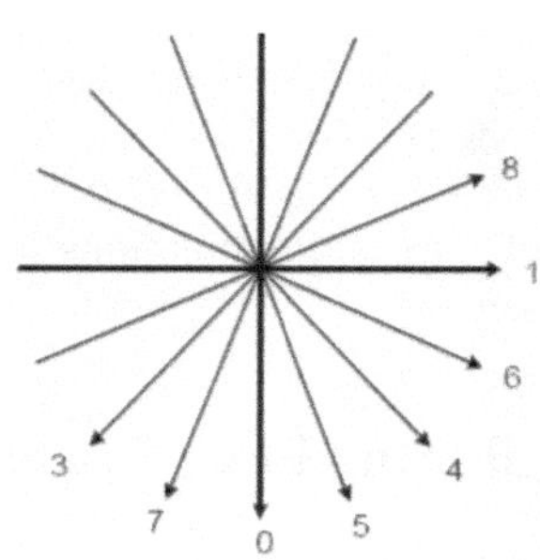

Fig. 1. The nine Luma 4x4 intra prediction modes and their corresponding directions

In H.264, to achieve better video quality and optimal bitrate compression, the RDO (Rate Distortion Optimization) is employed but with more computational cost. It compares the RD costs for different modes to determine which mode is optimal for the macroblock. The H.264 encoding process is illustrated in Figure.2.

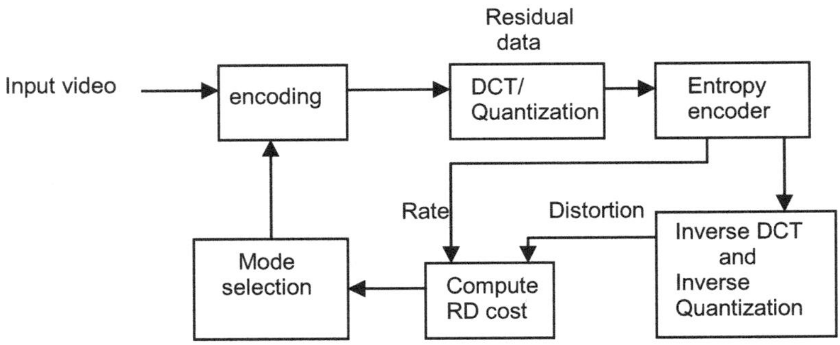

Fig. 2. H.264 encoding flowchart

The RD cost is computed with the following formula.

$$J(s,c,MODE \mid QP,\lambda_{MODE}) \\ = SSD(s,c,MODE \mid QP) + \lambda_{MODE} \cdot R(s,c,MODE \mid QP) \tag{1}$$

Where s and c are the source video signal and the reconstructed video signal, respectively, QP is the quantization parameter, λ_{MODE} is the Lagrange multiplier, MODE indicates a macroblock mode, such as P16x16, P16x8, P8x16, P8x8, I16x16, I4x4, etc., SSD is the sum of the square differences between s and c, R(s,c,MODE|QP) is the number of bits associated with the chosen macroblock MODE and QP.

When it starts to encode a macroblock, as shown in the above flow chart, it needs to check all the mode combinations to choose the one with the minimal RD cost in the mode selection procedure. In I-frame, it only needs to do intra coding to decide the intra mode, and the total number of intra mode combinations is C8*(L4*16+L16), where C8, L4, and L16 denote the numbers of the Chroma8x8 modes, Luma4x4 modes and Luma16x16 modes, respectively. Thus, the total number of mode combinations is 4*(9*16+4)=592. This will take a considerable amount of time to compute the RD costs for all mode combinations, hence we need to reduce the total number of mode combinations in the mode decision process to speed up the computation.

3 Neighboring Block Mode and Image Features

3.1 Neighboring Block Mode

Now, let us illustrate why the encoding block is related to its neighboring block modes in intra mode decision. The intra 4x4 mode for each macroblock is collected when JM 10.2 [8] encodes the sequence. Figure 3 and 4 depict examples of intra 4x4 mode maps from two video sequences. As we see from these two examples, the encoded block mode is closely related to its neighboring block modes and its own image content gradient features. So if we can utilize this characteristic to predict the mode of a block, we can estimate which mode may achieve lower bitrate and better video quality. This can also be applied to intra 16x16 mode and Chroma 8x8 mode.

Fig. 3. image and 4x4 intra mode map (the fiftieth frame of Forman CIF sequence)

Fig. 4. image and 4x4 intra mode map (the fiftieth frame of CarPhone QCIF sequence)

3.2 Image Gradient Feature

Feature based algorithms [2-5] have been commonly used for intra mode decision. It is critical to extract representative image features very fast. Several previous algorithms compute edge features to reduce modes in the search, but they usually lead to higher bitrates and larger distortion.

In this work, we extract very simple image features for intra mode decision. These image gradient features are the convolutions with the gradient mask shown in Figure 5. Wang et al. [5] also used similar gradient masks for extracting features for intra mode prediction.

$$\begin{bmatrix} 1 & -1 \\ 1 & -1 \end{bmatrix}, \begin{bmatrix} 1 & 1 \\ -1 & -1 \end{bmatrix} \qquad \begin{bmatrix} 1 & -1 \\ 1 & -1 \end{bmatrix}, \begin{bmatrix} 1 & 1 \\ -1 & -1 \end{bmatrix}, \begin{bmatrix} 1 & -1 \\ -1 & 1 \end{bmatrix}$$

(a) (b)

Fig. 5. Gradient masks for image feature extraction, (a) two and (b) three masks

We apply the above masks for convolution with a 4x4, 8x8, or 16x16 block. Let us take an NxN block for example:

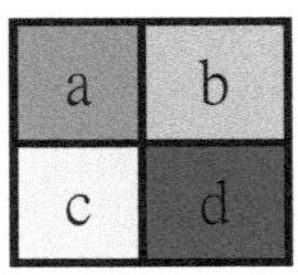

a,b,c,d are all the mean of N/2 * N/2 block

Fig. 6. 2x2 matrix for applying the mask

In our implementation, we quantize the computed gradient features for computing the conditional probability by using the following two different schemes:
Scheme (a):

1. Compute the correlation between the 2x2 matrix and the two masks in Figure 5(a) to obtain the two values S_v and S_h, respectively.
2. Normalize S_v and S_h to obtain the normalized coefficients Q_1 and Q_2 as follows:

$$Sum=abs(S_v) + abs(S_h) \tag{2}$$

$$Q_1=S_v/Sum,\ Q_2=S_h/Sum \tag{3}$$

3. Quantize Q_1 and Q_2 to the levels inx_1 and inx_2, respectively.

Scheme (b):

1. Compute the correlation between the 2x2 matrix and the three masks in Figure 5(b) to obtain the three values S_v, S_h and S_{diag}, respectively.
2. Normalize S_v, S_h and S_{diag} to obtain the normalized coefficients Q_1, Q_2, and Q_3,, respectively, as follows:.

$$Sum=(abs(S_v) + abs(S_h))+abs(S_{diag}) \tag{4}$$

$$Q_1=abs(S_v)/Sum,\ Q_2=abs(S_h)/Sum,\ Q_3=abs(S_{diag})/Sum \tag{5}$$

3. Quantize Q_1, Q_2 and Q_3 to inx_1, inx_2 and inx_3, respectively.

Note that we quantize the gradient features in scheme (a) and (b) into 8 and 4 levels, respectively. Figure 7 shows the uniform quantization used in our implementation.

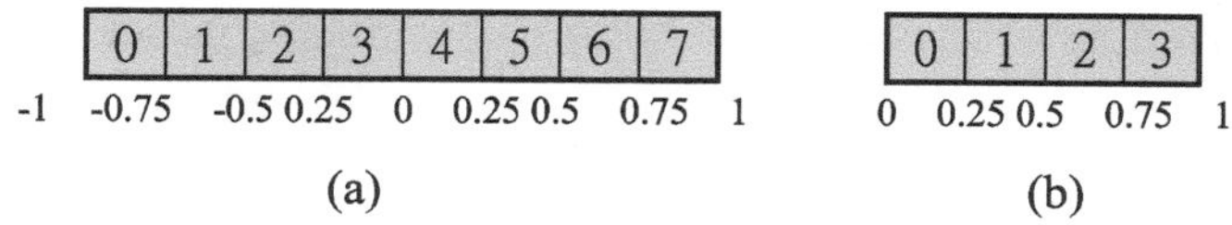

Fig. 7. Uniform quantization for (a) 8 and (b) 4 levels

4 Proposed Intra Mode Decision Algorithm

The proposed algorithm consists of the training and execution phases. We first describe the procedure for training in the following.

Step 1. Apply the exhaustive search to determine the optimal intra modes and extract the image gradient features for each macroblock in some training video sequences to obtain the training data.

Step 2. From the training data, we count the occurrence of joint event for the optimal modes for the current block and its neighboring blocks and the associated image features, Let the count of joint event be denoted by $C(m_c, \mathbf{m}_p, \mathbf{g})$, where m_c is the optimal intra mode for the current block, $\mathbf{m}_p$ is the vector containing the optimal modes in the left and upper blocks, and $\mathbf{g}$ is gradient feature vector computed from section 3.2.

Step 3. Compute and store the conditional mode probability distribution $p(m_c \mid \mathbf{m}_p, \mathbf{g})$ by normalizing the counts of occurrences of joint events as follows:

$$p(m_c|\mathbf{m}_p,\mathbf{g}) = \frac{C(m_c,\mathbf{m}_p,\mathbf{g})}{\sum_{m_c \in M} C(m_c,\mathbf{m}_p,\mathbf{g})} \tag{6}$$

where M is the set of all possible modes. For Luma 4x4, it contains mode 0 to 8. For Luma 16x16 and Chroma 8x8, the set M only contains mode 0 to 3.

After we have the above mode conditional probability learned from the training data set, we can use it to determine the most probable candidate modes from the encoded neighboring modes and the associated gradient features. Then, the search for the optimal mode is reduced to only these candidate modes, thus the computational cost for the intra mode decision is significantly reduced. To be more specific, we compute the gradient features and quantize them for each block as described in section 3.2. Then, the mode conditional probability distribution given these gradient features as well as the intra modes of the left and upper neighboring blocks is used to decide the most probable modes as the candidates in the refined search for the optimal intra modes from their RD cost values. In our implementation, we select four candidate modes in the refined search for the case of 4x4 blocks, and only two candidate modes are selected for 16x16 blocks and 8x8 blocks.

The flowchart of the proposed algorithm is depicted in Figure 8. We give the process flowcharts the training and encoding process.

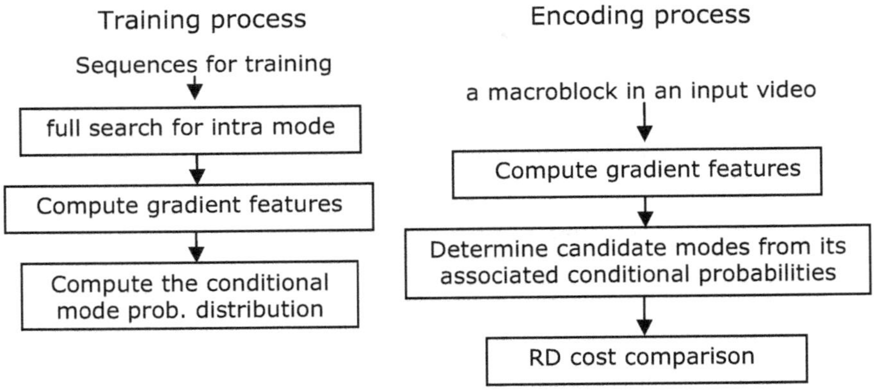

Fig. 8. The flowchart of the proposed algorithm

5 Experimental Results

We implement our algorithm in JM 10.2. The option for transform 8x8 is off, and the new intra 8x8 for luma component is also off. Based on the same experimental setting, we compare the efficiency and compression performance of the proposed intra mode decision algorithm with other methods [4-5].

Table 2-5 summarize the experimental results of these different intra mode decision methods for some benchmarking CIF and QCIF video sequences. The numbers in parentheses denotes the number of frames in the sequences. The sequence name with gray background means this sequence was included in our training dataset. In our experiments, we encode all video sequences in all I-frames. From the

Table 2. Experimental comparison on QCIF (176x144) sequences

Note. QP=28		Akiyo (300)	Carphone (96)	Claire (494)	Foreman (300)	Grandma (870)	Hall_monitor (300)
JM 10.2	PSNR	39.6648	38.7239	41.0825	37.8954	37.991	38.8264
	BITRATE(KB/s)	544.46	325.228	355.115	729.723	634.201	674.943
	TIME(ms)	138655	46959	210396	152354	414618	150699
Pan et al.[4]	PSNR↓	-0.0988	-0.0959	-0.141	-0.1006	-0.1569	-0.0983
	BITRATE↑	17.34%	14.40%	25.75%	10.58%	8.09%	11.86%
	TIME SAVING	52.46%	52.60%	53.87%	53.44%	54.48%	52.50%
Wang et al. [5]	PSNR↓	-0.0563	-0.0464	-0.1165	-0.1012	-0.0625	-0.0634
	BITRATE↑	8.79%	6.87%	9.86%	10.26%	4.74%	6.14%
	TIME SAVING	60.96%	59.96%	61.36%	59.88%	61.17%	59.59%
Proposed algorithm	PSNR↓	-0.029	-0.0464	-0.0728	-0.0613	-0.0667	-0.0691
	BITRATE↑	2.68%	2.38%	3.70%	2.08%	2.20%	1.97%
	TIME SAVING	64.50%	64.49%	64.37%	64.35%	64.67%	64.72%

Table 3. Experimental comparison on QCIF (176x144) sequences (cont.)

Note. QP=28		mother-daughter (300)	News (300)	Salesman (449)	Silent (300)	Suzie (150)
JM 10.2	PSNR	39.1073	38.5508	37.248	37.2562	39.4939
	BITRATE(KB/s)	467.291	791.906	843.803	791.274	442.549
	TIME(ms)	136670	157224	241274	157249	67846
Pan et al.[4]	PSNR↓	-0.1432	-0.0569	-0.1467	-0.1383	-0.145
	BITRATE↑	14.33%	12.85%	10.90%	10.89%	10.55%
	TIME SAVING	54.08%	53.99%	54.46%	55.71%	54.68%
Wang et al. [5]	PSNR↓	-0.0667	-0.0158	-0.0625	-0.052	-0.0506
	BITRATE↑	7.87%	6.37%	4.51%	5.94%	5.80%
	TIME SAVING	61.11%	61.90%	61.00%	60.27%	59.79%
Proposed algorithm	PSNR↓	-0.0609	-0.0651	-0.0883	-0.0621	-0.0596
	BITRATE↑	3.55%	2.49%	2.07%	2.46%	3.15%
	TIME SAVING	64.39%	65.41%	65.35%	65.17%	65.09%

Table 4. Experimental comparison on CIF (352x288) sequences

Note. QP=28		Coastguard (300)	Container (300)	Foreman (300)	Highway (2000)	Stefan (90)	Tempete (260)
JM 10.2	PSNR	37.2135	38.1535	38.393	39.1406	37.4565	36.9332
	BITRATE(KB/s)	3155.139	2466.599	2310.821	1062.933	4287.33	4447.909
	TIME(ms)	703916	639519	613121	3621431	218673	645080
Pan et al.[4]	PSNR↓	-0.1649	-0.1138	-0.1022	-0.0558	-0.1399	-0.1656
	BITRATE↑	10.76%	11.13%	10.58%	16.83%	10.13%	8.72%
	TIME SAVING	56.96%	56.99%	54.54%	52.14%	56.53%	56.34%
Wang et al. [5]	PSNR↓	-0.0749	-0.0639	-0.0811	-0.0288	-0.1012	-0.0827
	BITRATE↑	4.68%	5.37%	8.56%	10.75%	4.85%	4.15%
	TIME SAVING	64.36%	64.44%	62.11%	63.08%	63.44%	63.54%
Proposed algorithm	PSNR↓	-0.0541	-0.0516	-0.0559	-0.0118	-0.1053	-0.1045
	BITRATE↑	0.85%	1.26%	1.87%	2.25%	1.85%	1.42%
	TIME SAVING	67.55%	67.05%	66.23%	66.51%	66.55%	66.96%

Table 5. Experimental comparison on SIF (352x240) sequences

		Football (125)	Garden (115)	Mobile (140)	Tennis (112)
JM 10.2	PSNR	35.6657	35.6175	35.2449	36.2946
	BITRATE(KB/s)	4395.85	6826.50	7547.33	3251.02
	TIME(ms)	280307	301705	373034	222486
Pan et al.[4]	PSNR↓	-0.1476	-0.2412	-0.1916	-0.0838
	BITRATE↑	4.90%	2.38%	4.80%	4.72%
	TIME SAVING	57.97%	59.87%	58.81%	55.65%
Wang et al. [5]	PSNR↓	-0.0829	-0.13	-0.1185	-0.0554
	BITRATE↑	2.77%	1.74%	2.49%	2.19%
	TIME SAVING	63.60%	63.98%	64.21%	63.21%
Proposed algorithm	PSNR↓	-0.0814	-0.1505	-0.1271	-0.0601
	BITRATE↑	1.25%	0.69%	1.24%	0.38%
	TIME SAVING	67.55%	67.43%	66.80%	66.68%

experimental results, it is obvious that the proposed algorithm can achieve slightly higher bitrate with significant computational reduction. Our algorithm provides much better bitrate reduction compared to the previous methods. Note that all of the experimental results are obtained by using scheme (a) in the gradient feature extraction. We show the performance of both scheme (a) and (b) in our algorithm from the RD curves for four different sequences in Figure 9.

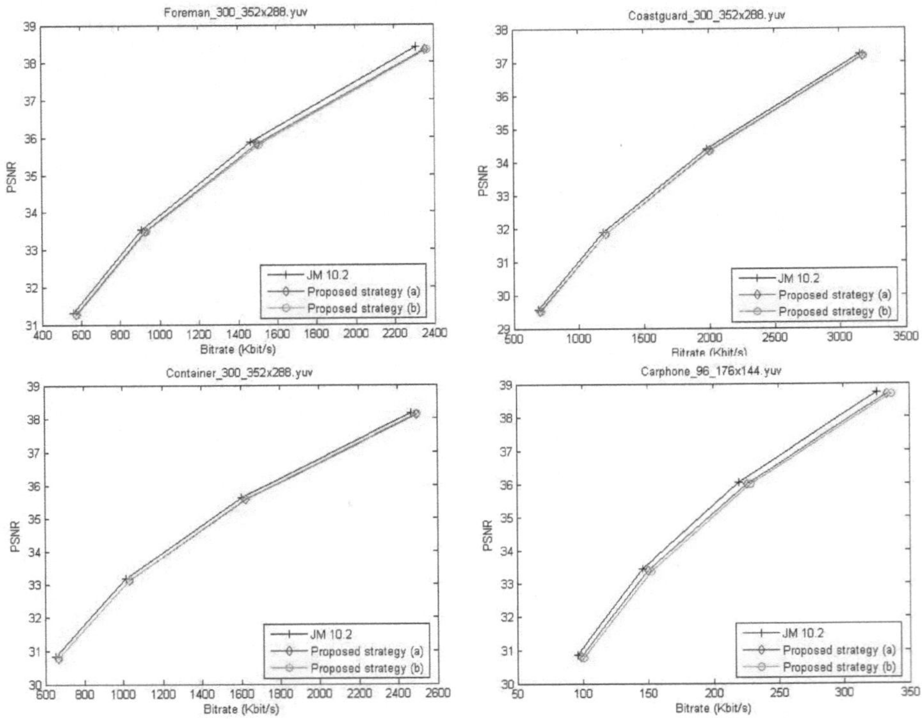

Fig. 9. RD-Curve comparison of the two schemes in the proposed algorithm with the JM reference program on four different video sequences. These RD curves are obtained with QP set to 28, 32, 36, and 40.

6 Conclusion

In this paper, we proposed a learning based algorithm for efficient intra mode decision. The conditional probability distribution of the optimal mode given the neighboring encoded modes and the image gradient features is learned from a collection of video sequences encoded with H.264. In the proposed fast mode decision algorithm, a small number of candidate modes are selected based on the associated mode conditional probability distribution to reduce the search for the optimal RD cost. Our experimental results show the proposed algorithm significantly reduces the computational cost with negligible bitrate increase. Compared with other previous methods, the proposed algorithm consistently outperforms the other methods on different video sequences.

Acknowledgements

This research work was supported in part by MOEA project under grant 95-EC-17-A-01-S1-034 and National Science Council, Taiwan, under grant 95-2220-E-007-028.

References

1. ITU-T Rec. H.264/SO/IEC 11496-10, Advanced video coding, Final Committee Draft, Document IVT F100 (December 2002)
2. Cheng, C.-C., Chang, T.-S.: Fast three step intra prediction algorithm for 4x4 blocks in H.264. In: Proc. IEEE Intern. Symp. Circuits and Systems, vol. 2, pp. 1509–1512 (2005)
3. Zhang, Y.-D., Feng, D., Lin, S.-X: Fast 4x4 intra-prediction mode selection for H.264. In: Proc. IEEE International Conf. Multimedia and Expo., vol. 2, pp. 1151–1154 (2004)
4. Pan, F., Lin, X., Rahardja, S., Lim, K.P., Li, Z.G., Wu, D., Wu, S.: Fast mode decision algorithm for intra prediction in H.264/AVC video coding. IEEE Trans. Circuits Systems for Video Technology 15(7), 813–822 (2005)
5. Wang, J.-F., Wang, J.-C., Chen, J.-T., Tsai, A.-C., Paul, A.: A novel fast algorithm for intra mode decision in H.264/AVC encoders. In: Proc. IEEE International Symp. Circuits and Systems (May 2006)
6. Sim, D.-G., Kim, Y.: Context-adaptive mode selection for intra-block coding in H.264/MPEG-4 Part 10. Real-Time Imaging 11, 1–6 (2005)
7. Huang, Y.-W., Hsieh, B.-Y., Chen, T.-C., Chen, L.-G.: Analysis, fast algorithm, and VLSI architecture design for H.264/AVC intra frame coder. IEEE Trans. Circuits and Systems for Video Technology 15(3), 378–401 (2005)
8. JVT Reference Software JM10.2, http://iphome.hhi.de/suehring/tml/download/old_jm/jm10.2.zip

Fast Mode Decision Algorithms for Inter/Intra Prediction in H.264 Video Coding

Ling-Jiao Pan, Seung-Hwan Kim, and Yo-Sung Ho

Gwangju Institute of Science and Technology (GIST)
1 Oryong-dong Buk-gu, Gwangju, 500-712, Korea
{hedypan, kshkim, hoyo}@gist.ac.kr

Abstract. In this paper, we propose fast mode decision algorithms for both intra prediction and inter prediction in H.264. In order to select the candidate modes for intra4x4 and intra16x16 prediction efficiently, we have used the spatial correlation and directional information. We have also applied an early block size selection method to reduce the searching time further. The fast inter mode decision is achieved by an early SKIP mode decision method, and a fast mode decision method for 16x16 and P8x8 modes. Extensive simulations on different test sequences demonstrate a considerable speed up by saving the encoding time up to 82% for intra prediction and 77% for inter prediction on average, compared to the H.264 standard, respectively. This is achieved at the cost of negligible loss in PSNR values and small increase in bit rates.

Keywords: H.264/AVC, video coding, fast mode decision.

1 Introduction

H.264 is the latest international video coding standard. Compared to previous video coding standards, it can achieve considerably higher coding efficiency. This is accomplished by a number of advanced features incorporated in H.264 [1]. One of the new features is multi-mode selection for intra-frames and inter-frames. In H.264, intra-frame mode selection dramatically reduces spatial redundancy in I-frames, while inter-frame mode selection significantly affects the output quality of P-/B-frames by selecting an optimal block size with motion vectors or a mode for each macroblock (MB). In H.264, the coding block size is not fixed. It supports variable block sizes to minimize the overall error.

H.264 provides a rate distortion optimization (RDO) technique to select the best coding mode among all the possible modes [2]. With this technique, we can maximize image quality and minimize coding bits by checking all the mode combinations for each MB exhaustively. However, the RDO technique increases the coding complexity drastically, which makes H.264 not suitable for real-time applications. Thus, fast mode decision methods are needed to reduce the encoding time.

Recently various efforts have been made to reduce coding complexity of H.264. Pan *et al.* [3] proposed a fast intra mode decision algorithm based on the edge direction information. However, they needed additional operations in calculating the

H.H.S. Ip et al. (Eds.): PCM 2007, LNCS 4810, pp. 158–167, 2007.

edge direction information. In other approach based on the idea of reducing possible candidate directions [4], RD costs of 6 to 7 out of 9 modes need to be computed in Intra4x4 prediction. This approach cannot select the best candidate mode efficiently because it examines unnecessary modes all the time. Recently, various fast inter mode decision algorithms have been proposed. Jeon *et al.* [5] proposed four conditions for the early SKIP mode decision. Another approach [6] not only considered the early SKIP mode, but also developed the early 16x16 mode decision using motion vectors of 16x16 and SKIP modes, reference frame, and the sub-optimal best mode. Although these methods provide fast and accurate mode decision for the SKIP mode and 16x16 mode, they still need to calculate J_{mode} (16x16) for the early SKIP mode decision. Furthermore, they do not include any fast mode decision algorithm for the P8x8 mode which consumes a large part of the encoding time.

In our work, we propose fast mode decision algorithms for both intra prediction and inter prediction. This paper is organized as follows. Section 2 describes the mode decision in H.264. Section 3 and Section4 describe fast mode decision algorithms for intra and inter prediction, respectively. Section 5 shows the simulation results, and we draw conclusions in Section 6.

2 Mode Decision in H.264

H.264 uses three different types of intra prediction for the luminance component Y. They are Intra4x4 (I4_MB), Intra8x8 (I8_MB, only for High profile) and Intra16x16 (I16_MB). In I4_MB, the prediction unit is a block of 4x4 pixels. The samples above and to the left (labeled A-M in Fig. 1(a)) have been coded and reconstructed previously and are therefore available both at the encoder and decoder to form a prediction reference. The pixels in the prediction unit are calculated based on the samples A-M by using one of the nine prediction modes. Fig. 1(b) shows the eight specific prediction directions for each mode. Mode 2 (DC mode) is not a directional mode, and all pixels are predicted by the mean of samples A-M. In I16_MB, only four prediction modes are applied to the whole macroblock. They are vertical prediction, horizontal prediction, DC prediction and plane prediction. The prediction method is similar to the I4_MB case. The only difference is that they are applied to the whole macroblock, instead of the 4x4 unit. The four chroma prediction modes are very similar to those of the I16_MB prediction, except that the order of modes is different.

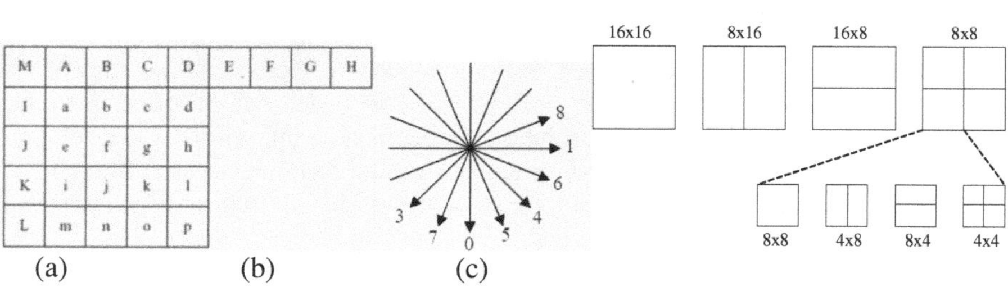

Fig. 1. (a) 4x4 intra block and neighboring pixels (b) Eight prediction directions for intra 4x4 prediction (c) Inter macroblock partitions and P8x8 sub-partitions

H.264 also supports inter prediction to reduce the temporal redundancy. H.264 uses seven different block sizes (16x16, 16x8, 8x16, 8x8, 8x4, 4x8, and 4x4) for interframe motion estimation/compensation. These different block size actually form a two-level hierarchy tree structure inside each MB. The first level includes the block size of 16x16, 16x8, and 8x16. In the second level, specified as the P8x8 type, each 8x8 block can be sub-divided into a smaller block size, such as 8x8, 8x4, 4x8 or 4x4. The relationship between these different block sizes is shown in Fig. 1(c). There is also a SKIP mode in P slice referring to the block size of 16x16, where no motion and residual information is encoded. In general, a homogeneous region of similar motions is more likely to be coded using a large block size, such as the SKIP or 16x16 mode. The area containing the boundaries of a moving object is more likely to be coded using a smaller block size. In order to decide the best motion vector (MV), the reference frame and the mode, H.264 uses the RDO method based on the Lagrangian function [2] to minimize the motion cost J_{motion} and the mode cost J_{mode}.

3 Fast Intra Mode Decision Algorithm

3.1 Intra Mode Decision for 8x8 Chroma Blocks

Since the choice of the prediction modes for chroma components is independent to the luma component, we can optimize chroma and luma components separately. Because the transformed coefficients are ultimately coded, we can achieve a better estimation of the mode cost using the Hadamard transform, instead of the DCT transform. SATD (the sum of absolute Hadamard transform differences) in H.264 is defined by:

$$SATD = \sum_{i}^{N} \sum_{j}^{N} \left| c_{ij} \right| \tag{1}$$

where c_{ij} denotes the (i, j)th element of C, which is the Hadamard transform of the residual block. The performance of SATD is close to the Lagrangian function, while the computational load is much lower [7]. In our work, we determine the best chroma mode by choosing the mode of the minimum SATD. Then, the following mode decision processes are performed with the best chroma mode.

3.2 Early Block Type Selection

We have observed that the block size depends mainly on the smoothness of a region. A large block size is likely to be used in homogeneous regions, while a small block size works well for complex texture regions. The main idea behind our approach is that the smooth filter does not affect the homogeneous area but will blur the details in the complex region. In our approach, we apply 1x5 and 5x1 mean-value filters to the top and left boundary of each macroblock separately. The filtered pixel value can be obtained by

$$p_{ij} = \frac{1}{5} \sum_{k=j-2}^{j+2} p_{ik} \qquad p_{ij} = \frac{1}{5} \sum_{k=i-2}^{i+2} p_{kj} \tag{2}$$

Then we calculate the sum of absolute differences between the original pixel value and the filtered pixel value (SADOF). Two thresholding operations, with the bottom threshold Th1 and up threshold Th2 are applied. If SADOF<Th1, the 16x16 intra prediction is further explored. If SADOF>Th2, the 4x4 intra prediction is adopted for the following mode decision. If SADOF is located between the two thresholds, both block sizes need to be checked. Since a large block size is preferred for higher QP, the threshold value should vary according to QP to reflect the quantization effect. Linear equations of QP in Eq. (3) and Eq. (4) are found to give a good performance, and a1, b1, a2, b2 are decided by extensive experiments.

$$Th1=a1*QP+b1 \tag{3}$$

$$Th2=a2*QP+b2 \tag{4}$$

3.3 Intra Mode Decision for 4x4 and 16x16 Luma Blocks

We have also observed that the pixels along the direction of the local edge normally have a similar value. This provides a clue for obtaining the directional information from the pixel values along the edge direction. Therefore, we can predict the best candidate mode roughly by checking NSAD (the normalized sum of absolute differences) for some selected pixel positions in the original block. Table 1 shows equations for calculating NSAD. In those equations, the pixel positions of "a" to "p" can refer to Fig.1 (a).

Table 1. NSAD for each intra prediction direction

Mode	Direction	NSAD
0	vertical	(|a-m|+|b-n|+|c-o|+|d-p|)/4
1	horizontal	(|a-d|+|e-h|+|i-l|+|m-p|)/4
3	diagonal down-left	(|b-e|+|d-m|+|l-o|)/3
4	diagonal down-right	(|a-p|+|i-n|+|c-h|)/3
5	vertical- right	(|a-j|+|b-k|+|c-l|)/3
6	horizontal- down	(|a-g|+|e-k|+|i-o|)/3
7	vertical-left	(|b-i|+|c-j|+|d-k|)/3
8	horizontal-up	(|e-c|+|i-g|+|m-k|)/3

Since Mode2 (DC mode) has no direction and are predicted by the mean of sample A-M, we apply Eq. (5) to deal with DC mode.

$$DDC = \sum_{i=0}^{3}\sum_{j=0}^{3}\left|p(x+i, y+j) - mean\right| \tag{5}$$

In Eq.(5), *mean* is the mean value of the samples A-M. If *DDC* (difference of the DC mode) is less than a threshold, the DC mode is selected as the best candidate mode for the current block and the mode with the smallest NSAD among the other eight modes is chosen as the second best mode. Otherwise, the mode with the smallest NSAD and the second smallest NSAD are selected as the best candidate mode and the second best candidate mode, respectively. Here we denote the best candidate mode by Mode C, and the second best candidate mode by Mode S.

Using NSAD and DDC, we can roughly predict the best mode. Further consideration of the spatial correlation information helps to evaluate the reliability of the best candidate. Observations show the best mode of the current block is highly correlated to its neighboring blocks. The most probable mode can be obtained from the left and above blocks. Fig. 2(a) shows the neighboring modes of the current block.

Through extensive experiments on various video sequences with different textures, we find the average probability of the current mode =L or the current mode=U is 80.86%. Under the condition of U=L, the probability of the current mode=U=L is up to 87.5%, which means that when U=L, the current mode has a very high probability to choose the same mode as U and L. Therefore, Mode U and L can be used to check the reliability of pre-predicted best candidate mode C. According to the reliability test we decide the number of candidate modes using Table 2.

Table 2. Candidate mode decision table

Condition	Reliability of mode C	Candidate modes
U=L=C	reliable	C
C=U&&C! =L	unreliable	C, S, L
C=L&&C! =U	unreliable	C, S, U
L=U&&C! =L	unreliable	C, S, L
C=!U&&C!=L&& L!=U	totally unreliable	C, S, L, U
U not available&& C=L	unreliable	C, S
U not available&& C! =L	totally unreliable	C, S, L
L not available&& C=U	unreliable	C, S
L not available&& C!=U	totally unreliable	C, S,U

The same idea is applied to the Intra16x16 luma block, except the different block size and the plane mode prediction. The plane prediction estimates a bilinear function from the neighboring pixels to the 16x16 block. It is not mathematically correct to associate the plane prediction to any directional edge. According to the plane prediction method used in the reference software [8], we use Eq. (6) to calculate the NSAD for plane prediction. In Eq. (6), Org (A_{diff}) and Org (B_{diff}) indicate the SAD of the original pixel values whose positions are pointed out by arrow A and arrow B (Fig. 2(b)), respectively. Est (A_{diff}) and Est (B_{diff}) indicate the SAD of estimated pixel values whose positions are pointed out by arrow A and arrow B (Fig. 2(b)), respectively.

$$NSAD= (A+B)/2$$
$$A= (Org\ (A_{diff}) - Est\ (A_{diff}))/7 \qquad B= (Org\ (B_{diff}) - Est\ (B_{diff}))/7 \tag{6}$$

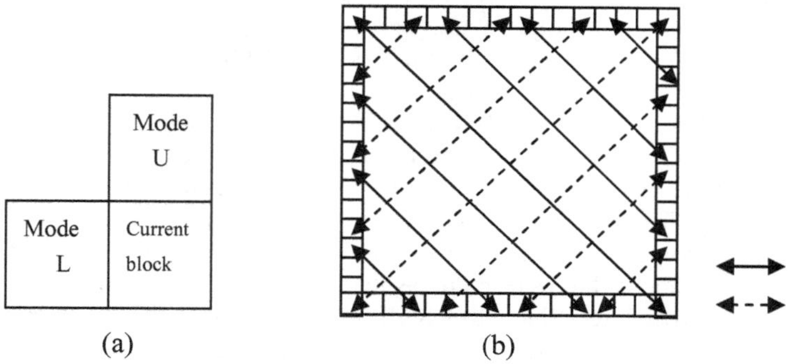

Fig. 2. (a) Neighboring blocks of the current block (b) NSAD for plane mode

3.4 Procedure of the Proposed Algorithm

Fig. 3 shows the overall structure of the proposed fast intra mode decision algorithm.

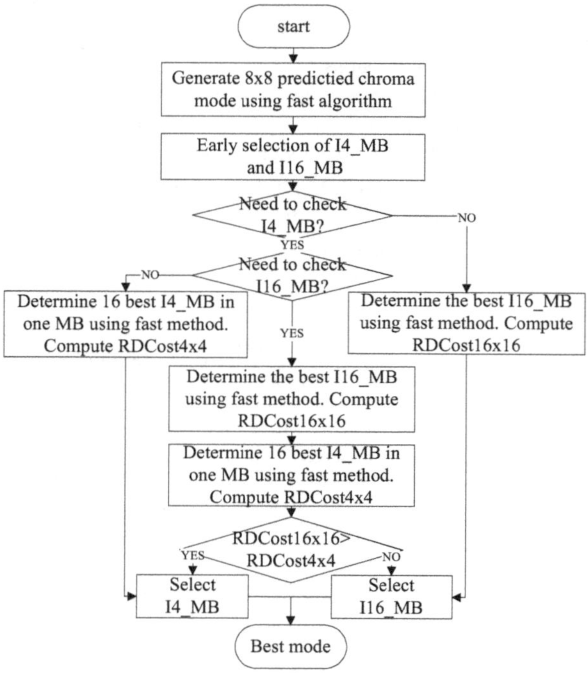

Fig. 3. Flowchart for the fast intra mode decision algorithm

4 Fast Inter Mode Decision Algorithm

In natural video sequences, we have lots of homogenous regions and when objects move, most parts of the object move in the similar direction. As we mentioned before, these areas are suitable for larger size inter mode coding. If we can detect these areas in the early stage, a significant time could be saved for the motion estimation and RDO computations of small size modes.

In our algorithm, we differentiate the SKIP mode from other block types and give it the highest priority. As mentioned before, SATD is close to the Lagrangian function while the computational load is much lower. Firstly, we calculate the SATD cost for the SKIP mode. The only information we need is the motion vector of the SKIP mode. Then, we compare the SKIP cost to the threshold value Th. If the SKIP cost is less than Th, we choose the SKIP mode as the best mode and terminate the following mode decision procedure. Since the SKIP mode is preferred for larger QP, the threshold value should vary with QP to reflect the quantization effect.

$$Th=a*QP+b \tag{7}$$

We also borrow the early 16x16 mode decision scheme from Ref. [6]. After performing motion estimation of the 16x16 block, calculating J_{mode} (16x16) and finding the SKIP motion vector (MV), we determine the best mode as the 16x16 mode when the following conditions are satisfied: (1) J_{motion} (16x16) is the smallest among J_{motion} (16x16), J_{motion} (16x8) and J_{motion} (8x16). (2) CBP (16x16) is zero. (3) SKIP MV is the same as 16x16 MV. Even though MB is not determined as the 16x16 mode, if both Condition (1) and Condition (2) are satisfied, we exclude the P8x8 mode for the best mode decision process.

Since the P8x8 mode is the most complex mode among all the modes and the frequency of the P8x8 mode increases at small QPs, it is necessary to consider fast decision for the P8x8 mode. We observe that the best prediction mode of a block is most likely to have the minimum SATD value. We simply select the P8x8 mode with the smallest SATD and inactivate the other P8x8 modes. Fig. 4 shows the flowchart of the fast inter mode decision algorithm.

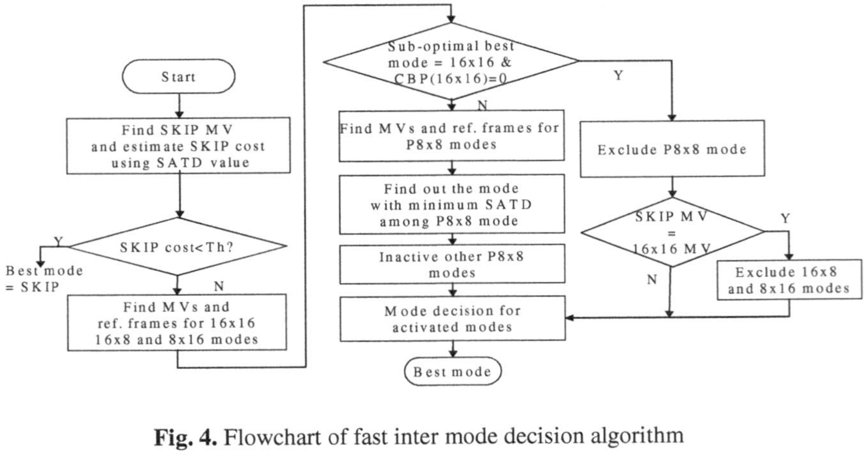

Fig. 4. Flowchart of fast inter mode decision algorithm

5 Simulation Results

The proposed algorithms are implemented on JM 11.0. We have tested several CIF (352x288) video sequences: Foreman, Bus, Coastguard, Mobile, City, Crew, Akiyo and Soccer. For each sequence, 100 frames are encoded. The frame rate is 30fps. Other simulation conditions [9] for fast intra mode decision algorithm and fast inter mode decision algorithm are shown in Table 3 and Table 4, respectively. For performance comparison, we have used the Bjonteggard delta PSNR values and Bjonteggard delta bit rates [10].

Table 3. Encoding parameters for fast intra mode decision algorithm

GOP Structure	IIII…	CABAC	Enable
Hadamard Transform	Used	QP	28, 32, 36, 40

Table 4. Encoding parameters for fast inter mode decision algorithm

GOP Structure	IPPP…	Reference Frames	5
Hadamard Transform	Used	QP	28, 32, 36, 40
Search Range	±16	FME Algorithms	UMHexagonS, CBFPS

Table 5 and Table 6 show the performance comparison of the fast mode decision algorithm for intra and inter prediction, respectively. They are relative to results by the H.264 standard. From Table 5 and Table 6, we observe that the proposed methods provide significant timesaving at the cost of negligible loss in PSNR values and a small increment in bit rates.

Fig. 5 and Fig. 6 display rate-distortion curves of "Foreman" and "Coastguard" sequences for the fast intra mode decision method and fast inter mode decision method separately. From Fig. 5 and Fig. 6, we note that the proposed methods provide a similar RD performance to the H.264 standard.

Table 5. Performance comparison for fast intra mode decision algorithm

Sequence	△PSNR_Y (dB)	△PSNR_UV (dB)	△Bits (%)	△Time (%)
Foreman	-0.03	0.18	3.645	-81.79
Bus	-0.08	0.15	2.93	-82.46
Coastguard	-0.05	0.30	2.055	-81.71
Mobile	-0.14	0.01	2.885	-83.31
City	-0.04	0.26	3.612	-80.91
Crew	-0.02	0.10	3.417	-81.57
Average	-0.06	0.17	3.091	-81.96

Table 6. Performance comparison for fast inter mode decision algorithm

Sequence	△PSNR_Y (dB)	△Bits(%)	△Time(%)
Foreman	-0.17	1.255	-80.95
Akiyo	-0.12	0.01	-91.86
Mobile	-0.12	0.397	-70.88
City	-0.08	0.456	-78.55
Crew	-0.12	0.838	-74.68
Bus	-0.11	1.256	-71.43
Soccer	-0.09	1.771	-78.40
Coastguard	-0.08	-0.68	-71.11
Average	-0.11	0.663	-77.23

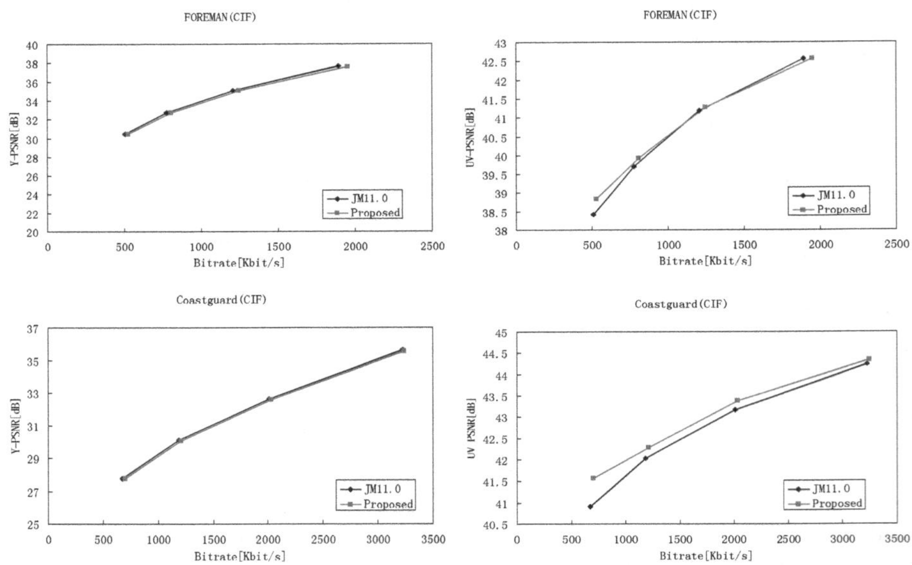

Fig. 5. RD performance of "Foreman" and "Coastguard" for intra mode decision

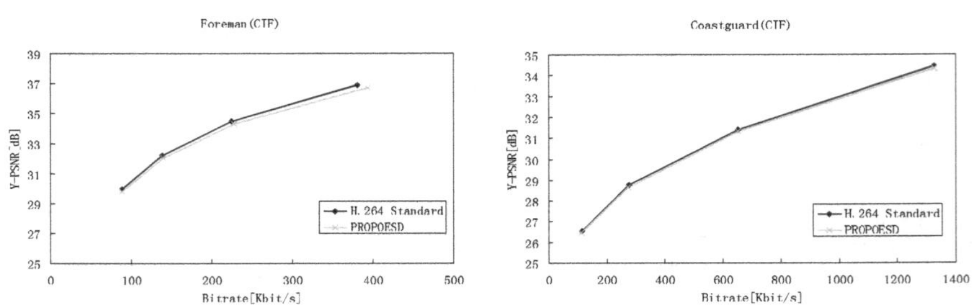

Fig. 6. RD performance of "Foreman" and "Coastguard" for inter mode decision

6 Conclusion

In this paper, we have proposed fast mode decision algorithms for both intra–frame and inter-frame to reduce the encoding complexity of the H.264 coding scheme. In the fast intra mode decision algorithm, we use the spatial correlation information and the directional information to reduce the candidate modes. We also apply an early block size selection method to reduce the computation complexity further. For the fast inter mode decision, an early SKIP mode decision method is applied in the first stage of mode decision by using SATD values. No additional information is required for the early selection. The early 16x16 mode decision and fast P8x8 mode decision methods are also developed to achieve further speedup. Results of extensive computer simulations demonstrate that the proposed algorithms can achieve time saving up to 82% and 77% in intra-coding and inter-coding, respectively, compared to the H.264 standard reference software. These considerable encoding time reductions are achieved at the cost of negligible loss in PSNR values and a small increase in bit rates.

Acknowledgments. This work was supported in part by the Institute for Information Technology Advancement (IITA), in part by the Ministry of Information and Communication (MIC) through the Realistic Broadcasting Research Center (RBRC) at Gwangju Institute of Science and Technology (GIST), and in part by the Ministry of Education (MOE) through the Brain Korea 21(BK21) project.

References

1. Wiegand, T., Sullivan, G.J., Bjontegaard, G., Luthra, A.: Overview of the H.264/AVC video coding standard. IEEE Trans. Circuits and Systems for Video Technology 13(7), 560–576 (2003)
2. Sullivan, G.J., Wiegand, T.: Rate-distortion optimization for video compression. IEEE Signal Processing Magazine 15, 74–90 (2003)
3. Pan, F., Lin, X., Rahardja, S., Lim, K.P., Li, Z.G., Wu, D., Wu, S.: Fast mode decision algorithm for intraprediction in H.264/AVC video coding. IEEE Trans. Circuits and Systems for Video Technology 15(7), 813–822 (2005)
4. Ri, S.H., Ostermann, J.: Intra-Prediction Mode Decision for H.264 in Two Steps. In: Picture Coding Symposium 2006 (April 2006)
5. Choi, I.C., Choi, W.I., Lee, J.Y., Jeon, B.W.: The Fast Mode Decision with Fast Motion Estimation. JVT Doc. JVT-N013
6. Kim, G.Y., Yoon, B.Y., Ho, Y.S.: A Fast Inter Mode Decision Algorithm in H.264/AVC for IPTV Broadcasting Services. In: Proc. SPIE, vol. 6508 (2007)
7. Lim, K.P., Sullivan, G.J., Wiegand, T.: Text description of joint model reference encoding methods and decoding concealment methods. JVT-N046, JVT of ISO/IEC MPEG and ITU-T VCEG (January 2005)
8. JVT Reference Software version JM11.0, http://iphome.hhi.de/suehring/tml/download/
9. Sullivan, G.J., Bjontegaard, G.: Recommended Simulation Common Conditions for H.26L Coding Efficiency Experiments on Low-Resolution Progressive scan Source Material. ITU-T Q.6/16, Doc. VCEG-N81 (2001)
10. Bjontegaard, G.: Calculation of Average PSNR Difference between RD-Curve. ITU-T Q.6/16, Doc. VCEG-M33 (2001)

A Novel Fast Motion Estimation Algorithm Based on SSIM for H.264 Video Coding

Chun-ling Yang[1], Hua-xing Wang[1], and Lai-Man Po[2]

[1] School of Electronic and Information Engineering, South China University of Technology, Guangzhou, Guangdong, 510641, China
[2] Department of Electronic Engineering, City University of Hong Kong, 83 Tat Chee Avenue, Kowloon Tong, Hong Kong, China
eeclyang@scut.edu.cn, washing2002@163.com, eelmpo@cityu.edu.hk

Abstract. H.264 achieves considerable higher coding efficiency compared with previous video coding standards, whereas the complexity is increased significantly. This paper proposed a novel fast algorithm based on structural similarity (SSIM) in motion estimation (ME) process (FMEBSS), which can greatly reduced the complexity of ME by eliminating the unnecessary search positions and reducing complex prediction modes. Simulation results demonstrate that the proposed method can averagely reduce the coding time by about 50%, and compression ratio is improved at the same time, while the degradation in video quality is negligible.

Keywords: Motion Estimation, H.264, Structural Similarity (SSIM).

1 Introduction

The complexity of H.264 is too high for real-time applications, and variable block size ME contributes most to the complexity of the encoder, it accounts for 60% (one reference frame) to 80 % (five reference frames) of the total encoding time of the encoder [1]. Thus, many fast algorithms have been proposed to reduce the complexity [1], [2], [3], [4], [5], [6]. [1] proposed an efficient prediction and early termination strategy based on the statistical characters of MV and SAD, which can decrease the computation complexity effectively. [2] proposed an early termination algorithm VBBMD, in which seven thresholds are defined respectively to the corresponding block-size. The thresholds are obtained by testing on a typical sequence and have to be adjusted according to the QP. In [3] a method was provided to reduce the complexity of ME by skipping the unnecessary SAD computations with adaptive threshold, the results seem promising. [4] also proposed a fast algorithm, it reduces the calculation by using partially computation to decide termination. [5] proposed to determine the early termination threshold adaptively according to the correlation between adjacent blocks, which is obtained from the block level motion intensity. The bound of the threshold is within a certain range, which is related to the block size. [6] takes advantage of the correlation between MVs in both spatial and temporal domains, controls to curb the

H.H.S. Ip et al. (Eds.): PCM 2007, LNCS 4810, pp. 168–176, 2007.

search, avoids of searching stationary regions, and uses variable shape search patterns to accelerate motion search. We can see that most fast algorithms are either based on skipping unnecessary calculations or shrinking searching region by a certain method in the ME process. Moreover, the early termination algorithm tries to reduce the complexity by setting thresholds in ME process to skip unnecessary computations and most thresholds are obtained by statistics.

The novel algorithm proposed in this paper is based on SSIM [7], [8], which is a newly developed approach to assess image quality. We also utilize SSIM as the distortion metric in the ME and mode decision process, and a fixed threshold relative to SSIM is used to early terminate the ME process. The rate distortion (RD) functions used in these processes are modified accordingly, and SSIM is also used to assess the whole encoding video quality.

The rest of this paper is organized as follows. Section 2 gives a brief introduction of SSIM and motion estimation process in H.264. The detail descriptions of the FMEBSS algorithm are specified in section 3. Simulation results and analysis are shown in section 4; Section 5 is the conclusion remarks.

2 SSIM and Mode Estimation Process in H.264

2.1 Structure Similarity (SSIM)

SSIM exhibits much more consistency with subjective measures compared with other image assessment methods. It is defined as follows:

$$SSIM = l(x,y)\cdot c(x,y)\cdot s(x,y) \tag{1}$$

Where $l(x,y)$ is luma comparison, $c(x,y)$ is contrast comparison and $s(x,y)$ is structure comparison, which are defined as follows:

$$l(x,y)=\frac{2\mu_x\mu_y+C_1}{\mu_x^2+\mu_y^2+C_1} \tag{2}$$

$$c(x,y)=\frac{2\delta_x\delta_y+C_2}{\delta_x^2+\delta_y^2+C_2} \tag{3}$$

$$s(x,y)=\frac{\delta_{xy}+C_3}{\delta_x\delta_y+C_3} \tag{4}$$

x, y are two nonnegative image signals. μ_x and μ_y are the mean of image x and y respectively, δ_x and δ_y are the corresponding standard deviation of image x and y, δ_{xy} is the covariance of image x and y. C_1, C_2 and C_3 are small constants to avoid the denominator being zero, and taken the same values as in [7]. SSIM is a decimal fraction between 0 and 1. And the larger of this value, the more similar of the corresponding blocks.

2.2 Motion Estimation in H.264

H.264 achieves higher coding efficiency by employing multiple inter-prediction modes and multiple reference frames. The inter mode decision process has two steps, the first step is to choose the best matching block of the current encoding MB for each inter prediction mode. Seven prediction modes are used in H.264 inter coding, including INTER16×16, INTER16×8, INTER8×16 and INTER8×8. If INTER 8×8 is selected as the best mode among these modes, it needs to further check the INTER8×4, INTER4×8 or INTER4×4 sub-modes too. The best matching block is selected through the RD function below:

$$MCOST(s,c) = SA(T)D(s,c) + \lambda_{MOTION} Bit(\Delta MV) \quad (5)$$

In the above formula, SA (T) D(s, c) is the sum of absolute differences between original block *s* and candidate matching block *c*. SAD is applied to integer pixel motion search, while SATD is for sub-pixel [9]. λ_{MOTION} is the Lagrange multiplier for motion estimation. ΔMV is the difference between the predicted motion vector (MV) and the actual MV. Bit (ΔMV) is the number of bits representing the ΔMV. The block(s) with the minimum MCOST will be selected as the best matching block(s) for the corresponding prediction mode.

The second step is to select the best mode among the candidate modes by the RD function below:

$$J(s,c,MODE \mid QP) = D(s,c,MODE \mid QP) + \lambda_{MODE} R(s,c,MODE \mid QP) \quad (6)$$

Where MODE is the prediction mode, *QP* is the quantization parameter. *D(s,c,MODE|QP)* is the sum of square differences (SSD) between original block *s* and reconstructed block *c*. *R(s,c,MODE|QP)* is the bit number used to encode the residue. The mode with the minimum RD cost will be chose as the best prediction mode for the coding MB.

3 FMEBSS

ME is the most time consuming process and sub-modes prediction (INTER8×8, INTER8×4, INTER4×8 or INTER4×4) increases the complexity even more. So we try to reduce the calculation by avoiding unnecessary searching positions and sub-modes prediction.

SSIM is a new image quality assessment method. The candidate block having larger SSIM implicates that it is more similar to the original one, and the residual block will be a lower frequency signal, which can be highly compressed. More over, the value of the SSIM just shows the similarity of the corresponding blocks, which is less correlated to the block size compared with SAD, this makes SSIM even more suitable to be used in early termination algorithm. So we propose a fast motion estimation based on SSIM (FMEBSS), which employs SSIM as the distortion metric in motion estimation process, and select a fixed value as the early termination threshold T for all the modes and QP.

Since we have changed the distortion metric, the related RD cost function has to be adjusted accordingly. The cost function of ME based on SSIM for each inter prediction mode is modified as:

$$MCOST(s,c) = K_1(1 - SSIM(s,c)) + \lambda_{MOTION} Bit(\Delta MV) \tag{7}$$

And the RDcost function based on SSIM for mode(s) decision is defined as:

$$J(s,c,MODE \mid QP) = K_2(1 - SSIM(s,c)) + \lambda_{MODE} R(s,c,MODE \mid QP) \tag{8}$$

λ_{motion} and λ_{mode} are the same as in formula (5) and (6). K_1 and K_2 are multipliers (shown in Table 1) to enlarge *(1-SSIM)*, which are obtained by intensive experiments. The new Lagrange multipliers in the above two formulas correspond to λ_{motion}/K_1 and λ_{mode}/K_2. *block_x* and *block_y* in Table 1 are the size of the current encoding block. We can see K_1 is an adaptive parameter and is correlated to the block size.

Table 1. Parameters used in RD functions

K \ *QP*	10	20	30
K_1	*block_x×block_y/4*	*block_x× block_y×3*	*block_x×block_y×4*
K_2	*85,000*	*260,000*	*490,000*

There are two new techniques in our proposed fast algorithm. The first one is early termination technique based on SSIM. If the SSIM between the searching block and the current encoding block is larger than the defined threshold T in the spiral full searching process, skip the other searching positions and choose the current searching block as the best matching block, because further searching contributes little to the quality improvements.

The other technique is trying to avoid unnecessary sub-modes prediction by using adaptive parameter K_1 in the motion estimation RD function. The parameter K_1 (shown in Table 1) is changing according to the block size. In this way, it increases the accuracy of the ME for larger blocks, so larger block is more inclined to be selected as best mode, and the unnecessary INTER8×8 and its sub-modes can be avoided rationally. This technique is more effective for the MBs with little motion or no motion at all. Only the macro blocks with dense and complex motion are likely to be further partitioned.

The major steps of the proposed FMEBSS are summarized as follows:

- **Step1: Select best matching block for each prediction mode in the searching region.**

  Step1.1. Initialize the minimum MV cost with a large value. The prediction motion vector position is selected as the first searching position.

Step1.2. Calculate the cost of encoding current searching position's MV ($\lambda_{MOTION} Bit(\Delta MV)$). If it is larger than the minimum MV cost, discard the current searching position, go to the next one and repeat step1.2. Otherwise, go to step1.3.

Step1.3. Calculate SSIM between the candidate block and the current encoding block, calculate the MV cost using equation (7), if it is larger than the minimum MV cost, this position is discarded, continue to the next searching position and repeat step1.2. Otherwise renew the best matching position and minimum RD cost and go to step1.4.

Step1.4. Compare the SSIM with the defined early termination threshold T. If it is smaller than T, go on to the next searching position and repeat step1.2-step1.4. Otherwise, terminate the searching process, the current searching position is selected as the best matching position and the minimum MV cost is renewed for later use.

- **Step2. Select the best prediction mode**

  For the best matching block(s) of each prediction mode, RD cost is calculated using equation (8), the mode with minimum RD cost will be selected as the best prediction mode. If the INTER 8×8 mode is selected as the best mode, then the sub-modes including INTER8×4, INTER4×8, INTER 4×4 need to be checked in the same way.

Simulation results demonstrate that the fixed SSIM threshold used in this algorithm creates desirable results, especially for the sequences with little motion.

4 Simulations and Results Analysis

4.1 Simulation Environment

All the experiments are carried out under the following conditions:

1. The proposed FMEBSS is implemented by modifying the H.264/AVC reference software JM11.0 [10]. Full search and spiral search pattern is selected. In order to compare the performance between the proposed FMEBSS and the original H.264 in inter coding, intra mode is forbidden in inter frame in both algorithms.
2. Experiments were conducted with three quantization parameters QP = 10, 20 and 30. 5 common test video sequences (QCIF 176×144) are selected to test our proposed algorithm, the first frame of the test sequences are shown in Fig 1. For each sequence, 50 frames are encoded with the first frame as I-frame with QP=10, and the rest 49 frames as P-frame.

Fig. 1. The first frame of the testing sequences

3. The results are performed on PD/2.8GHz personal computer with a 512×2M RAM and Microsoft Windows XP as the operation system.

4. Mean SSIM (MSSIM) is applied to assess the reconstructed video quality. It is measured frame by frame, and then average MSSIM of all frames as the whole sequence quality. The MSSIM of each frame is obtained by averaging all 8×8 sliding windows. The window starts from the top-left corner of the frame, moves pixel by pixel horizontally and vertically through all the rows and columns of the frame until the bottom-right corner is reached. We can assess the video quality even more strictly in this special way. The SSIM of the sliding 8×8 widow is calculated as follow:

$$SSIM = 0.6 \times SSIM_y + 0.2 \times SSIM_u + 0.2 \times SSIM_v \,. \tag{9}$$

Where $SSIM_y$, $SSIM_u$, and $SSIM_v$ represent the $SSIM$ of the component y, u and v of the current block respectively.

5. The value of parameters K_1 and K_2 are listed in Table1 and the early termination threshold T is defined as 0.99 for all the prediction modes and all the QP value.

4.2 Results Analysis

The coding performances are compared in terms of output Bit/Pic and MSSIM of the reconstructed videos. The encoding time is used to compare the complexity of encoding algorithm. MSSIM and Time is the average of all the P-frames' SSIM and Time correspondingly. The comparison results are tabulated in table 2, 3 and 4.

As is clearly shown in the tables, the proposed FMEBSS has greatly reduced the coding time. Compared with the H.264 standard full search, the maximum reduction of coding time is 70.14%. The average time savings of the proposed method is up to 62.62%, 50.11% and 27.45% for QP=10, 20 and 30 respectively. And the compression ratio is improved at the same time, the average reductions in Bit/Pic are 13.33%, 9.89%, 5.74%, while the MSSIM degradations are negligible. In order to compare video perceptual quality between our FMEBSS and H.264, we show the fiftieth reconstructed frame of the sequence "mobile" in Figure 2, from which we can see that FMEBSS has the same visual quality with the H.264 full search although the MSSIM decrease is the largest among all the test sequences.

We can also see that the proposed algorithm is even more efficient when applying to the sequences with little motion or large area of static background, such as "akiyo" and "grandma". The coding result of "grandma" at QP =20 is even more desirable, in which

H.264

FMEBSS

Fig. 2. Coding result comparison of the 50th frame "Mobile"

Table 2. Results comparison with parameter QP=10

Sequence	Algorithm	Bit/Pic	MSSIM	Time (ms)	△Bit/Pic (%)	△MSSIM (%)	△Time (%)
Akiyo	H.264	10358	0.9965	3259	-32.51	-0.05	-63.73
	FMEBSS	6991	0.9961	1182			
carphone	H.264	39141	0.9951	5958	-7.04	-0.04	-65.67
	FMEBSS	36386	0.9947	2045			
mobile	H.264	92689	0.9979	7687	-7.52	-0.06	-59.58
	FMEBSS	85723	0.9973	3107			
grandma	H.264	27013	0.9948	4982	-8.65	-0.06	-70.14
	FMEBSS	24677	0.9941	1488			
trevor	H.264	39077	0.9966	4831	-10.92	-0.07	-53.99
	FMEBSS	34809	0.9959	2223			
Average					-13.33	-0.06	-62.62

Table 3. Results comparison with parapeter QP=20

Sequence	Algorithm	Bit/Pic	MSSIM	Time (ms)	△Bit/Pic (%)	△MSSIM (%)	△Time (%)
Akiyo	H.264	2419	0.9942	2307	-19.64	-0.03	-49.41
	FMEBSS	1944	0.9939	1167			
carphone	H.264	8695	0.9848	5016	-5.32	-0.01	-56.46
	FMEBSS	8232	0.9848	2184			
mobile	H.264	37485	0.9887	7405	-11.06	-0.11	-46.40
	FMEBSS	33340	0.9877	3969			
grandma	H.264	3166	0.9881	3305	-6.90	0.01	-58.25
	FMEBSS	2948	0.9881	1379			
trevor	H.264	12693	0.9879	4492	-6.53	-0.06	-40.02
	FMEBSS	11864	0.9873	2694			
Average					-9.89	-0.04	-50.11

Table 4. Rsults comparison with parameter QP=30

Sequence	Algorithm	Bit/Pic	MSSIM	Time (ms)	ΔBit/Pic (%)	ΔMSSIM (%)	ΔTime (%)
Akiyo	H.264	498	0.9902	1812	-10.39	-0.01	-33.90
	FMEBSS	447	0.9901	1198			
carphone	H.264	1932	0.9669	3781	-7.75	0.15	-34.26
	FMEBSS	1783	0.9684	2486			
mobile	H.264	7800	0.9604	6730	-14.19	-0.15	-17.99
	FMEBSS	6693	0.9589	5519			
grandma	H.264	529	0.9818	2069	7.13	0.02	-33.24
	FMEBSS	567	0.9820	1381			
trevor	H.264	3440	0.9631	4020	-3.53	-0.05	-17.89
	FMEBSS	3319	0.9626	3301			
Average					-5.74	-0.01	-27.45

FMEBSS can save coding time by 58.25%, save bit number by 6.9% and the image quality is improved a little at the same time. So we predict that there is still a lot of room to optimize, if choosing more reasonable parameters in the RD functions.

And we also notice that the time saving decreases as QP increases. That is because the video quality declines as QP increases, fewer blocks can satisfy the threshold T. if adjusting the threshold lower, the time saving will be even more, but the reconstructed video quality may deteriorate.

5 Conclusion

In this paper, a fast algorithm FMEBSS was proposed to reduce the computation complexity of H.264. Compared with H.264 reference software, Simulation results show that the average time saving for all sequences is up to 46.73%. The proposed algorithm also averagely improve compression ratio by 9.65% at the same time, the coding quality MSSIM averagely declined only by 0.03%, which is negligible.

The parameters used in the RD functions are obtained by extensive experiments, so further improvement can be achieved by optimizing the RD functions parameters. And the proposed method also can be applied to the fast searching algorithm of H.264 to save more encoding time.

Acknowledgements

The work described in this paper was substantially supported by research project from National Natural Science Foundation of China [Project No. 60402015], and research project from Guangdong Natural Science Foundation of China [project No. 06025642].

References

[1] Xu, J.F., Chen, Z.B., He, Y.: Efficient Fast ME predictions and early-termination strategy based on H.264 statistical characters. In: ICICS-PCM 2003, Singapore, vol. 1, pp. 218–222 (2003)

[2] Yang, L.B., Yu, K.M., Li, J., Li, S.P.: An Effective Variable Block-Size Early Termination Algorithm for H.264 Video Coding. IEEE Transactions on Circuits And Systems for Video Technology 15(6), 784–788 (2005)

[3] Al Qaralleh, E.A., Chang, T.S.: Fast Motion Estimation by Adaptive Early Termination, Signal Processing Systems Design and Implementation, pp. 678–681 (2005)

[4] Ivanov, Y.V., Bleakley, C.J.: Skip Prediction and Early Termination for Fast Mode Decision in H.264/AVC. In: ICDT 2006. International Conference on Digital Telecommunications, pp. 7–7 (2006)

[5] Liang, Y.F., Ahmad, I., Luo, J.C., Sun, Y., Swaminathan, V.: On Using Hierarchical Motion History for Motion Estimation in H.264/AVC. IEEE Transactions on Circuits and Systems for Video Technology 15(12), 1594–1603 (2005)

[6] Ahmad, I., Zheng, W.G., Luo, J.C., Liou, M.: A Fast Adaptive Motion Estimation Algorithm. IEEE Transactions on Circuits and Systems for Video Technology 16(3), 439–446 (2006)

[7] Wang, Z., Bovik, A.C., Sheikh, H.R., Simoncelli, E.P.: Image quality assessment: from error visibility to structural similarity. IEEE Trans. Image Processing 13(4), 600–612 (2004)

[8] Wang, Z., Lu, L., Bovik, A.C.: Video quality assessment using structural distortion measurement. In: Proceedings of the IEEE International Conference on Image Processing, pp. 65–68 (September 2002)

[9] Wiegand, T., Sullivan, G.J., Bjontegaard, G., Luthra, A.: Overview of the H.264/AVC Video coding Standard. IEEE Trans. on CAS for video Technology 7(13), 560–576 (2003)

[10] http://iphome.hhi.de/suehring/tml/download/

Shot Boundary Detection for H.264/AVC Bitstreams with Frames Containing Multiple Types of Slices

Sarah De Bruyne[1], Wesley De Neve[1], Davy De Schrijver[1], Peter Lambert[1], Piet Verhoeve[2], and Rik Van de Walle[1]

[1] Ghent University - IBBT
Department of Electronics and Information Systems - Multimedia Lab
Gaston Crommenlaan 8, B-9050 Ledeberg-Ghent, Belgium
{sarah.debruyne,wesley.deneve,davy.deschrijver,
peter.lambert,rik.vandewalle}@ugent.be
http://www.multimedialab.elis.ugent.be/
[2] Televic, Izegem, Belgium
p.verhoeve@televic.com

Abstract. In this paper, a novel shot boundary detection algorithm is introduced for H.264/AVC bitstreams. This algorithm relies on features present in a compressed video bitstream, i.e., macroblock types and reference directions. In contrast to existing algorithms, the proposed technique is able to analyze bitstreams with frames containing different types of slices. To deal with such frames, formulas are presented that work on inter- and intra-coded slices. The results obtained for the different types of slices are combined by calculating a linear combination, taking into account their size. This way, a metric is found that can be used for the automatic detection of shot boundaries. Results show that the proposed algorithm has a high accuracy in terms of recall and precision for video sequences with frames containing multiple slice types.

1 Introduction

A prerequisite for video analysis is the automatic structuring of video content into visually-coherent segments. Therefore, shot boundary detection has generally been accepted as the first step in high-level video analysis [1]. Algorithms for shot boundary detection can typically be classified into two major groups, depending on whether the operations are performed on uncompressed data or whether they work with compressed domain features. Although algorithms in the uncompressed domain generally obtain better results, they are computationally demanding as a complete decompression step is required [2]. To avoid this computational overhead, we focus on methods operating in the compressed domain. Existing techniques in this domain mostly concentrate on previous MPEG standards like MPEG-2 and MPEG-4 Visual; they are based on the correlation of DCT coefficients, prediction type information, or motion-prediction statistics [3].

H.H.S. Ip et al. (Eds.): PCM 2007, LNCS 4810, pp. 177–186, 2007.

More and more video content is coded using the H.264/AVC video coding standard [4]. As this specification possesses features like intra prediction and multi-picture motion-compensation, shot boundary detection methods used for previous video coding formats can no longer be applied [5,6]. An algorithm based on the distribution of intra-coded macroblocks was discussed in [5], while the authors of this paper described a method in [6] using the distribution of intra-coded macroblocks and temporal macroblock prediction types. Liu *et al.* proposed a similar technique using a Hidden Markov Model [7].

The H.264/AVC specification allows constructing coded pictures consisting of a mixture of different types of slices. In [8], Undheim *et al.* use this feature to minimize bit rate variations by inserting I slices at specific positions in inter-coded frames, as an alternative to inserting fully intra-coded frames at a regular time basis. In addition, H.264/AVC offers a new tool called Flexible Macroblock Ordering (FMO) [9] which allows to encode slices with arbitrary shapes. Within the scope of error resilience, this tool can for example be used to better protect Regions Of Interest (ROIs) against transmission errors. This can be achieved by inserting more intra-coded slices to represent important regions.

However, none of the above-mentioned shot boundary detection algorithms is able to deal with multiple slice types in one frame as they work on completely intra- or inter-coded frames. In this paper, formulas are presented to deal with a mixture of inter- and intra-coded slices in a frame. First, formulas are introduced for the different types of slices. Second, the results obtained for the different slices are combined by making use of linear combinations, taking into account the percentage of macroblocks belonging to the different types of slices.

The remainder of this paper is organized as follows. In Sect. 2, a shot boundary detection algorithm is discussed that works on a frame basis, meaning that each frame consists of only one type of slice. Based on this algorithm, Sect. 3 subsequently proposes an algorithm capable of dealing with frames consisting of multiple types of slices. Next, the accuracy of our proposed method is discussed in terms of recall and precision. Finally, Sect. 5 concludes this paper.

2 Shot Detection on a Frame Basis

Within a video sequence, a strong correlation exists between successive frames. This results in specific characteristics of the motion prediction information and the distribution of intra-coded macroblocks, since an encoder usually tries to exploit temporal and spatial redundancy to a maximum extent. Based on these characteristics, a metric can be defined that is able to automatically locate possible shot boundaries in the compressed domain.

2.1 Shot Boundaries Located at Inter-Coded Frames

P and B frames[1] use temporal prediction to exploit similarities with previously coded frames. However, when the current frame is the starting frame of a

[1] We refer to fully I, P, or B slice-coded pictures as I, P, and B frames, respectively.

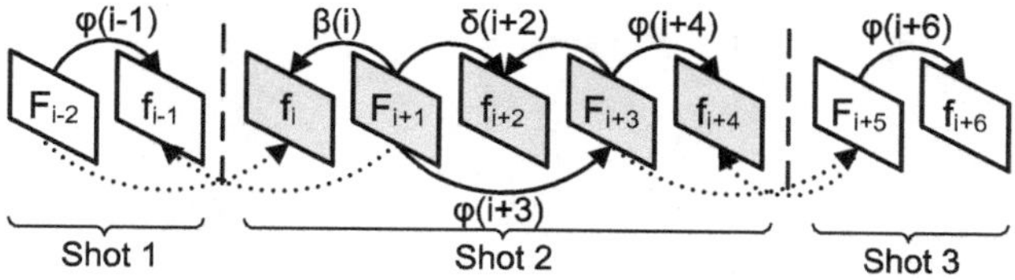

Fig. 1. Example of a video sequence consisting of three shots. In the figure, the frames are depicted in display order. F_j and f_j correspond to a reference and a non-reference frame, while the arrows represent the avaible reference frames. Full arrows indicate that the corresponding reference frame is frequently used.

new shot, this frame will hardly have any resemblance with previously depicted frames. Therefore, an encoder will prefer to mainly use intra-coded macroblocks or macroblocks referring to following frames (called backward prediction), as can be seen in Fig. 1 for frames f_i and F_{i+5}. The previous frame, in its turn, will hardly have any correlation with frames belonging to the next shot; it will therefore mainly contain macroblocks referring to previously depicted frames (called forward prediction) and intra-coded macroblocks (e.g., frames f_{i-1} and f_{i+4}).

In prior standards, there was a strict dependency between the ordering of pictures for motion compensation referencing purposes and the ordering of pictures for display purposes. In H.264/AVC, these restrictions are mostly removed, allowing the decoupling of referencing order from display order [4]. Therefore, in order to determine the reference directions, it is not sufficient to only investigate the macroblock types; the display numbers of the reference frames and the current frame also need to be considered. In [6], a new concept was proposed, which we called *temporal prediction type* of a macroblock; it represents the reference direction of a macroblock. Based on a comparison between the display numbers of the reference frames and the current frame, the temporal prediction types of the macroblocks in the current frame can be determined. In case the display numbers of all reference frames are prior (resp. next) to the current frame, we speak of forward (resp. backward) temporal prediction. In case reference frames are located before as well as after the current frame, a macroblock is coded using bi-directional temporal prediction. Finally, a macroblock can also be intra-coded.

Based on the percentage of macroblocks coded with these four different temporal prediction types, a metric can be defined for determining possible shot boundaries located at a P or B frame. Let $\iota(i)$, $\varphi(i)$, $\beta(i)$, and $\delta(i)$ be the number of macroblocks coded using intra, forward, backward, and bi-directional temporal prediction, respectively, of the current frame f_i; let f_{i-1} be the previous frame and let $\#_{MB}$ denote the number of macroblocks in a frame. A shot boundary is then declared at the current P or B frame when

$$\frac{1}{\#MB}(\iota(i-1)+\varphi(i-1)) > T_1 \ \wedge \ \frac{1}{\#MB}(\iota(i)+\beta(i)) > T_1, \qquad (1)$$

where T_1 represents a predefined threshold. In Sect. 4, we will elaborate on the selection of the optimal value for this threshold.

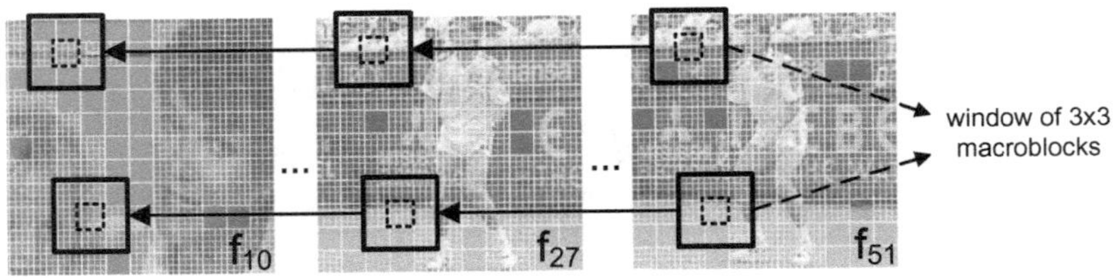

Fig. 2. Distribution of Intra_4×4 and Intra_16×16 macroblocks in successive I frames

2.2 Shot Boundaries Located at Intra-coded Frames

In the H.264/AVC standard, spatial prediction is used to code I frames. The specification supports several types of intra macroblock types, of which Intra_4×4 and Intra_16×16 are the most commonly used. Intra_4×4 is generally preferred by an encoder in case a part of a picture contains a significant amount of detail, whereas Intra_16×16 is more suited for coding smooth areas.

In case the frame preceding the current I frame is inter-coded, this frame contains hardly any spatial information. Therefore, it is not useful to compare these two frames. Instead, the current frame is compared with the previous I frame in the bitstream (e.g. frames f_{27} and f_{51} in Fig. 2).

When two successive I frames belong to different shots, the distribution of the intra prediction modes in both frames will highly differ, as shown in Fig. 2. By comparing the intra prediction modes in both frames at corresponding positions, the dissimilarity between these frames can be calculated. However, due to the movement of objects or the camera, this approach will lead to a high number of false alarms. Therefore, instead of comparing corresponding macroblocks, a window is selected for each macroblock. In this paper, we work with a window of 3×3 macroblocks, but other dimensions could be used as well. This window is compared with the corresponding window in the previous I frame by taking into count the different amounts of Intra_4×4 and Intra_16×16 macroblocks. Let f_i and f_j be the current and previous I frame, $w(f_i, m)$ the window belonging to the mth macroblock in frame f_i, and $I_4(w(f_i, m))$ and $I_{16}(w(f_i, m))$ the amount of macroblocks in $w(f_i, m)$ coded using Intra_4×4 and Intra_16×16. The dissimilarity metric $\Omega(i)$ for two I frames can then be defined as follows:

$$\Omega(i) = \frac{1}{\#_{MB}} \sum_{\forall m \in f_i} W(f_i, m) \quad with \tag{2}$$

$$W(f_i, m) = \frac{\left|I_4(w(f_i, m)) - I_4(w(f_j, m))\right| + \left|I_{16}(w(f_i, m)) - I_{16}(w(f_j, m))\right|}{2 \cdot size\_in\_macroblocks(w(f_i, m))}. \tag{3}$$

Based on this metric for the current frame f_i and the percentage of macroblocks coded using intra and forward temporal prediction in the previous frame f_{i-1}, a shot boundary is declared at an I frame when the following two conditions are met:

$$\frac{1}{\#_{MB}}(\iota(i-1) + \varphi(i-1)) > T_1 \ \wedge \ \Omega(i) > T_2, \tag{4}$$

where T_2 represents a second predefined threshold (see Sect. 4).

3 Shot Detection on Frames with Multiple Slice Types

In the previous section, two formulas are developed to locate shot boundaries depending on the coding type of the current frame. However, as discussed in Sect. 1, it is allowed in H.264/AVC to construct coded pictures consisting of a mixture of different types of slices. As a result, the likelihood of a shot boundary needs to be calculated for every slice type separately. Afterward, the computed results for the different types of slices are then combined, taking into account the size of each slice.

Depending on the application area, a slice can have a different size and shape. In the following sections, we focus on slices with a limited number of macroblocks in raster-scan order, as well as slices corresponding to ROIs. Note that these algorithms can also be applied to other subdivisions of pictures into slices.

3.1 Shot Detection on a Slice Basis

Formulas for Inter-coded Slices. The formula for P and B slices can be derived in a similar way as for P and B frames (Formula 1). Instead of computing the percentage of macroblocks coded using intra, forward, backward, and bi-directional temporal prediction in a frame, these percentages are calculated for a slice.

Formulas for Intra-coded Slices. For I slices, on the other hand, a more complex approach is needed as it is possible that I slices are not always located at the exact same position or differ in size [8]. For example, in Fig. 3, ROIs are coded as I slices more frequently, while the background remains inter-coded. Since an object of interest may move, ROIs can change in terms of shape and position. Another example is given in Fig. 4, where macroblocks are assigned to slices in raster-scan order, after which the obtained slices are intra-coded alternately across the different frames. In Sect. 2.2, the dissimilarity between two I frames was calculated by comparing the intra prediction modes of macroblocks within a window at corresponding positions. However, this method cannot directly be applied to slices as the previous I slice is not necessarily located at the same position or has the same size as the current I slice. This can for example be seen in Fig. 3. Furthermore, comparing the windows of the current I slice with the previous fully I slice-coded frame is not a good approach either as a lot of spatial information originating from intermediate I slices is discarded. To overcome this problem, an extended approach is needed.

Instead of only taking into account the macroblock modes of the previous I slice, it is possible to compare the current macroblocks with the macroblocks in all previous I slices. As the content of closely located pictures is typically more similar than pictures located further away, the co-located macroblocks are selected from the closest I slice covering this position. An example is given in Fig. 3. Here, the bottom six macroblocks of the window in frame f_{18} are compared with the co-located macroblocks in the previous I slice, which belongs to f_{12}. The upper three macroblocks, on the other hand, belong to an inter-coded

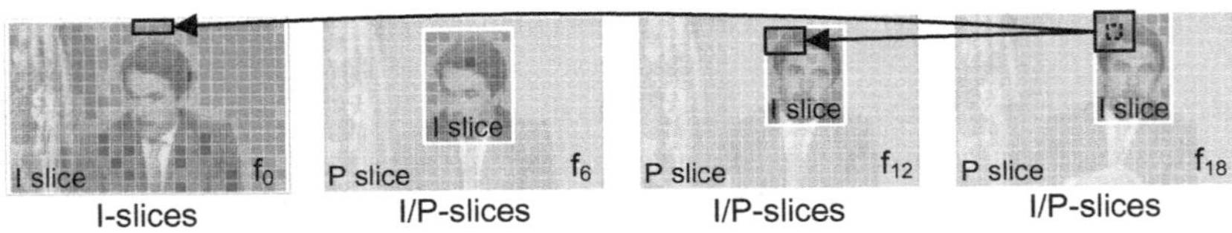

Fig. 3. Part of a video coded using multiple types of slices. Every six frames, an I slice is used for coding the ROI while the background is inter-coded. The nine macroblocks in the selected window in f_{18} are compared with macroblocks in previous I slices.

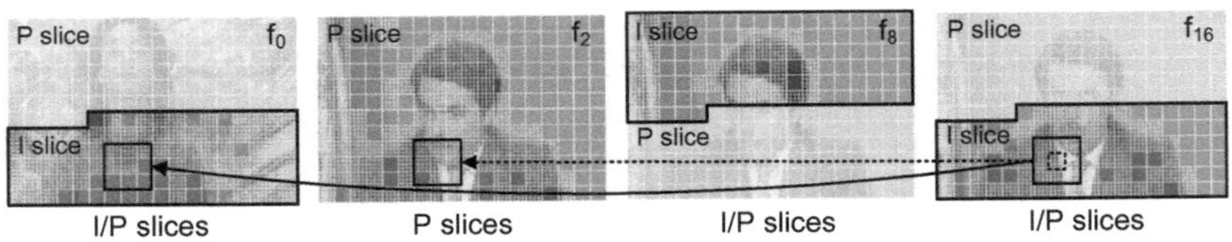

Fig. 4. Video sequence where every eight frames, one of the slices is alternately coded as an I slice. Although f_2 does not contain I slices, it is depicted as well as it is the first frame of a new shot. The full arrow points to the co-located macroblocks in case f_2 is not used, while the dotted arrow represents the new technique.

slice in frame f_{12}. Therefore, we go back in the video sequence until we find an I slice that covers this area, i.e., an I slice in frame f_0.

At a first glance, it looks like all previous I slices need to be stored for the successful execution of our algorithm. However, it is only necessary to know for each macroblock what its prediction mode was in the last covering I slice. As a result, this information can be stored in an *intra prediction map* M_i, having the dimension of a frame. After processing an I slice, the map M_i is updated with the information retrieved from this I slice.

To calculate the dissimilarity $\Omega(s_i)$ between the current slice s_i and the map M_i, which contains information from the previous frames, Formulas 2 and 3 need to be adjusted in order to be able to work on a slice basis. For this, we use the same conventions as in Sect. 2.2.

$$\Omega(s_i) = \frac{1}{\#_{MB}} \sum_{\forall m \in s_i} W(s_i, m) \quad with \tag{5}$$

$$W(s_i, m) = \frac{\left|I_4(w(s_i,m)) - I_4(w(M_i,m))\right| + \left|I_{16}(w(s_i,m)) - I_{16}(w(M_i,m))\right|}{2 \cdot size(w(s_i,m))}. \tag{6}$$

In certain applications, video sequences are coded using fixed GOP structures. This means that fully I slice-coded pictures are inserted on a regular time basis independent of the content of the video. As a result, it can be expected that the first encoded frame of a new shot will be coded using P or B slices mainly containing intra-coded macroblocks, as can be seen in Fig. 4. This shot boundary will normally be detected using the formulas for P and B slices. However, as the content of the video highly changes due to the shot boundary, spatial information in following I slices will highly differ from the spatial information present in the map. This is due to the fact that the map still contains information corresponding to the previous shot. As a result, the dissimilarity metrics for following slices will indicate that the probability of a shot boundary is high. This is incorrect because the map still contains old information, although a new shot has already been started. Therefore, when a new shot boundary is detected on a P or B slice coded frame, the intra-coded macroblocks of this frame are inserted into the map as well. The content of the map will then be updated with the new shot information, resulting in less false positives.

Fig. 4 illustrates the update step for the intra prediction map M_i. When processing the macroblocks in the I slice of f_{16}, the map contains macroblock information from f_8 and f_0. However, the information from f_0 is out-dated. When comparing the macroblocks from f_{16} with the information from f_0, it results in a high dissimilarity. Therefore, one could falsely conclude that the possibility of a shot boundary at f_{16} is high. Instead, a new shot will typically be declared at f_2 as this frame only contains intra-coded macroblocks. When inserting the intra-coded macroblocks of a frame corresponding to a shot boundary into the map, the number of false alarms is reduced.

3.2 Combining Different Types of Slices in One Frame

As a frame can consist of different types of slices, the formulas for inter- and intra-coded slices need to be combined. Therefore, we propose to combine the results obtained for the different types of slices, as explained in the previous section, by calculating a linear combination. In this formula, the size of each slice in terms of macroblocks is also taken into account. This means that the result for relatively small slices has a minor impact on the final result compared to relatively large slices. Let $v(Intra_i)$ and $v(Inter_i)$ be the values obtained for the intra- and inter-coded slices in the current frame i (i.e., the dissimilarity metric $\Omega(s_i)$ for the I slices and the percentage of intra-coded and backward referring macroblocks for the inter-coded slices). Let $s(Intra_i)$ and $s(Inter_i)$ denote the corresponding relative sizes. The current frame will then coincide with a shot boundary in case:

$$s(Inter_i) \cdot v(Inter_i) + s(Intra_i) \cdot v(Intra_i) > s(Inter_i) \cdot T_1 + s(Intra_i) \cdot T_2 \quad (7)$$

As shown in the next section, the optimal threshold for inter-coded slices, T_1, is higher than the threshold for intra-coded slices, T_2. As a result, large values for $v(Inter_i)$ could undermine the results for I slices. Therefore, we rescale the part of Formula 7 corresponding to the I slices so that both parts are compared with the same threshold, i.e., T_1. This is done by multiplying the parts corresponding to I slices with $\frac{T_1}{T_2}$. After reducing this formula, we obtain the following formula:

$$s(Inter_i) \cdot v(Inter_i) + s(Intra_i) \cdot v(Intra_i) \cdot \frac{T_1}{T_2} > T_1 \quad (8)$$

As can be seen in Formulas 1 and 4, there are always two conditions that need to be fulfilled in case a shot boundary is detected. The first condition considers the previous frame, while the second condition corresponds to the current frame.

As Formula 8 corresponds to the second condition, an extra formula needs to be added for the previous frame. This can be done in a similar manner. In case the formulas for both the current and previous frame exceed the thresholds, a shot boundary is detected. Note that in case these formulas are applied to sequences with frames containing only one type of slice, exactly the same results are obtained as the formulas presented in Sect. 2.

For the detection of gradual transitions, a similar approach as described in [6] is adopted. This technique compares the amount of intra-coded macroblocks within a frame with the average amount of intra-coded macroblocks in a number of previous frames. This technique can be used for frames containing different types of slices as well.

4 Results

To evaluate the accuracy of our algorithm, experiments have been carried out on three trailers with a resolution of 848×352 pixels, a frame rate of 25 fps, about 9500 frames, and brimmed with all kinds of shot changes, variations in light intensity, and motion. These sequences were coded a number of times with slices corresponding to ROIs as well as with slices containing a fixed number of macroblocks in raster-scan order. Furthermore, different fixed GOP structures (IPP^* and $I(BBP)^*$) were used.

In the first case, different choices for the ROIs were used, as can be seen in Table 1. As the center of a video sequence generally contains the most important information, 25%, resp. 50%, of the macroblocks located in the middle were indicated as ROI. In addition, the ROIs were also selected manually to evaluate their influence on the algorithm. This way, ROIs can move around and change in size, which was not possible in the previous configuration. I slices corresponding to ROIs were inserted every three or fifteen frames (indicated by ΔROI_I).

In the second case, the sequences were coded using regular slices each containing 250 macroblocks. As a result, each frame is divided in five slices. Every three, resp. six, frames, an I slice was inserted alternately (indicated by ΔI_slice). This means that the distance between two frames containing an I slice at the same position is 15, resp. 30, frames. This is similar as in Fig. 4, where ΔI_slice is equal to eight. Results for this configuration are shown in Table 2.

In the previous sections, the obtained results were compared to thresholds in order to detect the shot boundaries. To optimize the performance of the algorithm, these thresholds were selected by comparing the recall and precision of the algorithm for different values. Preliminary work has shown that the optimal values for T_1 and T_2 are equal to 80 % and 22 %. This technique is also used by Kim *et al.* in [5] to calculate the optimal value of a threshold.

The results obtained with our proposed algorithm were compared with the ground truth and are tabulated in Table 1 and Table 2. For this purpose, the "recall" and "precision" ratios are applied, based on the number of correct detections (*Detects*), missed detections (*MDs*), and false alarms (*FAs*):

$$Recall = \frac{Detects}{Detects + MDs} \quad and \quad Precision = \frac{Detects}{Detects + FAs}.$$

Table 1. Performance of the algorithm using precision (Pr) and recall (Re) ratios (%) on sequences coded with slices corresponding to ROIs

Test sequences	# original shots	0% ROI		25% ROI		50% ROI		moving ROI	
		Pr	Re	Pr	Re	Pr	Re	Pr	Re
Little miss sunshine									
IBBP (ΔROI_I = 3)	106	93.3	99.0	91.4	99.0	91.4	100.0	96.2	99.0
IBBP (ΔROI_I = 15)	106	93.3	99.0	91.4	99.0	95.2	100.0	97.1	97.1
IPPP (ΔROI_I = 3)	106	97.1	93.6	96.2	96.2	94.3	100.0	99.0	95.4
IPPP (ΔROI_I = 15)	106	97.1	93.6	96.2	96.2	95.2	96.2	97.1	93.6
Accepted									
IBBP (ΔROI_I = 3)	124	98.4	95.3	98.4	93.8	99.2	94.6	100.0	93.2
IBBP (ΔROI_I = 15)	124	98.4	95.3	98.4	93.8	99.2	93.1	99.2	91.0
IPPP (ΔROI_I = 3)	124	98.4	93.8	97.6	95.2	96.7	96.0	100.0	95.3
IPPP (ΔROI_I = 15)	124	98.4	93.8	97.6	93.8	98.4	93.1	99.2	93.1
Friends with money									
IBBP (ΔROI_I = 3)	50	93.3	99.0	95.9	100.0	93.9	100.0	98.0	98.0
IBBP (ΔROI_I = 15)	50	93.3	99.0	91.8	100.0	93.9	100.0	98.0	100.0
IPPP (ΔROI_I = 3)	50	97.1	93.6	93.9	97.9	91.8	100.0	95.9	97.9
IPPP (ΔROI_I = 15)	50	97.1	93.6	89.8	97.8	91.8	97.8	95.9	95.9

Table 2. Performance of the algorithm using precision (Pr) and recall (Re) ratios (%) on sequences coded with slices each containing 250 of macroblocks in raster-scan order

Test sequences	# original shots	no extra I slices		ΔI_slice = 3		ΔI_slice = 6	
		Pr	Re	Pr	Re	Pr	Re
Little miss sunshine							
IBBP	106	93.3	99.0	92.4	99.0	96.2	98.1
IPPP	106	97.1	93.6	97.1	100.0	97.1	96.2
Accepted							
IBBP	124	98.4	95.3	99.2	96.1	99.2	95.3
IPPP	124	98.4	93.8	99.2	94.6	99.2	93.8
Friends with money							
IBBP	50	93.3	99.0	100.0	100.0	100.0	98.0
IPPP	50	97.1	93.6	100.0	100.0	95.9	97.9

To compare the results with sequences with frames containing only one type of slice, a column representing *0% ROI*, resp. *no extra I slices*, was added as well. Here, no I slices were inserted, resulting in traditional coding patterns.

The results show that the proposed algorithm is characterized by a high accuracy for different encoder settings and different subdivisions of a picture into slices. Nearly all cuts were correctly detected, whereas the gradual changes caused more problems.

The major part of the missed detections is caused by long gradual changes, which is a problem most algorithms cannot cope with [3]. As the difference between successive frames is minimal, it is difficult to detect these transitions.

Falsely detected cuts are mostly caused by sudden changes in light intensity. Furthermore, fast motion covering a major part of the scene results in falsely detected gradual changes as the characteristics of the macroblocks are similar.

Note that the accuracy of the algorithm is encoder dependent as the algorithm relies on the coding choices made by the encoder.

5 Conclusions

This paper introduced an algorithm for shot boundary detection on H.264/AVC compressed bitstreams. In contrast to existing algorithms, the approach is able to deal with frames that consist of different types of slices. To deal with such frames, formulas are presented for inter- and intra-coded slices that make use of the distribution of the different macroblock types and the reference directions. To combine the results of the different types of slices, a linear combination of the obtained results is calculated, taking into account the size of each slice. Experimental results show that our algorithm is characterized by a high accuracy in terms of recall and precision for conventional video sequences, as well as for sequences with frames that consist of different types of slices.

Acknowledgments. The research activities that have been described in this paper were funded by Ghent University, the Interdisciplinary Institute for Broadband Technology (IBBT), the Institute for the Promotion of Innovation by Science and Technology in Flanders (IWT-Flanders), the Fund for Scientific Research-Flanders (FWO-Flanders), and the European Union.

References

1. Hanjalic, A.: Shot-Boundary Detection: Unraveled and Resolved? IEEE Transactions on Circuits and Systems for Video Technology, 90–105 (2002)
2. Lienhart, R.: Comparison of automatic shot boundary detection algorithms. Proceedings of SPIE Storage and Retrieval for Image and Video Databases VII 3656, 290–301 (1999)
3. Gargi, U., Kasturi, R., Strayer, S.: Performance Characterization of Video-Shot-Change Detection Methods. IEEE Transactions on Circuits and Systems for Video Technology 10(1), 1–13 (2000)
4. Wiegard, T., Sullivan, G., Bjontegaard, G., Luthra, A.: Overview of the H.264/AVC Video Coding Standard. IEEE Transactions on Circuits and Systems for Video Technology 13(7), 560–576 (2003)
5. Kim, S.M., Byun, J., Won, C.: A scene change detection in H.264/AVC compression domain. In: Ho, Y.-S., Kim, H.J. (eds.) PCM 2005. LNCS, vol. 3768, pp. 1072–1082. Springer, Heidelberg (2005)
6. De Bruyne, S., De Neve, W., De Wolf, K., De Schrijver, D., Verhoeve, P., Van de Walle, R.: Temporal video segmentation on H.264/AVC compressed bitstreams. In: Cham, T.-J., Cai, J., Dorai, C., Rajan, D., Chua, T.-S., Chia, L.-T. (eds.) MMM 2007. LNCS, vol. 4351, pp. 1–12. Springer, Heidelberg (2006)
7. Liu, Y., Wang, W., Gao, W., Zeng, W.: A novel compressed domain shot segmentation algorithm on H.264/AVC. In: Proceedings of ICIP 2004, vol. 4, pp. 2235–2238 (2004)
8. Undheim, A., Lin, Y., Emstad, P.J.: Characterization of Slice-based H.264/AVC Encoded Video Traffic. In: Proceedings of the ECUMN 2007 (2007)
9. Lambert, P., De Neve, W., Dhondt, Y., Van de Walle, R.: Flexible macroblock ordering in H.264/AVC. Journal of Visual Communications & Image Representation 17, 358–375 (2006)

A Lexicon-Guided LSI Method for Semantic News Video Retrieval*

Juan Cao[1, 2], Sheng Tang[1], Jintao Li[1], Yongdong Zhang[1], and Xuefeng Pan[1,2]

[1] Key Laboratory of Intelligent Information Processing, Institute of Computing Technology, Chinese Academy of Sciences, Beijing 100080, China
[2] Graduate University of the Chinese Academy of Sciences, Beijing 100039, China
{caojuan, ts, jtli, zhyd, xfpan }@ict.ac.cn

Abstract. Many researchers try to utilize the semantic information extracted from visual feature to directly realize the semantic video retrieval or to supplement the automated speech recognition (ASR) text retrieval. But bridging the gap between the low-level visual feature and semantic content is still a challenging task. In this paper, we study how to effectively use Latent Semantic Indexing (LSI) to improve the semantic video retrieval through the ASR texts. The basic LSI method has been shown effective in the traditional text retrieval and the noisy ASR text retrieval. In this paper, we further use the lexicon-guided semantic clustering to effectively remove the noise introduced by news video's additional contents, and use the cluster-based LSI to automatically mine the semantic structure underlying the terms expression. Tests on the TRECVID 2005 dataset show that the above two enhancements achieve 21.3% and 6.9% improvements in performance over the traditional vector-space model(VSM) and the basic LSI separately.

Keywords: ASR text, LSI, Semantic video retrieval.

1 Introduction

In video retrieval, the users' need is not only the visually similar content, but the semantic similar content. So low-level features are now becoming insufficient to build efficient news video retrieval systems. Many works have done to bridge the gap between low-level features and semantic content, but this is still a challenging task in the future. In this paper, we try an alternative way to mine the video's semantic information from its automatic speech recognition (ASR) text. One reason is that ASR text is the direct semantic description about video content. The other is that the technologies of text retrieval are more mature than the ones of visual features process. But news video's ASR texts have their own characteristics, and we should adopt the traditional information retrieval methods, LSI, for it.

* This paper is supported by National Basic Research Program of China (973 Program, 2007CB311100), Beijing Science and Technology Planning Program of China (D01060-08040291) and National High Technology and Research Development Program of China (863 Program, 2007AA01Z416).

H.H.S. Ip et al. (Eds.): PCM 2007, LNCS 4810, pp. 187–195, 2007.

Many works have done to prove the effectiveness of LSI in common text retrieval [5][9][13]. Moreover, L.Hollink et al. demonstrated the feasibility of the basic LSI method in the noisy ASR texts[1]. In TRECVID 2005 ASR texts, the word error rate(WER) is 33.8%[14], and the average length of shot document is about 14.5, while the counterpart in TREC collection is 84.6(after pre-processing) [13]. These data are a challenge to the basic LSI. By enhancing the basic LSI to fit ASR texts, we further affirmed the validity of the LSI approach in video's ASR texts retrieval.

1.1 Related Work

In semantic video retrieval field, much of prior work focused on extracting semantic information from videos' multi-modality resources to supplement the video's ASR text. Neo[2] integrates event-related high-level features (HLFs) to provide the additional context and knowledge. The event-related HLFs are relevant visual features detected by a machine learning approach. The improvement of the performance is significant. But the HLF detectors' training need a large scale annotated corpus, and the detection confidence is unstable when the test collection is inconsistent with the training collection. Many researchers try to use the data mining technology to automatically mine the semantic information directly from the video's low-level visual features. In [3] and [4], authors perform LSI separately on the region-level and low-level visual features, and try to automatically bridge the gap from low-level visual features to the semantic content. But these approaches need a rigorous experimental environment: [3] assume that a video shot is well represented by its key frames. In [4]'s experiment, the corpus must be standard and contain limited semantic categories. However, all these assumptions are unpractical.

1.2 Our Work

We parse a corpus in three level hierarchical structures, initially keywords(term-document matrix), topics(LSI semantic space) and semantic clustering, and retrieve under this structure.

Generally, ASR texts include two main errors: one is the word error imported by speech recognition step, and the other is the matching error induced when mapping the ASR text to the video's shot. To reduce the negative influence imported by errors, we retrieve the text by using LSI approach instead of using the common term-matching algorithm. LSI can map the keywords space to a reduced-dimension semantic concept space and ignore the unimportant details. These features make the LSI very compelling and useful in semantic retrieval.

Besides, the video's shot ASR text is very short (in our experiment, the shot text's average length is 14.5). Much important information may appear as rarely as the real noises do. Furthermore, news videos not only include the real-life events shots (valuable news content), but also include some additional shots (redundant content), such as led-in/out, advertisement, special graphic effects, etc. So we mine semantic structure in this impure corpus is unadvisable. We utilize lexicon–guided semantic clustering to remove the redundant contents in news video, and perform LSI in the semantic class instead of the whole document collection. As confirmed by our experiments, the introduction of lexicon can get an improvement of 6.9%.

The rest of this paper is organized as follows: In section 2, we give a brief review of LSI, and describe its importance to ASR texts retrieval. Next we present the lexicon-guided semantic clustering and the cluster-based LSI in the section 3. Then we set up the experimental framework to compare the adaptive LSI to traditional methods in section 4 and discuss two open questions in section 5. Finally, conclusion and future work are given in the last section.

2 Latent Semantic Indexing

2.1 LSI

In natural langue analyzing field, a certain word can be interpreted in different ways within different contexts (polysemy); while the same concept can be described using different terms(synonymy). LSI was proposed to solve these problems. The key idea is clustering the **co-occurring keywords**, and mapping documents and queries into a lower dimensional space(latent semantic space)[5]. The advantage of retrieval in this space is that a query can be similar to a document even when they share no words.

The LSI technique makes use of the singular value decomposition(SVD) to mine the total collection's semantic structure. Firstly, we represent the document collection as a term-document matrix $M_{t\times d}$, then the SVD decompose $M_{t\times d}$ into the product of three matrices:

$$M_{t\times d} = T_{t\times r} S_{r\times r} \left(D_{d\times r}\right)^T \tag{1}$$

where t is the number of terms, d is the number of documents. r is the rank of M. T and D are the matrices with orthonormal columns. S is a diagonal matrix of M's singular values sorted in decreasing. The singular value is larger, the corresponding dimension is more important. By restricting the matrixes T,S,D to their first k rows , we can get a approximate matrix M':

$$M'_{t\times d} = T'_{t\times k} S'_{k\times k} \left(D'_{d\times k}\right)^T \tag{2}$$

Where k< r.

Discarding the less important dimensions can remove much of the noise, and transform the term space to the reduced-dimension latent semantic space.

In retrieval period, through the formula(3) we transform the q to latent semantic space:

$$q' = q^T T'_{t\times k} S^{-1}{}_{k\times k} \tag{3}$$

We use the standard cosine measure(4) to compute the similarity between the query and document:

$$LSI\left(q, doc_i\right) = \frac{q' \bullet (D')_i}{|q'||(D')_i|} \tag{4}$$

$(D')_i$ is the i-th column of matrix D'.

2.2 LSI in ASR Texts

In the ASR text retrieval, the contribution of LSI is not limited in polysemy and synonymy problems, it can reduce the negative effect brought by speech recognition errors. LSI reduces the importance of the individual terms, and pays more attention to the latent structure underlying the whole document collection. So the individually term recognition error can not influence the retrieval precision in LSI.

Furthermore, LSI is a completely automatic unsupervised statistical learning approach, and is free of hand-labeled training data. This factor overcomes the drawback that the confidence depends on the training collection. This problem lies in most of the traditional machine learning approaches used to extract HLFs from visual feature, and hinders the HLFs' application in semantic video retrieval.

The other problem in practical application is the efficiency. [5] shows that decomposing a matrix with 70,000 documents and 90,000 terms requires about 18 hours of CPU time on a SUN SPARCstation 10 workstation. This cost is a too horrendous to bear. Note that the term-document matrix is quite sparse. In our experiment, the matrix contains only 0.17% non-zero entries. So we select the SVDPACK[6] to quickly compute the SVD. This software package implements Lanczos and subspace iteration-based methods for determining several of the largest singular triplets (singular values and corresponding left- and right-singular vectors) for large sparse matrices. For a matrix with the size of 20932×8410, only require about 1 minute of CPU time on a P4 PC. Meanwhile our semantic clustering in next section will be used to reduce the dimension of the matrix, and to further increase the performance efficiency.

3 Lexicon Guided Semantic Cluster

Based on the characteristics of news videos, we predefined four semantic classes: politics, sports, finance, and general [10]. The general class is designed to remove the redundant shots described in the above section. The initial cluster centroids are pre-constructed pseudo samples based on the HowNet's relevance calculator[7][11]. Then we use the k-means approach to continually adjust the initial cluster centers to really reflect the current collection's characteristics. The detail process is as follows:

- In step1, we utilize the HowNet's relevance calculator to separately produce three relevant word lists for politics, sports and finance. Then we transform these lists to term vector space of the Term-Document Matrix $M_{t\times d}$.. These vectors are the initial cluster centers $Center = \{C_0, C_1, C_2, C_3\}$. Where C_0 is the initial center of general class, and we set it's values with zero.
- In step2, we use the iterative computation to adjust the pseudo centers to the real corpus, and produce the final cluster centers : $Center' = \{C_0', C_1', C_2', C_3'\}$.
- In step3, we classify the corpus to four classes based on $Center'$.
- In step4, by measuring the distance between the query and the three new cluster centers C_1', C_2', C_3', we get the scores of the query belonging to the corresponding semantic classes: α_1 , α_2 , α_3 .

– In step5, we separately perform the LSI analysis in three semantic classes, and fuse the results based on the scores in step4:

$$Sim(q,D)=\sum_{k=1,2,3}\alpha_k LSI_k(q,D_k) \tag{5}$$

By deeply analyzing the original data and the classified results, we found that the general class can effectively remove the additional shots. In the 20932 documents, only 2228 shot documents are clustered into general class, and these snippets are very short, or their contents are irrelevant to any news classes.

The comparison experiments tell us that classifying the document collection only based on the HowNet's cluster centers or the k-means centers performs worse than the above approach. Because the HowNet's cluster centroids are produced by its corpus and rules, and the terms' distribution is somewhat different from the current collection. So the strategy of using lexicon to guide the k-means clustering is reasonable and hence effective.

4 Empirical Validation

We choose the TRECVID 2005's English test collection as our experimental data. After pre-processing, the total number of the shot documents is 20932, the number of the unique terms is 8410, and 305529 non-zero entries in the term-document matrix.

We select 12 topics from the 2005 search task to test our methods, and the choice criterion is the number of the relevant documents in the test collection bigger than 50. Table.1 is the topics' information:

149="Find shots of Condoleeza Rice";
160="Find shots of something (e.g., vehicle, aircraft, building, etc) on fire with flames and smoke visible";
161="Find shots of people with banners or signs";
162"Find shots of one or more people entering or leaving a building";
163="Find shots of a meeting with a large table and more than two people";
164="Find shots of a ship or boat";
165="Find shots of basketball players on the court";
166="Find shots of one or more palm trees";
168="Find shots of a road with one or more cars";
169="Find shots of one or more tanks or other military vehicles";
170="Find shots of a tall building (with more than 5 floors above the ground)";
172="Find shots of an office setting, i.e., one or more desks/tables and one or more computers and one or more people";

Table 1. Statistics of topics

topic	149	160	161	162	163	164	165	166	168	169	170	172
Rel-Num	72	90	255	162	95	64	130	159	548	286	135	487
Pre-Rank	9	17	12	22	14	5	13	18	7	11	19	16

Where the Rel-Num is the topics' relevant documents number in the test collection; and the Pre-Rank is the topics' mean average precision ranking among the 24 topics, the average ranking is 13.5.

The version of HowNet we used in our experiments includes 158849 words.

4.1 Evaluation Method

To determine the accuracy of the methods' retrieval results, we use *average precision*, following the standard in TRECVID evaluations. Let $L^k = \{l_1, l_2, ..., l_k\}$ be a ranked version of the retrieval results set S. At any given rank k let R_k be the number of relevant shots in the top k of L, where R is the total number of relevant shots in a set of size S. Then average precision is defined as:

$$\text{Average Precision} = \frac{1}{R}\sum_{k=1}^{|S|}\frac{R_k}{k}f(l_k) \tag{6}$$

Where function $f(l_k) = 1$ if $l_k \in R$ and 0 otherwise. The average precision favors highly ranked relevant shots.

We use the truths provided by NIST to evaluate our methods. But we found that the truths are only subsets of the whole test collection, and many of the documents returned by our system were not judged for relevance. The same obstacle of evaluation is also encountered by[9]. So we only evaluate the performance of submitted results with relevance judgments.

4.2 Pre-processing

Firstly, we matched the ASR texts with the shots based on the shot temporal boundaries, and expanded the shot boundaries to include up to 3 immediate neighbors on either side to compensate for speech and visual misalignment.

Then we remove the stopwords using the SMART's English stoplist. Additionally, we computed all the terms' document frequency (DF) occurred in the whole collection, and add the terms with highest DF to the user-defined stop word list.

To decrease the matrix total size and to enhance the efficiency, we extract only nouns and verbs. This step can decrease the term dimension from 8410 to 7159.

We also used the Porter's well-established stemming algorithm [8] to unify terms, which allows several forms of a word to be considered as a unique term.

4.3 Primary Results

In our experiment, we realized three runs to compare our method's effect. Where:

Run1: the vector space model(VSM)
Run2: LSI
Run3: lexicon-guided cluster + LSI

The three methods have the same pre-processing. In Run2 the dimension of LSI is 306, and in Run3 the dimensions of three LSI respectively are 206, 206 and 214.

Fig. 1 displays the performance curves for the retrieval average precisions of three methods for 12 topics.

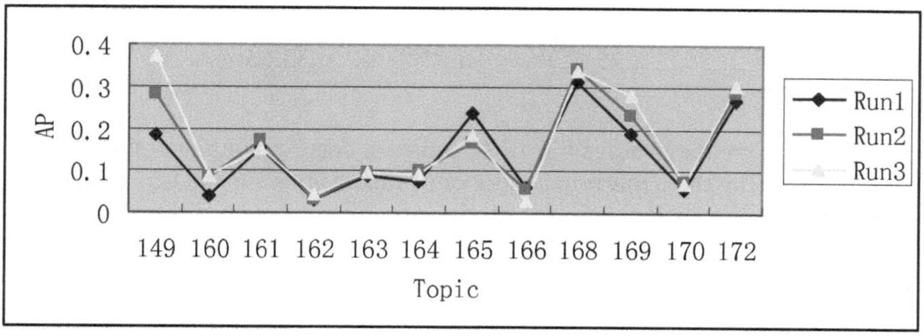

Fig. 1. Average precision of three methods

Table.2 displays the mean average precision(MAP) of the three runs:

Table 2. Evaluation Results in MAP

Runs	Run1	Run2	Run3
MAP	0.141	0.160	0.171

In Run2, we noted that applying LSI in semantic retrieval can increase the performance by about 13.5% than VSM, and Run3 shows that the lexicon-guided semantic cluster can increase the performance by about 6.9% than LSI.

5 Discussion

On the deeper analysis, we find that LSI is designed as a recall enhancing method by expanding the terms in retrieving process. The enhancement can easily find in the second row of Table.3. But the other result of expansion is that there are highly ranked but irrelevant documents in the LSI's result list(Run2 in Top10 is 1.08, and Run1 in Top10 is 1.16). The lexicon-guided semantic cluster can partially alleviate this problem(the Run3 in Top10 is 1.75). But the hits in the top ranking is still too low, and we'll seek some more effective approach to distinguish what should be expanded from what should not be expanded, such as the syntactic or statistically-derived phrases, part of speech parsing, etc.

Table 3. The average hits at depths 10,50,100,300 and 500

	Top10	Top50	Top100	Top300	Top500
Run1	1.16	6.66	11.33	35.83	58.58
Run2	1.08	7.33	15.75	42.91	69.91
Run3	1.75	8.25	16	33.83	36.67

Where the scores are the average hits of 12 topics at corresponding depths.

Besides, choosing the appropriate number of dimensions for the LSI representation is an open research question. In our experiments, we set *k* with different values such as 100, 200, 300, 500, 800 and 1000. We find that the performance improves as *k* increases for a while, and then decreases, and reach the best results on from 200 to 300.

6 Conclusion

In this paper, we proposed a method of using lexicon knowledge to guide the semantic clustering, and using semantic cluster to restrict the LSI's expansion. The experiments show that the proposed approach can improve the retrieval performance significantly. Prior works have proved the validity of the basic LSI in common texts retrieval, and our works further affirmed the validity of the enhanced LSI approach in video's ASR texts retrieval. In the future we'll try to fuse multi-modality video features to a uniform representation space, and to learn the semantic in this space.

References

1. Hollink, L., Nguyen, G.P., Koelma, D.C., Schreiber, A.T., Worring, M.: Assessing user behaviour in news video retrieval. IEE proceedings on Vision, Image and Signal Processing, 911–918 (2005)
2. Neo, S-Y., Zhao, J., Kan, M-Y., Chua, T-S.: Video Retrieval Using High-level features: Exploiting Query-matching and Confidence-based Weighting. In: Sundaram, H., Naphade, M., Smith, J.R., Rui, Y. (eds.) CIVR 2006. LNCS, vol. 4071, Springer, Heidelberg (2006)
3. Souvannavong, F., Merialdo, B., Huet, B.: Latent Semantic Indexing for Semantic Content Dectection of Video Shots. In: ICME 2004, Taipei, Taiwan (June 27th - 30th, 2004)
4. Zhao, R., Grosky, W.I.: From Features to Semantics: Some Preliminary Results. In: ICME 2000, New York, USA (July 30th - August 30th, 2000)
5. Rosario, B.: Latent Semantic Indexing: An overview [A]. INFOSYS 240 (Spring 2000)
6. Berry, M.W.: SVDPACK: A Fortran-77 software libray for the sparse singular value decomposition. Technical Report CS-92-159, University of Tennessee, Knoxville, TN (June 1992)
7. Dong, Z., Dong, Q.: HowNet, http://www.keenage.com/
8. Porter, M.F.: An Algorithm for Suffix Stripping Program, vol. 14, pp. 130–137 (1980)

9. Dumains, S.T.: Latent Semantic Indexing(LSI)and TREC-2[C]. In: Harman, D. (ed.) The Second Text Retrieval Conference(TREC2).National Institute of Standards and Technology Special Publication, pp. 105–116 (1994)
10. Chua, T.-S., Neo, S.-Y., Goh, H.-K., Zhao, M., Xiao, Y., Wang, G.: TRECVID 2005 by NUS PRIS. In: TRECVID 2005, NIST, Gaithersburg, Maryland, USA (November 14-15, 2005)
11. Qun, L., Su-Jian, L.: Computing word similarities based on IqowNet? Computational Linguistics and Chinese Language Processing? 7(2), 59–76 (2002)
12. Cao, J., Li, J., Zhang, Y., Tang, S.: A Novel Method for Spoken Textual Feature Extraction in Semantic Video Retrieval. In: Zhuang, Y., Yang, S., Rui, Y., He, Q. (eds.) PCM 2006. LNCS, vol. 4261, Springer, Heidelberg (2006)
13. Dumais, S.: Latent Semantic Indexing (LSI): TREC-3 Report. In: Harman, D. (ed.) The Third Text Retrieval Conference, National Institute of Standards and Technology Special Publication 500–226, pp. 219–230 (March 1994)
14. Garafolo, A., Voorhees, E.M.: The TREC Spoken Document Retrieval Track: A Success Story. In: Proceedings of the RIAO 2000 Conference: Content-Based Multimedia Information Access, Paris, pp. 1–20 (2000)

3D Tracking of a Soccer Ball Using Two Synchronized Cameras

Norihiro Ishii[1], Itaru Kitahara[2], Yoshinari Kameda[2], and Yuichi Ohta[2]

[1] University of Tsukuba, Graduate School of System and Information Engineering, Tennodai 1-1-1, Tsukuba-shi, Ibaraki, 305-8577, Japan
ishii@image.esys.tsukuba.ac.jp
http://www.image.tsukuba.ac.jp/
[2] {kitahara,kameda,ohta}@iit.tsukuba.ac.jp

Abstract. We propose an adaptive method that can estimate 3D position of a soccer ball by using two viewpoint videos. The 3D position of a ball is essential to realize a 3D free viewpoint browsing system and to analyze of soccer games. At an image processing step, our method detects the ball by selecting the best algorithm based on the ball states so as to minimize the chance to miss the ball and to reduce the computation cost. The 3D position of the ball is then estimated by the estimated 2D positions of the two camera images. When it is impossible to obtain the 3D position due to the loss of the ball in an image, we utilize the Kalman Filter to compensate the missing position information and predict the 3D ball position. We implemented a preliminary system and succeeded in tracking the ball in 3D at almost on-line speed.

1 Introduction

Live broadcasting of sports is considered as one of the promising applications in multimedia literature. Among the various kinds of sports, soccer is one of the most popular sports and it is worth broadcasting and making innovative multimedia content for that. While traditional live broadcasting system is designed to send a video stream that is just taken by cameras, new style of browsing the sports, live 3D video browsing, is going to be in reality. In the 3D video browsing, audience can virtually fly over the soccer field and see the game from any preferred viewpoint.

Kanade et al. have developed a pioneering system for 3D sport browsing, named Eye Vision System[1]. It can produce a video stream in which the camera virtually revolves around a player in focus though viewers cannot choose the player to see in the system. Some of the research works succeeded in providing a true 3D browsing system for games held in a soccer stadium[2][3].

The 3D position of the soccer ball is very important to enjoy watching soccer games, especially in 3D browsing system. This is because audience usually watches the soccer games by chasing the ball. In addition, its 3D position information can contribute to analyze sport scenes and to improve strategies of soccer team.

H.H.S. Ip et al. (Eds.): PCM 2007, LNCS 4810, pp. 196–205, 2007.

However, the 3D position estimation of a ball is not an easy task because it is usually very small in an image and it could be easily lost due to the occlusion caused by players. *D'Orazio et al.* have detected the ball by using the Circle Hough Transform[4]. *Shimawaki et al.* have extracted the candidate balls by using the size and color attributes and then selected the one as the true ball over some frames[5]. *Ren et al.* have tracked a soccer ball using the Kalman Filter and succeeded in obtaining the ball trajectory in a single camera image[6]. But, these methods cannot estimate 3D position of a ball. *Yan et al.* and *Misu et al.* have proposed a ball tracking algorithm by particle filter[7][8]. *Choi et al.* and *Saito et al.* have used the template matching to detect a ball[9][10]. Unfortunately, these methods need much calculation cost to realize the real time detection. *Iizuka et al.* have developed the real time 3D position measurement system[11]. But it needs the large object in a image. In this paper, we propose an efficient ball tracking method that can estimate the 3D position of the soccer ball at almost on-line speed. We use two video images captured simultaneously at two stable cameras. In order to reach the real-time processing speed, the search area of a ball in a video image is narrowed according to ball states and an appropriate image processing method is selected to detect the ball. When the 3D position cannot be estimated because of the lack of the two-view information of the ball, we exploit the Kalman Filter to compensate the missing information and predict the 3D position of the ball.

The rest of the paper is organized as follows. In section 2, we explain our ball detection method at an image processing stage. Then, we discuss the algorithm to narrow the search area of the ball that can contribute to reduce the computation cost in section 3. We exploit the Kalman Filter to estimate the 3D position of the ball even in the case where one of the cameras misses the ball in section 4. We conducted an experiment and showed the efficiency of our proposed method in section 5. Finally, we conclude our paper and discuss future works in section 6.

2 Ball Detection in an Image

Ball detection on a video image is essential to estimate the 3D position of a ball. In this section, we propose a method that can extract a ball region effectively for the most of the time of a soccer game.

2.1 Detection of Moving Objects

In soccer games, a ball is moving for the most of the time. Therefore, we first extract moving objects by frame subtraction operation. Pixel-wise subtraction of two successive images can extract moving object regions. However, the pairwise subtraction of two successive frames ($k-1$ and k) extracts not only moving objects in a current frame but also the one in the previous frame. Hence, we exploit the result of the next frame pair to eliminate the moving object region that belongs to the previous frame. Only the moving object region at the current frame k can survive when we conduct logical AND operation for the subtraction frames of $I_{k-1,k}$ and $I_{k,k+1}$.

2.2 Elimination of Player Regions

The motion object regions detected by the method described in section 2.1 includes both the ball and players. Therefore, player regions must be removed from the regions so as to extract the ball region.

One of the most significant differences between a ball and a player on an image is their size. Therefore, we can eliminate the player regions by setting the threshold of area size appropriately. Unfortunately, however, the motion object regions may be split into small pieces because of the subtraction method. Therefore, we exploit background subtraction method. The background subtraction method can extract relatively large segments and we can obtain player segments by selecting the segments that are larger than a threshold value. Then, the motion object regions that overlap the player segments are eliminated because they are considered to be a part of player regions.

Note that the background subtraction method is useful only when we extract relatively large objects because wide range of intensity threshold can be accepted for that. Since the ball region is usually very small, it is hard to set the intensity threshold appropriately to preserve the ball region in the extracted foreground segments. Our hybrid method can extract the ball regions stably during the soccer game.

Fig.2 shows the image processing steps to extract ball regions. Fig.1(a)is a background image, (b) is an input image, and (c) is the foreground segments. (d) shows the motion object regions obtained by the method of section 2.1. By

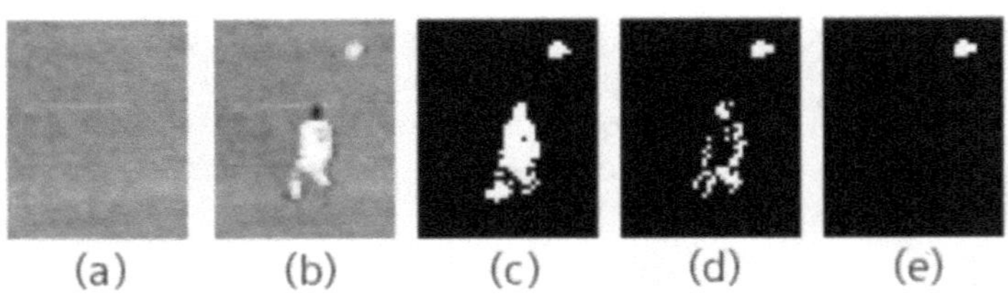

Fig. 1. Extraction of ball region

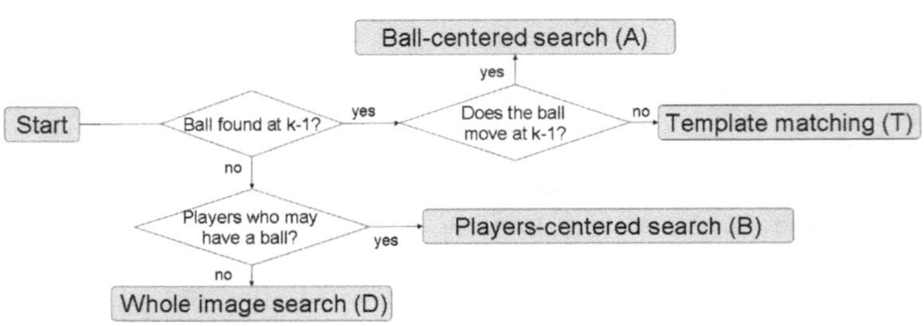

Fig. 2. Selection of Ball Extraction Methods

referring (c), we can remove player regions and obtain ball-like regions shown in (e). We call the extracted regions ball candidates.

2.3 Ball Detection

Since some of the ball candidates are false ball regions due to noise and/or small objects that can be found around the soccer field, we need one more step to remove those false candidates. We count for the speed of the soccer ball to remove false candidates.

Suppose the maximum speed of soccer ball is 100km/h, the diameter of the ball is 22cm, and the frame rate of our video system is 30fps. Then, the ball goes for 90cm at one frame interval. That means the ball movement for one frame is within the several times of the apparent size of the ball in an image. We denote the maximum distance on an image as R.

The elimination algorithm is as follows. Suppose the current frame is k. First, the ball candidates of frame k that have at least one ball candidate of frame $k-1$ within the maximum distance R are selected. If more than one ball candidates are selected, we then examine whether the selected ball candidates of frame $k-1$ have at least one corresponding ball candidates at frame $k-2$ or not within R. We repeat this process until only one ball candidate remains. The remained ball candidate is considered to be the true ball region.

3 Selection of Ball Extraction Methods

The disadvantage of the ball detection method described in section 2 is the computation cost because it requires both the frame subtraction process and background subtraction process. It also has the other disadvantage that it works well only when the ball is moving though the ball is moving for the most of the time in a game.

In order to diminish these two disadvantages, we propose to reduce the search area as much as possible and to exploit a template matching method if the ball is considered to move very slowly or stops. The selection algorithm of the ball extraction methods is shown in Fig.2. Suppose the current frame is k. If the ball is found at $m_{k-1} = (u_{k-1}, v_{k-1})$ at frame $k-1$, it means the ball should be observed within the distance R from m_{k-1}. We choose the proposed method (A) if the ball is moving, otherwise we use a template matching method (T).

If the ball has been already lost at frame $k-1$, we find all the possible players who may hold the ball and set the search area around them (B). If there are no players around the location where the ball is observed for the last time, we conduct the whole image search (C) though it consumes computation cost.

(A) Ball-Centered Search

When the ball is detected in frame $k-1$, the search area in frame k can be narrowed within a circle the center of which is m_{k-1} and its radius is R.

(T) Template Matching

When the ball speed is considered to be very slow, the method proposed in section 2 may not succeed in finding the ball region because the frame subtraction may not extract the ball region as motion object regions. Therefore, in this case, the template matching is employed in the same search area of (A). The ball region extracted at frame $k-1$ is used as the template.

(B) Players-Centered Search

When the ball is detected in frame $k-2$ (or before) and is lost in frame $k-1$, we can say that one of the players (at $p_{s,k-1}$) who were close to m_{k-2} should have the ball in frame $k-1$, and then one of the players (at $p_{t,k}$) who are close to one of $p_{s,k-1}$ probably hides or keeps the ball. In this case, the search area in frame k can be narrowed to the area of multiple circles. The center of each circle is the location of a player who stands within the distance R from $p_{s,k-1}$ and the radius of the circle is R. As there may be several players within R from $p_{s,k-1}$, the search area should include all the corresponding circles. Fig.3 shows the search area of players-centered search in frame k. Circle 1 is defined by the player (not shown in the image) who stood within the distance R from m_{k-2}. The center of the circle 1 can be denoted as $p_{s,k-1}$. Then the search area in frame k is the circles 2I and 2J that are defined by the players $P_{i,k}$ and $P_{j,k}$ because they are found within circle 1.

(C) Whole Image Search

When there are no players around the location where the ball is observed for the last time, it means the ball has disappeared by some reasons. Hence the search area is the whole image in this case.

4 3D Tracking by the Kalman Filter

When the ball positions for the both cameras are estimated, its 3D position can be easily calculated by a wide baseline stereo method (Fig.4). Unfortunately, we

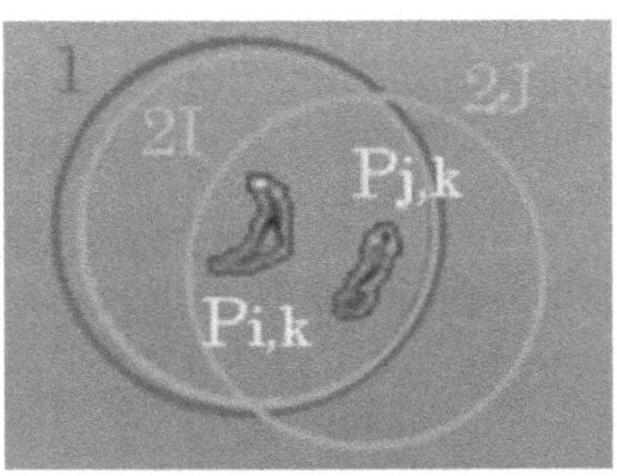

Fig. 3. Players-Centered Search

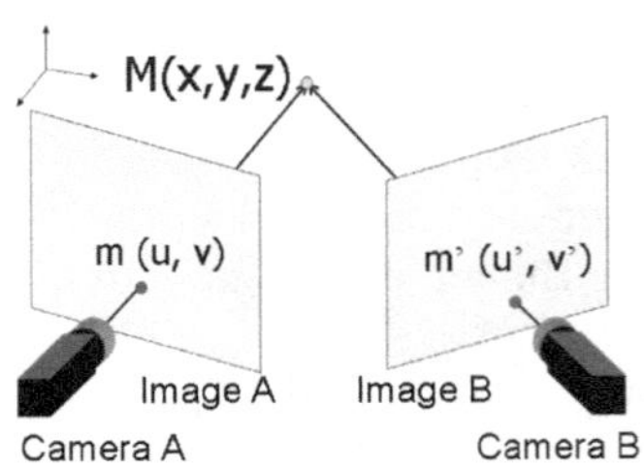

Fig. 4. Estimation of ball position in 3D

cannot expect to detect the ball regions for the both cameras for every frame due to some occlusions or overlaps with players, and some noise also matters.

We model the ball motion model three dimensionally and exploit the Kalman Filter to compensate the status of the ball-missing frame. Since our method aims to build up on-line system that broadcasts the real soccer game in virtual fashion[2], we need to exploit a deterministic method that can uniquely estimate the ball position. Hence we use the Kalman-Filter which costs small calculation and is deterministic, and we avoid the Particle-Filter[9][10] for that reason. Note that we assume the cameras are calibrated in advance and they are synchronized.

4.1 The Prediction of 3D Ball Position

Let us denote the state vector $\mathbf{X}_k$ as the 3D position, the velocity, and the acceleration of the ball at frame k and the measurement vector $\mathbf{Y}_k$ as the 3D position calculated according to the two ball regions on the two camera images. $\mathbf{X}_k$ and $\mathbf{Y}_k$ are defined by:

$$\mathbf{X}_k = [x_k, y_k, z_k, \dot{x}_k, \dot{y}_k, \dot{z}_k, \ddot{x}_k, \ddot{y}_k, \ddot{z}_k]^T \tag{1}$$

$$\mathbf{Y}_k = [p_k, q_k, r_k]^T \tag{2}$$

Where (x_k, y_k, z_k) and (p_k, q_k, r_k) are the 3D position vector in the soccer field. The transition equation and the observation equation are:

$$\mathbf{X}_{k+1} = A\mathbf{X}_k + \gamma \tag{3}$$

$$\mathbf{Y}_k = C\mathbf{X}_k + \omega \tag{4}$$

Where A is the state transition matrix, C is the measurement matrix, and γ and ω are the process noise and measurement noise that are modeled by the Gaussian distribution. We assume horizontal velocity and the vertical acceleration as constant. Therefore, A and C are given by:

$$A = \begin{bmatrix} 1 & 0 & 0 & \delta_t & 0 & 0 & 0 & 0 & 0 \\ 0 & 1 & 0 & 0 & \delta_t & 0 & 0 & 0 & 0 \\ 0 & 0 & 1 & 0 & 0 & \delta_t & 0 & 0 & 0 \\ 0 & 0 & 0 & 1 & 0 & 0 & 0 & 0 & 0 \\ 0 & 0 & 0 & 0 & 1 & 0 & 0 & 0 & 0 \\ 0 & 0 & 0 & 0 & 0 & 1 & 0 & 0 & \delta_t \\ 0 & 0 & 0 & 0 & 0 & 0 & 0 & 0 & 0 \\ 0 & 0 & 0 & 0 & 0 & 0 & 0 & 0 & 0 \\ 0 & 0 & 0 & 0 & 0 & 0 & 0 & 0 & 1 \end{bmatrix} \quad C = \begin{bmatrix} 1 & 0 & 0 & 0 & 0 & 0 & 0 & 0 & 0 \\ 0 & 1 & 0 & 0 & 0 & 0 & 0 & 0 & 0 \\ 0 & 0 & 1 & 0 & 0 & 0 & 0 & 0 & 0 \end{bmatrix} \tag{5}$$

Where δ is the interval between two successive frames. When the 3D position of the ball cannot be obtained because of the failure of ball detection in any of the two cameras, we compensate it with the predicted vector by the Kalman Filter. If the prediction of vertical position component is negative, it is regarded as a bounce and the vertical component value is changed to satisfy the complete elastic collision on the ground.

5 Experiment

5.1 Image Acquisition

We set up video cameras for taking images of soccer scene in the national Kasumigaoka stadium of Japan. As shown Fig.5, half of the field can be captured by camera A and camera B. We use two NTSC cameras (SONY DXC-9000). The cameras are synchronized by GPS signals. The size of the captured image is 640x480 and the frame rate is 30 fps. We implement the proposed method and run it on the PC that has Intel(R) Core(TM)2 CPU and 2,048 MB memory with Vine Linux 4.1.

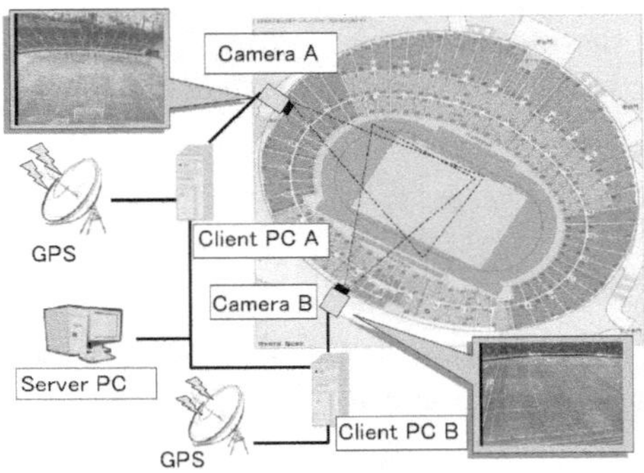

Fig. 5. Image Acquisition

Fig. 6. Camera (SONY DXC-9000)

5.2 The Ball Detection Result

We took short videos in 4 scenes during the games of the inter-university championship of Japan. Fig.7 shows the estimated trajectories of the ball. The result of image processing step is shown in Table.1. f_{total} indicates the total frames in each scene. $f_{visible}$ indicates frames in which the ball is visible. Our method successfully detected the ball for $f_{success}$ frames. The result shows our method detects the ball for more than 80% of frames.

The method failed to detect the ball for some situations. The method missed the ball for $f_{failure1}$ frames though it is visible, and it incorrectly estimated the position of the ball in the images for $f_{failure2}$ frames. it also incorrectly reported the detection of ball for $f_{failure3}$ frames in which the ball is invisible. Our method can not detect the ball when a part of player is recognized as a ball. It also fails if its speed is very slow when the ball comes to be visible.

When the ball was invisible or involved in player regions, the system tried to detect the ball with the (C) players-centered search because several players were often found around the ball. Note that the ball detection is impossible when the ball visibility is no, if any of the cameras was in this status, we need the Kalman Filter step to compensate the 3D position of the ball.

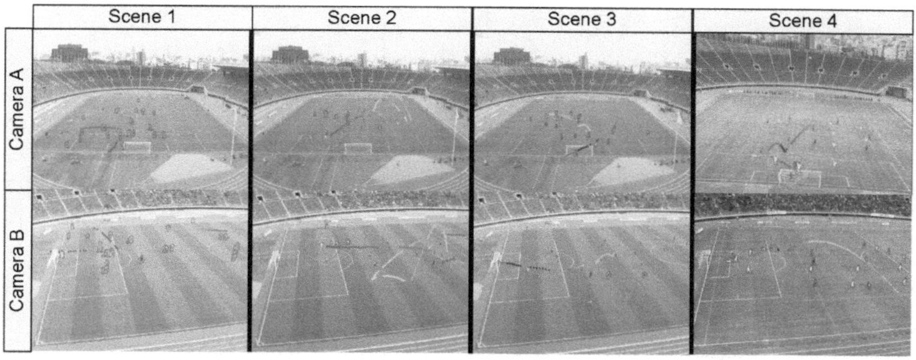

Fig. 7. Trajectory of detected ball

Table 1. Ball detection result

	Camera A				Camera B			
Scene	Scene 1	Scene 2	Scene 3	Scene 4	Scene 1	Scene 2	Scene 3	Scene 4
f_{total}	350	430	300	217	350	430	300	217
$f_{visible}$	74	195	79	101	67	253	79	116
$f_{success}$	73	171	76	101	54	224	71	116
$f_{failure1}$	0	24	3	0	13	29	7	0
$f_{failure2}$	1	0	0	0	0	0	1	0
$f_{failure3}$	0	1	2	0	0	1	1	0

The average time of the ball detection methods are shown in Table.2. Note that we succeeded in speeding up the ball detection for 8.5 (A) and 2.1 (B) times faster than the normal whole image search (C). As the frame interval for NTSC video is 33.3 [m-sec], we can say that our method can sufficiently achieve the real-time speed.

5.3 3D Position Estimation of the Ball

We calculated the 3D ball positon from the above results. The blue small squares in Fig.8, Fig.9, and Fig.10 show the calculation result of the 3D position in

Table 2. Average time and frequencey of the ball detection methods

The method	Average time [m-sec]	Frequency [%]
(A) Ball-Centered Search	3.08	29.6
(T) Template Matching	10.49	2.1
(B) Players-Centered Search	12.49	35.1
(C) Whole Image Search	26.17	33.2

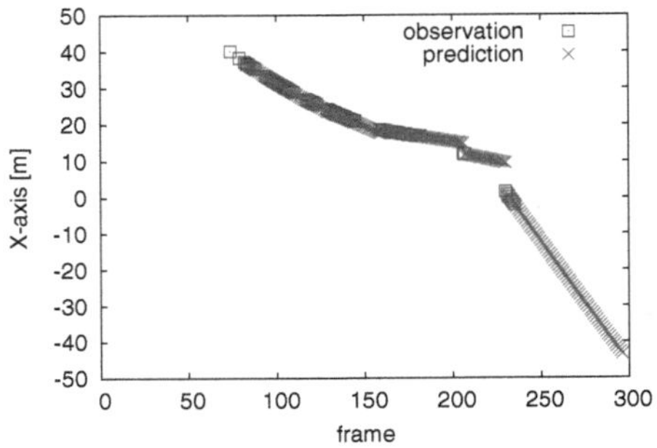

Fig. 8. X-axis

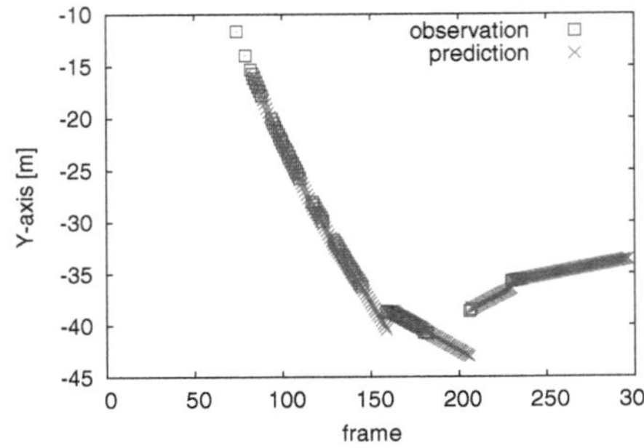

Fig. 9. Y-axis

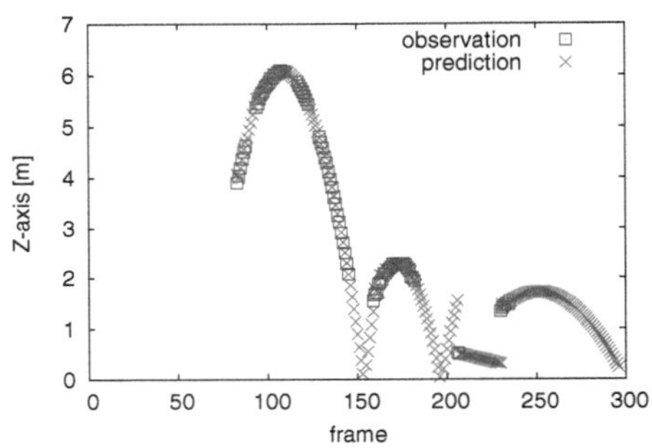

Fig. 10. Z-axis

Fig. 11. Plot of 3D position of the ball

scene 4. Each figure shows the result of 3D position in X, Y (horizontal), and Z (vertical) axis respectively. We utilized the Kalman Filter to estimate the 3D position of the ball for the frames at which the ball position cannot be directly calculated because of the failure of the ball detection in the two cameras. The results are shown in red crosses in the same figures. The estimation was acceptable for the most of the video sequence. However, in the sequence from frame 200 to frame 230, the prediction was failed due to the insufficient number of frames for observation. Fig.11 shows the 3D plot of the ball trajectory. The white ball indicates the directly calculated positions and the red wire ball indicates the estimated position given by the Kalman filter.

6 Conclusion

We propose an adaptive method that can estimate 3D position of a soccer ball by using two viewpoint videos. At an image processing step, our method can detect the ball by selecting the best algorithm based on the ball states so as to minimize the chance to miss the ball. The 3D position of the ball is then calculated with the estimated 2D positions of the two camera images. We utilize the Kalman Filter to estimate the 3D ball position even when the ball was lost on the image processing step.

Since the ball cannot be detected when the ball is in front of the players in the proposed method, the ball detection method could be improved. Experiments for long video sequence are also needed to verify our proposed method.

References

1. `http://www.ri.cmu.edu/events/sb35/tksuperbowl.htm`
2. Koyama, T., Kitahara, I., Ohta, Y.: Live Mixed-Reality 3D Video in Soccer Stadium. ISMAR, 178–187 (2003)
3. Hayashi, K., Saito, H.: Synthesizing Free-Viewpoint Images from Multiple View Videos in Soccer Stadium. In: IEEE International Conference on Computer Graphics, Imaging and Visualisation 26-28, pp. 220–225 (2006)
4. D'Orazio, T., Ancona, N., Cicirelli, G., Nitti, M.: A Ball Detection Algorithm for Real Soccer Image Sequences. In: 16th International Conference on Pattern Recognition, vol. 1 (2002)
5. Shimawaki, T., Miura, J., Sakiyama, T., Shirai, Y.: Ball Route Estimation in Broadcast Soccer Video. In: Leonardis, A., Bischof, H., Pinz, A. (eds.) ECCV 2006. LNCS, vol. 3954, pp. 26–37. Springer, Heidelberg (2006)
6. Ren, J., Orwell, J., Jones, G.: Generating Ball Trajectory in Soccer Video Sequences. ECCV on Computer Vision Based Analysis in Sport Environments (2006)
7. Yan, F., Christmas, W., Kittler, J.: A Tennis Ball Tracking Algorithm for Automatic Annotation of Tennis Match. In: BMVC 2005. Proceedings of the British Machine Vision Conference, pp. 619–628 (2005)
8. Misu, T., Matsui, A., Naemura, M., Fujii, M., Yahi, N.: Distributed Particle Filtering For Mutiocular Soccer-ball Tracking. In: ICASSP. Distributed and Cooperative Adaptive Processing (2007)
9. Choi, S., Seo, Y., Kim, H., Hong, K.: Where are the ball and players?:Soccer Games Analysis with Color-based Tracking and Image Mosaik. In: Proc. of ICIAP, pp. 196–203 (1997)
10. Matsumoto, K., Sudo, S., Saito, H., Ozawa, S.: Optimized Camera Viewpoint Determination System for Soccer Game Broadcasting. In: IAPR. Workshop on Machine Vision Applications, pp. 115–118 (2000)
11. Iizuka, T., Nakamura, T., Wada, T.: Real Time 3-D Position Measurement System Using a Stereo Camera. In: MIRU 2004. Proceedings I, pp. 111–112 (2004)(Japan)

Object Tracking Based on Parzen Particle Filter Using Multiple Cues

Lei Song, Rong Zhang, Zhengkai Liu, and Xingxing Chen

MOE-Microsoft Key laboratory of Multimedia Computing and Communication
Department of Electronic Engineering and Information Science
University of Science and Technology of China
230027 HeFei, P.R. China
polosong@mail.ustc.edu.cn, {zrong, zhengkai}@ustc.edu.cn,
chenstar@mail.ustc.edu.cn

Abstract. Particle filtering provides a general framework for propagating probability density functions in non-linear and non-Gaussian systems. However, generic particle filter (GPF) is based on Monte Carlo approach and sampling is a problematic issue. This paper introduces a parzen particle filter (PPF) which uses a general kernel approach to better approximate the posterior distribution rather than Dirac delta kernel in GPF. Furthermore, we adopt multiple cues and combine texture described by directional energy from multi-scale, multi-orientation steerable filtering with color to characterize our tracking targets. The advantages of tracking with multiple cues compared to individual ones are demonstrated over experiments on artificial and natural sequences.

Keywords: object tracking, parzen particle filter, steerable pyramid.

1 Introduction

Object tracking is required in many vision applications such as human-computer interface, video communication, traffic control, security and surveillance systems, etc. Often the goal is to obtain a record of the trajectory of single or multiple moving targets over time and space. Object tracking in video sequences is a challenging task because of changing appearances, non-rigid motion, dynamic illumination, etc. Moreover, most of the models encountered in visual tracking are nonlinear, non-Gaussian, multi-modal or any combination of these. Much work has been done in the object tracking area. Comaniciu in [1] modeled the object by a kernel density estimation of the target's color region then the tracking problem is solved by mean shift procedure [2][3], this algorithm has an advantage due to its small computational cost and can handle some occlusions, however it generally cannot recover from a failure. Probabilistic trackers based on Kalman filtering are introduced to improve on this problem [4], but these methods can only model unimodal probability distribution. To address this weakness, Isard [5] develops an algorithm based on particle filter which can solve non-linear and non-Gaussian state estimation problems, but as sampling times increase, the algorithm fails to represent the posterior distributions of

H.H.S. Ip et al. (Eds.): PCM 2007, LNCS 4810, pp. 206–215, 2007.

interest adequately. Recently many variations of particle filter have been proposed. UPF [6] (Unscented Particle Filter) relies on UKF [7] (Unscented Kalman Filter) to produce the importance distribution. Rao-Blackwellis particle filter [8] which can be interpreted as an efficient stochastic mixture of Kalman filters effectively debases the dimension of sampling space. Under the assumption that the process noise distribution can be approximated by a mixture of Gaussians, the family of Gaussian sum particle filters [9] arises.

In this paper, we introduce parzen density estimator into GPF and adopt a general kernel approach to replace Dirac delta kernel, through which the posterior distribution approximation can be improved without increasing the number of the particles. Furthermore, we adopt multiple cues to characterize our tracking targets. Traditional object tracking methods rely on a single cue, for example, color; and their greatest weakness is the ambiguity in scenes with objects or regions whose color features are similar to those of the object of interest. So far, texture cues have not been widely used for video based tracking. Based on steerable pyramid decomposition, we obtain the texture cue actually directional energy of the tracking targets. Combining the texture with the color cue, the tracking performance gets better than individual ones.

The paper is organized as follows. Section 2 states the GPF and the PPF. Section 3 introduces multiple cues to be used for tracking, color and texture. In Section 4 the filters' performance is investigated and validated over different scenarios. We will show the advantage of tracking using combined cues compared to single ones on artificial and natural video sequences. Our conclusions are briefly drawn in Section 5.

2 Generic Particle Filter and Parzen Particle Filter

2.1 Generic Particle Filter

Generally the filtering problem can be simply formulated as:

$$x_k = f(x_{k-1}) + v_{k-1} \tag{1}$$

$$z_k = h(x_k) + w_k \tag{2}$$

where x_k is state vector and z_k is observation vector, v_k , w_k are i.i.d process noise and observation noise. Due to Bayesian formula we have:

$$p(x_k \mid z_{1:k-1}) = \int p(x_k \mid x_{k-1}) p(x_{k-1} \mid z_{1:k-1}) dx_{k-1} \tag{3}$$

$$p(x_k \mid z_{1:k}) = p(z_k \mid x_k) p(x_k \mid z_{1:k-1}) / p(z_k \mid z_{1:k-1}) \tag{4}$$

$$\text{where } p(z_k \mid z_{1:k-1}) = \int p(z_k \mid x_k) p(x_k \mid z_{1:k-1}) dx_k \tag{5}$$

(3) and (4) constitute the Bayesian optimum solution, but the integral can not be calculated analytically, hence we need some way of estimating the distribution

$p(x_k \mid z_{1:k-1})$. Based on Monte Carlo methods, we can independently sample N samples: $\{x_{0:k}^i; i=1,2\cdots,N\}$ from the importance distribution function: $q(x_k^i \mid x_{0:k-1}^i, z_{1:k})$, then the distribution can be estimated as:

$$p(x_{0:k} \mid z_{1:k}) = \sum_{i=1}^{N} \tilde{\omega}_k^i \delta(x_{0:k} - x_{0:k}^i) \tag{6}$$

where $\tilde{\omega}_k^i = \omega_k^i / \sum_{i=1}^{N} \omega_k^i$, $\omega_k^i = \omega_{k-1}^i \, p(z_k \mid x_k^i) p(x_k^i \mid x_{k-1}^i) / q(x_k^i \mid x_{0:k-1}^i, z_{1:k})$ (7)

Generally, the generic particle filtering is composed of three steps: sampling, weighting and re-sampling. The re-sampling step is crucial in the implementation of particle filtering because without it, the variance of the particle weights quickly increases, i.e., very few normalized weights are substantial.

2.2 Parzen Particle Filter

As described above in section 2.1, the re-sampling step in GPF is crucial and problematic. Yet it is a posterior distribution approximation and propagation problem essentially. In GPF Dirac delta kernel is utilized to estimate the probability density function. The basic concept to improve GPF is using a better density estimate. With a parzen density estimator [10] a distribution can be approximated arbitrarily close by a number of identical kernels centered on points chosen from the distribution. So we can replace Dirac delta kernels with general ones such as the Gaussian kernels [11].

From (1) the state transition density $p(x_k \mid x_{k-1})$ is fully specified as:

$$p(x_k \mid x_{k-1}) = p_v(x_k - f(x_{k-1})) \tag{8}$$

Based on the kernel representation equation, (3) can be written as:

$$p(x_k \mid z_{1:k-1}) = \sum_{i}^{N} \omega_{k-1}^i \int p_v(x_k - f(x_{k-1})) K(A_{k-1}^i (x_{k-1} - x_{k-1}^i)) dx_{k-1} \tag{9}$$

where A^i is a transformation matrix used to keep track of distortions of the kernel. Each kernel can be propagated through the mapping $p(x_k \mid x_{k-1})$ by using a local linearization. All kernels in (9) are assumed that they are small compared to the dynamic in the non-linearity such that f can be locally linearized. The Jacobian $J|_{x_{k-1}^i} = \frac{\partial f}{\partial x}|_{x_{k-1}^i}$ is obtained by linearizing f around x_{k-1}^i, $A_k^i = A_{k-1}^i J|_{x_{k-1}^i}^{-1}$. Then the following change of variables can be employed:

$$\hat{x}_{k-1} = x_k - f(x_{k-1}^i) - J|_{x_{k-1}^i} (x_{k-1} - x_{k-1}^i) \tag{10}$$

Inserting (10) in the integral from equation (9) yields:

$$|J|_{x_{k-1}^i}|^{-1}\int p_v(\hat{x}_{k-1})K(A_{k-1}^i J|_{x_{k-1}^i}^{-1}(x_k - f(x_{k-1}^i) - \hat{x}_{k-1}))d\hat{x}_{k-1} \quad (11)$$

(11) is an expectation over p_v, it can be approximated by a sample mean. In the extreme case a single sample drawn from p_v can be used:

$$E_{p_v}[K(A_{k-1}^i J|_{x_{k-1}^i}^{-1}(x_k - f(x_{k-1}^i) - \hat{x}_{k-1}))] \approx K(A_{k-1}^i J|_{x_{k-1}^i}^{-1}(x_k - f(x_{k-1}^i) - v_{k-1})) \quad (12)$$

So for a given particle set $\{(x_k^i, \omega_k^i)_{i=1,2,\cdots,N}\}$, we can get:

$$p(x_k \mid z_{1:k}) = \sum_i^N \omega_k^i K(A_k^i(x_k - x_k^i)) \quad (13)$$

Due to (3), (4), (9) and (11), the weights update can be obtained as follow:

$$\omega_k^i = \omega_{k-1}^i p(z_k \mid x_k^i) | J|_{x_{k-1}^i}|^{-1} \quad (14)$$

For a Gaussian kernel, the transformation matrix can use the covariance matrix. So the update of the transformation matrix A_k^i can be replaced with an update of the covariance matrix as follows:

$$\sum{}_k^i = J|_{x_{k-1}^i} \sum{}_{k-1}^i J|_{x_{k-1}^i}^T \quad (15)$$

The approximation of the stochastic integral based on Gaussian kernel using particles includes an inherent re-sampling step at each iteration, which allows the particle filter accuracy to survive longer than the standard version and a further advantage is that the density estimate becomes continuous and hence improves the particle posterior distribution without increasing the number of the particles.

3 Target Representation Using Multiple Cues

To characterize the target, first a feature space should be chosen. In this paper, we use both color and texture features to describe the target. Assuming the features being used as cues are independent, the overall likelihood is a product of the likelihoods of the separate cues, in our case color and texture, as shown below:

$$w(z_k \mid x_k) = w_{color}(z_{color,k} \mid x_k) w_{texture}(z_{texture,k} \mid x_k) \quad (16)$$

where z_k denotes the measurement vector, composed by $z_{color,k}$ from the color cue and $z_{texture,k}$ from the texture cue. Sections 3.1 and 3.2 will give more details for the particular cues considered.

3.1 Color Cue

The color likelihood model has to be defined in a way to favor candidate color histograms close to the reference histogram. The histogram $h_x^c = (h_{1,x}^c, \cdots, h_{N,x}^c)$, for a region R_x corresponding to state x is given by:

$$h_{i,x}^c = C_N \sum_{u \in R_x} \delta_i(b_u^c), i = 1, 2 \cdots, N \tag{17}$$

where $b_u^c \in \{1, 2 \cdots, N\}$ is the histogram bin index associated with the intensity at pixel $u = (x, y)$ in channel c of the color image and C_N is a normalizing constant such that $\sum_{i=1}^{N} h_{i,x}^c = 1$.

A distance metric which is appropriate to make decisions about the closeness of two histograms $\hat{h}_1$ and $\hat{h}_2$ is the Bhattacharyya similarity distance [1]:

$$d(\hat{h}_1, \hat{h}_2) = \sqrt{1 - \rho(\hat{h}_1, \hat{h}_2)} = \sqrt{1 - \sum_{i=1}^{m} \sqrt{\hat{h}_{1,i} \hat{h}_{2,i}}} \tag{18}$$

where $\rho(\hat{h}_1, \hat{h}_2)$ is the Bhattacharyya coefficient. The larger the coefficient $\rho(\hat{h}_1, \hat{h}_2)$ is, the more similar the distributions are. Based on this distance, the color likelihood model can be defined as:

$$w_{color}(z_{color} \mid x) \propto \exp(-\sum_{c \in \{r,g,b\}} d^2(h_x^c, h_{ref}^c) / 2\sigma_c^2) \tag{19}$$

where the standard deviation σ_c specifies the Gaussian noise in the measurements, h_x^c is the current histogram of the target, and h_{ref}^c is the reference histogram. Small Bhattacharyya distances correspond to large weights in particle filter.

3.2 Texture Cue

Texture is an appealing feature to be used as a basis for an observation model because of its intuitive definition. Although there is no unique definition of texture, it is generally agreed that texture describes the spatial arrangements of pixel levels in an image, which may be stochastic or periodic, or both. Wavelet transform has been widely used in texture analysis; however it is sensitive to both translation and rotation of the signal. Steerable pyramid is a multi-scale, multi-orientation image decomposition method and has a translation and rotation invariant property. In video sequences objects especially non-rigid objects often change their appearances or sometimes rotate, so we introduce the steerable pyramid for texture analysis and show how it improves the tracking performance in later experiments.

The concept of steerable filter is first proposed by William T. Freeman [12]. It describes a class of filters in which a filter of arbitrary orientation can be synthesized as a linear combination of a set of "basis filters" (Figure 1 displays the steerable filter architecture). Moreover, it may be designed in quadrature pairs to allow adaptive control over phase as well as orientation.

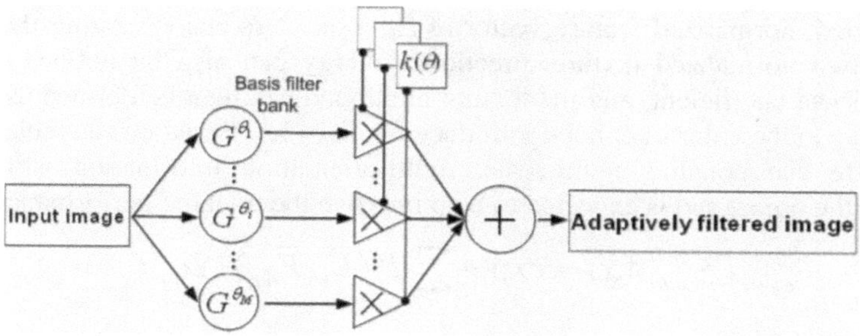

Fig. 1. Steerable filter architecture

$$G^{\theta}(x,y) = \sum_{i=1}^{M} k_i(\theta) G^{\theta_i}(x,y) \tag{20}$$

Figure 1 and (20) explain how to construct an oriented filter. $G^{\theta_i}(x,y)$ is basis filter, $k_i(\theta)$ is interpolation function and $G^{\theta}(x,y)$ is the synthesized filter oriented along direction θ. For more details about the design of steerable filter, you can refer to [12]. Next we will describe the steerable filter used in our later experiments.

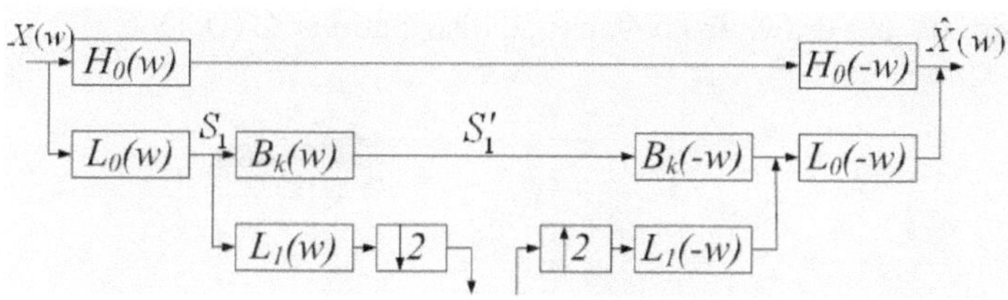

Fig. 2. Steerable pyramid structure

Figure 2 is the steerable pyramid's structure, $H(w)$, $L(w)$ and $B_k(w)$ are respectively high-pass, low-pass and oriented band-pass filter; S_i is the output image of $L(w)$ and S_i' is sub-band images obtained through oriented filtering. We construct a 3-layer steerable pyramid, there are 4 oriented band-pass filters along 0°, 45°, 90° and 135° each layer. Then for each S_i we calculate the energy along the above 4 directions:

$$E_{ij} = \frac{1}{M_i \times N_i} \sum_{x=1}^{M_i} \sum_{y=1}^{N_i} (| S_i(x,y) * G_j(x,y) |^2 + | S_i(x,y) * H_j(x,y) |^2) \tag{21}$$

where $i = 1,2,3$; $j = 1,2,3,4$; and G_j represents the four oriented filters. H_j is G_j's Hilbert transform. The texture of the region using this scheme is represented by directional energy vector with 12 elements: $E=\{E_{11},E_{12}\cdots;E_{ij,}\cdots;E_{34}\}$. We notate the mean-shifted, normalized feature vector as $\overline{E}$, a measure characterizing the distance between two normalized texture directional energy can also be defined using the Bhattacharyya coefficient, and the texture likelihood can then be defined as (22) in a similar way to the color likelihood introduced in Sect 3.1. Based on steerable filtering, our texture cue contains multi-scale, multi-orientation information which better describes the object and is expected to help improve the tracking performance.

$$w_{texture}(z_{texture} \mid x) \propto \exp(-\sum d^2(\overline{E}_x, \overline{E}_{ref})/2\sigma_t^2) \qquad (22)$$

4 Experiments

4.1 Simulation on One Dimensional Problem

In this section, the performance of PPF is compared with that of GPF based upon a one dimensional problem:

$$x_k = 0.5x_{k-1} + 25\, x_{k-1}/(1+x_{k-1}^2) + 8\cos(1.2k) + v_k \qquad (23)$$

$$z_k = 10\arctan(0.1x_k) + w_k \qquad (24)$$

where v_k and w_k are drawn from Gaussian distributions $G(0,1)$.

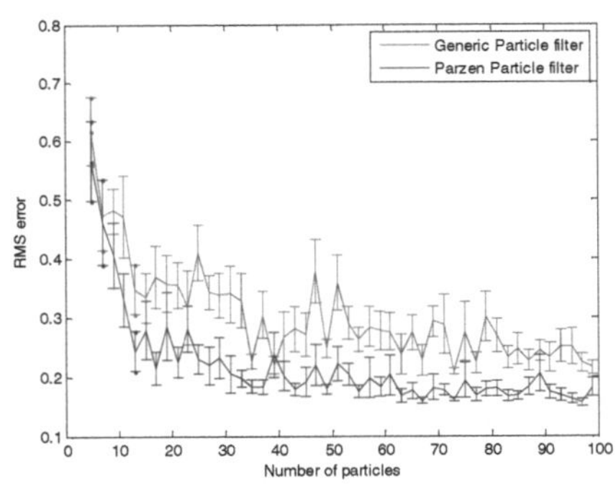

Fig. 3. Performance of PPF and GPF on one dimensional problem

In figure 3 above, the root mean square error (RMSE) is plotted as a function of the number of particles. It can be seen that with few particles the two filters perform equally good (or bad), but as the number of particles increases the PPF show its advantage. Note that the RMSE of PPF with about 24 particles equals to that of GPF with about 50 particles, PPF can drastically reduce the number of particles by improving the particle posterior distribution.

4.2 Object Tracking Tests with Artificial and Natural Sequences

To demonstrate the effectiveness of methods we proposed, experiments of PPF and GPF based object tracking will be carried out on artificial and natural sequences separately. In all these experiments, the target is initialized in a rectangular manually and a random walk is assumed for the object motion model. To tackle self-occlusion of the tracked objects, the feature vector representing the tracked object should be updated over time: $F_{next} = (1-\alpha)F_{prev} + \alpha F_{cur}$, where $\alpha \sim (0,1)$ (we set 0.6) weighs the contribution of the current state feature vector F_{cur}, and F_{prev}, F_{next} represent the target's reference feature vector of previous and next frame (F refers to histogram h and directional energy $\overline{E}$ for color and texture cues respectively).

4.2.1 Artificial Sequences

To intuitively evaluate the performance of the color, texture and combined color and texture cues, the tests are carried out on artificial sequences with known object motion.

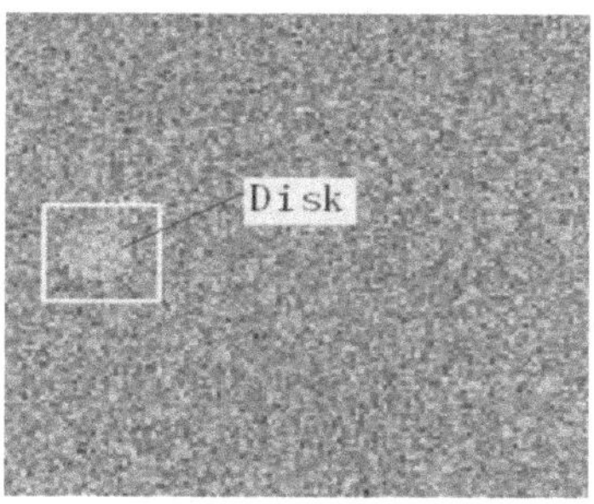

(a)

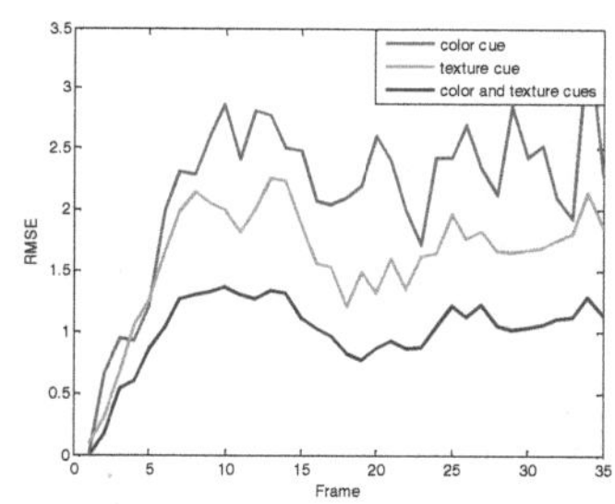

(b)

Fig. 4. (a) 'disk' for tracking (b) RMSE for color, texture and combined cues

Figure 4(a) shows the 'disk' for tracking, a 10 pixels radius circle. The sequences are artificially synthesized that the target disk has its own special texture and is a little brighter compared with the background. As we know the correct location of the target object (x_i, y_i) in each frame and n is the number of realizations, the RMSE at a given frame is:

$$RMSE = \sqrt{\frac{1}{n}\sum_{i=1}^{n}((x_i - \tilde{x}_i)^2 + (y_i - \tilde{y}_i)^2)} \tag{25}$$

The results of tests with individual cue and combined cues are presented in figure 4(b) according to RMSE over 35 frames. It can be seen that the color (gray) cue tracks the disk with a much lower degree of accuracy than texture or combined cues. Texture provides good tracking results, however tracking with combined cues is more accurate and robust.

4.2.2 Natural Sequences

Our natural sequences are video sequences from part of a basketball match. we construct our experiments as follows: i) GPF with color cue only, ii) GPF with combined cues and iii) PPF with combined cues.

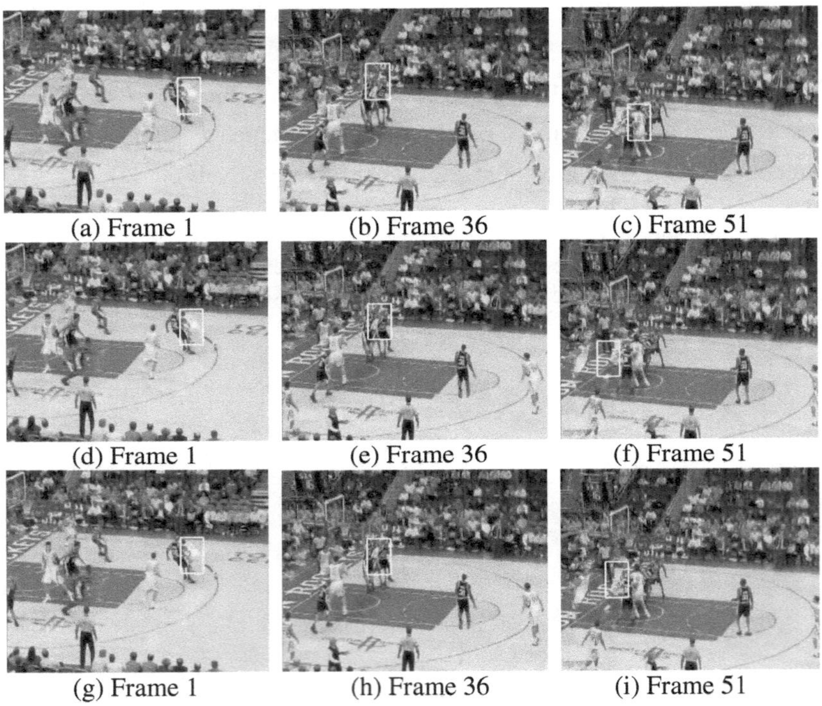

Fig. 5. Tracking a basketball player (in yellow rectangular): Figures (a)-(c) are based on GPF with color cue only, (d)-(f) GPF with combined cues and (g)-(i) PPF with combined cues

There are mainly two difficulties for tracking in these sequences: little camera induced motion and confusion from teammates or audiences near the floor. The impact of camera induced motion is partially debased due to feature vector update model and motion model described at the beginning of section 4.2, while the confusion avoidance depends highly on the cues characterizing the target.

Displayed in figure 5, a basketball player dressed in white (in yellow rectangular) is tracked on the floor. By GPF with only color cues we could not track the player accurately, as is demonstrated by figure 5(b), at 5(c) even the player is lost. At frame 51, the color distribution nearby the target player is almost similar to that of itself, so color cue only could not handle it. With combined cues of both color and texture, the tracking results are generally good. From figure 5(d) to 5(i) we can see GPF nearly performs as well as PPF except for a little drift away from the target at figure 5(f), however PPF uses fewer particles than GPF, according to our experiments, one would need to run the GPF using about 300 particles to obtain a comparable result with PPF using 100 samples.

5 Conclusions

This paper has presented a parzen particle filter using multiple cues for object tracking. The PPF is based on parzen density estimates and particle filter like propagation of the kernel through local linearization of the nonlinear function. Demonstrated though the experiments, PPF can drastically reduce the number of particles while get more robust results compared to GPF. The advantages of combined color and texture cues compared with individual ones are improved accuracy and robustness. Though only color and texture are the cues described here, other possible cues such as edges and illumination can be introduced too. In this paper only the Gaussian kernel is examined, however it is expected that other kernels would be well suited. Current and future areas for research include the comparison between different kernels, the investigation of other cues, different feature fusion schemes, automatic detection and multiple objects tracking.

References

1. Comaniciu, D., Ramesh, V., Meer, P.: Kernel-Based Object Tracking. IEEE Transactions on Pattern Analysis and Machine Intelligence 25(5), 564–577 (2003)
2. Cheng, Y.: Mean shift, mode seeking, and clustering. IEEE Transactions on Pattern Analysis and Machine Intelligence 17(8), 790–799 (1995)
3. Bradski, G.R.: Real time face and object tracking as a component of a perceptual user interface. In: Proceedings of Fourth IEEE Workshop on Applications of Computer Vision, vol. 4, pp. 214–219 (1998)
4. Kiruluta, A., Eizenman, M., Pasupathy, S.: Predictive head movement tracking using a Kalman filter. IEEE Transactions on Systems, Man and Cybernetics, Part B 27(2), 326–331 (1997)
5. Isard, M., Blake, A.: Condensation–conditional density propagation for visual tracking. International Journal on Computer Vision 29(1), 5–28 (1998)
6. Julier, S.J., Uhlmann, J.K.: A new method for the nonlinear transformation of means and covariance in filters and estimators. IEEE Trans on Automatic Control 45(3), 477–482 (2000)
7. van der Merwe, R., Doucet, A., de Freitas, N., Wan, E.: The Unscented Particle Filter. In: NIPS13. Advances in Neural Information Processing Systems, MIT Press, Cambridge (2000)
8. de Freitas, N.: Rao-Blaekwellised particle filtering for fault diagnosis. In: IEEE Aerospace Conference Proceedings, vol. 4, pp. 1767–1772 (2002)
9. Jayesh, H.K., Petar, M.D.: Gaussian Sum Particle Filtering. IEEE Transactions on Signal Processing 51(10), 2602–2612 (2003)
10. Parzen, E.: On estimation of a probability density function and mode. Ann. Math. Stat. 27, 1065–1076 (1962)
11. Lehn-Schiøler, T., Erdogmus, D., Principe, J.C.: Parzen Particle Filters. In: ICASSP 2004, vol. 5, pp. 781–784 (2004)
12. Freeman, W.T., Adelson, E.H.: The design and use of steerable filters[J]. IEEE Trans Pattern Anal. Machine Intell. 13(9), 891–906 (1991)

Random Convolution Ensembles

Michael Mayo

Dept. of Computer Science
University of Waikato
Private Bag 3105, Hamilton, New Zealand
mmayo@cs.waikato.ac.nz

Abstract. A novel method for creating diverse ensembles of image classifiers is proposed. The idea is that, for each base image classifier in the ensemble, a random image transformation is generated and applied to all of the images in the labeled training set. The base classifiers are then learned using features extracted from these randomly transformed versions of the training data, and the result is a highly diverse ensemble of image classifiers. This approach is evaluated on a benchmark pedestrian detection dataset and shown to be effective.

Keywords: Image Classification; Random Convolution; Pedestrian Detection.

1 Introduction

Methods for the automatic classification of multi-dimensional data objects are one of the central themes in pattern recognition research. Although the most common class of such object is the two-dimensional array, or image, methods should ideally scale to data objects in any number of dimensions.

In contrast to this, machine learning deals with techniques for classifying one-dimensional objects, referred to variously as "instances", "records", or "feature vectors". The most recent machine learning techniques to date, such as support vector machines [1], random forests [2], and instance-based methods (see, e.g. [3]), have proven to be extremely effective feature vector classifiers. The main difficulty that arises is usually deciding which of the techniques (along with its associated parameters) to actually use: currently, this is an empirical problem.

When it comes to designing image classifiers, there is a second significant degree of freedom: how to map the high-dimensional objects in the dataset onto one-dimensional feature vectors, in order to use machine learning for classification. Typically a direct one-to-one mapping of pixels to features is not the best option. Numerous solutions have therefore been proposed in the past, from classical colour histograms (of which there are many variants, e.g. the colour coherence vector [4]), to spatial pyramids [5], to locally receptive fields [6,7]. However, like the problem of classifier selection, there are no hard and fast rules when it comes to a particular problem.

For the remainder of this paper, the term "image classifier", therefore, will be used to denote a system comprising these two main components: a feature extraction

H.H.S. Ip et al. (Eds.): PCM 2007, LNCS 4810, pp. 216–225, 2007.

function for transforming a multi-dimensional object into a one-dimensional feature vector, along with a machine learning classifier for making a prediction about the image's class given the feature vector.

The main contribution of this paper, then, is to propose a new ensemble method called Random Convolution Ensembles (RCEs) for enhancing the performance of a base image classifier. This method works with any machine learning classifier and feature mapping function. The basic idea is that each base image classifier is trained on a randomly (but consistently) transformed copy of the entire training image set. Each base classifier consequently "sees" a different set of feature vectors extracted from the same training images. When all of the base classifiers are trained, the result is a diverse set of image classifiers whose performance as an ensemble outperforms the performance of any one of the base classifiers individually.

The basic details and motivation underlying RCEs are given in the next section. Section 3 discusses the benchmark pedestrian detection image dataset [7] used to evaluate this technique, and Section 4 describes an experiment on the benchmark dataset, showing that RCEs are effective image classifiers. In Section 5, we add an element of selection to the generation of random image transformations, and describe a second experiment showing that performance improves as a result. Section 6 concludes the paper and discusses the way forward.

2 Random Convolution Ensembles

Ensemble methods are extremely popular in machine learning. The rationale behind them is to learn not a single classifier, but a group of them, where each member of the group is designed to solve the same classification problem. It is important to ensure somehow that each individual classifier is different from the others in the group, because the more similar their structure (and therefore their predictions), the less effective overall the ensemble will be.

Methods for ensuring ensemble diversity include training each classifier with only a random subset of the feature vectors, a method known widely as bagging [8]; weighting the feature vectors in the training data differently for each classifier (e.g. boosting [9]); or even training completely different types of classifier and then combining their predictions in some way (e.g. voting [10] and stacking [11]).

All of these methods work with one-dimensional data. While standard ensemble methods can be used with images (for example, images can be bagged), such approaches do not take advantage of the multi-dimensional nature of the data in its original form (because, for example, bagging images is the same as bagging the feature vectors derived from the images).

The RCE approach proposed here overcomes this problem by generating diversity *before* the feature extraction step, by producing multiple randomly transformed copies of the training images. The basic idea is to take the complete set of training images and make n copies of them. N random image transformations are then generated, and all the images in the ith copy of the training set (where $1 \leq i \leq n$) are transformed by the corresponding ith transformation. The result is n copies of the original training set, each transformed in a random but consistent way. We then learn n base machine learning classifiers, one on each of the feature vector sets extracted from the transformed copies of the training images. When a test image is to be classified, all of the *n* base image classifiers make a prediction, and the results are combined by a meta-classifier to produce a single, final prediction.

Figure 1 depicts the architecture of an RCE, from the perspective of a test image *I* about to be classified. In the figure, the random image transformation is convolution [13] by a randomly generated kernel, and these kernels are specified by op_1, ops_2, ... The *Conv(..)* function denotes the application of one of them to *I* to produce a new, distorted image. We also assume a uniform feature extraction function *Features(.)* for transforming images into feature vectors. The diversity in the ensemble derives from the fact that each of the base machine learning classifiers ($Class_1..Class_n$) in the figure is trained on a different but complete set of feature vectors. In the figure, there are *n* feature vectors $F_1...F_n$ derived from the test image *I*. A meta-classification step at the end combines all of the predictions for each feature vector.

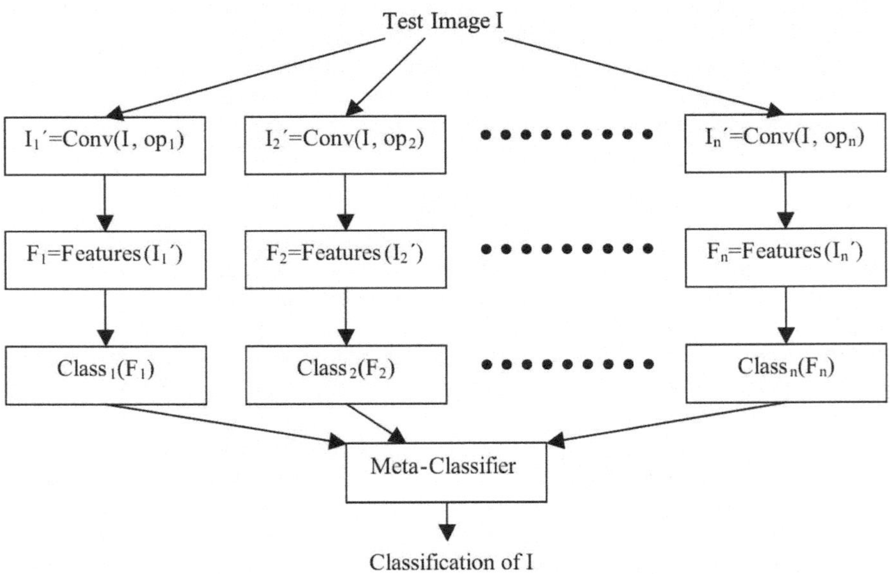

Fig. 1. Architecture of a Random Convolution Ensemble when presented with test image *I*

3 Benchmark Dataset

This new approach to image classification was evaluated against a benchmark image dataset developed by Munder & Gavrilla [7]. The dataset was proposed in order to compare different solutions to the problem of pedestrian detection in images captured from urban, outdoor environments. The classification problem is binary, in that images either depict a pedestrian (the positive class) or they do not (the negative class).

The basic version of the benchmark data consists of three training sets and two test sets. Each of these sets comprises 800 positive pedestrian images and 5000 negative, non-pedestrian images. To equalize the classes, the positive images were copied, mirrored and shifted by a few pixels in a random direction to produce five new, slightly different, positive examples for each of the original positive examples. This resulted in 4800 positive images in total. Figure 2 gives examples of some of the images in the datasets. Note that the negative examples were deliberately chosen to be challenging, with many vertical lines similar to those in the positive class (as opposed to an easier negative class with many uniform textures, which would be straightforward to distinguish). The size of each image is a uniform 18x36 grey scale pixels.

To perform an experiment using this dataset, a classifier should trained on the union of two of the three training datasets, and tested on one of the test datasets. Thus, there are six possible different train/test experiments. The results over all six runs should be averaged in order to obtain an overall more reliable and final estimate of any classifier's performance.

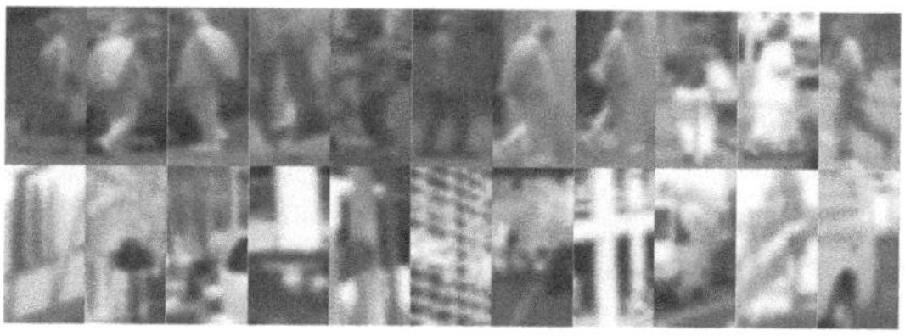

Fig. 2. Examples of positive (top row) and negative (bottom row) images in the pedestrian detection dataset proposed by [7]

4 Random vs. Standard Convolution Operators in the Ensemble: A Comparison

An RCE classifier as described in Section 2 was implemented in the Java programming language, within the WEKA (version 3.5.5) machine learning framework [12].

The random image transformation implemented was convolution [13] using a randomly generated 3x3 convolution operator or kernel. For the random operators used in this paper, we set each element in the 3x3 kernel to a random number sampled uniformly in the range -2.5…2.5.

The features used in this experiment (extracted by the *Features(.)* function in Fig. 1) were determined by the following process. Firstly, the image was divided into square blocks of size $s*s$ pixels. The blocks were allowed to overlap by 50% in both horizontal and vertical directions, thus ensuring that any important features would not be lost due to the boundary between two blocks. The block size parameter s was set to one of the values from the set {18, 9, 6}.

For each block, the sum, mean, variance, skewness, and kurtosis of the pixel values were calculated. These statistics basically describe the intensity histogram for the block. A feature vector was then constructed for each image by concatenating the statistics for all of the blocks in the image. This results, for block size s=18, in 25 features per image; for s=9 it results in 105 features; and for s=6, there are 275 features.

In the experiments performed in this section and the next, the base classifier was set to bagged random forests. Random forests [2] are an ensemble classifier in which each individual classifier is a decision tree learned from a random subset of the features in the dataset. Individual decision trees in the forest average their predictions to give a final prediction for the entire ensemble.

Bagging random forests considerably speeds up the training process, whilst (in our initial tests) only slightly impairing performance compared to a single random forest classifier trained on the entire dataset. In this experiment, each bag contained 5% of the training data, randomly selected. There were 30 bags, meaning that feature vectors could be selected for more than one bag. Each random forest classifier consisted of ten decision trees.

The meta-classifier used to combine all of the individual image classifier's predictions was voting [10], which is straightforward averaging.

The question that the first experiment set out to answer was: does this new method work at all? In other words, does randomly convolving the training data in the way described actually produce sufficiently variable sets of feature vectors for the purpose of creating a diverse ensemble of image classifiers? Or would simply convolving the images with standard operators such as edge detectors do just as well? Indeed, does this new approach provide any gain at all over the simplest possible approach, that of extracting the features directly from the original image and learning only a single base image classifier, without any image convolution at all? (This latter approach is actually the most common taken in the literature.)

$$ID = \begin{bmatrix} 0 & 0 & 0 \\ 0 & 1 & 0 \\ 0 & 0 & 0 \end{bmatrix} \qquad PK = \begin{bmatrix} -1 & -1 & -1 \\ -1 & 8 & -1 \\ -1 & -1 & -1 \end{bmatrix}$$

$$G_x = \begin{bmatrix} -1 & 0 & 1 \\ -2 & 0 & 2 \\ -1 & 0 & 1 \end{bmatrix} \qquad G_y = \begin{bmatrix} 1 & 2 & 1 \\ 0 & 0 & 0 \\ -1 & -2 & -1 \end{bmatrix}$$

Fig. 3. Common standard convolution operators: the null filter (ID), which does nothing; a Laplacian peak point detector (PK), which detects bright points; and the Sobel operators for edge detection (G_x and G_y)

Table 1. Convolution operator sets used in Experiment 1

OPS_1	{ID}
OPS_2	$\{ID, G_x, G_y, PK\}$
OPS_3	$\{R_1, R_2, R_3, R_4\}$
OPS_4	$\{ID, G_x, G_y, PK, R_1, R_2, R_3, R_4\}$
OPS_5	$\{R_1, R_2, R_3, R_4, R_5, R_6, R_7, R_8\}$

To set the experiment up, four different convolution operators as depicted in Figure 3 were grouped, along with some randomly generated operators, into five sets as shown in Table 1. Each set in Table 1 effectively defines an RCE of size *n*, where *n* is the size of the set. OPS_1 is clearly the simplest, corresponding to an ensemble with a single base image classifier (i.e. n=1 in Figure 1) and no image convolution. OPS_2 corresponds to the set of standard image convolution kernels shown in Figure 3, and OPS_3 is four randomly generated convolution kernels. OPS_4 is the set of size n=8 obtained by taking the union of OPS_2 and OPS_3, and this set is a mixture of both random and standard convolution operators. OPS_5, the last of them, consists of eight randomly generated convolution operators. Note that only OPS_3 and OPS_5 define "true" RCEs as per the definition given in the Section 2; the other ensembles are the baselines for comparison.

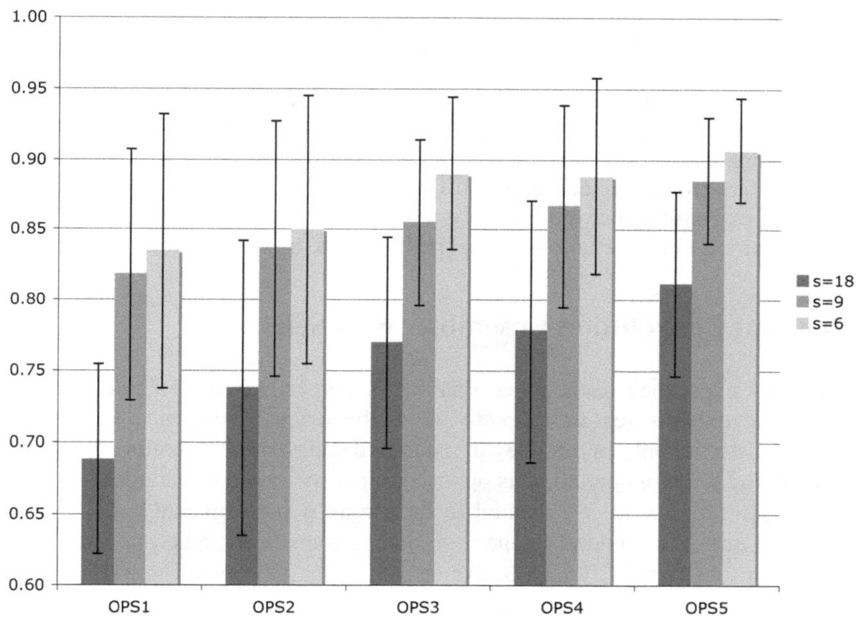

Fig. 4. Results of Experiment 1. The set of convolution operators used to construct the ensemble is specified on the x-axis, and average AUC after six independent train/test experiments is given on the y-axis. The error bars on the columns depict the standard deviation. Results are shown for features extracted using blocks of size sxs where $s \in \{18, 9, 6\}$.

For each experiment, the Area Under the ROC Curve (AUC) was calculated [14]. When using AUC, the worst possible classifier (i.e. a random classifier) should have an AUC of 0.5, while the best possible classifier (i.e. a 100% perfect classifier) should have an AUC of 1.0. Six train/test runs were performed for each combination of convolution operator set OPS_i and block size s, and Figure 4 depicts the average results.

First of all, the results clearly show that performance depends on the block size s. In every case, RCEs with a smaller block size for feature extraction have a higher final AUC. Interestingly, the ensemble with a single base image classifier without convolution (as specified by OPS_1) is the worst overall performer: AUC values for this classifier range from 0.69 to 0.84, and in every case, larger ensembles beat it.

Most importantly, Figure 4 also shows that the "true" RCEs always outperform ensembles defined using standard convolution operators, or mixtures of random and standard operators. For example, using OPS_3 as the set of convolution operators results in considerably better performance than using the set of standard operators, OPS_2 (the difference is 0.89 AUC compared to 0.85 when the block size s=6). And when the ensemble size is n=8, the completely random set OPS_5 consistently outperforms the set OPS_4, a mixture of random and standard operators (compare 0.91 AUC to 0.89 when s=6).

A second way important way in which Figure 4 shows that RCEs are superior to the other methods is the variance. In Figure 4, each average AUC column is depicted with an error bar showing the standard deviation of the AUC over the six train/test runs. It turns out that whenever only random operators are used, the standard deviation is much smaller. For example, the OPS_3 ensemble has a standard deviation of 0.06 compared to 0.10 for OPS_2, and for the larger ensembles, the standard deviation is 0.04 for OPS_5 compared to 0.07 for OPS_4. This implies that OPS_3 and OPS_5 define ensembles that are not only more accurate than the others, but they are also less sensitive to the variations in the quality of the training and testing data.

5 Random Convolution Ensembles with Selection

The previous experiment established that RCEs outperform (i) a single base image classifier that extracts features directly from the original images, and (ii) similar ensembles, differing only in that they use standard convolution operators, or a mixture of standard and random operators, as opposed to purely random operators.

In the next experiment, we wanted to determine if performance could be further improved by not only randomly generating image transformations, but also selecting them. Previously, if an RCE was of size n, then n random operators were generated. No consideration was given to the fact that one or more of the operators could potentially be useless, therefore impairing the entire ensemble. For example, a randomly generated convolution operator in which all the entries were nearly zero would effectively erase the images, making the learning task impossible for that particular member of the ensemble.

To add selection to the generation process, therefore, we performed the following steps. For every base image classifier that was required, two base image classifiers were considered, each one with a different randomly generated convolution operator. Both of them were then evaluated in a stratified two-fold cross-validation experiment on the training data. The classifier with the least number of classification errors was then retained in the final ensemble, while the other classifier was discarded. In other words, if the ensemble size was n, then $2n$ base image classifiers were generated and trained, but only half of them were retained in the final ensemble.

We considered RCEs of size n=4 and n=8 in order to compare the results of this second experiment to the first. Let OPS_3* and OPS_5* be the final set of convolution operators arrived at using generation with selection. The performance of ensembles defined by these sets on the pedestrian dataset is depicted in Figure 5, alongside the performance of the corresponding ensembles created without selection from the previous experiment.

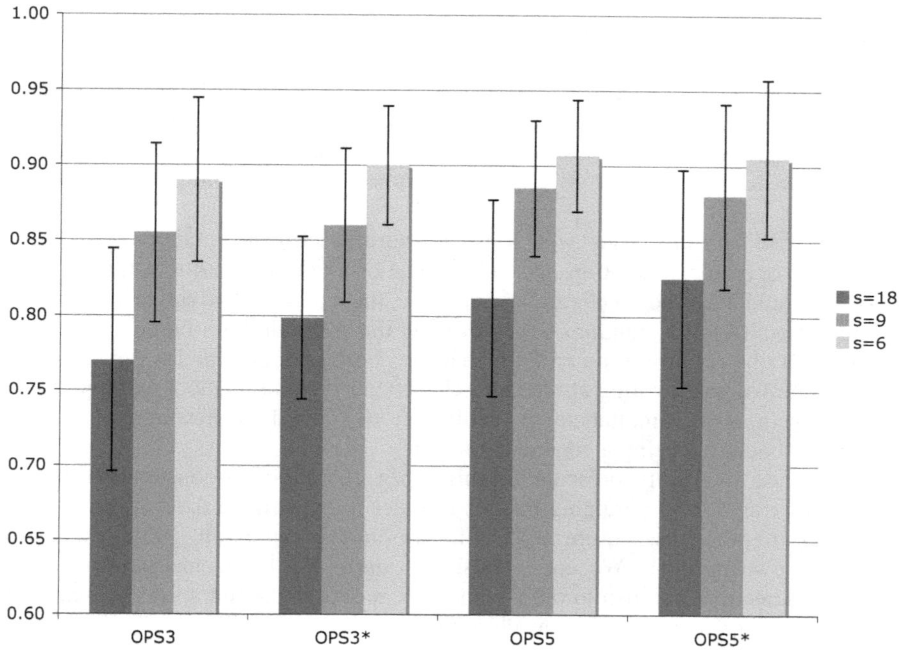

Fig. 5. Results of Experiment 2. The set of convolution operators used to construct the ensemble is specified on the x-axis, and average AUC after six independent train/test experiments is given on the y-axis. The error bars on the columns depict the standard deviation. Results are shown for features extracted using blocks of size sxs where $s \in \{18, 9, 6\}$.

The results show that adding selection to the generation process does sometimes improve the final performance. For block size s=18, selection always leads to an improvement in average AUC, while for the smaller block sizes, selection only leads to slight improvements in AUC for the n=4 ensemble (i.e., *OPS3** performs better than *OPS3*).

Although the gain due to selection is only slight in this experiment, it is suggestive that more sophisticated selection methods would produce much greater gains.

6 Concluding Remarks

This main contribution of this paper is a new method for enhancing the performance of a base image classifier. RCEs were compared to a more traditional image classifier in which features are extracted directly from the original image without using convolution and classified, and also to the strategy of extracting features from versions of the image convolved in standard ways (e.g. edge-detected versions of the training images). Furthermore, adding selection to the random operator generation process sometimes improves performance even more.

We did not compare the results obtained here directly to those of Munder & Gavrilla [7], primarily because their focus was on searching for the best features and classifier for the sole purpose of pedestrian detection. In contrast, we used different, less computationally expensive features and classifier, so as to evaluate this new approach. However, the best result (0.91 AUC) is comparable to Munder & Gavrilla's result for same version of the dataset, which they report as a 90% detection rate for a 10% false positive rate. It would be interesting to implement the same features and classifier as Munder & Gavrilla to determine if RCEs can further enhance performance.

Future work in this area will look at more intelligent methods of random convolution operator generation and selection. For example, a simple hill-climbing algorithm could be used to iteratively improve the quality of a single convolution operator after its initial random generation. If this hill-climbing-based classifier is then boosted, the result will be an RCE that uses both selection, and weighted voting rather than unweighted voting at the meta-classification stage. A more extreme idea in the same vein is to simultaneously evolve, from a random starting point, the n convolution operators using a genetic algorithm.

To conclude, the results presented in this paper are a proof-of-concept that the idea of randomly transforming training images in order to construct a diverse ensemble of image classifiers works. Future work will continue to build on and evaluate this promising new approach. We are interested in applying this technique not only to pedestrian detection, but also to other standard datasets in the literature, in areas such as object detection and natural scene classification.

References

1. Keerthi, S., Shevade, S., Bhattacharyya, C., Murthy, K.: Improvements to Platt's SMO algorithm for SVM classifier design. Neural Computation 13(3), 637–649 (1999)
2. Breiman, L.: Random Forests. Machine Learning 45(1), 5–32 (2001)
3. Atkeson, C., Moore, A., Schaal, S.: Locally Weighted Learning. AI Review 11, 11–73 (1996)
4. Pass, G., Zabih, R., Miller, J.: Comparing images using color coherence vectors. In: Aigrain, P., et al. (eds.) Proceedings of the 4th ACM international conference on Multimedia, pp. 65–73 (1997)
5. Lazebnik, S., Schmid, C., Ponce, J.: Beyond Bags of Features: Spatial Pyramid Matching for Recognizing Natural Scene Categories. In: Proceedings of the 2006 IEEE Computer Society Conference on Computer Vision and Pattern Recognition, pp. 2169–2178 (2006)
6. Fukushima, K., Miyake, S., Ito, T.: Neocognitron: A neural network model for the mechanism of visual pattern recognition. IEEE Trans. on Systems, Man, and Cybernetics 13, 826–834 (1983)
7. Munder, S., Gavrilla, D.: An experimental study on pedestrian classification. IEEE Transactions on Pattern Analysis and Machine Intelligence 28(11), 1863–1868 (2006)
8. Breiman, L.: Bagging Predictors. Machine Learning 24(2), 123–140 (1996)

9. Freund, Y., Schapire, R.: Experiments with a new boosting algorithm. In: Proc. of the 13th International Conference on Machine Learning, pp. 148–156 (1996)
10. Kittler, J., Hatef, M., Robert, P., Duin, W., Matas, J.: On combining classifiers. IEEE Transactions on Pattern Analysis and Machine Intelligence 20(3), 226–239 (1998)
11. Wolpert, D.: Stacked generalization. Neural networks 5, 241–259 (1992)
12. http://www.cs.waikato.ac.nz/ ml/
13. Seul, M., O'Gorman, L., Sammon, M.: Practical Algorithms for Image Analysis. Cambridge University Press, Cambridge (2000)
14. http://en.wikipedia.org/wiki/Receiver_operating_characteristic

A Hybrid Content-Based Image Authentication Scheme

Kai Chen, Xinglei Zhu, and Zhishou Zhang

Institute for Inforcomm Research, 21 Heng Mui Keng Terrace,
119613, Singapore
{kchen,xzhu,zszhang}@i2r.a-star.edu.sg

Abstract. In this paper, we propose a hybrid content-based image authentication scheme that integrates two complementary algorithms: Robust content-based authentication and semi-fragile crypto-hash based authentication. The former uses global features and is quite robust against various types of noise. The latter uses local features and therefore is able to identify the tempered area in case the image is attacked. The proposed scheme takes advantage from both algorithms and provides more information to guide the decision maker. In addition, we also propose two improved algorithms based on Fridrich's content-based and Sun's crypto-hash based authentication. Experiments show that the improved algorithms are more secure than the original algorithms. Another contribution of this paper is that, by concatenating the signatures generated with two different authentication algorithms, the fuzzy area in authentication decision can be further quantized, which provides more choices for authentication decision.

Keywords: Image Authentication, Digital Signature, Watermarking, Content hash, ECC.

1 Introduction

Effective image authentication is an increasing important issue in networked environments. To exchange images between two parties on the network, it is very important to provide integrity protection and non-repudiation.

Image authentication differs from the traditional data authentication in that the image content, rather than a specific representation of the image, is the authentication goal. Content-preserving manipulations like lossy compression should be able to pass the verification, while the malicious modification (which changes the image content) should fail the verification. However, content preserving is difficult to be specified precisely, thus it is hard to formalize the modification in the notions of the image content. As a result, there is no sharp boundary between the authentic and unauthentic images. Following the illustration in [2], the region of surely authentic images is separated from the region of surely unauthentic images by a fuzzy region, in which the authenticity of the modified image is difficult to judge. In Fig. 1, these regions are illustrated as circles to facilitate characterization, although they should have more complicated shapes. Thus there are three answers when authenticating an image: authentic, unauthentic or don't know.

H.H.S. Ip et al. (Eds.): PCM 2007, LNCS 4810, pp. 226–235, 2007.

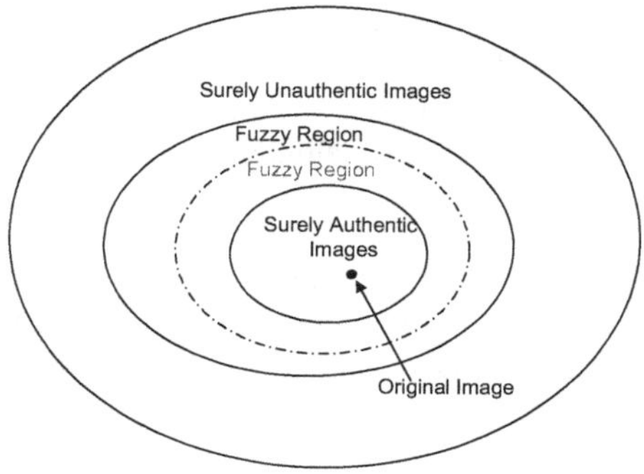

Fig. 1. Diagram illustrating the relationship between the original image, surely authentic images, surely unauthentic images and the fuzzy region inside which the authentication decision is uncertain. The dashed line represents the further quantization of the fuzzy region by proposed scheme.

In this paper we propose a hybrid content-based image authentication scheme. The system consists of a robust content-based authentication component and a semi-fragile crypto-based one, which are obtained by revising two existing content-based algorithms respectively. These algorithms are chosen because they are different in robustness and error locating properties. The revised algorithms overcome some weaknesses of the original work under certain attacks. The signature of these two components are concatenated together to form a new signature. By combining two different authentication algorithms, it is helpful to further reduce the fuzzy authentication region. In this paper, concatenating the two signatures quantizes the fuzzy authentication region as illustrated using dashed circle in Fig 1. How to choose the most appropriate authentication algorithms and how to fuse them to achieve maximal authentication benefits are beyond the scope of this paper and we leave them for future work.

The paper is organized as follows. In Section 2, we survey related works and give special attention to two closely related authentication algorithms. The proposed scheme is presented in Section 3. Results and discussions are given in Section 4. Finally, Section 5 concludes the paper.

2 Related Works

Many algorithms have been proposed to deal with the content authentication problem. Depending on the applications, some operations on the image are considered to be acceptable such as JPEG compression, format converting and watermark embedding. The first two operations could be considered as re-quantization and watermarking could be modeled as adding white Gaussian noise. The goal of designing authentication algorithm is to be robust against the content-preserving operations and be sensitive to content modification to achieve security. Lin and Chang's algorithm [3,4] is designed to survive JPEG compression up to a certain level. Lin-Podilchuk-Delp [5] proposes a method which is robust against almost all non-malicious signalprocessing operations, except for smoothing. Eggers-Girod [7] is very robust against JPEG compression. Queluz [8] is robust against many signal-processing operations. Fei and Kundur [1] propose a new approach, called MSB-LSB decomposition method which tolerates small amount of distortion, and is fragile to low quality JPEG compression.

In the rest part of this section, two representative algorithms, which will be improved to be used in constructing the proposed scheme in Section 3, are described in details. One is a content-based global authentication scheme proposed by Fridrich [6] and another is a crypto-based local authentication scheme proposed by Sun [10,12]. Their limitations are presented by analyzing several attacks on these two algorithms.

2.1 Fridrich's Content-Based Hashing Algorithm

Fridrich [6] proposes a content-based hash function, which is the most robust scheme to the best of our knowledge. The goal is to design a hash function to generate a bit sequence W that sensitively depends on a secret key K and robustly depends on the image I. With the same K, similar images should generate closely related Ws and dissimilar images should generate independent Ws. To make the procedure dependent on a key, N random matrices with entries uniformly distributed in the interval [0, 1] is generated. Then, a low-pass filter is repeatedly applied to each random matrix to obtain N random smooth patterns P_j, $1 \leqslant j \leqslant N$. All patterns are then made DC-free by subtracting the mean from each pattern. Considering the block and the pattern as vectors, the image block B_i is projected on each pattern P_j, $1 \leqslant j \leqslant N$ and its absolute value is compared with a threshold T to obtain N bits $b_{i,1},\ldots,b_{i,N}$. The total length of the bit sequence is decided by the number of blocks and the number of patterns.

Fridrich's algorithm has high robustness but is weak in security. Specially, we show two possible attacks on Fridrich's algorithm.

- *Smooth Block Attack*

Since feature projections only depend on the variations in the block itself. Experiments result demonstrates that this method is not suitable to detect those attacks which replace a smooth region of an image with another smooth region. Thus, it is possible to modify the smooth region of an image which changes the visual appearance of the image. For example, Fig. 2 shows that the hash bits of the modified block (top-right corner of the image) could be same with that of the original block.

- *Boosting substitution attack*

Fig. 2. Smooth Block Attack

In [11], Radhakrishnan proposes boosting substitution attack. If an attacker knows the features from which the hash bits are generated along with the hash bits themselves for a single image, then with sufficient training data, the attacker can then use boosting method to learn the behavior of the random vector. Then the attacker probably can forge an attacked image, replacing original blocks in the image with others which has the same projection hash bit. An example is shown in Fig. 3.

Fig. 3. Boosting Substitution Attack

Fridirich's algorithm is revised in Section 3.2 against the above two attacks. The improved version is used as the content-based component of the proposed scheme.

2.2 Sun's Crypto-Based Authentication Algorithm

A semi-fragile image authentication scheme which survives the JPEG compression by integrating error correction code (ECC), watermarking and cryptographic hash is proposed by Sun *et al* [10,12]. The image authentication method is robust against JPEG compression using quality factor of 10% or higher and additive white Gaussian noise (AWGN) with standard variance less than 10. The basic idea is to apply ECC coding to content features such that the bit errors introduced by content-preserving manipulations can be recovered. One DC and seven AC components are selected from the zig-zag scan of the 8 x 8 DCT block as DCT feature. The selection of the AC coefficients is based on a random sequence generated from a secret key. The ECC code is embedded into the first 20 AC components in the range of low to middle frequency band. Crypto signature scheme is used to generate the signature with all block features. At the receiver side, the content features are extracted from the received image and corrected by ECC decoding. By comparing the original content features (decrypted from signature) and the content features recovered from the received image, the verification process makes verification decision and identifies possible attacked area.

The above algorithm is not secure under counterfeit attack. Although the probability of guessing the 7 out of 20 coefficients using exhaustive attempt is small, DCT coefficients replacement attack can detect the correct locations of the 7 coefficients without knowledge of the key. Using this attack, attackers can modify all or part of an image and the modified image still passes verification. An example is shown in Fig. 4. After finding out the position of the protected DCT coefficients, the unprotected DCT coefficients of each block of the image "Lena" shown in Fig. 4(a) are replaced with the corresponding coefficients of the image "Flight" shown in Fig. 4(b), leaving the protected coefficients for feature extraction and watermark embedding unchanged. The attacked image shown in Fig. 4(c) can still pass the authentication verification system of [10,12], while the visual appearance of the image is obviously damaged.

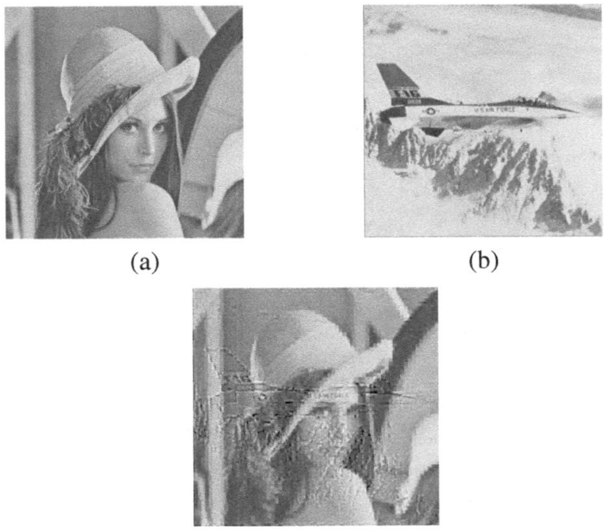

(a) (b) (c)

Fig. 4. An counterfeit attack designed to survive semi-fragile authentication (a) image "Lena"; (b) image "Flight"; (c) tampered image by replacing unprotected DCT coefficient with corresponding coefficients from the image "Flight"

Sun's algorithm is revised in Section 3.3 to prevent the counterfeit attack. The improved version is used to construct the crypto-based component of the proposed scheme.

3 Proposed Scheme

3.1 Framework

The system diagram of the proposed scheme is shown in Fig. 5. The authentication system composes of two components: a content-based authentication component and a crypto-based authentication component. The signatures generated from these two components are concatenated to form the final signature. The details of these two components will be given in the next two subsections.

The verification process first splits the concatenated signature into two parts and then verifies them separately as in their respective verification process. Since the two authentication algorithms have different robustness, the combination of their verification results gives a finer description of the position of the modified image in

Fig. 1. In other words, the fuzzy region is further quantized by combining verification results from different authentication algorithms. Such a finer quantization could be helpful in the decision of the authentication. Since the definition of content preserving is application dependent, we do no give a final judgment here. Instead, the proposed scheme provides more information to guide the decision maker.

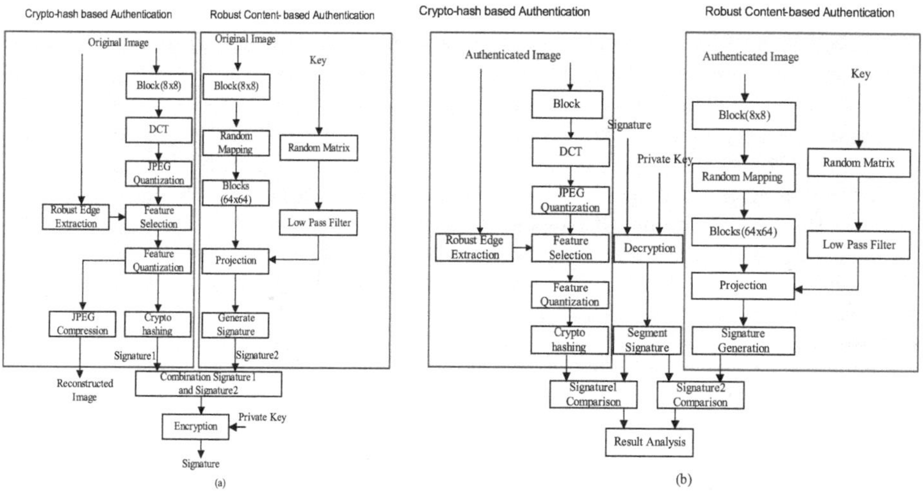

Fig. 5. System diagram of the proposed content-based JPEG image authentication scheme (a) signature generating process (b) Image verification process

3.2 Content-Based Authentication Component

The content-based authentication component is shown in the right part of Fig. 5(a) and its verification process is shown in the right part of Fig. 5(b). To improve the security of Fridrich's algorithm, we propose a simpler and straightforward solution. The basis of the smooth block attack is that feature projections only depend on the variations in the block itself. If the number of smooth blocks is reduced in the image, the attack can be prevented. The preliminary requirement of boosting substitution attack is the availability of the hashing code of each block of the image. Therefore, a pre-processing step, named random blocks mapping (RBM), is performed before feature projection. RBM divides an image into small blocks and randomizes their order by a key, which can be the same one used in pattern generation. Then the small blocks are grouped into larger hash blocks (64*64) and are further projected on to the low-passed random patterns to generate the robust signature. RBM greatly reduces the number of smooth blocks and makes the hash bits of each block unknown to the attackers. Thus the improved algorithm should be able to detect the aforementioned two attacks.

3.3 Crypto-Based Authentication Component

The crypto-based authentication component is shown in the left part of Fig. 5(a) and its verification process is shown in the left part of Fig. 5(b). Besides the algorithm presented in Section 2.2, we employ the edge feature of the original image to improve the security. Taking image edges as the features for image authentication can be found in some publications such as [8]. Edges in a natural image have important effects on the subjective visual quality and they are always associated with the boundary of an object or with marks on the object, thus edges can characterize the local significances in image. However, edge feature along is not suitable to authenticate those attacks such as adding gradual changing part of the image. Combine the edge feature with the semi-fragile authentication algorithm [10,12] solves the problem.

The input original image is firstly partitioned into non-overlapping 8x8 blocks. DCT coefficients are computed for each block and then quantized according to JPEG compression. With the fuzzy edge detector [13], which is robust to many image processing methods, edge features are extracted from the original image and further classified within each block. Thus each block is assigned an edge pattern. The selection of protected DCT coefficients is dependent on the secret key, edge pattern and block position. Thus if the modification on the block changes the edge pattern, the selected DCT coefficients from the received image will not be at the same position as the protected DCT coefficients from the original image. The Block-based invariant features are then extracted and the ECC code is embedded into the image as a watermark. Finally crypto hashing is used to generate the signature with all block features concatenated.

4 System Performance Analysis and Discussion

4.1 Performance of the Content-Based Component

To test the robustness change by adding the RBM module into Fridrich's algorithm, we randomly select 2000 images from Corel Gallery database. The authentication bits are generated as a robust visual hash of the 64x64 image blocks. Each block is projected onto $N=30$ Patterns. For each image, we apply a set of common image processing and calculate the similarity between the bit sequences generated with and without RBM module. Here the similarity is defined as the $R = 1-D(S_1, S_2)$ where $D(S_1,S_2)$ is the normalized hamming distance between bit sequences S_1 and S_2. The statistical result is shown in Table 1.

From Table 1 we can see that after adding RBM module, the generated bit sequence does not change much, which means that the robustness of the original Fridrich's algorithm is maintained.

As we analyzed in Section 3.2, RBM module is introduced into the content-based component to protect the content against smooth block attack and boosting substitution attack, by eliminating the smooth blocks and conceal the hashing code of each blocks respectively. Thus the content-based component module achieves better security while maintaining the robustness.

Table 1. The average and Standard deviation of normalized similarity results

Modification	Average similarity	Standard deviation (std)
JPEG (Q=90%)	0.9991	0.0012
JPEG(Q=80%)	0.9993	0.0012
JPEG(Q=70%)	0.9959	0.0029
JPEG(Q=60%)	0.9943	0.0039
JPEG(Q=50%)	0.9934	0.0042
JPEG(Q=40%)	0.9918	0.0050
JPEG(Q=30%)	0.9892	0.0060
AWGN5	0.9964	0.0028
AWGN 10	0.9949	0.0036
AWGN 20	0.9927	0.0046
AWGN 30	0.9912	0.0052
AWGN 40	0.9899	0.0058
AWGN 50	0.9885	0.0066
Increase Brightness	0.9990	0.0015
Decrease Brightness	0.9989	0.0014
Increase Contrast	0.9470	0.0326
Decrease Contrast	0.9989	0.0014
Low Pass Filter	0.9634	0.0187
Median Filter	0.9846	0.0100
Sharpen	0.9466	0.0301
Histogram Equalization	0.8933	0.0676

4.2 Performance of the Crypto-Based Component

By introducing the edge information into the DCT coefficient selection process, the modified crypto-based algorithm is sensitive to counterfeit attack and thus the security is enhanced. The same attack shown in Fig. 4 does not pass the verification process using the improved semi-fragile authentication. Fig. 6 shows the detection results, where the marked blocks indicate the modified area.

Fig. 6. Modification locating result under counterfeit attack

On the other hand, by considering the DCT coefficients, the crypto-based component successfully detects some gradual changes, which is unable to be detected using edge only features. An example is shown in Fig. 7. More clouds are added to

Fig. 7. Authentication test: (a) Original image; (b) Tampered image; (c) Tampering location image

the image in Fig. 7(a) on the upper-right site to form the image in Fig. 7(b). Although the edges of Fig. 7(a) and Fig. 7(b) are almost the same, the crypto-based authentication algorithm still locates the modified blocks, as illustrated in Fig. 7(c).

4.3 Discussions

In this section we further discuss the benefits of combining the content-based authentication and crypto-based authentication.

First, by employing the hybrid scheme, the fuzzy area between surely authentic area and surely unauthentic are is further divided into smaller areas, as illustrated in Fig. 1. For instance, if the image falls in the inner fuzzy area in Fig. 1, it is more likely to be authentic; on the other hand, if it falls in the outer fuzzy area, it is more likely to be unauthentic. Therefore, the proposed scheme further quantizes the fuzzy area to provide users with more information to facilitate decision making process.

Second, the content-based authentication module exploits global features, which makes it sensitive to cropping attack. On the other hand, the crypto-based authentication module exploits local block-based features, and hence it is able to locate the tampered region of the image. Therefore, the proposed scheme is able to locate tampered region while being sensitive to copping attack. In case that the received image falls in fuzzy decision space, the tamper-locating capability can alarm users to further investigate the suspicious area of the image.

5 Conclusion and Future Works

A hybrid content based image authentication scheme is proposed. The proposed hybrid system integrates a robust content-based authentication component and a semi-fragile crypto-based authentication component, which are obtained by revising two existing algorithms respectively. The revised algorithms achieve enhanced security over the original algorithms. By integrating two authentication algorithms, additional authentication benefits are obtained and it is helpful to further explore the fuzzy authentication region. For future work, we will examine the problem of how to fuse the verification results obtained from the two authentication components.

References

1. Fei, C., Kundur, D., Kwong, R.: Analysis and Design of Secure Watermark-based Authentication Systems. IEEE Transactions on Information Forensics and Security 1(1), 43–55 (2006)
2. Wu, C.W.: On the Design of Content-Based Multimedia Authentication Systems, IBM Research Report (2001)
3. Lin, C.Y., Chang, S.F.: A Robust Image Authentication Method Distinguishing JPEG Compression from Malicious Manipulation. IEEE Trans. on Circuits and Systems for Video Technology (2001)
4. Lin, C.Y., Chang, S.F.: Semi-Fragile Watermarking for Authenticating JPEG Visual Content. In: EI 2000. SPIE Security and Watermarking of Multimedia Contents II (2000)
5. Lin, E.T., Podilchuk, C.I., Delp, E.J.: Detection of image alterations using semi-fragile watermarks. In: ISNN 2006, vol. 3971, pp. 152–163 (2000)
6. Fridrich, J.: Robust Bit Extraction From Images. In: Proc. IEEE ICMCS 1999, Florence, Italy, vol. 2, pp. 536–540 (1999)
7. Eggers, J.J., Girod, B.: Blind watermarking applied to image authentication. In: ICASSP 2001. Intern. Conference on Acoustics, Speech and Signal Processing (2001)
8. Queluz, M.P.: Authentication of digital images and video: Generic models and a new contribution. Signal processing: Image communication 16, 461–475 (2001)
9. Queluz, M.P.: Spatial Watermark for Image Content Authentication. Journal of Electronic Imaging 11(2), 275–285 (2002)
10. Sun, Q., Tian, Q., Chang, S.F.: A Robust and Secure Media Signature Scheme for JPEG Images. IEEE MMSP (2002)
11. Radhakrishnan, R., Xiong, Z., Memom, N.: On the security of the visual hash function. In: Proceedings SPIE - Security and Watermarking of Multimedia Contents V, vol. 5020 (2003)
12. Ye, S., Sun, Q., Chang, E.-C.: Error Resilient Content-based Image Authentication Over Wireless Channel. In: ISCAS. IEEE International Symposium on Circuits and Systems (2005)
13. Chou, W.: Classifying Image Pixels into Shaped, Smooth and Textured Points. Pattern Recognition 32(10), 1697–1706 (1999)

Implementing DRM over Peer-to-Peer Networks with Broadcast Encryption

Yao Zhang, Chun Yuan, and Yuzhuo Zhong

Department of Computer Science and Technology, Tsinghua University, Beijing 100084, China
zhyao06@mails.tsinghua.edu.cn,
yuanc@sz.tsinghua.edu.cn,
zyz-dcs@mail.tsinghua.edu.cn

Abstract. P2P networks play a promotive role in distribution and transmission of digital multimedia content by providing high availability, fault tolerance, bandwidth efficiency and dynamic scalability. At the same time, however, it facilitates illegal pirate and unauthorized access towards copyright media content which may violate possessor ownership and result in economic loss. Conventional client/server model for DRM has difficulties coping with the challenge of secure communication in P2P environment. In this paper, we propose a strategy to incorporate DRM mechanism into P2P network architecture and construct a system which ensures efficient content sharing as well as reliable media protection. Our approach implements a revocable key management scheme based on broadcast encryption and enables cryptographic information for session key processing to be distributed among users within the same authorized domain in peer-to-peer mode. Mathematical analysis has demonstrated that the new strategy outperforms traditional solutions on alleviating communication overhead of License Server, minishing peer latency of authorization, and importing security modules without much modification to original peer-to-peer infrastructure.

Keywords: P2P Networks, DRM, Broadcast Encryption, Authorized Domain.

1 Introduction

P2P network is a self-organizing decentralized system in which every participant contributes its upstream bandwidth, processing ability and storage capacity in a collaborative manner. It greatly helps to establish multimedia communication networks and enables efficient distribution of digital content at a large scale. In the absence of security mechanism, however, P2P networks lack the ability to maintain content protection and access control towards copyright material, hence leading to piracy commitment, copyright infringement, and even revenue damnification. Therefore, it's of paramount importance to build an integrated platform which accomplishes both efficient delivery and legal consumption for digital content.

DRM refers to a set of policies, techniques and tools that monitor appropriate use of digital content [1]. Pertinent research has brought forth many DRM applications for

H.H.S. Ip et al. (Eds.): PCM 2007, LNCS 4810, pp. 236–245, 2007.

commerce, such as Windows Media DRM of Microsoft, Helix DRM of RealNetworks, and iTunes of Apple. Although the technology has been sufficiently developed and matured, traditional client/server model for DRM does not satisfy the requirements of P2P network architecture. Reasons for incompatibility mainly rest with intrinsic property of P2P framework and consideration of performance maintenance. On the one hand, centralized control may result in system bottleneck while meeting rigorous security requirements. On the other hand, security scheme can potentially adapt to peer-to-peer configuration and probably benefit from the sharing features.

In this paper we present a novel implementation of DRM for P2P networks. It takes full advantage of P2P architecture and exchanges information in a cooperative manner. The information flow traversing the entire system can be classified into two categories. One is the digital content, and the other is rights object which contains data for access control and session key processing. Our system organizes legal peers in form of authorized domain according to granted rights. Peers within the same cluster are able to exchange ciphertext in a peer-to-peer manner without disturbing License Server. The key scheme inherited from broadcast encryption [18] guarantees that privileged users can process session key successfully while illegal ones outside domain obtain nothing even if ciphertext was available. As a result we are able to accomplish several advancements beyond traditional solutions. First, authorization is achieved through decreasing communication between License Server and peer nodes. Second, licensing operations arouse shorter response delay for peer customer. Third, security modules can be conveniently integrated into existent peer-to-peer framework without intervening intrinsic configuration and performance of the entire system is improved compared with traditional combination.

This paper is organized as follows. Section 2 introduces previous work on the security management for P2P networks and discusses the motivation of our study. Section 3 analyses essential nature of P2P framework and possible challenge to security incorporation. It also outlines general broadcast encryption scheme and prefigures its potential for peer-to-peer application. Section 4 outlines the architecture of P2P-based DRM system. After that, implementation of revocable key scheme and its integration with peer-to-peer platform are detailed. Section 5 evaluates system performance and illustrates application scenarios. Finally, section 6 makes some conclusion remarks.

2 Related Work and Motivation

So far security issue with P2P networks has received much attention and investigation. It covers a wide range of aspects, such as trust and reputation, anonymity and privacy, content protection and rights management.

Malicious nodes and futile information pose a threat to the availability of P2P networks. [2-5] aim at building trust and reputation infrastructure so that querying peers can decide which candidate to interact with or whether suspectable information should be accepted.

Anonymity and privacy have a bearing upon customer experience. [6] presents a secure underlying protocol for trust management and provides mutual anonymity for both querist and respondent. [7] compares different realizations of mutual anonymity in the presence of trusted third party and otherwise. [8] implements anonymous lookup and information exchange with minimal modifications to most P2P substrate.

[9-11] are dedicated to legitimate content distribution. [9] provides detection and tracing mechanism against copyright infringement by identifying characteristics of P2P traffic. [10] and [11] prevent illegal publication by maintaining protected content list and utilizing fingerprinting and cryptographic hash technologies, respectively.

Conventional solutions for P2P security generally rely on Trusted Third Party (TTP) and Public Key Infrastructure (PKI) for fairness, integrity and confidentiality. Nevertheless, this may result in concentrated supervision and inapplicability to decentralized nature of P2P framework. Recent work has achieved certain innovation on dispensing with central administrator. [12] constructs a Ticket and Credit based Multimedia Commerce system for legal trading among peer customers and [13] proposes mutual authentication protocol for federated P2P environment. Both of them employ tamper-resistant hardware to enforce security strategies. [14] and [15] adopt Byzantine fault tolerant agreement and implement authentication without mediation of trusted third party. [16] and [17] implements security mechanisms for P2P home network by means of broadcast encryption. A collection of compliant devices makes up an authorized domain within which newcomer is authorized and content is shared. Content cryptography is bound to device cluster and authorization is carried out in a tree-based hierarchy.

With regard to content protection and rights management, central administrator is yet a necessity. It takes charge of content capsulation, identity registration, and rights authorization. Since centralized monitoring may conflict with decentralized nature of P2P architecture, security mechanisms should be migrated in a cost-effective way. Thus the major concern of this paper is to supply P2P architecture with scalable and adaptive security management. Every participating node shall be able to partake and balance the server load so as to alleviate possible congestion due to licensing operations. In reciprocation participants will also gain quick response of authorization information.

3 P2P Networks and Broadcast Encryption

3.1 Features of P2P Networks

P2P network is not only a collection of heterogeneous decentralized resources but also a congregation of active cooperation. While receiving service from system, peer node can propagate the information to other participants, sharing its link capacity, processing power and memory space likewise.

Owing to complete utilization of network resources, P2P model fits well the multimedia dissemination which normally involves huge amount of data transfer. Meanwhile, participating nodes behave autonomously, leaving and joining dynamically. Thus embedding security functionalities into such framwork demands comprehensive consideration. Centralized configuration can consolidate loosly coupled control, but may also place heavy burden upon the system. Thereby making security modules adaptive to peer-to-peer distributed nature might be a wise choice.

3.2 Broadcast Encryption and Its Applicability for P2P Networks

The technique of broadcast encryption was spawned by Amos Fiat and Moni Naor in [18] with a motivation of addressing key agreement via one-way communication. Broadcast encryption allows a central organization to broadcast secure transmissions to an arbitrary set of privileged recipients. The scheme guarantees that only legal users are able to process information correctly while unauthorized ones get nothing valuable. Broadcast encryption intends to minimize the communication overhead for key management while some PKI-based schemes require a two-way handshake to agree on a session key[19]. The one-way nature of broadcast encryption may also raise opportunities for peer-to-peer security framework.

Firstly, broadcast encryption is able to enforce compliance without identification and authentication in certain scenarios. P2P networking is outstanding for its sharing and collaboration. If we uniform the authentication and authorization to a confined range, the scope of cooperation will be extended by a large margin.

Secondly, broadcast encryption affords more robust and reliable key negotiation mechanism. Both License Server and normal peers can benefit from this robustness and reliability.

Lastly, broadcast encryption enables resilient secrecy against coalition to a certain extent. It is desirable that cryptographic information can be distributed in similar way as content data under peer-to-peer circumstances. Due to the autonomous behavior of peer-to-peer nodes, such practice seems to be sort of risky. Fortunately, however, we can rely on the resilience provided by broadcast encryption scheme. It guarantees that authorization object is safely disseminated among the peers in the same authorized domain.

4 P2P-Based DRM Implementation

4.1 System Architecture

The system architecture can be analyzed from two points of view. One is data transfer over peer-to-peer networks; the other is organization and collaboration of function modules. Figure 1 depicts data flow and interaction of function modules in our system. We only illustrate major components for clarity. The central server of the entire system consists of License Server and Content Provider which work cooperatively to provide rights management for content distribution.

Content Encapsulation
Content Classifier classifies multimedia content into categories in terms of intrinsic value and consumption rights. That is to say, each content category can be regarded as a binary tuple consisting of one content ID and certain rights. Then Content Packager chooses a content encryption key for each content category and encapsulates the content with symmetrical encryption.

Authentication and Authorization
License Server organizes peer nodes into authorized domain to which the same content and rights are endowed. Meanwhile, symmetrical key and authority license

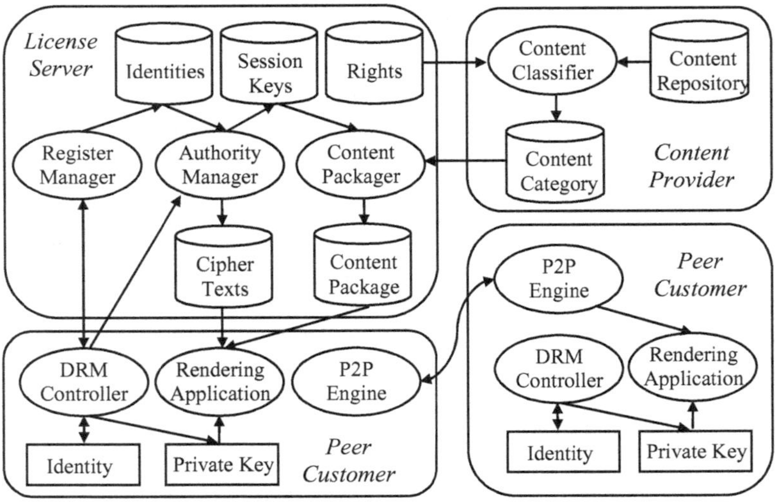

Fig. 1. Organization and interaction of function modules for secure P2P system. Arrows indicate data flow and control flow. We assume that the customer on the right has completed registration and authentication, thereby receiving ciphertext and content from others.

are also shared among peers within the same authorized domain. Register Manager deals with registration and assigns a private key to the customer, together with an identity. Any registered customer must request with its identity and verify to Authority Manager for any content category it intends to access. Such policy makes DRM implementation flexible and adaptable to various applications since verification can turn into payment, trading, or virtual cashing.

Ciphertext denotes the cryptographic information for session key processing. For successful authentication, Authority Manager updates corresponding ciphertext by performing group operations on set difference, marking the result with timestamp, embedding supplementary information and disseminating the up-to-date information. So far authentication and authorization have been accomplished.

Content Access Management

Since publish of public key, domain membership and even ciphertext won't pose any threat to system security, cryptographic information can be disseminated among users in a peer-to-peer manner. P2P Engine sees to the search and exchange of multimedia content as well as cryptographic information. Searching and tracking mechanisms for P2P networks are all available to achieve efficiency. We employ Distributed Hash Table (DHT) for data indexing and searching.

4.2 Key Management

Our key management scheme is derived from the collusion resistant broadcast encryption devised in [20]. We mainly accommodate the primary algorithm to peer-to-peer applications. The modifications to primary notion merely consist of parameter initialization and process scheduling.

Table 1. Useful notations and descriptions for key management scheme

Notation	Description
n	a value much larger than maximum number of users
G	a bilinear group of prime order p
g	a random generator of G, $g \in G$
α, γ	random of Z_p
g_i	g^{α^i}
υ	g^{γ}
PK	public key for system
d_i	private key for user i which equals to g_i^{γ}
K	session key for symmetrical content encryption
Hdr	broadcast ciphertext for processing session key
S	set of members within the same authorized domain

Useful notations of the scheme are described in Table 1. Then we can detail conformed key scheme for the secure peer-to-peer framework. n circumscribes the upper limit of users in the peer-to-peer networks and it should be assigned a reasonably large value in consideration of the dynamic growth. At the beginning, License Server will choose an n large enough for upper limit of customers. Then PK can be calculated once for all or gradually with renewal. At any one time, for j users registered with License Server, PK will be g, $g_{n-j+1}, \ldots, g_n, g_{n+2}, \ldots, g_{n+j}, \upsilon$. Whenever a new user joins the system we only append two more elements to PK. Optionally, License Server can calculate the whole PK in advance, $g, g_1, \ldots, g_n, g_{n+2}, \ldots, g_{2n}, \upsilon$, sparing PK renewal during runtime.

To create a new session key K, we choose a random $t \in Z_p$ and perform the bilinear map $K = e(g_{n+1}, g)^t$. Multimedia content are classified into categories and we oblige each category to be symmetrically encrypted with one unique session key. Thus more than one K should be generated for multiple instances.

Each registered customer holds a private key which is only known to License Server and the owner itself. As soon as License Server successfully authenticates a customer's request for certain multimedia category, it will bind the customer to corresponding S and construct a Hdr based on generation of corresponding K and membership in authorized domain:

$$Hdr = \left(g^t, (\upsilon \cdot \prod_{j \in S} g_{n+1-j})^t \right) \in G^2$$

It's implicated that authorized domain S , multimedia category and symmetrical K form a mapping relationship. In other words, all the participants in S are authorized equally, thereby sharing the same instance of Hdr , S and K . When the querist receives from other participating nodes Hdr , as well as PK and S , it is able to process ciphertext and obtain K for rendering protected content:

$$Hdr = (C_0, C_1)$$

$$K = e(g_i, C_0) \;\; / \;\; e(d_i \cdot \prod_{\substack{j\in S \\ j\neq i}} g_{n+1-j+i}, C_1)$$

Only authenticated customers bound to the cluster can process Hdr successfully.

4.3 Management of Cryptographic Information

On arrival of new customers, Hdr shall be updated and accommodated to variation of S . Optimization can be applied with previous computation. Since original Hdr is available, $Hdr' = \prod_{j\in S'} g^{t}_{n+1-j}$ for S' can be computed from $\prod_{j\in S} g^{t}_{n+1-j}$ with just δ group operations, where δ is the set difference between S and S'. Decryption on client side can benefit from similar optimization in respect that $\prod_{\substack{j\in S' \\ j\neq i}} g_{n+1-j+i}$ can be computed from $\prod_{\substack{j\in S \\ j\neq i}} g_{n+1-j+i}$ easily if S and S' are similar. Furthermore, system performance can be optimized with precomputed $\prod_{j=1}^{n} g^{t}_{n+1-j}$ on condition that receiver sets tend to be large.

Although cryptographic information can occupy corresponding entries in DHT as multimedia content, dynamic variations of PK , S and Hdr demand special management. Substantially, Authority Manager should maintain the mapping relationship between S and Hdr . On occurrence of update, set difference, partial PK and temporary Hdr are combined into a message marked with timestamp. P2P Engine searches for original messages as well as the up-to-date one, checks timestamps, and computes new Hdr with collected information.

5 Performance Evaluation and Application Scenarios

In virtue of our scheme, License Server doesn't have to encapsulate and transmit session key for every verification separately. License Server computes $\prod_{j\in \Delta S} g^{t}_{n+1-j}$ for set difference ΔS as temporary Hdr on update. The value can serve as many as ΔS customers while consuming License Server only one transmission. Since Hdr is of constant size, average overhead of communication shall be Hdr's division by ΔS . In a word, the more requests are submitted to License

Server at a time, the more customers can obtain expected ciphertext from one update. Obviously, too rare requests will degrade the system into client/server networking.

We will make comparison between our system and traditional solutions. Typical DRM over P2P networks are centralized and based on PKI. Each registered customer keeps a private key while License Server maintains the public one. It sends to License Server a license request and goes through a verification routine optionally. If the authentication is successful, License Server will encrypt session key with customer's public key and encapsulate it into a certificate with certain rights. In consideration of integrity, License Server normally appends to the certificate a signature with its private key and then sends back the licensing message to the customer.

Table 2. Performance comparison between P2P DRM based on broadcast encryption and centralized DRM based on PKI. n is the number of customers. The comparison mainly focuses on consumption of authorization for Lisence Server.

	P2P DRM Based on Broadcast Encryption	Centralized DRM Based on PKI
Storage Requirement	$O(n)$ for domain membership, public key, and ciphertexts	$O(n)$ for public keys
Number of Transmissions	Not more than One in average for each authorization	One for each authorization
Computation Cost	One group operation for each new participant	One public key operation for each new participant
Communication Overhead	One PK for the entire system; One S for an authorized domain; One Hdr and timestamp for each update	n public keys for the entire system; One encapsulation of session key for each user

Table 2 presents the performance comparison between P2P DRM based on broadcast encryption and typical centralized DRM based on PKI. Performance is evaluated in terms of storage requirement, number of transmissions, computation cost and communication overhead. P2P DRM based on broadcast encryption consumes more storage than typical one for cluster information management. Both schemes perform equally on computation complexity. Since cryptographic information is shared within authorized domain and disseminated in a peer-to-peer mode, S for certain cluster is published gradually but just once in all and Hdr is only distributed on update which usually handles several authorizations. Consequently novel DRM outperforms the typical one on average transmission times and communication overhead. License Server can then be load-balanced, communication accelerated, response latency shortened and overall performance improved.

Moreover, the novel scheme involves little modifications to original peer-to-peer infrastructure. It can be flexibly and efficiently adapted to various P2P applications, such as on-line business, virtual-cash trading, e-commerce and DRM for P2P streaming where users demanding the same channel natually fall into one authorized domain.

6 Conclusion and Future Work

Large-scale distribution of digital content has benefited a lot from high availability and dynamic scalability of P2P networks. Since the decentralized nature facilitates pirate and illegality, DRM over P2P networks will be a necessity to satisfy both access control over valuable materials and efficient distribution of media content.

In this paper we have proposed an efficient and flexible implementation of DRM over P2P networks. Our novel strategy takes full advantages of peer-to-peer features, derives the key scheme from broadcast encryption and allows the cryptographic information to be disseminated around in peer-to-peer mode, thereby reducing communication overhead and balancing work load for License Server. Mathematical analysis shows that novel DRM outperforms the traditional solution on alleviating server bottleneck, shortening response latency, and maintaining high scalability. In addition, our DRM places little impact on original peer-to-peer infrastructure and can be incorporated into various P2P applications, such as e-business, on-line trading, virtual cashing and DRM for P2P live streaming.

Our future work consists of providing fast recovery from dynamic variation, abbreviating cryptographic messages for collecting up-to-date ciphertext, enhancing robustness against abrupt fluctuation and adapting the system to more general peer-to-peer applications.

References

1. Subramanya, S.R., Yi, B.K.: Digital Rights Management. IEEE Potentials 25(2), 31–34 (2006)
2. Kumar, V.: Trust and Security in Peer-to-Peer System. In: Proceedings of the 17th International Conference on Database and Expert Systems Applications, pp. 703–707 (2006)
3. Yu, F., Zhang, H., Yan, F.: A Fuzzy Relation Trust Model in P2P System. In: International Conference on Computation Intelligence and Security, vol. 2, pp. 1497–1502 (2006)
4. Griffiths, N., Chao, K.-M., Younas, M.: Fuzzy Trust for Peer-to-Peer Systems. In: Proceedings of the 26th IEEE International Conference on Distributed Computing Systems Workshops, pp. 73–78 (2006)
5. Song, S., Hwang, K., Zhou, R., Kwok, Y.-K.: Trusted P2P Transactions with Fuzzy Reputation Aggregation. IEEE Internet Computing 9(6), 24–34 (2005)
6. Singh, A., Liu, L.: TrustMe: Anonymous Management of Trust Relationships in Decentralized P2P Systems. In: Proceedings of the Third International Conference on Peer-to-Peer Computing, pp. 142–149 (2003)
7. Xiao, L., Xu, Z., Zhang, X.: Low-Cost and Reliable Mutual Anonymity Protocols in Peer-to-Peer Networks. IEEE Transactions on Parallel and Distributed Systems 14(9), 829–840 (2003)
8. Nandan, A., Pau, G., Salomoni, P.: GhostShare – Reliable and Anonymous P2P Video Distribution. In: IEEE Global Telecommunications Conference Workshops, pp. 200–210 (2004)
9. Mee, J., Watters, P.A.: Detecting and Tracing Copyright Infringements in P2P Net-works. In: Proceedings of the International Conference on Networking, International Conference on Systems and International Conference on Mobile Communications and Learning Technologies, pp. 60–65 (2006)

10. Chen, K., Deng, Q.: Legitimate Peer-to-Peer Content Distribution Network. In: Proceedings of the Fifth International Conference on Grid and Cooperative Computing Workshops (2006)
11. Schmucker, M., Ebinger, P.: Promotional and Commercial Content Distribution based on a Legal and Trusted P2P Framework. In: Proceedings of the Seventh IEEE International Conference on E-Commerce Technology, pp. 439–442 (2005)
12. Chu, C.-C., Su, X., Prabhu, B.S., Gadh, R., Kurup, S., Sridhar, G., Sridhar, V.: Mobile DRM for Multimedia Content Commerce in P2P Networks. In: 2006 3rd IEEE Consumer Communi-cations and Networking Conference, vol. 2, pp. 1119–1123 (January 2006)
13. Neelima Arora, R.K., Shyamasundar, R.K.: PGSP: A Protocol for Secure Communication in Peer-to-Peer System. In: IEEE Wireless Communications and Networking Conference, vol. 4, pp. 2094–2099 (2005)
14. Pathak, V., Iftode, L.: Byzantine Fault Tolerant Public Key Authentication in Peer-to-Peer Systems. Computer Networks. Special Issues on Management in Peer-to-Peer Systems: Trust, Reputation and Security 50(4), 579–596 (2006)
15. Palomar, E., Estevez-Tapiador, J.M., Hernandez-Castro, J.C., Ribagorda, A.: Certificate-based Access Control in Pure P2P Networks. In: Proceedings of the Sixth IEEE International Conference on Peer-to-Peer Computing, pp. 177–184 (2006)
16. Pestoni, F., Lotspiech, J.B., Nusser, S.: xCP: Peer-to-Peer Content Protection. IEEE Signal Processing Magazine 21(2), 71–81 (2004)
17. Zhou, Y.C., Cerruti, J.A., Ma, L., Ma, L., Myles, G.: CPWCT: Making P2P Home Network Secure Virtual Multimedia Device. In: Proceedings of the IEEE Conference on Local Computer Networks 30th Anniversary (2005)
18. Fiat, A., Naor, M.: Broadcast Encryption. In: Proceedings of the 13th Annual International Cryptology Conference on Advances in Cryptology, pp. 480–491 (August 1994)
19. Lotspiech, J., Nusser, S., Pestoni, F.: Broadcast Encryption's Bright Future. Computer 35(8), 57–63 (2002)
20. Boneh, D., Gentry, C., Waters, B.: Collusion Resistant Broadcast Encryption with Short Ciphertexts and Private Keys. In: Shoup, V. (ed.) CRYPTO 2005. LNCS, vol. 3621, pp. 258–275. Springer, Heidelberg (2005)

A New Video Encryption Scheme for H.264/AVC

Yibo Fan[1], Jidong Wang[1], Takeshi Ikenaga[1],
Yukiyasu Tsunoo[2], and Satoshi Goto[1]

[1] Graduate School of Information, Production and Systems, Waseda University
2-7 Hibikino, Wakamatsu, Kitakyushu, Fukuoka, 808-0135, Japan
[2] Internet Systems Research Laboratories, NEC Corp.
Kawasaki, Kanagawa 211-8666, Japan
fanyibo@ruri.waseda.jp, wangjidong@fuji.waseda.jp,
ikenaga@waseda.jp,
tsunoo@bl.jp.nec.com, goto@waseda.jp

Abstract. With the increase of video applications, the security of video data becomes more and more important. In this paper, we propose a new video encryption scheme for H.264/AVC video coding standard. We define Unequal Secure Encryption (USE) as an approach that applies different cryptographic algorithms (with different security strength) to different partitions of video data. The USE scheme includes two parts: video data classification and unequal secure video data encryption. For data classification, we propose 3 data classification methods and define 5 security levels in our scheme. For encryption, we propose a new stream cipher algorithm FLEX and XOR method to reduce computational cost. In this way, our scheme can achieve both high security and low computational cost. The experimental results show that the computational cost of the USE scheme is very low. In security level 0, the computational cost is about 18% of naive encryption. The USE scheme is very suitable for high security and low cost video encryption systems.

Keywords: Video, Encryption, H.264/AVC.

1 Introduction

With the increase of multimedia applications in communication, the data transmission and information security become more and more important. For video data compression, there are several important standards such as MPEG-1, MPEG-2/H.262, MPEG-4 and H.264/AVC. H.264/AVC video compression standard is the newest international video coding standard, which is jointly developed by ITU-T Video Coding Experts Group (VCEG) and the ISO/IEC Moving Picture Experts Group (MPEG) [1].

For information security, a common video encryption standard does not exist. To protect the video content, there are three major security technologies: (1) Encryption technology to provide end-to-end security when distributing video over internet or other public communication channel. (2) Watermarking technology to achieve copyright protection, ownership trace, and authentication. (3) Access control

H.H.S. Ip et al. (Eds.): PCM 2007, LNCS 4810, pp. 246–255, 2007.

technology to prevent unauthorized access. In this paper, we focus on video data encryption technology, especially for H.264/AVC video data encryption.

Most of existing video encryption schemes is designed for previous video coding standards, and there are few video encryption schemes designed for H.264/AVC. According to these video encryption schemes, they can be classified into two major encryption types: whole video data encryption and selective video data encryption. The whole video data encryption method has two different approaches: (a) Video scrambling technology. Permuting the video in the time domain or the frequency domain, however, the security is low. (b) Encryption. Encrypting the entire video data using standard cryptographic algorithms, it is often referred to as "naive approach". This method can provide substantial high security. However, it needs huge computational cost.

Most of researches are about selective video data encryption, which can reduce computational cost as it just encrypts only a part of video data. However, the security becomes problem in many proposed schemes. Some schemes only achieved moderate to low security and only few of the proposed methods achieved substantial security.

In this paper, an Unequal Secure Encryption (USE) scheme is proposed for video secure systems. There are three major targets in the USE scheme: security, feasibility, and low computational cost. In the USE scheme, we encrypt the total video data using standard cryptographic algorithms to make our scheme highly secure. In order to make the USE scheme can be used in most of the video security systems, we perform all of the encryption operations after entropy coding. In this way, the video coding system and the video encryption system can be separated with each other. The remaining problem is computational cost. As computational cost of "naive approach" is huge, we need to make some optimization to reduce the computational cost. Here we use two methods: (1) *Data classification*. We classify the total video data into two data partitions, important data partition and unimportant data partition. Many new features in H.264/AVC make this procedure easy to implement. Normally, important data partition has smaller size than unimportant one. (2) *Unequal secure encryption*. We use AES [13] to encrypt important data partition and proposed FLEX algorithm to encrypt unimportant data partition. The computational cost of FLEX is only 1/5 of AES. In this way, we can keep our scheme highly secure with low computational cost.

The rest of this paper is organized as follows. The existing video encryption schemes are discussed in Section 2. The USE scheme is proposed in Section 3. Our experimental results are presented in Section 4. Finally, the conclusion is given in Section 5.

2 Video Encryption Methods

The most secure way of protecting video data is naive algorithm, which encrypts the entire video data by standard cryptosystem. However, larger computational overhead makes it inefficient or impossible in lots of applications. As a result, selective encryption becomes popular in most of the video encryption researches.

Liu and Eskicioglu in [3], Furht, Socek and Eskicioglu in [6] have presented a comprehensive classification include most of the presented selective video encryption algorithms. According to their work, these encryption schemes can be further classified into three types: frequency domain schemes, spatial domain schemes and entropy coding schemes. Frequency domain scheme selects frequency domain data in video such as motion vector, DCT coefficients, I blocks, I frames and so on. Most of the selective encryption methods are based on frequency domain. Spatial domain schemes make use of spatial information in video data. Entropy coding schemes use special entropy codec to do encryption.

There are three main problems in these encryption schemes.

A. Security Problem

A lot of cryptanalysis work has been done in proposed video encryption schemes [5, 7-11]. From the view points of these researches, the security of schemes which don't use standard cryptographic algorithms is very low. For example, Permutation is highly risky shown in [5, 8-10]. Even using standard cryptographic algorithms such as DES or AES in video encryption scheme, there are also many security problems existing. The corresponding cryptanalysis can be found in [5, 7, 11].

B. Computational Cost Problem

Some methods can provide substantial security. However, computational overhead and data overhead become worse. For example, VEA scheme [12] is *"very close to the security of encryption scheme E that is internally used"* [6]. However, it needs to encrypt half of video data using internal encryption scheme E and transfer a large amount of additional keys to receiver.

C. Feasibility Problem

Feasibility is another problem existed in many schemes. A lot of existing schemes are so called *"Integrated video compression and encryption system"*. It means that the video encryption module must be integrated into video compression system. For example, permutation of AC, DC coefficients should be done before entropy coding. In this way, the encryption should break the procedure of video compression, and the encryption module must be integrated into video compression system. That is why the standard decoder can't work when decoding encrypted video data. The corresponding decoder to this secure encoder should be *"Integrated video decompression and decryption decoder"*. This causes such kind of scheme very hard to be widely used in commercial applications.

3 Unequal Secure Encryption (USE) Scheme

3.1 USE Scheme Introduction

The purpose of designing Unequal Secure Encryption scheme is to provide substantial security with low computational cost for video encryption. As discussed in Section 1, a lot of existing video encryption schemes target low computational cost while ignoring security problems, many proposed schemes are so *called "Integrated video compression and encryption system"* which is hard to be widely used in video security systems. Some proposed schemes can achieve high security level. However, the computational cost is bad.

Figure 1 shows the idea of the USE scheme.

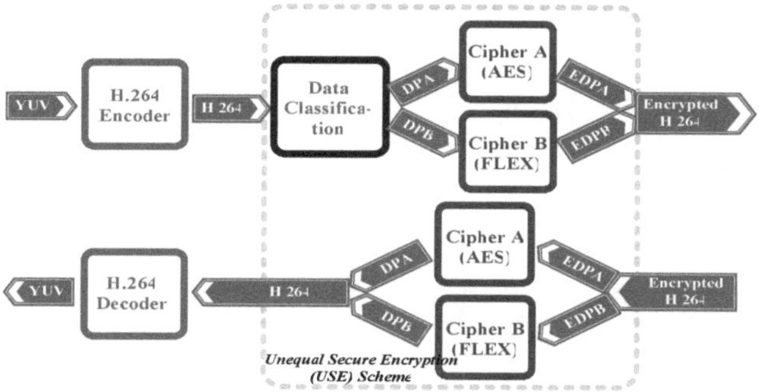

Fig. 1. Unequal Secure Encryption scheme

The USE scheme includes two major steps: The first step is video data classification. The purpose of classification is to divide video data into two partitions: important video data partition and unimportant video data partition. The importance is evaluated by how difficult to reconstruct a picture. As shown in Figure 1, after data classification, H.264/AVC video data is parted into DPA (Data Partition A, important) and DPB (Data Partition B, unimportant).

The second step in the USE scheme is unequal secure encryption. Unlike the existing selective encryption scheme, the USE scheme encrypts total video data, and different cryptographic algorithms are selected to encrypt different part of video data. As discussed in Section 1, from the view points of cryptanalysis, the best way to keep security is to encrypt the total video data by standard cryptographic algorithms, other than some other methods whose security can not be approved. As shown in Figure 1, two algorithms are used in the USE scheme. DPA is encrypted by cipher A, and DPB is encrypted by cipher B. Different algorithm has different security level and computational cost. In the USE scheme, we use AES as cipher A, and FLEX as cipher B. FLEX is based on AES, the hardware implementations of AES can also support FLEX, and the speed of FLEX is faster than AES. Besides AES and FLEX, some other *cryptographic* algorithms also can be used in the USE scheme.

The computational cost for USE *scheme* depends on data classification and cryptographic algorithms.

3.2 Data Classification Methods

There are many data classification methods in the USE scheme. As the USE scheme is designed for H.264/AVC, some new features in H.264/AVC can be used in data classification.

Data Partitioning (Extended Profile): This is a new feature in H.264/AVC *Extended Profile*, which can do data partition automatically. As shown in Figure 2, the coded data that makes up a slice is placed in three separate Data Partitions (A, B and C). Partition A contains the slice header and header data *for* MBs. Partition B contains intra coding MBs' residual data, Partition C contains inter coding MBs' residual data. Obviously, the information in Partition A is more important than B and C. Normally, intra data (Partition B) is considered more important than inter data (Partition C).

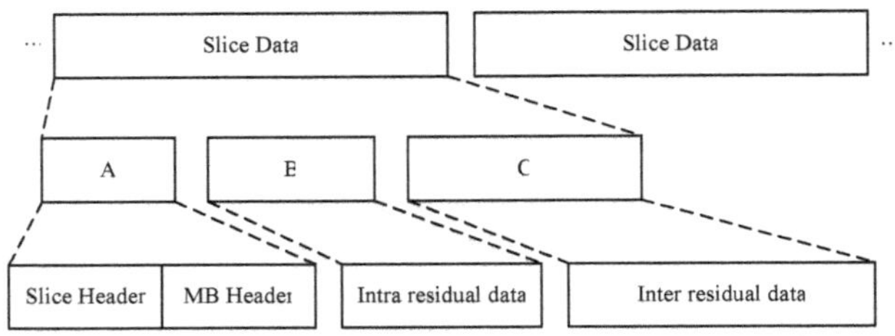

Fig. 2. Slice syntax of H.264/AVC Extended Profile

FMO (Baseline Profile, Extended Profile): FMO is a new feature in H.264/AVC. It has ability to partition the picture into regions called slice groups. In H.264/AVC standard, *FMO* consists of seven different partition types. All of these types make it easy to partition pictures. In the USE scheme, there are two kinds of partition modes (shown in Figure 3). The first partition mode is *Region Based FMO*. In this mode, the picture is partitioned into two slice groups: Secret regions and Normal regions. The shape of secret regions can be decided by other pre-processing tools such as object recognition and extraction. This mode can support extraction of any interesting shapes in picture, so object based encryption can be realized. The second partition mode is *Mode Based FMO*. In this mode, the picture is partitioned into two slice groups: Intra MBs and Inter MBs. As Intra MBs is more important than Inter MBs to reconstruct picture, the Intra MBs should use highly secure encryption algorithms.

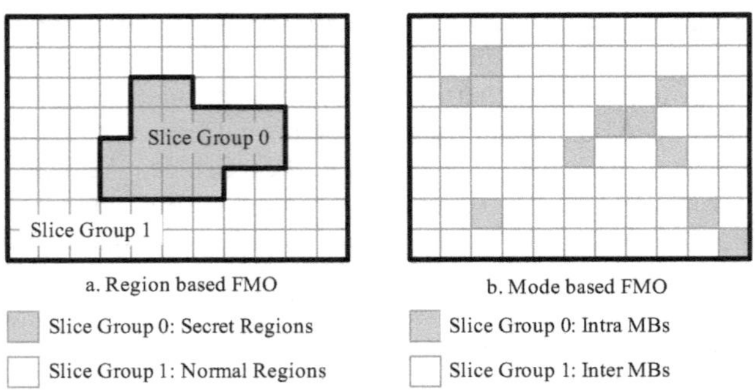

Fig. 3. Data Partitioned Slices by FMO

Parameters Extraction (All Profiles): Since *Data Partitioning* method and *FMO* method are profile limited methods, a common method which can be used in any profiles is needed. The *Parameter Extraction* method which is shown in Figure 4 is such kind of method. The effect of this method is like *Data Partitioning* method. The difference is that *Data Partitioning* method can be automatically done by codec.

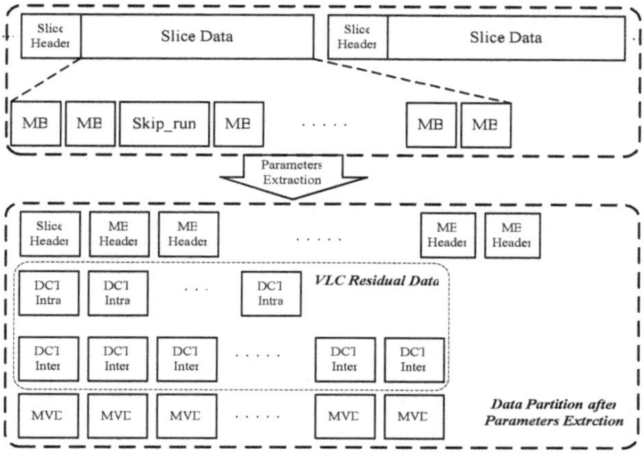

Fig. 4. Data Partitioning by Parameters Extraction

3.3 Security Levels

There are 5 security levels in the USE scheme (Shown in Table 1). The definitions are listed as following:

Level 0: Headers are encrypted by AES, and the remained data are encrypted by FLEX. In level 0, the computational cost is the lowest. The *Parameters Extraction* method can be used in this level.

Level 1: Headers and MVDs (in H.264/AVC, MVD corresponds to motion vector) are encrypted by AES, and the remained data are encrypted by FLEX. The *Data Partitioning* method and *Parameters Extraction* method can be used in this level.

Level 2: Headers, MVD and Intra MBs are encrypted by AES, and Inter MBs are encrypted by FLEX. All of three data classification methods can be used in this level.

Level 3: The entire video is encrypted by AES. Level 3 has the highest computational cost and security.

Level x: This is an extra security levels for the USE scheme. Only FMO methods can be used in this level. It can be used in object-based encryption applications.

3.4 Encryption Methods

A. FLEX Algorithm

FLEX (which stands for Fast Leak EXtraction) is a stream cipher algorithm based on the round transformation of AES. FLEX provides the same key agility and short message block performance as AES while handling longer messages faster than AES. In addition, it has the same hardware and software flexibility as AES, and hardware implementations of FLEX can share resources with AES implementations. The FLEX algorithm is shown in Figure 5.

Table 1. Security levels in the USE scheme

Secure Levels	Algorithm	Video content	Data Classification Methods
Level 0	AES	Headers	Parameters Extraction
	FLEX	Inter, Intra, MVD	
Level 1	AES	Headers, MVD	Data Partitioning
	FLEX	Inter, Intra	Parameters Extraction
Level 2	AES	Headers, MVD, Intra	Data Partitioning Parameters Extraction FMO
	FLEX	Inter	
Level 3	AES	All	-
Level x	AES	Secret Region	FMO
	FLEX	Normal Region	

Firstly, the given IV is encrypted by AES invocation: $S=AES_{Key}(IV)$. The 128-bit result S together with encryption Key constitutes a 256-bit secret state of the stream cipher. Secondly, we use result S as a new input data to AES: $S'=AES_{Key}(S)$. The cipher stream will be generated as this process continues. The output of FLEX is not S or S', it comes from internal states of AES. As shown in Figure 6, 4×4 array of bytes constitutes the internal state of AES. In every round function of AES, a part of AES *States* is output. In FLEX algorithm, $b_{0,0}$, $b_{0,2}$, $b_{1,1}$, $b_{1,3}$, $b_{2,0}$, $b_{2,2}$, $b_{3,1}$, $b_{3,3}$ are output in odd rounds, $b_{0,1}$, $b_{0,3}$, $b_{1,1}$, $b_{1,3}$, $b_{2,1}$, $b_{2,3}$, $b_{3,1}$, $b_{3,3}$ are output in even rounds. It totally outputs 80 *States* of AES (640 bits) in every AES encryption round. The speed of FLEX is exactly 5 times faster than AES.

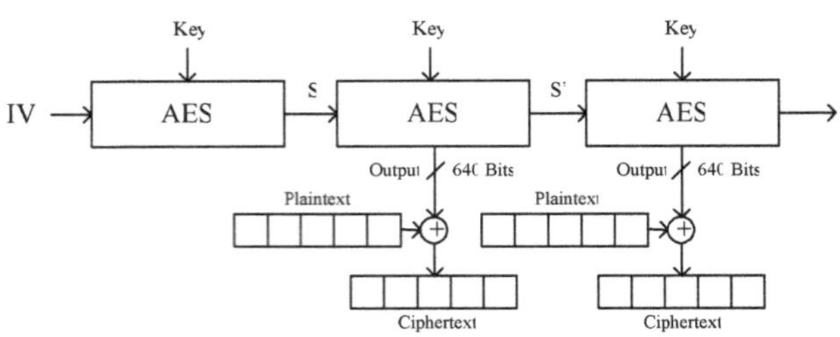

Fig. 5. FLEX encryption algorithm

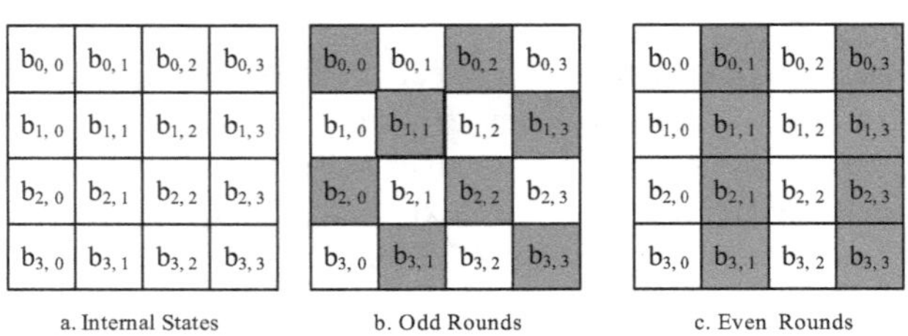

Fig. 6. Leak position in the even and odd rounds

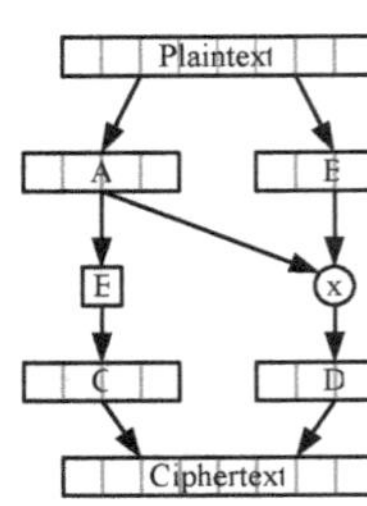

Fig. 7. XOR Method

B. XOR Method

In order to further reduce computational cost, we use XOR method to reduce 50% of computational cost. This method is shown in Figure 7. There are three steps of this method:

Step 1: Divide total plaintext into two partitions A and B (with the same size),
Step 2: Encrypt partition A while XOR partition A with partition B bits by bits,
Step 3: Partition C and D are ciphertext.

By using XOR method, we can just encrypt half of video data to achieve low computational cost. The security of total plaintext is equal to partition A.

6 Experimental Results

Table 2 shows the experimental results for several H.264/AVC QCIF sequences. It lists the header information size, MVD size, Intra MBs residue size and Inter MBs residue size in 10 QCIF test sequences. In every test sequence, it begin with I frame, followed by P or B frames. Totally 100 frames are included in each test sequence.

From these 10 sequences, the average ratios of data size for Header is about 20%, MVD is about 20%, Intra residue is about 15%, and Inter residue is about 45%.

Table 3 shows the computational cost and encrypted data percentage comparison of our USE scheme with other's proposals. The comparison is under the experimental results listed in table 2. We use the average percentage of 10 sequences. The computational cost is measured by *n*@AES. We consider that the "naive encryption" by AES is 100%@AES. For example, the computational cost for SECMPEG level 1 is 20%@AES. It means that the computational cost of SECMPEG level 1 is 20% of "naive encryption". The encrypted data percentage reflects the security strength of

Table 2. Video data partition size (QCIF@100 Frames, I Frame followed by P or B Frames)

Video Sequence	Header		MVD		Intra MBs Residue		Inter MBs Residue		Total size (bits)
	Header (bits)	Header/Total (bits)	MVD (bits)	MVD/Total (%)	Intra (bits)	Intra/Total (%)	Inter (bits)	Inter/Total (%)	
Canoa	375761	14.41%	300816	11.58%	769777	29.62%	1152357	44.34%	2608088
CarPhone	163807	26.56%	150868	24.85%	55551	9.15%	236802	39.01%	616672
Claire	57026	32.47%	38300	23.18%	10801	6.54%	59111	35.77%	175640
Container	63771	29.28%	32468	15.68%	23877	11.53%	86899	41.98%	217832
Football	435313	15.84%	390128	14.25%	866291	31.64%	1046531	38.22%	2747592
Foreman	180379	26.50%	195606	29.13%	43971	6.55%	251588	37.46%	680648
Grandma	60164	30.29%	39218	20.86%	17903	9.52%	70763	37.63%	198600
Mobile	247232	19.59%	207090	16.54%	54242	4.33%	743504	59.38%	1261768
News	97174	21.37%	86012	19.35%	55332	12.45%	206017	46.34%	454736
Table	147555	18.55%	165196	21.03%	78360	9.98%	394422	50.21%	795512

Table 3. Comparison with other symmetric cryptographic algorithms based video encryption schemes

Encryption Schemes		Content to be encrypted	Computational overhead (@ AES)	Encrypted Data
SEC MPEG [15]	Level 1	Header	20% @ AES	20%
	Level 3	Header and Intra	35% @ AES	35%
	Level 4	All	100% @ AES	100%
Aegis [16,17]		Header, I frame	35% @ AES	35%
VEA [12]		All	50% @ AES	100%
RVEA [18, 19]		Sign Bit of DCT and motion vectors	10% @ AES	10%
Alattar [20]	Method 0	Header, Intra and MVD	55% @ AES	55%
	Method 1	Every n^{th} I MB	1/n*15%@AES	1/n*15%
	Method 2	+ Header	(1/n*15 + 40)% @ AES	(1/n*15 + 40)%
	Method 3	+ n^{th} Header	(1/n*15 +1/n*40)%@ AES	(1/n*15 +1/n*40)%
Ours	Level 0	All	18% @ AES	100%
	Level 1	All	26% @ AES	100%
	Level 2	All	32% @ AES	100%
	Level 3	All	50% @ AES	100%

each video encryption schemes. As all of the schemes use AES to encrypt the selected important data, the security can be evaluated by the amount of encrypted data.

From table 3, it can be seen that our scheme can achieve both high security and low computational cost compared to others' work. For example, the computational cost of Level 0 in our USE scheme is just about 18% of naive encryption, and the encrypted data percentage is 100%.

7 Conclusion

In this paper, an unequal secure encryption scheme for H.264/AVC is proposed. This scheme mainly includes two parts: *Data classification* and *Unequal secure encryption*. Some new ideas are proposed in this scheme, such as Data classification methods, FLEX algorithm, XOR method and so on. The experimental results show that our scheme can achieve both high security and low computational cost. It is very suitable to be used in low power and high security video encryption systems.

Acknowledgement

This research is supported by CREST, JST.

References

1. Ostermann, J., Bormans, J., List, P., Marpe, D., Narroschke, M., Pereira, F., Stockhammer, T., Wedi, T.: Video coding with H.264/AVC: tools, performance, and complexity. IEEE Circuits and Systems Magazine 4(1), 7–28 (2004)
2. Furht, B., Socek, D.: Multimedia Security: Encryption Techniques, IEC Comprehensive Report on Information Security, International Engineering Consortium, Chicago, IL (2003)
3. Liu, X., Eskicioglu, A.M.: Selective Encryption of Multimedia Content in Distribution Networks: Challenges and New Directions. In: CIIT 2003. IASTED International Conference on Communications, Internet and Information Technology, Scottsdale, AZ, (November 17-19, 2003) pp. 17–19 (2003)

4. Lookabaugh, T., Sicker, D.C., Keaton, D.M., Guo, W.Y., Vedula, I.: Security Analysis of Selectively Encrypted MPEG-2 Streams. In: Multimedia Systems and Applications VI Conference, Orlando, FL (September 7-11, 2003)
5. Qiao, L., Nahrstedt, K.: Comparison of MPEG Encryption Algorithms, International Journal on Computer and Graphics. Special Issue on Data Security in Image Communication and Network 22(3) (1998)
6. Furht, B., Socek, D., Eskicioglu, A.M.: Fundamentals of multimedia encryption techniques. In: Multimedia Security Handbook, ch. 3, pp. 93–131. CRC Press, Boca Raton (2004)
7. Agi, I., Gong, L.: An Empirical Study of Secure MPEG Video Transmission. In: Proceedings of the Symposium on Network and Distributed Systems Security, IEEE, Los Alamitos (1996)
8. Qiao, L., Nahrstedt, K., Tam, I.: Is MPEG Encryption by Using Random List Instead of Zigzag Order Secure? In: IEEE International Symposium on Consumer Electronics, Singapore (December 1997)
9. Bhargava, B., Shi, C., Wang, Y.: MEPG: Video Encryption Algorithms (August 2002), available at http://raidlab.cs.purdue.edu/papers/mm.ps
10. Seidel, T., Socek, D., Sramka, M.: Cryptanalysis of Video Encryption Algorithms. In: TATRACRYPT 2003. Proceedings of The 3rd Central European Conference on Cryptology, Bratislava, Slovak Republic (2003)
11. Alattar, A., Al-Regib, G.: Evaluation of selective encryption techniques for secure transmission of MPEG video bit-streams. In: Proceedings of the IEEE International Symposium on Circuits and Systems, vol. 4, pp IV-340-IV-343, (1999)
12. Qiao, L., Nahrstedt, K.: A New Algorithm for MPEG Video Encryption. In: CISST 1997. Proceedings of the 1st International Conference on Imaging Science, Systems and Technology, Las Vegas, NV, pp. 21–29 (July 1997)
13. National Institute of Standards and Technology (U.S.). Advanced Encryption Standards (AES). FIPS Publication 197 (2001)
14. Biryukov, A.: A New 128-bit Stream Cipher LEX, ECRYPT Stream Cipher Project Report, 2005, Available at http://www.ecrypt.eu.org/stream/lex.html
15. Meyer, J., Gadegast, F.: Security Mechanisms for Multimedia Data with the Example MPEG-1Video, Project Description of SECMPEG, Technical University of Berlin, Germany (May 1995)
16. Maples, T.B., Spanos, G.A.: Performance study of selective encryption scheme for the security f networked real-time video. In: Proceedings of the 4th International Conference on Computer and Communications, Las Vegas, NV (1995)
17. Spanos, G.A., Maples, T.B.: Security for Real-Time MPEG Compressed Video in Distributed Multimedia Applications. In: Conference on Computers and Communications, pp. 72–78 (1996)
18. Shi, C., Bhargava, B.: A Fast MPEG Video Encryption Algorithm. In: Proceedings of the 6th International Multimedia Conference, Bristol, UK (September 12-16, 1998)
19. Shi, C., Wang, S.-Y., Bhargava, B.: MPEG Video Encryption in Real-Time Using Secret key Cryptography. In: PDPTA 1999. 1999 International Conference on Parallel and Distributed Processing Techniques and Applications, Las Vegas, NV (June 28 - July 1, 1999)
20. Alattar, A.M., Al-Regib, G.I., Al-Semari, S.A.: Improved Selective Encryption techniques for Secure Transmission of MPEG Video Bit-Streams. In: ICIP 1999. Proceedings of the 1999 International Conference on Image Processing, Kobe, Japan (October 24-28, 1999) vol. 4, pp. 256–260 (1999)

Tattoo-ID: Automatic Tattoo Image Retrieval for Suspect and Victim Identification

Anil K. Jain, Jung-Eun Lee, and Rong Jin

Computer Science and Engineering, Michigan State University,
East Lansing, Michigan 48824, USA
{jain, leejun11, rongjin}@cse.msu.edu

Abstract. Tattoos are used by law enforcement agencies for identification of a victim or a suspect using a false identity. Current method for matching tattoos is based on human-assigned class labels that is time consuming, subjective and has limited performance. It is desirable to build a content-based image retrieval (CBIR) system for automatic matching and retrieval of tattoos. We examine several key design issues related to building a prototype CBIR system for tattoo image database. Our system computes the similarity between the query and stored tattoos based on image content to retrieve the most similar tattoos. The performance of the system is evaluated on a database of 2,157 tattoos representing 20 different classes. Effects of segmentation errors, image transformations (e.g., blurring, illumination), influence of semantic labels and relevance feedback are also studied.

Keywords: Human Identification, Content-based Image Retrieval, Tattoos, Forensics.

1 Introduction

People have used tattoos in order to represent themselves and to be identified as distinct from others for over 5,000 years [1]. Until recently, practice of tattooing was limited to particular groups, such as motor bikers, sailors and members of criminal gangs. But, now, tattoos are no longer associated with such unsavory reputations, and as a result, the size of the tattooed population is rising rapidly. The rising popularity of tattoos among the younger section of the population is even more surprising. A study published in the Journal of the American Academy of Dermatology in 2006 reported that about 36% of Americans in the age group 18 to 29 have at least one tattoo [2].

Tattoos are a useful tool for person identification in forensic applications. There has been an increased emphasis on the use of "soft biometric" traits [3] (e.g., tattoos) in identification tasks when primary biometric traits (e.g., fingerprints) are either no longer available, or corrupted. Tattoo pigments are embedded in the skin to such a depth that even severe skin burns often do not destroy a tattoo; tattoos were used to identify victims of 9/11 attacks [4] and Asian tsunami in 2004 [5]. Criminal identification using tattoos is another important application, because tattoos often

H.H.S. Ip et al. (Eds.): PCM 2007, LNCS 4810, pp. 256–265, 2007.

contain useful information, such as gang membership, religious beliefs, previous convictions, years spent in jail, etc. [1] (Fig. 1). A study by Burma [6] suggested that delinquents are significantly more likely to have tattoos than non-delinquents.

(a) (b) (c)

Fig. 1. Examples of Criminal Tattoos: (a) Teardrop tattoo (person has killed someone or had a friend killed in prison), (b) Texas Syndicate (TS) gang member tattoo, (c) Three dots tattoo found on the prisoner's back of the hand [7-8]

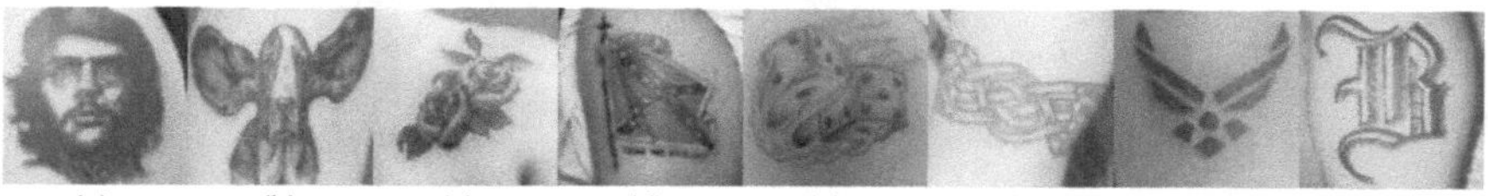

(a) (b) (c) (d) (e) (f) (g) (h)

Fig. 2. Sample tattoos from the eight major classes in ANSI/NIST-standard: (a) Human, (b) Animal, (c) Plant, (d) Flag, (e) Object, (f) Abstract, (g) Symbol, and (h) Other

Law enforcement agencies routinely photograph and catalog tattoo patterns for the purpose of identifying victims and convicts (who often use aliases). The ANSI/NIST-ITL 1-2007 standard [9] defines 8 major class labels, e.g., human face, animal, and symbols for tattoos (Fig. 2). Manual searches are performed by matching the class labels of query and database tattoos. The tattoo matching process based on human-assigned class labels is subjective, has limited performance and time-consuming. Further, simple class description in textual query ("find a dragon tattoo") does not include all the semantic information in tattoos [10] as evident by the large intra-class variability (Fig. 3). Finally, the classes in ANSI/NIST standard are not adequate to describe increasing variety of new tattoo designs.

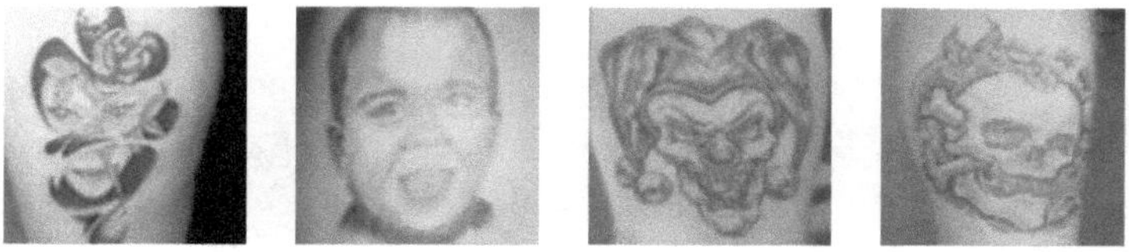

Fig. 3. Different images belonging to HUMAN category

We describe the preliminary design and implementation of a CBIR system for tattoo images, called Tattoo-ID. While, successful CBIR systems for a variety of application domains such as satellite, trademark, vacation, and medical images have been reported [12], [13], to our knowledge, this is the first attempt to build a system for tattoo images. Compared to the general CBIR systems, which retrieve images similar to the given query, the goal of our Tattoo-ID system is driven by the specific application requirements. Since tattoo images are used for human identification, the system is expected to retrieve all the images in the database that are some minor variations of the specific tattoo in the given query image. In this sense, each tattoo is unique. Any variation in its multiple images is caused by the imaging environment and the condition of the tattoo on the skin (e.g., fading over time). Therefore, the challenges of this application domain are not only the large intra-class variability, but also a large number of potential image variations. We currently limit ourselves to variations introduced by image transformation, such as blurring and illumination (Fig. 4).

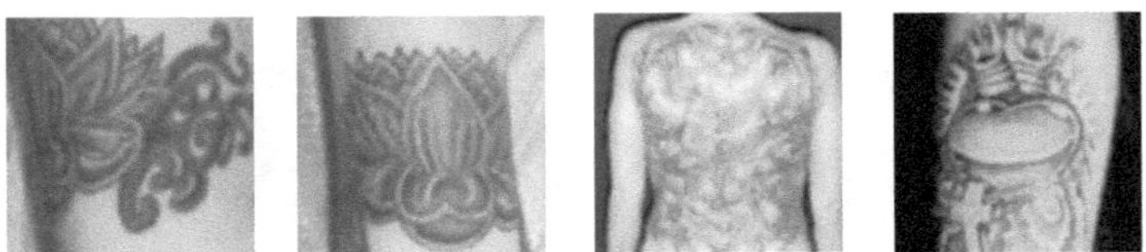

(a) (b) (c) (d)

Fig. 4. Examples of difficult tattoos: (a) and (b) same tattoo from two different viewpoints, (c) and (d) multi-object tattoos

2 Tattoo Image Database

We have downloaded 2,157 tattoo images from the Web [14] belonging to eight main classes and 20 subclasses based on ANSI/NIST standard [9]. Tattoo images are often captured under non-ideal conditions (e.g., by a surveillance video camera). We classify the resulting image transformations as: blurring, additive noise, changes in illumination, color, aspect ratio and rotation (Fig. 5). For each image transformation, we generate 20 different variations of a tattoo as follows: two different intensities of blurring, additive noise and illumination; six different aspect ratios, four different rotations, and four different color changes. This results in a total of 43,140 transformed images of 2,157 original tattoo images.

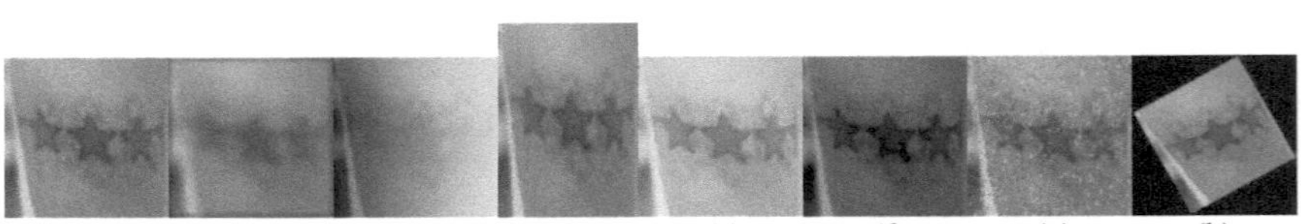

(a) (b) (c) (d) (e) (f) (g) (h)

Fig. 5. Examples of tattoo image transformations: (a) original, variations due to (b) blurring, (c) illumination, (d) aspect ratio, (e) and (f) color, (g) additive noise, and (h) rotation

3 Tattoo-ID System

In our design of a tattoo CBIR system (Fig. 6), we examine and evaluate the following issues: (i) types of transformations that mimic the reality in capturing tattoo images and their effects on image retrieval, (ii) choice of image features and similarity measure, and (iii) effect of user relevance feedback.

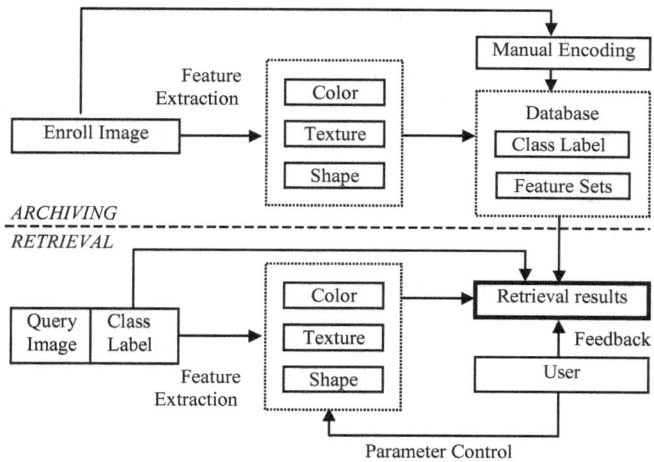

Fig. 6. Tattoo-ID system

3.1 Preprocessing

Since tattoos appear on uniform regions of skin, edge based operations generally perform well for foreground segmentation (region of interest). We used 3 × 3 Sobel operator to obtain the magnitude and direction of gradient at each pixel. By thresholding the gradient, followed by a morphological closing and opening operations, foreground is obtained (Fig. 7).

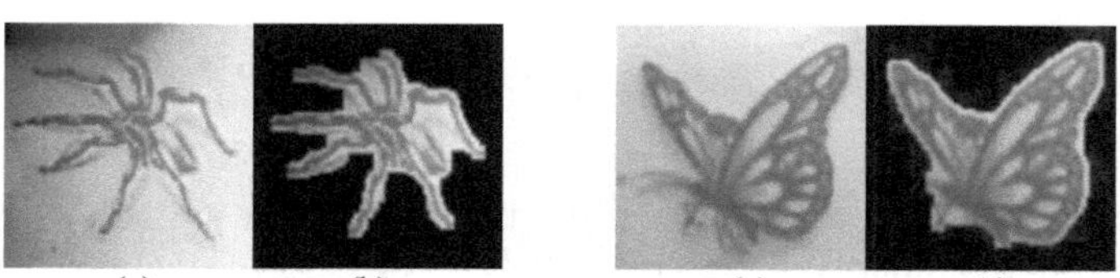

Fig. 7. Examples of tattoo segmentation: (a) and (c) are input images, (b) and (d) are corresponding segmented images

3.2 Image Features

Our choice of features for capturing low-level image attributes (color, shape and texture) is based on the extensive literature on content-based image retrieval [11], [12], [13], [16], [19]. Specific features chosen depend on our application domain of tattoo images.

Color. We used the RGB space to extract two color descriptors, namely color histogram and color correlogram [11], [15]. A color correlogram is a table indexed by a pair of colors, where the k-th entry for (i, j) specifies the probability of finding a pixel of color j at a distance k from a pixel of color i in the image. In our experiments, the color histogram and correlogram are calculated by dividing each color component into 20 and 63 bins, respectively, resulting in total of 60 and 189 total bins for the color histogram and correlogram, respectively. For computational efficiency, we compute color autocorrelogram between identical colors in a local neighborhood, i.e., $i = j$ and $k = 1, 3, 5$.

Shape. Classical 2D shape representation uses a set of moment invariants. Based on 2nd and 3rd order moments, a set of seven features that are invariant to translation, rotation, and scale are obtained [16]. Two feature sets are extracted from the segmented grayscale and the gradient tattoo images, respectively [11].

Texture. Edge Direction Coherence Vector that stores the ratio of coherent to non-coherent edge pixels with the same quantized direction (within an interval of 10°) is used [12]. A threshold (0.1% of image size) on the edge-connected components in a given direction is used to decide the region coherency. This feature discriminates structured edges from randomly distributed edges.

3.3 Matching

To decide a match between two tattoo images, we first compute a similarity score for each attribute (color, shape and texture) separately. Since each of the features is in the form of a vector, we regarded the vectors as histograms and apply histogram intersection method [17] to compute the similarity. Given two normalized histograms H^1 and H^2, the similarity is defined as:

$$S_{H^1,H^2} = \sum_{i}^{B} \min(H^1(i), H^2(i)) \quad (1)$$

where B is the number of bins. When the two histograms are completely disjoint (overlapping), the similarity score equals 0 (1). For color histogram, the similarity scores are calculated by averaging the similarities in individual color components (R, G, B). We currently assign the same weight to all the features, so that the overall matching score between two images is calculated as the sum of similarity scores from individual attributes.

3.4 Relevance Feedback

A simple relevance feedback approach is implemented to improve the retrieval accuracy. A straightforward approach for relevance feedback is to modify the query by the centroid of the images that are marked as relevant [18]. However, the problem with this approach is that it assumes a single mode for the set of images that the user considers relevant to the query. Given the large image variation, it is more likely for the relevant images to exhibit multi-modal distribution than uni-modal distribution. To address this problem, we first compute the similarity of every image in the database to each of the relevant images and then retrieve images based on this new similarity. The user can continue refining the retrieved images by running the feedback procedure iteratively until all the matched tattoo images are found. A graphical user interface is designed to allow a user to provide relevance judgments for the retrieved images.

4 Experimental Results

To evaluate the retrieval performance of the Tattoo-ID system, three sets of experiments are conducted with following scenarios: (I) high quality query images that are taken by police officers when booking suspects in prison, and (II) query images of victims/suspects that are captured at crime scenes. We simulate the second category of query images by applying the image transformations (see Fig. 5) to the high quality query images. In the third experiment, (III) we repeated experiments I and II by including semantic (class) labels associated with query and database to determine if retrieval performance can be improved. Table 1 summarizes the database and the query size for the experiments I and II.

Table 1. Database and query size for Experiments I and II

Experiment	Number of queries	Database size
I	2,157 high quality tattoos	43,140 transformed images
II	43,140 transformed images	2,157 high quality tattoos

Experiment I aims to evaluate the Tattoo-ID system with high quality query images. A retrieved image is deemed to be relevant when it is a transformed version of the query image. Both precision and recall are used as the evaluation metrics. Fig. 8(a) shows the average precision and recall curve of this experiment; the precision at ranks 1, 10 and 20 are 84.6%, 60.4%, and 51.2%, respectively. Among all the images in the database, the transformed images that are blurred and undergo changes in illumination and color component modification are the most difficult to retrieve (Fig. 8(b)). This is because both blurring and uneven illumination makes it difficult to correctly automatically segment a tattoo image from its background (Fig. 9). This issue can be partially addressed by the user relevance feedback. Overall, the average precision at rank 20 is improved from 51.2% to 64.7%, 68.7%, and 69.2% after the first three iterations of user relevance feedback.

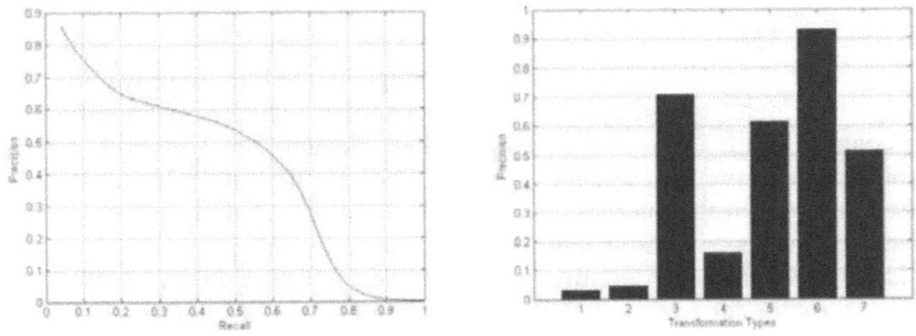

(a) (b)

Fig. 8. Experiment I results: (a) Precision & recall curve, (b) precision of each transformation at rank 20 (transformations are labeled as follows. 1: blurring, 2: illumination, 3: additive noise, 4: color, 5: rotation, 6: aspect ratio, and 7: overall).

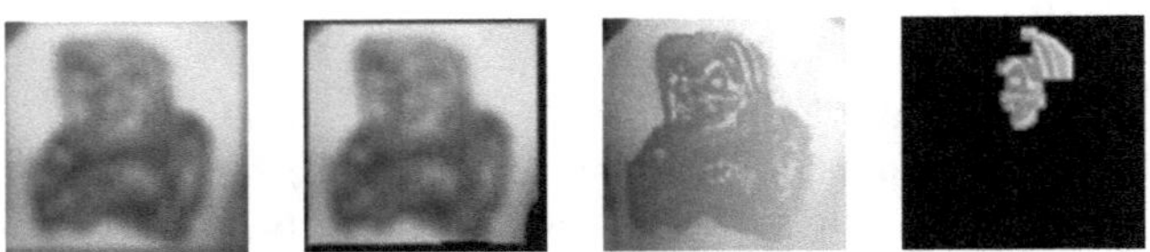

(a) (b) (c) (d)

Fig. 9. Examples of segmentation errors: (a) blurred image, (b) segmentation, (c) uneven illuminated image and (d) its segmentation. For the blurred image in (a), the entire image is found as foreground.

In addition to the synthetic transformation of the tattoo images, we also evaluated our approach on multiple images of a tattoo captured under different imaging environments. One such example is shown below (Fig. 10). Seven different images of the fish tattoo were captured and added to our tattoo database of 2,157 images; each image was then used as a query to find the other six images among the 2,163 images. Our system successfully found one similar image at rank 1 for five out of the seven queries; the average number of correctly retrieved images at rank 20 is three. Queries that posed problems are those that have severe distortions (Figs. 10(c) and (d)).

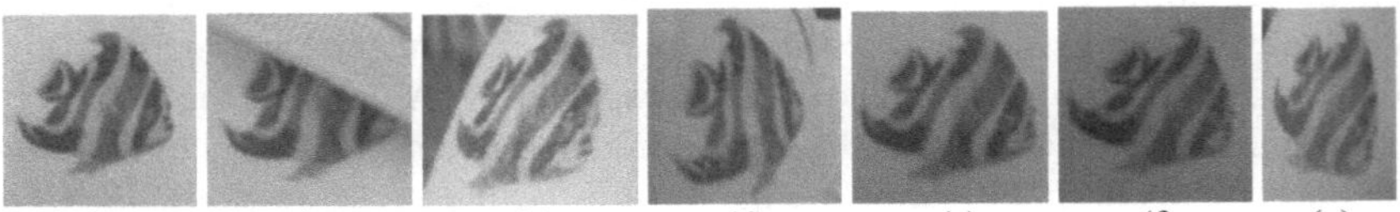

(a) (b) (c) (d) (e) (f) (g)

Fig. 10. Seven different images of the fish tattoo taken under different imaging conditions

Experiment II aims to evaluate the retrieval accuracy of the Tattoo-ID system when the query images are noisy. Now a retrieved image is deemed to be relevant when the query image is generated from the retrieved one by one of the image transformations shown in Fig. 5. Since there is only one truly "similar" image in the database for every transformed query image, we adopted the cumulative matching curve (CMC) [20] as the evaluation metric for this experiment. Fig. 11(a) shows the CMC curve. Overall, the chance of retrieving the correct image in the database is ~60% when we only look at the first retrieved image, and is increased to ~80% when we examine the top 20 retrieved images. Similar to the Experiment I, queries that are blurred, have uneven illumination and whose color components have been changed are the most difficult (Fig. 11(b)) for the system and we attribute the problem to the errors in automatic image segmentation. We confirm this hypothesis by manually segmenting the two images in Fig. 9 (that could not be segmented correctly by our algorithm) and running the retrieval experiment using the manually segmented images as queries. The rank of the correct database image is now increased from 83 to 21 for 9(a) and from 1,157 to 32 for 9(c) when using the manually segmented images.

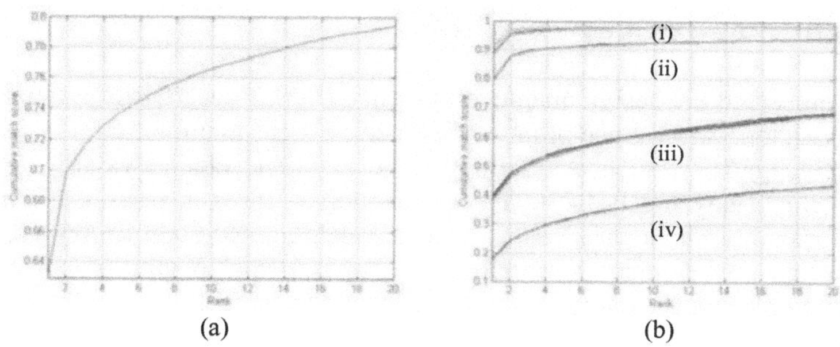

Fig. 11. Experiment II results: (a) Cumulative Matching Curve, (b) CMC for each transformation types: (i) noise and aspect ratio, (ii) rotation, (iii) color and blurring, (iv) illumination

Experiment III. Tattoo-ID system can optionally accept the semantic class label(s) of a query image from users. By using the class label(s), if available, as a part of the query, we are able to narrow down the candidate tattoo images in the database and therefore enhance the retrieval performance. Fig. 12 compares the retrieval performances of our CBIR system with and without using class labels as a part of the query: Figures 12 (a) and (b) show the precision and recall curves of experiment I and CMC of experiment II with and without class labels. By including class labels in the query, we are able to improve the retrieval performance significantly for both experiment I and II. In particular, for experiment I, the average precision at rank 20 is improved from 51.2% to 90.8% by using class labels, and the cumulative match score at rank 20 in experiment II is improved from 79.4% to 94.5%. We thus conclude that the incorporation of class labels in the query can significantly improve the retrieval performance. However, it is important to note that query class label alone (without image attributes) is not enough to retrieve the correct match in the database since there are ~100 images/class in our database. Hence, a combination of image based features and class label is needed for good retrieval performance.

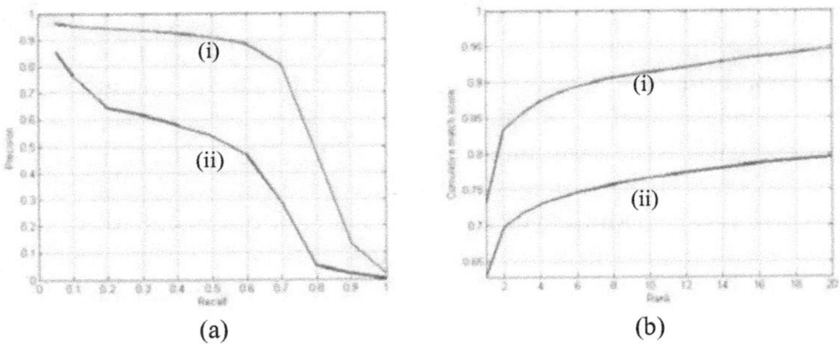

Fig. 12. Comparison between retrieval performance with and without class label: (a) Average Precision and Recall curve ((i) with class label and (ii) without class label), and (b) CMC ((i) with class label and (ii) without class label)

5 Conclusions and Future Work

We have presented the design and development of a prototype CBIR system for tattoo images. With the growing use of tattoos for person identification by forensics and law enforcement agencies, such a system will be of great societal value. While tattoo matching alone may not be sufficient to uniquely identify a person, it can provide useful information about the person's identity such as the group (religious, criminal, etc.) to which he belongs. Our preliminary experimental results based on a set of relatively simple image features are promising. However, the complex nature of the tattoo images requires that we develop robust image segmentation and feature extraction algorithms to further improve the retrieval performance. We have also shown that including the tattoo class information in the query improves the retrieval performance. Our ongoing work addresses (i) expanding the database (to 10,000 tattoos), (ii) capturing multiple images of a tattoo under different imaging conditions, (iii) finding additional salient features and designing a robust matcher, (iv) building a complete user interface, and (v) developing a more sophisticated user relevance feedback mechanism.

Acknowledgements

The authors would like to thank Yi Chen, Unsang Park and Chris Samiadji-Benthin for their assistance in preparing this manuscript. This research was supported by NSF IUC on Identification Technology Research (CITeR).

References

1. A Brief History of Tattoos, http://www.designboom.com /history/tattoo_history.html
2. Tattoo Facts and Statistics (October 2006), http://www.vanishingtattoo.com/ tattoo_facts.htm
3. Jain, A.K., Dass, S.C., Nandakumar, K.: Can Soft Biometric Traits Assist User Recognition? In: Proc. SPIE, Orlando, vol. 5404, pp. 561–572 (April 2004)

4. Lipton, E., Glanz, J.: Limits of DNA Research Pushed to Identify the Dead of Sept. 11, NY Times (April 22, 2002)
5. Decay Challenges Forensic Skills, The Standard-Times (January 8, 2005)
6. Burma, J.H.: Self-Tattooing among Delinquents: A Research Note, Sociology and Social Research 43, 341–345 (1959)
7. Texas Prison Tattoo, http://www.foto8.com/issue09/reportage/AndrewLichtenstein/prisontattoos01.html
8. Prison Tattoos and Their Meaning, http://www.tattoo-designs.dk/prison-tattoos.html
9. ANSI/NIST-ITL 1-2007 standard: Data Format for the Interchange of Fingerprint, Facial, & Other Biometric Information (2007)
10. GangNet: A 21st Century Solution to the Gang Problem (December 2006) http://psd.orionsci.com/Products/Gangnet.asp
11. Long, F., Zhang, H.J., Feng, D.D.: Fundamentals of Content-Based Image Retrieval. In: Multimedia Information Retrieval and Management- Technological Fundamentals and Applications, Springer, Heidelberg (2003)
12. Jain, A.K., Vailaya, A.: Shape-Based Retrieval: A Case Study with Trademark Image Databases. Pattern Recognition 31(9), 1369–1390 (1998)
13. Shih, P., Liu, C.: Comparative Assessment of Content-Based Face Image Retrieval in Different Color Spaces. International Journal of Pattern Recognition and Artificial Intelligence 19(7), 873–893 (2005)
14. Online Tattoo Designs, http://www.tattoodesing.com/gallery/
15. Huang, J., Kumar, S.R, Mitra, M., Zhu, W., Zabih, R.: Image Indexing using Color Correlogram. In: Proc. IEEE Computer Society Conf. on CVPR, pp. 762–768 (1997)
16. Hu, M.K.: Visual Pattern Recognition by Moment Invariants. IEEE Trans. Information Theory 8, 179–187 (1962)
17. Swain, M.J., Ballard, D.H.: Indexing via Color Histograms. In: Proc. 3rd International Conference on Computer Vision, pp. 309–393 (1990)
18. Rui, Y., Huang, T.S., Ortega, M., Mehrotra, S.: Relevance Feedback: A Power Tool in Interactive Content-based Image Retrieval. IEEE Trans. on Circuits and Systems for Video Technology 8(5), 644–655 (1998)
19. Flickner, M., Sawhney, H., Niblack, W., Ashley, J., Huang, Q., Dom, B., Gorkani, M., Hafner, J., Lee, D., Petkovicand, D., Steele, D., Yanker, P.: Query by Image and Video Content: The QBIC system. IEEE Computer 38, 23–31 (1995)
20. Moon, H., Phillips, P.J.: Computational and Performance Aspects of PCA-based Face Recognition Algorithms. Perception 30, 303–321 (2001)

Auto-Annotation of Paintings Using Social Annotations, Domain Ontology and Transductive Inference

Liza Marchenko Leslie[1], Tat-Seng Chua[1], and Ramesh Jain[2]

[1] National University of Singapore
{marchenk,chuats}@comp.nus.edu.sg
[2] University of California, Irvine
jain@ics.uci.edu

Abstract. Knowledge of paintings domain includes a variety of sources such as essays, visual examples, ontologies of artistic concepts and user- provided annotations. This knowledge serves several purposes. First, it defines a wide range of concepts for annotation and flexible retrieval of paintings. Second, it serves to bootstrap auto-annotation and disambiguate the generated candidate labels. Third, the user-provided annotations serve to discover folksonomies of concepts and vernacular terms. In this paper, we propose a framework for paintings auto-annotation that incorporates user provided images and annotations, domain ontology and external knowledge sources. We utilize these sources of information to bootstrap and support the auto-annotation task, which is based on transductive inference mechanism that combines probabilistic clustering and multi-expert approach to generate labels. We further combine user-provided annotations with generated labels and domain ontology to disambiguate the concepts. In our experiments, we focus on the auto-annotation of painting and demonstrate that the user-provided annotations significantly increase annotation accuracy.

Keywords: Transductive Inference, Multi-expert Approach, Probabilistic Clustering, Domain Ontology, Paintings, Annotation, Concept Disambiguation, Learning, Social Network.

1 Introduction

Extensive digitization of the paintings domain facilitates such applications as digital libraries and authoring of resources for learning and appreciating arts. Various studies proposed systems for the annotation and retrieval of paintings. Early paintings retrieval systems such as QBIC and ARTISTE facilitate example-based retrieval of paintings. Corridoni et al. [2] focused on the limited set of artistic color concepts, where the authors back-projected image colors onto the artistic sphere and extracted color temperature and color contrast concepts. Herik et al. [4] and Li et al. [6] performed annotation of artist names based on low-level features using Neural networks and 2D-HMM. Such approaches have several disadvantages. First, they yield limited accuracy since they do not incorporate domain knowledge about concepts [15]. Second, they require large manually prepared datasets. Existing studies

H.H.S. Ip et al. (Eds.): PCM 2007, LNCS 4810, pp. 266–275, 2007.

propose various solutions to these problems. To incorporate concept relationships, Schreiber et al. [12] employed concept ontologies such as AAT [10]. To reduce the need for labeled data, various studies proposed semi-supervised classification and clustering techniques [3]. In our previous work [9], we combined these approaches to perform annotation of paintings. However, such framework is still limited: 1) it still requires sufficient number of manually labeled samples; b) it does not incorporate any feedback information about quality of annotation; and c) it currently relies on the pre-defined range of concepts and does not incorporate any external information to improve the annotation performance. These limitations can be minimized by utilizing additional information in form of social annotations and artistic essays. Such essays are available online, while Web 2.0-like systems offer a wide range of tools to implicitly gather such social annotations as training samples and manually assigned concepts.

To incorporate such information, we propose a novel framework that includes three major parts: social annotations, domain knowledge and auto-annotation framework. Using this framework, we aim to: a) gather additional training samples; b) facilitate feedback from large scale user annotations to discover new concepts/relationships and evaluate annotation quality; and c) bootstrap and disambiguate auto-annotation. In this paper we first propose the overall layout of this annotation framework and then propose a transductive inference mechanism that incorporates social annotations and domain knowledge to annotate samples.

The rest of the paper is organized as follows. Sections 2 and 3 present the proposed framework for annotation of paintings. In Section 4 we discuss how the proposed framework combines the user input and domain ontology to perform concept disambiguation. Section 5 focuses on the prototype for learning and appreciating of arts. Section 6 presents the experiment results and Section 7 outlines the conclusions and future work.

2 Auto-Annotation of Paintings Using Web 2.0

In this section, we propose a framework for auto-annotation of paintings that relies on domain knowledge, social annotations and external information to support auto-annotation task. To gather social annotations, it utilizes Web 2.0 site, where the user contributes annotations in two ways: 1) visually by uploading new image and providing spatial annotations; and 2) textually by providing tagging and comments to uploaded images. Domain ontology represents the hierarchical organization of concepts; it combines AAT and ULAN [10] arts-oriented ontologies. In our system social annotations and online essays serve to discover new visual examples, new concepts and concept relationships, while ontology serves as a platform to relate this newly discovered information to the existing knowledge. Our framework exploits these types of information to: 1) discover new concepts and relationships; and 2) bootstrap and disambiguate auto-annotation task. Figure 1 demonstrates the overall framework.

To discover new concepts and relationships, our framework exploits social annotations and external knowledge. It runs the *keyword extractor* pipeline to process textual information. For this task, it: a) applies morphological analysis to extract such constructs as *[adj+] noun.*; and b) it checks whether these constructs are already present in domain ontology and stores information about their co-occurrence and proximity-based distance [7]. The concepts with high co-occurrence count and low proximity-based distance are further used within a feedback mechanism to update the concept relationships within the domain ontology and add new concepts.

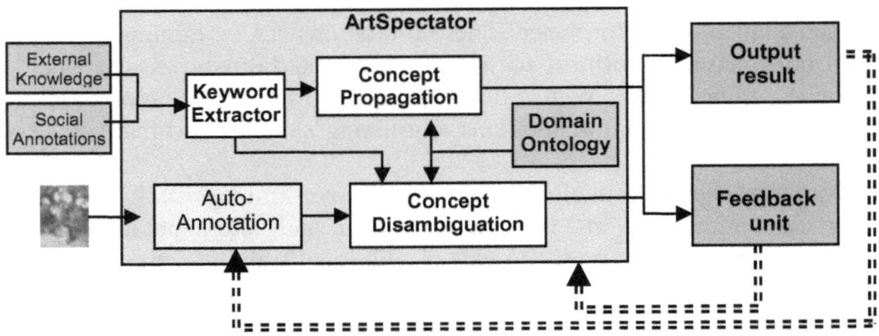

Fig. 1. High-level scheme of ArtSpectator

To bootstrap and disambiguate auto-annotation, the system relies on social annotations and domain ontology. Social annotations serve to gather additional training samples and disambiguate generated candidate labels. The system performs auto-annotation that leverages on training samples and domain ontology, which includes visual and high-level concepts. Visual level concepts include brushwork, colour temperatures, palettes and contrasts. High-level concepts include semantics used by both expert and novice users such as the artist names, painting style and various abstract concepts. Visual-level concepts serve as cues to annotation of high-level concepts. Our system utilizes this fact and performs hierarchical concept annotation, where it first utilizes low-level features to annotate visual-level concepts and then combines the low-level features with visual-level concepts to infer high-level concepts. To disambiguate the annotated visual and high-level concepts, the framework performs a two-step procedure, in which it exploits social annotations and concept relationships from domain ontology. First, it ensures that the auto-annotation results correlate well with user provided annotations. Second, it ensures that auto-annotated concepts are in line with existing formal knowledge available from domain ontology. We discuss auto-annotation and concept disambiguation methods in Sections 3 and 4 respectively. Based on the annotated concepts, the system performs concept propagation through domain ontology to extract more related terms. For example, the propagation of concept *Cezanne* results in *Impressionism*, *European*, *French*, *Modern*, *Fine Art* terms.

To re-use the user-provided information, the framework incorporates a feedback mechanism to update the knowledge base with newly discovered information. Our framework performs update of the base classifiers with newly added training samples. To update domain ontology, it adds newly discovered concepts and relationships.

lastly, it updates the collection of already generated indexes based on the modifications of ontology.

Overall, the proposed framework performs annotation of paintings with a wide range of concepts. It relies on extensive domain knowledge that incorporates knowledge from expert and layman users. These annotations facilitate both spatial and image-level indexing of paintings collections.

In this paper we focus on the auto-annotation and disambiguation component of this framework. We will work on the discovery of new knowledge, concept propagation and feedback components in our future work.

3 Auto-Annotation of Artistic Concepts

3.1 Auto-Annotation of Paintings

The majority of paintings in WWW are annotated manually with partial information such as artist name, painting title, date and/or medium. Such information offers a limited basis for navigation. Also, it does not facilitate spatial retrieval and querying by various visual and high-level concepts. While artistic essays discuss such detailed information, they are mostly cover only a small fraction of well-known paintings. In our work we aim to perform annotation with various artistic concepts for large-scale painting collections. Our system utilizes several strategies to handle large-scale collections: 1) it gathers additional training samples and bootstraps classifiers by adopting on-line mode of learning; 2) it relies on social annotations and arts-oriented ontologies to perform annotation and disambiguation; and 3) it iteratively extends ontology and improves the set of base classifiers using the newly acquired data. To generate labels, we employ our earlier proposed transductive inference method that aims to minimize the required training datasets. It performs probabilistic soft clustering [3] over the combined labeled and unlabelled data samples. This enables us to benefit from the distribution of feature values from unlabelled samples and generate more accurate clusters. This transductive inference procedure results in a large number of clusters that include a mixture of labeled and unlabelled samples. Some clusters are pure in a sense that we are able to use the labeled samples within the cluster to make classification decision of the unlabelled samples within this cluster. However, many clusters are impure or have no labeled samples. To perform disambiguation of such clusters, we perform iterative clustering based on the manually pre-defined decision hierarchy.

3.2 Tansductive Inference of Concepts Using Multi-Expert Approach

Figure 2 demonstrates the overall view of the transductive inference method. The decision process iteratively splits the whole dataset into the most dissimilar subsets of classes until it reaches the individual classes. The similarity information is manually pre-defined within the decision hierarchy. Figure 3 shows the decision hierarchy for artist name and brushwork concepts.

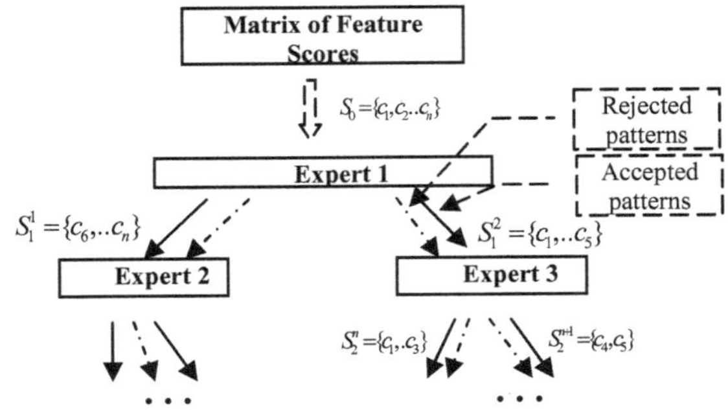

Fig. 2. Transductive Inference Method

In Figure 2, each node of the decision hierarchy is associated with an individual classifier or *expert*. Individual experts implement transductive inference of the labels using soft probabilistic clustering based on GMM models. An expert evaluates the resulting clusters using *the cluster purity* measure. We define *pure* cluster of class X as the cluster in which more than 75% of the labeled patterns are of class X. The cluster purity measure represents the degree to which the generated cluster contains labels of class X and is defined as $p(c)=N_X/N_{all}$, where N_X and N_{all} denote the number of labeled patterns of class X and the overall number of patterns in cluster c respectively.

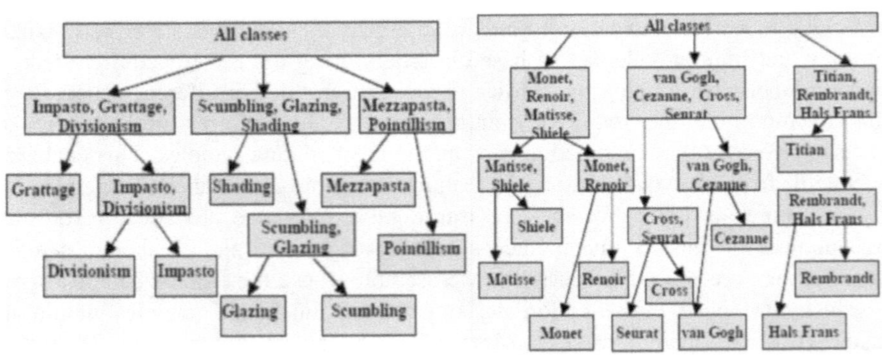

Fig. 3. Decision hierarchy for brushwork and artist name concepts

Unlabelled patterns that fall in the pure clusters will receive the candidate class labels of these clusters. The unlabelled patterns in impure or rejected clusters are reevaluated in the subsequent levels of the decision hierarchy. If such patterns reach the leaf nodes, the system assigns the final concepts to such patterns using the highest posterior probability generated by the individual experts. To achieve the least erroneous clustering model, each individual expert performs the model selection step. During this step, it trains several cluster models using a varying number of parameters and subsets of features and selects the least erroneous model using Vapnik's combined bound [3].

Each individual expert uses the feature relevance information, which is calculated prior to the overall inference process. To calculate feature relevance scores we employ Chi-square statistics [16]. Intuitively, if the distributions are similar, then the analyzed feature is not representative of the cluster and its Chi-square statistics is comparatively low. We represent the feature distributions using the normalized histograms of each feature in the cluster and the whole dataset. To measure the similarity of distributions, we employ Pearson's Chi-Square test: $X^2=\Sigma(O_i- E_i)^2/E_i$, where we treat the *i-th* histogram bin of the feature distribution in a cluster and the overall dataset as the observed counts O_i and expected counts E_i respectively. Using the Chi-square statistics we obtain the relevance score of each individual class, which is further utilized by individual experts.

3.3 Annotation of Visual and High-Level Concepts

The auto-annotation framework performs two major steps. First, we perform annotation of image blocks with visual color and brushwork concepts. For annotation of color concepts, we utilize Itten's theory [5] that proposes the mapping between colors and artistic color concepts such as color temperature concepts (*warm, cold* and *neutral*), color palette concepts (primary, *complimentary* and *tertiary*) and color contrasts (*complimentary*, *light-dark* and *temperature*). To annotate image with visual color concepts, we employ our earlier proposed method [8] that: 1) back-projects the image colors and extracts the domain-specific features such as the distribution of various color temperature and palettes; and 2) employs probabilistic SVM method [14] to perform annotation. For brushwork analysis, we employ eight brushwork classes often used in Medieval and Modern periods of art [1] such as *divisionism, pointillism, grattage, mezzapasta, scumbling impasto, glazing* and *shading*. We extract a wide range of texture features such as gradient, edge and intensity statistics, energy-based features from multi-scale Gabor transform and wavelet transforms, fractal based features and Zernike moments. To annotate brushwork concepts, we rely on transductive inference method discussed above.

Second, we perform the annotation of image blocks with high-level concepts. For this we combine color and brushwork concepts with low-level features and again utilize the transductive inference method. To disambiguate visual-level and high-level concepts, we rely on the concept disambiguation method to be discussed in Section 4.

4 Concept Disambiguation Using Social Annotations

The proposed concept disambiguation method performs disambiguation of both visual-level and high-level concepts. It uses social annotations and, second, combines social annotations and concept relationship information to disambiguate concepts. The system first uses social annotations to propagate the annotated terms via domain ontology and extract the list of related concepts. Useful social annotations for paintings usually include year of painting, artist name, brushwork and color techniques etc. Thus, knowing the year of painting, the system will be able to infer art period. Using this information, it in turn is able to generate a list of most likely brushwork concepts, which includes *shading, glazing and mezzapasta.* The proposed method then performs weighting of the posterior probabilities of the concepts generated by the base classifiers. Since visual-level concepts within an image are defined spatially, this step: a) ensures that these concepts are well correlated with user-provided social annotations; and b) serves as an intermediate step to generate final set of image-level labels.

Next, the system integrates block-level annotations to generate the final set of image-level labels. To resolve conflicts among block-level labels, we design a disambiguation method that generates the most likely concepts, which satisfy both domain knowledge constraints and social annotations for this image. Domain knowledge constraints arise from ontological relationships among the high-level concepts. For example, domain ontology associates *van Gogh* with *Modern* art period and *Post-Impressionism* painting style, but not with *Medieval* art period and *Renaissance* or *Rococo* painting styles. To incorporate social annotations, the system utilizes posterior probabilities of annotated high-level concepts that are weighted based on the social annotations during the previous step. To disambiguate concepts, the system first back-projects the block-level labels onto their respective images and calculates the distribution of annotated high-level concepts. We currently perform the annotation of artist name, painting style and art period concepts; however this list can be extended depending on the base classifiers currently available within the system. Based on these distributions we form all possible concept combinations, in this case <artist name–painting style–art period>. This gives rise to a constraint satisfaction problem, which can be solved using the integer linear programming approach [11, 13]. The constraint satisfaction problem includes three classification tasks $CT = \{CT_1, ...CT_3\}$ that correspond to artist name, painting style and art period classification. Each task CT_i assigns a label from the *set* $L_i = \{l_{i1}, ...,l_{imi}\}$ to an image, where each label is associated with weighted posterior probability. We model the assignments as the variables of linear cost function and aim to optimize each of the auto-annotated concept combinations <artist name-painting style-art period> with respect to the weighted posterior probabilities and domain constraints. The formulation of the cost function and constraints is presented in our previous work [9].

5 ArtSpectator: Learning Arts in Web 2.0

The proposed framework serves as a platform for interactive learning of arts. Such platform facilitates various modes of interaction such as collaborative authoring and sharing of resources, goal-setting, result discussions etc. Large-scale annotated collection paired with multimodal taxonomies support various user activities. First, it offers rich context for navigation and browsing of the collection. Second, it facilitates reports for in-depth learning of painting styles, art periods, cultures and artists. For example, a report about painting technique includes the definition of this technique, visual examples from various known paintings and curatorial essays about it. Third, a wide range of annotated visual-level concepts serves to perform comparative analysis of paintings. Fourth, the combination of the concept definitions from domain ontology and auto-annotation results serves to compose textual summaries of paintings. We aim to further develop this system into a fully functional learning portal to help teachers to compose lessons, set and track learning goals, create collaborative exhibitions and curatorial essays.

6 Experiments

For our experiments we utilize dataset of 1050 paintings from WebMuseum [15], which includes paintings by 11 artists in 7 painting styles from both Modern and Medieval art periods. Five expert users provided visual-level concepts for the randomly sampled subset of this collection. The users marked regions within paintings and entered their annotations in form of free text. We gathered high-level concept annotations, which are usually supplied by the expert users, from the WWW. This information was extracted from the semi-structured text that accompanied gathered images.

We resize the painting images by preserving the aspect ratio of each painting with the smallest side fixed at 580 pixels. We employ the fixed-size blocks of size 32x32 for the concept analysis. To measure the accuracy of labeling with visual-level concepts, we employ 5,000 randomly sampled blocks from painting regions annotated by the expert users. The earlier provided annotations of visual-level concepts served as the ground truth for this experiment. To annotate color temperature and palette concepts, we utilize 75% of the blocks to train probabilistic SVM classifiers and achieve the accuracy 91.2% and 93.7% during annotation of color temperature and color palette concepts respectively. We did not evaluate the annotation of blocks with color contrast concepts due to the lack of ground truth, but we have demonstrated its performance for region-based retrieval task in our previous work [8]. For brushwork annotation, we utilize the transductive inference framework and achieve 94% of annotation accuracy.

For annotation of application-level concepts we employ the full dataset using 315 and 735 images for the training and testing respectively. We perform two sets of experiments to evaluate the proposed framework, which performs two-level annotation with visual and high-level concepts and then disambiguates high-level concepts. We first evaluate this framework with no account for partial user annotations and then evaluate the performance of this framework with partial user annotations. In the first set of experiments, we compare the proposed framework with three baseline methods as shown in Table 1: (a) Baseline 1 (B1): inductive inference methods using low-level features only, (b) Baseline 2 (B2): transductive inference using low-level features and visual-level concepts and (c) Baseline 3 (B3): the proposed two-level annotation. For all baselines we utilize the majority vote strategy to generate image-level results. We implement inductive inference using probabilistic SVM method. The results demonstrate that the use of visual-level concepts facilitates more accurate annotation as compared to the use of low-level features only. The two-step painting annotation (Baseline 3) achieves higher accuracy as compared to Baseline 1 and 2 because of the improvements related to the use of visual-level concepts, semi-supervised inference, and adaptive model and feature selection. Further, the use of OCD with our auto-annotation framework method further improves these results by over 10% for artist name and painting style concepts. The annotation of art period concepts results in significantly higher annotation accuracy as compared to the annotation of artist name and painting styles since these concepts can be easily distinguished using color/texture features.

Table 1. Performance of the auto-annotation framework

Concepts\Strategy	B1	B2	B3	Proposed Framework
Artist Name	40%	57%	73%	86%
Painting Style	42%	61%	74%	88%
Art Period	81.48%	93.56%	98.71%	99.5%

In the second set of experiments we utilize social annotations and evaluate our framework within real-life scenario. In this scenario, we would like to publish our collection online and we require all three concepts (artist name, painting style and art period) concepts to be correctly annotated for each image. For example, combination "da Vinci, Renaissance, Medieval" is correct, while combination "da Vinci, Abstractionism, Medieval" is not. We evaluate image-level annotations generated by our framework using block-level labels and three disambiguation strategies: 1) Majority vote (MV); 2) Concept disambiguation using ontology relationships (CDO); and 3) Concept disambiguation using ontology relationships and social annotations (CDOSA). To introduce social annotations, the system utilized artist name annotations supplied by the end users. We consider image as *correct*, if all three concepts are annotated correctly in accordance to the ground-truth.

Table 2 presents the experiment results and demonstrates that the use of social annotations (CDOSA) method results in higher F1 rates as compared to both CDO and MV methods. This improvement is due to the fact that partial annotations offer additional evidence for disambiguation of high-level concepts.

Table 2. Performance of concept disambiguation strategies

Strategy	F1,%
Majority vote	57
CDO	72
CDOSA	89

This experimental set-up utilizes relatively controlled data from the end expert users. The real-life scenario with both the expert and novice users annotating in form of free text is likely to be different. To facilitate this scenario in our framework, we need to consider the following important key points: 1) account for the distribution of annotations for each painting and contextual cues to minimize the impact of the annotation errors by novice users and the errors appeared during the mining from the Web; 2) usability of general terms during the disambiguation step; and 3) automatic construction and update of the decision hierarchy for transductive inference using domain-specific information such as the arts timeline.

7 Conclusions

In this paper we presented an auto-annotation framework for paintings domain. This framework incorporates social annotations with domain knowledge to perform auto-annotation and disambiguation of a wide range of artistic concepts. It serves as a platform to facilitate learning of arts within a social network scenario. We presented experiments with auto-annotation of concepts and concept disambiguation. These experiments demonstrate that the use of domain ontology and social annotations significantly improves the annotation accuracy. In our future work, we first aim to focus on the discovery of folksonomies and their integration with the proposed auto-annotation framework to support auto-annotation. Second, we aim to release our Web 2.0 site that utilizes the proposed framework to support learning of arts as discussed in Section 5. This site facilitates authoring, re-use and dynamic content generation for both the expert and novice users, and utilizes the social network resources to enrich the knowledge base and support the auto-annotation task.

References

1. Canaday, J.: Mainstreams of Modern Art. Saunders College Publishing (1981)
2. Corridoni, J.M., Del Bimbo, A.: Retrieval of Paintings Using Effects Induced by Color Features. In: CAIVD, pp. 2–11 (1998)
3. El-Yaniv, R., Gerzon, L.: Effective Transductive Learning via PAC-Bayesian Model Selection. Technical Report CS-2004-05, IIT (2004)
4. Herik, H.J., van den Postma, E.O.: Discovering the Visual Signature of Painters. Future Directions for Intelligent Systems and Information Sciences , 129–147 (2000)
5. Itten, J.: The Art of Color, Reinhold Pub. Corp (1961)
6. Li, J., Wang, J.Z.: Studying Digital Imagery of Ancient Paintings by Mixtures of Stochastic Models. IEEE Trans. on Image Proc 13(3) (2004)
7. Lin, D.: Using Syntactic Dependency as Local Context to Resolve Word Sense Ambiguity, ACL, pp. 64–71 (1997)
8. Marchenko, Y., Chua, T.-S., Aristarkhova, I., Jain, R.: Representation and Retrieval of Paintings based on Art History Concepts. IEEE ICME (2004)
9. Marchenko, Y., Chua, T.-S., Jain, R.: Ontology-Based Annotation of paintings using Transductive Inference Framework. In: Int'l Conf on MultimediaModelling (2007)
10. Paul Getty Trust. Art and Architecture Thesauri and United List of Artist names (2000)
11. Punyakanok, V., Roth, D., Yih, W., Zimak, D.: Semantic role labeling via integer linear programming inference. In: Proceedings of International Conference on Computational Linguistics (2004)
12. Schreiber, A.T., Dubbeldam, B., Wielemaker, J., Wielinga, B.J.: Ontology-based photo annotation. IEEE Intelligent Systems 16, 66–74 (2001)
13. Tsai, T.-H., Wu, C.-W., Lin, Y.-C., Hsu, W.-L.: Exploiting Full Parsing Information to Label Semantic Roles Using an Ensemble of ME and SVM via Integer Linear Programming. In: The CoNLL-2005 Shared Task on Semantic Role Labeling
14. Vapnik, V.: Estimation of Dependences Based on Empirical Data. Springer, Heidelberg (1982)
15. Web Museum. Available at http://www.ibiblio.org/wm/
16. Wu, S., Flach, P.A.: Feature selection with labelled and unlabelled data. CML/PKDD 2002, pp.156–167, http://www.cs.bris.ac.uk/Publications/pub_info.jsp?id=1000659

Value Combination Technique for Image Authentication

Jie Zhang, Fenlin Liu, Ping Wang, and Guodong Wang

Institute of Information Science and Technology, Zhengzhou 450002, China
zhangjacker@163.com, liufenlin@sina.vip.com,
pingwang1109@yahoo.com.cn,Wgdguodong2006@163.com

Abstract. Value Combination Technique is proposed for a novel bitmap exact authentication. It combines the pixel values in an image block with the block position, and the combined values are used as the initial state of chaotic system to generate watermark. Furthermore, a general rule is given to analyze the reliability of algorithm, and another rule is presented to design an algorithm with high reliability in this paper. Then, a concrete algorithm illustrates our proposed authentication system. Extensive experiments show that this system can effectively resist such as feature extraction attack, vector quantization attack and so on, and be very sensitive to tamper.

1 Introduction

Multimedia authentication techniques are used to verify the information integrity, the alleged source of data, and the reality of data. Recently, image authentication has been researched actively [1, 2, 3]. With the development of digital watermark, image authentication based on fragile watermark has the following advantages compared with the authentication art in traditional cryptography [4]: no use for excess data management, tamper localization and so on.

Walton in [5] was firstly proposed an image authentication algorithm based on fragile watermark, which generated fragile watermark by calculating the check sum of pixel values. This method was not secure and didn't accurately localize tamper, although it's simple and effective. The given icon was used as watermark and embedded into a natural image in [6]. This method had the ability to localize tamper, but it's easy to undergo collusion attack. Since image features can reflect image content, many existing methods used block average [7], transform coefficients [8] and so on as watermark and embedded them into images. Thus, this kind of algorithms can resist collusion attack effectively, because the watermark is relative with image. However, it is easy to undergo feature extraction attack [9]. Ref. [10] divided an image into blocks, and then watermark was respectively embedded into each block. They can powerfully detect and localize tamper, but suffer from vector quantization (VQ) attack because the other blocks were not used when generating and embedding watermark into one block.

In this paper, the proposed authentication system based on fragile watermark combines the pixel values in a block with the block positions. And the watermark is then generated by the cascading multiple chaotic systems with the combined value as its initial state. At last, watermark is embedded into the redundancy of natural image.

H.H.S. Ip et al. (Eds.): PCM 2007, LNCS 4810, pp. 276–285, 2007.

This scheme can not only resist aforementioned attacks due to its unique combined value by value combination technique (VCT), but also guarantee the quality of the watermarked image and the localization accuracy.

2 Algorithm Descriptions

The block-wise idea is introduced into our proposed algorithm to detect and localize tamper. Moreover, we still adopt the method that watermark is generated by the most significant bits and embedded into the least significant bits to guarantee the quality of image.

This system composes of the embedding algorithm and the authentication algorithm shown in Fig. 1. During embedding, the higher bit planes are used to generate watermark W, which is embedded into the least bit planes in an image I, so as to produce the watermarked image I'. During authenticating, we generate W' from the higher bits of the considered image I'', extract W'' from the low bits of I'', and compare W' with W'' to determine whether the image is tampered or not. The frame is presented in Fig.1.

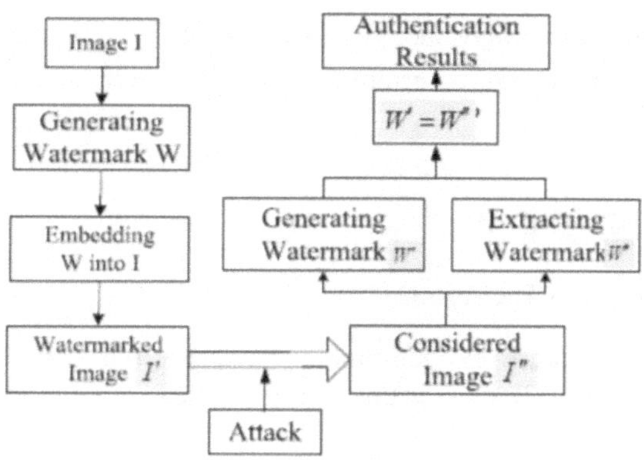

Fig. 1. Authentication system

2.1 Embedding Process

For each $m \times n$ block, embedding process is given as follows:

1) Initialize a seed key K and introduce the vector function $\xi(\bullet)$ that satisfies $\xi(\bullet)=\left(\xi_1^T(\bullet),\xi_2^T(\bullet),\hbar\ ,\xi_c^T(\bullet)\right)^T$, where c denotes the total number of blocks, and then generate the key of block I_i $K_i : K_i = \xi_i^T(K)$.

2) Combine the higher seven bit planes of pixel values under the control of K_i.

A. set the lower p bits to zero in block I_i, supposing that watermark is embedded into the lower p bit planes, and then get the image $\hat{I}_i$.

B. set a vector $B_i = \left(\hat{I}_i^1, \hat{I}_i^2, \hbar\ , \hat{I}_i^{m\times n}\right)^T$, where $\hat{I}_i^j$ is the higher $8-p$ bits of the jth pixel in $\hat{I}_i$, $j = 1,2,\hbar\ , m\times n$ .We compute the combined value V_i by $\varphi(\bullet)$, that is, $V_i = \varphi(B_i, K_i)$. Note that $\varphi(\bullet)$ satisfies that $\varphi(B_i, K_i) = \varphi(B_i', K_i)$ if $\forall B_i = B_i'$.

3) Combine the position values and get $P_i : P_i = (X_i, Y_i)^T$ in I_i , which X_i , Y_i correspondingly denote row and column. The position-combination operation $\phi(\bullet)$ will be constructed to generate the position-combination value $L_i : L_i = \phi(P_i)$.

4) Combine V_i with L_i under the control of key K_i , and thus generate watermark $w_i = f(V_i, L_i, K_i)$

5) Embed w_i into I_i to produce a watermarked block $I_i' : I_i' = E(I_i, w_i, p)$.

2.2 Authentication Process

Similarly, the authentication process also regards block as operation unit. Its details are as follows:

1) Generate watermark w_i' from the authenticated image I'' by the same function and key in the embedding process.

2) Extract the embedded watermark w_i'' from the lower p bit planes of image I''.

3) Compare w_i' with w_i'' to determine whether the authenticated image block I_i'' is tampered or not.

3 Algorithm Analysis

3.1 Value Combination Technique

The precondition of feature extraction attack is that the extracted features can't indicate all information of image, or the modified image has the same features as the original.

Proposition1: The pixel-combination operation $\varphi(\bullet)$ in the embedding process can resist feature extraction attack.

Proof: Given a block I_i and key K_i , generate a vector B_i . Then, I_i is randomly modified to get I_i' . Afterwards, vector B_i' is generated from I_i' . Besides, $\varphi(B_i, K_i) \neq \varphi(B_i', K_i)$ holds certainly for $\forall B_i \neq B_i'$. Thus, using $\varphi(B_i , K_i)$ as features can put resistance against feature extraction attack.

Note 1: The combination value as features can resist feature extraction attack in theory. However, it is noticeable that the combination values will go beyond the computer precision. In order to solve this problem, this thesis groups each block by the granularity of k , and combines the values in each group.

Proposition2: The position-combination operation $\varphi(\bullet)$ can resist vector quantization attack, and get the tampering location precision of $m\times n$.

Proof: During embedding, the position P_i of a block I_i is combined by $\phi(\bullet)$, generate the position-combination value L_i. Since $\phi(\bullet)$ is one-to-one mapping, L_i holds the same when P_i is different. In this way, the generated watermark w_i is related with the block position, so VQ attack can be resisted.

Note 2: Many an algorithm based on block-wise independence often suffer from VQ attack. The popular methods against VQ attack are realized by making the watermark in each block dependent on other blocks. But this will decrease the localization accuracy. Nevertheless, the position-combination value has been utilized as an input of the watermark generator so as to resist VQ attack without decreasing localization accuracy.

3.2 Security Analysis

We evaluate the performance of image authentication system according to forgery authentication. We will give a detailed instance to show that it is difficult to attack our proposed system in this paper.

Let the size of each block I_i is $m \times n$, and k is the group granularity. Assuming that watermark is embedded in the lower p bit planes, then these p bits will be set 0 to get $\hat{I}_i$. From these, it is known that watermark w_i is with the size of $m \times n \times p$ bits. Besides, key K_i, represented by $K_i = K_{i,1}K_{i,2}K_{i,3}K_{i,4}$, is used to control $\varphi(\bullet)$, $\phi(\bullet)$ and the watermark generator $f(\bullet)$. Noting that $K_{i,1}$, $K_{i,2}$, $K_{i,3}$, $K_{i,4}$, the decimal integers with $d_{i,1}$, $d_{i,2}$, $d_{i,3}$, $d_{i,4}$ lengths, respectively control $\varphi(\bullet)$, $\phi(\bullet)$, the choice of the initial variable of $f(\bullet)$ and the iteration times of $f(\bullet)$.

For block I_i, denote the position vector by $P_i : P_i = (X_i, Y_i)^T$, make position-combination operation $\phi(P_i, K_i) \triangleq x_1 x_2 \triangleq L_i$, thus x_a $(a = 1,2)$ correspond to the position X_i or Y_i; similarly, there are $\frac{m \times n}{k}$ combination values in a block that will be put as the initial variable of $f(\bullet)$ with L_i to generate watermark w_i.

A. While attackers know $\varphi(\bullet)$, the first element in the combination vector has $C_{m\times n}^k \times k!$ possibilities, the second element has $C_{m\times n-k}^k \times k!$ possibilities, thus the $\frac{m \times n}{k}$ th element has $C_k^k \times k!$ possibilities. Therefore, the pixel-combination value has $(C_{m\times n}^k \times k!) \times (C_{m\times n-k}^k \times k!) \times \hbar \times (C_k^k \times k!) = (m \times n)!$ possibilities. Similarly, the position-combination value has $2!$ possibilities

B. While attackers know $f(\bullet)$, the initial variable has $(\frac{m \times n}{k} + 1)!$ possibilities because there are $\frac{m \times n}{k} + 1$ inputs of chaotic iteration. Due to that $K_{i,4}$ is a decimal integer with $d_{i,4}$ length, the chaotic iteration times will be $10^{d_{i,4}}$ possibilities, thus there may be $(\frac{m \times n}{k} + 1)! \times 10^{d_{i,4}}$ watermarks.

In summary, the probability of the successful forgery authentications is $1/[(m\times n)\times 2\times(\frac{m\times n}{k}+1)\times 10^{d_{i,4}}]$ with knowing $\varphi(\bullet)$, $\phi(\bullet)$ and $f(\bullet)$ for attackers. From this, the security of our system can be markedly improved, and the accuracy of tamper detection increases by 2 times than that of paper [11].

Note 3: The attack difficulty is related with not only the key K_i, but also the block size of $m\times n$ in the case of knowing $\varphi(\bullet)$, $\phi(\bullet)$ and $f(\bullet)$.

3.3 Reliability Analysis

Because "watermark is generated by the most significant bits and embedded into the least significant bits" method possesses multiple-to-one mapping, then it is possible that the tampered image can still pass authentication. Therefore, we will analyze the reliability of our system from the view of forgery authentication.

Definition 1: If the tampered block can pass authentication, it is called "missing".

Definition 2: If all D tampered blocks can pass authentication, then it is called "D-blocks missing".

During authenticating, the first step is to judge whether image is tampered or not, the second step is to localize the tampered blocks. When one of D tampered blocks is detected, we can assert that this image is attacked. It is concluded that there exists image missing just when all the tampered blocks can pass authentication. From **Definition 2**, if the probability of "D-blocks missing" is P, the detection accuracy will be $1-P$.

For a $m\times n$ block I_i, embedding watermark into the lower p bit planes can be denoted by $\Omega:\Gamma\rightarrow\mathbf{M}$, where Γ is the higher $(8-p)$ bit plane space, $\mathbf{M}$ is the watermark space, and $|\Gamma|=2^{m\times n\times(8-p)}$, $|\mathbf{M}|=2^{m\times n\times p}$. Besides, Γ can be parted into $|\mathbf{M}|$ categories:

$$\Gamma=\bigcup_{i=1}^{|\mathbf{M}|}\pi_i,\ \pi_i\cap\pi_j=\begin{cases}\pi_i, & i=j\\ \phi, & i\neq j\end{cases} \tag{1}$$

Here $\pi_i=\{\alpha\mid\alpha\in\Gamma\wedge\Omega(\alpha)=\beta_i,\beta_i\in\mathbf{M},i=1,2,\ldots,|\mathbf{M}|\}$. The higher $(8-p)$ bit plane space must belong to π_j. If α_μ is the higher $(8-p)$ bit and $\alpha_\mu\neq\alpha_\nu$, $\alpha_\mu,\alpha_\nu\in\pi_i$, the alterative still pass authentication when α_ν is replaced by α_μ. We denote the probability of forgery authentication by $P_{ij}=P(I_i)=\frac{|\pi_j|}{|\Gamma|}$. There are several properties as follows:

Properties 1: If blocks $I_{i1},I_{i2},\ldots,I_{iD}$ are tampered, then the missing probability is $\prod_{j=1}^{D}P_{ij}$.

Proof: If the missing probability of a block I_{ij} $(j=1,2,\hbar\ ,D)$ is P_{ij}, and the missing of each block is independent, the missing probability of all the tampered blocks will be $P = P_{i1} \times P_{i2} \times \hbar\ \times P_{iD} = \prod_{j=1}^{D} P_{ij}$.

Properties 2: If blocks $I_{i1}, I_{i2}, \hbar\ , I_{iD}$ are tampered, the probability on localizing all D tampered blocks will be $\prod_{j=1}^{D}(1-P_{ij})$.

Proof: The missing probability of a block I_{ij} $(j=1,2,\hbar\ ,D)$ is P_{ij}, so the probability on detecting malicious manipulation is $1-P_{ij}$. And the missing of each block is independent, and then the probability on localizing all D tampered blocks will be $(1-P_{i1})\times(1-P_{i2})\times\hbar\ \times(1-P_{iD}) = \prod_{j=1}^{D}(1-P_{ij})$.

In fact, the attack difficulty mainly depends on the system design rule and the performance of the proposed algorithm. If the mapping Ω makes $|\pi_i|(i=1,2,\hbar\ ,|\mathbf{M}|)$ uniform, namely, $P(I_i) = \frac{|\pi_j|}{|\Gamma|} = \frac{|\Gamma|/|\mathbf{M}|}{|\Gamma|} = \frac{1}{|\mathbf{M}|}, i=1,2,\hbar\ ,|\Gamma|$, the probability on tampering each block is the same, which means that it is equally difficult to attack each block; otherwise, $P(I_i) > \frac{1}{|\mathbf{M}|}$ for a certain block, which indicates that it cut down the difficulty to attack some certain blocks. For example, assuming that the block size is 64×64, the block granularity is $m\times n = 8\times 8$, $p=1$ and $|\pi_i|(i=1,2,\hbar\ ,64)$ will be uniform by Ω, thus the missing probability of each block is 2^{-64}. When $D=10$, the missing probability of image is $(2^{-64})^{10} = 2^{-640} \approx 10^{-193}$, the detection accuracy is $1-2^{-640} \approx 1$, and the localization accuracy probability is $(1-2^{-64})^{10} \approx 1$.

Note 4: Because the principal point in fragile watermark algorithm is to detect whether an image is tampered or not, the reliability of the algorithm lies on the missing probability $\prod_{j=1}^{D} P_{ij}$. When D increases, $\prod_{j=1}^{D}(1-P_{ij})$ will decrease, or the localization probability of each block decreases. Moreover, $1-\prod_{j=1}^{D} P_{ij}$ will increase with the augment of D, indicating that the detection results become more reliable with the increase of the tampered blocks.

Note 5: The watermark design rule satisfies that each of $|\pi_i|(i=1,2,\hbar\ ,|\mathbf{M}|)$ should the same as one another in order to make attack more difficult. Besides, the embedded bits p also influence the reliability of the algorithm. When $p \ge 4$, “the higher bits are used to generate watermark, the lower bits are used for embedding” method may be one-to-one mapping that results in no missing, thus the reliability of our algorithm will amount to 100% . However, we choose $p \le 2$ to guarantee the quality of the watermarked image.

4 Example of Algorithm

We will use an example to illustrate our proposed algorithm implemented by ***C++Builder6.0***. Due to the limited space, we only show the experimental results of grayscale man.bmp.

The chaotic system is designed with seventeen inputs and one output, of which sixteen inputs are the pixel-combination values and one as the position-combination values. Thereafter, we choose the cascading multiple chaotic system as the watermark generator described in Fig.2.

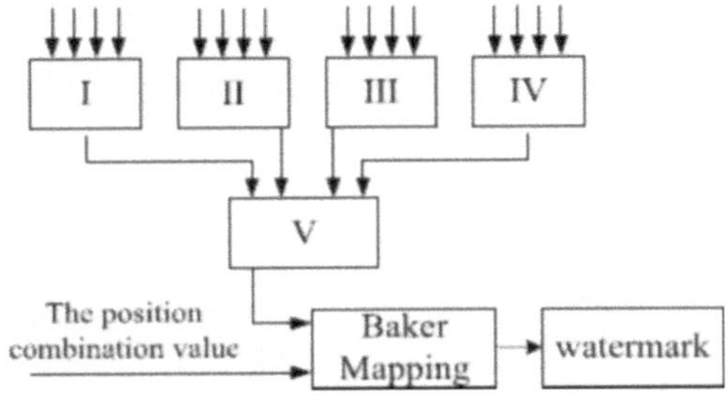

Fig. 2. The cascading multiple chaotic system

Baker mapping is introduced to iterate for 2-dimension chaotic system. The iterative equations of Baker mapping are as follows:

$$\begin{cases} x_u(n+1) = \begin{cases} 2\times x_u(n) & x_u(n)\in[0,0.5) \\ 2\times x_u(n)-1 & x_u(n)\in[0.5,1) \end{cases} \\ x_v(n+1) = \begin{cases} 0.5\times x_v(n) & x_u(n)\in[0,0.5) \\ 0.5\times x_v(n)+0.5 & x_u(n)\in[0.5,1) \end{cases} \end{cases} \tag{2}$$

All 4-dimention chaotic systems have the same iteration equations and control parameters. The 4-dimension iteration equations are extended from 1-dimension ***Bernoulli*** mapping, which are given by

$$x_q(n+1) = \begin{cases} 2\times x_q(n) & x_q(n)\in[0,0.5) \\ 2\times x_q(n)-1 & x_q(n)\in[0.5,1) \end{cases} \tag{3a}$$

$$x_r(n+1) = \begin{cases} 2\times x_r(n) & x_r(n)\in[0,0.5) \\ 2\times x_r(n)-1 & x_r(n)\in[0.5,1) \end{cases} \tag{3b}$$

$$x_s(n+1) = \begin{cases} 2\times x_s(n) & x_s(n)\in[0,0.5) \\ 2\times x_s(n)-1 & x_s(n)\in[0.5,1) \end{cases} \tag{3c}$$

$$x_t(n+1)=\begin{cases}0.125\times x_t(n) & x_q(n+1)\in[0,0.5)\hbar\ x_r(n+1)\in[0,0.5)\hbar\ x_s(n+1)\in[0,0.5)\\ 0.125\times x_t(n)+0.125 & x_q(n+1)\in[0.5,1)\hbar\ x_r(n+1)\in[0,0.5)\hbar\ x_s(n+1)\in[0,0.5)\\ 0.125\times x_t(n)+0.25 & x_q(n+1)\in[0,0.5)\hbar\ x_r(n+1)\in[0.5,1)\hbar\ x_s(n+1)\in[0,0.5)\\ 0.125\times x_t(n)+0.375 & x_q(n+1)\in[0.5,1)\hbar\ x_r(n+1)\in[0.5,1)\hbar\ x_s(n+1)\in[0,0.5)\\ 0.125\times x_t(n)+0.5 & x_q(n+1)\in[0,0.5)\hbar\ x_r(n+1)\in[0,0.5)\hbar\ x_s(n+1)\in[0.5,1)\\ 0.125\times x_t(n)+0.625 & x_q(n+1)\in[0.5,1)\hbar\ x_r(n+1)\in[0,0.5)\hbar\ x_s(n+1)\in[0.5,1)\\ 0.125\times x_t(n)+0.75 & x_q(n+1)\in[0,0.5)\hbar\ x_r(n+1)\in[0.5,1)\hbar\ x_s(n+1)\in[0.5,1)\\ 0.125\times x_t(n)+0.875 & x_q(n+1)\in[0.5,1)\hbar\ x_r(n+1)\in[0.5,1)\hbar\ x_s(n+1)\in[0.5,1)\end{cases} \quad (3d)$$

In this example, the block size is 8×8, the group granularity $k=4$, and watermark is embedded in LSB, namely, $p=1$. To facilitate the implementation, we choose the same key for each block.

The pixel-combination value is computed by $\varphi(\bullet)$. Firstly, set all the LSB zero; secondly, the ***Arnold*** transform times is set by $K_{i,1}$, and then I_i will be scrambled by ***Arnold*** transform. Here, we set $K_{i,1}=10$; thirdly, combine pixels to get the vector $V_i=(0.y_1y_2y_3y_4,\ 0.y_5y_6y_7y_8,\ \hbar\ ,\ 0.y_{61}y_{62}y_{63}y_{64})^T$, which y_a represents the a th element in $\hat{I}_i$, and $a=1,2,\hbar\ ,64$.

We combine all elements in $P_i : P_i=(X_i, Y_i)^T$ to get the position-combination value $L_i : L_i=0.X_iY_i$ by $\phi(\bullet)$, which is controlled by $K_{i,2}$. We respectively show the cover image and the watermarked image in Fig.3 and Fig.4.

Fig. 3. the Cover Image—Man.bmp

Fig. 4. The watermarked image

Image Fidelity

The image fidelity is weighted by $MPSNR=10\times\log_{10}(255^2/E^2)[dB]$, of which N represents the image size and $E=MN\max\limits_{m,n} I_{m,n}^2 \Big/ \sum\limits_{m,n}(I_{m,n}-I'_{m,n})^2$. The *MPSNR* between Fig.3 and Fig.4 is 49.6422. It is concluded that that the embedded image has the higher fidelity.

Detecting and Localizing the tampered blocks

Fig.4 is subtracted by the pixel value at the 100th row and the 100th column to get Fig.5. Fig.6 shows the results on localizing the tampered blocks after being authenticated, of which the black denotes the successful authentication and the white indicates the authentication failure. It is obvious that our proposed algorithm can detect tamper and the localization accuracy is 8×8 block.

Fig. 5. The tampered image

Fig. 6. Authentication Result of Fig.5

VQ Attack

When the position is involved in generating watermark, we can detect VQ attack and localize it. The block at the 8th row and the 10th column is exchanged with the block at the 25th row and the 20th column in Fig.4 to get Fig.7, and its tamper localization is shown in Fig.8.

Fig. 7. The watermarked image with block exchanges

Fig. 8. The tampering localization of Fig.7

When the position is not involved in generating watermark, there exist forgery authentications in Fig.9-10. We exchange the block at the 8th row and the 10th column with the block at the 25th row and the 20th column to get Fig.9. Fig.10 shows its authentication result.

Fig. 9. VQ attack

Fig. 10. Authentication Results of Fig.9

5 Conclusion

In this paper, a novel image authentication algorithm is proposed against the existing attacks. Theoretical analysis and experimental results show that the algorithm can effectively thwart feature extraction attack owing to VCT; when the block position is involved in generating watermark, our algorithm not only put resistance against quantization attack, but also doesn't decrease the tampering localization granularity.

References

1. Zhu, B.B., Swanson, M.D., Tewfik, A.H.: When Seeing Isn't Believing. IEEE Signal Processing Magazine 21(2), 40–49 (2004)
2. Zhu, B.B., Swanson, M.D.: Multimedia authentication and watermarking. In: Feng, D., Siu, W.C. (eds.) Multimedia Information Retrieval and Management, pp. 148–177. Springer, Heidelberg (2003)
3. Albanesi, M.G., Ferretti, M., Guerrini, F.: A taxonomy for image authentication techniques and its application to the current state of the art. In: Proceedings of the 11th International Conference of Image Analysis, Palermo, Italy, pp. 535–540 (2001)
4. Wu, J.H, Lin, F.Z.: Image Authentication Based on Digital Watermarking. Chinese Journal of Computers 27(9), 1153–1160 (2004)
5. Walton, S.: Image authentication for a slippery new age. Dr.Dobb's Journal 20(4), 18–26 (1995)
6. Yeung, M., Mintzer, F.: An invisible watermarking technique for image verification. In: Processings of the IEEE International Conference on Image Processing, Santa Barbara, USA, pp. 680–683 (1997)
7. Bassali, H., Chhugani, J., Agarwal, S., Aggarwal, A., Dubey, P.: Compression tolerant watermarking for image verification. In: Proceedings of the IEEE International Conference on Image Processing, Vancouver, Canada, pp. 430–433 (2000)
8. Lin, C.Y., Chang, S.F.: Semi-fragile watermarking for authenticating JPEG visual content. In: Proceedings of the SPIE International Conference on Security and Watermarking of Multimedia Contents II, San Jose, USA, pp. 140–151 (2000)
9. Wu, J., Zhu, B., Li, S., Lin, F.: New attacks on SARI image authentication system. In: Proceedings of the SPIE. Security and Watermarking of Multimedia Contents VI, San Jose, California, USA, vol. 5306, pp. 602–609 (2004)
10. Wong, P., Memon, N.: Secret and public key image watermarking schemes for image authentication and ownership verification. IEEE Transactions on Image Processing 10(10), 1593–1601 (2001)
11. Li, S., Chen, G.: On the Dynamical Degradation of Digital Piecewise Linear Chaotic Maps. The Tutorial-Review section of International Journal of Bifurcation and Chaos 10(15), 3119–3151 (2005)

A Novel Multiple Description Approach to Predictive Video Coding

Zhiqin Liang, Jiantao Zhou, Liwei Guo, Mengyao Ma, and Oscar Au*

Department of Electronic and Computer Engineering
Hong Kong University of Science and Technology
{zhiqin,eejtzhou,eeglw,myma,eeau}@ust.hk

Abstract. Multiple description coding (MDC) is a source coding technique that exploits path diversity to combat packet losses over error-prone channels. In this paper, we proposed a novel drift-free multi-state MDC method. At the encoder side, the original video is compressed into multiple independently decodable H.263 streams, each with its own coding structure and prediction process, such that if one stream is lost, the other stream can still be used to produce video with acceptable quality. At the decoder side, each description is considered as a noisy observation of the original video. A Least square-error (LSE) based merge algorithm is proposed to combine the descriptions. The experimental results show that the proposed algorithm has similar coding efficiency to [1], yet with improved error resilience.

Keywords: Multiple description coding (MDC), least square-error estimator (LSE), H.263, PB Frame.

1 Introduction

Transmission of video over non guaranteed Qos network is a challenging task, especially for real-time interactive multimedia applications where re-transmission is not feasible. Multiple description coding (MDC) has emerged as a promising approach to overcome such difficult situation. The basic idea is to encode the original signal into multiple coded streams, called descriptions, and transmit them over different channels. At the destination, each description alone provides low but acceptable quality and all descriptions together lead to better quality. This structure takes advantage of the fact that error/loss occurred in different channel is independent and it provides adequate quality without requiring re-transmission of any lost packets.

During the past decade, various MD compression algorithm have been proposed. Comprehensive reviews of the MD technique can be found in [2]. However, incorporating MDC for video compression is still a challenge. The reason is that all conventional video compression standards adopt a predictive coding

* This work has been supported by the Innovation and Technology Commission of the Hong Kong Special Administrative Region, China (project no. GHP/033/05).

H.H.S. Ip et al. (Eds.): PCM 2007, LNCS 4810, pp. 286–295, 2007.

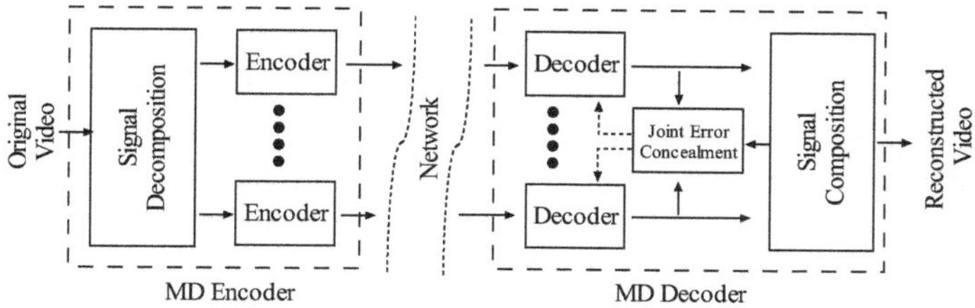

Fig. 1. System Architecture of Multi-state MDC

technique and encoding the prediction error using MDC is not straightforward. Moreover, a frame that uses two descriptions, for example, have three possible reconstructions at the decoder. The encoder may use a signal for prediction that is unavailable to the decoder (due to loss of one or more descriptions) and error will occur and accumulate in the following motion-compensated frames. Such phenomenon is called drifting and it is a fundamental design concern in MD Video coders.

One class of MDC methods, known as multi-state MDC, is gaining popularity in practical application. The system architecture is shown in Figure 1. The idea is to decompose the original signal into subsets, either in the spatial [3] and temporal [1,4] domain. Each subset is then encoded into an independently decodable description using a separate predictive coder. One obvious advantage is that conventional video standards, such as H.263 [5] and MPEG4 [6], can be adopted into the system directly. Furthermore, there will not be any drifting because every description has its own prediction loop. These features make such class of MDC methods extremely appealing for practical systems. However, the accumulate error varies a lot in each description due to the independent prediction loop and the signal composition process is not straightforward. A simple merge method will result in flickering video outputs for human eyes. And very unfortunately, an efficient postprocessing method to eliminate such flickering effect is missing from the literature.

In this paper, we introduce a new scheme based on the beneficial system structure of multi-state MDC. Instead of decomposing the signal into subsets, we encode the original video signal into multiple descriptions directly at the MD coder stage. Each description is generated by the same encoding scheme but with different initial configuration parameters (i.e. with different GOP structure, motion estimation methods, rate-control methods, etc.). Then at the MD decoder side, each description is treated as a noisy observation of the original video signal. A least square-error (LSE) based merge algorithm is developed and applied at the signal composition stage to improve the reconstructed video quality.

The paper is organized as follows. Section II will derive the theory for the merge algorithm at the MD decoder and describe its implementation issues. The strategy to optimize the coding efficiency at the MD encoder is then discussed in section III. Simulation results for the Rate Distortion performance is shown in section IV. Finally, section V concludes this work.

2 The Proposed LSE Based Merge Algorithm

In this section, we describe the theory and implementation of the LSE merge algorithm based on the assumption that H.263 [5] is used to encode each description with varying initial configuration. We treat each description as a noisy observation of the original video and an optimal linear estimator based on the LSE criteria is applied in the DCT domain to combine multiple descriptions. In order to facilitate this, we first develop a model to estimate the mean square error of each DCT coefficient reconstructed from a particular description. And then the LSE merge algorithm is presented.

Throughout this section, we denote the kth video frame as F_k. Let $x_i(F_k)$ be the ith DCT coefficient in the original video, and let $\tilde{x}_i(F_k, V_l)$ be the ith DCT coefficient in the reconstructed video of the lth description V_l.

2.1 The H.263 Quantization Scheme

Let $Q(I, Q_p)$ and $DeQ(L, Q_p)$ be the quantization and dequantization mapping with inputs I, L and quantization step Q_p. In most of the H.263 codec implementations, quantization mapping for intra-coded and inter-coded blocks are different. Let $Q_{intra}(I, Q_p)$ and $Q_{inter}(I, Q_p)$ be the quantization mappings for intra-coded and the inter-coded blocks respectively. The one suggested in the reference software [7] can be expressed as follows

$$Q(I, Q_p) = \begin{cases} Q_{intra}(I, Q_p) \text{ if intracoded} \\ Q_{inter}(I, Q_p) \text{ otherwise} \end{cases} \tag{1}$$

$$Q_{intra}(I, Q_p) = floor(\frac{|I|}{2Q_p}) \cdot sign(I), \tag{2}$$

$$Q_{inter}(I, Q_p) = floor(\frac{|I| - Q_p/2}{2Q_p}) \cdot sign(I), \tag{3}$$

where $floor(\cdot)$ rounds the input to the nearest integer that is smaller than the input and $sign(\cdot)$ return the sign of the input. In particular, $Q_p = 8$ for the DC coefficient of intra-coded blocks.

The dequantization mapping is specified in the H.263 standard [5]. The mapping $DeQ(L, Q_p)$ is the same for both intra-coded and inter-coded blocks as shown below.

$$DeQ(L, Q_p) = \begin{cases} Q_p \cdot (2 \cdot L + 1) & \text{if } Q_p \text{ is odd} \\ Q_p \cdot (2 \cdot L + 1) - 1 & \text{otherwise} \end{cases} \tag{4}$$

From (1)-(4), we define the reconstruction of I as

$$Rec(I, Q_p) = DeQ(\ Q(I, Q_p), Q_p\ ). \tag{5}$$

For a particular reconstructed value $\tilde{I}$, let $LB(\tilde{I}, Q_p)$ and $UB(\tilde{I}, Q_p)$ be the minimum and maximum values of I satisfying $Rec(I, Q_p) = \tilde{I}$. Therefore, with a quantizer of Q_p, if I is reconstructed to $\tilde{I}$, the cell (range) of the original signal I is

$$I \in [\ LB(\tilde{I}, Q_p)\ ,\ UB(\tilde{I}, Q_p)\ ]. \tag{6}$$

2.2 Distribution of the DCT Coefficient for Intra-Coded Blocks

If $x_i(F_k)$ is intra-coded, the reconstructed coefficient is

$$\tilde{x_i}(F_k, V_l) = Rec(\ x_i(F_k), Q_p\ ). \tag{7}$$

According to [8], the AC coefficients for I-blocks obey a zero-mean Laplacian probability distribution. The Laplacian probability density function (PDF), $f^i_{F_k,V_l}(x)$ for each coefficient can be expressed as

$$f^i_{F_k,V_l}(x) = \frac{1}{2\lambda^i_{F_k,V_l}} e^{-|x|/\lambda^i_{F_k,V_l}}, \tag{8}$$

where $\lambda^i_{F_k,V_l}$ is the rate parameter of the distribution of the ith coefficient of F_k in V_l. The rate parameter of $f^i_{F_k,V_l}(x)$, can be estimated in a similar method stated in [9] by observing the distribution of $\tilde{x_i}(F_k, V_l)$.

2.3 Distribution of the DCT Coefficient for Inter-Coded Blocks

If $x_i(F_k)$ is inter-coded, let $p_i(V_l)$ denote the ith DCT coefficient of the prediction block generated by available reference frame in the decoder, no matter from the previous frame (P block) or the future frames (B blocks and PB blocks). In addition let $r_i(F_k, V_l)$ be the ith DCT coefficient of the residual signal where

$$x_i(F_k) = p_i(V_l) + r_i(F_k, V_l). \tag{9}$$

In this way, the quantized version of the ith DCT coefficient of the residual of V_l can be expressed as

$$\tilde{r_i}(F_k, V_l) = Rec\big(r_i(F_k, V_l), Q_p\big). \tag{10}$$

And the ith reconstructed DCT coefficient of the block is

$$\tilde{x_i}(F_k, V_l) = p_i(V_l) + \tilde{r_i}(F_k, V_l). \tag{11}$$

As stated in [8], the distribution of $r_i(F_k, V_l)$ is also Laplacian. The PDF can be specified as (8) with a different rate parameter. Again, the rate parameter can be obtain from the statistics of $\tilde{r_i}(F_k, V_l)$.

2.4 MMSE Reconstruction and the Corresponding MSE

For the ease of notation, we drop the subscript i. And the parameters F_k and V_l corresponds to each coefficient in F_k of V_l. From the distribution of the coefficient, together with the knowledge of the quantizer applied, we can obtain the minimum MSE (MMSE) reconstruction by the Lloyd-Max method.

For intra-coded block, the optimal reconstruction is as follows

$$x_{opt} = \frac{\int_l^u x f(x)dx}{\int_l^u f(x)dx} \tag{12}$$

where $l = LB(\tilde{x}, Q_p)$, $u = UB(\tilde{x}, Q_p)$, Q_p is the quantizer stepsize, and $f(x)$ is the distribution of the DCT coefficient of the block in the form of (8).

For inter-coded block, the MMSE reconstruction of the residual is specified below,

$$r_{opt} = \frac{\int_{l'}^{u'} r f(r) dr}{\int_{l'}^{u'} f(r) dr} \tag{13}$$

where $l' = LB(\tilde{r}, Q_p)$, $u' = UB(\tilde{r}, Q_p)$, Q_p is the quantizer stepsize, and $f(r)$ is the distribution of the DCT coefficient of the residual block in the form of (8). In this way, the optimal reconstruction of the video signal is

$$x_{opt} = p + r_{opt}. \tag{14}$$

Now, the MSE of the MMSE reconstruction of the DCT coefficient for intra-blocks and inter-blocks can be expressed as $MSE_I(x_{opt})$ and $MSE_P(x_{opt})$ respectively as shown below.

$$MSE_I(x_{opt}) = \int_l^u (x - x_{opt})^2 f(x) dx \tag{15}$$

$$\begin{aligned} MSE_P(x_{opt}) &= \int_{l'}^{u'} \left((p + r) - (p + r_{opt})\right)^2 f(r) dx \\ &= \int_{l'}^{u'} (r - r_{opt})^2 f(r) dx \end{aligned} \tag{16}$$

2.5 The LSE Based Merge Algorithm

Suppose we have n different descriptions $(V_1, \cdots, V_n)$ of the same original video. For each description V_l, from (12) and (14), we can obtain its DCT coefficients in the MMSE sense. For the ease of notation, we drop the subscript i corresponding to each DCT coefficient. Let $X_{\mathrm{MMSE}} = (x_{opt1}, \cdots, x_{optn})^T$ be the column vector of the MMSE reconstructions of the collocated DCT coefficient from $(V_1, \cdots, V_n)$. Let $Err = (e_1, \cdots, e_n)^T$ be the column vector of the random variables corresponding to the reconstruction error from each video stream.

Then, the least square-error estimate (LSE) of the original signal x is

$$x_{\mathrm{LSE}} = X_{\mathrm{MMSE}}^T \cdot W \tag{17}$$

where W=$(w_1, \cdots, w_n)$ is the weights subjecting to the constrain that $\Sigma_{i=1}^n w_n$=1, and minimizing

$$E[(x - x_{\mathrm{LSE}})^2] = E[(Err^T \cdot W)^2] \tag{18}$$

The solution of W can be obtained by differentiating (18) with respect to w_i and solving the n equations together with the constrain.

3 Optimizing Coding Efficiency at the Encoding Stage

We will consider the case for generating two descriptions in this section. In particular, H.263 video standard is assumed to be applied in the proposed system architecture. However, other contemporary predictive compression standards can be applied as well, with small modification to the quantization noise model analyzed in the previous section.

In order to achieve high coding efficient (rate-distortion performance), the initial configurations of the two H.263 encoders must be carefully selected. In this section, we first present three guidelines and then develop the configurations that maximize the coding efficiency for the proposed multiple description coding method.

3.1 Factors Critical to the Performance of Merge Algorithm

If we have two descriptions, for example, let $\sigma_1^2 = E[e_1^2]$, $\sigma_2^2 = E[e_2^2]$ be the error variances of the two reconstructions of a particular DCT coefficient and $\rho = E[e_1 e_2]/\sigma_1\sigma_2$ be the error correlation coefficient. Then the weights are

$$W = \left(\frac{\sigma_2^2 - \sigma_1\sigma_2\rho}{\sigma_1^2 + \sigma_2^2 - 2\sigma_1\sigma_2\rho}, \frac{\sigma_1^2 - \sigma_1\sigma_2\rho}{\sigma_1^2 + \sigma_2^2 - 2\sigma_1\sigma_2\rho}\right). \tag{19}$$

where σ_1 and σ_2 of can be calculated with respect to (15) and (16). The error correlation can be obtained from statistics. Details refer to the following section.

With the optimal weights, the expected mean square error of the LSE estimation is

$$E[(x - x_{\text{LSE}})^2] = \frac{\sigma_1^2\sigma_2^2(1-\rho^2)}{\sigma_1^2 + \sigma_2^2 - 2\sigma_1\sigma_2\rho}. \tag{20}$$

From (20), the performance of the LSE decoding algorithm depends on two factors: the error variances of the two reconstructions and their correlation. If $\rho \approx 0$ and $\sigma_1 \approx \sigma_2$, the resulting expected error variance is $\sigma_1^2/2$, which corresponds to $3dB$ gain in the PSNR measure.

Therefore, in order to get the maximum performance out of the merge algorithm, we have the following three guidelines in configuring the two encoders.

1. *The two descriptions should have similar noise levels.*
2. *The error correlation coefficient between the two must be kept small.*
3. *The configurations should not degrade the coding efficiency for side encoders.*

3.2 The Encoder Configuration and The Error Correlation

In the previous section, we have found the three criteria to optimize the performance of the merge algorithm. In this section, we will investigate on the encoder configurations for H.263 encoder [7] that fulfill the three criteria. without loss of generality, we assume two descriptions to be generated in this section.

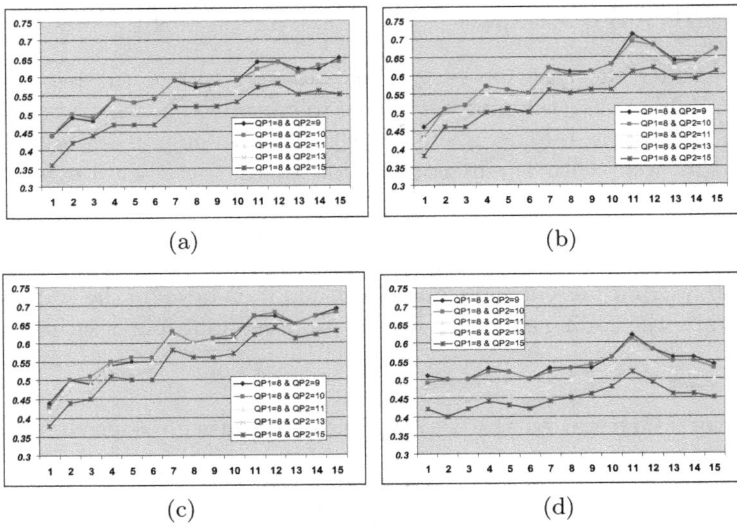

Fig. 2. Error correlation ρ for the first 16 DCT Coefficients (in Zigzag order) for two description using Conventional IPPP coding structure with quantization parameters set to QP_1 for description 1 and QP_2 for description 2. (a) *Foreman* QCIF @ $15fps$ (b) *Foreman* CIF @ $30fps$ (c)*City* QCIF @ $15fps$ (d)*Stefan* QCIF @ $15fps$.

As there is no close form expression for the error correlation coefficient ρ, we use experimental methods to gain insights of the relationship between encoder configurations of the two descriptions and the corresponding ρ.

We first investigate what effect would have on ρ if we vary the quantization factors. The two descriptions are generated with the conventional IPPP coding structure but with different quantization parameters. The resulting ρ are plotted in fig.2 for four test sequences with different levels of motion activities and texture complexity. It can be seen that if the more the quantization step varies, the smaller the error correlation coefficient. However, if QP varies a lot, the noise level in the two description will not be similar (i.e. rule 1 is violated). Therefore, by just varying the QP of the two encoder configurations is not enough to achieve good performance.

We then consider the effect that would have on ρ if we change the coding type (i.e intra-coded or inter-coded). Fig 3(a) shows the resulting ρ of the two descriptions with same QP but different coding structure. Description 1 is coded using the normal $IPPP$ structure while description 2 only utilizes intra-coding. It can be observed that ρ is kept low which satisfied rule 2. Nevertheless, since a lot of intra-frames is coded for description 2, the coding efficiency is extremely low.

From the previous two observations, the authors come up with the idea of applying PB coding to the two descriptions as depicted in fig 4. In a PB frame, a P frame and a B frame are coded as one unit. As discussed in [10], the PB coding increases the temporal resolution without increasing the bitrate too much. A more detailed discussion about PB coding can be found in [11]. For PB coding

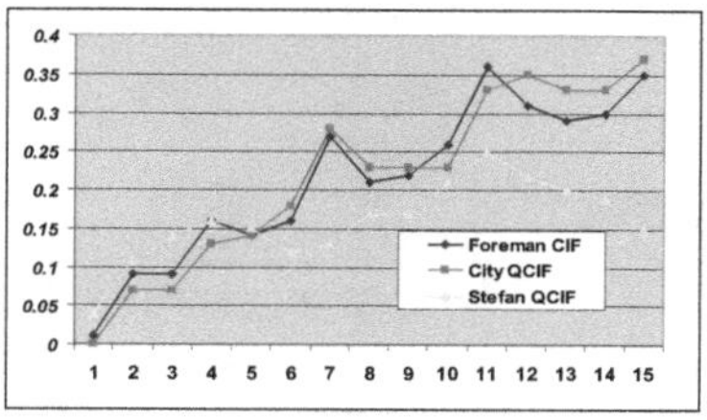

(a)

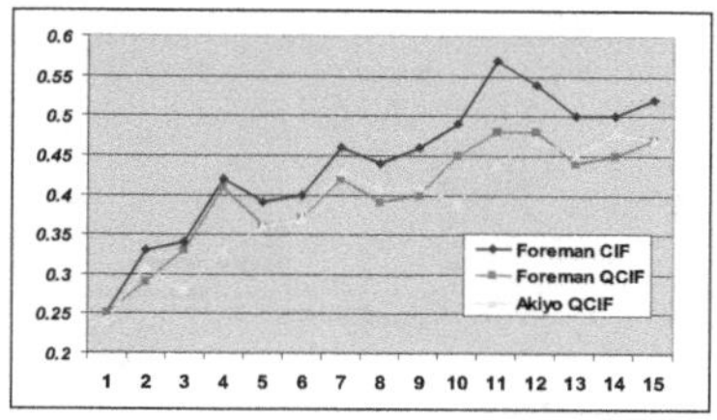

(b)

Fig. 3. Error correlation ρ for the first 16 DCT Coefficients (in Zigzag order). (a) IPPP structure for description 2 with $QP_2 = 8$ and all I-frames coding structure for description 1 with $QP_1 = 8$ (b) The two descriptions are coded using the PB coding structure shown in figure 4 with $QP_1 = QP_2 = 8$ and $QP_B = QP_1 + 2$.

structure, the quantization step for B frame is intentionally set to be higher than that in P frames, $QP_B = QP_P + 2$, to maintain the coding efficiency. With the alternating frame coding type, as well as the different quantizers applied, the resulting ρ should be low. Fig 3(b) shows the simulation results which confirms our reasoning.

4 Simulation Results

In this section, we will present the simulation results for the proposed system with two descriptions. The proposed PB coding structure is applied at the MD encoder side and the proposed LSE merge algorithm is performed at the MD decoder side.

Fig 5 shows the rate-distortion (RD) curves for four sequences with different levels of motion and texture complexity. The RD curves of the temporal sub-sampling method discussed in [1] are also presented for comparison. It can be seen that the coding performance of the proposed method is a little bit better the temporal sub-sampling method. However, despite of the extra complexity, the proposed system greatly improves the error resilient capability since every frame is coded twice. Moreover, the proposed method can be applied in parallel with the temporal and spatial subsampling methods to generate multiple description

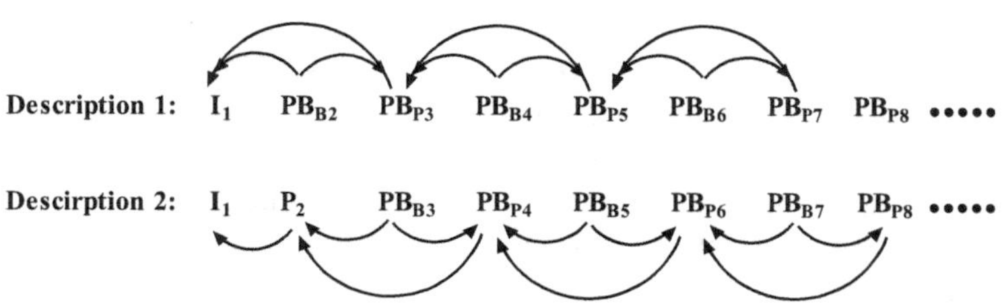

Fig. 4. PB Coding Structure of the Two Descriptions

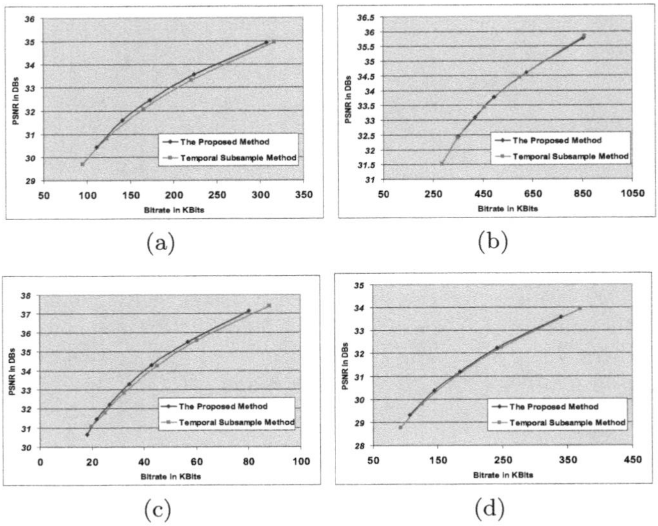

Fig. 5. Rate Distortion Performance Comparison (a) *Foreman* QCIF @ 30*fps* (b) *Foreman* CIF @ 30*fps* (c) *Akiyo* QCIF @ 15 *fps* (d) *City* QCIF @ 15*fps*

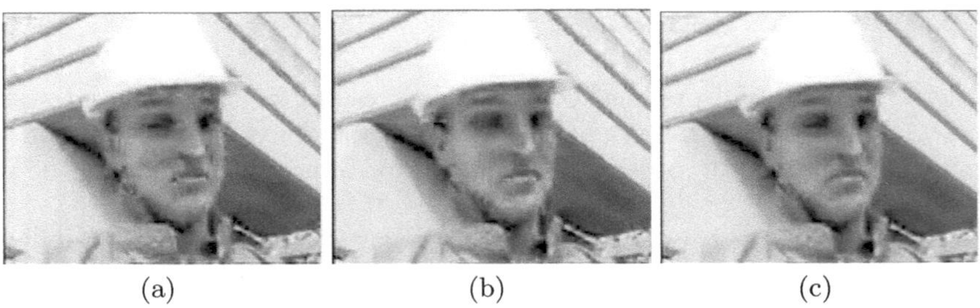

Fig. 6. Visual comparison for the 72nd frame of *Foreman* QCIF @ 30*fps*. A post-processing deblocking filter [6] is applied. (a) The frame in description 1 (b) The frame in description 2 (c) The output of the proposed algorithm combining description 1 and description 2.

more efficiently, especially in the case that more than three descriptions are required.

In terms of visual quality, Fig 6 shows a selected frame from the foreman sequence. Figure 6(a) and 6(b) show the results that only one description is decoded. Figure 6(c) shows the output of the proposed LSE merge algorithm, which is much more visually pleasing. Furthermore, there is no flickering effects which will accompany with the temporal subsampling method.

5 Conclusions

In this paper, we proposed a new scheme for multiple description coding of video. At the encoder side, we encode the original video into multiple H.263 video streams with different initial encoder configurations. At the decoder side, we treat each description as an noisy observation of the original signal. A LSE based merge algorithm is proposed to jointly decode the multiple H.263 video streams. With the proposed MDC method, each side encoder is performed in its optimal rate-distortion performance. There is no drifting in the case that only one description arrives. Furthermore, no flickering effect can be perceived by human eyes as compared to [1].

Experimental results show that the proposed scheme archives very high coding efficiency. As each frame is coded and transmitted twice, we believe that the proposed MDC method has extremely good error resilient capability. The error concealment methods based on the proposed architecture would be an interesting research problem.

More importantly, the proposed method complements the temporal and spatial sub-sampling methods. Each method alone may not be capable to generate a large number of descriptions efficiently. However, a combination of these methods might be a way to resolve the problem.

References

1. Wenger, S.: Video redundancy coding in h.263+. In: Proc. AVSPN (1997)
2. Wang, Y., Reibman, A., Lin, S.: Multiple description coding for video delivery. Proceedings of The IEEE 93, 57–70 (2005)
3. Franchi, N., Fumagalli, M., Lancini, R., Tubaro, S.: Multiple description video coding for scalable and robust transmission over ip. IEEE Transactions On Circuits And Systems For Video Technology 15, 321–334 (2005)
4. Apostolopoulos, J.: Error resilient video compression through the use of multiple states. In: Proc. IEEE International Conference on Image Processing, vol. 3, pp. 352–355 (2000)
5. ITU Telecom. Standardization Sector of ITU: Video Coding for Low Bitrate Communication (2007) ITU-T Recommendation H.263
6. ISO/IEC MPEG: 14496-2: Information Technology-Coding of audio visual objects–Part 2 Visual (2001)
7. Signal Processing and Multimedia Lab, University of British Columbia: TMN8 (H263+) Encoder/decoder Version 3.1.3 (1998)
8. Pa, I.M., Sun, M.T.: Modeling dct coefficients for fast video encoding. IEEE Transactions on Circuits and Systems for Video Technology 9, 608–616 (1999)
9. Turaga, S., Chen, D., Caviedes, Y.: No reference psnr estimation for compressed pictures. Signal Processing: Image Communication 19, 173–184 (2004)
10. Girod, B., Steinbach, E., Farber, N.: Performance of the h.263 video compression standard. The Journal of VLSI Signal Processing 17, 101–111 (1997)
11. Cote, G., Erol, B., Gallant, M., Kossentini, F.: H.263+: Video coding at low bit rates. IEEE Transactions on Circuits and Systems for Video Technology 8, 849–866 (1998)

Video Multicast over Wireless Ad Hoc Networks Using Distributed Optimization

Yifeng He, Ivan Lee, and Ling Guan

Department of Electrical and Computer Engineering,
Ryerson University, Toronto, Canada
{yhe, ilee, lguan}@ee.ryerson.ca

Abstract. Video multicast over wireless ad hoc networks is a quite challenging task. In this paper, we propose an optimized video multicast scheme. Firstly, we apply prioritized coding scheme and network coding scheme to eliminate the decoding hierarchy and delivery redundancy. Then, we maximize the aggregate throughput at all the receivers by jointly optimizing both the source rate allocation and the routing scheme. The proposed algorithm is fully distributed, thus very suitable for wireless ad hoc networks. Simulation results show that the proposed video multicast scheme yields a superior video quality compared to the double-tree routing scheme.

Keywords: Video multicast, wireless ad hoc network, network coding, convex optimization, distributed algorithm.

1 Introduction

Wireless ad hoc networks consist of a collection of wireless nodes which dynamically exchange data among themselves. Recently, there is a compelling need to support real-time video multicast in wireless ad hoc networks. For example, soccer fans in a stadium may like to receive real-time TV broadcast using their portable devices, while watching the World Cup matches. A TV operator, requiring no preexisting infrastructure, can provide this service to the subscribers via wireless ad hoc networks. As a result, video streaming over ad hoc networks provides a flexible solution to users with a reduced cost.

In this paper, we study the problem of how to simultaneously deliver a real-time video from a single source to multiple users over wireless ad hoc networks. Multicast over ad hoc networks is bandwidth-efficient compared to multiple-unicast sessions. However, there are some challenges for video multicast over wireless ad hoc networks. First of all, routing is challenging due to the dynamic topology and variable channel conditions. Multi-path routing can potentially provide a higher throughput to the receiver [1]. However, how to optimally split the traffic over multiple paths is a problem that requires further investigation. Secondly, source rate allocation is another important problem for video multicasting over wireless ad hoc networks. If the source rate exceeds the network capacity, congestion will occur. On the other hand, if the source rate is too small, some users may not receive the video at maximum quality levels.

H.H.S. Ip et al. (Eds.): PCM 2007, LNCS 4810, pp. 296–305, 2007.

Multicast routing has been an active research area for many years. Some algorithms aim to find a single tree using network layer performance metrics, such as delay, loss, or throughput. Recently, multiple tree routing algorithms are proposed to explore the path diversity for each receiver. Two typical multiple-tree video multicast in wireless ad hoc networks are given in [2, 3]. In [2], two multicast tree are constructed to deliver two descriptions, each description is layered encoded to meet the heterogeneous capacity of the receivers. The authors minimize the expected distortion when constructing multiple trees using genetic algorithm. The drawbacks of this approach are the dependence of a centralized computation and the complexity of the algorithm. In [3], the authors propose a multiple tree construction protocol to build two nearly disjoint trees simultaneously in a distributed way. These multicast trees are built based on the network layer metrics, and the system does not guarantee to achieve an optimal performance. Optimization techniques have been applied in the network utility maximization over wireless ad hoc networks [4, 5]. Zhu *et al* [6] examine an approach which jointly optimizes the source rate and routing scheme for multiple unicast video streams in the wireless ad hoc networks.

In this paper, we propose a distributed algorithm to jointly optimize the source rate allocation and the routing scheme for video multicasting over wireless ad hoc networks. The proposed algorithm is fully decentralized, making it extremely suitable for video streaming over wireless ad hoc networks.

2 Prioritized Coding Scheme and Network Coding

For video multicast over wireless ad hoc networks, each receiver may receive a different throughput. A scalable source coding can provide different quality levels for these heterogeneous receivers. Inspired from [12], we use a prioritized coding scheme shown in Fig. 1(a). The prioritized coding scheme consists of two steps. At the first step, each frame of a video sequence is encoded into N layers. The source bits in layer i (i=1,...,N) is denoted as R_i. At the second step, the source bits R_i is split into i equal source blocks, each containing bits R_i/i. Then (N-i) redundant blocks of 0s are padded to construct N blocks. In this way, N source packets, denoted from M^1 to M^N, are generated.

We notice that the source packet is hierarchical. The decoding of a packet requires the existence of all the corresponding lower-layer packets. This hierarchical relationship can be removed with network coding [8]. With random linear network coding [13], the source node sends out encoded packets that are linear combinations of the original source packets as shown in Fig. 1(b), and the intermediate nodes forwarding the encoded packets that are linear combinations of previously received packets. The receiving nodes decode the received packets to get the original source information.

The padding pattern of the 0s blocks is broadcasted to all the nodes before video transmission. If a receiver receives k packets, the receiver can recover the source bits from R_1 till R_k, thus reconstructing k-layer video quality. Even if some of the packets in a frame are lost, that frame can still be constructed to a partial video quality.

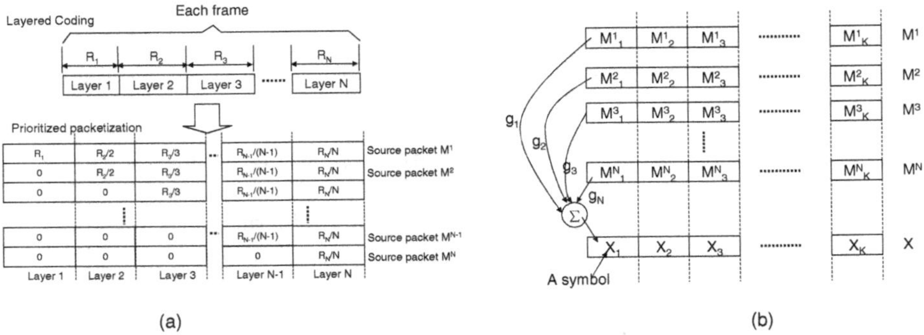

Fig. 1. Coding techniques for video multicast over wireless ad hoc networks: (a) prioritized coding scheme, and (b) network coding at the source node

In random linear network coding, each node in the network selects uniformly at random the encoding coefficients over the field $\mathbf{F}_{2^s}$, in a completely independent and decentralized manner [13]. It has been shown that the probability of selecting linearly dependent combinations is negligible even for a small field sizes (for example, s = 8) [14]. In other words, network coding statistically eliminate the redundant packets. Each received packet is useful for the video reconstruction.

The combination of prioritized coding scheme and network coding is superior to multiple-description coding (MDC) in terms of redundancy elimination. MDC is a coding scheme performed only at the source node. In mesh networks, there is risk that a node may receive redundant descriptions, thus wasting the bandwidth.

With prioritized coding scheme and network coding, a receiver with a larger throughput can reconstruct the video at a higher quality since all the received packets are distinct. For video multicasting over wireless ad hoc networks, our objective can be placed on the maximization of the aggregate throughput received at all the receivers.

3 Optimization Problem and Distributed Solution

3.1 The Model

We represent the topology of a wireless ad hoc network by a directed graph. In this model, a collection of nodes are labeled with m=1,...,M. A wireless link is presented as an order pair (i, j) of distinct nodes. We label the links with integers l=1,...,L. The network topology can be represented by a node-link incidence matrix $\mathbf{A} \in \mathbf{R}^{M \times L}$, whose element is given by

$$a_{ml} = \begin{cases} 1, & \text{if } m \text{ is the start node of link } l, \\ -1, & \text{if } m \text{ is the end node of link } l, \\ 0, & \text{otherwise.} \end{cases}$$

With network coding, a multicast link rate is feasible in a directed network if and only if it is feasible from the source node s to each receiver independently, as a unicast [8]. Therefore a multicast flow from s to H receivers can be viewed as H conceptual unicast sessions [7]. The multicast rate at a link is the maximum among H conceptual unicast rates at this link. Each conceptual unicast session follows the flow conservation law as follows.

$$\sum_{l} a_{ml} x_{hl} = \eta_m^h, \qquad h = 1,\ldots,H;\ m = 1,\ldots M, \tag{1}$$

where x_{hl} is the link rate at link l for conceptual unicast session h. Let s_h denote the source rate for conceptual unicast session h. η_m^h is equal to s_h if node m is the source, or $-s_h$ if node m is the receiver, or 0 for all other cases.

We adopt Gaussian broadcast channel with FDMA as the communication model. Therefore there is no interference among links. Link l is assigned disjoint frequency band with bandwidth W_l and transmit power P_l. Based on Shannon theory, the capacity of link l can be formulated as follows.

$$c_l = W_l \log_2\left(1 + \frac{G_l P_l}{\sigma_l W_l}\right), \quad l = 1,\ldots,L, \tag{2}$$

where σ_l is the power spectral density of additive white Gaussian noise at the receiver of link l, G_l represents the path gain from the transmitter to the receiver at link l.

To simulate data communications over a fading channel, the failure process of a link can be modeled with a two-state Markov chain. When a link (link l) is in a Good (G) state, the packets transmitted over this link will be successfully received at the destination. When link l is in a BAD (B) state, the transmitted packets will be lost. The probability of obtaining a G state from a G state is denoted by γ_l, and the probability of obtaining a B state from a B state is denoted by β_l. The steady state analysis shows that the packet loss rate p_l at link l is given by $p_l = (1-\gamma_l)/(2-\gamma_l-\beta_l)$.

For conceptual unicast session h, there are J_h paths, labeled with j_h=1,2,…,J_h, from the source to the receiver. Let $T(j_h)$ denote the set of the links in path j_h. Path j_h carries a normalized portion z_{j_h} of the total traffic, we have $z_1 + z_2 + \ldots + z_{j_h} = 1$. We define a binary variable $Q_l^{j_h} \in \{0,\ 1\}$ for link l:

$$Q_l^{j_h} = \begin{cases} 1, \text{ if } l \in T(j_h), \\ 0, \text{ if } l \notin T(j_h). \end{cases} \tag{3}$$

For path j_h, the end-to-end packet loss rate can be computed as follows.

$$p_{j_h}^E = 1 - \prod_l \left(1 - Q_l^{j_h} p_l\right). \tag{4}$$

Typically, the packet loss rate p_l at each link is very small (e.g., $p_l \ll 1$). Thus, the end-to-end packet loss rate for path j_h can be approximated as

$$p_{j_h}^E \approx \sum_l \left(Q_l^{j_h} p_l\right). \tag{5}$$

With multi-path routing, the source traffic is disseminated over J_h paths. Therefore, the end-to-end packet loss rate for conceptual session h is given by

$$p_h^E = \sum_{j_h} \left(z_{j_h} p_{j_h}^E \right) \approx \sum_{j_h} \left(z_{j_h} \sum_l \left(Q_l^{j_h} p_l \right) \right) = \sum_l \left(p_l \sum_{j_h} \left(z_{j_h} Q_l^{j_h} \right) \right) = \sum_l \left(p_l \frac{x_{hl}}{s_h} \right). \tag{6}$$

3.2 Problem Formulation

As described in section 2, the combination of the prioritized coding scheme and network coding eliminates the decoding hierarchy and delivery redundancy. Therefore, our objective for video multicast over wireless ad hoc networks is to maximize the aggregate throughput received at all the receivers. The problem can be formulated as a linear program (**LP**) as below:

$$\begin{aligned} \text{maximize:} \quad & \sum_h s_h \left(1 - p_h^E\right) = \sum_h \left(s_h - \sum_l x_{hl} p_l \right) \\ \text{subject to:} \quad & \sum_l a_{ml} x_{hl} = \eta_m^h, \quad h = 1,\ldots,H,\ m = 1,\ldots M, \\ & 0 \le x_{hl} \le c_l, \quad h = 1,\ldots,H,\ l = 1,\ldots,L, \\ & s_h \ge 0, \quad h = 1,\ldots,H, \end{aligned} \tag{7}$$

where link capacity c_l is given by equation (2).

The **LP** can be solved with centralized algorithms, such as the simplex method or interior point method [9]. However, centralized algorithm requires a central computation node, which may not be available in wireless ad hoc networks. Therefore, we look for a distributed algorithm to solve the above optimization problem. We approximate the problem (7) to the following formulation.

$$\begin{aligned} \text{minimize:} \quad & \sum_h \left(-s_h + \sum_l x_{hl} p_l + \varepsilon s_h^2 + \delta \sum_l x_{hl}^2 \right) \\ \text{subject to:} \quad & \text{the same constraints as given in (7),} \end{aligned} \tag{8}$$

where ε and δ are small positive numbers. When ε and δ are sufficiently small, the term $\left(\varepsilon s_h^2 + \delta \sum_l x_{hl}^2 \right)$ is close to 0, therefore the solution for problem (8) is arbitrarily close to the solution for problem (7).

3.3 Distributed Solution

Since the objective function is strictly convex and the constraints are linear, the problem (8) represents a strictly convex optimization problem. By using the Lagrangian duality properties, we can develop a distributed algorithm to solve problem (8).

By introducing dual variables v_{hm} (h=1,…,H, m=1,…,M), we have the Lagrangian of the primal problem (8) as below

$$\begin{aligned} L(\mathbf{s},\mathbf{x},\mathbf{v}) &= \sum_h \left(-s_h + \sum_l x_{hl} p_l + \varepsilon s_h^{\ 2} + \delta \sum_l x_{hl}^{\ 2} \right) + \sum_h \sum_m v_{hm} \left(\sum_l a_{ml} x_{hl} - \eta_m^h \right) \\ &= \sum_h \left(-s_h + \varepsilon s_h^{\ 2} - \sum_m v_{hm} \eta_m^h \right) + \sum_h \sum_l \left(\delta x_{hl}^{\ 2} + x_{hl} \left(p_l + \sum_m v_{hm} a_{ml} \right) \right), \end{aligned} \tag{9}$$

where $\mathbf{v} \in \mathbf{R}^{H \times M}$ is the dual variable matrix, $\mathbf{s} \in \mathbf{R}^H$ is the vector of the conceptual source rates, and $\mathbf{x} \in \mathbf{R}^{H \times L}$ is the matrix of the conceptual link rates.

The Lagrange dual function $G(\mathbf{v})$ is the minimum value of the Lagrangian.

$$\begin{aligned} G(\mathbf{v}) &= \inf_{\mathbf{s},\mathbf{x}} \{ L(\mathbf{s},\mathbf{x},\mathbf{v}) \} \\ &= \sum_h \inf_{s_h} \left(-s_h + \varepsilon s_h^{\ 2} - \sum_m v_{hm} \eta_m^h \right) + \sum_h \sum_l \inf_{x_{hl}} \left(\delta x_{hl}^{\ 2} + x_{hl} \left(p_l + \sum_m v_{hm} a_{ml} \right) \right). \end{aligned} \tag{10}$$

The dual function can be evaluated separately via the conceptual source rate s_h and the link rate x_{hl}. The Lagrange dual problem associated with the primal problem (8) is given by

$$\text{maximize} \quad G(\mathbf{v}) = G_{source}(\mathbf{v}) + G_{routing}(\mathbf{v}). \tag{11}$$

Since the dual function $G(\mathbf{v})$ is always convex, the Lagrange dual problem is therefore a convex optimization problem [10]. In optimization problem (8), Slater's condition for strong duality holds [10]. The primal variables s_h and x_{hl} converge to the optimal solution to the primal problem (8) when the dual variables v_{hm} converge to the optimal solution to the dual problem (**11**).

At the k-th iteration, the optimal primal variables can be obtained from dual variables.

$$s_h^{(k)} = \arg \inf_{s_h \geq 0} \left\{ -s_h + \varepsilon s_h^{\ 2} - \sum_m v_{hm}^{\ (k)} \eta_m^h \right\}, \quad h = 1, \ldots, H, \tag{12}$$

$$x_{hl}^{(k)} = \arg \inf_{0 \leq x_{hl} \leq c_l} \left\{ \delta x_{hl}^{\ 2} + x_{hl} \left(p_l + \sum_m v_{hm}^{\ (k)} a_{ml} \right) \right\}, \quad h = 1, \ldots, H, \ l = 1, \ldots, L. \tag{13}$$

We use subgradient method [11] to solve the dual problem (**11**). Since the dual function is continuously differentiable due to the strictly convexity of the primal objective function, we can find a subgradient from the gradient. The subgradient of the negative dual function $-G(\mathbf{v})$ at v_{hm} is given by

$$g_{hm}^{(k)} = \eta_m^{h\ (k)} - \sum_l a_{ml} x_{hl}^{\ (k)}, \quad h = 1, \ldots, H, \ m = 1, \ldots M. \tag{14}$$

We update the dual variables by

$$v_{hm}^{(k+1)} = v_{hm}^{(k)} - \alpha^{(k)} g_{hm}^{(k)}, \quad h = 1, \ldots, H, \ m = 1, \ldots M, \tag{15}$$

where $\alpha^{(k)} > 0$ is a scalar step-size at the k-th iteration. One simple convergence condition requires that the step-size sequence satisfies

$$\alpha^{(k)} \to 0, \quad \sum_{k=1}^{\infty} \alpha^{(k)} = \infty .$$

The step-size we use in our algorithm is: $\alpha^{(k)} = \omega / \sqrt{k}$, where ω >0.

The above algorithm is fully distributed in the following senses. First, the source node computes each conceptual source rate using its dual variable and the dual variable of the receiver. Second, each node computes the conceptual link rates of its outgoing links, using the packet loss rates of its outgoing links, the local dual variable, and the dual variables of its neighboring nodes. The proposed distributed algorithm only requires information exchange in the neighborhood, thus greatly reducing the overhead.

In wireless ad hoc networks, the nodes may join or leave the networks dynamically due to mobility or channel failures. To handle the network dynamics, our algorithm can run in a discrete-time manner (e.g. every 10 seconds). At the beginning of each time slot, a node updates and sends its new dual variables to its neighbors if it has detected any topology change. A node that has not experienced any change in its local topology will also need to update its dual variables. In this way, local changes will propagate throughout the network, and the optimal source rate and routing scheme will be recomputed. The proposed distributed algorithm has a fast convergence speed, which enables a fast adaptation to the network changes.

4 Simulations

We generate a wireless ad hoc network by placing 15 nodes at random locations in a square region of 400m * 400m. Two nodes are able to communicate if their distance is smaller than the coverage threshold 150m. Node 1 is chosen as the source node. Four nodes (node 6, 7, 10 and 11) are chosen as the receivers. For every link, the transition probability from a GOOD state to the next GOOD state is uniformly distributed in [0.90, 0.95], and the transition probability from a BAD state to the next BAD state is uniformly distributed in [0.05, 0.10]. We encode Foreman QCIF sequence into 8 layers using SNR-scalable extension of H.264/AVC [15]. Each GOP consists of 16 frames. The source bits are packetized into 8 descriptions, each having an average bit rate of 67.0 Kbps. No error-concealment is used for the lost frames. In the communication model, the bandwidth allocated for each link is 15 KHz. The transmit power at each link is fixed at 0.70 W. The power spectral density σ_l of additive white Gaussian noise at each receiver is uniformly distributed in [0.05, 0.10] W/Hz. The path gain G_l for link l is given by $G_l = 0.01 / d_l^{\,2}$, where d_l is the distance in meters between the transmitter and the receiver at link l. In the optimization, ε and δ are both set to 0.05. The step-size at the k-th iteration is $\alpha^{(k)} = 0.2 / \sqrt{k}$.

With the predefined convergence threshold of 10^{-4}, all the primal variables (the conceptual source rates and link rates) converge within 135 iterations. The fast convergence speed makes fast re-routing possible when the network topology changes due to mobility or channel failures. The iteration of the conceptual source rates is shown in Fig. 2(a). The maximum among all the optimal conceptual source rates is the optimal multicast source rate, which is 0.565 Mbps. There are totally 80 links in the ad hoc network. The multicast link rate at each link is the maximum among four conceptual unicast link rates. We randomly select 9 multicast link rates and show their convergences in Fig. 2(b). We can see that the selected 9 link rate variables all converge within 135 iterations.

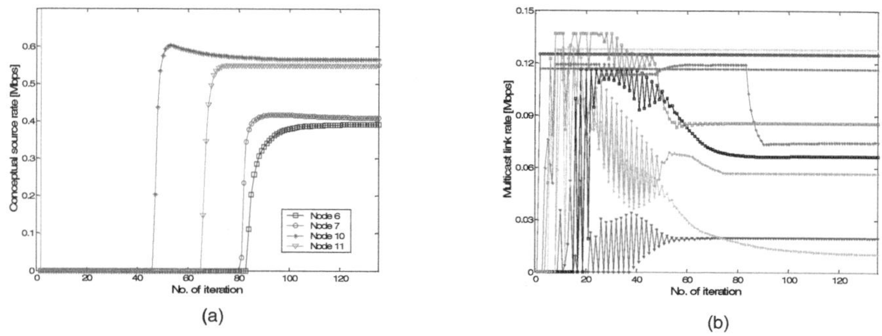

Fig. 2. The iteration of primal variables: (a) conceptual source rates, and (b) randomly selected 9 multicast link rates

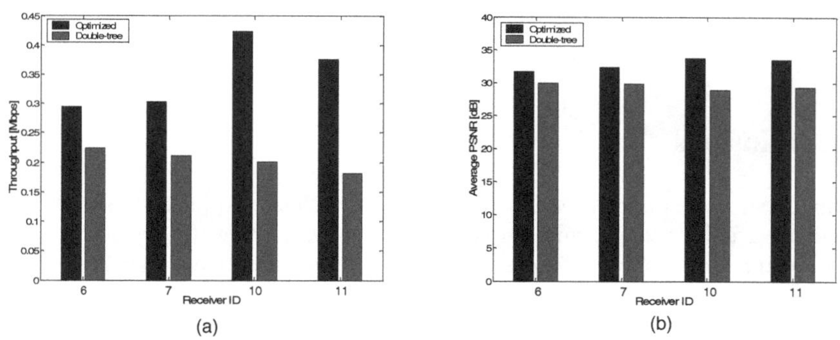

Fig. 3. Comparison between the optimized routing scheme and the double-tree routing scheme: (a) throughput comparison, and (b) average PSNR comparison

We compare the proposed optimized routing scheme to the double-tree routing scheme. In the double-tree routing scheme, we construct the double trees as follows: All the nodes except the source are classified into two categories: group 0 and group 1. Within each group, we construct a single tree from the source to the receivers by using the link throughput metric $c_l(1\text{-}p_l)$. The source rate for each conceptual session in the double-tree scheme is equal to the end-to-end available bandwidth. In order for fair comparison, the bandwidth consumption and power consumption at each node are kept the same in both schemes. Fig. 3 shows the comparison between these two schemes. As shown in Fig. 3(a), the optimized routing scheme achieves a much larger end-to-end throughput over the double-tree scheme because it makes optimal use of the link bandwidth with path diversity. With the prioritized coding scheme and network coding, a larger throughput leads to a higher average PSNR. Therefore, the optimized routing scheme outperforms the double-tree scheme in terms of average PSNR. The frame PSNR comparison of the reconstructed Foreman QCIF sequence at node 11 is illustrated in Fig. 4. The optimized routing scheme yields higher PSNR values since it yields an improved end-to-end throughput.

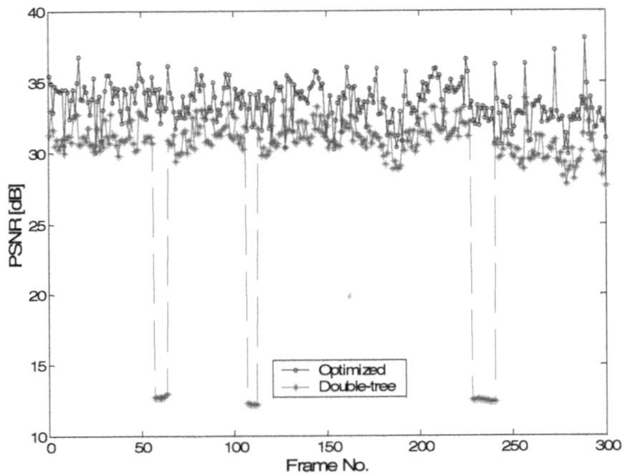

Fig. 4. Frame PSNR comparison at node 11

5 Conclusions

In this paper, we study the video multicast in wireless ad hoc networks. We apply prioritized coding scheme and network coding to eliminate the decoding hierarchy and delivery redundancy. Then we develop a fully distributed algorithm using the Lagrangian duality properties to jointly optimize the source rate and the routing scheme. The simulation results illustrate significant improvements in video quality over the double-tree routing scheme.

References

1. Mao, S., Lin, S., Panwar, S.S., Wang, Y., Celebi, E.: Video transport over ad hoc networks: Multistream coding with multipath transport. IEEE Journal on Selected Areas in Communications 21(10), 1721–1737 (2003)
2. Mao, S., Cheng, X., Hou, Y.T., Sherali, H.D.: Multiple description video multicast in wireless ad hoc networks. In: Proc. of IEEE BROADNETS, pp. 671–680 (2004)
3. Zakhor, A., Wei, W.: Multiple Tree Video Multicast over Wireless Ad Hoc Networks. In: Proc. of IEEE ICIP (2006)
4. Xiao, L., Johansson, M., Boyd, S.: Simultaneous routing and resource allocation via dual decomposition. IEEE Transactions on Communications 52(7), 1136–1144 (2004)
5. Chen, L., Low, S.H., Chiang, M., Doyle, J.C.: Joint optimal congestion control, routing, and scheduling in wireless ad hoc networks. In: Proc. of IEEE INFOCOM (2006)

6. Zhu, X., Singh, J.P., Girod, B.: Joint Routing and Rate Allocation for Multiple Video Streams in Ad Hoc Wireless Networks. Journal of Zhejiang University, Science A 7(5), 727–736 (2006)
7. Li, Z., Li, B., Jiang, D., Lau, L.C.: On Achieving Optimal Throughput with Network Coding. In: Proc. of IEEE INFOCOM, vol. 5, pp. 2184–2194 (2005)
8. Ahlswede, R., Cai, N., Li, S.Y., Yeung, R.W.: Network information flow. IEEE Transactions on Information Theory 46, 1204–1216 (2000)
9. Vanderbei, R.J.: Linear programming: foundations and extensions, 2nd edn. Springer, Heidelberg (2001)
10. Boyd, S., Vandenberghe, L.: Convex Optimization. Cambridge University Press, Cambridge (2004)
11. Bertsekas, D.P., Nedic, A., Ozdaglar, A.E.: Convex Analysis and Optimization. Athena Scientific (2003)
12. Chou, P.A., Wu, Y., Jain, K.: Practical network coding. In: Proc. of 41st Annual Allerton Conference on Communication, Control, and Computing (2003)
13. Ho, T., Koetter, R., Medard, M., Karger, D.R., Effros, M.: The benefits of coding over routing in a randomized setting. In: Proc. of IEEE ISIT, pp. 442–442 (2003)
14. Wu, Y., Chou, P.A., Jain, K.: A comparison of network coding and tree packing. In: Proc. of IEEE ISIT, pp. 143–143 (2004)
15. Schwarz, H., Marpe, D., Wiegand, T.: SNR-scalable extension of H.264/AVC. In: Proc. of IEEE ICIP, vol. 5, pp. 3113–3116 (2004)

Acoustic Features for Estimation of Perceptional Similarity

Yoshihiro Adachi[1,2], Shinichi Kawamoto[1], Shigeo Morishima[1], and Satoshi Nakamura[1]

[1] ATR Spoken Language Communication Research Laboratories, 2-2-2 Keihanna, Science City, Kyoto, 619-0288 Japan
[2] Science and Engineering, Waseda University, 3-4-1 Okubo Shinjuku-ku Tokyo, 169-8555 Japan
xyadachi@toki.waseda.jp, shinichi.kawamoto@atr.jp, shigeo@waseda.jp, satoshi.nakamura@atr.jp

Abstract. This paper describes an examination of acoustic features for the estimation of perceptional similarity between speeches. We firstly extract some acoustic features including personality from speeches of 36 persons. Secondly, we calculate each distance between extracted features using Gaussian Mixture Model (GMM) or Dynamic Time Warping (DTW), and then we sort speeches based on the physical similarity. On the other hand, there is the permutation based on the perceptional similarity which is sorted according to the subject. We evaluate the physical features by the Spearman's rank correlation coefficient with two permutations. Consequently, the results show that DTW distance with high STRAIGHT Cepstrum is an optimum feature for estimation of perceptional similarity.

Keywords: Perceptional similarity, Physical similarity, Acoustic features, Spearman's rank correlation coefficient.

1 Introduction

With the technological advances in computer graphics, we recently can generate a Computer Graphics (CG) character which resembles a real person. A new visual entertainment system which enables anyone to easily appear in a pre-recorded film as an instant CG movie star have been developed [1]. Audience can watch the movie that performed by themselves as a cast without actually performing, and a pre-recorded voice of either an actor or actress is substituted for each character's voice. Therefore, discrepancies between the character's voice and the audience member's own can produce feelings of dissatisfaction.

One of the solutions for this dissatisfaction is to assign visitor's voice to characters. However, it requires immense amount of time and is impossible to record every visitor's voice in advance. There is another solution; to convert the voice quality of the recorded speeches to similar voice quality of each visitor [2]. However this is neither realistic, since the present synthesis technology has not been

H.H.S. Ip et al. (Eds.): PCM 2007, LNCS 4810, pp. 306–314, 2007.

improved enough to achieve high voice quality and natural sounds. For these reasons, we generate a character whose voice is more similar to the participant's own by following processes; recording many audio tracks in advance, selecting the most similar voice and assigning the audio track of the selected voice to the character.

Speaker recognition which deals with similarity of speeches have been researched and applied to several fields such as security field. In the security field, the similarity of speaker is generally determined based on likelihood of Gaussian Mixture Model (GMM) between speakers. However, we focus on the perceptional similarity rather than the similarity of speaker models. Additionally, the aim of speaker recognition is to perceive oneself without consideration of the similarity between other speakers. Meanwhile, as for the relation between perceptional similarity and physical distance, Amino et al. [3] proved the strong correlation between cepstral distance and perceptional similarity. Nagashima et al. proved the strong correlation between spectrum distances at 2 - 10 kHz and perceptional similarity with speeches in which utterance speed and intonation were controlled by speaker [4]. Therefore we examine the physical similarity for the estimation of perceptional similarity between speeches, the personality of which appears not only in voice quality but also in utterance speed or prosodic intonation.

The purpose of our study is to reveal the relation between calculated physical similarity with acoustic features and perceptional similarity in sentence. We deal with Mel Frequency Cepstral Coefficient (MFCC), STRAIGHT Cepstrum, spectrum, STRAIGHT-Ap (aperiodic component) which is an analysis parameter of STRAIGHT [5], fundamental frequency, utterance speed, formants and spectrum slope. We demonstrate what feature is related to perceptional similarity most in the following sections.

Firstly, we introduce how to extract the acoustic features in section 2. In section 3, we explain how to extract the physical similarity based on the acoustic features. In section 4, we describe the way of evaluating physical similarity for perceptional similarity and demonstrate the result of this evaluation. In section 5, we conclude this paper and discuss our future work.

2 Extraction of Acoustic Features

2.1 MFCC

MFCC is one of acoustic features which is robust in noisy environments, and is commonly used for not only speech recognition but also speaker recognition using GMM [6]. In our study, MFCC is represented by the vector of 25 dimensions (12 static, 12 dynamic, 1 dynamic power). We set 16 as the number of mixture of GMM, and extract acoustic features except for the silent part: a pause.

2.2 STRAIGHT Cepstrums

Many researchers have engaged in discovering the speech parameter which implies personality the most [7][8]. Kitamura described that the perception of personality is influenced by the high STRAIGHT Cepstrum and the first STRAIGHT

Cepstrum which represent the fequency characteristic of vocal sound source and that gradient respectively [9]. Therefore, we decided to focus on the relation between perceptional similarity and the high STRAIGHT Cepstrum or first STRAIGHT Cepstrum.

We extract Cepstrum by STRAIGHT analysis and define that of over 35 dimensions as the high STRAIGHT Cepstrum (CepH). The first STRAIGHT Cepstrum (Cep1) is the first dimension of the calculated STRAIGHT Cepstrum.

2.3 Spectrum

High frequency bandwidth of spectrum has also the strong relation with personality. Furui et al. [10][4] demonstrated the strong relation between a high frequency bandwidth of spectrum and personality. Therefore, we research the relation between high log spectrum and perceptional similarity. In this paper, the high spectrum means over 2.6 kHz [9] spectrum frequency.

2.4 STRAIGHT-Ap

Saito et al. [11] discovered the information of personality in STRAIGHT-Ap (Ap) under 2 kHz. In other words, they indicated such information in characteristic of vocal sound source. Therefore, we focus on the relation between Ap and perceptional similarity.

2.5 Fundamental Frequency

We investigated the relation between fundamental frequency (F0) and perceptional similarity, because Hashimoto et al. [12][13] have proved that F0 has an effect on the personality perception. We extracted F0 every 10 ms using STRAIGHT-TEMPO which is a part of STRAIGHT analysis.

2.6 Utterance Speed

As for the relation between utterance speed and personality perception, Francis et al proved that the utterance speed is changed depending on the personality of a speaker [14]. Therefore we research the relation between utterance speed and perceptional similarity. In our research, the utterance speed is the average duration of mora.

2.7 Formants, Spectrum Slope

Voice quality is a critical acoustic feature to assess the similarity of speech. Kido et al. [15][16] described that formants (Formant) and spectrum slope (SpecSlope) are indispensable features for expression of voice quality. By using those features, we examine the physical similarity. In this paper, Formant composite is from 1st to 4th formant, and SpecSlope is a gradient from 0 kHz to 3 kHz log Spectrum.

3 Extraction of Physical Similarity

In this section, we explain the calculation of physical similarity. We calculate the physical similarity based on GMM likelihood and DTW distance using acoustic features described above, except for the utterance speed. In case of the utterance speed, we define the difference of utterance speed of two speeches as the physical similarity.

3.1 GMM Likelihood

Speaker identification, the aim of which is to search the target speaker, and likelihood of GMM is commonly used in speaker identification [17]. Remarkable advantages of using GMM are to be able to represent the complex feature vector, to be robust in noisy environments, and to be independent from the context of speeches. Therefore, GMM is effective in speaker identification and verification [18][19][20]. In this study, we investigate the similar speaker from voice actor database; not searching audiences voice. We examine GMM likelihood defined as the physical similarity to reveal the relation between GMM likelihood and perceptional similarity.

If M is the model of speaker, and $X = \{x_1, ...x_T\}$ is the observational time-series acoustic feature, the likelihood of GMM is represented in the following.

$$logP(X|M) = \frac{1}{T}\sum_{t=1}^{T} logP(x_t|M) \tag{1}$$

where

$$P(x|M) = \sum_{i=1}^{N} w_i p_i(x) \tag{2}$$

$$P_i(x) = \frac{exp\{-\frac{1}{2}(x - \mu_i)'(\Sigma_i)^{-1}(x - \mu_i)\}}{(2\pi)^{D/2}|\Sigma_i|^{1/2}} \tag{3}$$

Where T is the number of frame of acoustic features, x is the acoustic feature vector of D dimension, and N is the number of mixtures. ω is the weight for mixtures, and Σ is a covariance matrix. $|\Sigma_i|$ is a determinant of the covariance matrix, and $(\Sigma_i)^{-1}$ is the inverse matrix for the covariance matrix. μ_i is the average vector of x. We define the above log likelihood as a similarity by GMM likelihood between a speaker of M and a speaker of x.

3.2 DTW Distance

We recognize DTW distance as a measure of the physical similarity between speeches. Sakoe et al. [21] have developed the DTW distance for matching of speeches with time warping. DTW is commonly used in a wide range of pattern recognition because of the simplicity of the theory, the ease of the implementation and a small amount of the calculation.

In this study, we recognize the DTW distance between acoustic features as the distortion of similarity. We firstly extract all acoustic features per every 10ms except for the utterance speed. Secondly we calculate the Euclidean distance of acoustic features by every affiliated frame based on DTW, and then we define the mean distance as the physical similarity calculated by DTW.

4 Evaluation of the Physical Similarity to Estimate the Perceptional Similarity

4.1 Experimental Evaluations

We evaluate physical similarity to reveal the relation between physical similarity and perceptional similarity. We firstly examine the perceptional similarity of speeches for evaluation of the relation. It is difficult for us to represent the perceptional similarity in numeric value because this similarity depends on the emotion of each person. However, we represent the perceptional similarity in numeric value with using Mean Opinion Score (MOS). We investigate the similarity by the score of five-grade evaluation (5: quite similar, 4: similar, 3: slightly similar, 2: rather not similar, 1:not similar) In this evaluation, the score '4' means not being twice of score '2', but just being bigger than score '2'. In other words, the subject just classifies the similarity into five-grade evaluation. The result is the relative score not the absolute score, even if we classify furthermore and subjects evaluate all the speech pair with different scores. Those relative scores are too untrustworthy for us to use as a perceptional similarity.

We therefore render the perceptual similarity with the permutation based on similarity. We sort speeches in our database based on perceptional similarity of the target speech as follows.

1. We define the target speech as X.
2. We select a speech randomly from our speech database and define this speech as A.
3. We divide these speeches into two groups (one is more similar to X than A and the other is opposite.)
4. We apply same processing (2 and 3) to each divided group.
5. We can sort speeches according the perceptional similarity by repeating this process recursively.

In the process 3, the similarity between two speeches is judged from comprehensive impression not just focusing one of the acoustic features (e.g. quality of voice, intonation and speaking rate). To judge which pair has more similarities for subjects is easy, though it is difficult to evaluate the difference of similarities between two pairs of speeches. In other words, the evaluation results using sorted permutation is more reliable compared with that of using absolute score data.

We evaluate the physical similarity using the perceptional similarity rendered by a permutation. We sort speeches based on the physical similarity as well as the perceptional similarity. Then we calculate Spearman's rank correlation coefficient with two permutations. We represent the Spearman's rank correlation coefficient ρ in equation (4).

$$\rho = 1 - \frac{6\sum_{i=1}^{N}(a_i - b_i)^2}{N^3 - N} \tag{4}$$

a is the permutation according to the perceptional similarity by the subject. b is the permutation according to the physical similarity. The bigger this rank correlation is, the stronger the relation between physical similarity and perceptional similarity becomes. Therefore we find out which physical similarity is useful to estimate the perceptional similarity.

4.2 Experimental Conditions

We analyze the Japanese sentence 'Arayuru genjitsu o subete jibun no hoe nejimageta noda.' uttered by 36 females whose age are from 18 years old to 59 years old. These speeches are quantized with 16 bit and sampled with 16 kHz. We randomly selected one speech for the target speech, and sorted other speeches based on the similarity to the subject. We conducted this experiment by alternating the target speech three times from 36 speeches and compared each result. The subject is supposed to have normal hearing ability. The subject has never heard the analysis speeches and met the speaker: the subject has no information of the speakers and analysis speeches in advance.

4.3 Experiment Results

Firstly, we examine the repeatability of sorting the similarity by the subject. The subject sorted the speeches twice for one target speech according to the similarity. We conducted the second experiment on a separate day for the purpose of preventing the subject from reminding of the order at the first experiment. We calculated the Spearman's rank correlation coefficient with two permutations. We represent this result in Fig.1. This result indicates that the subject can sort

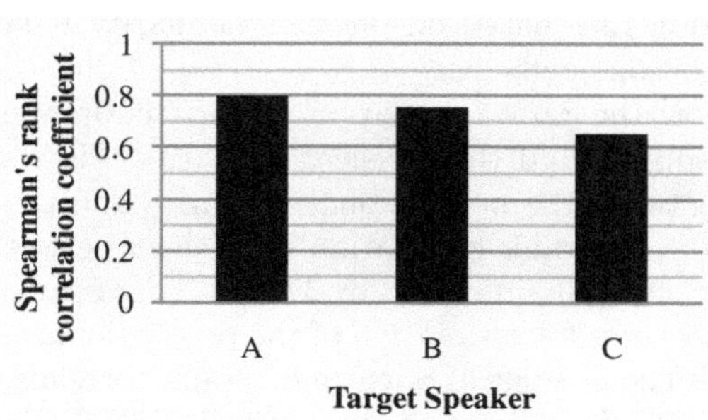

Fig. 1. Spearman's rank correlation coefficient of two rank arrays arranged by the subject

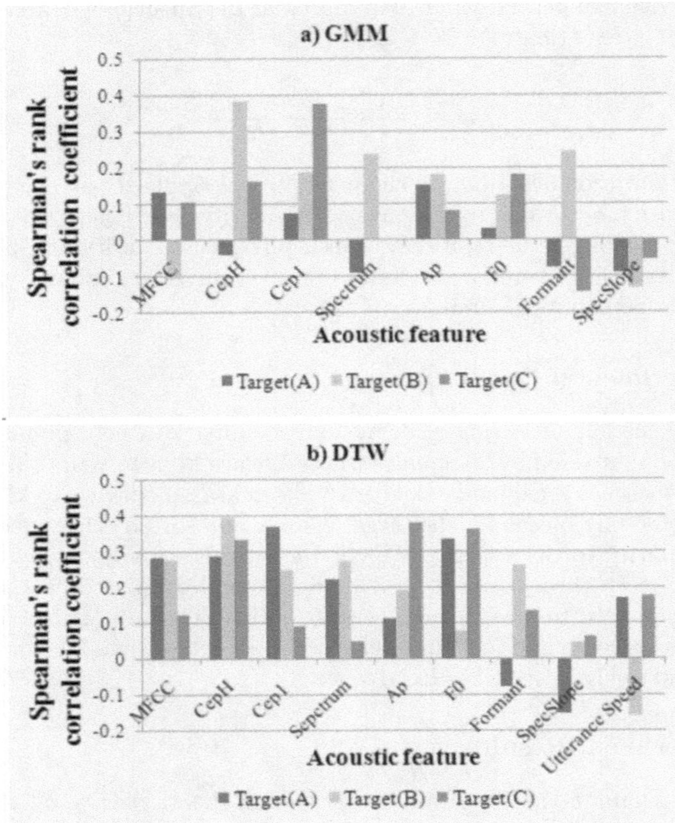

Fig. 2. Spearman's rank correlation coefficient of two rank arrays arranged by the subject and the physical similarity

the speeches same similarity order regardless of the target speech. Additionally, the target estimation rate based on physical similarity is around from 0.65 to 0.80 on rank correlation coefficient.

In Fig.2, we show the rank correlation coefficient between the perceptional similarity by the subject and the physical similarity. Fig.2-a is the rank correlation coefficient between the perceptional similarity and the physical similarity by GMM. Fig.2-b is the rank correlation coefficient between the perceptional similarity and the physical similarity by DTW. This result indicated that the effective acoustic features for estimation of the perceptional similarity depend on the target speaker. The average of Spearman's rank correlation coefficients of all acoustic features is 0.130, and the maximum is 0.391(DTW, CepH). We proved that the CepH distance based on DTW is the most effective physical similarity to estimate the perceptional similarity, because the result of the CepH distance based on DTW is stable and has high correlation coefficient (Target A:0.287,

Target B:0.391, Target C:0.332). However it is clear that the result of CepH distance is not enough by comaring Fig.1 and Fig.2. One of the reasons is that the subject focuses on the same acoustic features at all times. The subject tends to pay much attention to the prosody information when the voice quality is similar to the target speech, and vice versa. Therefore, we need to select the physical similarity depending on speeches and estimate the perceptional similarity by using the selected similarity.

5 Conclusions

We examined the relation between physical similarity and perceptional similarity. The experimental result with 36 speeches uttered by 36 females indicates that DTW distance with high STRAIGHT Cepstrum (CepH) is the most effective physical similarity for estimating perceptional similarity.

We have researched with the perceptional similarity answered by one subject. The purpose of this research is to maintain an evaluation standard for the same combination. However, the similarity of the subject is not always equal to other subjects. As future work, we need to increase the number of subjects and research for discovering the universal similarity. To estimate the similarity which many people can share enables us to apply our technology to the system such as Future Cast System [1]. Additionally, we need to select the acoustic features depending on the speech with consideration of the new physical similarity to improve the accuracy of the perceptional similarity estimation.

Acknowledgments. This research is supported by the Special Coordination Funds for Promoting Science and Technology of Ministry of Education, Culture, Sports, Science and Technology.

References

1. Morishima, S., Maejima, A., Wemlera, S., Machida, T., Takebayashi, M.: Future Cast System. ACM SIGGRAPH 2005 Sketch. ACM SIGGRAPH 2005 Full Conference DVD-ROM Disc 2 (2005) ISBN 1-59593-099-X.020-morishima.pdf
2. Toda, T., Saruwatari, H., Shikano, K.: High Quality Voice Conversion Based on Gaussian Mixture Model with Dynamic Frequency Warping. In: Proc. INTERSPEECH2001-EUROSPEECH, Aalborg, Denmark, pp. 349–352 (September 2001)
3. Amino, K., Sugawara, T., Arai, T.: Speaker Similarities in Human Perception and their Spectral Properties. In: Proc. of WESPAC (2006)
4. Nagashima, I., Takagiwa, M., Saito, Y., Nagao, Y., Murakami, H., Fukushima, M., Yamnagwa, H.: An investigation of speech similarity for speaker discrimination. In: Acoustical Society of Japan 2003 Spring Meeting, pp. 737–738 (2003)(in Japanese)
5. Kawahara, H.: STRAIGHT: An extremely high-quality VOCODER for auditory and speech perception research. In: Greenberg, Slaney (eds.) Computational Models of Auditory Function, pp. 343–354. IOS Press, Amsterdam (2001)

6. Reynolds, D.A.: Robust Text-Independent Speaker Identification Using Gaussian Mixture Speaker Models. IEEE Trans. On Acoust. Speech and Audio Processing 3(1) (1995)
7. Abe, M.: Speech morphing by gradually changing spectrum parameter and fundamental frequency. In: ICSLP 1996, pp. 2235–2238 (1996)
8. Kasuya, H., Zhu, W., Matsuda, M., Yang, C.S.: Voice quality conversion based on an ARX speech analysis-synthesis method and its application to the study of speaker individualilty. J. Acoust. Soc. Am. Pt.2 100(4), 2600 (1996)
9. Kitamura, T., Saitou, T.: Contribution of acoustic features of sustained vowels on perception of speaker characteristic. Acoustical Society of Japan 2007 Spring Meeting , 443–444 (2007) (in japanese)
10. Furui, S., Akagi, M.: Perception of voice individuality and physical correlates. Journal of the Acoustical Society of Japan J66-A, 311–318 (1985)
11. Saitou, T., Kitamura, T.: Factors in /VVV/ concatenated vowels affecting perception of speaker individuality. Acoustical Society of Japan 2007 Spring Meeting , 441–442 (2007) (in Japanese)
12. Higuchi, N., Hashimoto, M.: Analysis of acoustic features affecting speaker identification. In: Proc. of EUROSPEECH 1995, pp. 435–438 (1995)
13. Higuchi, N., Hashimoto, M.: Analysis of acoustic features affecting speaker identification. J. Acoust. Soc. Jpn (E) 17(1), 33–35 (1996)
14. Francis, A.L., Nusbaum, H.C.: Paying attention to speaking rate. In: Proc. of ICSLP 1996 (1996)
15. Minowa, Y., Kido, H., Kasuya, H.: The acoustic parameters associated with the expression of voice quality -a preliminary study. In: Proc. Spring Meeting Acoust. Soc. Japan, pp. 363–364 (2000)
16. Kido, H., Kasuya, H.: Voice quality expressions of speech utterance and their acoustic correlates. Technical report of IEICE, SP2002-95, WIT2002-35 (2002)
17. Martin, A., Przybocki, M., Doddington, G., Reynolds, D.: The NIST speaker recognition evaluation - overview, methodology, system, results, perspectives. Speech Communication 31, 225–254 (2000)
18. Weber, F., Manganaro, L., Peskin, B., Shriberg, E.: Using Prosodic and Lexical Information for Speaker Identification. In: Proc. ICASSP, vol. 1, pp. 141–144 (2002)
19. Reynolds, D.A.: Speaker Identification and Verification using Gaussian Mixuture Speaker Models. Speech Communication 17, 177–192 (1995)
20. Sukkar, R.A., Gandhi, M.B., Setlur, A.R.: Speaker Verification Using Mixture Decomposition Discrimination. IEEE Trans. Speech Audio Proc. 8(3), 292–299 (2000)
21. Sakoe, H., Chiba, S.: A Dynamic Programming Algorithm Optimization for Spoken Word Recognition. IEEE Trans. on ASSP 26(27), 43–49 (1978)

Modeling Uncertain Speech Sequences Using Type-2 Fuzzy Hidden Markov Models

Xiao-Qin Cao, Jia Zeng, and Hong Yan

Department of Electronic Engineering,
City University of Hong Kong, P.R. China
{xiaoqcao,jiazeng,h.yan}@cityu.edu.hk

Abstract. The automatic speech recognizor (ASR) based on hidden Markov models (HMMs) is very sensitive to multi-talker, non-stationary babble noise, which consists of a large number of speakers talking simultaneously. One major reason is due to mismatches between the training and testing conditions, which makes the accurate parameters of the HMM incapable of describing the uncertain distributions of the observations in speech signals. This paper applies one extension of the HMM referred to as the type-2 fuzzy hidden Markov models (T2 FHMMs) to modeling uncertain speech sequences. More specifically, we use the type-2 fuzzy set (T2 FS) to describe uncertain parameters of the HMM that may vary anywhere in an interval with uniform possibilities. As a result, the likelihood of the T2 FHMM becomes an interval rather than a precise real number, which can be processed by the generalized linear model (GLM) for final classification decision-making. Experimental results of phoneme classification in the babble noise demonstrate a significant improvement compared with the HMM in terms of the robustness and classification rate.

Keywords: Uncertain speech sequences, hidden Markov models, type-2 fuzzy sets, babble noise.

1 Introduction

The performance of the automatic speech recognizor (ASR) based on hidden Markov models (HMMs) degrades seriously in multi-talker, non-stationary babble noise that consists of a large number of speakers talking simultaneously. One major reason is that the HMM parameters estimated from training sequences is insufficient and mismatched with test sequences corrupted by the babble noise from multi-speakers. Therefore, an effective method is needed to handle uncertain parameters of the HMM for modeling uncertain speech sequences.

The HMM [1] has N hidden states where the first and final states are non-generating as shown in Fig. 1. The transition probability, $a_{ij} = P(s_j|s_i)$, $\sum_{j=1}^{N} a_{ij} = 1$, $1 \leq i,j \leq N$, determines the relationship between two states s_i and s_j. Each state is associated with a Gaussian mixture model (GMM)

H.H.S. Ip et al. (Eds.): PCM 2007, LNCS 4810, pp. 315–324, 2007.

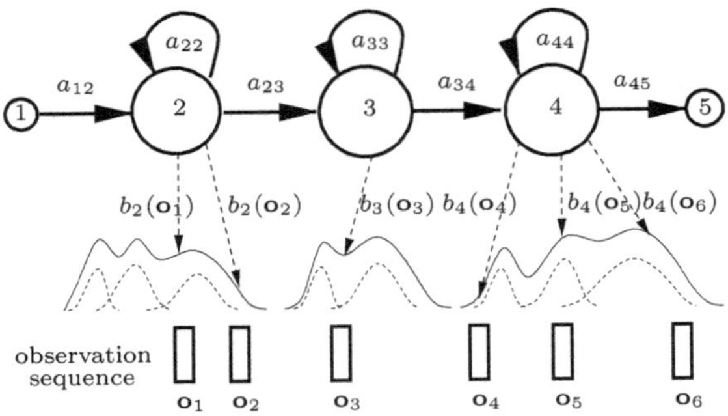

Fig. 1. The left-right non-skip Gaussian mixture HMM

$b_j(\mathbf{o}_t)$ to describe the likelihood of the jth state with respect to the observation $\mathbf{o}_t, 1 \leq t \leq T$, where T is the length of the observation sequence. To model speech signals, the left-right non-skip HMM is often used where no transitions are allowed to states whose indices are lower than the current state in Fig. 1. The GMM with M mixture components is

$$b_j(\mathbf{o}_t) = \sum_{m=1}^{M} w_{jm} N(\mathbf{o}_t; \boldsymbol{\mu}_{jm}, \boldsymbol{\Sigma}_{jm}), \tag{1}$$

where the mixing wight, $\sum_{m=1}^{M} w_m = 1, w_m > 0$. The multivariate Gaussian distribution $N(\mathbf{o}; \boldsymbol{\mu}, \boldsymbol{\Sigma})$ with the mean vector $\boldsymbol{\mu}$ and covariance matrix $\boldsymbol{\Sigma}$ is

$$N(\mathbf{o}; \boldsymbol{\mu}, \boldsymbol{\Sigma}) = \frac{1}{\sqrt{(2\pi)^d |\boldsymbol{\Sigma}|}} e^{-\frac{1}{2}(\mathbf{o}-\boldsymbol{\mu})' \boldsymbol{\Sigma}^{-1} (\mathbf{o}-\boldsymbol{\mu})}, \tag{2}$$

where d is the dimensionality of $\mathbf{o}$. For simplicity, we use only the diagonal covariance matrix, $\boldsymbol{\Sigma} = diag(\sigma_1^2, \dots, \sigma_d^2)$.

The *Baum-Welch* algorithm and the *Viterbi* search algorithm are efficient algorithms for HMM-based training and recognition [1]. The Baum-Welch algorithm can iteratively and automatically adjust parameters $\boldsymbol{\mu}$ and $\boldsymbol{\Sigma}$ in the mth mixture component of the HMM according to the maximum-likelihood (ML) criterion [2]. The Viterbi algorithm decodes the maximum likelihood state sequence Q, since the best state sequence Q may represent words or phonemes in speech recognition.

The HMM is completely certain once its parameters, $\{a_{ij}, w_{jm}, \boldsymbol{\mu}_{jm}, \boldsymbol{\Sigma}_{jm}\}$, are specified. However, those parameters may not accurately reflect the underlying distribution of the observations according to the ML estimation because of insufficient or noisy data in real-world problems. In addition, it may seem problematical to use likelihoods that are themselves precise real numbers to evaluate uncertain HMMs with respect to the observation. Although this does not pose a serious problem for many applications, it is nevertheless possible to describe the uncertain parameters of the HMM to allow for the uncertain likelihoods.

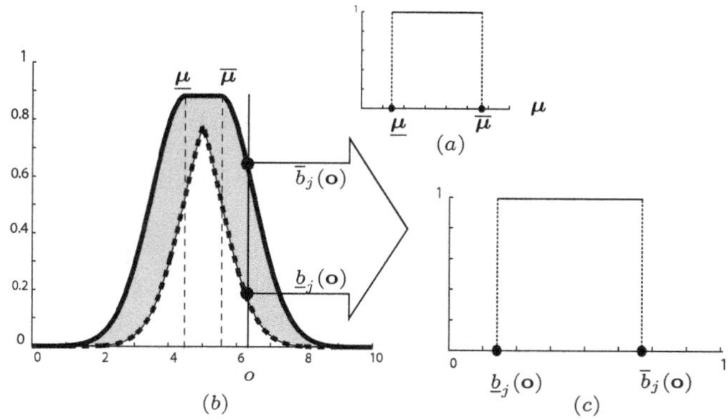

Fig. 2. The Gaussian type-2 fuzzy membership function with uncertain mean in (a) has lower (thick dashed line) and upper (thick solid line) boundaries in (b). The likelihood with respect to $\mathbf{o}$ becomes an interval, $[\overline{b}_j(\mathbf{o}), \underline{b}_j(\mathbf{o})]$, with uniform possibilities in (c).

Zeng and Liu [3] integrated the type-2 fuzzy set (T2 FS) with the HMM referred to as the type-2 fuzzy hidden Markov model (T2 FHMM) to handle uncertain parameters of the HMM. In the T2FHMM, the parameters of the GMM are assumed to vary anywhere in the interval with uniform possibilities as shown in Fig. 2 (a), where the mean vector $\boldsymbol{\mu} \in [\underline{\boldsymbol{\mu}}, \overline{\boldsymbol{\mu}}]$. Such a representation of uncertain mean vector is called the Gaussian type-2 fuzzy membership function [4]. The ensemble of all possible Gaussian distributions form the shaded region called the footprint of uncertainty (FOU) in Fig. 2 (b). Practically we are not sure which one in the FOU is the best, so that we need to keep all the possibilities until the final decision-making. As a result, the likelihood of the Gaussian type-2 membership function becomes an interval with uniform possibilities in Fig. 2 (c) [5]. This conclusion is easy to justify because the interval likelihood is composed of every likelihood of the embedded distribution in the FOU with uniform weighting. According to the interval arithmetic, the result of the calculation between interval likelihoods is also an interval with uniform possibilities [5]. For example, if two interval likelihoods are $[\underline{b}_1(\mathbf{o}), \overline{b}_1(\mathbf{o})]$ and $[\underline{b}_2(\mathbf{o}), \overline{b}_2(\mathbf{o})]$, then the sum and product are $[\underline{b}_1(\mathbf{o})+\underline{b}_2(\mathbf{o}), \overline{b}_1(\mathbf{o})+\overline{b}_2(\mathbf{o})]$ and $[\underline{b}_1(\mathbf{o})\underline{b}_2(\mathbf{o}), \overline{b}_1(\mathbf{o})\overline{b}_2(\mathbf{o})]$, respectively. More details of the T2 FSs and their applications to pattern recognition can be found in [6, 7].

In this paper, we apply the T2 FHMM to modeling uncertain speech signals. There are three major differences from [3]. First, we simplify the training process of the T2 FHMM in [3]. Here we think of the T2 FHMM as the HMM with uncertain parameters, which means that we can train the HMM and then add the description of uncertain parameters as a kind of prior knowledge. Second, because the output likelihood of the T2 FHMM is an interval, we propose the generalized linear model (GLM) to make the classification decision rather than the heuristic interval ranking method in [3]. Third, we use the T2 FHMM to model more complex speech signals corrupted by the real-word babble noise instead of the simple additive white Gaussian noise in [3].

2 Type-2 Fuzzy Hidden Markov Models

In this section, we briefly introduce the T2 FHMM framework, which has been described in detail in [3].

Given a d-dimensional observation vector $\mathbf{o}$, the corresponding mean vector $\boldsymbol{\mu}$, and the diagonal covariance matrix $\boldsymbol{\Sigma} = diag(\sigma_1^2, \ldots, \sigma_d^2)$, the multivariate Gaussian with uncertain mean vector or covariance matrix is

$$N(\mathbf{o}; \tilde{\boldsymbol{\mu}}, \boldsymbol{\Sigma}) = \frac{1}{\sqrt{(2\pi)^d |\boldsymbol{\Sigma}|}} \exp\left[-\frac{1}{2}\left(\frac{o_1 - \mu_1}{\sigma_1}\right)^2\right] \ldots \exp\left[-\frac{1}{2}\left(\frac{o_d - \mu_d}{\sigma_d}\right)^2\right],$$
$$\mu_1 \in [\underline{\mu}_1, \overline{\mu}_1], \ldots, \mu_d \in [\underline{\mu}_d, \overline{\mu}_d], \quad (3)$$

or

$$N(\mathbf{o}; \boldsymbol{\mu}, \tilde{\boldsymbol{\Sigma}}) = \frac{1}{\sqrt{(2\pi)^d |\boldsymbol{\Sigma}|}} \exp\left[-\frac{1}{2}\left(\frac{o_1 - \mu_1}{\sigma_1}\right)^2\right] \ldots \exp\left[-\frac{1}{2}\left(\frac{o_d - \mu_d}{\sigma_d}\right)^2\right],$$
$$\sigma_1 \in [\underline{\sigma}_1, \overline{\sigma}_1], \ldots, \sigma_d \in [\underline{\sigma}_d, \overline{\sigma}_d], \quad (4)$$

where $\tilde{\boldsymbol{\mu}}$ and $\tilde{\boldsymbol{\Sigma}}$ denote uncertain mean vector and covariance matrix, respectively. Indeed, each exponential component in (3) and (4) is the Gaussian primary membership function with uncertain mean or standard deviation (std) [5]. Obviously the multivariate uncertain Gaussian is accumulated by all of its d dimensional uncertain exponential components. The factor k controls the interval range in which the parameters vary,

$$\underline{\mu} = \mu - k\sigma, \quad \overline{\mu} = \mu + k\sigma, \quad k \in [0, 3], \quad (5)$$

$$\underline{\sigma} = k\sigma, \quad \overline{\sigma} = \frac{1}{k}\sigma, \quad k \in [0.3, 1]. \quad (6)$$

we constrain $k \in [0, 3]$ in (5) and $k \in [0.3, 1]$ in (6), because a one-dimensional gaussian has 99.7% of its probability mass in the range of $[\mu - 3\sigma, \mu + 3\sigma]$.

Replacing Eq. (2) with Eq. (3) and Eq. (4) in Eq. (1), we obtain the T2 FHMM with uncertain mean vector and uncertain variance (T2 FHMM-UM and T2 FHMM-UV). If we assume the factor k as a constant according to prior knowledge, we can first train the HMM using the Baum-Welch algorithm, and then add k to produce the corresponding T2 FHMM-UM and T2 FHMM-UV. Hence the training process of the T2 FHMM is the same with that of the HMM. However, to decode the single best state sequence, $Q = \{q_1^*, \ldots, q_T^*\}$, we need to modify the Viterbi algorithm to handle the interval likelihoods passing between states, which involve only interval arithmetic as explained in Section 1. For the given observation sequence, $\mathbf{O} = \{\mathbf{o}_1, \ldots, \mathbf{o}_T\}$, and T2 FHMM $\tilde{\lambda}$, we define the variable of the likelihood lower bound as

$$L_t(i) = \max_{q_1, \ldots, q_{t-1}} P(q_1, \ldots, q_t = s_i, \mathbf{o}_1, \ldots, \mathbf{o}_t | \tilde{\lambda}), \quad (7)$$

input : $\mathbf{O}, \tilde{\lambda}$.
output : $[L_T(N), U_T(N)], Q$.
initialize: $L_1(1) \leftarrow 1, L_1(j) \leftarrow a_{1j}\underline{b}_j(\mathbf{o}_1), U_1(j) \leftarrow a_{1j}\overline{b}_j(\mathbf{o}_1), \psi_1(i) \leftarrow 1,\ 2 \leq i, j \leq N-1$.
begin
  for $t \leftarrow 2$ **to** T **do**
    for $j \leftarrow 2$ **to** $N-1$ **do**
      $L_t(j) \leftarrow \max_i[L_{t-1}(i)a_{ij}]\underline{b}_j(\mathbf{o}_t)$;
      $U_t(j) \leftarrow \max_i[U_{t-1}(i)a_{ij}]\overline{b}_j(\mathbf{o}_t)$;
      $\psi_t(j) \leftarrow \arg\max_i\left[\frac{1}{2}(L_t(i) + U_t(i))a_{ij}\right]$;
    end
  end
  $L_T(N) \leftarrow \max_i[L_T(i)a_{iN}]$;
  $U_T(N) \leftarrow \max_i[U_T(i)a_{iN}]$;
  $q_T^* \leftarrow \arg\max_i\left[\frac{1}{2}(L_T(i) + U_T(i))a_{iN}\right]$;
  for $t \leftarrow T$ **to** 2 **do**
    $q_{t-1}^* \leftarrow \psi_t(q_t^*)$;
  end
end

Algorithm 1. The type-2 fuzzy Viterbi algorithm

where $L_t(i)$ is the highest probability of the lower bound for the first t observations and ends in state i along a single path. Similarly we can define the variable of the upper bound $U_t(i)$. The variable $\psi_t(i)$ keeps track of the best state at each time slot t. For each state i, it stores the best previous state that has the maximum average value of the two recursive bounds, $[L_{t-1}(i) + U_{t-1}(i)]/2$. In this paper we suggest the average value because we believe the center of the interval may be stabler than its two ends. As a summary, Algorithm 1 shows the type-2 fuzzy Viterbi algorithm, which outputs the best state sequence Q and the interval likelihood, $[L_T(N), U_T(N)]$.

3 Generalized Linear Model (GLM) for Decision-Making

In T2 FHMM pattern recognition, we would have a number of T2 FHMMs, one for each category $1 \leq c \leq C$, and classify a test sequence according to the model with the best interval likelihoods $[L_T(N), U_T(N)]$ in Algorithm 1. To make classification decision from interval likelihoods, we adopt the GLM,

$$\mathbf{y} = f_a(\mathbf{wx} + \mathbf{b}), \tag{8}$$

where $\mathbf{w}$ is the weight matrix, $\mathbf{b}$ is the bias vector, f_a is the logistic activation function, and $\mathbf{x} = [L^1, U^1, \ldots, L^C, U^C]$ is the vector of output interval likelihoods of C classes of T2 FHMMs. The iterated re-weighted least square algorithm [8, Chapter 4.5] estimates the GLM parameters from all feature vectors $\mathbf{x}$ of training data. This estimated GLM is in turn used to classify the interval likelihood features with respect to test data. As a summary, Fig. 3 shows the pattern classification system based on T2 FHMMs.

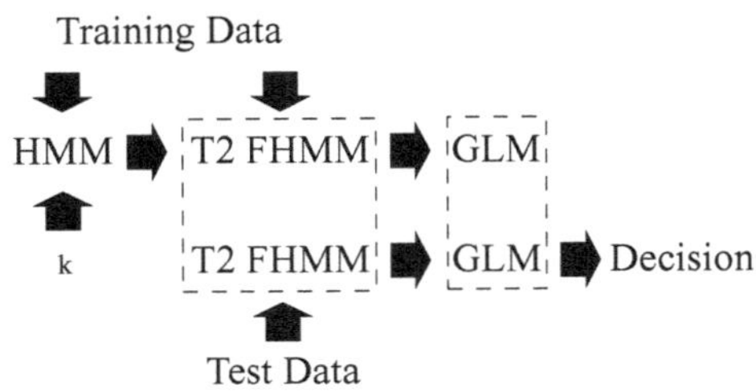

Fig. 3. The pattern classification system based on the T2 FHMM. We adopt the GLM to make the classification decision from interval likelihoods.

4 Experiments

To confirm the effectiveness of the T2 FHMM for modeling uncertain speech sequences, we carried out extensive experiments on TIMIT [9] speech database. TIMIT contains 6300 utterances produced by 630 speakers from eight major dialect divisions of the United States. It provides phonetic transcriptions to all utterances. We broke up 6300 utterances into phonemes according to the transcriptions, and obtained totally 61 phonemic and phonetic classes including silence and closure intervals of stops. We combined six closure intervals of stops, *bcl, dcl, gcl, pcl, tcl, kcl*, into one class, and combined "silence" symbols, *pau, epi, h#*, into another class. We removed eight phonemic classes, *ax-h, b, d, dx, em, eng, nx, zh*, because they have less than 500 samples. Finally, we obtained totally 46 phonemic classes for classification.

The speech signal, sampled at 16KHz, was processed in frames of 25ms with a 15ms overlapping (rate=100Hz). We first pre-emphasized speech frames with an FIR filter ($HZ = 1 - az^{-1}, a = 0.97$), and weighted them with a Hamming window to avoid spectral distortions. After pre-processing, we extracted Mel Frequency Cepstral Coefficents (MFCCs) [10] as the acoustic features. Each acoustic feature vector consists of 12 MFCCs, the energy term, and the corresponding velocity and acceleration derivatives. The dimensionality of acoustic feature vector is 39 for each frame. Thus each observation sequence is a $T \times 39$ matrix. In all experiments, we did not consider the observation sequences with $T \leq 3$. We added the babble noise to all test speech data.

To compare the phoneme classification performance in the babble noise, we used five states and three mixtures in the HMM to model phonemes [10]. For each class, we selected 300 training samples from clean data and 200 test samples from data corrupted by the babble noise with signal-to-noise ratio (SNR) 20dB, 10dB, 5dB, 0dB, −5dB, and −10dB. As discussed in Section 3, we trained the GLM by the vector with $2C$ length, $[L^1, U^1, \dots, L^C, U^C]$, where C is the number of classes. In the 46 phoneme classification, we have to estimate the GLM using the vector with 92 length, which is a high dimension leading to bad estimation of the GLM. Hence we reduced the dimension 92 to 46 using principle component analysis (PCA) [2]. To show the classification performance, we grouped the correct samples classified by the HMM and the T2 FHMM into seven general

Table 1. The number of correct samples classified by the HMM

SNR	S	A	F	N	G	V	O
clean	676	238	913	367	846	1794	217
20dB	520	198	708	285	673	1742	21
10dB	299	124	355	116	326	1601	0
5dB	158	64	199	46	207	1404	0
0dB	67	31	77	11	117	1110	0
-5dB	27	13	21	1	50	809	0
-10dB	6	1	3	0	11	525	0

Table 2. The number of correct samples of the T2 FHMM-UM with $k = 1$

SNR	S	A	F	N	G	V	O
clean	694	248	928	378	891	1972	210
20dB	547	164	706	275	737	1916	28
10dB	297	96	391	102	366	1659	0
5dB	169	60	234	33	259	1369	0
0dB	97	35	124	8	164	1040	0
-5dB	46	18	74	1	95	719	0
-10dB	16	7	39	0	57	487	0

classes: S—Stops, *g, p, t, k, q*; A—Affricates, *jh, ch*; F—Fricatives, *s, sh, z, f, th, v, dh*; N—Nasals, *m, n, ng, en*; G—Semivowels and Glides, *l, r, w, y, hh, hv, el*; V—Vowels, *iy, ih, eh, ey, ae, aa, aw, ay, ah, ao, oy, ow, uh, uw, ux, er, ax, ix, axr*; and O—Others, *bcl, dcl, gcl, pcl, tcl, kcl, pau, epi, h#*.

Table 1 shows the correct test samples classified by the HMM. The number of correct samples of "silence" drops significantly when the SNR decreases, which results in many "insertion" errors in continuous speech recognition [10]. Besides "silence", the classification rate of nasals degrades quickly with the decrease of the SNR. The vowels are relatively less influenced by the babble noise.

Table 2, Table 3, and Table 4 show the correct test samples classified by the T2 FHMM-UM with $k = 1, 2, 3$, respectively. Compared with Table 1, the number of correct samples on clean test data is more than that of the HMM. In particular, the classification of the vowels and glides have been greatly improved by additionally classifying about 200 test samples correctly. Table 5 shows that the average classification rate in clean test data increases 2.94%, 3.23%, and 2.05% when $k = 1, 2, 3$, respectively. Furthermore, when $k = 2$, the T2 FHMM-UM outperforms the HMM by increasing the average classification rate 2.28%, 1.04%, 1.13%, 1.49%, 0.70%, and 1.02% in all SNRs. The T2 FHMM-UM is robust to the babble noise in classifying fricatives. As shown in Table 2 and Table 3, the classified fricatives are 124 and 150 samples in 0dB compared to 77 samples in Table 1. When the SNR decreases to -5dB, the classified fricatives still have 74 and 78 samples compared to 21 samples of the HMM.

Table 6, Table 7, and Table 8 show the number of correct samples classified by the T2 FHMM-UV with $k = 0.9, 0.7, 0.5$, respectively. The T2 FHMM-UV

Table 3. The number of correct samples of the T2 FHMM-UM with $k = 2$

SNR	S	A	F	N	G	V	O
clean	683	261	927	376	886	2002	213
20dB	531	157	676	285	716	1941	52
10dB	278	100	399	115	365	1656	3
5dB	156	67	251	46	245	1417	0
0dB	79	38	150	10	168	1105	0
-5dB	31	19	78	2	107	748	0
-10dB	17	7	22	1	73	519	0

Table 4. The number of correct samples of the T2 FHMM-UM with $k = 3$

SNR	S	A	F	N	G	V	O
clean	686	256	911	361	861	1951	213
20dB	529	158	640	277	689	1903	53
10dB	285	85	319	111	324	1679	0
5dB	157	48	158	42	221	1429	0
0dB	82	29	73	9	155	1117	0
-5dB	43	14	23	2	114	757	0
-10dB	21	6	1	0	88	527	0

Table 5. The comparison of classification rate (%)

SNR	HMM	T2 FHMM-UM		
		k = 1	k = 2	k = 3
clean	54.90	57.84	58.13	56.95
20dB	45.08	47.53	47.36	46.18
10dB	30.66	31.64	31.70	30.47
5dB	22.59	23.09	23.72	22.34
0dB	15.36	15.96	16.85	15.92
-5dB	10.01	10.36	10.71	10.36
-10dB	5.93	6.59	6.95	6.99

Table 6. The number of correct samples of the T2 FHMM-UV with $k = 0.9$

SNR	S	A	F	N	G	V	O
clean	681	240	952	362	873	1929	209
20dB	551	155	687	273	712	1874	61
10dB	320	92	390	98	362	1656	3
5dB	212	56	264	34	243	1414	0
0dB	128	32	155	4	153	1076	0
-5dB	81	20	90	0	103	751	0
-10dB	42	7	47	0	39	510	0

Table 7. The number of correct samples of the T2 FHMM-UV with $k = 0.7$

SNR	S	A	F	N	G	V	O
clean	684	238	928	370	881	1943	209
20dB	548	159	705	266	697	1905	81
10dB	315	103	418	103	377	1658	9
5dB	191	62	260	36	255	1385	0
0dB	108	35	154	5	153	1074	0
-5dB	51	19	72	2	92	757	0
-10dB	20	5	24	0	43	506	0

Table 8. The number of correct samples of the T2 FHMM-UV with $k = 0.5$

SNR	S	A	F	N	G	V	O
clean	675	247	923	367	889	1934	208
20dB	541	156	723	271	696	1915	69
10dB	315	89	414	113	353	1670	5
5dB	185	48	232	38	245	1409	0
0dB	105	26	120	10	150	1078	0
-5dB	55	13	41	1	82	760	0
-10dB	24	2	7	0	48	507	0

Table 9. The comparison of the classification rate (%)

SNR	HMM	T2 FHMM-UV		
		k = 0.9	k = 0.7	k = 0.5
clean	54.90	57.02	57.10	56.99
20dB	45.08	46.88	47.40	47.51
10dB	30.66	31.75	32.42	32.16
5dB	22.59	24.16	23.79	23.45
0dB	15.36	16.83	16.62	16.18
-5dB	10.01	11.36	10.79	10.35
-10dB	5.93	7.01	6.50	6.39

is more robust to the babble noise to classify the class "O" than the HMM and T2 FHMM-UM. Even in 10dB babble noise, it can still classify 3, 9, and 5 samples correctly in class "O" with $k = 0.9, 0.7, 0.5$, respectively. Table 9 shows the comparison of average classification rate between the HMM and HMM-UV with $k = 0.9, 0.7, 0.5$.

5 Conclusions

Experimental results on TIMIT database are encouraging. Overall, T2 FHMMs consistently outperform HMMs in the babble noise of different SNRs. The best results show that the T2 FHMM-UM ($k = 2$) outperforms the HMM 1.56% on average, and T2 FHMM-UV ($k = 0.9$) outperforms the HMM 1.50% on average in terms of classification rates. Furthermore, for fricatives, glides, and "silence" phonemes, both T2 FHMM-UM and T2 FHMM-UV are more robust to babble noise than the HMM. Besides, the classification performance seems insensitive to the factor k, which offers convenience in handling real-world problems.

Currently, the proposed system is suitable for short speech sequences. Although in continuous speech recognition phoneme boundaries are not known, we may apply the GLM directly to word models to decide which model is the best for the test sequence. Future works include the design of the decision method from uncertain likelihoods for continuous speech recognition.

References

1. Rabiner, L.R.: A tutorial on hidden Markov models and selected applications in speech recognition. Proc. IEEE 77, 257–286 (1989)
2. Duda, R.O., Hart, P.E., Stork, D.G.: Pattern Classification, 2nd edn. John Wiley & Sons, New York (2001)
3. Zeng, J., Liu, Z.Q.: Type-2 fuzzy hidden Markov models and their application to speech recognition. IEEE Trans. Fuzzy Syst. 14(3), 454–467 (2006)
4. Mendel, J.M.: Uncertain Rule-based Fuzzy Logic Systems: Introduction and New Directions. Prentice-Hall, Englewood Cliffs (2001)
5. Liang, Q., Mendel, J.M.: Interval type-2 fuzzy logic systems: Theory and design. IEEE Trans. Fuzzy Syst. 8(5), 535–549 (2000)
6. Mendel, J.M.: Advances in type-2 fuzzy sets and systems. Information Sciences 177, 84–110 (2007)
7. Zeng, J., Liu, Z.Q.: Type-2 fuzzy sets for pattern recognition: The state-of-the-art. Journal of Uncertain Systems 1(3), 163–177 (2007)
8. Nabney, I.T.: NETLAB: Algorithms for Pattern Recognitions. Springer, London (2002)
9. Garofolo, J.S., Lamel, L.F., Fisher, W.M., Fiscus, J.G., Pallett, D.S., Dahlgren, N.L.: DRAPA TIMIT acoustic-phonetic continuous speech corpus CD-ROM. In: NISTIR, vol. 4930 (1992)
10. Young, S., Evermann, G., Kershaw, D., Moore, G., Odell, J., Ollason, D., Povey, D., Valtchev, V., Woodlands, P.: The HTK Book for HTK Version 3.2. Cambridge University Engineering Department, Cambridge, UK (2002)

A New Adaptation Method for Speaker-Model Creation in High-Level Speaker Verification

Shi-Xiong Zhang and Man-Wai Mak*

Dept. of Electronic and Information Engineering,
The Hong Kong Polytechnic University, Hong Kong
{zhang.sx, enmwmak}@polyu.edu.hk

Abstract. Research has shown that speaker verification based on high-level speaker features requires long enrollment utterances to be reliable. However, in practical speaker verification, it is common to model speakers based a limited amount of enrollment data. To minimize the undesirable effect of insufficient enrollment data on system performance, this paper proposes a new adaptation method for creating speaker models based on high-level features. Different from conventional methods, the proposed adaptation method not only adapts the phoneme-dependent background model but also the phoneme-independent speaker model. The amount of adaptation in the latter is adjusted by a proportional factor derived from the phoneme-independent background models. The proposed method was compared with traditional MAP adaptation under the NIST2000 SRE framework. Experimental results show that the proposed method can solve the data-spareness problem effectively and achieves a better performance when compare with traditional MAP adaptation.

1 Introduction

Text-independent speaker verification systems typically extract speaker-dependent features from short-term spectra of speech signals to build speaker-dependent Gaussian mixture models (GMMs) [1]. To increase the ability to discriminate between client (target) speakers and impostors, a GMM-based background model is used to represent the characteristics of impostors. The background model can be trained using the speech of non-target background speakers from large speech corpora. Therefore, finding enough speech to train the background model is usually not too difficult. However, obtaining a large number of client utterances is difficult and impractical because most clients are not willing to spend a long time for enrollment. To address this problem, various adaptation methods, such as maximum a posteriori (MAP) [1], maximum-likelihood linear regression (MLLR) [2], kernel eigen-space MLLR (KEMLLR) [3], and adaptation of phoneme-independent speaker models [4] have been proposed for creating low-level acoustic speaker models from a small amount of client data. It has been

* This work was supported by the Research Grant Council of the Hong Kong SAR Project No. PolyU5230/05E and HKPolyU Project No. A-PA6F.

H.H.S. Ip et al. (Eds.): PCM 2007, LNCS 4810, pp. 325–335, 2007.

shown that KEMLLR outperforms other adaptation methods when the amount of enrollment data is very limited and that when a large amount of enrollment data is available, MAP is a better candidate for creating speaker models [5].

Recently, to improve the robustness of speaker verification systems, researchers have started to investigate the possibility of using long-term, high-level features to characterize speakers [6]. One problem of using high-level features is that it requires a large amount of speech data for creating reliable speaker models. Although Leung et al. [7] have shown in their articulatory feature-based pronunciation model (AFCPM) that this problem can be tackled by classical MAP adaptation, the client models that they created are essentially a linear weighted sum of enrollment data's distribution and background models. It was found that the modeling capability of the AFCPMs drops rapidly when the amount of enrollment data decreases [8].

To alleviate this problem, we propose to adapt not only the phoneme-dependent background models but also the phoneme-independent speaker models to create client speaker models. A scaling factor, which is derived from the ratio between the phoneme-dependent background model and the phoneme-independent background model, will also be used to adjust the phoneme-independent speaker models during adaptation. The results show that the proposed adaptation method, which uses as much information as possible from the training data, significantly outperforms the classical MAP adaptation method.

2 Phoneme-Dependent AFCPM

Articulatory features (AFs) are representations describing the movements or positions of different articulators during speech production. In Leung et al. [7], manner and place of articulation were used for pronunciation modeling. The manner property has 6 classes, $\mathcal{M}$ ={Silence, Vowel, Stop, Fricative, Nasal, Approximant-Lateral}, and the place property has 10 classes, $\mathcal{P}$ ={Silence, High, Middle, Low, Labial, Dental, Coronal, Palatal, Velar, Glottal}. The AFs were automatically determined from speech signals using AF-based multilayer perceptrons (MLPs). See [7] for detail description of AFCPM approach.

In phoneme-dependent AFCPM, N phoneme-dependent universal background models (UBMs) are trained from the AF and phoneme streams of a large number of speakers to represent the speaker independent pronunciation characteristics. Each UBM comprises the joint probabilities of the manner and place classes conditioned on a phoneme. The training procedure begins with aligning two AF streams (l_t^{M} and l_t^{P}) obtained from the AF-MLPs and a phoneme sequence q_t obtained from a null-grammar recognizer. The joint probabilities corresponding to a particular phoneme q is given by

$$\begin{aligned} P_b(m,p|q) &= P_b(L^{\mathrm{M}}=m, L^{\mathrm{P}}=p|\text{Phoneme}=q, \text{Background}) \\ &= \frac{\#((m,p,q) \text{ in the data of all background speakers})}{\#((*,*,q) \text{ in the data of all background speakers})}, \end{aligned} \tag{1}$$

where $m \in \mathcal{M}, p \in \mathcal{P}, (m, p, q)$ denotes the condition for which $L^{\mathrm{M}} = m, L^{\mathrm{P}} = p$, and Phoneme $= q$, $*$ represents all possible members in that class, and $\#()$ represents the total number of frames with phoneme labels and AF labels fulfill the description inside the parentheses. The unadapted speaker models $P_s(m, p|q)$ are created in the same way:

$$\begin{aligned} P_s(m, p|q) &= P_s(L^{\mathrm{M}} = m, L^{\mathrm{P}} = p|\text{Phoneme} = q, \text{speaker} = s) \\ &= \frac{\#((m, p, q) \text{ in the enrollment utterrence of speaker } s)}{\#((*, *, q) \text{ in the enrollment utterrence of speaker } s)}. \end{aligned} \tag{2}$$

We can see for each phoneme, a total of 60 probabilities can be obtained. These probabilities are the products of 6 manner classes and 10 place classes.

3 Adaptation Methods for AFCPMs

Here, we review the classical MAP adaptation and propose three MAP-based adaptation methods that use as much information obtainable from training data as possible (see Fig. 1).

Method A: Adapted from phoneme-dependent background models(classical MAP used in [7]).
Method B: Adapted from phoneme-independent speaker models.
Method C: Adapted from phoneme-independent speaker models with a phoneme-dependent scaling factor.
Method D: Adapted from phoneme-dependent background models and phoneme-independent speaker models with a phoneme-dependent scaling factor.

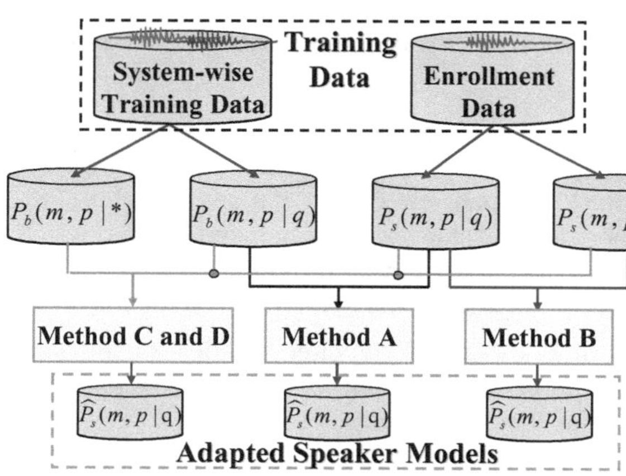

Fig. 1. Data-set utilization in different adaptation methods. Methods A and B only use part of available models. Methods C and D fully utilize all of the possible models that can be obtained from training data. '*' means that the corresponding model is phoneme-independent.

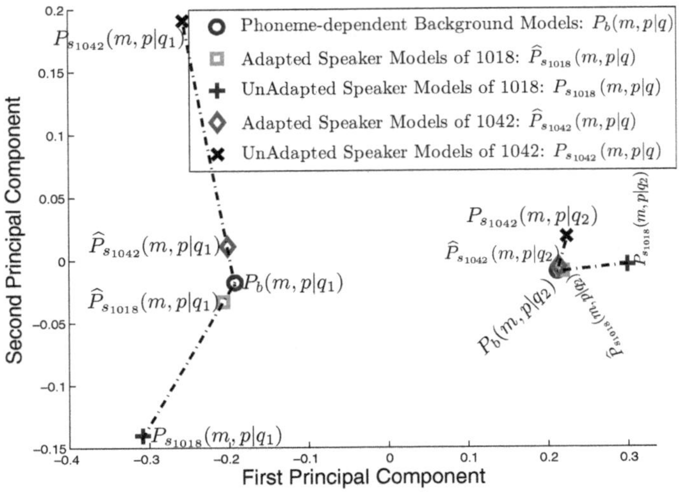

Fig. 2. *Method A.* Relationship (based on real data) between the background, unadapted, and adapted AFCPMs in classical MAP (q_1=/jh/, q_2=/uw/). The linear combination in Eq. 3 suggests that the adapted model will lie along the straight line passing through the unadapted model and the background model.

Method A: In [7], MAP adaptation is applied as follows:

$$\widehat{P}_s(m,p|q) = \beta_s^q P_s(m,p|q) + (1 - \beta_s^q) P_b(m,p|q) \quad (3)$$

where, $\beta_s^q \in [0,1]$ is a phoneme-dependent adaptation coefficient controlling the contribution of the enrollment data and the background models (Eq. 1) on the MAP-adapted model. It is obtained by

$$\beta_s^q = \frac{\#((*,*,q) \text{ in the enrollment utterances of speaker } s)}{\#((*,*,q) \text{ in the enrollment utterances of speaker } s) + r} \quad (4)$$

where r is a fixed relevance factor common to all phonetic classes and speakers. The relationship between the adapted, unadapted and background models is illustrated in Fig. 2. When enrollment data is sufficient, MAP adaptation can create client models that capture the phoneme-dependent characteristics of speakers. However, when the amount of enrollment data is limited, this speaker-model creation method may have three fundamental problems:

Problem 1: The method will make the client models of the same phoneme too close to the background model of the corresponding phoneme, even though the clients may have very different pronunciation characteristics. This will cause the client models fail to discriminate the true speakers from the imposters.

Problem 2: The method does not fully utilize the information available in the training data.

Problem 3: The method imposes too much constraint on the adaptation.

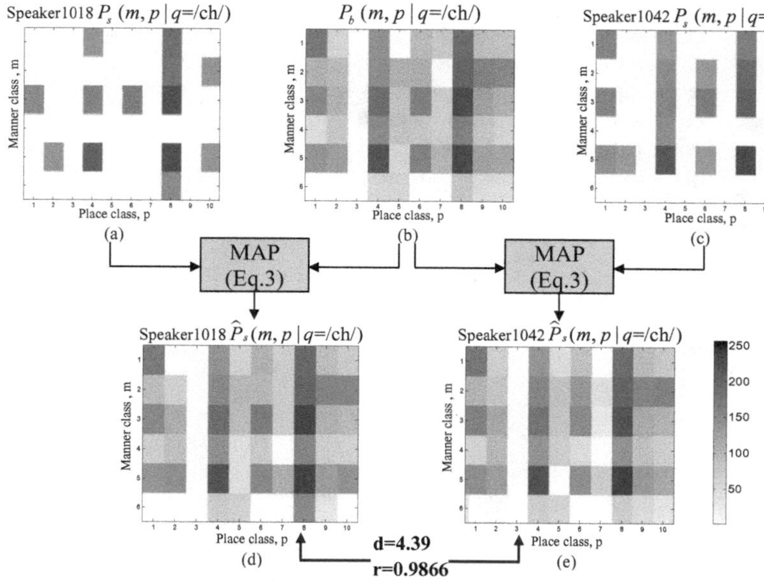

Fig. 3. Phoneme-dependent AFCPMs correspond to phoneme /ch/ of (a) speaker 1018 from NIST00, (b) background speakers from NIST99, and (c) speaker 1042 from NIST00. (d) and (e): Phoneme-dependent speaker models of the two speakers adapted from (b) using the traditional MAP adaptation (see Method A in section 3). d and r represent the Euclidean distance and the correlation coefficient between the models pointed to by arrows. The 60 discrete probabilities corresponding to the combinations of the 6 manner and 10 place classes are nonlinearly quantized to 256 gray levels using log-scale, where white represents 0 and black represents 1.

Problem 1 is exemplified in Fig. 3, where the adapted models of two speakers are very similar because they are very close to the background model. Comparison between Figs. 3(d) and 3(e) reveals that the model of speaker 1018 are very similar to that of speaker 1042. This will make the speaker models fail to discriminate the true speakers from impostors. For Problem 2, the method only uses two out of four possible models for adaptation. Fig. 1 shows the possible models from which the target models can be adapted. Method A uses the phoneme-dependent models only and ignores the fact that the phoneme-independent models ($P_b(m,p|*)$ and $P_s(m,p|*)$) can also be used to create target speaker models. For Problem 3, the method uses all of the background speakers' data to train phoneme-dependent background models from which phoneme-dependent target speaker models are created by MAP adaptation. Creating a phoneme-dependent speaker model from the corresponding phoneme-dependent background model means that the resulting speaker model is constrained by the articulatory properties of a single phoneme. In other words, the method does not allow cross-phoneme adaptation. Note that the classical MAP adaptation for

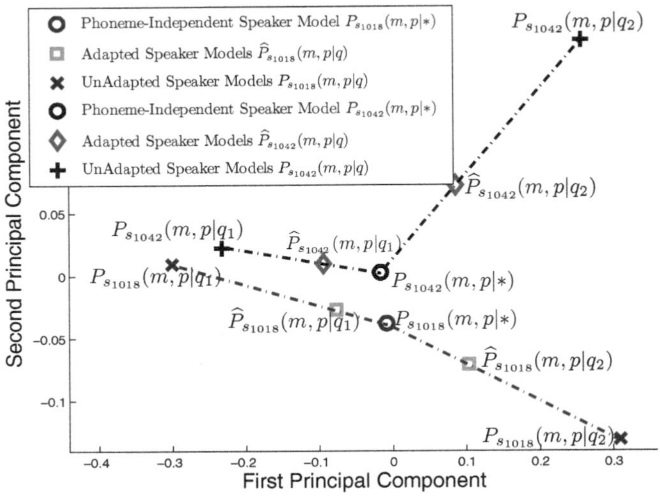

Fig. 4. *Method B.* Relationship between the phoneme-independent speaker model, unadapted speaker models, and adapted speaker models for speakers 1018 and 1042 (q_1=/jh/, q_2=/uw/)

acoustic GMMs does not have such a hard constraint. Instead, a soft constraint is implicitly imposed by the posterior probabilities of the mixture components.

Method B: Instead of adapting from the phoneme-dependent UBM, we can create the speaker model $\widehat{P}_s(m,p|q)$ by adapting the speaker-dependent, phoneme-independent speaker model $P_s(m,p|*)$, i.e.,

$$\widehat{P}_s(m,p|q) = \beta_s^q P_s(m,p|q) + (1-\beta_s^q) P_s(m,p|*). \tag{5}$$

While this method can help solve Problems 1 and 3 mentioned in Method A, it does have its own problem. The problem is that for a particular client, all of his/her phoneme-dependent models are adapted from the same phoneme-independent model, causing loss of phoneme-dependence in the client model. In fact, the method uses enrollment data only, as illustrated in Fig. 1. This loss of phoneme-dependence, however, violates the requirement of the scoring procedure (see Section 4) where the speaker and background models are assumed to be phoneme-dependent. Fortunately, the phoneme-dependence in the client models can be easily retained by introducing a phoneme-dependent scaling factor in the adaption equation. This is to be discussed next.

Method C: In this method, a phoneme-dependent scaling factor is added to the adaptation formula in Eq. 5:

$$\widehat{P}_s(m,p|q) = \beta_s^q P_s(m,p|q) + (1-\beta_s^q) \cdot \left[\frac{P_b(m,p|q)}{P_b(m,p|*)} \cdot P_s(m,p|*)\right] \tag{6}$$

where $P_b(m,p|*)$ represents the phoneme-independent background model and $\frac{P_b(m,p|q)}{P_b(m,p|*)}$ is the scaling factor. With this factor, the model to be adapted becomes $\frac{P_b(m,p|q)}{P_b(m,p|*)}P_s(m,p|*)$. Therefore, the resulting target model $\widehat{P}_s(m,p|q)$ is now adapted from a model with certain degree of phoneme-dependence instead of adapting from a purely phoneme-independent model $(P_s(m,p|*))$.

Note that $\frac{P_b(m,p|q)}{P_b(m,p|*)}P_s(m,p|*)$ in Eq. 6 can also be written as $\frac{P_s(m,p|*)}{P_b(m,p|*)}P_b(m,p|q)$. In that case, we can interpret $\frac{P_s(m,p|*)}{P_b(m,p|*)}$ as a phoneme-independent scaling factor for the classical MAP adaptation in Eq. 3. This factor can help alleviates Problems 2 and 3 in classical MAP mentioned earlier, because it implicitly incorporates the speaker-dependent articulatory properties of other phonemes into the adaptation equation.

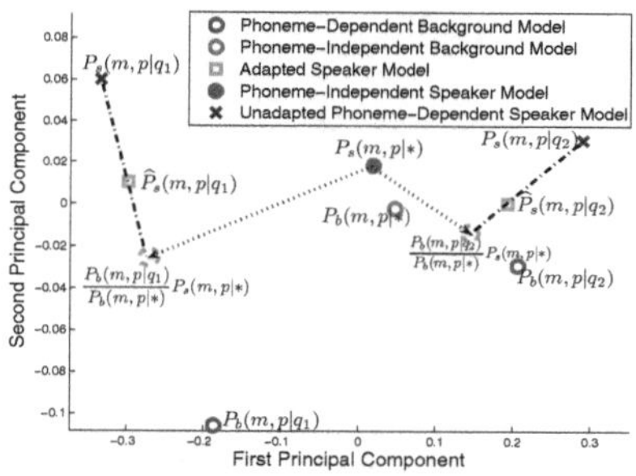

Fig. 5. *Method C.* Relationship between the phoneme-independent speaker model, unadapted speaker models, and adapted speaker models for speaker 1018 (q_1=/jh/, q_2=/uw/).

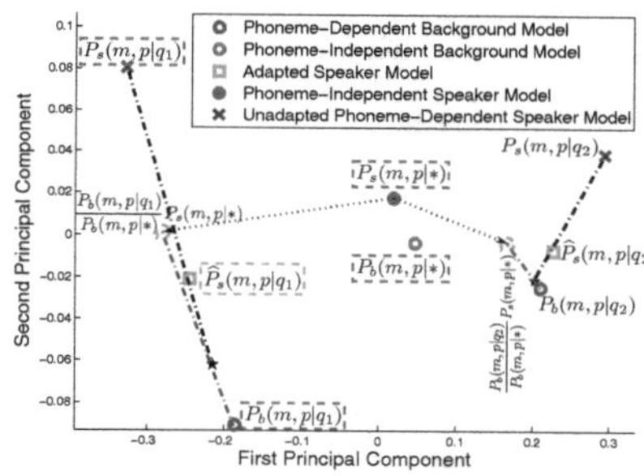

Fig. 6. *Method D.* Relationship between the phoneme-independent speaker model, unadapted speaker models, and adapted speaker models for speaker 1018. (q_1=/jh/, q_2=/uw/ and the marker '★' represents the term inside the square brackets in Eq. 7.)

Method D: It becomes clear that Method A is likely to impose too much constraint on the adaptation. Method B aims to relax such constraint by introducing a phoneme-independent model in its adaptation equation. However, the relaxation may be too far so that the phoneme-dependent scaling factor in Method C is necessary to limit the loss of phoneme-dependence. Nevertheless, the target models created by Method C depend implicitly on the phoneme-dependent background models $P_b(m,p|q)$ through the scaling factor. To strengthen the dependence of these background models while allowing certain degree of phoneme-independence, we may combine Methods A and C. We refer to the resulting adaptation as Method D whose adaptation equation is written as:

$$\widehat{P}_s(m,p|q)=\beta_s^q P_s(m,p|q)+(1-\beta_s^q)\left[\alpha_b^q P_b(m,p|q)+(1-\alpha_b^q)\frac{P_b(m,p|q)}{P_b(m,p|*)}P_s(m,p|*)\right] \quad (7)$$

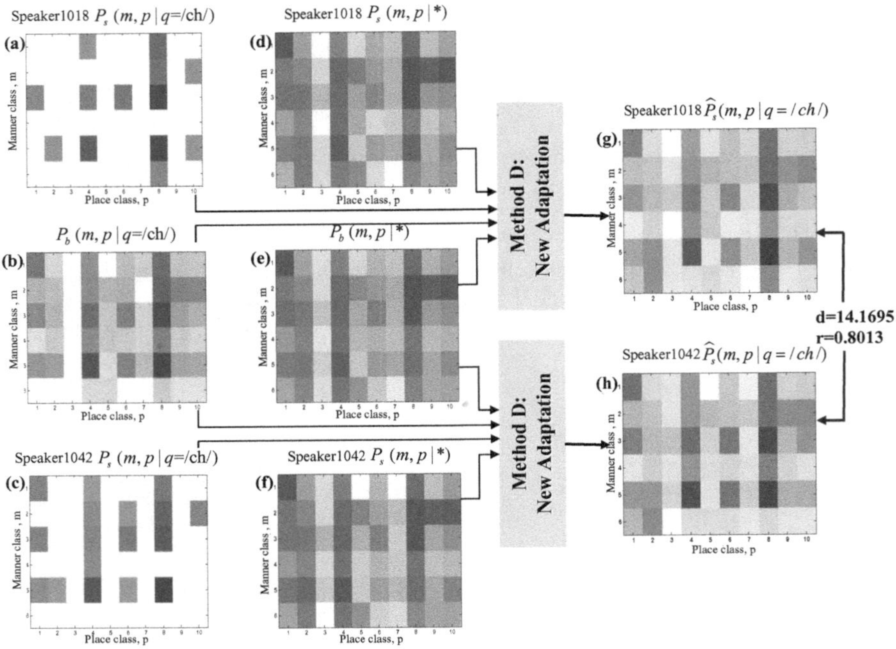

Fig. 7. Phoneme-dependent AFCPMs ((g) and (h)) of speakers 1018 and 1042 created by Method D. (a) and (c): Unadapted speaker models. (b) Phoneme-dependent background model. (d) and (f): Phoneme-independent speaker models. (e) Phoneme-independent background model. d and r represent the Euclidean distance and the correlation coefficient between the adapted models pointed to by arrows.

where, $\alpha_b^q \in [0,1]$ is a phoneme-dependent adaptation coefficient. It is obtained by

$$\alpha_b^q = \frac{\#((*,*,q) \text{ in the utterances of all background speakers})}{\#((*,*,q) \text{ in the utterances of all background speakers}) + r_\alpha} \tag{8}$$

where r_α is also a fixed relevance factor.

Fig. 6 illustrates the relationship between different models in Method C, and Fig. 7 explains why this method is better than Method A via an illustrative example.

Comparing Figs. 3 and 7 reveals that the Euclidean distance and dissimilarity between the AFCPM models of speakers 1018 and 1042 become larger (the distance increases from 4.39 to 14.17 and the correlation coefficient reduces from 0.9966 to 0.8013). Therefore Method D makes the speaker models easier to discriminate speakers.

4 Scoring

We follow the scoring method in [1]. Specifically, we define the verification score of a test utterance $X = \{X_1, \ldots, X_t, \ldots, X_T\}$ as:

$$S(X) = \sum_{t=1}^{T} (\log \widehat{p}_s(X_t) - \log p_b(X_t)) \tag{9}$$

where the speaker models $\widehat{P}_s(m,p|q)$ and background models $P_b(m,p|q)$ created by using different adaptation methods discussed in Section 3 are used to compute the scores:

$$\widehat{p}_s(X_t) = \widehat{P}_s(l_t^{\mathrm{M}}, l_t^{\mathrm{P}}|q_t) = \widehat{P}_s(L^{\mathrm{M}} = l_t^{\mathrm{M}}, L^{\mathrm{P}} = l_t^{\mathrm{P}}|\mathrm{Phoneme} = q_t, \mathrm{Speaker} = s) \tag{10}$$

$$p_b(X_t) = P_b(l_t^{\mathrm{M}}, l_t^{\mathrm{P}}|q_t) = P_b(L^{\mathrm{M}} = l_t^{\mathrm{M}}, L^{\mathrm{P}} = l_t^{\mathrm{P}}|\mathrm{Phoneme} = q_t, \mathrm{Background}), \tag{11}$$

In Eqs. 10 and 11, q_t is the phoneme of frame t in the test utterance recognized by a null gram phoneme recognizer, and l_t^{M} and l_t^{P} are the AF labels determined by the AF-MLPs [7].

5 Experiments and Results

5.1 Procedures

NIST99, NIST00, SPIDRE [9], and HTIMIT [10] were used in the experiments. NIST99 was used for creating the background models, and the female part of NIST00 was used for creating speaker models and for performance evaluation. HTIMIT and SPIDRE were used for training the AF-MLPs and the null-grammar phone recognizer, respectively.

The phone recognizer uses standard 39-D vectors comprising MFCCs, energy, and their derivatives. The training part of NIST99 was used for creating phoneme-dependent AF-based UBMs. We followed the evaluation protocol of NIST00. Specifically, for each female client speaker in NIST00, her phoneme-dependent speaker models were created using Methods A to D.

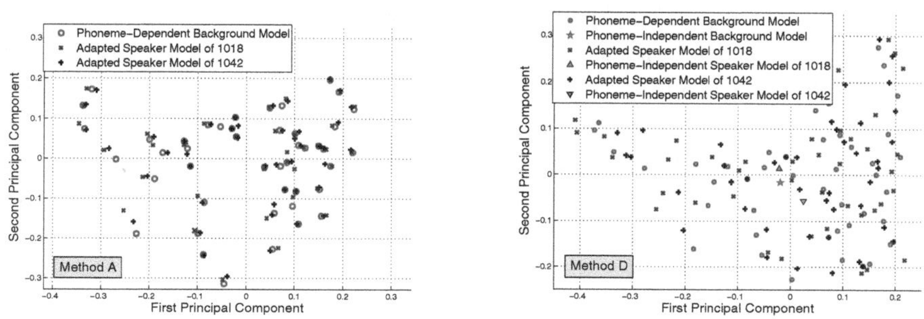

Fig. 8. The distribution of all adapted phoneme-dependent speaker models and phoneme-dependent background models in principal component space for speaker 1018 and 1042 based on Method A (left) and Method D (right).

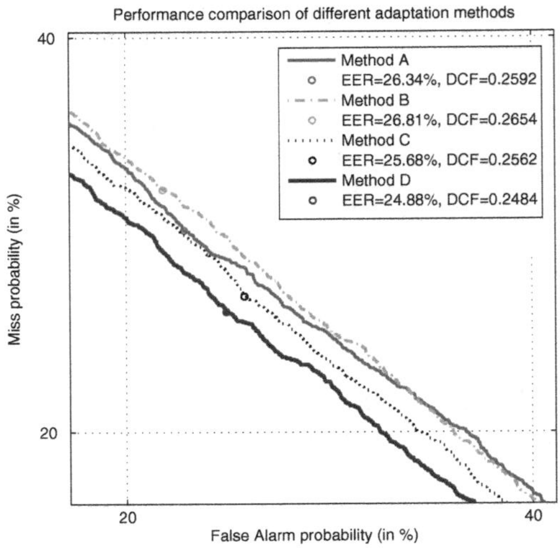

Fig. 9. DET performance of AFCPM-based speaker verification systems using different adaptation methods.

Table 1. EERs obtained by phoneme-dependent AFCPMs created by MAP-based adaptation methods described in Section 3. The p-values between the classical MAP and the new adaptation methods are listed in the last column.

Adaptation Method	EER (%)	p-values
Method A	26.34	–
Method B	26.81	0.04560
Method C	25.68	0.00008
Method D	24.88	0.00000

5.2 Results and Discussion

Fig. 8 shows the relationship between the phoneme-dependent background and adapted models (corresponding to 46 phonemes) of two speakers for Methods A and D. Apparently, Problem 1 in Method A (left figure) mentioned in Section 3 does not appear in Method D (right figure).

Table 1 shows the equal error rate (EER) and p-values [11] (with respect to Method A) achieved by different adaptation methods. It shows that Methods C and D achieve a lower error rate as compare to the classical MAP adaption. This confirms our earlier argument that better speaker models can be obtained by adapting the phoneme-independent models in addition to the phoneme-dependent models.The DET plots corresponding to Table 1 are shown in Fig. 9. Evidently, Method D achieves the best performance across a wide range of decision threshold. It was found that the proposed adaptation approaches can effectively solve the data sparseness problem, resulting in a significantly lower error rate. Apparently, Problem 2 and 3 in Method A have also been overcome by method D.

References

1. Reynolds, D.A., Quatieri, T.F., Dunn, R.B.: Speaker verification using adapted Gaussian mixture models. Digital Signal Processing 10, 19–41 (2000)
2. Leggetter, C.J., Woodland, P.C.: Maximum likelihood linear regression for speaker adaptation of continuous density hidden Markov models. Computer Speech and Language 9(2), 171–185 (1995)

3. Mak, B., Ho, S., Hsiao, R., Kwok, J.T.: Embedded kernel eigenvoice speaker adaptation and its implication to reference speaker weighting. IEEE Transactions on Speech and Audio Processing 14, 1267–1280 (2006)
4. Matsui, T., Furui, S.: Concatenated phoneme models for text-variable speaker recognition. In: Proc. ICASSP 1993, vol. 1, pp. 391–394 (1993)
5. Mak, M.W., Hsiao, R., Mak, B.: A comparison of various adaptation methods for speaker verification with limited enrollment data. In: ICASSP 2006, pp. 929–932 (2006)
6. Reynolds, D., et al.: The superSID project: Exploiting high-level information for high-accuracy speaker recognition. In: Proc. International Conference on Audio, Speech, and Signal Processing, Hong Kong, vol. 4, pp. 784–787 (April 2003)
7. Leung, K.Y., Mak, M.W., Kung, S.Y.: Adaptive articulatory feature-based conditional pronunciation modeling for speaker verification. Speech Communication 48(1), 71–84 (2006)
8. Zhang, S.X., Mak, M.W., Meng, H.M.: Speaker verification via high-level feature based phonetic-class pronunciation modeling. IEEE Trans. on Computers, Vol. 56, No. 9, pp. 1189-1198, (September 2007)
9. Campbell, J.P., Reynolds, D.A.: Corpora for the evaluation of speaker recognition systems. In: Proc. ICASSP 1999, vol. 2, pp. 829–832 (1999)
10. Reynolds, D.A.: HTIMIT and LLHDB: Speech corpora for the study of handset transducer effects. In: Proc. ICASSP 1997, vol. 2, pp. 1535–1538 (1997)
11. Gillick, L., Cox, S.: Some statistical issues in the comparison of speech recognition algorithms. In: Proc. ICASSP 1989, pp. 532–535 (1989)

Dynamic Sound Rendering Based on Ray-Caching

Ken Chan[1,2], Rynson W.H. Lau[2,3], and Jianmin Zhao[3]

[1] Department of Computer Science, City University of Hong Kong, Hong Kong
[2] Department of Computer Science, University of Durham, United Kingdom
[3] College of Math., Physics and Info. Engineering, Zhejiang Normal University, China

Abstract. Dynamic sound rendering is attracting a lot of attention in recent years due to its applications in computer games and architecture simulation. Although physical based methods can produce realistic outputs, they typically involve recursive tracing of sound rays, which may be computationally too expensive for interactive dynamic environments. In this paper, we propose a ray caching method that exploits ray coherence to accelerate the ray-tracing process. The proposed method is tailored for interactive sound rendering based on two approximation techniques: spatial and angular approximation. The ray cache supports intra-frame, inter-frame and inter-observer sharing of rays. We show the performance of the new method through a number of experiments.

1 Introduction

Real-time spacious sound synthesis in dynamic virtual environments is important in many applications, such as computer games and architecture simulation. It does not only provide a sense of presence to the users, but also allow the users to experience the sound effect of a virtual environment.

The main process of generating real-time spacious sound is sound rendering, which generates impulse responses to an observer from all the input sound sources of an environment. The inputs to the sound rendering process include the geometry of the environment, position and orientation of the observer, and position and waveform of each sound source. An approach to generate impulse responses is the physical approach [Gard98], which deals with the geometrical modeling of sound wave transmission. First, the paths of sound sources are traced to obtain a set of virtual sound sources. The Head-Related Transfer Functions (HRTFs) at the virtual sound source positions are then convolved with the sound waves to produce spacious sound.

In general, the physical approach is not efficient as it requires recursive tracing of sound paths in the environment. A popular method for tracing sound paths is ray-tracing, by which rays are projected from the observer in all directions. When a ray hits an object surface, a reflected ray is typically generated. For a transmissive surface, a transmitted ray may also be generated. Each new ray is further projected to the environment and recursively traced until either the ray hits a sound source or its effect to the observer becomes too small. As this approach traverses logarithmic number of surfaces for each ray, it is generally too expensive for real-time use.

H.H.S. Ip et al. (Eds.): PCM 2007, LNCS 4810, pp. 336–346, 2007.

In this paper, we propose a method that exploits ray coherence of sound to accelerate the sound ray tracing process. Our method is based on the ray-history concept [Sber04]. It incorporates multi-resolution approximation of rays in both spatial and angular dimensions to maximize the caching performance. Experimental results show that our method offers a significant performance improvement, making it suitable for use in interactive dynamic environments.

The rest of the paper is organized as follows. Section 2 describes related work on sound rendering and acceleration techniques. Section 3 presents an overview of our ray caching method. Section 4 presents the ray caching method. Section 5 shows the performance of the proposed method with a number of experiments. Section 6 briefly summarizes this paper and suggests possible future work.

2 Related Work

There are a few sound rendering methods proposed which are based on the physical approach. For example, [Funk98] proposes a beam tracing method that considers the preprocessing of reflection paths. [Funk99] accelerates the method by applying priority driven and estimation techniques. This method can achieve good results of discovering reflection paths, but has to deal with expensive beam intersections. [Muel99] proposes a scalable PC-based software sound rendering system based on ray tracing. Unfortunately, their experimental results indicate that the system cannot be used for real-time applications. [CATT] is a software system targeted for architectural acoustic simulation but it is not for interactive purpose. [LTL] is a hardware/software system for multi-purpose sound rendering. It makes use of dedicated DSPs to generate real-time spatialized sounds. Unfortunately, it is expensive and not scalable.

Our method is based on tracing sound rays. There are already a lot of acceleration techniques proposed for ray-tracing in computer graphics to exploit coherence. These techniques can be roughly classified into four categories [Rein02, Suth74]:

Object Coherence: It exploits position adjacency between objects. It works by pre-processing data structures including grids, BSPs (binary space partitions) and BVHs (bounding volume hierarchies) [Arvo89] to group related objects together. With these data structures, the number of intersection tests for each ray can be reduced.

Image Coherence: It exploits local constancy between neighboring pixels. In [Mart01, Havr03], caching methods are proposed to cache intersection points of previous primary rays in object space with their corresponding pixels in image space. The cache is then used to direct new rays towards objects that have been previously hit. In [Havr03], an additional cache storing object orders is maintained, providing information on which nearest object that a new ray is intersected with. Each entry in the cache, indexed by pixel position, stores a reference to the nearest intersected object and the number of times that it is referenced by neighboring pixels. If this number exceeds a threshold, the same pixel in the next frame would be reprojected to the same object. Otherwise, the traditional ray tracing technique is applied.

Ray Coherence: It exploits similarity between adjacent rays on traveling directions and intersected objects. [Wald01] employs parallelism provided by SIMD instructions and careful memory layout for the BSP data structure to improve the ray tracing performance. Packets of rays are traversed and intersected in parallel since they have high chance of intersecting the same objects. Ray coherence can be further extended by tracking the ray paths across consecutive frames. [Sber04] proposes a fast global illumination method to support moving light sources. As a preprocessing step, all direct and reflected paths to light sources are traced. The illumination by the traced paths and the first hit points from the light sources are cached. Then, all the traced paths are weighted among all frames for indirect illumination and the weighed paths are cached. During frame generation, direct illumination is recomputed for each frame while the weighted paths are reused from cache to produce the final image. With this method, direct illumination should be recomputed while indirect illumination requires only computing the weighted impact of all virtual light sources. Path splitting and joining are useful ideas of ray caching. However, the method benefits mostly on indirect illumination due to its aim on caching shadow paths. As it is based on preprocessing, it is only suitable for predefined animations.

Frame Coherence: It exploits similarity of the projected rays between consecutive frames. One approach to frame coherence is spatial subdivision. [Mura90] proposes a ray-object intersection tree structure with voxel traversal history, which is a list of all voxels traversed by a path segment, and intersection history, which is a list of intersection points that hit a moving object. The intersection history helps eliminate unnecessary intersection tests to non-moving objects. Due to the voxels architecture, this method has high memory cost and does not support moving camera. In [Davi99], frame coherence is applied to accelerate animation. It subdivides the scene into regular voxels and involves a preprocessing step to test all object movements in an animation against the voxels. All voxels passed through by objects are marked with frame numbers. During ray tracing, primary and higher order rays are projected from a pixel, intersecting the voxels. The lowest frame number of all passed through voxels is referenced and marked in a cache structure called t-buffer, which is then used to determine the next frame number that the pixel should project rays again. Caching of rays is inherently achieved by the voxel structure and reuse of rays is inherently achieved by the t-buffer. This method suffers from the costly preprocessing step, and is less useful in moving cameras as coherence is only exploited for static background.

3 Method Overview

The core of a sound rendering process based on the physical approach is the search for virtual sound sources. In our method, this is done by ray tracing. Rays are projected from the observer in different directions to search for the nearest intersected objects or sound sources. If an object surface is hit, a reflected ray is generated from the surface, which further intersects other objects. New rays would be generated until one hits a sound source. A *reverberation path* is a sequence of projected rays starting from the observer until reaching a sound source. By mirroring the reverberation path, we could locate the position of the virtual sound source at the end of the path. Each observer maintains a virtual source map in each frame, storing information of all the virtual sound sources reaching him/her. During the auralization process, we generate spacious impulse responses by convoluting the virtual source map with HRTFs.

Spacious waveform can then be generated by multiplying the spacious impulse responses with the input sound sources.

In a dynamic environment, observer and sound sources may move around. For each observer or sound source movement, we need to update all reverberation paths. With a traditional ray tracing method, we need to perform all the intersection tests again, making it difficult to achieve real-time response. Our research objective here is to discover and exploit the coherencies between observer/sound source movements. Typically, an observer moves step by step, rather than jumps abruptly, from his current position. During each frame, there are likely a lot of rays with similar directions to the rays projected in the previous frame, intersecting the same objects at similar angles and reflecting in a similar way. If we could cache the intersection history of previous rays and reuse them, we may save a lot of computations.

Our method employs the ray coherence concept for acceleration. Intersection history of traced rays is cached for future reuse. Rays with similar starting points and projection directions as previously projected rays do not have to be retraced again. To cache the intersection history, we subdivide the objects into discrete patches. Ray transmission is represented by pointers from one patch to another. Thus, the ray cache is a graph with all the patches as nodes and the rays as edges. When a ray intersects a previously intersected patch, we can easily locate the next patch to be intersected from the cache, replacing the costly intersection tests with memory referencing operations. However, there are a number of issues to be considered when designing a ray cache. For example, schemes have to be set up to fully utilize the ray cache in dynamic environments with moving observers, sound sources, and objects.

3.1 Patch Subdivision

We subdivide each object into patches small enough that we may treat all incident rays the same way if they hit the same patch at the same direction, even at different intersection points. For rays hitting the same patch from the same direction, all of their reflected rays will be projected from the center of the patch. In this way, the original reflective rays of the incoming rays are *spatially approximated* by the outgoing ray. In addition, each patch is also subdivided into a number of angular divisions. Incoming rays falling within the same angular division would be reflected by the same ray. In this way, the incoming rays are *angularly approximated* by the outgoing reflected ray.

3.2 Multi-resolution Patches

The nature of ray tracing is that spatial resolution decreases along with increasing distance of each projected ray as the separation between two neighbor rays is proportional to their ray lengths. Missing hits may occur for distant sound sources if the angular width between neighbor rays is too high or the diameter of the sound source is too small. To avoid missing hits without adjusting the initial ray sampling rate, we may increase the diameter of the sound source as the path length increases.

We apply this concept to the size of the patches. Without adjusting the sampling rate of the projected rays, we may increase the patch size as the path length increases. This may increase the probability of reusing projected rays without increasing the approximation error. When a ray hits a patch, we apply spatial approximation and re-project the ray from the patch center. To support variable patch sizes, we apply multi-resolution modeling techniques here. Each surface of an object is subdivided into a hierarchy of patches. Although many different multi-resolution methods have been proposed [To01], we have adopted a simple method in our implementation. For each surface, we uniformly subdivide it recursively to form a quad-tree. This means that the patch length reduces by half as we move down the quad-tree from one level to the next. Hence, when a ray interests a surface patch, we determine the appropriate resolution of the patch according to its path length.

3.3 Intra-frame, Inter-frame and Inter-observer Coherencies

Intra-frame coherence occurs when a re-projected ray is shared by more than one reverberation path within the same frame. This could be due to, for example, neighboring rays that hit the same patch at similar angle. These rays will then have the same reverberation path, making it possible to reuse the traced paths.

Inter-frame coherence occurs when ray history of previous frames are reused. This could happen easily if an observer is moving step by step. Figure 1 shows that an observer moves forward by one step. Paths traced for patches B, C, and E in the last frame can be reused in the current frame since the rays in both frames intersect the same patches at similar angles. We may observe that it is more likely to reuse rays intersecting distant patches than those intersecting nearby patches. For example, the angle between the dashed arrow and the solid arrow hitting D is larger than that of E. Hence, there is a higher chance that the two rays intersecting E fall within the same angular division used in angular approximation, hence reusing the rays intersecting E.

Inter-observer coherence occurs when ray history of another observer is reused. One scenario of inter-observer coherence is when a group of observers move in a similar direction, e.g., in a virtual touring.

4 Ray Cache

The ray cache is composed of a tree and a graph attached to the tree. Each object is composed of a number of surfaces. Each surface is divided into multiple levels of patches and each patch is further divided into angular divisions. Figure 2 shows an example object tree, starting from object at the root to angular divisions at the leaves. Typically, there is only a small amount of angular division nodes which are ever accessed. To save run-time memory, only the accessed angular division nodes are instantiated during ray-tracing. We reference each leaf node in the tree by a multiple-component division index, (object, surface, {patch, patch, ...}, division), which will simply be referred to as *division* in remaining text.

When a surface is intersected by a ray, it is recursively subdivided into smaller patches until the patch length is just small enough proportional to the path length of the ray. To save memory, only the patches containing intersection points are further subdivided. When we reach the appropriate patch level, we calculate the angular division to approximate the incoming ray direction. Figure 3 shows the patch hierarchy of surface **W** found in Figure 2. For clarity, we only show the reflective

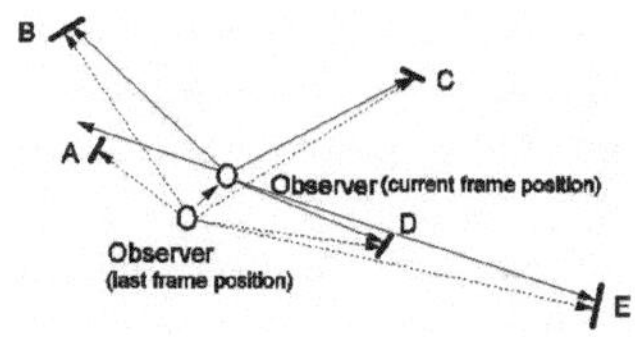

Fig. 1. Inter-frame coherence

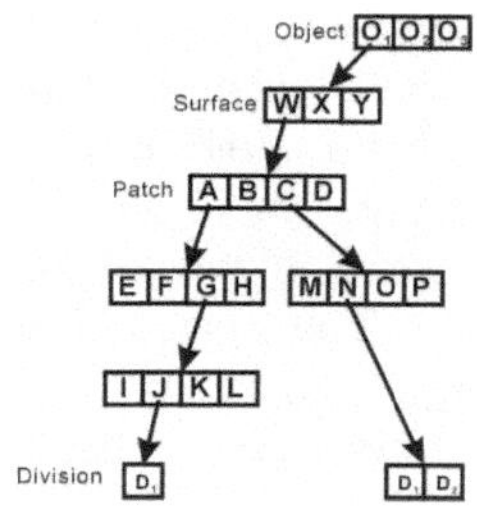

Fig. 2. The ray cache tree

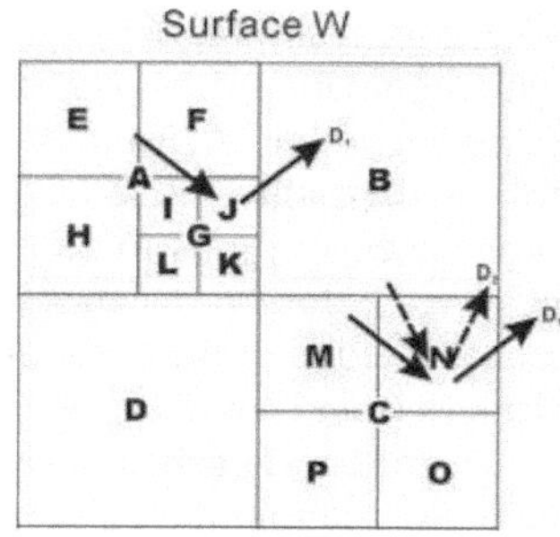

Fig. 3. Patch hierarchy of surface **W** in Fig. 2

property of the patch. There should be another patch hierarchy to represent the transmissive property. For each ray we stored in cache, we also store the backward version of the ray to facilitate path finding in backward direction. This is particularly useful for locating paths from sound source to observer, in a sound source movement.

4.1 Constructing the Ray Cache

We use an example to illustrate how the ray cache is being constructed. To simplify the description, we assume in this example that all rays are equidistant and each ray intersection happens to cause the patch resolution to reduce by one level.

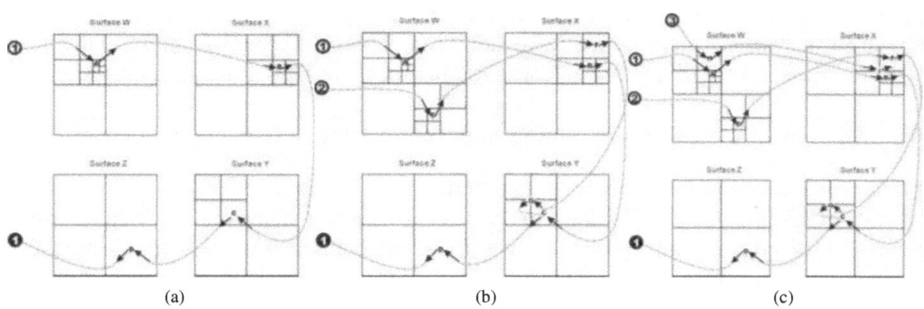

Fig. 4. Constructing the ray cache (white circles are observers; black circles are sound sources)

Initially the ray cache is empty. The first path is constructed by tracing the reverberation path from the observer to the sound source as in Figure 4(a). The intersected *divisions* are instantiated in the tree. The division intersection sequence is recorded by creating an edge entry from one *division* to another. This intersection sequence is retained in the ray cache even if the path does not hit a sound source. In this example, the path traced for observer 1 intersects 4 surfaces via patches A, B, C and D. The path finally reaches sound source 1. When another path is to be traced, in addition to instantiating the new *divisions* and caching the new rays, the process will seek reuse opportunities as in Figure 4(b). (Note that the patch resolution is reduced whenever a ray intersects a patch.) If we reach a patch of required patch resolution, which contains child patches, we search the child patches for cached records of the same incoming *division*. If the same incoming *division* exists, we may reuse and follow the cached edge from the child patch. In other words, each edge entry can be propagated upwards to parent patches for reuse. In the example, a path is traced for observer 2 through patches E, F and G. In patch G, a child patch C is found which has a cached edge of the same *division*. Thus, patch G is connected to patch C and finally reaches sound source 1 by reusing the cached path.

The reuse of cached edges follows a policy that only the nearest child patches will be chosen to minimize the spatial error as in Figure 4(c). Since the re-projection point of the parent patch is at the center of the patch, the child patch which is nearest to the center will be chosen. In the figure, observer 3 traces a path through patches H and I. In patch I, 2 reusable cached edges are found in child patches B and F. The cached edge in patch B is chosen for reuse since patch B is nearer to the center of patch I.

4.2 Ray Cache Purging

In a dynamic environment, the size of the ray cache will continue to grow in time as the number of rays projected increases in time. When the cache is full, we need to remove some of the cached rays. Our experiments (as will be shown in Section 5.2) show that most of the reused rays are computed in the recent frames. Thus, we may use time-stamping to keep track of the usage of cached rays for purging.

Each ray in the ray cache is time-stamped during its creation or when it is revisited. A pointer list is created in each frame to reference to all rays which are created or reused in that frame. When the ray cache is full, purging of rays need to be carried out starting from those with earlier frame numbers. The pointer lists of the earlier frames are used to find out rays which have not been reused in recent frames. These rays, with their associated divisions, patches, and parent patches, will be all removed.

4.3 Movement of Observers, Sound Sources and Scene Objects

Observer Movement: An observer is a node that initiates sound rays in all directions to the initial intersected *divisions* to form edges. When it moves, its virtual source map and all edges connecting it to the initial intersected *divisions* are cleared. We reconstruct new edges from the new position of this observer by projecting new rays to all direction to find the initial intersected *divisions*. Once a new ray hits a cached *division*, we follow the path starting from the cached edge. If a sound source can be reached finally, a new path is completed and a new virtual source map entry would be created. If the initial intersected *division* has no cached edges, the new path will be further traced until it reaches a cached *division* or its effect becomes insignificant.

The main cost of observer movement is on updating the reverberation paths from the observer. The ray cache helps reduce the number of intersection tests if the newly projected rays hit a cached *division*.

Sound Source Movement: A sound source is the reverse version of an observer. A sound source attaches backward edges to all *divisions* linked to it. When it moves, all forward and backward edges linked to it will need to be removed. Then, new initial rays will be projected from the sound source to search for intersections. When a surface is intersected by a ray, we need to check if it contains any cached *divisions*. We start from the surface level, search down the tree for the patch node that contains the intersection point, until we reach the lowest level. If we find a node with cached *divisions* matching the outgoing direction, an edge is created to link that node to the sound source. A backward edge is also created.

Scene Object Movement: With the ray cache, when a scene object is moved, only a small number of rays may need to be re-traced in typical situations. To do this, we first remove the edge entries of all patches of the moved object. We then test all the remaining edge entries in the cache for intersection with the moved object. If an edge is found intersecting the moved object, it is removed. At the same time, we also test all the edges initiated from each of the observers and sound sources for intersection with the moved object. All the intersected edges would be removed. Finally, we check all the previously constructed reverberation paths starting from all observers to see whether there are broken links. If a broken link is found, we apply ray-tracing from the broken point to re-trace the remaining path.

5 Results and Discussions

To study the performance of the proposed method, we have conducted a number of experiments, all on a single PC with a P4 2.0GHz CPU and 512MB of memory. There are a total of 20 sound sources used.

5.1 Inter-frame Coherence vs. Different Enclosure Volumes

As stated in Section 3.3, the degree of inter-frame coherence depends on how far away the patch is from the observer. To verify this statement, we study the ray cache usage in 3 different environments with a room of different dimensions but of the same architecture. Within each of the environments the observer walks into the room from outdoors, walks around the room and then leaves it.

Figure 5 shows the experimental results. In both the initial and the final frames, there are only a few projected rays that intersect objects in the environment in all three cases. This is because the observer is outdoors during these frames. In the middle frames, where the observer is inside the room, the number of intersected rays increases significantly. This is due to both the intersection of rays with the room interior surfaces, and the generation of reflective rays from these surfaces. If we look at the quantity difference between the two curves in each diagram, i.e., number of projected rays vs. number of rays reused, we can see that in a small room, the proportion of rays reused from the ray cache is smaller than that in a large room. This agrees with our discussion earlier that there is a higher degree of inter-frame coherence if the objects (or room surfaces) are further away.

5.2 Cache Reuse Performance

To study how the ray cache grows in time, we have plotted the number of projected rays and the number of cached edges in the ray cache as a function of the frame number as shown in Figure 6. The memory consumption of the ray cache is proportional to the total number of edges cached. We can see that the size of the ray cache grows sub-linearly with the total number of projected rays, while the memory consumption is continuously growing with the frame number.

We have analyzed the distribution of reused rays, as shown in Figure 7. The test scene is similar to the one used in Section 5.1, where an observer moves from outdoors to inside a room, walks around and then leaves the room. There are a total of 100 frames and we divide them into three groups: the initial frames when the observer is outdoors, the middle frames when the observer is inside the room and the final frames when the observer is again outdoors. The height of each bar in Figure 7 indicates the average number of rays being reused from the cache within a frame

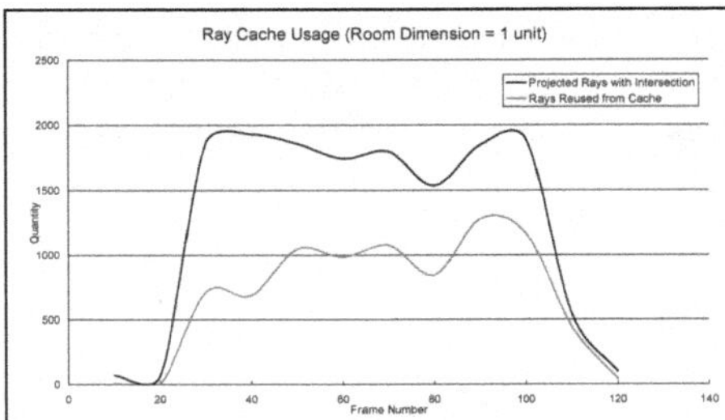

(a) Room dimension = 1 unit.

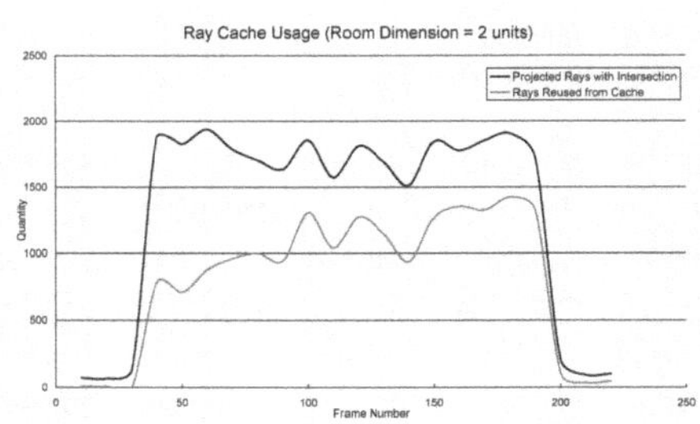

(b) Room dimension = 2 units.

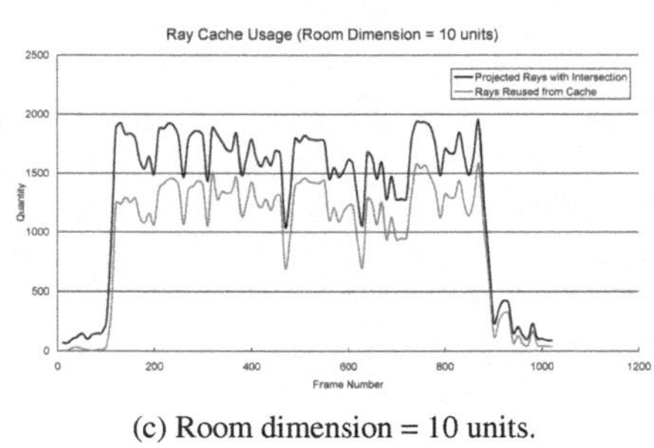

(c) Room dimension = 10 units.

Fig. 5. Ray cache usage

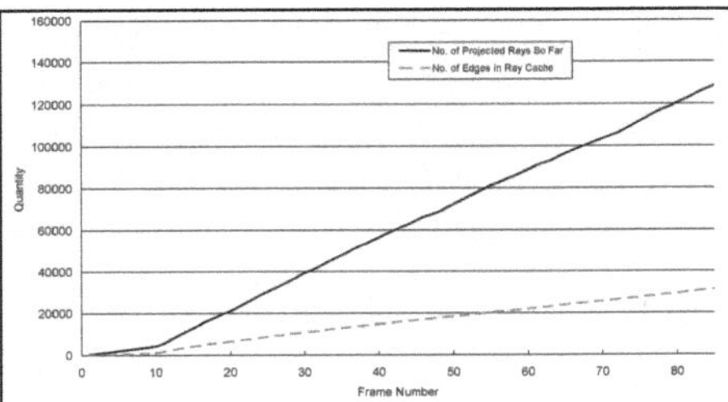

Fig. 6. Growth of the ray cache

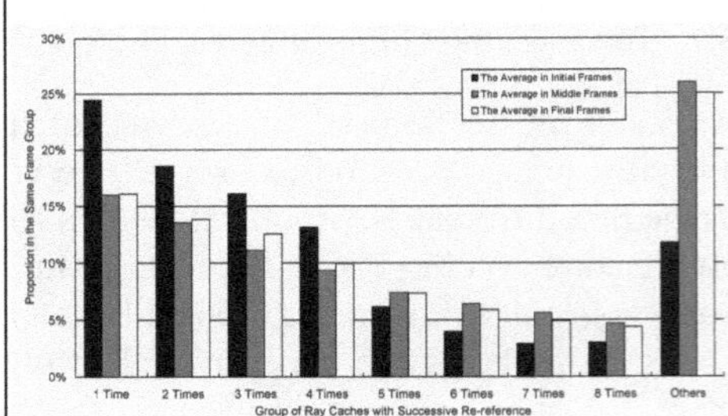

Fig. 7. Amount of reused rays

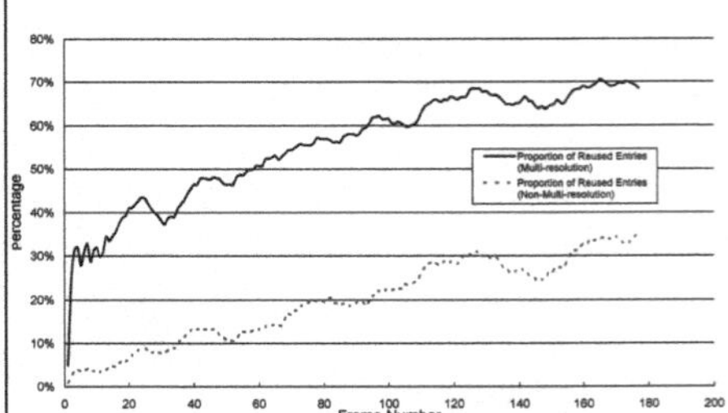

Fig. 8. Percentage of reused rays with/without multi-resolution patch subdivision

group. In general, there are more than 74% of the reused rays that are reused within 8 consecutive frames. This high percentage of reused rays is due to the inter-frame coherence of observer movement. Hence, we may conclude that if we apply the time-stamping approach to purge the cache up to the last 8 frames, we may still be able to keep about 74% of reused rays in the cache.

5.3 Multi-resolution vs. Non-multi-resolution Patches

We presented our spatial approximation technique based on multi-resolution patch subdivision in Section 3.2,. In this experiment, we compare the percentage of reused rays from the ray cache with and without applying the multi-resolution patch subdivision technique. The same test scene and same observer movement (only within the room) are used here. Figure 8 shows the results of the ray cache usage. As the observer is moving inside the room only, the two percentage reuse curves (with and without multi-resolution patch subdivision) are increasing as the frame number. This means that in time, more and more reverberation paths in the ray cache are reused. We can see that with the multi-resolution technique, the percentage of reused rays is much higher, meaning that the technique allows more efficient use of the ray cache.

5.4 Performance in Multi-observer Environments

In this experiment, we would like to study the performance improvement of our method with and without ray caching. We compare the performance by measuring the average time spent on projecting a single ray in a multi-observer environment. A number of observers are set to move inside the same room randomly for a period of 25 frames and the response time of the sound rendering server is recorded. Table 1 shows our experimental results. We can see from the table that in general, the ray caching method could speed up ray-tracing by 38% of the original time when there is only one observer. The speed up increases as the number of observers increases, due to more cached rays being reused among the observers.

Table 1. Ray-tracing time with and without ray cache in a multi-observer environment

No. of observers	Time per ray (Non-cached)	Time per ray (Cached)	Speed-up
1	0.0876 ms.	0.0542 ms.	38%
2	0.0822 ms.	0.0486 ms.	41%
3	0.0806 ms.	0.0455 ms.	44%
4	0.0819 ms.	0.0444 ms.	46%

6 Conclusions and Future Work

Sound rendering for dynamic environments based on the physical approach poses a great challenge due to the high computational cost in computing the reverberation paths. In this work, we have successfully improved the performance of the physically based sound rendering process by exploiting ray coherence. Our method is based on two approximation techniques in caching traced rays for reuse: spatial approximation and angular approximation. Our experimental results show that significant performance improvements are achieved by using the ray cache. The new method is particularly beneficial to multi-user, interactive environments, in which a higher percentage of rays can be reused.

We have attempted to extend our proposed method to a multi-server environment. However, we observe from our experimental results that networking overheads can significantly affect the performance. As a future work, we would like to investigate an efficient scheme to share the cached information. Such a sharing scheme is essential if the ray caching method is to be used in a multi-server environment.

References

[Arvo89]Arvo, J., Kirk, D.: A Survey of Ray Tracing Acceleration Techniques. In: Glassner (ed.) An Introduction to Ray Tracing, Academic Press, London (1989)

[CATT]CATT-Acoustic, CATT, Sweden, http://www.netg.se/ catt/

[Davi99]Davis, T., Davis, E.: Exploiting Frame Coherence with the Temporal Depth Buffer in a Distributed Computing Environment. In: Proc. IEEE Symp. on Parallel visualization and graphic (1999)

[Funk98]Funkhouser, T., Carlbom, I., et al.: A Beam Tracing Approach to Acoustic Modeling for Interactive Virtual Environments. In: Proc. ACM SIGGRAPH, pp. 21–32 (1998)

[Funk99]Funkhouser, T., Min, P., Carlbom, I.: Real-Time Acoustic Modeling for Distributed Virtual Environments. In: Proc. ACM SIGGRAPH, pp. 365–374 (1999)

[Gard98]Gardner, B.: Reverberation Algorithms. In: Applications of Digital Signal Processing to Audio and Acoustics, Kluwer Academic Publishers, Dordrecht (1998)

[Havr03]Havran, V., Bittner, J.: Exploiting Temporal Coherence in Ray Casted Walkthroughs. In: Proc. Spring Conf. on Computer Graphics (2003)

[LTL]Lake Technology Limited, Huron acoustic virtual reality

[Mart01]Martin, W., Parker, S., Reinhard, E., Shirley, P., Thompson, W.: Temporally Coherent Interactive Ray Tracing. Technical Report UUCS-01-005, University of Utah (2001)

[Muel99]Mueller, W., Ullmann, F.: A Scalable System for 3D Audio Raytracing. In: Proc. IEEE ICME (1999)

[Mura90]Murakami, K., Hirota, K.: Incremental Ray Tracing. In: Proc. EG Workshop on Photosimulation, Realism and Physics in Computer Graphics, pp. 15–29 (June 1990)

[Rein02]Reinhard, E.: Parallel Global Illumination Algorithms. Practical Parallel Rendering, AK Peters (2002)

[Sber04]Sbert, M., Lászl6, S., Lászl6, S.: Real-time Light Animation. In: Proc. Eurographics (2004)

[Suth74]Sutherland, I., Sproull, R., Schumacker, R.: A Characterization of Ten Hidden-Surface Algorithms. ACM Computing Surveys 5(1), 1–55 (1974)

[To01]To, D., Lau, R., Green, M.: An Adaptive Multi-Resolution Method for Progressive Model Transmission. Presence 10(1), 62–74 (2001)

[Wald01]Wald, I., Slusallek, P., Benthin, C., Wagner, M.: Interactive Rendering with Coherent Ray Tracing. In: Proc. Eurographics, pp. 153–164 (2001)

Spread-Spectrum Watermark by Synthesizing Texture

Wenyu Liu, Fan Zhang, and Chunxiao Liu

Huazhong University of Science and Technology, Wuhan, 430074, P.R. China
{liuwy, zhangfan}@hust.edu.cn,
liucx@smail.hust.edu.cn

Abstract. Image watermarking is a mapping from watermark message to a set of image counterparts, where every version conveys the same meaning with the original image. Since textures that present single perceptual meaning have certain diversity, an intuitive idea of watermarking is to replace the texture region of an image with a similar-looking synthetic texture containing the watermark. We propose a spread-spectrum watermarking scheme by integrating existent work on texture extraction, segmentation and synthesis, and obtain suggestive results, including (1) the synthetic watermarks can resist adaptive Wiener filtering attack due to its power spectrum similar with the original image; (2) if using the spread-spectrum carrier which is designed elaborately according to the subspace spanned by the textures, hiding capacity can be improved by 20%, while effective hiding capacity under Wiener filtering attack can be doubled; (3) the proposed watermarking scheme also enlighten a sophisticate strategy for watermark attack.

1 Introduction

Watermarking, also called steganography, is to discreetly embed information into media signals without eliciting noticeable distortion. For the applications which do not demand strict media fidelity, such as covert communication or rights management for entertainment media, *unnoticeablity* of distortion is reasonable to be ruled as no changing or confusing the perceptual meaning of the media. In this way, image watermarking is a mapping from watermark message to a set of image counterparts, where every counterpart conveys the same meaning with the original image.

In his tutorial literature on data-hiding codes [1], Moulin suggested an idea of connecting image modeling and image watermarking: *"A sophisticated embedder or attacker could replace a textured portion of an image (say a grass field) with a similar-looking synthetic texture, introducing negligible perceptual degradation."*

To realize the idea, this paper designs a watermarking-by-synthesizing scheme, which integrates existent work of texture extracting, segmenting and synthesizing.

Recent work of Balakrishnan [8] propose a image representation method called Hybrid ICA-Mixture of PPCA Algorithm (HIMPA), which use an independent component analysis (ICA) model for edge representation followed by a mixture of probabilistic principal components analyzers (MPPCA) for surface representation. We use a variant of HIMPA for texture extraction and segmentation.

A number of texture synthetic algorithms [3] create texture by clever resampling from the original texture. Although the results are visually stunning, they do not

H.H.S. Ip et al. (Eds.): PCM 2007, LNCS 4810, pp. 347–356, 2007.

provide an explicit model for texture and their cooperation with watermarking seem unsystematic, e.g., the method in [4], known as texture block coding, which inserts a textured patch into an area of the image with the same appearance. Founded on certain texture model, some texture synthetic algorithms [5] ~ [7] adopt synthesis-by-analysis methodology to create texture by matching statistical feature with the original texture. We model the spread-spectrum watermarking as an optimization problem with a linear object and nonlinear distortion constraints, and use the algorithm in [7] to pursue the watermarked image.

The proposed scheme is introduced in section 2. Experimental results and analysis are presented in section 3. The paper closes with concluding remarks in section 4.

2 Proposed Scheme

Our scheme is shown in Figure 1. Without loss of generality, we embed one bit of message m whose value is either –1 or +1. Generated according to secret key k, $\boldsymbol{p}$ is a pseudorandom sequence with zero mean and unit variance. Modulated by m, the sequence $\boldsymbol{p}$ yields the watermark pattern $m\boldsymbol{p}$. Pseudorandom sequence $\boldsymbol{p}$ plays the role of the spread-spectrum *carrier* for watermark m.

The host image $\boldsymbol{x}$ can be divided into texture part and nontexture part, that is

$$\boldsymbol{x} = \boldsymbol{x}_{\mathrm{T}} + \boldsymbol{x}_{\mathrm{N}} \ . \tag{1}$$

The core of the watermarking scheme is to synthesize a texture part $\boldsymbol{x}_{\mathrm{T}}'$, which has the maximal inner product with $m\boldsymbol{p}$ and meanwhile shares the same texture features with $\boldsymbol{x}_{\mathrm{T}}$, as the description of (2)

$$\boldsymbol{x}_{\mathrm{T}}' = \arg\max < \boldsymbol{x}_{\mathrm{T}}', m\boldsymbol{p} > \tag{2}$$

$$\text{s.t. } \phi_k(\boldsymbol{x}_{\mathrm{T}}') = \phi_k(\boldsymbol{x}_{\mathrm{T}}),\ k = 1 \ldots N_C \tag{3}$$

where $<\boldsymbol{A}, \boldsymbol{B}>$ denotes correlation, i.e., the inner product of sequence $\boldsymbol{A}$ and sequence $\boldsymbol{B}$. Φ_k is a set of feature functions of texture, which establish texture equivalence between $\boldsymbol{x}_{\mathrm{T}}'$ and $\boldsymbol{x}_{\mathrm{T}}$. Given $m\boldsymbol{p}$ and $\boldsymbol{x}_{\mathrm{T}}$, the problem above is an optimal program with linear object (2) and nonlinear constraints (3). After finding the optimal $\boldsymbol{x}_{\mathrm{T}}'$, the watermarked image is generated as

$$\boldsymbol{y} = \boldsymbol{x}_{\mathrm{T}}' + \boldsymbol{x}_{\mathrm{N}} \tag{4}$$

The watermarked image is possibly corrupted by an attacker's noise. We only consider the additive noise, as formula (5)

$$\boldsymbol{z} = \boldsymbol{y} + \boldsymbol{n} \ . \tag{5}$$

The receiver knows the secret key k and can recover the $\boldsymbol{p}$, and then the detection is performed. Firstly, the (normalized) correlation is calculated as

$$r = \frac{<\boldsymbol{z}, \boldsymbol{p}>}{\sigma_z \sigma_p} = \frac{<\boldsymbol{x}_{\mathrm{T}}', \boldsymbol{p}> + <\boldsymbol{x}_{\mathrm{N}}, \boldsymbol{p}> + <\boldsymbol{n}, \boldsymbol{p}>}{\sigma_z}, \tag{6}$$

where σ_z^2 and σ_p^2 is respectively the variance of z and $\boldsymbol{p}$. The two latter terms of numerator in (6) can be neglected due to independency between $\boldsymbol{x}_{\mathrm{N}}$ and $\boldsymbol{p}$ and independency between $\boldsymbol{n}$ and $\boldsymbol{p}$, so the one-bit watermark is estimated by the sign of r in formula (7),

$$\hat{m} = \text{sign}(r) \; . \tag{7}$$

Absolute value of r determines the error probability of detection and thereby the effective rate of watermark. In this paper, we use *averaged normalized correlation* $|r|/L$ to measure the hiding capacity of watermarking scheme, where L is the amount of pixels.

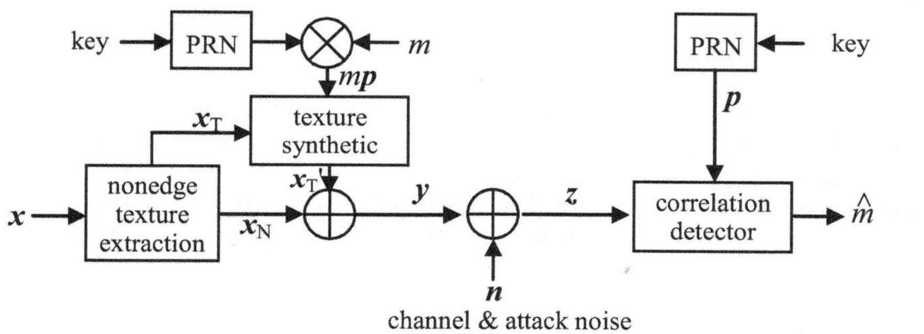

Fig. 1. The proposed watermarking scheme

How should one go about extracting the texture from natural image and synthesizing a watermarked texture? We explain the methods in following sections.

2.1 Texture Extraction

For texture extraction, we propose a three-factor image model. Three factors are assumed to contribute to the appearance of nature image: (*a*) objects' intrinsic luminance and shading effects, (*b*) structural edges, and (*c*) texture. Different from HIMPA model [9], our model isolates low frequency band of image $\boldsymbol{x}_{\mathrm{L}}$ as the factor (*a*), and uses HIMPA model to divide the residual high frequency band $\boldsymbol{x}_{\mathrm{H}}$ into edge region and surface region. The reason for isolating factor (*a*) is that texture clustering will not be affected by local average luminance, and thereby will depend more on local contrast.

According to HIMPA [9], we use independent component analysis (ICA) to extract texture from the high frequency band of image. An image patch $\boldsymbol{x}_{\mathrm{H}}$ is represented as a linear superposition of columns of the mixing matrix $\boldsymbol{A}$ and a residue noise which can be neglected.

$$\boldsymbol{x}_{\mathrm{H}} = \boldsymbol{A}\boldsymbol{s} \; . \tag{8}$$

The columns of $\boldsymbol{A}$ are learned from nature images by making the components of the vector $\boldsymbol{s}$ statistically independent. In the learning algorithm, $\boldsymbol{A}$ is constrained to be an orthogonal transformation. So the vector $\boldsymbol{s}$ is calculated by

$$s = A^T x_H \ . \tag{9}$$

The elements of s with large magnitudes signify the presence of structure in an image block, corresponding to edges, oriented curves, etc. The elements of s with smaller magnitudes represent the summation of a number of weak edges to yield texture. For each image block, we divide A into two groups, A_E and A_T, keeping all the absolute values of s corresponding to columns of A_E are larger than A_T. The image block is also decomposed into two subcomponents.

$$x_H = x_E + x_T \ . \tag{10}$$

where

$$x_E = A_E (A_E{}^T A_E)^{-1} A_E^T x_H \ . \tag{11}$$

The ratio between the column amounts of A_T and A is determined by ICA threshold. For example, if ICA threshold is 0.2, A_E has 128 columns while A_T has 32 columns. Because of ratio control, texture is the residual after removing the relatively dominant edge instead of the absolutely sharp edge in HIMPA [9], and much intenser texture will be extracted from the rough region than the smooth region. Fig. 2 illustrates the process of texture extraction.

2.2 Texture Segmentation

Suggested by [9], MPPCA is able to model complex textures in a real image scene due to texture clustering. The textures can be assumed to sample from a limited number of clusters. Each cluster is assumed homogenous, where a texture block from cluster k is generated using the linear model

$$x_k = W_k s_k + \mu_k + \varepsilon_k, \quad k = 1, \ldots, K \ . \tag{12}$$

where $s_k \in \mathbf{R}^q$ is a column vector elongated from the host image block and has a dimension of a, $s_k \in \mathbf{R}^q$ is the lower dimensional subspace assumed to be Gaussian distributed with zero mean and identity covariance. Note that, in this section, image block always refers to the texture block. The dimension of s_k is q and $a > q$. W_k is a mixing matrix of a by q. μ_k is the cluster observation mean, ε_k is Gaussian white isotropic noise with zero mean, i. e. $\varepsilon_k \sim \mathrm{N}(0, \sigma^2\mathbf{I})$.

W_k, s_k, μ_k, and ε_k are hidden variables that can be estimated from the data of observed texture. Meanwhile, posterior probability of membership $R(x \mid k)$ can also be calculated, which measures how likely a block x belongs to cluster k and conforms to the condition $\sum_k R(x \mid k) = 1$. Right middle of Figure 2 shows the posterior probability of three clusters using a trinary image.

2.3 Texture Synthesis

Given a set of feature functions $\{\Phi_k\}$, and their corresponding values $\Phi_k(x_T)$, the problem of synthesizing watermarked texture becomes one of looking for image x_T', which has the maximal projection across watermark, from the associated texture

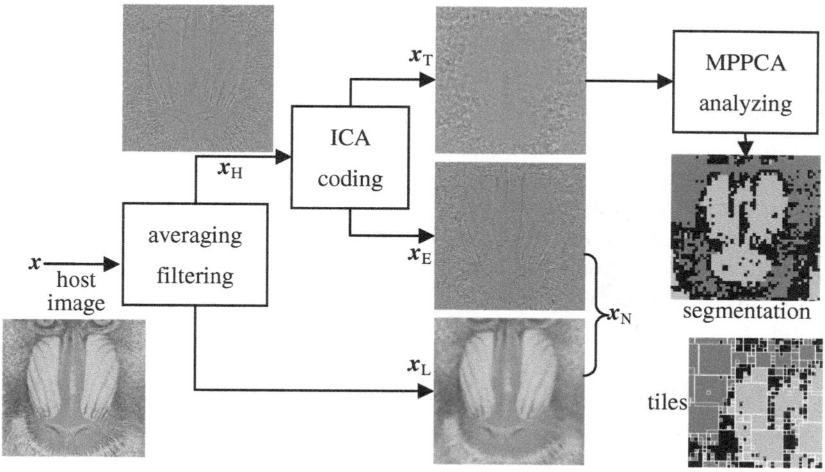

Fig. 2. Three-factor model for nonedge extraction and features learned by MPPCA

ensemble $S_\Phi = \{\boldsymbol{x} : \Phi_k(\boldsymbol{x}) = \Phi_k(\boldsymbol{x}_\mathrm{T}), \ \forall k\}$. The complexity of the feature functions $\{\Phi_k\}$ in a realistic model of a texture makes it difficult to find the solution directly. We consider an iterative solution, in which the texture to be synthesized is initialized as the carrier ***mp*** (a random noise) and the constraints are imposed on the texture sequentially, rather than simultaneously. According to [7], we repeatedly utilize

$$\boldsymbol{x}_{t+1} = \boldsymbol{x}_t + \sum_k \lambda_k \nabla \Phi_k(\boldsymbol{x}_t) \tag{13}$$

to make the texture's features approach $\Phi_k(\boldsymbol{x}_\mathrm{T})$, where ∇ is gradient operator, and λ_k is a scalar solved to satisfy or come to closest to satisfying $\Phi_k(\boldsymbol{x}_{t+1}) = \Phi_k(\boldsymbol{x}_\mathrm{T})$. And we also repeatedly use

$$\boldsymbol{x}_{t+1} = \boldsymbol{x}_t + \varepsilon \boldsymbol{mp} \tag{14}$$

To Whom It May Concern: drive $\boldsymbol{x}_{t+1}$ has a larger projection across ***mp***. ε goes to 0 as the iteration goes to the end. A rigorous theory for the algorithm convergence has yet to be found, nevertheless, the algorithm has not failed to get close to convergence for many examples tested.

We use parts of the feature functions Φ_k proposed in [7], which first decomposes the image by steerable pyramid transform [7,15] and then defines the features on the statistics of the transform coefficients and the statistics of pixel values.

The statistical operators which we selected from literature [7] include

- S_1 coarse marginal statistics. Variance, minimum and maximum of image pixels.
- S_2 fine marginal statistics. Skewness and kurtosis of image pixels and low-pass bands at each scale, and variance of the high-pass band.
- S_3 raw coefficient correlation. Auto-correlation of the low-pass bands. These characterize the salient spatial frequencies and the regularity of the structures.

- S_4 coefficient magnitude statistics. Auto-correlation of magnitude of each subband, cross-correlation of each subband magnitudes with those of other orientations at the same scale, and cross-correlation of subband magnitudes with all orientations at a coarser scale. These represent edges, bars, corners, etc.

Textures having been segmented in Section 2.2 always have irregular shape, so we use a few of rectangle tiles with size of $2^m \times 2^m$ (m = 3, 4, 5, 6) to make up the texture shape, followed by synthesizing every regular tile instead of the whole irregular texture. A greedy algorithm is used to fill irregular shape with the tiles as large as possible, so that the amount of tiles is close to minimal. (Right bottom of Figure 2 shows the tiles). During synthesis of the larger tile, we use more constraint parameters and iterate synthesis by more steps as shown in Table 1.

Table 1. Feature parameters and algorithm parameter for different tile size

tile size 2^m	transform parameters		statistical operators				iteration steps
	scale	orientation	S_1	S_2	S_3	S_4	
64	3	4	√	√	√	√	50
32	2	4	√	√	√	×	25
16	1	4	√	√	×	×	10
8	1	4	√	×	×	×	1

3 Experimental Results and Analysis

ICA mixing matrix is estimated using samples from a training set of 13 natural images downloaded with the FastICA package [12]. Note that ICA mixing matrix is independent with host images and need not be held by watermark detector.

At the watermark encoder, after 8x8 averaging filtering, texture is extracted by ICA coding, and then, partitioned into 8x8 blocks, vectorized into 64x1 vectors, and fed to MPPCA for clustering. Texture is classified into three clusters with 4 principal components in each cluster, where each cluster is divided into regular tiles and synthesized tile by tile. Finally, watermarked image is generated by summarizing the synthetic texture, the edge part and the low-pass band. The program code was developed based on NETLAB Matlab package [11] and Texture Analysis/Synthesis Matlab package [8].

At the watermark decoder, only correlation detection is enough to extract the watermark message.

3.1 Watermarked Image

We test our scheme on typical images in Figure 3. Our scheme has followed advantages. Firstly, it does not incite watermark intensity at sharp edges due to the three-factor image coding before watermarking. Secondly, it prefers to embed watermark into rough region rather than smooth region because texture segmentation and texture synthesis keep texture features. The characters are clearly exhibited on the

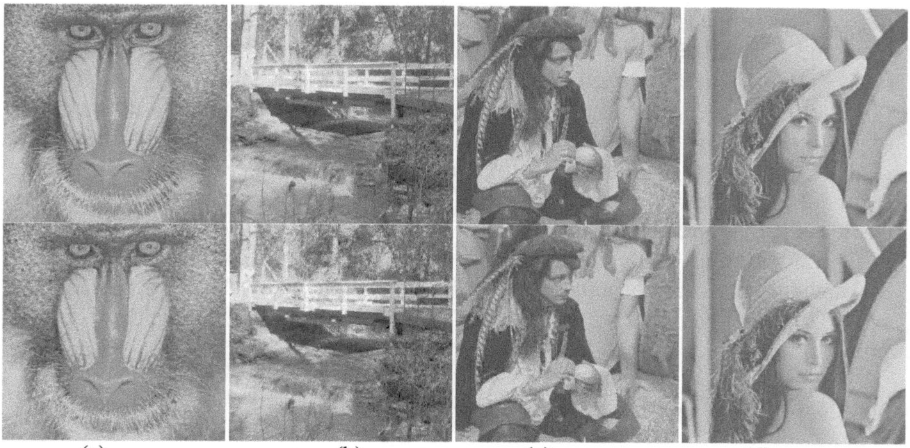

(a) (b) (c) (d)

Fig. 3. Original images (top) and watermarked images (bottom). (a) *Baboon*. $|r|$=0.254, SNR=17.4dB. (b) *Bridge* $|r|$=0.150, SNR=18.2dB. (c) *Man* $|r|$=0.103, SNR=21.9dB. (d) *Lena* $|r|$=0.074, SNR=27.1dB.

(a) (b) (c)

Fig. 4. Synthetic watermark. (a) original texture $\boldsymbol{x}_T$. (b) synthetic texture $\boldsymbol{x}_T'$. (c) watermark signal $\boldsymbol{x}_T' - \boldsymbol{x}_T$. White is positive signal and black is negative signal.

watermark signal in Figure 4. However, because our scheme exploits texture region, its advantages disappear in images with sparse texture, e.g. image *Lena*.

3.2 Carrier Pruning Based on Prior Information

Spread-spectrum watermark detection utilizes the projection of watermarked image on the carrier. Larger is the projection, higher hiding capacity can be achieved. Since watermarked images always locate in the subspace spanned by the similar-looking image counterparts, if the designed carrier approaches the said subspace, it has more possibility to generate a large projection on the watermarked image. Here, we give an example of carrier pruning, by which hiding capacity is proved to be improved in the experiments of section 4.3 (to see Figure 5).

The proposed method of carrier pruning exploits the homogenous feature of texture, that is, different blocks within a texture look similar. In another word, block permutation alert texture appearance little. So we generate the carrier by means of 8×8 block permutations within each cluster of x_T, and the permutation is controlled by a key. The pruned carrier still keeps uncorrelated with original image due to their averaged normalized correlation of about 10^{-4}, while the texture can be synthesized fairly *similar* with the pruned carrier (modulated by watermark).

Given the x_T in a 512×512 image, the amount of possible carrier is about $(512^2/(3\times8^2))!^3\approx10^{11068}$, where texture block permutation is controlled within each one of three clusters. Although a monotone image or an awful permutation algorithm may reduce the uncertainty of carrier, the cryptographic attack of brute-force searching the carrier is still a burdensome work.

Carrier pruning here implies the watermarking scheme is not blind one, because the detector need x_T during detection. However, one may design a more elaborate scheme, where only concise prior information and special side information are used to prune the carrier.

3.3 Robustness Against Wiener Filtering Attack

Sophisticate attackers can make estimation-based attack if they can obtain some prior knowledge of host image or watermark's statistics [13]. Image denoising provides a natural way to develop estimation-based attacks, where watermark is treated as a noise. Given the power spectrum of host image and watermark, one of the most malevolent attacks is the denoising by adaptive Wiener filter. So the most robust watermark should have a power spectrum directly proportional to the power spectrum of the host image [13]. We compare the power spectrum of watermark under different schemes in Figure 5. We have found that spread-spectrum watermark under spatial JND (just-noticeable-distortion) mask has a white power spectrum (Figure 5d) and watermark under wavelet JND mask concentrate its power in the middle frequency (Figure 5e) in the former literature [14]. However, synthetic watermark (Figure 5b and 5c) by our scheme has more similar power spectrum with the original image (Figure 5a), especially the watermark modulating the pruned carrier (Figure 5c).

(a) (b) (c) (d) (e)

Fig. 5. Power spectrum by Fourier analysis. (a) host image *Baboon*. (b) synthetic watermark from Gaussian carrier. (c) synthetic watermark from pruned carrier. (d) spatial watermark modulating binomial carrier. (e) wavelet watermark modulating Gaussian carrier. Signal is normalized to 0 mean and unit variance before Fourier analysis. The grey level denotes logarithmic amplitude of Fourier components. Zero-frequency component is shifted to the center.

We compare our scheme with spatial JND scheme in robustness against Wiener filtering attack. The comparison is made in different situations of using common carrier and pruned carrier, and using 3×3 Wiener filter and 5×5 one. Robustness can be measured by the survival rate of correlation $|r|$. From the results in Figure 6, we can draw following conclusions. 1. Survival rate of correlation in our scheme is larger than spatial JND scheme by 30%~40%, so our scheme is more robust. 2. Robustness can be improved by using pruned carrier for either our scheme or spatial JND scheme. 3. Hiding capacity of our scheme can be improved by 10%~25% under no attack, and by 100%~200% under Wiener filtering attack if pruned carrier is used. However, pruned carrier is no helpful for spatial JND scheme under no attack.

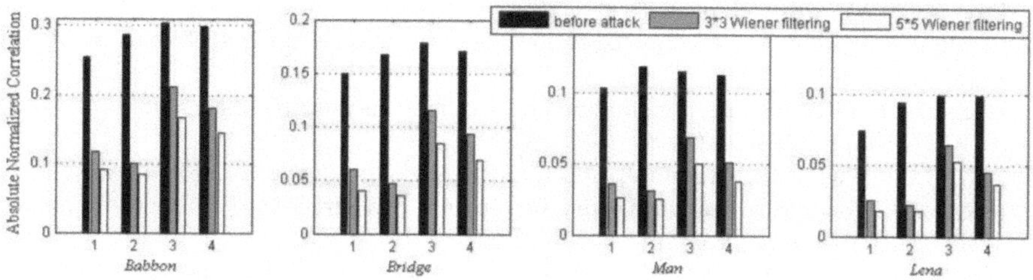

Fig. 6. Wiener attack' effect on hiding capacity under different scheme. 1 synthetic scheme using Gaussian carrier, 2 spatial JND scheme using binomial carrier, 3 synthetic scheme using pruned carrier, 4 spatial JND scheme using pruned carrier.

4 Conclusion

We have formulated the spread-spectrum watermarking as an optimization problem with a linear object and nonlinear distortion constraints, and presented a watermarking-by-synthesizing solution. Several properties of the scheme are noteworthy. First, pursuing the watermarked signal by optimization algorithm can obtain the suboptimal, if not optimal, solution with highest hiding capacity. Second, texture segmentation facilitates estimation of the *narrow* subspace where homogenous textures focalized, and is helpful to prune the carrier so as to improve hiding capacity. Last, synthetic watermarked image has a similar power spectrum with original image and thus robustness against adaptive filtering attack.

Moreover, the scheme enlightens a method of watermark attack. Under attacking-by-synthesizing, the SNR of attacked image can be fairly low, so that many traditional watermarks are hard to survive.

Property of the scheme also follows common heuristics: intensity change of low frequency band or edges in an image is easy to be noticed therefore is not suitable to utilized by watermarking scheme. Therefore, we believe it is necessary of discrimination on low frequency band, structural edges and texture for image watermarking. Watermark in structures has yet to be designed conforming to distortion measure of shape and skeleton.

Acknowledgement. This work is supported by NSFC (NO: 60572063), Doctoral Fund of Ministry of Education of China (NO: 20040487009), and the Cultivation Fund of the Key Scientific and Technical Innovation Project, Ministry of Education of China (NO: 705038).

References

1. Moulin, P., Koetter, R.: Data-hiding codes. In: Proc. of the IEEE, vol. 93, pp. 2083–2126 (December 2005)
2. Cox, I.J., Kilian, J., Leighton, F.T., Shamoon, T.: Secure spread spectrum watermarking for multimedia. IEEE Trans. Image Proc. 6, 1673–1687 (1997)
3. Wei, L.Y., Levoy, M.: Fast texture synthesis using tree-structured vector quantization. In: Proc. ACM SIGGRAPH, pp. 479–488 (2000)
4. Bender, W., Gruhl, D., Morimoto, N., Lu, A.: Techniques for data hiding. IBM Syst. J. 35(3/4), 313–336 (1996)
5. Heeger, D., Bergen, J.: Pyramid-based texture analysis/synthesis. In: Proc. ACM SIGGRAPH, pp. 229–238 (1995)
6. Zhu, S.C., Wu, Y.N., Mumford, D.B.: Filter, Random fields, and Maximum Entropy (FRAME) -Towards a Unified Theory for Texture Modeling. Int'l Journal of Computer Vision 27, 107–126 (1998)
7. Portilla, J., Simoncelli, E.P.: A parametric texture model based on joint statistics of complex wavelet coefficients. Int'l Journal of Computer Vision 40, 49–71 (2000)
8. Portilla, J., Simoncelli, E.: Texture Synthesis (April 2001), http://www.cns.nyu.edu/ lcv/texture/
9. Balakrishnan, N., Hariharakrishnan, K., Schonfeld, D.: A new image representation algorithm inspired by image submodality models, redundancy reduction, and learning in biological vision. IEEE Trans. Pattern Analysis & Machine Intelligence 27, 1367–1378 (2005)
10. Tipping, M., Bishop, C.: Mixtures of Probabilistic Principal Component Analyzers. Neural Computation 11(2), 443–482 (1999)
11. Nabney, I., Bishop, C.: Netlab Neural Network Software (2003), http://www.ncrg.aston.ac.uk/netlab
12. Hyrarinen, A.: Fast ICA Matlab package (April 2003), http://www.cis.hut.fi/projects/ica
13. Voloshynovskiy, S., Pereira, S., Pun, T., et al.: Attacks on Digital Watermarks: Classification, Estimation-Based Attacks, and Benchmarks. IEEE Communications Magazine 39, 118–126 (2001)
14. Zhang, F., Liu, W.Y., Liu, C.X.: High capacity watermarking in nonedge texture under statistical distortion constraint. In: Asian Conf on Computer Vision, LNCS 4843, pp. 282-291, 2007
15. Simoncelli, E.P., Freeman, W.T.: The Steerable Pyramid: A Flexible Architecture for Multi-Scale Derivative Computation. In: IEEE Int'l Conf on Image Processing, pp. 444–447 (October 1995)

Design of Secure Watermarking Scheme for Watermarking Protocol

Bin Zhao[1], Lanjun Dang[1], Weidong Kou[1], Jun Zhang[2], and Xuefei Cao[1]

[1] The State Key Laboratory of ISN, Xidian University, Xi'an, 710071, China
{binzhao, ljdang, wdkou, xfcao}@mail.xidian.edu.cn
[2] School of CSSE, University of Wollongong, Wollongong, NSW 2522, Australia
jz484@uow.edu.au

Abstract. Watermarking technique enables to hide an imperceptible watermark into a multimedia content for copyright protection. However, in most conventional watermarking schemes, the watermark is embedded solely by the seller, and both the seller and the buyer know the watermarked copy, which causes unsettled dispute at the phase of arbitration. To solve this problem, many watermarking protocols have been proposed using watermarking scheme in the encrypted domain. In this paper, we firstly discuss many security aspects in the encrypted domain, and then propose a new method of homomorphism conversion for probabilistic public key cryptosystem with homomorphic property. Based on our previous work, a new secure watermarking scheme for watermarking protocol is presented using a new embedding strategy in the encrypted domain. We employ an El Gamal variant cryptosystem with additive homomorphic property to reduce the computing overload of watermark embedding in the encrypted domain, and RA code to improve the robustness of the watermarked image against many moderate attacks after decryption. Security analysis and experiment demonstrate that the secure watermarking scheme is more suitable for implementing the existing watermarking protocols.

1 Introduction

With rapid development of information technology, most multimedia contents have become available in digital form, which makes it possible to reproduce perfect copies of digital image, video, and other multimedia contents. The increasing concern about copyright protection is due to the fact that a large number of digital multimedia contents have been illegal distributed at the cost of a huge amount of valid profit. A promising technique for copyright protection is digital watermarking that enables to hide an imperceptible watermark into a multimedia content while preserving quality. In most conventional watermarking schemes, the watermark is embedded solely by the seller in behalf of intellectual property, and then the seller send the watermarked copy to the buyer. Since both the seller and the buyer know the watermarked copy, it causes unsettled dispute at the phase of arbitration. Thus, the watermark could not be considered as legally sufficient evidence for accusing copyright violation.

It is significant in the sense that the watermarking framework needs protocols to solve both the resolution of the rightful ownership problem and the protection of the

H.H.S. Ip et al. (Eds.): PCM 2007, LNCS 4810, pp. 357–366, 2007.

customer's right problem, which is first introduced by L. Qiao and K. Nahrstedt [1]. An effective buyer-seller watermarking protocol is expected to mostly satisfy the following important requirements.

1. No Repudiation (Seller's Security): A guilty buyer producing unauthorized copies should not repudiate the fact and not able to claim that the copies were possibly made by the seller.
2. No Framing (Buyer's Security): An honest buyer should not be falsely accused for reparation by a malicious seller who can reuse the embedded watermark to frame.
3. Traceability: A guilty buyer (traitor / copyright violator) who has illegally distributed digital contents can be traced.
4. Anonymity: A buyer should be able to purchase digital contents anonymously.

For these reasons, many watermarking protocols have been proposed based on the watermarking scheme in the encrypted domain. In such a condition, the seller can not produce copies containing the watermark identifying the buyer, because he can not know the exact watermark from the ciphertext in the embedding procedure. When an illegal copy is found, the seller can prove to a third party that the buyer is certainly guilty. N. Memon and P. W. Wong [2] presented a buyer-seller watermarking protocol to resolve both the pirate tracing problem and the buyer's right problem. Successively, Chin-Laung Lei *et al.* [3] pointed out the unbinding problem and proposed an efficient and anonymous buyer-seller watermarking protocol. Recently, J. Zhang *et al.* [4] proposed a secure buyer-seller watermarking protocol based on the idea of sharing a secret. Additionally, M. Kuribayashi and H. Tanaka [5] presented an anonymous fingerprinting protocol and a quantization-based scheme for embedding encrypted watermark bits by additive homomorphic property.

We aim to promote watermarking schemes and watermarking protocols into real-world application. In this paper, we take many security aspects into consideration and propose a new secure watermarking scheme for watermarking protocol based on our previous work. Our contributions to the secure watermarking scheme involve many facets. (1) A new method of homomorphism conversion between multiplicative and additive are proposed for probabilistic public key cryptosystem with homomorphic property. (2) A new embedding strategy in the encrypted domain is presented to simplify embedding steps and provides another secret key. (3) An El Gamal variant cryptosystem with additive homomorphic property is employed to reduce the computing overload of watermark embedding in the encrypted domain. (4) RA code is used to deal with the synchronization issue and bit errors, and it also improves the robustness of the watermarked image against many moderate attacks after decryption.

2 Security Aspects in the Encrypted Domain

2.1 Probabilistic Public Key Cryptosystem with Homomorphic Property

The conventional public key cryptosystem has been considered as functions $E(\bullet)$ in such a way that the message M presumably cannot be computed from the encryption $E(M)$. However, even if the adversary cannot identify M exactly, he may be able to obtain some partial information about M, for example tell whether M is an even number or odd, etc. An extreme case of this problem exist in watermarking schemes in the encrypted domain, because the watermark represented by 0 and 1 is encrypted bit by bit separately, and the adversary knows each encrypted bit is one of two possibilities, 0 or 1. Since the same public key is employed to encrypt each watermark bit, what the adversary needs to do is compare $E(0)$ and $E(1)$ with each ciphertext $E(M)$. Hence, he can know the entire watermark bits by this means, which causes both framing issue and repudiation issue as mentioned before. Therefore, deterministic public key cryptosystems could not be used in the watermarking protocols, for example, the plain RSA cryptosystem [6].

Probabilistic public key cryptosystem, first introduced by Shafi Goldwasser and Silvio Micali [7], could be employed to solve this problem. Instead of $E(M)$ being a single determinate ciphertext, the same message M has many different ciphertexts at different time, and the ciphertexts of different messages is indistinguishable, because $E(M)$ involves a random number r during encryption.

A public key cryptosystem used in watermarking protocols should have homomorphic property, either additive or multiplicative homomorphism, which means multiplying two ciphertexts $E(x,r_1)$ and $E(y,r_2)$ leads to addition or multiplication of two plaintexts x and y after decryption.

$$D(E(x,r_1)\ E(y,r_2)) = D(E(x+y,r')) = x+y \mod n \tag{1}$$

$$D(E(x,r_1)\ E(y,r_2)) = D(E(x\ y,r')) = x\ y \mod n \tag{2}$$

It is known that El Gamal cryptosystem [8], Paillier cryptosystem [9] and Okamoto-Uchiyama cryptosystem [10] are probabilistic with homomorphic property. El Gamal cryptosystem is multiplicative homomorphism, while Paillier cryptosystem and Okamoto-Uchiyama cryptosystem are additive homomorphism.

2.2 New Method of Homomorphism Conversion and El Gamal Variant Cryptosystem

In many watermarking protocols, watermark embedding relies significantly on the public key cryptosystem with additive homomorphic property. In some scenarios, the constraint on the type of cryptosystem limits the flexibility of watermarking protocol. For instance, El Gamal cryptosystem, a well-known public key cryptosystem with multiplicative homomorphism, appears unsuitable for the watermarking protocol based on the additive homomorphic property in [5]. As for practical applications, it is necessary to provide more types of public key cryptosystem for watermarking schemes in the encrypted domain.

Fortunately, a simple exponential-logarithmic method can mutually convert homomorphism between multiplicative and additive. homomorphism conversion from multiplicative to additive could be achieved by means of replacing x by an exponential operation based on g.

$$\begin{aligned} D(E(g^x,r_1)\ E(g^y,r_2)) &= D(E(g^x\ g^y,r')) \\ &= D(E(g^{x+y},r')) \\ &= g^{x+y} \mod n \end{aligned} \tag{3}$$

The inverse conversion from additive to multiplicative could be achieved by means of replacing x by a logarithmic operation based on g.

$$\begin{aligned} D(E(\log_g x, r_1)\ E(\log_g y, r_2)) &= D(E(\log_g x + \log_g y, r')) \\ &= D(E(\log_g (x\ y), r')) \\ &= \log_g (x\ y) \quad \bmod n \end{aligned} \tag{4}$$

Essentially, a variant of original El Gamal cryptosystem has the same additive homomorphic property. Let n be a secure large prime number and g be a generator of $\mathbf{Z}_n^*$. A public key y is defined by $y = g^x$ mod n where $x \in \mathbf{Z}_{n-1}$ is a private key.

[Encryption] Let g^m be a plaintext to be encrypted, where $0 \le g^m \le$ (n-1), and r be a random number chosen from $\mathbf{Z}_{n-1}$.

$$E(m,r) = (B;C) \quad \text{where } B = g^m\ y^r \bmod n \text{ and } C = g^r \bmod n \tag{5}$$

[Decryption] Extract the two parts c and d from the ciphertext, the decrypted plaintext is:

$$D(E(m,r)) = B\ C^{-x} = g^m\ y^r\ g^{-x\ r} = g^m\ g^{x\ r}\ g^{-x\ r} = g^m \quad \bmod n \tag{6}$$

Then compute the original message m from a logarithmic operation without modular arithmetic.

$$m = \log_g (g^m) \tag{7}$$

The El Gamal variant cryptosystem is as secure as the original El Gamal cryptosystem [8] based on the difficulty of the discreet logarithm problem in finite fields, which is too difficult to solve. This variant cryptosystem is of ideal semantic security, because the plaintext m is just replaced by a power of g in a cyclic group [11]. The additive homomorphic property of this variant cryptosystem can be represented as following.

$$\begin{aligned} D(E(x, r_1)\ E(y, r_2)) &= D((B;C)\ (F;G)) \\ &= D((B\ F; C\ G)) \\ &= D(E(x+y, r_1+r_2)) \\ &= x+y \quad \bmod n \end{aligned} \tag{8}$$

3 Secure Watermarking Scheme for Watermarking Protocol

In the watermarking protocols [2]-[5], for the sake of no repudiation and no framing, watermark bits should be encrypted by the buyer's public key unexposed to the seller. As watermark embedder, the seller usually has the original image and the encrypted watermark bits. Using the watermarking scheme in the encrypted domain, the seller can embed the encrypted watermark bits into the encrypted host image, and then he sends the encrypted watermarked image to the buyer.

This work is a further extension of our previous research [12], which enhances the original SEC scheme in [13] and then applies the enhanced scheme in the encrypted domain using the embedding method proposed in [5]. Here, we propose a new embedding strategy to embed encrypted watermark bits into encrypted selected coefficients, and apply it to our previous work. Compared with the embedding method in [5], the new embedding strategy in the encrypted domain simplifies embedding steps and provides the odd-even information of cutoff result as another secret key. In this section, we briefly summarize a new secure watermarking scheme for watermarking protocol, and the detailed steps can be referred to [12].

3.1 Watermark Embedding

In watermark embedding procedure, the seller should save many parameters as a set of secret keys, such as a positive integer threshold t for the threshold criterion, the value of designated QF, the number N of candidate coefficients per block in a fixed low frequency band ($1 \le k \le N$), a random permutation $P(\,)$, and the odd-even information *INFO* of cutoff result.

After 8x8 block partition, DCT, division by the quantization table at designated QF and zig-zag scanning, in a fixed low frequency band ($1 \le k \le N$), the quantized coefficient c_k whose magnitude lies between threshold t and $(t+1)$ are rounded to the nearest integer as a preprocessing.

$$c_k = \begin{cases} \pm t, & \text{if } t < |c_k| < (t+\frac{1}{2}), \text{ and } 1 \le k \le N, \\ \pm(t+1), & \text{if } (t+\frac{1}{2}) \le |c_k| < (t+1), \text{ and } 1 \le k \le N, \\ c_k, & \text{otherwise.} \end{cases} \tag{9}$$

The new embedding strategy is employed in the following steps. The quantized coefficients c_k in a fixed low frequency band ($1 \le k \le N$) whose magnitude $|c_k|$ is greater than threshold t as the threshold criterion are selected and cutoff to the nearest integer $\overline{c_k}$ whose magnitude is less than c_k. The odd-even information *INFO* of cutoff result $\overline{c_k}$ is saved for watermark extracting.

$$\overline{c_k} = \text{int}_{cutoff}(c_k), \quad \text{for } |c_k| > t, \text{ and } 1 \le k \le N. \tag{10}$$

All the selected coefficients $\overline{c_k}$ are inverse zig-zag scanned to obtain $\overline{c_{ij}}$ and then every $\overline{c_{ij}}$ is encrypted with the buyer's public key and a random number b_n to calculate the encrypted coefficient $E(\overline{c_{ij}}, b_n)$. Note that each embedding position is represented by subindex ij in that block.

In the embedding positions, the encrypted watermarked coefficients $E(\overline{d'_{ij}}, r')$ can be calculated by multiplying two ciphertexts $E(\overline{c_{ij}}, b_n)$ and $E(w_p, a_m)$.

$$\begin{aligned} E(\overline{d'_{ij}}, r') &= (E(\overline{c_{ij}}, b_n)\ E(w_p, a_m))^{M_{ij}^{QF}} \\ &= (E(\overline{c_{ij}} + w_p, b_n + a_m))^{M_{ij}^{QF}} \\ &= E((\overline{c_{ij}} + w_p)\ M_{ij}^{QF}, (b_n + a_m)\ M_{ij}^{QF}) \end{aligned} \tag{11}$$

In the other positions, the unwatermarked coefficients are rounded to the nearest integer by the following operations.

$$\overline{d_{ij}} = \begin{cases} \mathrm{int}_{near}(c_{ij}), & \text{for } 0 \le |c_k| < t, \text{ and } 1 \le k \le \mathrm{N}, \\ \pm t\ M_{ij}^{QF}, & \text{for } |c_k| = t, \text{ and } 1 \le k \le \mathrm{N}, \\ \mathrm{int}_{near}(c_{ij}), & \text{for } \forall |c_k|, \text{ and } k = 0 \cup \mathrm{N} < k \le 63. \end{cases} \tag{12}$$

Then, each $\overline{d_{ij}}$ is encrypted with the same public key as encrypted watermark and a random number *r* to obtain ciphertext $E(\overline{d_{ij}}, r)$. After block-by-block processing, seller obtains all the encrypted DCT coefficients of the watermarked image, and then he sends them to buyer. Finally, buyer obtains the watermarked image by decrypting all the DCT coefficients and employing IDCT to gain his image in plaintext.

3.2 Watermark Extracting

In watermark extracting procedure, watermark extractor uses the same threshold criterion and secret keys as the watermark embedder to extract the watermark bits.

After 8×8 block partition, DCT, division by the quantization table at designated QF and zig-zag scanning, in a fixed low frequency band ($1 \le k \le \mathrm{N}$), all the quantized DCT coefficients are rounded to the nearest integer. The quantized DCT coefficient integers $\overline{d_k}$ whose magnitude is greater than the threshold *t* as the same threshold criterion are considered as embedding a watermark bit. Hence, every watermark bit w_p can be readily extracted using the following judgments.

If *INFO* is odd, then

$$w_p = \begin{cases} 0, & \text{if } \overline{d_k} \text{ is odd}, \quad |\overline{d_k}| > t, \text{ and } 1 \le k \le \mathrm{N}, \\ 1, & \text{if } \overline{d_k} \text{ is even}, \quad |\overline{d_k}| > t, \text{ and } 1 \le k \le \mathrm{N}. \end{cases} \tag{13}$$

Else *INFO* is even, then

$$w_p = \begin{cases} 1, & \text{if } \overline{d_k} \text{ is odd}, \quad |\overline{d_k}| > t, \text{ and } 1 \le k \le \mathrm{N}, \\ 0, & \text{if } \overline{d_k} \text{ is even}, \quad |\overline{d_k}| > t, \text{ and } 1 \le k \le \mathrm{N}. \end{cases} \tag{14}$$

4 Security Analysis

For the El Gamal variant cryptosystem, the security certification relays sufficiently on the following testimonies. (1)The El Gamal variant cryptosystem is based on the difficulty of the discreet logarithm problem in finite fields. (2) The El Gamal variant cryptosystem is of semantic security. (3) The El Gamal variant cryptosystem is probabilistic cryptosystem with additive homomorphic property.

For both seller's security and buyer's security, firstly, because the watermark is embedded in the encrypted domain, the seller can not know the exact watermark from the ciphertext. In addition, only the buyer can obtain the watermarked image, since the watermarked image is encrypted by the buyer's public key and no one knows the private key to decrypt it. On the one hand, the seller can not reproduce the watermarked image, and a guilty buyer making unauthorized copies could not repudiate the fact. On the other hand, the seller can not obtain the embedded watermarked, and an honest buyer can not be framed by a malicious seller.

For traceability, if the buyer never redistributes an unauthorized copy to the market, he is innocent and the watermark is concealed. If the buyer's watermark is found in an illegal copy, the seller can trace the buyer's identity and prove that the buyer is certainly guilty using watermark as legally sufficient evidence.

For anonymity, it is supplied by watermarking protocol, not by watermarking scheme in the encrypted domain.

5 Experimental Results

All the tests were performed on the 256×256 grayscale image "Lena", the same test image reported in [5]. The enciphering rate of both El Gamal variant cryptosystem and Paillier cryptosystem is 1/2, which is higher than that of Okamoto-Uchiyama cryptosystem 1/3. For the sake of less ciphertext length and higher computing efficiency, $|n|$=512-bit El Gamal variant cryptosystem with additive homomorphic property is employed in our experiments. One benefit of this variant cryptosystem is that the computing overload of watermark embedding is reduced to a large extent by multiplying two times the corresponding ciphertext parts with half ciphertext length, rather than multiplying two ciphertexts with full ciphertext length at one time.

Error correction code with powerful erasure and error correction is proved to be a good solution to deal with the synchronization issue and bit errors in the previous watermarking scheme in the encrypted domain [12]. RA code [14], an effective error correction code, is used in our experiments because of flexible coding rate, simple realization and near-capacity correction performance in erasure channels. At a specified rate $1/q$, RA encoding involves q-repetition, random interleaving, and bitstream accumulation. Decoding employs the soft-decision iterative sum-product algorithm [15]. The length of RA code is defined by the range of candidate coefficients in a fixed low frequency band ($1 \le k \le N$) (this parameter N can be changed, and it is independent of the host image). In our experiments, 20 DCT coefficients per block are used in a given low frequency band ($1 \le k \le 20$), and then the total watermark bitstream length of a 256×256 image with 1024 8×8 blocks is 20×1024=20480.

5.1 Watermarking Capacity Without RA Coding

The secure watermarking scheme has a flexible watermarking capacity in a given host image by adjusting many parameters. Watermark bits are embedded into the image "Lena" at designated QF 50 in different low frequency bands ($1 \le k \le N$). All of the embedded watermark bits are equiprobably and independently generated with $p(1) = p(0) = 0.5$, and each result is the average over a large number of repeated tests. Table 1 reports the number of embedded watermark bits and corresponding PSNR of watermarked images after decryption. Note that the number of watermark bits reported here is actually the number of uncoded bits.

Table 1. The number of embedded watermark bits and PSNR with different parameters

QF=50	N=9		N=14		N=20	
Threshold *t*	Embed bits	PSNR (dB)	Embed bits	PSNR (dB)	Embed bits	PSNR (dB)
0	5450	39.41	7011	36.86	8051	34.76
1	3277	42.24	3828	40.78	4095	39.67
2	2382	43.86	2628	42.89	2724	42.24
3	1826	44.87	1948	44.28	1979	44.02
4	1438	45.85	1502	45.45	1511	45.33
5	1178	46.55	1208	46.29	1211	46.28

5.2 JPEG Compression Resistance

Since the previous watermarking scheme in the encrypted domain [12] is tuned to JPEG quantization table [16], the embedded watermark bits are efficient enough for free bit-error recovery against the JPEG compression less severe than the designated QF. As for the secure watermarking scheme, RA code can further improve the resistance against the JPEG compression more severe than the designated QF to a limited extent. For example, at RA coding rate 1/20, all the 1024-bit information in a watermarked image with parameters of QF=50, t=1, N=20 can be perfectly retrieved at the QF value of JPEG compression greater than 40, which is the same performance of the one with parameters of QF=25, t=3, N=14 in the previous watermarking scheme.

5.3 Image Tampering Tolerance and Detection

The secure watermarking scheme with RA coding can resist a limited amount of image tampering on the watermarked image and detect the tampered area in block level. If the watermarked image has undergone tampering, the tampered area in the watermarked image can be easily located. First, original information bits are retrieved by decoding the watermark bitstream from the tampered image. Second, the originally embedded RA bitstream is reconstructed by encoding the retrieved information bits again with the same parameters as original coding. Finally, by comparing the extracted watermark bitstream with the original RA bitstream, the tampered areas are indicated by where the errors exist.

In order to resist limited image tampering, the RA coding rate designated in watermark generation phase should be low enough to withstand limited erasures and errors and to decode information bits successfully. For example, at RA coding rate 1/40, all the 512-bit information in a watermarked image with the parameter of QF=50, t=1, N=20, PSNR=39.4083dB can withstand a global tampering with the gray value 128. In another case, at RA coding rate 1/32, all the 640-bit information in a watermarked image with the parameter of QF=50, t=1, N=20, PSNR=39.2729dB can withstand a local tampering with block shifting in an unobvious manner. Fig. 1 (a) and (c) display the watermarked images with global tampering (PSNR=24.8906) and local tampering (PSNR=26.9398) respectively. Fig. 1 (b) and (d) show the localization of tampered area in block level according to the tampered image.

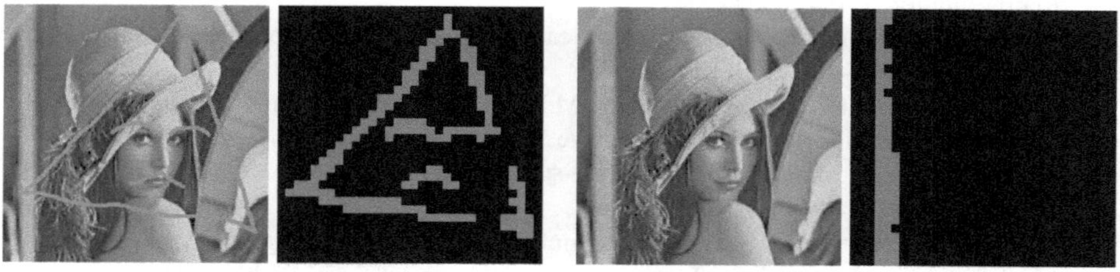

(a) (b) (c) (d)

Fig. 1. Watermarked image with global tampering and local tampering

5.4 Other Attacks Resistance

The secure watermarking scheme presented in this paper can also resist many moderate attacks on the watermarked image after decryption. For example, additive noise, low-pass filtering, gaussian filtering, median filtering and image resizing. The lower RA coding rate designated in watermark generation phase, the higher ability to survive more intense attacks. However, this watermarking scheme fails to withstand several geometric attacks, such as rotation and cropping.

6 Conclusion

In this paper, we discuss some security aspects in the encrypted domain and propose a new method of homomorphism conversion for probabilistic public key cryptosystem with homomorphic property. Based on our previous work [12], a new secure watermarking scheme for watermarking protocol is presented, in which we employ a new embedding strategy in the encrypted domain. It simplifies embedding steps and provides another secret key. The El Gamal variant cryptosystem with additive homomorphic property is used to reduce the computing overload of watermark embedding in the encrypted domain. RA code deals with the synchronization issue and bit errors, and it also improves the robustness of watermarked image against many moderate attacks after decryption. As security analysis and experiment shows, the secure watermarking scheme is more suitable for implementing the existing watermarking protocols.

Acknowledgments

This work was supported by the National Natural Science Foundation of China under Grant 90304008, the College and University Subject of Doctors Specific Scientific Research Foundation of China under Grant 2004071001, and the Graduate Innovation Fund of Xidian University 05017 and 05019.

References

1. Qiao, L., Nahrstedt, K.: Watermarking schemes and protocols for protecting rightful ownerships and customer's rights. Journal of Visual Communication and Image Representation 3, 194–210 (1998)
2. Memon, N., Wong, P.W.: A buyer-seller watermarking protocol. IEEE Trans. Image Processing 4, 643–649 (2001)
3. Lei, C.L., Yu, P.L., Tsai, P.L., Chan, M.H.: An efficient and anonymous buyer-seller watermarking protocol. IEEE Trans. Image Processing 12, 1618–1626 (2004)
4. Zhang, J., Kou, W., Fan, K.: Secure buyer-seller watermarking protocol. IEE Proceeding of Information Security 1, 15–18 (2006)
5. Kuribayashi, M., Tanaka, H.: Fingerprinting protocol for images based on additive homomorphic property. IEEE Trans. Image Processing 12, 2129–2139 (2005)
6. Rivest, R., Shamir, A., Adleman, L.: A method for obtaining digital signatures and public key cryptosystems. Communications of the ACM 2, 120–126 (1978)
7. Goldwasser, S., Micali, S.: Probabilistic encryption. Journal of Computer and System Sciences 2, 270–299 (1984)
8. El Gamal, T.: A public key cryptosystem and a signature scheme based on discrete logarithms. IEEE Trans. Inform. Theory 4, 472–649 (1985)
9. Paillier, P.: Public key cryptosystems based on composite degree residuosity classes. In: Stern, J. (ed.) EUROCRYPT 1999. LNCS, vol. 1592, pp. 223–238. Springer, Heidelberg (1999)
10. Okamoto, T., Uchiyama, S.: A new public-key cryptosystem as secure as factoring. In: Nyberg, K. (ed.) EUROCRYPT 1998. LNCS, vol. 1403, pp. 308–318. Springer, Heidelberg (1998)
11. Mao, W.: Modern Cryptography: Theory and Practice. Prentice-Hall, Englewood Cliffs (2003)
12. Tong, X., Zhang, J., Wen, Q.-Y.: New Constructions of Large Binary Sequences Family with Low Correlation. In: Lipmaa, H., Yung, M., Lin, D. (eds.) INSCRYPT 2007. LNCS, vol. 4318, Springer, Heidelberg (2007)
13. Solanki, K., Jacobsen, N., Madhow, U., Manjunath, B.S., Chandrasekaran, S.: Robust image-adaptive data hiding using erasure and error correction. IEEE Trans. Image Processing 12, 1627–1639 (2004)
14. Divsalar, D., Jin, H., McEliece, R.J.: Coding theorems for turbo-like codes. In: Proc. 36th Allerton Conf. Communications, Control, Computing, pp. 201–210 (1998)
15. Kschischang, F.R., Frey, B.J., Loeliger, H.-A.: Factor graphs and the sum-product algorithm. IEEE Trans. Inform. Theory 2, 498–519 (2001)
16. Wallace, G.K.: The JPEG still picture compression standard. Communications of the ACM 4, 30–44 (1991)

Digital Watermarking Based on Stochastic Resonance Signal Processor

Shuifa Sun[1,2,3], Sam Kwong[2], Bangjun Lei[3], and Sheng Zheng[1,3]

[1] College of Electrical Engineering and Information Technology, China Three Gorges University, Yichang 443002, China
{watersun, zsh}@ctgu.edu.cn
[2]Department of Computer Science, City University of Hong Kong, Kowloon, Hong Kong SAR, P.R. China
CSSAMK@cityu.edu.hk
[3]Institute of Intelligent Vision and Image Information, China Three Gorges University, Yichang 443002, China
Bangjun.Lei@ieee.org

Abstract. A signal processor based on an bi-stable aperiodic stochastic resonance (ASR) is introduced firstly. The processor can detect the base-band binary pulse amplitude modulation (PAM) signal. A digital image watermarking algorithm in the discrete cosine transform (DCT) domain is implemented based on the processor. In this algorithm, the watermark and the DCT alternating current (ac) coefficients of the image are viewed as the input signal and the channel noise of the processor input, respectively. In conventional watermarking systems, it's difficult to explain why the detection bit error ratio (BER) of a watermarking system suffering from some kinds of attacks is lower than that of the system suffering from no attack. In the present watermarking algorithm, this phenomenon is systematically analyzed. It is shown that the DCT ac coefficients of the image as well as the noise imported by the attacks will cooperate within the bi-stable ASR system to improve the performance of the watermark detection.

Keywords: digital watermarking; stochastic resonance; signal processing.

1 Introduction

The concept of digital watermarking has been put forward for more than 10 years [1-4, 15]. Digital watermarking plays a very important role in preventing multimedia works from being pirated. Its idea is to embed some critical information by replacing parts of original media data with certain so-called watermark. The watermark can then be detected purpose by the receiver. Two approaches to digital watermarking were proposed for grayscale images in [1]. In the first approach, a watermark in the form of a sequence-derived pseudo noise (PN) codes is embedded in the least significant bit (LSB) plane of the image data. A frequency-domain watermarking was introduced by Cox and Kilian [2]. The watermark contains a sequence of numbers with a normal distribution with zero mean and a variance of one. The watermark is inserted into the

H.H.S. Ip et al. (Eds.): PCM 2007, LNCS 4810, pp. 367–376, 2007.

image in the frequency-domain to produce the watermarked image. To verify the presence of the watermark, the similarity between the recovered watermark and the original watermark is measured. A blind watermarking detection algorithm based on the correlation detection was further proposed by Barni [3]. Barni computed the global DCT transformation for a given image, and then selected some middle and low frequency DCT coefficients to embed the marker. Quantization-index modulation (QIM) methods, introduced by Chen and Wornell [4], possess attractive practical and theoretical properties for watermarking. The method consists on coding the message by modifying the original data itself, where the elements of the message act as an index that select the quantizer used to represent them. Imperceptivity and robustness are two basic requirements to digital watermarking. Imperceptivity means that the difference between the embedded media and the original media should be imperceptible. For instance, the difference should not be easily perceived by humans' eyes for an image watermarking. Robustness means that the watermarking system should be able to survive some attacks. From the signal processing perspective, however, digital watermarking involves detecting weak signals in the presence of strong background noises.

Stochastic resonance (SR) is an effective approach for signal processing [5-11]. From this perspective, SR effect is commonly understood as first an increase and then a decrease in the signal-to-noise ratio (SNR) at the output with varying noise level at the input. Other quantitative measures, such as bit error ratio (BER), can also be employed. In this study, a signal processor based on ASR [7-10] is investigated. A digital image watermarking algorithm in the discrete cosine transform (DCT) domain is then implemented based on this ASR signal processor.

The paper is organized as follows. A signal processor based on the nonlinear bi-stable dynamic system is investigated in Section 2. A digital image watermarking algorithm in DCT domain is implemented based on the ASR signal processor in Section 3. Experimental results are presented in Section 4 and conclusions are drawn in Section 5.

2 Bi-stable ASR signal processor

From the signal processing perspective, the mathematical model of a nonlinear bi-stable dynamic system can be written as

$$dx/dt = -dV(x)/dx + Input(t), \tag{1}$$

where $V(x)$ is the quartic potential function and can be written as $V(x) = -ax^2/2+\mu x^4/4$. The parameters a and μ are positive and given in terms of the potential parameters. The quartic potential function $V(x)$ represents a bi-stable nonlinear potential with two wells and a barrier. The input can be written as $Input(t) = h(t) + \xi(t)$, where $h(t)$ is the input signal and $\xi(t)$ is the noise. If the signal $h(t)$ is an aperiodic signal and the SR effect occurs, it is called an ASR system [4].

This bi-stable system was used by Hu *et al.* [7], Godivier & Chapeau-Blondeau [8] and Duan & Xu [9] to detect the base-band pulse amplitude modulated (PAM) aperiodic binary signal $h(t)$ in the presence of the channel noise $\xi(t)$. The signal waveforms can be represented as $h_1(t)=-A$ and $h_2(t)=A$ for $(n-1)T_s \leq t < nT_s$, $n=1,2,\ldots$

If the amplitude of the aperiodic signal A is not larger than the critical value $A_{CR} = \sqrt{4a^3/27\mu}$ [11], then the input signals is called sub-threshold signal and supra-threshold signal otherwise. Here, a parameter Q_{SR} called SR-Degree is defined as follows:

$$Q_{SR} = A/A_{CR}. \quad (2)$$

When the SR-Degree $Q_{SR} < 1$, the aforementioned nonlinear bi-stable dynamic system corresponds to the sub-threshold system and supra-threshold system otherwise. This study is limited in the sub-threshold system, i.e. $A < A_{CR}$. The time interval T_s is termed as bit duration and the code rate $r=1/T_s$. The BER of the system is $P_e = P(1)P(0|1) + P(0)P(1|0)$. Readers should refer to [7-10] for more details about this signal processor.

3 Watermarking Based on ASR Signal Processor

In the remainder of this paper, a digital image watermarking algorithm based on the aforementioned ASR signal processor is implemented. The watermark sequence and the DCT alternating current (ac) coefficients of the image are viewed as the weak signal and the noise of the ASR signal processor, respectively, making up the input of the ASR signal processor.

3.1 Watermark Embedding

Referring to Eq. (1), the DCT ac coefficients can be viewed as the sampled noise $\xi^E(l)$ ($0 \leqslant l < L$ and L is the total number of DCT ac coefficients used) and the watermark as the signal $h_i^E(j) \in \{1,-1\}$ ($i \in \{1,2\}$, $h_1^E = 1$, $h_2^E = -1$, $0 \leqslant j < J$, and J is the length of the binary watermark sequence). The steps for the watermark embedding are as follows:

STEP 1. Forward DCT
For a image A^S of size $N_1 \times N_2$, applying global DCT to it, we get a DCT coefficient matrix B^S of the same size, where N_1 and N_2 are the width and the height of the image, respectively.

STEP 2. Selecting DCT ac coefficients
Selecting the DCT ac coefficients from matrix B^S line by line and sorting them according to their absolute values, we get a vector C^S. Those coefficients whose absolute values lie between M and $M+L-1$ elements in the vector C^S is picked up and form a vector C^E of length L. In this process, $1 \leqslant M$ and $(M+L) < N_1 \times N_2 - 1$. This means that the DCT direct current (DC) coefficient is not used, which is usually the biggest one in all the DCT coefficients and at the position 0 in the vector C^S. It is because that a change in this coefficient during the watermarking process will modify the mean level of the image and thus makes it perceptible. In fact, the same logic also holds for the first few DCT ac coefficients. Such as for the simulations given in Sec.4, M is 1000. At the same time, the position of the selected coefficients C^E in matrix B^S is recorded for later use.

STEP 3. Randomization of the selected DCT ac coefficients
The DCT ac coefficients of image are rearranged after the DCT transformation. The magnitudes of the low frequency coefficients are usually larger than those of the high frequency coefficients. In order to make the DCT ac coefficients more like the white noise, the selected DCT coefficients should be disordered. The method used is described as follows:

A. Given a random seed k, we generate a sequence of random numbers, which will be recorded and served as position index information in following step.
B. For an empty vector ξ^E with the same size of C^E, we select the DCT ac coefficients from C^E one by one, and put them at certain position of the vector ξ^E according to the position information obtained in the previous Step A.

It is clear that the position index sequence changes according to the random seed k. So, the parameter k can work as the key of the watermarking system. The parameter M and L can also work as the key of the watermarking system if necessary. But it is more appropriate to transmit it as the side information of the system.

STEP 4. Spreading the watermark sequence
Spreading the watermark sequence from one of length J to one of length L with an up-sample function and making $h_i^E(j_q\Delta t) = h_i^E(j)$ $(0\leqslant q<Q$, where $Q\times J=L$ and $Q\ \Delta t$ equals to the duration of a binary watermark code), we then obtain a spread watermark sequence. To simplify, we remove Δt of $h_i^E(j_q\Delta t)$ in the numerical simulation, which means that $h_i^E(j_q)$ is the qth sample of the jth watermark code.

STEP 5. Embedding watermark
The watermarked sequence $\xi^M(l)$ is obtained according to the following Eq. (3)

$$\xi^M(l) = f\times h_i^E(j_q) + \xi^E(l), \tag{3}$$

where f is the scaling parameter. Using the positions recorded in STEP 3 and STEP 2 accordingly, we can replace the selected coefficients in the matrix B^S with the watermarked sequence $\xi^M(l)$ one by one and get the watermarked matrix B^M.
STEP 6. Inverse DCT
Applying the inverse DCT on the matrix B^M, we obtain the watermarked image A^M.

3.2 Watermark Detection

The first three steps for the watermark detection are the same as those in the above embedding procedure. The whole procedure for watermark detection is as follows:

STEP 1. Forward DCT
Given a $N_1\times N_2$ image matrix A^U, applying DCT, we get a DCT coefficient matrix B^U.

STEP 2. Selecting DCT ac coefficients
Using the position information recorded in STEP 2 of subsection 3.1, we can select DCT ac coefficients at those positions from the matrix B^U and get a vector C^U.

STEP 3. Randomization of the selected vector
Using the random seed k to randomize the selected vector C^U with the same method given in STEP 3 of subsection 3.1, we obtain a vector $\xi^U(l)$ to test.

STEP 4. Detection
Substituting the sequence $\xi^U(l)$ into Eq.(1) as the sampled input *Input*(t) of the bi-stable system, we get the following Eq. (4) [14]

$$x(l+1) = \Delta t(ax(l) - bx^3(l) + \xi^U(l)) + x(l). \tag{4}$$

Without loss of generality, we may assume that $x(0)=0$ in the numerical simulation. We can then get the detected sequence $h_i^D(j_q) = x(l+1)$ and recover the watermark h_i^D by using the sample at the end time of each bit duration [8] or use the statistical method proposed in [10] to improve the detection performance of the system. Comparing h_i^D with h_i^E, the total bit error number and *BER* of the watermarking system are obtained.

For both watermarking algorithms in [2] and [3], the DCT ac coefficients of the image are actually viewed as the additive white Gaussian noise because the correlation detector, which is the optimal detector for the communication system in the presence of this kind of noise, is used. In the present watermarking system, not only the selected DCT ac coefficients sequence but also the noise imported by the attack is viewed as the additive white Gaussian noise. If the image A^U is the watermarked image A^M, which means that the watermarking system has not been attacked, the aforementioned ASR signal processor works well. If indeed the watermarking communication system suffers from some kinds of attack, $\xi^U(l)$ is still a white Gaussian noise because it is a combination of two additive white Gaussian noises. Therefore, the aforementioned ASR signal processor will work well in both cases.

4 Numerical Simulations and Results

In this section, the numerical simulations on the above implementation are introduced. The original image is the standard gray-scale image "Lena" with a size of 512×512, as shown in Fig. 1(a). The watermark is a PN sequence h_i^E generated by a linear feedback shift register with 8 registers. The length of the watermark code J is 255. The first 10 codes are shown in Fig. 1(b). The parameters M and L for the simulations were 1000 and 255×500, respectively. This means that the parameter Q=500. The scaling parameter f was 5. The watermarked image is shown in Fig. 1(c) and the peak signal to noise ratio (*PSNR*) was 37.28 dB. Comparing it with the original image in Fig. 1(a), we hardly can see any difference. From Fig.2 one can clear see that the parameter-induced stochastic resonance phenomenon happened in the watermarking system. In the following attack tests, the optimal value a_{SR} (=39) will be used to detect the watermark.

4.1 Adding Salt and Pepper Noise Attack Test

Some pulse noises are added into the image when the image is transmitted or processed. This kind of noises are often called salt and pepper noises and make the

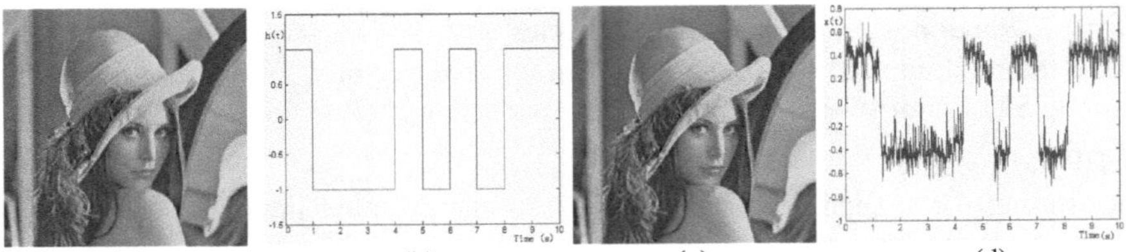

(a) (b) (c) (d)

Fig. 1. (a) Original image 'Lena'. (b) Original watermark code. (c) Watermarked image. (d) Detected sequence from (c) when the bi-stable system parameter a=39. Other simulation parameters are the same as those in Fig. 2.

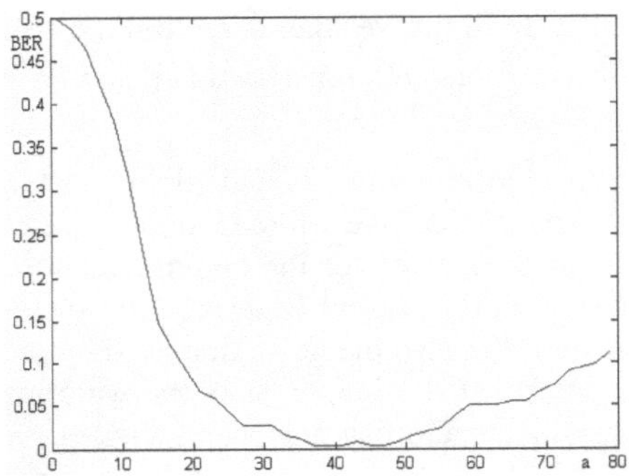

Fig. 2. Relationship between the *BER* and the parameter a of the bi-stable system. The SR-Degree Q_{SR} is 0.86. The parameter a changes from 1 to 80 with a step of 2. The sample interval Δt in Eq. (4) is 0.002. The recovered waveform for the first 10 codes is shown in Fig. 1 (d) where the bi-stable system parameter a =39.

image looking quite dirtier and older. Fig. 3(a) is the image when the watermarked image was corrupted by the salt and pepper noise with density of 2.5%, the peak signal to noise ratio (PSNR) was 21.37 dB. Comparing it with the watermarked image in Fig. 1(c), the difference is obvious. As shown in Fig. 3(b), however, the trace of the watermark is clear and there are only 8 error codes among all 255 transmitted codes.

4.2 Adding Gaussian Noise Attack Test

Another typical noise in the image transmission or processing is Gaussian noise, which makes an image blurry. Fig. 3 (c) is the image when the watermarked image is corrupted by a Gaussian noise whose mean and covariance are 0 and 0.01, respectively. Comparing it with the watermarked image in Fig.1 (c), we can see the difference between them clearly and *PSNR*=20.06 dB. But the trace of the watermark is still obvious as shown in Fig.3 (d) and there were only 9 error codes among all 255 transmitted codes.

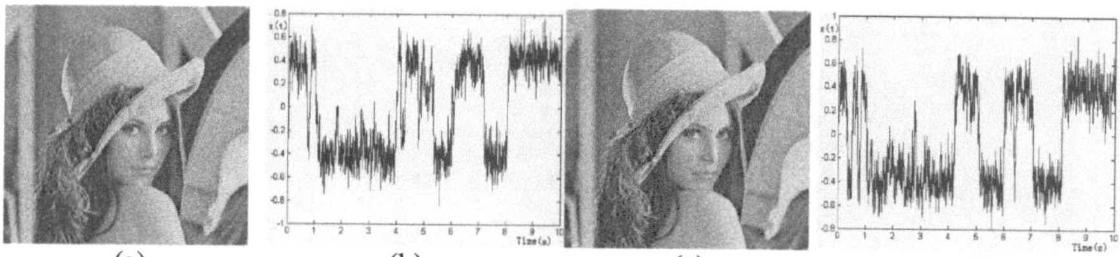

(a) (b) (c) (d)

Fig. 3. Adding salt and pepper noise attack case and adding Gaussian noise attack case. (a) Attacked image after adding spiced salt noise. (b) Detected waveform from (a) for the first 10 codes. (c) Image after adding Gaussian noise. (d) Detected waveform from (c) for the first 10 codes. Other simulation parameters are same with those of Fig. 2.

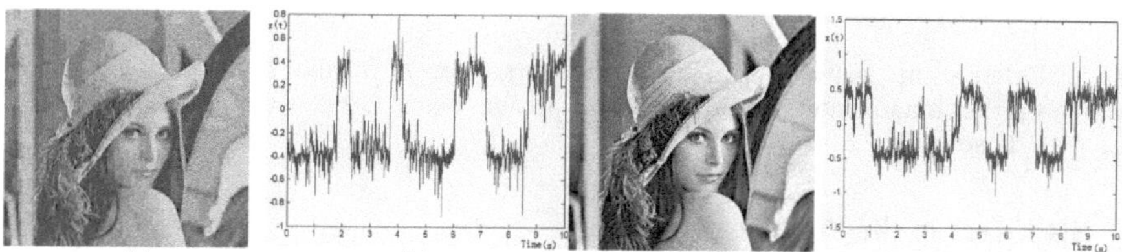

(a) (b) (c) (d)

Fig. 4. JPEG compression attack case and histogram equalization attack case. (a) Image after JPEG compression. (b) Detected waveform from (a) for the first 10 codes. (c) Image after histogram equalization. (d) Detected waveform from (c) for the first 10 codes. Other simulation parameters are the same as those in Fig. 2.

4.3 JPEG Compression Attack Test

JPEG compression is a widely used image processing method. Fig. 4(a) is the image when the watermarked image was compressed using JPEG with a quality factor 5. Comparing it with the watermarked image in Fig. 1 (c), the difference caused by block effect is obvious and *PSNR*=26.95 dB. But from the detected result shown in Fig. 4(b), there was still a trace of the watermark and the *BER* is 39.6%. Our explanation is given as follows: the JPEG compression forced many high frequency DCT ac coefficients to zeros and the watermark embedding in these coefficients were then removed. It is why that many digital watermarking algorithms do not use high frequency DCT ac coefficients as the carrier of watermark. Embedding watermark only into the low frequency DCT ac coefficients will overcome this defect of the watermarking system.

4.4 Histogram Equalization Attack Test

In the image processing, histogram equalization is usually used to increase the contrast of an image. Fig. 4(c) is the resulting image when the histogram of the watermarked image was equalized. The difference between them can be easily told by comparing it with the watermarked image in Fig. 1(c) (*PSNR*=19.18dB). But from the detected result shown in Fig. 4(d), there were trances of the watermark code and there were only 6 error codes among all 255 transmitted codes.

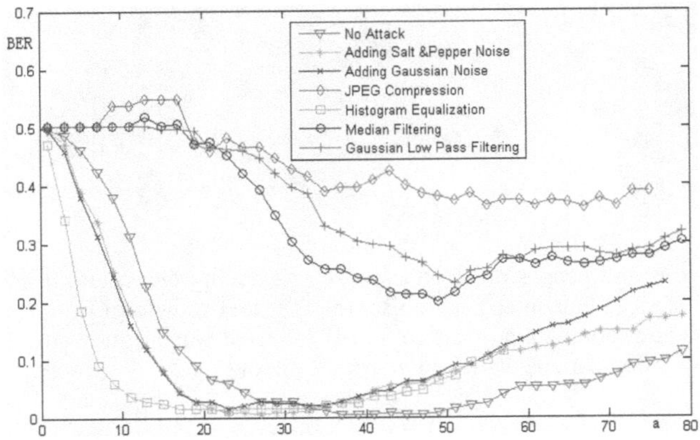

Fig. 5. Relationship between *BER* and the parameter *a* of the bi-stable system in the watermarking communication systems for the image Lena. Other simulation parameters are same with those of Fig. 2.

4.5 SR Effect in the Presence of Attack

Figure 5 shows the relationship between the parameter a and the *BER* for all of the preceding attacks cases, as well as the no attack case. one can clearly see that the parameter-induced stochastic resonance effect in some of the watermarking communication systems being attacked. So, not only the DCT ac coefficients of the image themselves but also the combination of them and the noise imported by the attacks will cooperate with the bi-stable system to improve the watermark detection performance. It is also clear that the number of erroneous bits when the system suffers from the pulse noise attack or the Gaussian noise attack is less than that when the system does not suffer any attack, such as a=17 in Fig.5. For both watermarking algorithms proposed by Cox and Kilian [2], and Barni *et al.* [3], the DCT ac coefficients of the image are also viewed as the noise of the watermarking communication system. Whereas, for watermarking algorithms based on the ASR signal processor, the detection BER when the system suffers from some kinds of attacks is lower than that when the system does not suffer from any attacks. This is unbelievable for conventional watermarking systems but is reasonable for the ASR signal processor based on the nonlinear system, which the conventional linear signal processor does not have [8].

4.6 Comparison with the Matched Filter

We next wish to compare the ASR signal processor with the matched filter. The matched filter is the optimal linear filter in the presence of additive Gaussian noise. The matched filter correlates with the received signal (the signal-noise mixture) $u(t)$ with a replica of a binary pulse of the watermark signal $h(t)$. In our case, the impulse response of the matched filter $r(t)$ is A if $t \in [0, T_s]$ and 0 otherwise. The signal at the output of the matched filter y (t) is $y(t) = \int_{-\infty}^{t} r(t-t')u(t')dt'$. At every time

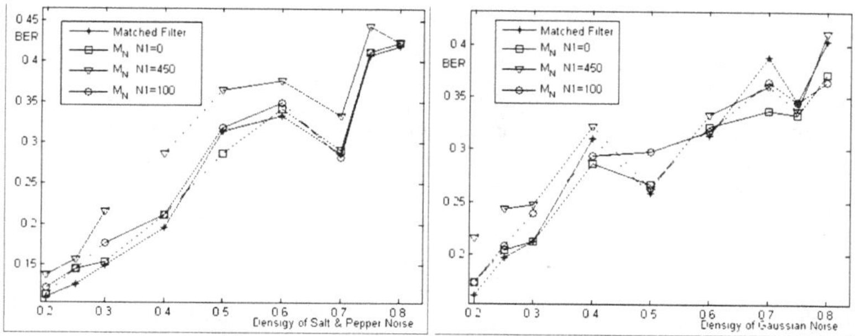

(a) (b)

Fig. 6. Comparison with the matched filter. The other parameters for the experiments are same with those of Fig. 2. M_N stand for the new method given in [10] and N1 is also defined in [10].

multiple of input pulse duration T_s, the output of the matched filter $y(t)$ was read and a decision was made that $u(t)= A+ \xi(t)$ if $y(t)>0$ and $u(t)= -A + \xi(t)$ otherwise (assuming $P_0=P_1$). Every decision was perfectly synchronized with the end of each binary pulse of the information-carrying signal $h(t)$. In Fig. 6, we compare the performance of the ASR signal processor to that of the matched filter, with these relevant conditions of detection. It can be seen from Fig.6 that the performance of the matched filter is not always better than that of the ASR signal processor, especially when the density of the noise is high. The results also show that the method proposed in [10] is an effective method when the noise density is high.

5 Conclusion

In this paper, a signal processor based on ASR was investigated. A digital image watermarking algorithm based on this ASR signal processor was then implemented. The experimental results showed that, under certain circumstances, extra amount of noises can in fact improve rather than deteriorate the performance of some communication systems. It was also found that the performance of a matched filter is not always better than that of the ASR signal processor. In the algorithm, both the selected DCT ac coefficients and the noise imported by the attacks are viewed as the additive white Gaussian noise. However, as shown by the results in [15], the characteristics of cover data (the selected DCT ac coefficients here) and the distortion vectors (the noise imported by the attack) are different for given images and attacks. So, further extension to this paper could be to study the ASR signal processor in the presence of other kinds of channel noises [16-17] and apply it to watermarking.

Acknowledgments. This work was supported partly by a grand from the National Natural Science Foundation of the People's Republic of China, No. 60572048. Shuifa Sun acknowledges the City University of Hongkong Strategic Grant 7001955.

References

1. Schyndel, R.G., Tirkel, A.Z., Osborne, C.F.: A Digital Watermark. In: Proc IEEE Int Conf on Image Processing, pp. 86–90. IEE Computer Soc. Los Alamitos (1994)
2. Cox, I., Kilian, J.: Secure spread spectrum watermarking for multimedia. IEEE Trans. on Image Processing 6, 1673–1687 (1997)
3. Barni, M., Bartolini, F., Capellini, V., Piva, A.: A DCT-domain system for robust image watermarking. Signal Processing 66, 357–372 (1998)
4. Chen, B., Wornell, G.: Quantization Index Modulation: A Class of Provably Good Methods for Digital Watermarking and Information Embedding. IEEE Trans. on Information Theory 47, 1423–1443 (1998)
5. Benzi, R., Sutera, S., Vulpiani, A.: The Mechanism of Stochastic Resonance. J. Phys. A 14, 453–457 (1981)
6. Collins, J., Chow, C., Imhoff, T.: Aperiod stochastic resonance in excitable systems. Phys. Rev. E. 52(4), R3321–R3324 (1995)
7. Hu, G., Gong, D., Wen, X., et al.: Stochastic resonance in a nonlinear system driven by an aperiod force. Phys. Rev. A 46, 3250–3254 (1992)
8. Godivier, X., Chapeau-Blondeau, F.: Stochastic resonance in the information capacity of a nonlinear dynamic system. Int. J. Bifurcation and Chaos 8, 581–590 (1998)
9. Duan, F., Xu, B.: Parameter-induced stochastic resonance and baseband binary PAM signals transmission over an AWGN channel. Int. J. Bifurcation and Chaos 13, 411 (2003)
10. Sun, S., Kwong, S.: Stochastic resonance signal processor: principle, capacity analysis and method. Int. J. Bifurcation and Chaos 17, 631–639 (2007)
11. Moss, F., Pierson, D., O'Gorman, D.: Stochastic resonance: Tutorial and update. Int. J. Bifurcation and Chaos 4, 1383–1398 (1994)
12. Xu, B., Duan, F., Chapeau-Blondeau, F.: Comparison of aperiodic stochastic resonance in a bistable system realized by adding noise and by tuning system parameters. Physical Review E 69, 061110, 1–8, (2004)
13. Gammaitoni, L., Hanggi, P., Jung, P., Marchesoni, F.: Stochastic resonance. Rev. Mod. Phys. 70, 223–287 (1998)
14. Mitaim, S., Kosko, B.: Adaptive stochastic resonance. Proc. IEEE. 86, 2152–2183 (1998)
15. Cox, I., Miller, M.L., McKellips, A.L.: Watermarking as communications with side information. Proc. IEEE 87, 1127–1141 (1999)
16. Jia, Y., Zheng, X., Hu, X., Li, J.: Effects of colored noise on stochastic resonance in a bistable system subject to multiplicative and additive noise. Phys. Rev. E 63 031107(2001)
17. Xu, B., Li, J., Duan, F.: Effects of colored noise on multi-frequency signal processing via stochastic resonance with tuning system parameters. Chaos, Solitons & Fractals 16, 93–106 (2003)

A DWT Blind Image Watermarking Strategy with Secret Sharing

Li Zhang, Ping-ping Zhou, Gong-bin Qian, and Zhen Ji

Faculty of Information Engineering, Shenzhen University, Shenzhen, China, 518060
wzhangli@szu.edu.cn, pingp_zhou@163.com, jizhen@szu.edu.cn

Abstract. A blind image watermarking scheme based on secret sharing in discrete wavelet transform domain is proposed. Watermark was divided into *n* shadows according to secret sharing scheme. And *t* or more of those shadows can reconstruct the watermark, while *t*-1 or less shadows could not do it. In order to achieve optimum embedding strategy, a closed loop embedding process is proposed, which is modified iteratively according to results of performance analysis. The convergence of closed loop watermarking is proved. Independent component analysis is utilized so that detector can not merely detect watermark but also can extract it. Before watermark reconstruction, one way hashing function is used to withstand cheating attacks. The experimental results show that it is robust against a wide range of attacks proposed by Stirmark and it is more safety than traditional watermarking techniques.

Keywords: blind image watermarking, secret sharing, closed loop, Stirmark.

1 Introduction

With the development of Internet, how to realize valid copyright protection and information security has become an important problem [1,2]. Digital watermarking technique is an effective means to resolve the problem by embedding additional information (i.e. watermark information) into digital media. Watermark embedded must have robustness to image manipulation and processing operations and must be perceptually invisible.

There are many literatures on the digital watermarking technique including that in spatial domain [3] and that in transform domain. The techniques in transform domain are usually implemented by Discrete Fourier Transform (DFT) [4] , Discrete Cosine Transform (DCT) [5] and Discrete Wavelet Transform (DWT) [6] . Since DWT can fit well with the characteristics of Human Visual System (HVS) and is consistent with the newly issued standard of image compression, JPEG 2000, it is used widely in digital watermarking.

Secret sharing is an important issue in confirming the security of secret information[7]. In a (t,n) secret sharing scheme, a secret is usually broken into n pieces called shadows, so that t or more of those shadows can reconstruct the secret, while t-1 or less shadows could not do it. Chin-Chen Chang proposed a way can deal with the

H.H.S. Ip et al. (Eds.): PCM 2007, LNCS 4810, pp. 377–384, 2007.

cheating attack with hidden a signature in least significant bits of image, so this scheme has poor robust[8]. Huiping Guo [9] proposed a watermarking algorithm that make use of a secret sharing scheme to address the problem of joint ownership verification for a digital image without a trusted dealer. Given that multiple owners create an image jointly, they collaboratively compute their own distinct keys without anyone else involved. For the watermark detection, only when certain numbers of owners present their keys can the ownership of the image be verified. Feng Hsing Wang[10] introduced a multi-user-based watermarking system for providing the function of secret sharing, which a user key generation procedure is used to generate one master key and several normal keys. By using either of these normal keys, a secret watermark is obtained firm the cover image.

The paper is organized as followings. Watermark embedding process is described in section 2, and in section 3 the watermark extraction is introduced in detail. Performance of the watermark is analyzed in section 4 and experimental results are showed in section 5. Finally, the conclusion is drawn in section 6.

2 Watermark Embedding Process

In this section, the method of watermark embedding process in DWT with secret sharing is described in detail. The detailed steps of watermarking embedding are as followings:

Step1. Initialized the watermark - The watermark is an image which is given before and is expressed by W , which is independent to the original image. It is beneficial to preprocess the watermark before embedding to enhance the security of the watermark. In this paper the preprocess is spread spectrum.

Step2. Divide the watermark- Divide the initialized watermark into N blocks, and transform their numerals so that they satisfies $(0,q-1)$. Where, q is a larger prime and larger than n. So the secret watermark can be obtained, which is expressed as M.

Step3. Create and distribute shadows- Use Shamir's (t,n) threshold scheme to distribute the shadows s_i to the users u_i, for $i=1,2\dots n$. Lagrange interpolation polynomial is used to realize it. Assume that a polynomial f of degree t-1 as form of:

$$f(x)=a_1x+a_2x^2+\hbar\ +a_{t-1}x^{t-1}+M\ . \tag{1}$$

Where, $a_1,a_2,\hbar\ ,a_{t-1}$ are random numbers. M is the hidden watermark image, which is a constant here. Suppose p is a large prime and it is larger that $a_1,a_2,\hbar\ ,a_{t-1}$. So it can be expressed as:

$$shadow(x_i)=f(x_i)\bmod p\ . \tag{2}$$

Let G be a group with n points $(x_1,f(x_1)),(x_2,f(x_2)),\hbar\ (x_n,f(x_n))$. And let T is a subset of G which has t points and each point satisfies $(x_i,f(x_i))\in G$. So all points in T can be used collectively to compute the secret through the Lagrange formula:

$$M = \sum_{j=1}^{t} shadow(x_i) \prod_{i \neq j} \frac{x - x^i}{x^j - x^i} . \tag{3}$$

While less t points could not do it. And more than t points will be wasted. In this paper, a (3,10) threshold scheme is used, that is, arbitrary 3 users of 10 can be used collectively to construct M. And set use p=13, $a_1 = 8$ and $a_2 = 7$ which are chosen arbitrarily, so it can be obtained that:

$$shadow(x_i) = (7x_i^2 + 8x_i + M) \bmod 13 . \tag{4}$$

Step4. Information hidden process - An implementation approach of the closed loop shadows image embedding process described in wavelet domain is proposed, which is depicted in Fig. 1.

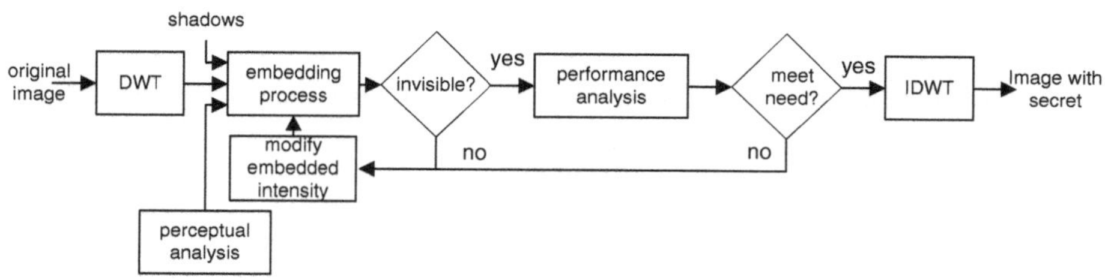

Fig. 1. Closed loop watermarking technique in wavelet domain

2.1 The Initial Embedded Intensity of the Watermark Embedding

From Fig. 1, it is known that the traditional watermarking is equal to the initial step of closed loop process. The initial embedded intensity α is usually determined by JND (Just Noticeable Difference) of the image [11].

2.2 Algorithm Description of the Closed Loop Watermarking in Wavelet Domain

Now the closed loop watermarking technique in wavelet domain will be described in detail. The steps of embedding process are as follows:

Step1: DWT - Discrete wavelet transform is done to the original image and the shadows are embedded with initial intensity α_0 . Suppose initial step size for modification of embedded intensity is q_0 . Set $q_0 = \rho\alpha_0$, where $0 < \rho < 1$. set $k = 1$.

Step2: Embedded the watermark with closed loop embedding process, which is already proposed by us in [12].

3 Watermark Extraction Process

3.1 Extract the Shadows with ICA

ICA process is the core of the intelligent detector accomplished by the FASTICA algorithm [14]. The watermark was utilized the intelligent watermark detector based on ICA proposed in [13].

3.2 Validate the Validity of the Users

In order to avoid cheating attack, validate the validity of the users before reconstructing the secret. One way hashing function is used for cheating detection. A one way hashing function *h(.)* has the following characteristics: (1) given an arbitrary length input, it always gives a fixed length output; (2)given an input, it is easy to compute the output though the function; (3) from an output, it is difficult to find another input such that the two inputs have the same output. So it is collision free, i.e., it is computationally infeasible to find distinct x and y with $h(x)=h(y)$; (4) from an output, it is difficult to derive the input.MD5 is a well-known one way hashing function which is used in this paper. It is known that [15], let $T=\sum_{i=1}^{n} a_i p^{i-1}$, where $0 \le a_i < p$. Then $\left\lfloor \frac{T}{p^{i-1}} \right\rfloor \bmod p = a_i$

So a one way hashing function $h(.)$ and a prime number p are choosen, such that $h(.)<p$ for all users in G. Present their possess shadows $shadow^{\bullet}(x_i)$ and compute:

$$T^{\bullet} = \sum_{G} h(shadow^{\bullet}(x_i))\, p^{2(i-1)} \,. \tag{5}$$

For each users in G, check $x = \left\lfloor \frac{T-T^{\bullet}}{p^{2(i-1)}} \right\rfloor \bmod p = h(shadow(x_i)) - h(shadow^{\bullet}(x_i))$. If the equation is equal to zero, then the user is honest. Otherwise, the user is a cheater.

3.3 Reconstruct the Secret Watermark

Since (3,10) threshold scheme is used, suppose use $shadow(x_i)$, $shadow(x_j)$ and $shadow(x_k)$ to reconstruct the secret:

$$\begin{aligned} p^{\bullet}(x) = {} & shadow(x_i)\frac{(x-x_k)(x-x_j)}{(x_i-x_k)(x_i-x_k)} + shadow(x_j)\frac{(x-x_k)(x-x_i)}{(x_j-x_k)(x_j-x_i)} \\ & + shadow(x_k)\frac{(x-x_i)(x-x_j)}{(x_k-x_i)(x_k-x_j)} \end{aligned} \tag{6}$$

So the secret can be reconstructed as:

$$\begin{aligned} M = {} & shadow(x_i)\frac{x_k x_j}{(x_i-x_k)(x_i-x_j)} + shadow(x_j)\frac{x_i x_k}{(x_J-x_i)(x_j-x_k)} \\ & + shadow(x_k)\frac{x_i x_j}{(x_k-x_i)(x_k-x_j)} \end{aligned} \tag{7}$$

Change it to according to the initialized step to get the real hidden image.

4 Performance of the Proposed System

4.1 Security Analysis

In Lagrange interpolation polynomial, the polynomial of degree t-1 requires t or more images which hidden the secret for the reconstruction of the whole secret polynomial. That means need any t or more images which hidden the secret to extract the secret, but t-1 or less images which hidden the secret could not do this work. Therefore we can confirm the security of our scheme.

4.2 Performance Analysis

So far, many proposed scheme can not be able to deal with the cheating attack and hiding image at the same time. To resist the cheating attacks, use the one way hashing function. Only t or more honest users can work collectively to reconstruct the secret, where dishonest users could not do it.

5 Experimental Results

Experiments are done to test the robust of the threshold watermarking scheme with secret sharing based on ICA in DWT proposed in this paper, and set $P_{f0} < 0.000001$ and $P_{d0} > 0.999998$. All the image operations are produced Stirmark, which popularly used to test watermarking technique. Experiments of several attacks combined to the stego image are also completed. The Normalization Correction (NC)[16] is used to express the similarity between the original watermark w and the extracted watermark w^* quantitatively:

$$NC = \sum_{i=1}^{256}\sum_{j=1}^{256} w(i,j)w^*(i,j) \Big/ \sum_{i=0}^{256}\sum_{j=0}^{256} (w(i,j))^2 . \tag{8}$$

5.1 Robust Against Image Compression

Experiments are done to test the robustness of the proposed watermarking to JPEG compression produced by Stirmark with different qualify factor from 90 to 10, and table 1 lists the results. The experimental results show that the proposed watermarking has a good robust to JPEG compression.

5.2 Robust Against Image Processing Produced by Stirmark

Experiments are done to test robustness of the proposed method with respect to single attack and combined attacks produced by Stirmark. Table 2 lists NC between original and extracted watermark from the image which has been attacked by Stirmark.

Table 1. Robust to JPEG compression produced by Stirmark

Qualify factor	90	80	70	60	50	40	30	20	10
NC	0.9948	0.9937	0.9931	0.9925	0.9901	0.9874	0.9498	0.9410	0.8554

Table 2. Robustness to attacks produced by Stirmark

Attacks	Remove1 row2 columns	Remove17 rows3 columns	Median filter	Convolution filter	Sharpening filtering	Skewx 5.0% y 5.0%	Random geometric distortion
NC	0.9967	0.9958	0.9993	0.9457	0.9426	0.9985	0.9754
Attacks	Scaling x 1.0 y 1.20	Scaling x 0.5 y 0.75	Scaling x 1.5y 1.75	Crop to 217×217	Crop to 192×192	Rotation 5 scale 2 crop	Add Gaussian noise
NC	0.9976	0.9947	0.9936	0.9935	0.9901	0.7954	0.9913

5.3 Robust Comparison with other Watermarking Technique

Compare the experimental results of the our method with ref. [4], which proposed a digital watermarking technique in DFT domain. The method proposed in this paper can be realized in any domain, and the detection will not need any information about attacks that stego image have encountered, original image, watermark and embedding process. It can be seen that this watermarking technique has a good robustness.

Table 3. Experiment results comparison between the methods proposed in this paper and [4]

Attack types	Results in [4]	Results in this paper	Attack types	Results in [4]	Results in this paper
Scaling	0.78	1	Rotation	1	1
Cropping	0.89	1	JPEG compression	0.74	1
Cancel row/column	1	1	Random geometric distortion	0	1

The results are compared with that of reference [17]. The authors in [17] adopt the ICA in spatial domain. Fig 2 shows the comparisons on the attack of scaling and rotation. The experimental results have shown that the proposed watermarking in this paper has a much better robustness.

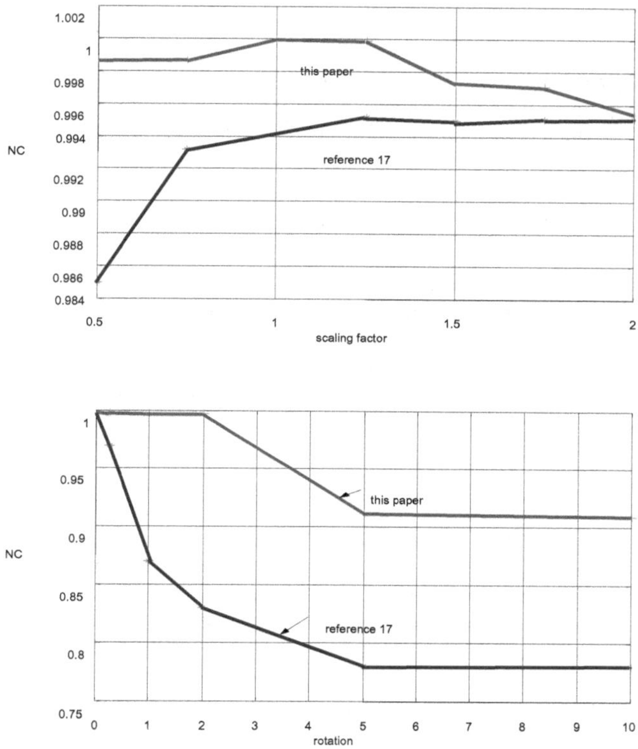

Fig. 2. NC comparison (scaling and rotation)

6 Conclusions

A novel (t,n) threshold watermarking scheme based on secret sharing is proposed in this paper. The secret watermark image was divided into n shadows according to secret sharing scheme to avoid betray the pot to the roses. In order to achieve optimum embedding strategy, a closed loop embedding process is used for watermarking technique. Combining the embedding process with the performance analysis, an implementation approach in discrete wavelet transform domain is given. The embedding process is modified iteratively according to the results of the performance analysis of watermarking so as to obtain optimal embedding effect. The convergence of the closed loop techniques is proved. During the secret detection, the independent component analysis technique is adopted so that the detector not need any information about the watermarking embedding process and attacks that maybe encountered during the stego image transmission, the detector can not merely detect the shadows watermark but also can extract the exact them. Before secret image reconstruction, one way hashing function is used to withstand cheating attacks. The experimental results show this strategy is robust against a wide range of image processing operation, such as filtering, compression, crop, rescale, shift, additive noise, which proposed by Stirmark-the popular watermarking test software.

Acknowledgement

This work is supported by National Nature Science Foundation of China (Grant No. 60502027).

References

1. Shieh, C.S., Gray, H.C., Wang, F.H., Pan, J.S.: Generic watermarking based on transform domain techniques. Pattern Recognition 37(3), 555–565 (2004)
2. Gunsel, B., Sener, S., Yaslan, Y.: An adaptive encoder for audio watermarking. WSEAS Transactions on Computer 4(2), 1044–1048 (2003)
3. Delaigle, J.F., De Vleeschouwer, C., Macq, B.: Watermarking algorithm based on a human visual model. Signal proceeding 66, 319–335 (1998)
4. Pereira, S., Pun, T.: Robust template matching for affine resistant image watermarks. IEEE Trans. On Image Processing 9(6), 1123–1129 (2000)
5. Wolfgang, R.B., Podichuk, C.I., Delp, E.J.: Perceptual watermarks for digital images and video. Proceedings of the IEEE 87(7), 1108–1126 (1999)
6. Kundur, D., Hatzinakos, D.: Digital watermarking for telltale tamper proofing and authentication. Proceedings of the IEEE 87(7), 1167–1180 (1999)
7. Shamir, A.: How to share a secret. Communications of ACM 22, 612–613 (1979)
8. Chang, C.-C., Lin, I.-C.: A new (t,n) threshold image hiding scheme for sharing a secret color image. In: Proceedings of ICCT, pp. 196–202 (2003)
9. Guo, H., Georganas, N.D.: Digital image watermarking for joint ownership verification without a trusted dealer. In: Proceedings of ICME, pp. 497–500 (2003)
10. Wang, F.H., Jain, L.C., Pan, J.S.: Design of hierarchical keys for a multi user based watermarking system. In: IEEE International Conference on Multimedia and Expo, pp. 919–922 (2004)
11. Watson, A.B., Yang, G.Y., Solomon, J.A., Villasensor, J.: Visibility of wavelet quantization noisep. IEEE Transactions on Image Processing 6(8), 1164–1174 (1997)
12. Li, Z., Gong-bin, Q., Li-min, C., Xia, L.: A Blind Information Hiding Scheme Based on Optimum Embedding Strategy. In: The fourth international symposium on multispectral image processing and pattern recognition, Wuhan University Wuhan, China (October 31 -November 2, 2005)
13. Li, Z., Kwong, S., Ji-hong, Z., et al.: The Design Intelligent Watermark Detection Decoder Based on Independent Component Analysis. In: Kalker, T., Cox, I., Ro, Y.M. (eds.) IWDW 2003. LNCS, vol. 2939, pp. 223–234. Springer, Heidelberg (2004)
14. Hyvarinen, A., Oja, E.: Independent component analysis: a tutorial. In: IJCNN 1999. Notes for International Joint Conference on Neural Networks, Washington D. C. (1999), http://www.cis.hut.fi/projects/iac/
15. Knuth, D.E.: The art of computer programming, semi-numerical algorithm, vol. 2. Addison Wesley, Reading (1981)
16. Hsu, C.T., Wu, J.L.: Hidden digital watermarks in images. IEEE Transactions on Image Processing 8(1), 58–68 (1999)
17. Yu, D., Sattar, F., Ma, K.K.: Watermark detection and extraction using independent component analysis method. EURASIP Journal on Applied Signal Processing (1), 92–104 (2002)

Using Enhanced Shape Distributions to Compare CAD Models

Xin Hou, XuTang Zhang, and WenJian Liu

School of Mechatronics Engineering, Harbin Institute of Technology, China
sonicwall@163.com, {zxt,cadcam}@hit.edu.cn

Abstract. This paper has discussed how to use feature and topology information to compare 3D CAD models represented by polygonal meshes. In this work we propose an enhanced method to compare CAD models based on shape distributions. A topology-preserving simplification method of polygonal meshes was used to simplify CAD model as the pretreatment for generation of sample points. We improved the method of sampling points and a pair of shape functions more sensitive to shape was employed to construct a 2D shape distribution. The experiential results showed that simplification has a positive effort on shape comparison and our method achieved more effective performance than the conventional one.

Keywords: shape retrieval; polygonal-mesh simplification; shape distribution.

1 Introduction

Since the use of Computer-Aided Design (CAD) models is now widespread throughout the design and manufacturing stages of product development, reusing and sharing the knowledge embedded in CAD models is becoming an important way to accelerate the design process, improve product quality, and reduce costs. However, as the industry has matured, CAD models have considerably increased in complexity and number so that a search system which is capable of retrieving similar 3D models based on their shape is greatly needed [1].

In this paper, an enhanced shape distribution-based shape retrieval methodology of CAD models represented by polygonal meshes is discussed in detail. The major contributions of this paper are:

- Using a topology-preserving simplification algorithm as the pretreatment of shape comparison. It facilitates shape distribution generation and shape classification.
- Improving the method of generating random sample points and utilizing an enhanced shape function to compare CAD models.

2 The Shape Similarity Comparison Algorithm

In our algorithm, we use the topology-preserving polygonal-mesh simplification algorithm of [4] as the pretreatment of models to reduce the computational cost for

H.H.S. Ip et al. (Eds.): PCM 2007, LNCS 4810, pp. 385–388, 2007.

their shape distributions. An improved effective algorithm called D-IA for comparing polygonal-mesh models is proposed. The major improvements are as follows.

Traditional method for sampling can not guarantee that each of the triangle facets is sampled. In this approach, the points to be used for shape distribution are sampled in what we call a semi-random full-sampling manner. First, if *n* points need to be sampled from the entire part faces, traverse all the triangle facets, get the number *m* of sample points of each target face by multiplying *n* by the ratio of the area of the target face to the entire area of the part faces. If $m < 1$, *m* is assigned 1, otherwise, *m* is assigned the least integer greater than *m*. Then sample *m* points on the target facet. We can construct a point **P** in a triangle with vertices (**A, B, C**) by generating two random numbers, t_1 and t_2, between 0 and 1.

$$\mathbf{P} = (1 - t_2)\,\mathbf{A} + t2\,(1 - t_1)\,\mathbf{B} + t_1 t_2\,\mathbf{C} \tag{1}$$

In order to generate points uniformly, we assign t_1 the values of 1 divided by $m+1$. t_2 can be generated randomly to make sure that the constructed points are of randomicity to some degree. According to [2], we create a base number (*n=1024*) of sample points. The actual number may be more than the base number, which can be meliorated by using simplified CAD models.

The shape signature is represented as a probability distribution sampled from a couple of shape functions based on [3], namely *D2 shape function* measuring the Euclidean distance between two random points on the surface and *Intersection angle shape function* measuring the angle formed by the triangle facets where a pair of sample points is positioned. The distances between two sample points can be normalized by the average distance. And we only calculate the pair of shape functions for two points that locates on different facets.

We plot a 2D histogram (see Fig.1) using the two independent variables above. There are three coordinates in shape distribution. The *x*-coordinate and *y*-coordinate represent the normalized distance between two sample points and the cosine value of intersection angle respectively. We evenly divide the *x*-coordinate and *y*-coordinate into *Lx* and *Ly* subparts respectively so that the *x-y* coordinate plane is decomposed to $Lx \times Ly$ cells. For each cell, we count up the probability of pairs of distance and intersection that fall in the cell, which is denoted by *z*-coordinate. We use L_1 norm to compare shape distributions to produce dissimilarity measures.

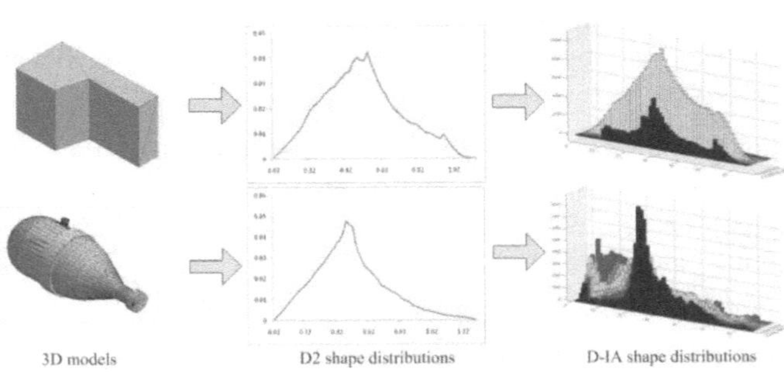

Fig. 1. D2 shape distributions and D-IA shape distributions of dissimilar models

3 Experimental Results

We have applied this method to a set of solid models of mechanical parts from the 3D engineering shape benchmark (ESB) developed by PRECISE [5]. The algorithm has been implemented in C++ and run on a Windows XP PC with a 2.40 GHz Pentium IV processor and 512MB of memory. We created an index to models from ESB in terms of the classification schema given by PRECISE and show how it can support a real-time query-by-example scenario.

From the Fig.2., we can notice that the query model is always the top match for each one. In these examples, the D-IA with simplification seems to perform better than the other two, for example, the D-IA seems to retrieve more similar models for Query1-4 than D2, and it has fewer models that look much different than D2. Moreover, the numbers in D-IA embody the dissimilarity more since the numbers vary directly as the shape of models, i.e. they are more sensitive to the model shape.

Table 1. Quantificational comparisons among different shape functions

Shape functions	Performance			Computational cost		
	FT	ST	NN	Model Simplification(s)	Function computation(s)	Retrieval Total(s)
D2	18%	29%	40%	0	0.39	1.64
D-IA without simplification	27%	38%	47%	0	0.78	2.05
D-IA with simplification	30%	41%	52%	0.001	0.50	1.86

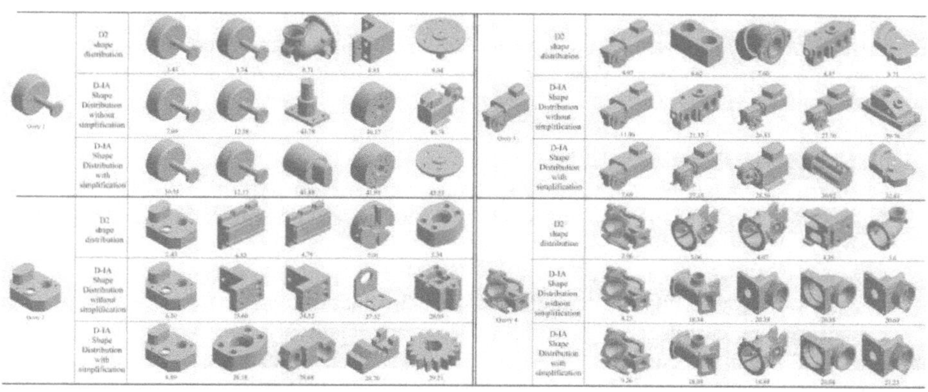

Fig. 2. Comparisons among query results obtained by different shape functions

Table.1. compares the average performances and computational costs among different shape functions quantificationally. The meanings of FT, ST and NN can refer to [3]. We can see that D-IA achieves better performance although the retrieval total time is a little greater than D2 since the sample points generated by semi-random full-sample manner are more than D2. The D-IA with simplification works best. Therefore, simplification has a positive effort on shape retrieval since simplification reduces the number of triangle facets so that sample points can reflect the shape more concentratedly.

4 Conclusion

In this paper, we improved the methodology for shape distribution of CAD models represented by polygonal meshes. We believe our method is the first that used a simplification algorithm for shape comparison to reduce the amount of triangles of CAD models with the topology of models preserved, which facilitates shape distribution generation and shape indexing and classification. In sampling phase, we exploited a semi-random full-sampling method to guarantee that the sample points are uniformly positioned on the surface so that sample points can represent the shape more sufficiently. We employed an enhanced shape function for triangle meshes, the distance-intersection angle shape function, to construct the shape distribution. The experiential results show that simplification acts a positive effort on shape retrieval and our method is effective and more sensitive to shape than D2.

There are two issues for discussion and future research. We hope the sample points can be adaptive to the shape without 'points explosion', so the simplification method for shape searching could be improved by controlling its end condition to make sure that each triangle has approximate area. And the method of comparing shape distributions can be studied more for 2D histogram to make full advantage of the information given by the shape distribution.

References

1. Iyer, N., Jayanti, S., Lou, K., Kalyanaraman, Y., Ramani, K.: Three-dimensional shape searching: state-of-the-art review and future trends. Computer-Aided Design 37, 509–530 (2005)
2. Osada, R., Funkhouser, T., Chazelle, B., Dobkin, D.: Shape Distributions. ACM Transactions on Graphics 21, 807–832 (2002)
3. Ohbuchi, R., Minamitani, T., Takei, T.: Shape-Similarity Search of 3D Models by using Enhanced Shape Functions. International Journal of Computer Applications in Technology, 70–85 (2005)
4. Kanaya, T., Teshima, Y., Nishio, K.: A Topology-Preserving Polygonal Simplification Using Vertex Clustering. In: Proceedings of the 3rd international conference on Computer graphics and interactive techniques in Australasia and South East Asia, 117–120 (2005)
5. Jayanti, S., Kalyanaraman, Y., Iyer, N., Ramani, K.: Developing an engineering shape benchmark for CAD models. Computer-Aided Design 38, 939–953 (2006)

Wavelet-Based Salient Region Extraction

Dong-Woei Lin[1,2] and Shih-Hsuan Yang[1]

[1] Department of Computer Science and Information Engineering
National Taipei University of Technology
1, Sec. 3, Chung-Hsiao E. Rd., Taipei, Taiwan
[2] Department of Electronic Engineering
Chin Min Institute of Technology, Miaoli, Taiwan
{s0669009, shyang}@ntut.edu.tw

Abstract. In this paper, we propose a new technique for extracting salient regions in an image. Identification of salient regions is useful for region/object based image processing. Previous works on salient regions/points typically involve complex detection and are not always reliable in terms of perceptual importance and robustness. This paper presents an efficient salient-region extraction algorithm based on the significance of accumulated wavelet coefficients. The proposed method is robust to common image processing such as compression, filtering, and geometric distortions. Experimental results substantiate the distinguished performance of the proposed method.

Keywords: Invariant image features, salient region extraction, wavelet transform, image understanding.

1 Introduction

One central issue for voluminous digital image data management is an efficient and effective method for automatic content-based image indexing and retrieval (CBIR). Another important issue is the digital rights management (DRM), including digital watermarking, image hashing, and other copyright-protection mechanisms. As digital images could be processed without noticeable loss in their semantic meanings, identification of invariant features in images is hence crucial to CBIR and DRM applications.

One of the appealing methods is to collect the salient points using low-level characteristics such as Harris detector [1] and scale-invariant feature transform (SIFT) [2]. Salient points can also be detected on the wavelet domain [3]. The problem for feature-point approaches is that the results may be vulnerable to small perturbations and a precise matching based on the scattered feature points. To increase the robustness and ease feature matching, salient regions have been proposed in the literature. Salient regions can be built from detected salient points (as vertex or centroid), but the region-growing process may be problematic. Shao and Brady [4] proposed a salient region selection algorithm by measuring the entropy of local attributes and the inter-scale saliency. The method has applied to object retrieval.

H.H.S. Ip et al. (Eds.): PCM 2007, LNCS 4810, pp. 389–392, 2007.

We propose an efficient wavelet-based salient region generation algorithm that provides sufficient invariance to common image manipulations. Section 2 presents the algorithm. In Section 3, the properties of proposed method are evaluated and compared to related works, followed by the concluding remarks in Section 4.

2 Salient Region Extraction

A wavelet coefficient summarizes the spatial/scale information of a region. We use the Daubechies (9,7) filter in this paper because of its excellent performance. The wavelet coefficients are often organized as a spatial-orientation tree, as shown in Fig. 1(b). The coefficients from the highest to the lowest levels of wavelet subbands depict a coarse-to-fine variation in scales (resolutions). We have thus determined to construct the "saliency map" by its accumulated significance. Let H_i, V_i, and D_i denote the wavelet coefficients of horizontal, vertical, and diagonal subbands at level i respectively. (A larger value of i indicates a coarser resolution.) The saliency map is organized into the smallest-scale detail subbands H_1, V_1, and D_1 (excluding the approximation subband), and the value of its entry is obtained by adding the magnitude of the corresponding wavelet coefficient and its ancestors.

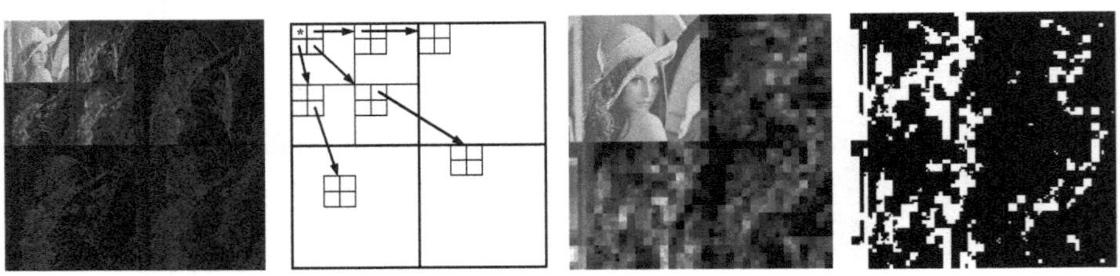

(a) (b) (c) (d)

Fig. 1. (a) Wavelet transform (b) spatial-orientation trees. (c) The saliency map for each subbands of Lena. (d) The corresponded significant coefficients using τ_{15}. Top left is the final salient region.

The significant coefficients are obtained by binarizing the saliency map. We use a universal threshold τ_x, whose value is determined by allowing $x\%$ entries in saliency map is declared significant (x = 15 in Fig.1(d)). The salient regions in the spatial domain are thus found by collecting and taking the union of the areas that correspond to significant coefficients in the horizontal, vertical, and diagonal directions. Fig. 1(d) demonstrates an example for the test image Lena.

3 Analysis and Evaluation

The proposed saliency by accumulating the magnitudes across scales provides a combined global/local significance, and is progressive in nature. It is manifest from Fig. 2 that visually important objects are preserved under different thresholds, and thus less sensitive to a specific τ_x. Moreover, the proposed region-based method *directly* identifies regions of interest while a point-based method usually extends from the salient points. It is questionable that a particular extension scheme (say a small disk) could be adequate. Another attractive characteristic of the proposed method is that there is notably a single parameter τ.

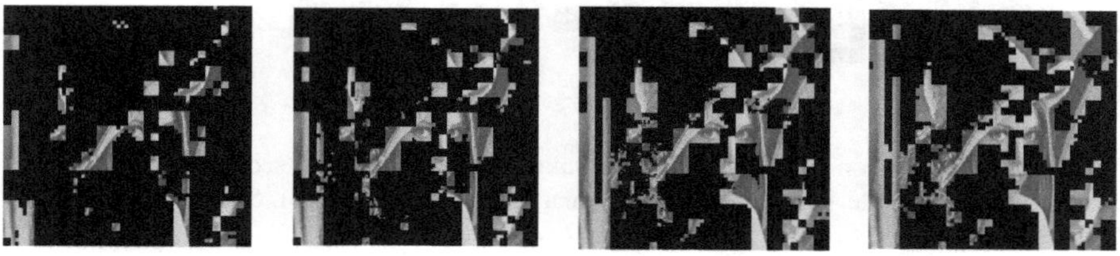

Fig. 2. Results of superimposing salient regions on the original image demonstrate the saliency in progressive under thresholds τ_5, τ_8, τ_{12}, and τ_{15} (from left to right)

To evaluate the effectiveness of proposed method, we make the comparison between proposed method and two point-based schemes: Harris detector [5], wavelet-based detector [3], and a region-based algorithm [4]. Fig. 3 illustrates the comparison results. A big difference on the point locations between [5] and [3] implies that the extension regions will be quite different. The proposed salient region algorithm provides a confined regions pertaining to the essence of image content instead of edges or points only. Fig. 3(c) illustrates a similar result of proposed method to Fig. 3(d). However, our method is based on a simple and efficient accumulation process, and thus is more attractive in database applications.

We evaluate the robustness of the proposed method against the Stirmark 3.1 benchmarking system [6]. Baboon, Lena, F16, and pepper are used as the test images. The attacks in Stirmark 3.1 can be separated into two distinct categories. For content preserving attacks, such as filtering, we compare the salient regions (bi-level masks) of the original and the attacked images by computing the normalized Hamming distance Δ_{SR}. The value Δ_{SR} calculates the ratio of spatially unmatched points. All salient regions of transformed images remain stable (with a tiny Δ_{SR} value) as in Table 1. For content lossy attacks, such as rotation with cropping, as the attack destroys the synchronization between the original and attacked images, some results of Lena are showed in Fig. 4 to reveal that the proposed method is general very robust and stable.

Table 1. Average Δ_{SR} of type I attacks for four test images. Threshold is set to τ_{10}

Attack description	Amount	baboon	F16	Lena	pepper
Convolution/rank filtering	5	0.1188	0.0783	0.0573	0.0298
JPEG	12	0.0449	0.0346	0.0210	0.0111
Scaling	6	0.0834	0.0498	0.0396	0.0287
Affine	8	0.0637	0.0350	0.0328	0.0240
Type I average Δ_{SR}		0.0860	0.0552	0.0416	0.0247

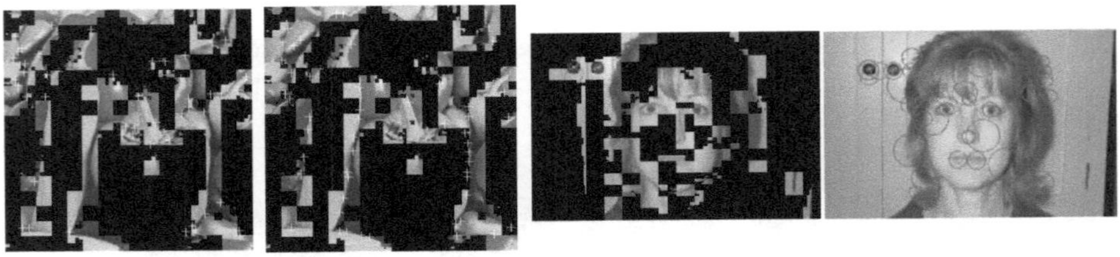

Fig. 3. The comparison between proposed salient region and points detected by (a) Harris detector [5], (b) wavelet-based detector [3] (marked as white crosses). Salient region detected by (c) our method and (d) Shao's method [4]. ((d) is cited from [4].)

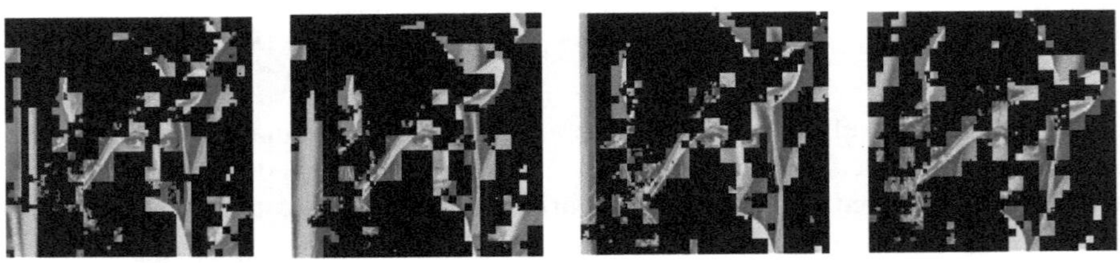

Fig. 4. The examples of proposed salient region for Lena under several manipulations

4 Conclusion

A wavelet-based salient region formation algorithm is proposed. The algorithm extracts salient region efficiently through an accumulation process and is invariant to common image manipulations. We evaluate the effectiveness of proposed method and verify the invariance to several image operations. Experimental results exhibit that the proposed salient region not only identifies the essence of image content but also provide proper stability.

References

1. Bas, P., Chassery, J.-M., Macq, B.: Geometrically invariant watermarking using feature points. IEEE Trans. Image Processing 11, 1014–1028 (2002)
2. Lee, H.-Y., Kim, H., Lee, H.-K.: Robust image watermarking using local invariant features. Optical Engineering 45, 1–11 (2006)
3. Tian, Q., Sebe, N., Lew, M., Loupias, S.E., Huang, T.S.: Image retrieval using wavelet-based salient points. J. Electronic Imaging 10, 835–849 (2001)
4. Shao, L., Brady, M.: Specific object retrieval based on salient regions. Pattern Recognition 39, 1932–1948 (2006)
5. Harris, C.G., Stephens, M.J.: A combined corner and edge detector. In: Proc. Fourth Alvey Vision Conf., Manchester, pp. 147–151 (1988)
6. StirMark version 3.1, http://www.cl.cam.ac.uk/ fapp2/watermarking/stirmark/

Color-Based Text Extraction for the Image

Jian Yi[1,2], Yuxin Peng[1,2,*], and Jianguo Xiao[1,2]

[1] Institute of Computer Science and Technology, Peking University, Beijing 100871, China
[2] State Key Laboratory of Text Processing Technology, Peking University, Beijing 100871, China
{yijian, pengyuxin, xjg}@icst.pku.edu.cn

Abstract. In this paper, we focus on the text extraction of image, and propose a new approach for it into two phases: Firstly, for the effective binarization of text region image, instead of performing the binarization in a constant color plane as in the existing methods, our approach adaptively selects the relatively best color plane for the binarization, which uses the text contrast difference among the color planes. Secondly, to remove the noise in the binary image, we consider the color difference between the text strokes and noises, and the color-based clustering is then utilized to remove the noise for the effective text recognition. The experimental result has shown that the proposed approach is better than the existing methods in terms of the performance of text extraction.

Keywords: Text extraction; binarization; noise removal; color-based clustering.

1 Introduction

Generally, text extraction of image includes two key steps: binarization of text region image, and noise removal of binary image. For the binarization of text region image, most existing methods binarize the text region image in a constant color plane [2][4][6]. However, the methods are not always reasonable, because other color plane is sometimes better for the image binarization. In addition, for the noise removal, two methods are proposed in [2][4][5], which are the connected component analysis (CCA) and the gray constant constraint (GCC). All these methods, however, do not consider the color difference between the text strokes and noises, which is extremely useful for noise removal. Based on the above analysis, we propose a new approach for the text extraction of image. The major contributions of our approach are as follows:

- *Color Plane Selection for Image Binarization*: Instead of performing the binarization of the text region image in a constant color plane as in [2][4][6], we adaptively select the best color plane with the strongest text contrast from the *YUV* color planes, and then the method in [1] is utilized to binarize the text region image, which improves the result of the binary image.

---

* Corresponding author.

H.H.S. Ip et al. (Eds.): PCM 2007, LNCS 4810, pp. 393–396, 2007.

- *Color-based Clustering for Noise removal*: For the effective text recognition, we consider the color difference between the text strokes and noises in the color image, and the color-based clustering, together with CCA and GCC, is employed for the effective noise removal.

2 Color Plane Selection for Image Binarization

Many existing methods binarize the text region image in the constant Y color plane [7], however, the Y is not always reasonable for the binarizaition. Take a text region image with the red text for example, text pixels of this image have relative large value in R and small value in G and B color planes, while the non-text pixels have relatively small value in R and large value in G and B color planes. According to Eqn (1), when this image is converted from RGB to V color plane, the text pixels with red color have high intensity in V, while the non-text pixels with non-red color have low intensity. So, for this image, there are two advantages in V: the text contrast is relatively high and the background is clear. Based on the above analysis, we propose a method to adaptively select the color plane with the strongest text contrast in YUV for the binarization, which is described as in Eqn (2) and (3).

$$V = 0.615\times R - 0.515\times G - 0.100\times B \tag{1}$$

$$C_\alpha = \max(C_Y, C_U, C_V),\ \alpha \in \{Y, U, V\} \tag{2}$$

$$C_Y = \sum_{\substack{w/3\le i\le w\times 2/3\\ h/3\le j\le h\times 2/3}} E_Y(i,j),\ C_U = \sum_{\substack{w/3\le i\le w\times 2/3\\ h/3\le j\le h\times 2/3}} E_U(i,j),\ C_V = \sum_{\substack{w/3\le i\le w\times 2/3\\ h/3\le j\le h\times 2/3}} E_V(i,j) \tag{3}$$

In Eqn (2), the color plane α is thought to have the strongest text contrast, and is selected for the image binarization. In Eqn (3), E_Y, E_U and E_V are the edge maps of the text image detected by the *Sobel* edge detector in YUV color planes respectively, w is the width and h is the height of the image.

3 Color-Based Clustering for Noise Removal

After the binarizaition, the text region image has been binarized into foreground and background, and the foreground is composed of text strokes and noises. CCA and GCC [2][4][5] are firstly employed for the noise removal, but these methods can not remove the noises which have the similar geometry property and gray value with the text strokes. So the color-based clustering is proposed to remove these noises. Initially, the connected components are assigned to be their corresponding color in the color image. Then the algorithm described in Fig. 1 is utilized. In our approach, C is clustered into two classes by k-means, and the class with more pixels is regarded as text, because the number of text pixels is generally more than that of noise pixels. In Fig. 1, P_i denotes a color connected component, $c(P_i)$ is the average color value of all pixels in P_i, c_{Add} is the average color value of the pixels in background. We add

c_{Add} into C to make sure there are at least two different colors in C, which avoids the texts strokes with homogenous color are separated into the different classes.

1. For each P_i, $P_i \in S$, S is the set of all the connected components
   $c(P_i) = avg(o(R\ G\ B))$, $o \in P_i$
2. $c_{Add} = avg(o'(R\ G\ B))$, $o' \notin P_i$
3. $C = \{c_{Add}\} \hbar \{c(P_i)\}$,
4. Cluster C into two classes by color: $Class_{text}$ and $Class_{noise}$
5. For each P_i
   If $c(P_i) \in Class_{text}$
      Then P_i is thought to be a text stroke
   Else
      Then P_i is thought to be the noise

Fig. 1. Color-based clustering for noise removal

4 Experiment Result

To evaluate the performance of the proposed approach, we set up a database that consists of 1621 text regions. Totally, there are 10594 Chinese characters in the 1621 text regions. The text regions are processed by the methods of text extraction, then they are input to the same OCR software for text recognition. So the result of text recognition can evaluate the performance of the text extraction methods. Three methods are implemented for comparison: I. Our approach. II. Our approach without noise removal by color-based clustering. III. Lyu's approach in [2]. The character recognition rate (CRR) and character recognition precision (CRP) are used to evaluate the performance of the text extraction methods, which are defined as the follows:

$$CRR = N_c \div N \qquad CRP = N_c \div N_r \tag{4}$$

Where N_c is the number of the correctly recognized characters, and N_r is the number of recognized characters. N is the number of characters in the text regions.

Table 1 shows the experimental results of the three methods. Overall, our two methods (I and II) achieve better result than Lyu's approach[2] (III) in terms of CRR and CRP. The reason mainly lies in two aspects: On one hand, our approach utilizes the adaptively selected color plane, which is better than only *Y* color plane for the binarization of text image in Lyu's approach [2]. Another hand, the proposed approach could remove noises more effective than the Lyu's method[2], which employ the color-based clustering, together with CCA and GCC. In addition, compared with our approach I and II, method I employ the color-based clustering while method II does not use it, and method I achieves better performance in terms of CRR and CRP, which shows the effectiveness of the proposed color-based clustering approach for noise removal. An example is illustrated in Fig. 2, in which our approach

Table 1. Experimental results for text extraction in image

	I	II	III
CRR	67.5%	60.4%	43.8%
CRP	82.9%	80.8%	58.7%

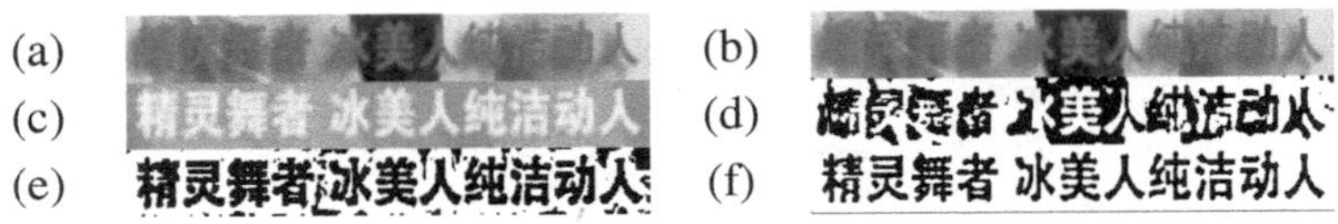

Fig. 2. (a): Original image. (b) and (c): The results of Y and the adaptively selected color planes in (a) respectively. (d) and (e): Binary images of (b) and (c) respectively, both processed by the improved method of Niblack's binarization algorithm in [1]. (f): The result based on (e), processed by the proposed approach for noise removal.

can effectively binarize the text region image in the adaptively selected color plane, and the noise in the binary image can be effectively removed by our approach.

5 Conclusion

This paper has proposed a new approach for text extraction in the images. In our approach, the text region image is binarized in the adaptively selected color plane, and the color-based clustering is employed to remove the noise in the binary image. The experimental results have shown the effectiveness of our approach.

Acknowledgments. The work described in this paper was fully supported by the National Natural Science Foundation of China under Grant No. 60503062, and the Program for New Century Excellent Talents in University (NCET).

References

1. Chen, X., Yuille, A.L.: Detecting and Reading Text in Natural Scenes. CVPR (2004)
2. Lyu, M.R., Song, J., Cai, M.: A Comprehensive Method for Multilingual Video Text Detection, Localization and Extraction. IEEE Transactions on CSVT 15(2) (2005)
3. Liu, C., Wang, C., Dai, R.: Text Detection in Images Based on Unsupervised Classification of Edge-based Features. In: ICDAR, pp. 610–614 (2005)
4. Ye, Q., Gao, W., Huang, Q.: Automatic Text Segmentation from Complex Background. In: International Conference on Image Processing, Singapore (2004)
5. Chen, D., Odobez, J., Bourlard, H.: Text Detection and Recognition in Images and Video Frames. Pattern Recognition 37(3), 595–608 (2004)
6. Lienhart, R., Wernicke, A.: Localizing and Segmenting Text in Images and Videos. IEEE Transactions on Circuits and Systems for Video Technology 12(4) (2002)
7. Jung, K., Kim, K.I., Jain, A.K.: Text Information Extraction in Images and Video: a survey. Pattern Recognition (2004)

Text Segmentation in Complex Background Based on Color and Scale Information of Character Strokes

Weiqiang Wang[1,2], Libo Fu[1], and Wen Gao[1,2]

[1] Institute of Computing Technology, CAS, Beijing, China, 100080
[2] Graduate School of Chinese Academy of Sciences, CAS, Beijing, China, 100039
{wqwang,lbfu,wgao}@ict.ac.cn

Abstract. This paper presents a robust approach to segmenting text embedded in complex background. Our approach consists of four steps: smart sampling, unsupervised clustering, the Bayesian decision, post-processing. The experimental results show that it works effectively, and is more efficient in removing complex background residues than the popular K-means method.

Keywords: text segmentation, character stroke, complex background.

1 Introduction

Text extraction in images and videos is very useful in automatic image/video annotation, indexing and retrieval etc. [1,2,3,4,5]. Once text regions are detected and located, text segmentation is required to identify text pixels in text regions so that the binary images generated can be effectively processed by most optical character recognition (OCR) software. Many text segmentation algorithms have been proposed, including the threshold-based method [1], the geometrical analysis techniques based on connected component analysis (CCA) [2], the Markov random field [3], the unsupervised clustering [5],.

In this paper we propose a text segmentation approach based on a hybrid probability model. Our method first smartly samples the pixels close to the edges in text regions, and then a clustering procedure is applied to identify the dominant color and the scale of text strokes. Finally a probability model is constructed online to characterize the color and the scale of text strokes, and those pixels fitting the model well based on color and scale are labeled as text. A post-processing is used to further remove background residues.

2 Our Text Segmentation Approach

In our system, text regions are first located using the text detection algorithm in [4]. The text lines are then scaled to a proper fixed size (60 pixels) through sub-pixel linear interpolation. The scaling can increase the resolution of small text regions, and make character strokes have similar expected thickness. Characters in a text line generally have homogeneous color, and character strokes also have consistent

H.H.S. Ip et al. (Eds.): PCM 2007, LNCS 4810, pp. 397–400, 2007.

thickness. Each pixel in text regions is represented as (c, s), where c is its color in the CIE-La*b* color space, and s denotes its scale. The scale of a pixel refers to the scale of the homogeneous region which the pixel belongs to. As shown in Fig.1, given a pixel P, a search is performed along six directions $d_i, i = 0,1,...,5$, outwards to collect the pixels with the similar color as P. The color similarity is measured by Euclidean distance. The search terminates if the similarity of two adjacent pixels is lower than a pre-defined threshold T_c. Let $n_i, i = 0,...,5$ denote the number of the pixels collected in each direction, the scale of the pixel P is defined as $\min_i \{n_i\}$.

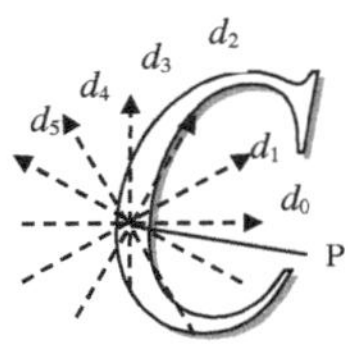

Fig. 1. Illustration of the scale of a pixel P

Text strokes generally have a strong contrast against their background, so the boundary of character strokes corresponds to strong edges. We sample the pixels along the normal on each side of edges in text regions (5 pixels in our experiments). It is reasonable that a dominant mode corresponding to text pixels exist in the feature space (c, s) of the sampled pixels. The samples are first clustered using the color reduction method [2]. Among the clusters generated, text samples are expected to distribute in one of two largest clusters. For each pixel in the two largest clusters, its scale is evaluated. The same color reduction method is applied to each reserved cluster based on the scales of sampled pixels. After this scale clustering, the largest one in each reserved cluster is finally chosen as candidate cluster containing text samples. As a result, we obtain two candidate clusters through color and scale clustering on sampled pixels.

For the two candidate clusters, we can estimate the conditional probability density $p(c, s \mid text; \theta)$ of text pixels in text regions respectively, where θ denotes the model parameter. Since the color and the scale of a pixel are independent, we have

$$p(c, s \mid text; \theta) = p(c \mid text; \theta_c)\, p(s \mid text; \theta_s)\,. \tag{1}$$

The Gaussian mixture model (GMM) is used to model text color, and each color component is assumed to be independent. The scale of text pixels is modeled by the Gaussian distribution. Our extensive experiments show that the number of Gaussians in GMM has very slight influence on the likelihood function and the final segmentation results for most text regions. Thus, our system only adaptively chooses 2 or 3, depending on which generates the maximum likelihood for all training samples.

Based on $p(c, s \mid text; \theta)$, the Bayesian rule is used to classify each pixel in text regions. Ideally $p(text \mid c, s; \theta)$ is preferred, but we have no knowledge about the prior $p(c,s)$. Assuming $p(c,s)$ conforms to the uniform distribution approximately, we can perform text segmentation based on $p(c,s \mid text)$ instead. Since the pixel-wise classification results in rough boundaries of extracted character strokes in some cases, our algorithm exploits the joint probability of the pixels in a certain neighborhood (shown in Fig.2) to segment text strokes.

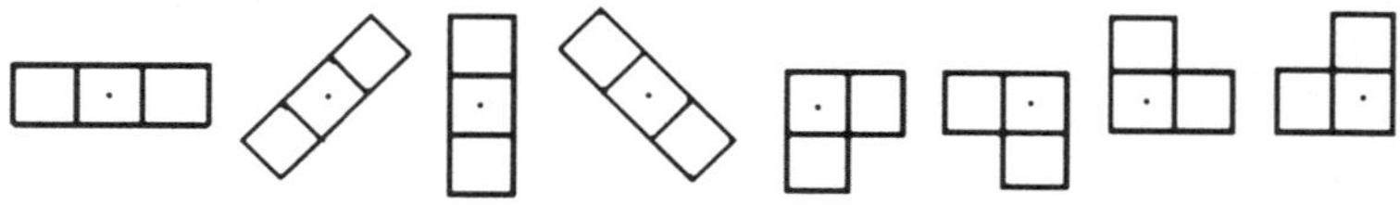

Fig. 2. Eight neighborhoods for computing the joint probability

To select a text image layer more accurately, a post-processing step is designed to further remove background residues. CCA is used to filter out some of them based on geometry properties (character size and aspect ratio). Furthermore, since the western characters are well aligned in a line, the baseline of characters can be located based on the projection profile [2], and the background residues far from the baseline are eliminated. For Chinese characters, the spatial relation constraints proposed in [6] is used to remove background residues. Finally, based on the periodical and symmetrical layout of characters in a text line, we use the x-axis projection profile [6] to select the true text image layer from two candidates. Its binary text image can be fed to an OCR engine for character recognition.

3 Experimental Results

Our approach is evaluated on two datasets. The first dataset (**FD**) consists of 620 text lines located from a MPEG-2 news video, and the second one (**SD**) consists of 465 text lines from a MPEG-1 news video. The two datasets contain 5437 Chinese characters and 4170 western characters overlaid on complex background respectively. The performance of the proposed approach is evaluated according to the character extraction rate (CER) and the character recognition rate (CRR). They defined as

$$CER = N_x / N, \quad CRR = N_c / N \tag{2}$$

where N_x is the number of characters completely extracted without obviously lost strokes or connected background residues, N_c is the number of characters correctly recognized by an OCR engine and N is the number of all the characters.

We compared our method with the K-means method. For the K-means method, we chose the best result for each text line under different K. Text recognition is carried out by HWOCR5.0. To evaluate the influence of the post-processing on the CRR, we measure the CRR respectively in the case of using post-processing and not. The experimental results are summarized in Table 1. The experimental results show the CER of our method is higher than that of the K-means method, especially on the second dataset. Since the color clustering in our algorithm is performed on a smaller set of samples, rather than the whole text regions, so it is less sensitive to the complexity of background, and can estimate text color more precisely. Additionally the characters segmented by the K-means method for **SD** is more easily connected with background residues due to blurry boundary of character strokes. The scale feature in our algorithm can remove the background regions with large scales. We see the CRR of our algorithm is slightly higher than that of the K-means, while our algorithm has much higher CRR in the case of no post-processing. It shows that our algorithm itself is more efficient in removing background regions of large scales. The relatively lower CRR for **SD** results from some lost or conglutinated strokes.

Table 1. Performance comparison using K-means and our method on the two datasets

Data	Algorithms	CER	CRR (No)	CRR (Yes)
FD	K-means	97.8%	68.4%	93.7%
	Our algorithm	98.1%	82.3%	94.1%
SD	K-means	88.5%	69.8%	73.9%
	Our algorithm	93.2%	73.6%	76.6%

4 Conclusion

We present a robust approach to segmenting text in complex background based on color and scale information of character strokes. In our approach, the smart sampling technique makes subsequent color clustering prone to give a more precise estimation of text color. The proposed scale feature can effectively improve completeness of the segmentation of text strokes, and thus increase the performance of character recognition. The comparison experiments show that our approach itself is very effective and robust for images with high quality, and always has better performance compared with the popular K-means approach.

Acknowledgement. The work is supported by "National 242 project: 2006A09" and the start-up research fund of graduate school, CAS.

References

1. Wu, V., Manmatha, R., Riseman, E.: Finding text in images. In: Proceedings of ACM International Conference on Digital Libraries, Philadelphia, pp. 1–10 (1997)
2. Jain, A.K., Yu, B.: Automatic text location in images and video frames. Pattern Recognition 31(12), 2055–2076 (1998)
3. Chen, D., Odobez, J-M., Bourlard, H.: Text detection and recognition in images and video frames. Pattern Recognition 3(37), 595–608 (2004)
4. Ye, Q., Gao, W., Wang, W., Zeng, W.: A robust text detection algorithm in images and video frames. In: 4th IEEE Pacific-Rim Conference on Multimedia, Singapore, pp. 802–806 (2003)
5. Gllavata, J., Ewerth, R., Stefi, T., Freisleben, B.: Unsupervised Text Segmentation Using Color and Wavelet Features. In: Proceedings of the 3rd International Conference on Image and Video Retrieval, Dublin, Ireland, pp. 216–224 (July 2004)
6. Fu, L., wang, W., Zhan, Y.: A robust text segmentation approach in complex background based on multiple constraints. In: Ho, Y.-S., Kim, H.J. (eds.) PCM 2005. LNCS, vol. 3768, pp. 594–605. Springer, Heidelberg (2005)

Design of a Decentralized Video-on-Demand System with Cooperative Clients in Multicast Environment

K.M. Ho and K.T. Lo

Department of Electronic and Information Engineering,
The Hong Kong Polytechnic Uninversity, Hong Kong
enkmho@eie.polyu.edu.hk,
enktlo@polyu.edu.hk

Abstract. Peer-to-Peer (P2P) communications have become a popular alternative solution to provide large-scale video-on-demand (VoD) services. Recent approaches are designed for streaming applications in a unicast infrastructure. As the successful deployment of IP broadcast delivery, the system could have a further improvement when broadcasting scheme can be coupled with P2P paradigm. In this paper, we develop a possible solution for building a VoD system using existing broadcasting protocol coupled with cooperative clients in multicast environment. The objective of this work mainly focuses on addressing one design issue in such framework: reliability. An analytical model is developed to determine the minimum number of cooperative clients required for the system. The results showed that 60 peers, each of which has the availability of 0.4, are enough to leverage the workload of the central server up to 95%, when the startup delay of the system is 10 minutes.

Keywords: multicast, video-on-demand, peer-to-peer.

1 Introduction

In this paper, we develop a possible solution for building a VoD system using existing broadcasting scheme coupled with P2P paradigm denoted Broadcast-based Peer-to-Peer Protocol (BPP). The general idea of BPP is to decentralize the broadcasting channels from the central server to a number of client denoted peer server which are willing to contribute their storages and processing powers to the system such that each peer is only responsible for broadcasting the video over one or several channels simultaneously. Thus, the bottleneck of the system is no longer on the server side. However, similar to other P2P applications, each peer server in the system is allowed to leave and enter the system at arbitrary time. To avoid the disruption of the services, a central server is still deployed in the system but the role of the central server just acts as a standby unit. Therefore, the objective of this work mainly focuses on addressing one design issues in such framework: reliability. An analytical model is developed to determine the minimize number of peer server required for the system. Our proposed policy and model is protocol-independent and thus any existing broadcasting protocols can also be applied. Staggered [3] broadcasting protocol (SB)

H.H.S. Ip et al. (Eds.): PCM 2007, LNCS 4810, pp. 401–404, 2007.

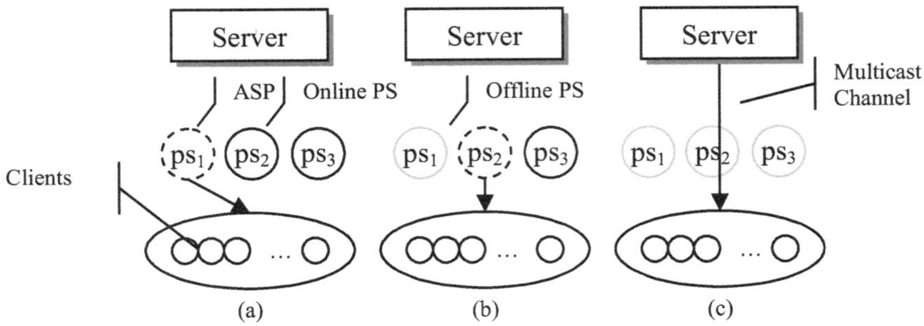

Fig. 1. Operation of the proposed system

will be used as an example to illustrate how the broadcasting scheme can be coupled with P2P paradigm.

2 Description of Proposed Scheme

Different from SB to handle all video channels in a single server, BPP distributes the video channels to a number of peer denoted peer server (PS) which are willing to contribute their storages and processing powers to the system such that each peer is only responsible for broadcasting the video over one or several channels simultaneously. Thus, the bottleneck of the system is no longer on the server side. However, similar to other P2P applications, each PS in the system is allowed to leave and enter the system at arbitrary time. Therefore, for each video channel, more than one PS may be deployed in order to increase the degree of reliability. Each PS handling the identical video channel forms a peer server group (PSG) and only one of them denoted active serving peer (ASP) will be responsible for broadcasting the video. When the system is launched, one of PS in each PSG will be selected as an ASP to broadcast the stored video over the network. As shown in Fig. 1, there are three PSs forming a PSG and ps1 is selected to broadcast video i (V_i). After some time has elapsed, the current ASP (ps1) departs. Then, another PS in the same PSG is picked to take over the service (i.e. ps2, see Fig. 1b). However, if all PSs for this video leave, the central server should handle the service in order to avoid disruption of service (see Fig. 1c). Once one of the PSs in the PSG is online again, the central server will return the duty to this PSG. In general, the central server provides the services to clients only when all PSs in the PGS are offline. Therefore, in order to leverage the workload of the central server, we should determine the minimum number of replica for each video channel.

3 System Modeling

Similar to original SB, a new video session for V_i is created every W_i seconds in BPP. Thus, the number of channel required for V_i (S_i) is $S_i = \lceil L_i / W_i \rceil$, where L_i is the length of V_i. Therefore, if each PS can contribute a bandwidth of X channels, the number of PSG for V_i (J_i) can be expressed by $J_i = \lceil S_i / X \rceil$. Since each PS can leave and enter the system at anytime, it is assumed that the mean up time and mean down time of each PS are independent and identically distributed with exponential function with the rate γ_{up} and γ_{down} respectively. Then, the availability of each PS (A) can be defined as $A = \gamma_{up}^{-1} / (\gamma_{up}^{-1} + \gamma_{diwb}^{-1})$ [1]. Because the video channels of V_i handled by PSG j (K_j^i) is served alternatively by the PSG j and the central server, it forms an alternating renewal process [1]. Let Z_1^{ij}, Z_2^{ij}, ... denote the successive serving time of K_j^i and also let D_1^{ij}, D_2^{ij}, ... denote the corresponding successive serving time of the central server. Obviously, more PSs for one video channel results in longer $Z_k^{ij}, \forall k$ and thus fewer central server resources are involved. Therefore, the operation of PSG j can be modeled as a reliability model with N_j PSs and thus the mean serving time of PSG j for V_i (Z^{ij}) can be expressed as $Z^{ij} = \frac{1}{\gamma_{up}} \sum_{m=1}^{N_j} \left(\frac{\gamma_{down}{}^{m-1} (N_j - 1)!}{m \gamma_{up}{}^{m-1} (N_j - m)!(m-1)!} \right)$ and the corresponding mean serving time of the central server (D^{ij}) is $D^{ij} = (N_j \gamma_{down})^{-1}$. Therefore, the mean time between renewals is $Y^{ij} = Z^{ij} + D^{ij}$. Then, the average bandwidth reserved by the central server for PSG j can be given by $B_S^{ij} = XB_i \cdot D^{ij} / Y^{ij}$, where B_i is the data rate of V_i. Therefore, the overall bandwidth required for the central server to support V_i is computed by $B_S^i = \sum_{j=1}^{J_i} B_S^{ij}$. In general, we want to determine the number of PSs required for the system for V_i (N) such that the central server resources for this video can reduce to rS_iB_i, where $N = \sum_{i=1}^{S_i} N_i$ and $0 < r \le 1$. Therefore, the optimization problem is to minimize N subject to $B_S^i \le rS_iB_i$ and $N_i \ge 1$, $i = 1,2,3\hbar\ , S_i$. The second constraint implies that at least one PS should be deployed in each PSG.

4 Results

In this section, we evaluate the performance of the proposed protocol. It is assumed that the video length is 7200 seconds long and each PS contributes a bandwidth of one video channel (i.e. $X=1$). For simplicity, we assume that B_i is equal to 1. Also, the availability of PS (A) is set as 0.4 and W_i is of 600 seconds. Therefore, there is 12 PSGs in the system. We investigate the number of PSs required for each PSG against various availabilities such that the target reduction of the central server resources can

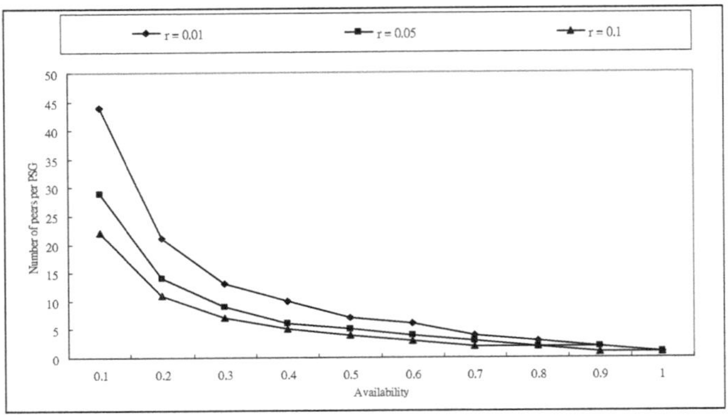

Fig. 2. Number of PS per PSG requirement against Availability of PS.

be achieved. In Fig.2, as we expected, the number of PSs requirement is decreasing when the availability of each PS is increased. With the same value of *r*, when the availability is increased, the lifetime of each PS is also increased and thus fewer PS are required for standby. It is found from the results that, the workload of central server can be reduced to 95% compared with the original SB when there are 60 peer servers deployed (it is reminded that there are 12 PSGs in the system), each of which has the availability of 0.4.

5 Conclusion

In this paper, we develop a possible solution for building a VoD system using existing broadcasting scheme coupled with P2P paradigm. The general idea of the proposed policy is to decentralize the broadcasting channels from the central server to a number of client denoted peer server, each of which is only responsible for broadcasting the video over one or several channels simultaneously. Thus, the bottleneck of the system is no longer on the server side. We use Staggered as an example to show how this policy can be accomplished. In order to tackle the dynamic nature in P2P environment, an analytical model is also developed to determine the minimize number of peer server required for the system. The results showed that 60 peers, each of which has the availability of 0.4, are enough to leverage the workload of the central server up to 95%, when the startup delay of the system is 10 minutes.

References

1. Hoyland, A., Rausand, M.: System Reliability Theory: Models and Statistical Methods. In: Williams, J.G. (ed.) Instantiation Theory. LNCS, vol. 518, Springer, Heidelberg (1991)
2. Arvind, K.: Probabilistic Clock Synchronization in Distributed Systems. IEEE Trans. On Parallel and Distributed Systems 5(5), 474–487 (1994)
3. Wong, J.W.: Broadcast delivery. Proceedings of IEEE. 76(12), 1566–1577 (1988)

Low Computing Loop Filter Using Coded Block Pattern and Quantization Index for H .264 Video Coding Standard

Kwon Yul Choi, Won-Seon Song, and Min-Cheol Hong

School of Electronic Engineering, Soongsil University, Seoul, 156-743, Korea
{tantis, won}@vipl.ssu.ac.kr, mhong@ssu.ac.kr

Abstract. We propose a low computing loop filter for reducing the blocking and ringing artifacts for H.264 video coding standard. One-dimensional regularized smoothing function and regularization parameters are newly defined. The experiment result shows that the proposed loop filter has the low computing complexity with similar performance.

Keywords: H.264, blocking artifacts, ringing artifacts, Loop Filter, Complexity.

1 Introduction

H.264 video coding standard has been jointly developed to obtain higher compressed ratio with better quality video [1]. As the other video coding standards, H.264 produces the blocking artifacts due to the information loss caused by the quantization [2]. To remove blocking artifacts, loop filter was added in H.264. However it has been pointed out that it is inefficient in view of computing complexity of the decoder.

So we propose a low computing loop filter in this paper. In Sect. 2, a new one-dimensional smoothing function to incorporate the smoothness to its two neighboring pixels into the solution is defined and the regularization parameters to control the trade-off between the local fidelity to the data and the smoothness are determined by available overhead information, such as, coded block pattern and quantization step size. And then, experimental results and conclusions are described in Sect. 4, 5.

2 Proposed Algorithm

2.1 Problem Formulation

The image compression process can be formulated by linear pixel based form. It is

$$g(i,j) = f(i,j) + n(i,j) , \tag{1}$$

where g , f , and n represent the compressed image, the original image, and the additive quantization noise, respectively [2]. In this work, we assume that the quantization noise is identically independent distributed (i.i.d). And (i,j) denotes the vertical and the horizontal coordinates in the two-dimensional imaging system.

H.H.S. Ip et al. (Eds.): PCM 2007, LNCS 4810, pp. 405–408, 2007.

Although the regularized iterative techniques used in image restoration problem are very efficient, for the simple and low computing cost filtering algorithm, we define the one-dimensional smoothing function as shown in Eq. (2) for example, horizontally regularized smoothing function.

$$M(f(i,j)) = M_p(f(i,j)) + M_n(f(i,j)), \tag{2}$$

where subsidiary regularization smoothing functions are written as

$$\begin{aligned} M_p(f(i,j)) &= (1-\alpha_p(i,j))(f(i,j)-g(i,j))^2 + \alpha_p(i,j)(f(i,j)-f(i,j-1))^2, \\ M_n(f(i,j)) &= (1-\alpha_n(i,j))(f(i,j)-g(i,j))^2 + \alpha_n(i,j)(f(i,j)-f(i,j+1))^2, \end{aligned} \tag{3}$$

where $\alpha_p(i,j)$ and $\alpha_n(i,j)$ represent regularization parameters to control the degree of smoothness to horizontally two neighboring pixels of (i,j)-th pixel. Assuming that local mean of quantization noise in spatial domain is equal to 0 namely,

$$\alpha_p(i,j)n(i,j-1) + \alpha_n(i,j)n(i,j+1) = 0, \tag{4}$$

the solution of Eq. (2) can be written as

$$\hat{f}(i,j) = \frac{(2-\alpha_p(i,j)-\alpha_n(i,j))\,g(i,j) + \alpha_p(i,j)g(i,j-1) + \alpha_n(i,j)g(i,j+1)}{2}. \tag{5}$$

by taking differential operator with respect to $f(i,j)$ and then setting it equal to 0. After the horizontal filtering, the vertical filtering is taken place in the similar way.

2.2 Regularization Parameters

The regularization parameters to control the trade-off between the local fidelity to the data and the smoothness are determined by available overhead information, such as, coded block pattern and quantization step size (QP_{step}) and prior information.

Visibility of the annoying artifacts is different depending on block coding type and pixel location. Based on such prior information, a block is classified as (1) intra-coded block (class 1), (2) block having large motion vector difference (class 2), (3) block having non-zero transform coefficients (class 3), or (4) block having zero transform coefficients (class 4). The block strength related with each class is assigned as

$$Strength = \begin{cases} 2 & for\ class\,1 \\ 1 & for\ class\,2\,and\,3 \\ 0 & for\ class\,4 \end{cases}. \tag{6}$$

According to well-known regularization theory, the regularization parameters can be written as

$$\frac{1-\alpha_p(i,j)}{\alpha_p(i,j)} = \frac{(f(i,j)-f(i,j-1))^2}{\phi_p(QP_{step})}, \quad \frac{1-\alpha_n(i,j)}{\alpha_n(i,j)} = \frac{(f(i,j)-f(i,j+1))^2}{\phi_n(QP_{step})}, \tag{7}$$

where $\phi_l(\cdot)$ (for $l = p,n$) can be defined as $\phi_l(QP_{step}) \approx K_l \times QP_{step}^2$, since QP_{step} represents the energy of the quantization noise. To incorporate the prior information into the solution, the tuning parameters (K_l) are defined, which are determined depending on block strength and pixel position such as

$$K_p = \begin{cases} (2\times(m+1))/16 & for\ class 3 \\ (4\times(m+1))/16 & for\ class 2, \\ (8\times(m+1))/16 & for\ class 1 \end{cases} \quad K_n = \begin{cases} (2\times(n+1))/16 & for\ class 3 \\ (4\times(n+1))/16 & for\ class 2 \\ (8\times(n+1))/16 & for\ class 1 \end{cases}. \tag{8}$$

Where m and n are determined by pixel location such as

$$m = \begin{cases} 1 & if\ g(i,j)\ and\ g(i,j-1) \in S_{HB} \\ 0 & otherwise \end{cases}, \quad n = \begin{cases} 1 & if\ g(i,j)\ and\ g(i,j+1) \in S_{HB} \\ 0 & otherwise \end{cases} \tag{9}$$

Where S_{HB} means the set of horizontal block boundary pixels. Finally, the regularization parameters can be approximated as

$$\alpha_p(i,j) = \frac{K_p QP_{step}^2}{(g(i,j)-g(i,j-1))^2 + K_p QP_{step}^2}, \quad \alpha_n(i,j) = \frac{K_n QP_{step}^2}{(g(i,j)-g(i,j+1))^2 + K_n QP_{step}^2} \tag{10}$$

under the assumption that $n(i,j) = n(i,j-1) = n(i,j+1)$.

To avoid floating-point operation, filtering process of Eq. (5) can be modified as

$$\hat{f}(i,j) = \frac{(2^9 - \beta_p(i,j) - \beta_n(i,j))\,g(i,j) + \beta_p(i,j)g(i,j-1) + \beta_n(i,j)g(i,j+1)}{2^9}$$

$$\text{where} \begin{cases} \beta_p(i,j) = \lfloor 2^8 \alpha_p(i,j) \rfloor = \left\lfloor \dfrac{2^8 K_p QP_{step}^2}{(g(i,j)-g(i,j-1))^2 + K_p QP_{step}^2} \right\rfloor \\ \beta_n(i,j) = \lfloor 2^8 \alpha_n(i,j) \rfloor = \left\lfloor \dfrac{2^8 K_n QP_{step}^2}{(g(i,j)-g(i,j+1))^2 + K_n QP_{step}^2} \right\rfloor \end{cases} \tag{11}$$

where $\lfloor . \rfloor$ represents the round-off operation.

Finally, using CBP(Coded Block Pattern), the recovery processing is switched as

$$\hat{f}(i,j) = \begin{cases} \hat{f}_p(i,j) & if\ g(i,j) \in not-coded\ block \\ Eq.\ (11) & otherwise \end{cases}, \tag{12}$$

where $\hat{f}_p(i,j)$ represents (i,j)-th pixel value of the restored previous frame and "not-coded block" represents the duplication of the block of previous decoded frame. If blocking and ringing artifacts of the previous frame are well removed, the corresponding not-coded block of the current compressed frame can be restored without filtering procedure, resulting in reduction of the computational cost.

3 Experimental Results

Fig. 1 shows that the proposed loop filter has relatively 30-40 % low computing cost than H.264 loop filter. On the other hand the proposed loop filter has the similar PSNR performance and removes the coding artifacts which H.264 loop filter misses.

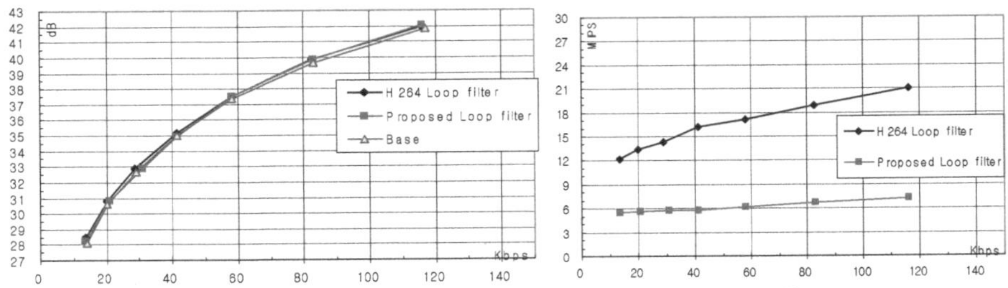

(a) (b)

Fig. 1. (a) PSNR and (b) Complexity comparison as a function of bit rate of QCIF News

(a) (b) (c)

Fig. 2. (a) News 97th reconstructed frame without loop filter, (b) corresponding reconstructed frame with H.264 loop filter, (c) corresponding reconstructed frame with proposed loop filter

4 Conclusion

This paper addresses a low computing loop filter to eliminate the blocking and ringing artifacts of H.264 compressed video. A pixel-based smoothing function with the regularization parameters which are determined from the prior knowledge is newly proposed. The novelty of the proposed algorithm is that the annoying artifacts and the computational cost are effectively reduced with similar PSNR performance.

Acknowledgments. This research was supported by Seoul Future Contents Convergence (SFCC) Cluster established by Seoul R\BD Program and Soongsil University Research Fund.

References

1. Draft ITU-T Recommendation and Final Draft International Standard of Joint Video Specification (ITU-T Rec. H.264/ISO/IEC 14496-10 AVC) (2003)
2. Katsaggelos, A.K., Galatsanos, N. (eds.): Signal Recovery Techniques for Image and Video Compression and Transmission. Kluwer Academic Publisher, Dordrecht (1998)

A Low Complexity Block-Based Video De-interlacing Algorithm for SIMD Processors

Yogesh Gupta and Sriram Sethuraman

Ittiam Systems (P) Ltd.,
Bangalore, India
{yogesh.gupta, sriram.sethuraman}@ittiam.com

Abstract. A low complexity video de-interlacing algorithm is presented in this paper which is suitable for SIMD (Single Instruction Multiple Data) processors to be used as a pre-/post-processing option in low-cost consumer electronic devices. It is a block-based motion-adaptive technique that converts an interlaced video to progressive, preserving the details in static or low motion areas while leaving no combing artifacts or without introducing any ghosting artifacts. It adapts to the content and chooses one amongst temporal, spatio-temporal or spatial filtering for de-interlacing on a block by block basis analyzing characteristics such as the extent of motion and the correlation across fields. The proposed scheme has been benchmarked against a recent low complexity motion-adaptive algorithm and the performance has been measured across a number of real and synthetic video sequences. The proposed algorithm offers an order of magnitude complexity reduction on SIMD processors over the reference low complexity algorithm while providing a significantly better fidelity towards the progressive source.

Keywords: Interlaced, progressive, de-interlacing, pre-/post-processing, SIMD processors, block-based, spatio-temporal, motion detection.

1 Introduction

The de-interlacing algorithms proposed in the literature range from simple spatial or temporal methods to moderately complex motion adaptive spatio-temporal methods to complex motion-compensation based methods [1]. The low complexity methods leave visual artifacts, while the others give better performance at a higher computational cost [2, 3]. But in low-cost DSP based consumer electronics products, it is desired to have a low complexity and minimal artifact de-interlacing. Hence, a motion-adaptive spatio-temporal algorithm becomes an obvious choice.

In this paper, a motion-adaptive spatio-temporal de-interlacing algorithm is proposed that achieves very good quality de-interlacing at a fairly low complexity on SIMD capable processors by tailoring the entire de-interlacing algorithm to work at a block level as opposed to on a per-pixel level. Further, the SIMD complexity and de-interlacing fidelity for the proposed algorithm has been benchmarked against a recent low complexity motion-adaptive algorithm [4].

H.H.S. Ip et al. (Eds.): PCM 2007, LNCS 4810, pp. 409–412, 2007.

2 Proposed De-interlacing Scheme

The proposed scheme adapts to the content and chooses one amongst temporal, spatio-temporal and spatial filtering for de-interlacing on a block by block basis by analyzing characteristics such as the extent of motion and the correlation across fields.

In this scheme, each field is broken into blocks of MxN (M rows x N columns) and processing is done separately on each of these blocks. For de-interlacing an MxN block from a field, pixel values from the spatially co-located previous and next fields are taken. The algorithm can be divided roughly into the following four steps:

2.1 Motion Detection and Weaving

If the current MxN block is stationary, i.e., it has low motion with respect to its temporal neighbors, the missing pixels can directly be picked from the opposite parity adjacent field instead of interpolating. To check the stationarity of a block, the Mean of Absolute Differences (MAD) is computed across spatially co-located regions in temporally adjacent previous and next fields of the opposite parity.

If the MAD is within a threshold limit, the block is considered to be stationary. The block level checks reduce the number of conditions considerably and also make the motion detection robust. This stationarity check is made more robust by using a content-adaptive threshold that adapts to the spatial variance of the block.

2.2 Combing Artifacts Check

The woven block generated in the previous step could have combing artifacts if motion detection failed. To check this, a combing-artifact-check (CAC) is applied to the woven block. Inside CAC, the frame and field correlations are computed within the block. For frame correlation, the pixel differences between adjacent rows are computed and accumulated across the MxN block, while for field correlation the same is done for alternate rows. To discriminate texture from combing artifact, separate row and column based accumulation techniques are employed. If the field correlation turns out to be more than the frame correlation, the block is considered to have combing artifacts and weaving is not chosen.

2.3 Edge-Adaptive Spatial Interpolation

If a block fails to qualify for weaving, it is interpolated using a block-based edge-oriented spatial method. The edge-oriented interpolation removes the jaggy-pattern in the areas having strong edges and makes it look pleasing. The MxN field block is divided into multiple sub-blocks. Then the prominent edge direction is estimated for a sub-block. The interpolation is done in that orientation for all pixels inside the sub-block. The block based operations make the directional checks more robust and keep the computational complexity low.

2.4 Spatio-temporal Interpolation

Even in low motion areas, it has been shown to be beneficial to apply a vertical-temporal interpolation filter [5]. The high vertical frequencies from the temporally adjacent fields are added to the spatially interpolated values to get a better approximation to the missing field. But in areas with high motion, adding the temporal information might degrade the quality of the interpolation.

In the proposed algorithm, the spatio-temporal interpolation (STI) is employed in the areas which are not stationary but do not exhibit high motion as determined using the second content adaptive fallback threshold.

In STI, a vertical filter is applied to each of the previous and next temporal adjacent fields. The outputs of the filter from both the adjacent fields are then added to the output of the edge-oriented spatial interpolation.

3 Complexity Comparison

The proposed algorithm has been benchmarked against a recent motion-adaptive spatio-temporal de-interlacing algorithm described in [4]. This algorithm uses a pixel by pixel approach. It adapts the weighting factor between spatial interpolation and temporal weaving according to the motion intensity measured at that pixel using frame difference over a 3x3 neighborhood window.

The complexity estimation has been done for both the algorithms on a SIMD processor. Overall, the benchmark algorithm turns out to be 13 times more complex than the proposed scheme. This is largely attributed to the per-pixel processing of the benchmark scheme as against the block-level processing of the proposed scheme. Also, the benchmark does one division operation per pixel, which in turn is done by several arithmetic and logical operations on a DSP.

Further, the proposed scheme does only 0.1 times the number of comparisons used by the benchmark scheme. This reduces the conditional processing drastically and hence helps the algorithm to be implemented on a processor with VLIW (Very Long Instruction Word) architecture. The VLIW processors take advantage of instruction level parallelism by executing multiple instructions in different stages of software pipeline. But conditional processing creates halts in the pipeline stages deteriorating the processing efficiency.

4 Experiments and Results

To measure and compare the performances given by the benchmark and the proposed methods, the progressive test sequences were converted to interlaced at half the frame-rate. As an objective measure, Peak Signal to Noise Ratio (PSNR) was computed on the de-interlaced sequences against the original progressive sequences.

Across the test sequences, the proposed scheme gives an average gain of 2.6 dB against the benchmark. Also, for the high motion sequences the gain is even higher (3.3 dB). This is probably because the benchmark method neglects the inter-field motion while doing the MAD calculation for motion detection.

Further, the output of the proposed method visually looks much more pleasing than that of the benchmark method. Here, the CAC in the proposed scheme detects all the visible artifacts, even if the motion-detection fails. Also, in the edge-oriented interpolation, the block-based direction check of the proposed method is much more robust than the pixel-level checks of the benchmark method which chooses random directions in textured regions.

5 Conclusions

The proposed method works better than the benchmark scheme in all the sequences considered for comparisons, while incurring only a fraction of the benchmark scheme's computational complexity. Subjective viewing has also shown that the proposed scheme produces far fewer visible combing artifacts for both real and synthetic sequences. This is attributable to the combing artifact check. In fact, the CAC can be applied even with motion compensated interpolation techniques.

The block based processing used in the proposed scheme is ideally suited for implementation on DSPs and other SIMD processors. In addition to that, with fewer comparisons per pixel, it is very much suitable for VLIW processors. But the benchmark scheme is not suitable for these kinds of processors because of the higher number of conditional operations and need for a division operation per pixel.

While performing quite satisfactorily as a motion adaptive de-interlacer, the proposed scheme lags behind the performance of a motion-compensated de-interlacer as expected. Future efforts will focus on lower complexity improvements to the existing scheme that can use motion information available at the decoding side.

References

1. de Haan, G., Bellers, E.B.: Deinterlacing – An Overview. Proc. Of the IEEE 86(9), 1839–1857 (1998)
2. Lin, S.-F., Chang, Y.-L., Chen, L.-G.: Motion Adaptive Interpolation with Horizontal Motion Detection for Deinterlacing. IEEE Transaction on Consumer Electronics 49(4), 1256–1265 (2003)
3. Deame, J.: Motion Compensated De-Interlacing: The Key to the Digital Video Transition. SMPTE 141st Technical Conference, New York (November 19-22, 1999)
4. Chung, R.H.Y., Wong, K.-Y.K., Chin, F.Y.L., Chow, K.P., Yuk, S.C.: Generalized Motion and Edge Adaptive Interpolation De-interlacing Algorithm. WSEAS Transaction on Computers 5(11), 2544–2551 (2006)
5. Interpolating Lines of a Video Signal, U.S. Patent 4789893 (December 1988)

Fast Normalized Cross Correlation Based on Adaptive Multilevel Winner Update

Shou-Der Wei and Shang-Hong Lai

Department of Computer Science, National Tsing Hua University, Hsinchu, Taiwan
{greco, lai}@cs.nthu.edu.tw

Abstract. In this paper we propose a fast normalized cross correlation (NCC) algorithm for pattern matching based on combining adaptive multilevel partition with the winner update scheme. This winner update scheme is applied in conjunction with an upper bound for the cross correlation derived from Cauchy-Schwarz inequality. To apply the winner update scheme, we partition the summation of cross correlation into different levels with the partition order determined by the gradient energies of the partitioned regions in the template. Thus, this winner update scheme can be employed to skip the unnecessary calculation. Experimental results show the proposed algorithm is very efficient for image matching under different lighting conditions.

Keywords: pattern matching, normalized cross correlation, winner update strategy, multi-level successive elimination, fast algorithms.

1 Introduction

The pattern matching problem can be formulated as follows: Given a source image *I* and a template image *T* of size *MxN*, the pattern matching problem is to find the best match of template *T* from the source image *I* with minimal distortion or maximal correlation. Several previous works on pattern patching have been proposed [1][2][3][4] based on the measure of sum of absolute differences (SAD) or sum of squared differences (SSD). The NCC measure is more robust than SAD and SSD under uniform illumination changes, so it has been widely used in image matching, object recognition and industrial inspection.

The NCC between two images *I* and *T* with displacement (*x*,*y*) is defined by

$$NCC(x,y) = \frac{\sum_{i=1}^{M}\sum_{j=1}^{N} I(i+x, j+y)\cdot T(i,j)}{\sqrt{\sum_{i=1}^{M}\sum_{j=1}^{N} I(i+x, j+y)^2}\cdot\sqrt{\sum_{i=1}^{M}\sum_{j=1}^{N} T(i,j)^2}} \tag{1}$$

The sum table scheme [6] was proposed to reduce the computation in the denominator. In addition, Cauchy-Schwarz inequality has been employed to reduce the computation in the numerator [5].

H.H.S. Ip et al. (Eds.): PCM 2007, LNCS 4810, pp. 413–416, 2007.

2 The Proposed Fast NCC-Based Image Matching Algorithm

In this paper, we propose a fast algorithm for NCC-based image matching by applying the adaptive block partition in the Cauchy-Schwarz inequality with the winner update scheme. As shown in equation (2), we can divide a block into many subblocks and calculate the summation of each block's upper bound to obtain tighter bound by Cauchy-Schwarz inequality for the cross correlation (CC). Following the uniform partitioning scheme of MSEA [1], we have many upper bounds for different partitioning levels and the relation between the upper bounds for different levels are given in equation (3) and (4). At the final level, the upper bound is equal to the cross correlation. In contrast to the uniform partition, we can determine the partition order by the sum of gradient magnitudes for the subblocks in the template. The block with the current largest sum of gradient magnitudes is divided into 2x2 sub-blocks for consideration of further partitioning. The adaptive block partitioning algorithm is given in Algorithm 1 and an example of adaptive block partition is depicted in Fig. 1.

$$\sqrt{\sum_{i=1}^{N} a_i^2}\cdot\sqrt{\sum_{i=1}^{N} b_i^2} \geq \sqrt{\sum_{i=1}^{k} a_i^2}\cdot\sqrt{\sum_{i=1}^{k} b_i^2} + \sqrt{\sum_{i=k+1}^{N} a_i^2}\cdot\sqrt{\sum_{i=k+1}^{N} b_i^2} \geq \sum_{i=1}^{N} a_i \cdot b_i \tag{2}$$

$$UB_l(x,y) = \sum_{a\in AllSubblock}\left(\sqrt{\sum_{i\in AllPixels} I_{a_i}(x,y)^2}\cdot\sqrt{\sum_{i\in AllPixels} T_{a_i}^2}\right) \tag{3}$$

$$UB_0 \geq UB_1 \geq \cdots \geq UB_{L=\log_2 N} = CC \tag{4}$$

$$BV(x,y) = \frac{UB(x,y)}{|I(x,y)|\cdot|T|} \tag{5}$$

Algorithm 1: Algorithm for determining adaptive block partitioning order

---

Push the largest block into the queue
Repeat until the queue is empty
1. Select the block with largest sum of gradient magnitudes from the queue.
2. Divide the selected block into four sub-blocks and calculate their sum of gradient magnitudes.
3. Check the four sub-blocks and push each sub-block into the queue if its sum of gradient magnitudes is greater than a given threshold T.

The proposed algorithm includes the adaptive block partitioning algorithm combined with the winner update scheme [4] for fast search of the location with maximal NCC. With the block partitioning, we have the relation of upper bounds for different levels as $UB_0 \geq UB_1 \geq \cdots \geq UB_{\max L} \geq CC$. We can calculate the boundary values from equation (5) and have the relation of boundary values of different levels as $BV_0 \geq BV_1 \geq \cdots \geq BV_{\max L} \geq NCC$. The BV_l value is closer to NCC as the level increases. Based on the above relation of BV_l, we can apply the winner update scheme to it. At first, we calculated BV_0 for all candidates, and then at each iteration we choose the candidate with the current maximal BV_l as the winner to update its level and recalculate the BV_{l+1}. This procedure is repeated until the chosen winner reaches the maximal level, thus its BV_{maxL} is the same as the maximal NCC value. This algorithm of applying winner update scheme with adaptive block partition for NCC is summarized in Algorithm 2. Similar to the winner update method in [4], we also use a hash table to find the temporary winner.

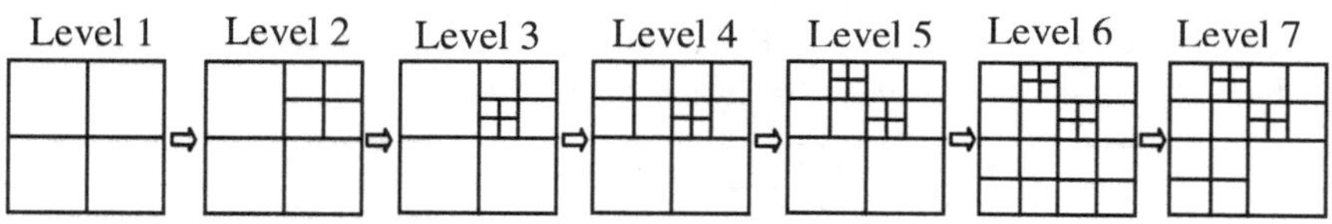

Fig. 1. An example of the adaptive block partitioning order

Algorithm 2: The proposed fast NCC pattern matching algorithm

---

Step 1: Determine the elimination order.
Step 2: Calculate the norm of template |T|
Step 3: Calculate the BV_0 of all candidate and initial the Hash Table
Repeat
Step 5: Select the candidate with maximal BV in hash table as the winner
Step 6: Update the level and BV of the winner

1. Retrieve the next partitioning next level l
2. Calculate the UB_l for level l. Compute $BV_l = UB_l / (|T|\,|C(x,y)|)$
3. Push candidate into Hash Table.

Until the winner reaches the maximal level.

---

3 Experimental Results

To compare the efficiency of the proposed algorithm, termed WUS_NCC, we also implemented the multi-level SEA with fixed partitioning scheme and the results are termed as MSEA_NCC. In our experiment, we used the sailboat image of size 512-by-512 as the source image and six template images of size 64x64 inside the sailboat image as shown in Figure 2. The experimental results of the proposed algorithms and the original NCC are shown in Table 1. All these three algorithms used the sum table to reduce the computation of denominator in NCC. For efficiently calculating the bound of the numerator, we also used the approach of BSPA [2] to build two block square sum pyramids for intensity image and the gradient map, respectively. The execution time shown in the table includes the time of memory allocation for sum table and pyramids, and building sum table, pyramids and the gradient map. These experimental results show the significant improvement in the efficiency of the proposed fast NCC-based pattern matching algorithm.

(a) (b) (c) (d) (e) (f)

Fig. 2. (a), (b), (c): The template images (64x64). (d), (e), (f): their brighter versions

Table 1. The execution time (in msec) of applying traditional NCC, MSEA_NCC and WUS_NCC on six templates shown in Figure2(a)~(f), Note that the NCC algorithm used the sum table to reduce the computation in the denominator of NCC.

Unit: msec	T(a)	T(b)	T(c)	T(d)	T(e)	T(f)
NCC	3235	3235	3235	3235	3235	3235
MSEA_NCC	281	203	656	234	219	563
WUS_NCC	109	94	94	94	94	94

4 Conclusion

In this paper, we proposed a very efficient algorithm for fast pattern matching in an image based on normalized cross correlation. To achieve very efficient computation, we partition the summation of cross correlation into different levels and apply the winner update scheme to find the location with maximal NCC. The block partition order is adaptively determined by the sum of gradient magnitudes for each partitioned regions in the template. Our experimental results show the proposed algorithm is very efficient and robust for pattern matching under linear illumination change.

References

1. Gao, X.Q., Duanmu, C.J., Zou, C.R.: A multilevel successive elimination algorithm for block matching motion estimation. IEEE Trans. Image Processing 9(3), 501–504 (2000)
2. Lee, C.-H., Chen, L.-H.: A fast motion estimation algorithm based on the block sum pyramid. IEEE Trans. Image Processing 6(11), 1587–1591 (1997)
3. Gharavi-Alkhansari, M.: A fast globally optimal algorithm for template matching using low-resolution pruning. IEEE Trans. on Image Processing 10(4), 526–533 (2001)
4. Chen, Y.S., Huang, Y.P., Fuh, C.S.: A fast block matching algorithm based on the winner-update strategy. IEEE Trans. Image Processing 10(8), 1212–1222 (2001)
5. Di Stefano, L., Mattoccia, S.: A sufficient condition based on the Cauchy-Schwarz inequality for efficient template matching. In: Proc. Intern. Conf. Image Processing (2003)
6. Lewis, J.P.: Fast template matching. Vision Interface, 120–123 (1995)

Hierarchical Intra-mode Restriction Technique in H.264/MPEG4-AVC Video

Donghyung Kim[1] and Jechang Jeong[2]

[1] Electronics and Telecommunications Reaserch Institute,
138 Gajeong, Yuseong, Daejeon, 305-700, Korea
[2] Dept. Of Electrical and Computer Engineering, Hanyang University,
17 Haengdang, Seongdong, Seoul, 133-791, Korea
kdh2465@gmail.com, jjeong@ece.hanyang.ac.kr

Abstract. The H.264/AVC standard uses new coding tools such as variable block size, multiple reference frames, intra prediction, etc. Using these coding tools, the coding efficiency has been significantly improved. However, the encoder complexity is greatly increased. We focus on the complexity reduction method of intra-mode decision. Our algorithm first restricts selective prediction modes of intra4×4 using a simple preprocessing. The prediction modes of intra4×4 are used for restricting those of the other intra-modes. Simulation results show that the proposed method outperforms other conventional methods.

Keywords: H.264/MPEG4-AVC Video, Fast Encoding, Hierarchical Intra-Mode Decision, Correlation of Prediction Modes, Rate Distortion Cost.

1 Introduction

In H.264/AVC, the use of new coding tools has enabled the standard to achieve higher coding efficiency. The encoder complexity, however, increases greatly [1].

Several researches have been proposed to reduce the complexity of intra-mode selection. Cheng et al. proposed three-step method [2]. They used the fact that there exists high correlation between the modes of adjacent macroblocks. Using the correlation, their method limits the candidate prediction modes (pmodes) hierarchically. Zhang et al. proposed the fast pmode selection method based on local edge information obtained by calculating edge feature parameters [3]. The method exploiting the correlation among pmodes of intra-modes was proposed by Park et al. They restricted selective pmodes of intra4×4 and chromaintra8×8 using a chosen pmode of intra16×16 [4]. Pan et al. proposed the method based on the distribution of the edge direction histogram [5]. Their method finds edge map prior to intra prediction, then only small part of intra prediction modes are chosen for rate-distortion optimization (RDO) calculation using edge map.

In this paper, the proposed method restricts selective pmodes of intra4×4 using edge estimation of 4×4 blocks in advance. The selective pmodes of intra16×16 depend on the best pmodes of sixteen 4×4 blocks in intra4×4, and those of chromaintra8×8 depend on the best pmode of intra16×16. It exploits the fact that there is much correlation between pmodes.

H.H.S. Ip et al. (Eds.): PCM 2007, LNCS 4810, pp. 417–420, 2007.

2 Encoding Process of Intra-block in the JVT Model

H.264/AVC uses the RDO technique to achieve the best coding performance. This means that the encoder has to encode an intra-block using all the mode combination and choose the best one that gives the minimum cost shown in Eq. (1).

$$RDcost = Distortion + \lambda \times Rate \tag{1}$$

where Distortion is computed by calculating the SNR of the block and the Rate is calculated by taking into consideration the length of the stream after the last stage of encoding, and λ is Lagrange multiplier. Refer to [1] for detail of the process of intra-mode prediction in JVT model.

3 Proposed Algorithm

3.1 Mode Decision in Intra4×4

The pixels along the direction of local edge normally have similar values. Therefore, a good prediction could be achieved if the pixels were predicted using those neighboring pixels that are in the same direction of the edge. For fast pmode decision of intra4×4, the proposed method estimates an edge direction of a 4×4 block, and limits selective pmodes that require the RDcost computation. In order to estimate the edge tendency of a 4×4 block, edge magnitude and angle are generated by Prewitt edge operators at seven positions located at left and upper boundaries in 4×4 blocks.

The proposed method sums up the edge magnitude with similar edge directions for seven convolution positions, and then the pmode with the maximum sum of edge magnitude is defined as primary edge mode (PEM), neighboring pmodes of PEM are defined as neighboring edge modes (NEMs). NEM_1 and NEM_2 are neighboring pmodes located at clockwise and counterclockwise direction of PEM, respectively. Also neighboring pmode of NEM_1 in clockwise direction is NEM_{11} and neighboring pmode of NEM_2 in counterclockwise direction is NEM_{22}.

After selection of PEM and NEMs, one of subsets of {DC, PEM, NEM1, NEM2, NEM11, NEM22} is used for selective pmodes of intra4×4 depending on three conditions.

Firstly, the proposed method only carries out the RDcost computation of two pmodes: {DC, PEM}. If the RDcost of PEM is bigger than that of DC enough, that is, Eq. (2) is satisfied, the proposed method does not consider any other pmodes. Therefore, in this case, two pmode candidates are only used.

$$\text{RDcost(DC)} \times \boldsymbol{K} < \text{RDcost(PEM)} \quad \text{where} \quad \boldsymbol{K} = (1 + \text{QP}/(51 \times 2)). \tag{2}$$

In Eq. (2), K depends on quantization parameter, so it could be 1 to 1.5.

If the first condition is not satisfied, the proposed method evaluates the RDcosts of two other pmodes: {NEM_1, NEM_2}. In case that the RDcost of PEM is the smallest among {PEM, NEM_1, NEM_2}, the proposed method does not consider any other pmodes. Therefore, in this case, four pmode candidates are used.

If the second condition is not satisfied, the proposed method evaluates the RDcost of NEM_{11} or NEM_{22}. In case that the RDcost of NEM_1 is equal to or less than that of

NEM_2, the proposed method considers NEM_{11}, otherwise NEM_{22} is considered as an additional pmode candidate. Therefore, in this case, five pmode candidates are used.

Consequently, one of {DC, PEM}, {DC, PEM, NEM_1, NEM_2}, {DC, PEM, NEM_1, NEM_2, NEM_{11}}, and {DC, PEM, NEM_1, NEM_2, NEM_{22}} is considered as selective pmode candidates for intra4×4 in the proposed method.

3.2 Mode Decision in Intra16×16 and Chromaintra8×8

In order to reduce the complexity of intra16×16, the proposed method restricts selective pmodes according to the results of intra4×4. Among the best pmodes of sixteen 4×4 blocks in intra4×4, the numbers of pmodes with DC, vertical, and horizontal prediction directions are defined as num(DC), num(V), num(H), respectively. And also the sum of the numbers of pmodes with diagonal-down-left and diagonal-down-right prediction directions is defined as num(P). If num(DC) is more than 80% of the number of counted blocks, the proposed method does not consider any other pmodes of intra16×16. Otherwise, one additional pmode which has maximum counted values is considered. Therefore, in intra16×16, the proposed method considers two pmodes at most.

For a chromaintra8×8 mode, the proposed method set the candidate pmode to DC. Then, the second candidate pmode is to the best pmode of intra16×16. If the best pmode of intra16×16 is DC, then the proposed method considers only DC as pmode. Therefore, similarly to intra16×16, the proposed method considers two pmodes in chromaintra8×8 at most.

4 Simulation Results

For the purpose of evaluation, the public reference encoder JVT Model was used. The reference software was tested on an Intel Pentium-IV based computer with 1,024 MB RAM under the Windows XP Professional operating system.

This simulation used RDO, quantization parameters (QP) of 20 to 30. The simulation was performed on six standard video sequences with different sizes. These included Coastguard (176×144), Table Tennis (176×144), Container (352×288), News (352×288), Mobcal (1280×720), and Shields (1280×720). The first 10 frames of each of these sequences were encoded to intra-frames only. The performance of the

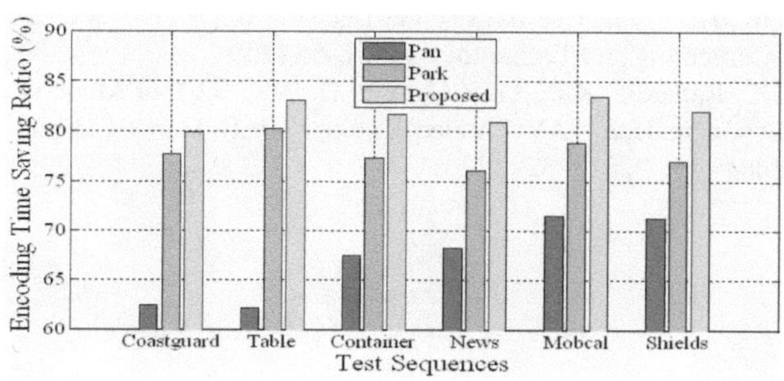

Fig. 1. Comparison of encoding time saving ratio when using Park's (78%), Pan's (67%) and our method (82%)

proposed method was compared with Park's method [4], Pan's method [5] and the reference implementation (JM 10.1).

Fig. 1 compares encoding time saving ratio compared with the reference implementation. As shown in this figure, total encoding time can save about 82% when using the proposed method. Though there is similar to or less PSNR drop and bitrate increase, the proposed method can save more encoding time than other two methods.

5 Conclusions

In this paper, a fast prediction mode selection in intra-frames is proposed by using the reduction method of the number of RDO process. For intra4×4, the edge information of the interested pixels is applied to figure out the best pmode, and for the intra16×16, the sixteen best modes of 4×4 sub-blocks are exploited to find the best pmode. Also, the best pmode of intra16×16 is referred to choose the best mode of a chromaintra8×8 block. When using the proposed method, total encoding time can be alleviated about 82% with a negligible PSNR drop and a bitrate increase.

Acknowledgement

This work was supported by the Ministry of Commerce, Industry and Energy with the project of Development of Personal Next Generation TV terminal.

References

1. JVT G050r1. Draft ITU-T Recommendation and Final Draft International Standard of Joint Video Specification (ITU-T Rec. H.264/ISO/IEC 14496-10 AVC) (2003)
2. Cheng, C.C, Chang, T.S.: Fast Three Step Intra Prediction Algorithm for 4x4 Blocks in H.264. In: ISCAS 2005. Proceeding of the IEEE International Symposium on Circuits and System, vol. 2, pp. 4–7 (2005)
3. Zhang, Y., Feng, D., Lin, S.: Fast 44 Intra-Prediction Mode Selection for H.264. In: ICME 2004. Proceeding of the IEEE International Conference on Multimedia Expo, vol. 1, pp. 1151–1154 (2004)
4. Park, J.S., Song, H.J.: Selective Intra Mode Decision for H.264/AVC Encoders. Trans. on Engineering. Computing and Technology 13, 51–55 (2006)
5. Pan, F., Lin, X., Rahardja, K.P., Li, Z.G., Wu, D., Wu, S.: Fast Mode Decision Algorithm for Intraprediction in H.264/AVC Video Coding. IEEE Trans. Circuits and Systems for Video Technology 15(7), 813–822 (2005)

A Fast Global Motion Estimation Method for Panoramic Video Coding

Jiali Zheng, Yongdong Zhang, and GuangNan Ni

Key Laboratory of Intelligent Information Processing, Institute of Computing Technology, Graduate School of the Chinese Academy of Sciences, Beijing, China
{zhengjiali, zhyd, ngn}@ict.ac.cn

Abstract. In this paper, a fast global motion estimation method is proposed for panoramic video coding. This method accelerates the procedure of global motion estimation (GME) during inter-frame prediction by using two techniques: 1) a compact motion model, which uses only three motion parameters to represent accurately the global motion among the successive panoramic frames. 2) A GME filter, which filters the blocks unreliable and contributing less to the GME, based on a threshold method. The experimental results show the proposed fast global motion estimation method manages to speed up the processing of estimating the motion vector field while maintaining the coding performance.

Keywords: global motion estimation (GME), motion model.

1 Introduction

The changes among successive panoramic frames are mainly caused by camera motions, such as translation and zooming. These camera motions are global motions. In previous work, some polynomial motion models [1]-[4] have been proposed to represent such global motions. These polynomial motion models can produce better quality of predicted image than the conventional translational-only motion model. However, computing costly is a disadvantage of applying these polynomial motion models. To overcome this problem, this paper proposes a compact motion model and a GME filter to simplify the GME in panoramic video coding.

2 Three-Parameter Motion Model

Considering in the panoramic video, the main global motions are camera translation and zooming. It is not necessary to employ complex motion models which consume much more computing, but the gain of the coding performance is not much better. In this paper, a 3-parameter motion model showed in following equations is proposed to simplify the processing of the GME while maintaining the accuracy of the global motion predicted compensation.

H.H.S. Ip et al. (Eds.): PCM 2007, LNCS 4810, pp. 421–424, 2007.

$$\begin{aligned}\Delta x &= a_1 x + a_2 \\ \Delta y &= a_1 y + a_3\end{aligned}. \quad (1)$$

Where (x, y) refer to the coordinates of the center point pixel in the current block, $(\Delta x, \Delta y)$ refer to the motion vectors of the current block. a_1 denotes the zooming motion parameter both on X coordination and Y coordination, because the focus parameters of the camera in the horizontal direction and the vertical direction are the same. a_2 denotes the translational motion parameter on the horizontal direction as well as a_3 denotes the translational motion parameter on the vertical direction.

Compared with the 4-parameter motion model proposed by Wu and Kittler [1], the 3-parameter motion model removes the rotation motion parameter, for considering the fact that less rotational camera motion occurs in most panoramic videos.

3 GME Filter

The main problem GME facing is how to exclude the unreliable and less contributive blocks from the GME effectively. These unreliable blocks mainly come from the smooth region and the moving objects in the foreground.

3.1 Filter the Smooth Region Blocks

In our scheme, the proposed filter is used to find out the blocks in smooth region before performing the GME. The principle of the proposed filter is to differentiate the smooth region blocks from all of the blocks by comparing the image intensity of the current block with a set threshold. The image intensity G_B of the current block B can be obtained by using following equation:

$$G_B = \sum_{i=1}^{m}\sum_{j=1}^{n} S_{i,j} / m\times n, \qquad 0 \le S_{i,j} \le 255. \quad (2)$$

Where $S_{i,j}$ denotes the image intensity of the pixel (i, j), which is calculated by using a Sobel operator [5]. And $m\times n$ is the block size.

The threshold T_g is set according to the following equation:

$$T_g = Max(\frac{1}{N}\sum_{i=1}^{N} G_i, C_g). \quad (3)$$

Where N is the number of the blocks in the current frame, G_i denotes the image intensity of the ith block and C_g is a constant limiting the threshold T_g. The value of the C_g is discussed at section 4 by using experimental results. Comparing the image intensity of the current block G_B with T_g, if G_B is smaller than T_g, the current block is marked as the smooth region block and is excluded from the GME.

3.2 Filter the Foreground Blocks

After filtering the smooth region blocks, an iterative minimization algorithm is used to filter the blocks composing the moving object in the foreground. The proposed algorithm is divided into following three steps:

A. *Block match*
Firstly, the motions of the blocks in current frame are estimated by a fast block matching algorithm [6], to find out the corresponding blocks in the reference frames. And a pair of motion vectors ($\Delta x, \Delta y$) of each block are obtained.

B. *Global motion parameter estimation*
Next, substituting the values of the motion vectors ($\Delta x, \Delta y$) into (1) to calculate motion parameters a_1, a_2 and a_3 of the central point pixel in each block. To estimate the values of the global motion parameters in the current frame, a global motion error function E is summarized in the following equation:

$$E_k = \sum_{i=1}^{N}((a_{1,k}x_i + a_{2,k} - \Delta x_i)^2 + (a_{1,k}y_i + a_{3,k} - \Delta y_i)^2). \tag{4}$$

Where $(a_{1,k}, a_{2,k}, a_{3,k})$ denote the kth set motion parameters, $k=1\sim N$. (x_i, y_i) denote the coordinates of the center point pixel in the ith block and ($\Delta x_i, \Delta y_i$) denote the motion vectors of the ith block. Substituting respectively the N sets of the motion parameters into (4), to calculate the global motion error function E. The set of the motion parameter which minimizes the function E, i.e. min $\{E_1, E_2, E_3 \ldots E_{k-1}, E_k\}$, is the best result of this iteration.

C. *Filter the foreground blocks*
In this step, a pair of global motion vectors ($\Delta x', \Delta y'$) of each block can be obtained by using the derived global motion parameters a_1, a_2 and a_3 from previous step. If the real movement of the ith block is independent from the global motion, the global motion vectors ($\Delta x_i', \Delta y_i'$) of the ith block will be distinguished from the motion vectors ($\Delta x_i, \Delta y_i$) which is estimated in the step of the block match. An error function D_i which measures the discrepancy between the real movement of the ith block and the global motion, is given in the following equation:

$$D_i = \sqrt{(\Delta x_i - \Delta x_i')^2 + (\Delta y_i - \Delta y_i')^2}. \tag{5}$$

If D_i is greater than a threshold T_d defined as following equation, the ith block is marked as the foreground block, and is excluded from the GME.

$$T_d = Min(\frac{1}{N}\sum_{i=1}^{N} D_i, C_d). \tag{6}$$

Where C_d is a constant limiting the threshold T_d. The value of the C_d is given in section 4. The GME result needs to be refined. Iterating step 2 and step 3 till the values of the global motion parameters converge at a stable result.

4 Experimental Results

In the experiments, the proposed techniques are integrated into the H.264/AVC reference software JM90 [7]. By coding cylindrical panoramic videos [8] with various formats, we can conclude that when the C_g is set as 105 in (3) and C_d is set as 2 in (6), the proposed GME filter can work effectively and maintain the accuracy of the GME in panoramic video coding. Compared with traditional scheme, the statistical results show that the proposed scheme speeds up the GME by 186%. In addition, the experimental results also prove that the proposed GME filter is a low complexity algorithm which only occupies small part of the total computing time.

5 Conclusion

This paper proposed a fast global motion estimation method for panoramic video coding. The main contribution of the presented work is the compact motion model and the effective GME filter. The GME filter also accommodates other motion models and can be integrated into the existing coders compatibly. Further work will focus on extending the proposed method for coding other virtual reality applications, such as light-filed rending and three-dimensional scenes.

Acknowledgments. This work is partially supported by the National Basic Research Program of China (973 Program, 2007CB311100), Beijing Science and Technology Planning Program of China (D0106008040291) and National High Technology and Research Development Program of China (863 Program, 2007AA01Z416).

References

1. Wu, S.F., Kittler, J.: A differential method for simultaneous estimation of rotation, change of scale and translation. In: Signal Processing: Image Communication, pp. 69–80. Elsevier, New York (1990)
2. Keesman, G.J.: Motion estimation based on a motion model incorporating translation rotation and zoom. In: Signal Processing IV: Theories and Applications, pp. 31–34. Elsevier, New York (1988)
3. Hoetter, M., Thoma, R.: Image segmentation based on object oriented mapping parameter estimation. In: Signal Process, vol. 15, pp. 315–334. Elsevier, Netherlands (1988)
4. ISO/IEC JTC1: Coding of audio-visual objects - Part 2: Visual. ISO/IEC 14496-2 (MPEG-4 Visual), Version 1 (April 1999), Amendment 1: Version 2 (February 2000)
5. Gonzales, R.C., Woods, R.E.: Digital Image Processing. Addison-Wisley, Massachusetts (1992)
6. Zhu, S., Ma, K.K.: A new diamond search algorithm for fast block matching motion estimation. IEEE Transaction on Image Processing 9, 287–290 (2000)
7. http://iphome.hhi.de/suehring/tml/download
8. ftp://ftp.tnt.uni-hannover.de/pub/3dav

Bisynchronous Approach for Robust Audio Watermarking Technology

Xiaoming Zhang[1] and Xiong Yin[1,2]

[1] Department of Computer, Beijing Institute of Petrochemical Technology, China
[2] College of Information, Beijing University of Chemical Technology, China
{zhangxiaoming,yinxiong}@bipt.edu.cn

Abstract. A kind of bisynchronous approach, including two processes of self-synchronization and additive synchronization, is proposed for audio watermarking to get the robust performance. The self-synchronous valley is created for watermark location rapidly, and the additive synchronous approach is adopted to locate the usable watermarks. Moreover, an adaptive matching approach is stated to obtain the final watermark from several candidates. The experimental results show that the valleys can be searched rapidly and effectively. The approach is robust against most common attacks.

Keywords: Bisynchronization, Self-synchronization, Adaptive matching, Audio watermarking, Robustness, Wavelet.

1 Introduction

There are two kinds of synchronous methods, additive synchronous message and self-synchronization, in locating watermarking. The former is easily implemented but weak in desynchronous attack [1,2]. The self-synchronous technology is based on the inner features of audio carrier [3]. These feature points only rely on the audio carrier, and none of change will bed occurred to the carrier in the synchronous designing process. Most of the researches focus on pitch technology [4] with complicated extracting process. While Zhang [5] proposed a kind of valley synchronous algorithm for effective audio watermarking. Based on the valley approach, an additive synchronous approach is followed to form a bisynchronous technology for audio watermarking. An adaptive matching approach is stated to measure the additive synchronous effects to obtain the final watermark from several watermark candidates. The approach is desired to get more robustness to the common attacks to the watermarked audio in signal processing and network transmission.

2 Principle of Bisynchronous Technology

The bisynchronous principle in audio watermarking is stated in Figure 1.

The self-synchronous positions V are searched along the audio, and the additive synchronous information S is followed behind the valley V. Then, the watermark W is followed the S. In order to get robustness to the audio attack, the same S and W are hidden behind the valleys for several times.

H.H.S. Ip et al. (Eds.): PCM 2007, LNCS 4810, pp. 425–428, 2007.

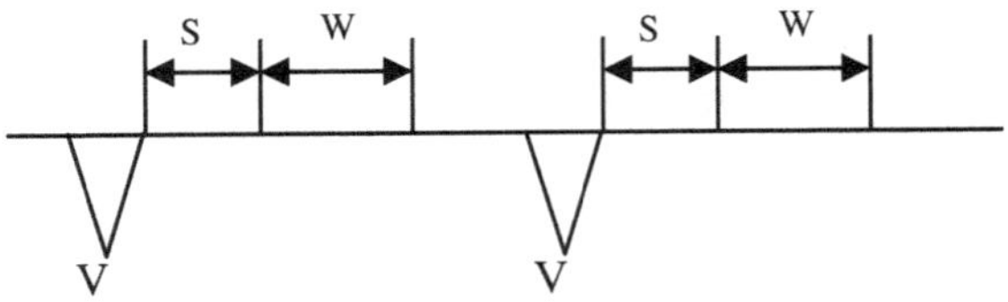

Fig. 1. Bisynchronous principle

The self-synchronous algorithm is explained in [5] in detail. The valleys can be seen as the first guard for the secrets. Owing to different attacks to the secret, especially the cropping attacking, even if the synchronous valley has been found, the followed secret may be distortion. Then, the extracted information is incorrect. Hence, following the synchronous valley, a kind of synchronous signal is added before the secret. Only if the adding synchronous position is located, the secret watermarking can be argued and obtained. Here, the sequence code is adopted for the adding synchronous bits.

3 Description of Bisynchronous Audio Watermarking Algorithm

Up to date, the discrete wavelet transforming is most popularly used in multimedia watermarking algorithms. The quantization approach is adopted in the DWT for watermark embedding and extracting.

The watermark embedding process is described in Figure 2.

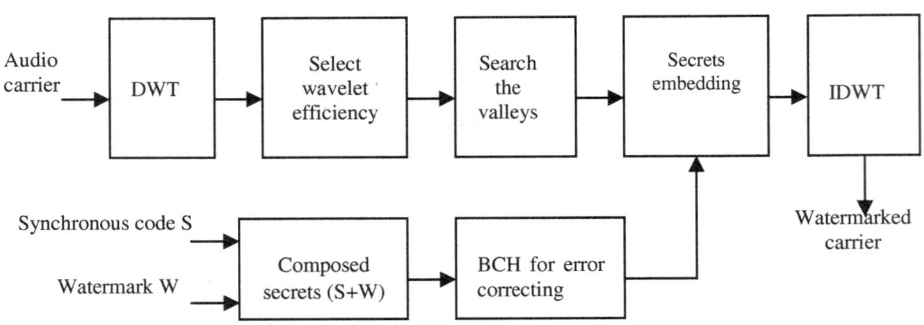

Fig. 2. Audio watermark embedding process with bisynchronous principle

The first three stages in the extraction process are the same as that in data embedding process. After the composed secrets (S+W) is obtained, the important stage is synchronous code matching. Due to many kinds of attacks, some synchronous bits may be damaged. When the matching number is more than half of the number of synchronous bits, the secrets are thought of hiding behind the synchronous bits.

However, this value is always unfit to the actual hiding situation because the matching number in extracting process often varied significantly.

For the synchronous coding matching, the extracted synchronous code will be compared with the code when embedding. Supposing the length of synchronous code is L_s, N_s is the number of duplicated synchronization segment, the initial synchronous code is $M=\{m_i|i=1,2,\ldots, L_s\}$, and the extracted synchronous code is $M'=\{m'_i|i=1,2,\ldots, L_s\}$. Then, the matching number L_m is defined as following:

$$L_m = | m_i \oplus m_i' |, i = 1, 2, \ldots, Ls \quad (1)$$

Given a rate R_{ma} for range of matching synchronous codes, the approach is stated below.

(1) Get the lowest tolerable matching number. If

$$L_m(i) < \left\lfloor \frac{L_s}{2} + 1 \right\rceil, (i = 1, 2, \ldots, N_s) \quad (2)$$

then declare the failure of the synchronization fragment.

(2) Find the maximum of extracted synchronization values:

$$\max M = \max(L_m(i)), (i = 1, 2, \ldots, N_s) \quad (3)$$

(3) Obtain the matching range as following:

$$rangeM = \{\lfloor R_{ma} \times \max M \rceil, \max M\} \quad (4)$$

(4) Get the number of usable synchronous segments:

$$N_w = | \{ L_m(i) \mid L_m(i) \in rangeM \} | \quad (5)$$

The *rangeM* will be adapted with the different value of *maxM*. When the synchronous ability is strong, the *maxM* often approaches to the Ls, and the secret can be extracted accurately. If some of synchronous segments are in distortion, the secret can also be corrected through the modification of *rangeM*.

The final watermark will be calculated by devoting from the candidates of extracted watermark. Supposing L_w is the length of watermark, $L_a(k)$ is the added number of the same bit position k for N_w candidates, then we have the following devoting rule:

$$L_a(k) = \sum_{j=1}^{N_w} w(k, j), k = 1, 2, \ldots, L_w \quad (6)$$

Then,

$$w(k) = (\frac{L_a(k)}{N_w} > 0.5)\,?\,1 : 0 \quad (7)$$

4 Experiments and Analysis

The proposed approach is tested on a 16-bit signed mono music sampled at 44.1 kHz with the length of about seconds in the WAVE format. The watermark is 32-bit binary sequence, and the BCH code is (17,7,2). Besides, the parameters of L, limEa, limEb, limR and limX are set as 128, 3, 3, 0.1 and 0.1, respectively. And, the Harr wavelet is selected to be decomposized at 6 levels.

Seven typical attacks on the watermarked audio are designed to verify the robustness of the algorithm. The six attacks are almost the same stated in [5]. The performance of common attacks shows robust in MP3 coding, re-sampling, re-coding, re-quantization, echo delay and adding noise of the bisynchronous technology.

For the cropping attack, the waveform is separated as 4 parts of P1, P2, P3 and P4. The ability against cropping is very strong, as shown in Table 1.

Table 1. Cropping results to the watermarked audio

Cut parts	Valley number	L_m	Adaptive matching	BER
P2+P3	5	31, 31, 63, 35, 32	63	0
P3+P4	4	63, 29, 63, 63	63, 63, 63	0
P2+P3+P4	2	32, 63	63	0
P1+P2	3	34, 21, 32	34	0.39

5 Conclusion

A bisynchronous algorithm is presented for audio watermarking with strong robustness against the attacks of cropping and common signal processing. The synchronous valley approach can help searching the secret locations accurately, and the adaptive matching approach is effective in finding usable candidates of watermark.

Acknowledgments. This work is supported by the Funding Project for Academic Human Resources Development in Institutions of Higher Learning Under the Jurisdiction of Beijing Municipality.

References

1. Gomes, L. d. C.T., et al.: Audio Watermarking and Fingerprinting for Which Applications? Journal of New Music Research 32(1), 65–82 (2003)
2. Kirovski, D., Attias, H.: Audio Watermark Robustness to Desynchronization via Beat Dectection. In: Proc. of the Int. Conf. on Information Hiding, pp. 160–176 (2002)
3. Coumou, D.J., Sharma, G.: Watermark synchronization for feature-based embedding: Application o speech. In: IEEE ICME (2006)
4. Celik, M., Sharma, G., Tekalp, A.M.: Pitch and duration modification for speech watermarking. In: Proc IEEE ICASSP, vol. II, pp. 117–120 (March 2005)
5. Zhang, X., Yin, X.: Feature-based self-synchronous audio watermarking technology. In: ICIP 2007. Workshop of NPC07, Dalian, China (September 2007)

Design and Implementation of Steganographic Speech Telephone

Zongyuan Deng, Zhen Yang, Xi Shao
Ning Xu, Chao Wu, and Haiyan Guo

Nanjing University of Posts and Telecommunications,
210003 Nanjing, China
{y050919,yangz, shaoxi, y050921, y050922, y050902}@njupt.edu.cn

Abstract. This paper explains the work to design an information hiding based secure communication system, named covert speech telephone (CST). The overall system is designed over the internet using UDP protocol. Based on a GUI (graphical user interface) software, CST is possible to execute two optional secure modes. It is a completely digital system with high speech quality. Practical effects show that CST can meet the requirement of real-time secure communication. This new technique can effectively guarantee information security in VoIP system.

Keywords: steganography, information hiding, Least Significant Bit (LSB).

1 Introduction

Different from conventional encryption-based secure communication [1], this paper explores the technique of information hiding to guarantee communicating securely by concealing both the contents of information and its existence during the transmission process [2], which ensures that it is not easy to detect the presence of a secret in the mixed message. The main strength of this paper is that we have implemented the whole system. We will discuss the detailed descriptions in the following section.

2 System Architecture

2.1 Proposed Steganographic Scheme

Based on the stegonagraphic and watermarking ideas, we successfully design two approaches optional for real-time CST.

Figure 1 shows the proposed schematic diagram. It can be readily seen from the figure that the first approach is the prevailing LSB-based (Least Significant Bit Substitution) steganograchic method [3] combined with modified CELP (Code Excitation Linear Prediction) codec. In addition, CST applies the technique of scrambling to improve security.

H.H.S. Ip et al. (Eds.): PCM 2007, LNCS 4810, pp. 429–432, 2007.

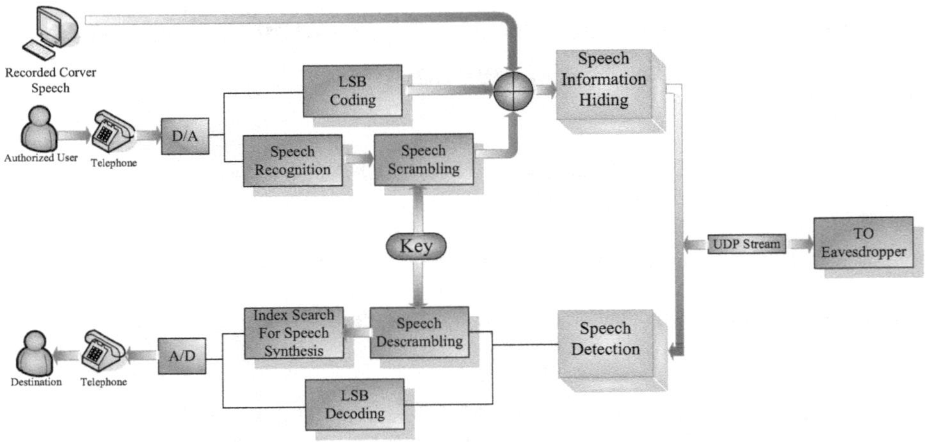

Fig. 1. CST Modular

To meet the requirement of real-time software implementation, some modifications is done on the basis of ITU G.729A [4]. These modifications do not obviously degrade the speech quality. Instead of applying a pre-selection process, the proposed scheme directly searches the optimum pitch gain by minimizing equation 1.

$$E=\left\|\mathbf{x}-g_p\mathbf{y}-g_c\mathbf{z}\right\|^2=\mathbf{x}^T\mathbf{x}+g_p^2\mathbf{y}^T\mathbf{y}+g_c^2\mathbf{z}^T\mathbf{z}-2g_p\mathbf{x}^T\mathbf{y}-2g_c\mathbf{x}^T\mathbf{z}+2g_pg_c\mathbf{y}^T\mathbf{z}\ . \quad (1)$$

Where **x** is the target vector, **y** is the filtered adaptive-codebook vector, and **z** is the filtered fixed codebook vector, g_p is the gain of adaptive-codebook, and g_c is the gain of fixed-codebook [4].

In addition, we also simplify the construct of matrix Φ in the subroutine of algebraic codebook search.

As viewed above, the most difficulty of the real-time voice information hiding system lies in real-time processing. On the other hand, many transparency and robust watermarking schemes suggest us converting the real-time steganographic message to watermarking information and using robust data hiding scheme to implement the steganographic system. Thus, the second idea is to use speech recognition (so the data rate is reduced dramatically) followed by a watermarking system to add the data to the non-secret speech. From the perspective of information theory, the reason why speech recognition can compress data is that human speech consists of both semanteme and some identity information of the speaker such as tone and emotion. In military secure communication system, these characteristics of speaker are redundant compared to the semanteme which is possible to be discarded. However, the accuracy of speech recognition cannot be guaranteed to be perfectly accurate at present. Therefore, we can make reasonable assumption that for military purpose, the transmitted orders are possible to be limited in definite vocabularies or phrases. In such scenario, the speech recognition algorithm is possible to reach high accuracy. In addition, a synthesized decision-feedback system is applied to avoid the false recognition. This system synthesizes speech according to the former recognition result, followed by a yes-or-no verification procedure. Generally, the recognition system can possibly achieve 100% recognition accuracy with the yes-or-no verification procedure. The subsequent information hiding step is not executed unless the verification result is "yes".

An improved watermarking algorithm is proposed which adaptively chooses embedding locations and applies the multi-nary modulation technique. The main differences between the traditional algorithm and the proposed algorithm are manifolds: (1) Embedded locations are varied by adaptively searching, which is controlled by an encryption key (K2). (2) For every embedded location selected, multi-states can be transmitted (i.e. four codes states for one modification). In this way, multi-nary modulation system can increase the embedding efficiency. (3) The proposed approach makes full use of the characteristic of human auditory system (HAS) to realize robustness against various interferences. Its detailed discussion appears in [5].

2.2 User Guide

CST is designed to work over the internet in accordance to the fast developing of real-time communication over internet in recent years. It focuses on applying various techniques of speech signal processing to ensure covert communication. It commonly consists of a voice fingerprint authorized system and a disguised communication system.

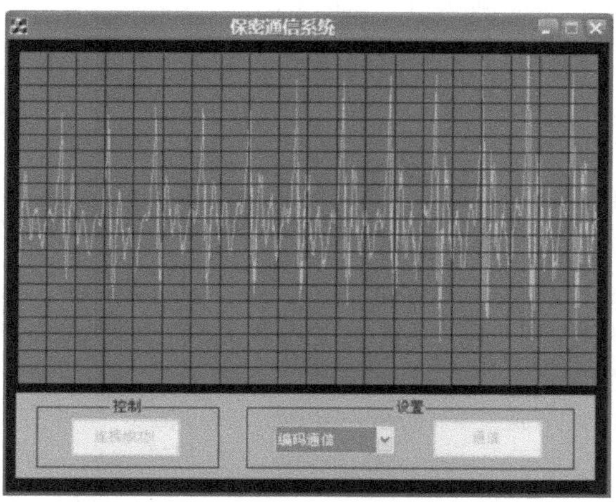

Fig. 2. Communication Interface of CST

Authorized user only needs to have a PC installed with CST-GUI software and follow the instructions. Then, secure connection is established using UDP protocol. CST works in full-duplex communication mode. This system only uses the μ/a-law based speech as the cover signal at 64kbps. As the system starts, user should pass the voice-fingerprint authentication procedure. We use the VQ-GMM-based approach for speaker identification in CST. Its detailed discussion can be found in [6]. Authenticated by the proposed system, the authorized user is possible to speak secret message via the transmitting interface shown in figure 2. The experimental results show the imperceptibility and robustness of the proposed watermarking system. It also is shown to be effective against steganalysis techniques [5].

3 Conclusion

In this paper, we present a novel covert speech communication system (CST). One approach uses LSB-based technique. In another way, the secret speech signal is converted into a sequence of indexes using a speech recognition algorithm. Then, this sequence of indices is embedded into a cover speech signal using a robust watermarking algorithm. At the receiver, the embedded data is retrieved and speech is synthesized from code book indices. Practical performance shows that CST can meet the requirement of real-time secure communication.

Acknowledgments. This work is supported by National 863 key project (2006AA010102).

References

1. Diez-Del-Rio, L., Moreno-Perez, S.: Secure speech and data communication over the public switching telephone network. In: ICASSP. Acoustics, Speech, and Signal Processing, 1994 IEEE International Conference on (April 19-22, 1994) vol. ii, pp.II/425–II/428
2. Eggers, J.J, Bauml, R.: Scalar Costa scheme for information embedding. [J], IEEE Transactions on Signal Processing 51(4), 1003–1019 (2003)
3. Wu, Z.-j., Niu, X.-x., Yang, Y.-x.: Design of Speech Information Hiding Telephone. In: Proc, IEEE Int. Conf. Tencon 2002, pp. 113–116 (2002)
4. Salami, R., Laflamme, C.: ITU-T G.729 Annex A: reduced complexity 8 kb/s CS-ACELP codec for digital simultaneous voice and data. IEEE Communication Magazine 35(9), 56–63 (1997)
5. Deng, Z., Yang, Z., Deng, L.: A Real-time Secure Voice Communication System Based on Speech Recognition. In: IEEE ICSNC 2006. IEEE International Conference on Systems and Networks Communication, Tahiti, France, p. 22 (2006)
6. He, J., Liu, L.: Palm: A discriminative training algorithm for VQ-based speaker identification. IEEE Transaction on Speech and Audio Processing 7(3), 353–356 (1999)

A Low Complexity Recovery Temporal Synchronization Signals Based on Local Variance Statistics

Ta-Te Lu[1], Wei-Lun Hsu[2], and Pao-Chi Chang[2]

[1] Department of Computer Science & Information Engineering, Ching Yun University, Chung-Li, Taiwan
ttlu@cyu.edu.tw
[2] Department of Communication Engineering, National Central University, Chung-Li, Taiwan
{wlshiu, pcchang}@vaplab.ee.ncu.edu.tw

Abstract. Temporal attacks will affect temporal synchronization signals loss. In this paper, we propose a low complexity temporal synchronization recovery method using local variance statistics in each group of picture (GOP), which is regarded as the feature parameters and sent as side information to recover synchronization signals. The temporal distortions can be identified by comparision of the feature parameters and the feature statistics of the received watermarked video data. Simulation results show that the proposed method is more robust against temporal attacks.

Keywords: Temporal attacks, synchronization, temporal distortions.

1 Introduction

Digital watermarking has been recognized as a helpful technology for copyright protection. However many video watermarking techniques are sensitive to synchronization attacks, e.g. dropping, insertion, and transposition [1]-[3]. Most of watermark extraction methods will fail to extract watermarks from incorrect frames after synchronization attacks. Therefore, the temporal synchronization is an important process of detecting the proper order of video frames [4]-[5].

Some video watermarking methods include embedding auxiliary synchronization signals into video sequences. Wang and Pearmain [4] partitioned video sequence into N scenes, then added the same redundancy bits against frame dropping in each frame within the same scene. Pickering *et al.* [5] changed the reordering key every N frames against frame dropping. Unfortunately, these techniques are weak against transposition and the same redundancy bits are easily removed by attacks.

In this paper, we propose a local variance statistics (LVS) method to process re-synchronization at the watermarking extraction end. The temporal synchronization mechanism is based on feature statistics, which are regarded as the synchronization signal and sent as side information. Furthermore, the synchronization mechanism can be used with a wide class of current video watermarking techniques.

H.H.S. Ip et al. (Eds.): PCM 2007, LNCS 4810, pp. 433–436, 2007.

2 Synchronization Feature Extraction

This work presents a feature extraction method based on local variance statistics (LVS) in order to obtain effective features in each frame. The feature parameters C in each frame can be extracted by LVS and recorded shown in Fig. 1. The detailed LVS process is described in Section 2.1.

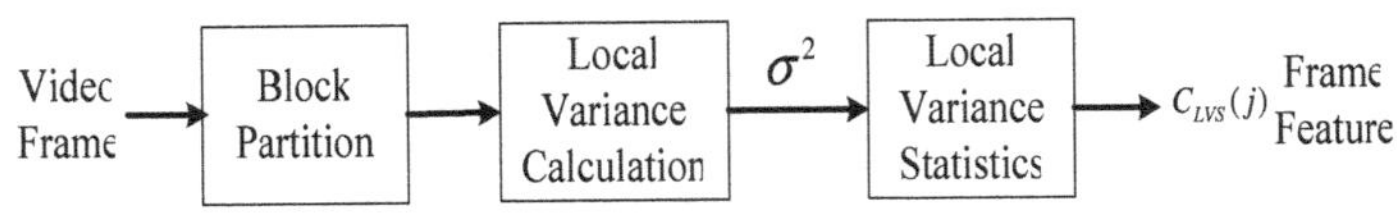

Fig. 1. The block diagram of local variance statistics

2.1 Local Variance Statistics

The successive video frames characteristics are very similar, but block features in local regions may be different from each other. Therefore, each frame can be identified by these block features.

The LVS process contains three block diagrams: block partition, local variance calculation and local variance statistics, as shown in Fig. 1. Each video frame is partitioned into m non-overlapping blocks by block partitions, with each block having n pixels, and then the block feature is extracted from its statistical characteristic using local variance calculation at each block. The local variance $\sigma^2 = \{\sigma_1^2, \sigma_2^2, \ldots \sigma_m^2\}$ is calculated and taken as the block feature, which is defined as (1).

$$\sigma_i^2 = \frac{1}{n}\sum_{l=1}^{n}[p_i(l) - u_i]^2 , \tag{1}$$

where $P_i(l)$ is the l-th pixel in the i-th block, u_i denotes the local mean in the i-th block, and n is the amount of pixels.

The frame feature $C_{LVS}(j)$ evaluates the statistical characteristics of local variance from all blocks in the j-th frame

$$C_{LVS}(j) = \frac{1}{m}\sum_{i=1}^{m}\left[\sigma_i^2 - \tilde{\sigma}_j\right]^2 , \tag{2}$$

where $\tilde{\sigma}_j$ represents the average of all blocks' local variances in j-th frame,

$$\tilde{\sigma}_j = \frac{1}{m}\sum_{i=1}^{m}\sigma_i^2 , \tag{3}$$

σ_i^2 represents the local variance in the i-th block, and m is the amount of blocks.

3 Temporal Re-synchronization

The received watermarked video stream is recovered back to the video sequence in the pixel domain by video decoding. Then the feature parameters C' are extracted.

The feature extraction process is the same as the embedding end, which was described in section 2.1. In the temporal detection procedure, the temporal recovery indexes T are used in re-synchronization processes in order to recover proper frame orders. The index T can be obtained by comparing C' and the received C. Details of temporal detection processes are described in Section 3.1.

3.1 Temporal Detection

The square errors, which are denoted $D_{SE}(C, C') = (C - C')^2$, between the received feature parameters C and the uncertain feature parameters C' in the received video are calculated. And then the temporal index parameter T_j in j-frame is determined by the minimum D_{SE}. The temporal recovery indexes T, which are defined by (4), are used to recover the proper frame order in the re-synchronization procedure.

$$T = \left\{ T_j;\ T_j = \min_{i \in \{1,\dots,N\}} D_{SE}(C_i, C_j');\ \text{for all j} \right\}, \tag{4}$$

4 Simulation Results

The temporal attacks, such as dropping, insertion, and transposition, are used to measure the temporal synchronization method. In this scheme, two video sequences are tested as experimental samples, e.g. Akiyo and Foreman (size of 176x144 and 100 frames, GOP=10). Re-synchronization with the GOP unit can decrease the amount of synchronization parameters, which is transmitted as side information. In these simulation cases: the 4-th GOP position is dropped; the 3-th GOP and the 7-th GOP positions are transpositions; and the 6-th GOP position is inserted by another GOP. Fig. 2 (a)-(b) shows of the effects watermark extraction without temporal re-synchronization. The NC values are small after temporal attacks. After re-synchronization processing, the performance of the watermarking system is improved significantly, as shown Fig. 3(a)-(b). In Fig. 3(a)-(b), the 4-th GOP is dropped information so this situation is denoted NC = 0 in this paper.

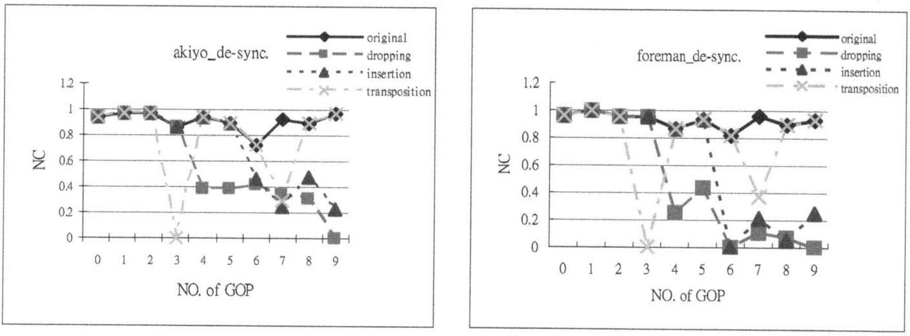

(a) (b)

Fig. 2. Watermark extraction NC results after temporal attacks without the LVS method (a) Akiyo (b) Foreman

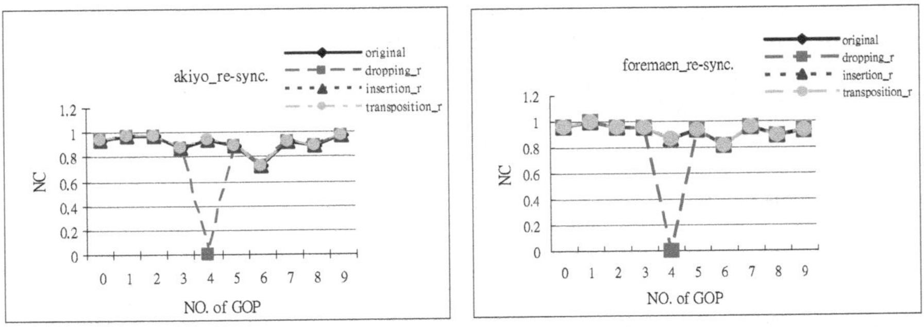

(a) (b)

Fig. 3. Watermark extraction NC results after temporal attacks with the LVS method (a) Akiyo (b) Foreman

5 Conclusions

This work presents a low complexity recovery synchronization method that is appropriate for real time applications. Simulation results show that the temporal synchronization mechanism can effectively resist temporal attacks. Furthermore, the synchronization mechanism can be used with a wide class of current video watermarking techniques.

References

1. Cox, I., Miller, M., Bloom, J.: Digital Watermarking. Morgan Kaufmann Publishers, San Francisco (2001)
2. Delannay, D., Macq, B.: Watermarking Relying on Cover Signal Content to Hide Synchronization Marks. IEEE Trans. on Information Forensics and Security, 87–102 (2006)
3. Sun, S.W., Chang, P.C.: Video Watermarking Synchronization Based on Profile Statistics. IEEE Aerospace and Electronic Systems Magazine 19(5), 21–25 (2004)
4. Wang, Y., Pearmain, A.: Blind MPEG-2 Video Watermarking Robust Against Geometric Attacks: A Set of Approaches in DCT Domain. IEEE Trans. on Image Processing 15, 1536–1543 (2006)
5. Pickering, M., Coria, L.E., Nasiopoulos, P.: A Novel Blind Video Watermarking Scheme for Access Control Using Complex Wavelets. In: IEEE Int. Conf. on Consumer Electronics, pp. 1–2 (2007)

An Efficient Video Watermarking Scheme with Luminance Differential DC Coefficient Modification*

Yun Ye, Xinghao Jiang, Tanfeng Sun, and Jianhua Li

School of Information Security Engineering, Shanghai Jiaotong University,
Shanghai, P.R. China, 200240
{sjtumary, xhjiang, tfsun, lijh888}@sjtu.edu.cn

Abstract. In this paper, an efficient video watermarking scheme is presented through modifying the third decoded luminance differential DC component in each selected macro block. The modification is implemented by binary dither modulation with adaptive quantization step. The proposed scheme is based on the observation that luminance differential DC components inside one macro block are generally space correlated, so the quantization step can be adjusted according to adjacent differential components, to utilize properties of human visual system (HVS). This method is very robust to gain attacks since amplitude scaling will have the same effect on differential components and the quantization step. Experimental results show that it can be implemented in real time with better visual quality than uniform-quantizing scheme.

Keywords: Video watermarking, real-time embedding, luminance differential DC coefficient, binary dither modulation, adaptive quantization step.

1 Introduction

Video watermarking is gaining popularity in information hiding community, along with rapid development of video industry [1~3]. However, some image-level schemes are not preferable when it comes to real-time embedding situations such as user labeling in VOD (video on demand) service, which requires instant operation on compression coded data with tolerable delay. In order to make better tradeoff among robustness, complexity, security and perceptibility [3~5], this paper exploits adjustment in differential DC components and presents an efficient video watermarking scheme with luminance differential DC coefficient modification. Only three VLC (variable length code) code words of the selected macro blocks' differential DC coefficients are decoded and two of them are modified. The modification is implemented by performing binary dither modulation on one differential DC coefficient, and the quantization step is made self-adaptive according to the neighboring unchanged two inside the same macro block.

* Supported by the National Natural Science Foundation of China (No.60702042).

H.H.S. Ip et al. (Eds.): PCM 2007, LNCS 4810, pp. 437–440, 2007.

2 Differential DC Coefficient Modification Model

Certain video compression codec standards, such as MPEG-2, MPEG-4, H.264, apply DCT to original sequential pictures on block level, and DC coefficients are handled with DPCM (differential pulse code modulation) before being encoded into VLC code words. Take MPEG-2 for example, Fig.1 (L) shows the predicting relation of four luminance (Y component) DC coefficients (after quantization), denoted as DC1, DC2, DC3, DC4, inside one 16×16 macro block, with corresponding VLC code words representing diff1=DC1-DC4', diff2=DC2-DC1, diff3=DC3-DC2, diff4=DC4-DC3.

The differential DC coefficient modification model is constructed based on the observation and experimental statistics, that in an I frame, luminance differential DC components inside one macro block are generally space correlated, as depicted in Fig.1 (R). For an explicit expression, the relation of three selected luminance differential DC components, diff2, diff3, and diff4, in one macro block is formulated with the following equation.

$$diff\,3 \approx \alpha * (diff\,4 + diff\,3 - diff\,2)\,, \tag{1}$$

where α is a proportional factor (around 0.7 for most tested macro blocks).

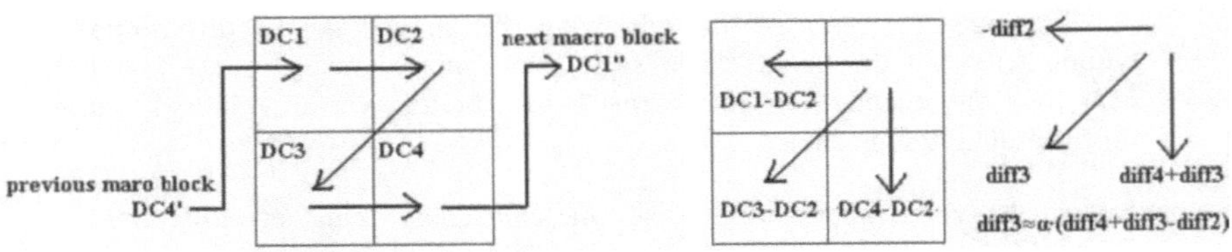

Fig. 1. Predicting relation of DC coefficients(L); Estimation of differential DC components(R)

Provided with above estimating relation, it is feasible to make the quantization step self-adaptive.

$$q = |\,q0 * (diff\,4 + diff\,3 - diff\,2)\,|\,, \tag{2}$$

where $q0$ is a pre-determined scaling factor and q is the quantization step. $|x|$ denotes the absolute value of x. Then diff3 is modified through binary dither modulation[4]. After modifying diff3, diff4 is modified to keep the original value of DC4 and not to influence the DC coefficients in following blocks:

$$diff\,4' = diff\,4 + diff\,3 - diff\,3'\,. \tag{3}$$

In this way, the quantization step, q, is constrained by (diff4+diff3) and –diff2. Both fidelity assurance and blind extraction are achieved, since only DC3 is actually modified and the quantization step can be accurately retrieved by the unchanged DC1, DC2 and DC4. Another advantage to apply dither modulation to differential DC components is that it is very robust to gain attacks [5], because amplitude scaling will have the same effect on diff2, diff3', diff4' and hence q.

3 Watermark Embedding and Extracting

Detailed embedding procedure is described as follows.

1) Obtain L-bit binary original message, and encrypt it by exclusive-or operation with the template generating seed, S, to get the watermark data to be embedded, W.
2) Use S to generate L templates containing random '0' and '1' signals, each template contains N signals, the same size with the m-block number of each I frame.
3) For the i-th I frame to be embedded, select macro blocks with signal '1' in the same position in the i-th template.
4) For each selected macro block, decode the three luminance differential DC coefficients' VLC code words to get diff2, diff3, diff4.
5) Calculate the quantization step q according to equation (2).
6) Modify diff3 and diff4 according to the i-th bit value of W.
7) Encode diff3', diff4' back to VLC code words and produce the embedded video.

The watermark extracting procedure is similar. Since diff3'+diff4' is equal to diff3+diff4 by equation (3), and diff2 is unchanged, the quantization step, q, is retrieved reliable by equation (2). The embedded bit value for each selected macro block is determined by the minimum distance criterion [4]. And the i-th bit value of W is identical to the majority of these bit values extracted from the i-th I fame.

4 Implementation of the Proposed Scheme

The proposed scheme is applied to four MPEG-2 video sequences, Flower garden (704×480, 6M bps), Mobile (704×480, 6M bps), Susan (352×240, 1.5M bps) and Table tennis (352×240, 1.5M bps), and compared with uniform-quantizing scheme.

In this experiment, q0 is set to 0.1 and 0.4 separately, for different embedding intensity test. The encrypted message is successfully extracted under both circumstances. Visual quality is greatly improved if proper upper bound is set for the quantization step, e.g., when the upper bound is 30.0, the visual quality of embedded *Susan* with q0=2.0 is equivalent to the non-limited embedded one with q0=0.1.

Table 1. MSE and PSNR (dB) calculation for the proposed scheme (upper MSE/PSNR) and the uniform-quantizing scheme (lower MSE/PSNR). Increased data size (byte) in embedded MPEG-2 files with the proposed scheme is provided in the last row.

Y pictures	Flower garden		Mobile		Susan		Table tennis	
	q0=0.1	q0=0.4	q0=0.1	q0=0.4	q0=0.1	q0=0.4	q0=0.1	q0=0.4
MSE	17.344	25.321	23.403	34.663	2.432	3.103	6.422	7.005
PSNR	35.739	34.096	34.438	32.732	44.271	43.212	40.054	39.677
MSE	25.213	38.870	35.601	59.101	3.144	4.749	6.369	10.562
PSNR	34.115	32.235	32.616	30.415	43.156	41.365	40.090	37.894
Size increase	-39	-71	-111	-79	-6	9	28	21

The proposed scheme and the uniform-quantizing one is compared through calculating the PSNR and MSE of the embedded data. For each scheme, the embedded and non-embedded MPEG-2 sequences are converted to YUV files and the correlations of their Y pictures are computed respectively. The experimental data in Table 1 show that the visual quality of the embedded pictures with the proposed scheme is satisfied, with smaller MSE and higher PSNR (about 2dB) than conventional one using uniform quantization step. This scheme can also be applied to other video format with similar compression coding mechanism.

5 Conclusion

In this paper, an efficient video watermarking scheme is presented with luminance differential DC coefficient modification. The modification is implemented by binary dither modulation without resorting to original DC coefficients, and the quantization step is made self-adaptive, according to the modified component's two neighbors. Thus visual quality of the embedded video is well maintained, while the provable robustness of dither modulation technology is reserved.

Experimental results verify the estimation relation of adjacent luminance differential DC components and display the superiority of the proposed scheme to conventional one using uniform quantization step. Watermark embedding and extracting procedures are based on independent macro blocks, and can easily be integrated with the video encoder and decoder. Therefore, it is suitable for real-time applications such as user labeling in VOD service, multimedia retrieval, and so on. More accurate formulation for the correlation of differential DC components and quantitative analysis on maximum embedding intensity are included in the future work.

References

1. Lie, W.-N., Lin, T.C.-I., Lin, C.-W.: Enhancing video error resilience by using data-embedding techniques. IEEE Transactions on Circuits and Systems for Video Technology 16(2), 300–308 (2006)
2. Wang, C.-C., Lin, Y.-C., Ti, S.-C.: Satellite interference detection using real-time watermarking technique for SMS. In: ICITA 2005. Third International Conference on Information Technology and Applications, 2005 , vol. 2, pp. 238–241(July 4-7, 2005)
3. Langelaar Gerrit, C., Lagendijk Reginald, L., Jan, B.: Real-time labeling of MPEG-2 compressed video. Journal of Visual Communication and Image Representation , 256–270 (1998)
4. Chen, B., Wornell, G.W.: Quantization index modulation: a class of provably good methods for digital watermarking and information embedding. IEEE Transactions on Information Theory 47(4), 1423–1443 (2001)
5. Perez-Gonzalez, F., Mosquera, C., Barni, M., Abrardo, A.: Rational dither modulation: a high-rate data-hiding method invariant to gain attacks. IEEE Transactions on Signal Processing, Part 2 53(10), 3960–3975 (2005)

Real-Time Secure Multimedia Communication System Based on Chaos Theory

Rogelio Hasimoto-Beltrán and Edmar Mota-García

Department of Computer Science, Center for Research in Mathematics (CIMAT),
Jalisco s/n, Col. Mineral de Valenciana, Guanajuato, Gto, México 36240
{hasimoto,edmar}@cimat.mx

Abstract. We propose a novel block-based symmetric encryption system based on an *n-array* of independently iterated chaotic logistic maps with global and local feedback as a diffusion process. Local feedback represents the temporal evolution of a single map, while global feedback represents the temporal evolution of the whole system (cross-map evolution). For security, the cryptosystem periodically modifies its internal configuration using a three-level random perturbation scheme, one at system-key (reset operation) and two at map array level (to increase the chaotic cycle length of the system). An analysis of the proposed scheme regarding its vulnerability to attacks, statistical properties and implementation performance is presented. To the best of our knowledge we provide a simple and secure scheme with the fastest software implementation reported in the literature.

Keywords: Discrete chaotic encryption, Block ciphers, symmetric encryption.

1 Introduction

Building secure multimedia communications demand new challenges difficult to handle by currently adopted encryption schemes (DES, RSA, AES, and IDEA) [1, 2]. Multimedia requires the processing of huge amounts of information at speeds going from Kilobits/sec (Kbs) to the order of Megabits/sec (Mbs), in particular those applications involving real-time audio and video transmission. Discrete chaotic dynamical systems (DCS) have been used since late 80's, but few proposals have emerged for voice and video data encryption (with limited real-time capabilities) [3-6]. Considering this, we propose a novel symmetric encryption system based on an *n-array* of independently iterated chaotic maps, along with a three-level periodic perturbation and a two-mode feedback (global and local feedback) for real-time multimedia communications. The perturbation scheme changes current system condition by modifying the system-key and the trajectory of the chaotic maps to increase system security against statistical and differential attacks. The system key is periodically modified using a random number generator, while every map trajectory is modified using the system's output itself (ciphertext) rather than a predefined perturbation equation. Since chaotic maps are iterated independently, ciphertext inter-dependency is created by adding global and local feedback to current ciphertext value.

H.H.S. Ip et al. (Eds.): PCM 2007, LNCS 4810, pp. 441–445, 2007.

Global feedback represents the temporal evolution of the entire system, while local feedback represents the temporal evolution of a single map.

2 Proposed Chaotic Encryption Scheme

Our scheme can be split into three main components:

A) System-key Generation: An initial seed is first created and used for the generation of the system-key (K) using a random number generator (RNG). For security, K is constantly modified using both fixed and forced updates. Fixed key update is part of the three-level perturbation scheme in which K is replaced periodically using RNG after a random number of iterations. Forced updates on the other hand are used as a resynchronization process between cipher and decipher in the case of data errors during transmission (or when security is compromised).

B) Encryption System: Once K of size $B \geq 128$ bits is generated, it is divided into *2n* equal parts, where each part is used to initialize a corresponding system variable and parameter of the n-array of logistic maps as follows:

$$\begin{aligned} &X_{i,0} = K(2i-1), \\ &\lambda_i = 3.73364 + [K(2i)/2^{B/2n} + K(2i)/10^{h_8} + (a \oplus b)/2^{B/4n}]/10, \\ &i \in \{1,2,3,\ldots, n\} \end{aligned} \tag{2}$$

where $X_{i,0}$ and λ_i are the ith map variable initial condition and parameter respectively, h_8 is the number of digits in the largest decimal number represented by B/8 bits ($K(k)/10^{h_8} = 0.(2^{B/8})$), $a \oplus b$ term is the exclusive-OR (XOR) of the most (*a*) and least (*b*) significant bits of *K(2i)* having both equal size bit representation of *B/4n*. $X_{i,0}$ and *K* are de-correlated by iterating $X_{i,0}$, $1 \leq i \leq n$ a random number of times *RT* over all maps:

$$\begin{aligned} &For \quad i \in \{1,2,3,\ldots, n\} \\ &\quad \gamma = X_{i,0}, \\ &\quad repeat \quad RT \quad times \\ &\quad\quad \gamma = \gamma.\lambda_1.(1-\gamma), \quad \gamma = \gamma.\lambda_2.(1-\gamma), \quad \gamma = \gamma.\lambda_3.(1-\gamma), \quad \gamma = \gamma.\lambda_4.(1-\gamma) \\ &\quad X_{i,0} = \gamma \end{aligned} \tag{3}$$

Even a one-bit change in *K*, will generate a completely different map orbits, which in turn generates different ciphertexts. Once $X_{i,j}$ and λ_i values have been obtained, the *n-array* of logistic maps can be written as:

$$X_{i,j} = \lambda_i . X_{i,j-1} . [1 - X_{i,j-1}], \qquad i \in \{1,2,3,\ldots n\} \tag{4}$$

where *i* and *j* represent the map and state indexes respectively. For a fixed state *j*, *n* map variables are obtained to encrypt their corresponding plaintext of size *B/n* using the following equation:

$$C_{i,k} = ([P_k + X'_{i,k}] \mod 2^{B/n}) \oplus X'_{i,k} \oplus ([C_{i-1,k} + C_{i,k-1}] \mod 2^{B/n}), \quad (5)$$
$$i \in \{1,2,3,\ldots,n\}, \qquad k = (j+i-1)$$

where k is the cipher iteration index ($k = nj$), X' is the corresponding integer representation of X using B/n bits, P_k is the kth plaintext input, $C_{i-1,k}$ is the previous cyphertext output ($i-1$) of the current iteration (k^{th}), and $C_{i,k-1}$ is the previous cyphertext output of the same i^{th} map, but from the ($k-1$) iteration. A total of B bits are encrypted per state iteration (B/n encrypted bits per map). $C_{i-1,k}$ and $C_{i,k-1}$ represent the global and local feedback respectively. The security of the system is increased by sending out not $C_{i,k}$, but its perturbation:

$$C^p_{i,k} = C_{i,k} + X'_T, \; X'_T = X'_{1,k} \oplus X'_{2,k} \oplus \hbar \; \oplus X'_{n,k} \quad (6)$$

Therefore, decipher cannot use $C^p_{i,k}$ directly to find its corresponding plaintext, it needs to know X'_T. For performance reasons we defined eq.5 as simple as possible, but it is possible to increase its complexity by adding more terms or combinations involving $X'_{i,k}$. The corresponding decryption system is:

$$P_k = [(C^p_{i,k} - X'_T) \oplus X'_{i,k} \oplus ([C_{i-1,k} + C_{i,j-1}] \mod 2^{B/n}) + 2^{B/n} - X'_{i,k}] \mod 2^{B/n}, \quad (7)$$
$$i \in \{1,2,3,\ldots,n\}, \qquad k = (j+i-1)$$

C) Three-Level Perturbation Scheme: To increase the cycle length of logistic maps, a three-level periodic perturbation scheme is proposed. In the first perturbation level, the trajectory of every map is slightly modified to increase its cycle length [5, 20] as follows:

$$X^p_{i,j} = X_{i,j} + \frac{1.1 + C_{n,j}(i)}{10^{h_{16}}}, \qquad i \in \{1,2,3,\ldots,n\} \quad (8)$$

where $C_{n,j}(i)$ is the ith element of the global feedback $C_{n,j}$ with size $B/4n$ bits, at the current state j. We post-process $X^p_{i,j}$ so that its first digit after the decimal point stays the same as in $X_{i,j}$; therefore $abs(X^p_{i,j} - X_{i,j}) < 10^{-1}$.

The second level perturbation replaces each map system variable by the resultant state of cross-iterating its value using all maps (same process as in eq. 3). For the ith map in state j, its new system variable is obtained by:

$$\begin{aligned} &\gamma = X_{i,j}, && i \in \{1,2,3,\ldots,n\} \\ &\gamma = \gamma.\lambda_k.(1-\gamma), && k \in \{[i \bmod n]+1, [(i+1) \bmod n]+1, [(i+2) \bmod n]+1\} \\ &X_{i,j} = \gamma \end{aligned} \quad (9)$$

New system variables are influenced by all maps, the output of the ith map is the input of the $[(i+1) \bmod n]+1$ map and so on and so forth. Third level perturbation replaces current system-key every random number of iterations. Every time the system-key is updated, the new key is sent to decipher to update system maps variables and parameters. The cycle of the perturbations represented by PT_i, $1 \leq i \leq 3$, can be randomly selected.

3 Experimental Results and Conclusions

Our proposed scheme is flexible regarding the system-key size and number of chaotic maps used for the encryption process, however there must be some congruency between their corresponding bit sizes. In general, B (size of K) can be a multiple of m bits (B_n) for $m \in \{8,16,32\}$, and the number of chaotic maps can be at least B_n/m (one map per m bits of K) and at the most $B_n/8$. A recommendation is not to use more than 32 bits of K for the generation of X_{i0} and λ_i (16 bits for each value).

We applied the proposed scheme to multimedia data with different sizes and statistical properties with the following setting: $B_{32} = 128$ bits, $n=4$ (four logistic maps), $RT = 20$, $PT_1 = 15$ iterations, $PT_2 = n_1\, PT_1$, and $PT3 = n_2 PT_2$, for $n_1 = n_2 = 3$. Fig.1a shows the histograms of plaintext and corresponding ciperhtext using two randomly chosen keys to prove statistical independence of the scheme. In all cases, the ciphertext histogram is uniform and independently of the shape of the plaintext histogram and system-key. As an average over all data files, 99.6% of the total bytes and 50% of the total bits were changed during the encryption process. The response of the scheme to slight changes (flipping of the least significant bit) of the system-key is immediate (Fig.1b), diverging drastically from the original sequence. Same behavior is found when the perturbation scheme is applied. To additionally complicate things out under an opponent attack, the correspondent random variable X_T (see eq. 6) is added to current ciphertext output; so in the case of an attack the opponent never has access to the real ciphertext values. If the opponent chooses brute force attack instead,

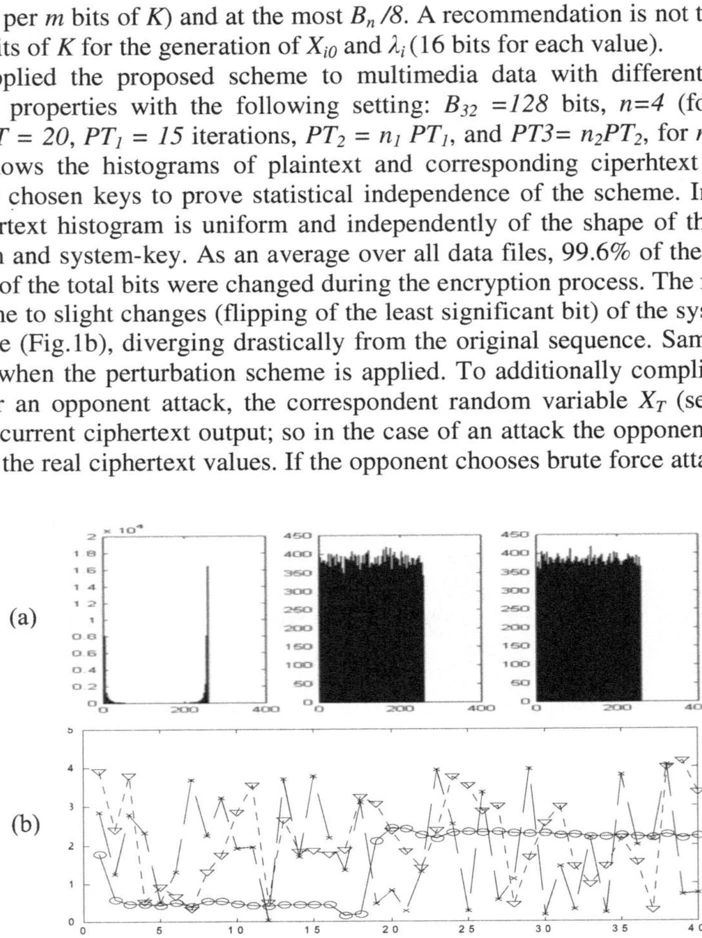

Fig. 1. (a) Histogram of plaintext (left column) and corresponding ciphertext for two different system-keys (middle and right columns). (b) Sensitivity to system key changes. Plaintext (circled continues line) encrypted with two different keys.

it will need to search for at least $2^{128} \approx 3.4 \times 10^{38}$ key possibilities in our current setting. Additionally, there are four more random numbers with 5-bit representation each, *RT, P_1, P_2, and P_3*; so brute force attack will need to consider a total space analysis of $(2^{128}).(2^{20})$. Finally, a C-language implementation of the cipher system on a 940Mhz Pentium®-III, with 190Mb of memory running Linux version 2.4.20-28.9, shows an average speed of 230Mbs (Megabits/sec); which is way faster than any other scheme reported in the literature. These reported speeds are fast enough for real-time multimedia communications.

References

1. Chen, G., Mao, Y., Chui, C.K.: A symmetric image encryption scheme based on 3D chaotic cat maps. Chaos Solit. & Fract. 21, 749–761 (2004)
2. Yang, M., Bourbakis, N., Li, S.: Data-image-video encryption. IEEE Potentials 23(3), 28–32 (2004)
3. Lian, S., Sun, J., Wang, Z., Dai, Y.: A fast encryption scheme based on chaos. In: 8th Int. Conf. Control, Automation, Robotics and Vision, pp. 126–131 (2004)
4. Paraskeve, T., Klimis, N., Stefanos, K.: Security of human video objects by incorporating a chaos-based feedback crytpography scheme. In: Proceedings of the 12th annual ACM international conference on Multimedia, New York, USA, pp. 352–355 (2004)
5. Roskin, K.M., Casper, J.B.: From Chaos to cryptography (1999), Available online at http://xcrypt.theory.org/paper
6. Tang, K.W., Tang, W.: A chaos-based secure voice communication system. In: ICIT 2005. IEEE Inter. Conf. Industrial tech, pp. 571–576 (2005)

A Remediable Image Authentication Scheme Based on Feature Extraction and Clustered VQ

Chin-Chen Chang [1,2], Chih-Chiang Tsou [1], and Yung-Chen Chou [2]

[1] Department of Information Engineering and Computer Science, Feng Chia University, Taichung 40724, Taiwan
ccc@cs.ccu.edu.tw, p9431570@fcu.edu.tw
[2] Department of Computer Science and Information Engineering, National Chung Cheng University, Chiayi 62102, Taiwan
jackjow@cs.ccu.edu.tw

Abstract. We present an image authentication scheme based on feature extraction and codeword clustering in this paper. The two-level detections can be performed progressively based on the requirements of the authenticator. In order to generate these two-level authentication codes, the quad-tree segmentation and clustered VQ techniques are used. Using the first-level authentication code, the malicious tampered areas can be detected and located. In the second-level, it not only provides a more rigid detection of tampered areas but also can further remedy them. According to the experimental results, our scheme can correctly detect the malicious tampering and tolerate some incidental modifications, and then successfully remedy the tampered area. In addition, the space cost of authentication code is quite little.

Keywords: Image authentication, quad-tree segmentation, tampering detection.

1 Introduction

Digital signature is one of those that can protect the integrity of images [1–3]. To store the authentication code as an independent file better than embeds it into the image because there is no distortion incurred and the authentication code can be used to remedy the tampered area. Hence, a trusted certification authority (CA) is required to allow the image owners register their images there by storing the authentication code of the image. Most of digital signature schemes are sensitive to the slight modification and cannot remedy the tampered area. The incidental modifications are usually incurred in the common image applications, such as image compression and image enhancement. These processes should be treated as legal processes.

This paper presents an image authentication scheme based on the digital signature approach, which can achieve the goals of malicious tampering detection and remedy with lower storage requirement. In the proposed scheme, the quad-tree segmentation technique is used to generate first-level authentication code. The second-level authentication code is generated by applying vector quantization technique with codeword clustering. For detection process, the first-level authentication code

H.H.S. Ip et al. (Eds.): PCM 2007, LNCS 4810, pp. 446–449, 2007.

(quad-tree structure) is employed to detect the malicious tampering and locate them. The second-level authentication code is used for the stricter detection and remedying.

2 Wang *et al.*'s Scheme

Wang *et al.*'s scheme [3] composes information hiding and the image authentication two processes. For information hiding process, first, the grayscale image is divided into non-overlapping blocks. Then the quad-tree structure of each block is built. The watermark W is permuted by a cryptographic hash function with user's private key. The quad-tree operation is then performed based on similarity rate and computed by $SR(A,B)=1-\sum_{i=1}^{m}\sum_{j=1}^{m}\left|a_{ij}-b_{ij}\right|/m\times m$, where A and B are two binary images sized $m\times m$. a_{ij} and b_{ij} are two binary elements of image A and B, respectively.

If the similarity rate of permuted watermark block and original watermark block is larger than or equal to a predefined threshold T, then the blocks are determined as similar and the quad-tree operation on the block is stopped. Otherwise, the permuted watermark block and original watermark block are divided into four equally sized quadrants, respectively, and then the same operation is performed individually to each pair of quadrants. All the pairs of quadrants will be divided until the quadrants are similar to each other, and the generated quad-tree structure is stored for the image authentication process.

For image authentication, first, the authenticator obtains authentication information. Then, the candidate image is divided into non-overlapping blocks. Then, the permuted watermark is generated by using the hash function with user's private key. Based on the feature of hash function, the watermark can be recovered by comparing with the retrieved validity quad-tree and candidate permuted watermark. If the candidate permuted watermark is more similar to original watermark, the recovered watermark will be more similar to the original watermark. In addition, the tampered areas can be located by the recovered watermark.

The shortcomings of Wang *et al.*'s scheme: 1) authentication code generation highly related to hash function; 2) heavy storage cost requirement for storing authentication code. Because hash function design and watermark format, the generated quad-tree is nearly a complete tree. Besides, the tampered areas cannot remedy when the area has been detected.

3 The Proposed Scheme

The proposed method utilizes quad-tree technique to generate first-level authentication code. Initially, two thresholds, TH_A and k, are preset, and the image is divided into non-overlapping blocks of $M\times M$ pixels. Here, k is the feature block size. The standard deviation $\sigma(X_i)$ for each block X_i is computed for feature blocks extracting. The value of $\overline{X}$ denotes the mean of block X_i. TH_A is used to determine the type of X_i. If $\sigma(X_i)<TH_A$, then stops the quad-tree segmentation of X_i, and the type of X_i is smooth. Otherwise, X_i is divided into four equally sized quadrants, and to examine the type of each quadrant. If quadrant size equals to k and the standard deviation of quadrant is larger than or equal to TH_A, then the type of the quadrant is

denoted as a feature block; otherwise, the type of block is smooth. The resulting quad-tree is stored as the first-level authentication code by the breadth-first traversal order.

The second-level authentication code is obtained by to computing mean value for smooth block, and using vector quantization (VQ) [4, 5] with codeword clustering for feature blocks. For economic consideration, the mean value of smooth block is quantized by $\overline{x}^* = \lfloor \overline{x}/q \rfloor$. For feature block, a VQ codewords are clustered into N_G groups using LBG algorithm [5] in order to reduce the storage requirement. Next, each feature block is performed by the VQ encoding procedure to find the nearest codeword c_i, and to record the index of G_j when $c_i \in G_j$.

For first-level detection, the authenticator obtains the first-level authentication code of the candidate image. The tampered blocks can be found by comparing the authentication codes from candidate image and the trusted certification authority. For second-level detection, the detection can be done by finding the difference between the second-level authentication codes from candidate image and trusted certification authority. TH_B is a predefined threshold for avoiding the incidental modifications on smooth blocks. $\overline{x}'$ denotes the quantized mean value of the candidate smooth block. If $|\overline{x}' - \overline{x}^*| > TH_B$, then the block is tampered. For the feature block detection, if the corresponding group index is not identical to its signature, then the block is tampered. Note that the blocks that have passed the first-level detection are still required to be checked again in the second-level.

The second-level authentication code is used to remedy the tampered blocks. For the smooth blocks, $\overline{x}^{\#} = \overline{x}^* \times q$ is used to remedy the tampered smooth block. Moreover, the tampered feature block is remedy by randomly choose a codeword in the corresponding group.

4 Experiments

Six grayscale images of 512×512 pixels used in these experiments. Peak signal-to-noise-ratio (PSNR) is used to measure the remedied image quality. Figs. 1(a)-(f) present the tampered images, and the PSNRs of tempered images are 25.26 dB, 31.19 dB, 31.66 dB, 28.69 dB, 24.49 db, and 34.49 dB, respectively. In our experimental results, the proposed method not only detected both adding object and erasing object but also remedied the tampered areas. Figs. 1(g)-(l) show the remedied images with the PSNR values: 34.32 dB, 38.19 dB, 40.59 dB, 41.38 dB, 35.36 dB, and 41.39 dB, respectively. The corresponding parameters TH_A, N_G, k, and TH_B are set as 8, 32, 4, and 10, respectively. Note that all tampered areas can be remedied using the second-level authentication code. Comparing Wang *et al.*'s method with the proposed scheme, only the proposed method can remedy the tampered areas. The quad-tree structure space cost of Wang *et al.*'s scheme requires an average of 1.3 bits/pixel. Our scheme needs only 0.03 to 0.06 bits/pixel to store the first-level authentication code. Furthermore, the second-level authentication code only requires 0.1 to 0.3 bits/pixel. Hence, the storage cost of the authentication codes in the proposed method is quite low. In the proposed scheme, several parameters are used to control performance. We set TH_B, k, and N_G to 10, 4, and 32, respectively. The storage cost has significant reduced when TH_A increases. The lower TH_A and k will increase the remedied image quality, and the larger N_G increases the remedied image quality.

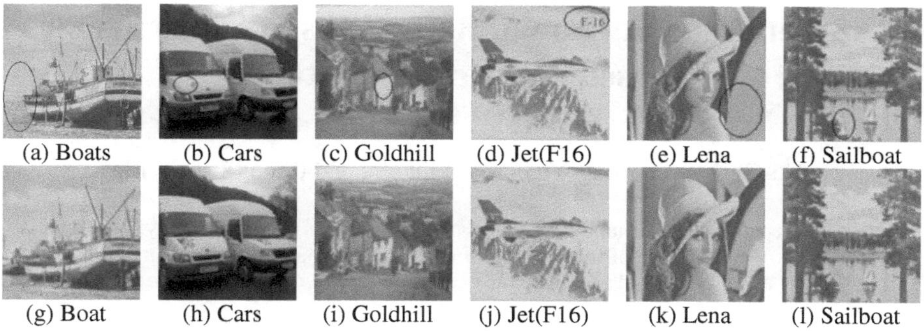

Fig. 1. Test images and results: (a)-(f) tampered images; (g)-(l) remedied images

5 Conclusions

This paper presents an image authentication scheme that provides two levels of authentication codes to detect malicious tampering and remedy tampered areas. The first-level authentication code detects the precise location of tampered areas. The second-level authentication code can be applied to detect changes to the image and remedy the tampered areas. From the experimental results, the quality of the remedied image achieves an average of 38 dB. The proposed method can also be used to filter out incidental modifications, such as non-geometric processes. Furthermore, the storage costs of the authentication codes are quite low. Our scheme requires only 0.03 to 0.06 bits/pixel to store the first-level authentication code and 0.1 to 0.3 bits/pixel to store the second-level authentication code. As far as trusted third party is concerned, the proposed scheme is suitable for large amounts of image registration due to the low storage cost.

References

1. Chan, C.S., Chang, C.C.: An Efficient Image Authentication Method Based on Hamming Code. Pattern Recognition 40(2), 681–690 (2006)
2. Lin, P.L., Hsieh, C.K., Huang, P.W.: A Hierarchical Digital Watermarking Method for Image Tamper Detection and Recovery. Pattern Recognition 38, 2519–2529 (2005)
3. Wang, H., He, C., Ding, K.: Quadtrees-based Image Authentication Technique," IEICE Transactions on Fundamentals. IEICE Transactions on Fundamentals E87-A(4), 946–948 (2004)
4. Gray, R.M.: Vector Quantization. IEEE Transactions on Acoustics, Speech, and Signal Processing 1, 4–29 (1984)
5. Linde, Y., Buzo, A., Gray, B.M.: An Algorithm for Vector Quantizer Design. IEEE Transactions on Communications 28(1), 84–95 (1980)

Segmentation of Human Body Parts in Video Frames Based on Intrinsic Distance

Yu-Chun Lai[1], Hong-Yuan Mark Liao[1,2], and Cheng-Chung Lin[1]

[1] Department of Computer Science, National Chiao-Tung University, Taiwan
[2] Institute of Information Science, Academia Sinica, Taiwan
{uglai,liao}@iis.sinica.edu.tw, cclin@cs.nctu.edu.tw

Abstract. We propose an intrinsic-distance based segmentation approach for segmenting human body parts in video frames. First, since the human body can be seen as a set of articulated parts, we utilize the moving articulated attributes to identify body part candidate regions automatically. The candidate regions and the background candidate regions are generated by voting and assigned to the spatiotemporal volume, which is comprised of frames of the video. Then, the intrinsic distance is used to estimate the boundaries of each body part. Our intrinsic distance-based segmentation technique is applied in the spatiotemporal volume to extract the optimal boundaries of the intrinsic distance in a video and obtain segmented frames from the segmented volume. The segmented results show that the proposed approach can tolerate incomplete and imprecise candidate regions because it provides temporal continuity. Furthermore, it can reduce over growing in the original intrinsic distance-based algorithm, since it can handle ambiguous pixels. We expect that this research can provide an alternative to segmenting a sequence of body parts in a video.

Keywords: Segmentation, Human body part, Intrinsic distance.

1 Introduction

In recent years, the field of computer vision has attracted a great deal of attention due to the advances of digital cameras and the new technologies developed in the field of multimedia. It can be used in several applications; for example, human motion recognition is a practical application. In this particular area, the proposed methods can be classified into two categories: 1) methods that recognize human movements based on information about the whole body; and 2) methods that separate information about the whole body into several body parts to identify and label them. Although many good solutions based on the first approach have been proposed, the second category remains challenging because of the difficulty of segmenting body parts. Thus, we focus on the second category in this paper. In [1], the authors introduced a silhouette-based approach to label and segment body parts, while a skeleton-based segmentation approach was proposed in [2]. In the latter method, the human shape is cut into several triangles, the centers of which are linked to the skeleton to segment the body parts. Some authors have tried to apply segmentation methods to videos to obtain temporal information. For example, in [3], the authors initially use edge templates to

H.H.S. Ip et al. (Eds.): PCM 2007, LNCS 4810, pp. 450–453, 2007.

detect torsos in video frames. Then, the relations between the torso and the body parts are used to search the body parts. However, exact body parts segmentation is very difficult using those methods, because of insufficient information of single image. Moreover, the appearance of the torso may vary from case to case. In this paper, we propose a spatiotemporal framework that yields reasonably good segmentation results since it considers both spatial and temporal continuity. We believe this approach provides a good alternative to segmenting body parts in a video. In the following sections, we describe candidate region location and intrinsic distance-based segmentation. We then present some concluding remarks.

2 Candidate Region Location

To segment body parts, we locate the candidate region of an articulated part. The method used to locate candidate regions is similar to the trajectory extraction method we proposed in [4]. The basic concept is that we identify articulated moving objects as foreground candidate regions by clustering sampling points with similar motions. We also extend our previous approach [4] by adding another voter to provide information about the background surrounding the articulated part. The voter is fan-shaped, but it does not include the center region because that is the object region. Moreover, the voting direction is indicated by the gradient direction.

3 Intrinsic Distance-Based Segmentation

In [5], Yatziv and Sapiro propose an intrinsic-based colorization method for coloring a grayscale image using scribble drawn by a user. The concept is that regions with similar luminance and a short intrinsic distance might imply similar chrominance. We adopt the concept of the intrinsic distance in our segmentation method. The intrinsic distance is defined as follows:

$$d(s,t) = \min_{C_{s,t}} \int_0^1 \left|\nabla Y \cdot \dot{C}(p)\right| dp \text{ ,} \tag{1}$$

where $C_{s,t}$ is a curve from point $s = C(0)$ to point $t = C(1)$, p is a point along the curve, and ∇Y is the gradient of the luminance. To assign the scribble automatically, we use the previously extracted candidate regions to provide foreground and background scribble. In the original algorithm, the scribble must be chosen carefully to ensure that the scribble do not extend beyond the object's boundaries; however, it is difficult to achieve this in an automatic assignment method. Thus, we modify the algorithm to compensate for this characteristic. The basic concept is that we delay the growing order of the ambiguous pixels which appears in both the foreground and the background candidate regions. We think that the delay should depend on the probability of the color in the opposite class as shown in Equation (2).

$$dist(p,q) = \begin{cases} p \in foreground & |L(p) - L(q)| + w_d * H_{background}(C(q)) \\ p \in background & |L(p) - L(q)| + w_d * H_{foreground}(C(q)) \end{cases} \text{,} \tag{2}$$

where p is one of the selected pixels in the priority queue; q is a neighboring pixel of p ; L is the grayscale intensity of a pixel; w_d is a weight of the delay range; $H_{background}$ and $H_{foreground}$ are the quantized histograms of the background and foreground respectively; and C is the color of the pixel. In our segmentation approach, we first align video frames with a 3D spatiotemporal volume. The volume provides temporal continuity that can be used if the scribble is incomplete. First, the candidate regions are assigned to this volume by frames. Then, the modified intrinsic distance-based algorithm is applied to grow the candidate regions in both the spatial and the temporal dimension. After all pixels have been designated to the appropriate classes, the grown volume can be seen as a sequence of separated frames that display the grown results.

4 Experiment Results

In the experiments, we used two video sequences to test the approach. The lengths of sequences were 44 and 35 frames respectively. Fig. 1 shows the frames of the testing video and the segmentation results. As the figures shown, our approach provided reasonably good segmentation results since we considered about both spatial and temporal continuity. However, the approach does have some limitations. First, it needs sufficient motion to support candidate region identification. Therefore, body parts with little motion may be incomplete. To resolve this problem, we may accumulate motions until we have sufficient and use a variable-sized volume. The second limitation is that trajectory clustering thresholds and the radius of the voting region still need to be assigned. However, since the thresholds have some relation to the size of the body part, the image difference between frames may provide some information about selecting the thresholds.

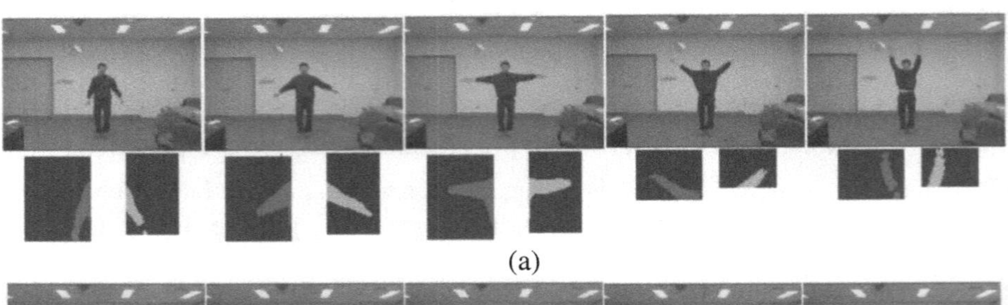

(a)

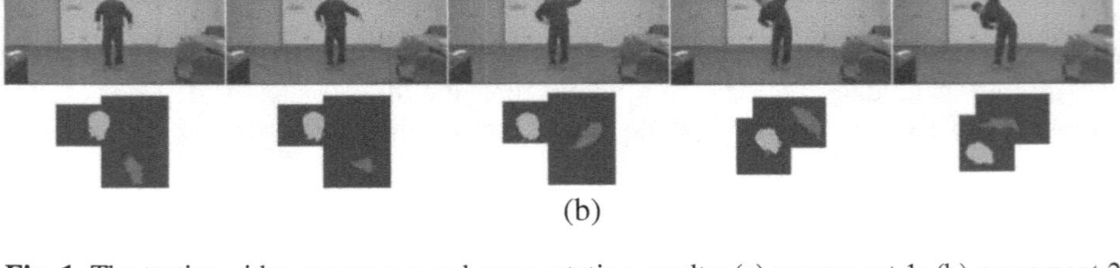

(b)

Fig. 1. The testing video sequences and segmentation results; (a) movement 1; (b) movement 2

5 Conclusion

We have proposed a human body part segmentation framework that automatically segments human body parts in videos. First, we cluster sampling points according to the moving parts' articulated attributes. Next, the clustered sampling points locate the approximate foreground and background region. The latter can be seen as candidate regions and assigned to a spatiotemporal volume. Then, we apply a modified intrinsic distance-based segmentation approach to a 3D spatiotemporal volume for determining the optimal boundaries of body parts in terms of the intrinsic distance. Although the automatically assigned candidate regions might be imprecise and incomplete, our modified segmentation approach can tolerate such conditions and still yield good segmentation results. In the future, we will conduct further experiments on using segmented body parts to recognize human motion.

Acknowledgments. The authors would like to thank the Department of Industrial Technology, Ministry of Economic Affairs, Taiwan for supporting this research under Contract No. 96-EC-17-A-02-S1-032.

References

1. Haritaoglu, I., Harwood, D., Davis, L.: Ghost: A Human Body Part Labeling System Using Silhouettes. In: Proc. International Conference of Pattern Recognition, pp. 77–82 (1998)
2. Hsieh, J.-W., Chen, C.-C., Hsu, Y.-T.: Segmentation of Human Body Parts Using Deformable Triangulation. In: IEEE International Conference on Pattern Recognition, vol. 1, pp. 355–358 (2006)
3. Ramanan, D., Forsyth, D.A., Zisserman, A.: Tracking People by Learning Their Appearance. IEEE Transactions on Pattern Analysis and Machine Intelligence 29(1), 65–81 (2007)
4. Lai, Y.-C., Liao, H.Y.M.: Human Motion Recognition Using Clay Representation of Trajectories. In: Proc. IEEE International Conference on Intelligent Information Hiding and Multimedia Signal Processing, USA (December 2006)
5. Yatziv, L., Sapiro, G.: Fast image and video colorization using chrominance blending. IEEE Transactions on Image Processing 15(5), 1120–1129 (2006)

A Distributed Remote Rendering Method Based on Awareness Model

Xiang-bin Shi[1,2], Jian-feng Su[2], Xian-min Chen[2], Ling Du[1], and Fang Liu[1]

[1] Department of Computer Science and Engineering,
Shenyang Institute of Aeronautical Engineering, Shenyang 110034, China
{sxb@syiae.edu.cn, lingdang820313@163, weilan2328@163.com}
[2] School of Information Science and Technology,
Liaoning University, Shenyang ,110036, China
{sjf800510@126.com, benjamin1983617@163.com}

Abstract. This paper proposes a kind of remote rendering method based on awareness model. This method takes the additional cost caused by the movement of the viewpoint into cost calculation and designs a cost prediction algorithm based on the vision field divided by awareness model. The simulation results show that the improved method can not only improve the quality of the remote rendering, but also make full use of the bandwidth of the network, as well as make the remote rendering more fluent when the viewpoint moves fast.

Keywords: Remote Rendering, Awareness Model, Cost Calculation, Cost Prediction.

1 Introduction

With the rapid development of network graphics technology and the enlarging of the application domain of virtual reality, the remote rendering [1] today has gradually become one of the research hotspot in the domain of virtual reality. Remote rendering means that remote user renders the virtual scene which stores in the server, and the effect is the same as the local rendering. That is, if a client doesn't have the rendering resources, it can download the rendering resources, and then walk through the virtual scene stored in the server. The self-adaptability of the remote rendering means that the sever optimizes and selectively transmits the resources which the rendering needs according to the following factors, including the characteristic of transmitting data, network latency, and the rendering characteristic of the client and so on.

During the remote rendering, the server looks the virtual scene as a set of 3D objects. Each of the objects has one or more model representations. The aim of the server is to gather the model representation sequence which provides the highest quality rendering. The model representation sequence is determined by the cost calculation and the cost prediction of the rendering. The existing cost calculation and the cost prediction algorithms ignore the added transmitting cost that is caused by movement of the viewpoint. Because the algorithm proposed in this paper analyzes the added transmitting cost caused by the movement of the viewpoint, the cost calculation is more reasonable and the cost prediction is more effective.

H.H.S. Ip et al. (Eds.): PCM 2007, LNCS 4810, pp. 454–457, 2007.

2 Cost Calculation and Cost Prediction

2.1 AM-MMOG Awareness Model

AM-MMOG[2] awareness model is an awareness model based on the behavior characteristics of vision. In AM-MMOG, the vision field is divided into comprehension area, identification area and detection area. This paper introduces the AM-MMOG awareness model into the remote rendering and uses its method for dividing the vision field area to divide the vision field area of remote user. In this paper n_{full} is the number of the full models in the comprehension area, n_{LOD} is the number of LOD models in the identification area, and n_{image} is the number of image models in the detection area.

2.2 Cost Calculation and Cost Prediction

In this paper, each object has three kinds of model representations which are full 3D models, a set of LOD models and image models [3, 4, 5, 6].

A large number of objects may be welling up when the viewpoint moves fast. This paper put the additional transmission cost caused by the movement of viewpoint into the cost calculation. FullModelSet is the set of full models, LODSet is the set of LOD models and ImageSet is the set of image models. Suppose that there are n objects, and C_{addi} is the additional cost of object i. The formula of additional cost is as formal (1).

$$C_{addi} = \begin{cases} FullCost_i * f(v_{viewport}), i \in FullModelSet \\ \left(LOD_{fulli} * \left(\max\left(\frac{a_i}{F_i}, 1\right) / \max\left(\frac{a_i}{f_i}, 1\right) \right) \right) * f(v_{viewport}), i \in LODSet \\ \left(Image_{fulli} * \left((h_{0i}/h_i) * (\min(\sin \alpha_i, \sin 60^{h}) / \sin 60^{h}) \right) \right) * f(v_{viewport}), i \in IamgeSet \end{cases} \quad (1)$$

LOD_{full} is the document size of LOD model. a is the area of the bounding box of the object on the screen, f is the number of faces in the LOD, and F is the number of faces in the full model of the objects. $Image_{full}$ is the document size of image model. h_0 is the height of the lower accuracy image model. h is the height of the object's image from the current viewpoint .α is the angle between the base line of image model. $FullCost_i$ is the size of full model. $f(v_{viewport})$ is a function that depends on the speed of viewpoint.

The overall additional cost can be calculated by the formula as follows:

$$C_{add_{total}} = \begin{cases} 0, V_{viewport} \leq V_{threshold} \\ \sum_{i=0}^{n} C_{addi}, V_{viewport} > V_{threshold} \end{cases} \quad (2)$$

Here, $C_{add_{total}}$ is the overall additional cost caused by the movement of viewpoint during walkthrough. $V_{viewport}$ is the instant speed of the viewpoint. $V_{threshold}$ is the threshold speed of the viewpoint.

When users walk through in the virtual scene remotely, the overall transmission cost of the remote walkthrough changes continuously. Therefore, the trend of the overall transmission cost at next moment can be predicted. This paper divides the vision field of remote rendering user based on the AM-MMOG. And the overall transmission cost is as follows:

$$C_{total}=\sum_{i=0}^{n_{full}} FullCost_i+\sum_{j=0}^{n_{LOD}}\left(LOD_{fullj}*\left(\max\left(\frac{a_j}{F_j},1\right)/\max\left(\frac{a_j}{f_j},1\right)\right)\right)+\sum_{k=0}^{n_{image}}\left(Image_{fullk}*\left(\frac{h_{0k}}{h_k}*\frac{\min\left(\sin\alpha_k,\sin 60^{h}\right)}{\sin 60^{h}}\right)\right)+C_{add_{total}} \quad (3)$$

Here, $FullCost_i$ is the transmission cost of the full model i in n_{full} full models. LOD_{fullj} is the transmission cost of the full accuracy LOD model j in n_{LOD} LOD models. $Image_{fullk}$ is the transmission cost of the full accuracy image model k in n_{image} image models. The algorithm of remote rendering cost prediction based on AM-MMOG awareness model is as follows:

Step1: After the viewpoint information of peer which sends the requirement of remote rendering is received, the view frustum is calculated, as well as the maximum transmission cost C_{max}, turn to Step2, or the remote rendering stops.

Step2: Calculating the overall transmission cost C_{total} according to formula (3). If $C_{total} \leq C_{max}$, turn to Step3. If $C_{total} > C_{max}$, turn to Step4.

Step3: If $C_{max} - C_{total}$ is less than the threshold value (decided according to current system), turn to Step6. If $C_{max} - C_{total}$ is more than the threshold value, turn to Step5.

Step4: Adjusting the partition of the visual field. R_{LOD} is reduced firstly. If still $C_{total} > C_{max}$, the range of comprehension area should be minished. If still $C_{total} > C_{max}$, the identification area will be adjusted again, turn to Step4. If $C_{total} \leq C_{max}$, turn to Step3.

Step5: Adjusting the partition of visual field. The range of comprehension area is enlarged firstly. If $C_{max} - C_{total}$ is still more than threshold value, the range of identity area should be enlarged. If $C_{max} - C_{total}$ is still more than threshold value, turn to Step5. If $C_{max} - C_{total}$ is less than threshold, turn to Step6.

Step6: Transmit the 3D model representation sequence. Turn to Step7 to predict the overall transmission cost at the next moment.

Step7: Record the overall transmission cost $C_{total_{t1}}$ and $C_{total_{t2}}$ at the moment t_1 and t_2. If $\Delta C > 0$, the area of LOD model should be minished preferentially. If $\Delta C < 0$, the area of full model should be increased preferentially. If $\Delta C = 0$, it's unnecessary to adjust the rendering area. Turn to Step1.

3 Experiments

This paper builds the P2P network structure with JXTA, and uses OpenGL graphic library to construct the 3D virtual world. In this paper, the model representations haven't been compressed when be transmitted. This paper tests a set of scenes. The data amount in the scene could be 120MB approximately.

In order to test the capability of the distributed remote rendering system, under three kinds of typical bandwidth user walks through the scene 240 seconds in the same way. The result is given as the Fig.1 and Fig.2. This paper defines the walkthrough quality at the moment t as the ratio between the sum of rendering cost of all model representations at the moment t and the sum of rendering cost of all full model representation. From these figures, it can be found out that the traditional cost

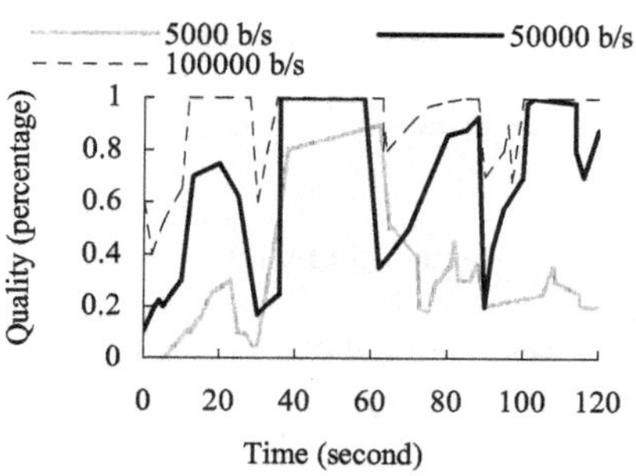

Fig. 1. Quality of our system of different b/s

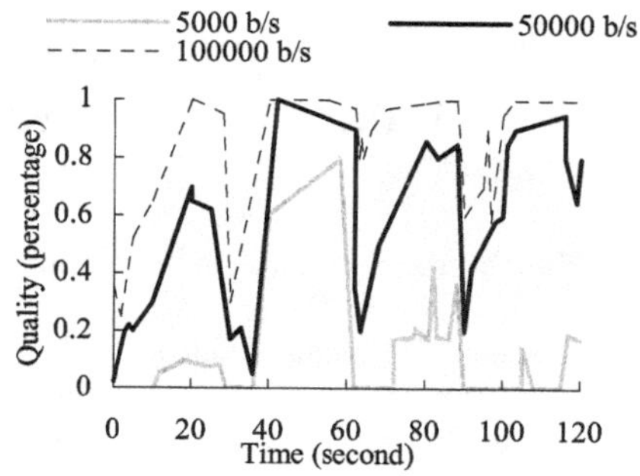

Fig. 2. Quality of traditional system of different b/s

calculation and cost prediction is restricted greatly by bandwidth to render remotely, and the improved cost calculation and cost prediction can take full advantage of bandwidth.

4 Conclusions

This paper analyses the additional cost caused by the movement of viewpoint, and introduces it into the cost calculation, as well as proposes the cost prediction algorithm based on the vision field divided by awareness model. The simulation results show that this system not only performs well under various bandwidths, but also improves the fluency of remote rendering during the fast movement of viewpoint.

References

1. Cheng, Z.Q., Dang, G., Jin, S.Y.: The Survey of Adaptive Real-time Remote Rendering on Geometric Model. In: The virtual reality conference of China (2005)
2. Shi, X.B., Li, Q., Wang, Y., Liu, F.: An Awareness Model for Interest Management in MMOG. MINI-MICRO SYSTEMS (2007) (Accepted and will be published in 2007)
3. Cui, L., Bei, J., Cui, Y.Y., Chen, L.J., Pan, J.G.: Research on Scalable Architecture of Remote Rendering. Journal of System Simulation 18(4), 1081–1083 (2006)
4. Yoon, I., Neumann, U.: Web-based remote rendering with ibrac (image-based rendering acceleration and 100 compression). Computer Graphics Forum 19(3), 321–330 (2000)
5. Tang, X.A., Cai, X.P., Sun, M.Y.: Study on hybrid render arithmetic based 3D-Warp. Journal of Image and Graphics 6(7), 710–714 (2001)
6. Eyal, T., Dani, L.: Streaming of complex 3d scenes for remote walkthroughs. In: EUROGRAPHICS 2001 Annual Conference (2001)

Signer Adaptation Based on Etyma for Large Vocabulary Chinese Sign Language Recognition

Yu Zhou[1], Wen Gao[1], Xilin Chen[2], Liang-Guo Zhang[2], and Chunli Wang[3]

[1] School of Computer Science and Technology, Harbin Institute of Technology, Harbin, 150001, China
[2] Institute of Computing Technology, Chinese Academy of Sciences, Beijing, 100080, China
[3] School of Computer Science and Technology, Dalian Maritime University, Dalian, 116026, China
{yzhou, wgao, xlchen, lgzhang, clwang}@jdl.ac.cn

Abstract. Sign language recognition (SLR) with large vocabulary and signer independency is valuable and is still a big challenge. Signer adaptation is an important solution to signer independent SLR. In this paper, we present a method of etyma-based signer adaptation for large vocabulary Chinese SLR. Popular adaptation techniques including Maximum Likelihood Linear Regression (MLLR) and Maximum A Posteriori (MAP) algorithms are used. Our approach can gain comparative results with that of using words, but we only require less than half data.

Keywords: SLR, signer adaptation, signer independency, MLLR, MAP.

1 Introduction

SLR aims to transcribe sign language to text so that the communication between deaf and hearing society can be convenient. SLR also helps to make the human computer interface more naturally.

By far the signer-dependent SLR has achieved remarkable results. T.Starner [1] achieved a correct rate of 91.3% for 40 signs based on the image. C.Vogler and D.Metaxas [2] described an approach to continuous, whole-sentence American SLR. C. Wang and W. Gao [3] realized a Chinese SLR system with a vocabulary of 5100 signs. But the signer-independent SLR is still a big challenge, especially in the large vocabulary SLR. The main obstacles in large vocabulary signer-independent SLR are the difficulty of availability to multi-signers' data and the vast variation of different signers' regions, habits, moods, etc. There are more than 5,000 words in Chinese sign language. It is impossible to constitute a database including all kinds of signers. Therefore, modeling one signer's sign language by sparse data becomes an urgent problem. We try to give an answer to this problem by signer adaptation based on etyma in this paper.

The rest of this paper is organized as follows. In Sect. 2, the signer adaptation method based on etyma is proposed. In Sect. 3, the experimental results are reported. Finally in Sect. 4, we give the conclusions and some possible future work.

H.H.S. Ip et al. (Eds.): PCM 2007, LNCS 4810, pp. 458–461, 2007.

2 Etyma-Based Signer Adaptation

We select etyma as the basic recognition units so as to decrease the adaptation data required, and etyma are modeled by HMMs. MLLR and MAP are used for adaptation. Now we briefly introduce MLLR and MAP, they are detailedly described in [4][5][6].

MLLR and MAP. MLLR supposes that model adaptation can be achieved by applying some affine transformations to the original model parameters. There is a regression class set in MLLR, and in each regression class the parameters share the same transformation. MLLR transforms HMMs' means by equation (1).

The conventional Maximum Likelihood (ML) estimation supposes the parameter that we want to estimate is fixed though it is not known. MAP estimation supposes that the parameter we want to estimate is under some probability distribution function, If conjugate priors are used, the MAP result of single Gaussian mixture's mean is as equation (2).

$$\hat{\mu} = A\mu + b = W\xi \tag{1}$$

$$\hat{\mu} = (N\overline{\mu} + \tau\mu)/(N + \tau) \tag{2}$$

where $\hat{\mu}$ is the adapted mean, μ is the original mean, A is the transformation matrix, b is the bias vector; $W = [A^T, b^T]^T$ is the extended transformation matrix, and $\xi = [\mu^T, 1]^T$ is the extended mean vector; τ is a weighting of the priori knowledge to the adaptation data, N is the occupation likelihood of the adaptation data, and $\overline{\mu}$ is the mean of the observed adaptation data.

Previous work. We have presented a method in which Chinese Sign Language can be recognized from models of etyma in [7]. In Chinese sign language, there are more than 5000 words in total. We break them down to about 2400 etyma. Each word is composed of 1 or more etyma in sequence. [7] has proven that the recognition accuracy of the approach based on etyma is comparable to that of the approach based on words.

Signer adaptation based on etyma. Since the approach based on etyma is comparable to that of the approach based on words, we can adapt the signer-independent system using the etyma data, whose vocabulary number is about half of the words data's vocabulary number. Our process is as below:

1) Train HMMs based on etyma;
2) Adapt HMMs using etyma data of the new speaker;
3) Generate HMM-Nets according to the word-etymon map list;
4) Recognize the test word data using HMM-Nets generated above.

Our experiments are executed with HTK [8]. Because we want to compare our method to conventional method on the level of word accuracy, we generate

HMM-Nets when we do experiments based on etyma. For more details about HMM-Nets, please read [8].

3 Experimental Results Comparison

We use etyma and words as basic units. Each etymon and word is performed four times by six signers. Four times data of all the other five signers except the test signer are used for training. The test signer's fourth time data is used for test, and the other times data are used for adaptation. We use cross validation and leave one out. The results of six signers are listed in Table 1. When we use MLLR, 1 time of adaptation data is used, and 3 times is used when we use MAP.

Table 1. The recognition accuracy comparison

Signer for test	Etyma based method			Words based method		
	SI%	MLLR%	MAP%	SI%	MLLR%	MAP%
S1	59.93	72.67	88.79	62.82	76.15	94.78
S2	56.28	68.74	90.35	60.03	73.59	95.43
S3	62.55	72.90	91.11	65.68	76.73	96.09
S4	62.55	72.87	90.99	65.36	76.46	95.80
S5	65.48	75.00	91.01	69.94	79.78	96.31
S6	59.13	71.79	88.75	62.67	74.84	94.10
Average	60.99	72.33	90.17	64.42	76.26	95.42

We only execute the global transformation adaptation during MLLR. We can find that all of the two methods improve the average recognition accuracy of words by about 12%, but the method of adaptation based on etyma only needs about half of the data compared to that of adaptation based on words.

MAP can gain better results when the adaptation data become rich, so we use 3 times data to execute MAP adaptation. Experiment results show that MAP can improve the average recognition accuracy by about 30%. Still the method we presented can save about half data.

We also experiment with different times of adaptation data and compare the accuracy improved by MLLR and MAP. Fig.1 shows the results. The improvements by MAP are much better than that of MLLR, because the adaptation data we used (even 1 time data) are plenty enough for MLLR global transformation but not for MAP.

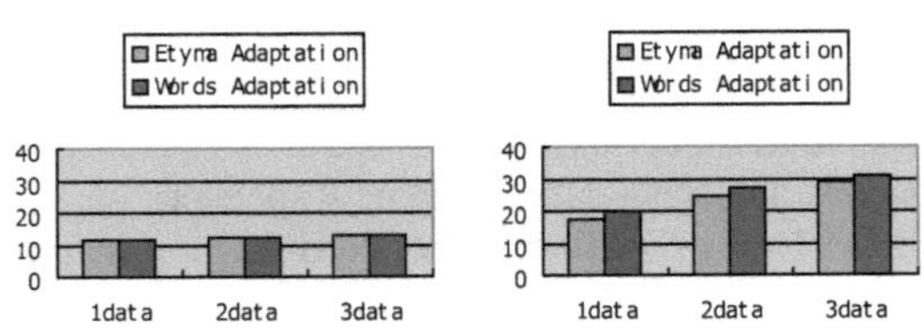

a) MLLR b) MAP

Fig. 1. The comparison between MLLR and MAP

4 Conclusions and Future Work

Adapting large vocabulary Chinese sign language based on etyma can save more than half data compared to adaptation based on whole words with both MLLR and MAP algorithms. MLLR should be adopted when adaptation data is not enough(for example only one time data or less), and MAP should be adopted after more adaptation data was collected. Breaking words to etyma is a proper way to solve signer-independent Chinese SLR.

In the future, we will break the etyma to phonemes to reduce the adaptation data required further; we will apply the adaptation to continuous Chinese SLR; we will also do some work on unsupervised adaptation.

Acknowledgment

This research is partially sponsored by Natural Science Foundation of China under contract No.60303018 and No.60603023, and Natural Science Foundation of Beijing Municipal under contract No.4061001.

References

1. Starner, T., Weaver, J., Pentland, A.: Real-Time American Sign Language Recognition Using Desk and Wearable Computer Based Video. IEEE PAMI 20(12), 1371–1375 (1998)
2. Vogler, C., Metaxas, D.: Toward scalability in ASL Recognition: Breaking Down Signs into Phonemes. In: Proceedings of Gesture Workshop, Gif-sur-Yvette, France, pp. 400–404 (1999)
3. Wang, C., Gao, W., Ma, J.: A Real-time Large Vocabulary Recognition System for Chinese Sign Language. Gesture and Sign Language in Human-Computer Interaction, 86–95 (April 2001)
4. Leggetter, C.J., Woodland, P.C.: Maximum likelihood linear regression for speaker adaptation of continuous density hidden Markov models. Computer Speech and Language, 171–185 (September 1995)
5. Gales, M.J.F.: Maximum Likelihood Linear Transformations for HMM-Based Speech Recognition. Computer Speech and Language, 75–98 (December 1998)
6. Gauvain, J.L., Lee, C.H.: Maximum a Posteriori Estimation for Multivariate Gaussian Mixture Observations of Markov Chains. IEEE Transactions on Speech and Audio Processing 2(2), 291–298 (1994)
7. Wang, C., Chen, X., Gao, W.: A Comparison Between Etymon- and Word-Based Chinese Sign Language Recognition Systems. In: Gibet, S., Courty, N., Kamp, J.-F. (eds.) GW 2005. LNCS (LNAI), vol. 3881, pp. 84–87. Springer, Heidelberg (2006)
8. Young, S., Evermann, G., Kershaw, D., Moore, G., Odell, J., Ollason, D., Povey, D., Valtchev, V., Woodland, P.: The HTK Book (for HTK Version 3.2), pp. 161–177. Cambridge University (December 2002)

The Photo News Flusher: A Photo-News Clustering Browser

Tatsuya Iyota and Keiji Yanai

Department of Computer Science,
The University of Electro-Communications
1–5–1 Chofugaoka, Chofu-shi, Tokyo, 182–8585 Japan
{iyota-t,yanai}@mm.cs.uec.ac.jp

Abstract. We propose a novel news browsing system that can cluster photo news articles based on both textual features of articles and image features of news photos for a personal news database which is built by accumulating Web photo news articles. The system provides two types of clustering methods: normal clustering and thread-style clustering. It enables us to browse news articles over several weeks or months visually and find out useful news easily. In this paper, we describe an overview of our system, some examples of uses and user studies.

1 Introduction

Many commercial news sites exist on the Web, and they deliver a lot of new articles to us every day. Since data on the Web can be collected automatically by crawler programs, we can accumulate news articles on the Web automatically and build a personal news database with almost no cost. We can gather more than one thousand articles a month, so that it is very difficult to watch all of them and find out interesting articles out of such huge news database.

In this paper, we propose a novel news browsing system which can cluster photo news articles based on both textual features of articles and image features of news photos for a personal news database on PC. The system provides two types of clustering methods: normal clustering and thread-style clustering. For the normal clustering, we can adjust weights of textual features and image features, and for the thread-style clustering, we can control width of thread branches with a novel method. Ide et al. [1] extracted topic threads from a large-scale TV news video corpus and created a thread-based interface which enables users to browse news articles related to the same topic along time series. This topic threading is helpful to browse a large amount of news articles, so that we import and modify it for our system as one of the clustering methods. By these functions, the proposed system enables us to browse news articles over several weeks or months visually and find out useful news easily. In this paper, we describe an overview of our system, examples of uses, and user studies.

2 Proposed System

Regarding Web news search, it is general to search for news articles without photos using only textual information. On the other hand, our targets are news

H.H.S. Ip et al. (Eds.): PCM 2007, LNCS 4810, pp. 462–466, 2007.

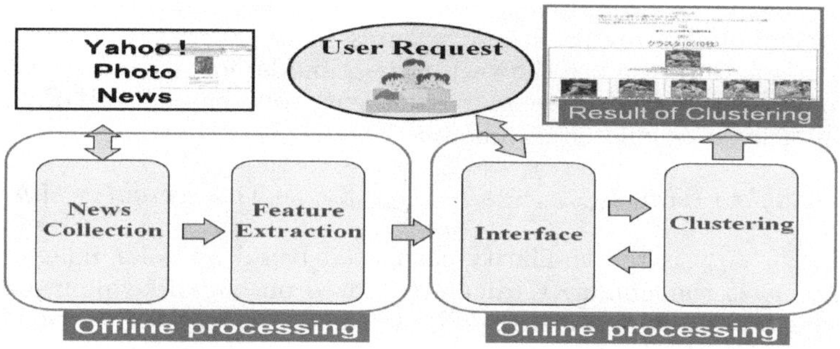

Fig. 1. Structure of the proposed system which consists of the four parts

articles with photos, which have a special characteristic that it can be understood intuitively with just a look without reading. Our purposed system cluster news articles using both textual information from text news articles and visual information from photo articles. Since photos have the advantage of being visually recognizable, results of clustering are also easy to understand visually with just a look. We aim to achieve a system which enables us to find interesting news articles easily taking advantage of photos as visual clues.

We collect news articles with photos from the Yahoo Photo News Japan. Being different from usual news articles, the main contents of articles of the Yahoo Photo News are photos. In addition to a photo, each article has a title and a short main text which explain the contents of the photo. Note that all articles are written in Japanese, since the Photo News site we use in our work is the Yahoo Photo News Japan. But our method did not rely on a specific language, so we can adjust our system for the other languages easily.

Our system consists of four parts: **News Collection Part**, **Feature Extraction Part**, **User Interface Part**, and **Clustering Part** (Fig.1). The News Collection Part and the Feature Extraction Part are carried out once a day as off-line preprocessing. The User Interface Part and the Clustering Part are carried out on-line.

News Collection. In the News Collection Part, we gather titles, main texts, and photos of news articles by following the links from the top page of Yahoo Photo News. If the Web page of the photo news includes a link to a usual news article which has no photos, we collect the main text of the normal news article as a "linked text" of the photo news article.

Next, we classify news articles collected into seven categories (domestic, international, business, entertainment, sports, computer, and local). The seven categories are already classified by the Yahoo Photo News and can be distinguished from the URL of news articles. In addition, we prepare "all" to which all articles belongs.

Feature Extraction. In the Extraction Part, we extract image features from the gathered photos and textual features from the titles, the main texts and the linked texts gathered in the Collection Part.

As image feature, we use color histograms computed in the Lu^*v^* color space as color image features. Each histogram quantizes the color space into 64 (4 for each axis) bins. In addition, we also use the bag-of-keypoints histogram [2] which consists of 300 bins as texture image features.

As textual feature, we use the vector space model for textual features. Each element of keyword vectors is weighted by the entropy-based TF-IDF. Similarity between articles is calculated as follows:

$$sim = weight * (sim_{img\_color} + sim_{img\_texture}) + (1 - weight) * sim_{text} \quad (1)$$

where sim_{img_color} is the similarity calculated based on color image features, $sim_{img\_texture}$ is the similarity calculated based on bag-of-keypoint-based texture image features, sim_{text} is the similarity calculated based on textual features, and $weight$ $(0 \leq weight \leq 1)$ is a weight of image features. $Weight$ is adjusted by a slider on the User Interface. Similarities based on both color and texture image features are calculated by the histogram intersection. Before calculating similarities, each feature vector is normalized so that the sum of its elements is 1. Similarity based on textual features is calculated by the cosine similarity.

User Interface (UI). A user selects a term and a category of news articles and set *weight* based on his/her preference on the Web-based UI. *Weight* is the ratio of the textual feature and the image feature used in similarity calculation for clustering. The Web-based user interface provides us with a slider to set a weight of textual features and image features.

Clustering. In the Clustering Part, the system clusters news articles according to similarity of feature vectors extracted in the Feature Extraction Part, and shows the article which is closest to the mean of the cluster as the representative article of each cluster. We can see all the images of the cluster by selecting "display all images" on the UI.

The proposed system provides two kinds of clustering: k-means-based normal clustering and time-series-based thread clustering.

Thread clustering groups articles related to the same topic and show them in the time order. Here, "thread" means series of articles which are related to the same one topic in the time order. If several articles are not similar each other but all of them are similar to a certain article, "branching" will be made. "Thread" can includes branches, and is composed as tree-structure in general.

By thread-clustering, we extract a thread which starts from a certain topic a user selects from the result of normal k-means clustering, and show several articles arranged as a short comic strip. They enable us to find out the flow or relation of affairs or events more easily. In the UI, a user also select a constant α which decides what extent of topic drift in a thread is allowed. "Topic drift" means that the main topic of a thread is changing gradually along time progress. This "topic drift" control by a constant is one of novelties of our system, compared to Ide et al. [1].

To find child articles which are highly related to the parent and their time stamps are always newer than the parent's. "Highly related" is defined by the following condition:

$$sim(v_n, V_{n-1}) \leq T \quad (2)$$

, where

$$V_n = \begin{cases} v_n & (n = 0) \\ v_n + \alpha V_{n-1} & (n \geq 1) \end{cases} \quad (3)$$

$$\left(\begin{array}{rl} \alpha & : \text{a constant which controls “topic drift”} \quad (0 \leq \alpha \leq 1) \\ T & : \text{a threshold} \\ v_n & : \text{a feature vector of } n\text{-th article} \\ V_n & : \text{an } n\text{-th accumulative mean vector} \end{array}\right)$$

3 Example Uses and a User Study

Use of Normal Clustering. We assume a user have an interest on the Japan national team of World Cup of soccer. At first, the user selects “two months” as the term of news articles and “sports” as the category. Next, the user selects “text 100%” as the weight of textual and image features so that the clusters are associated with a sub-category of sports such as soccer and golf (Fig.2). The representative image in the third cluster is soccer, so we can estimate the third cluster contains many soccer articles.

In the next step, the user carries out re-clustering for the third cluster with text 50% and image 50% in order to divide soccer articles into some clusters. As a result, the user find out a "Japan Soccer W-cup" cluster which includes a lot of articles related to the Japan National Soccer Team (Fig.3).

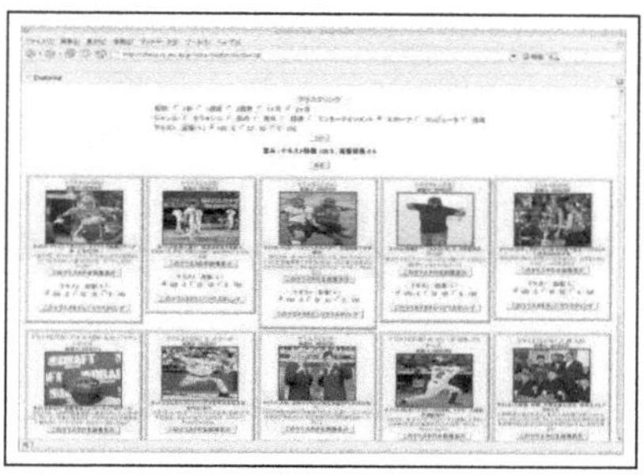

Fig. 2. Clustering result of sport news articles

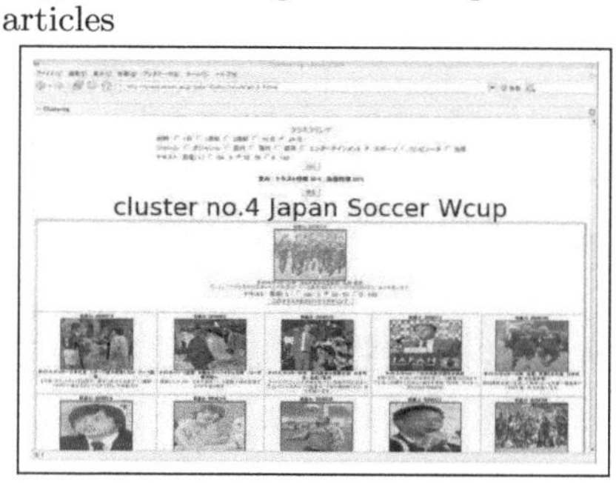

Fig. 3. "Japan Soccer W-cup" cluster

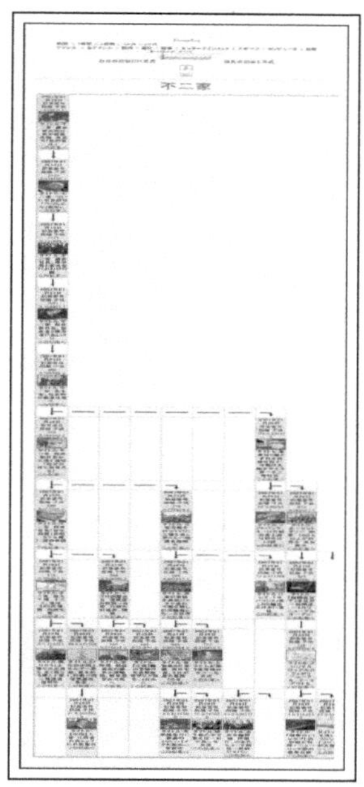

Fig. 4. Thread ($\alpha = 0$)

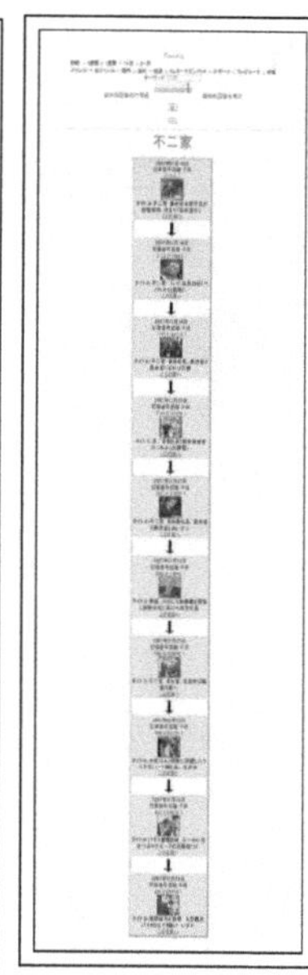

Fig. 5. Thread ($\alpha = 0.9$)

Use of Thread Clustering. We assume that the thread clustering is used for searching for related articles along time series after a user find out an interesting article by the normal clustering.

Fig.4 shows the thread on the food poisoning affair in the Japanese Domestic news which was one of biggest news in early 2007 in case that α is 0, while Fig.5 shows the thread on the same topic in case that α is 0.9. These results indicates the extent of branching is adjusted by varying the value of α.

User Study. We made the brief user study on the proposed system. We asked seven subjectives to compare the proposed system with a baseline system regarding how easily to search for interesting articles based on their own preferences. The interface of the baseline system is similar to the Yahoo Photo News site. The subjectives evaluated both the baseline and the proposed system with a score from 1 to 5. As a result, the proposed system and the baseline system obtained 3.86 and 2.43 on average, respectively. By applying Student's T-test, the difference on the average scores was proved to be significant.

4 Conclusions

We proposed a new photo news clustering browser which provided normal and thread clustering. Its effectiveness was proved by the user study.

References

1. Ide, I., Mo, H., Katayama, N.: Threading news video topics. In: Proc. of ACM SIGMM MIR, pp. 239–246 (2003)
2. Csurka, G., Bray, C., Dance, C.R., Fan, L.: Visual Categorization with Bags of Keypoints. In: Proc. of ECCV WS on Stat. Learn. in CV, pp. 1–22 (2004)

Multimedia-Learning in a Life Science Workflow Environment

Carsten Ullrich[1], Ruimin Shen[1], and Su-Shing Chen[2]

[1] Shanghai Jiaotong University
[2] PICB, Shanghai
ullrich_c@sjtu.edu.cn, rmshen@sjtu.edu.cn,
suchen@cise.ufl.edu

The Taverna workbench allows constructing highly complex analyses over life sciences data and computational resources. It provides access over 1000 of bioinformatic services, e.g., analysis algorithms for comparing genome sequences, and facilitates the construction of bioinformatic workflows. These workflows make tacit procedural bioinformatics explicit and as such lend themselves for being used in bioinformatics education. However, until now, no Taverna e-learning service exists. In this paper, we describe how Taverna can be used for learning and the services that need to be integrated in Taverna for that purpose. This includes a digital library of multimedia resources since multimedia, especially visualization, plays an important role in bioinformatics. Equally important is an intelligent educational service that automatically assembles learning activities and resources into a pedagogically coherent whole.

1 Introduction

The Taverna workbench [7] facilitates the composition and execution of workflows for the life sciences community and allows a biologist or bioinformatician with limited computing background to construct highly complex analyses over public and private data and computational resources. Currently, Taverna provides access over 1000 of bioinformatic services, e.g., analysis algorithms for comparing genome sequences.

Bioinformatics or, more general, biomedicine is a very rich field of multimedia information. Resources include texts, images and videos obtained by a variety of methods such as X-Ray, ultrasound and magnetic resonance devices. However, despite the fact that bioinformatics is highly multi-medial in nature, Taverna has no explicit support for multi-media resources and services.

Additionally, the workflow-based approach realized in Taverna lends itself for being used for learning. Workflows make tacit, i.e., implicit, knowledge explicit and represent skills and activities that students in bioinformatics need to learn. But again, there is no Taverna service that realizes learning support.

In this paper, we will describe what it takes to use Taverna for multimedia learning. We start with a general overview on the Taverna workbench (Section 2),

H.H.S. Ip et al. (Eds.): PCM 2007, LNCS 4810, pp. 467–474, 2007.

followed by a brief introduction on state-of-the-art adaptive learning technologies (Section 3), namely course generation. Section 4 then sketches Taverna multimedia services that we are currently developing: VIACIPA, a digital library service of multimedia objects, and a course generator learning service based on VIACIPA.

2 A Workflow Environment in Life Sciences

The Taverna workflow workbench environment [7] allows a user (typically a biologist or bioinformatician) to specify and execute scientific workflows. The workflows model "in silicio" experiments: they involve the combination of data and analyses made available by the research teams. In bioinformatics, this type of experiments complements lab-based experiments and allows to generate new information from the publicly available data and to form hypothesis which can be assessed in lab studies.

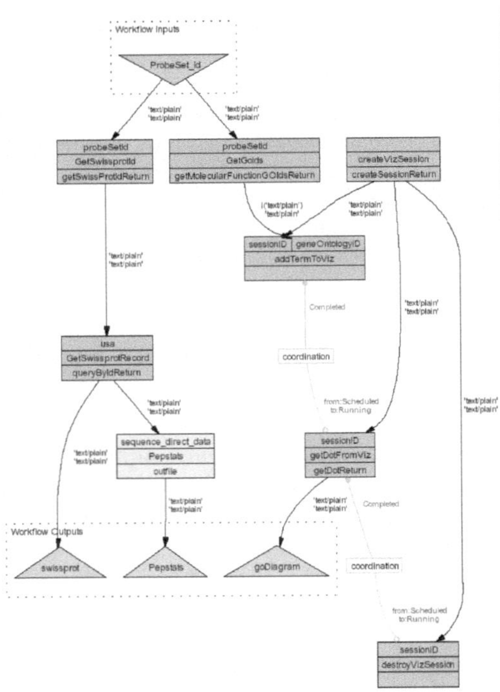

Fig. 1. An example of a Taverna workflow

Taverna integrates more than 1000 bioinformatical services, ranging from applications such as analysis algorithms for comparing sequences, over databases arising from species-specific genome projects or holding cross species data sets for proteins or nucleotides, to visualization tools for protein structures, simulations of heart excitation models. Extensibility was one major design goal in Taverna. New services (called processors) can be easily plugged-in based on Web-service interfaces and similar means.

Workflows as realized in Taverna enable a scientist to model and execute their experiments in a repeatable and verifiable way (see Fig. 1 for an example of a workflow). Just like experiments can be repeated by other research groups, Taverna workflows can be exchanged and are resources in their own right. Thus, workflows capture the essential aspects of "in silicio" experiments and, what makes them so valuable for learning, they make tacit procedural knowledge explicit.

The components of a Taverna workflow consists of the following: a set of data inputs; a set of outputs (the exit points); a set of processors each of which represents an individual step within a workflow: a processor receives data on its input ports, processes the data internally and produces data on its output ports. The final components of a workflow are links between the data sources and/or the processors, which, for instance, specify that the output of one data source serves as the input of another one.

3 Technology-Supported Learning

Technology-enhanced learning uses computers to support the learning process. Examples range from very basic Learning Management Systems that primarily administer learning to Intelligent Learning Environments (ILE). An ILE helps the learner during the complete learning process, by selecting and annotating learning content (resources), by suggesting what resources to read etc. The ActiveMath system is an example of a state-of-the-art ILE.[1] It is a Web-based, multi-lingual, user-adaptive learning system for mathematics that operates on semantically encoded learning objects annotated with metadata for providing advanced adaptive features. One of its main components is a course generator that automatically assembles individual courses according to a learner's learning goal, learning scenario, competencies, learning context and preferences. The following section takes a closer look at the course generator.

3.1 Assembling Sequences of Learning Activities

Course generation uses pedagogical knowledge to generate structured sequences of educational activities that are adapted to the learners' competencies, individual variables, and learning goals [1]. The educational activities include viewing of learning objects but also using tools and services that support learning or that the student needs to master (e.g., computer algebra systems and function plotters for mathematic students, and bioinformatic services as available in Taverna for students of biomedicine). The generation process uses pedagogical knowledge, information about the resources and tools and, if available, information about the learner to select and sequence the resources that are to be studied and the tools to be used, and their order.

Paigos [10] is a course generator that was developed for ActiveMath. Its distinguishing features are a complex model of pedagogical knowledge and a

[1] www.activemath.org

service-oriented architecture. Its pedagogical knowledge allows *Paigos* to generate courses that support a learner in achieving a number of learning goals, such as discovering new content ("discover" in short), rehearsing, and training specific competencies. For these learning goals, *Paigos* generates complete courses which contain all the learning material required by a learner to achieve the goals. *Paigos* is also used to retrieve single elements that specifically fulfill a given purpose, such as presenting an example or exercise adequate for the current the learner. This functionality is important for remedial, e.g., if a learner fails to solve a task, then the presentation of an example might help the learner to overcome that difficulty.

Paigos contains about 300 rules that determine the selection, ordering and structuring of resources. This "expensive" functionality lends itself to being "outsourced": if the course generator is available as a service then other learning environments can access the functionality without having to re-implement it. Thus, *Paigos* makes its functionality available as a Web-Service (CGWS). Clients send a learning goal to the CGWS and receive a structured sequence of resource identifiers (URI) as a result. The sequence is represented using a standard representation called IMS Manifest. The CGWS implements a mediator architecture that enables a client to easily register its own repository and thus make it available to *Paigos*. At registration time, a client has to provide the name and the location of its repository, together with an ontology that describes the metadata structure used in the repository and a mapping of the metadata used in the CG onto the repository ontology. The metadata in *Paigos* consists of an ontology of instructional objects that describes LO from a pedagogical point of view sufficiently precise in order to allow for intelligent automatic pedagogical services.

After receiving a learning goal, *Paigos* automatically assembles the sequences of resources, without any human intervention. However, this requires that the resources are annotated in a way that allows for pedagogical reasoning. This means that the resource repository needs to able to answer questions about the existence of resources, e.g., whether there exists an example of a domain concept. The following section will further elaborate on the required metadata.

3.2 Requirements on Metadata

Educational services need to have access to information about the resources that are to be included in the learning process. This information is called metadata. Metadata describes characteristics of resources relevant to the application domain the resources are used in.

The most basic and most relevant aspect of a resource is the domain concept it describes (or explains, exercises, defines). This information can be given as simple keywords or as pointer to concept defined in a separate concept space, which contains the domain concepts additionally annotated with relationships among them, such as "prerequisite-of", "part-of", etc.

In the case of educational services, a widely employed standard is LOM [2], which includes metadata such as difficulty, typical learning time, etc. However, LOM was primarily designed for human actors, e.g., authors and teachers. It does not describe resources precise enough for pure software services, i.e., services that automatically perform operations on it, such as course generation. For instance, in LOM it is not possible to express that a resource is of the type “example”. An alternative metadata vocabulary is defined by the OIO (Ontology of Instructional Objects [9][10]. The OIO defines a set of about 20 classes and several relationships that allow representing the “instructional semantics” of resources. The classes include “definition”, “law”, “process”, “interactivity”, “exercise”, “evidence”, “example”, etc.

Ideally, resources are described using the OIO and LOM. The more precise the metadata, the higher the quality of service that tools like a course generator can offer.

Despite the fact that *Paigos* was developed for the ActiveMath system, which is primarily used for mathematics, the pedagogical knowledge formalized within *Paigos* is independent of the mathematical domain but can be applied to other domains as well. Previous work investigated the usage of *Paigos* within a workflow-oriented proactive delivery of educational resources in order to support learning at an office workplace [8]. In the following, we will explore what it takes to use *Paigos* within a truly multimedia environment for bioinformatics.

4 Multimedia Services in Taverna

The current version of Taverna is focused on bioinformatical services. Bioinformatics or, more general, biomedicine is a very rich field of multimedia information (see Figure 2 for examples). Resources include texts, images and videos obtained by a variety of methods such as X-Ray, ultrasound and magnetic resonance devices. However, despite the fact that bioinformatics is highly multi-medial in nature, Taverna has no explicit support for multi-media resources and services.

In the following, we will first describe a digital library for fusion of multimedia information resources that can be used as an important service for mediating multimedia information in Taverna. We then describe how the resources can be used for learning purposes.

4.1 Digital Library Server for Fusion of Multimedia Information

In [2,3], a digital library server for fusion of multimedia information has been developed that addresses the problem that biomedical information has disparate information sources. In [2], Chen used an ontology-based approach for fusion of different multimedia sources, such as the Gene Ontology (GO), Clinical Bioinformatics Ontology (CBO) and the Foundational Model of Anatomy (FMA). An even higher level integration was developed in [3] which handled various system level issues. Ontology deals with concept level issues of the information content. For examples, anatomy deals with the human body, while cells are substructures within the organ structures of the human body. Ontology relates these concepts in a tree like structures. However multimedia information are different representations of possibly the same concept. For examples, a single organ can be imaged by both ultrasound and X-ray media. Thus we need to address the integration issue of these two kinds of information. In [2], Chen has addressed this issue, which has been a key topic of the multimedia research community.

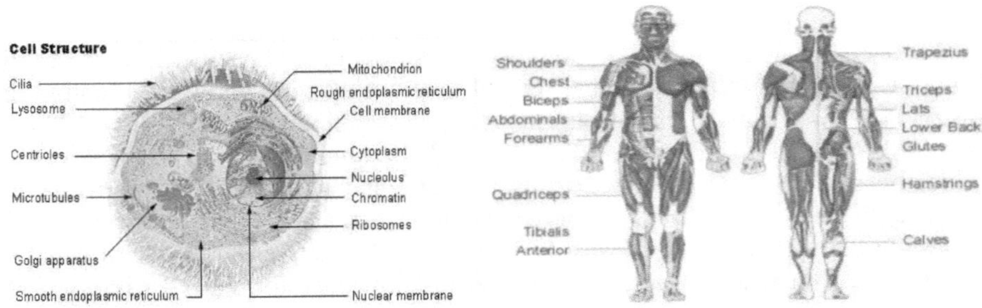

Fig. 2. Example of multimedia information for bioinformatics

4.2 Learning in a Workflow Environment

In this section, we make two suggestions of how these multimedia resources can be used for learning within a workflow environment as exemplified by Taverna. The first approach corresponds to the "traditional" usage of course generation, while the latter is an innovative approach directly based on workflows and the embedded services.

4.2.1 Traditional Course Generation

In this approach, the course generator takes a learning goal (given by the learner or set by a teacher) and assembles a sequence of resources and tool usages that supports the learner in achieving the goal.

In an open environment as Taverna, which is not specifically geared towards learning, the quality of the educational resource metadata will differ significantly. This reflects on the educational services: they have to be able to cope with such limited metadata, but at the same time use good metadata, if available. We developed a specific type of course for these situations, called "guided tour". The guided tour is based on guidelines from instructional design [6] and multimedia learning [5] and is structured as follows. For each concept given in the goal task, and for each unknown prerequisite concept, the following sections are created:

- **Introduction.** This section arises a learner's interest by presenting educational resources of the type introduction.
- **Problem.** This section inserts a real world problem for the concept.
- **Concept.** This section presents the concept.
- **Explanation.** This section contains educational resources that provide explaining and deepening information about the concept.
- **Illustration.** This section provides opportunities for the learner to examine demonstrations of applications of the concepts.
- **Practice.** This section enables a student to actively apply what he has learned about the concept.
- **Conclusion.** This section presents educational resources that contain concluding information about the concept.
- **Reflection.** This section provides the learner with an opportunity to reflect and discuss his new knowledge.

If no resource was found for a specific section, then the section is skipped. As an example, we will assume *A*, *B* and *C* are concepts and that concept *A* is a prerequisite of concept *B*. If the learning goal is *(guidedTour (B,C))*, then the resulting course will consists of three sections, one for each concept *A*, *B*, and *C*, and each of these sections will consist of up to 8 subsections corresponding to the list above. The course generator will automatically retrieve the prerequisites, the concept *A* in the above example.

From the viewpoint of the course generator, the services that are integrated in Taverna are modeled using resources stored in the library. The specific type of such a service resource depends on how they are used. If they are used for illustrative purposes, e.g., showing how to access a service and what results to expect, then they would be of type example. If the user should use them interactively to come up with a specific result, then they would be classified as exploration. For each of these service usages, a resource needs to be created.

The result of the course generation is a structured sequence of links to resources. They can be presented in Taverna's enactor invocation window.

4.2.2 Workflow Instantiation

As elaborated in Section 2, workflows form an integral part of the knowledge of an experienced biologist and bioinformatician. Workflows make tacit procedural knowledge about experiments and data analyses explicit and thus offer a way of communicating this knowledge to students. Taverna treats workflows as resources in their own rights and as such they can serve to guide learning processes. Recall that a workflow essentially consists of input and output nodes and of processor nodes that perform operations on data, such as multiple sequence alignment. For learning, a processor node can be seen as an example of the application of the service it represents. Thus, when studying a workflow, a learner should be able to select a processor node and request educational resources that elaborate on this service and its specific operation. This requires a corresponding set of resources that are annotated with the service they illustrate. Resources can thus play a double role. They describe a specific phenomenon and at the same time they are examples of the usage of the service they were created with.

Since the resources are annotated with the service name, each usage of this specific service can be linked to the corresponding resource, regardless of the workflow. Take as an example a workflow that takes in a protein sequence and then runs the InterProScan service to find family domians.[2] If the resources are annotated with the service name (*InterProScan_proteinraw*), then the learner can request information about this service in each workflow that uses it. In this way, a workflow is annotated with additional information that may help to understand it, and in addition, a workflow is an example of how to use services.

This type of learning support will benefit significantly from multimedia resources: since here the goal is to give examples of tool usage, presenting video sequences allows illustrating the complete process of the usage, including the results.

[2] Workflow example by Paul Fisher (http://www.cs.man.ac.uk/~fisherp/).

5 Conclusion

In this paper, we described how to employ multimedia services to a workflow environment used in bioinformatics. We sketched two services that add a new layer of functionality to the Taverna workflow workbench: VIACIPA, a web-based digital library service of multimedia objects, and *Paigos*, a course generator that assembles sequences of resource with the goal of supporting the learning process. *Paigos* can be used in Taverna in two ways: in the traditional, course-based way, but also within a workflow to illustrate the different processes employed in the workflow.

References

[1] Brusilovsky, P., Vassileva, J.: Course sequencing techniques for large-scale webbased education. International Journal of Continuing Engineering Education and Lifelong Learning 13(1/2), 75–94 (2003)
[2] Chen, S.: Fusion of Multimedia Information in Biomedicine, this Conference
[3] Kim, H., Choo, C., Chen, S.: Generating a Meta-DL by Federating Search on OAI and Non-OAI Servers. Journal of Intelligent Systems
[4] IEEE Learning Technology Standards Committee. 1484.12.1-2002 IEEE standard for Learning Object Metadata (2002)
[5] Mayer, R.: Multimedia Learning. Cambridge University Press, New York (2001)
[6] Merrill, M.D.: First principles of instruction. Educational Technology Research & Development 50(3), 43–59 (2002)
[7] Oinn, T., Greenwood, M., Addis, M., Alpdemir, M.N., Ferris, J., Glover, K., Goble, C., Goderis, A., Hull, D., Marvin, D., Li, P., Lord, P., Pocock, M.R., Senger, M., Stevens, R., Wipat, A., Wroe, C.: Taverna: Lessons in creating a workflow environment for the life sciences in Concurrency and Computation: Practice and Experience. Grid Workflow Special Issue 18(10), 1067–1100 (2005)
[8] Rostanin, O., Ullrich, C., Holz, H., Song, S.: Project TEAL: Add adaptive e-learning to your workflows. In: Tochtermann, K., Maurer, H. (eds.) Proceedings: I-KNOW 2006. 6th International Conference on Knowledge Management, Graz, Austria, pp. 395–402 (September 2006)
[9] Ullrich, C.: The learning-resource-type is dead, long live the learning- resource-type! Learning Objects and Learning Designs 1(1), 7–15 (2005)
[10] Ullrich, C.: Course Generation as a Hierarchical Task Network Planning Problem. Unpublished Doctoral Thesis, Department of Computer Science, Saarland University (2007)

Visualization of High-Dimensional Biomedical Image Data

Peter Serocka

CAS-MPG Partner Institute of Computational Biology, Shanghai Institutes of Biological Sciences, Chinese Academy of Sciences, Shanghai 200031, China
Max-Planck-Institute for Mathematics in the Sciences, Inselstraße 22, 04103 Leipzig, Germany
pserocka@picb.ac.cn

Abstract. A new challenge to data visualization has arisen from a new laboratory technique that is capable of imaging a large number of biomedical relevant molecule types in a single tissue probe, termed the Toponome. While aiming at deciphering the biochemical interactions of the molecules, and thus their biological functions as well their roles in diseases, no current methods of image analysis are fully suited for this new quality of high-dimensional image data. To overcome this problem we demonstrate a novel framework for interactive real-time visualization, making use of standard graphics acceleration hardware. We show a sample implementation of a threshold-based visualization technique that is connected to the original work of the Toponome authors, improving it by means of fast user interaction.

Keywords: Protein interaction networks, Toponome, multi-variate image data, hardware-accelerated computer graphics.

1 Introduction

Visualization has driven medical research since the inventions of microscope and X-ray imaging. While the microscope as an optical instrument gives a merely enlarged view of the reality, it provides a real and live sight, and thus insight to the object under examination. X-ray images give far less real pictures, however it is still intuitively clear how the three-dimensional reality is mapped to a two-dimensional image space through, mathematically speaking, a projection.

Today, Ultrasonic Imaging can display moving living three-dimensional subjects in real-time, allowing for studying processes in time as well as for changing the perspective, or navigating, to get a clearer view of spatial shapes and structures. In addition, Computer Tomography lets you first record data from a space volume and later generate the optimal view in the computer. Augmented Reality techniques combining real and computer generated images help in carrying out more accurate and less invasive surgery techniques.

Thus, biomedical imaging has always been challenging our visual perception: By re-scaling reality, projecting shapes to flat canvases, by capturing and re-presenting

H.H.S. Ip et al. (Eds.): PCM 2007, LNCS 4810, pp. 475–482, 2007.

sequences in time as well as in space. Over the time, the need for intermediating stages (ergo: media) has increased from simple lenses over X-ray film and video towards mathematical algorithms in form of computer software. The resulting challenges have been mastered, mostly because the resulting images still have an understandable link to reality and because adopting to different scales, mapping the three-dimensional world to our two-dimensional retina and acting within the flow of time still appear natural to us.

In this paper we try to continue and extent this long, successful path of emerging visualization techniques that challenge our perception. The paper is organized as follows: First we will motivate the underlying biological and medical questions. Then we describe a new laboratory technique addressing these questions und discuss the data structures involved, as well as difficulties arising from analyzing such data. We motivate the need of new, intuitive visualization methods and sketch the outline of a suitable programming framework. Its usefulness is demonstrated by implementing an example algorithm, which is then applied to actual data from a laboratory experiment.

2 Fundamental Questions in Biomedicine

To understand the new challenge we deal with in this paper we draw our attention to the fundamental questions that are asked today in biology and medicine. These questions appear on the level of molecules.

While we are not reviewing the principles of molecular genetics, that deal with the function of the famous double-helix DNA molecule, we should be aware of the DNA acting as a master plan for 30.000 or more (in human) different types of molecules, called the proteins. The ways proteins are build from the DNA and how they interact with each other and with other molecules widely determine the ways of growth and development of organisms, how organisms multiply, age and die. In particular, many diseases can be understood as malfunctioning of these fundamental interactions, in addition to attacks of microbes.

Because for proteins to interact they must come close to each other in an organism's body, a key approach to understanding the complex chains and networks of their interactions lies in detecting which groups of proteins appear together in each part of living organisms and which do not.

3 Imaging the "Toponome" of an Organism

Ideally one would like to know the positions of all molecules within an organism in one point of time. While this is technically infeasible, recently a new imaging technique has been described [1] that performs this detection task for a least 100 protein types at a time. It utilizes standard fluorescent microscopy on prepared tissue samples, where individual types of proteins are biochemically dye-marked and imaged through a microscope and a CCD camera.

The novelty lies in applying this process to 100 different protein types in a single tissue specimen one after the other, bleaching away the fluorescent dye of each previous imaging cycle. Thus, the output is a set of 100 aligned microscope images of the same tissue location, one image for each protein. Such an image set is referred to as a record of the *Toponome* of the organism under investigation.

Seen as a data structure, these sets of images resemble multi-spectral or multi-modal image data from space or land exploration much more than data representing time series or three-dimensional volumes. With the Toponome, each pixel is given by a 100-dimensional vector of protein abundances measured by the CCD camera at that pixel's location.

4 Analysis of High-Dimensional Image Data

To analyze Toponome data sets many methods of visualization, image processing, statistics and machine-based learning can be in principle applied to reduce the high-dimensionality of the data to low-dimensional, comprehensive structures. We briefly review the problems we have found when applying these methods to Toponome data.

A standard procedure of visualizing high-dimensional images data is through false-color composition where each image channel is assigned a distinct color and all images are finally superimposed. As this is helpful for less then 10 image channels one looses in general too much information when mapping 100-dimensional image sets into the three-dimensional Red-Green-Blue space as done in Fig. 2.

Classical image processing is based on applying filters in the spatial domain, and features such are edges or textures can be detected or images are segmented into possibly relevant sub-regions. Typically, these methods operate on single-valued or gray-scale images with extensions to technical and natural color spaces such as RGB and CIE. However to our knowledge no practical framework has been developed that covers image data of arbitrary dimensions.

While principal component analysis (PCA) can be applied to Toponome data in a canonical way, it regards the image data merely as an unordered set of pixels, not taking into account their actual positions in the image domain and so an important information, all spatial relations, never contribute to the analysis.

The same is true for general machine-based learning methods (when used without spatial filtering), either unsupervised clustering or supervised classification techniques. In addition the vast number of algorithms and their parameters make their choice and the interpretation of the results somewhat incomprehensible if not arbitrary.

Though all these methods may reduce the high number of dimensions inherent in Toponome data sets, the difficulty seems to be in controlling which part of the original information will be lost.

5 A Framework for Interactive Visualization

As a practical approach, and while keeping in mind the great success of visualization outlined in the first section, we demand for visual methods that result in descriptive images being generated and controlled in a natural and intuitive way. We regard interactive control in real-time is necessary to allow for quick data visualization, in-depth feature extraction, as well as for concisely comparing multiple data sets. An excellent review and discussion of related ideas is given by [4].

In the following we first derive the cornerstones for possible implementations from the proposed real-time constraint, then we give an overview of our framework design and in the next section we show an example of an implemented technique.

As a typical Toponome data set has 100 images of 1000x1000 pixels each, its total size is about 100 Megapixels. Processing these at 10 frames per second or faster gives a pixel-rate of at least 1 Gigapixel per second. Today, such and higher rates can be achieved by off-the-shelf hardware when utilizing strong graphics cards as produced for the gaming and the multi-media markets, typically based on chip technologies by ATI and Nvidia. When used for image processing at high pixel rates, the built-in processing parallelism must be fully exploited, so only a limited set of operations should be used:

- (A) mapping pixel values to new pixel values by applying look-up tables
- (B) adding, subtracting, multiplying or comparing pixel values
- (C) composing any fixed sequence of operation types (A) and (B)

It should be noted that applying image (convolution) filters does not appear in this list.

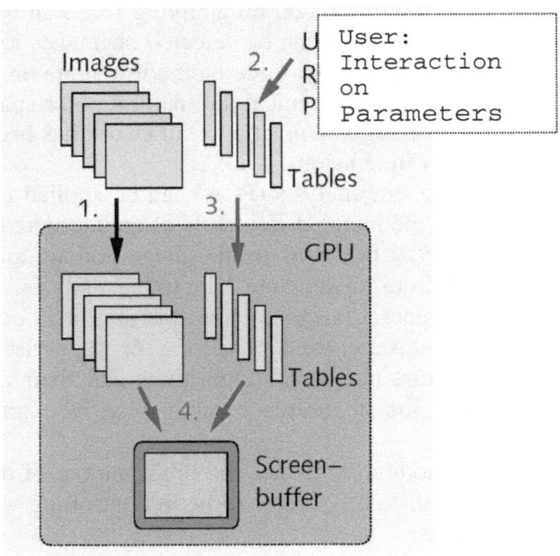

Fig. 1. Architecture of our visualization framework (GPU=Graphics Processing Unit). Phase 1: Initialization, transferring image data to GPU. Phase 2: Pre-processing user's interaction. Phase 3: Transferring interaction parameters to CPU. Phase 4: Generating the result image by the GPU.

Using the standardized and widely available *OpenGL* [2] programming interface for the C/C++ languages we have designed and implemented a framework that clearly distinguishes between the normal CPU with its main memory and the Graphics Processing Unit (GPU) with its own memory. The aim is to have as many operations from the list (A), (B) and (C) as possible being performed by the graphics unit for fastest execution while minimizing the programming efforts for users of the framework.

The architecture of the framework is outlined in Fig 1. It allows for loading an entire Toponome data set as 8-bit texture images into the graphics units memory at the initialization phase 1. In the interaction phase 2, any control parameters changed by the user can be pre-processed by the regular CPU and are then transferred as a set of one-dimensional tables into the graphics unit (phase 3). By keeping the amount of parameter data small compared to the Toponome data, the CPU can handle its part in real-time. In phase 4 the final image is generated from the Toponome data set and the parameter tables solely by the graphics unit under the control of an OpenGL *pixel shader*, which is coded in a standardized instruction format dedicated to performing operation of types (A)-(C) on the graphics unit. Only phases 2-4 are repeated over the interaction cycles and are therefore time-critical.

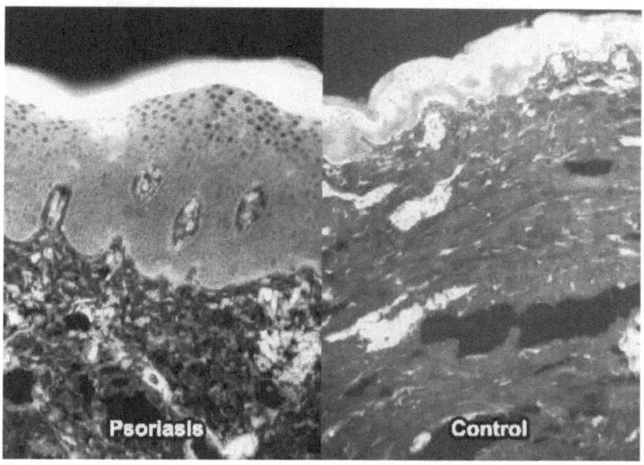

Fig. 2. False color images comparing two Toponome data sets. Left: human skin involved in Psoriasis, a widespread inflammatory skin disease, right: uninvolved skin from same individual. (Original image sets published as online supplementary data to [1] by Schubert et al.)

6 Example: A Threshold-Based Visualization Technique

Within this framework we have implemented a simple visualization technique that is closely related to the threshold-based method described in the original Toponome publication [1]. However we enhance the original power by adding full interactive control of the threshold parameters as opposed to determining them statically. In the original paper the data complexity is reduced by applying to each of the 100 images in the data set an individual threshold value, transforming the Toponome data set into binary or black/white images for further processing. In our framework, we achieve this step by building look-up tables of binary values according to the user-controlled

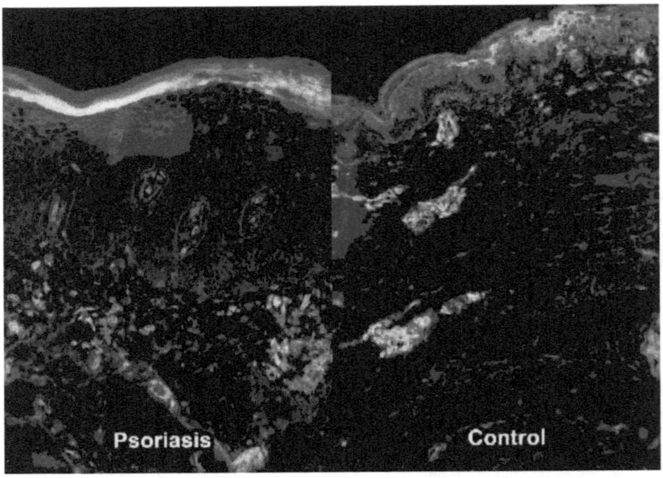

Fig. 3a. Data sets from Fig 2 visualized by our combined threshold/false-color method. Example threshold values and colors according to Fig 3b.

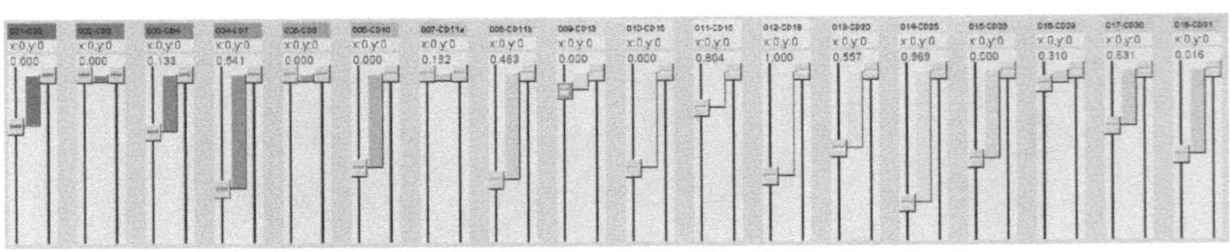

Fig. 3b. Threshold values (as set for Fig 3a.) in the graphical user interface. The colors of the threshold bars are used for the false-color representations in Fig 2 and Fig 3a. Only 18 out of 100 threshold values and colors are shown.

threshold values. The final image is composed at the user's choice either through AND logic, resulting in white pixels in regions where all thresholds are met by the image data, or through false-color superposition of the binarized images. By carefully choosing the threshold values the amount and the exact stage of information reduction can be controlled.

To follow the intended aim of finding groups of interacting proteins based on this interactive threshold-setting technique we suggest the following workflow, which clearly should be based on and guided by in-depth biological knowledge (that is beyond the scope of this paper):

1. From individual original, non-binarized images, choose regions of potential interest.
2. For each such region:
- 2a. Set thresholds for the proteins with highest abundance in that region such that it appears as separated from other images regions.

- 2b. Fine-tune the thresholds sets, while visually optimizing the overall shape of composed output image to either match expected substructures in the tissue, or to reveal the most unexpected, surprising spatial patterns.
- 2c. The set of the highest thresholds denote the proteins that are most likely to interact with each other in the region.

3. Compare the protein lists obtained for different regions as well the regions' shapes and their relative positions to draw conclusions on possible biochemical relations and biological functions.

Compared to a regular false-color image (Fig 2.) we believe much more insight is provided through the interactive process with the intermediate pictures giving clearer information (Fig 3a+b). When compared to the original authors' work we find that comparing and fine-tuning thresholds for several image data channels guided by composite visualization output may help in more precisely finding the relevant threshold values.

The great power of Toponome imaging and the need to overcome threshold-based analysis methods have already been pointed out by other authors [3]. While binarizing the images is only a first step towards comprehensive visualization of high-dimensional Toponome data it already shows the technical validity of our framework. One can also see how a concrete method can be conceptually linked with and compared to previously established ones, rising expectations to new promising principles of interaction.

With the design of novel techniques that will act on the full range of pixel values instead of binarizing the image data we expect to further boost the visual experience and understanding of high-dimensional Toponome data sets.

7 Conclusion

We have shown that a new laboratory technique for imaging biological samples lead to new challenges of data visualization and analysis, because image sets of 100 or more images representing different modes of the same subject come into play. The need for an intuitive visualization has been emphasized in contrast to abstract processing algorithms.

For mapping high-dimensional data to a two-dimensional display we have suggested the use of new interactive processes and we have derived a design of a suitable framework for real-time visualization. Modern standard graphics hardware and software interfaces have been used to implement such a framework. Its fitness has been demonstrated with an example of a threshold-based technique.

In the future we expect more sophisticated algorithms and visualization metaphors to be designed and implemented within this framework, allowing for new insights into high-dimensional image data sets and the biomedical phenomena they cover. Maintaining a good balance between challenging and utilizing the capabilities of our visual perception will effectively guide this development.

References

1. Schubert, W., et al.: Automated multidimensional fluorescence microscopy. Nature Biotechnol. 24(10), 1270–1278 (2006)
2. Shreiner, D., et al.: OpenGL Architecture Review Board, OpenGL Programming Guide: The Official Guide to Learning OpenGL, 5th edn. Addison-Wesley Professional, Reading (2005)
3. Murphy, R.F.: Putting proteins on the map. Nat. Biotechnol. 24(10), 1223–1224 (2006)
4. Nattkemper, T.W.: Multivariate image analysis in biomedicine: a methodological review. Journal of Biomedical Informatics 37(5), 380–391 (2004)

Moving Object Segmentation Using the Flux Tensor for Biological Video Microscopy

Kannappan Palaniappan, Ilker Ersoy, and Sumit K. Nath*

Department of Computer Science, University of Missouri-Columbia,
Columbia MO 65211, USA**

Abstract. Time lapse video microscopy routinely produces terabyte sized biological image sequence collections, especially in high throughput environments, for unraveling cellular mechanisms, screening biomarkers, drug discovery, image-based bioinformatics, etc. Quantitative movement analysis of tissues, cells, organelles or molecules is one of the fundamental signals of biological importance. The accurate detection and segmentation of moving biological objects that are similar but *non-homogeneous* is the focus of this paper. The problem domain shares similarities with multimedia video analytics. The grayscale structure tensor fails to disambiguate between stationary and moving features without computing dense velocity fields (i.e. optical flow). In this paper we propose a novel motion detection algorithm based on the *flux tensor* combined with multi-feature level set-based segmentation, using an efficient additive operator splitting (AOS) numerical implementation, that robustly handles deformable motion of non-homogeneous objects. The flux tensor level set framework effectively handles biological video segmentation in the presence of complex biological processes, background noise and clutter.

1 Introduction

High throughput screening environments using time lapse video microscopy combined with robotically assisted image sequence data collection systems, quickly generate large volumes of gigabyte- to terabyte-sized image sequence archives. Such imaging collections are being used to discover a wide range of mechanisms and pathways of cellular behavior, screening for biomarker molecules, drug discovery, cancer biomedicine, image-based bioinformatics, etc. [1, 2]. Precise reproducible motion analysis of tissues, cells, organelles, molecules or aggregate assemblies is one of the primary biologically significant signals especially for mechanical transduction signaling for which computational scientists can develop automatic algorithms in collaboration with wet-bench biologists; see [3] and the references therein. Live cell imaging in particular is undergoing a paradigm shift from the study of isolated, static, equilibrium macromolecular properties to disease contextual, dynamic, non-equilibrium cellular states and pathways [4, 1]. Algorithm development for the mining of video microscopy data shares many

* SKN currently at Rensselaer Polytechnic Institute, Troy, New York 12180 USA.

** Research partially supported by the U.S National Institute of Health NIBIB award R33-EB00573.

H.H.S. Ip et al. (Eds.): PCM 2007, LNCS 4810, pp. 483–493, 2007.

similarities and challenges with multimedia applications in video analytics including scalable techniques for image and video feature extraction, classification, clustering, and indexing. Large scale image and video analysis algorithms can take advantage of parallelization and web-based workflows like Taverna.

A wide range of techniques have been applied for detecting and segmenting biological objects of interest in video microscopy imagery including spatially adaptive thresholding, morphological watershed, mean shift, active contours, graph cuts, clustering, multidimensional classifiers like neural networks, genetic algorithms, etc. The classical spatiotemporal orientation or 3D grayscale structure tensor has been widely utilized for low-level motion detection, segmentation and estimation [5], since it does not involve explicit feature tracking or correlation-based matching. The structure tensor fails to disambiguate between stationary and moving features without an explicit (and expensive) eigen-decomposition step at every pixel to estimate a dense image velocity or optical flow field. In this paper we propose a new motion detection algorithm based on the novel *flux tensor* that successfully discriminates between stationary and moving image structures more efficiently than structure tensors using only the trace.

The basic Chan and Vese level set image segmentation method was extended by our group, in a series of papers, to combine both image intensity and edge information as well as incorporate spatial coupling constraints between objects using a graph theoretic approach for cell segmentation and tracking [6, 7, 8, 9, 3]. These algorithms established the feasibility of segmenting and tracking a large number of homogeneous objects. However, in biological video microscopy and multimedia video analysis applications the moving objects are seldom homogeneous in appearance. The motion energy then becomes an important feature for segmentation [10]. The novel idea for segmentation of moving non-homogeneous objects is to combine flux tensors for moving object detection, with a multi-feature level set-based active contour algorithm for refinement and object segmentation.

2 Detecting Moving Objects Using Flux Tensors

Grayscale structure tensor-based approaches have been used for segmenting root image sequences and estimating velocity profiles of growth at micron scale resolution [5, 11]. But neither the classical structure tensor or the proposed flux tensor, have been applied to the segmentation of other biological data such as cell migration [7,6], or bacterial pathogenesis studies [12] as shown in this paper.

Under the constant illumination model, the optic-flow (OF) equation of a spatiotemporal image volume $\mathrm{I}(\mathbf{x})$ centered at location $\mathbf{x} = (x, y, t)$ is given by,

$$\frac{d\mathrm{I}(\mathbf{x})}{dt} = \frac{\partial \mathrm{I}(\mathbf{x})}{\partial x} v_x + \frac{\partial \mathrm{I}(\mathbf{x})}{\partial y} v_y + \frac{\partial \mathrm{I}(\mathbf{x})}{\partial t} v_t = \nabla \mathrm{I}(\mathbf{x}) \cdot \mathbf{v}(\mathbf{x}) = 0 \tag{1}$$

where, the inner product operator between vectors is, $\cdot$, $\mathbf{v}(\mathbf{x}) = [v_x, v_y, v_t] = [\frac{\partial x}{\partial t}, \frac{\partial y}{\partial t}, v_t]$ is the optic-flow vector at $\mathbf{x}$. In order to estimate $\mathbf{v}(\mathbf{x})$, we minimize Eq. 1 over a local 3D image volume centered at $\mathbf{x}$, and filtered using the convolution kernel $W(\mathbf{x}, \mathbf{y}, \sigma_I)$, and subject to the condition that the orientation vector is of unit length $||\mathbf{v}(\mathbf{x})|| = 1$, leads to the standard minimum eigenvalue problem, $\mathbf{J}(\mathbf{x}, W)\ \hat{\mathbf{v}}(\mathbf{x}) = \lambda\ \hat{\mathbf{v}}(\mathbf{x})$, for the best estimate of $\mathbf{v}(\mathbf{x})$, denoted as $\hat{\mathbf{v}}(\mathbf{x})$, where, $\mathbf{J}(\mathbf{x}, W) = \int \left\{ \nabla \mathrm{I}(\mathbf{y}, \sigma_D)\, \nabla \mathrm{I}^T(\mathbf{y}, \sigma_D) \right\} W(\mathbf{x} - \mathbf{y}, \sigma_I)\, d\mathbf{y}$ is the integral of an outer product matrix, and the numerical dependence of the gradient computation on a scale parameter σ_D, using spatially invariant convolutions, is explicitly shown. This is the classical 3D grayscale structure tensor for the spatiotemporal volumetric window centered at $\mathbf{x}$. Fig. 1 shows a synthetic example of a moving disk and stationary rectangle with additive white Gaussian noise added. The circle experiences a constant translational motion of positive one pixel/frame in both horizontal and vertical directions over nine frames. The thresholded $\mathrm{Tr}(\mathbf{J})$ in Fig. 1b shows strong responses to both moving and stationary edges.

The shortcoming of the structure tensor is related to the fact that although the elements of $\mathbf{J}$ include information relating to gradient changes, the temporal variation of these gradients is not fully incorporated. Using temporal variations in terms of partial derivatives with respect to time, we develop a new approach to motion detection based on extending the grayscale structure tensor which we refer to as the flux tensor, that is fast and robust. We demonstrate that the flux tensor can be used to disambiguate between stationary and moving image features without expensive eigen-decomposition analysis and with more sensitivity to small slowly moving objects. Under the brightness constancy and locally constant velocity model, the partial derivative of Eq. 1 with respect to t,

$$\begin{aligned}\frac{\partial}{\partial t}\frac{d\mathrm{I}(\mathbf{x})}{dt} &= \frac{\partial^2 \mathrm{I}(\mathbf{x})}{\partial x \partial t} v_x + \frac{\partial^2 \mathrm{I}(\mathbf{x})}{\partial y \partial t} v_y + \frac{\partial^2 \mathrm{I}(\mathbf{x})}{\partial t^2} + \frac{\partial \mathrm{I}(\mathbf{x})}{\partial x} a_x + \frac{\partial \mathrm{I}(\mathbf{x})}{\partial y} a_y \\ &= \nabla_t \mathrm{I}(\mathbf{x}) \cdot \mathbf{v}(\mathbf{x}) + \nabla \mathrm{I}(\mathbf{x}) \cdot \mathbf{a}(\mathbf{x}) \end{aligned} \tag{2}$$

where the spatiotemporal derivative operator is defined as, $\nabla_t \equiv \frac{\partial}{\partial t}\nabla$, $\mathbf{v}(\mathbf{x})$ is the velocity field and $\mathbf{a}(\mathbf{x}) = [a_x, a_y, 0]$ the acceleration of the pixel at $\mathbf{x}$. We use a locally constant motion model for $\mathbf{v}(\mathbf{x})$, as in the traditional structure tensor, and the error functional simplifies to, $e_{ls}^{\mathrm{F}}(\mathbf{x}) = \int \left\{ \nabla_t \mathrm{I}(\mathbf{y}, \sigma_D) \cdot \mathbf{v}(\mathbf{x}) \right\}^2 W(\mathbf{x}, \mathbf{y}, \sigma_I)\, \mathbf{y} + \lambda \left\{ 1 - \mathbf{v}(\mathbf{x}) \cdot \mathbf{v}(\mathbf{x}) \right\}$. Similar to the 3D grayscale structure tensor, $\mathbf{J}$, we denote the tensor quantity, $\mathbf{J}_{\mathrm{F}}$, as the *flux tensor* which is the filtered temporal variation of the image gradient fields using (spatially invariant) convolution, $\mathbf{J}_{\mathrm{F}}(\mathbf{x}, W) = \int \left\{ \nabla_t \mathrm{I}(\mathbf{y}, \sigma_D)\, \nabla_t^T \mathrm{I}(\mathbf{y}, \sigma_D) \right\} W(\mathbf{x} - \mathbf{y}, \sigma_I)\, d\mathbf{y}$. The flux tensor, $\mathbf{J}_{\mathbf{F}}$, can be written in expanded matrix form, as shown below, with some convolution and integration parameters omitted for clarity,

$$\mathbf{J}_{\mathrm{F}} = \begin{bmatrix} \int \{\frac{\partial^2 \mathrm{I}}{\partial x \partial t}\}^2 W d\mathbf{y} & \int \frac{\partial^2 \mathrm{I}}{\partial x \partial t}\frac{\partial^2 \mathrm{I}}{\partial y \partial t} W d\mathbf{y} & \int \frac{\partial^2 \mathrm{I}}{\partial x \partial t}\frac{\partial^2 \mathrm{I}}{\partial t^2} W d\mathbf{y} \\ \int \frac{\partial^2 \mathrm{I}}{\partial y \partial t}\frac{\partial^2 \mathrm{I}}{\partial x \partial t} W d\mathbf{y} & \int \{\frac{\partial^2 \mathrm{I}}{\partial y \partial t}\}^2 W d\mathbf{y} & \int \frac{\partial^2 \mathrm{I}}{\partial y \partial t}\frac{\partial^2 \mathrm{I}}{\partial t^2} W d\mathbf{y} \\ \int \frac{\partial^2 \mathrm{I}}{\partial t^2}\frac{\partial^2 \mathrm{I}}{\partial x \partial t} W d\mathbf{y} & \int \frac{\partial^2 \mathrm{I}}{\partial t^2}\frac{\partial^2 \mathrm{I}}{\partial y \partial t} W d\mathbf{y} & \int \{\frac{\partial^2 \mathrm{I}}{\partial t^2}\}^2 W d\mathbf{y} \end{bmatrix} \tag{3}$$

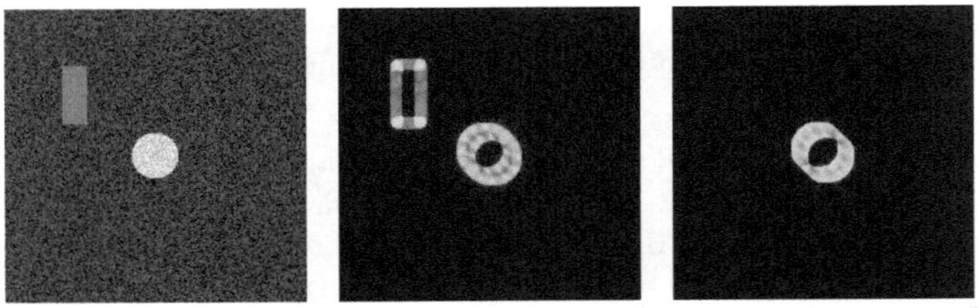

(a) Noisy Frame 5 of 9 (b) $\mathbf{J}, k_{trace} = 5 \times 10^{-2}$ (c) $\mathbf{J}_{\mathrm{F}}, k_{trce} = 5 \times 10^{-3}$

Fig. 1. Synthetic moving disk and stationary rectangle sequence with eigenvalue-based feature maps using structure and flux tensors. Frames corrupted by white Gaussian noise with statistics $\mathcal{N}(0, 1)$.

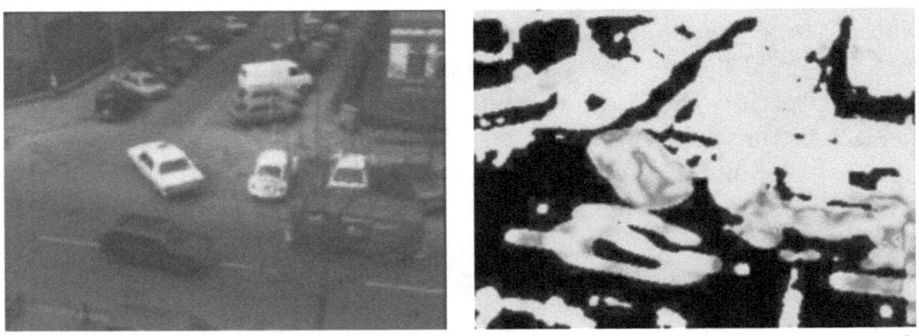

(a) Hamburg Taxi Frame 37 (b) Struc. Tensor $k_{trace} = 5 \times 10^{-3}$

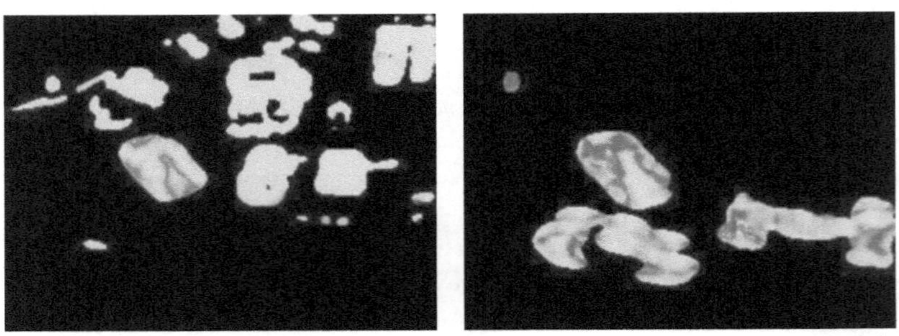

(c) Struc. Tensor $k_{trace} = 5 \times 10^{-2}$ (d) Flux Tensor $k_{trace} = 1 \times 10^{-4}$

Fig. 2. A frame from the "*Hamburg Taxi*" sequence. Scaled eigenvalue confidence measures are shown as RGB color; the color scheme will be described elsewhere. When the trace threshold of $\mathbf{J}$ is increased, useful features are not detected.

The 3D convolutions for both the derivative and averaging filters can be efficiently implemented as separable 1D convolutions with a ring-buffer for memory management of the streaming block of video frames needed for temporal filtering as shown in [10], where a more complete derivation of 3D structure tensors and flux tensors is also given. The trace of $\mathbf{J}_{\mathrm{F}}$ is sufficient to discriminate between moving and stationary portions of the scene as shown in the following examples. Fig. 1(c) shows the correct detection of only the moving circle and the flux tensor has noise suppression performance comparable to the 3D structure tensor – that is the second derivative calculation for the flux tensor does *not* lead to increased noise sensitivity. Increasing the trace threshold for **J** is problematic as shown using frame 37 of the "*Hamburg taxi*" video sequence (http://i21www.ira.uka.de/image_sequences) in Fig. 2(a). Using a trace threshold of $k_{trace} = 5 \times 10^{-3}$ for **J** results in Fig. 2(b) where the stationary background clutters the output. Increasing the trace threshold reduces clutter significantly but high contrast stationary cars and buildings still remain (Fig. 2(c)), and importantly the low contrast car moving to the right is not detected. Using the flux tensor all four moving objects are correctly identified including the low contrast person, while suppressing information from stationary objects in the scene. The reliable performance of the flux tensor extends to biological objects with deformable motion and complex non-homogeneous internal (foreground) textures that are often difficult to distinguish from the background (see Results section).

3 Multi-feature Active Contour Level Set Segmentation

The flux tensor-based moving object detection results in Fig. 2 highlight the need for further refining the flux tensor detector output in an explicit segmentation step in order to obtain more compact solid blobs that accurately correspond to visual object boundaries. Motion blobs are usually larger than the objects themselves and elongated along the direction of motion. The motion blobs may also be incomplete (i.e. motion boundary may not match object boundary), fragmented (i.e. broken boundaries due to multiple motion blobs for a single object), or contain holes/concavities due to the lack of internal structure within moving homogenous objects. A multi-feature multi-class level set approach with a flux tensor mask initialization is used to improve segmentation accuracy.

An active area of image and video segmentation research is the use of geometric partial differential equation based level set methods in combination with 3D structure tensors [13]. One widely used level set-based algorithm, to segment 2D images into two-classes, was proposed by Chan and Vese and is well suited for segmenting nearly homogeneous biological objects which often do not have distinct edges as discussed in [7]. The speed of convergence and stability of the Chan and Vese active contour algorithm depends on the initialization of ϕ, the size of the dynamical evolution time step Δt and the numerical update procedures, among other factors. Here, we use the flux tensor to accurately initialize the curve in a region that is close to the desired segmentation to ensure consistently fast object extraction. The trace of the flux tensor is a motion energy map that gives a good approximation of the moving objects in the frame, and is used to create the initialization for the level set evolution. Accurate flux tensor-based initialization also significantly reduces the number of iterations.

The original Chan and Vese formulation enforces an homogeneity constraint on the segmented regions in terms of the average gray value. This effectively evolves the curve to find the interface which separates darker regions from lighter regions. This assumption although seeming intuitive, is not always satisfied in

(a) Original Frame (b) $\mathbf{J}$, $k_{trace} = 5 \times 10^{-3}$ (c) $\mathbf{J}$, $k_{trace} = 5 \times 10^{-2}$

(d) $\mathbf{J}_{\mathrm{F}}$, $k_{trace} = 2 \times 10^{-4}$ (e) Level Set Segmentation (f) Segmented root

Fig. 3. Maize roots grown in vermiculite. Scaled measures are represented in color channels. Thresholding the 3D structure tensor can lead to useful features being discarded. The flux tensor successfully isolates the root. When used as weights for the level set segmentation result (1500 iterations for non-AOS implementation), the root is correctly isolated (after boundary smoothing), while background vermiculite information is suppressed to a large extent.

real world imagery – for example, in some phase contrast microscopy images of cells the average cell gray value is not significantly different from the background (as seen in Fig. 5), phase halos are bright regions adjacent to cell boundaries that are of the same intensity as rounded-up cells beginning mitosis, subtle illumination gradients can confuse the two phases of the level set, etc.

Instead of using only the mean image intensity within a phase, additional image-based features can be used to improve the object segmentation including distributions of image intensity, variance, color, texture, shape, etc. Using a Bayesian inference approach for $N-$features leads to the energy functional [13],

$$E(p_{1j}, p_{2j}, \phi) = -\sum_{j=1}^{N} \Big(\int_{\Omega} \lambda_{1j} \, \log p_{1j}(\mathrm{I}_j(\mathbf{x})) \, H(\phi(\mathbf{x})) d\mathbf{x} + \lambda_{2j} \, \log p_{2j}(\mathrm{I}_j(\mathbf{x})) \, (1 - H(\phi(\mathbf{x})) d\mathbf{x}) + \mu \int_{\Omega} |\nabla H(\phi(\mathbf{x}))| \, d\mathbf{x} \tag{4}$$

where p_{ij} corresponds to the conditional probability density function of observing feature value $\mathrm{I}_j(\mathbf{x})$ within region Ω_i (i.e. for two classes foreground and background), $\phi(\mathbf{x})$ is the embedding Lipschitz functional, $H(\phi)$ is a regularized Heaviside function that defines the interior and exterior regions of level set contours and the last term measures the length of all contours. Minimizing this functional with respect to ϕ, leads to the associated Euler-Lagrange equations and provides a gradient descent multi-feature optimization update equation,

$$\frac{\partial \phi}{\partial t} = \delta(\phi) \left(\sum_{j=1}^{N} \lambda_{1j} \log p_{1j}(\mathrm{I}_j(\mathbf{x})) - \lambda_{2j} \log p_{2j}(\mathrm{I}_j(\mathbf{x})) + \mu \,\mathrm{div} \frac{\nabla \phi}{|\nabla \phi|} \right) \quad (5)$$

Equations 4 and 5 simplify to the standard two-class Chan and Vese level set model (or equivalently the Mumford-Shah cartoon model where the smoothness term has infinite weight) in the case when both region intensities are from Gaussian distributions with $\mathcal{N}(c_1, \sigma_1)$, $\mathcal{N}(c_2, \sigma_2)$, and $\sigma_1 = \sigma_2 = \sqrt{0.5}$. The extension from the two-class multi-feature case to the $M-$class multi-feature case is straightforward but computationally demanding since there are either $M-$level sets using one level set per object class, or $\log M-$level sets to update using a multi-phase approach. When the gradient descent equation is solved using an explicit numerical scheme, the time steps need to be relatively small (e.g. $\Delta t = 0.1$) for stable convergence and consistency in order to satisfy the Courant-Friedrichs-Levy condition relating numerical waves to physical waves. Consequently, many iterations are needed to converge to an accurate solution. A semi-implicit scheme named *additive operator splitting* (AOS) was derived for non-linear diffusion filtering that is numerically stable even with large time steps. AOS also surprisingly decomposes the multi-dimensional updating into independent one dimensional updates. The Euler-Lagrange update Eq. 5 can be put into the AOS form, $\frac{\partial \phi}{\partial t} = a(\phi) + \mathrm{div}(b(\phi)\nabla\phi)$, and so can be efficiently implemented using the AOS numerical scheme. Due to space limitations details will be described elsewhere and we refer the reader to [14] for a description of the AOS implementation for minimizing the level set active contour functional.

4 Results for Biological Video Microscopy Datasets

The flux tensor multi-feature level set framework effectively handles motion detection and moving object segmentation in the presence of complex biological behavior (e.g., cell crawling, cell division/mitosis, cell death/apoptosis, touching cells, entering and exiting objects), spatially varying illumination, noise and

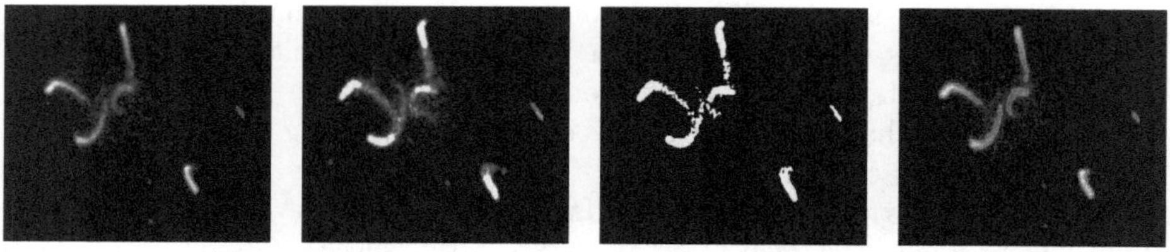

(a) Bacterial pathogenesis (b) Flux Tensor (c) Initial Mask (d) Segmentation (120 iterations)

Fig. 4. Phase contrast image showing Listeria bacteria actin motility (data from J. Theriot website [12]). Trajectories, or "comet tails", of the bacterial pathogen moving in the cytoplasm of an infected cell for studying actin-based motility.

background clutter. Experimental results demonstrating versatile and robust estimation of root tissue velocities, cancer cell migration trajectories and movement of bacterial pathogens are shown.

Figure 3(a) shows the fifth frame in a nine frame sequence of a maize root grown in vermiculite to study velocity profiles along the midline of the root meristem tissue. Estimation of accurate longitudinal root growth profiles requires suppression the background responses from mostly stationary vermiculite particles. Figures 3(b) and 3(c) are the 3D structure tensor-based detection results showing the difficulty of selecting a threshold in the presence of strong stationary features – at low trace thresholds stationary vermiculite is segmented as moving, while at higher thresholds useful features about the root contours are lost. Using the *flux tensor* with $k_{trace} = 2 \times 10^{-4}$ gives Fig. 3(d) which preserves features from the root, while the stationary vermiculite is mostly suppressed. Using the Chan and Vese single-feature explicit level set algorithm leads to the segmentation in Fig. 3(e), with the foreground regions highlighted by bright boundaries. Once accurate boundaries are available the flux tensor response $\mathbf{J}_{\mathrm{F}}(\mathbf{x})$ can be used to compute confidence weights for each pixel in the image and aggregated for each blob. The final segmentation combining the weighted flux tensor responses with the level set refinement is shown Fig. 3(f). Fig. 4 shows motile Listeria bacteria infecting and moving around within a host cell visible as actin "comet tails" in phase contrast images that resolve polystyrene beads coated with ActA [12]. Trajectories of the bacterial pathogen moving in the infected cell are sufficiently uniform to be accurately detected using flux tensors and segmented using the intensity image alone.

The sequence in Fig. 5 shows a few frames from one field in the T25 plastic culture flask of a control experiment with a low density culture of human melanoma cell line WM793 to assess any toxicity to the high-throughput imaging system [4]. Pixel resolution is 0.67 micron $\times$ 0.59 micron in X and Y using a 20$\times$ objective lens. The flux tensor detects moving cells reliably and provides an initial coarse segmentation for refinement. Although mean intensities within cells and the background are nearly the same, using the local image variance feature leads to successful multi-feature level set-based segmentation – intracellular variance is higher than the background variance. The variance feature image also does not have sharp boundaries so geodesic active contours that depend on an edge-based stopping function would not produce reliable cell segmentation. Using the flux tensor initialization and the semi-implicit AOS scheme with $\Delta t = 30$, the level set segmentation converges in less than 150 iterations. We highlight the fact that complex contours of the three dividing cells, in the middle of each frame, are accurately extracted from the initial compact bright rounded-up circular stage through elongated dark flattened-out post-cytokinesis final stages. The proposed segmentation algorithm works successfully on both homogeneous and non-homogeneous biological objects in a variety of video microscopy datasets.

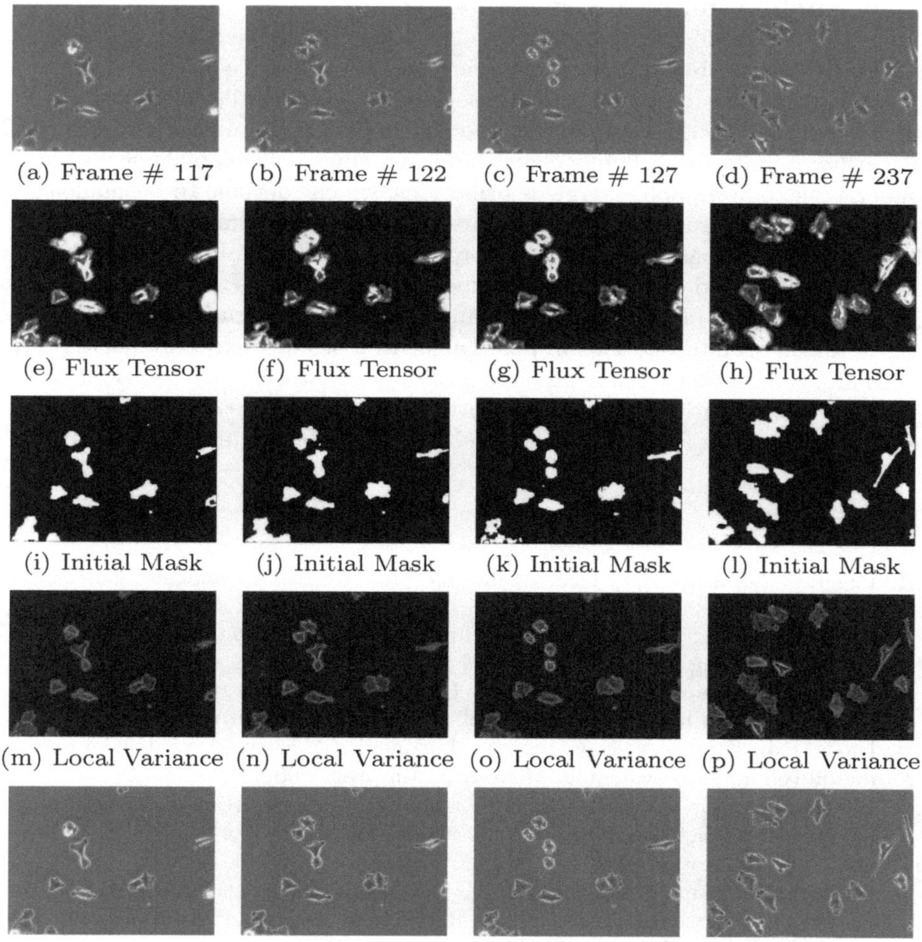

(a) Frame # 117 (b) Frame # 122 (c) Frame # 127 (d) Frame # 237

(e) Flux Tensor (f) Flux Tensor (g) Flux Tensor (h) Flux Tensor

(i) Initial Mask (j) Initial Mask (k) Initial Mask (l) Initial Mask

(m) Local Variance (n) Local Variance (o) Local Variance (p) Local Variance

(q) Segmentation (100 iterations) (r) Segmentation (100 iterations) (s) Segmentation (100 iterations) (t) Segmentation (100 iterations)

Fig. 5. Four frames from a sequence of human melanoma cells in a control experiment (data from LSDCAS, M. Mackey and F. Ianzine, U. Iowa [4]). Flux tensor detects moving cells reliably and provides an initial coarse segmentation for refinement. Although mean intensities within cells and the background are nearly the same, using the local image variance feature leads to successful multi-feature level set-based segmentation. Complex contour evolution of the three dividing cells, in the middle region of each frame, is accurately extracted. Frames show the early stage when cells shrink and round up for division in prophase/metaphase (i.e. become compact, spherical/circular, textureless and brighter in phase contrast) through elongated cytokinesis when cells flatten out (i.e. become elongated/ellipsoidal, textured and darker in phase contrast) in anaphase/telophase/interphase.

5 Conclusions and Future Work

A new flux tensor-based motion detection and multi-feature level set segmentation algorithm was developed for the segmentation of motile biological objects that is suitable for high-througput live cell microscopy studies. The proposed algorithm handles both homogeneous and non-homogeneous biological objects, undergoing complex split-merge deformations, which continue to be challenging research areas in tracking. The flux tensor detects both homogeneous and non-homogeneous biological objects, and provides a good initialization for the fast AOS level set based active contour segmentation. Flux tensor masks are used to initialize the evolving level set curve and to guide the segmentation to isolate active regions of interest. The proposed algorithm produces accurate, fast, reproducible segmentations of moving biological objects. Non-homogeneous biological objects with mean intensity similar to the background are handled in a novel way using variance features for the level set active contour evolution process.

References

1. Eggert, U.S., Mitchison, T.J.: Small molecule screening by imaging. Curr. Opin. Chem. Biol. 10, 232–237 (2006)
2. Zhou, X., Wong, S.: High content cellular imaging for drug development. IEEE Signal Processing Magazine 23, 170–174 (2006)
3. Nath, S., Palaniappan, K., Bunyak, F.: Four-color level set segmentation using generalized Voronoi neighborhoods for cell migration. Medical Image Analysis (2007)
4. Davis, P.J., Kosmacek, E.A., Sun, Y., Ianzine, F., Mackey, M.A.: The large scale digital cell analysis system. J. Microscopy (in press, 2007)
5. Palaniappan, K., Jiang, H., Baskin, T.: Non-rigid motion estimation using the robust tensor method. In: IEEE Comp. Vision. Patt. Recog. Workshop on Articulated and Nonrigid Motion, Washington DC, USA, pp. 25–32 (2004)
6. Nath, S., Palaniappan, K., Bunyak, F.: Cell segmentation using coupled level sets and graph-vertex coloring. In: Larsen, R., Nielsen, M., Sporring, J. (eds.) MICCAI 2006. LNCS, vol. 4190, pp. 101–108. Springer, Heidelberg (2006)
7. Bunyak, F., Palaniappan, K., Nath, S., Baskin, T., Dong, G.: Quantitative cell motility for *in vitro* wound healing using level set-based active contour tracking. In: ISBI. Proc. 3rd IEEE Int. Symp. Biomed. Imaging, pp. 1040–1043 (2006)
8. Nath, S., Bunyak, F., Palaniappan, K.: Robust tracking of migrating cells using four-color level set segmentation. In: Blanc-Talon, J., Philips, W., Popescu, D., Scheunders, P. (eds.) ACIVS 2006. LNCS, vol. 4179, pp. 920–932. Springer, Heidelberg (2006)
9. Nath, S., Palaniappan, K., Bunyak, F.: Accurate spatial neighborhood relationships for arbitrarily-shaped objects using Hamilton-Jacobi GVD. In: Ersbøll, B.K., Pedersen, K.S. (eds.) SCIA 2007. LNCS, vol. 4522, pp. 421–431 (2007)
10. Bunyak, F., Palaniappan, K., Nath, S., Seetharaman, G.: Fux tensor constrained geodesic active contours with sensor fusion for persistent object tracking. J. Multimedia (in Press, 2007)
11. Weele, C., Jiang, H., et al.: A new algorithm for computational image analysis of deformable motion at high spatial and temporal resolution applied to root growth. Plant. Phys. 132, 1138–1148 (2003)

12. Shenoy, V., Tambe, D., Prasad, A., Theriot, J.: A kinematic description of the trajectories of *listeria* monocytogenes propelled by actin comet tails. In: Proc. Natl. Acad. Sci., USA, vol. 104, pp. 8229–8234 (2007)
13. Cremers, D., Rousson, M., Deriche, R.: A review of statistical approaches to level set segmentation: Integrating color, texture, motion, shape. Intern. J. Computer Vis. 72, 195–215 (2007)
14. Jeon, M., Alexander, M., Pedrycz, W., Pizzi, N.: Unsupervised hierarchical image segmentation with level set and additive operator splitting. Patt. Recog. Letters 26, 1461–1469 (2005)

Fusion of Multimedia Information in Biomedicine

Su-Shing Chen

CAS-MPG Partner Institute of Computational Biology, Shanghai Institutes of Biological Sciences, Chinese Academy of Sciences, Shanghai 200031, China
suchen@picb.ac.cn

Abstract. Biomedicine is a very rich field of multimedia information. It is also a fruitful ground for information fusion and integration about scientific research data as well as clinical records of digital medical systems. In this paper, we present a global overview of these ideas, which have not been realized so far and could be interesting to the multimedia research community. We exemplify the complex information resources in terms of Gene Ontology (GO), Clinical Bioinformatics Ontology (CBO) and the Foundational Model of Anatomy (FMA). GO is a biomedical scientific research system used to describe genes and gene products, but no cellular components. CBO is a clinical oriented ontology of information, which potentially include many multimedia images: X-Ray, ultrasound and magnetic resonance images. FMA is a foundational clinical source used to describe the anatomy of the human body as well as cellular components. While scientists in each sector may use these systems to help develop their own information, it is very difficult for a layman or broad-spectrum researcher to integrate the two different languages into one interface. We will attempt to address these issues to describe how information fusion can be achieved.

Keywords: Ontology, GO, CBO, FMA, information fusion.

1 Introduction

Biomedicine is a very rich field of multimedia information. It is also a fruitful ground for information fusion and integration about scientific research data as well as clinical records of digital medical systems. In this paper, we present a global overview of these ideas, which have not been realized so far and could be tackled by the multimedia research community. We exemplify the complex information resources in terms of Gene Ontology (GO), Clinical Bioinformatics Ontology (CBO) and the Foundational Model of Anatomy (FMA). GO is a biomedical scientific research system used to describe genes and gene products, but no cellular components. CBO is a clinical oriented ontology of information which potentially include many multimedia images: X-Ray, ultrasound and magnetic resonance images. FMA is a foundational clinical source used to describe the anatomy of the human body as well as cellular components. While scientists in each sector may use these systems to help develop their own information, it is very difficult for a layman or broad-spectrum researcher to integrate the two different languages into one interface.

H.H.S. Ip et al. (Eds.): PCM 2007, LNCS 4810, pp. 494–500, 2007.

We will attempt to address this issue to describe how information fusion can be achieved. First, we will integrate these two languages into an ontology editor-Protégé. Then, we will present the Unified Medical Language System, which converts various data sets into a single language, which can input various data formats to a SQL database. With a front-end interface for access and search, we have the basic idea of developing information fusion systems.

The organization of the paper is as follows. We first present FMA, GO and CBO. These information content and their multimedia content can be understood from these ontologies. Next we will develop various technological aspects of information fusion: Protégé, Unified Language System (UMLS) and LexGrid. Other techniques, which have not covered here, are those fusion methods of multimedia information. However they have been the key research areas of the multimedia research community.

2 Foundational Model of Anatomy (FMA)

FMA was developed by Todd Detwiler and SIG (Structural Informatics Group) at the University of Washington. FMA includes methods for representing spatial and symbolic information about the physical organization of the body (see Figures 1 and 2), and for using these structural representations as a basis for organizing non-structural information, under the hypothesis that structure is a logical foundation for organizing and inter-relating most information in biomedicine. FMA develops web-accessible computer programs, which utilize these representations to solve practical problems in clinical medicine, research and education. Initially, it applies these methods to the domains of biological structure and neuroscience, including macroscopic, microscopic, cellular and subcellular anatomy, the structure of biological macromolecules, and the relationship of these structures to functional properties of the brain.

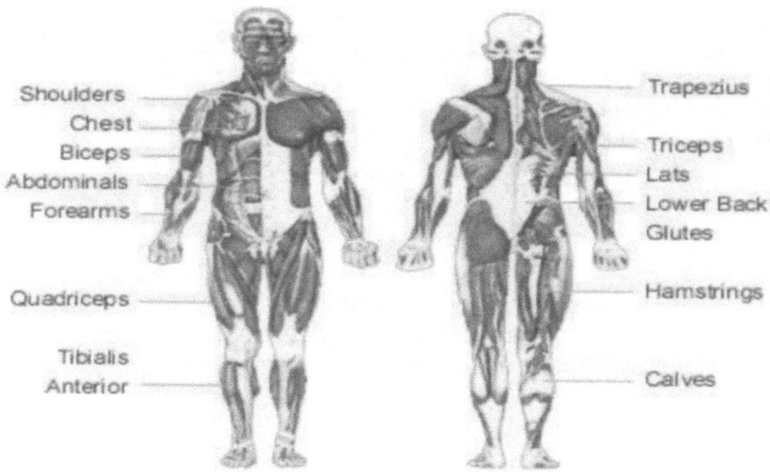

Fig. 1. A FMA Anatomy Structure

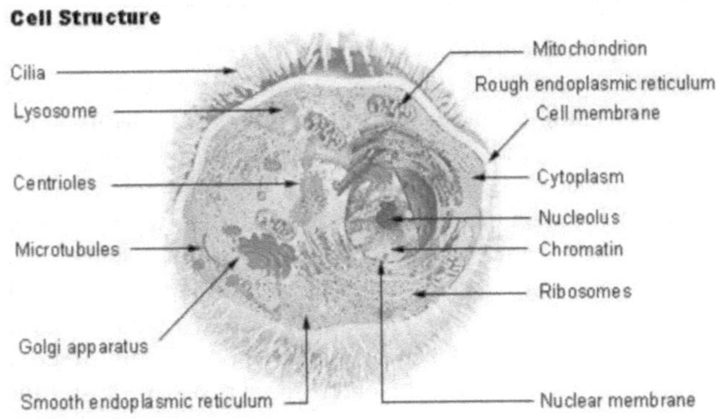

Fig. 2. A FMA Cell Structure

3 Gene Ontology (GO)

The Gene Ontology project provides a controlled vocabulary to describe gene and gene product attributes in any organism. GO envelops the type of information we might capture about a gene product. This includes the biochemical material, either ribonucleic acid (RNA) or protein, resulting from expression of a gene. The amount of gene product is used to measure how active a gene is. In general, the gene ontology captures what the gene product does, why does it perform these activities and where does it act. GO contains three sub-ontologies that define these concepts. The Molecular Function Ontology captures what the gene product does, the Biological Process Ontology captures what processes the gene product is involved in and the Cellular Component Ontology captures where the gene ontology acts. Figure 3 demonstrates how a gene ontology term is arranged. It contains an id, a term and a definition. Unfortunately there are areas that the GO does not cover. This includes no pathological processes, no experimental conditions, no evolutionary relationships and no gene products. GO is not a system of nomenclature. As of 2006, the GO contained 20623 terms, 95.7% of which had definitions. There were 11360 biological processes, 1806 cellular components and 7457 molecular functions. There are 1007 terms not included in the aforementioned statistics.

term: gluconeogenesis

id: GO:0006094

definition: The formation of glucose from noncarbohydrate precursors, such as pyruvate, amino acids and glycerol.

Fig. 3. Example of a GO Term

4 The Clinical Bioinformatics Ontology (CBO)

Existing medical vocabularies lack rich terms to describe findings generated by molecular diagnostic and cytogenetic techniques. Bioinformatics resources were not designed to support the needs of the clinical community. Clinical Bioinformatics Ontology (CBO) was initiated to address these gaps and covers the areas of molecular genetics, molecular pathology, cytogenetics and infectious disease.

The Clinical Bioinformatics Ontology includes a controlled vocabulary with uniquely identified concepts. It is machine-readable and comes in many formats such as the RDF format which is a format recognizable by Protégé. It also includes a semantic network, which provides biological context to clinical findings. Furthermore, the CBO is a curated resource. This means that there is consistent application of content creation methodology, quality control process. The CBO is focused on current clinical practice in a controlled scope. As of 2006 the CBO contained 8155 concepts, 18946 relationships, 4304 Facets and 13341 terms.

5 Information Fusion Tools

The following subsections contain some basic tools for information fusion.

5.1 Digital Library Server for Fusion of Multimedia Information

In [1], a digital library server for fusion of various information sources has been developed which handled various system level issues. At present, we address more basic issues within the information content. First, biomedical information has disparate information sources. We use an ontology-based approach for fusion of different multimedia sources, such as GO, CBO and FMA. Ontology deals with concept level issues of the information content. For examples, anatomy deals with the human body, while cells are substructures within the organ structures of the human body (Figures 1 and 2). Ontology relates these concepts in a tree like structures (FIGURE 3). However multimedia information are different representations of possibly the same concept. For examples, a single organ, such as the brain, can be imaged by both MRI and CT media. Thus we need to address the integration issue of these two kinds of information. This important issue has been a key topic of the multimedia research community. In this paper, we only address the ontology approach and leave the image-level fusion for future research. Our ongoing VIACIPA (Video Image Archive of Cell Images for Protein Activities) is such a research project.

5.2 Protégé

The Protégé is a semantic integration system, which is potentially useful for information fusion. However there are difficulties to use it at present. For example, the Foundational Model of Anatomy's website does not have a downloadable format that is compatible with Protégé (OWL or OBO files), though the GO website provides a downloadable OBO file. One of the beneficial features of Protégé is the graphical

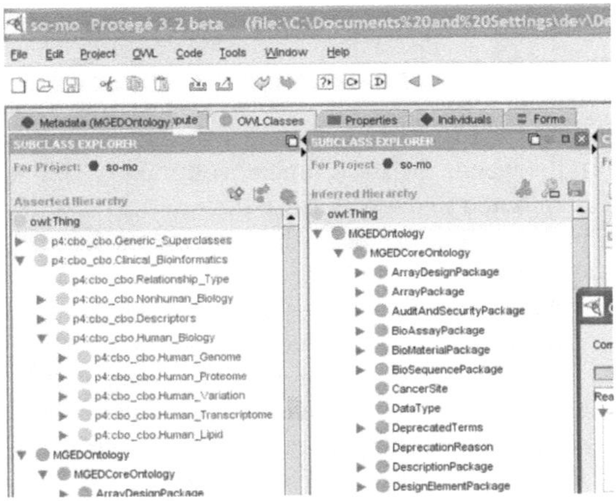

Fig. 4. A Protege Interface

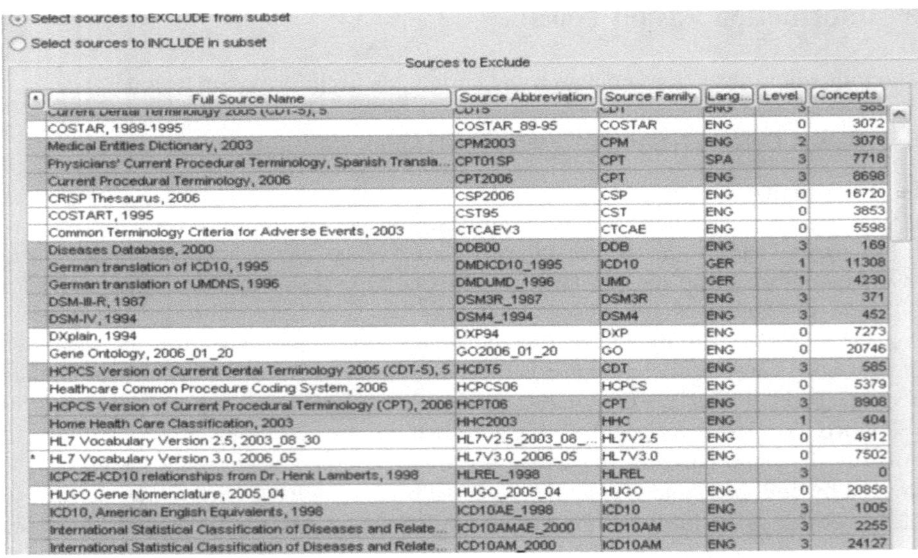

Fig. 5. A UMLS Screeshot

interface, which models relationships and entities in a tree structure (see Figure 4 for a Protégé interface).

5.3 Unified Medical Language System

The purpose of NLM's Unified Medical Language System (UMLS) is to facilitate the development of computer systems that behave as if they "understand" the meaning of the language of biomedicine and health (Figure 5). The UMLS contains hundreds of different ontologies, though the only few used here are the FMA, CBO and GO.

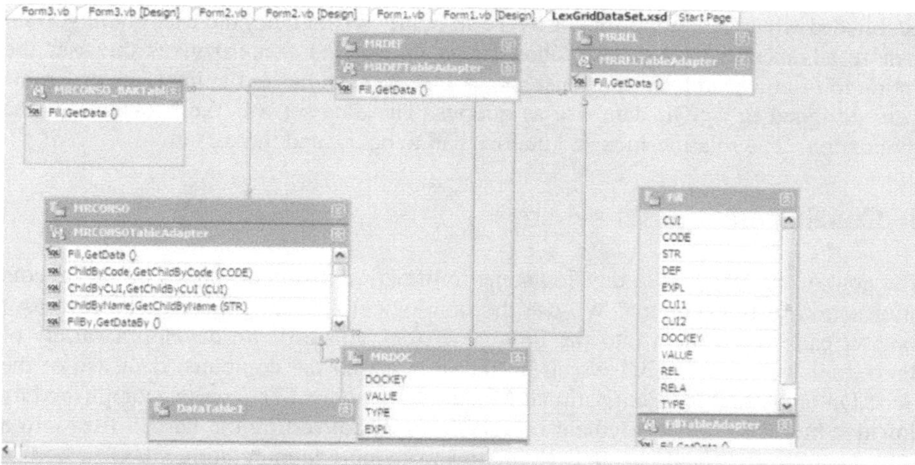

Fig. 6. An Experimental Frontend Interface

These files are installed onto the system as RRF (Rich Release Files), which are very similar to the standard ontology RDF files. These files can be viewed through the UMLS Browser, which gives basic searching abilities. The drawback to this system is that while it provides search tools, it makes no attempts to integrate any ontologies together or give any reasoning capabilities.

5.4 LexGrid

LexGrid is a software tool provide by the Mayo Clinic, which provides for the conversion between various formats (UMLS's RRF, OBO files, OWL files) and various SQL databases (MySQL, AccessSQL, etc.). Once the UMLS had been installed, LexGrid was used to convert the FMA and GO RRF files into an MS Access SQL database. This database contained seven tables, each detailing a specific facet of the dual ontologies. There was one main table, which had column headings for several attribute fields, which could be looked up in one of the other tables.

The relationships between the data tables can be created easily, since no pre-defined relationships existed. These relationships are used to create a variety of queries based on the Search Term's Name, ID number or relationships. We can delve deeper into the SQL queries, for information fusion as the relationships established.

5.5 Frontend Interfaces

Once the data was converted into a SQL database, it was very easy to access and search the data. The one thing that was missing was a good interface from which to do this. Therefore, a GUI can be written to allow the user to view and search terms in multiple ontologies with ease.

In Figures 6, we have developed some preliminary results of information fusion. The first frame of the application displays the basic information about a term. On the right, the user can search by Code, CUI (some sort of Identifier – it was never established what CUI stood for) or by Term name. From here, the user could go into a more advanced search. The second frame (Advanced Search) gives the user the option to filter a search by relationships. All of the searches in the interface programs were designed in a SQL database as queries. The data set was the backbone of the application. The relationships and queries had to be created there.

6 Conclusion

The goal of this paper is to develop some information fusion examples of multimedia information in biomedicine. We use the ontological approach. Ideally, Protégé as a tool set can import them into the Protégé system. Instead, we develop a variety of direct tools to create a GUI which let the user search the combined database of the Gene Ontology and the Foundational Model of Anatomy. This was accomplished by downloading the Unified Medical Library System, converting the UMLS files into a SQL database and finally using SQL queries to support an integrating GUI.

References

[1] Kim, H., Choo, C., Chen, S.: Generating a Meta-DL by Federating Search on OAI and Non-OAI Servers. Journal of Intelligent Systems

[2] Yandell, M.D., Majoros, W.H.: Genomics and natural language processing. Nature Reviews Genetics 3(8), 601–610 (2002)

[3] McCray, A.T., Browne, A.C., Bodenreider, O.: The Lexical Properties of the Gene Ontology (GO). In: Proc. of AMIA Annual Symposium, pp. 504–508 (2002)

[4] Raychaudhuri, S., Chang, J.T., Sutphin, P.D., Altman, R.B.: Associating Genes with Gene Ontology Codes Using a Maximum Entropy Analysis of Biomedical Literature, vol. 12(1), pp. 203–214 (January 2002)

[5] Smith, B., Williams, J., Schulze-Kremer, S.: The Ontology of the Gene Ontology, In Biomedical and Health Informatics: From Foundations to Applications. In: Proceedings of the Annual Symposium of the American Medical Informatics Association, Washington DC (2003)

Websites

The Gene Ontology, www.geneontology.org
The Clinical Biomedical Ontology, https://www.clinbioinformatics.org/cbopublic/
The Microarray Ontology, http://mged.sourceforge.net/ontologies/MGEDontology.php
Protégé, http://protege.stanford.edu, http://www.cise.ufl.edu/~doliver/geneontology/.
LexGrid, http://informatics.mayo.edu/LexGrid/index.php?page=aboutlg
UMLS, http://www.nlm.nih.gov/research/umls/about_umls.html
Foundational Model of Anatomy, http://sig.biostr.washington.edu/projects/fm/AboutFM.html
National Library of Medicine: MEDLINE Fact Sheet. http://www.nlm.nih.gov/pubs/factsheets/med line.html.

Channel-Aware Adaptive Multi-RPS Scheme for Video Error Resilient Transmission over Wireless OFDM Channel

Yanzhuo Ma and Yilin Chang

National Key Lab. on ISN, Xidian University, Xi'an, Shaanxi, 710071, China
yzma@mail.xidian.edu.cn, ylchang@xidian.edu.cn

Abstract. Orthogonal Frequency Division Multiplexing (OFDM) is a promising technique in broadband wireless communication systems. This paper presents a novel multi-reference scheme based on 3D interleaving for video coding and transmission over OFDM channel. Initially, a combining interleaving method in spatial, frequency and temporal domains, called SFTI, is proposed. With SFTI, different slices within one frame are transmitted in different sub-channels of OFDM, whose SNR can be estimated, and the transmission status of slices through these sub-channels are real-time feedback to the encoder. Based on the feedback information, a multi-reference scheme for video coding is proposed where the well-transmitted slices are selected as the reference picture of its consequent pictures in inter-frame coding to eliminate the impairment caused by error propagation in video transmission over wireless OFDM channels. Extensive experimental results have demonstrated the effectiveness of the proposed methods in error resilience.

Keywords: OFDM, multi-reference picture selection (multi-RPS), Spatial Frequency Temporal Interleaving (SFTI).

1 Introduction

Due to the parallel, slower bandwidth nature, Orthogonal Frequency Division Multiplexing (OFDM) is widely used in broad-band wireless channels to combat Inter Symbol Interference (ISI). Video transmission over OFDM channels, however, still faces the challenges of channel errors and error propagation as in other wireless channels. Besides forward error correction (FEC), error resilient video coding schemes, e.g. intra-refreshment or multi-reference picture selection (multi-RPS) can serve as effective tools to reduce the impairment caused by channel errors and error propagation.

Multi-RPS, which can provide higher coding efficiency and better error resilient capability, is firstly proposed in H.263+ standard annex N [1] [2], and later is subsumed in annex U of H.263++. Now it has been integrated in H.264 standard [3]. The principle of multi-RPS is to restrain error propagation by selecting known-as-correct reference frames in motion compensation during video transmission over error-prone channels. Much work has been carried out to utilize the multi-RPS in

H.H.S. Ip et al. (Eds.): PCM 2007, LNCS 4810, pp. 501–509, 2007.

real-time error resilient video transmission. In [4] the end-to-end distortion is estimated by error tracking and then used to decide the optimal mode, motion vector and reference frame for the current macroblock (MB). In [5], the distortion at the decoder is estimated by simulating the channel behavior at the encoder. [6] follows a similar spirit as in [4] in distortion estimation to select the optimal reference frame.

These methods are all based on distortion estimation, which unavoidably introduces high computational burden to the encoder and in addition, may not be accurate. A heuristic frame restriction method has also been proposed in [7], where the actual transmission status of reference frames is not considered.

The approaches of combining end-to-end feedback with multi-RFC are also designed and evaluated in [2], [4] and [8], where the advantage of combination of multi-RPS and low delay feedback has been demonstrated. However, in most actual environments, low delay feedback is hard to obtain, and the long delay of end-to-end feedback will inevitably degrade the performance gain.

In this paper a novel channel-aware adaptive multi-RPS scheme is proposed, taking advantage of the low delay feedback from OFDM channels. In fact, the feedback information of OFDM channel estimation at physical layer can be real-time, and reflects the real-time state of the wireless channel. The proposed adaptive multi-RPS scheme is based on a Spatial Frequency Temporal Interleaving (SFTI) method, and utilizes the real time feedback of OFDM channel together with the interleaving information to inform the encoder of the transmission status of a slice in a reference frame. Therefore, the error-prone slices are avoided to be used as reference in inter-prediction. In consequence, the impairment of channel errors and error propagation can be well reduced. In addition, the complexity of the proposed scheme for cross layer control can be negligible and no delay will be introduced.

The rest of this paper is organized as follows. Section II describes the proposed interleaving method (SFIT) and the adaptive multi-RPS method based on SFTI. Section III demonstrates the experimental results. Conclusion and future work is given in section IV.

2 Proposed Adaptive Multi-RPS Scheme Based on SFTI

2.1 Proposed SFTI

Mobile radio channels are time varying and multi-path fading channels, so burst bit-errors are frequently encountered in wireless channels. OFDM, which divides one wide-band channel into numbers of sub-channels resulting in slower transmission speed over each sub-channel, is often used to alleviate ISI in these channels.

At the OFDM receiver, given the channel impulse response $\mathbf{H}(t)$ at time t, the received signal can be expressed as

$$\mathbf{S_r} = \mathbf{H}(t)\mathbf{S_t} + \mathbf{N} . \tag{1}$$

where $\mathbf{N}$ is the channel noise, and $\mathbf{S_t}$ is the transmitted signal. $\mathbf{H}(t)$ is time varying and frequency-selective, which is illustrated in Fig.1.

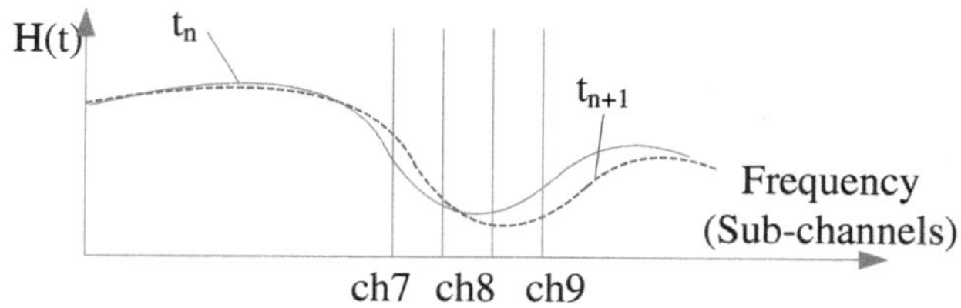

Fig. 1. Time-varying frequency-selective fading OFDM channel

It is widely known that in most video coding standards, such as H.263+/264[1],[3], a frame can be divided into several slices, and each slice can be encoded or decoded independently. Based on this feature and the characteristics of OFDM, a novel 3D-interleaving method, namely SFTI, is proposed. In this method, spatial interleaving operates after channel coding on bit level to enhance the performance of FEC. Frequency interleaving, on the other hand, is performed on slice level to limit the influence of sub-channels fading to a few slices. Temporal interleaving is also performed on slice level to facilitate efficient multi-RPS and error concealment.

The bit level spatial interleaving is the same as generally used interleaving methods with the purpose of enhancing the efficiency of FEC. Spatial interleaving rearranges channel coded bits so that the contiguous data is separated and reassembled into a non continuous stream. After deinterleaving the burst bit errors will be dispersed, and then the source data can be retrieved more efficiently by FEC.

The frequency interleaving is designed to transmit slices in a frame over different interleaved sub-channels of OFDM. And by assigning adjacent slices into un-adjacent sub-channels to avoid the simultaneous corruption of adjacent slices, which will facilitate spatial error concealment. An example of the interleaving process for coded video data in frequency domain is given in equation (2). This process is also visualized in Fig.2 (a). In this example, the contiguous slices such as slice 1 and 2 of the n th frame have been assigned into un-adjacent sub-channels 1 and 3. There are many other interleaving algorithms which can implement this function, too.

$$Z_i = \begin{cases} (i+1)/2, & \text{while } i \text{ is odd} \\ i/2 + N/2, & \text{while } i \text{ is even} \end{cases}, \quad i = 1, \cdots, N \ . \tag{2}$$

where Z_i denote the serial numbers of slice data transmitted over the i th sub-channel. Here N is the number of slices in one frame.

The temporal interleaving is to re-interleave the slices of the subsequent frames in frequency domain to avoid that co-located slices may suffer from burst errors in the same sub-channels. Also an example of the corresponding process is shown in equation (3) and Fig. 2.

$$Z_{t+1,i} = \left(Z_{t,i} + r\right) \bmod N + 1 \ . \tag{3}$$

where r is a random integer.

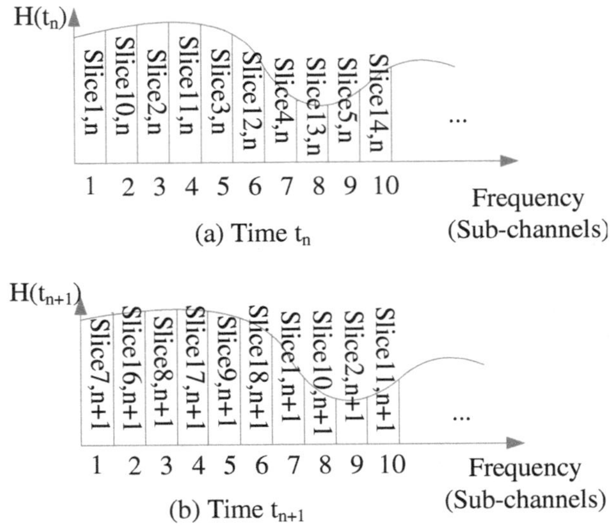

Fig. 2. Example of temporal interleaving over slices between time t_n(a) and time t_{n+1}(b). And at the same time, (a) and (b) show frequency interleaving at time t_n and t_{n+1}, respectively.

The proposed 3D interleaving method utilizes frequency and time diversity, so that the performance of any pre-used FEC can be enhanced. The corresponding performance gain obtained by SFTI is evaluated in section III. The proposed SFTI also facilitate the operation of error concealment, since slice-level interleaving permutes the corresponding relationship of slice with sub-channels, and consecutive loss of slices can be avoided.

2.2 Proposed Multi-RPS Scheme with SFTI

According to the real-time feedback of OFDM sub-channels and interleaving mechanism of SFTI, the reception status of each slice after transmission (successfully received or lost) can be obtained. Then the encoder can utilize this information in reference frame selection.

Fig. 3 shows the system diagram of the proposed adaptive multi-RPS scheme. At the receiver of an OFDM channel, channel characteristics are estimated by pilots.

Then corresponding information such as SNR of each sub-channel is fed back to the encoder. Utilizing the feedback information and SFTI parameters, the reception status of each slice is determined by the following steps.

1. The SNR of each sub-channel $\hat{\mathbf{\rho}} = \left[\hat{\rho}_1, \ \hat{\rho}_2, \dots, \hat{\rho}_N\right]$ at time t_n is obtained by feedback.
2. An error-free threshold $\hat{\rho}_{\mathrm{t}}$ is selected according to the FEC and modulation scheme.

3. The serial numbers of transmitted slices in each sub-channel at time t_n by SFTI is obtained.
4. For the nth sub-channel, if $\hat{\rho}_{\text{n}} < \hat{\rho}_{\text{t}}$, the reception status of corresponding slice is denoted as "unsuccessful", other wise, i.e. $\hat{\rho}_{\text{n}} \geq \hat{\rho}_{\text{t}}$, it is denoted as "successful".

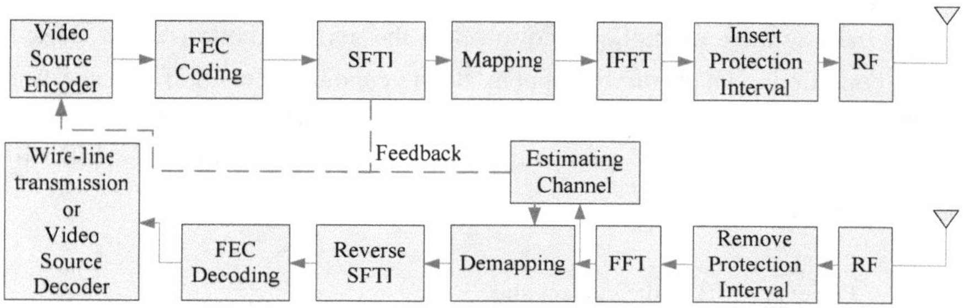

Fig. 3. System diagram

After the reception status of all slices of the frame transmitted at time t_n is obtained, this information is used in adaptive multi-RPS. Based on the reception status of slices, encoder performs multi-RPS as shown in Fig. 4. In this figure, the shadowed blocks show the coding MB in the current frame (n^{th}) and the most matched MB's in its reference frames, with the serial number of from $n-r$ to $n-1$ (supposed that there are r reference pictures for the current picture). The candidate MB in a lost slice, such as slice m of the $n-r+2$ th frame will be excluded in motion search.

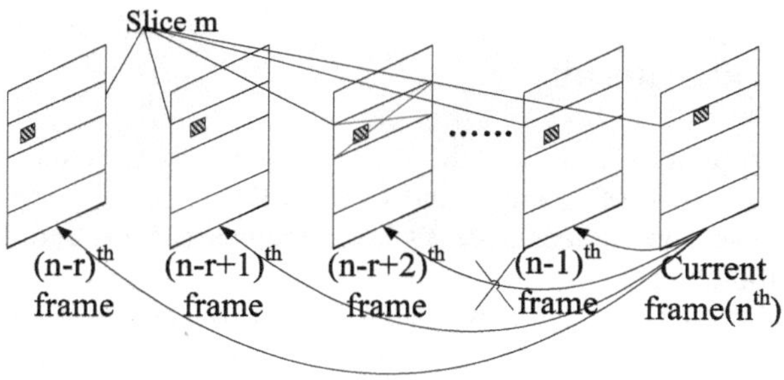

Fig. 4. Multi-RPS scheme

The pseudo code of RPS MV-searching is shown in Fig.5. In an RD optimized environment such as in the reference software of H.264 (JM series) [3], this process is incorporated in the motion estimation process, as shown in equation (4).

$$\begin{aligned}(mv, ref)_{opt} &= \arg\min\{J(mv, ref)\} \\ &= \arg\min\{D_{DFD}(mv, ref) + \lambda_{motion} R(mv, ref)\}\end{aligned} \quad (4)$$

Here motion estimation is performed in slices with the reception status of slice ref as "successful". In the equation, J is the Lagrangian cost. D_{DFD} denotes the displaced frame difference obtained in motion estimation, R denotes the coded bit rate, and λ_{motion} is the Lagrange multiplier used to select the optimal motion vector. Note that in some conditions, which rarely happen, all the candidates of the reference frames may have been denoted as "unsuccessful" ones, then the optimal motion estimation $(mv, ref)_{opt}$ cannot be found out by equation (4). In such conditions, the MB will be coded in intra modes.

```
For every MB in the current slice
{
    For every sub-block in the MB
    {
      Find the most fit reference MB among the slices in status
      of " successful" of usable reference frames by selecting
      the minimum cost J_min, avoid using the slices in status of
     " unsuccessful" ;
    }
    Add up the cost of sub-blocks, obtain J_MB;
    Record the information of MV, and reference frame;
}
```

Fig. 5. Multi-RPS motion search

3 Simulation and Results

In the following simulations, we use JM 10.2 [9] to encode the QCIF format standard test sequence Foreman (300 frames) and Claire (400 frames) using a fixed QP=28 without rate control. The number of MB's in a slice is set to 11, and there are 9 slices in a QCIF format picture.

To simulate the wireless channels, TU in COST207 [10] is selected as wireless channel simulation model, which represents the typical urban environments. The maximum Doppler frequency drifting is set as $f_{D\max} = 150\text{Hz}$, which presents vehicle speed 80Km/h with modulation carrier $f_0 = 2\text{GHz}$.

Parameters in the OFDM systems are set as follows: $T_s = 100\mu s$, $N_{FFT} = 64$, $N = 52$, $T_g = 20\mu s$ [11]. The interval of sub-carriers is $\Delta f \approx 10\text{KHz}$, and QPSK modulation is used. The convolutional encoder at the physical layer encodes on the coding rate of $R=1/2$.

The first frame of each sequence is intra-coded, and all subsequent frames are inter-coded. In order to improve error resilient performance besides channel coding, three MB's are intra updated in each frame, corresponding to an intra-frame updating period of $N=99/3=33$ frames. The number of reference frames is set to 10.

At the decoder, those MB's which cannot be decoded due to noise corruption in a slice will be discarded. After resynchronization with the next slice header, the decoder starts decoding the next slice, and conceals the damaged slices using the co-located slices in the former picture. Experimental results under different channel conditions (SNR) are shown in Tab.1 and Tab.2.

There are fours schemes have been simulated and compared as follows:

a. General interleaving without feedback.
b. SFTI without feedback.
c. General interleaving with adaptive multi-RPS,1 frame-delay feedback.
d. SFTI with adaptive multi-RPS, the proposed scheme.

Table 1. Performance Evaluation for Claire over different channel conditions (SNR)

	SNR 15dB		SNR 20dB		SNR 25dB		SNR 30dB	
	PSNR	Bit rate	PSNR	Bit rate	PSNR	Bit rate	PSNR	Bit rate
a	36.19	59.58	37.44	59.58	38.09	59.58	38.74	59.58
b	36.50	59.58	38.64	59.58	39.21	59.58	39.66	59.58
c	37.24	59.69	37.73	59.53	38.85	59.62	34.79	59.65
d	39.51	61.92	39.66	59.99	39.72	59.67	39.72	59.85

Note: PSNR in dB, Bit rate in Kbps.

Table 2. Performance Evaluation for Foreman over different channel conditions (SNR)

	SNR 15dB		SNR 20dB		SNR 25dB		SNR 30dB	
	PSNR	Bit rate	PSNR	Bit rate	PSNR	Bit rate	PSNR	Bit rate
a	23.75	179.61	27.14	179.61	28.83	179.61	28.89	179.61
b	25.71	179.61	29.66	179.61	34.05	179.61	31.85	179.61
c	24.34	179.84	28.69	179.42	30.59	179.75	31.53	179.88
d	34.91	188.47	35.29	182.22	35.49	180.57	35.51	180.37

Note: PSNR in dB, Bit rate in Kbps.

It can be seen that the proposed combination of SFTI with adaptive multi-RPS, i.e. *scheme d*, obtains the best performance in all compared methods, with little increase of bit rate than other schemes (only up to 5%).

It outperforms SFTI without feedback (*scheme b*) by up to 3 dB for Claire, and up to 9 dB for Foreman. This indicates that the *adaptive multi-RPS* is very effective in transmission of video over lossy channels. On the other hand, we can see the contribution of *SFTI* alone (*scheme b*), compared with general interleaving (*scheme a*), which can bring about 1 dB improvement for transmission of Claire, and 2~3 dB for Foreman, with no increase of bit rate.

Although when combined with the proposed adaptive multi-RPS, the performance of the general interleaving can be improved (*scheme c*), which can be seen up to more than 1 dB for both Claire and Foreman with 1 frame-delay feedback, however, the improvement is limited due to its dependency on end-to-end feedback, and the requirement of the end-to-end feedback with long delay is not preferred in video transmission. While comparing the proposed combination of SFTI and adaptive multi-RPS (*scheme d*) with this scheme (*scheme c*), up to more than 2 dB performance gain of the proposed method for Claire, and up to 10 dB for Foreman can be observed.

It is noticeable that the quality gain of Foreman is mostly greater than Claire because Foreman has more intensive movement and is more sensitive to the errors. This interesting phenomenon also demonstrates the advances of the proposed method in error sensitive cases.

4 Conclusion

This paper addresses the issue of how to transport video effectively and robustly over wireless OFDM channels. An adaptive multi-RPS scheme based on SFTI is proposed.

By introducing the SFTI method, slices of one frame are transmitted separately over interleaved sub-channels of OFDM. The performance of FEC is therefore enhanced. The real-time feedbacks of OFDM channel are utilized in combination with SFTI to obtain transmission status of slices within previously coded frames. Therefore, multi-RPS can be implemented efficiently to alleviate propagation error.

Experimental results demonstrate that the proposed scheme can obtain better performance than conventional transmission methods and more graceful quality degradation with the decrease of channel SNR.

References

1. ITU Telecom. Standardization Sector of ITU. Video Coding for Low Bit Rate Communication. ITU-T Recommendation H.263 Version 3 (2000)
2. Wenger, S., Knorr, G.D., Ott, J., Kossentini, F.: Error resilience support in H.263+. IEEE Trans. Circuits Syst. Video Technol. 8(7), 867–877 (1998)
3. Joint Video Team of ITU-T and ISO/IEC JTC 1. Advanced video coding for generic audiovisual services. Draft ITU-T Recommendation and Final Draft International Standard of Joint Video Specification (ITU-T Rec. H.264 | ISO/IEC 14496-10 AVC) (2003)
4. Wiegand, T., Färber, N., Stuhlmüller, K., Girod, B.: Error-Resilient Video Transmission Using Long-Term Memory Motion-Compensated Prediction. IEEE JSAC 18(6), 1050–1062 (2000)
5. Stockhammer, T., Kontopodis, D., Wiegand, T.: Rate-Distortion Optimization for JVT/H.26L Coding in Packet Loss Environment. In: Proc. PVW, Pittburgh, PY (2002)
6. Liang, Y.J., Girod, B.: Network-Adaptive Low-Latency Video Communication Over Best-Effort Networks. IEEE Transactions on Circuits and Systems for Video Technology 16(1), 72–81 (2006)
7. Stockhammer, T., Kontopodis, D.: Error robust macroblock mode and reference frame restriction. Joint Video Team (JVT) of ISO/IEC MPEG and ITU-T VCEG, JVT-B102 (2002)

8. Thomas Stockhammer Video Coding and Transport Layer Techniques for H.264/AVC-based Transmission over Packet-Lossy Networks. In: icip2003 (2003)
9. Office for Publications of the European Communities, Digital land mobile radio communications. Luxembourg, Final Rep. COST 207 (1989)
10. Harada, H., Prasad, R.: Simulation and software radio for mobile communication. Bk&CD-Rom, pp. 29–61,165–202. Artech House Publishers (2002)

An Improved Marking Mechanism for Real-Time Video over DiffServ Networks

Lishui Chen, Guizhong Liu, and Fan Zhao

School of Electronics and Information Engineering, Xi'an Jiaotong University, 710049, Xi'an, China
liugz@xjtu.edu.cn, chenls@mail.xjtu.edu.cn, zhaofan@mail.xjtu.edu.cn

Abstract. As is well known, in video applications the former P frames are more important than the subsequent P frames in coding/decoding order due to the inter-prediction architecture adopted by the advanced video coding standards. A source marking mechanism based on this fact is proposed accordingly in this paper, along with an improved two rate three color maker (ITRTCM) scheme, which takes into account both the source mark value of a packet and the current network status. The results of ITRTCM are compared with those of the two rate three color marker (TRTCM), the enhanced token bucket three color marker (ETBTCM) and the TypeMapping method.

Keywords: DiffServ, TRTCM, ETBTCM, TypeMapping and ITRTCM.

1 Introduction

With the rapid development of multimedia applications over Internet like distant learning, video conference, Voice over IP (VoIP), and Video on Demand (VoD), it is more and more needed for Internet to provide Quality of Services (QoS). However, current IP networks provide only the Best Effort Service. Although those applications are loss-tolerant, packet loss and packet delay still have great impact on the end-to-end video quality and even make it unacceptable sometimes. Therefore, IETF defined two service models, namely the IntServ model [1] and the DiffServ model [2], to offer QoS in IP networks. Due to the simplicity, availability and scalability, DiffServ is more attractive to be applied in IP networks.

There are many mapping schemes [4,5,6], a simple one is TypeMapping which maps I frame packets to green, P frame packets to yellow and B frame packets to red, however, as described in [7], there is no policing algorithm involved at the edge of DiffServ domain to check the conformance of the incoming packets and the importance indication of a packet may be disregarded if legacy packet markers such as Two Rate Three Color Marker (TRTCM) [8], which marks the video packets only according the network condition and never taking the relative importance of the packets into account, are applied at the ingress of the DiffServ domain. So Chih-Heng Ke et. al. propose a two marker system in [7], application-level source marker and Enhanced Token Bucket Three Color Marker (ETBTCM), considering both the

H.H.S. Ip et al. (Eds.): PCM 2007, LNCS 4810, pp. 510–519, 2007.

relative importance of packets and the network condition, to improve the delivery quality of MPEG video streams. There, if there are sufficient tokens in the bucket, all frame packets are marked as green. However, when there are insufficient tokens for the packet to pass, less important packets are marked with a higher drop probability, i.e. red for B frame packets and yellow for P or I frame packets.

Many video coding standards, e.g., MPEG-x and H.26x, use motion-compensated prediction in order to gain better coding efficiency at the expense of inducing a dependency structure among the encoded video frames. A frame may use its former frames in coding/decoding order as references. Generally speaking, a Group of Pictures (GoP), which usually contains one I frame, several P frames and several B frames, are coded one time when an encoder is encoding a video sequence. P frame uses one I frame or its former decoded P frame as a reference and B frame uses at most two previously-decoded frames as references. So timely delivery of packets of a frame does not guarantee a good video quality to end-users, except that all the frames to which this particular predicted frame references are received and decoded correctly. Even if there is an error concealment mechanism which can recover the frames with wrong or one or more of whose packets are lost in their way, the difference (resulting error) between the frame recovered by error concealment scheme and its original frame will propagate along the subsequent frames in decoding order and this may have greatly impact on the video quality. From the description above, we can find the fact that not all the frames in a GoP have the same importance. In the DiffServ architecture, the simplest way of mapping packets importance to Differentiated Services Code Point (DSCP) is green to I slice packets, yellow to P slice packets and red to B slice packets based on the fact above [4]. However, we think that although all the B slice packets have the same importance, the slice packets of different P frames in a single GoP have different importance. For the previously-decoded P frames may have impact on all subsequent frames in decoding order in a GoP due to the prediction structure of video coding standards and those subsequent fames use its former P frame as a reference. In order to mapping more than three types of source marks (16 kinds in this study) to three classes drop precedence in a single Assured Forward (AF) class, we develop a new marker called Improved Two Rate Three Color Marker (ITRTCM) which will be placed at the ingress of the DiffServ domain to complete this mapping according to the source marks, which represent the relative importance of the packets, and the network condition when the packets get to the edge router.

The remainder of this paper is organized as follows. The delivery system proposed is presented in details in Section 2. In Section 3 the simulation model is introduced and our experimental results are also presented and discussed in this section, and a brief conclusion is presented in Section 4.

2 The Novel Delivery System

The video packets delivery system consists of the source marking scheme and the edge marking scheme, and we will illustrate them in details as follows. It is important to note that we only consider the video streaming application and never consider the QoS of audio which goes with the video in a multimedia application in this study.

2.1 The General Novel Source Marking Scheme

The basic idea of this source marking scheme is based on the observation that packets of different P frames have different impacts on the quality of their subsequence frames in the decoding order. In a single GoP the first P frames are more important. Let N denotes the size of a GoP with one I frame, Np P frames and $N-Np-1$ B frames. We define 16 importance grades for video packets, ranging from 1 to 16. 1's are assigned to the I frame packets, which are the most important packets; 16's are assigned to the B frame packets. The other 14 values from 2 to 15 are assigned to the P frame packets in terms of their relative importance. The greater values are assigned to the less important P frame packets.

Let i be the number of P frames in a GoP. $prior[i]$ stands for the mark value, which represents the importance of the packets of the ith P frame, defined by

$$prior[i] = \lceil \frac{14}{Np} * i \rceil + 1, \quad (i = 1 \ldots Np) \tag{1}$$

where $\lceil T \rceil$ represents the smallest integer greater than T, and $prior[i]$ ranges from 2 to 15.

2.2 Improved Two Rate Three Color Marker

There are totally 16 types of source marks in our proposed source marking algorithm, but there are only 3 colors in a single AF class. So we should develop a reasonable mapping between the source marks and colors. Considering the fact that different source marks stand for different importance of packets, and at the same time the variable network condition, we use a viable algorithm for metering and marking at the edge of a DiffServ domain. In our marking algorithm, there are 4 traffic parameters: a Peak Information Rate (PIR) and its associated Peak Burst Size (PBS) and a Committed Information Rate (CIR) and its associated Committed Burst Size (CBS), which is the same as TRTCM [8]. PBS is the size of token bucket P and PIR is the rate of token produced in P, and CBS is the size of token bucket C and CIR is the rate of token produced in C. As is well known, the token count of the bucket reveals current network status; the less the token count is in the bucket, the busier the network is. We use 5 thresholds ($CBS/5$ and 0 for bucket C, $PBS/2$, $PBS/4$ and 0 for bucket P in our study) for dividing the network status into 6 different grades according to the vacancy degrees of the buckets P and C, with each grade being associated with a special marking scheme. Assume that the edge begins to work at time 0, the token count in P at time t is represented by $Tp(t)$ and the token count in C at time t is represented by $Tc(t)$, then $Tp(0) = PBS$ and $Tc(0) = CBS$. Supposing a packet with size B arrives at the edge at time t and the edge route use the algorithm ITRTCM shown in Fig. 1 to mark it. It is worthwhile to note that $prior$ represents the value of the source mark of a packet.

```
If Tc(t) - B > CBS/5
        The packet is green;
        Tp is decremented by B;
        Tc is decremented by B;
Else if 0 < Tc(t) - B ≤ CBS/5
    If prior < 1 + 3*14*(Tc(t) - B)/CBS
            The packet is green;
            Tp is decremented by B;
            Tc is decremented by B;
    Else
            The packet is yellow;
            Tp is decremented by B;
    End
Else if Tp(t) - B > PBS/2
    If prior == 1
            The packet is green;
            Tp is decremented by B;
            Tc is decremented by B;
    Else if prior == 16
            The packet is red;
    Else
            The packet is yellow;
            Tp is decremented by B;
    End
Else if PBS/4 < Tp(t) - B ≤ PBS/2
    If prior > 1 + 4*14*[(Tc(t) - B)/CBS - 1/4]
            The packet is red;
    Else
            The packet is yellow;
            Tp is decremented by B;
    End
Else if Tp(t) - B ≤ PBS/4
    If prior == 1
            The packet is yellow;
            Tp is decremented by B;
    Else
            The packet is red;
    End
Else
    The packet is red;
End
```

Fig. 1. Metering and Marking of ITRTCM

3 Simulation

3.1 Design of the Simulation Experiment

We use the Network Simulation 2 (NS2) simulator [12] to complete our experiment. Fig. 2 shows the simulation network topology. It is a simple network topology with a DS region consisting of two DS domains. The egress, named Edge router, of DS domain 1 is the ingress of DS domain 2, and each of the DS domains has a bottleneck, bottleneck 1 and bottleneck 2.

Due to the fact that we need a long time simulation but there are no video sequences longer than 5000 frames in [13], as the test video we choose a QCIF (size 176X144) format sequence which has about 5000 frames from the movie Star War. The sequence is encoded into an H.264 bit-stream with a mean bit rate of 384kb/s (represented by R_1). Each frame is divided into 5 slices, and the bit stream data of each of the slices is encapsulated into one Network Abstraction Layer Unit (NALU). At the same time the encoder generates a trace file, which contains the main information of all the NALUs such as the type, the length, the index and so on, to be used by the network simulator. A traffic generator uses the trace file as an input to generate a video flow. In domain 1, there are two competing traffics, a CBR traffic flow 1 with a rate of 350kb/s (R_2), and an on-off background traffic flow with an exponential distribution with the mean packet size of 1000 bytes, the burst time interval 100 ms, the idle time interval 50 ms and the rate of 250kb/s (R_3). All of the three stream sources are connected to the Ingress router 1. There is a CBR traffic flow 2, with a rate of 200kb/s (R_4) generated by the CBR background traffic sender 2 which connects with the ingress of the DS domain 2. The senders and their corresponding receivers are shown in Fig. 2.

We can change the bandwidth of the bottleneck to obtain 5 different levels of input load (110, 120, 130,140 and 150% of the bottleneck's capacity), needing not to change the input load actually. For instances, the total input load ($Total_{input1}$) of domain 1 in this simulation is 984kb/s ($R_1 + R_2 + R_3$) and that ($Total_{input2}$) of domain 2 is 834kb/s ($R_1 + R_3 + R_4$), and according to the input load demand the corresponding five levels' bandwidthes of bottleneck 1 ($BW1$) and bottleneck 2 ($BW2$) are respectively 895kb/s and 758kb/s, 820kb/s and 695kb/s, 757kb/s and 642kb/s, 703kb/s and 596kb/s, and 656kb/s and 556kb/s. For each input load level, five subscription levels (R_{af}) of DiffServ AF (40 60, 80, 100 and 120% of the bottleneck's capacity) are considered. Here the level of DiffServ AF stands for the rate of "green" packets committed to the network to carry [4]. The marker in the ingress use parameters as follows:

$$CIR = R_{af} * BW * R / Total_{bitrate}, \tag{2}$$

where $BW = BW1, BW2$, $R = R_1, R_2, R_3, R_4$ and $Total_{bitrate} = Total_1, Total_2$,CBS, PIR and PBS parameters according to $PIR = \alpha \cdot CIR$, $CBS = \beta \cdot CIR$, $PBS = \beta \cdot PIR$ with $\alpha = 2$ and $\beta = 1.5$ which are recommended in [10]. For example, when $R_{af} = 80\%$

and the level of input load is 120%, the CIR, CBS, PIR and PBS for the Video sender in domain 1 is respectively 256kb/s ($80\%*(820kb/s)*(384kb/s)/(984kb/s)$), 48k bytes ($\beta*CIR/8$), and 512kb/s ($\alpha*CIR$) and 96k bytes. The core routers in the two DS domains implement the Weighted Random Early Detection (WRED) mechanism for the active queue management. In our experiment the WRED parameters, namely the minimum threshold, the maximum threshold and the drop probability, are specified respectively as 10, 15 and 0.02 for the green packets, 7, 10 and 0.10 for the yellow packets and 3, 6, and 0.20 for the red packets.

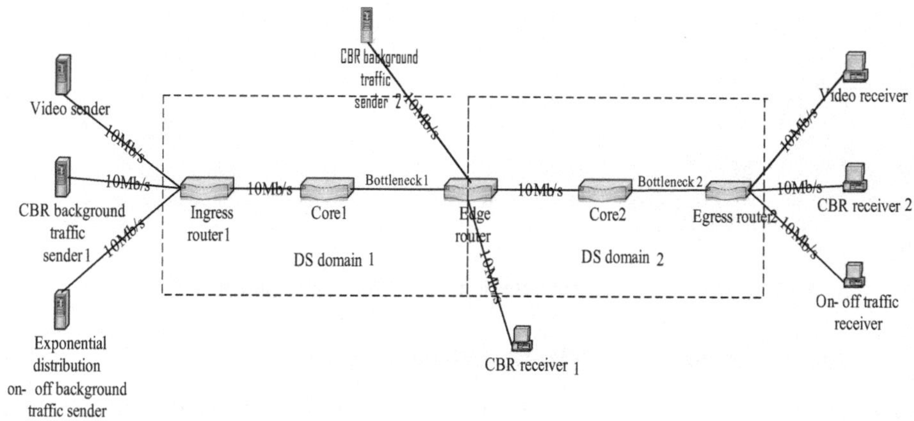

Fig. 2. Simulation Network Topology

3.2 Comparison on Different Marking Schemes with Different Packet Loss Ratios

Fig. 3 shows the video flows' receipt rate for each of the subscription levels of DiffServ with R_{af} =60%. The three subfigures are the receipt rates of the I slice packets, P slice packets and B slices packets respectively. The four marking schemes are TRTCM, ETBTCM, TypeMapping which is the direct mapping from the three frame types (I, P and B) to three colors [4], and ITRTCM. The TypeMapping scheme can obviously protect the I-type packets, but the loss rate of P-type packets and that of B-type packets become larger and larger as the network load increases, even reaches a quantity greater than 70% when the network load is 150% of its bottleneck capacity. We can easily imagine what the video quality becomes when using this marking scheme when the network is badly in congestion. In Fig.3, the receipt rate of the I-type packets when using ITRTCM scheme is greater than the other two schemes and the effect is more and more distinct as the payload of the network increases. When R_{af} =60%, although our results of the P-type packets and the B-type packets are sometimes lower than those of the other methods, there are no significant difference along them. The same results are obtained when R_{af} =40%, 80% and 100%. So a simple conclusion can be drawn: ITRTCM can effectively protect more important packets and never has great impact on the transmission of less important packets and it is more adaptive for marking video flow packets before they enter DiffServ networks.

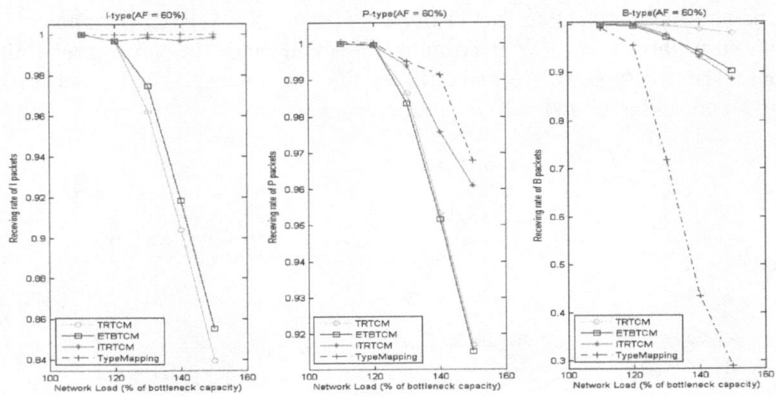

Fig. 3. Comparison of the receipt rates among the four mark scheme with R_{af} =60%

3.3 Objective Quality of End-To-End Video Delivery

Results presented in 3.2 only show the different receipt rates of the different marking schemes at different network payloads. Although the results with the scheme we proposed are better than those of the other schemes, it does not fully present the advantage of our scheme for video delivery. Because the final purpose is to provide a better video quality and our source marking scheme is designed not only for protecting I-type packets but for protecting all the correspondingly important packets which contain not only I slice packets but the anterior P slice packets in decoding order.

Here we only present the results of a scenario of R_{af} =60% with 5 network payloads for end-to-end objective quality of video delivery. The reason we choose R_{af} =60% are that the results of ITRTCM with R_{af} =40% is obviously better than those of the other schemes for all the receipt rates are higher than those of the other and the case R_{af} =60% can well stand for the other two cases. Fig. 4 shows the PSNRs of the frames from 1500 to 2000 with their respective network payload from 140%. We only consider three schemes in the figures except the TypeMapping method because there are so many P frame packets lost in their way while adopting the TypeMapping method that its resulting bit stream can not be correctly decoded using JM11.0 [14]. When the TypeMapping method is used, there are only 1200 fames which are correctly decoded when network the payload is 140% of the bottleneck capability, and 850 frames correctly decoded when the network payload is 150% of the bottleneck bandwidth. We can see from those figures, that the line labeled "ITRTCM" is higher and higher than the other two lines, that is, with the network payload increasing our scheme can still better protect the important information and get a better end-to-end objective quality. The mean PSNRs of Y, U and V of the 4 schemes when R_{af} =60% is listed in Table 1, Table 2 and Table 3 respectively. It is worth to mention that only the frames which have been correctly decoded are considered while we compute the mean PSNR of using TypeMapping scheme. Results in these tables show the same conclusion drawn above. When the network payload is 150% of the bottleneck capability, the PSNR of Y component using ITRTCM is even 5.5978 greater than that using ETBTCM and 6.0825 greater than that TRTCM, and even 10.0045 greater than that using TypeMapping method; the PSNRs of U and V components are also greater than those using the other methods.

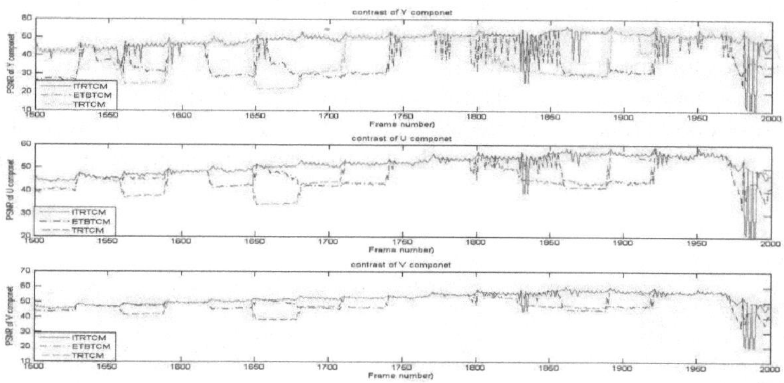

Fig. 4. Comparison of PSNR at network load 140% of the bottleneck bandwidth (R_{af} =60%)

Table 1. Mean PSNR of Y component

Payload Psnr Schemes	110%	120%	130%	140%	150%
ITRTCM	42.3418	42.1673	41.1083	39.1970	37.1724
ETRTCM	42.3418	42.0676	39.0226	34.1555	30.5746
TRTCM	42.3418	42.1265	38.8825	34.5791	31.0899
TypeMapping	42.2750	41.3826	36.4745	29.7828	27.1179

Table 2. Mean PSNR of U component

Payload Psnr Schemes	110%	120%	130%	140%	150%
ITRTCM	45.2046	45.1256	44.8817	44.2310	43.6584
ETRTCM	45.2046	45.0976	44.1862	42.5171	41.1196
TRTCM	45.2046	45.1261	44.0705	42.6282	41.0003
TypeMapping	45.1523	44.9581	43.4666	36.3833	34.7379

Table 3. Mean PSNR of V component

Payload / Psnr / Schemes	110%	120%	130%	140%	150%
ITRTCM	45.9521	45.8980	45.6991	45.2086	44.7275
ETRTCM	45.9521	45.8766	45.1112	43.9649	42.7901
TRTCM	45.9521	45.8966	45.0581	44.1458	42.7435
TypeMapping	45.9105	45.7489	44.4405	40.2234	39.1763

3.4 Subjective Quality of End-To-End Video Delivery

In order to provide a more intuitive end-to-end quality comparison, subjective visual qualities with different delivery schemes are shown in Fig. 5. The numbers on the left of the pictures are the frame numbers in the display order and the marks above the pictures represent the marking schemes which are used. Obviously, the visual quality obtained by using ITRTCM is better than those using TRTCM and ETBTCM. Due to the reason mentioned in 3.3 above, we do not compare the results with TypeMapping in use.

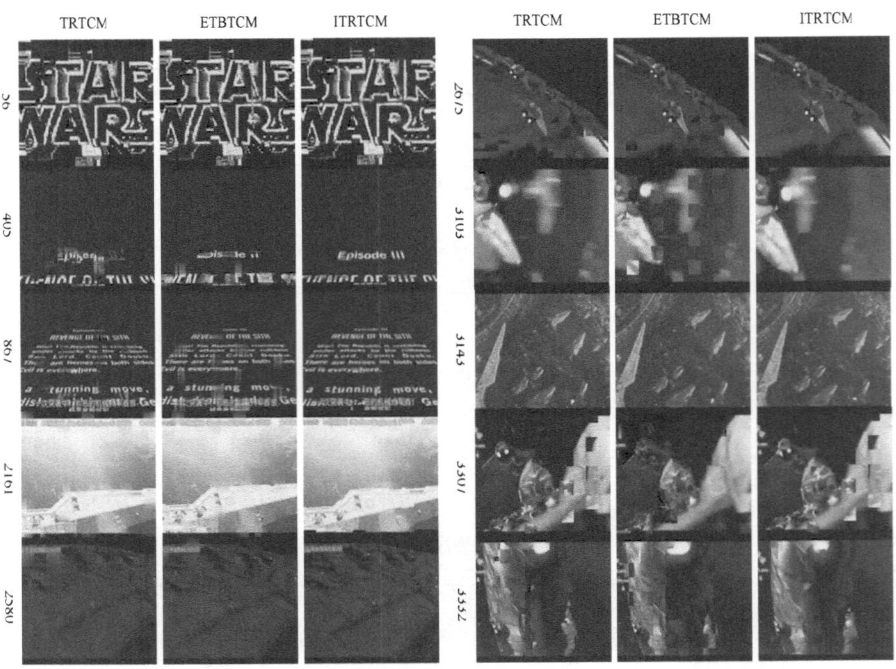

Fig. 5. Comparison of visual quality when the network payload is 150% of the bottleneck bandwidth (R_{af} =60%)

4 Conclusion

In this study we first developed a source marking at the application level according to the different importance of I, P and B frame packets, the relative importance of the different P frame packets in a GoP. Then we designed a novel marking algorithm for the edge routers of a DS domain. At last, we compared the effects not only in the network loss rate in different scenarios, but also the end-to-end objective video quality and the subjective visual quality with the other three methods. From the simulation results we can draw the conclusions that our proposed method can protect the more important packets in a more effective way, and that the end-to-end video quality is greatly improved due to the former P frame packets in the coding/decoding order receive a better protection.

References

[1] Braden, R., Clark, D.D., Shenker, S.: Integrated services in the Internet architecture: an overview. RFC 1633 (June 1994)

[2] Blake, S., et al.: An architecture for differentiated services. RFC 2475 (December 1998)

[3] Heinanen, J., Baker, F., Weiss, W., Wroclawski, J.: Assured Forwarding PHB Group. Internet Standards Track. RFC 2597, IETF (June 1999)

[4] Orozco, J., Ros, D.: DiffServ-Aware Streaming of H.264 video. In: PV 2004. Proceedings of 14th International Packet Video Workshop, Irvine (CA), USA (December 2004)

[5] Wenger, S., Horowitz, M.: Flexible macroblock ordering; a new error resilience tool for IP based video. In: Das, S.K., Bhattacharya, S. (eds.) IWDC 2002. LNCS, vol. 2571, Springer, Heidelberg (2002)

[6] Wenger, S.: H.264/AVC over IP. IEEE Transactions on Circuits and Systems for Video Technology 13(7), 645–656 (2003)

[7] Ke, C.-H., Shieh, C.-K., Hwang, W.-S., Ziviani, A.: Two Markers system for improved MPEG video delivery in a DiffServ Network. IEEE Communication Letters 9(9) (April 2005)

[8] Heinanen, J., Gu´erin, R.: A two rate three color marker. RFC 2698 (September 1999)

[9] Wiegand, T., Sullivan, G.J., Bj¢ntegaard, G., Luthra, A.: Overview of the H.264/AVC Video Coding Standard. IEEE Trans. Circuits Syst. Video Technol. 13(7), 560–576 (2003)

[10] Medina, O., Orozco, J., Ros, D.: Bandwidth sharing under the Assured Forwarding PHB. Annales des Telecommunications 59(3-4) (March-April 2004)

[11] Casner, S., Frederick, R., Jacobson, V.: A Transport Protocol for Real-Time Applications. RFC 3550 (July 2003)

[12] NS, http://www.isi.edu/nsnam/ns

[13] Video Quality Meter, Institute for Telecommunication Sciences, USA, http://www.jts.bldrdoc.gov/n3/video/vqmdownload_US.htm

[14] JM11.0, http://ftp3.itu.int/av-arch/jvt-site/

Priority Ordering and Packetization for Scalable Video Multicast with Network Coding*

Song Xiao[1,2], Hui Wang[2], and C.-C. Jay Kuo[2]

[1] ISN key Lab, Xidian University, Xi'an, Shaanxi, 710071, China
[2] Ming Hsieh Dept. of Electrical Engineering, University of Southern California
Los Angeles, CA, 90089, USA
xiaosong@mail.xidian.edu.cn, wanghui@usc.edu, cckuo@sipi.usc.edu

Abstract. The integration of scalable video representation and network coding (NC) offers an excellent solution to robust and flexible video multicast over IP networks. In this work, we examine one critical component in this system, *i.e.* video priority ordering and packetization at the source of the multicast tree. First, a GOP-adaptive layer-based packet priority ordering algorithm is proposed to allow flexible prioritized video transmission with unequal error protection. Then, a packetization scheme tailored to NC delivery is discussed. Simulation results are given to demonstrate that the proposed algorithms offer better performance in video quality and bandwidth efficiency as compared the SNR-based packetization method.

Keywords: scalable video coding (SVC), network coding (NC), robust.

1 Introduction

With the maturity of video coding technologies, networking infra-structures and the rapid growth of computing power, digital video such as video-conferencing, multimedia chatting, video on demand (VoD), IPTV has reached us over wired and wireless IP networks. Video transmission over broadband networks in general and wireless networks in particular suffers from time-varying bandwidth and packet delay and loss. The scalable video coding (SVC) standard [1],[2], developed as an extension of H.264/MPEG-4 AVC, has attracted a lot of research interests for its flexible scalability and adaptability to a wide range of varying network conditions, applications and terminals. An efficient and robust SVC transmission system is expected to overcome these challenges for reliable video transmission.

Research has been conducted to achieve robust video transmission over wired or wireless IP networks extensively for years. Unequal error protection (UEP) [3], [4], [5] based on priority encoding transmission (PET) [6] offers one of the most promising techniques among numerous proposed methods. For example, the data partition mode in H.264 divides a bit stream into three types of data of different importance so that different channel coding rates can be applied to them. Rate

* This project is supported by the NSFC (No. 60702058) and Chinese Scholarship Council.

H.H.S. Ip et al. (Eds.): PCM 2007, LNCS 4810, pp. 520–529, 2007.

allocation to minimize the distortion or power as well as maximize video quality was considered by Xiao *et al.* in [3]. For SVC transmission, Fang and Chau [4] proposed a scheme to allocate an unequal amount of protection based on Reed-Solomon codes to different frames of a GOP (*i.e.*, temporal scalability) or the progressive bit stream in each frame (*i.e.*, SNR scalability) using the genetic algorithm. Schierl *et al.* [5] used the Raptor forward error correction (FEC) codes to protect SVC layers of different importance. Only source and channel coding methods have been considered in these methods. While packets are transmitted in the network, they are delivered by the traditional store-and-forward (S/F) mechanism in intermediate nodes.

More recently, network coding (NC) [7]-[9] has been extensively studied by researchers in the information theory community. NC allows packets to be encoded at intermediate nodes and can achieve the maximum multicast information rate. The application of NC to wireless video multicasting using the H.264/SVC video format was studied by Wang, Xiao and Kuo [7]. However, a critical component in the whole system was not well addressed in [7]; namely, video packetization at the source node, due to the space limit. This work serves as a companion paper to [7] by focusing on the source video packetization problem.

In this research, a GOP-adaptive layer-based priority ordering algorithm is proposed to organize the H.264/SVC video bitstream, which makes the whole system more robust under the same bandwidth condition than the default SVC ordering scheme or the SNR-based ordering algorithm. Then, the packetization algorithm optimized for NC delivery is discussed.

The rest of this paper is organized as follows. Sec. 2 presents an overview of the NC-based video multicast system. Sec. 3 describes the packet priority ordering algorithm and the packetization algorithm in detail. The proposed ordering scheme is compared with other ordering algorithms in Sec. 4. Concluding remarks and future research directions are given in Sec. 5.

Fig. 1. The proposed SVC video multicast system using the NC technique in the network

2 Video Multicast with Network Coding

The proposed SVC video multicast system using the NC technique is shown in Fig. 1. First, SVC video coding and packetization are performed at the source node. Then, the random linear network coding (RLNC) technique is conducted at intermediate nodes of a multicast tree with multiple in-degrees. Finally, the Gaussian elimination method is used for random linear network decoding, which is followed by packet reconstruction at all receiving nodes. In this work, we focus on the task on the first stage, *i.e.*, source video packetization. For more details in RLNC encoding and decoding, we refer to [7].

There are three major steps in preparing packets at the source node as detailed below.

Step 1: SVC bitstream generation and priority layering

The prioritized layers of H.264/SVC are represented as $L_0,\dots,L_{M-1}$. Each layer is composed by symbols $s_j \in L_i$ over the finite Galois field F.

Step 2: Packet mapping

Different amounts of redundant protection bits are assigned to layers of different priority, and these data are interleaved into packets. Most of the PET-based methods [3], [4] adopt the *(n,k)* Reed-Solomon code, where *n-k* redundant packets to protect *k* source packets. With NC, we can use zeros rather than RS codes [7] to simplify the packetization process. For example, some packets are concatenation of symbols from all layers $(P_i = s_{1,i} \,\|\, s_{2,i} \,\|\, \dots, \|\, s_{M-1,i})$ while others are concatenation of symbols from some layers and redundant protection bits $(P_j = 0 \,\|\, 0 \,\|\, s_{m,j} \,\|\, \dots, \|\, s_{M-1,j})$. By interleaving data this way, it helps equalize the importance of different packets. As a result, there is no need for intermediate nodes to differentiate the importance of each packet in the NC mixing process, which simplifies the design and maintenance of multicast trees.

Step 3: Packet loading

Consider a video stream of N packets. Due to the finite input bandwidth, we do not pump all N packets into the source node simultaneously. Instead, they are organized into multiple groups, and each group is sent to the source node per unit time. This group of packets is represented by G^t where t is the time index. Packets within the same group are mixed in intermediate nodes of the network using the RLNC algorithm. The loading time τ is the total time required for the source node to transmit all the packets of the video stream. There are two factors that determine the loading time. One is the capacity of out-going links of source node denoted by C_s, which limits the amount of data to be sent to the network. The other is the bottleneck of the network, which corresponds to the minimum cut of the graph denoted by $C_{\min}$. If $C = \min(C_s, C_{\min})$, we need $\tau = N/C$ time units to send out all N packets to the receiver.

In the following sections, we describe Step 1 and Step 2 in detail; namely, the packet priority ordering and packtization algorithms.

3 Priority Ordering and Packetization

3.1 Priority Ordering

When transmitting SVC video over the network, the source content is encoded once with the highest resolution and bit-rate. If there is no error and/or packet loss during the transmission, different receivers can extract a bit stream of different resolutions according to its own capability. However, if some errors and/or packet loss occur, reconstructed video quality may degrade.

The default ordering of the SVC bit stream is done according to the temporal layer (frame) in the unit of GOP. Each temporal layer contains several spatial layers that may contain one base SNR layer and several enhancement SNR layers. The frontal portion is the base layer. At the same time, SVC uses the network abstraction layer (NAL) packet as its basis unit for transmission over the network. When one NAL packet is lost, all packets that depend on this NAL packet will be affected. Sometimes, it may make the subsequent bit stream un-decodable at the receiver. As a result, the impact of packet loss to SVC video transmission over networks must be considered carefully.

A 3D layer based ordering algorithm is proposed in this work to organize SVC video with prioritization within one GOP. It can have the highest quality (or least distortion) under a certain number of correctly received NAL packets. In other words, the impact of NAL packet loss to the overall performance of the GOP can be significantly reduced by the proposed ordering algorithm. The method can be applied to bandwidth adaptation. When the target resolution is determined, the method can provide optimal performance to the receivers under different bandwidth conditions.

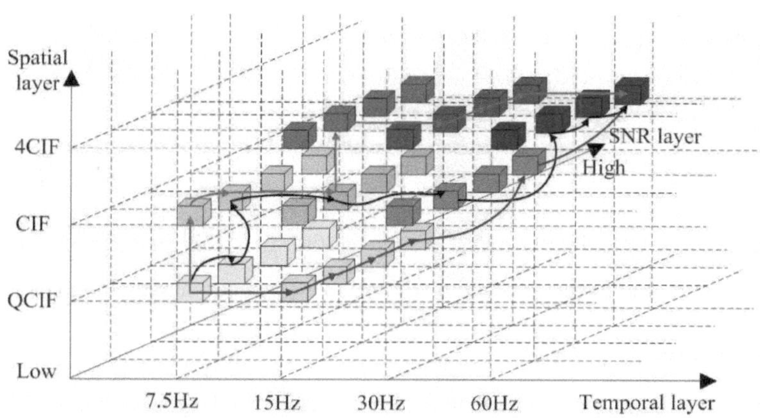

Fig. 2. Illustration of the path selection process, where lines with different colors represent different paths from the start point to the destination point

The objective of the method is to find the optimal path in the 3D coordinates to get the optimal rate-distortion (RD) performance, where the 3D co-ordinates are formed by temporal, spatial and SNR layers as shown in Fig. 2. By the optimal path, we mean the optimal rate distortion performance from the lowest spatial, temporal and SNR resolution (*i.e.,* the base layer) to the highest resolution (*i.e.,* the inclusion of all enhancement layers). We see from the figure that there are many candidate paths for selection. Since each GOP of different video sequences may have different characteristics, the path may vary from one GOP to the other. The basic idea of the proposed algorithm is to choose several candidates under certain constraints at each local step and then integrate these local decisions to form a path that provides the optimal RD performance.

Let (s,t,q) be the 3D integer layer indices, where s, t and q are spatial, temporal and quality layer indices, respectively. The lowest resolution is (0,0,0) while the highest resolution is (s^*,t^*,q^*). By ordering, we map the 3D coordinates into 1D array, *i.e,*

$$L(s,t,q)=i,$$

where L represents a specific ordering scheme. We use L_j to denote the jth element of the 1D array ordered by scheme L. It is clear that a legitimate order has to meet the following criterion:

$$PSNR_{L_i} > PSNR_{L_j}, \quad \forall i > j.$$

In other words, video quality improves if an additional layer is added into existing video.

A greedy algorithm to select a legitimate path is described below.

- **Initialization** ($i = 0$)
  The lowest layer $(0,0,0)$ is chosen as the start point of the path.
- **Iteration** ($i = 0,1,...$)
  Suppose that $L(s,t,q) = i$ is the current 1D index. We consider three possible positions $(s+1,t,q)$, $(s,t+1,q)$ and $(s,t,q+1)$ as the possible next 1D index denoted by $j=i+1$. Then, we choose the following one:

$$L_j^* = \arg\max \frac{\partial PSNR_{L_j}}{\partial R_{L_j}},$$

where ∂R_{L_j} is the rate increase due to the addition of this new layer. The above process is repeated until the maximum resolution along each dimension is reached.

3.2 Packetization Algorithm

After priority ordering, we consider the packetization problem. Assuming all NALs in the pth GOP are partitioned into M layers $L_i, i = 0,1,...M-1$. These M layers are packetized into N packets, each of which has K bytes as shown in Fig. 3. The width and the height of each layer are w_i and h_i bytes respectively. Then, we have

$$\sum_{i=0}^{M-1} w_i h_i = R_p \tag{1}$$

$$\sum_{i=0}^{M-1} h_i + H = K \tag{2}$$

$$w_i \le w_j \ when \quad i < j \tag{3}$$

where R_p is the total bit rate of the pth GOP.

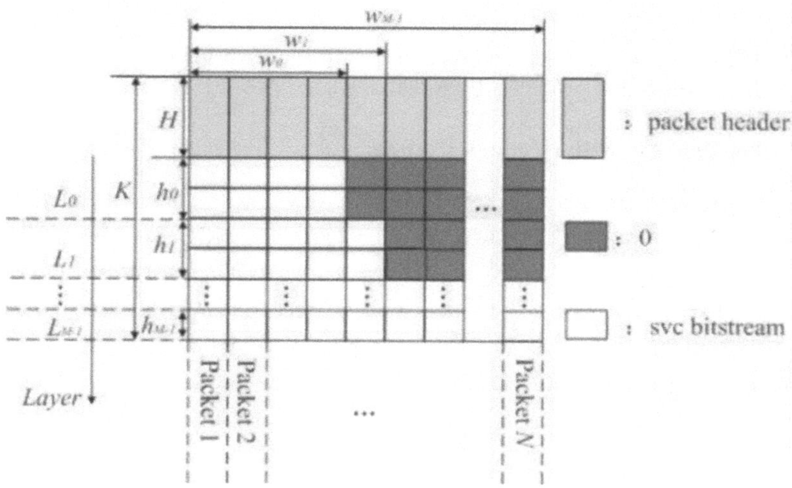

Fig. 3. The packetization structure

Usually, H and K are fixed parameters. N is always smaller or equal to C_s, which is the capacity of outgoing channel of source node. We show how to find parameters w_i and $h_i, i = 0,1,...,M-1$, below.

The distortion function can be written as

$$D(p) = \sum_{i=0}^{M-1} (\Delta D_i \cdot P(.)), \tag{4}$$

where $\Delta D_i = \begin{cases} D_i & i = 0 \\ D_i - D_{i-1} & 0 < i \le M-1 \end{cases}$, and $P(.)$ is the probability that the ith layer could be correctly received. The objective is to find parameters to minimize the overall distortion or maximize the quality of decoded video. This constrained optimization problem can be formulated as

$$\min_{w_i \in w_{opt}, h_i \in h_{opt}} D \text{ subject to constraints (1)-(3)} \tag{5}$$

By using random linear network coding (RLNC), the source information is distributed among different packets. For example, for the *ith* layer, w_i source information is distributed among N packets. The more the source information is distributed, the higher the probability of correct reception. Then, we can relate $P(.)$ in (4) with the ratios of w_i and replace the objective function in (5) by the following:

$$\Delta = \sum_{i=0}^{M-1} \left(\frac{D_0}{D_i} - \frac{w_0}{w_i}\right) \tag{6}$$

$$\min_{w_i \in w_{opt}, h_i \in h_{opt}} \Delta \quad \text{subject to constraints (1)-(3)} \tag{7}$$

The fast bidirectional local search algorithm with iterative improvement can be used to solve the optimization problem. For details, we refer to [3].

3.3 Packet Delivery with Network Coding

After priority ordering and packetization, we have w_{M-1} source symbol vectors, denoted by $x_j = [x_{j,1}, x_{j,2,} ... x_{j,K}]$, $j = 0,1,...w_{M-1} - 1$, for one GOP. To transmit them, we can follow the standard network coding framework as stated in [8]-[9]. Consider an acyclic graph (V, E), a sender $s \in V$ and a set of receivers $T \subseteq V$. Then, each edge $e \in E$ dispersed from a node $V = in(e)$ carries a symbol $y(e)$ that is a linear combination of source symbols, *i.e.*

$$y(e) = \sum_{j=0}^{w_{M-1}-1} f_j(e) x_j \text{ ,}$$

where the vector of coefficients $f(e) = [f_0(e), f_1(e)...f_{w_{M-1}-1}(e)]$ is known as the global kernel vector on edge e. It can be determined recursively by local kernel vectors that are randomly chosen from finite field F and entering symbols. Any receiver $t \in T$ receiving w_i $(i = 0,1...M-1)$ or more incoming symbols in form

$$\begin{bmatrix} y(e_0) \\ y(e_1) \\ ... \\ y(e_{w_i}) \end{bmatrix} = \begin{bmatrix} f(e_0) & f_1(e_0) & ... & f_{w_i}(e_0) \\ f(e_1) & f_1(e_1) & ... & f_{w_i}(e_1) \\ ... & ... & ... & ... \\ f(e_{w_i}) & f_1(e_{w_i}) & ... & f_{w_i}(e_{w_i}) \end{bmatrix} \begin{bmatrix} x_0 \\ x_1 \\ ... \\ x_{w_i} \end{bmatrix} = F_e \begin{bmatrix} x_0 \\ x_1 \\ ... \\ x_{w_i} \end{bmatrix} \tag{8}$$

can recover source symbols $x_0, x_1 ... x_{w_i}$ as long as matrix F_e of global kernel vectors $f(e_0), f(e_1)...f(e_{w_i})$ has rank w_i. This implies that i source layers (including all layers small or equal to i) can be decoded correctly. During the package procedure, the global kernel vector is recorded at each packet header so that it can reach any receiver via received packets. This can be implemented by appending the jth global kernel vector to the jth source vector $x_j, 0 = 1,2..., w_{M-1} - 1$. Any receiver can recover the source vector by applying the Gaussian elimination algorithm to w_{M-1} or more received packets.

4 Simulation Results

To verify the efficiency of the proposed priority ordering and packetization algorithms, the bit stream generated by the SVC reference source code JSVM6 [2] was used. The standard sequences of mother&daughter(class A), foreman(class B) and football(class C) sequence of size 352×288, 30 frames per second and 300 frames in total were tested. The test sequences were coded by H.264/SVC with 2 spatial layers, 3 temporal layers and 2 SNR layers. The GOP size was 32, where the first frame of each GOP was intra-coded. A 3-tier multicast tree with 5 receive nodes with increasing access capacity were adopted to simulate the single source multicast network. The maximum in-degree of any intermediate node was 3. The finite field was of size 256. We set the target resolution to be full spatial, temporal and SNR resolutions. If the bit stream cannot be decoded due to the packet loss, error concealment of frame copy in the temporal domain and AVC half-sample interpolation filter ({1,-5, 20, 20,-5, 1}/32 of luminance and {16, 16}/32 of chrominance) in the spatial domain was used to achieve the target resolution.

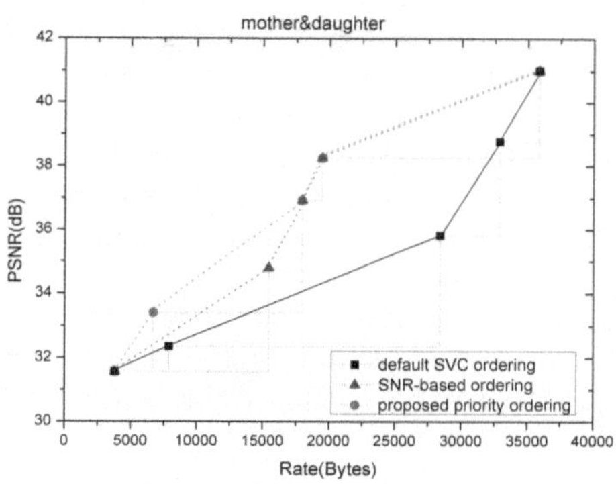

(a) Mother&daughter sequence

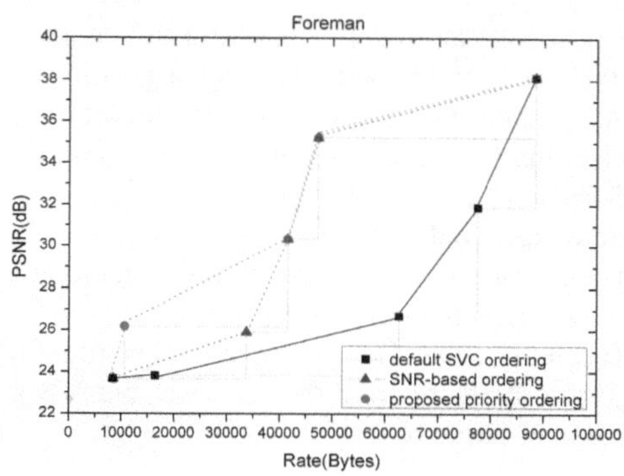

(b) Foreman sequence

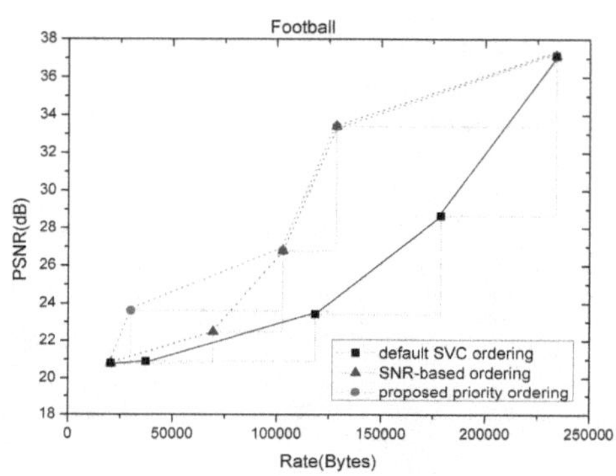

(c) Football sequence

Fig. 4. R-D performance Comparison of three priority ordering methods

In Fig. 4, we compare the R-D performance of three sequences using the default SVC ordering, the SNR-based ordering and the proposed priority ordering, where the averaged PSNR value of multiple simulation runs were shown. From the highest resolution layer to the lowest one, the bit stream is arranged first by the SNR layer, then the temporal layer and finally the spatial layer for the SNR-based ordering while it is arranged first by the temporal layer, then the spatial layer and finally the SNR layer for the default SVC ordering. When the bit rate is low, the proposed ordering method can provide better performance than the SNR-based ordering and the default SVC bit stream for all three sequences. As the bit rate reaches certain bit rate (about 18Kbytes for mother&daughter, 41Kbytes for foreman and 103Kbytes for football), the gap between the proposed ordering algorithm and the SNR-based ordering algorithm becomes very small, because the SNR layer contributes more to the R-D performance at this time and the proposed method will chose SNR layer as its increment direction. However, they are still much better than the default SVC ordering. When the bit rate reaches the highest spatial, temporal and SNR resolution, the difference among the three ordering methods disappears. It is also shown in the figures that the R-D performances of three priority ordering methods are content sensitive. For sequences with low spatial detail and low amount of movement (mother&daughter), the performance gap between the proposed ordering algorithm and the SNR-based ordering algorithm is the smallest (up to 1.8dB) among three sequences. For sequences with medium spatial detail and low amount of movement (foreman), the coding gain of proposed method beyond SNR-based method (up to 3.7dB) is even higher than that of the sequences with medium amount of movement and high spatial detail (football) (up to 2.8dB). This is probably because that, when the bit rate is small, the spatial enhancement layer often contributes more to the R-D performance, while the foreman (class B) sequence has less spatial details than the football (class C) sequence, when the full resolution is required but small bits are correctly decoded at the receiver, class B sequences will have better performance than class C sequences.

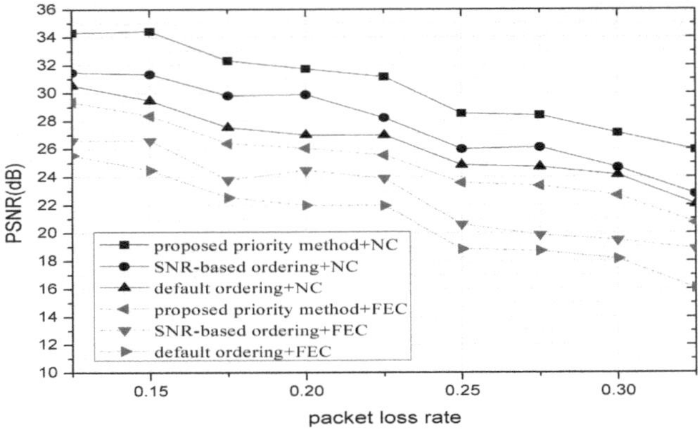

Fig. 5. Comparison of NC and S/F delivery mechanism using three orderings

The performance of the default SVC ordering, the SNR-based ordering and the proposed priority ordering at different packet loss rates for video transmission over a multicast network using NC and the store/forward (S/F) delivery with Reed Solomon codes is shown in Fig. 5. 1000 runs were used to verify the validity of the method. We see that NC delivery outperforms the S/F delivery by about 5dB in all packet loss rates for the same ordering. With the same delivery mechanism, the proposed ordering gives the best performance while the default SVC ordering method the worst. Our priority ordering outperforms the SNR based ordering by 3dB under different packet loss rates either the NC or the S/F delivery mechanism.

5 Conclusion and Future Work

A new priority ordering scheme and a packetization algorithm for H.264/SVC video multicasting using NC was proposed. The excellent performance of the proposed priority ordering and packetization with NC or S/F delivery was demonstrated by computer simulation. The proposed priority method can provide better performance than SNR-based and default SVC methods. The performance can be further improved by NC as compared to those using S/F with FEC. Our preliminary study reveals the significant advantage of integrating NC and H.264/SVC in video multicasting. More test cases, including different network topologies and video sequences, will be conducted in the near future.

References

1. Wiegand, T., Sullivan, G., Reichel, J., Schwarz, H., Wien, M.: Joint Draft 8 of SVC Amendment, ISO/IEC JTC/SC29/WG11 and ITU-T SG16 Q.6. Hangzhou, China (October 20-27, 2006)
2. Reichel, J., Schwarz, H., Wien, M.: Joint scalable video model JSVM-6, ISO/IEC JTC/SC29/WG11 and ITU-T SG16 Q.6, Geneva, Switzerland (31 March-7 April 2006)
3. Xiao, S., Wu, C., Du, J., Yang, Y.: Reliable transmission of H.264 video over wireless network. In: Proceedings of the 20th International Conference on Advanced Information Networking and Applications, Vienna, Austria vol. 2, pp. 84–88 (April 18-20, 2006)
4. Fang, T., Chau, L.P.: GOP- based channel rate allocation using genetic algorithm for scalable video streaming over error-prone networks. IEEE Trans. Image processing 15(6), 1323–1329 (2006)
5. Schierl, T., Ganger, K., Hellge, C., Wiegand, T.: SVC-based multisource streaming for robust video transmission in mobile ad hoc network. IEEE Wireless Comm. 13(5), 96–103 (2006)
6. Albanese, A., Blömer, J., Edmonds, J., Luby, M., Sudan, M.: Priority encoding transmission. IEEE Trans. Inf. Theory 42(6), 1737–1744 (1996)
7. Wang, H., Xiao, S., Jay Kuo, C.-C.: Robust and flexible wireless video multicast with network coding (accepted for publication in Globecom 2007)
8. Chou, P.A., Wu, Y., Jain, K.: Practical network coding. In: 51st Allerton Conference on Communication, Control, and Computing, Monticello, IL (October 2003)
9. Li, S-.Y.R., Yeung, R.W., Cai, N.: Linear network coding. IEEE Trans. On Information Theory 49(2), 371–381 (2003)

Error Concealment for INTRA-Frame Losses over Packet Loss Channels

Mengyao Ma[1], Oscar C. Au[2], Liwei Guo[2], Zhiqin Liang[2], and S.-H. Gary Chan[1]

[1] Dept. of Computer Science and Engineering
[2] Dept. of Electronic and Computer Engineering
Hong Kong University of Science and Technology
{myma,eeau,eeglw,zhiqin,gchan}@ust.hk

Abstract. In this paper, we propose an *Error Concealment* algorithm for INTRA-frame losses over packet loss channels. The novelty is that not only the INTRA-frame but also the subsequent INTER-frames are error concealed. We use the received INTRA-MBs to refine their neighbors based on the strong correlation between adjacent pixel values. In addition, *Motion Compensation* is used to reconstruct the INTER-pixel which has an INTRA-pixel in its motion trajectory. Both subjective and objective simulation results are given to demonstrate the performance of our proposed algorithm.

Keywords: Error Concealment, Error Propagation, Motion Compensation, Spatial Interpolation.

1 Introduction

Delivering video of good quality over the Internet or wireless networks is very challenging today, due to the use of predictive coding and *Variable Length Coding* (VLC) in video compression [1]. In block-based video coding method, if we use INTER-prediction mode, each macroblock (MB) is predicted from a previously decoded frame by *Motion Compensation.* If data loss occurs during the transmission, the corresponding frame will be corrupted, and this error will propagate to the subsequent frames because of INTER-prediction, until the next INTRA-coded frame is correctly received. In addition, a simple bit error in VLC can cause desynchronization; as a result, all the following bits cannot be used until a synchronization code arrives. Due to these facts, it is useful to develop some *Error Resilience* (ER) or *Error Concealment* (EC) techniques to control the errors in video transmission. Error resilience is usually applied at the encoder side. The coding efficiency of an ER codec is lower than a normal codec, because the encoder needs to introduce some redundancy to the stream. In the case of error, the decoder would use this additional information to reconstruct the video. On the other hand, error concealment is applied at the decoder side. It requires no

H.H.S. Ip et al. (Eds.): PCM 2007, LNCS 4810, pp. 530–538, 2007.

change to the encoder and does not increase the bit rate, so it is more preferable for low bit-rate applications [2][3].

Lots of EC algorithms have been developed for video communication, such as spatial interpolation using some smoothness measure and temporal compensation based on inter-frame correlation [4][5]. Boundary matching algorithm (BMA) is also developed to estimate the lost motion vectors (MV) [6][7]. Most of current EC methods assume that only a few MBs or slices in a video frame are lost. However, in low bit-rate applications, one frame is usually carried in one data packet in order to save transmission overhead. As a result, the loss of one packet will lead to the loss of one entire frame [3]. When frame loss occurs, we can copy the previous received frame to reconstruct the lose one. More sophisticated methods recover the motion vectors (MVs) in pixel or block level based on the assumption of translational motion, i.e. motion remains constant along motion trajectory [3][8][9].

As in most of the block-based video coding systems all the INTER-frames are encoded based on the preceding INTRA-frame, the protection and restoration of INTRA-frames is especially important for the decoding of subsequent frames. However, as far as we know, most of the EC algorithms in the literature focus on the restoration of INTER-frames, and only a few works deal with the EC of INTRA-frames. In addition, almost all these algorithms assume that only part of the INTRA-frame is corrupted so that the lost MBs can be reconstructed using the information from the neighbors [10][11]. Since in low bit-rate video transmissions the loss of a packet usually results in the loss of a whole frame, an error concealment algorithm for INTRA-frame losses is necessary in reality. In this paper, we will focus on this problem and propose an algorithm to improve the reconstructed video quality when INTRA-frame loss occurs. The novelty is that not only the INTRA-frame but also the subsequent INTER-frames are refined using the received INTRA-MBs.

Random INTRA Refresh (RIR) scheme has been used in both earlier and current standards such as MPEG-4, H.263 and H.264, where INTRA-coded MBs are randomly inserted into the bitstream to remove artifacts caused by error and INTER-prediction drift. Although coding efficiency is reduced a little, RIR with a low INTRA-rate is more practical than inserting periodic INTRA-frames due to the bit-rate constraint [12]. As the RIR scheme is implemented in the encoder and does not introduce any decoding overhead, it is often jointly used with other ER or EC schemes. In our algorithm we assume that the received bitstream contains such INTRA-MBs. When an INTRA-frame is lost, the received INTRA-MBs in the subsequent frames can be used to refine their INTER-neighbors based on the strong correlation between adjacent pixel values. In addition, an INTER-pixel can also be refined by *Motion Compensation* (MC) if there is an INTRA-pixel in its motion trajectory.

The rest of this paper is organized as follows. In Section 2, we describe the proposed EC algorithm. Its performance is demonstrated in Section 3 by both subjective and objective results. Section 4 is conclusion.

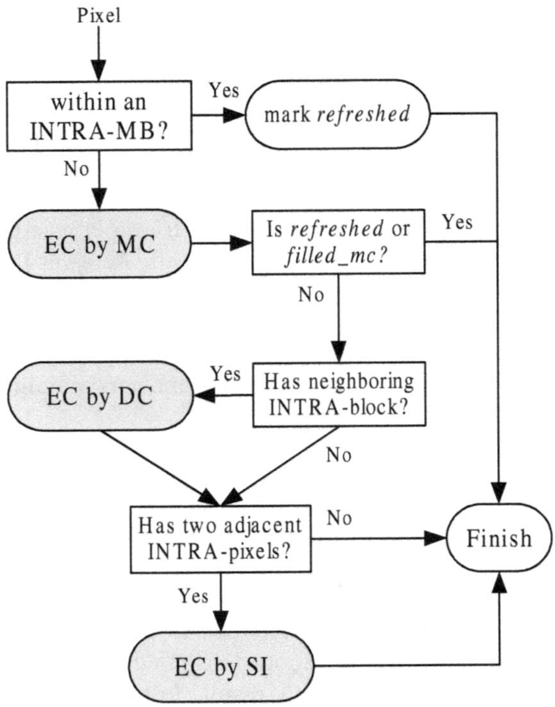

Fig. 1. The flow chart of the proposed EC algorithm for INTRA-frame loss

2 The Proposed EC Algorithm

In conventional EC algorithms, only the corrupted (lost) frames are error-concealed. Although the subsequent frames can be decoded as usual, some annoying artifacts will exist due to the drifting errors and the video quality can be even worse in the case of INTRA-frame loss. In this work, we propose to use four ways to reconstruct the subsequent INTER-pixels after a lost INTRA-frame:

- Decoding directly as in the conventional codec;
- Error concealment by motion compensation (MC);
- Error concealment by the DC of INTRA-MB (DC);
- Error concealment by spatial interpolation (SI).

Each INTER-frame is decoded and then error concealed pixel by pixel, using the algorithm in Figure 1. We will describe the three EC ways in the following subsections and then summarize the algorithm. As the INTRA-MBs coded by *Random INTRA Refresh* (RIR) can help to stop the propagated error, for each pixel we use one mark to represent whether it is error-free (*refreshed*) or not. For a lost frame, all the pixels are set to be *non_refreshed*. And when an INTRA-MB is received later, the corresponding pixels are marked *refreshed*. So a status map

(M_f) needs to be maintained for each frame in the frame buffers, one bit for one pixel. In addition, we also maintain a small map M_s (size 16×16) for the pixels in an INTER-MB. The initial status of each pixel is *non_filled_mc*. Whenever a pixel is refined by MC, its status in M_s is changed to *filled_mc*.

2.1 EC by MC

Suppose there are L frames in the reference frame buffer. For each INTER-pixel p, we have its motion vector MV_0 and the corresponding reference frame index k_0, $k_0 \in \{1, 2, \ldots, L\}$. Then p can be refined by motion compensation (MC) if there is a *refreshed* pixel in its motion trajectory. In detail,

1. Mark the status of p in M_s as *non_filled_mc*. Use MV_0 to find the reference pixel of p, i.e. q_0. If q_0 lies at an integer-pixel position marked as *refreshed*, or if q_0 lies at a sub-pixel position surrounded by *refreshed* pixels, mark p as *refreshed* in M_f and stop. Otherwise, set $k = 0$ and go to 2).
2. Increase k by 1. If k is great than L, i.e. all the reference frames have been checked, stop. Otherwise, go to 3).
3. If k equals k_0, go to 2). Otherwise, estimate the MV of p to the kth reference frame based on the constant velocity model, i.e. $MV_k = MV_0 \times k/k_0$. Then use MV_k to find the corresponding pixel q_k in the kth reference frame. If q_k lies at an integer-pixel position marked as *refreshed*, or if q_k lies at a sub-pixel position surrounded by *refreshed* pixels, replace p by the pixel value of q_k and set the status of p as *filled_mc* in M_s; stop. Otherwise, go to 2).

2.2 EC by DC

Divide the video frame into blocks with size $D \times D$, $D \in \{4, 8, 16\}$. Suppose pixel p lies in block B_c. We first check the eight neighbor blocks of B_c. If one neighbor lies in an INTRA-MB, p will be refined by the DC of this block, i.e. DC_{nb}. In other words, the value of p is changed to

$$p = w_{dc} \times DC_{nb} + (1 - w_{dc}) \times p, \qquad (1)$$

where w_{dc} is the weighting factor to control the emphasis on DC.

2.3 EC by SI

For an INTER-pixel p, two nearest *refreshed* pixels are searched within a window, which is centered at p with size $(2S + 1) \times (2S + 1)$. If there is no or just one such pixel, the condition of *EC by SI* is not satisfied. Otherwise, suppose the two pixels found are p_1 and p_2, with distance d_1 and d_2 from p, respectively. Then an interpolated value for p from its spatial neighbors can be

$$\hat{p} = \frac{p_1 \times d_2 + p_2 \times d_1}{d_1 + d_2}. \qquad (2)$$

Using weight w_{si} to control the strength of spatial interpolation, we obtain the final value of p:

$$p = w_{si} \times \hat{p} + (1 - w_{si}) \times p. \qquad (3)$$

2.4 Summary for the EC Algorithm

If an INTRA-frame (I_0) is lost, all the pixels inside are filled by grey color, i.e. 128 for all the YUV components. Each of the subsequent N frames is decoded and then error concealed as follows until an INTER-frame is lost. Here N is an integer to control the number of frames for EC.

- For the first INTER-frame (P_1), compute the DC of the INTRA-MBs within this frame, i.e. DC_{intra}. Fill the reference frame of P_1 (the buffer for I_0) and all the INTER-pixels of P_1 by DC_{intra}. Then for each INTRA-MB in P_1, use its DC to fill the eight neighboring INTER-MBs.
- For the subsequent frames, the INTER-pixels are error concealed as in Figure 1.

If an INTER-frame is lost, it is reconstructed by copying the previous frame (*copy-previous*).

3 Simulation Results

We use the JVT reference software version 11.0 (baseline profile) for the simulations [13]. The first 300 frames of video sequences *Foreman* and *News* (QCIF) are encoded at 7.5fps, and only the first frame is I frame. Two reference frames are used for INTER-prediction. Parameter *UseConstrainedIntraPred* is set to be 1 in the reference software, i.e. INTER pixels are not used for the prediction of INTRA-MB. And the INTRA-rate for RIR is 3%. The compressed video is supposed to be transmitted though a packet loss channel, and one packet contains the information of one frame. So the loss of one packet will lead to the loss of one entire frame. The simulated packet loss patterns are obtained from [14], with loss rate P = 3%, 5%, 10%, or 20%. Decoder PSNR is used as the objective measurement, which is computed using the the original uncompressed video as reference. Given a packet loss rate P, the video sequence is transmitted 40 times, and the average PSNR for the 40 transmissions is calculated at the decoder side. Three EC algorithms are evaluated, which will act as follows in the case of INTRA-frame loss:

- *EC_F0_128*: The lost INTRA-frame is filled by grey color, i.e. 128 for all the YUV components. And the subsequent frames are decoded directly.
- *EC_F01_DC*: The EC approach is the same as *EC_MV_DC_SI*. However, only the lost INTRA-frame and the first INTER-frame are error concealed.
- *EC_MV_DC_SI*: The proposed algorithm in section 2.4, with parameter w_{dc}= 1/2, w_{si} = 1/3 and S = 16. Suppose the video frames are I_0, P_1, P_2, P_3, P_4.... We use D = 16 for P_1, P_2 and D = 4 for P_i, $i \geq 3$.[1]

The lost INTER-frame is error concealed by *copy-previous* for all these three algorithms.

[1] Note that when *EC by SI* is applied in *EC_MV_DC_SI*, with $w_{dc} = 1/2$ in Eqn. (1) and $w_{si} = 1/3$ in Eqn. (3), an INTER-pixel p is reconstructed by the average of the DC_{nb}, the interpolated pixel and the decoded one.

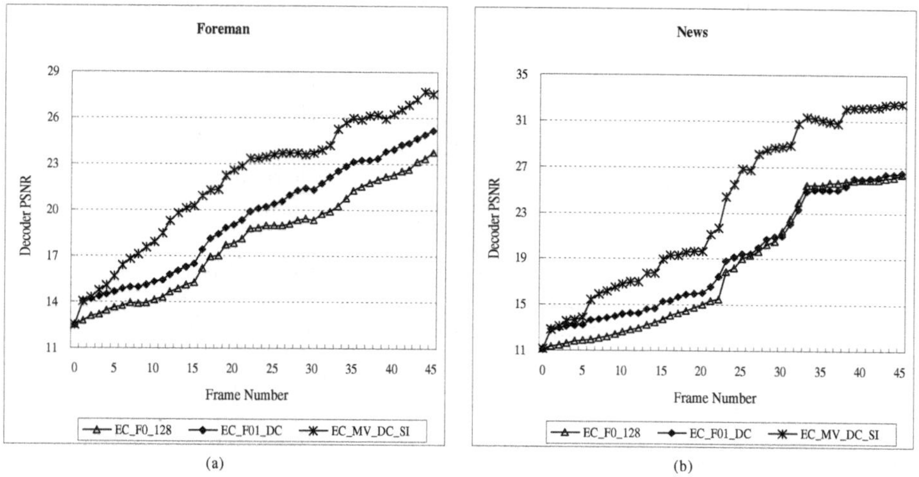

Fig. 2. The decoder PSNR of different EC algorithms for INTRA-frame loss

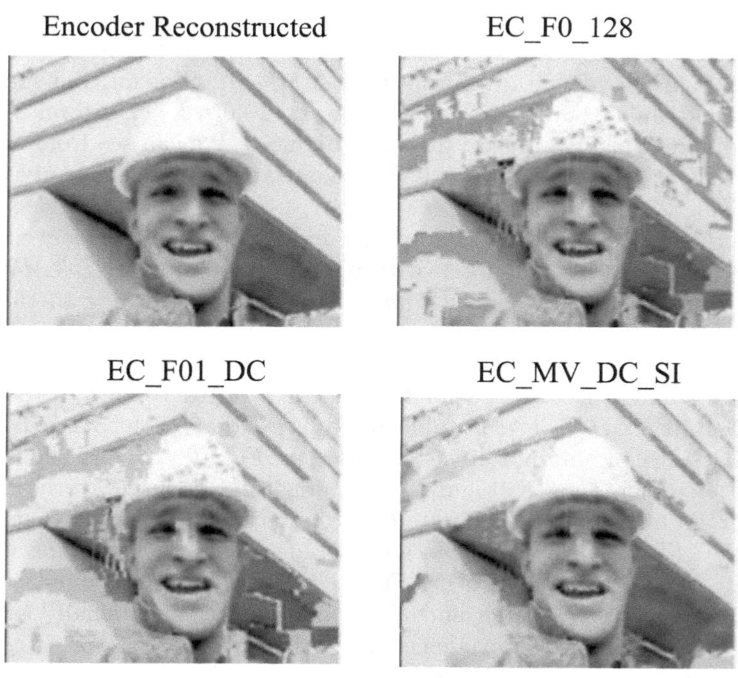

Fig. 3. The 30th INTER-frame of *Foreman* in different EC algorithms for INTRA-frame loss

Table 1. The average decoder PSNRs for different loss rate P

Foreman (QP=30)								
	Decoder PSNR				Delta-PSNR			
P	3%	5%	10%	20%	3%	5%	10%	20%
EC_F0_128	29.41	26.52	23.82	20.24	0.00	0.00	0.00	0.00
EC_F01_DC	29.47	26.59	23.94	20.51	0.06	0.07	0.12	0.27
EC_MV_DC_SI	29.54	26.70	24.02	20.60	0.13	0.18	0.20	0.36
News (QP=30)								
	Decoder PSNR				Delta-PSNR			
P	3%	5%	10%	20%	3%	5%	10%	20%
EC_F0_128	32.37	30.61	28.28	24.08	0.00	0.00	0.00	0.00
EC_F01_DC	32.40	30.64	28.36	24.38	0.03	0.03	0.08	0.30
EC_MV_DC_SI	32.58	30.86	28.52	24.50	0.21	0.25	0.24	0.42

We first simulate the case of INTRA-frame loss, and all the subsequent frames are assumed to be received. Parameter N of *EC_MV_DC_SI*, i.e. the number of frames for EC, is selected to be $N = 75$ for a better illustration. Constant QP (QP=30) is used to encode both *Foreman* and *News*. The decoder PSNR is plotted in Figure 2. As shown in the figure, the video quality can be improved by just error concealing the first two frames, i.e. filling with the DC of received INTRA-MBs. However, with the proposed *EC_MV_DC_SI* algorithm, much more improvement can be obtained. The reconstructed 30th INTER-frames of *Foreman* by different algorithms are shown in Figure 3. We can see from the figure that *EC_MV_DC_SI* can suppress the propagated error more efficiently than the other two algorithms.

The performances of the EC algorithms under random packet loss conditions are given in Table 1 and Figure 4, with parameter $N = 30$ for *EC_MV_DC_SI*. Both INTRA-frames and INTER-frames can be lost according to the packet loss rate (P). Table 1 shows the average decoder PSNRs for different P. To give a clearer illustration, we also present the difference between *EC_F01_DC*/ *EC_MV_DC_SI* and *EC_F0_128* for the same loss rate, as shown in the column named Delta-PSNR. From the table we can see that both *EC_F01_DC* and *EC_MV_DC_SI* can obtain a higher PSNR than *EC_F0_128*, and the difference increases with increasing P. Figure 4 compares the RD curves of the three EC algorithms for a given packet loss rate P. From the figure we can see that by using *EC_MV_DC_SI* at $P = 5\%$, we can gain about 0.19dB for *Foreman* and about 0.26dB for *News*, compared to using *EC_F0_128*. For $P = 20\%$, about 0.4dB can be obtained for both *Foreman* and *News*. In addition, for a small loss rate P, i.e. $P = 3\%$ or 5%, the performance (decoder PSNR) of *EC_F01_DC* is closer to *EC_F0_128* than to *EC_MV_DC_SI*. And when P increases, the performance of *EC_F01_DC* gets closer to *EC_MV_DC_SI*. This can be observed from both Table 1 and Figure 4.

Not that in Table 1 and Figure 4, the gap between *EC_MV_DC_SI* and *EC_F0_128* is smaller than that in Figure 2. As in the case of INTER-frame losses, the two algorithms have the same action, i.e. *copy-previous*, and the

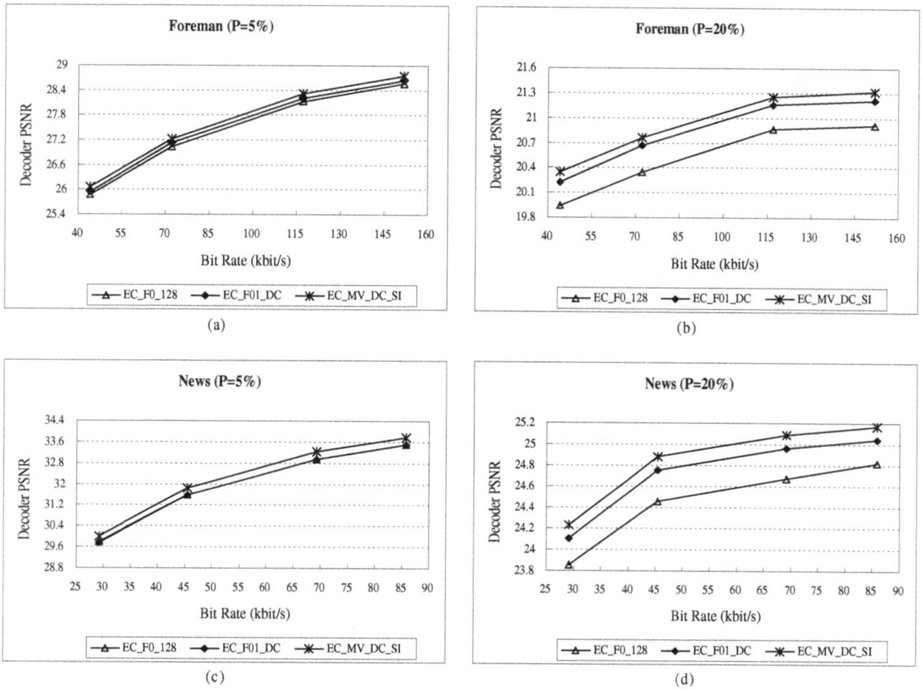

Fig. 4. The RD curves of different EC algorithms with loss rate $P = 5\%$ and $P = 20\%$

advantage of *EC_MV_DC_SI* over *EC_F0_128* is not obvious. Actually in such conditions, the received INTRA-MBs can also be used to refine the subsequent INTER-frames. We will take this as a future work.

4 Conclusion

In this paper, we propose an EC algorithm for INTRA-frame losses over packet loss channels. Both motion compensation and spatial interpolation are used to refine the INTER-pixels in the subsequent frames. As a result, the propagated error can decrease much faster than just error-concealing the lost INTRA-frame.

Acknowledgments. This work has been supported by the Innovation and Technology Commission of the Hong Kong Special Administrative Region, China (project no. GHP/033/05).

References

1. Wang, Y., Zhu, Q.F.: Error control and concealment for video communication: a review. In: Proc. IEEE, pp. 974–997 (May 1998)
2. Al-Mualla, M., Canagarajah, C., Bull, D.: Multiple-reference temporal error concealment. In: Proc. IEEE ISCAS, pp. 149–152 (May 2001)

3. Chen, Y., Yu, K., Li, J., Li, S.: An error concealment algorithm for entire frame loss in video transmission. In: Proc. PCS (December 2004)
4. Zhu, W., Wang, Y., Zhu, Q.-F.: Second-order derivative-based smoothness measure for error concealment in DCT-based codecs. IEEE Trans. Circuits Syst. Video Technol. 8, 713–718 (1998)
5. Hsia, S.-C., Cheng, S.-C., Chou, S.-W.: Efficient adaptive error concealment technique for video decoding system. IEEE Trans. Multimedia 7, 860–868 (2005)
6. Lam, W.M., Reibman, A.R., Liu, B.: Recovery of lost or erroneously received motion vectors. In: Proc. IEEE ICASSP, pp.417–420 (1993)
7. Su, C.-Y., Tsay, S.-H., Huang, C.-H.: Error concealment using direction-oriented candidate set and predicted boundary matching criteria. In: Proc. IEEE ICIP, pp.2221–2224 (2006)
8. Belfiore, S., Grangetto, M., Magli, E., Olmo, G.: Concealment of whole-frame losses for wireless low bit-rate video based on multiframe optical flow estimation. IEEE Trans. Multimedia 7, 316–329 (2005)
9. Wu, Z., Boyce, J.M.: An error concealment scheme for entire frame losses based on H.264/AVC. In: Proc. IEEE ISCAS, pp. 4463–4466 (May 2006)
10. Nasiopoulos, P., Coria-Mendozal, L., Mansour, H., Golikeri, A.: An improved error concealment algorithm for intra-frames in H.264/AVC. In: Proc. IEEE ISCAS, pp. 320–323 (May 2005)
11. Wang, H., Lv, J.: A novel error concealment scheme for intra frames of H.264 video. In: Proc. IEEE Int. Workshop VLSI Design & Video Tech., pp. 300–303 (2005)
12. Kumar, S., Xu, L., Mandal, M.K., Panchanathan, S.: Error resiliency schemes in H.264/AVC standard. Elsevier J. Vis. Commun. Image Represent. 17(2), 425–450 (2006)
13. Jvt reference software, version 11.0. [Online]. Available: `http://iphome.hhi.de/suehring/tml/download/`
14. Wenger, S.: Error patterns for internet experiments in ITU-T SG16 Doc. Q15-I-16r1 (October 1999)

Information Delivery Systems for Car Passengers Without Networking Capabilities

Chun-Hsiang Huang[1], Po-Wei Chen[1], Ping-Yen Hsieh[1], and Ja-Ling Wu[1,2]

[1] Department of Computer Science and Information Engineering, National Taiwan University, Taipei, Taiwan
[2] Graduate Institute of Networking and Multimedia, National Taiwan University, Taipei Taiwan
{bh, doublech, kukki, wjl}@cmlab.csie.ntu.edu.tw

Abstract. In this paper, audio data-hiding schemes and speaker/recorder devices are employed to deliver information within nearby areas where connection and networking capabilities are expensive or even unavailable. Conventionally, information delivery in this way suffers from low data rate, questionable robustness and, most seriously, the limited transmission distance. Here, we alleviate the constraint of short transmission distance by devising a novel application scenario where widely available speaker/recorder devices move around together with the recipient – the information delivery service based on car radio systems. To be more specific, passengers in cars can receive additional visual information broadcasted through radio channels using devices capable of audio recording. To achieve sufficient data rate and necessary robustness, existing audio watermarking schemes have been enhanced. Furthermore, empirical on-road tests are performed to evaluate the robustness of the proposed scheme in real-world environments. According to our experimental results, enhanced audio watermarking schemes can be practically adopted to provide visual information without introducing additional costs or specific receivers in the client end. The proposed scheme can bring new business opportunities and commercial values for existing radio channels and car radio systems.

Keywords: audio data-hiding, information delivery using car radio systems, data capacity.

1 Introduction

In the past decade, digital watermarking technologies were once regarded as a promising solution against copyright infringements of all kinds of multimedia. However, until now, the systems have not been widely deployed and accepted yet. It is due to the doubts about the security of watermarking schemes, as well as improper market timings and business models. Fortunately, many interesting applications other than copyright protection have been devised.

Recently, communications over acoustic channels via messages hidden in audio signals [1-3] have received more and more attentions. In these schemes, a speaker is

H.H.S. Ip et al. (Eds.): PCM 2007, LNCS 4810, pp. 539–548, 2007.

used as a transmitter and a microphone is adopted as a receiver. Messages hidden in audio signals are transmitted acoustically and then extracted in the receiving end. In [1], the authors suggest that discounts information in shopping malls and flight times in airports can be delivered via music played around. In [2], bootleg copies of live performances distributed over Internet can be automatically traced according to the messages embedded into played sounds. In addition, identities of audiences who illegally record live performances can be verified using the scheme introduced in [3] and related seat information.

One of the major advantages of communication systems based on audio data-hiding schemes is the backward compatibility. Since speakers (music-playing devices) and microphones (recording devices) are commonly available in our daily life, it is convenient and cost-effective to deliver information by acoustic channels without the need for networks or connections, as claimed in [1].

However, the aforementioned schemes also suffer from several serious drawbacks. First, the information transfer distance is constrained by the physical characteristics of sound waves, i.e. the hidden information can only be received within the areas where the played music is audible. Therefore, in order to get the additional information transferred via acoustic channels, information recipients must move to positions near a speaker and then watch the information displayed in their own devices. Furthermore, data transmission rate of existing schemes are in fact too low to be practically used for delivering useful information. For example, the authors of [1] claim that messages are delivered at the highest bit rate of 213 bits/minute while keeping the error rate under 10%. In other words, delivering a simple message like "30% off, the last 2 days!" requires more than 60 seconds! Apparently, the prescribed information-delivery systems would never be practically deployed due to such low data transmission rate.

To extend the applicability of audio data-hiding systems, we devise a practical usage of audio data hiding schemes – visual information delivery based on car radio systems. Section 2 illustrates the basic ideas and system requirements of the proposed applications. Implementation details that boost the capacity of existing schemes are described in Section 3. Section 4 gives the empirical experimental results of our information delivery system, including real-world on-road tests. Limits and potential extensions of the proposed scheme are discussed in Section 5. Section 6 concludes this paper.

2 Delivering Visual Information Via Existing Car Radio System

As mentioned in Section 1, though speakers are commonly available in our living environment, expecting a recipient to move close to a fixed speaker and wait for a certain period for receiving information is unrealistic. However, there is a very common scenario that people inevitably stay close to speakers for a certain period – traveling by cars equipped with radio systems. Since almost each car has a built-in radio system, the backward-compatibility advantage of audio data-hiding can be fully retained. As long as messages carried by audio signals can survive the intermediate D/A–A/D conversions and the environmental noises during car moving, passengers can use audio recording-enabled devices, such as laptops or intelligent mobile phones, to extract the hidden information. Furthermore, if the data transmission rate can be increased significantly, useful visual information for car passengers can be delivered as Fig. 1.

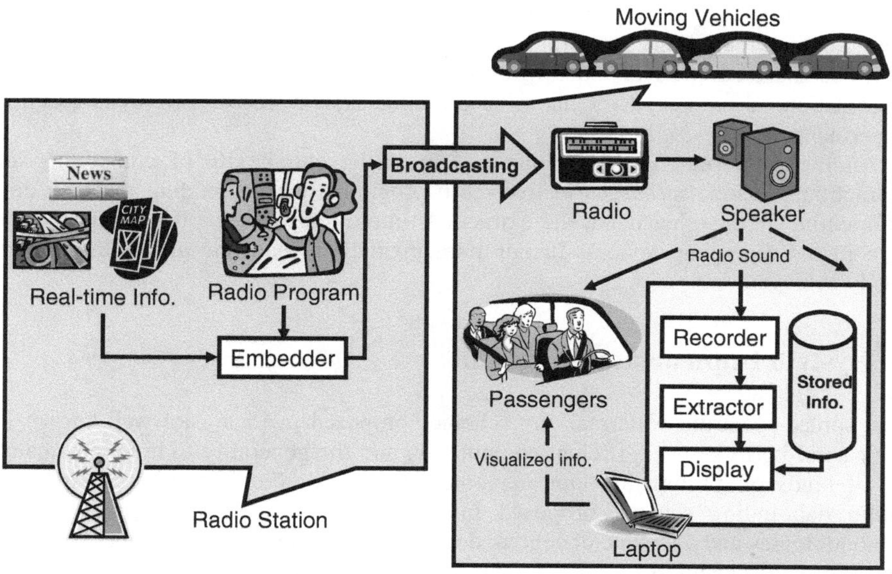

Fig. 1. The proposed information delivery system based on car radio system

Many kinds of useful information can be delivered to car passengers in visualized form via acoustic channels. For example, textual description of real-time news together with simple illustrations, newest traffic conditions labeled in pre-stored maps, tour recommendations or emergency instructions with routes and accompanying descriptions, as well as e-coupons or advertisements, are good candidates of hidden messages. Though conventional radio programs can also convey some of these messages by sounds, there are several advantages of the proposed scheme: (1) broadcasted music does not have to be interrupted by annoying reports or advertisements. (2) Passengers can actively decide whether he or she would like to receive the embedded information, rather than conventional "no advertisement, no music" radio-listening style. (3) The received information can be stored for time-shifted usage. (4) New commercial values of audio broadcast channels and business models can be developed.

Currently, some information service providers cooperated with car manufacturers have provided similar information-delivery services together with their GPRS services. However, the customers have to purchase and install additional devices and continuously pay a monthly fee. The proposed system has the advantage that the end users can spend least additional expenses and still enjoy the existing services. Note that the service of providing local information based on positioning capability of GPRS devices can be implemented based on different information actively delivered by different regional radio stations.

Radio Data System [4], or denoted as RDS, is a standard for sending digital information using conventional FM radio broadcasts and has been applied in Europe and the United States. However, specialized devices must be purchased to receive and decode additional information. Different from the RDS systems, the proposed scheme can be facilitated by legacy car radio systems and widely available receiving devices with common recording capabilities.

Since the data rates of existing implementations are too low to provide useful information, a high-capacity audio data-hiding system based on spread-spectrum watermarking is devised.

Another important issue for this system is the complexity of embedding and extraction. To hide messages in live radio programs, the embedding must be done efficiently. On the other hand, the extraction time directly affects the required buffer size in the receiving devices. In our implementation, real-time embedding can be easily achieved.

3 System Implementation Details

The spread-spectrum watermarking schemes proposed in [5, 6] are well-known for their good performance, efficient computation and the generality to hide information in all kinds of multimedia. Our implementation is similar to the spread-spectrum audio data-hiding scheme proposed in [1], but now additional synchronization methodologies and adequate codebook designs are adopted to improve the robustness and the data transmission rate. In addition, messages are embedded to the middle-frequency coefficients, instead of all the transform coefficients of host audio signal. Therefore, the fidelity performance can also be improved.

3.1 Embedding

In our implementation, DCT coefficients of host audio signals are divided into consecutive n-components frames. We denote the kth coefficient of the ith frame as $X_i[k]$, k=1,…,n. Messages are represented by codewords in a m-element codebook, and each codeword C_j in a codebook is a pseudo-randomly generated binary sequence consisting of l bits. The data transmission rate is partially determined by the codebook size m since log$m$ is the number of bits that will be hidden in each frame of the host audio signal. On the other hand, the length of codeword l affects the robustness of the data hiding system since the auto-correlation characteristic of pseudo-random sequences is better when l is larger. In addition, l also controls the fidelity performance.

Throughout our experiments, l is deliberately chosen to be substantially smaller than n so that only portions of coefficients will be modified. The embedding process for embedding the jth message codeword into the ith DCT frame can be described by:

$$Y_i[\Delta+k] = X_i[\Delta+k] + a_i[\Delta+k]\cdot C_j[k], k = 1,\ldots,l \tag{1}$$

where Δ denotes the number of unmodified low-frequency coefficients, i.e. only middle-frequency coefficients from $X_i[\Delta+1]$ to $X_i[\Delta+l]$ will be altered during the embedding process. a_i is the scale factor that determines the fidelity of marked signal and takes the masking effect of each critical band into consideration:

$$a_i[k] = \bigcup_{b\in B} a_{i,b}[k] \tag{2}$$

B is the set of all the middle-frequency critical bands b. $a_{i,b}[k]$ is the scale factor for the ith-frame coefficients within the critical band b, and is defined as:

$$a_{i,b}[k] = p \cdot \max_{k \in b} Y_{i-1,b}[k] \tag{3}$$

where $Y_{i-1,b}[k]$ is the coefficient possessing the largest magnitude within the critical band b in the previous marked frame. Calculating adequate scale factor according to characteristics of the previous frame is mainly due to the real-time constraint of the proposed application. Finally, p is a given parameter that determines the degree of coefficient alternations. The relationships between all the specified system parameters and the system performances will be clearer when subsequent experimental results are presented.

3.2 Extraction

The received DCT frame $Y_i'[k]$ is firstly divided by the scale factor $a_i'[k]$ so that the auto-correlation properties of pseudo-random sequences degraded by the perceptual scaling operation employed in the embedding process can be improved. Then, as in common spread-spectrum watermarking schemes, the correlation values between $Y_i'[k]$ and all the codewords are calculated. At last, the codeword corresponds to the highest correlation value is regarded as the embedded message.

3.3 Synchronization

Since the embedded audio signals will be transmitted in the form of sound waves and may suffer from environmental noises, the hidden messages may easily get out of synchronization. Therefore, a two-stage synchronization scheme is adopted to prevent the out-of-sync problem. Initially, a buffer provided by the receiving device is used to store the first s frames. All the n possible offsets, i.e. from 0 to n-1, are iteratively tested by calculating all the sums of correlation values between the synchronizing codeword and the s received coefficient frames shifted according to each offset. The offset corresponds to the highest correlation value are used to rearrange the forthcoming audio signals. Throughout all experiments, s is empirically set as 10.

Furthermore, a periodic synchronization operation is performed regularly each time an interval t has elapsed. The periodic synchronization process is similar to the initial synchronization but the range of tested offsets is significantly reduced to avoid buffer overflow. In our experiments, t is set as 1 second and the range of tested offset is limited to 4 samples before and after corresponding signal samples.

4 Experimental Results

Our experimental results can be classified into two parts. In the first part, detection performances are evaluated in indoor areas without noises. In the second part, the proposed system is empirically tested in a moving car to see whether the proposed scheme can resist noises during car moving. Experiments on freeways and urban roads are performed to evaluate the effects of different driving conditions.

All the embedding processes in the experiments are performed in real-time using a desktop computer with 3.4GHz CPU. The extraction processes are done using an

Acer TravelMate 3001 laptop equipped with a built-in sound card. And all the on-road experiments are performed within a Suzuki SX4 hatchback car [7].

All the necessary implementation parameters will be provided when necessary to help reproduce the experimental results. Nevertheless, the uncontrollable variances in actual environmental noises and traffic conditions may slightly affect the experimental results.

4.1 Experimental Results of Indoor Tests

Five 20-second mono audio clips recorded from daily radio programs are used as the host audio signals. The sampling rate is set to 44.1 kHz. Table 1 lists the characteristic of each audio clip.

Table 1. Audio clips adopted as host signals

Audio Clips	Description
SMNY	Symphony played by an orchestra.
POP1	Chinese POP music soloed by a female singer.
POP2	English POP music played by a band.
Speech1	10-second traffic condition reports with subsequent music.
Speech2	DJ talking with apparent background music.

Fig. 2 lists the indoor detection performance of the adopted audio clips. The parameters are set as follows: n=512, m=16, 32, l=128, Δ=128, and p=0.3. The achieved bit-rates are therefore 344 and 430 bps respectively. All experimental results are obtained by calculating the average value of detection results of three repeated tests for each audio clip.

Note that the pure-music clips SMNY, POP1, and POP2 show relatively good detection performance over clips containing speech signals. This is reasonable since the underlying data-hiding scheme is designed for audio signals, rather than speech signals. Since one of the design goals is to eliminate the need of speech reporting or advertisement, the low performance of extracting from speech signals does not limit the feasibility of our scheme at all.

On the other hand, as expected, the detection performance degrades as the data rate increases. In other words, a feasible communication system shall decide the reasonable trade-offs between the data rate and the detection performance according to its application scenario.

Table 2 lists the SNR values for all embedded audio clips. Note that since the bit-rate increases is obtained by increasing the codebook size only, the SNR values of each signal for both experiments are the same. In addition to the objective measurements of SNR, subjective fidelity tests of embedded audio signals also show satisfying results.

When devices with better recording capability are employed, the performance can be improved accordingly. For example, when we repeated the experiments of the SMNY clip using a desktop equipped with a Creative Sound Blaster Audigy card, the detection performance increases to 89.5% and 86.8% respectively, as compared to 83% and 77% in the laptop's case.

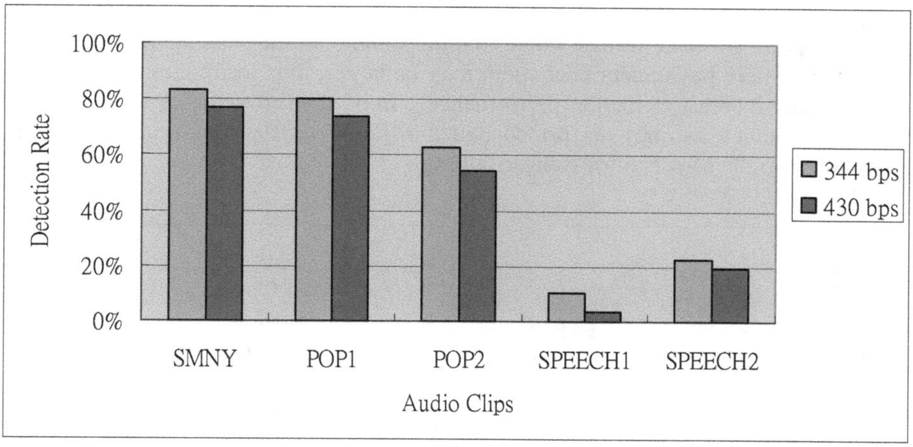

Fig. 2. Detection performance for indoor tests

Table 2. SNR values of marked audio clips

Audio Clips	SMNY	POP1	POP2	Speech1	Speech2
SNR (dB)	20.9	17.2	19.6	28.8	26.6

4.2 Experimental Results of the On-Road Tests

To evaluate whether the proposed scheme can actually resist noises occurred during driving, empirical on-road tests are performed. Throughout all experiments, there are always one driver and two other passengers in the car. Furthermore, all the tests are performed using the prescribed laptop. Similarly, all the results are average values of results obtained by repeating each test for three times.

According to the indoor tests, speech signals are inadequate for the audio data hiding scheme. Therefore, only the SMNY, POP1 and POP2 clips are used in on-road tests. Fig. 3 shows the detection results for freeways (the average speed is between 70 km/hr and 80 km/hr) and urban roads (the average speed is under 50km/hr) while the data rate is 344 bps (m=16). Other experimental parameters are the same as aforementioned ones. According to these experimental results, the noises introduced during car moving degrade the detection performance moderately. Therefore, technologies such as error-correcting codes could be incorporated to enhance the error resilience of the proposed scheme. Note that there is no obvious difference between the results obtained in freeway and those in urban roads.

Though asking car passengers to stop talking so that information can be smoothly delivered is undoubtedly an annoying constraint, we try to enhance the detection performance by eliminating controllable noises caused by chatting between passengers. However, the test results do not improve for all the cases as we originally expected. This seemingly counterintuitive phenomenon is mainly due to the difficulties to reproduce the road conditions of the previous experiments. Although the on-road experiments are performed on the same segment of freeway and the nearby urban areas, the traffic conditions for each test cannot be perfectly controlled or reproduced. To make things worse, the environmental noises occurred during the experiment where passengers kept silent may be larger, thus leading to the illusion of "chatting can increase detection performance". In other words, the experiments shall be merely viewed as ones performed under different traffic conditions, rather than trying to grasp the effects of passenger talking.

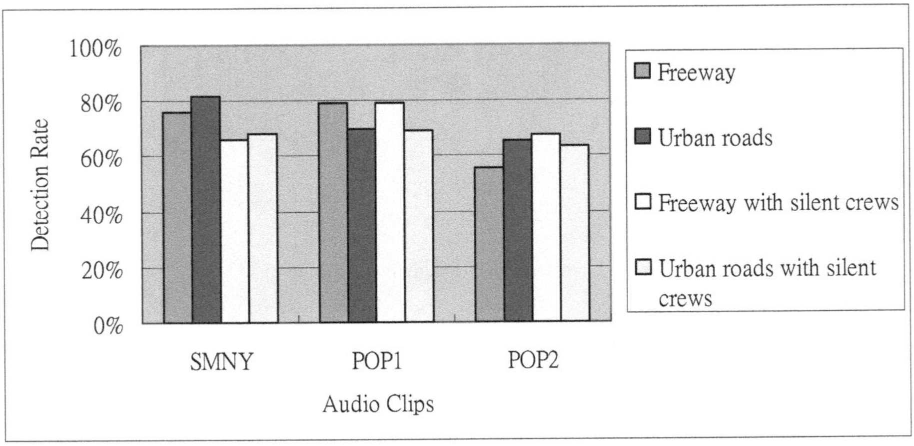

Fig. 3. On-road experimental results when the bit-rate is 344 bps

4.3 Computation Time and Required Storage

The extraction processes requires about 8.3 seconds and 11.5 seconds for the initial synchronization procedure in the two experiments whose results are represented by Fig. 2. Subsequent extraction function can be performed in a real-time manner. Besides, corresponding average buffer sizes in the receiver are 0.747M bytes and 1.035M bytes.

5 Discussions

5.1 Challenges Faced in On-Road Tests

According to the experimental results, the proposed system does possess good robustness against noises occurred in indoor environments and moving cars. However, due to the difficulty of controlling the traffic conditions, as well as the constraints on human power and research equipments (e.g. to obtain experimental results for another test car or in other areas), the experimental results cannot be easily generalized. We hope that more "real-world" tests could be performed so that the feasibility of the proposed scheme could be proved on a more solid basis.

Moreover, audio signals used in all experiments are played and recorded using devices attached to desktops or laptops. The actual distortions caused by AM/FM broadcasting and car sound systems are not completely reproduced. Therefore, seeking the opportunities for collaborative researches with campus radio stations or car sound system manufactures would be an important part of our future work.

5.2 Legislative Constraints on Broadcast Channels

Due to the rarity of broadcast bandwidth and political concerns, governments in many countries have imposed constraints on the usage of broadcast signal, or even prohibiting embedding any information in broadcasted audio signals. Such regulations could seriously limit the usage of the proposed scheme.

5.3 Potential Extensions

According to the experimental results, we successfully boost the transmission rate of audio data-hiding scheme to about 400 bps with acceptable error rate. However, though our works are much faster than existing works, there is still a significant gap in transmission rate between our works and current short-distance data transmitting technologies like infrared or Bluetooth. If the data transmission rate based on audio data hiding can be further improved, audio data-hiding schemes could be a convenient and cost-effective alternative to existing data communication schemes without physical connection mediums. Therefore, more advanced watermarking approaches, such as spread-transform dither modulation (STDM) [8] and improved spread-spectrum (ISS) [6] schemes, will be adopted and tested in order to achieve better system performance.

6 Conclusions

In this paper, an information delivery system for car passengers is proposed. The proposed system shows the advantages of sufficient data capacity, strong robustness against driving noises and backward capability with legacy car radio systems. Both indoor tests and on-road experiments are performed to evaluate the system performance of the proposed car information delivery system.

Acknowledgement. This work was supported by the National Science Council of ROC under NSC95-2622-E-002-018. The authors also appreciate the help provided by Shang-Chih Chuang for document preparation.

References

[1] Lazic, N., Aarabi, P.: Communication over Acoustic Channel Using Data Hiding Techniques. IEEE Transactions on Multimedia 8(5) (October 2006)
[2] Tachibana, R.: Sonic Watermarking. EURASIP Journal on Applied Signal Processing 2004(13), 1955–1964 (2004)
[3] Nakashima, Y., Tachibana, R., Nishimura, M., Babaguchi, N.: Estimation of Recording Location Using Audio Watermarking. In: ACM Multimedia and Security Workshop 2006, Geneva, Switzerland (September 2006)

[4] Kopitz, D., Marks, B.: RDS: Radio Data System (Mobile Communications Library) ISBN 0-89006-744-9
[5] Cox, I.J., Kilian, J., Leighton, T., Shamoon, T.: Secure Spread Spectrum Watermarking for Multimedia. IEEE Transactions on Image Processing 6(12) (December 1997)
[6] Marvar, H.S., Florencio, A.F.: Improved Spread Spectrum: A New Modulation Technique for Robust Watermarking. IEEE Transactions on Signal Processing 51(4) (April 2003)
[7] The official website of Suzuki SX4, http://www.globalsuzuki.com/sx4/index.html
[8] Chen, B., Wornell, F.: Quantization Index Modulation: A Class of Provably Good Methods for Digital Watermarking and Information Embedding. IEEE Transactions on Information Theory 47, 1423–1443 (2001)

Predictable Processing of Multimedia Content, Using MPEG-21 Digital Item Processing

Chris Poppe, Frederik De Keukelaere*, Saar De Zutter, Sarah De Bruyne, Wesley De Neve, and Rik Van de Walle

Ghent University - IBBT
Department of Electronics and Information Systems - Multimedia Lab
Gaston Crommenlaan 8, B-9050 Ledeberg-Ghent, Belgium
{chris.poppe, frederik.dekeukelaere, saar.dezutter, sarah.debruyne, wesley.deneve, rik.vandewalle}@ugent.be
http://www.multimedialab.elis.ugent.be/

Abstract. Within an MPEG-21 architecture, the two key concepts are the Digital Item, representing multimedia content, and Users, interacting with this content. MPEG-21 introduced Digital Item Processing to allow content authors to describe suggested processing of their Digital Items. It standardizes ways to insert functionality into a Digital Item, as such, creating a dynamic and interactive multimedia format. Moreover, if a terminal wants to support Digital Item Processing, it needs to provide an execution environment offering basic functionality. The semantics of this functionality have been standardized, however there is significant room for interpretation. Consequently, a Digital Item author may not be aware of the actual processing when using this functionality. In this paper, a system is proposed, compliant with the Digital Item Processing specification, to give content creators full control on the processing. This allows creating advanced predictable multimedia systems in an MPEG-21 environment.

1 Introduction

ISO/IEC 21000, better known as MPEG-21, is a standards suite developed by MPEG. It envisions to create a multimedia framework for the creation, delivery, and consumption of multimedia content across a wide range of networks and devices [1]. An MPEG-21-compliant terminal is a terminal that provides the necessary functionality to process MPEG-21 content and will further be called MPEG-21 terminal. A content author will create a Digital Item (DI), containing references to multimedia content and metadata. Embedded functionality in the DI allows the author to define the way the content should be processed when an MPEG-21 terminal is used to consume it.

* The work considered in this paper has been partially conducted while Frederik De Keukelaere was a PhD student at Multimedia Lab. Since October 1, 2006 he is working at IBM Japan Tokyo Research Laboratory.

H.H.S. Ip et al. (Eds.): PCM 2007, LNCS 4810, pp. 549–558, 2007.

This paper focuses on the processing part, defined in part 10 of the MPEG-21 Multimedia Framework, named Digital Item Processing (DIP)[2]. DIP allows the execution of script code inserted in the DI. Moreover, it provides basic functionality with standardized interfaces, available on any DIP-compliant terminal (called DIP terminal). DIP has been succesfully applied in the Los Alamos National Library for the dissemination of digital objects and as means to create services, linked to the digital objects, which can be executed by agents [3]. In this case the DIP terminals were all implemented by the same person and known to the DI authors. Contrarily, in a more open environment, different DIP terminals might interprete the standardized interfaces differently. Regarding an MPEG-21 environment, these possible implementations may lead to potential issues for the creation of DIs containing DIP functionality. The paper shows how these different implementations prevent a DI creator to know how his content is processed.

Accordingly, a system is presented to allow the content author to take full control of the processing by using standardized DIP functionality. The proposed system allows an author to implement his own set of basic functionality which can be used on a client device when the content is consumed. As a result, the author exactly knows how his content will be processed, while still maintaining MPEG-21 compliance.

The outline of the paper is as follows. The next section elaborates on the MPEG-21 standard, specifically on DIP. Section 3 recapitulates the issues arising within an ubiquitous MPEG-21 environment and in Section 4, we present our solution. Section 5 elaborates on new use cases that become achievable by the proposed system. Finally, Section 6 formulates a number of conclusive remarks.

2 MPEG-21

The aim of MPEG-21, the so-called Multimedia Framework, is to enable transparent and augmented use of multimedia resources across a wide range of networks, devices, and communities. In this framework, the fundamental unit of transaction is a Digital Item (DI) as defined in part 2, named Digital Item Declaration (DID) [1]. This part defines the structure of a DI, which can contain (references to) multimedia content and metadata. The declaration of a DI uses an XML-based language, called Digital Item Declaration Language (DIDL), which defines the structure of the items. A DI can, for example, represent a music collection including audio files, descriptive information of every song, graphical elements representing CD-covers, etc. This is a static presentation, meaning there is no information available on how a DI should be processed by a consumer.

DIP has been created to permit the author of a DI to add explicit information on how the item should be processed [2]. This way, an author can, for instance, add a method to the item which shows the cover of the CD, whilst playing a song and displaying a textual description. DIP allows the addition of interaction to the static declaration of a DI by means of Digital Item Methods (DIMs). These methods are written in the Digital Item Method Language (DIML), which extends ECMAScript [5]. They are essentially code fragments inserted in the

XML representation of the DI. A DIP terminal will most likely contain a module, called a DIP engine, capable of executing these methods.

To extend the scripting functionality, DIP provides specific multimedia processing by defining a standardized set of functions. As such, similar behavior can be obtained on different terminals. These functions, called Digital Item Base Operations (DIBOs), form a library, available on any DIP terminal, which can be called from within a DIM. MPEG-21 has standardized the interfaces and semantics of this functionality and the developer of the DIP engine is responsible for providing an implementation. This has as advantage that different vendors can compete in their implementation. The DIBOs are divided into different categories, relating to different parts of the MPEG-21 framework. Moreover, the DOM Level 3 Core API and the DOM Level 3 Load and Save API [6] are included in DIML, allowing access, manipulation, loading, and serializing of the DID at the XML level. For a detailled description of the DIBOs, the reader is referred to [1].

An example of a DI containing DIP functionality is shown in Fig. 1. The XML representation shows two Components. The first component (identified by the id "movieResource") defines a movie resource and a descriptor stating this element represents a Movie object. The second component (identified by the id "DIM") contains a resource that represents a DIM. The first descriptor in this component is used to indicate the presence of a DIM. The second descriptor is used to denote the type of arguments the DIM takes. Consequently, the figure shows a DIM which takes a Movie object as argument and then executes a DIBO (DIP.play() in the example) on this object. The play DIBO is one of the DIP-related DIBOs and renders the element, passed as an argument, into a transient and directly perceivable presentation. When the functionality provided by the DIBOs on a DIP terminal is not sufficient, a DI author can make use of Digital Item eXtension Operations (DIXOs). A DIXO is externally generated code which can be included in the DI. DIP defines ways to invoke DIXOs from inside a DIM and a DIXO has access to the entire DIBO set through standardized bindings. So DIBOs are part of a DIP terminal, but DIXOs are typically externally created by a DI author. The language of the DIXOs can be chosen freely, but currently only DIXOs written in the Java language, called J-DIXOs, are standardized. The J-DIXO itself is a Java class (if necessary included in a Java archive) which implements a pre-defined J-DIXO interface. A specific DIBO has been defined, called runJDIXO, which invokes the J-DIXO.

Fig. 2 shows the different components of an MPEG-21 terminal from a DIP point of view. We can see that the DIP engine takes a central position; interacts with the User and is connected to additional modules related to the different MPEG-21 parts. A DID engine parses item and forward the DIP elements to the DIP engine. Through the DIBOs, an interface is created for a DI to utilize (part of) the underneath platform. However, there is room for interpretation of the semantics of the DIBOs and this vagueness can introduce several problems in real life scenarios, as will be discussed in the next section.

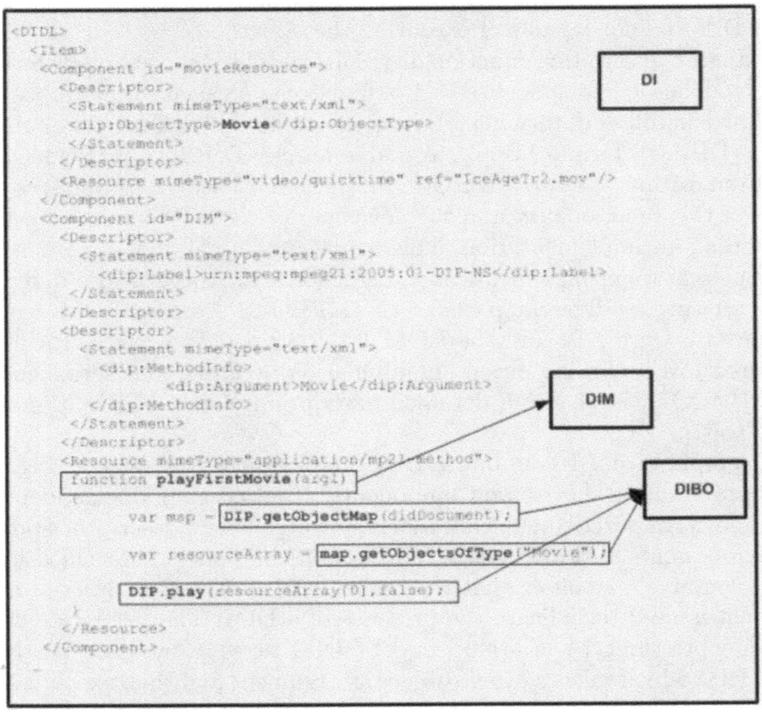

Fig. 1. Example Digital Item

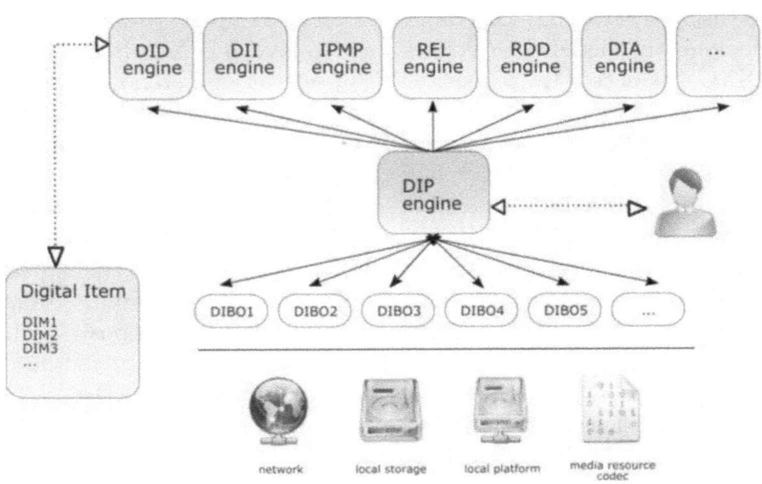

Fig. 2. MPEG-21 terminal

3 Problem Description

Given that every DIP terminal can have its own implementation of the DIBOs, a number of problems arise. Although the semantics of the function are determined, the actual implementation can vary considerably, making it hard for a DI author to compose his content without knowledge of the client application.

A short example is the alert DIBO, which takes a string as parameter and alerts the User. The semantics of this DIP-related DIBO are defined as "provide simple textual feedback to the User" [1]. It is obvious that the actual interpretation of alerting a User is rather vague and can be synchronously showing a popup message on the screen, displaying a warning on the media player, or even just adding some information to a log file. This might issue a problem for a content author if his application relies on the reaction of the user on this alert. For the other DIBOs similar problems can be found.

Several of the DIBOs can only be used to their full capacity if the creator of the DI is aware of the actual implementation of the DIBOs at client side. Clearly a mechanism is needed that allows DI authors to control the processing of their content in a more detailled manner.

4 System for Predictable Digital Item Processing

The solution we propose makes use of the existing technology defined by DIP, therefore allowing full compliance with the standard. The basic idea is that a DI author provides an own implementation for a set of DIBOs (further called authorDIBOSet), encapsulated in a DIXO, which will then be used whenever a DIBO is called from within the DI.

To accomplish this, a DI author adds a specific method which can be called by the DIP engine. By adding the attribute "autoRun" to the definition of the DIM and by setting its value to "true", a DIP Engine will automatically execute this method when processing the DI. The method invokes a DIXO provided by the content author, containing the authorDIBOSet. The DIXO itself can be transported along with the DI or can be made available online. The execution of the DIXO starts with changing the occurrences of the desired DIBO calls into calls to the DIXO itself, as shown in Fig. 3. Since the DIXO can make use of the DIBOs and more specifically the DOM functionality, we can easily replace the textual occurrence of the DIBO calls by calls to the DIXO. The first four arguments of runJDIXO() are used to identify the element containing the Java archive or class, while the fifth argument (given the value "DIXOSet" in Fig. 3) is needed to define the appropriate class to be executed. The last argument is an array of arguments which is passed to the class. In our system, we use the first element in this array to identify the DIBO call, which was replaced by using the specific name of the DIBO (in this case the play DIBO, noticeable by the "play" argument of the DIXO call). The rest of the array is used to pass the original arguments of the DIBO to the DIXO. This ends the initialization phase, corresponding to step 1, shown in the sequence diagram in Fig. 4. The

```
<Resource mimeType="application/mp21-method">
  function playMovie(arg1)
  {
    DIP.play(arg1,false);
  }
</Resource>
```

```
<Resource mimeType="application/mp21-method">
  function playMovie(arg1)
  {
    DIP.runJDIXO("dii","urn:dii:jdixos","dii",
    "urn:dii:dixoSet","DIXOSet",new Array(
    "play", arg1, false));
  }
</Resource>
```

Fig. 3. Conversion of DIBO calls to DIXO calls

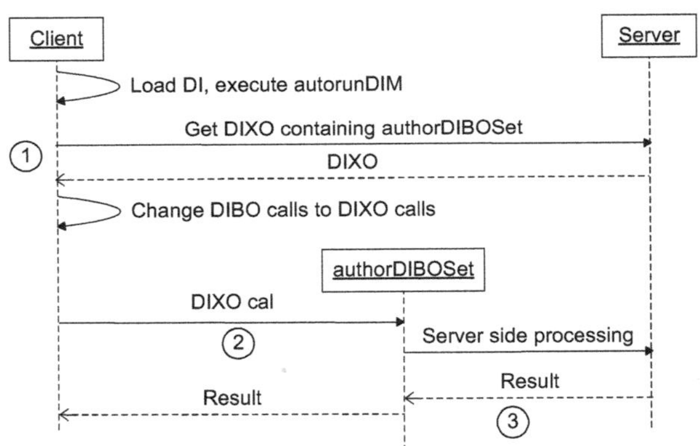

Fig. 4. Sequence diagram of the use of an authorDIBOSet

DIXO will then allow the User to choose a DIM in the updated document. If a DIBO is invoked within that DIM, a direct call to the DIXO containing the authorDIBOSet is performed, with the appropriate arguments (step 2 in Fig. 4). At this point, the execution of the appropriate DIBO, provided by the DI author, starts and return values, if any, are passed back to the invoking DIM. As such, the content author can be sure that his implementation of the DIBO set is used and can uniquely determine the outcome. This system is transparent to the user, since he is not involved with the internal working of the methods, but only with the perceivable outcome.

The DI author can deliver an implementation for every DIBO or restrict himself to the most relevant ones and reuse a number of the DIBOs available in the client application. As shown in step 3 of Fig. 4, the author can even choose to place the DIBO implementation on a centralized server, or provide the DIBO functionality throug a web service, thereby reducing the processing effort on the client device.

To increase the performance of the system, a simple check might be added in the DIM which loads the DIXO, to see if the set is already present in the client application. Since a content author typically produces numerous diverse DIs, there is a clear benefit to get the authorDIBOSet only once and consequently refer to it in those DIs.

The described system gives an author full control of the processing, allowing to exploit his in-depth understanding of the content. Therefore, the possibilities for different DIBOs are extended in the following ways.

The DIBO related to Digital Item Adaptation (DIA) allows to adapt elements of the DI. According to the DIBO requests that an attempt is done to adapt a specific element. This attempt might fail if the DIP engine has no adaptation capabilities, or it does not know how to interpret the input arguments. Since the DI author is aware of the actual format of the input arguments, he is more equiped to create the adaptation. Our system allows that the author can introduce specific adaptation tools steered by associated metadata. MPEG-21 DIA defines tools to adapt DIs based on context information. Resources can be adapted according to descriptions of the usage environment, introducing an advanced quality of service. For example, within DIA, means are defined to describe the preferences of the user. This way, scenes of interest within a movie can be identified and could be displayed at higher quality [7]. The rich variety of adaptations introduced in DIA can only be used if appropriate software is available and if the format of the arguments is exactly known. Our system allows to execute this adaptation since the DI author himself will implement it. If high consuming adaptations cannot be run on the client device, the author can choose to place them on a server.

The DIBOs related to part 2 of MPEG-21, Digital Item Declaration (DID), provide means to allow the end-user to make specific choices when dealing with a DI (for example the choice of a specific movie to be shown). The way that these choices are presented to the user is not defined. Through our system the DI author can present the choices in a consistent and structured way, according to his own preferences.

The DIBOs related to part 3 of MPEG-21, Digital Item Identification (DII), specify means to retrieve elements from a DI according to a specific identification. The DI author is better suited to provide an implementation of these DIBOs, since he has a priori knowledge about the structure of the DI and the location of several identified elements. This way, high cost XML processing can be avoided to increase the systems performance [8].

The DIP-related DIBOs, which mostly interact with the User, can be extended with rich user interfaces allowing consistent presentation of different DIs from the same content author. Playback of specific content can be achieved, by providing appropriate codecs and even entire players which offer advanced control to the User.

The DIBOs related to part 5 of MPEG-21, Rights Expression Language (REL), can now be used according to the intention of the DI author. The author can set up his own license server and has, consequently, more control on the usage of his content.

A DI author can use an alternative to our proposed system. Upon creation of the DIMs within his DI, he might choose to use DIXOs instead of DIBOs. The playMovie DIM, in Fig. 3, will then directly contain a DIXO call instead of the play DIBO call. This is similar to the DI formed after the initialization phase (step 1 in Fig. 4). The creation of DIs in such a manner has as an advantage that there is no need to reconvert the DI at the Users' side. However, when the DI author wants to change the inserted functionality this has to be done for all the produced DIs. Our system collects the DIBO implementations in a set and allows easy updates. The author can also choose between DIBO implementations on the DIP terminal or implementations from the authorDIBOSet, whereas this is not possible in the alternative system, since this is hard-coded.

5 Discussions

Our system allows to accomplish new use cases and service delivery. In this section, the use case of a museum equipped with an interactive multimedia infrastructure is presented.

In the case of a closed environment, meaning a system in which the client applications and the provided content are known to the DI author, the author is aware of the actual processing. This might be the case in an interactive museum, where people get a museum-owned PDA containing an MPEG-21 terminal, which can be used to consume content provided by the museum (this was the use case of the European project DANAE[1]). Since the client application is known by the museum, several assumptions can be made on what the values are for the different arguments of the DIBOs and what happens within the processing. If we want to achieve the goal of MPEG-21 and broaden the environment in a way that the content authors do not need to have knowledge about the client MPEG-21 terminals, we foresee difficulties for the content authors as mentioned above.

Consider a museum with the infrastructure to present interactive multimedia content. A central server stores MPEG-21 content and is responsible for delivering this to available terminals. If a user enters the museum, carrying his own PDA, cell phone or other multimedia device, containing an MPEG-21 terminal, he will be able to consume the museum content. Context about the consumers is collected and processed to generate advanced quality of service and user experience.

We can work out the use case through the system presented in this paper. The museum creates an authorDIBOSet, implementing the relevant DIBOs, which will be used on all client devices. By using this authorDIBOSet, a specific user

[1] http://danae.rd.francetelecom.com/

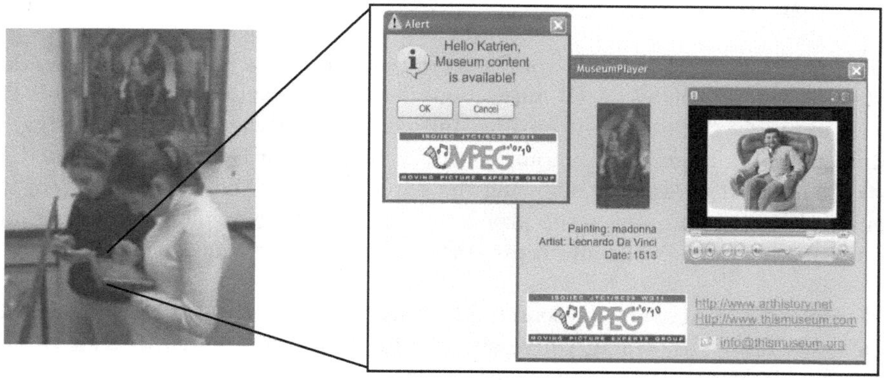

Fig. 5. Multimedia application using DIP

interface can be created for communication with the user (see Fig. 5). Advertisements can be added to the user interface, without having to incorporate these in the media content itself . A consistent uniform user interface is provided in any interaction and on any device. Control of the play DIBO allows to play proprietary content with a specific codec or player according to the needs of the museum (in the figure, the player is a multimedia player able to show rich multimedia presentations including text, graphics, sound, and movies).

A full implementation of the license related DIBOs, making use of internal licensing and registration servers can be used to deliver specific content to appropriate users. As such, customers with a subscription to the museum can get access to additional content or services.

Heavy processing, like the adaptation of content is done on server side, allowing even the most constrained devices to consume the multimedia. Information is gathered on the number of consuming clients, the maximum bandwidth, and the capacity of the museum's infrastructure. Consequently, this is taken into account when performing adaptations or delivering content. By using a centralized server, context can be collected and made available to each application. For example the figure shows the name of the consumer, "Katrien", when starting an interaction. The name is just a simple example of various contextual information, which can be collected when a consumer enters a museum. This use of context creates a more personalized approach to multimedia processing; it focuses on the key player in an interactive multimedia application, namely the user.

The presented solution allows introduction of any MPEG-21 terminal into the multimedia infrastructure of the museum. Visitors can use their own multimedia devices resulting in reduced costs for the museum. The use case presented in this section can be extended to other domains wherein a multimedia infrastructure can be exploited, e.g., warehouses, educational environments, and cultural events. By providing the appropriate DIBO sets and domain-specific content, the existing client application can be used in other settings.

6 Conclusions

The major contribution of our work is the development of an MPEG-21-compliant system to extend the way a DI author can define the actual processing of his DI. The system gives the content authors full control over the actual processing. A number of advantages throughout the different parts of DIP were presented. A use case has been presented, showing the applicability of the system in a real-life scenario. Our system makes the processing of Digital Items more appealing and interesting for industrial content providers, allowing advanced service delivery.

Acknowledgments. The research activities that have been described in this paper were funded by Ghent University, the Interdisciplinary Institute for Broadband Technology (IBBT), the Institute for the Promotion of Innovation by Science and Technology in Flanders (IWT-Flanders), the Fund for Scientific Research-Flanders (FWO-Flanders) and the European Union.

References

1. Burnett, I., Pereira, F., Van de Walle, R., Koenen, R.: The MPEG-21 Book, pp. 195–204. Wiley, Chichester (2003)
2. De Keukelaere, F., De Zutter, S., Van de Walle, R.: MPEG-21 Digital Item Processing. IEEE Transactions on Multimedia 7, 427–434, 809–830(2005)
3. Bekaert, J., Balakireva, L., Hochstenbach, P., Van de Sompel, H.: Using MPEG-21 DIP and NISO OpenURL for the Dynamic Dissemination of Complex Digital Objects in the Los Alamos National Laboratory Digital Library D-Lib Magazine, vol.10 (2004)
4. Poppe, C., De Keukelaere, F., De Zutter, S., Van de Walle, R.: Advanced Multimedia Systems Using MPEG-21 Digital Item Processing. In: Proceedings of Eighth IEEE International Symposium on Multimedia, pp. 785–786 (2006)
5. ECMA, Standard ECMA-262 ECMAScript Language Specification, 3rd edn. `http://www.ecma-international.org/publications/standards/Ecma-262.htm`
6. The W3C Document Object Model `http://www.w3.org/DOM/`
7. Devillers, S., Timmerer, C., Heuer, J., Hellwagner, H.: Bitstream Syntax Description-Based Adaptation in Streaming and Constrained Environments. IEEE Transactions on Multimedia. 7, 463–470 (2005)
8. De Zutter, S., De Keukelaere, F., Poppe, C., Van de Walle, R.: Performance analysis of MPEG-21 technologies on mobile devices. In: Proceedings of Electronic Imaging, vol. 6074 (2006)

A Novel Pipeline Design for H.264 CABAC Decoding

Junhao Zheng[1,2], David Wu[3], Don Xie[3], and Wen Gao[1,2,4]

[1] Institute of Computing Technology, Chinese Academy of Sciences, 100080 Beijing, China
[2] Graduate University of Chinese Academy of Sciences
[3] Spreadtrum Communication Corporations
[4] Institute of Digital Media, Peking University
{jhzheng, wgao}@jdl.ac.cn, {david.wu, don.xie}@spreadtrum.com

Abstract. H.264/AVC is the newest international video coding standard. This paper presents a novel hardware design for CABAC decoding in H.264/AVC. CABAC is the key innovative technology, but it brings huge challenge for high throughput implementation. The current bin decoding depends on the previous bin, which results in the long latency and limits the system performance. In this paper, the data hazards are analyzed and resolved using the algorithmic features. We present a new pipeline-based architecture using the standard look-ahead technique where the arithmetic decoding engine works in parallel with the context maintainer. An efficient finite state machine is developed to match the requirement of the pipeline controlling and the critical path is optimized for the timing. The proposed implementation can generate one bin per clock cycle at the 160-MHz working frequency.

Keywords: CABAC, H.264/AVC, pipeline, VLSI.

1 Introduction

H.264/AVC [1] is the new emerging video compression standard. It uses a combination of novel advanced coding technologies based on the mature hybrid block-based coding framework and achieves up to 50% coding gains compared with MPEG-2 standard [2].

Among these technologies, Context-based Adaptive Binary Arithmetic Coding (CABAC) is one of the most important tools of the H.264/AVC standard Based on the traditional Q-coder family [3], CABAC adopts the adaptive context models to obtain non-stationary symbol statistics and the table-driven engine to avoid the slow multiplicative calculation during the interval subdivision. However, the control intensive operations combined with the arithmetic carry feedback in the CABAC algorithm result in the high calculation time which becomes the bottleneck of the H.264 decoder system. The computational requirements for CABAC decoding are a huge challenge and exceed the capabilities of today's generic CPUs [4], especially for the High Definition (HD) Video in the consumer electronics. Real-time applications, such as Set Top Box, require a stable, high-throughput hardware implementation.

There are various architectures of CABAC decoding proposed in literature [5-7]. Reference [5] takes averagely 2 to 3 cycles to decode one bit. Reference [6]

H.H.S. Ip et al. (Eds.): PCM 2007, LNCS 4810, pp. 559–568, 2007.

concatenated two regular bins or two bypass bins decoding and [7] used the MPS (Most Probable Symbol) prediction to accelerate the bin processing. Their schemes do improve the decoding performance in the normal cases, but they don't really break the limitation of feedback loop. In their designs, the number of clock cycles required to decode one bin is variable and only the average statistic data are provided for the normal cases. But for actual product development, the system performance in the worst case must be considered.

In this paper, a high throughput design for CABAC decoding is proposed. The proposed design can process one bin per clock cycle at the 160-MHz working frequency. The original sequential decoding is replaced by a novel pipeline-based scheme using the standard look-ahead technique. An efficient finite state machine (FSM) is developed to achieve the flexible control of the algorithm processing. The critical path involved the renormalization operation is optimized based on the characteristics of the arithmetic decoding algorithm. Our implementation results show that the proposed design can meet the requirement of CABAC real-time decoding for 1080i video. This paper will concentrate on the coefficient group decoding in CABAC, as further explained in Section II.

The remainder of the paper is organized as follows. The CABAC decoding algorithm is briefly described in Section II. Section III illustrates the details of the hardware design. VLSI implementation results will be given in Section IV. Finally, we draw a conclusion in Section V.

2 CABAC Decoding Algorithm

The decoding process of CABAC is composed of two major steps: the context modeling and the arithmetic decoding. In the first stage, based on which syntax element (SE) to be decoded, CABAC decoder selects the context by referring to the neighboring or previously decoded SEs. Afterwards, the bit value along with its associated model is passed to the regular decoding engine, where the arithmetic decoding together with subsequent model updating takes place. For some bits with the equal probability, the bypass decoding mode is chosen in order to allow a speedup of the whole decoding process.

2.1 Syntax Group

The standard [1] specifies 18 kinds of SEs which need to be coded using CABAC. They can be classified to two classes based on occurrence probability. Most of them occur a few times per picture. Oppositely, a few SEs produce a long bin string and need to be decoded hundreds of times per picture. As expected, the coefficient related SEs contribute to most of the arithmetic decoder workload, especially in high quality applications. These SEs are mainly residual coefficients and significance maps. The bin rate of the coefficient group is up to 60% according to our statistics for many high bitrate streams. A dedicated hardware accelerator is needed for these SEs. For other SEs with low frequency of occurrence, the software solution may provide the higher flexibility. In this paper, both the algorithm analysis and hardware design are focused on the coefficient related decoding. Furthermore, all proposed methods in this paper can also be extended to the hardware implementation of other SEs decoding because of the CABAC algorithmic consistency and similarity.

In the bitstream, coded_block_flag(*CBF*), significant_coeff_flag(*MAP*), last_significant_coeff_flag(*LAST*), coeff_abs_level_minus1 and coeff_sign_flag (*LEVEL*) [1] make up of the coefficient group. Each group includes full map and residual information which can generate the exact 4, 16, or 64 coefficient values depending on the coded block size: 2x2, 4x4, or 8x8. Fig. 1 shows the decoding flow for one coefficient group.

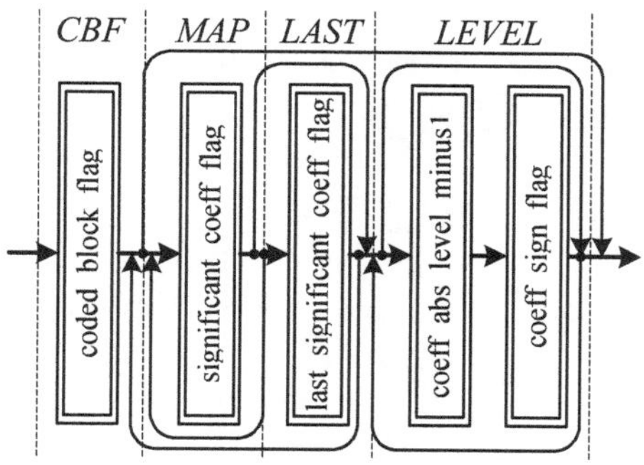

Fig. 1. Decoding flow for one coefficient group

2.2 Binarization

All syntax elements in one coefficient group all use the fixed length coding except *LEVEL*. The *LEVEL* binarization applies the concatenated unary/0-th order Exponential-Golomb Unary (UEG0) method [4]. Its whole range is divided into several sub-ranges, as denoted in equation (1). *m* and *n* denotes the bit number of the middle bin (*Mid-bins*) and the Exp-Golomb coded bin (*EG-bins*) respectively.

$$\begin{cases} \{1st, Sign\} & if\ 1\ or -1; \\ \{1st, \{n\{Mid\}\}, Sign\} & if \in [-14,-2]or[2,14]; \\ \{1st, \{n\{Mid\}\}, \{m\{EG\}\}, Sign\} & if < -14\ or > 14. \end{cases} \quad (1)$$

1st-bin plus *Sign-bin* is set to denote +1/-1. The absolute value between 2 to 14 needs the additional unary bins which are called as the *Mid-bins*. The others require 4 parts: *1st-bin*, *Mid-bin*, *EG-bin*, and *Sign-bin*. The bigger the value of the residual coefficient is, the longer the bin string of the coefficient is. For example, assume that the current residual coefficient is equal to +2038 whose bin string is composed of 36 bins including 1 *1st-bin*, 13 *Mid-bins*, 21 *EG-bins*, and 1 *Sign-bin*. The decoding control becomes quite complicated because of the long bin string and the context switch.

2.3 Context Models

Each kind of SE has its own context models. The scanning position decides the context index for both *MAP* and *LAST*. For *CBF*, the neighboring *CBFs* from left and above macroblocks (MBs) are used to calculate the context index. For one *LEVEL*, 5 models (called One_Ctx) are used for the *1st-bin* and another 5 models (called Abs_Ctx) for all *Mid-bins*. Both *EG-bins* and *Sign-bin* are decoded through the equal probability estimation. The context index of One_Ctx is determined by the accumulated number of decoded trailing 1 and will be reset to 0 immediately once the current coefficient is greater than 1. The context index of Abs_Ctx is decided by the accumulated number of decoded levels with absolute value greater than 1. Both of the indices have the maximum value of 4. Decoding one coefficient needs the corresponding contexts which will be updated after the current decoding. This adaptive context scheme results in a long feedback loop which strongly affects the design for a high throughput system.

3 Hardware Design

Fig. 2 depicts the block diagram of the proposed hardware design. It consists of 3 main logic blocks.

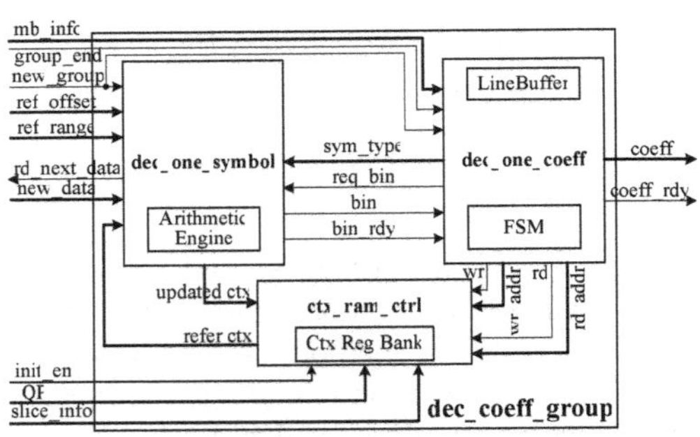

Fig. 2. Coefficients decoder block diagram

The *dec_one_coeff* module controls the coefficient decoding flow through a *FSM*. In this module, a *line buffer* is adopted to store the *CBF* data from the above MB row. The *dec_one_symbol* module implements an optimized arithmetic decoding engine to generate the bin result. The *ctx_ram_ctrl* module is responsible for the context initialization and maintains the context tables which are stored into a *context register bank*.

Firstly, *dec_one_coeff* module knows that which bin in one specific SE will be decoded and informs *ctx_ram_ctrl* module to fetch the corresponding context information from *context register bank*. Secondly, the bitstream data from the outside stream buffer are read to *dec_one_symbol* module and the current context information is passed to *dec_one_symbol* module too. Through the arithmetic calculation, the decoded bin will be outputted to *dec_one_coeff* module. Thirdly, the correct coefficient will be sent out depending on the combination of the current bin value and the previous bin string. At the same time, the current context table will be updated for future operations. Then the next loop will continue until the end of bitstream.

3.1 FSM for Coefficient Group

From the previous analysis, decoding one coefficient group involves 4 major kinds of SEs, which are *CBF*, *MAP*, *LAST*, and *LEVEL*. Each SE contains one or more bins. A dedicated *FSM* is designed to control the whole procedure which is given in Fig. 3. The SEs decoding in Fig. 1 is mapped to different stages. *CBF* for a single block, *MAP*, and *LAST* are the one-bin SEs and thus only one stage is assigned. *LEVEL* is disassembled to 5 stages based on the UEG0 binarization rules. *dcbf*, *dmap*, and *dlast* are the decoded values. *tot* is the total coefficient number and *cnt* for the coefficient counter which is used to record the scanning position of *MAP* and *LAST*. *dbin* is the decoded bin of one *LEVEL* value and *bcnt* is the bin counter to accumulate the number of *Mid-bins* or *EG-bins*. The *De_IDLE* state is the special state used to control the beginning and end of the group.

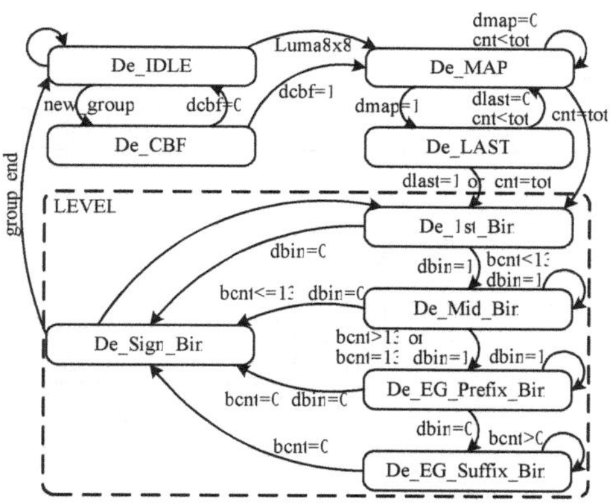

Fig. 3. State transition of coefficient decoding

The precise context management can be obtained through the above *FSM* as well. Based on the state transition, the probability information of the next state can be pre-fetched from the context tables. For example, if the next state is *De_1st_Bin*, the probability information of *1st_bin* is pre-fetched from the *context register bank*. If the state will leave the *De_Mid_Bin*, the updated state and MPS are written back into the context tables. The context index of *CBF* is calculated using the neighboring *CBF* values from above MBs and left MB. Thus when the next state is the *De_CBF*, the *CBFs* of above MB will be loaded from the *line buffer*. After finished, the decoded *CBF* of current MB will be stored to the *line buffer* for the future calculation in next MB row. Besides, the transition from *De_Sign_Bin* to *De_1st_Bin* can guarantee for the successive coefficient decoding in one group. Consequently all bins in one coefficient group can be generated consecutively without stalling under the control of the *FSM*.

3.2 Pipeline Scheme

Pipelining is one effective implementation technique to improve the system throughput. But in CABAC, there exists the strong data dependency between two neighboring bins. In order to solve this problem, the data hazards must be analyzed firstly.

Decoding one regular bin needs 5 major phases:

1) Generate the context index;
2) Look up the context table to obtain the context model;
3) Look up the probability table based on the current context model;
4) Arithmetic decoding using the current probability value where the main calculation occurs;
5) Update the context table.

Data processing in the sequential fashion limits the throughput of the decoder which is depicted in Fig. 4 (a). If the previous bin has not been totally decoded, the context model of the current bin can not be obtained. So the bin dependency constitutes a major obstacle for the pipeline design. Decoding a bin needs a long calculation time and results in the low throughput of the decoder system.

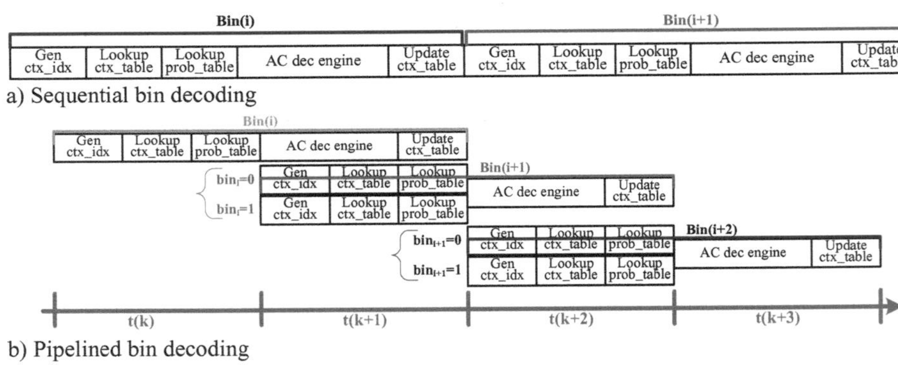

Fig. 4. Bin decoding flow

In our implementation, a novel decoding pipeline is designed using the look-ahead technique to solve the data hazards, as illustrated in Fig. 4 (b). The long processing is separated into two stages. Stage I including phase 1 to 3 is responsible to provide the probability information. Stage II consisted of phase 4 and 5 fulfills the arithmetic decoding and context updating. The key point is that there are two instances of Stage I. Because for each bin, only 0 and 1 are probable values, two instances working in parallel can cover all situations. When the bin[i] is calculated in the arithmetic engine, the probability information of bin[i+1] is prepared simultaneously based on the estimating values of the bin[i]. So the probability estimating of the next bin works in parallel with the arithmetic decoding of the current bin. Once the current bin is generated, the exact probability estimation for the next bin can be obtained immediately only through a simple selection. The proposed pipeline can obtain twice throughput and generate one bin per clock cycle compared with the conventional design. In other words, the sequential design can also achieve a bin per clock cycle, but it needs double the clock cycle time just shown in Fig. 4.

The most crucial challenge of the pipeline design is to balance the workload of each stage and obtain fluent pipeline flow without introducing too much hardware overhead. In our design, Stage I includes three phases and only two phases for Stage II. The reason is that phase 4 requires the complicated arithmetic calculation and occupies two time slots. So the workload of two stages is the same approximate. On the other hand, only a small number of hardware circuits need be built twice. The context tables in our implementation are stored in the *context register bank*. It's not necessary to adopt two same context tables because the register-based scheme can easily support two reading and one writing operations simultaneously. The logic of generating the context index is naturally designed for two situations: one for bin 0 and another for bin 1. For the probability tables, it needs two instances, as further described in subsection 3.3. One *rLPS* table size is 256×8 bits. The implementation of Stage I doesn't bring much area overhead.

3.3 Arithmetic Engine

The key limitation of the CABAC algorithm comes from the arithmetic engine. There exists the data dependency for *Offset* and *Range* values. The straightforward mapping implementation will result in the long propagation paths.

- Optimization for Lookup Tables

In our design, the look-ahead technique is also adopted to the circuit level in order to reduce delays on critical paths, which is illustrated in Fig. 5. The partial calculation logics are doubled in order to achieve the concurrency of both MPS and LPS branches. All decisions are made at the end of the decoding iteration through *Mux1~5* as depicted in Fig. 5. Thus the partial parallel processing can be achieved.

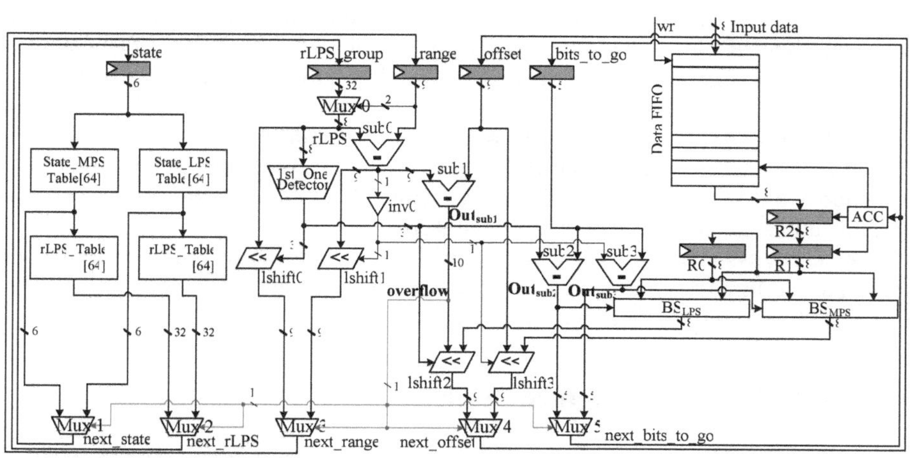

Fig. 5. Arithmetic decoding engine

The output of *sub0* is (*range* – *rLPS*) which is used in both MPS and LPS path. The output of *sub1* is the value of (*offset - (range - rLPS)*). The overflow bit, the most significant bit of Out_{sub1}, works as the final selecting signal and is used to determine which logic path will be chosen. *LPS* is the Least Probable Symbol. *Range* is the current length of the subinterval and *offset* for the offset position. *rLPS* is the size of subinterval associated to the LPS.

The operations of looking up the transTables (*State_MPS_Table* and *State_LPS_Table*) and the arithmetic calculation of *sub0* and *sub1* are performed in parallel. Two same transIdxLPS tables (*rLPS_Table*) are looked up concurrently. The 32-bit output is latched to the *rLPS_group* register firstly. The final *rLPS* value is selected by range [7:6] through *Mux0*. So the operation of looking up the 256 entries is split into two stages to reduce the propagation time.

- Optimization for Renormalization

Renormalization procedure is the computationally expensive part of CABAC. Each time a renormalization operation must be carried in one or more bits depending on the current interval range value. Exactly, the numerical difference between 8 and the bit index of the most significant bit (MSB) in the range value determines the times of the renormalization loop.

In our design, the renormalization operation is optimized using the algorithm features. For MPS, at most one bit is shifted since the MPS probability is never less than 0.5. Only the highest bit should be checked and it's enough using a simple inverter *inv0* to fulfill this task. For LPS, the range of the shifting bits is from 1 to 7 bits because the maximum range is 240 and minimum is 2. A First One Detector circuit (*FOD*) is employed to perform the leading one detection.

- Barrel Shifter

A *Data FIFO* is used to store the input bitstream. It can fetch more data from the external memory once its space is half full. The register *R2* latches the output of the *Data FIFO* in order to improve the timing. When the accumulator generates a carry, it indicates that the data in *R0* is useless, so *R0* loads the data from *R1* immediately. At the same time, *R1* loads the new word from *R2* and *R2* is updated using the *FIFO* output. Two *barrel shifters* storing a 16-bit window of the data from *R0* and *R1* are served for MPS and LPS branch respectively. The outputs of *sub2* and *sub3* are the accumulated length of decoded code words which decide how many bits should be shifted in the *barrel shifters*. Thus the shifters output always begin with the first bit of the code word to be decoded. Therefore, using the *FOD* and *barrel shifters*, the normalization can be finished in one single step.

For the bypass mode, the logic circuits of MPS branch can be reused to reduce the area. An additional subtraction is required to calculate the value of (*{offset, 1'b0/1'b1} - range*). No more operations are involved.

4 Simulation and Implementation

We have described the design in Verilog HDL at RTL level. According to H.264/AVC verification model [8], a C-code model of coefficient group decoding is also developed to generate simulation vectors. By testing with the conformance bitstreams including SD and HD sequences, Synopsys VCS simulation results show that our Verilog code is functionally identical with the H.264/AVC verification model.

The validated Verilog code is synthesized using 0.18-μm CMOS cells library by Synopsys Design Compiler. The gate count of each functional block is listed in Table 1. The circuit totally costs about 30.2K logic gates exclusive the register bank when the working frequency is set to 160-MHz. The register bank including 2,200 registers costs about 16,200 logic gates.

Table 1. Gate count profile

Functional block	Gate count
ctx_ram_ctrl	10,483
dec_one_coeff	7,615
dec_one_symbol	12,028
Total	30.2K+16.2K

Table 2. Comparison of Synthesized Results

	[5]	[6]	[7]	Proposed
Technology	0.13-μm	0.18-μm	0.18-μm	0.18-μm
Working frequency	200 MHz	/	/	160 MHz
Critical path	/	6.7 ns	3.3 ns	6.2 ns
Gate count	138K gates (logic + table)	30.0K gates ($0.3mm^2$) + 32×105 bits RAM	/	30.2K gates + 2,200 registers
Throughput	0.33~0.5 bit/cycle (averagely)	1~3 bins/cycle (averagely)	0.33 bin/cycle (exactly)	1 bin/cycle (exactly)
Capacity	CIF (Normal Case) at FPGA platform	SDTV (Normal Case) (720×576, 25fps)	/	HDTV (Worst Case) (1920×1080, 30fps)

The comparison between our proposed design and other designs in literature is presented in Table 2. The table shows the synthesized results and performance. Reference [5] can finish one bit decoding in 2~3 clock cycles averagely. But the H.264/AVC standard doesn't specify the maximum bit-to-bin rate. It's possible that one bit can produce a long bin string based on the algorithm features. These bins in the worst case will drop down its performance. Reference [6] can achieve 1~3 bins per clock cycle and support the SDTV application. However, it didn't provide any performance analyses in the worst case as well. Decoding 3 bins in one cycle can be fulfilled only in some special situations. Reference [7] needs 3 cycles to decode one bin, that is, 10 ns per one bin. The proposed implementation can guarantee decoding one bin per cycle even in the worst case and achieve the high throughput of 160M bins/s. According to the binrate constrains specified in the H.264/AVC standard, it's enough for real-time 1080i video decoding of H.264 High Profile at Level 4.1. Its critical path is well optimized and the pure data path is about 5.6 ns if the clock uncertainty (0.35 ns) and the library setup (0.26 ns) don't be counted in. Exactly, the proposed design does cost more silicon area. But the additional cost is controlled in a reasonable range through our optimization in both architecture level and circuit level.

5 Conclusion

This paper presents the design and VLSI implementation of a high throughput CABAC decoder for H.264/AVC. The proposed design is based on a 2-stage pipeline. As it is known, pipeline is the important technique for fast system design. But the potential data hazards in CABAC limit the system performance and it is impractical to adopt the pipeline method to the CABAC design directly. In this paper, the features of CABAC algorithm and the bin dependency is analyzed firstly. An efficient FSM is employed to control the whole procedure. Through the look-ahead estimation, the data hazards are solved. The pipeline-based architecture is proposed that can obtain the fluent data processing flow. In addition, the critical path at the circuit level is optimized to reduce the propagation time. The renormalization procedure can be finished in one step in the proposed circuit. Finally, we gave out simulation results and synthesis reports. Our design is verified with the standard video test sequences and it can achieve the throughputs of 160M bins/s. It can support the real-time CABAC decoding of HDTV 1080i H.264/AVC video. The architecture can be easily integrated into H.264/AVC CODEC SoC.

References

1. ISO ITU-T: advanced video coding for generic audio visual services. ITU-T Recommendation H.264 | ISO/IEC 14496-10 (MPEG-4 AVC) (2005)
2. Wiegand, T., Sullivan, G.J.: Overview of the H.264/AVC Video Coding Standard. IEEE Transactions on Circuits And Systems For Video Technology, 560–566 (2003)
3. Pennebaker, W.B., Mitchell, J.L., G, G.L., Arps, R.B.: An overview of the basic principles of the Q-Coder adaptive binary arithmetic coder. IBM J. Res. Develop., 717–726 (1988)
4. Marpe, D., Schwarz, H., Wiegand, T.: Context-based adaptive binary arithmetic coding in the H.264/AVC video compression standard. IEEE Transactions on Circuits and Systems for Video Technology, 620–636 (2003)
5. Chen, J.W., Chang, C.R., Lin, Y.L.: A hardware accelerator for context-based adaptive binary arithmetic decoding in H.264/AVC. In: ISCAS 2005. IEEE International Symposium on Circuits and Systems, pp. 4525–4528 (2005)
6. Yu, W., He, Y.: A high performance CABAC decoding architecture. IEEE Transactions on Consumer Electronics, 1352–1359 (2005)
7. Kim, C.H., Park, I.C.: High speed decoding of context-based adaptive binary arithmetic codes using most probable symbol prediction. In: ISCAS 2006. IEEE International Symposium on Circuits and Systems, pp. 1707–1710 (2006)
8. Suhring, K.: JVT H.264/AVC Reference Software, JM 9.8. (2005) http://bs.hhi.de/suehring/tml

Efficient Segment Based Streaming Media Transcoding Proxy for Various Types of Mobile Devices

Yoohyun Park[1], Yongju Lee[1], Hagyoung Kim[1], and Kyongsok Kim[2]

[1] Digital Home Research Division, Electronics and Telecommunications Research Institute, 161 Gajeong-Dong, Yuseong-Gu, Daejeon, Korea
[2] School of Computer Science and Engineering, Pusan National University, San-30, Jangjeon-Dong, Geumjeong-Gu, Busan, Korea
{bakyh, yongju, h0kim}etri.re.kr, gimgs@asadal.cs.pusan.ac.kr

Abstract. Streaming media has contributed to a significant amount of today's Internet Traffic. One solution of to solve this problems is using streaming proxy. There are two categories in streaming proxy; that is for homogeneous and heterogeneous client. The transcoding proxy can be used for heterogeneous client. The traditional proxy considers only a single version of the objects, whether they are to be cached or not. However the transcoding proxy has to evaluate the aggregate effect from caching multiple versions of the same object to determine an optimal set of cache objects. And recent researches about multimedia caching frequently store initial parts of videos on the proxy to reduce playback latency and archive better performance. Also lots of researches manage the contents with segments for efficient storage management. In this paper, we propose the efficient proxy policy that combines the segment-based caching mechanism and aggregate effect at transcoding proxy. The results demonstrate that the proposed algorithm outperforms in delay time, byte-hit ratio and the amount of transcoding data than other methods.

Keywords: Transcoding, Proxy Caching, Multimedia Caching, Segment based caching.

1 Introduction

Proxy caching has been widely used to cache static objects on the Internet so that subsequent requests to the same objects can be served directly from the proxy without contacting the original content server. However, the proliferation of multimedia content makes caching challenging due to the typical large size and the low latency and continuous streaming demands of media objects[1].

To solve the problems caused by large size media objects, researchers have developed a number of segment-based proxy caching strategies that cache partial segments of media objects instead of entire media objects[2].

And currently, most cache architectures are designed for end users with similar network links and device profiles. Differential content delivery must be based on users' network and computing environments. Users who are connected to a high-speed network prefer high-quality video wile users with low-bandwidth wireless links

H.H.S. Ip et al. (Eds.): PCM 2007, LNCS 4810, pp. 569–578, 2007.

may not enjoy the same quality of videos, since the delay is too large to be acceptable. Therefore, many web sites provide streaming video clips at several different bit-rates to serve users with different connection bandwidths. However, existing media caching systems still take each version of a video object as an independent object, rather than considering the aggregate effect from caching multiple versions of the same video object[3].

In this paper, we propose the segment-based caching algorithm for efficiently caching multiple versions of the same multimedia object. The main contributions of this paper are as follows: 1) the events in the transcoding proxy using segment-based caching technologies are defined; 2) we combine the profit based transcoding proxy and segment-based proxy.

The remainder of this paper is organized as follows. In section 2, we define about the events in transcoding proxy and describe about the transcoding graph that is based in this paper. In section 3, we provide the main idea of this paper that is segment based streaming media in transcoding proxy. And in section 4, we evaluate the simulation results. Finally in section 5, we summarize our work and conclude the paper.

2 Related Work

Much work has focused on adapting multimedia content delivery by various means. With regard to Web content and mobile client capabilities, the InfoPyramid[4] has two key components that define a representation scheme to provide multimodal, multi-resolution, and the selection method is achieve via client capabilities. In addition, the InfoPyramid contains individual components of the multimedia content, such as text, images, video, and audio, that has to be adapted to different client devices, and customizes its characteristics and processes via off-line transcoding, not by caching or streaming[5].

Traditional partial caching schemes store initial parts of popular videos on the proxy to reduce playback latency and achieve better performance via consideration of the IP network, the prefix size, and so on. In content layering or versions, the video streaming of multiple versions is compared to that of multiple layers in a caching environment, and mixed distribution/caching strategies have been shown to provide the best overall performance. However, layer-encoded formats may not always be available in the real world. TranSquid[6] maintains the server-directed transcoding information as part of meta-data and uses this information to convert its fidelity, modes, and user heuristics, while considering three distinct events(miss, partial hit, and hit). When the cache already contains a higher fidelity variant but no object, a partial hit event occurs. Outstanding transcoding-enabled algorithm for adaptive content delivery are the full version only(FVO) and transcoded version only (TVO) schemes, and TEC. FVO and TVO[7] utilize caching algorithms with transcoding capabilities, in which the video object is cached in the proxy. Under the TEC scheme, Transcoding-enabled Caching(TeC)[8], which is defined by TEC-11, TEC-12 and TEC-2, also defines three distinct events(exact hit, transcode hit, and miss) in a TeC proxy. TeC-11 and TeC-12 cache at most one version of a video object at the proxy at any time. On the other hand, TeC-2 may cache multiple versions of the same video and hence reduces the processing load on the transcoder. Tests of their performance using a synthesized and enterprized trace-driven simulation showed that TEC-11 and TEC-12 perform better than TEC-2 under similar network capacity conditions, and that the performance of TEC-2 is superior with heterogeneous network connectivity. However, all TEC algorithms evict one complete version even if the newly transcoded version is sufficiently smaller than the size of the victim[4].

Cheng-Yue et al. formulated a generalized Profit Function(PF) to evaluate the profit obtained by caching each version of an object[9]. However, their approach considers only the aggregate caching efficiency from caching multiple versions of small web objects, rather than video objects which need much more space for caching. Additionally, it employs only the delay saving ratio as a metric, whereas in fact the byte-hit ratio must also be considered, since the byte-hit ratio is important for streaming content caching. Chi-Feng et al. formulated a generalized Video Profit Function(VPF) to estimate the benefit of caching partial or whole clips of various versions of video objects[3].

3 Segment-Based Cache Replacement Algorithm for Streaming Media in Transcoding Proxy

3.1 Events in a Transcoding Proxy

We had defined the events in a transcoding proxy in [4]. But, we had assumed the proxy manage the content by the half-size unit of the content. So it isn't satisfied whole events at transcoding proxy with partial caching. In this paper, we define the events for partial caching in transcoding proxy.

When a client request a version of a content, transcoding proxy decides the event by caching status. Traditional proxy has only two events such as cache hit and miss. Some researches about transcoding proxy often include more events such as transcoding hit. We define these events(Hit, Miss, Transcoding Hit) as atomic events. To define events in a transcoding proxy using partial caching, we divide the content as 1 ~ 3 parts. If all parts are cached, it is defined as H(Hit). And if prefix part is cached, middle part isn't cached but there is a version that is able to transcode to the version, and suffix part isn't cached any version of that content, it is defined as HTM(Hit/Transcoding Hit/Miss). The second column in Table 1 shows the atomic events in each part. For example, in case of HT(Hit/Transcoding hit), the cached content is divided by 2 part(prefix/suffix). Atomic event in prefix part is Hit and that in suffix part is TransCoding Hit. The third column shows the next actions. For example, in case of event HTM, the proxy has to transcode(T) the middle part from original version in the transcoding proxy to the requested version and fetch/transcoding(F&T) the suffix part(Missed part) from original server.

All events in transcoding proxy are shown in Table 1. and Fig. 1. There are 7-events using these 3-atomic events such as H(Hit), M(Miss), T(Transcoding hit), HM(Hit/Miss), HT(Hit/Transcoding hit), HTM(Hit/Transcoding hit/Miss) and TM(Transcoding hit/Miss). In cases of M and HM, each has 2 cases whether the requested version is 0 or not. In case of M or HM with version 0, proxy has to fetch

Table 1. Events in a transcoding proxy

Event name	Atomic events in each range			Next action
H	Hit			No act
M(F[1])	Miss			F
M(F&T[2])	Miss			F&T
T[3]	TCH[4]			T
HM(F)	Hit	Miss		F
HM(F&T)	Hit	Miss		F&T
HT	Hit	TCH		T
HTM	Hit	TCH	Miss	T/F&T
TM	TCH	Miss		T/F&T

[1]: Fetch [2]: Fetch and Transcoding [3]: Transcoding [4]: TransCoing Hit

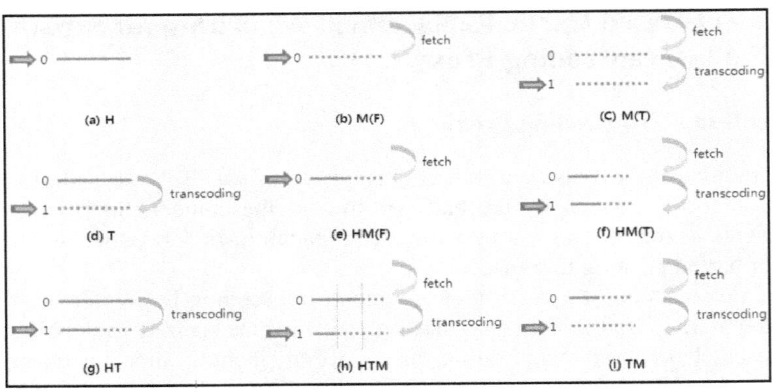

Fig. 1. Events in transcoding proxy

the data from original server. And the other case, proxy has to fetch the version 0 from original server and transcodes it to requested version simultaneously. Consequently, there are 9-cases events in transcoding proxy using partial caching.

3.2 The Weighted Transcoding Graph

[3] and [9] presented a weight transcoding graph of the transcoding relationship. As shown in Fig. 2, a weighted transcoding graph, G_i, is a directed graph of the transcoding relationship among transcodable versions of object i. For each vertex $v \in E[G_i]$, v represents a version of object i, Version x of object i is transcodable to version y iff there exists a directed edge $(x, y) \in E[G_i]$. The transcoding cost from version x to version y is represented as $w_i(x, y)$, so the cache algorithm must find the subgraph G_i' of the weighted transcoding graph G_i that minimizes the aggregate transcoding cost for object i. Fig. 3 presents an example, Fig. 3(a) plots the directed weithgted transcoding graph of object i. If versions 1 and 2 of object i are already

cached, then the transformation from the directed weighted graph of object I into such a subgraph is as shown in Fig. 3(b). When a client requests version 3 or 4, they will be transcoded from version 2 instead of version 1, because the transcoding cost of each transformation is smaller.

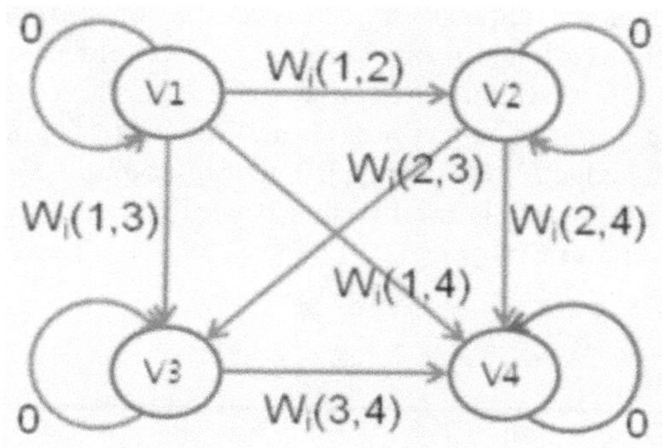

Fig. 2. Directed weighted transcoding graph of object *i*

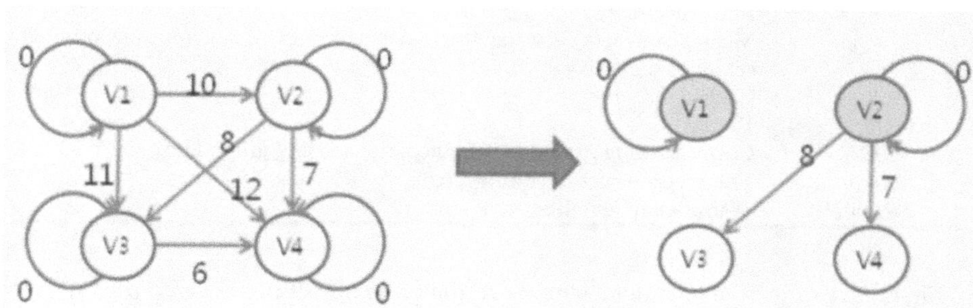

Fig. 3. Example of transformation from the directed transcoding graph into a subgraph

3.3 The Segment Based Profit Function(SPF)

The generalized SPF is almost same with generalized VPF in [3], but some meaning of variable is different. VPF use the mean reference rate and average duration of access to certain version. But SPF use total reference rate and cached size of certain version. The generalized SPF is composed of two factors – delay time saving and reduction in the number of bytes transmitted. In the proposed algorithm, this function is adopted to assign the eviction priorities of each object. Initially, the individual profit function is derived to estimate the profit from caching a single version of a video object. Then, the aggregate profit function is derived to estimate the profit when caching multiple versions of a video object simultaneously. Finally, depending on the aggregate profit function, the complete profit function is formulated for estimating the profit from caching a version of a video object when other versions of the object are already cached.

Let $o_{n,v}$ denote version v of video object n. The reference rates to different versions of objects are assumed to be statistically independent of each other and denoted by $r_{n,v}$, which is the number of accesses of version v of object n. The mean fetching delay for first several frames of version v of video object n from the original server to the transcoding proxy is denoted by $d_{n,v}$. The fetching delay is defined as the interval between the sending of the request and the receiving of sufficient data to play the film. The cache size of version v of object n is $S_{n,v}$. The number of cached segment of $S_{n,v}$ is $N_{n,v}$ and the bitrate of version v of object n is $R_{n,v}$. The corresponding extended weighted transcoding graph of object n is G_n and the cost of transcoding from $o_{n,v}$ to $o_{n,v'}$ is the value on the edge (v, v') in $E[G_n]$. The transcoding length from $o_{n,v}$ to $o_{n,v'}$ *is* $TRL(v, v')$. Table 2 lists symbols used in this paper. They are used in estimating the profit from caching version v of object n.

Table 2. List of Symbols

Symbol	Description
v_0	The original version of v and v'
$o_{n,v}$	Version v of object n
$o_{n,v}'$	Version v' that has the longest runtime more than $o_{n,v}$
$r_{n,v}$	Reference rate to $o_{n,v}$
$d_{n,v}$	Mean fetch delay for the first several frames of $o_{n,v}$ from the original server to the proxy
$S_{n,v}$	Cached size of $o_{n,v}$
$R_{n,v}$	Bitrate of $o_{n,v}$
G_n	Corresponding extended weighted transcoding graph of $o_{n,v}$
$w_n(v,v')$	Transcoding cost of from $o_{n,v}$ to $o_{n,v'}$
$TRL(v,v')$	Transcoding length from $o_{n,v}$ to $o_{n,v'}$

First, the profit from caching a single version of an object in the video proxy, when no other versions are cached, is considered. For client users, as optimal cache replacement algorithm is expected to minimize the response time. Thus, the individual profit from caching the partial version v of object n is calculated from the delay saving and bandwidth saving as follow.

Definition 1. SPF($o_{n,v}$) is a function used to calculate the individual profit for caching $S_{n,v}$ size of $o_{n,v}$, when no other version of object n is cached.

$$SPF(o_{n,v}) = \frac{\sum_{(v,v')\in E[G_n]} r_{n,v} \times TRL(v,v') \times R_{n,v'} \times (d_{n,v_1} + w_n(v_0,v') - w_n(v,v'))}{S_{n,v}}$$

Definition 2. SPF($o_{n,m1}, o_{n,m2,\dots}, o_{n,mk}$) is a function used to evaluate the aggregate profit for simultaneously caching $o_{n,m1}, o_{n,m2},\dots, o_{n,mk}$, where G_n' is the subgraph obtained by the MPTC procedure[3].

$$SPF(o_{n,m1}, o_{n,m2}, \ldots, o_{n,mk}) = \sum_{v,V[G_n']} \frac{\sum_{(v,v')\in E[G_n']} r_{n,v} \times TRL(v,v') \times R_{n,v'} \times (d_{n,v_0} + w_n(v_1,v') - w_n(v,v'))}{S_{n,v}}$$

Definition 3. SPF($o_{n,m}| o_{n,m1}, o_{n,m2,\ldots,} o_{n,mk}$) is a function used to calculate the individual profit for caching $S_{n,v}$ size of $o_{n,v}$, when $o_{n,m1}, o_{n,m2,\ldots,} o_{n,mk}$ are already cached, where m ≠m1, m2, …, mk.

$$SPF(o_{n,m} \mid o_{n,m1}, o_{n,m2}, \ldots, o_{n,mk}) = SPF(o_{n,m}, o_{n,m1}, o_{n,m2}, \ldots, o_{n,mk,}) - SPF(o_{n,m1}, o_{n,m2}, \ldots, o_{n,mk,})$$

3.3 Design of Cache Replacement Algorithm

Based on the generalized segment based profit function (SPF) formulated in 3.3, cache-replacement algorithm is designed. The replacement is happened when the new segment is needed at transcoding or fetching a content from original server. In other algorithms such as FVO, TVO, TeC, and transcoding graph based methods, they reserve a space area in advance at saving the first parts of the content. They are simple, but waste the storage because the speeds of fetch or transcoding are not fast to occupy the reserved space at that time. In our proposed segment based algorithm, it reserves a segment at new data as a small size unit. So, more different data can store in transcoding proxy than other methods. But it needs much more replacement operations.

Table 3. Replacement Algorithm for Segment based Transcoding Proxy

```
replacement(n,v,s)
{
   if(!is_room()) {
     find_profit_victim(victim_n, victim_v)
     delete_last_seg(victim_n, victim_v)
   }
   add_seg(n, v, s)
   update_profit(n)
}
is_room()
{
   if(capacity + SEG_SIZE > CAPACITY)
     return FALSE;
   else
     return TRUE;
}
```

4 Simulation Results

We implemented a simulator for performance analysis. In the client model, client devices can be partitioned into 5 classes (15%, 20%, 30%, 20%, 15%). That is, each data item can be transcoded to 5 different versions by the transcoding proxy to satisfy the users' requirements. The bit rate of the 5 versions of each media object are assumed to be 512, 256, 128, 64 and 32 kbps. The transcoding delay for the first sufficient segments of version from i to j is determined to $(j - i) * 500$ ms. The popularity of the video object follow a Zipf distribution with a skew factor α of 0.47. And we use 500 CBR video clips, whose lenghs are uniformly distributed (30 sec – 12 min). The simulation lasts 400 simulation hours with 100,000 accesses that follow a random Poisson distribution. The delays for fetching the first several segments of video objects from the original server are exponentially distributed ($\mu = 1.5$) and the ratio of the access duration to the total duration of a video sequence in a partial viewing environment is random distributed. The cache capacity is assumed to be (0.3 ~ 0.9) * ($\sum$ 128 kbps bit-rate object size) [3]. We assume the fetch speed from original server to proxy server is the same with the bit-rate of version 0 and the transcoding speed is 512 kbps. And the default segment size is 64 kbyte.

In our simulation, the variation of the performance of the proposed cache-replacement algorithm with cache capacity is investigated. We thought that the startup delay time and byte-hit ratio is important to client and the amount of transcoding data is important to the proxy system because of transcoding is CPU-intensive task[10]. So we simulate that factors as following figures. Fig. 4 and Fig. 5 plot the results of the evaluations of SVF and other policies such as TeC2[8], VPF-complete[3] and VPF-partial[3]. In each figure, X-axis is the relative cache size rate of the sum of 128 kbps bit-rate object size.

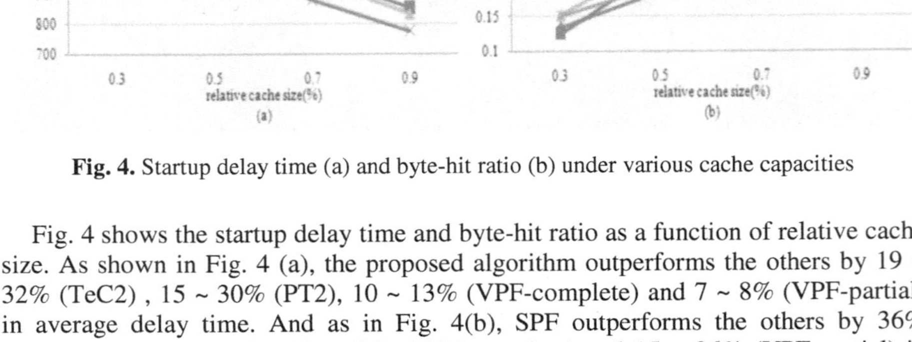

Fig. 4. Startup delay time (a) and byte-hit ratio (b) under various cache capacities

Fig. 4 shows the startup delay time and byte-hit ratio as a function of relative cache size. As shown in Fig. 4 (a), the proposed algorithm outperforms the others by 19 ~ 32% (TeC2) , 15 ~ 30% (PT2), 10 ~ 13% (VPF-complete) and 7 ~ 8% (VPF-partial) in average delay time. And as in Fig. 4(b), SPF outperforms the others by 36% (TeC2), 28 ~ 35%(PT2), 16 ~ 40% (VPF-complete) and 15 ~ 26% (VPF-partial) in byte-hit ratio. Byte hit ratio is defined as the number of bytes served from the cache to clients over the number of bytes requested from the clients. Specially, TeC system has worst performance in delay time, because it is based on LRU algorithm ignore the size and the popularity of the objects as well as the delay.

Fig. 5 shows the total jitter count that sum of jitter of each users and the amount of evicted data. Jitter count is increased when the client cannot receive some of data in play time. The evicted data is the sum of dumped data at replacement time for new caching data. The amount of evicted data is almost same with sum of the amount of fetching and transcoding data. As shown Fig. 5, SPF has fewer jitters and evicts data less than other algorithms.

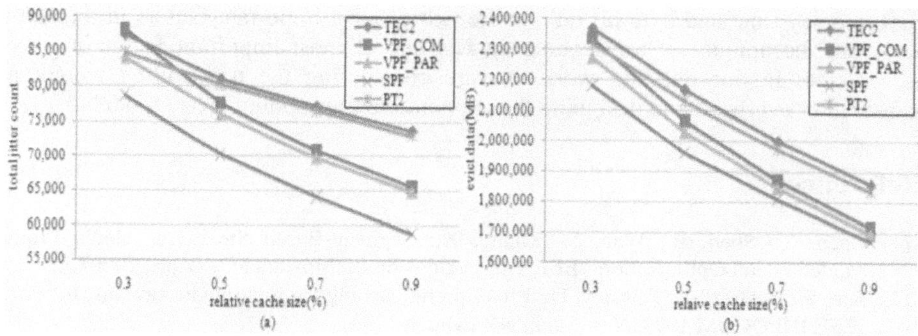

Fig. 5. Total jitter count(a) and the amount of evicted data(b)

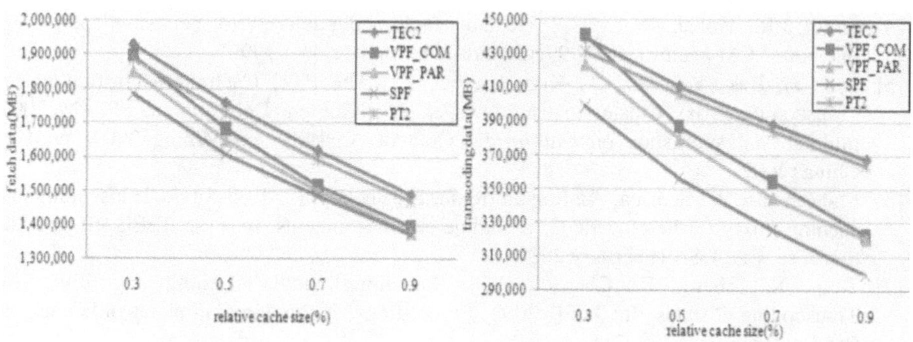

Fig. 6. Amount of transcoding data under various cache capacities

Fig. 6 shows the amount of fetching(a) and transcoding data(b). In this figure(b), the proposed algorithm outperforms the others by 10 ~ 23% (TeC2) , 8 ~ 21%(PT2), 8 ~ 11% (VPF-complete), 6 ~ 7% (VPF-partial) in the amount of transcoding data. Since transcoding is a CPU-intensive task[10], it is the better method that has less the amount of transcoding data. Also SPF less fetchs data from original server than other algorithms, as shown Fig. 6(a).

As a result, SPF caches and evicts data by segment-size unit, so it managed data by fine-grained unit than others, therefore it increases byte hit ratio and decreases the fetch, transcoding and evicted data in the proxy. And because SPF also consider the startup delay time, transcoding length and content size, it reduce the startup delay time than others.

5 Conclusions

In this paper, we first define 9-events at the transcoding proxy using atomic events such as Hit, Miss and Transcoding Hit. And we propose a segment based caching algorithm using aggregate profit values in streaming media transcoding proxy. The simulation results demonstrate that the proposed algorithm outperforms the competing algorithms in delay time, byte hit ratio and the amount of transcoding data. The startup delay time and byte-hit ratio is the two of most important factors in the client side, and the amount of transcoding data is one of most important factor in proxy server side. In our ongoing work, we are considering the transcoding weight as transcoding overhead and designing the cooperative transcoding proxy models.

References

[1] Chen, S., Shen, B., Wee, S., Zhang, X.: Segment-Based Streaming Media Proxy: Modeling and Optimization. IEEE Transactions on Multimedia 8(2) (April 2006)

[2] Sen, S., Rexford, J., Towsley, D.: Proxy prefix caching for multimedia streams. In: Proc. IEEE INFOCOM 1999, New York, NY (March 1999)

[3] Kao, C.-F., Lee, C.-N.: Aggregrate Profit-Based Caching Replacement Algorithms for Streaming Media Transcoding Proxy Systems. IEEE Transactions on Multimedia 9(2) (February 2007)

[4] Smith, J.R., Mohan, R., Li, C-S.: Scalable multimedia delivery for pervasive computing. In: Proc. ACM Multimedia 1999, Orlando, Florida (October 1999)

[5] Lee, Y., Bak, Y., Min, O., Kim, H., Lee, C.: The PT-2 Caching Algorithm in the Transcoding Proxy Cluster to Facilitate Adaptive Content Delivery. In: MCAM 2007. International Workshop on Multimedia Content Analysis and Mining 2007, WeiHai, China (2007)

[6] Maheshwari, A., Sharma, A., Ramamrithan, K., Shenoy, P.: TransSquid:Transcoding and caching proxy for heterogeneous e-commerce environments. In: Proc. IEEE RIDE 2002, San Jose, CA, USA (February 2002)

[7] Tang, X., Zhang, F., Chanson, S.T.: Streaming Media Caching Algorithms for Transcoding Proxies. In: ICPP 2002. Proceedings of the International Conference on Parallel Processing (2002)

[8] Shen, B., Lee, S.-J., Basu, S.: Caching Strategies in Transcoding-Enabled Proxy Systems for Streaming Media Distribution Networks. IEEE Transactions on Multimedia 6(2) (April 2004)

[9] Chang, C.-Y., Chen, M.-S.: On Exploring Aggregate Effect for Efficient Cache Replacement in Transcoding Proxies. IEEE Transactions on Parallel and Distributed Systems 14(6) (June 2003)

[10] Liu, D., Chen, S., Shen, B.: AMTrac:Adaptive Meta-caching for Transcoding. In: NOSSDAV 2006. Proceedings of ACM International Workshop on Network and Operating Systems Support for Digital Audio and Video, Newport, Rhode Island (May 22-23, 2006)

Distributed Streaming for Video on Demand

Ramesh Yerraballi and Shraddha Rumade

Department of CSE, University of Texas at Arlington,
P.O. Box 19015, Arlington TX 76019, USA
ramesh@cse.uta.edu, shraddha.rumade@ge.com

Abstract. Implementing reliable Video on Demand (VoD) systems over the Internet, which is inherently best-effort, is a challenge. Distributed streaming for Video on Demand addresses this challenge with a combination of two techniques. The first, Distributed Video Streaming using Multicast (DVSM) involves video streaming from multiple servers to overcome path congestion by exploiting path diversity. The second technique, Asynchronous Hybrid mechanism for Video on Demand, implements a segmentation-based periodic broadcast to effectively utilize network bandwidth and decrease latency. The combination involves devising new algorithms for bandwidth estimation, segment partitioning and scheduling. A simulation of our proposed solution demonstrates its effectiveness. Specifically the results show, the prompt reaction of our strategy to congestion, and, the effect the various parameters have on system performance. The results shed light on parameters that can be fine-tuned for an effective VoD system.

Keywords: Video on Demand, Patching, Scheduling, Distributed Streaming, Multicast.

1 Introduction

Video on demand (VoD) systems allow users to choose what videos to play and when to play them. A user interacts with the server with playback, pause, forward and rewind operations. The basic components of a generic VoD system are users, service providers, program providers and the network. The users request videos from the service providers who in turn get the video from program providers and make it available to the clients via the network. A single program provider or server might lead to large access latency for clients. Thus there is a need to distribute the content on a group of linked VoD servers for shorter access times. Content distribution is determined by both video popularity load distribution[1].

Implementing streaming video over the Internet requires that the video servers continuously stream the video while coping with network congestion. To address this issue, standards are now available to reserve bandwidth and buffer resources along the network path. Multicasting is also used to further reduce network bandwidth requirements [2]. Further, clients implement buffering to store out of sync packets. Buffer size limitations result in overflow or underflow if the desired transmission rate is not sustained. Additional protocols are used to manage

H.H.S. Ip et al. (Eds.): PCM 2007, LNCS 4810, pp. 579–589, 2007.

timing issues. Although adequate for low bit rate applications, systems using bit rates greater than about 1Mbps still require "tuning" to achieve optimum and reliable performance.

Current research in distributed VoD, focuses on selecting among replicated servers to serve a client request completely[5,9]. That is, once a request is directed to a server, that server takes care of the entire video transmission to the client or a multicast group of clients. In our work a single video is streamed from different servers in an interleaved fashion to overcome path congestion as well as provide continuous streaming to avoid breaks in the video playback.

We propose a design based on distributed streaming of fragmented videos. New algorithms for deciding the streaming sequence of segments are designed. A mathematical relation between the streaming time of a segment and its playback duration is derived to ensure continuous playback even in case of path congestion. The proposed solution is validated with a simulation study conducted using the OPNET Modeler[15].

2 Related Work

Batching and patching are two commonly used techniques in traditional VoD systems. We look at recently reported research that combines these two. In Maximum Factored Queue Length (MFQL)[3], a batching approach and a threshold-based patching scheme are combined to propose two hybrid multicast algorithms. Their idea is to link up small VoD servers to a network so servers with excess retrieval bandwidth help servers that are temporarily overloaded.

In [4], the Virtual Interface Architecture (VIA) communication protocol and the interval cache algorithm are used to minimize the time required to transfer data across the connecting network. In [5], server selection techniques for a system of replicated batching VoD servers is reported. All of these works focus on efficient ways for selecting one amongst the distributed servers and streaming the video with minimum delay. But the issue of delay due to network congestion has not been considered, which is the focus of our work. Also lower startup delay is one of our other main design concerns.

In other related work, implementation of Distributed VoD servers such as the Yima [6] and VoDKA [7] demonstrate cost effective solutions for Video on Demand services.

3 Preliminaries

Two of the techniques that form the basis of our research are presented in this section. Distributed Video Streaming using Multicast (DVSM) [8] employs multiple servers to stream video to a group of receivers. It provides path diversity [9,10] via multiple servers and provides efficient bandwidth utilization via multicast streaming. DVSM comprises of three main algorithms, bandwidth estimation, rate allocation and packet partitioning. Receivers send asynchronous feedback in the form of control packets indicating current bandwidth and loss estimates.

Servers process the feedback and change sending rates and sending sequences. Bandwidth estimation is done at a receiver using a TCP-friendly sending rate estimation formula [11]. When one of the paths from a server to a receiver gets congested above a predefined threshold, the receiver sends out control packets notifying all the servers about the change in network status. Each server then computes a new consistent bandwidth distribution and adjusts its sending rate and the packets to be sent accordingly.

Rate allocation in DVSM tries to compensate the sending rate of a congested sender by leveraging the rates of less congested sender(s). If a sender's available bandwidth falls below the equally (initially) divided sending rate, increasing the rates of other servers compensates for the loss in bandwidth of the server. Distributed Streaming for VoD does not require rate allocation for two reasons. Firstly the receivers always start buffering the segment before its playback begins. So it is not required to stream the segment with a higher rate in case of path congestion. Secondly the rates of the channels are set in a way to maintain playback continuity at the receiver. Changing these rates would disrupt the segment schedule. Thus rate adjustment is neither required nor permissible.

Packet partitioning algorithm ensures that the received packets arrive in an interleaved fashion from multiple senders, so as to reduce the startup delay. The goals of the packet-partitioning algorithm are to maximize the difference between the playback and arrival time of a packet received at the receiver, to avoid missing and minimize duplicate packets.

Asynchronous hybrid VoD implements a segmentation-based periodic broadcast [12] technique that combines the best features of broadcasting [13] and patching[14]. If a request comes when the broadcast of a video has already begun, then the part that the request has missed is patched in such a manner, as to ensure that the request is able to catch up soon with the broadcast. Using segmented video and periodic broadcasting limits the amount of patching to a maximum of one segment. There is no constraint of synchronicity on the video streams which reduces the implementation complexity of the system. Further, the system provides VCR like functionality very efficiently.

4 System Model

Our system comprises of a Central Server, subordinate servers (senders), and, receivers (clients). The senders store all the video content of M popular videos. The central server controls the distribution of requests from receivers to the senders. It takes care of streaming the first video segment as well as patching the part of the first segment to receivers that have missed it. One or more secondary servers which will stream the remaining video. A receiver joins the multicast of a number of senders to receive different segments of the video from different servers.

A video of length L is divided into K segments of equal size. A Segment is further divided into packets to fit the maximum segment size of the transport layer. Scheduling takes place at the Segment level though retransmission happens at the Packet level. The Central Server schedules the multicast of the first

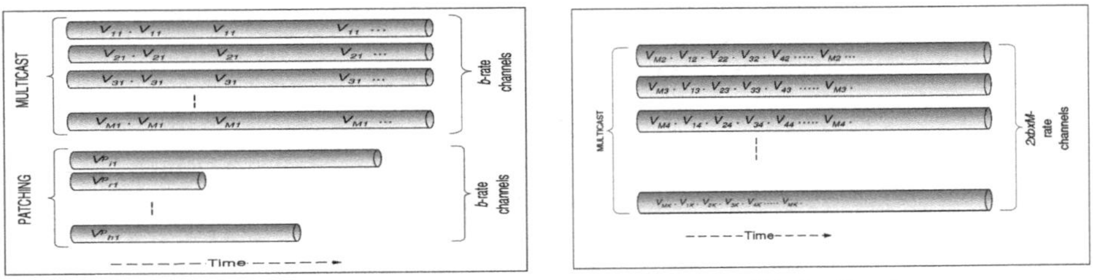

(a) At Central Server (b) At Senders

Fig. 1. Channel Partitioning

segment of all popular videos cyclically over M channels each of bandwidth b. Segment V_{X1} is the first segment of the Xth video. Figure 1(a). shows the channel partitioning on the Central Server. The Senders simultaneously schedule the multicast of the remaining $K-1$ segments of all the videos on $K-1$ channels each of bandwidth $2 \times b \times M$. As shown in Figure 1(b), the ith channel carries the $(i+1)^{th}$ segments of all the M videos in a cyclic manner. It is important to note that out of the M video segments that are scheduled only those which are being requested and assigned to this sender by the Central Server are actually multicast, the remaining are scheduled only as place holders. At time t, a client sends a video request to the Central Server. The central server (CS) calculates its *estimated wait time* (w^e) for the request. This is given by the time until the next scheduled multicast of the requested video. Recall that the first segment of each popular video is being repeatedly multicast on a dedicated channel. This estimate is used in deciding how to deal with the request as follows:

- *Case A*: If the estimated wait time (w^e) for the request falls within a threshold δ seconds of the end of the current multicast of the first segment then the request is made to wait till the start of the next cycle of multicast of the first segment of the requested video.
- *Case B*: If the estimated wait time (w^e) is longer than the threshold, the Central Server patches the part of the first segment of the current multicast that the request has missed.

4.1 Multicast Schedule on Senders

When the Central Server receives a client request it notifies the receiver to join the multicast of N channels where N segments starting from the second segment are scheduled for multicast, one on each after an interval of one segment-playback time. After $N-1$ segment-playback intervals with respect to the end of the current segment transmission, each sender schedules the multicast of a segment which is calculated as the currently streamed segment number $+N$. For example. Suppose that video 2 is requested and the Central Server notifies senders 1,2 and 3 to schedule the 2nd, 3rd and 4th segment. The 1st server schedules the multicast of the 5th segment after two playback durations since streaming the 2nd segment.

So when the receiver starts getting the 4th segment it also starts buffering the 5th segment, to maintain continuity in playback. Similarly sender 2 and 3 schedule multicast of segments 3 and 6 and segments 4 and 7 respectively and so on.

4.2 Control Packets and Synchronization Sequence Number

When a sender receives a control packet it has to identify the receiver that has sent it in order to determine the segment streaming sequence of which video multicast has to be changed. The control packet format is modified from that in DVSM to include information about the multicast group, the segment number and the packet number within the segment that the receiver expects to receive next. The packet contains, delay (D_i) and loss-rate(L_i) values for each of the

D_1	L_1	D_2	L_2	...	D_n	L_n	M	*Packet*	*Sync*

N senders. M is the multicast group of the receiver, which is received from the central server at the start. *Sync* represents the synchronization sequence number and is the next segment requested by the receiver.The receivers buffer the segment next to the one which is currently being played, in order to maintain continuity in playback. When it finds packet loss in the reception of a segment it sends a control packet with the *Sync* field set to that segment number. As the segment size is large, the complete requested segment is unlikely to be in transit and not yet reached the receiver. Thus the receiver notifies the exact segment number using the *Sync* field, while it uses the *Packet* field to convey an estimate of the packet number that has to be sent next by the senders based on what may already be in transit.

4.3 Segment Partitioning Algorithm (SPA)

When a sender receives a control packet, it immediately runs the SPA to determine the next sequence of segments in the video stream to be sent. All of the senders arrive at the same conclusion since they use the same copy of the control packet to run the same algorithm. All senders use the segment number in the control packet to initialize the segment partitioning algorithm. Each sender calculates the estimated time difference between arrival and playback time of the requested packet number in the control packet. The calculation of this estimate is based on the Delay values corresponding to each sender as reported by the receiver via the control packet. All the senders can determine the sender who maximizes this time difference, and then that sender sends the requested part of the segment. Every time a sender is selected to stream the next segment the segment count is incremented by 1. After that, the segment partitioning algorithm runs every half a segment playback interval by selecting a sender to send the next segment.

4.4 Playback Continuity

In order to maintain continuity in play the user must be able to start buffering the second segment before the first segment completes play. It is required that the receiver be able to buffer the next segment even in case of congestion where it has to receive the segment from a different sender after receiving a part from the first sender. The following constraint must be satisfied: $\frac{L_s}{b} \geq 2 \times \frac{L_s}{\frac{(B_m - b \times M)}{K-1}} \times M$

The time that it takes to playback a segment must be greater than or equal to twice the time that it takes for the server to start transmission of the next segment. This ensures that in one segment playback time the next segment is scheduled for multicast twice. Thus during a segment transmission, if the receiver notifies congestion on the path from one sender the remaining part of the segment is streamed from another sender within the previous segment playback time. This condition gives the value of K, the number of segments to fragment the video into: $K \leq \frac{B_m - b \times M}{2 \times b \times M} + 1$

5 Simulation Study and Results

The model was implemented using OPNET Modeler [15] for validation and performance study. "OPNET Modeler is the industry's leading environment for network modeling and simulation, allowing one to design and study communication networks, devices, protocols, and applications with unmatched flexibility and scalability". Finite state machine (FSM) modeling was used to simulate the protocol behavior. Process and node models with full functionality for the Central Server, Senders and Receivers were designed and implemented. Figure 2 shows the network model with the positioning of the Central server, senders and receivers. NSFNet backbone network (July 1989-November 1992) was used for the network topology. In each scenario, there exist congestion links shared with other TCP traffic. All the links are 100Mbps except the congestion links which are 100Kbps each. During the simulation period, a burst of TCP traffic is started and stopped to test how Distributed Streaming for Video on Demand compares to DVSM [8]. A video of length 120 minutes is streamed to the receiver(s). Each receiver is assumed to have buffering capability of $2L_s$. In the first scenario we look at how the system adjusts to congestion in case of 3 and 6 servers respectively. Table 1 lists the simulation parameters used. First we consider 3 senders $S1$, $S2$ and $S3$ to be streaming video to the receivers. We shall

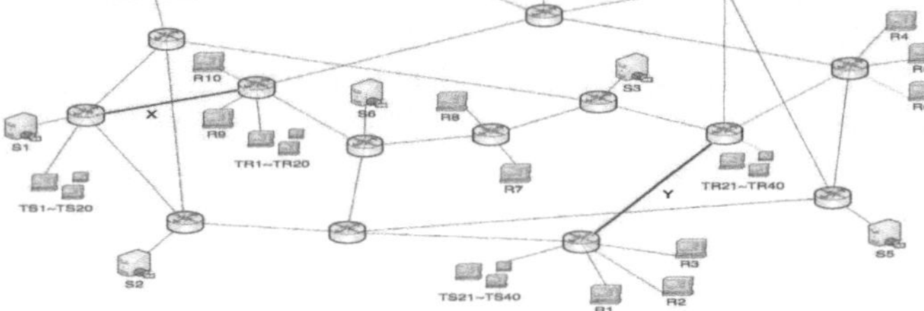

Fig. 2. NSFNet Backbone Network for Simulation

Table 1. Simulation Parameters

Video length, L	120 min
Total Bandwidth, B	200Mbps
Video coding rate, b	1.5Mbps
Number of segments, K	4
Length of a segment, Ls	30 min
Patching threshold, δ	Ls/8 - Ls/3
Multicast to patching ratio, α	0.5-0.8
Number of patching channels	53
Number of videos when N = 3	10
Number of videos when N = 6	20

look at the behavior of the system for the receivers falling in the same multicast group. Receivers $R1$, $R2$, $R7$ and $R8$ send video requests at 103, 108, 110 and 112 seconds respectively for the same video (say video 2) and so fall in the same multicast group as decided by the Central Server. There are two groups of TCP connections sharing a congestion path with S1 and S3. Congestion paths are represented with thicker lines. Link X is a congestion link shared with receivers $R7$ and $R8$ and link Y is a congestion link shared with receivers $R1$ and $R2$. $TS1 \sim TS20$ and $TS21 \sim TS40$ represent the TCP servers and $TR1 \sim TR20$ and $TR21 \sim TR40$ represent the TCP clients. TCP transmissions start and stop during the simulation to simulate congestion and to see if $S1$ and $S3$ adjust accordingly. The simulation results demonstrate the impact of the various parameters on the performance of our strategy, and the responsiveness of the strategy to congestion in the network.

5.1 Performance Study

Important performance metrics for a VoD system are, the average startup latency for a client and the capacity of the system to handle client requests. These metrics will be studied in the following. All the statistics are in a $\pm5\%$ confidence interval with a confidence level of 95% [16]. Figure 3(a) shows the impact of bandwidth partitioning on latency. For a given value of α as we increase the arrival rate we observe that the latency stays steady till a point after which it increases rapidly. Till the point where the latency remains steady, a video request finds a patching channel available on arrival, after that it has to wait for patching channels to be free before it is serviced. Values of α below 0.6 give poor performance, as the bandwidth assigned to the multicast component is less. Thus the latency offset which is due to the multicast delay is larger. When α is 0.6 we get a very good performance, as the multicast delay component is around 25 seconds and we are able to support up to 0.1 arrivals per second (6 arrivals per minute) with a latency of no more than 120 seconds.

The impact of δ on latency is shown in figure 3(b). During less popular times when the request arrivals are few we can use smaller values of δ ($1/8^{th}$ Ls) , as this would keep the latency low (less than 15 seconds). Higher values of threshold

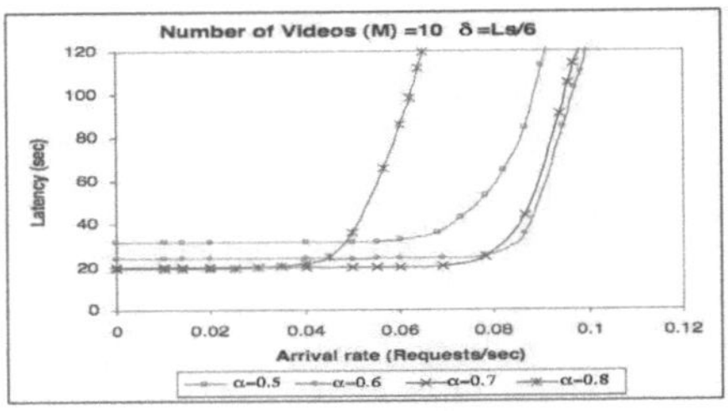

(a) Impact of Bandwidth Partitioning

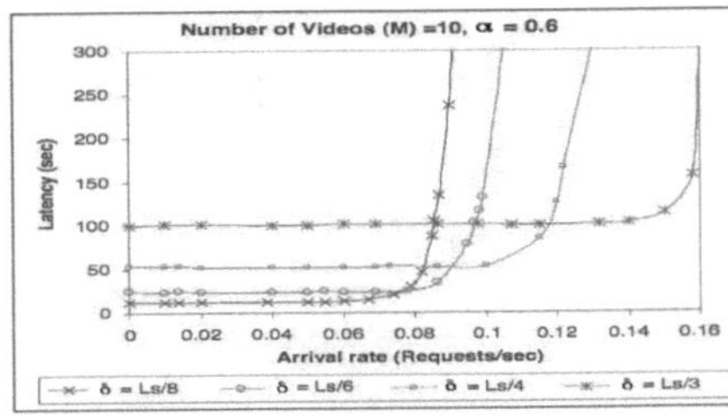

(b) Impact of Threshold

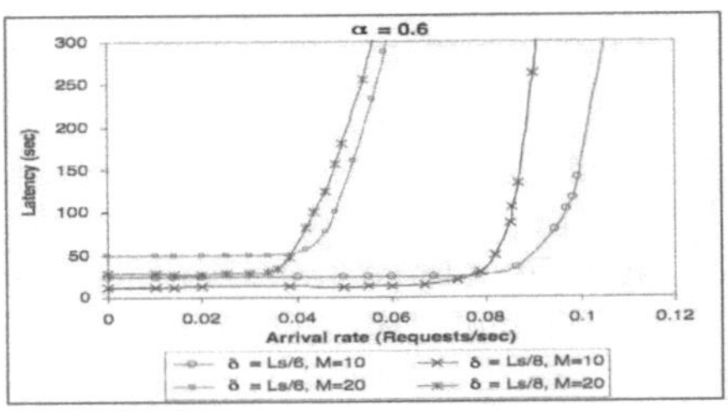

(c) Impact of Supporting more Videos

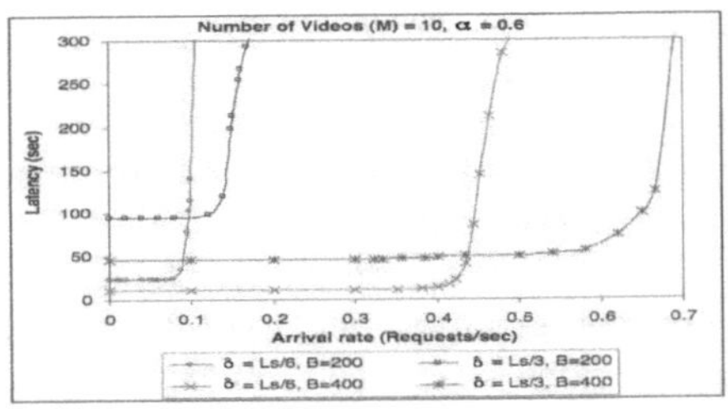

(d) Impact of more Net Bandwidth.

Fig. 3. Latency Results

are desirable for busier times (up to $1/3^{rd}$ Ls) with a tolerable latency of 100 seconds.

The system can also support more videos with a compromise on the maximum number of supported arrivals. If the number of popular videos, M, is 20 as opposed to 10 then we can still support a reasonable number of arrivals, about 3 per minute. Here we can choose δ such that we can handle more requests by compromising on the latency. Figure 3(c) shows the latency plots for supporting more videos.

Increasing the total bandwidth also affects the latency. Figure 3(d) shows that with an increase (doubling) in bandwidth the number of requests that can be handled increases around five-fold (0.08 to 0.4 and 0.13 to 0.58). This indicates that bandwidth enhancements are efficiently utilized by the system to improve capacity (support more request arrivals).

5.2 Response to Network Congestion

We observe that the senders adjust their sending sequence in response to the network congestion ensuring continuous playback at the receivers. Figure 4(a) and 4(b) show the loss rates and throughputs with three senders $S1$, $S2$ and $S3$ (not shown) measured at receivers $R7$ and $R8$ (not shown). High loss rate for $S1$ is observed when there are TCP connections (to simulate congestion, twenty TCP sources and receivers start transmitting) competing on the shared link X after t=455s (7 minutes 35 seconds) till t=487s (8 minutes 7 seconds). That

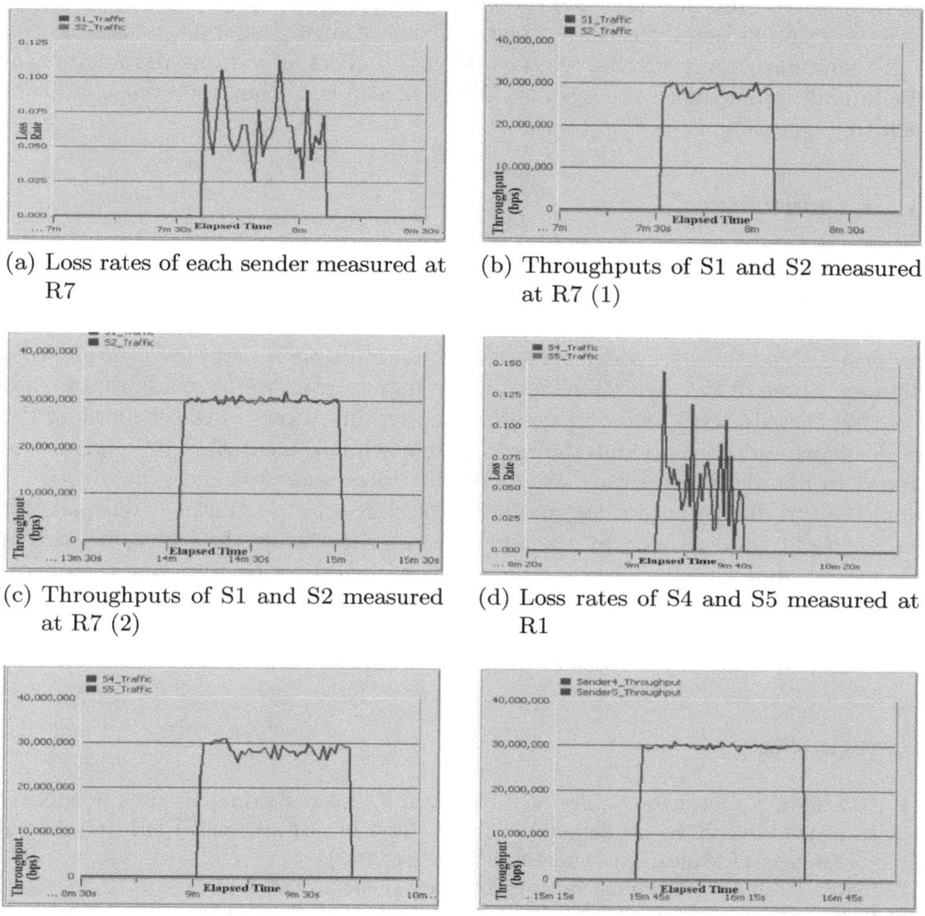

(a) Loss rates of each sender measured at R7

(b) Throughputs of S1 and S2 measured at R7 (1)

(c) Throughputs of S1 and S2 measured at R7 (2)

(d) Loss rates of S4 and S5 measured at R1

(e) Throughputs of S4 and S5 measured at R1 (1)

(f) Throughputs of S4 and S5 measured at R1 (2)

Fig. 4. Network Congestion Results

is, congestion on link X causes the loss rate for $S1$ at receivers $R7$ and $R8$ to increase. The throughput of S1 continuously drops also. In response, $R7$ and $R8$ send out control packets to notify the senders to change the segment sending sequence. Consequently S2 (figure 4(c)) is selected to stream the remaining part of the second segment. Next we consider six senders $S1 \sim S6$ while supporting 20 videos (Figures 4(d), 4(e) 4(f)). Videos 1 to 10 are replicated on S1, S2 and S3 while videos 11 to 20 are replicated on S4, S5 and S6. In this case R1 and R2 request for video 12 while R7 and R8 still request video 2. Thus S1, S2 and S3 service requests from R7 and R8 while S4, S5 and S6 handle those from R1 and R2. R7 and R8 do not experience any congestion in this case and senders $S1 \sim S3$ continue with the initial segment schedule to stream all the segments of video 2. R7 and R8 face congestion on link Y due to TCP connections. We observe a similar reactiveness to cope with congestion as in the previous scenario.

To summarize our results, we have seen the effect of various parameters on the latency provided by the system. We have also seen that the system adjusts well to congestion.

6 Conclusion

This paper extends existing research on Video on Demand systems by presenting a combination of two techniques, viz. DVSM and Asynchronous Hybrid mechanism for Video on Demand. Distributed streaming for Video on Demand has proposed algorithms for video streaming from multiple servers in an interleaved manner. Some of the algorithms in the two base techniques were adapted to suit the new Distributed Video on Demand Architecture. Roles of the sender and the receiver are modified to suit the new system while a Central Server was introduced to handle initial setup. We were able to provide low access latencies for requests arriving in an ad hoc manner. The derived mathematical relations for latency hold good as seen by the simulation results while the characteristics of the system match well with those of DVSM with respect to adjusting to congestion. As a part of the future work we can devise a technique for the distributed streaming of the first segment. Also selective placement of the video content and scalability are two other areas to look into.

References

1. Gonzalez, S., Navarro, A., Lopez, J., Zapata, E.: Load sharing based on popularity in distributed video on demand systems. In: Proceedings of IEEE International conference on Multimedia and Expo (August 2002)
2. Sigma Designs, Streaming video technology (February 2005)
3. Gonzalez, S., Navarro, A., Lopez, J., Zapata, E.: Two hybrid multicast algorithms for optimizing resources in a distributed vod system. In: Proceedings of the 10th International Multimedia Modeling Conference (January 2004)
4. Oh, S., Chung, S.: A distributed vod server based on via and interval cache. In: Proceedings of the 12th international workshop on Network and operating systems support for digital audio and video (May 2002)
5. Guo, M., Ammar, M.H., Zegura, E.F.: Selecting among replicated batching video-on-demand servers. In: Proceedings of the 12th international Workshop on Network and Operating Systems Support For Digital Audio and Video (May 2002)
6. Zimmermann, R., Fu, K., Shahabi, C., Yao, D., Zhu, H.: Yima: Design and evaluation of a streaming media system for residential broadband services. In: Proceedings of the VLDB 2001 Workshop on Databases in Telecommunications (September 2001)
7. Barreiro, M., Gulas, V.M., Freire, J.L., Snchez, J.J.: An erlang-based hierarchical distributed vod. In: EUC2001. Proceedings of the 7th International Erlang/OTP User Conference, Ericsson Utvecklings, AB (September 2001)
8. Lee, B.: Distributed video streaming using multicast, M.S. thesis (2004), ISBN: 0-496-22963-0

9. Nguyen, T.P., Zakhor, A.: Distributed video streaming over the internet. In: Proceedings of Multimedia Computing and Networking (January 2002)
10. Nguyen, T.P., Zakhor, A.: Path diversity with forward error correction (pdf) system for packet switched networks. In: Proceedings of INFOCOM (2003)
11. Floyd, S., Fall, K.: Promoting the use of end-to-end congestion control in the internet. IEEE/ACM Transactions on Networking (TON) 7(4), 458–472 (1999)
12. Yerraballi, R., Zhao, X., Kanabar, J.: A new asynchronous hybrid mechanism for video on demand. In: Proceedings of 29th Euromicro Conference (September 2003)
13. Bradshaw, M.K., Wang, B., Gao, L., Kurose, J., Shenoy, P., Towsley, D., Sen, S.: Periodic broadcast and patching services: implementation, measurement, and analysis in an internet streaming video testbed. In: Proceedings of the International Conference on Multimedia (August 2001)
14. Hua, K., Cai, Y., Sheu, S.: Patching: A multicast technique for true video-on-demand services. In: Proceedings of ACM Multimedia (1998)
15. OPNET Inc., OPNET Modeler: Accelerating Network R&D, www.opnet.com
16. Jain, R.: The Art of Computer Systems Performance Analysis. Wiley-Interscience, New York, NY (1991)

Context Aware Body Area Networks for Telemedicine

V.M. Jones[1], H. Mei[1], T. Broens[1], I. Widya[1], and J. Peuscher[2]

[1] University of Twente/Department of Computer Science, Enschede, The Netherlands
{V.M.Jones, H.Mei, T.H.F.broens, I.Widya}@utwente.nl
[2] Twente Medical Systems International, Enschede, The Netherlands
Jan.Peuscher@tmsi.com

Abstract. A Body Area Network (BAN) is a body worn system which provides the user with a set of mobile services. A BAN incorporates a set of devices (eg. mp3 player, video camera, speakers, microphone, head-up display, positioning device, sensors, actuators). A BAN service platform for mobile healthcare and several health BANs targetting different clinical applications have been developed at the University of Twente. Each specialization of the BAN is equipped with a certain set of devices and associated application components, as appropriate to the clinical application. Different kinds of clinical data may be captured, transmitted and displayed, including text, numeric values, images and multiple biosignal streams. Timely processing and transmission of such multimedia clinical data in a distributed mobile environment requires smart strategies. Here we present one approach to designing smart distributed applications to deal with multimedia BAN data; namely the context awareness approach developed in the FREEBAND AWARENESS project.

Keywords: Telemonitoring, multimedia medical data, Body Area Networks, Context awareness, power management.

1 Introduction

With the development of mobile and high capacity personal computing devices, miniature wearable sensors and ever improving wireless communication infrastructures, mobile healthcare (m-health) is becoming a realistic prospect from the technical point of view [1-4]. The potential now exists for healthcare professionals and patients to transfer health related data anywhere anytime. Furthermore, the healthcare systems of different healthcare providers are increasingly interconnected. Consequently, ubiquitous access to and availability of healthcare information is becoming technically feasible. However current mobile devices and wireless communications still suffer from certain limitations which restrict the ability to store, process and transmit large volumes of multimedia clinical data in real time. Mobile devices still have limited memory and processing power, and are especially restricted by of battery life. State of the art wireless communications technologies now handle high bandwidth applications, however transmission of some kinds of (multimedia) clinical data strains or exceeds the capacity available today. Furthermore applications need to adapt to the dynamically changing communications environment and to the changing needs and

H.H.S. Ip et al. (Eds.): PCM 2007, LNCS 4810, pp. 590–599, 2007.

situation of the user. For this and other reasons m-health applications need to be context aware. In this paper we describe the AWARENESS approach to context awareness for BAN-based m-health applications.

The University of Twente and partners have been developing mobile health systems based on Body Area Networks (BANs) since 2001 [5]. A number of BANs and a BAN service platform targeted at the healthcare domain were developed during the course of several European and Dutch projects. We define a *health BAN* as a network of communicating devices (sensors, actuators, multimedia devices etc.) worn on, around or in the body which provides mobile health related services to the user.

The generic health BAN has been specialised for different m-health applications targeted at different clinical conditions, to provide a variety of telemedicine services. Each specialization of the BAN is equipped with a certain set of BAN devices and associated application components as appropriate to the clinical application.

A BAN for health monitoring incorporates one or more sensors capturing biosignals, which are transmitted to a remote healthcare location for viewing by health professionals. One of the BAN devices, the Mobile Base Unit (MBU), acts as a communication gateway to other networks and takes care of local storage and processing. The MBU has been implemented on a number of different PDAs and smart phones (e.g. IPAQ 3870, Qtek 9090). BAN data has been transmitted to the remote location via a range of wireless network technologies including WiFi, GPRS and UMTS. Typically multiple biosignals will be captured and, depending on the measurement, will be displayed as numeric readouts or as biosignal traces along a time axis. In some cases visualisations of biosignal data will be combined with video or medical images. BAN output is often therefore multimedia in nature, incorporating text, numeric data, sensor data to be presented graphically and possibly streaming video or still images.

The first application envisaged for health BANS was the trauma application, where an accident victim would have a trauma patient BAN attached to them by the ambulance paramedics. This BAN would incorporate vital signs sensors and would transmit the casualty's vital signs to the hospital emergency room. At the same time the paramedics would wear BANs which would transmit video of the scene to the hospital and provide two way audio communications between the paramedics and the hospital staff. The intention was to enable a distributed team such that the emergency room team could collaborate with the paramedics at the scene and could assess the condition of the casualty in order to better prepare for their reception at the hospital.

During the European IST project MobiHealth [6] the first BAN service platform and a number of variants of the health BAN were developed and trialled in four European countries, with various biosignals monitored and transmitted to remote healthcare centers over GPRS and UMTS. The nine trials in MobiHealth included telemonitoring for cardiology and respiratory insufficiency (COPD) patients, for pregnant mothers and in trauma care. In the trauma trial both the anticipated trauma patient BAN and paramedic BAN were implemented but the latter using still images rather than video.

BAN development subsequently continued in the Dutch FREEBAND AWARENESS project [7] and the European eTEN project HealthService24 [8].

In AWARENESS the innovation lies in applying context awareness to build smart BAN applications for neurology. In this paper, we discuss why context awareness is important for health BANs and the processing of multimedia medical data and give an example of how context awareness may be used to address the problem of power management in mobile devices.

In Section 2 we introduce our concept of health BAN. In Section 3 we describe specializations of the generic health BAN for clinical applications in neurology and in Section 4 we discuss some issues relating to context awareness. In Section 5 we give an example of context awareness relating to power management as applied in AWARENESS. In Section 6 we discuss some challenges and possible future directions.

2 Health BANs

Figure 1 shows the general configuration of the BAN service platform. The patient wears a set of devices which communicate via the MBU with a user (or with a software application) at a remote location via the BAN Backend server. Some sensors are standalone, others are front-end supported. In the latter case the sensors are connected to a sensor front end or 'sensor-box' which powers the sensors and performs some signal processing and filtering. At the remote location a health professional can view biosignals and other BAN data and send control commands to the BAN. IntraBAN communication may be wireless (eg via BlueTooth) or wired, or a mixture of the two, and extraBAN communication is wireless (over GPRS, UMTS, WiFi etc.)

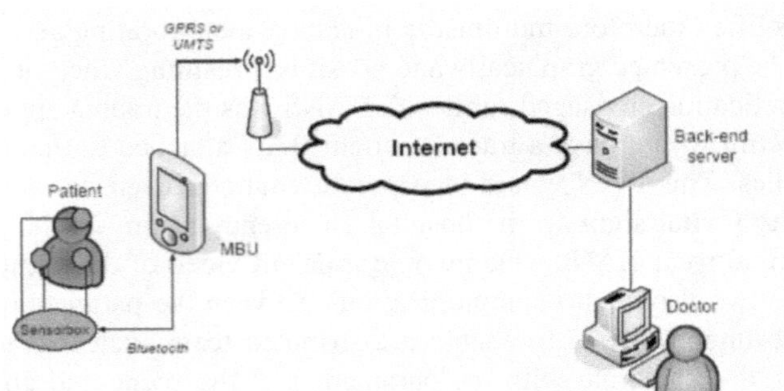

Fig. 1. A health BAN Network for Telemedicine

Figure 2 shows one variant of the BAN. In this case the MBU is implemented on a Qtek PDA. The sensors are electrodes and a respiration sensor, examples of front end supported sensor systems. In the centre is the sensorbox (the Mobi from TMSI). Figure 3 shows a visualisation of output from the patient trauma BAN. The upper part shows ECG output from three electrodes; below that the derived QRS complex is displayed. Lower we see respiration, then pulse plethysmogram and the lowest trace in the top part of the display is a sawtooth reference signal. The lower part of the display shows: oxygen saturation, heart rate, mean heart rate, heart rate variability, heart rate variability short, heart rate variability long, sensor status, and marker

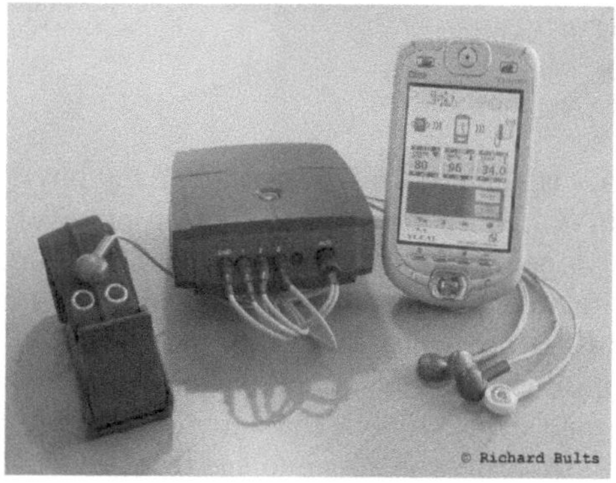

Fig. 2. BAN with electrodes and respiration sensor

output (a button used for alarms or notifications). Blood pressure (systolic) and blood pressure (diastolic) are measured externally and values are input manually. To the right of the graphical representation, current values of the parameters are presented textually (eg. 96% for oxygen saturation). Bottom right there is a panel of text showing further information relevant in trauma care, including: fluids administered, left and right pupil size and reaction, and injury type, by timestamp.

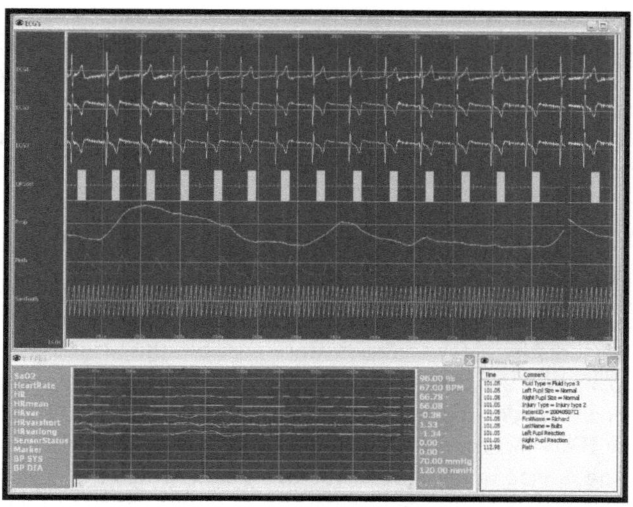

Fig. 3. Display of BAN data from multiple biosignal sources

In AWARENESS we develop context aware BAN applications for neurology, with specializations of the BAN for telemonitoring of epilepsy and spinal cord lesion patients and for teletreatment of patients with chronic pain. The corresponding specialisations of the BAN are described in the next section.

3 BANs for Neurology

3.1 Chronic Pain BAN

One variant of the BAN is planned for investigating daily physical activity patterns in chronic low back pain (CLBP) patients in relation to physical fitness, psychological variables and subjective perceived activity level [9]. The ultimate objective is to use BANs to provide teletreatment by monitoring physical activity in daily life and giving real time feedback to CLBP patients, adapted to the context of the patient (e.g. location, current activity), in terms of advice on adapting activity levels to an optimum lying between hyper- and hypoactivity. The chronic pain BAN incorporates the following devices: MBU, Mobi sensor front end and the Xsens MT9 inertial 3-D motion tracker. The MT9 measures 3-D rate-of-turn and acceleration.

3.2 Motor Disorder BAN

It is proposed to use this variant of the BAN for the management of motor disorders, specifically spasticity in spinal cord lesion patients [10]. Spasticity is a sensory-motor disorder characterised by involuntary muscle activity, resulting in restrictions in function, deformities and pain. Spasticity fluctuates over time and is known to be influenced by contextual factors. The BAN is used for long-term monitoring and will also yield important research data concerning the fluctuation of spasticity over time and its relationship with various context parameters.

In addition to the MBU and the Mobi, the Motor Disorder BAN will incorporate one or more sensors to measure surface EMG and, possibly, sensors to measure the (angular) position or displacement of the knee or force exerted by spastic muscle contractions. The EMG sensors will be positioned on the upper thigh muscles, preferably on more than one muscle.

3.3 Epilepsy BAN

Epilepsy is a serious chronic neurological condition characterized by recurrent unprovoked seizures. Seizures may happen anywhere and at any time. If detection or even prediction of seizures by a few seconds were possible this would give the patient a chance to prepare and the care network of health professionals and informal caregivers the chance to render appropriate assistance and/or advice.

The epilepsy BAN incorporates electrodes (for measuring ECG), an activity sensor and a positioning device in addition to the MBU and Mobi [11]. The Epilepsy BAN has been used to test a novel seizure detection algorithm based on analysis of HRV (heart rate variability) in the context of information about the patient's activity levels as derived from the activity sensor. Information from the positioning device can be used to determine the location of the patient in case assistance needs to be dispatched. This BAN is used in the remainder of this paper as a case example to discuss the AWARENESS context awareness extension to health BANs.

4 Context Awareness for m-Health

Health professionals may now access patient information from their office PC or from a mobile device when they are on the move. However, especially if the mobile device is a phone or PDA rather than a laptop, retrieving relevant information for a specific patient may become tedious and awkward, due to the situation (professional on the move) and to the limitations of the device. This example illustrates the need to pay attention to two aspects of context; namely the situation of the user and the capabilities of the device in use [12].

Smart healthcare applications need to adapt to the situation of the user in order to provide timely and tailored information in a way suited to the moment and to the context of use. In the AWARENESS project we are developing an infrastructure to support this type of smart context aware application. AWARENESS takes a service-oriented approach to context usage [13]. The AWARENESS approach considers two classes of entity relevant for context exchange: context producers and context consumers. Context producers create and offer context information services while context consumers (typically a context aware application) discover and use services provided by the producers. Context related aspects incorporated into the AWARENESS infrastructure are:

- Context discovery, acquisition and transfer
- Context reasoning
- Security, privacy and trust.

AWARENESS validates its context aware infrastructure with the telemedicine prototypes based on the BAN and the m-health service platform. We provide several approaches to enable context-awareness. For example, we provide a rule language and engine to automatically react to context changes [14]. Furthermore, we provide an infrastructure to discover [15] and dynamically bind sources [16] of context with context-aware applications.

In the epilepsy application for example we see context information used in order to interpret biosignals. HRV is derived from ECG but cannot be reliably interpreted in the absence of context information relating to patient activity, since changes in HR may be due to motion rather than to imminent seizure. Furthermore, context information on the location of the patient and the location of possible caregivers (to determine nearby caregivers), combined with the availability of caregivers is used to effect the dispatch of specific caregivers to patients having an epileptic seizure. First of all, this saves dispatch time because only available caregivers are contacted and secondly, this reduces time to reach the patient. These aspects may improve "golden-hour" effectiveness in medical emergencies.

Another kind of context awareness relates to the technical aspects of the system. One example is the use of knowledge of changing traffic loads in the communications infrastructure to support dynamic routing; another example involves migrating the execution of (selected) software components to compensate for breaks in connectivity, or to cope with low battery power in mobile devices given the fact that biosignal processing often places heavy demand on resources. In the following section we focus on the latter example and describe the AWARENESS strategy for using context information to enable smart power management.

5 Context Aware Power Management

An epilepsy detection algorithm based on real-time ECG measurement is being tested in AWARENESS using the Epilepsy BAN [17]. At a high level, the algorithm consists of six biosignal processing units (BSPUs) as shown in Figure 4. First, the patient's ECG data is filtered to remove signal artifacts and environment noise. Thereafter, beat-to-beat heart rate is derived and HRV in the frequency domain is calculated. The frequency spectrum of the HRV is then used to calculate the probability of an upcoming or occurring seizure. To reduce the chance of false alarms, the patient's activity information is monitored as well and correlated with the analyzed spectrum in the final stage.

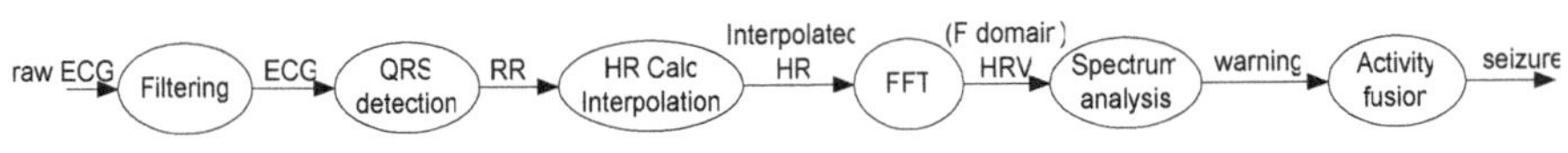

Fig. 4. Epileptic seizure detection algorithm

In the epilepsy BAN, four devices are capable of executing BSPUs: (1) the sensorbox, (2) the MBU, (3) the backend server and (4) the health professional's terminal (c.f. Figure 1). The sensorbox and MBU are resource-scarce mobile devices local to the BAN; the other two are resource-full devices and located remotely. To do smart power management, the BAN may shift certain BSPUs to execute remotely, for instance if the user is away from a charging point and battery power is getting low. The context aware power management strategy as applied in AWARENESS is illustrated by the following scenario:

Sandra suffers epileptic seizures and she wears an Epilepsy BAN. All the computation tasks are executed on her MBU. Once a seizure is detected, her MBU can send an alarm to the back-end server. One day when she is out shopping, the power management component on her MBU detects that battery power is running low. In order to prolong system life time, it decides to shift some computation tasks, e.g. the BSPUs of "FFT", "Frequency analysis" and "activity fusion" (Figure 4), onto the back-end server and terminal. Thus, system lifetime can be extended giving a better chance of functioning until Sandra returns home and charges the battery.

A key to this solution is to know which BSPU should be assigned to which device in different situations. This requires investigation of the optimal BSPU assignment with the objective of maximizing system life time.

The problem described above can be generalized as a chain-to-chain mapping problem as studied by Bokhari [18]. An example of such an assignment is illustrated in Figure 5. In the series of studies on the *chain-to-chain* assignment problem [18-21], algorithms are proposed to obtain an optimal assignment to minimize the bottleneck processing speed. In this section, we show how to apply a similar approach to finding the optimal assignment in order to maximize system life time.

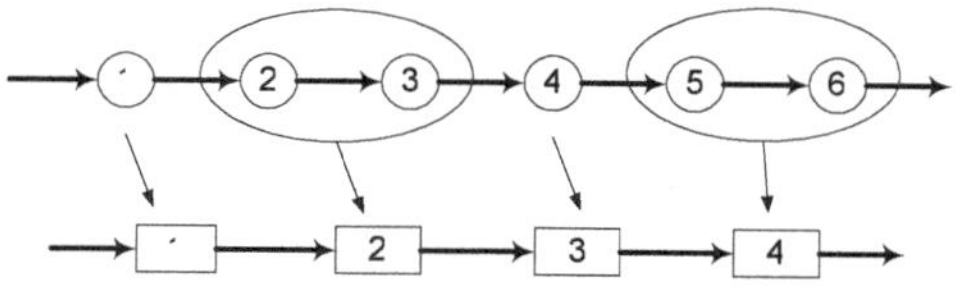

Fig. 5. An example of assigning a BSPU chain to a device-chain

First a layered directed graph (Figure 6) is built, in which each layer corresponds to a device and the label on each node corresponds to a possible sub-chain of BSPUs assigned to a device. Any path connecting nodes <S> to <T> therefore corresponds to a feasible assignment of BSPUs to devices. For example, the thick path in Figure 6 corresponds to the assignment of Figure 5. We further weight each node with the battery support time of running the sub-chain on the corresponding device with both computation and communication power consumptions in mind. For example, node "<2,3>" in the second level (device 2) is weighted with the battery support time of running BSPU 2 and 3 on device 2. Node <S> is weighted zero. In the last step, each arc inherits the weight of its departure node. Now the largest capacity path [22] in the graph corresponds to the BSPU assignment that maximizes the system lifetime.

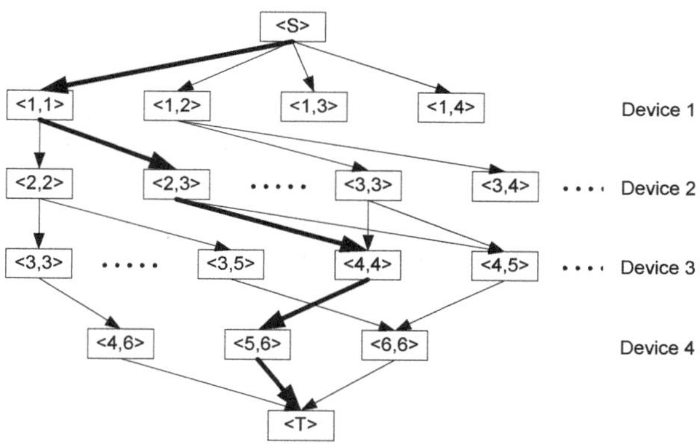

Fig. 6. The assignment graph for a problem with six BSPUs and four devices

Similar to Bokhari's method [18], a faster procedure with $O(m^2n)$ exists based on the special layered feature of this labeled assignment graph, where m is the number of BSPUs and n is the number of devices: We visit every node layer by layer from layer 1. For each node we visit, we compare the maximum of the incoming arc' weights with the node's weight. The smaller value is re-labeled to this node and copied to all of its outgoing arcs as their weights. After all the nodes are visited in the assignment graph, we can find the incoming arc to node <T> with the maximum weight. By tracing back through this link, it is possible to identify the optimal assignment.

The method of power management described above is being implemented in the current BAN service platform and represents one of the mechanisms developed in AWARENESS for augmenting BAN-based applications with context awareness. It is however a generic approach which could be applied in any clinical application or indeed in other applications processing multimedia data in a mobile environment.

6 Conclusions and Future Directions

We have described the m-health BAN and service platform and three variants of the health BAN aimed at applications in neurology. Following this we discussed the importance of context awareness and outlined the approach taken in the AWARENESS project. The example given of applying context information to achieve smart power management addresses one of the most critical problems faced today in mobile services, namely the severe constraints imposed on use of mobile devices by battery life limitations.

Development of the Awareness framework for context awareness continues, along with development of new clinical applications for the BAN. Many challenges remain, however. Future success of BAN-based m-health systems will depend on the intelligence of the BAN services, and this in turn relies, amongst others, upon development of more sophisticated context aware mechanisms. One such mechanism was discussed, namely the dynamic relocation of biosignal processing across the m-health platform in response to the fluctuating mobile environment. Such process relocation strategies can be applied to more general multimedia processing systems where multimedia streams can be processed at different nodes.

Another challenge relates to usability of the BAN itself. The development team have made enormous progress in BAN and BAN service platform development, however current generation BANs have not yet reached desirable levels of unobtrusiveness and user friendliness, due to various limitations of current technologies. It is not convenient for patients to wear current generation BANs for long periods, for one because they have to wear or carry and manage a collection of different devices including a PDA or smart phone. We envisage several directions in which BANs may evolve in the long term to overcome some of these shortcomings. Three directions of possible future evolution are enabled by *wearable microelectronics, micro implants and bio-nanotechnology*. We envision increasing miniaturization eventually enabling the "disappearing BAN", incorporating micro- and nano-scale devices, processes and materials, possibly implanted, communicating with the Ambient Intelligent Environment to provide cost-effective, unobtrusive, pervasive, context aware services.

Acknowledgment

This work is part of the Freeband AWARENESS project (http://awareness.freeband.nl). Freeband is sponsored by the Dutch government under contract BSIK 03025.

References

[1] Rasid, M.F.A., Woodward, B.: Bluetooth telemedicine Processor for multichannel biomedical signal transmission via mobile cellular networks. IEEE Transactions on Information Technology in Biomedicine 9, 35 (2005)

[2] Rodriguez, J., Goni, A., et al.: Real-Time Classification of ECGs on a PDA. IEEE Transactions on Information Technology in Biomedicine 9, 23–34 (2005)

[3] Yuan-Hsiang, L., Jan, I.C., et al.: A wireless PDA-based physiological monitoring system for patient transport. IEEE Transactions on Information Technology in Biomedicine 8, 439 (2004)

[4] Hung, K., Yuan-Ting, Z.: Implementation of a WAP-based telemedicine system for patient monitoring. IEEE Transactions on Information Technology in Biomedicine 7, 101 (2003)

[5] Jones, V.M., Bults, R.G.A., et al.: Healthcare PANs: Personal Area Networks for trauma care and home care. In: WPMC. presented at Fourth International Symposium on Wireless Personal Multimedia Communications, Aalborg, Denmark (2001)

[6] MobiHealth, MobiHealth project webpage, http://www.mobihealth.org/

[7] Freeband AWARENESS project, http://www.freeband.nl/project.cfm?id=494&language=en

[8] eTen HealthService 24 project, http://www.healthservice24.com

[9] Methods for ambulatory monitoring of activity and personalized feedback in chronic pain patients, Awareness deliverables (2006)

[10] Voerman, G.E., Fleuren, J.F.M, et al.: Long-term monitoring of biosignals in spasticity and other motor disorders: A systematic review, Awareness deliverables (2006)

[11] Tönis, T., Hermens, H.J., et al.: Context aware algorithm for discriminating stress and physical activity versus epilepsy, AWARENESS deliverables (2006)

[12] Panigrahi, D., Panigrahi, T D., et al.: Battery life estimation of mobile embedded systems. In: Presented at 14th International Conference on VLSI Design (2001)

[13] van Sinderen, M.J., van Halteren, A.T., et al.: Supporting context-aware mobile applications: an infrastructure approach. Communications Magazine, IEEE 44, 96 (2006)

[14] Dockhorn Costa, P., Pires, L., et al.: Controlling Services in a Mobile Context-Aware Infrastructure. In: CAPS 2006. Second Workshop on Context Awareness for Proactive Systems, Kassel, Germany (2006)

[15] Hesselman, C., Tokmakoff, A., et al.: Discovery and Composition of Services for Context-Aware Systems. In: EuroSSC 2006, Enschede, the Netherlands (2006)

[16] Broens, T., Quartel, D., et al.: Towards a Context Binding Transparency. In: presented at 13th EUNICE Open European Summer School, Enschede, the Netherlands (2007)

[17] Huis in 't Veld, M.H.A., Ordelman, S.C.M.A., et al.: Context aware algorithm for epileptic seizure detection, Awareness deliverables (2005)

[18] Bokhari, S.H.: Partitioning problems in parallel, pipelined, and distributed computing. IEEE Transactions on Computers 37, 48–57 (1988)

[19] Nicol, D.M., O'Hallaron, D.R.: Improved Algorithms for Mapping Pipelined and Parallel Computations. IEEE Transactions on Computers 40, 295–306 (1991)

[20] Ashraf Iqbal, M., Bokhari, S.H.: Efficient algorithms for a class of partitioning problems. IEEE Transactions on Parallel and Distributed Systems 6, 170 (1995)

[21] Woeginger, G.J.: Assigning chain-like tasks to a chain-like network. In: Presented at Proceedings of the twelfth annual ACM-SIAM symposium on Discrete algorithms (2001)

[22] Christofides, N.: Graph theory: An algorithmic approach. Academic Press, London (1975)

M-LTW: A Fast and Efficient Non-embedded Intra Video Codec*

O. López[1], M. Martínez-Rach[1], P. Piñol[1], J. Oliver[2], and M.P. Malumbres[1]

[1] Miguel Hernández University, Avda. Universidad s/n, Elche, Spain 03202
{otoniel,mmrach,pablop,mels@umh.es}
[2] Technical University of Valencia, Camino de Vera s/n, Valencia, Spain 46022
{joliver@disca.upv.es}

Abstract. Intra video coding is a common way to process video material for applications like professional video editing systems, digital cinema, video surveillance applications, multispectral satellite imaging, HQ video delivery, etc. Most practical intra coding systems employ JPEG encoders due to their simplicity, low coding delay and low memory requirements. JPEG2000 is the main candidate to replace JPEG in this kind of applications due to the excellent R/D performance and high coding flexibility. However, its complexity and computational resources required for proper operation could be a limitation for certain applications. In this work, we propose an intra video codec, M-LTW, which is able to reach very good R/D performance results, as well as JPEG2000 or H.264 INTRA, with faster processing and lower memory usage.

Keywords: image and video coding, tree-based wavelet coding, integer lifting transform, low complexity coding.

1 Introduction

A wide variety of video compression schemes have been reported in the literature. Most of them are based on the DCT transform and motion estimation/compensation techniques. However, a lot of research interest was focused on developing still image and video wavelet coders due to the great properties of wavelet transform. Most wavelet-based video encoding proposals are strongly based on inter-coding approaches, which require high-complexity encoder designs as counterpart to the excellent R/D performance benefits. However, some applications like professional video editing, digital cinema, video surveillance applications, multispectral satellite imaging, HQ video delivery, etc. would rather use an intra coding system that is able to reconstruct a specific frame of a video sequence as fast as possible and with high visual quality.

So, the strength of an intra video coding system relies on the ability to efficiently exploit the spatial redundancies of each video sequence frame avoiding complexity in the design of the encoding/decoding engines. There are several still image codecs that

* This work was funded by Spanish Ministry of education and Science under grant TIC2003-00339 and by Valencia Government under grant ARVIV/2007/045.

H.H.S. Ip et al. (Eds.): PCM 2007, LNCS 4810, pp. 600–608, 2007.

get very good R/D (Rate/Distortion) results. Unfortunately, most of them propose complex algorithms to achieve the pursued R/D performance. As a consequence of the higher computational complexity demanded by these coders, their software (even hardware) implementations would require powerful processors with enough computational resources to cope with the algorithm requirements. For example, the JPEG2000 [1] standard uses a large number of contexts and an iterative time-consuming optimization algorithm (called PCRD) to improve coding efficiency, increasing the complexity of the encoding engine. Something similar happens with H.264/AVC [2] INTRA coding, where a powerful spatial prediction scheme with context modeling and rate-distortion optimization is employed in order to efficiently exploit spatial redundancies.

In this paper, we propose a new lightweight and efficient intra video coder, M-LTW (Motion Lower-Tree Wavelet), based on the LTW algorithm [3]. The main contribution of LTW is the way that it builds the significance map when coding each video frame. As other tree-based wavelet coders, it is based on the construction and efficient coding of wavelet coefficient trees. However, it does not use an iterative loop in order to determine the significant coefficients and to assign them bits. It builds the significant map in only one step by using two symbols for pruning tree branches, and codes the significant coefficients also in one step.

Several rate control schemes have been reported in the literature. Most of them are applied to DCT transform like Test Model Near-term version 5 (TMN5) [4] used in H.263 standard or the MPEG Test Model 5 (TM5) [5]. In [6] the authors propose a new rate control scheme based on Game Theory and a deep introduction to rate control is made.

Since the LTW encoding engine is non-embedded and it is based on DWT transform, we have proposed a low complexity rate control tool to encode the original video sequence to a user-defined target bitrate, in order to increase the flexibility of M-LTW video encoder and allowing LTW to work with rate-adaptive applications. Also, we have changed the overall codec to work with fixed point arithmetic. So, the DWT transform may use the original lifting floating-point approach or an equivalent DWT integer lifting version which will speed up the DWT transform step. As a secondary benefit, the required memory space is halved (16-bit integer data types instead of 32-bit floats).

The organization of the paper is the following one: in section 2 the M-LTW algorithm is described, making special emphasis in the LTW spatial coding and the proposed rate control tool. In section 3, we show some evaluation results using as performance metrics rate/distortion, complexity and memory requirements. Finally, in section 4 some conclusions and future work are drawn.

2 M-LTW Coder Description

As shown in figure 1, the proposed M-LTW intra video encoder is composed of (a) DWT module, which computes the Discrete Wavelet Transform, (b) the proposed rate control tool, which adjusts quantization parameters to fit a user-specified target bitrate, (c) the coding engine, which is based on the LTW still image encoder, (d) an arithmetic entropy encoder, which is fully integrated with the LTW encoder, and (e) a format bitstream module to multiplex the info delivered by rate control (quantization parameters) and the two data sets delivered by LTW (entropy encoded significant map symbols and the raw coefficient values as explained later).

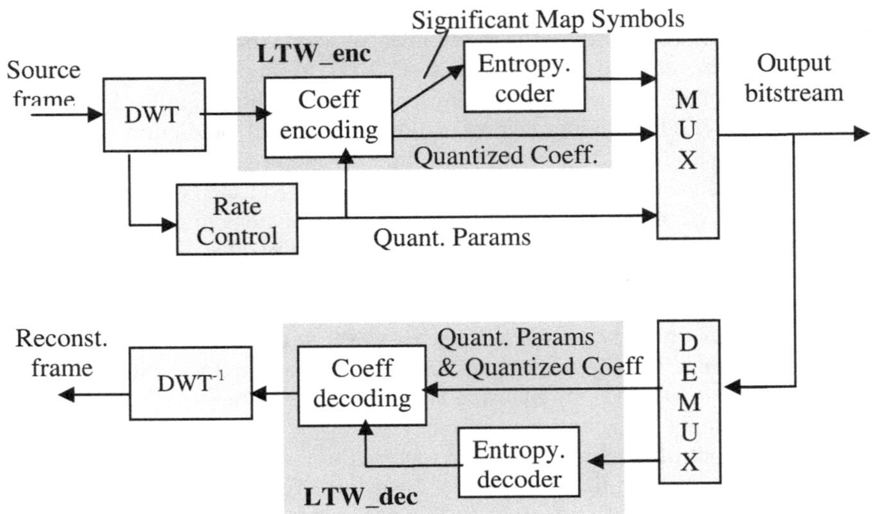

Fig. 1. M-LTW block diagram

We have also developed two versions of the DWT transform module: (a) a standard lifting version based on 7/9 biorthogonal filter (as many other wavelet encoders use) and (b) a version of the former one using an integer-to-integer lifting scheme based on [8] and [9]. We have performed the expansion factor of DWT by an approximation to integer operations (multiplication and shift). In this manner we avoid three extra lifting steps at the expense of making the DWT not reversible. The proposed approximation does not introduce a meaningful error, being the difference respect to the regular lifting scheme negligible.

The M-LTW is designed to work with fixed point arithmetic, with the exception of the standard lifting version of DWT transform module, that uses float data types for its computations.

2.1 LTW: The Intra Coding Engine

In LTW, the quantization process is performed by two strategies: one coarser and another finer. The finer one consists in applying a scalar uniform quantization, Q, to wavelet coefficients. The coarser one is based on removing the least significant bit planes, *rplanes*, from wavelet coefficients.

A tree structure (similar to that of [7]) is used not only to reduce data redundancy among subbands, but also as a simple and fast way of grouping coefficients. As a consequence, the total number of symbols needed to encode the image is reduced, decreasing the overall execution time. This structure is called lower tree, and it is a coefficient tree in which all its coefficients are lower than $2^{rplanes}$.

Our algorithm consists of two stages. In the first one, the significance map is built after quantizing the wavelet coefficients (by means of both *Q* and *rplanes* parameters). The symbol set employed in our proposal is the following one: a *LOWER* symbol represents a coefficient that is the root of a lower-tree, the rest of coefficients in a lower-tree are labeled as *LOWER_COMPONENT*, but they are never encoded because they are already represented by the root coefficient. If a coefficient is insignificant but it does not belong to a lower-tree because it has at least one significant descendant, it is labeled as an *ISOLATED_LOWER* symbol. For a significant coefficient, we simply use a symbol indicating the number of bits needed to represent it.

Let us describe the coding algorithm. In the first stage (symbol computation), all wavelet subbands are scanned in 2×2 blocks of coefficients, from the first decomposition level to the Nth (to be able to build the lower-trees from leaves to root). In the first level subband, if the four coefficients in each 2×2 block are insignificant (i.e., lower than $2^{rplanes}$), they are considered to be part of the same lower-tree and they are labeled as *LOWER_COMPONENT*. Then, when scanning upper level subbands, if a 2×2 block has four insignificant coefficients, and all their direct descendants are *LOWER_COMPONENT*, the coefficients in that block are labeled as *LOWER_COMPONENT*, increasing the lower-tree size.

However, when at least one coefficient in the block is significant, the lower-tree cannot continue growing. In that case, a symbol for each coefficient is computed one by one. Each insignificant coefficient in the block is assigned a *LOWER* symbol if all its descendants are *LOWER_COMPONENT*, otherwise it is assigned an *ISOLATED_LOWER* symbol. On the other hand, for each significant coefficient, a symbol indicating the number of bits needed to represent that coefficient is employed.

Finally, in the second stage, subbands are encoded from the LL_N subband to the first-level wavelet subbands. Observe that this is the order in which the decoder needs to know the symbols, so that lower-tree roots are decoded before its leaves. In addition, this order provides resolution scalability, because LL_N is a low-resolution scaled version of the original image, and as more subbands are being received, the low-resolution image can be doubled in size. In each subband, for each 2×2 block, the symbols computed in the first stage are entropy coded by means of an arithmetic encoder. Recall that no *LOWER_COMPONENT* is encoded. In addition, significant bits and sign are needed for each significant coefficient and therefore binary encoded.

2.2 M-LTW Rate Control Tool

The proposed rate control is founded on the definition of a simplified model of LTW coding engine. Applying this idea to the LTW encoder, the simplified coding model will lead us to get an initial and fast bitrate estimation for different values of the coarser quantizer *rplanes* (from 2 to 7). This estimation is computed as follows: for each specific value of *rplanes*, the probability distribution of significant and insignificant symbols is calculated. Then, the bit rate estimation (E_{bpp}) for each *rplanes* value is calculated, taking into account: (a) an estimation of the bit-rate that the arithmetic encoder will produce, and (b) the number of bits required to store the sign and significant bits (which are binary coded). The resulting estimation gives a biased measure of the real bit rate for all operative bit-rate range (from 0.0625 to 1 bpp), so we will reduce the error by means of a correction factor calculated from the Kodak image set [10].

After that, the target bit-rate, T_{bpp} will establish the proper value of the quantization parameter *rplanes* ($E_{bpp}(rplanes) > T_{bpp} > E_{bpp}(rplanes+1)$). In order to determine the proper value of the quantization parameter *Q*, the bit rate progression from the current *rplane* to the next one follows a second order polynomial curve with a common minimum. So, with the estimated values ($E_{bpp}(rplanes)$ and $E_{bpp}(rplanes+1)$), we can build the corresponding expression that will supply the estimated value of *Q* for a given target bitrate.

To perform the rate control in the overall video sequence, we have extended the rate control explained above by using a very simple approach. Firstly, we apply the proposed rate control algorithm to the first frame, in order to estimate the values of *rplanes* and *Q* quantization parameters that produce the frame bitrate budget. After coding the first frame, we compute the estimation error, so we will try to compensate it when coding the following frames. We will do that keeping the same value of *rplanes* and estimating the appropriate values for *Q* based on the observed error. When the estimated error reaches a threshold, the algorithm detects a scene change and runs the initial estimation algorithm in order to re-estimate more suitable *rplanes* and *Q* parameters. Then, the accumulated error will be corrected gradually in order to avoid great R/D alterations. After several experiments, the accuracy of the proposed error control was always better than 98.5% (worst case at very low target bitrates).

3 Numerical Results

In addition to R/D performance we will also employ other performance metrics like coding delay and memory consumption. All the evaluated encoders have been tested on an Intel PentiumM Dual Core 3.0 GHz with 1Gbyte RAM Memory. We have selected H.264 (Baseline, JM10.2), M-JPEG2000 (Jasper 1.701.0), M-LTW and M-LTW_Int (the integer version of M-LTW), since their source code is available for testing. The correspondent binaries were obtained by means of Visual C++ (version 2005) compiler with the same project options and under the above mentioned machine. The test video sequences used in the evaluation are: Foreman (QCIF and CIF), Hall (QCIF and CIF), Container (QCIF and CIF), News (QCIF and CIF), Mobile (ITU→576p30) and Station2 (HD→1024p25).

Table 1 shows the R/D evaluation of the proposed encoders. In general, the M-LTW obtains the best results (about 0.5 dB with respect to M-JPEG2000 in Foreman QCIF). The difference is higher with ITU and HD formats (around 2 dB with respect to H.264). At these sizes, optimal DWT decompositions can be exploited. The M-LTW_Int encoder has slightly lower PSNR results than H.264. The lower performance of the integer version is mainly due to the arithmetic precision loss, which is more noticeable at lower compression rates.

Table 2 shows the encoding delay for all encoders under evaluation. As expected, H.264 is the slowest encoder and M-LTW is one of the fastest encoders. All M-LTW versions are faster than M-JPEG2000, specially the integer version that performs the encoding process six times faster on average than M-JPEG2000.

In Table 3, the memory requirements of different encoders under test are shown. The M-LTW needs only the amount of memory to store the source image (in-line processing is another feature of LTW encoder) and an extra of 1.2 KB basically used to store the histogram of significant symbols, required by the rate control algorithm. M-JPEG2000 requires two times the memory of M-LTW, and H.264 needs six times the memory of M-LTW for QCIF size and eight times for CIF size. Note that M-LTW_Int could be implemented using 16-bit integer, reducing to the half the amount of needed memory.

Table 1. PSNR (dB) with different bit-rate and coders

Codec/Bitrate (Kb/frame)	H.264	M-JPEG 2000	M-LTW	M-LTW _Int
Foreman (QCIF 176x144, 30Hz)				
2.36	22.86	19.99	**23.03**	23.01
7.40	**28.72**	28.00	28.69	28.58
20.49	**35.36**	34.53	34.99	34.40
33.73	39.24	38.78	**39.37**	37.62
Mobile (ITU 640x512, 30Hz)				
38.08	27.04	28.42	**28.59**	28.48
119.93	32.29	32.39	**32.57**	32.26
213.36	35.29	35.07	**35.40**	34.75
386.23	38.59	38.41	**38.87**	37.21
Station2 (HD 1920x1024, 25Hz)				
93.92	30.49	32.35	**32.45**	32.19
180.00	32.58	34.36	**34.49**	34.06
604.64	37.55	38.66	**39.02**	37.73
1117.53	40.37	40.76	**41.38**	39.08

Table 2. Execution time comparison of the coding process including DWT (time in seconds)

Codec/Bitrate (Kb/frame)	H.264	M-JPEG 2000	M-LTW	M-LTW _Int
CODING Hall (QCIF 176x144, 30Hz)				
2.70	121.92	4.04	0.86	0.51
7.77	137.18	4.39	1.07	0.71
19.54	165.67	4.55	1.57	1.10
29.50	184.67	4.87	1.97	1.41
CODING News (CIF 352x288, 30Hz)				
14.91	531.40	15.63	3.96	2.62
23.62	559.45	15.20	4.26	2.81
57.73	650.47	15.54	5.98	3.94
89.91	720.44	16.43	7.17	4.95

Table 3. Memory requirements for evaluated encoders (KB) (Results obtained from Windows XP task manager, peak memory usage column)

Codec/ Format	H.264	M-JPEG 2000	M-LTW	M-LTW _Int
QCIF	6508	2264	1104	1104
CIF	13016	3920	1540	1540

Figure 2 shows the maximum frame rate for all evaluated encoders at different sizes for an average PSNR video quality of 30 dB. The integer version of M-LTW is the fastest of all encoders and it can encode an ITU size sequence in real time.

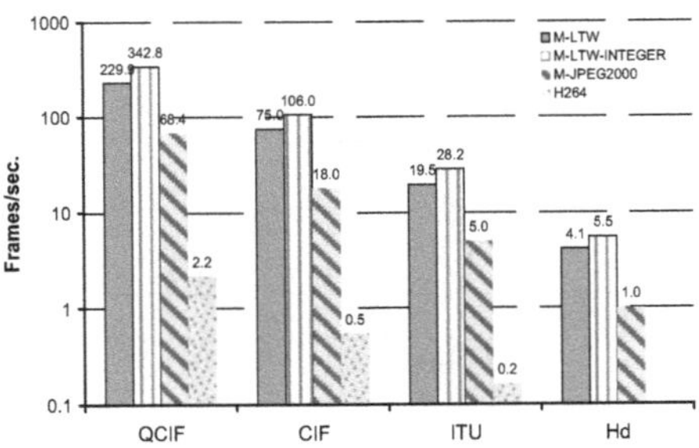

Fig. 2. Maximum frame rate for an average R/D of 30dB

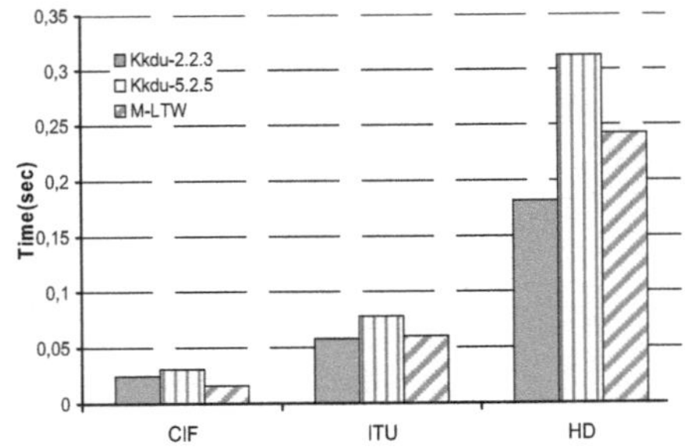

Fig. 3. Execution time comparison (end-to-end) of the coding process

The M-LTW implementation was developed finding the optimizations for maximizing R/D performance, so its software code is not optimized, just like H.264 and JPEG2000 reference software. However, we have compared its performance with respect to a fully optimized implementation of JPEG2000: Kakadu [12], in order to evaluate if a full optimization of M-LTW will be worth the effort. For that purpose, we have used two versions of Kakadu software: (a) version 2.2.3, compiled without optimization options, and (b) the last version 5.2.5 which is fully optimized including multi-thread multi-core hardware capabilities.

Table 4. PSNR (dB) comparison between Kakadu and M-LTW

Codec/ (Kb/frame)	KKDU 2.2.3	KKDU 5.2.5	M-LTW
News (CIF, 30Hz)			
14,91	27.63	27.44	**27.74**
23,62	30.27	29.96	**30.42**
36.75	33.33	33.31	**33.36**
57,73	**37.26**	37.10	36.89
Mobile (ITU, 30Hz)			
38.08	28.59	28.39	**28.61**
119.93	32.56	32.52	**32.62**
213.36	35.34	35.34	**35.47**
386.23	38.85	38.89	**38.90**
Station2 (HD, 25Hz)			
93.92	**33.79**	33.70	33.62
180.00	**36.16**	36.15	36.08
604.64	**41.11**	41.11	40.96
1117.53	**43.18**	43.18	42.94

As shown in figure 3, M-LTW is a very fast encoder even though not being fully optimized. The speed of M-LTW lies on the simple engine coding model. M-LTW is approximately 2 times faster than Kkdu-5.2.5 for News CIF sequence for a PSNR of 32dB. For HD images, M-LTW is slower than Kkdu-2.2.3, due to the cache page miss fail of the lifting DWT implementation. In terms of R/D, there are slightly differences between all codecs as shown at table 4. For small and medium size images M-LTW outperforms KKDU at medium and high compression rates. For larger images, M-LTW has slightly lower PSNR than both versions of Kakadu, but these differences are not perceptible when PSNR is over 38dB as concluded in [11].

Regarding to memory requirements, M-LTW needs only the amount of memory required to store the source image, while Kakadu memory requirements are independent of the image size due to its DWT block-based implementation.

5 Conclusions

In this paper we have presented a fast an efficient intra video coder, M-LTW, which is based on the non-embedded LTW image coder. We have proposed a fast rate control algorithm to both M-LTW encoder versions. After evaluating M-LTW performance in terms of R/D, execution time and memory consumption, it exhibits the best trade-off between R/D performance, coding delay (3 times faster than M-JPEG2000 and 108 times faster than H.264) and overall memory usage (half the memory of M-JPEG2000 and 6 times less than H.264). Also, the M-LTW coder is able to encode in real time an ITU video signal with very low memory demands and good R/D performance at moderate to high compression rates (up to 2 dB with respect to H.264 in the HD sequence).

For further evaluation, we have compared M-LTW coder with a highly optimized version of JPEG2000 (Kakadu), being also competitive in terms of coding delay (up to 2 times faster than Kkdu for small and medium size images) and R/D performance (0.4 dB for CIF, and 0.1 dB for ITU at medium and high compression rates). So, a fully optimization process will make M-LTW even faster and with lower memory requirements (with line-based or block-base DWT implementations).

References

1. ISO/IEC 15444-1. Jpeg 2000 image coding system. Part 1: core coding system (2000)
2. ISO/IEC 14496-10:2003. Coding of audiovisual objects part 10: advanced video coding for generic audiovisual services (2003)
3. Oliver, J., Malumbres, M.P.: Fast and efficient spatial scalable image compression using wavelet lower trees. In: Proc. IEEE Data Compression Conf., Snowbird, UT (March 2003)
4. Video Codec Test Model for the Near-Term 5 (TMN5), ITU-T SG 15 Experts Group for Very Low Bitrate Visual Telephony (1995)
5. Test Model 5 (TM5), ISO/IEC JTC1/SC29/WG11, Document N400 (1993)
6. Ahmad, I., Luo, J.: On using Game Theory for Perceptually Tuned Rate Control Algorithm for Video Coding. IEEE Transactions on Circuits and Systems for Video Technology 16(2), 202–208 (2006)

7. Said, A., Pearlman, A.: A new, fast, and efficient image codec based on set partitioning in hierarchical trees. IEEE CSVT 6(3), 243–250 (1996)
8. Calderbank, A.R., Daubechies, I., Sweldens, W., Yeo, B-L.: Wavelet transforms that map integers to integers. Applied & Computational Harmonic Analysis 5(3), 332–369 (1998)
9. Daubechies, I., Sweldens, W.: Factoring wavelet transforms into lifting steps. Journal of Fourier analysis and applications 4(3), 247–269 (1998)
10. Center for Image Processing Research - Electrical, Computer, and Systems Engineering Dept - Rensselaer Polytechnic Institute, http://www.cipr.rpi.edu/resource/stills/ kodak.html
11. Martinez-Rach, M., López, O., Piñol, P., Oliver, J., Malumbres, M.P.: A Study of Objective Quality Assessment Metrics for Video Codec Design and Evaluation. In: Proc. IEEE Computer Society, pp. 517–524 (2006)
12. Kakadu Software, http://www.kakadusoftware.com/

Intra Frame Encoding Using Programmable Graphics Hardware

MC Kung, Oscar Au, Peter Wong, and Chun-Hung Liu

Department of Electronic and Computer Engineering, The Hong Kong University of Science and Technology
{mckung,eeau,eepeter,hungsiu}@ust.hk
http://www.ece.ust.hk/

Abstract. In this paper, we propose a parallel algorithm for H.264/AVC intra frame encoding by using the graphics processing unit (GPU). The proposed algorithm can handle 4x4 intra block prediction and reconstruction. By rearranging the encoding order of 4x4 blocks and modifying the architecture of H.264/AVC encoder, thirty times speed up can be achieved which utilizing the computing power of GPU without any loss in coding efficiency.

Keywords: Intra Prediction, GPU, Graphics Hardware.

1 Introduction

With the development of Internet and wireless network, multimedia information, especially video content, becomes more and more popular. However, since the size of uncompressed videos is usually quite large. It is impractical to transmit videos without compression.

H.264 is the newest international coding standard developed by Joint Video Term (JVT) [1] which consists of the experts from the members in ITU-T's video coding experts group (VCEG) and ISO/IEC's moving picture experts group (MPEG). It contains a number of new features to achieve video compression in a more effective way, e.g. multiple reference frames, sub-pixel motion estimation and a variety of intra mode. With such advanced intra mode decisions, the rate distortion performance of intra frame is greatly improved. However, the coding complexity increases at the same time. To reduce the computation complexity, many recent researches focus on fast intra prediction [2] [3]. But those methods usually introduce PSNR loss as a trade-off.

On the other hand, over the past few years, graphics hardware technology has grown in an unprecedented rate. It is because multi-billion dollar video game market is a pressure cooker that drives innovation and the specialized nature of graphics hardware makes it easier to use additional transistors for computation instead of cache. Nowadays, the graphics hardware is not only a specialized hardware for accelerating three-dimensional graphics processing and rendering but also a co-processor, which equips a Graphics Processing Unit (GPU), to process data stream with user developed program. According to the Moore's

H.H.S. Ip et al. (Eds.): PCM 2007, LNCS 4810, pp. 609–618, 2007.

Law, the performance of CPUs is improved with an annual growth rate 1.4x. However, the annual growth rate of the performance of GPUs is 1.7x (pixel/sec) to 2.3x (vertices/sec), which is much faster than that of CPUs. GPUs grow with significant improvement on the quality of computation and programmability. It provides a very powerful data parallel mechanism and more flexibility for general-purpose computing. Recently, quite a lot of works have used GPU for both graphics and non-graphics applications, such as HDR [4], watermarking [5], linear algebra [6], FFT [7], etc.

Nowadays, many researches focus on applying GPU to video compression framework, e.g. GPU-based decoding [8] and inter frame motion estimation [9] [10] [11]. However, there are few related works on accelerating intra frame encoding. In this paper, we present an efficient intra frame encoding which not only perform intra block prediction but also generate the reconstructed blocks by re-arranging the encoding order of 4x4 block on GPU without losing any coding efficiency.

The rest of the paper is organized as follows. In section 2, we discuss the Programmable Graphics Pipeline and Intra Block Encoding in H.264/AVC. Then, we go through the detail of GPU-based implementation in section 3. In section 4, we evaluate the performance of the proposed method. Finally, we draw a conclusion in section 5.

2 The Programmable Graphics Pipeline and Intra Block Encoding in H.264/AVC

2.1 The Programmable Graphics Pipeline

Figure 1 shows a high-level diagram of modern graphics pipeline. The typical use of graphics hardware is to process 3D data. The applications use an API (for example OpenGL or Direct3D) to send the graphics geometry description as a stream of vertices to the GPU. These vertices are transformed to their final screen location by the vertex processor which also assigns each vertex a color based on the scene lighting. The Rasterizer converts geometry presentation (vertex) to image presentation (fragment) and it interpolates per-vertex quantities across pixels. Then the fragment processor which is multiple in parallel will compute the final color for each pixel and store back into the frame buffer. The user can implement customized operations by writing program called shaders on both vertex processor and fragment processor for per-vertex and per-fragment computing. They are fully programmable and perform SIMD like operations on a vector with 4 components.

In general purpose computation (GPGPU), the GPU is a stream processor to provide independent parallel process. It executes a number of kernels on data streams. The kernel is like a function applied on each data element of the stream. For the proposed intra block processing, kernel is used for 4x4 block prediction and intra mode selection, image reconstruction processes including forward Integer Cosine Transform(ICT), quantization, inverse ICT, De-Quantization and

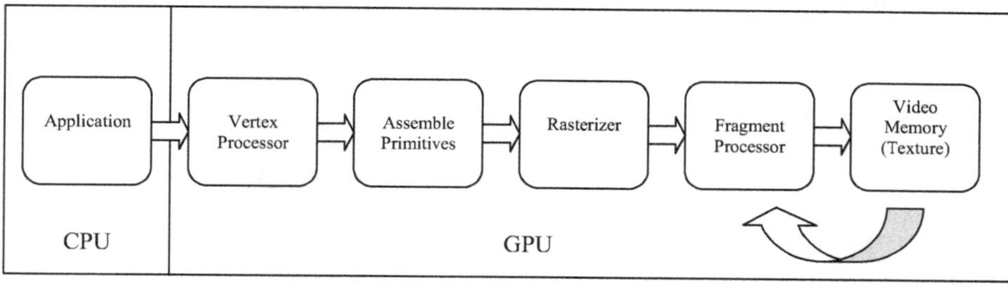

Fig. 1. High-level diagram of modern graphics pipeline

inverse prediction. Textures are used to store the original frame and the previous reconstructed neighbors block information. The detail will be described in Section 3.

2.2 Intra Prediction in H.264/AVC

In 4x4 block prediction, each 4x4 block is predicted from the spatially neighboring sample(Figure 2.b) where symbols **a** to **p** are the current block pixels and symbols **A** to **L** and **X** are the neighbor's block pixels for generate the prediction block. There are 9 prediction modes: one DC prediction mode and 8 directional prediction modes(Figure 2.b).

In the mode decision part, the cost function composes of the sum of absolute different(SAD) and Mode Cost. It is a rate-constrained optimization problem and the best mode is selected that minimizes the Lagarangian cost function. The Mode Cost is a function of 4x4 block prediction mode m, Most Probable Mode(MPM) and the Lagrangian multiplier λ. λ imposes rate constraint of coding mode information which is QP dependent. The cost function is shown in the following equation. Where C is the original 4x4 block, P_m is the predict block with corresponding mode m and MPM donate the Most Probable Mode which is computed from the Intra mode of left and up 4x4 block.

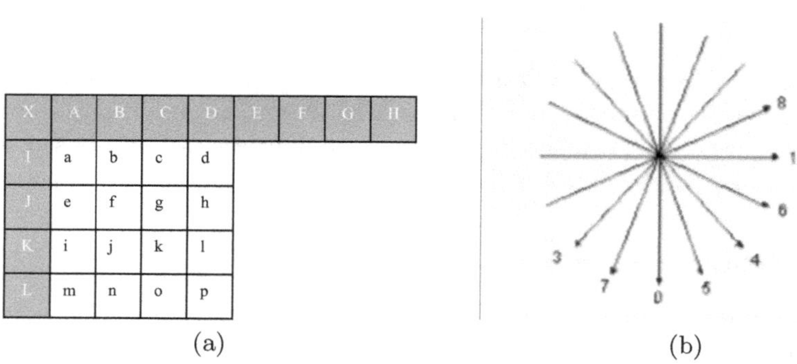

Fig. 2. 4X4 block Intra Prediction

$$COST(m, \lambda, MPM) = SAD(C, P_m) + Mode\_COST(m, \lambda, MPM)$$
$$SAD(C, P(m)) = \sum_{y=1}^{4} \sum_{x=1}^{4} |C[y, x] - P_m[y, x]|$$
$$Mode\_COST(m, \lambda, MPM) = (m! = MPM) \times \lambda$$

As the intra prediction requires the previous coded neighbors block information: reconstructed pixels for building predict block and block modes for computing MPM. The dependency among adjacent block is introduced.

2.3 CPU Working Flow for Intra Frame Processing

In the reference software JM8.2, the MB coding in raster scan order. The high-level block diagram is shown in Figure 3. The prediction block needs to use the previous coded neighbors MB. The process of next MB must wait until current MB finish. High dependency is introduced between MBs. Weak data parallelism due to the MB coding order. In section 3, we propose a modified MB and 4x4 block coding order to maximum the throughput of data parallel processing on GPU.

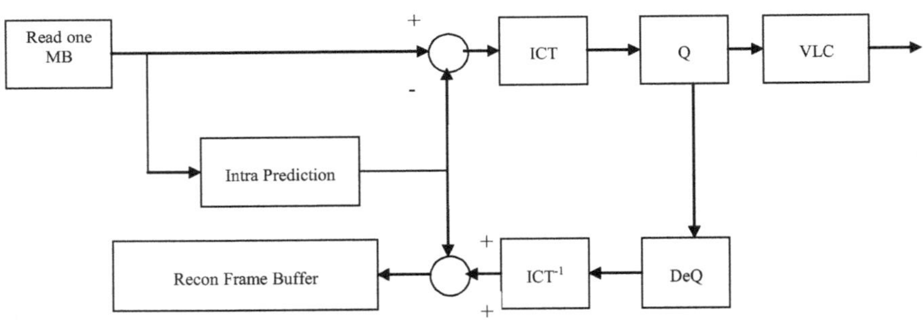

Fig. 3. High-level diagram of intra frame processing on H.264/AVC

3 Proposed GPU-Based Intra Frame Processing

The proposed GPU-Based Intra Frame Processing performs 4x4 intra block prediction and generates the reconstruction block as the predict information for future blocks. Figure 4 is shown the high-level block diagram of GPU-based Intra Frame Processing and the detail will be discussed in the following subsections.

3.1 Data Representation in Graphics Hardware

For the input data, current original 4x4 block and previous coded neighbors block information (pixel values and 4x4 intra prediction modes) is needed and also the current block availability. All of them can be represented as texture objects and stored in texture memory but the bandwidth for memory access

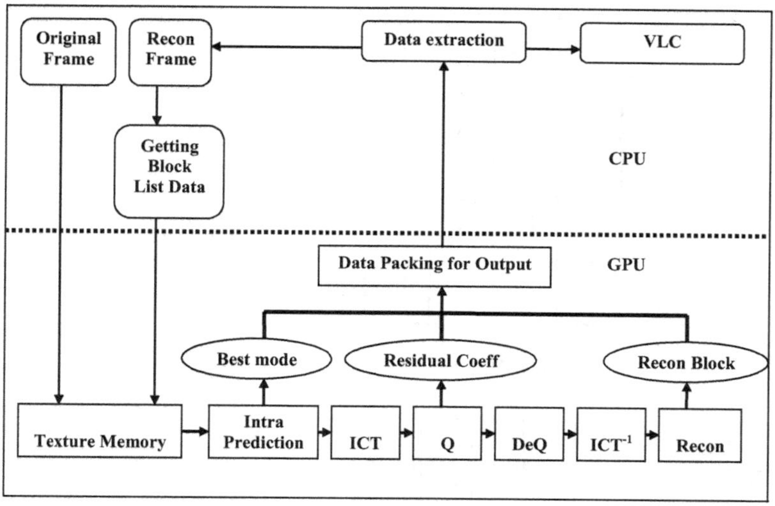

Fig. 4. Encoding order of 4x4 block within MB

from CPU to GPU is expensive. We use GL_RGBA as the input data type, it is a vector containing of 4 float data. The current original frame is loaded into the texture memory once and the rest of the data is packed into one buffer and loaded into the texture memory for each process.

3.2 Data-Level Parallelism

In section 2.2, it point out the dependency among adjacent block. Figure 5 is shown the original encoding order of 16 4x4 blocks within one MB. Symbols **A** to **D** donate 4 up 4x4 blocks, **E** donate the up-right 4x4 block, **F** to **I** donate 4 left 4x4 blocks and **X** donate the up-left 4x4 block. The small blocks represent the 4x4 blocks inside MB and the number in the block represents the encoding order. Recently some researches focus on better parallel and pipelined execution of 4x4 intra prediction. **Genhua Jin** [12] and **Wonjae Lee** [13] proposed to rearrange the 4x4 block coding order to provide parallel processing between 4x4 blocks within the same MB. But associate with the large number of stream processors inside GPU, the parallel process is not only target on 4x4 blocks within same MB but also the 4x4 blocks within same frame.

We propose to divide the frame into many diagonal 4x4 block lists. Figure 6 is shown the division of 4x4 block list, the 4x4 blocks with the same number belong to the same block list and the number also represent block list encoding order. For each 4x4 block in the block list, the necessary neighbor's data is available after the previous block list process finished and they are independence with each other. The encoder processes the 4x4 diagonal block list from top-left to bottom-right. Thanks to the parallelism of GPU, the encoding of all 4x4 block can be done at the same time. This method solves the dependency problem and provides a high degree parallelism.

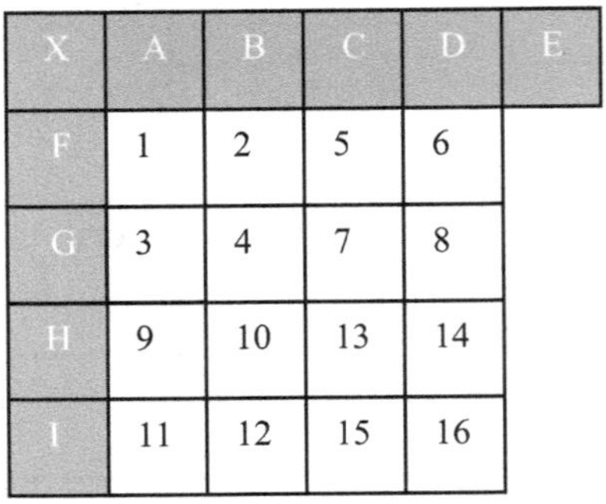

Fig. 5. Encoding order of 4x4 block within MB

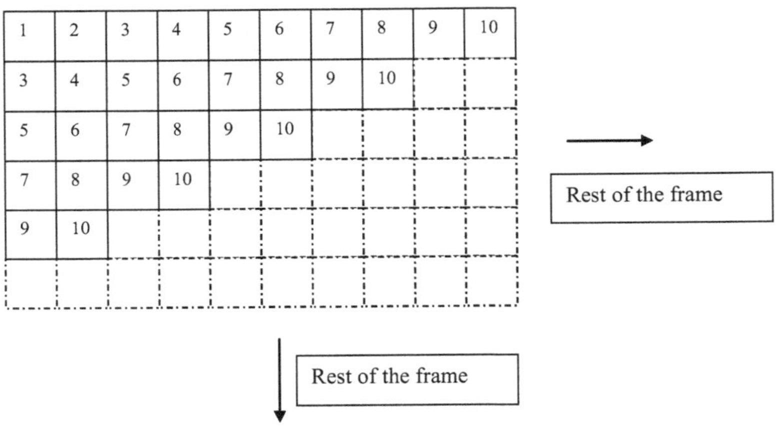

Fig. 6. Rearrangement of 4x4 block encoding order

3.3 Output Data Packing

The latest high-end graphics hardware can support maximum 1024 bits as output and the consumer-level graphics hardware usually supports 512 bits as output. It has 4 vectors with 4 components and use 32 bits float as the data type for each component. For the output data, we have one 4x4 reconstruction block, one 4x4 residual coefficients block and current block mode. The GPU provides totally 16 floating number(32 bits for each) to store the output data. Inside the kernel, bit shifting operations is not supported. We cannot directly embed the data into high 16 bits. As a floating point number can represent as one integer number plus one decimal number least than one. We embed the output data into both integer and decimal place by multiple and divide the data. For the 4x4 reconstruction block, it is all positive and within the range from 0 to 255. It is more suitable to embed into the decimal place. Figure 7 is shown the data packing process.

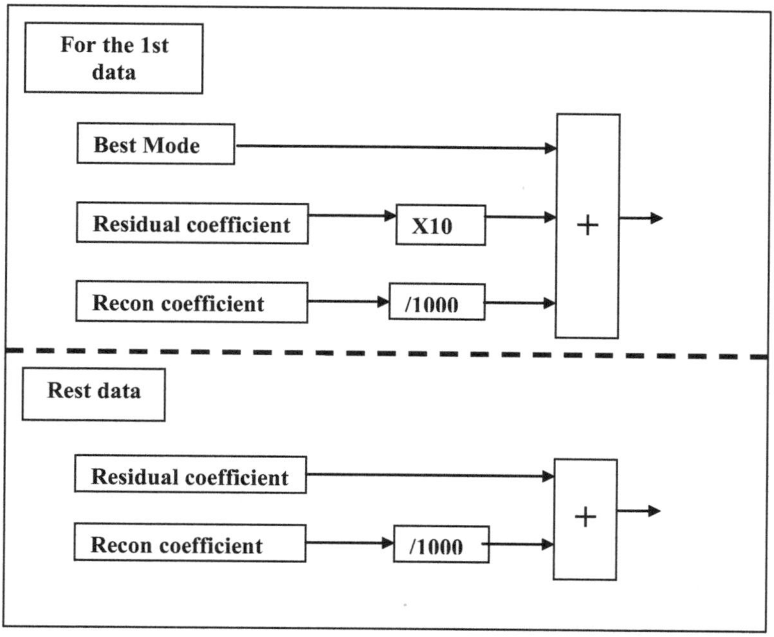

Fig. 7. Method of Data Packing

4 Performance Evaluation

We use one PC equipped GeForce 8800 GTS PCIe graphics card with 96 stream processors(1200Mhz for each) and Intel Pentium 4 3.2GHz processor with 1 GB DDR2 memory as the testing platform. The shaders were programmed OpenGL API and the Cg computer language. Experiments are conducted to evaluate the performance of proposed method, the impact on limited download bandwidth from GPU to CPU and the speed up ratio compare with CPU implementation.

We performance all the experiments to measure the execution time begin at the intra prediction and end at the generating reconstruction image. In order to show how download bandwidth limit from GPU to CPU impact the performance, both with and without readback data from GPU to CPU also be tested. We first find out the execution time for different size of block list. Figure 8 is shown the result. For short block list, less blocks can be processed parallel, the overhead of data I/O becomes significant. But for the long block list, the gain on process it on GPU is significant from the benefit of parallel mechanism it also diminishes the effect of setup overhead of GPU. The longer block list, the larger speed up. We obtain the optimal block list size S_o(speed up ratio is greater than 1 when block list size is longer then S_o) for different testing condition.

Finally, we adjust the selection of processing block lists by using CPU or GPU. If the sizes of block list smaller than S_o, the processing will be running on CPU, otherwise on GPU. Figure 9 is shown the performance of CPU or GPU selection with using S_o as the threshold.

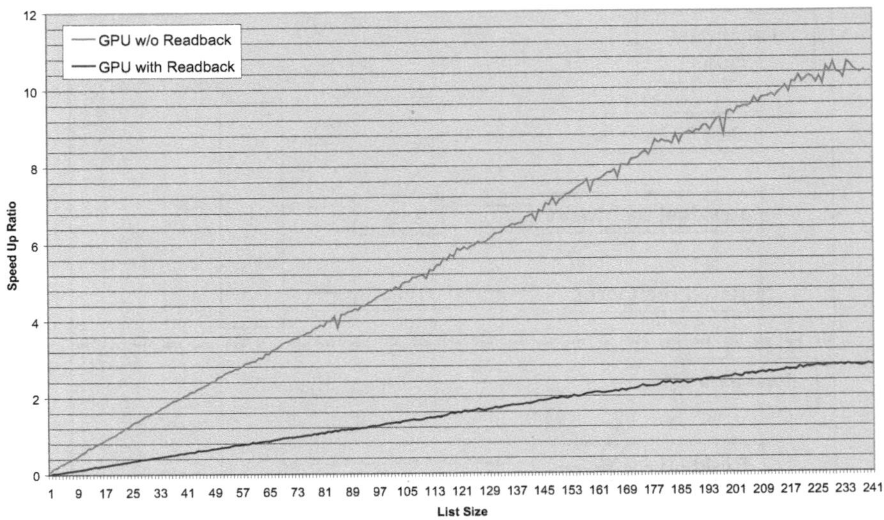

Fig. 8. Speed up ratio of GPU vs CPU for different 4x4 block list size

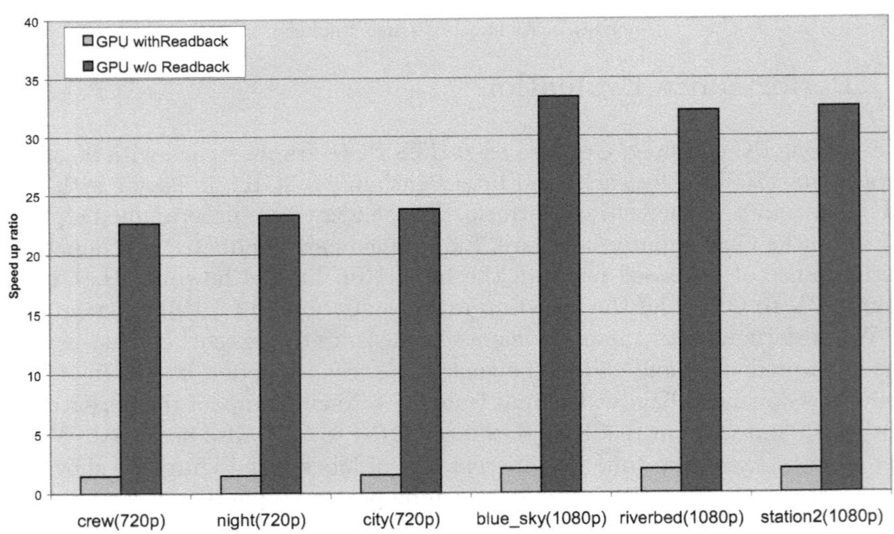

Fig. 9. Speed up ratio of different test case on GPU

From the experiment result, the speed up ratio of readback and w/o readback has about 16 times different. It shows that the readback data from GPU to CPU is the main bottleneck. The overhead of readback data from GPU to CPU is the domain of the process.

5 Conclusions and Discussion

We proposed a GPU-based intra frame processing implementation to offload the computation loading from CPU to GPU. By rearranging the 4x4 block encoding order, the process can favor from the parallel mechanism on GPU. With using the optimal block list size for the selection. Up to thirty times speed-up can be achieved. However, the performance improvement is limited by the download bandwidth limitation. The proposed method does not support 16x16 intra prediction. This is due to output data for one 16x16 MB exceed the limit of output data size. Possible solution is to compress the data prior to the output process. This is left for the future works.

Acknowledgments. This work has been supported by the Innovation and Technology Commission of the Hong Kong Special Administrative Region, China (project no. GHP/033/05).

References

1. Joint Video Team (JVT) of ISO/IEC MPEG and ITU-T VCEG: Draft ITU-T recommendation and final draft international standard of joint video specifictio (ITU-T Rec. H.264/ISO/IEC 14 496-10 AVC). JVT-G050 (2003)
2. Gang-yi, J., Shi-ping, L., Mei, Y., Fu-cui, L.: An efficient fast mode selection for intra prediction. In: Proc, IEEE VLSI Design and Video Technology, pp. 357–360 (2005)
3. Lin, Y.K., Chang, T.S.: Fast block type decision algorithm for intra prediction in h.264 frext. In: IEEE International Conference on Image Processing, pp. 585–588 (2005)
4. Goodnight, N., Wang, R., Humphreys, G.: Computation on Programmable Graphics Hardware. IEEE Computer Graphics and Applications 25(5), 12–15 (2005)
5. Brunton, A., Zhao, J.: Real-time video watermarking on programmable graphics hardware. In: Canadian Conference Electrical and Computer Engineering, 2005, pp. 1312–1315 (2005)
6. Kru"ger, J., Westermann, R.: Linear algebra operators for gpu implementation of numerical algorithms. In: International Conference on Computer Graphics and Interactive Techniques (2005)
7. Fialka, O., Cadik, M.: Fft and convolution performance in image filtering on gpu. In: Information Visualization, pp. 609–614 (2006)
8. Shen, G., Gao, G.P., Li, S., Shum, H.Y., Zhang, Y.Q.: Accelerate video decoding with generic gpu. In: IEEE Transactions on Circuits and Systems for Video Technology, vol. 15, pp. 685–693 (2005)
9. Ho, C.W., Oscar, A., Gary, C., Yip, S.K., Wong, H.M.: Motion estimation for h.264/avc using programmable graphics hardware. In: IEEE International Conference on Multimedia and Expo, pp. 2049–2052 (2006)
10. Kelly, F., Kokaram, A.: General purpose graphics hardware for accelerating motion estimation. In: Irish Machine Vision and Image Processing Conference (2003)

11. Lin, Y.C., Li, P.L., Chang, C.H., Wu, C.L., Tsao, Y.M., Chien, S.Y.: Multi-pass algorithm of motion estimation in video encoding for generic gpu. In: Proc. IEEE International Conference on Circuits and Systems (2006)
12. Jin, G., Lee, H.J.: A Parallel and Pipelined Execution of H.264/AVC Intra Prediction. In: IEEE International Conference on Computer and Information Technology, p. 246 (2006)
13. Lee, W.L., Seongjoo Kim, J.: Pipelined intra prediction using shuffled encoding order for h.264/avc. In: IEEE Region 10 Conference TENCON, pp. 1–4 (2006)

Error Concealment Techniques for Multi-view Video Sequences

Taeyoung Chung, Kwanwoong Song, and Chang-Su Kim

School of Electrical Engineering, Korea University,
Seoul, Korea
{lovelool17, kwsong71, changsukim}@korea.ac.kr

Abstract. In this work, we investigate error patterns in compressed multi-view video signals and propose three error concealment algorithms, which can hide the effects of transmission errors efficiently. The proposed algorithms conceal a lost block by choosing and combining the best candidate blocks in the temporally adjacent frames or the inter-view frames at the same time instance. Simulation results demonstrate that the proposed algorithms effectively protect the quality of reconstructed videos against transmission errors.

1 Introduction

The advances of diverse multimedia technologies make the acquisition, coding, transmission and display of multi-view video sequences possible. A multi-view video sequence provides multiple views of the same scene, thus it can offer interactivity as well as rich experience. However, in spite of these advantages, a typical multi-view sequence requires a huge amount of storage space, which is proportional to the number of available views. Therefore, the compression algorithm is being standardized jointly by ISO/IEC and ITU-T to reduce the data rates of multi-view video sequences [1].

Unlike a single-view sequence, a multi-view sequence exhibits high correlations between views as well as spatio-temporal correlations within a view. To achieve a high coding gain, the inter-view and spatio-temporal correlations are exploited by predictive coding schemes. However, if an error occurs, it propagates to adjacent views as well as to subsequent frames, degrading the picture quality severely. Whereas various approaches have been proposed to protect the qualities of single-view sequences against transmission errors, little effort has been made for the robust transmission of multi-view sequences. In this work, we analyze the hierarchical B prediction structure [2,3] for multi-view video coding and the corresponding error propagation patterns. Then, we propose several error concealment (EC) algorithms to hide the effects of block losses in multi-view video transmission.

The rest of this paper is organized as follows. Section 2 briefly explains the hierarchical B structure for multi-view video coding. Section 3 describes the proposed algorithms, and Section 4 evaluates their performances. Finally, Section 5 gives concluding remarks.

H.H.S. Ip et al. (Eds.): PCM 2007, LNCS 4810, pp. 619–627, 2007.

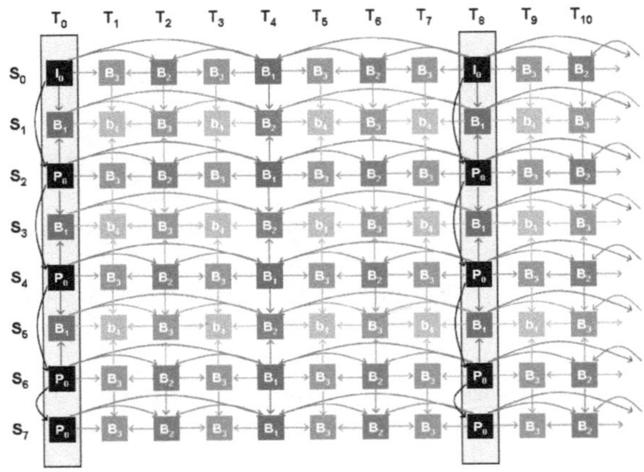

Fig. 1. The prediction structure for multi-view sequences, proposed in [3]. T_i denotes time, while S_j denotes a view. In this example, a group of pictures (GOP) contains 8 temporal frames in 8 different views.

2 Prediction Structure for Multi-view Sequences

The hierarchical B picture mode in the H.264/AVC standard enables the efficient compression of video sequences using the bi-directional prediction in a hierarchical manner [2]. It decouples the coding order of frames from the display order. Using the hierarchical B picture mode, various predictive structures can be designed for multi-view video sequences, since a frame can be predicted using different view frames and/or temporally adjacent frames.

Merkle *et al.* [3] proposed a prediction structure for multi-view sequences, which is shown in Fig. 1. This structure is used in this work for its effectiveness. The vertical axis represents different camera views, while the horizontal axis represents the temporal axis. The first view S_0 is encoded using only the temporal correlations. The other even views S_2, S_4 and S_6 are also encoded based on the temporal prediction, but their first frames are encoded using the inter-view prediction. In the odd views S_1, S_3 and S_5, both the temporal and inter-view predictions are jointly used to improve the compression performance. The last view can be an even or odd view depending on the number of views. In this example, a group of pictures (GOP) contains pictures at 8 different time instances, but the other GOP lengths are also possible, such as 12 or 15.

3 Proposed Algorithms

3.1 Error Patterns

We apply different concealment methods according to error patterns. In this work, a view is referred to as I-view, P-view or B-view according to the type of its first key frame. For example, in Fig. 1, S_0 is I-view, the other even views

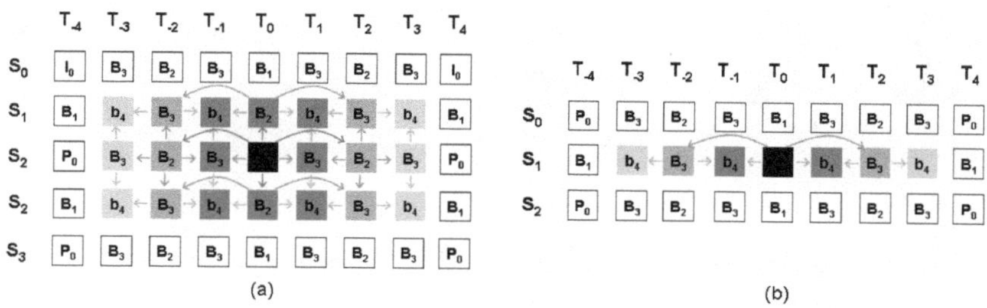

Fig. 2. Error propagation effects according to the error patterns. The loss of a frame in (a) a P-view sequence and (b) a B-view sequence.

S_2, S_4 and S_6 are P-view, and the odd views S_1, S_3 and S_5 are B-view. Note that the last view S_7 is P-view, since its first frame is predicted from a single neighbor only.

Frames in an I-view or P-view sequence are used for the prediction of frames in a B-view sequence. Therefore, if an error occurs in an I-view or P-view, it propagates temporally within the same view and also to the frames in the adjacent views. In contrast, frames in a B-view sequence are never used for the prediction of the other view frames. Thus, errors in a B-view sequence are confined within that view and propagate in the temporal direction only.

Fig. 2(a) illustrates the temporal and inter-view error propagation when frame T_0 in a P-view S_2 is lost during the transmission. On the other hand, Fig. 2(b) shows the temporal propagation when frame T_0 in a B-view S_1 is corrupted. We see that the loss of an I-view or P-view frame has more devastating effects than that of a B-view frame.

3.2 Elementary Concealment Modes

In general, error concealment schemes estimate lost information using the intact information in neighboring blocks or frames. According to an error pattern, different information is available for the concealment. Therefore, we utilize several concealment modes depending on the error patterns.

We use two temporal modes to conceal the loss of blocks.

- Temporal EC-forward (TEC-F): a lost block is replaced by another block in the nearest preceding frame within the same view, which has been already decoded.
- Temporal EC-backward (TEC-B): a lost block is replaced by another block in the nearest subsequent frame within the same view, which has been already decoded.

Moreover, we use two additional inter-view modes.

- Inter-view EC-left (IEC-L): a lost block in a B-view (or P-view) sequence S_n is replaced by a block in the adjacent view S_{n-1} (or S_{n-2}) at the same time instance.

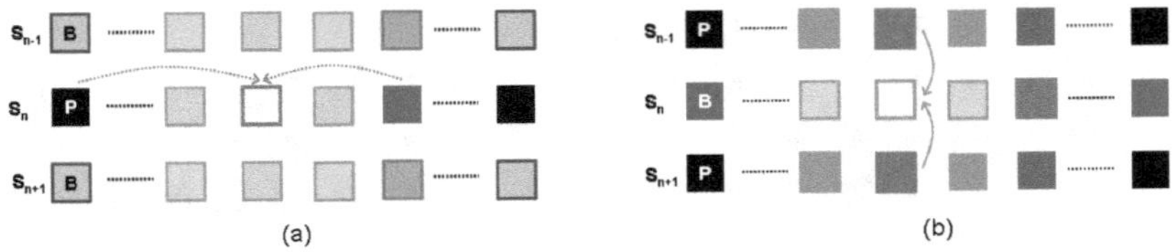

Fig. 3. Four elementary concealment modes: (a) temporal EC modes and (b) inter-view EC modes

- Inter-view EC-right (IEC-R): a lost block in S_n is replaced by a block in S_{n+1} at the same time instance.

The IEC-R mode cannot be applied to blocks in I-view or P-view sequences because of the decoding order. Also, note that we implement the decoder to store S_{n-2} in order to employ the IEC-L mode for a P-view sequence S_n. Fig. 3(a) illustrates the temporal EC modes, and Fig. 3.(b) illustrates the inter-view EC modes.

Using the four modes, a lost block is replaced by a block in the future, past, left or right reference frame. To find an appropriate concealment block, the decoder can estimate the motion vector of the lost block using the neighboring pixel values, as done in the decoder motion vector estimation (DMVE) [4,5] or the block matching algorithm (BMA) [6]. In DMVE, the motion vector of the neighboring pixels is estimated and then used for the lost block. In BMA, the motion vector is selected such that it minimizes the side matching distortion between the recovered block and the neighboring pixels.

As in DMVE, the proposed algorithm first estimates the motion vector for the lost block, which minimizes the sum of absolute differences (SAD). In the SAD calculation, we use the left two lines and the upper two lines of the lost block. The conventional DMVE selects the motion vector, yielding the smallest SAD, and replaces the lost block with the block in the past frame specified by the motion vector. However, the computation of SAD is based on the neighboring pixels, not on the lost block itself. Therefore, the estimated motion vector is not reliable and may not effectively represent the motion of the lost block. In this work, we achieve more reliable concealment by finding multiple candidates in the four (future, past, left and right) reference frames and combining them efficiently.

3.3 Three Error Concealment Algorithms

We propose three error concealment algorithms, which are described in detail subsequently.

Single-Hypothesis EC: As mentioned previously, there are three and four elementary EC modes for blocks in P-view and B-view sequences, respectively. In the first algorithm, called single-hypothesis EC (SHEC), we find the best matching block in each mode. Specifically, when a block is lost in a P-view sequence, we employ the DMVE algorithm to find the best matching blocks in the future, past and left frames, respectively. Then, we choose the final block, which yields the minimum SAD, among the three best blocks, and then replace the lost block with the final block. A lost block in a B-view sequence is concealed in a similar way.

Multi-Hypothesis EC 1: In multi-hypothesis EC, more than two candidate (or hypothesis) blocks are combined to reconstruct a lost block. In [7], Park *et al.* proposed an algorithm, which finds a candidate block in each of the N previous frames and combines the N candidate blocks to form the concealing block. In [8], Kung *et al.* proposed an adaptive EC algorithm, which combines multiple candidate blocks to minimize error propagation. The underlying assumption of multi-hypothesis EC is that individual reconstruction errors of candidate blocks cancel one another, and thus the energy of the final reconstruction error is stochastically lower than that of the reconstruction error of each hypothesis.

In this work, we propose two novel multi-hypothesis EC algorithms for error concealment of multi-view video sequences. In the first multi-hypothesis EC (MHEC1) algorithm, a block in a B-view sequence is concealed in the following way.

1. Find out the block with the minimum SAD in each of the four elementary modes: TEC-F, TEC-B, IEC-L and IEC-R.
2. Between TEC-F and TEC-B, select the block, denoted by B_1, with a smaller SAD.
3. Between IEC-L and IEC-R, select the block, denoted by B_2, with a smaller SAD.
4. Replace the lost block with $(B_1 + B_2)/2$.

On the other hand, in the case of P-view, we cannot use the IEC-R mode. Thus, the inter-view concealment may not be as reliable as the temporal concealment, and we adopt a different scheme for P-view concealment as follows.

1. Find out the block with the minimum SAD in each of the three elementary modes: TEC-F, TEC-B and IEC-L.
2. If the IEC-L mode provides the smallest SAD, conceal the lost block by averaging the IEC-L block and the temporal block with the second smallest SAD. Otherwise, conceal the lost block by averaging the two temporal blocks.

Multi-Hypothesis EC 2: The next algorithm, called multi-hypothesis EC 2 (MHEC2), has the same procedure as MHEC1, but it adaptively changes weighting factors when combining two candidate blocks.

In [9], Song *et al.* showed that the optimally weighted multi-hypothesis EC provides better concealment performances for single-view video sequences than the equally weighted multi-hypothesis EC. Especially, in the double-hypothesis case, the optimal weights are approximately $\frac{2}{3}$ and $\frac{1}{3}$ for the best matching block and the second best matching block, respectively.

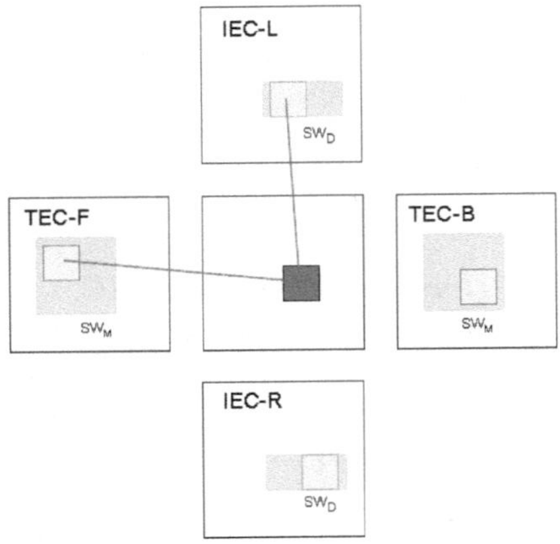

Fig. 4. MHEC1, when the TEC-F and IEC-L modes have the smallest SAD values in the temporal and inter-view directions, respectively

In MHEC2, we classify a lost block according to its estimated motion vector, which yields the minimum SAD in the TEC-F or TEC-B mode. If the magnitude of the motion vector is larger than a pre-specified threshold, the lost block is called a fast block; otherwise, it is a slow block. For a fast block, the inter-view concealment modes are more effective than the temporal concealment modes in general. On the other hand, for a slow block, the temporal concealment modes are more effective. Therefore, the concealment procedure for a B-view sequence in MHEC1 is modified in order to adaptively change the weighting coefficients.

Table 1. The PSNR performance of the proposed algorithms when the error rate is 10%

Sequences		Error	SHEC	MHEC 1	MHEC 2
P	Ballroom	17.87	27.77	28.00	28.12
	Exit	19.65	31.39	31.63	31.86
B	Ballroom	18.54	29.78	30.02	30.31
	Exit	19.44	32.11	31.85	32.28

Table 2. The PSNR performance of the proposed algorithms when the error rate is 5%

Sequences		Error	SHEC	MHEC 1	MHEC 2
P	Ballroom	21.19	30.23	30.48	30.51
	Exit	22.92	33.63	33.70	33.85
B	Ballroom	21.94	31.72	31.89	32.08
	Exit	22.79	34.07	33.88	34.22

1. Find out the block with the minimum SAD in each of the four elementary modes: TEC-F, TEC-B, IEC-L and IEC-R.
2. Between TEC-F and TEC-B, select the block, denoted by B_1, with a smaller SAD.
3. Between IEC-L and IEC-R, select the block, denoted by B_2, with a smaller SAD.
4. If the lost block is a fast block, use $\frac{1}{3}B_1+\frac{2}{3}B_2$ for the concealment; otherwise, use $\frac{2}{3}B_1+\frac{1}{3}B_2$ for the concealment.

The concealment procedure for a P-view sequence is modified in a similar way.

4 Simulation Results

We test the performances of the proposed algorithms on two test sequences: the "Ballroom" and "Exit" sequences. Each sequence is encoded by the joint multi-view video model (JMVM) 3.0 codec using the hierarchical B prediction structure [1]. All the encoding parameters are set according to the JVT common test condition [10]. B-view S_3 or P-view S_4 is corrupted in the test, and a slice is lost randomly within the corrupted view with a loss rate 5% or 10%. Since concealment performances depend heavily on the error locations, we test 10 different slice error locations and present the average PSNR.

Tables 1 and 2 show the performances of the proposed algorithms in the cases of 5% and 10% error rates, respectively. The column "Error" gives the PSNRs when a lost slice is filled with black pixels. We see that the proposed algorithms

(a) (b) (c) (d)

Fig. 5. The reconstructed 55th frame of the B-view S_3 in the "Ballroom" sequence: (a) error locations - 15.43 dB, (b) SHEC - 26.51 dB, (c) MHEC1 - 27.28 dB, and (d) MHEC2 - 28.79 dB

(a) (b) (c) (d)

Fig. 6. The reconstructed 144th frame of the P-view S_4 in the "Exit" sequence: (a) error locations - 20.17 dB, (b) SHEC - 26.56 dB, (c) MHEC1 - 28.90 dB, and (d) MHEC2 - 29.37 dB conceal losses effectively and provides much higher PSNRs than the black pixel filling scheme. Also, note that MHEC2 shows the best performance among the three proposed algorithms by exploiting the inter-view and temporal correlations adaptively.

Fig. 5 shows the 55th frame of the B-view S_3 in the "Ballroom" sequence, when its several slices are lost during the transmission. SHEC provide an acceptable performance, but it shows artifacts around the orange dress of the dancing woman. MHEC1 and MHEC2 reduce those artifacts and provide higher quality reconstructions. Fig. 6 shows the 144th frame in the P-view S_4 in the "Exit" sequence. Again, MHEC1 and MHEC2 provide high quality reconstructed images without any noticeable artifacts.

5 Conclusion

In this work, we proposed three EC algorithms for multi-view video sequences. The proposed algorithms use four elementary modes, which can exploit inter-view correlations as well as temporal correlations. The first algorithm, SHEC, selects the best matching block among all candidates blocks. It provides an acceptable performance. Moreover, the advanced algorithms, MHEC1 and MHEC2, combines multiple candidate blocks to hide the effects of transmission errors more effectively. Simulation results demonstrated that the proposed algorithms can reconstruct high quality sequences even in severe error conditions.

Acknowledgments. This research was supported by the MIC, Korea, under the ITFSIP (IT Foreign Specialist Inviting Program) and the ITRC support program (IITA-2006-C1090-0603-0017), both of which are supervised by the IITA.

References

1. ISO/IEC JTC1/SC29/WG11 and ITU-T SG16 SQ.6, Joint Multiview Video Model (JMVM) 3.0, JVT-V207, Marrakech, Morocco (2007)
2. Schwarz, H., Marpe, D., Wiegand, T.: Analysis of hierarchical B Pictures and MCTF. In: Proc. ICME, pp. 1929–1932 (2006)
3. Merkle, P., Muller, K., Smolic, A., Wiegand, T.: Efficient compression of multi-view video exploiting inter-view dependencies based on H.264/MPEG4-AVC. In: Proc. ICME, pp. 1717–1720 (2006)
4. Zhang, J., Arnold, J.F., Frater, M.R.: A cell-loss concealment technique for MPEG-2 coded video. IEEE Trans. Circuit Syst. Video Technol. 10(4), 659–665 (2000)
5. Tsekeridou, S., Pitas, I.: MPEG-2 error concealment based on block-matching principles. IEEE Trans. Circuit Syst. Video Technol. 10(4), 646–658 (2000)
6. Lam, W., Reibman, R., Liu, B.: Recovery of lost or erroneously received motion vectors. Proc. ICASSP 1993 5, 417–420 (1993)
7. Park, Y.O., Kim, C.-S., Lee, S.-U: Multi-hypothesis error concealment algorithm for H.26L video. In: Proc. ICIP-2003, pp. 465–468 (2003)

8. Kung, W.-Y., Kim, C.-S., Kuo, C.-C.J.: Spatial and temporal error concealment techniques for video transmission over noisy channels. IEEE Trans. Circuit Syst. Video Technol. 16(7), 789–802 (2006)
9. Song, K.W., Chung, T.Y., Kim, C.-S., Park, Y.O., Kim, Y.D., Joo, Y.H., Oh, Y.J.: Efficient Multi-Hypothesis Error Concealment Technique for H.264. In: ISCAS-2007 (2007)
10. ISO/IEC JTC1/SC29/WG11 and ITU-T SG16 SQ.6, Common Test Conditions for Multiview Video Coding, JVT-U207, Hangzhou, China (2006)

Consistent-Quality Distributed Video Coding Framework

Geming Wu[1], Lifeng Sun[2], and Feng Huang[2]

[1] School of Software, Tsinghua University,
Beijing 100084, China
Wgm05@mails.tsinghua.edu.cn

[2] Department of Computer Science, Tsinghua University,
Beijing 100084, China
{sunlf, huangf}@tsinghua.edu.cn

Abstract. In this paper, we address the problem of quality control for distributed video coding (DVC). In a pure DVC framework, the compression performance conflicts with the consistency of the video quality. A hybrid framework is proposed to solve this problem. Wyner-Ziv video coding and zero vector motion compensation are combined to keep the visual quality in consistency while maintaining satisfied compression efficiency. Simulation results show that the proposed framework can effectively reduce the variance of the video quality, and the compression performance is 1-5dB better than pure DVC framework worked in constant quality mode. We also evaluate the decoding efficiency of two multistage decoding (MSD) strategies in Wyner-Ziv coding. Simulate results show that passing soft decision from low level to high level works better in DVC.

Keywords: Distributed Video Coding (DVC), Wyner-Ziv Coding, low-density parity-check (LDPC).

1 Introduction

Distributed video coding (DVC) is a fundamentally new paradigm for video compression [1][2][3], which contains a light video encoder. In a DVC framework, frames are divided into intra frames and Wyner-Ziv frames, the intra frames are coded using conventional intra frame coder while the Wyner-Ziv frames are coded using Wyner-Ziv coder. The Wyner-Ziv encoder generates the syndrome bits of the Wyner-Ziv frames and sends them to the decoder. The decoder uses these syndrome bits to correct the virtual errors in the side information, i.e. an approximation of the current frame.

The peak signal-to-noise ratio (PSNR) of a reconstructed Wyner-Ziv frame relies on the quality of the side information. Different solutions have been proposed to get better side information. In [4], hash is send to the decoder to guide the selection of the side information. In [5], universal prediction is proposed to generate the side information by extrapolation from previously decoded frames.

H.H.S. Ip et al. (Eds.): PCM 2007, LNCS 4810, pp. 628–637, 2007.

In [6], the authors deal with video quality control in multi-view video coding, frames captured by the neighbor cameras are sent to the decoder to improve the quality of the reconstructed frame.

In this paper, we address the problem of quality control for DVC and propose a DVC framework based on zero vector motion compensation. The residual frame (the difference between the current frame and the previous frame) is intra-coded and the low-frequency coefficients are sent, these low-frequency coefficients are used to perform block match, and we control the video quality by changing the percentage of the low-frequency coefficients be sent. In[4] high-frequency coefficients of the current frame are sent as hash, the idea is similar to ours, but the authors only consider the compression performance while we aim to design a consistent quality video coding framework. Also in our framework the percentage of the coefficients is variable according to the motion level. We describe the detail of this framework in Section II and demonstrate its performance in Section III. The second contribution of this paper is that we evaluate the decoding efficiency of two multistage decoding (MSD) strategies in Wyner-Ziv coding, simulation results are displayed in section III.

2 Proposed Framework

2.1 Quality Consistency of Wyner-Ziv Video Coding

For most real-world video applications, it is desirable to have consistent video quality. This can be satisfied easily in conventional video coding standards like H.26x because they exploit the temporal correlation at the encoder, and entropy codes helps them to work in variable rate mode naturally.

Under Wyner-Ziv setup, quantization step of the Wyner-Ziv frame must be chosen according to the motion level, coarse quantization has to be taken when the motion is large. We explain this by a simple test. We encode the second frame of foreman sequence in QCIF format using both H.263 intra codec and Wyner-Ziv coder. We compare the compression efficiency of these two schemes. Under Wyner-Ziv setup, we assume that the first frame is perfectly reconstructed at the decoder and help decoding the second frame as the side information. The results are illustrated in TABLE I. Wyner-Ziv coding becomes less efficient than intracoding as the quantization level increases. This is because a Wyner-Ziv encoder achieves compression gain by sending M syndrome bits instead of K information bits, the compression rate is K/M, where M is a monotonically increasing function of E and can be written as $M(E)$. K is often fixed in real application and it can not be too large because long block length can cause high delay. So as E increases, the compression efficiency $K/M(E)$ decreases. When the motion between two successive frames is large, coarse quantization has to be taken to reduce the virtual errors E, otherwise the compression efficiency must be poor. The motion level of a sequence often varies with time, so a Wyner-Ziv encoder has to change the quantization step according to the motion level so as to achieve high average compression gain. In application, quantization step can be chosen proportioned to sum of absolute differences (SAD) between two successive frames [1]. This makes the video quality of a Wyner-Ziv video coder's output varies with time.

Table 1. Coding results of wyner-ziv coding and intracoding

Quantization Level	8	16	32
LDPC syndrome (bits)	10200	30650	68280
Intracoding (bits)	14008	31181	65400
PSNR (dB)	30	35	40

Due to this natural drawback of Wyner-Ziv video coder, there is a contradiction between compression performance and quality control in pure DVC framework. So we propose to combine Wyner-Ziv coding with zero vector motion compensation. The detail is discussed in the following subsection.

2.2 Hybrid Distributed Video Coding Framework

The structure of the proposed DVC framework is illustrated in Fig. 1 and Fig. 2. This framework combines a Wyner-Ziv coder and an intraframe coder. The intraframe coder is used to compress the residual frame between the current frame and the previous frame. We use this zero vector motion compensation technique to generate better side information at the decoder, and save the syndrome bits needed to be sent.

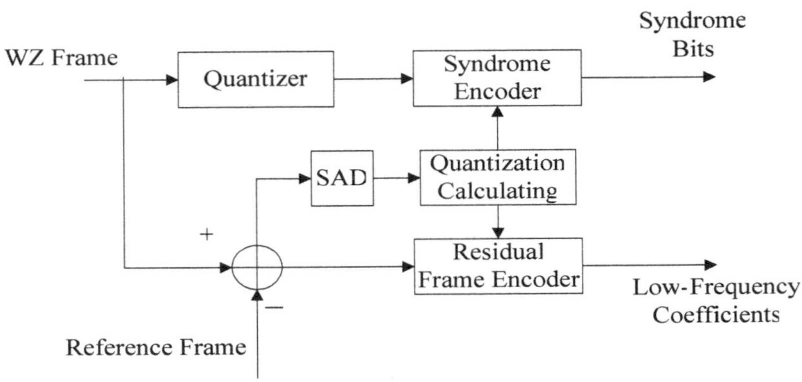

Fig. 1. The structure of the encoder in the proposed framework

Let the current to-be-encoded frame and the previous frame denoted by X and Y respectively. First we calculate the residual frame: $N = X - Y$, and then N is intracoded using 8×8 DCT and entropy codes. Unlike the work in [4] where high-frequency coefficients are sent as hash, we send low-frequency coefficients. We consider that low-frequency coefficients carry most of the information, so more accurate block match results can be expected, further, we observe in experiments that it's not efficient to compress the high-frequency coefficients without doing motion estimation.

At the decoder side, the side information is generated in the following way:

1. IDCT is applied to the received low-frequency coefficients producing a coarse residual frame T.
2. Add up T and the previous decoded frame we get a coarse version of the current frame T', at this time, T' does not contain any high-frequency information.
3. Use T' to perform motion search in the previous frame to find the best match denote by T''. This step is the same as the motion search in H.26x. Integrate the low-frequency coefficients of T' and the high-frequency coefficients of T'', we get the final side information.

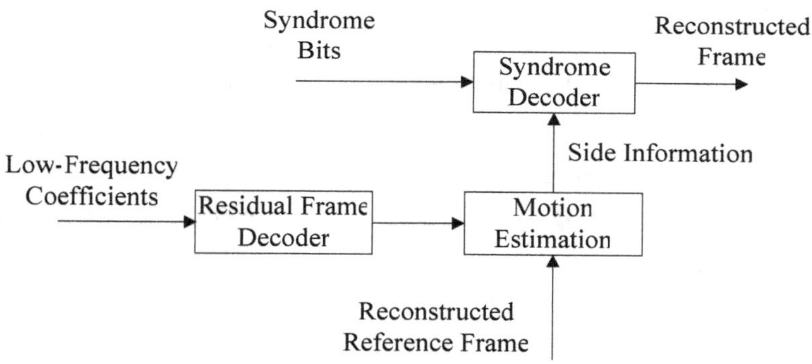

Fig. 2. The structure of the decoder in the proposed framework

The flowchart can be seen in Fig. 3. In our scheme, the low-frequency coefficients sent by the encoder are used directly to generate the side information, so the quantization step of the residual frame is chosen according to the quality requirements. The percentage of the to-be-sent low-frequency is chosen according to the motion level. In practice, this percentage is chosen proportioned to the SAD which can be calculated without adding much complexity to the encoder.

The syndrome conception is first introduced in [1] by Ramchandran *et al.* Our Wyner-Ziv scheme is based on the scheme proposed in [2] by Aaron *et al.* Each pixel in a Wyner-Ziv frame is quantized by a uniform scalar quantizer. The quantized symbols are then converted to bitplanes. LDPC encoding is applied to these bitplanes producing syndrome bits which are sent to the decoder.

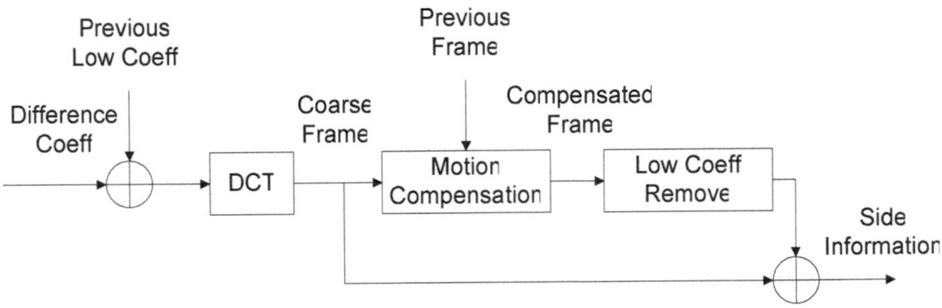

Fig. 3. The decoding procedure

The quantizer in the proposed framework consists of a uniform scalar quantizer concatenated by a modular quantizer. First, pixel data ranging from 0 to 255 are quantized to M_1 levels codewords, $M_1 \in \{2,4,8,16...\}$. Then codewords are quantized again by a M_2 level modular quantizer. Both quantizations can be view as binning, the whole range 0-255 is partitioned into several bins, and the bin index is the quantization result. For the scalar quantizer, there are $256/M_1$ elements in the same bin having the minimum distance 1 from each other, for the lattice quantizer, there are $256/(M_1 * M_2)$ elements in a modular bin having the minimum distance $256/(M_1 * (M_2 - 1))$ from each other. M_1 is chosen proportioned to the SAD of the difference frame N such that the number of the virtual error won't excess the capacity of the error correcting codes. Lager M_2 brings higher compression rate, but too large M_2 can result in reconstruction error.

In pure Wyner-Ziv framework, the syndrome quantization level has to be small when the motion is large, so the quantized symbols Q carry not enough information which leads to poor quality of the decoded frame. In our scheme, better quality side information can be generated by sending more low-frequency coefficients. Because the reconstruction of a Wyner-Ziv frame W is a function: $W = E(W \mid Q, S)$, better side information will give a better estimation of W , thus reducing the syndrome bits needed to be sent.

2.3 Encoding Complexity and Multistage Decoding

The syndrome encoder in our scheme is based on the framework in [3], its main calculation is the multiplication of the bitplanes and the LDPC matrix. The residual encoding has the same complexity as intracoding. The calculation of the percentage of the to-be-sent coefficients can be accomplished by several times of multiplication, so it brings little complexity.

In [8], bitplanes are decoded from low level (less important bitplane) to high level (more important bitplane) using multistage approach [9]. After the bitplane of level i

is decoded, the decoding results are passed to high levels, and the initial log-likelihood of level $i+1$ is calculated with the help of previous i levels decoding results:

$$L_{i+1}^{ch} = Ln \frac{\sum_{\{J|j_{i+1}=1, j_1=\hat{x}_1 \hbar, j_i=\hat{x}_i\}} \exp(-\frac{d^2(Y,4J)}{2\sigma^2})}{\sum_{\{J|j_{i+1}=0, j_1=\hat{x}_1 \hbar, j_i=\hat{x}_i\}} \exp(-\frac{d^2(Y,4J)}{2\sigma^2})} \quad (1)$$

Where d^2 denotes the Euclidean distance, σ^2 denotes the variance of the residual frame, Y denotes the side information, and $\hat{x}_i$ denotes the previously decoded results.

Multistage decoding is first introduced as modulation technique used in communication. And it's used in Wyner-Ziv coding to avoid the use of non-binary error correcting codes which can bring huge computing burden and high delay. We consider that the application of multistage decoding in DVC is different from that in communication for two reasons. First, bitplanes are dependent while bits are assumed to be independent in channel codes. Error propagation from low levels to high levels [10] will cause PSNR loss. Second, multilevel coding is directly applied to the original data in DVC while signal mapping is taken before multilevel coding in modulation. So in our decoding scheme, soft decision results is passed to higher levels instead of hard decision results. In practice, the initiate log-likelihood of each bitplane is calculated as follows:

$$\begin{aligned} L_{i+1}^{ch} &= Ln \frac{\Pr(x_{i+1}=1 | Y, L_l^{ap})}{\Pr(x_{i+1}=0 | Y, L_l^{ap})} \\ &= Ln \frac{\sum_{\{J|J_{i+1}=1\}} \exp(-\frac{d^2(Y,4J)}{2\sigma^2}) \prod_{n=1}^{l} P(\hat{x}_i)}{\sum_{\{J|J_{i+1}=0\}} \exp(-\frac{d^2(Y,4J)}{2\sigma^2}) \prod_{n=1}^{l} P(\hat{x}_i)} \end{aligned} \quad (2)$$

Where $P(\hat{x}_i)$ is the probability of the i-level bit x_i being $\hat{x}_i$ which is called soft decision results.

3 Experimental Results and Discussion

First, the comparison of decoding success rate using soft decisions passing and hard decisions passing is illustrated in Fig. 4. The carphone sequence is used as test sequence. The block length K of LDPC and the quantization step is chosen as 25536 and 16 respectively. We adjust the LDPC rate and record the decoding success rate. Results show that passing soft decisions from low level to high level can improve the decoding efficiency. In the following simulations, soft decisions passing scheme is adopted.

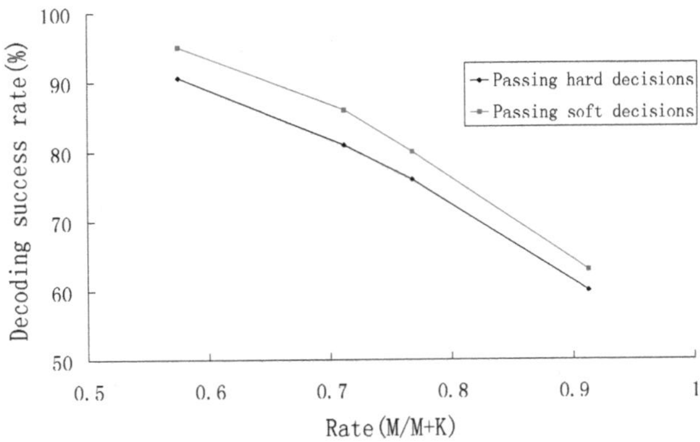

Fig. 4. Efficiency comparison of two multistage decoding strategy

We took salesman and carphone sequences in QCIF format to test our framework, which represent small and large motion scenes respectively. We compared the compression efficiency of the proposed framework with H.263+ intracoding, intercoding and pure DVC. In pure DVC framework, the previous frame is directly used as the side information. For the plots in the figure, the bits for both key frames and WZ frames are counted, and only the PSNR of the luminance component is considered.

A modified version of Radford Neal's package for LDPC encoding/decoding [7] was used for simulations. Different quantization levels $2^M \in \{4,8,16,32,64\}$ are used. I-P-P-P structure was applied in our experiments. The percentage of the to-be-sent coefficients varies from 0-40%.

In Fig. 5 and Fig. 6, the performance of our framework is between H.263 intercoding and intracoding. The gap below H.263+ is about 1.5dB for salesman and about 2-3 dB for carphone. Both the pure DVC framework and the proposed framework perform better in low motion sequences. It's because for high motion sequences, it's difficult to setup a proper correlated model for the to-be-decoded frame and its side information. Second, for high motion sequences, the true motion vectors are far from zero, so the zero vector compression technique can not exploit the temporal correlation efficiently. Similar results can be observed in [2][3][4].

We also display the compression performance of the pure DVC framework in Fig. 5 and Fig. 6, where we fixed the quantization levels to make it work in consistent quality mode. The proposed framework outperforms the pure DVC for 1-5dB.

In Fig. 7 and Fig. 8 the PSNR of the first 100 frames of salesman and carphone is displayed. Both the proposed framework and pure DVC have almost the same average compression performance, but there is high variance of quality in pure DVC framework (up to 4 dB) while the quality variance in the proposed framework is quite small (within 1 dB).

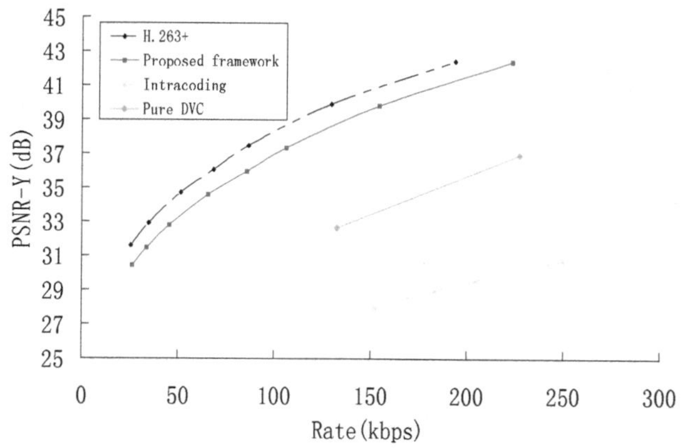

Fig. 5. Rate vs. PSNR at 15 fps for salesman

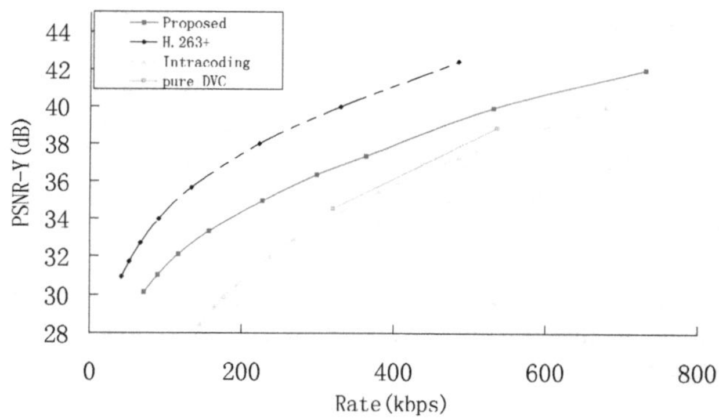

Fig. 6. Rate vs. PSNR at 15 fps for carphone

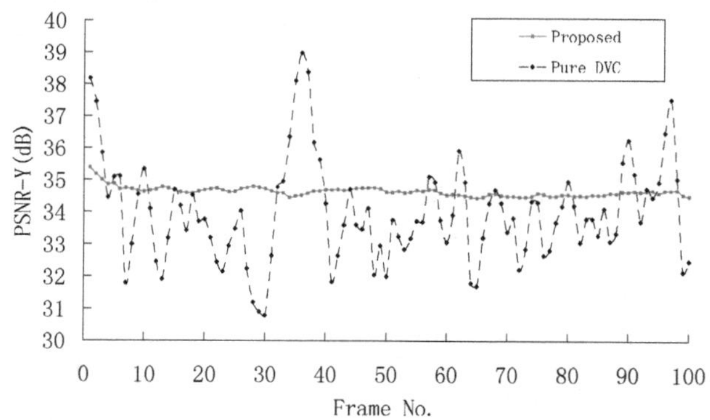

Fig. 7. The PSNR of the first 100 frames of salesman

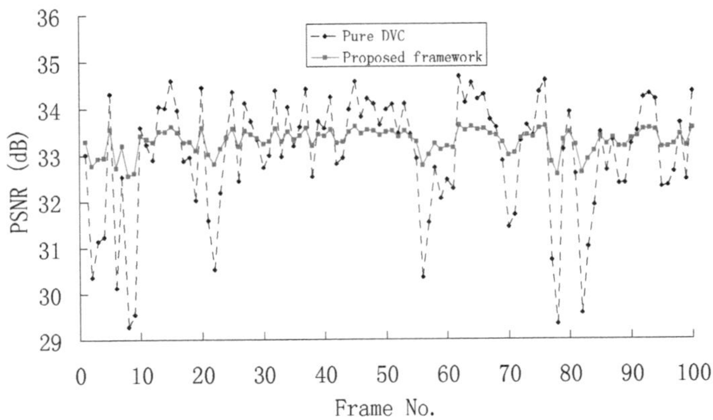

Fig. 8. The PSNR of the first 100 frames of carphone

4 Conclusions and Future Work

In this paper, we propose a distributed framework combining zero vector compression and Wyner-Ziv video coding. Simulation results show that the proposed framework can effectively reduce the variance of decoded video quality while maintaining satisfied compression performance. The soft decision passing and hard decision passing scheme in multistage decoding for Wyner-Ziv coding is also discussed in this paper.

More effective residual frame coding method remains our future work. Current quantization coefficients and the codebook of entropy codes are designed to work with block search, so it must have some potential for improvement. The work includes the designing of quantization coefficients and the codebook of the entropy codes.

Acknowledgements. This work is supported by the Natural Science Foundation of Beijing under Grant No.4063037 and 973 Program under Grant No. 2006CB303103.

References

1. Puri, R., Ramchandran, K.: PRISM: A New Robust Video Coding Architecture Based on Distributed ompression Principles. In: 40th Allerton Conference on Communication Contr ol and Computing, vol. 6, pp. 379–381 (2002)
2. Aaron, R.Z., Girod, B.: Wyner-Ziv coding of motion video. In: Proc. Asilomar Conference on Signals and Sys tems, Pacific Grove, California (November 2002)
3. Aaron, A., Varodayan, D., Girod, B.: Wyner-Ziv Residual Coding of Video. In: Proc. International Picture Coding Symposium, Beijing, P. R. China (April 2006)
4. Aaron, A., Rane, S., Girod, B.: Wyner-Ziv video coding with hash-based motion compensation at the receiver. In: Proc. IEEE International Conference on Image Processing, San Fran cisco, CA (2004)

5. Li, Z., Liu, L., Delp, E.J.: Wyner-Ziv video coding with universal prediction. IEEE Trans on Circuits and Systems for Video Technology 16, 1430–1436 (2006)
6. Sun, J., Li, H.: A Wyner-Ziv coding approach to transmission of interactive video over wireless channels. In: Proc. IEEE Interna tional Conference on Image Processing, vol. 2, p. II-686-9 (September 2005)
7. Neal, R.: Software for low-density parity-check (LDPC) codes. http://www.cs.toronto.edu/ radford/ldpc.software.html
8. Lan, C.F., Liveris, A.D., Narayanan, K., Xiong, Z.: Slepian-Wolf coding of multiple M-ary sources using LDPC codes. In: Proc. DCC (2004)
9. Calderbank, A.R.: Multilevel codes and multistage decoding. IEEE Transactions on Communication, 222–229 (1989)
10. Isaka, M., Imai, H.: On the iterative decoding of multilevel codes. IEEE Journal on Selected Areas in Communications, 935–943 (2001)

Laplacian Distortion Model (LDM) for Rate Control in Video Coding

Long Xu[1], Xiangyang Ji[1], Wen Gao[1], and Debin Zhao[2]

[1] Institute of Computing Technology, Chinese Academy of Sciences, Beijing 100080, China
{lxu,xyji,wgao,dbzhao}@jdl.ac.cn

[2] Department of Computer Science and Technology, Harbin Institute of Technology, Harbin 150001, China

Abstract. In many rate control models, a uniform weighted distortion has been assumed; that is, the DCT coefficients of the motion-compensation difference frames (residues) conform to a uniform distribution. However, the residue after transform does not conform to a uniform distribution but approximate to a Laplacian distribution. In this paper, we first deduce a new distortion model with the assumption of Laplacian distribution of quantized DCT coefficients (called Laplacian distortion model, LDM), and then a more accurate rate-distortion model is proposed based on LDM. Experimental results on H.264/AVC show that our proposed method can improve PSNR up to 0.8dB compared to that of traditional TMN8; meanwhile, the mismatch of target bit rate and actual bit rate generated for coding can be controlled below 2.5%.

1 Introduction

The rate control plays an important role in video coding and communication systems. Without rate control, any video coding encoder would be practically hard to use. Therefore, any video coding standard usually develops their own non-normative rate control scheme during the standardization process, such as TM5 for MPEG2 [1], TMN8 for H.263 [2,3] and VM8 for MPEG4 [4]. In [5], Li *et al.* presents an adaptive rate control scheme for H.264/AVC, where the linear prediction model and quadratic rate-distortion model are employed, as well as the hypothetical reference decoder (HRD) is considered. The key of equation-based rate control methods above is to find the relation between rate and distortion, namely rate-distortion (R-D) model. Traditionally, both the rate and distortion models are considered as functions of quantization parameter (QP), so that the traditional R-D model is the function of QP. For example, in TM5, a simple linear R-D model, i.e., $R(QP) = X/QP$ is adopted, where X is the complexity measure of a picture, QP is the quantization parameter and R is the coded bits for the picture. In VM8 and H.264/AVC, a more accurate quadratic rate-distortion (R-D) model, i.e., $R(QP) = a_1 \times X/QP + a_2 \times X/QP^2$ is employed. In TMN8, an R-D model $R_i = A(K\sigma_i^2/QP_i^2 + C)$ is used. Besides, a novel R-D model is directly represented with the relation between rate and ρ, where

H.H.S. Ip et al. (Eds.): PCM 2007, LNCS 4810, pp. 638–646, 2007.

ρ indicates the percentage of zero coefficients after quantization [7]. Conventionally, a uniform distortion model is considered in many rate control models. However, the uniform distortion model suffers from relatively large estimation and control error as the DCT coefficients after quantization does not conform to a uniform distribution but a Laplacian distribution [3,6]. In this paper, we first deduce a distortion model with the assumption of Laplacian distribution of quantized DCT coefficients (called Laplacian distortion model, LDM), which can represent the actual distortion more accurately. And then, we incorporate the Laplacian distortion model into the traditional TMN8 [3,8], and derived a more accurate R-D model. The newly proposed R-D model can control the bit rate more accurately and improve PSNR significantly. The rest of this paper is organized as follows. Section 2 describes the deduced LDM. Section 3 presents the proposed new R-D model. Section 4 gives the simulation results of the new methods. Section 5 concludes this paper.

2 Laplacian Distortion Model (LDM)

As we know, the residue after transform for inter-frames conforms to the Laplacian distribution. However, in practice, it is very complex to use Laplacian distribution to combine bit rate and distortion, thus, a uniform distortion model is usually considered in most of rate control schemes, such as TMN8 and ρ-domain.

Assumed that the random variable X at the quantizer input conforms to a density function $f_y(y)$, and then the quantizer maps it into a discrete-valued random variable Y. In [9], the minimum entropy of Y represented as

$$H_{min} \approx H_0 - \log Q, \tag{1}$$

and the corresponding distortion coming with the quantizer represented as

$$D(Q) = Q^2/12, \tag{2}$$

can be obtained when a uniform quantizer is applied, where Q is the step size of quantizer, and H_0 is the entropy of the continuous distribution of random variable X. Generally, the DCT coefficients of the motion-compensated are approximately uncorrelated and Laplacian distributed with variance σ^2 as

$$f_y(y) = \frac{\lambda}{2} e^{-\lambda|y|} (\lambda = \frac{\sqrt{2}}{\sigma}). \tag{3}$$

Then H_0 can be calculated as

$$H_0 = -\int_{-\infty}^{+\infty} \frac{\lambda}{2} e^{-\lambda|y|} \log(\frac{\lambda}{2} e^{-\lambda|y|}) dy = \log \frac{2e}{\lambda}, \tag{4}$$

From (1) and (4), we can obtain the minimum entropy of the random variable Y as

$$H_{min} = \log \frac{2e}{\lambda} - \log Q = \log \frac{2e}{\lambda Q} (\log \frac{\sqrt{2} e\sigma}{Q}), \tag{5}$$

which represents the minimum bits used for coding the quantized DCT coefficients. And then, based on (2) and (5), the rate-distortion (R-D) model is derived as follow,

$$R = \log \frac{\sqrt{2}e\sigma}{Q} = \log (\frac{\sigma}{\sqrt{D}}) + C (C = \log \frac{e}{\sqrt{6}}). \tag{6}$$

When uniform distortion model is considered, the distortion in each macroblock (MB) is introduced by uniformly quantizing its DCT transform coefficients with a quantizer of step size Q as shown in (2). When Laplacian distribution is assumed, we deduce the LDM as follows.

In H.264/AVC, a total of 52 quantization values (QP) are supported [10,11]. From (2) and (3), the theoretical distortion $D(Q)$ is

$$D(Q) = \sum_{-\infty}^{+\infty} \int_{Q(i-0.5}^{Q(i+0.5)} (y - Q(i))^2 \frac{1}{\sqrt{2}\sigma} e^{\frac{\sqrt{2}}{\sigma}|y|} dy, \tag{7}$$

where $Q(i)$ is the reconstructed y value derived after quantization and inverse quantization. Equation (7) is an even function of Q. Thus, it can be re-written as

$$D(Q) = \sum_{i=1}^{+\infty} 2 (\int_{Q(i-0.5)}^{Q(i+0.5)} (y - Q(i))^2 \frac{1}{\sqrt{2}\sigma} e^{\frac{\sqrt{2}}{\sigma} y} dy)$$
$$+ 2 (\int_{0}^{0.5Q} (y - Q(i))^2 \frac{1}{\sqrt{2}\sigma} e^{-\frac{\sqrt{2}}{\sigma} y} dy). \tag{8}$$

Since

$$\begin{cases} \int y e^{-ay} dy = -\frac{e^{-ay}}{a^2}(ay+1) + c \\ \int y^n e^{-ay} dy = -\frac{1}{a} e^{-ay} y^n + \frac{n}{a} \int y^{n-1} e^{-ay} dy \end{cases}, \tag{9}$$

$D(Q)$ can be derived from (8) using (9) as

$$D(Q) = \sigma^2 - \frac{\sqrt{2}Q\sigma}{e^{\frac{Q}{\sqrt{2}\sigma}} - e^{-\frac{Q}{\sqrt{2}\sigma}}} = \sigma^2 (1 - \frac{\frac{Q}{\sqrt{2}\sigma}}{\frac{1}{2}(e^{\frac{Q}{\sqrt{2}\sigma}} - e^{-\frac{Q}{\sqrt{2}\sigma}})})$$
$$= \sigma^2 (1 - \frac{\frac{Q}{\sqrt{2}\sigma}}{\sinh \frac{Q}{\sqrt{2}\sigma}}) = \sigma^2 (1 - \frac{\beta}{\sinh \beta}), \tag{10}$$

where $\beta = \frac{Q}{\sqrt{2}\sigma}$, the sinh(.) is defined as

$$\sinh \beta = \frac{\beta}{1} + \frac{\beta^3}{3!} + \frac{\beta^5}{5!} + \ldots. \tag{11}$$

(11) can be approximated by $\beta + \beta^3/6$ when $\beta < \sqrt{e}$ corresponding to high bit rate [3] is true. Then, the (10) can be replaced by

$$D(Q) \approx \sigma^2 \frac{Q^2}{12\sigma^2 + Q^2}. \tag{12}$$

3 Rate-Distortion (R-D) Model

Based on our proposed LDM, we can get a new R-D model as follows. The rate control problem, which compromises between the whole distortion and bit rate budget, can be formulated as an optimization problem as

$$\begin{cases} Q_1^* Q_2^* \cdots Q_N^* = argmin \frac{1}{N} \sum_{k=1}^{N} D_k \\ \sum_{k=1}^{N} B_k < B, B_i \approx A(K \frac{\sigma_i^2}{Q_i^2} + C) \end{cases} . \tag{13}$$

where B_i represents the expected number of bits produced by coding the i-th macroblock in current frame, B is the bits budget of current frame, K is the model parameter, A is the number of pixels in a macroblock, and σ_i is the standard deviation of the residue in the i-th macroblock, C is the overhead rate. Here, B_i can be represented by the experimental entropy of quantized DCT coefficients [3] as

$$H(Q) = \begin{cases} \frac{1}{2} \log_2 (2e^2 \frac{\sigma^2}{Q^2}) , & \frac{\sigma^2}{Q^2} > \frac{1}{2e} \\ \frac{e}{\ln 2} \frac{\sigma^2}{Q^2} & , \frac{\sigma^2}{Q^2} < \frac{1}{2e} \end{cases} , \tag{14}$$

which is based on the assumption that the DCT coefficients of residue are approximately uncorrelated and Laplacian distributed. According to the Lagrange algorithm [12,13],

$$\begin{aligned} f(Q) &= Q_1^* Q_2^* \cdots Q_N^* \lambda^* \\ &= argmin \frac{1}{N} \sum_{k=1}^{N} \alpha_k^2 \sigma_k^2 \frac{Q_k^2}{12\sigma_k^2 + Q_k^2} + \lambda [\sum_{k=1}^{N} (A(K \frac{\sigma_k^2}{Q_k^2} + C)) - B] \end{aligned} \tag{15}$$

From (1) and (15), the traditional TMN8 [3,8] selects the values of the quantization parameter of the i-th macroblock in a frame is calculated as

$$Q_i^* = \sqrt{\frac{AK}{B - ANC} \frac{\sigma_i}{\alpha_i} \sum_{k=1}^{N} \alpha_k \sigma_k} \tag{16}$$

where A is the number of pixels in each MB, N is the number of MB in a frame, K is a distortion model parameter, C is the overhead rate, σ_i and α_i is the standard deviation and distortion or importance weight of the i-th MB respectively. From (12) and (15), i.e., based on LDM, we can get the quantization parameters of the macroblock as

$$Q_i = \sqrt{\frac{12\sigma_i^2 AK \sum_{k=1}^{N} \alpha_k \sigma_k}{\alpha_i \sigma_i [AKN + 12(B - ANC)] - AK \sum_{k=1}^{N} \alpha_k \sigma_k}} \tag{17}$$

where the parameters have the same meanings as in (16). Formula (17) requires about the same computational complexity as formula (16). And its bit rate control accuracy or quality is better than when applying formula (17).

4 Experiments and Discussions

In [14], Yin *et al.* has provided a new rate control scheme for H.264/AVC, where the TMN8 model is employed, and the pre-analysis only using 16x16 inter mode is performed to get the variance σ^2 of each MB. In this paper, we implemented the proposed LDM based rate control scheme(called LDM for short in the following content) and TMN8 in H.264/AVC encoder (JM9.8). The encoder employs the frame-layer bit allocation as in [5] to select a target number of bits for the current frame, and the macroblock-layer QP control using LDM and TMN8 to select the values of the QPs for the macroblocks in that frame. Besides, the pre-analysis only using 16x16 intra mode for I frame, and 16x16 inter mode for P frame is adopted here.

For evaluating the performance of our proposed R-D model, the experiments both on LDM and TMN8 are performed on a set of video sequences. Experimental results for "Foreman" (CIF: 352x288) and "Football" (CIF: 352x288) are tabulated in Table 1 and Table 2 respectively. According to Table 1, we can see that the PSNR improvement for sequence "Football" can be up to 0.7dB; meanwhile, little mismatch of target bits and real bits generated below 1% can be observed.

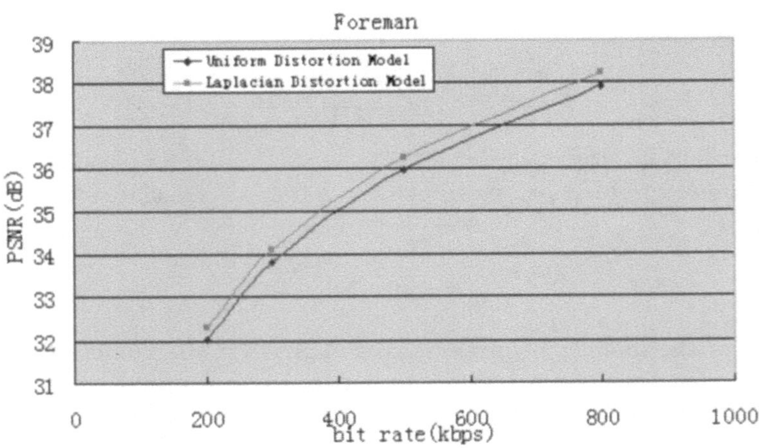

Fig. 1. PSNR vs bit rate of "Foreman"

The R-D curves are explicitly shown in Fig.1 and Fig.2 for "Foreman" and "Football" respectively. From Fig.1 and Fig.2, our proposed LDM achieves about 0.3-0.5dB PSNR improvements in average over TMN8 scheme. In addition, using

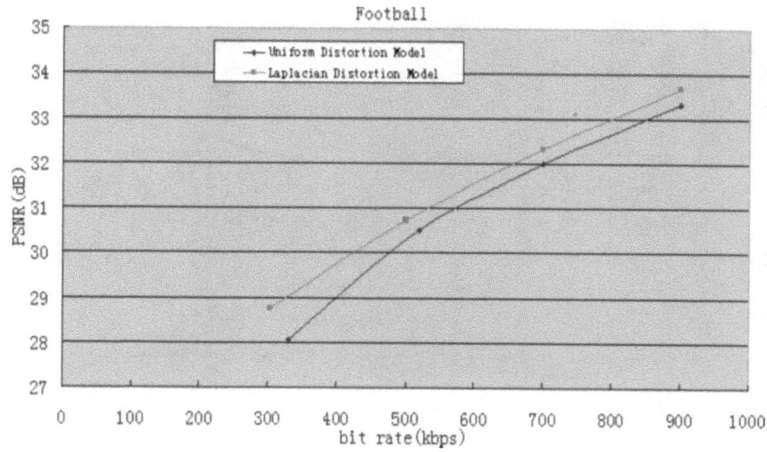

Fig. 2. PSNR vs bit rate of "Football"

Table 1. Coding performance with uniform and laplacian distortion models for "Foreman"

Bit Rate (kbps)	Uniform Distortion			Laplacian Distortion			ΔPSNR
	PSNR(Y)	REAL-BR	ΔBR	PSNR(Y)	REAL-BR	ΔBR	
200	32.02	199.93	-0.07	32.30	200.10	0.10	0.28
300	33.80	300.05	0.05	34.11	300.10	0.10	0.31
500	35.95	499.84	-0.16	36.24	500.09	0.09	0.29
800	37.90	799.90	-0.10	38.20	800.09	0.09	0.30

Table 2. Coding performance with uniform and laplacian distortion models for "Football"

Bit Rate (kbps)	Uniform Distortion			Laplacian Distortion			ΔPSNR
	PSNR(Y)	REAL-BR	ΔBR	PSNR(Y)	REAL-BR	ΔBR	
300	28.06	330.14	30.14	28.76	302.47	2.47	0.71
500	30.50	519.42	19.42	30.73	500.12	0.12	0.23
700	32.00	700.70	0.70	32.33	700.03	0.03	0.33
900	33.32	900.13	0.13	33.68	900.12	0.12	0.36

LDM proposed, there is just a little gap of mismatch between the target bit rate and the real bit rate generated. In our experiments, the mismatch of target bits and generated bits does not exceed 2.5% for all test sequences. Furthermore, the rate control can brings PSNR improvement in the large range of bit rate.

For illustrating the quality fluctuation of each frame, the PSNR per frame for "Foreman" and "Football" is shown in Fig.3 and Fig.4 respectively, where the buffer size is 2 seconds, the size of group of picture (GOP) is 30, intra refresh period is 1 second and only I/P frame is considered. From Fig.3, the PSNR

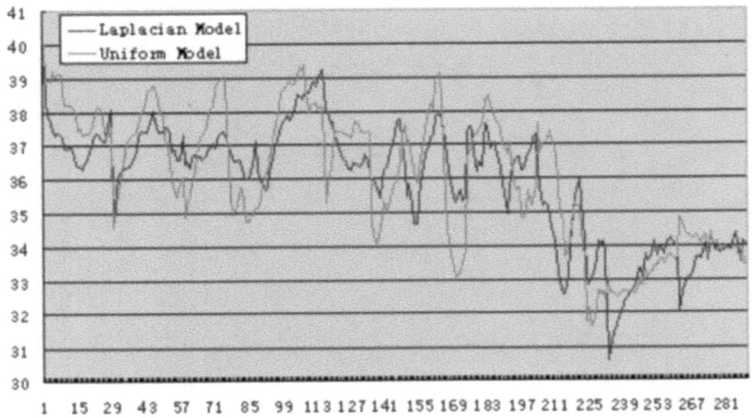

Fig. 3. PSNR per frame of "Foreman" (CIF, 30Hz). (Target bit rate is 500kbits/s, and real bit rate generated is 500.17kbits/s and 508.21kbits/s for our proposed LDM scheme and TMN8 scheme respectively. And, the average PSNR is 36.02dB and 35.96dB for our proposed LDM scheme and TMN8 scheme respectively).

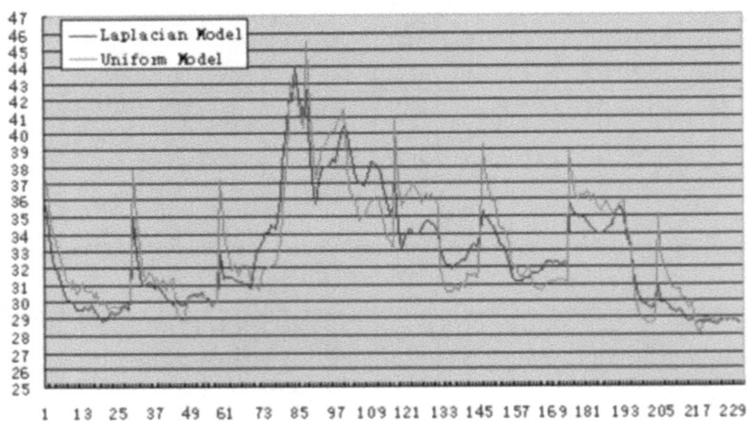

Fig. 4. PSNR per frame of "Football" (CIF, 30Hz). (Target bit rate is 800kbits/s, and real bit rate generated is 800.49kbits/s and 831.21kbits/s for our proposed LDM scheme and TMN8 scheme respectively. And, the average PSNR is 32.78dB and 33.05dB for our proposed LDM scheme and TMN8 scheme respectively).

fluctuation of our proposed LDM is less than that of TMN8 based on uniform distortion model; meanwhile, the mismatch between target bit rate and real bit rate generated is less than that of TMN8 when our proposed LDM is employed. Fig.4 shows the experimental results for "Football" (CIF), and the higher coding performance as "Foreman" can be also observed.

From our experience, the variation of quality of pictures will be magnified if the bit rate controls badly. In addition, the quality of subsequent frames deteriorate much more when high motion or big scene change resulting in much bits consumed occurs. To the accuracy of bit rate controlling, our proposed LDM and TMN8 in MB-level is better than the rate control scheme in H.264/AVC [5]. In our experiments, the mismatch between target bit rate and real bit rate generated of each GOP can't exceed 5% when our proposed LDM is employed; in addition, the bits consumed of each frame also nears to the bits quota allocated. From Fig.3 and Fig.4, our proposed LDM can obtain the smoother picture quality compared to the TMN8 scheme. However, the higher performance of our proposed LDM is somewhat dependent on the better bit allocation strategy. Otherwise, the bad bit allocation strategy will yield the big quality fluctuation, which will deteriorate the subjective and objective quality of pictures coded ultimately. Thus, we introduce a QP constraint strategy for each MB and frame, to get the higher coding performance and the better picture quality.

5 Conclusions

In this paper, we first present a distortion model using Laplacian density approximation to the DCT coefficient distribution. Experimental results show that LDM is more accurate than that from the uniform distribution. Second, we propose a new R-D model based on LDM in H.264/AVC. The simulation results show that not only PSNR improvement but also better matching of target bits and real bits generated for coding can be obtained. Moreover, the LDM can be easily applied to other rate control schemes and the improved coding and the best matching performances can expect to be achieved.

References

1. ISO/IEC JTC1/SC29/WG11, Coding of Moving Pictures and Associated Audio, Test model 5, MPEG (1994)
2. ITU-T/SG15, Video codec test model, TMN8, Portland (June 1997)
3. Corbera, J.R., Lei, S.: Rate Control in DCT Video Coding for Low-Delay Communications. IEEE Trans. on CSVT 9(1) (February 1999)
4. Chiang, T., Zhang, Y.-Q.: A new rate control scheme using quadratic rate distortion model. IEEE Trans. on CSVT 7 (February 1997)
5. Li, Z.G., Gao, W., Pan, F., Ma, S.W., Lim, K.P., Feng, G.N., Lin, X., Rahardja, S., Lu, H.Q., Lu, Y.: Adaptive Rate Control for H.264. Journal of Visual Communication and Image Representation 17(2), 376–406 (2006)
6. Bellifemine, F., Capellino, A., Chimienti, A., Picco, R., Ponti, R.: Statistical analysis of the 2D-DCT coefficients of differential signal for images. Signal Processing: Image Commun. 4, 477–488 (1992)
7. He, Z.: ρ-domain rate-distortion analysis and rate control for visual coding and communication, Ph.D. dissertation, Elect. Comput. Eng. Univ. California, Santa Barbara
8. Chang, T.J., Heh, H.C.: Modified TMN8 rate control for low-delay video communications. IEEE Trans. on CSVT 14(6) (June 2004)

9. Gish, H., Pierce, J.N.: Asymptotically efficiency Quantizing. IEEE Trans. on Inf. Theory IT-14(5) (September 1968)
10. Gray, R.M., Neuhoff, D.L.: Quantization. IEEE Trans. on Inf. Theory 44(6) (October 1998)
11. H.264/MPEG-4 Part 10, Transform & Quantization, [Online] Available: http://www.vcodex.com
12. Sullian, G.J., Wiegand, T.: Rate-Distortion optimization for video compression. IEEE Signal Process. Mag. 15(6) (November 1998)
13. Wiegand, T., Girod, B.: Lagrange multiplier selection in hybrid video coder control. In: Proc. Int. Conf. Image Processing, Thessaloniki, Greece (October 2001)
14. Yin, P., Boyce, J.: A new rate control scheme for H.264 video coding. In: IEEE Proc. Conf. on ICIP, Singapore, pp. 449–452 (October 2004)

Acquiring Critical Light Points for Illumination Subspaces of Face Images by Affinity Propagation Clustering

Senjian An, Wanquan Liu, and Svetha Venkatesh

Department of computing,Curtin University of Technology
Perth, WA 6102, Australia
{s.an,w.liu,s.venkatesh}@curtin,edu.au

Abstract. Previous work has shown that human faces under variable lighting conditions can be modeled by low-dimensional subspaces called illumination subspaces that can be computed using images under a universal lighting configuration. This configuration can be estimated using Harmonic images. However, harmonic images can only be obtained by using 3D information, and thus can be restrictive. In this paper, we overcome this limitation by presenting a completely data-driven method to find good universal lighting configurations. Motivated by the fact that affinity propagation clustering finds the cluster centers from the real images, we use affinity propagation clustering on real images taken under variable lighting conditions to find the cluster centres and use them to determine the lighting configuration. The illumination subspace for each individual is spanned by their images acquired in this lighting configuration. Matching is performed by comparing the distances to these individual illumination subspaces. Further, kernel methods are used to explore the non-linear structures of the illumination cone and carry out the illumination subspace methods in the kernel induced feature space. Experiments conducted on the Extended Yale Face B database demonstrate that the configuration obtained by our method is better than earlier recommended configurations. We also demonstrate that our technique is robust to pose variations using the CMU PIE database.

Keywords: Face Recognition, Illumination Subspace, Affinity Propagation.

1 Introduction

Face recognition under variable lighting and pose is a challenging problem and has attracted tremendous attention in the computer vision community over the past few decades. Many new techniques [1,4,5,7,9], have been developed to overcome the lighting variation problem. [1] has shown that the images from one person under any lighting condition but with fixed pose can be well-approximated by a low-dimensional subspace spanned by a few Harmonic images. To acquire these Harmonic images, one needs to know the 3D information of faces such as surface normals and albedos. In order to avoid potential complex 3D reconstruction, [5] proposed finding a good lighting configuration with a small number of lighting directions and using real images under this

H.H.S. Ip et al. (Eds.): PCM 2007, LNCS 4810, pp. 647–654, 2007.

lighting configuration to estimate the subspace spanned by the Harmonic images. However, to train the lighting configurations, the Harmonic images and thus 3D information are still required.

In this paper, we propose a completely data-driven method to estimate the lighting configuration. For a small number of people, we assume that the real images under sufficiently diverse lighting directions are available. By applying affinity propagation (AP) clustering [3] on these real images, we can obtain the cluster centers which are real images. Motivated by the fact that a low-dimensional subspace can be estimated by a few vectors in this subspace and that the cluster centers are good representations of their neighbors, we use the lighting directions associated with these central images as the lighting configuration. We then apply this configuration to face recognition of larger set of people. The proposed method completely avoids using 3D information and only requires a large amount of training images for a small number of people.

Though the images under variable lighting can be well approximated by a low-dimensional subspace, these images constitute a nearly convex cone [4] but not exactly a subspace. To better approximate this illumination cone, we proposed to use kernel method by approximating it as a subspace in the kernel-induced feature space. Since kernel methods can exploit the nonlinear structure of face images, it has potential to improve performance of the recognition system.

There are two major contributions in this paper. First, a novel method is proposed to find good lighting configurations. The proposed method is computationally simple. It is data-driven and thus 3D information is not required, increasing its applicability; Second, a nonlinear extension of the subspace method is proposed that has the potential to better approximate the illumination cone constituted by the images under all lighting conditions. Experimental results are provided to demonstrate the effectiveness of the proposed methods.

The layout of the rest in this paper is as follows. In Section 2, we briefly review the background on the illumination models of the images under all possible lighting conditions. Section 3 addresses the clustering method to find good lighting configurations and Section 4 addresses the kernel method to estimate the illumination cone. Experimental results are provided in Section 5 for comparison.

2 Illumination Subspace of Face Images

Let $\mathcal{C}$ denote the images of one person (with fixed pose) taken under all possible lighting conditions. By assuming that the object is convex and Lambertian, [7,4] shows that $\mathcal{C}$ is polyhedral cone in the image space, called illumination cone. Moreover, [1,9] prove that the set $\mathcal{C}$ can be effectively approximated by a nine dimensional linear subspace which is spanned by nine virtue images. These nine virtue images, called Harmonic images, can be computed from the 3D information of the object. However, the Harmonic images are not images under real lighting conditions.

To avoid using 3D information such as surface normal and albedo, instead of Harmonic subspace, it was suggested to find a subspace spanned by images under real lighting conditions to approximate the illumination cone well. To find the critical lighting conditions, the earlier proposed method minimizes the distances of the images under these lighting conditions to the Harmonic subspace. To do so, one still needs to know the 3D information: surface normals and albedos. For convenience, we refer illumination subspace to the space spanned by the real images taken under the critical lighting directions.

In the next section, we present a completely data-driven method to find the critical lighting conditions under which the associated images span a subspace which can approximate the illumination cone well.

3 Finding the Critical Images by Affinity Propagation Clustering

The problem is formulated as follows: given a collection $\{L_1, L_2, \cdots, L_n\}$ of lighting conditions or equivalently the associated images $\{I_1, I_2, \cdots, I_n\}$ under these lighting conditions, we want to find a few (say nine) images such that the subspace spanned by these images approximates all the images in this collection well, i.e., the projections of these images onto this subspace is maximized.

To find l from n images, we have C_n^l choices. Let $G_i, i = 1, 2, \cdots, N$ be N sets, each of which has l images randomly selected from the n images. This computation could be very expensive if one uses exhaustive search. Note that the distribution of the images is usually not uniform across the given lighting directions, for example, images with frontal lighting often dominate. With uniformly distributed lighting directions, the images may have several clusters. Motivated by the fact that the cluster centers are most likely independent and good representations for images of their clusters, we hypothesis that they are the good candidates for estimating the basis of the low-dimensional subspace spanned by all the images under variable lighting. We propose the use of affinity propagation clustering to find the clusters of the training images of a small number of people. The lighting directions associated with the cluster centres are then identified to be the critical lighting directions, thus estimating the illumination subspace. When estimating the illumination subspace, if the number of clusters (c) is large, a lower dimensional (d)subspace can be produced by principal component analysis, which is used for recognition later for recognition. Each person then has their own subspace spanned by their images taken in these critical lighting directions. At recognition stage, the query image is projected to the illumination subspaces for each person, and matched with the one with the minimal distance. We call this method the *Linear Subspace* method, to differentiate it from the nonlinear extension we describe later.

For AP clustering, we define the similarity of two images x_i, x_j as the negative of the square of their Euclidian distance, i.e., $s(x_i, x_j) = -\|x_i - x_j\|^2$. Although the number of clusters need not to be specified in AP clustering, one can specify input preferences for each data point, which then in turn controls the number of clusters [3]. By AP clustering on the images from 10 people on the Yale Face Database B under 64 light source directions, we find nine critical lighting directions. The images for one person under these lighting conditions are shown in Figure 1.

Similar as the configurations recommended in [5], this configuration includes one near front lights and six (there pairs of) symmetric side lights but the angles are larger than those recommended in [5]. The critical difference of these two configurations is that this configuration includes one lighting above the head. We note that [5] focus on 45 lights with good quality images and the configuration suggested is based on the analysis of these good quality images. Our experiments demonstrate that the images under all 64 lighting conditions are possible candidates for the illumination subspace. In addition, this freedom to incorporate bad images in the definition of the subspace allows poor images in similar lighting to be recognized. Also, being data driven, the method can be used to estimates the subspace from available images, and thus it has potential to be applied when the lights are not under strict control.

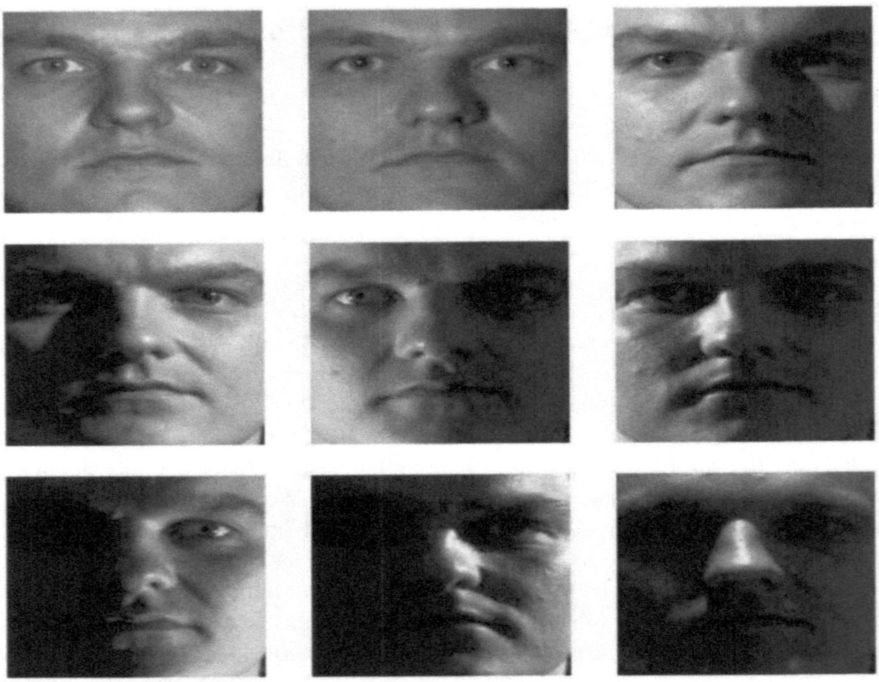

Fig. 1. The Nine Central Images

4 Nonlinear Extensions Using Kernel Trick

Though the images under variable lighting can be approximated well by a low-dimensional subspace, these images constitute a positive, convex cone but not exactly a subspace. Kernel methods can explore the nonlinear structure while maintaining the computational cost similar to the linear case. By exploring the nonlinear structure of the illumination cone, kernel methods have the potential to improve the approximation in the kernel-induced feature space.

In order to extend the illumination subspace method using kernel trick, we reformulate it as follows. Let $x_1, x_2, \cdots, x_l$ be l images (represented as vectors) for one person and denote $X = [x_1, x_2, \cdots, x_l]$. If these vectors are independent, one orthogonal basis u of $span(X)$ can be computed via the singular value decomposition of $X = u\Sigma v^T$.

The confidence level of a query image x (normalized to be unit norm) to be identified as this person is defined as the norm of its projection onto $span(X)$, i.e.,

$$\begin{aligned} c(x) &= \|x^T u\| \\ &= \|x^T X \Sigma^{-1} v^T\| \end{aligned} \tag{1}$$

where Σ and v satisfy

$$X^T X = v\Sigma^2 v^T.$$

Hence, the confidence level $c(x)$ can also be obtained by doing singular value decomposition on $X^T X$ and applying equation above. With this formulation, it is easy to generalize the illumination subspace method to a nonlinear extension using the kernel trick [10]. The data is now replaced with the feature vectors: $x_i \rightarrow \Phi_i = \Phi(x_i)$ induced by a kernel where $k(x_i, x_j) = \Phi(x_i)^T \Phi(x_j)$. By replacing the inner products $< x_i, x_j >$ with $k(x_i, x_j)$, $X^T X$ is replaced by K with $K_{i,j} = k(x_i, x_j)$, $x^T X$ is replaced by $\kappa(x) = [k(x, x_1), k(x, x_2), \cdots, k(x, x_9)]$ and one can perform the illumination subspace method in the kernel-induced subspace via singular value decomposition of K $(= v\Sigma^2 v^T)$. The confidence level of a query image can be computed directly as $c(x) = \kappa(x)\Sigma^{-1}v^T$. We note that the proposed method does not actually need to access either the feature vectors $\Phi(x_i)$ or the basis of the subspace spanned by these vectors. This method is called *Kernel subspace* method.

For kernel functions $k(\cdot, \cdot)$, one typically uses linear $k(x_i, x_j) = x_i^T x_j$, polynomial $(x_i^T x_j + 1)^d$ or Gaussian $k(x_i, x_j) = \exp\left(-\|x_i - x_j\|^2/\sigma^2\right)$. Recently, a new type of kernel called fractional kernel defined as

$$k(x_i, x_j) = sign(x_i^T x_j) \mid x_i^T x_j \mid^{\mu}$$

is suggested and applied successfully in face recognition [6]. In our experiments, we applied fractional kernel and the results demonstrate that it is useful to improve performance compared to the linear subspace method.

5 Experimental Results

Experiments were conducted with both the linear and kernel subspace methods on two databases: CMU PIE [11] and The Extended Yale Face Database B (YaleB) [4,5] to test the performance of the proposed algorithm. The CMU PIE face database contains 68 individuals with 41368 face images. The face images were captured by 13 synchronized cameras and 21 flashes, under varying pose, illumination and expression. The extended Yale Face Database B [5] contains 16128 images of 28 human subjects under 9 poses and 64 illumination conditions. The data format of this database is the same as the original Yale Face Database B [4]. From CMU PIE, we choose the five near frontal poses (C05,C07,C09,C27,C29) with images under different illuminations, lighting and expressions where each individual has 170 images except for a few bad images. All test image data used in the experiments are manually aligned, cropped, and then re-sized to 32x32 images.

Our first experiment is implemented on the Extended Yale Face Database B using the linear subspace approach. Since there are a few bad images for 7 persons, the order

Table 1. Performance (error rate %) on the Extended Yale Face Database B using Linear subspace method

$d \backslash c$	7	8	9	11	13	15	9([5])
5	7.36	7.09	7.80	7.61	6.77	5.46	8.86
6	6.17	3.74	4.28	6.57	5.69	4.87	7.33
7	3.06	2.88	2.70	2.98	4.49	2.96	6.45
8		2.36	2.05	1.95	3.42	2.04	6.33
9			2.11	1.70	1.71	1.12	6.10

Table 2. Performance (error rate %) on the Extended Yale Face Database B using Kernel subspace method

$d \backslash c$	7	8	9	11	13	15	9([5])
5	6.28	6.85	7.39	7.06	6.77	5.46	8.86
6	4.75	3.46	3.23	5.17	5.31	4.61	6.92
7	3.06	2.65	2.05	2.56	3.42	2.90	6.22
8		2.36	2.05	1.83	1.64	1.25	6.04
9			2.05	1.58	1.08	0.99	5.69

of lighting conditions of the images for these persons do not coincide with the images for other people, we exclude the images of these persons and use the images for 31 people. The results obtained by using the AP configuration setup proposed in this paper are compared to the results in [5].

The performance is illustrated in Table 1, where d denotes the dimension of the subspace used to formulate the recognition system and c is the number of cluster centers used for estimating the illumination subspace. The last column of Table 1 shows the performance using the earlier suggested lighting configuration ($c = 9$) in [5]. From this table, one can see that the error rate is significantly better when $d \geq 6$ compared to the performance in [5], and is better when $d = 5$. Note that we tested all the 64 images for each person while in [5] only used the 45 images of good quality.

Further, we also noted that with larger number of clusters (critical images) and larger number of dimension, better performance will be achieved. This indicates that nine harmonic images may not be the optimal choice in practice and we will investigate this issue further in the future.

The second experiment is done on the same database of Extended Yale Face Database B but we use the proposed kernel approach. It can be seen that the performance of the kernel approach is better in general.

The third experiment is done with the CMU PIE face database. Since there are a few bad images for one person, the order of lighting conditions of the images for this person do not coincide with the images for other people, we exclude the images of this person and use the images for 67 people. This database not only has different lighting but also has different poses (5 poses for each person in our experiment). In this case, the configuration setup in [5] will not be applicable and Table 3 shows the results. We note that very low errors are obtained when the number of cluster centers and the number

Table 3. Performance (error rate %) on CMU PIE face database using linear subspace method

$d \setminus c$	9	11	13	17	20
5	15.06	14.38	12.71	9.31	8.49
7	12.97	11.95	10.11	6.32	5.73
9	12.10	10.75	8.72	5.15	4.14
11		9.92	7.77	4.55	3.46
13			7.38	4.20	3.08
17				4.07	2.95
20					2.98

Table 4. Performances (error rate %) of Kernel subspace method versus Linear subspace method on the Extended Yale Face Database B with randomly selected training images

Methods $\setminus(Ntr, d)$	(10,9)	(20,9)	(20,13)	(30,9)	(30,15)
Linear	17.99	9.66	8.40	6.92	5.64
Kernel	14.58	7.85	7.04	5.64	4.96

of dimensions is increased ($c = 20, d = 20$), which indicates the robustness of the proposed method to pose variations.

In order to compare the performance of linear and kernel approaches for randomly selected training samples, we did an experiment on the Extended Yale Face Database B. A random subset with $Ntr(= 10, 20, 30)$ images per individual was taken with labels to form the training set, and the rest of the database was considered to be the testing set. For each given Ntr, we average the results over 50 random splits and we used the same splits and the same matlab data files[1] which were used in [2]. Table 4 reports the comparison of the linear and kernel subspace methods for randomly selected training samples, as obtained by examining the average performance of 50 randomly selected training samples. Here d denotes the dimension of the subspace. We used the fractional kernel and the parameter of the kernel is selected using the cross validation [8] on 5 random selected training samples. The increase in performance is observable. This shows that the kernel method is preferred in general case and thus is likely to be more applicable in real world settings where it is difficult to control the lighting conditions. Also, it shows when the dimension d is larger than 9, the performance can be improved which demonstrates that 9 dimensional subspace approximation may not be the best.

6 Conclusions

In this paper, we proposed a new approach of face recognition to deal with variational lighting and poses. First, based on affinity propagation clustering, we have proposed a new method to find the good lighting and pose configurations for face recognition under variable lighting and poses. Further, the fractional kernel approach is used to improve the current subspace approach for face recognition. Experimental results demonstrate

[1] Which were downloaded from http://ews.uiuc.edu/ dengcai2/Data/data.html

the proposed configuration setup performs better than earlier recommended configuration [5]. In addition, our method can also handle pose variations. Further the proposed kernel subspace method is more robust than the linear subspace method to the selection of training samples.

Also our approach is data-driven and is not depending on the 3D information of face model. The computational cost is usually lower, which we will investigate theoretically further in future. Since it is usually hard to control the lighting and pose variations in practice, the proposed approach is applicable broadly.

References

1. Basri, R., Lambertian, J.D.W.: reflectance and linear subsapce. IEEE Trans. Pattern Anal. Mach. Intelligence 25(2), 218–232 (2003)
2. Cai, D., He, X., Z.H., -J.: Orthogonal laplacianfaces for face recognition. IEEE Trans. Image Processing 15(11), 3608–3614 (2006)
3. Frey, B., D.D.: Clustering by passing messages between data points. Science 315, 972–976 (2007)
4. Georghiades, A., Belhumeur, P., Kriegman, D.: From few to many: Illumination cone models for face recognition undervariable lighting and pose. IEEE Trans. Pattern Anal. Mach. Intelligence 23(6), 643–660 (2005)
5. Lee, K., Ho, J., Kriegman, D.: Acquiring linear subspaces for face recognition under variable lighting. IEEE Trans. Pattern Anal. Mach. Intelligence 27(5), 684–698 (2005)
6. Liu, C.: Capitalize ondimensionality reduction increasing techniques from improving face recognition grand challenge performance. IEEE Trans. Pattern Anal. Mach. Intelligence 28(5), 725–737 (2006)
7. P., B., Kriegman, D.: What is the set of images of an object under all possible lighting conditions. Int. J. Computer Vision 28, 245–260 (1998)
8. Press, W., Teukolsky, S., Vetterling, W., Flannery, B.: Numerical recipes in C: the art of scientific computing. Cambridge University Press, Cambridge (1993)
9. R., R., Hanrahan, P.: A signalprocessing framework for inverse rendering. In: Proc. Of SIGGRAPH, pp. 117–228 (2006)
10. Saunders, C., Gammerman, A., Vovk, V.: Ridge regression learning algorithm in dual variables. In: ICML 1998. Proc. Of the 15th International Conference on Machine Learning, pp. 515–521. Madison-Wisconsin (1998)
11. Sim, T., Baker, S., Bsat, M.: The CMU pose, illumination, and expression (PIE) database. In: Proceedings of the Fifth IEEE International Conference on Automatic Face and Gesture Recognition, p. 215. IEEE Computer Society Press, Los Alamitos (2002)

Random Subspace Two-Dimensional PCA for Face Recognition

Nam Nguyen, Wanquan Liu, and Svetha Venkatesh

Department of Computing, Curtin University of Technology, WA 6845, Australia
{Thanh.Nguyen,W.Liu,S.Venkatesh}@curtin.edu.au

Abstract. The two-dimensional Principal Component Analysis (2DPCA) is a robust method in face recognition. Much recent research shows that the 2DPCA is more reliable than the well-known PCA method in recognising human face. However, in many cases, this method tends to be overfitted to sample data. In this paper, we proposed a novel method named random subspace two-dimensional PCA (RS-2DPCA), which combines the 2DPCA method with the random subspace (RS) technique. The RS-2DPCA inherits the advantages of both the 2DPCA and RS technique, thus it can avoid the overfitting problem and achieve high recognition accuracy. Experimental results in three benchmark face data sets – the ORL database, the Yale face database and the extended Yale face database B – confirm our hypothesis that the RS-2DPCA is superior to the 2DPCA itself.

1 Introduction

Face recognition is an active research area recently because of its numerous applications in authentication and surveillance systems. Given a human face image, a face recognition algorithm needs to identify the person with his information stored in the database. Otherwise, it needs to figure out that the person is new to the database. Building such algorithm is challenging because of the similarity of people faces and large variance of the face images belonging to the same person. Moreover, a person can change hair style or glasses when the face image is taken. Camera noise and poor image quality could also add trouble to the process of recognizing human face. For these reasons, a robust face recognition algorithm is still the goal of current research in face recognition.

One of the well-known methods for face recognition is the PCA (or Eigenfaces) method, which was originally proposed by Sirovich and Kirby [1,2] and then developed by Turk and Pentland [3]. The PCA converts the intensity of face image to a vector and uses the Karhunen-Loeve transform to construct an expressive subspace for face recognition. The face image vector is projected along the axes of the subspace to extract image features with lower dimension and maximize the variance among face images. Extensions of the PCA include the Nonlinear PCA [4], Independent Component Analysis (ICA) [5] and Kernel PCA [6].

H.H.S. Ip et al. (Eds.): PCM 2007, LNCS 4810, pp. 655–664, 2007.

The PCA represents image intensity as a vector, thus the size of the vector could be very large. For example, for a face image with size of 195×231 in the Yale face database, the size of the vector is $195 \times 231 = 45045$. This large size of vector creates problem to the PCA implementation when estimating the eigenvectors of the covariance matrix of the sample data. To avoid such drawback, Yang *et al.* [7] proposed the two-dimensional PCA (2DPCA), which works directly with the 2-D matrix of the image intensity. This makes the computational cost to extract the image features less expensive than PCA. Experimental results on various face data sets have showed that the 2DPCA is more reliable than the PCA in face recognition [7,8,9,10].

Both the PCA and 2DPCA rely on a single projection subspace. The subspace dimension d significantly affects the recognition accuracy of these methods. If d is small, the images could lose valuable discrimination information when projected onto the subspace. A large value of d could make the projected images overfitted to the sample data and reduce the recognition accuracy. The overfitting problem could be solved by using the random subspace (RS) technique as demonstrated in [11] for decision tree classification. The main idea of this technique is that, instead of using a single subspace for classification, multiple subspaces are constructed from the original space by a random procedure. The RS technique produces a classifier using each random subspace. Then, the final classification decision is achieved by combining all classification results. Although each classifier may not produce a good classification, their combination can be much better than using a single subspace. The RS technique has been applied successfully by Wang and Tang [12] to improve the recognition accuracy of the Fisherface [13] and Null Space Linear Discriminant Analysis (N-LDA) [14] algorithms. However, their work suffers the same drawback of the PCA, that is, inefficiency in computing eigenvectors of the covariance matrix of the sample data.

Inspired by [12], we present a novel method that combines the 2DPCA and RS technique in face recognition. This integrated method is named as the RS-2DPCA. Instead of using a single subspace that maximizes the discrimination of the projected images as 2DPCA method, the RS-2DPCA uses multiple subspaces obtained by a randomly sampling procedure. When a testing image arrives, it is projected onto the multiple random subspaces to extract the image features. These features are matched with image features of the sample images for classification. This method inherits the advantages of both the 2DPCA and RS techniques, which are efficient in computation and can avoid of overfitting. We test the RS-2DPCA on three popular data sets: the ORL database, the Yale face database and the extended Yale face database B. Experimental results on these data sets show that the RS-2DPCA outperforms the 2DPCA.

The remaining of the paper is as follows. Section 2 presents the 2DPCA algorithm. Section 3 describes the proposed algorithm – RS-2DPCA. Next, the experimental results to evaluate the performance of the RS-2DPCA are showed in Sect. 4. Section 5 gives some discussions on the RS-2DPCA and conclusions are followed in Sect. 6.

2 Two-Dimensional Principal Component Analysis (2DPCA)

Assume that the sample data consists of M training face images with size of $m \times n$. $A_1, \ldots, A_M$ are the matrices of the sample image intensity. The 2DCPA proposed by Yang *et al.* [7] is as follows:

1. Obtain the average image A of all training samples: $A = \frac{1}{M}\sum_1^M A_i$
2. Estimate the image covariance (scatter) matrix G:

$$G = \frac{1}{M}\sum_{j=1}^{M}(A_j - A)^T \times (A_j - A)$$

3. Compute d orthonormal vectors $X_1, X_2, \ldots, X_d$ corresponding to the d largest eigenvalues of G. $X_1, X_2, \ldots, X_d$ construct a $d-$dimensional projection subspace. Yang *et al.* [7] have showed that $X_1, \ldots, X_d$ are the d optimal projection axes, such that when projecting the sample images on each axis X_i, the total scatter of the projected images is maximum.
4. Project $A_1, \ldots, A_M$ on each vector $X_1, \ldots, X_d$ to obtain the principal component vectors:

$$Y_i^j = A_j X_i,\ i = 1, \ldots, d,\ j = 1, \ldots, M$$

5. When a testing image with 2D intensity matrix B arrives, compute the principal component vectors of the new image:

$$Y_i^B = BX_i,\ i = 1, \ldots, d$$

6. Compute the Euclidean distance between $(Y_1^B, \ldots, Y_d^B)$ and $(Y_1^j, \ldots, Y_d^j)$ $(j = 1, \ldots, M)$:

$$dist(B, A_j) = \sum_{i=1}^{d} ||Y_i^B - Y_i^j||_2$$

where $||Y_i^B - Y_i^j||_2$ is the Euclidean distance between Y_i^B and Y_i^j.
7. Use $dist(B, A_j)$ $(j = 1, \ldots, M)$ and a threshold θ to decide the label of the testing image.

The constructed image of a sample image A_j is defined as: $\tilde{A}_j = \sum_{i=1}^{d} Y_i^j X_i^T$. In the 2DPCA, the dimension d of the subspace has a great impact on the energy of the constructed image. According to Yang *et al.* [7], the energy of the constructed image is concentrated on first small number of component vectors corresponding to the larger eigenvalues. Thus, choosing the dimension d small is enough to obtain a high accuracy rate for the 2DPCA.

3 Random Subspace Two-Dimensional PCA (RS-2DPCA)

Based on the 2DPCA and random subspace (RS) technique, we proposed the Random Subspace Two-Dimensional PCA (RS-2DCPA) algorithm. The RS-2DPCA first computes the image covariance matrix G from sample images $A_1, \ldots, A_M$ as in 2DPCA. Then, it constructs K subspaces $\Gamma_1, \ldots, \Gamma_K$ by randomly selecting the eigenvectors of G. A classifier Ω_k is created using each random subspace Γ_k. To classify a testing image, the RS-2DPCA first labels the image by sequentially using each classifier Ω_k $(k = 1, \ldots, K)$. Then, it combines the labeled results of K classifiers using majority rule to achieve the final label of the testing image. Detail of the RS-2DPCA is as follows:

1. Obtain the average image A of the training images:$A = \frac{1}{M}\sum_1^M A_i$
2. Estimate the image covariance (scatter) matrix G:

$$G = \frac{1}{M}\sum_{j=1}^{M}(A_j - A)^T \times (A_j - A)$$

3. Obtain K random subspaces $\Gamma_1, \ldots, \Gamma_K$ as:
   (a) Select N_0 eigenvectors $X_1, \ldots, X_{N_0}$ corresponding to N_0 largest eigenvalues of G. These vectors are fixed in all random subspaces. Usually, N_0 is small.
   (b) Select N_1 eigenvectors $X^{(k)}_{N_0+1}, \ldots, X^{(k)}_{N_0+N_1}$ randomly corresponding to the remaining non-zero eigenvalues of G.
   (c) Random subspace Γ_k $(k = 1, \ldots, K)$ is constructed from $N_0 + N_1$ eigenvectors $X_1, \ldots, X_{N_0}, X^{(k)}_{N_0+1}, \ldots, X^{(k)}_{N_0+N_1}$.
4. When a testing image with 2D intensity matrix B arrives, label the testing image by using each classifier Ω_k derived from subspace Γ_k:
   (a) Compute principal component vectors of the sample images $A_1, \ldots, A_M$ by projecting them onto Γ_K:

$$Y_i^{j(k)} = A_j X_i^{(k)},\ i = 1, \ldots, N_0 + N_1, k = 1, \ldots, K$$

   (b) Compute the principal component vectors of the testing image:

$$Y_i^{B(k)} = BX_i^{(k)},\ i = 1, \ldots, N_0 + N_1, k = 1, \ldots, K$$

   (c) Obtain the distance between $(Y_1^{B(k)}, \ldots, Y_d^{B(k)})$ and $(Y_1^{j(k)}, \ldots, Y_d^{j(k)})$:

$$dist^{(k)}(B, A_j) = \sum_{i=1}^{d} ||Y_i^{B(k)} - Y_i^{j(k)}||_2$$

   (d) Use $dist^{(k)}(B, A_j)$ $(j = 1, \ldots, d)$ to label the testing image.
5. The final label of the testing image is the majority label obtained from the K classifiers.

4 Experimental Results

4.1 Experiments on the ORL Database

We use the ORL database[1] to test the performance of the RS-2DPCA algorithm in face recognition. The ORL database has 400 face images with the size of 112×92. There are 40 people in the database, each has 10 face images. The images are gray scaled and normalized before applying the RS-2DPCA algorithm. The face images of a person in the database are shown in Fig. 1(a).

We use the first five images of each person for training and the remaining images for testing. The RS-2DPCA is run with parameters $N_0 = 3$, $N_1 = 10$ and $K = 20$, where N_0 is the number of fixed eigenvectors, N_1 is the number of random eigenvectors and K is the number of random subspaces. Each random subspace has $N_0 + N_1 = 13$ dimensions. The RS-2DPCA creates K (= 20) classifiers with the random subspaces. The recognition accuracy of the 20 classifiers in a run of the RS-2DPCA is showed in Fig. 1(b). The RS-2DPCA combines all classifiers to label a test image using majority rule, that is, the most popular label obtained from the classifiers is taken as the final label of the test image. Figure 1(b) shows that the accuracy of the combination classifier (93.5%) is higher than the accuracy of most component classifiers (around 92%).

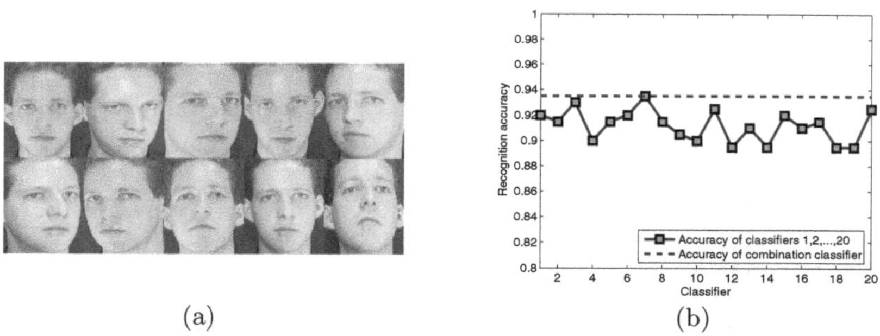

Fig. 1. (a) Face images of a person in the ORL database. (b) Comparison of the component classifiers with the combination classifier. The RS-2DPCA is run with parameters $N_0 = 3$, $N_1 = 10$, $K = 20$, and on the 5-train data set.

We compare performance of the RS-2DPCA with the 2DPCA on the ORL database. We construct five data sets from the ORL database: 1-train, ..., 5-train. The i-train data set ($i = 1, \ldots, 5$) is created by taking first i images of each person for training and the taking the remaining images for testing. We run the RS-2DPCA and the 2DPCA on the five data sets. The RS-2DPCA is run ten times on each data set with parameters $N_0 = 3$, $N_1 = 10$ and $K = 20$ to obtain the mean, variance, minimum and maximum of the recognition accuracy. Table 1 shows the performance of the RS-2DPCA on each data set.

[1] http://www.cl.cam.ac.uk/research/dtg/attarchive/facedatabase.html

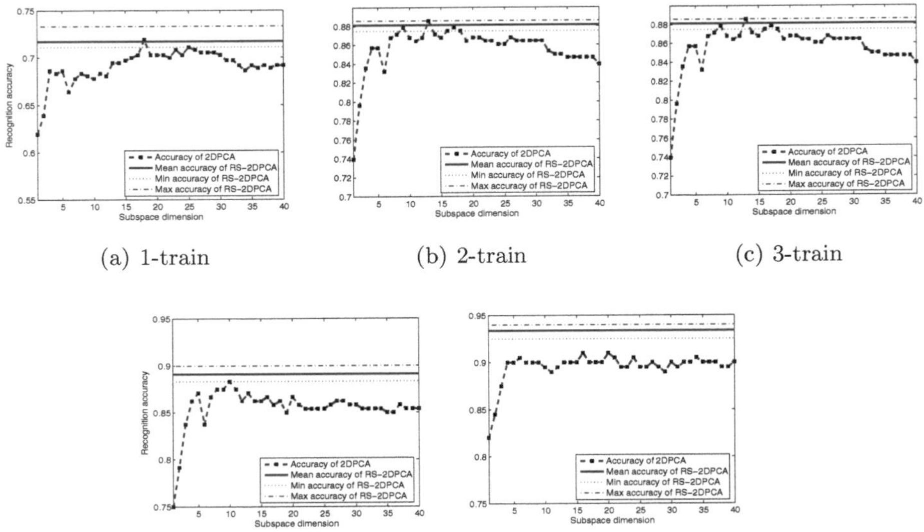

(a) 1-train (b) 2-train (c) 3-train

(d) 4-train (e) 5-train

Fig. 2. Comparison of RS-2DPCA with 2DPCA on the ORL database. The RS-2DPCA is run with parameters $N_0 = 3$, $N_1 = 10$ and $K = 20$, while 2DPCA is run with $d = 1, \ldots, 40$.

Table 1. The performance of the RS-2DPCA on the ORL database

Data set	1-train	2-train	3-train	4-train	5-train
Mean (%)	71.72	80.18	88.14	89.13	93.40
Variance	0.71	0.61	0.47	0.54	0.46
Minimum (%)	71.11	79.06	87.50	90.00	92.50
Maximum (%)	73.33	80.94	98.57	88.33	94.00

We run the 2DPCA on the five data sets with the subspace dimension d varying from 1 to 40. Figures 2(a)-(e) compare the performance of the RS-2DPCA with 2DPCA on the five data sets 1-train, 2-train, . . . , 5-train, respectively. The figures show that, most of time the mean accuracy of the RS-2DPCA is higher than the accuracy of the 2DPCA. Consider the results on the 5-train data set (Fig. 2(e)), the mean accuracy of the RS-2DPCA (93.40%) is much higher than the top accuracy of the 2DPCA (91%, when $d = 16$). Moreover, the minimum accuracy of the RS-2DPCA in ten runs (92.50%) is still higher than the top accuracy of the 2DPCA (91%). We conclude that, the RS-2DPCA outperforms 2DPCA on the ORL database.

4.2 Experiments on the Yale Database

The Yale face database[2] has 165 face images of 15 people. Each person has 11 face images with size of 231× 195. We test the performance of the RS-2DPCA with the 2DPCA on the five data sets 1-train, 2-train, ..., 5-train of the Yale face database. We run the RS-2DPCA ten times on each data set to obtain the mean and variance of the recognition accuracy. We set the parameters $K = 20$, $N_1 = 15$ and $N_0 = 2$ in the cases that the RS-2DPCA is run on the data sets 1-train, 4-train and 5 train, while $K = 20$, $N_1 = 15$ and $N_0 = 4$ in the other cases. We run the 2DPCA on the five data sets 1-train, 2-train, ..., 5-train with the subspace dimension d varying from 1 to 40. The mean recognition accuracy of the RS-2DPCA compared with the accuracy of the 2DPCA is shown in Figs. 3(a)-(e). The figures show that the RS-2DPCA outperforms the 2DPCA in all experiments on the Yale face database.

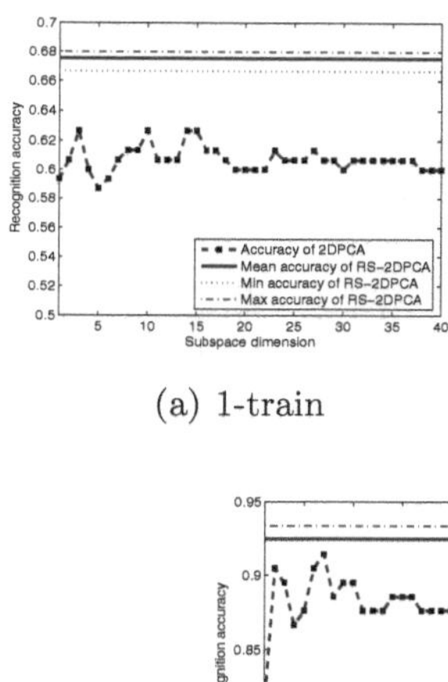

(a) 1-train

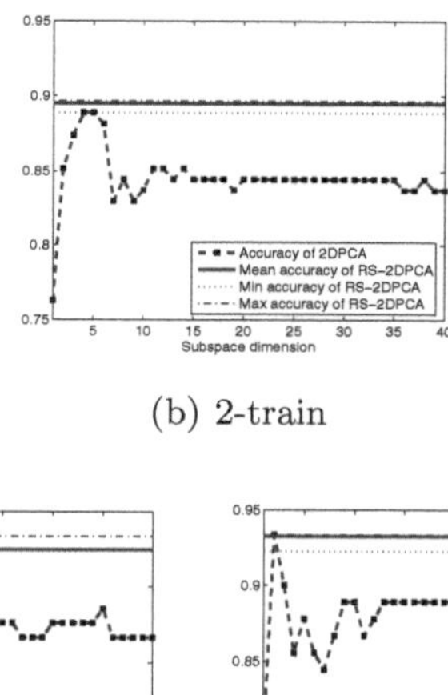

(b) 2-train

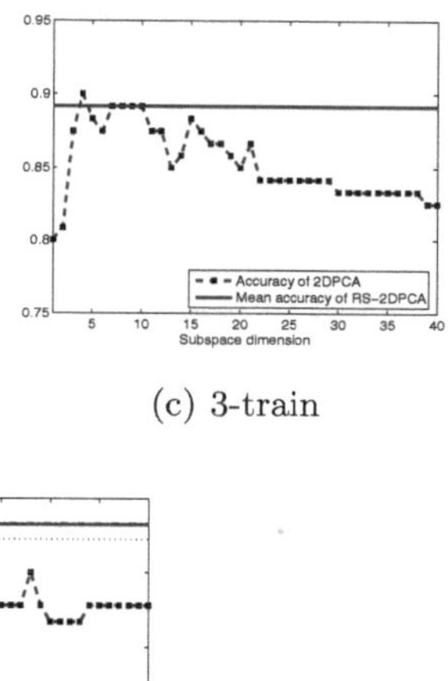

(c) 3-train

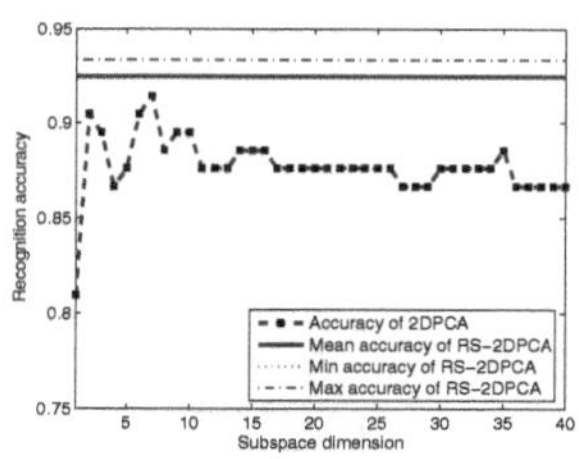

(d) 4-train

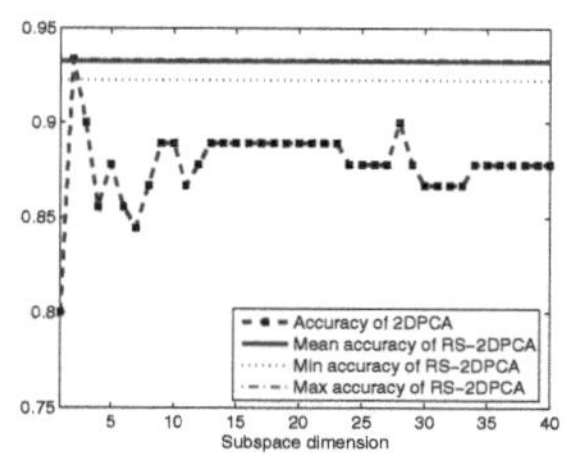

(e) 5-train

Fig. 3. Comparison of RS-2DPCA with 2DPCA on the Yale face database

4.3 Experiments on the Extended Yale Face Database B

We use the cropped images of the extended Yale face database B[3] [15,16]. The database contains face images of 38 people under 64 illumination conditions. The size of each image is 192×168. The light source direction with respect to

---

[2] http://cvc.yale.edu/projects/yalefaces/yalefaces.html

[3] http://vision.ucsd.edu/~leekc/ExtYaleDatabase/ExtYaleB.html

the camera axis varies from −130 to +130 degrees azimuth and −40 to +90 degrees elevation. We select a subset of the extended Yale face database B as follows. With each person, seven face images of which the light source is from −20 to +20 degrees azimuth and from −20 to +20 degrees elevation are randomly selected. We again create five data sets 1-train, 2-train, ...,5-train from this subset. Similar to the experiments conducted on the ORL and Yale face database, the RS-2DPCA is run ten times on each of the five data sets to obtain the mean recognition accuracy. The parameters of the RS-2DPCA are $N_0 = 1$, $N_1 = 15$ and $K = 20$. We also run the 2DPCA with the subspace dimension d varying from 1 to 60 (in the case of running on the 1-train data set) and from 1 to 40 (in the other cases). The mean recognition accuracy of the RS-2DPCA compared with the accuracy of the 2DPCA is shown in Figs. 4(a)-(e). The figures show that the RS-2DPCA is superior to the 2DPCA in all cases.

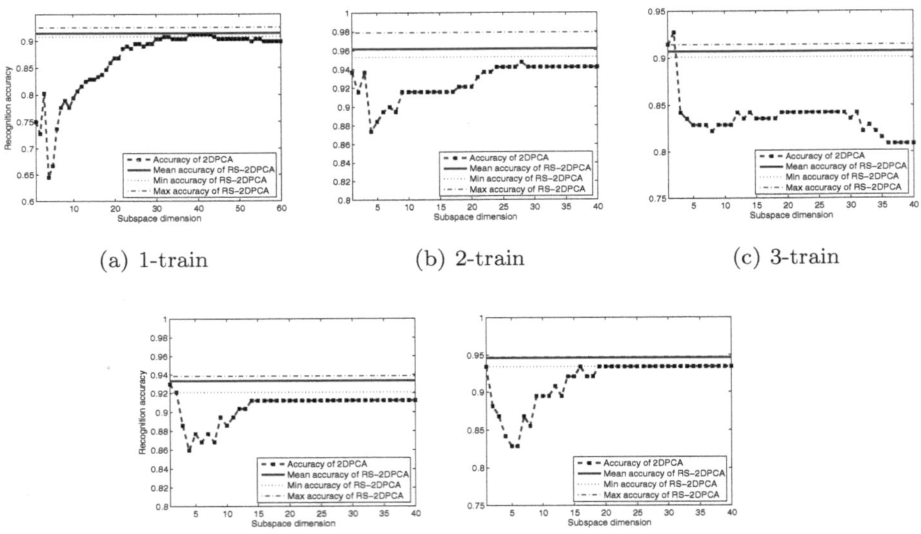

(a) 1-train (b) 2-train (c) 3-train

(d) 4-train (e) 5-train

Fig. 4. Comparison of RS-2DPCA with 2DPCA on a subset of the extended Yale face database B

5 Discussions

The number of random subspaces K affects significantly the performance of the RS-2DPCA. Figure 5(a) shows the recognition accuracy of the 2DPCA tested on the 5-train data set of the ORL database. The parameters N_0 and N_1 are fixed ($N_0 = 3$,$N_1 = 10$), but K is varied from 1 to 30. Figure 5(a) shows that, at the beginning, the recognition accuracy increases significantly when K

increases, then it stays roughly stable when K is above a certain high value. This is because when K is small, the RS-2DPCA cannot maintain well the discrimination information when projecting a face image onto the K random subspaces. But when K is large enough, most discrimination information has been retained and cannot be improved further by increasing K.

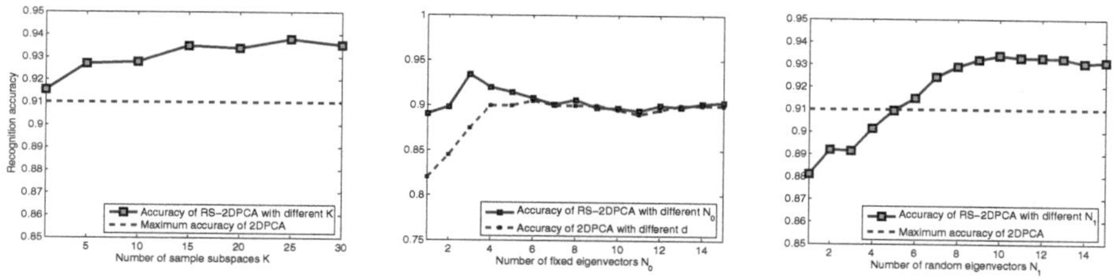

(a) (b) (c)

Fig. 5. Impact of parameters K, N_0 and N_1 on the performance of the RS-2DPCA. The RS-2DPCA is run on the 5-train data set of the ORL database and with (a) K varied from 1 to 30, $N_0 = 3$, $N_1 = 10$, (b) N_0 varied from 1 to 15, $N_1 = 10$, $K = 20$ and (c) N_1 varied from 1 to 15, $N_0 = 3$, $K = 20$.

The number of fixed eigenvectors N_0 also has great impact on the performance of the RS-2DPCA. Figure 5(b) shows the recognition accuracy of the 2DPCA running with the same values of N_1 (= 10) and K (= 20) but different values of N_0. The figure shows that when N_0 is small, the RS-2DPCA performs much better than 2DPCA with parameter $d = N_0$. However, when N_0 is large, the performance of the RS-2DPCA is the same as the 2DPCA. This is because when N_0 is high, the N_0 fixed eigenvectors make the RS-2DPCA overfit to the training data. Thus, the choice of the N_1 random eigenvectors does not affect significantly to the performance of the RS-2DPCA.

The recognition accuracy of the RS-2DPCA also depends on the choice of the number of random eigenvectors N_1. We test the RS-2DPCA running with the same value of $N_0(= 3)$ and $K(= 20)$ but with different value of N_1. The results are shown in Fig. 5(c). The maximum accuracy rate of the RS-2DPCA is achieved when $N_1 = 10$. When $N_1 > 10$, increasing N_1 does not improve the recognition accuracy of the RS-2DPCA. To obtain high accuracy rate for the RS-2DPCA, we suggest to choose small N_0, and large N_1 and K.

6 Conclusions

In this paper, we have presented a novel algorithm for face recognition – the RS-2DPCA. This is an integrated algorithm that combines the 2DPCA and random subspace (RS) method. The RS-2DPCA defines a set of classifiers by using random subspace technique. The classifiers are combined to obtain the final classification result. We have tested our algorithm in three data sets: the ORL database, Yale face database and the extended Yale face database B. The experimental results show that the RS-2DPCA is more reliable than the 2DPCA in face recognition. In the future work, alternative fusion methods for the classifiers will be investigated to improve the performance of the RS-2DPCA.

References

1. Kirby, M., Sirovich, L.: Application of the KL procedure for the characterization of human faces. IEEE Transactions on Pattern Analysis and Machine Intelligence 12(1), 103–108 (1990)
2. Sirovich, L., Kirby, M.: Low-dimensional procedure for characterization of human faces. Journal of the Optical Society of America 4, 519–524 (1987)
3. Turk, M., Pentland, A.: Eigenfaces for recognition. Cognitive Neuroscience 3(1), 71–86 (1991)
4. Kramer, M.A.: Nonlinear principle component analysis using auto-associative Neural networks. American Institution Chemical Engineering Journal 32(2) (1991)
5. Yunen, P., Lai, J.: Face representation using independent component analysis. Pattern recognition 35, 1247–1257 (2002)
6. Yang, M., Ahuja, N., Kriegman, D.: Face recognition using kernel Eigenfaces. In: Proceedings of International Conference of Image Processing, vol. 1, pp. 37–40 (2000)
7. Yang, J., Zhang, D., Frangi, A.F., Yang, J.: Two-dimensional PCA: A new approach to appearance-based face representation and recognition. IEEE Transactions on Pattern Analysis and Machine Intelligence 26(1), 131–137 (2004)
8. Kong, H., Wang, L., Teoh, E.K., Li, X., Wang, J., Venkateswarlu, R.: Generalized 2D principal component analysis for face image representation and recognition. Neural Networks 18, 585–594 (2005)
9. Visani, M., Garcia, C., Laurent, C.: Comparing robustness of two-dimensional PCA and Eigenfaces for face recognition. In: Campilho, A., Kamel, M. (eds.) ICIAR 2004. LNCS, vol. 3211, pp. 717–724. Springer, Heidelberg (2004)
10. Wang, L., Wang, X., Zhang, X., Feng, J.: The equivalence of two-dimensional PCA to line-based PCA. Pattern Recognition Letters 26(1), 57–60 (2005)
11. Ho, T.K.: The random subspace method for constructing decision forests. IEEE Transactions on Pattern Analysis and Machine Intelligence 10(8), 832–844 (1998)
12. Wang, X., Tang, X.: Random sampling for subspace face recognition. International Journal of Computer Vision 70(1), 91–104 (2006)
13. Belhumeur, P., Hespanda, J., Kiregeman, D.: Eigenfaces vs. Fisherfaces: Recognition using class specific linear projection. IEEE Transactions on Pattern Analysis and Machine Intelligence 19(7), 711–720 (1997)
14. Chen, L., Liao, H., Ko, M., Liin, J., Yu, G.: A new LDA-based face recognition system which can solve the small sample size problem. Pattern recognition 33(10), 1713–1726 (2000)
15. Georghiades, A., Belhumeur, P., Kriegman, D.: From few to many: Illumination cone models for face recognition under variable lighting and pose. IEEE Trans. Pattern Anal. Mach. Intelligence 23(6), 643–660 (2001)
16. Lee, K., Ho, J., Kriegman, D.: Acquiring linear subspaces for face recognition under variable lighting. IEEE Trans. Pattern Anal. Mach. Intelligence 27(5), 684–698 (2005)

Robust Speaking Face Identification for Video Analysis

Yi Wu[1,2], Wei Hu[2], Tao Wang[2], Yimin Zhang[2], Jian Cheng[1], and Hanqing Lu[1]

[1] National Laboratory of Pattern Recognition,
Institute of Automation, Chinese Academy of Science
{ywu, jcheng, luhq}@nlpr.ia.ac.cn
[2] Intel China Research Center, Beijing, P.R. China
{wei.hu, tao.wang, yimin.zhang}@intel.com

Abstract. We investigate the problem of automatically identifying speaking faces for video analysis using only the visual information. Intuitively, mouth should be first accurately located in each face, but this is extremely challenging due to the complicated condition in video, such as irregular lighting, changing face poses and low resolution etc. Even though we get the accurate mouth location, it's still very hard to align corresponding mouths. However, we demonstrate that high precision can be achieved by aligning mouths through face matching, which needs no accurate mouth location. The principal novelties that we introduce are: (i) proposing a framework for speaking face identification for video analysis; (ii) detecting the change of the aligned mouth through face matching; (iii) introducing a novel descriptor to describe the change of the mouth. Experimental results on videos demonstrated that the proposed approach is efficient and robust for speaking face identification.

Keywords: SIFT, watershed, speaking face identification, change detection, mouth alignment, video analysis.

1 Introduction

Speaker identification is a crucial step in many video analysis problems such as automatic annotation of characters [1], [10], [11], audio-visual speech recognition [2], user interfaces based on vision [3], [9], etc. In this paper, we address the speaking face identification problem in teleplay or movie video, only using the visual information. It is a challenging problem due to the following reasons: 1) face pose and expression change; 2) lip deformation; 3) changing illumination; 4) background clutters and 5) other factors, such as motion of the camera.

In recent years, many techniques have been proposed for speaker identification. Saenko et al. [2] use SVM to train a discriminative classifier to locate the lip and then train another strong classifier to detect the subclass of lip appearance corresponding to the presence of speech. However, they only consider frontal and upright faces under the controlled environment which is not practical in teleplay or movie video. In [3] Murphy et al. use Bayesian network model as an attractive statistical framework for cue fusion to detect speaker. The model combines four simple vision sensors: face

H.H.S. Ip et al. (Eds.): PCM 2007, LNCS 4810, pp. 665–674, 2007.

detection, skin color, skin texture, and mouth motion. Their aim is to build a human centered user interface and they assume that the face detector can only detect frontal faces. The assumption may be useful to construct a robust user interface, but again it is not true when dealing with teleplay or movie video.

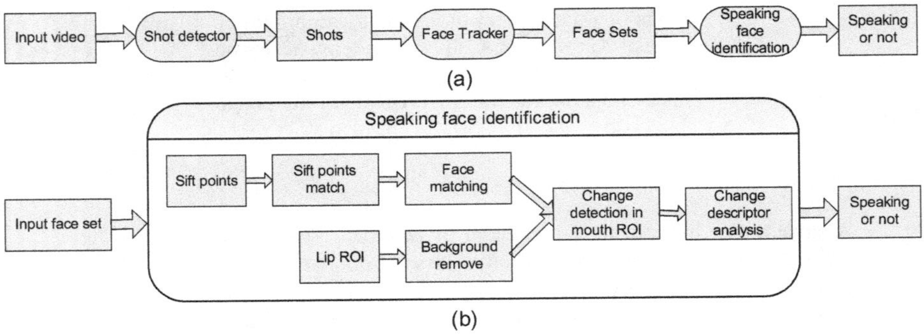

Fig. 1. (a) The flowchart of the proposed speaking face identification system; (b) The flowchart of the speaking face identification module

Everingham et al. [1] use speaking face identification as one module of automatic naming of characters in TV video. They achieved this by finding face detections with significant lip motion. A rectangular mouth region within each face is identified using the located mouth corners, and a mean squared difference of the pixel values in consecutive mouth regions is computed to determine if the shape of the mouth is changing or not. To achieve translation invariance the difference is computed over a search region around the mouth in the current frame and the minimum is taken. Two thresholds on the difference are set to classify face into 'speaking', 'non-speaking' or 'refuse to predict'. There are many constraints in their approach. First, they detect and track frontal upright faces which only occupy about 40% of the total faces in telefilm videos. The statistical number is got in our experiments by using multi-view face detector. Second, the detected mouth corners are used to locate the mouth and align the mouths, but to locate mouth corners precisely and stably is still a difficult problem, especially in profile face and moving mouth. Finally, they only consider translate transformation between two consecutive mouths. In this paper, we will try to resolve these problems and construct a robust speaking face identification system.

Despite many works have been proposed for speaker detection, most of the existing methods limit their use in indoor situations with controllable lighting condition, and their experiments are based on full frontal upright faces in good quality images. Few of them mentioned possible solutions to robust multi-view speaking face identification in real media such as teleplay or movie.

To address the problems mentioned above, we propose a framework for speaking face identification in this paper. The proposed framework is illuminated in Fig. 1. Video is first segmented into shots [4]. Then face sets in each shot are got by multi-view face detector and tracker [5]. Finally each face is labeled to be speaking or not roughly as following steps. First, the mouth Region-of-Interest (ROI) is located using the information got from the face detection and tracking module. The watershed segmentation [8] is then applied to remove non-face background pixels. Second, SIFT feature points are extracted in current face image and previous one, then these two sets of SIFT points are matched. Third, we use the matched SIFT points to calculate the transformation model to wrap the current face to the previous face image plane. The change in the aligned mouth ROI can be used to judge if the face is speaking. Here, we use a novel descriptor, which we call *Normalized Sum of Absolute Difference* (NSAD), to describe the change in the mouth ROI. Thus we get a vector of NSAD for each face set and use it to label if the face is speaking. Finally, we post-process the label vector and get the final smooth identification result. Experimental results on videos demonstrate that the proposed approach is efficient and robust for speaking face identification.

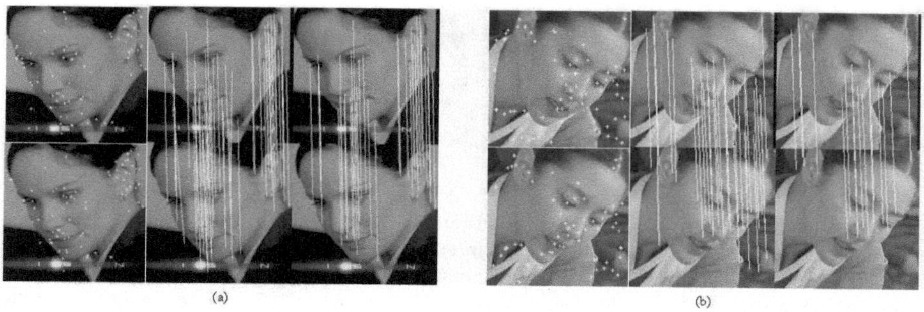

Fig. 2. Left column of each entry: the result of SIFT feature points detection; Middle: feature matching result before RANSAC; Right: matching result after RANSAC

The paper is organized as follows. Section 2 describes our approach for speaking face identification for video analysis. The experimental results are demonstrated in Section 3, followed by the conclusions in Section 4.

2 Speaking Face Identification

The speaking face identification is performed in two steps. The first step aligns the consecutive mouths through face matching. At the same time, the mouth ROI is extracted and background pixels in the ROI are removed. In the second stage the speaking face identification is achieved by capturing the change of the mouth using a novel descriptor.

2.1 Mouth Alignment

We observed the fact: it is much easier to match two consecutive whole faces robustly than to match two mouths directly, because face is more informative than mouth, and with less deformation. It is true especially when the resolution is low or the face size is small. Through matching two faces, the corresponding mouth alignment can be achieved naturally: when the two consecutive faces are well matched, the mouth on each face is also well aligned. Moreover, the translation limitation will be eliminated by using a four parameter affine transformation model when matching the faces.

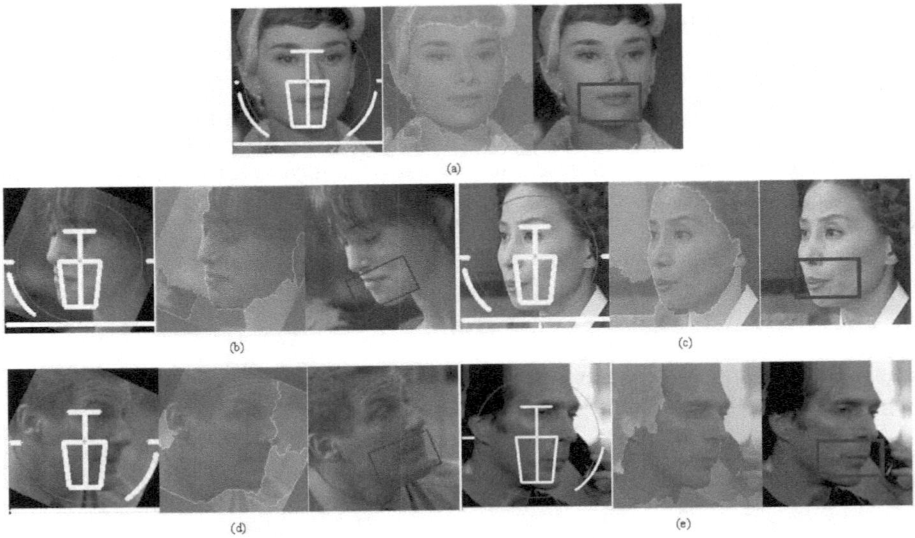

Fig. 3. Mouth ROI extraction and background remove. Left image of each example: the green point is the center of the face and the red circle reflects the face scale. The white lines are connected components for watershed segmentation. Middle image of each example: the segmentation result of the watershed algorithm. Right image of each example: the blue rectangle is the mouth ROI.

2.1.1 SIFT Feature Points Detection

For each face set, the current face image and its previous one are fed to the feature detector. The feature detector should be able to work reliably in demanding natural environments. It should be robust against illumination variations, imaging noise, image rotation and scaling. We tested different approaches presented in the literature [12], [13], and found that the SIFT feature [7] performs best. See [7] for details of SIFT points detection.

Left columns of Fig. 2(a) and (b) illustrate detected SIFT points using the SIFT detector. After the feature points have been detected, they are forwarded to the feature matching stage.

2.1.2 SIFT Feature Points Matching

For the two sets of feature points got in the consecutive faces, respectively, we seek for two closest by using the Euclidean distance as the similarity measure. If the two distances are too close to each other, the matching cannot be done reliably and the feature is discarded. Otherwise, the closest match is included to the match set. This procedure effectively removes the duplicate matches. In our experiments, we ignore the feature if the ratio of the two closest distances is bigger than 0.6. The feature matching stage outputs a set of feature matches between the current face image and the previous one. See Fig. 2 for examples of SIFT points matching.

2.1.3 Estimation of Geometric Transformation

After the feature matching stage, we have a set of feature correspondences between the current face image and the previous one. Most of the duplicate features are removed during the matching process, but there is still a possibility that some outliers, such as mismatched feature points, are included in the set. In order to achieve a reliable estimate for the transformation model, these outliers need to be removed. We adopt a well known and robust algorithm, the RANdom SAmple Consensus (RANSAC) [6]. The matching result after RANSAC is shown in Fig. 2.

In this work, a four parameter affine model is used. It is considered as sufficient for approximating transformation between consecutive faces as it can represent 2-D transformation consisting of translation, rotation, and scaling:

$$\begin{pmatrix} x' \\ y' \\ 1 \end{pmatrix} = \begin{pmatrix} s\cos\theta & -s\sin\theta & x_0 \\ s\sin\theta & s\cos\theta & y_0 \\ 0 & 0 & 1 \end{pmatrix} \begin{pmatrix} x \\ y \\ 1 \end{pmatrix}$$

where (x, y) is a coordinate in the current face image and (x', y') is its correspondence in the previous image. x_0, y_0 are related to common translational motion and s, θ are 2-D scale and rotation respectively.

The transformation model can now be used to transform the current face image to the previous face image plane. After that, the mouth would be aligned.

2.2 Mouth ROI Extraction

To detect the change of the mouth on consecutive images, we need to locate the mouth on each face first. However, accurate mouth location directly is a challenging task, especially in teleplay or movie video, because the environment is so complicated that there is no uniform color space to describe the lip/mouth, and the difference between lip and face may be very small in color or intensity. Fortunately, we can make use the face information acquired from the face detector and tracker to help to locate the mouth. Although the mouth location is somewhat coarse, it works very well for our purpose of speaking face identification.

The multi-view face detector and tracker [5] we used can provide the following information for each face: the center location of the face, the scale, in-plane rotation angle and out-of-plane rotation angle. From observation, some simple heuristic rules can be outlined and used to locate the mouth ROI. Example of location result is shown in Fig. 3 (the blue box).

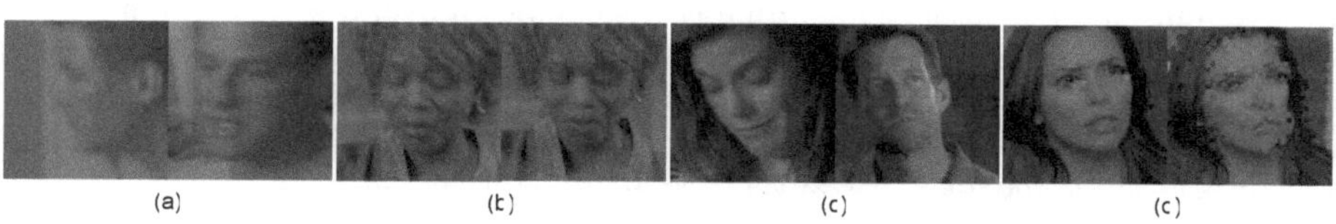

Fig. 4. Example images that can not be aligned well. (a) (b) motion blur; (c) shot detection error; (d) the poor quality of the video.

Let (x_{lf}, y_{lf}) denote the left top point of the mouth ROI and w, h denote the width and the height of the ROI respectively. The center and the radius (scale) of the face are denoted by (x_c, y_c) and r, respectively. We employ a simple empirical formulas to locate the mouth ROI as follow:

$$w = r, h = 0.6 \times r, y_{lf} = y_c + 0.2 \times h$$

$$x_{lf} = \begin{cases} x_c - 0.67 \times w & left-profile \\ x_c - 0.5 \times w & frontal \\ x_c - 0.33 \times w & right-profile \end{cases}$$

x_{lf} is changed according to the different face poses (out-of-plane rotation). If the face has in-plane rotation the mouth ROI should rotated according to the degree, as illustrated in the left of Fig. 3(b), (d).

2.3 Background Remove

The mouth ROI acquired in above step may contain some non-face region such as background clutters, especially for profile face. This will greatly influence the result of the change detection in the mouth ROI. Thus, these non-face regions should be removed before the mouth change detection. However, face segmentation is a challenging problem, especially in teleplay or movie video, due to the complicated illumination and background clutters. In this paper, face is segmented by watershed algorithm [8] which can easily make use the prior knowledge, e.g. the face information got from the face detector and tracker.

Connected component region selection is the most critical stage of the watershed method. Based on the information from the face detector and tracker, an empirical connected component mask is designed to separate the face pixels from the clutter backgrounds, for each of the three face poses respectively, as illustrated in Fig. 3. Although this kind of segmentation is somewhat coarse, it works well. After the segmentation, most non-face background pixels near the mouth are removed.

2.4 Mouth Change Description

After consecutive mouths are aligned and non-face background has been removed, we now describe the change in the mouth ROI. This change is a strong cue for speaking face identification. In [1], mean squared difference of the pixel values in the mouth region is computed between the current and previous frame to describe the change. To achieve translation invariance the difference is computed over a search region around the mouth region in the current frame and the minimum is taken. There are two main limitations of this approach: 1) the descriptor is not normalized according to the illumination and the scale of the face or the mouth; 2) it only considers translation transformation of the face. However, the motion of the face is not that simple, especially in teleplay or movie video. We have solved the second problem by the geometric transformation which can represent 2-D transformation consisting of translation, rotation, and scaling. Here, we will describe our proposed change descriptor which is illumination and scale normalized.

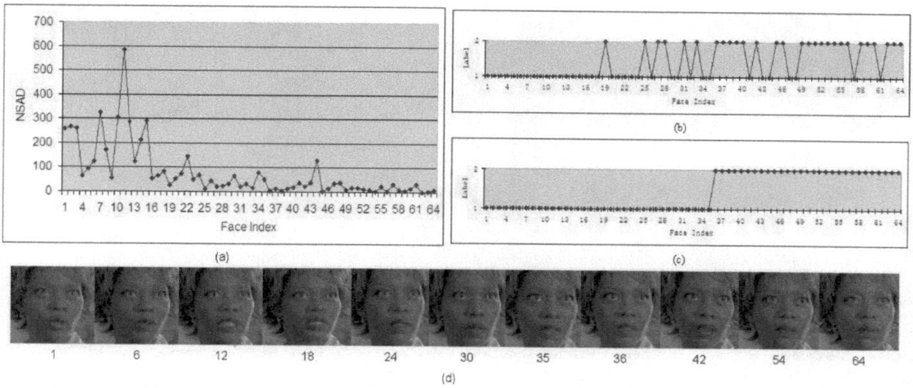

Fig. 5. (a) Illustration of the vector of change descriptor; (b) Illustration of speaking face labeling; (c) Label smoothing; (d) sample images from the face set. The character is speaking between frames 1-35 and remains silent for the rest of the track.

Denote the intensity in the previous face image and the current face image by I_p and I_c respectively. We can get the ordinary *Sum of Absolute Difference* (SAD) in the mouth ROI as follows:

$$d_{SAD} = \sum_{ROI} \left| I_p - I_c \right|$$

Then the average and standard deviation for the previous face region (μ_p, σ_p) and (μ_c, σ_c) for the current face region are calculated. The *Illumination Normalized SAD* (INSAD) and *Scale Normalized SAD* (SNSAD) are calculated as follows:

$$d_{INSAD} = \sum_{ROI} \left| \frac{I_p - \mu_p}{\sigma_p} - \frac{I_c - \mu_c}{\sigma_c} \right|$$

$$d_{NSAD} = d_{SNSAD} = d_{INSAD} \times s_0 / s$$

$$s = w \times h$$

We normalize the INSAD from scale s to scale s_0 and let the *Normalized SAD* (NSAD) $d_{NSAD} = d_{SNSAD}$. w, h stand for the width and the height of the previous face image respectively. In our experiments, we let $s_0 = 160 \times 160$.

In real-world environment, there are cases that the number of matched SIFT points in the consecutive faces is small, thus there is no reliable alignment between these two images. This always occurs when there are motion blur or shot detection error, as shown in Fig. 4. In these cases, we let the NSAD equal to 2000 and refuse to judge if the face is speaking.

After normalization, we can label each face if it is speaking according to the NSAD value, regardless of the illumination or the scale changes.

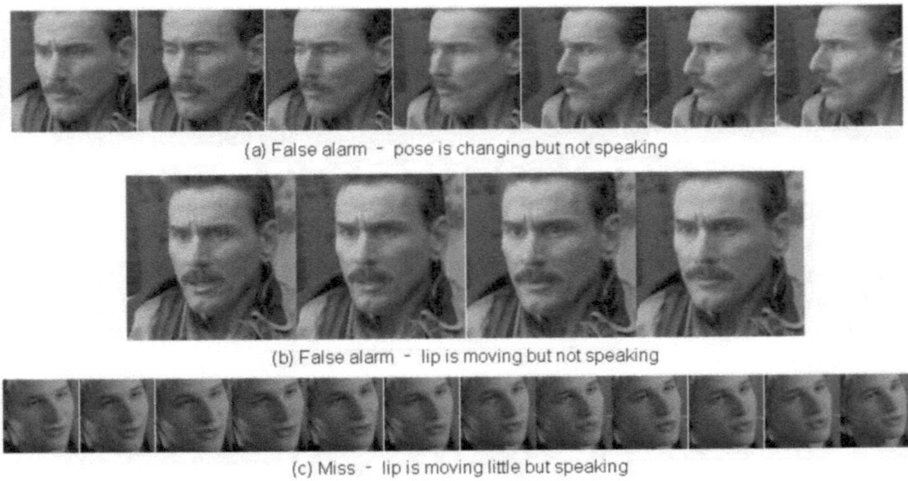

Fig. 6. The example face images of false alarm and misses

2.5 Speaking Face Labeling

In a face set, we calculate a NSAD value for each pair of consecutive face images, and then we get a vector of change descriptor, as illustrated in Fig. 5(a). When the NSAD is small, which means there is a reliable alignment between two face images, and at the same time the mouth is not moving, we can label it as 'non-speaking'. If the NSAD is relatively large, we label it as 'speaking'. If the NSAD is too large, we label it as 'refuse to predict'. In most cases, the too large NSAD values come from the wrong alignment of faces or out-of-plane rotation of the face. Following is the labeling criterion.

$$L = \begin{cases} 1 & t_1 \le d_{NSAD} \le t_2 \\ 2 & d_{NSAD} < t_1 \\ 3 & d_{NSAD} > t_2 \end{cases}$$

1: speaking; 2: non-speaking; 3: refuse to predict.

In all of our experiments, $t_1 = 30, t_2 = 700$. Fig. 5(b) shows the labeling result.

In the label vector of each face set, some label value may be different from its neighbors. This does not make sense in practice. To solve this problem, we can smooth the NSAD vector before labeling. Here we smooth the label vector instead, since it is semantic and meaningful. We use a median filter with the window size setting to five. The result is illustrated in Fig. 5(c).

3 Experimental Results

Experiments are carried out on five videos, including *episode 22 of Prison Break season 2, episode 21 of Desperate Housewives season 2, episode 31 of Dae Jang Geum, 25-minute clip of Roman Holiday* and *one hour clip of Pride and Prejudice.*

(In the following we use *PB, DH, Dae, Roman* and *Pride* for short respectively) We do not care those face sets that are not long enough (less than 40 frames), or contain very small faces, e.g., the scale (radius) of the face is less than 35 pixels. About ninety percent of the ignored face sets are non-speaking. Details of the data are shown in Table 1.

In order to quantitatively evaluate the proposed method we randomly select twenty face sets of each video to label each face if it is speaking, totally 13,527 faces, and 6,348 faces among them are labeled as speaking. Table 2 shows the precision/recall result. The term 'precision' and 'recall' are defined as follows:

$$precision = \frac{\#correctly\ identified\ speaking\ face}{\#identified\ speaking\ face}$$

$$recall = \frac{\#correctly\ identified\ speaking\ face}{\#total\ ground\ truth\ speaking\ face}$$

Note that the criterion is stricter than that used in [1]. We evaluated the result in 'frame' level while their evaluation is in 'track' level.

In our experiments, false alarm usually happens when the character's head is out-of-plane moving or the lip is moving but the character is not speaking. Miss detection of the speaking face always happens when the character is speaking but the lip doesn't move or move slightly. These incorrect cases are hardly eliminated through only the visual information, even if we can get the accurate contour of the lip. Some false identification examples are shown in Fig. 6.

When we fuse visual information with audio cues, the false alarm and miss would mostly be eliminated. This is our on-going work and will be reported elsewhere.

Table 1. The information of each video

	Frames	Resolution	Face Sets	Faces	Filtered sets	Filtered faces
PB	62127	608*336	953	34415	243	17113
DH	60856	608*336	908	53167	285	25669
Dae	67023	352*288	822	67444	346	38980
Roman	37372	528*384	507	58960	107	17440
Pride	104458	640*272	959	85069	320	37697

Table 2. The precision/recall result of each video

	PB	DH	Dae	Roman	Pride
precision	81.2%	89.1%	91.5%	85.2%	86.8%
recall	88.3%	81.9%	86.7%	83.4%	85.1%

4 Conclusion

Automatically identifying speaking faces for video analysis based solely on visual input is a challenging problem. In this paper, the speaking face identification is formulated as a change detection problem. We align the mouths through face matching and propose a novel change descriptor which is illumination and scale normalized. It can describe the change of the mouth effectively and we can get accurate speaking face identification through the analysis of the NSAD. The proposed method is tested on five videos and the experimental results demonstrate that the approach is reliable and robust.

Acknowledgements

This work is partially supported by the National Hi-Tech Research and Development Program of China (863 Program, Grant No. 2006AA01Z315), and the National Natural Science Foundation of China (Grant No. 60121302).

References

1. Everingham, M., Sivic, J., Zisserman, A.: Hello! My name is.. Buffy - Automatic Naming of Characters in TV Video. In: Proc. of the BMVC, pp. 889–908 (2006)
2. Saenko, K., Livescu, K., Siracusa, M., Wilson, K., Glass, J., Darrell, T.: Visual Speech Recognition with Loosely Synchronized Feature Streams. In: Proc. of the ICCV (2005)
3. Rehg, J.M., Murphy, K.P., Fieguth, P.W.: Vision-Based Speaker Detection Using Bayesian Networks. In: Proc. of the CVPR (1999)
4. Yuan, J., Zhang, W., et al.: Shot boundary detection and high-level feature extraction. In: TRECVID Workshops (2004)
5. Li, Y., Ai, H.Z., Huang, C., Lao, S.H.: Robust Head Tracking with Particles Based on Multiple Cues Fusion. In: HCI/ECCV, pp. 29–39 (2006)
6. Fischler, M.A., Bolles, R.C.: Random sample consensus: a paradigm for model fitting with applications to image analysis and automated cartography. Commun. ACM 24(6), 381–395 (1981)
7. Lowe, D.G.: Distinctive Image Features from Scale-Invariant Keypoints. International Journal of Computer Vision (2004)
8. Meyer, F.: Color image segmentation. In: Proc. of the ICIP, pp. 303–306 (1992)
9. Waters, K., Rehg, J.M., Loughlin, M., Kang, S.B., Terzopoulos, D.: Visual sensing of humans for active public interfaces. In: Computer Vision for Human-Machine Interaction, pp. 83–96 (1998)
10. Arandjelovic, O., Zisserman, A.: Automatic face recognition for film character retrieval in feature-length films. In: Proc. of the CVPR, pp. 860–867 (2005)
11. Everingham, M., Zisserman, A.: Identifying individuals in video by combining generative and discriminative head models. In: Proc. of the ICCV, pp. 1103–1110 (2005)
12. Shi, J., Tomasi, C.: Good features to track. In: Proc. of the CVPR, pp. 593–600 (1994)
13. Harris, C., Stephens, M.: A combined corner and edge detector. In: 4th Alvey Vision Conference, pp. 147–151 (1988)

Incremental AAM Using Synthesized Illumination Images

Hyung-Soo Lee, Jaewon Sung, and Daijin Kim

Department of Computer Science and Engineering
Pohang University of Science and Technology
{sooz, jwsung, dkim}@postech.ac.kr

Abstract. Active Appearance Model is a well-known model that can represent a non-rigid object effectively. However, since it uses the fixed appearance model, the fitting results are often unsatisfactory when the imaging condition of the target image is different from that of training images. To alleviate this problem, incremental AAM was proposed which updates its appearance bases in an on-line manner. However, it can not deal with the sudden changes of illumination. To overcome this, we propose a novel scheme to update the appearance bases. When a new person appears in the input image, we synthesize illuminated images of that person and update the appearance bases of AAM using it. Since we update the appearance bases using synthesized illuminated images in advance, the AAM can fit their model to a target image well when the illumination changes drastically. The experimental results show that our proposed algorithm improves the fitting performance over both the incremental AAM and the original AAM.

1 Introduction

Active Appearance Model (AAM) is a generative model that allows both the shape and appearance variations[1]. These variations are represented by linear models such as Principal Component Analysis (PCA), which finds a subspace reserving maximum variance of given data. The AAM has been widely used and has many application areas such as face modelling, medical image modelling and so on.

However, since the AAM uses the fixed appearance model, the fitting results are often unsatisfactory especially when the illumination condition of the target image is far different from that of training images which are used to learn the appearance model. This problem can be solved by collecting a large number of training images that contain every possible illumination conditions, but collecting such training images is impossible. To alleviate this problem, Lee et al.[2] proposed to use adaptive linear appearance model that update its appearance bases using the incremental PCA. However the update of appearance bases using ill-fitted images can worse their fitting performance of the AAM than that of original AAM. Hence they used modified adaptive observation model (AOM)[3] as a measure to determine whether to update the appearance bases or not when

H.H.S. Ip et al. (Eds.): PCM 2007, LNCS 4810, pp. 675–684, 2007.

a new fitting result is given. By this scheme, they first fit the AAM to the input image, then determine the goodness of the fitting result by computing the percentage of outlier pixels. If the fitting result is good, the AOM parameters are updated and the new appearance bases of the AAM are computed using the incremental PCA. Then, the updated AOM and AAM are used for the next frame image. This algorithm works well under the gradual change of illumination. However, when the illumination condition changes drastically, the AOM judges the entire warped pixel as outlier pixels. In a consequence, neither the AOM nor the AAM is updated and the fitting performance is not improved.

To overcome the drawback of the incremental AAM, we propose a novel scheme to update the appearance bases. The drawback of the incremental AAM is the AOM cannot adapt to the rapid change of illumination, as a result, no update of appearance bases is take place. Therefore, we do not use AOM. Instead, when a new person appears in the input image, we synthesize illuminated face images of that person and update the appearance bases using it. By doing this, the appearance bases can fit to the input image accurately. In addition, even when the illumination condition changes drastically, the AAM fit to the input image well by the virtue of the appearance bases which are updated using the synthesized illuminated face images. The advantage of the proposed algorithm over the incremental AAM is that since we update the appearance bases only once when a new person appears, we do not need to determine the goodness of the fitting result during the image sequences. The experimental results show that our proposed algorithm improves the fitting performance over both the incremental AAM and original AAM.

2 Theoretical Backgrounds

2.1 Active Appearance Models

In 2D AAM[1], the 2D shape is represented by a triangulated 2D mesh with l vertices, which correspond to the salient points of the object. Mathematically, the shape vector $\boldsymbol{s}$ consists of the 2D coordinate of the vertices that make up the mesh as $\boldsymbol{s} = (x_1, y_1, \ldots, x_l, y_l)^t$ and shape variation is expressed by a linear combination of a mean shape $\boldsymbol{s_0}$ and n shape bases $\boldsymbol{s_i}$ as

$$\boldsymbol{s} = \boldsymbol{s}_0 + \sum_{i=1}^{n} p_i \boldsymbol{s}_i, \tag{1}$$

where p_i are the shape parameters. A standard approach to compute the linear shape model is to apply the principal component analysis (PCA) to a set of shape vectors that are gathered from the manually landmarked training images and aligned using Procrustes analysis, where the ith shape basis $\boldsymbol{s}_i$ is the ith eigenvector that corresponds to the ith largest eigenvalue.

Once a mean shape $\boldsymbol{s}_0$ is obtained, the training images are warped to the mean shape using the piece-wise affine warp that is defined between the corresponding triangles in the landmarked shape of the training images and the mean shape. Then, we can define the appearance as a shape normalized image $A(\boldsymbol{x})$ over the pixels $\boldsymbol{x}$ that belong to the inside of the $\boldsymbol{s}_0$. The appearance variation is expressed by a linear combination of a mean appearance $A_0(\boldsymbol{x})$ and m appearance bases $A_i(\boldsymbol{x})$ as

$$A(\boldsymbol{x}) = A_0(\boldsymbol{x}) + \sum_{i=1}^{m} \alpha_i A_i(\boldsymbol{x}), \tag{2}$$

where α_i are the appearance parameters. As with the shape model, the appearance model is computed from the manually landmarked training images by collecting the shape normalized images and applying PCA to them, where the ith appearance basis image $A_i(\boldsymbol{x})$ is the ith eigenvector that corresponds to the ith largest eigenvalue.

2.2 Incremental Principal Component Analysis

To incrementally update the appearance bases such that the updated linear appearance model can represent a new appearance data, the traditional PCA requires to keep all the training images, which is very inefficient. Instead we use incremental subspace learning algorithm[4] that is more efficient than traditional PCA.

Suppose that a set of d-dimensional data vectors is $D = \{\boldsymbol{d}_1, \ldots, \boldsymbol{d}_N\}$. The eigenspace of the data set can be obtained by solving the singular value decomposition (SVD) of the covariance matrix $\mathbf{C}$. Then, the given data set can be represented by $k(< d)$-dimensional coefficient vectors $\boldsymbol{a}_i$ by projecting the data vector $\boldsymbol{d}_i$ to a subspace spanned by k eigenvectors corresponding to k largest eigenvalues. For the ease of the explanation, we will use a matrix $\mathbf{U} = [\boldsymbol{u}_1 \cdots \boldsymbol{u}_k] \in \mathbb{R}^{d \times k}$ that contains the k eigenvectors and a diagonal matrix $\mathbf{\Lambda} \in \mathbb{R}^{k \times k}$ that contains k large eigenvalues as the diagonal elements in the descending order.

When a new data vector $\boldsymbol{d}_{N+1}$ is given, the incremental PCA updates the mean and the basis vector as follows. Since the total amount of the data is changed, we should update the mean and the basis vector to represent the data including a new data. The mean is updated as $\bar{\boldsymbol{d}}' = \frac{1}{N+1}(N\bar{\boldsymbol{d}} + \boldsymbol{d}_{N+1})$. Then, the orthogonal residual vector $\boldsymbol{b}_{N+1}$ is computed as $\boldsymbol{b}_{N+1} = (\mathbf{U}\boldsymbol{a}_{N+1} + \bar{\boldsymbol{d}}) - \boldsymbol{d}_{N+1}$. Let a normalized vector be

$$\hat{\boldsymbol{b}}_{N+1} = \frac{\boldsymbol{b}_{N+1}}{\|\boldsymbol{b}_{N+1}\|_2}. \tag{3}$$

We acquire the new basis set $\mathbf{U}'$ by rotating the basis set $[\mathbf{U} \quad \hat{\boldsymbol{b}}_{N+1}]$ so that the i-th basis of the new basis represents the i-th largest maximal variance as the $\mathbf{U}' = [\mathbf{U} \quad \hat{\boldsymbol{b}}_{N+1}]\, \mathbf{R}$. The rotation matrix can be obtained by solving SVD for $\mathbf{D}$ matrix:

$$\mathbf{D}\,\mathbf{R} = \mathbf{R}\,\mathbf{\Lambda}', \tag{4}$$

when we compose $\mathbf{D} \in \mathbb{R}^{(k+1)\mathrm{x}(k+1)}$ as

$$\mathbf{D} = \frac{N}{N+1}\begin{bmatrix} \mathbf{\Lambda} & \mathbf{0} \\ \mathbf{0}^T & 0 \end{bmatrix} + \frac{N}{(N+1)^2}\begin{bmatrix} \boldsymbol{a}\boldsymbol{a}^T & \boldsymbol{\beta}\boldsymbol{a} \\ \boldsymbol{\beta}\boldsymbol{a}^T & \boldsymbol{\beta}^2 \end{bmatrix}, \tag{5}$$

where $\boldsymbol{\beta} = \hat{\boldsymbol{b}}_{N+1}^T(\boldsymbol{d}_{N+1} - \bar{\boldsymbol{d}})$ and $\boldsymbol{a} = \mathbf{U}^T(\boldsymbol{d}_{N+1} - \bar{\boldsymbol{d}})$.

2.3 Bilinear Model

The bilinear model is categorized into two types: symmetric model and asymmetric model. In symmetric model, the bilinear model interacts with the style and content using an interaction matrix that makes them independent. We used the symmetric model for the synthesis of illuminated face images.

A symmetric bilinear model represents the observation vector $\mathbf{y}$ as

$$\mathbf{y} = \sum_{i=1}^{I} \sum_{j=1}^{J} \mathbf{w}_{ij} a_i b_j, \tag{6}$$

where $\mathbf{w}$ is a basis vector which interacts with style factor a and content vector b and the size of the two vectors is K. To use the symmetric bilinear model, we need to learn the interaction basis vector $\mathbf{w}$. Assume that we have $S \times C$ training samples and we build the observation matrix $\mathbf{Y}$ by stacking them:

$$\mathbf{Y} = \begin{pmatrix} \mathbf{y}_{11} & \cdots & \mathbf{y}_{1C} \\ \vdots & \ddots & \vdots \\ \mathbf{y}_{S1} & \cdots & \mathbf{y}_{SC} \end{pmatrix}, \quad \mathbf{Y}^{VT} = \begin{pmatrix} \mathbf{y}_{11} & \cdots & \mathbf{y}_{1S} \\ \vdots & \ddots & \vdots \\ \mathbf{y}_{C1} & \cdots & \mathbf{y}_{CS} \end{pmatrix}, \tag{7}$$

where the superscript VT means vector transpose and each element $\mathbf{y}_{ij}$ is a K-dimensional observation vector. The observation matrix $\mathbf{Y}$ has a size of SK $\times$ C. Then, the symmetric bilinear model can be represented in a compact form as

$$\mathbf{Y} = \left(\mathbf{W}^{VT}\mathbf{A}\right)^{VT} \mathbf{B} \quad or \quad \mathbf{Y}^{VT} = (\mathbf{W}\mathbf{B})^{VT} \mathbf{A}, \tag{8}$$

where $\mathbf{A}$ and $\mathbf{B}$ represent the stacked style and content factor matrices whose size are $I \times S$ and $J \times C$, respectively:

$$\mathbf{A} = (\mathbf{a}_1, \cdots, \mathbf{a}_S), \quad \mathbf{B} = (\mathbf{b}_1, \cdots, \mathbf{b}_C) \tag{9}$$

and $\mathbf{W}$ is the stacked interaction matrix.

Usually, the optimal style and content matrices $\mathbf{A}$ and $\mathbf{B}$ are estimated by an iterative computation using singular value decomposition(SVD), because it tends to get the global and non-localized features. The detailed algorithm is given in [5].

3 Illumination Image Synthesis and Its Application to Incremental AAM

3.1 Illumination Image Synthesis

Many researches have been tried to synthesize new illuminated image from input image which is captured under arbitrary illumination condition. Sim and Kanade[6] proposed a model and example based method to synthesize a new illuminated image. Belhumeur and Kriegman[7] introduced the illumination convex cone. They argued that the images under all possible illumination conditions built a convex cone in the image space and the reconstructed shape and albedo of the face from a small number of samples served as a generative model for synthesizing images of the face under novel poses and illumination conditions. However this algorithm requires at least three images of the same face taken under different lighting conditions. Shashua[8] introduced the quotient image that uses class-based re-rendering and recognition with varying illuminations. They defined an illumination invariant signature image that enables an analytic generation of images with varying illuminations. However, their approach might fail in obtaining the illumination invariant feature when the input image has a shadow.

We propose a novel illumination image synthesis method which adopts ratio image concept into bilinear model framework. First, we assume that the face has the Lambertian surface: a face image can be represented by the product of the albedo, the surface normal, and a light source. Then the intensity of a pixel at the position (x, y) in the image is represented as

$$I(x,y) = \rho(x,y)\mathbf{n}(x,y)^T \cdot \mathbf{s}, \tag{10}$$

where, $\rho(x,y)$ is the albedo of pixel (x,y), $\mathbf{n}(x,y)$ is the surface normal, and $\mathbf{s}$ is the point light source, respectively. In addition, we warp the input face image into a predefined mean shape by means of AAM. Therefore we also assume that all the people have the same surface normal. Denote the input face image under an arbitrary illumination s as $I_{in}^s = \rho_{in}(x,y)\mathbf{n}(x,y)^T \cdot \mathbf{s}_s$. Ratio image of input face between two different illumination A, B is defined as follows:

$$R_{in}^{AB}(x,y) = \frac{I_{in}^B(x,y)}{I_{in}^A(x,y)}. \tag{11}$$

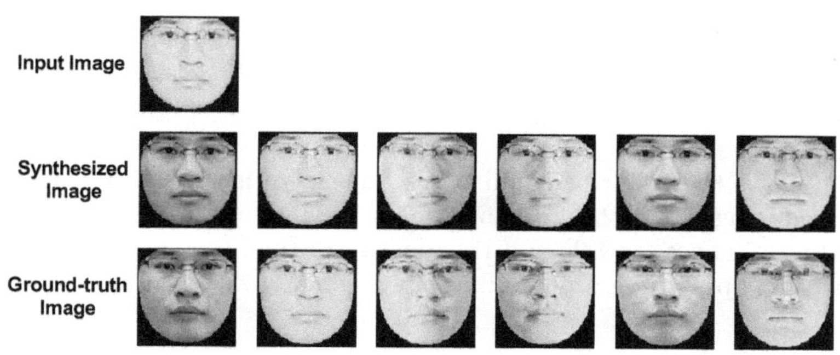

Fig. 1. The result of illumination image synthesis

From Eq. 10, we have

$$R_{in}^{AB}(x,y) = \frac{\rho_{in}(x,y)\mathbf{n}(x,y)^T \cdot \mathbf{s}_B}{\rho_{in}(x,y)\mathbf{n}(x,y)^T \cdot \mathbf{s}_A} = \frac{\mathbf{n}(x,y)^T \cdot \mathbf{s}_B}{\mathbf{n}(x,y)^T \cdot \mathbf{s}_A}. \tag{12}$$

Here, we can see that surface normal and light source determine the ratio image. Moreover, since we assume that all the people have the same surface normal, ratio image between two different illumination is the same for all the people. From now, we represent the ratio image between two illumination A and B as R^{AB} by dropping person-specific term from Eq. 11.

Our goal is to synthesize a face image I^t_{in} under a novel light source t, given input face image I^s_{in} under light source s and a reference image I^t_{ref} under target light source t. From the ratio image,

$$R^{st}(x,y) = \frac{I^t_{in}(x,y)}{I^s_{in}(x,y)} = \frac{I^t_{ref}(x,y)}{I^s_{ref}(x,y)}. \tag{13}$$

The target image I^t_{in} can be calculated if we can estimate $I^s_{ref}(x,y)$ which is the reference image under input light source s. We adopt symmetric bilinear model for estimating $I^s_{ref}(x,y)$ and treat the facial identity and the lighting as a content factor and a style factor of bilinear model, respectively. First we factorize the input face image into the identity factor and the lighting factor. Then we can synthesize the reference face image under the input lighting condition by multiplying the identity factor of the reference face image, the lighting factor of the input face image, and the interaction matrix of bilinear model. Here, we used mean of the training face images as the reference face image.

The detailed explanation of the overall procedure of the proposed illumination image synthesis method is given below.

1. Factorize the input face image into identity factor and lighting factor as $I^s_{in} = a_{in}Wb_s$, where a_{in} is the identity factor, b_s is the lighting factor, and W is interaction matrix, respectively.
2. Obtain the reference face image under the input lighting condition $I^s_{ref} = a_{ref}Wb_s$ using the identity factor of the reference image a_{ref} and the lighting factor of the input image b_s.
3. Obtain the ratio image between lighting s and t: $R^{st}(x,y) = \frac{I^t_{ref}(x,y)}{I^s_{ref}(x,y)}$.
4. Compute the target face image $I^t_{in}(x,y) = R^{st}(x,y)I^s_{in}(x,y)$.

Fig. 1 shows the result of illumination image synthesis. We can see that the synthesized images (row 2) have almost identical illumination condition with the ground-truth images (row 3) and the identity of the input face is not changed. Hence we can apply the proposed illumination image synthesis method to incremental AAM.

3.2 Incremental AAM Using Synthesized Illumination Face Images

To improve the fitting performance of AAM, incremental AAM updates the appearance bases as the imaging condition changes. However, when the illumination condition changes drastically, the AOM judges the entire warped pixel as outlier pixels. In a consequence, neither the AOM nor the AAM is updated

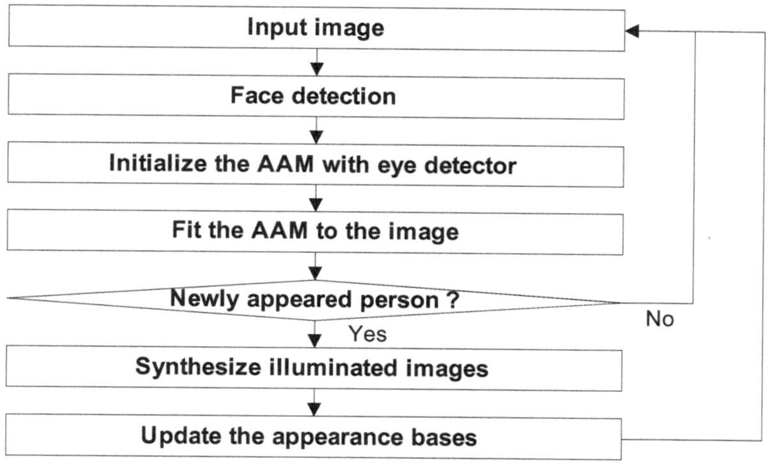

Fig. 2. The procedure of the incremental AAM using synthesized illumination images

and the fitting performance is not improved. To solve this problem, we first synthesize illuminated face images and update the appearance bases using it. As a result, we expect the fitting performance of AAM to improve.

Fig. 2 shows the procedure of the incremental AAM using synthesized illuminated images. For a new image, the AAM is initialized using a face and eye detector and fitted to the input image. Next, the algorithm determines whether the fitted face is a newly appeared person using the face tracker. If the fitted face is a newly appeared person, the illuminated face images are synthesized as explained in section 3.1 and the appearance bases of AAM is updated using theses images. Then, the updated AAM is used for the next input image.

4 Experimental Results

4.1 Data Setup

For constructing active appearance model, we used the face image database that were gathered from 28 people in our lab. For each person, 6 images are registered in the database and the images contain four facial expression variations(three neutral images, a happy image, a surprise image, and a angry image) at frontal view. Therefore there are 168 images and we manually landmarked all the images. Then we constructed the model and it is built using 37 appearance bases and 28 shape bases. Each number of bases is selected to account for 95% shape and appearance variations.

For training the bilinear model, we also gathered another face image database which consists of 15 people. For each person, 6 images under different lighting directions are registered. Therefore there are 90 images and we manually landmarked all the images. Then we warped each face image into the mean shape of the AAM and we used this warped face image to train the bilinear model. We built the observation matrix $\mathbf{Y}$ by stacking the warped face images. Each column of $\mathbf{Y}$ has the warped face image of a specific subject with all illuminations and each row has the warped face image of all the subject with a specific illumination. We take $S = 6$, $C = 15$, and $K = 6237$ for Eq. 7, where K is the dimension of the warped face image.

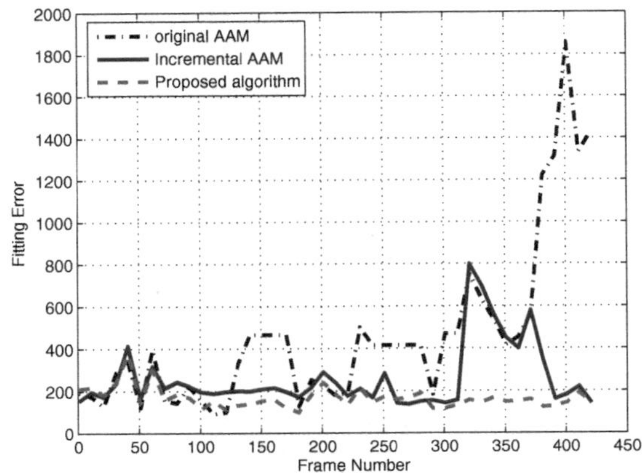

Fig. 3. Fitting error of each algorithm

4.2 Comparison of Fitting Performance

We compared the fitting performance of the original AAM, incremental AAM and proposed method. For evaluating the fitting performance of each algorithm, we recorded a image sequence which has varying illumination. It has gradual illumination change at the middle of the sequence, then sudden illumination change starts near frame index 300. Fig. 3 shows the fitting error of each algorithm. The fitting error is measured as the sum of squared error between the fitted shape point and the ground-truth shape point:

$$Error = \sum_{i=1}^{N} \sqrt{(x_i^{fit} - x_i^g)^2 + (y_i^{fit} - y_i^g)^2}, \tag{14}$$

where (x_i^{fit}, y_i^{fit}) is the i-th fitted shape point, (x_i^g, y_i^g) is the i-th ground-truth shape point, and N is the number of shape points[1]. From the figure, we can see that the fitting error of original AAM increases as the illumination changes. On the contrary, the fitting error of incremental AAM does not increase under the gradual change of illumination(from frame index 120 to 180 and from frame index 220 to 290), since the AOM adapts to the change of appearance variation of the face image and the update of appearance base is take place. However,

[1] In this experiment, we used 70 shape points.

when the illumination changes drastically after the frame index 300, the AOM cannot adapt to the change and as a result the fitting error increases like the original AAM. In case of the proposed algorithm, the fitting error is not changed much through the entire image sequence.

Fig. 4 shows the fitting result of each algorithm when the illumination changes drastically. We can see that the original AAM cannot fit the model to the input face image since the trained appearance bases do not contain illumination variations. The incremental AAM also cannot fit the model to the input face since the AOM cannot adapt to the rapid change of the illumination. However, the fitting result of the proposed algorithm is stable since we updated the appearance bases using the synthesized illumination face images at the first frame.

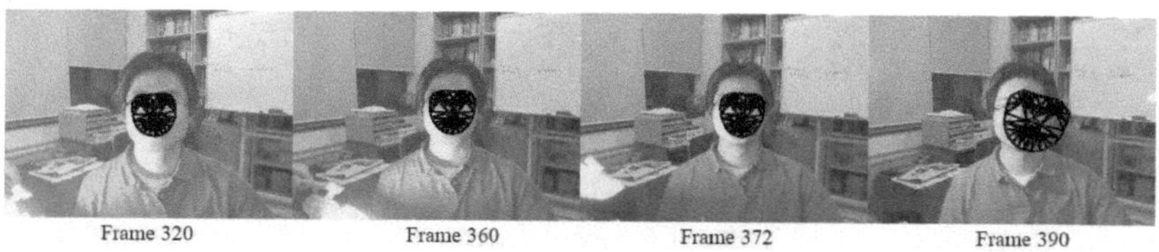

(a) Fitting result of original AAM

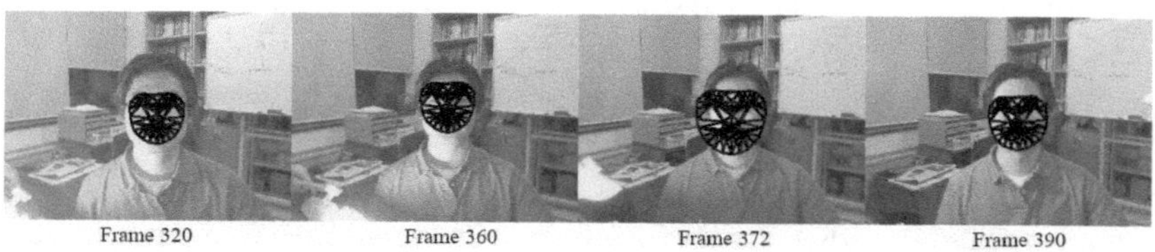

(b) Fitting result of incremental AAM

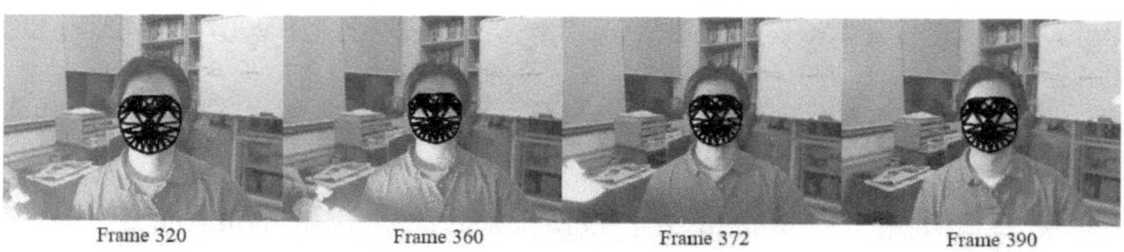

(c) Fitting result of incremental AAM using synthesized illuminated images

Fig. 4. Comparison of the fitting result of each algorithm

There were 32 updates of appearance bases for incremental AAM, while only 7 updates (1 for input image and 6 for synthesized illumination images) were take place for the proposed algorithm. Moreover, the incremental AAM should determine the goodness of the fitting result and update the AOM parameters for every frame. Thus, our proposed algorithm has less computation time than the incremental AAM.

5 Conclusion

In this paper, we proposed a novel scheme to update the appearance bases. First, for a new image, the AAM is initialized using a face and eye detector and fitted to the input image. Next, the algorithm determines whether the fitted face is a newly appeared person. If the fitted face is a newly appeared person, the illuminated face images are synthesized and the appearance bases of AAM is updated using theses images. Then, the updated AAM is used for the next input image. By doing this, the appearance bases can fit to the input image accurately, even when the illumination condition changes drastically. The experimental results show that our proposed algorithm improves the fitting performance over both the incremental AAM and original AAM.

Acknowledgements

This work was partially supported by the Korea Science and Engineering Foundation (KOSEF) through the Biometrics Engineering Research Center (BERC) at Yonsei University. Also, it was partially supported by the Intelligent Robotics Development Program, one of the 21st Century Frontier R&D Programs funded by the Ministry of Commerce, Industry and Energy of Korea.

References

1. Cootes, T., Edwards, G., Taylor, C.: Active appearance models. In: Burkhardt, H., Neumann Ed.s, B. (eds.) Proc. of European Conference on Computer Vision, pp. 484–498 (1998)
2. Lee, S., Sung, J., Kim, D.: Incremental update of linear appearance models and its application to aam: incremental aam. In: Proc. of ICIAR 2007 (to be published, 2007)
3. Zhou, S., Chellappa, R., Moghaddam, B.: Visual tracking and recognition using appearance-adaptive model in particle filter. IEEE Trans. on Image Processing 13, 1491–1506 (2004)
4. Hall, P., Marshall, D., Martin, R.: Incremental eigenanalysis for classification. In: British Machine Vision Conference (1998)
5. Tenenbaum, J., Freeman, W.: Separating style and content with bilinear models, neural computation. Neural computation 12, 1247–1283 (2000)
6. Sim, T., Kanade, T.: Combining models and exemplars for face recognition: An illuminating example. In: Workshop on Models versus Exemplars in Computer Vision (2001)
7. Belhumeur, P., Kriegman, D.: What is the set of images of an object under all possible illumination conditions. International Journal of Computer Vision 28, 245–260 (1998)
8. Shashua, A., Riklin-Raviv, T.: The quotient image: class-based re-rendering and recognition withvarying illuminations. IEEE Transactions on Pattern Analysis and Machine Intelligence 23, 129–139 (2001)

Content-Based 3D Model Retrieval Based on the Spatial Geometric Descriptor

Dingwen Wang[1,2], Jiqi Zhang[2], Hau-San Wong[2], and Yuanxiang Li[1]

[1] Computer Science School, Wuhan University
430079 Wuhan, China
wdingwen@gmail.com,yxli@whu.edu.cn
[2] Department of Computer Science, City University of Hong Kong
999077 Hong Kong, China
jzhang@cs.cityu.edu.hk, cshswong@cityu.edu.hk

Abstract. In this paper, we propose a novel shape descriptor for 3D objects, called spatial geometric descriptor (SGD), to represent the spatial geometric information of a 3D model by mapping its furthest distance, normal and area distribution onto spherical grids in a sequence of concentric shells. Then these spherical distribution functions are transformed to spherical harmonic coefficients which not only save the storage space but also provide multi-resolution shape description for any 3D model by adopting different dimensions for the coefficients. The feature vector extraction time can be reduced by adopting a single scan scheme on the mesh surface for a given 3D model. The retrieval performance is evaluated on the public Princeton Shape Benchmark (PSB) dataset and the experimental results show that our method not only outperforms Light Field Descriptor which is regarded as the best shape descriptor so far but also maintains an advantage of fast feature vector extraction procedure.

Keywords: 3D Model Retrieval, Shape Descriptor, Spherical Harmonincs.

1 Motivation

3D models become more and more popular in many modern application domains such as computer aided design, virtual reality, medicine, molecular biology, and entertainments. The conventional retrieval approach based on keyword annotation can't satisfy the retrieval requirement when the number of un-annotated 3D model becomes huge.The MPEG group also develops an MPEG-7 international standard for the description of multimedia data, but there is little description about 3D models [14]. In recent years, a variety of methods for characterizing 3D models have been proposed, such as Light Field Descriptor (LFD) [1], Spherical Harmonic Descriptor (SHD) [3], Radialized Spherical Extent Function (REXT) [5], Extended Gaussian Image (EGI) [11], SECSHELL [9], Voxel [6], D2 Shape Distribution [12] and so on. In [4], 12 shape descriptors have been evaluated on the Princeton Shape Benchmark (PSB) dataset of 3D objects including

H.H.S. Ip et al. (Eds.): PCM 2007, LNCS 4810, pp. 685–694, 2007.

LFD, which costs more computation time than the other shape descriptors, but provides the best retrieval precision based on 2D views in the experiments. It is reported that the shape descriptor based on 2D views is more discriminating than the other shape descriptors that capture 3D geometric relationships. However, there are few evidences to support this assertion. In this paper, we tend to propose a novel retrieval approach to capture 3D geometric relationships as much as possible, so that this spatial information can describe the 3D object as detailed as possible.

The next section contains a summary of related work. Section 3 describes the detailed procedures of 3D model retrieval system based on SGD. The experimental results are presented in section 4. Finally, Section 5 addresses the conclusion and future work.

2 Related Work

In general, a 3D model is consisted of many polygon surfaces with normal, area and distance from the center of mass to surfaces' centers. Most of the existing shape descriptors based on 3D geometric shape only represent certain single character. For example, REXT only gives distance information about the extent of an object from the center of gravity along radial directions; the multi-shell extended Gaussian Image (MSEGI) [13] mainly describes the normal distribution; The SECSHELL [9] proposed by Ankerst et al, is primarily used to classify 3D protein data by describing the vertices distribution and Voxel [6] represents the area distribution on 3D grid by subdividing the bounding cube of an object into equally-sized voxel cells.

In addition, some other methods have been proposed to improve the retrieval performance by combining multiple shape descriptors into a new one in recent few years. In [7], Vranic proposes the composite feature vector formed by concatenating the basic feature vectors together with longer dimensions to represent more effective shape descriptors. However, the shape descriptors with small dimension lose a lot of information and are not good enough to represent the 3D object. In [10], the query processing is based on the pairwise rankings of the objects, which are monotonically related to the pairwise distances, to eliminate the influence of the size of different feature vectors. However, this method may shorten or lengthen the real distance of the pairwise objects since the relevance scores generally contain more information than the mere ranking: the ranked ordering can be computed from the relevance scores, but not vice-versa.

3 The Proposed Method

In this section, we describe the detailed workflow of 3D model retrieval system based on SGD as follows (Fig. 1).

1. 3D objects are normalized in the same canonical frame to fix translation, rotation and scale variant problems.

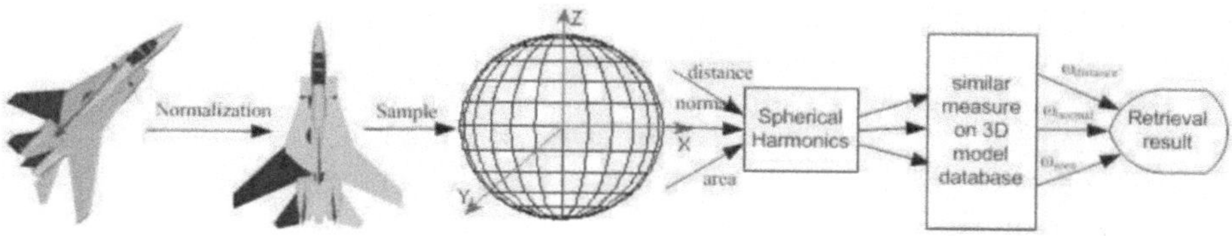

Fig. 1. The workflow of 3D model retrieval system

2. Uniformly decompose the 3D object into multi-concentric shells and split the surface of each shell into $N \times N$ cells.
3. Obtain the distribution function $f(r, \theta, \phi)$ by capturing the furthest distance, normal and area of the 3D object along longitude and latitude angle pairs in each concentric shell.
4. The distribution functions $f(r, \theta, \phi)$ are used to perform spherical harmonics transform to attain the feature vectors of 3D objects.
5. The similarity metrics is used to measure the similarity of two objects.

For the convenience of further discussion, we first give some definitions of a 3D model. For a given 3D triangular mesh model, we denote it by a set of triangles T_i which is represented by a set of three vertices.

$$T = \{T_1, \cdots, T_m\}, \quad T_i = \{P_{A_i}, P_{B_i}, P_{C_i}\} \tag{1}$$

We denote the center of triangle T_i by g_i and surface area with S_i, while the total area of the mesh model is S:

$$g_i = (P_{A_i} + P_{B_i} + P_{C_i})/3 \tag{2}$$

$$S_i = |(P_{C_i} - P_{A_i}) \times (P_{B_i} - P_{C_i})|/2, \quad S = \sum_{i=1}^{m} S_i \tag{3}$$

3.1 Normalization

The normalization step transforms the 3D models into a uniform canonical frame. The goal of this procedure is to eliminate the effect of transforming a 3D object by a different scale, position, rotation or orientation. Pose normalization can improve the performance of the shape descriptors.

Translation: models are translated to the center of mass.

$$O_I = (O_x, O_y, O_z) = \frac{1}{S} \sum_{i=1}^{m} S_i g_i \tag{4}$$

Rotation: we apply the principle component analysis method to normalize the 3D models for orientation. The eigenvectors and associated eigenvalues of the covariance matrix C_I are obtained by integrating the quadratic polynomials

$P_i \cdot P_j$, over the centers on the surface of all polygons. Three eigenvectors sorted by decreasing associated eigenvalues are the principal axes and can be used to fix the models after rotation. The ambiguity between positive and negative axes is resolved by choosing the direction of the axes so that the area of model on the positive side of the x-, y-, and z-axes is greater than the area on the negative side.

$$C_I = \frac{1}{12S}\sum_{i=1}^{m}(f(P_{A_i}) + f(P_{B_i}) + f(P_{C_i}) + 9f(P_{g_i}))S_i \tag{5}$$

$$f(v) = (P_i - O_I)\cdot(P_i - O_I)^T \tag{6}$$

Scale: 3D object is isotropically rescaled so that the average distance from the vertices to the center of mass is 0.5.

3.2 Sampling

After normalizing the object, we uniformly decompose a 3D space into concentric shells with radii $r_c = 1, 2, \cdots, N_s\,(c = 1, 2, \cdots, m)$ and divide the surfaces of each shell into $N \times N$ cells. Then we capture the furthest distance, normal and area on each cell in concentric shells. For normal, we map a triangle surface T_i to $Cell(r, i, j)$ according to its normal direction and distance d_k, where d_k is the normal distance of the surface to the origin in the direction of the surface normal. The $f_{normal}(r, i, j)$ counts the area of the triangle surface whose normal is mapped on $Cell(r, i, j)$. Since it is difficult to directly compute the furthest distance and area on each cell, we adopt an approximate approach. At first, as shown in the Fig. 2, a 3D model is subdivided into the P_{total} sub-surfaces if the number of a 3D model's surface is smaller than P_{total}, where P_{total} is a predefined value. Then we compute the center of each surface, and map it to certain cell according to its longitude, latitude and distance from the origin. Then, the $f_{area}(r, i, j)$ counts the approximate area on each spherical grid, and the $f_{distance}(r, i, j)$ records the furthest distance on each cell.

$$Cell(r, i, j) = \{r_n, [\theta_i, \theta_{i+1}], [\phi_i, \phi_{i+1}]\}, \quad i, j = 0, 1, 2, \cdots, N-1 \tag{7}$$

$$\theta_i = 2\pi i/N, \phi_i = \pi i/N, \quad i = 0, 1, 2, \cdots, N \tag{8}$$

$$r_i = \lceil \frac{d_k - \min(d_k)}{\max(d_k) - \min(d_k)} \times N_s \rceil, \quad i = 1, 2, \cdots, m \tag{9}$$

Obviously, if P_{total} is larger, the computation of the furthest distance and area on spherical grids is more accurate, but will cost more extraction time. In practice, P_{total} is valued at 40000 by balancing the retrieval performance and the extraction time. The whole extraction algorithm is summarized as following:

1. A triangle surface is mapped to the $Cell(r, i, j)$ according to its normal direction. The $f_{normal}(r, i, j)$ records the area of the triangle surface which normal is mapped on $Cell(r, i, j)$.

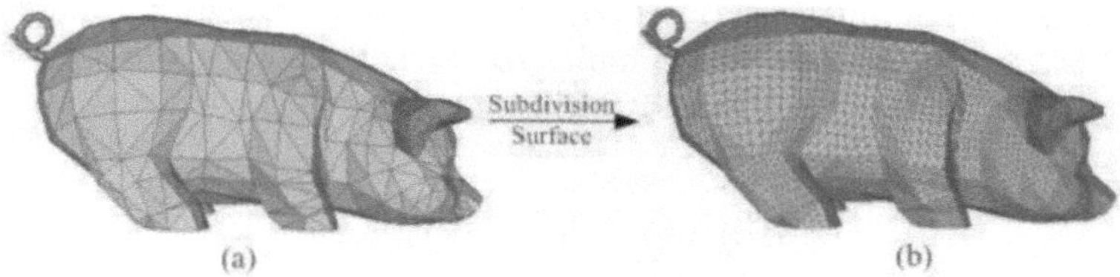

Fig. 2. subdivision

2. If $S_i > S/P_{total}$, then go to next step, otherwise the triangle surface is subdivided into $P_{total} \times (S_i/S)$ sub-triangle surfaces.
3. The $f_{distance}(r,i,j)$ and $f_{area}(r,i,j)$ respectively record the furthest distance and area of the triangle or sub-triangle surface which center is mapped to the $Cell(r,i,j)$.
4. Repeat above steps until all surfaces are scanned.

3.3 Spherical Harmonic Transform

Spherical harmonics transform is introduced as a useful tool for 3D model retrieval in [8]. The theory of spherical harmonics says that any spherical function $f(\theta,\phi)$ can be represented by the sum of its harmonics:

$$f(\theta,\phi) = \sum_{l=0}^{\infty} \sum_{m=-l}^{m=l} \tilde{f_{l,m}} Y_l^m(\theta,\phi) \tag{10}$$

Where $\tilde{f_{l,m}}$ denotes the Fourier coefficient and $Y_l^m(\theta,\phi)$ is the spherical harmonic base, calculated by certain products of Legendre functions and complex exponentials. Fig. 3 illustrates the spherical harmonics $Y_l^m(\theta,\phi)$ which are complex functions defined on spherical, up to degree 3.

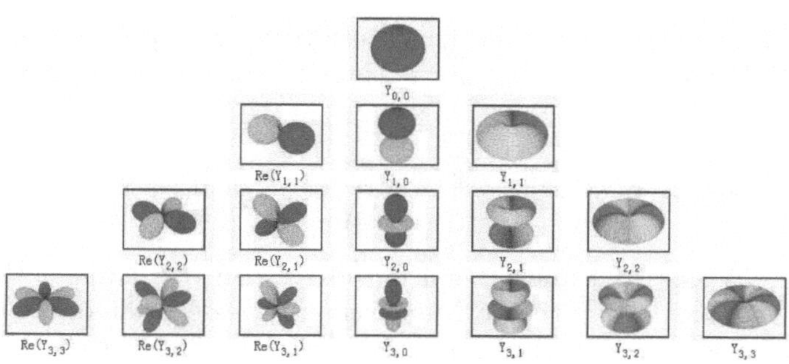

Fig. 3. Spherical Harmonics basis functions $Y_l^m(\theta,\phi)$: a visualization of complex functions defined on spherical, are up to degree 3

The distribution functions $f(r,\theta,\phi)$ of furthest distance, normal and area are used to perform spherical harmonics to extract their feature vectors. Since $f(r,\theta,\phi)$ is band-limited with bandwidth $N/2$, then we can express $f(r,\theta,\phi)$ as:

$$f(r,\theta,\phi) = \sum_{l=0}^{N/2} \sum_{m=-l}^{m=l} \tilde{f_{l,m}} Y_l^m(r,\theta,\phi) \tag{11}$$

Where l is the degree of spherical harmonics. In the practical application, feature vectors can be extracted from the first $l+1 (l < N/2)$ rows of coefficients, which can provide the multi-resolution feature descriptors for 3D models by choosing different value of l. Two important properties of spherical harmonics, which are used to extract different 3D shape feature vectors of based on a function on the spherical S^2.

Property 1. Let $f \in L^2(S^2)$ be a real-valued function, i.e., $f : S^2 \to \mathbb{R}$. Then, the following symmetry between the coefficients exists:

$$\tilde{f_{l,m}} = (-1)^m \overline{\tilde{f_{l,-m}}} \Rightarrow |\tilde{f_{l,m}}| = |\tilde{f_{l,-m}}| \tag{12}$$

Where, $\tilde{f_{l,m}}$ and $(-1)^m \overline{\tilde{f_{l,-m}}}$ are conjugate complex numbers.

Property 2. A subspace of $L^2(S^2)$ of dimension $2l+1$, which is spanned by the harmonics $Y_l^m (-l \leq m \leq l)$ of degree l, is invariant with respect to rotation of the sphere S^2.

We can use the absolute values of $\tilde{f_{l,m}}$ as components of our feature vectors to obtain the feature vector F_1. According to Property 1, if $f(\theta,\phi)$ is a real-valued function, then the symmetry relationship between the coefficients exists. Thus, the feature vector F_1 is composed by the first $l+1 (l < N/2)$ rows of the obtained coefficients.

$$F_1 = (|\tilde{f_{0,0}}|, |\tilde{f_{1,0}}|, |\tilde{f_{1,1}}|, \cdots, |\tilde{f_{l,0}}|, \cdots, |\tilde{f_{0,0}}|) \quad dim(F_1) = l(l+1)/2 \tag{13}$$

In addition, we can also obtain the feature vector F_2 with rotation invariance according to Property 2, without normalizing the orientation of a 3D model.

$$F_2 = (\|f_0\|, \cdots, \|f_{dim-1}\|), \quad \|f_i\| = \sqrt{\sum_{m=-l}^{m=l} |\tilde{f_{l,m}}|^2}, \quad dim \leq N/2 \tag{14}$$

However, F_2 loses the information on degree l, which hamper the retrieval performance of the feature vector. Moreover, each tessellation of the unit sphere is not uniform. As a result, the irregular sampling limits the rotation invariance of the shape descriptors. In [13], we have compared the retrieval performance of F_1 and F_2 extracted by two properties.

3.4 Feedback Overall Similarity Measure

The furthest distance, normal and area respectively represent different geometric information of a 3D model, and have different sizes. Bray Curtis distance is used to eliminate the influence of different sizes. Then, considering their feedback retrieval performance, we should choose an appropriate weight to obtain an overall similarity. To investigate the influence of different combined weights on the retrieval performance, we define the sum of their weights always to be 1. Fig. 4 shows the retrieval performance influenced by different combined weights, where the weight of furthest distance (FD) is respectively 0, 0.2, 0.4, 0.6, 0.8 and 0.9 while the ratio of the normal and area's weight changes from 0 to 5.

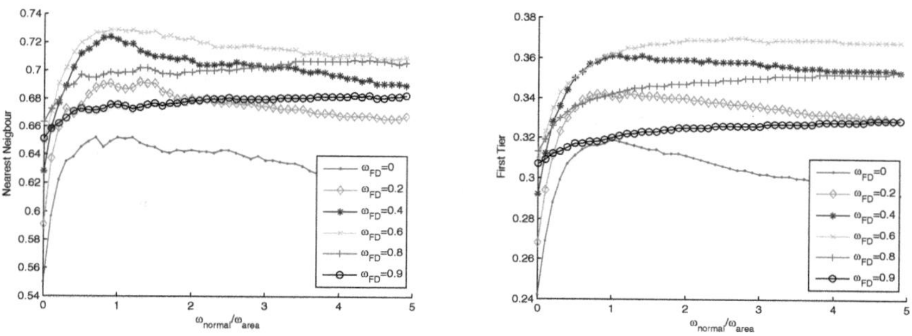

(a) (b)

Fig. 4. Performance (Nearest Neighbor and First Tier) versus different combined weights of distance, normal and area

4 Experiments and Results

In the experiments, we adopt the public Princeton Shape Benchmark (PSB) dataset [4] to compare SGD, LFD [1], FD (Furthest Distance on concentric spheres), REXT [5], MSEGI [13], EGI [11], AD (Area Distribution on concentric spheres), SECSHELL, SECTOR, SHELL [9], and the method in [10] that combines FD, MEGI and AD shape descriptors. We merge the train and test dataset of PSB into a larger dataset by combining the same classes and removing the classes with few models, which are 1280 3D models spanning 108 categories such as plane, ship, car, human, animal, plant, furniture etc. The experiments were run on a Windows PC with 3.4GHz Pentium 4 processor and 1G MB of memory.

We use precision vs. recall curves, a standard evaluation metrics for retrieval systems, to compare the effectiveness of our algorithms (Fig. 5), and also evaluate these shape descriptors on the following measurements: (1) Extraction Time, which represents the time of extracting the shape descriptors; (2) Nearest-Neighbor (NN) measure, which represents the percentage of the closest matches that belong to the same class as the query; (3) First-tier (FT) and Second-tier (ST), which represent the percentage of models in the query's class that appear

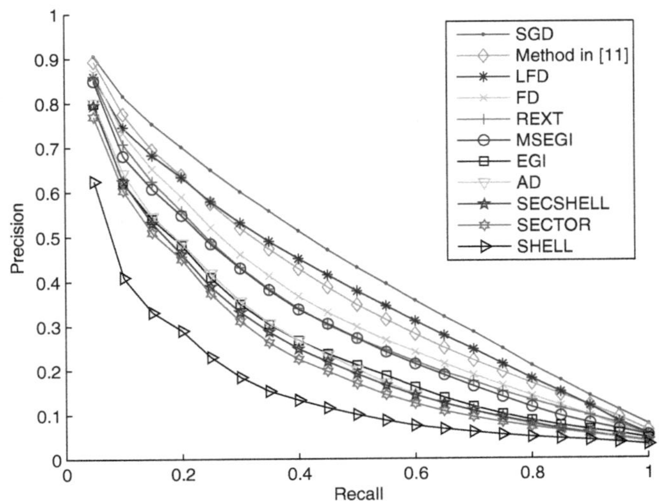

Fig. 5. Precision vs. recall curves computed for 11 approaches on the public Princeton Shape Benchmark dataset

Table 1. Retrieval measurements of 11 different shape feature vectors on the public Princeton Shape Benchmark dataset

Descriptors	Times(s)	NN	FT	ST	E-Measure	DCG
SGD	0.132	72.6%	36.7%	48.1%	29.2%	67.9%
LFD	2.016	67.1%	32.7%	43.0%	25.8%	64.3%
Method in [10]	0.343	65.1%	31.0%	42.2%	25.4%	67.1%
FD	0.125	62.7%	28.8%	38.6%	22.8%	60.4%
REXT	0.436	60.3%	26.2%	36.2%	21.4%	58.8%
MSEGI	0.185	56.1%	25.8%	34.9%	20.8%	57.8%
AD	0.123	55.0%	24.3%	33.5%	19.6%	57.6%
SECSHELL	0.091	49.1%	20.0%	28.0%	16.3%	52.8%
SECTOR	0.087	46.1%	18.3%	26.0%	15.7%	51.5%
EGI	0.079	45.5%	21.2%	29.8%	17.6%	53.7%
SHELL	0.078	26.3%	10.6%	16.7%	9.2%	42.7%

within the top K matches, where K depends on the size of the query's class, Specifically, for a $|C|$ class with members, $K = |C| - 1$ for the first tier, and $K = 2(|C| - 1)$ for the second tier; (4) E-Measure (EM) represents a composite measure of the precision and recall for a fixed number of retrieved results; (5) Discounted Cumulative Gain (DCG), which represents a statistic that weights correct results near the front of the list more than correct results later in the ranked list under the assumption that a user is less likely to consider elements near the end of the list. For NN, FT, ST, EM and DCG, higher values indicate better results.

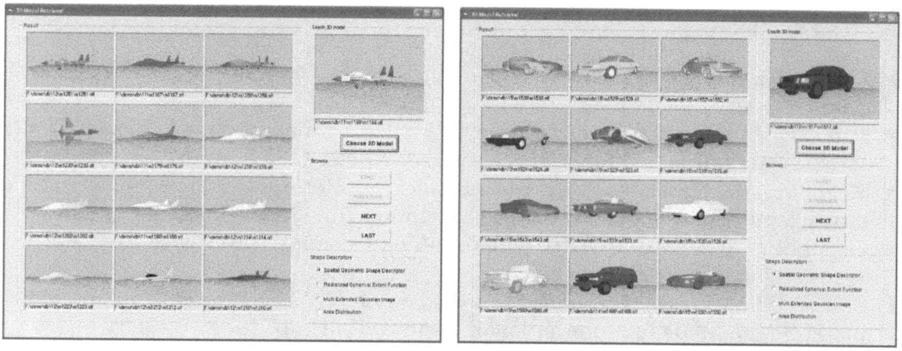

(a) (b)

Fig. 6. The retrieval results of a fighter and a car as the query

From the experimental results, we can summarize the main contributions of our method: (1) SGD not only significantly outperforms LFD and other popular shape descriptors, even the combined rank method in [10]; (2) The average extraction time of SGD is 0.132s, which is less than the best shape descriptors such as LFD, REXT etc.

We develop a 3D model retrieval system based on SGD and other shape descriptor. In the current version, the user first presents a 3D model file to the retrieval system. Then by choosing different shape descriptors, the system will display the query model and it's most 144 similar models in the database. Fig. 6 illustrates the retrieval results based on SGD on our 3D model retrieval system when a fighter and car model are given as queries.

5 Conclusion and Future Work

In this paper, we propose a new shape descriptor, called Spatial Geometric descriptor which represents the spatial geometric relationships of 3D object by extracting the furthest distance, normal and area distribution on each spherical grid in concentric shells. SGD significantly outperforms the other popular shape descriptor on the precision-recall, NN, First Tier, Second Tier and DCG measurements. Among the best shape descriptors, the extraction time of SGD is the least, so it is suitable for an online 3D model search engine. Bray Curtis distance is adopted as the similarity measurement metric to eliminate the influence of different sizes, and the feedback weight optimizes the retrieval performance. This weighted combined feature vector significantly outperforms the method which just directly combines the retrieval result of different shape descriptors.

In the future, we will further consider how to combine different shape descriptors more effectively and further investigate how the retrieval performance is affected by different similarity measurements.

References

1. Chen, D.Y., Tian, X.P., Shen, Y.T., Ming, O.Y.: On visual similarity based 3D model retrieval. Computer Graphics Forum 22, 223–232 (2003)
2. Brou, P.: Using the Gaussian Image to Find the Orientation of Objects. The International Journal of Robotics Research 3, 89–125 (1984)
3. Kazhdan, M., Funkhouser, T., Rusinkiewicz, S.: Rotation invariant spherical harmonic representation of 3D shape descriptors. In: Proceedings of the 2003 Eurographics/ACM SIGGRAPH symposium on Geometry processing, Aachen, Germany, vol. 43, pp. 156–164 (2003)
4. Shilane, P., Min, P., Kazhdan, M., Funkhouser, T.: The Princeton Shape Benchmark. Shape Modeling International, Genova, Italy, pp. 167–178 (2004)
5. Vranic, D.V.: An improvement of rotation invariant 3D-shape based on functions on concentric spheres. In: International Conference on Image Processing, vol. 3, pp. 757–760 (2003)
6. Vranic, D.V.: 3D Model Retrieval. University of Leipzig, Germany (2004)
7. Vranic, D.V.: DESIRE: a composite 3D-shape descriptor. In: IEEE International Conference on Multimedia and Expo, Amsterdam, The Netherlands (2005)
8. Vranic, D.V., Saupe, D., Richter, J.: Tools for 3D-object retrieval: Karhunen-Loeve transform and spherical harmonics. In: IEEE Fourth Workshop on Multimedia Signal Processing, pp. 293–298 (2001)
9. Ankerst, M., Kastenmuller, G., Kriegel, H.P., Seidl, T.: 3D shape histograms for similarity search and classification in spatial databases. In: Güting, R.H., Papadias, D., Lochovsky, F.H. (eds.) SSD 1999. LNCS, vol. 1651, pp. 207–226. Springer, Heidelberg (1999)
10. Atmosukarto, I., Wee Kheng, L., Zhiyong, H.: Feature Combination and Relevance Feedback for 3D Model Retrieval. In: Proceedings of the 11th International Multimedia Modelling Conference, pp. 334–339 (2005)
11. Horn, B.K.P.: Extended Gaussian images. Proceedings of the IEEE 72, 1671–1686 (1984)
12. Osada, R., Funkhouser, T., Chazelle, B., Dobkin, D.: Shape distributions. ACM Trans. Graph. 21, 807–832 (2002)
13. Wang, D., Zhang, J., Wong, H.-S., Li, Y.: 3D Model Retrieval Based on Multi-Shells Extended Gaussian Image. In: 9th International Conference on Visual Information Systems, Shanghai, China (2007)
14. Jeannin, S., Cieplinski, L., Ohm, J.R., Kim, M.: MPEG-7 Visual Part of Experimentation Model Version 7.0, ISO/IEC JTCI/SC29/WG11/N3521. Beijing, China (2000)

A Practical Server-Side Transmission Control Method for Multi-channel DTV Streaming System

Yuanhai Zhang[1,2] and Wei Huangfu[1]

[1] Institute of Software, Chinese Academy of Sciences, Beijing 100080, China
[2] Graduate University of Chinese Academy of Sciences, Beijing 100039, China
{yuanhai02, huangfuwei}@ios.cn

Abstract. In this paper, we propose a practical design and implementation of multi-channel High Definition (HD) and Standard Definition (SD) MPEG-2 video streaming system using server-side video rate adaptation and rate shaping over digital community network. For video rate adaptation, we employ Program Clock Reference (PCR) embedded in the MPEG-2 streams to enhance packet timing control precision and regulate the transmission rate in a refined way. For rate shaping, we introduce Traffic Control (TC) ingeniously to separate streams of different channels at the network card of server and avoid bandwidth contesting between them. Experimental results show that the proposed system can mitigate the quality degradation of video streaming due to the fluctuations of time-varying channel and simultaneously support 33-channel HDTV streams.

Keywords: Adaptive Video Streaming, PCR, HD, Traffic Control.

1 Introduction

With the rapid deployment of broadband community network access to Internet like FTTH (Fiber-To-The-Home), high quality video streaming service has now become an indispensable application for Internet Service Providers (ISPs). As the community network is often constructed at the area of dense residence and the number of customers subscribing to digital video program is expected to increase, one-to-many content distribution via IP multicast will be a key solution in terms of network and server resource efficiency [1]. In order to distribute video streams via IP multicast smoothly, lots of rate control mechanisms at both sender and receiver side have been presented [2, 3, 4]. From the receiver point of view, adaptive media playout (AMP) is proposed in [2] to vary the playout rate of media frames according to the receiver buffer occupancy as soon as the target buffer level is reached, which may cause jitter at the critical point of two adjacent buffer levels. As to the server-side technology, a multi-buffer scheduling scheme is proposed in [3] to schedule the transmission based on the source buffer priority. A Proportional-Integral-Derivative (PID) controller is adopted in [4] to have better tradeoff between spatial and temporal quality. But the above two schemes only consider the sender buffer state without taking into account the end-to-end delay constraint of multimedia applications. In addition, packet transmission rates are usually adjusted to the decoding rate of their content in multicast-based streaming system to avoid overflow and underflow of server and

H.H.S. Ip et al. (Eds.): PCM 2007, LNCS 4810, pp. 695–703, 2007.

client buffers [5]. However, typical implementation of multicast server may have problems because of poor packet timing control precision especially when transmitting High Definition (HD) streams which contain more high-motion frames and are encoded at a much higher bit rate with larger variation range. In [6], Program Clock Reference (PCR) values embedded in the video streams are used to enhance timing control precision and regulate transmission rate. It reduces the receiver buffer requirement at the cost of higher transmission rate because of the use of coarse regulation time scale [7].

This paper focuses on server-side technologies. We improve the PCR-based rate control algorithm to regulate the transmission rate using more precise timing control mechanism. For supporting more concurrent channels, TC-based rate shaping is also used to avoid bandwidth contesting between different channels. Compared to traditional solutions, our approach is unique in that it takes into account the video stream type as well as the stream characteristics to enhance the timing control precision and optimize an average quality of service for all the clients and is successfully incorporated into a practical multi-channel streaming system.

The rest of paper is organized as follows. Section 2 reviews the architecture of previously proposed service-integrated community network. Section 3 describes the components of our practical server-side transmission control method. In Section 4, we present experimental results. Conclusions and future work are given in Section 5.

2 Architecture of Broadband Community Network

Community broadband access network for integrated services is a very complicated system depicted in Fig. 1. It is first proposed in [8] and the main idea is to offer convergent services of Internet, IP phone and Digital TV (DTV) through combined network of fiber and LAN. In this paper, we place our emphasis on the design and

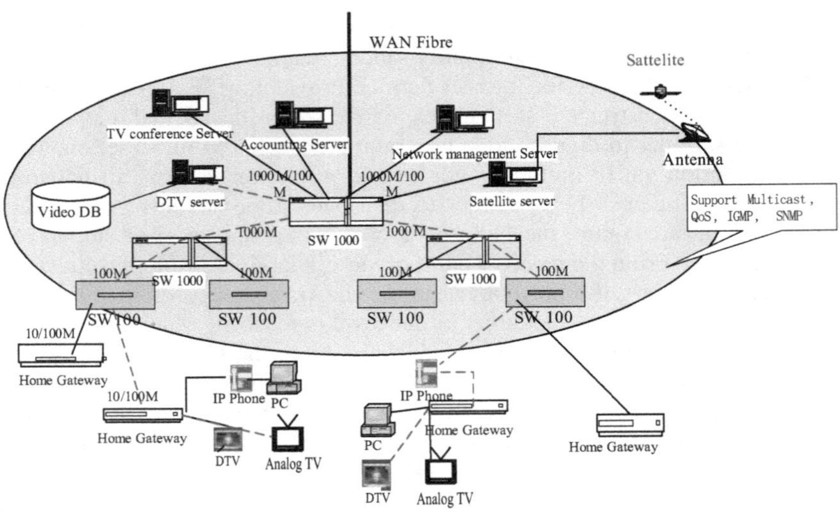

Fig. 1. IP-based broadband community network

implementation of DTV streaming that is shown by dashed line in Fig. 1. As mentioned in the above section, we adopt multicast with UDP as the streaming protocol.

The DTV multicast system involves DTV server, switches and home gateway devices. DTV server controls output rate of multicast streams by rate control and rate shaping algorithms while home gateway is used for playback. We will give a detailed description in the next section.

For supporting multiple channels, the IGMP modules in home gateway cooperate with IGMP Snooping modules in switch to implement the dynamic join and exit of a multicast group. This dynamic group management is the basic idea of dynamic selection of channel. Demanding one channel in fact means that a user joins the multicast group corresponding to this channel while exiting one channel stands for the exit of the multicast group. Switching from one channel to another is actually made up of the above two operations. In this way, multi-channel DTV IP multicast system can be implemented.

3 Server-Side Transmission Control Method

Server-side transmission control method is composed of two parts. One is PCR level rate controller and the other is TC-based rate shaper. Individual components of the method are described in the remainder of this section.

3.1 PCR Level Rate Controller

The problem of timing control precision is especially significant in case of high bit-rate contents. For example, given a MPEG-2 TS encoded HDTV stream whose average bit rate is approximately 24Mbps, the transmission application must maintain a precise time interval of 500 microseconds with Ethernet maximum transfer unit (MTU) constraint of 1500 bytes. To enhance the timing control precision, PCR-based solutions are proposed [6] to regulate transmission rate. PCR is the timing information embedded in the video stream by the encoder to keep clock synchronization. The traditional PCR-based schemes [6] use the PCR values to make sure that the PCR-containing packets are sent out at the correct time. For simplicity, they assume that there is only one PCR in one frame interval. However it is often not the case for VBR compressed videos especially for those with high bit rates, which leads to unprecise sending time and bad quality of playback. In [7], we propose a frame level scheme that considers the case of several PCRs in one frame interval and develop an analytical model. The model demonstrates that the more accurate the decided rate is, the smaller the required client buffer is, which can lighten the burden on the clients and improve the playback quality.

The above approaches only change the transmission rate when they observe a PCR or when the value of the time counter reaches the value of the most recently observed PCR. For a more refined rate control, repacketization process is needed to divide the PCR interval further. Assume that in the ith PCR interval (PCR_i, PCR_{i+1}) within a frame, the bit streams are divided into n_i individually decodable packets denoted as $P=\{P_{i,1},...,P_{i,j},...,P_{i,n_i}\}(1\le j\le n_i)$. A header is appended for each packet which contains a timestamp indicating the correct transmission epoch denoted as

$T = \{T_{i,1},...,T_{i,j},...,T_{i,n_i}\}(1 \le j \le n_i)$. The values of the timestamp can be calculated through two consecutive PCR values and the length of packets between them.

$$T_{i,j} = \begin{cases} PCR_i & j = 1 \\ PCR_i + \dfrac{\sum_{k=1}^{j-1} L(P_{i,k})}{\sum_{m=1}^{n_i} L(P_{i,m})} \times (PCR_{i+1} - PCR_i) & 2 \le j \le n_i \end{cases} \tag{1}$$

where $L(P_{i,j})(1 \leq j \leq n_i)$ is the length of $P_{i,j}(1 \leq j \leq n_i)$. The value of $L(P_{i,j})$ here can be variable below 1500 bytes which is the length of MTU. During the period of high bit rate, $L(P_{i,j})$ is set as a smaller value to minimize the visual impact because of packet loss in network congestion. A larger value of $L(P_{i,j})$ is set when the bit rate is low. The sum of $L(P_{i,j})$ should be equal to the amount of data between PCR_i and PCR_{i+1} as shown in the following equation.

$$\sum_{j=1}^{n_i} L(P_{i,j}) = b(PCR_{i+1}) - b(PCR_i) \tag{2}$$

where $b(PCR_i)$ and $b(PCR_{i+1})$ are the byte-order of ith and $(i+1)$th PCR in a video stream.

Table 1. The description of PCR level rate control algorithm

```
read the first packet P_{i,1} during interval (PCR_i, PCR_{i+1})
get the timestamp T_{i,1} of P_{i,1}
set the value of T_{i,1} as the BaseT_i
set the epoch when T_{i,1} is observed as the BaseTime
for packet P_{i,j} (2≤j≤n_i) in (PCR_i, PCR_{i+1}) do
  get the timestamp T_{i,j} of P_{i,j}
  get current epoch CurrentTime and calculate the current timestamp
    CurrentT_i, CurrentT_i = BaseT_i +(CurrentTime-BaseTime)
  update the BaseT_i, BaseT_i = CurrentT_i
  update the BaseTime, BaseTime=CurrentTime
  if CurrentT_i >= T_{i,j} then
    update BaseT_i, BaseT_i = T_{i,j}
  else
    wait for a period of T_{i,j}–CurrentT_i
  end if
  put the packet into the sender buffer
end for
```

The operation of PCR level rate allocation is shown in Table 1, where $BaseT_i$ denotes the reference timestamp used to calculate the current timestamp $CurrentT_i$, and *BaseTime* and *CurrentTime* are the timing information got from operation system respectively. To reduce the computation error, $BaseT_i$ and *BaseTime* are updated during each cycle of packet transmission. Also the protocol of Network Time Protocol (NTP) should be used to regulate the system time accuracy periodically. Fig. 2 depicts the transmission of packet $P_{i,j}$, where solid line represents the case of ahead of schedule while dashed line represents the case of behind schedule. Different cases will yield the regulation of transmission rate accordingly.

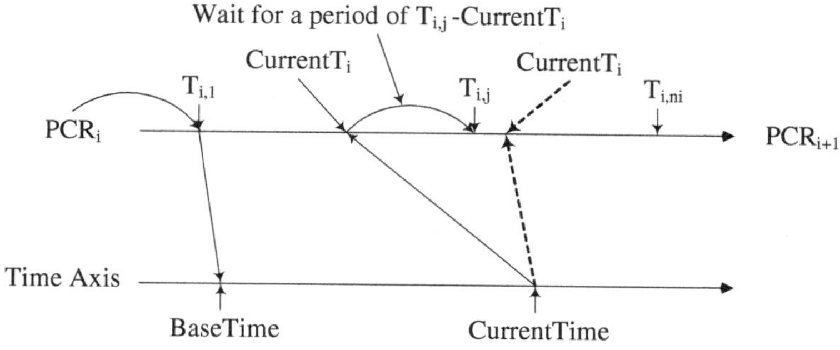

Fig. 2. The transmission of packet $P_{i,j}$

The refined mechanism of PCR level rate controller makes the decided rate reflect the variation of video streams more detailedly and reduces the difference between the decided rate and the real bit rate. This is more important for the transmission of HD streams.

3.2 TC-Based Rate Shaper

To perform rate shaping in multicast streaming system, [5] realizes a traffic shaper with the support of hardware components in layer-2 switch which enables bandwidth limitation of its links. This method is lack of flexibility and increases the production costs of switches at the same time.

Our rate shaping mechanism is performed at the DTV server with Traffic Control (TC) software [9] provided by Linux system. TC is the user level program which can

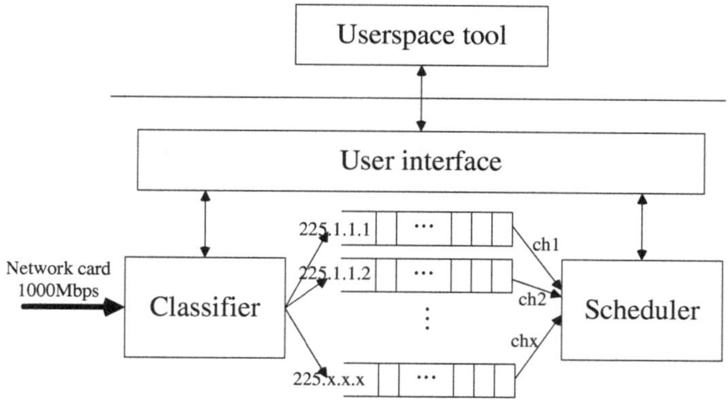

Fig. 3. TC-based rate shaper

be used to create and associate queues with the network devices. It is usually used in routers for network management to set up various kinds of queues and associate classes with each of those queues. It is also used to set up filters by which the packets are classified. However, we introduce it ingeniously into the multicast-based streaming system for flow control at network card of DTV server. The shaper is configured as shown in Fig. 3 to separate the multi-channel streams into different queues according to the destination multicast addresses with each queue having a certain bound determined by stream type. For SDTV streams, we set a lower bound while a higher bound is set for HDTV streams. In our experiments, the bounds are set to 7Mbps and 30Mbps respectively. Note that we also set it disable to borrow the bandwidth of other channels when one channel's bandwidth is insufficient, which can ensure the overall quality and concurrent numbers of video streams.

4 Performance Evaluation

4.1 Experimental Setup

We implement a prototype as a HDTV streaming system which is depicted in Fig. 4. The streaming system consists of a video server (Intel Pentium IV Xeon 3.0G, 2G RAM), a layer-2 switch and two Set-Top-Box (STB) clients (VIA C7 1.0G, 512M RAM, one for playback and the other for background traffic generation). For input video stream, we adopt both SD and HD MPEG-2 TS streams, the parameters of which are listed in Table 2. As to the client, we use the Fedora system and the popular MPlayer software [10] for decoding.

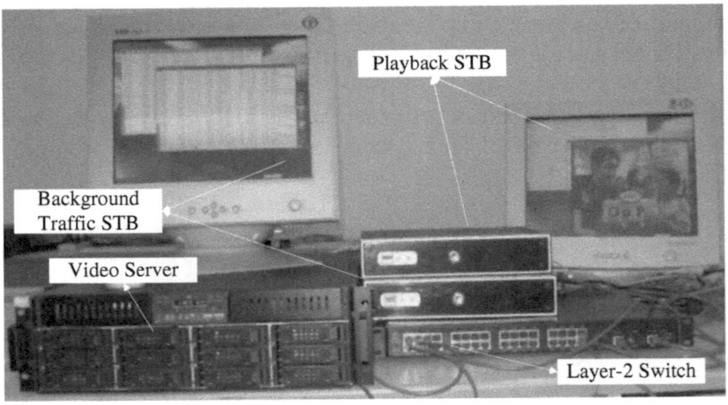

Fig. 4. Practical experimental system

For fair comparisons, all the experiments are performed under the same condition and the duration of 500s. In order to make the time-varying channel condition, a client generates an up-link TCP traffic between 100s and 200s. The sender and receiver buffer sizes are set to 1MB. To illustrate the advantages of our approach, we compare our proposed algorithm, denoted as PCR, with the adaptive media playout algorithm

[2], denoted as AMP. As the performance evaluation metrics, we measure three parameters: sender buffer occupancy, receiver buffer occupancy and PSNR values at the receiver.

Table 2. Video stream parameters

Parameter	Value	
Video Name	TVB-8 Program	Under-Water
Encoding	MPEG-2 TS	MPEG-2 TS
Video Length	6.639min	4.266min
Resolution	720×576	1920×1080
Average Bit Rate	5.8Mbps	19.6Mbps
Picture Pattern	$IBB(PBB)^4$	$IBB(PBB)^4$
Frame Rate	29.97fps	24.66fps
Level	SDTV	HDTV

4.2 Experimental Results

It can be predicted that the bandwidth will be decreased between 100s and 200s because of the completing TCP flows. From Fig. 5, we can find that for the SDTV trace, AMP and PCR can both maintain the sender buffer and receiver buffer

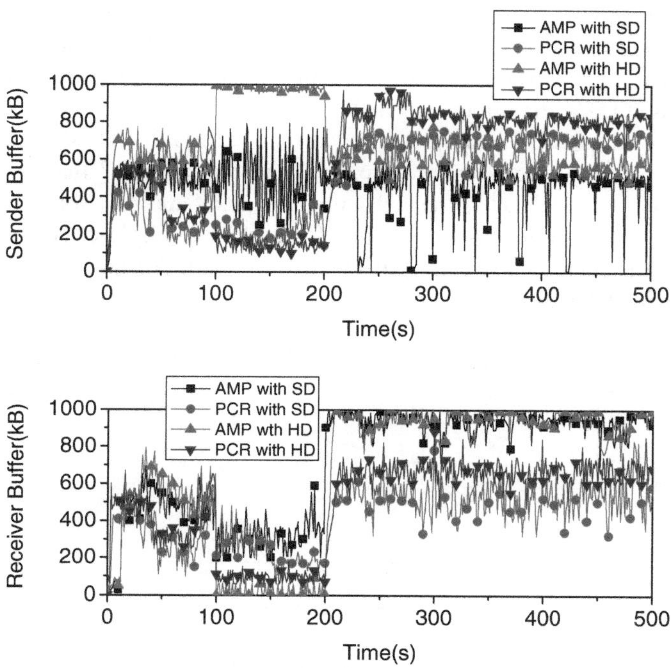

Fig. 5. The sender and receiver buffer occupancies

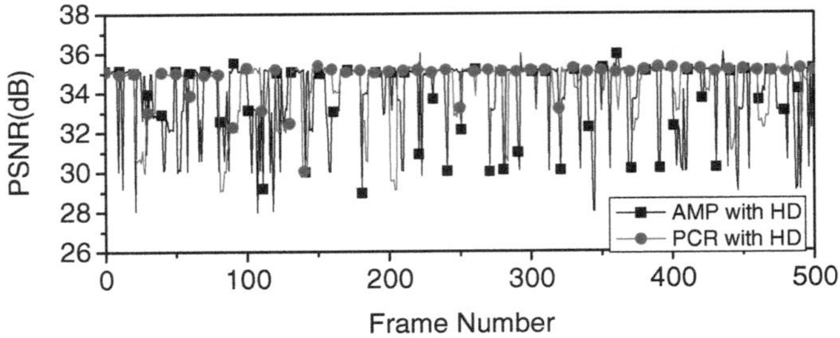

Fig. 6. PSNR comparison of AMP and PCR

occupancy around the normal range during the congestion period while the receiver buffer of AMP tends to overflow when the network condition is improved because of the lack of source rate control. For the HDTV trace, the sender and the receiver buffer of AMP tend to overflow and underflow respectively during the congestion period because the bit rates of HDTV are much higher and more variable, which makes the transmission of HDTV streams need more bandwidth while the AMP can not send the data timely at this time. After 200s, the receiver buffer of AMP increases burstly, which is expected to produce the video quality degradation. On the contrary, as PCR integrates source rate control with rate shaping, it can schedule the transmission rate according to the stream structure and significantly reduce the variation of the buffer, and thus achieve higher average PSNR and smaller PSNR variation than AMP, the values of which are depicted in Fig. 6. This experiment also demonstrates that it is more efficient to perform server-side rate control than receiver-side rate control in the multicast-based DTV streaming system.

We also evaluate the number of concurrent MPEG-2 HDTV channels on the premise of ensuring video quality. It can be seen from Fig. 7 that our system can support as many as 33 HDTV channels simultaneously and parallel channel numbers raise with the increase of server memory. However, it has little effect after the server memory is larger than 4G, which means that the bottleneck transfers to hard disk and available network bandwidth.

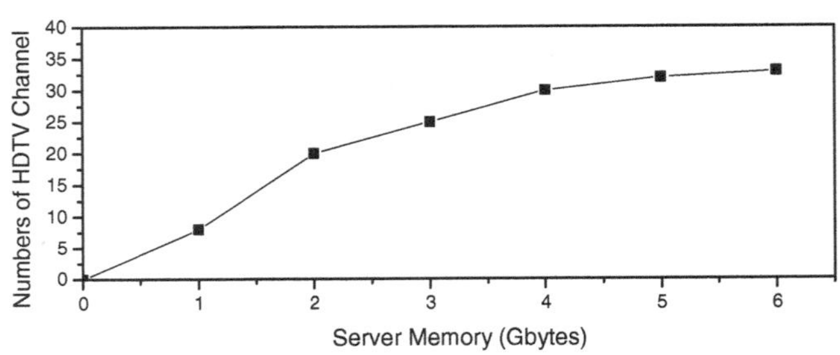

Fig. 7. Evaluation of concurrent channel number

5 Conclusions and Future work

In this paper, we propose a server-side approach for quality-optimal DTV streaming. PCR-based rate controller is used to regulate the transmission rate according to the timing information calculated by the PCRs in a refined way and TC-based rate shaper is ingeniously introduced to separate different channel streams to avoid bandwidth contesting. We also implement an experimental system and practical evaluation results have shown that the proposed algorithm can significantly improve the video quality and quality smoothness by reducing the overflow and underflow of both sender and receiver buffers. We will make enhancements to our home gateway devices so that the gateway can support playback rate adjustment in our future work.

Acknowledgments. This work was supported by the National Natural Science Foundation of China under Grant No.60434030, 60673178, 60472076 and the National Grand Fundamental Research 973 Program of China under Grant No.2007CB307106.

References

1. Williamson, B.: Developing IP Multicasting Networks (January 2000), ISBN 1-57870-077-9
2. Kalman, M., Steinbach, E., Girod, B.: Adaptive media playout for low-delay video streaming over error-prone channels. IEEE Trans. on Circuits and System for Video Technology 14(6), 841–851 (2004)
3. Luo, H., Shyu, M.-L., Chen, S.-C.: A multi-buffer scheduling scheme for video streaming. In: ICME. Proceedings of the IEEE International Conference on Multimedia & Expo, Amsterdam, The Netherlands, pp. 1218–1221 (July 2005)
4. Wong, C.-W., Au, O.C., Lam, H.-K.: PID-based real-time rate control. In: ICME. Proceedings of the IEEE International Conference on Multimedia & Expo, Taiwan, China, pp. 221–224 (June 2004)
5. Kamimura, K., Hasegawa, T., Hoshino, H., Ano, S., Hasegawa, T.: A practical multicast transmission control method for multi-channel HDTV IP broadcasting system. In: Proceeding of the Pacific Rim Conference on Multimedia, Jeju Island, Korea, pp. 429–440 (November 2005)
6. November, H.C., Jenwei, H., Juing, L.H., Chang, T.: PCR-Assist CBR for delivering pre-recorded MPEG-2 transport streams. In: ICMCS. Proceedings of the IEEE International Conference on Multimedia Computing and System, Ottawa, Canada, pp. 646–647 (June 1997)
7. Zhang, Y., Huangfu, W., Li, K., Xu, C.: Integrated rate control and buffer management for scalable video streaming. In: ICME. Proceedings of the IEEE International Conference on Multimedia & Expo, Beijing, China, pp. 248–251 (July 2007)
8. Wu, Z., Zhang, H., Wang, J.: Community network with integrated services. Journal of Software 14, 23–28 (2003)
9. Zhang, H., Wu, Z.: Traffic Control in Linux-Based Routers. Journal of Software 16(3), 462–471 (2005)
10. MPlayer software, http://www.mplayerhq.hu

Using Irradiance Environment Map on GPU for Real-Time Composition

Jonghyub Kim, Yongho Hwang, and Hyunki Hong

Dept. of Image Eng., GSAIM Chung-Ang Univ.
{hyubi00, hwangyh}@wm.cau.ac.kr, honghk@cau.ac.kr

Abstract. For the seamless integration of synthetic objects within video images, generating consistent illumination is critical. This paper presents an interactive rendering system using a Graphics Process Unit-based (GPU) irradiance environment map. A camcorder with a fisheye lens captures environmental information and constructs the environment map in real-time. The pre-filtering method, which approximates the irradiance of the scene using 9 parameters, renders diffuse objects within real images. This proposed interactive common illumination system based on the GPU can generate photo-realistic images at 18 ~ 20 frames per second.

Keywords: environment map, GPU, real-time rendering, irradiance, common illumination.

1 Introduction

The seamless integration of synthetic objects into real images is one of the most important areas in computer vision and graphics. In order to provide the illusion that virtual objects are parts of a real scene, the illumination of the environment should be taken into account when rendering virtual objects. Hence, to generate a photo-realistic scene, we use the global illumination (GI) models that simulate various light propagations [1]. However, these burden the system with high computation load and memory requirements. As the performance of GPU (Graphics Process Unit) continually improves, with increases of speed greater than that of the CPU, leveraging the GPU enables us to include a GI model and retain interactive frame rates [2].

In previous studies, the environment map was used as a classical technique of approximating specular reflections of the virtual object in interactive rendering [3]. Since the environment map stores the radiance incident from all directions at a reference point, it is widely used to generate environmental illumination in the real world. In addition, recent methods extended the environment map to work with complex materials, lighting and shadows [4-9]. However, there have been few methods that use the image sequence captured in real-time as the radiance texture for dealing with dynamically changing environmental illumination.

This paper proposes a method for the interactive common illumination of synthetic objects in video sequences through GPU-based irradiance environment mapping. The proposed system uses the camcorder with a fisheye lens, having a wide view angle, to

H.H.S. Ip et al. (Eds.): PCM 2007, LNCS 4810, pp. 704–713, 2007.

capture environmental information. In order to render the diffuse object in the dynamic environment map, a pre-filtering method is performed at every frame [4,5]. Experimental results show that, by using the irradiance environment map from the video camera, photo-realistic rendering images can be dynamically generated.

2 Related Work

Environment mapping was originally proposed for rendering ideal mirror surfaces with a perfect specular reflection. To include diffuse reflections of Lambertian surface in the environment map, irradiance information needs to be considered, which is reflected by the object surface owing to the Bi-directional Reflection Distribution Function (BRDF). Brute-Force technique is the traditional method of calculating irradiance. However, it is impossible implement in real-time because of a large number of instructions it requires.

To decrease the number of instructions and computational load, J. Kautz *et. al.* proposed an irradiance environment map [4]. Their method, aimed at real-time applications, generates the irradiance map in advance by prefiltering the environment map. This prefiltered environment map stored the radiance of light reflected towards the viewing direction, which is computed by weighting the incoming light from all directions with the BRDF. By using fast hierarchical prefiltering and GPU programming, they decreased precomputation time.

R. Ramamoorthi *et. al.* proposed a method which compresses the radiance environment map into 9 spherical harmonics coefficients in frequency space [5]. Using the spherical harmonic approximation allowed them to include complex materials under environmental illumination with little precomputation. Furthermore, because the irradiance environment map could be generated from only 9 coefficients, rendering was more efficient. Their research, not only introduced the diffuse property, but also glossy reflections [9]. J. Kautz *et. al.* presented a method rending system for VR applications [6] and G. King introduced a technique replicating the above methods on the GPU [7].

The aforementioned researches have dealt mainly with static situations in a fixed illumination environment. V. Havran *et. al.* proposed an interactive system to handle HDR image-based lighting captured in dynamic, real world conditions, with complex shadows and arbitrary reflectance models [6]. However, they focused mainly on the issues of temporal coherence and control over the number of sample lights [8]. In this paper we modify the environment mapping on the GPU to generate photo-realistic rendered images at interactive frame rates in dynamic environment.

3 Proposed System

The calibration information of the fisheye lens converts every frame of the image sequence captured by the camcorder to the environment map. The resulting environment map, which provides the environmental radiance, is represented by 9 spherical harmonics coefficients [10]. According to the object surface normal vector, diffuse reflections from the reconstructed irradiance function are obtained [5]. By using a reflection direction calculated from the surface normal and the viewing vector, a texel is obtained, which in turn is, used to create a specular reflection on the environment map [11]. In the final step, the computed specular and diffuse reflection values are interpolated linearly to include two surface properties, specular and diffuse. For real-time compositing, the entire process is iterated at every frame.

3.1 Omni-Directional Image Conversion

Since the environment map needs to capture incident radiance from a fixed position, the system uses a fisheye lens due to its wide Field of View (FOV). The omni-directional image is converted into perspective-transformed textures consisting of the environment map. For dynamically updating the environment map, we use a Look-Up Table (LUT) that stores a mapping of position vectors in the omni-directional image with its corresponding textures.

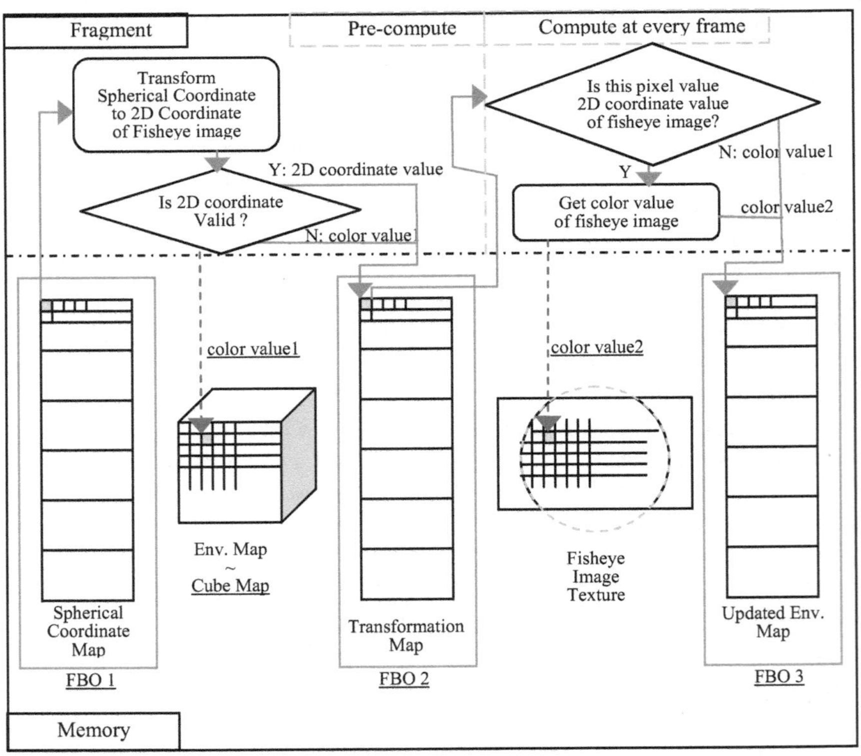

Fig. 1. Process of generating the environment map from video images

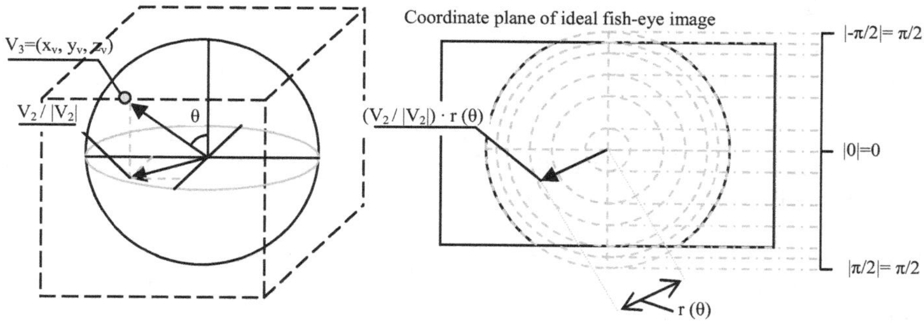

Fig. 2. Transformation of spherical coordinate to omni-directional image

$$V_3 = (x_v, y_v, z_v) \rightarrow F = (x_f, y_f) \qquad V_2 = (x_v, y_v) \ , \theta = \arccos(z_v)$$

$$r(\theta) = \sin\theta, \quad F(V_2, \theta) = \begin{pmatrix} x_f \\ y_f \end{pmatrix} = \begin{pmatrix} s_u & 0 \\ 0 & s_v \end{pmatrix} * \left(\frac{V_2}{|V_2|} \cdot r(\theta) \right) - \begin{pmatrix} t_u \\ t_v \end{pmatrix} \qquad (1)$$

In order to map the omni-directional image to a cube map, we use texture images, with resolutions of N×6N (width×height), as shown in Fig. 1. By normalizing the positional vector at the center of the cube, spherical coordinates are determined, and the spherical map is constructed. In Equation (1), the sine function of r transforms the spherical coordinates on the map to pixel coordinates on the omni-directional image. Compared to sine function, calibration of the omni-directional imaging system enables the estimation of a more precise projection model [12]. In Equation (1), s and t represent the scale and the translation parameters in u and v, respectively. Fig. 1 shows our process for generating the environment map using Frame Buffer Object (FBO) in the fragment program of the GPU.

After comparing the computed coordinates derived from Equation (1) with the width and height of the texture image and the radius of the omni-directional image, we determine a coordinate applicable to the environment map. When the obtained coordinates are in the effective image region, the omni-directional image pixel is stored in the environment map. Since a 180-degree fisheye lens is used in this paper, the entire 360-degree environment from the reference point is not updated. Hence, the computed coordinate located outside of the fisheye lens's FOV is not updated in real-time. Unseen regions are filled with initial images captured beforehand from the reverse reference point. For dynamic coverage of 360 degrees, a specially designed video camera may be equipped.

Fig. 1 shows generation of the transformed map from every texel of the spherical coordinate map, obtained through equation (1). This operation is performed in the fragment program, where all processes are parallel in each fragment. Using 3D vectors, the cube environment map of the fragment program is accessed efficiently. Fig. 3 shows the use of 3D and 2D environment maps. Transforming a 2D environment map to a 3D cube map requires significant computation time. We use the cube map for converting 3D vectors to 2D texture coordinates for real-time applications, in order to update the environment map with every frame of the omni-directional video.

In the environment map, the neighboring environment is usually at a large distance from the reference point [11]. Assuming this, we access the texel value using the reflection vector, regardless of the position of the object surface. However, coping with the reflection change due to the object motion is problematic, thus, a localizing method is utilized to address this [13].

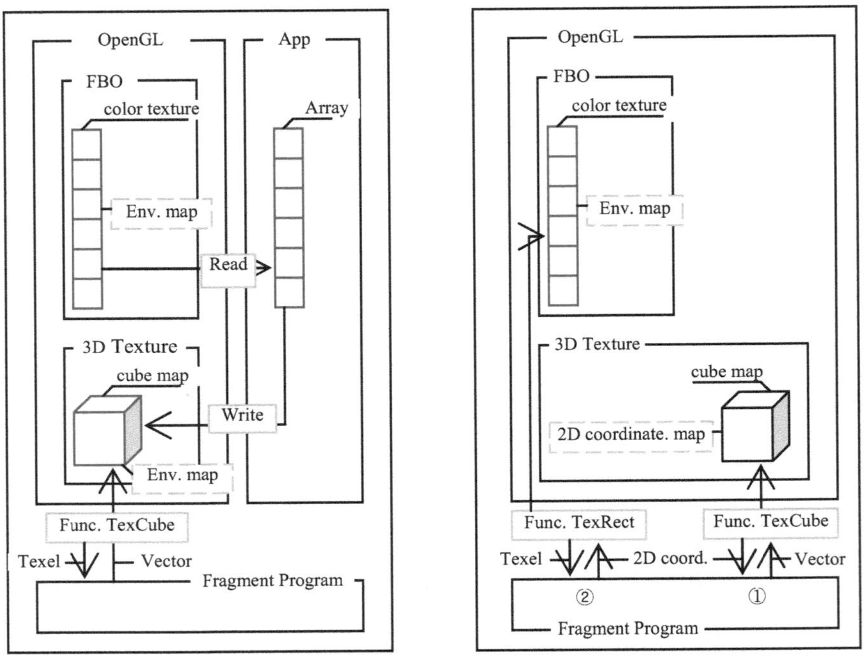

Fig. 3. Using 3D environment map (left) and 2D environment map (right)

3.2 Spherical Harmonic

The method we apply for calculating 9 spherical harmonics coefficients, Equation (2), was first proposed in [5]. We use L and Y_{lm} to denote the radiance environment map and the weight function for the spherical harmonic. Y_{lm}, therefore, represents the sum of the values of all pixels of the radiance environment map, which is weighted by the spherical harmonic as follows:

$$L_{lm} = \int_{\theta=0}^{\pi} \int_{\phi=0}^{2\pi} L(\theta,\phi) Y_{lm}(\theta,\phi) \sin\theta \, d\theta \, d\phi \tag{2}$$

The first step is to transform the texture coordinates of the environment map to spherical coordinates. This transformation is stored as a coordinate map, which is referenced in every frame by the fragment programs on the GPU. Second, three texture maps, to integrate the weighted radiance environment map according to the spherical harmonics, are generated [14]. This integration is performed rapidly on the GPU because every pixel computation on the fragment program runs in parallel. Although 9 coefficients can be directly computed from 9 textures, our system generates three textures at most due to the specification of the graphics driver. That is, 4 color-attachment textures of FBO are used [14, 15] at most by the graphics driver. Among these 4 textures, three are used to store the weighted environment map and one is utilized for sum-reduction of the integration of texture values [16].

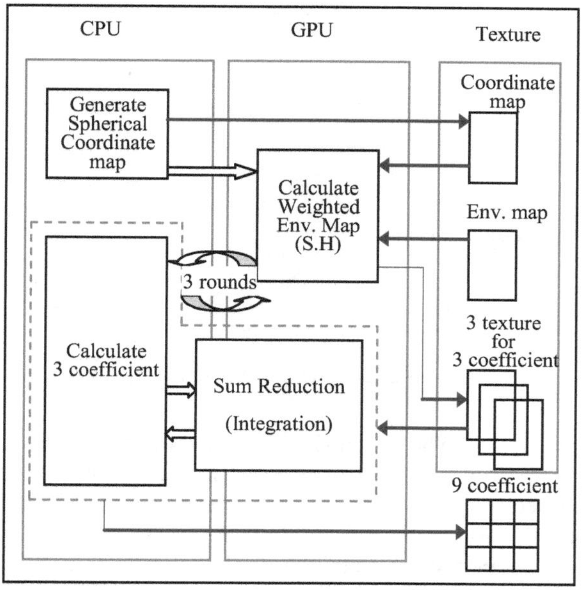

Fig. 4. Computing 9 coefficients

The coefficients are computed from the sum of every pixel value of the texture, and our system uses a reduction technique for this process [16]. This technique hierarchically decreases the range of computation by switching between the input and the output texture buffers. Among the 4 textures of the FBO, three are previously generated, and the unused one is designated as the output texture. In this case, 9 coefficients are computed from procedures repeated for three cycles in generation of the three textures, and from these generated textures, values of the weighted radiance of the textures are integrated.

4 Experimental Results

The image capture equipment used in our experiments for the environment map are, a video camera (SONY PD-150) with fisheye lens (Raynox DCR-CF185PRO), and the resolution of the rendered image is 1024×768. The computation equipment is an Intel Core 2 Duo CPU with an nVIDIA Geforce 7950 GPU, and the openGL Utility

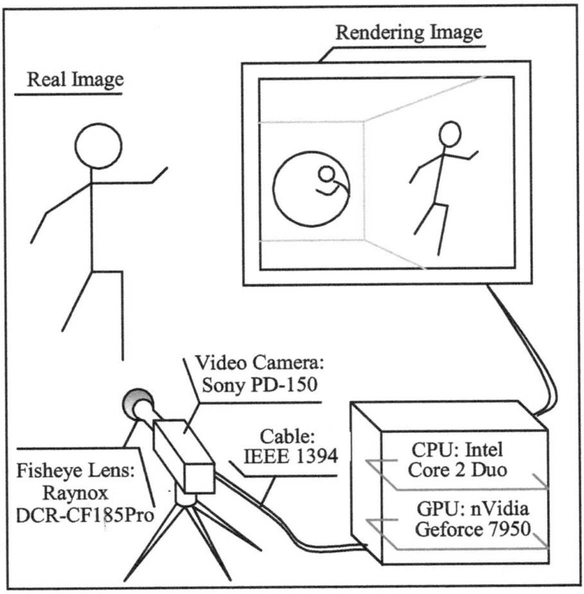

Fig. 5. System construction

Toolkit (GLUT) was used. The car model has 52,194 polygons and Fig. 5 shows the setup for dynamic environment mapping. For dynamically updating the environment map, the position vector of each pixel of the input image had to be calculated using the calibration information of the fisheye lens. Fig. 6 shows the rendered images of the object with the specular, diffuse and the combined reflections.

A callback function in GLUT to display the rendered image was called at 60 frames per second (fps). Table 1 shows that the frame rate when updating the environment map (UEM) with the omni-directional image is 60 fps. Since the NTSC camcorder (CAM) captures the video images at 30 fps, the overall rendering speed decreases to the frame rate of the imaging system. In addition, the computation of spherical harmonics affects the performance of the system, lowering frame rate to 20 fps.

Table 1. Comparison of rendering times in each process

UEM	CAM	SH	FPS
O	X	X	60
O	O	X	29~30
O	X	O	18~20
O	O	O	18~20

In the case of the spherical harmonics, 9 textures with 480×2880 (= 480×6×480) resolution are generated, and the summation operation at each texel of the texture is performed. If the computation load of these operations is K, the weight computation,

Fig. 6. Rendered images. Colored model (upper-left), diffuse reflection (upper-right), specular reflection (middle-left), combined reflections (middle-right, down).

and the summation operation using the sum reduction method, are 480×2880×K and 480×2880×K×(1+1/3). Yielding a total system computation time of 480×2880×(2×9+1/3)×K. Additionally, the computation complexity of the spherical harmonics coefficients is O(N2) when the environmental texture is N×6N. Therefore, system performance largely depends on the resolution of the environmental texture.

In the rendered images, the neighboring regions between the updated image in real-time and the initial textures, where the real-time captured image and the composited reverse 180-degree image meet, form a distinct border. Using a special imaging system allows us to capture 360 degrees at the reference point, and to compensate for these border problems. The proposed interactive system generates photo-realistic rendered images of the object including the specular and diffuse reflections in a dynamic illumination environment at 18 ~ 20 fps.

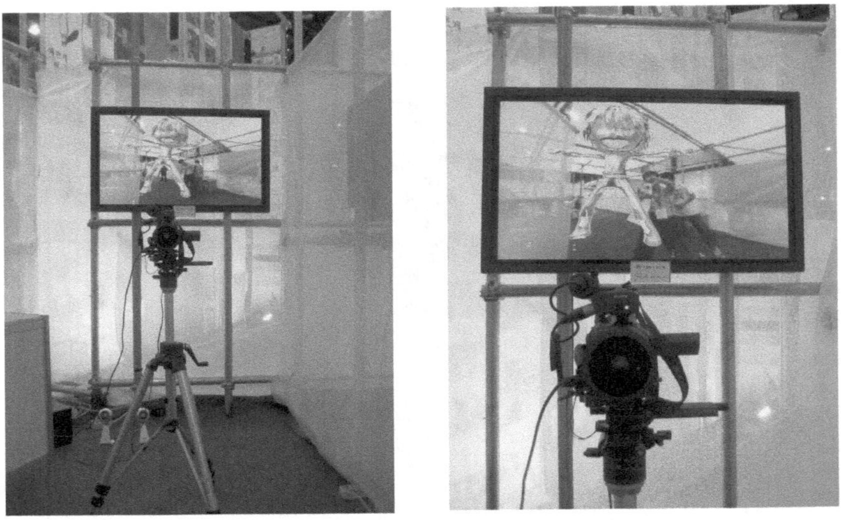

Fig. 7. Exhibition of interactive irradiance mapping system [17]

5 Conclusion

This paper presents a novel system that can generate specular and diffuse reflections in a dynamic illumination environment. In order to render these composite images in real-time, we dynamically implement the irradiance environment mapping on the GPU. Experimental results demonstrate that the proposed common illumination system can generate photo-realistic images at interactive frame rates. In near future, we shall include more efficient prefiltering techniques to reduce computation load, and introduce additional measures to overcome the motion parallax problem.

Acknowledgments. This research was supported by Seoul Future Contents Convergence (SFCC) Cluster established by Seoul R&BD Program, and by the Korea Culture and Content Agency on the CT project.

References

1. Fournier, A., Gunawan, A., Romanzin, C.: Common illumination between real and computer generated scenes. In: Proc. of Graphics Interface, pp. 254–262 (1993)
2. Szirmay-Kalos, L., Szécsi, L., Sbert, M.: GPUGI: Global illumination effects on the GPU. Eurographics Tutorial (2006)

3. Greene, N.: Environment mapping and other applications of world projections. IEEE Computer Graphics and Applications 6(11), 21–29 (1986)
4. Kautz, J., Vazquez, P., Heidrich, W., Seidel, H.P.: A unified approach to prefiltered environment maps. In: EuroGraphics Rendering Workshop, pp. 185–196 (2000)
5. Ramamoorthi, R., Hanrahan, P.: An efficient representation for irradiance environment maps. In: Proc. of SIGGRAPH, pp. 497–500 (2001)
6. Kautz, J., Daubert, K., Seidel, H.P.: Advanced environment mapping in VR applications. Computers & Graphics 28, 99–104 (2004)
7. King, G.: Real-time computation of dynamic irradiance environment maps; GPU Germs, vol. 2(4), pp. 98–105. Addison-Wesley Professional, London, UK (2005)
8. Havran, V., Smyk, M., Myszkowski, K., Seidel, H.P.: Interactive system for dynamic scene lighting using captured video environment maps. In: Proc. of Eurographics Symposium on Rendering, pp. 31–42 (2005)
9. Ramamoorthi, R., Hanrahan, P.: Frequency space environment map rendering. In: Proc. of SIGGRAPH, pp. 517–526 (2002)
10. Dempski, K., Viale, E.: Spherical harmonic lighting; advanced lighting and materials with shaders, pp. 157–210. Wordware Publishing, Inc. (2005)
11. Fernando, R., Kilgard, M.: Environment mapping techniques. The Cg Tutorial: The Definitive Guide to Programmable Real-Time Graphics. Addison-Wesley Professional, pp. 169–197 (2003)
12. Kannala, J., Brandt, S.: A generic camera calibration method for fish-eye lenses. In: Proc. Of ICPR, vol. 1, pp. 10–13 (2004)
13. Bjorke, K.: Image-based lighting. GPU Germs, vol. 1, pp. 307–321. Addison-Wesley Professional, London, UK (2004)
14. OpenGL.org.: The Framebuffer, http://www.rush3d.com/reference/opengl-redbook-1.1/chapter10. html
15. Shreiner, D., Woo, M., Neider, J., Davis, T.: OpenGL Programming Guide. Addison-Wesley Professional, London, UK (2005)
16. Göddeke, D.: GPGPU Reduction Tutorial, http://www.mathematik.uni-dortmund.de/~goeddeke /gpgpu/tutorial2.html
17. Kim, J., Hong, H.: Plastic fairy. Seoul International Cartoon & Animation Festival, Seoul Korea (May 23-27, 2007)

Ranking Using Multi-features in Blog Search

Kangmiao Liu, Guang Qiu, Jiajun Bu*, and Chun Chen

College of Computer Science, Zhejiang University
Hangzhou 310027, China
{lkm, qiuguang, bjj, chenc}@zju.edu.cn

Abstract. Blog has received lots of attention since the revolution of Web 2.0 and has attracted millions of users to publish information on it. As time goes by, information seeking in this new media becomes an emergent issue. In our paper, we take multiple features unique in blogs into account and propose a novel algorithm to rank the blog posts in blog search. Coherence between the query type and blogger interest, document relevance and freshness are combined linearly to produce the final ranking score of a post. Specifically, we introduce a user modeling method to capture interests of bloggers. In our experiments, we invite volunteers to complete several tasks and their time cost in the tasks is taken as the primary criteria to evaluate the performance. The experimental results show that our algorithm outperforms traditional ones.

Keywords: Blog search, ranking, multiple features, interest model.

1 Introduction

With the increase in the web's accessibility to the masses in recent years, the web content is changing. Especially since the revolution of Web 2.0, more and more web users participate in web activities, showing themselves off through the Internet. Blog, short for web-log, is a representative web application in which people record their daily lives, publish personal views on popular issues, or some other personal things. According to "Chinalabs.com", there are sixteen million blogs in China while the number is one hundred million around the world in September 2005. Thus, as time goes by, huge amount of information is collected in the blogosphere -- the collection of all blogs. The information seeking efficiency and effectiveness become a crucial issue.

Solutions to problems should be proposed according to requirements. So it is with the information seeking issue in blogosphere. As summarized in [1], it is assumed that any blog search engine should provide better-than usual searches in three specific domains which in other words describe the intentions of users using the engines: topic search, blogger search and reputation search. The topic search means to find interesting/funny topics mainly for entertainment purpose, the blogger search means to find blogger with similar interests or preferences and the reputation search means to find reviews or experiences of a specific product or service. Aside from these three aspects, we've also observed another user requirement that to find the degree of the

* Corresponding author, +86 571 87952148.

H.H.S. Ip et al. (Eds.): PCM 2007, LNCS 4810, pp. 714–723, 2007.

popularity of one's own or other's blog on the Internet. Some people are eager for being famous in some area and being concerned by others. We call this requirement as popularity search.

There's already lots of work done on the information seeking problem in blogosphere, such as the blog search services provided by Google (http://blogsearch.google.com) and Baidu (http://blogsearch.baidu.com) which are the leading search engines for English and Chinese respectively. However, their demonstration of search results, which meanwhile reflects the retrieval mechanism and ranking strategy, is quite similar to ordinary web search and thus fails to meet the requirements of blog search mentioned above.

In this paper, we propose a novel ranking algorithm, considering the categories of queries, the interest of bloggers and the text relevance and freshness, to fulfill the requirements in information seeking in blogosphere taking the unique features of blogs into consideration. We adopt a classical text classification approach to handle the query classification and a novel user modeling algorithm to describe user's interest. Text relevance and freshness are measured based on the vector space model and time stamp respectively.

The rest of the paper is organized as follows. In section 2, we describe related work in brief. Then we elaborate our proposed ranking algorithm in section 3. Experiments and results are demonstrated in section 4. Finally, we give the conclusions and future work in section 5.

2 Related Work

Lots of work has already been done on search result ranking in retrieval systems for web pages. A classical algorithm in web page ranking is PageRank proposed by the two founders of Google ([1]). Let *E(u)* be some vector over the Web pages that corresponds to a source of rank. Then the PageRank of a set of Web pages is an assignment, *R*, to the Web pages which satisfies:

$$R(u) = c\sum_{v\in B_u}\frac{R(v)}{N_v} + cE(u) \tag{1}$$

such that c is maximized and the L_1 norm of R equals 1. In the equation, B_u is the set of pages that point to page u and N_v is the number of links from page v. They propose a random surfer model to explain their algorithm. Imagining a user making a surfer on the web, he may keep clicking on successive links at random. However, if he gets into a small loop of web pages, it is unlikely that he will continue in the loop forever. Instead, he will jump to some other page with some probability. The factor E in the equation can be viewed as a way of modeling this behavior: the probability user jumps to a random page.

In previous work on blog search, they do not take use of the characteristic of blog fully ([2], [3], [4], [5]). Authors in [2] take the blog search needs into account and propose a multi-faceted blog search engine to provide different kinds of services to meet different needs. Their work in [3] proposes an algorithm called "EigenRumor" to rank the blog entries (posts). The algorithm scores each blog entry by weighting the hub and authority scores of the bloggers based on eigenvector calculations. It enables a higher score to be assigned to the blog entries submitted by a good blogger but not yet linked to by any other blogs based on acceptance of the blogger's prior work. However, neither of them takes the types of queries and the interests of the bloggers into consideration.

Query type identification can be considered as a specified type of text classification task in which the text is a query consisting of few words. There is already lots of work done on this identification task, which can be roughly divided into two categories: unsupervised and supervised learning classification. Authors in [6] use the common click-through documents to discover the latent relationships between queries, and further cluster similar queries together. However, this clustering approach has no idea of what kinds of types will be gained in the end and also requires expensive computation. Supervised learning classification has also been widely adopted in this area. Luis Gravano et al. in [7] use three machine learning methods to experiment the query classification based on geographical locality, including PIPPER, log-linear regression and SVMs. Dou Shen et al. implement the SVMs classification method to classify queries into predefined 67 categories ([8]). In [9], the perceptron with Margins algorithm is adopted, which is stated to be competitive with state-of-the-art algorithms such as SVMs in text classification and computationally efficient.

Another work related is personalization, particularly the usage-based Web personalization. The goal of web personalization is to provide users with the information they want or need, without expecting from them to ask for it explicitly ([11]). As described in [10], a typical personalization process consists of five modules: User profiling, Log analysis and Web usage mining, Content management, Web site publishing and Information acquisition and searching. In our work, we concern more about user profiling. This module gathers information specific to each visitor, either explicitly or implicitly. It includes demographic information about the user, his interests and even his behavior when browsing a web site. All the previous work done on user profiling can be divided into two categories: knowledge-based and behavior-based ([12]). Knowledge-based approaches engineer static models of users and dynamically match users to the closest model. Questionnaires and interviews are often employed to obtain this user knowledge. Behavior-based approaches use the user's behavior as a model, commonly using machine learning techniques to discover useful patterns in the behavior ([13]). In our paper, we propose a novel user modeling approach to capture the interest of a blogger. Machine learning methods are employed in our method.

3 Ranking Using Multi-features

In our ranking algorithm, three factors are considered, including query type, blogger interest, and document attribute consisting of relevance and freshness. The ranking score of a document (named as "post" in blogs) is formulated as follows:

$$Score = \alpha \times \frac{documentRelevance}{documentFreshness} + \beta \times typeCoherence\,, \tag{2}$$

where *alpha* and *beta* are two parameters that have to be estimated empirically to balance the importance of different factors.

documentRelevance is the relevance between the query and document determined by the classical cosine similarity measure. Given a query Q represented by an n-dimensional vector $<q_1, q_2, q_3, \ldots, q_n>$ and a document D represented by another n-dimensional vector $<d_1, d_2, d_3, \ldots, d_n>$, the cosine similarity is measured by following formula:

$$documentRelevance(Q, D) = \frac{\sum_{i=1}^{n} q_i d_i}{\sqrt{\sum_{i=1}^{n} q_i^2}\sqrt{\sum_{i=1}^{n} d_i^2}}, \tag{3}$$

where q_i and d_i is the weight of the words carrying in the query and document respectively, quantified by TFIDF.

documentFreshness represents the freshness of the document to measure how "recent" the document is to the query time. Gilad Mishne mentions in [14] the usage of temporal properties of blog search. They conduct a study on a blog search engine log ([15]) and show that a substantial amount of blog queries are *recency queries* – queries which favor recent documents rather than having an even distribution of relevance. Therefore in the ranking strategy, it seems to be useful to assign a higher ranking score to blog posts which were "recent" at the time the query was issued ([14]). In our paper, given a document D posted on the date T_{post}, the degree of "recent" – freshness is measured as follows:

$$documentFreshness(D) = \log_2(2 + T_{issue} - T_{post}) \tag{4}$$

Where T_{issue} is the date when the query is issued. A smoothing const 2 is added in case of zero divider.

Table 1. Categories defined in our work

Categories	Examples
IT	ipod price
Finance	shanghai stock market
Health	SARS
Education	early learning
Military	USA military budget
Trip	Hong Kong Disney
Sports	NBA Yaoming
Culture	Harry Potter
Job	software engineer Hangzhou

typeCoherence measures the coherence between the type of the query and the interest of the blogger, which has never been considered in previous work. We take this factor into account because of the prevailing intention in blog search, that to find out bloggers of some interest. However, in a search process, users can only describe their interest needs through the query issued, thus we measure the coherence between the interest of the query (type) and that of the blogger. Based on the categories defined in our paper (as shown in table 1), query type and blogger interest are both represented as a vector of categories, with the value in every dimension measured by the probabilities the query/blogger interest belongs to the corresponding category. Then the coherence is measured by the cosine similarity between these two vectors as given in equation 2. Consequently, two questions arise in measuring this factor: how to obtain the query type and how to model the blogger. Sections below show our solutions in details.

3.1 Query Classification

As mentioned above, query classification can be regarded as a specified task of text classification. Therefore, typical text classification approaches can be adopted in this task, such as Naive Bayes classifier and SVMs (Support Vector Machines). Considering the state-of-the-art performance in classification, we take use of the SVMs classifier to do the classification. The popular toolkit libsvm[1] is employed in our work.

For machine learning approaches, training data are indispensable. In our work, a training data set consisting of a number of labeled queries is needed. However, building such a corpus would be a tedious and heavy job. Therefore in our current work, we take use of an available data set – the sogou[2] text classification corpus which consists of approximate one hundred thousand web pages labeled manually with the same category definition mentioned above. Another more profound reason is that queries always contain only limited number of words, sometimes only one or two words, which can not fully reflect features of a category. Thus the classifier trained from these queries will not be able to predict new ones correctly as it self has not captured features of categories yet. However, we believe a classifier trained from web pages, which contain adequate words and features of categories, would be competent for the task. In our training phase, we set about 1330 web pages for one category, resulting in about 11970 pages totally as the training data.

3.2 Blogger Modeling

Lots of features exist in a blog reflecting the interest of a blogger, such as his job, his hobbies (if he provides in his blog) and the blog posts which are also the most common evidence that can be accessed conveniently. In our work, we take advantage of these posted texts to model the interest of the blogger.

Firstly, we categorize each post into one of the nine categories defined in our work. This is a typical text classification task and thus we employ the SVM method to do the categorization. The classifier trained for query classification can be used. Each post will be assigned with the probabilities it belongs to different categories. Given a post P and the category set $\{C\}$, we represent P as a vector:

---

[1] http://www.csie.ntu.edu.tw/~cjlin/libsvm/

[2] http://www.sogou.com

$$P = < w_1, w_2, w_3, \ldots, w_n > , \tag{5}$$

where w_j is the probability P belongs to category C_j.

Then, considering a situation that the blogger only has one post in his blog which is posted on sometime T_i, we introduce a *1-n interest matrix* ***IM*** to model the interest of that blogger:

$$IM = [m_{i1} \quad m_{i2} \quad m_{i3} \quad \ldots \quad m_{in}], \tag{6}$$

where the row of the matrix represents a time stamp, a column j represents the interest of the blogger to the corresponding category C_j and m_{ij} takes the value of w_j.

As time goes by, the blogger publishes more and more posts. Suppose he has got totally t posts in his blog by a given time stamp T_k, we construct the *interest matrix* ***IM*** of him as follows:

$$IM = \begin{bmatrix} m_{11} & m_{12} & \ldots & m_{1j} & \ldots m_{1n} \\ m_{21} & m_{22} & \ldots & m_{2j} & \ldots m_{2n} \\ \ldots & \ldots & \ldots & \ldots & \ldots \ldots \\ m_{i1} & m_{i2} & \ldots & m_{ij} & \ldots m_{in} \\ \ldots & \ldots & \ldots & \ldots & \ldots \ldots \\ m_{t1} & m_{t2} & \ldots & m_{tj} & \ldots m_{tn} \end{bmatrix}, \tag{7}$$

in which m_{ij} denotes his interest to category C_j at time T_i.

Finally, given the *interest matrix* describing user's interests at different time stamps, we propose two approaches to model his overall interests by far. One simple approach is just to sum all the rows together and the resulting vector will be the quantified description of his interests. In other words, this vector is the *interest model* ***M*** of the user and each entry is calculated as follows:

$$M_j = \sum_{i=1}^{t} m_{ij} \tag{8}$$

However, considering the nature of memory attenuation of human beings, we reduce the importance of posts published long ago in describing the interests. A second approach is therefore proposed to model the overall interests of bloggers with this factor included. Specifically, we introduce an *attenuation factor* $F(t_k)$ to quantify the degree of attenuation of the post published at time t_k. The factor is given by following formula:

$$F(t_k) = e^{-\frac{\log_2(t_0 - t_k)}{hl}}, \tag{9}$$

where t_0 is current time and hl is the period of time after which the blogger will only remain half of the interest compared with that he showed when the post was written at

t_k. Consequently, we update the calculation of each entry in our first *interest model* ***M*** as follows:

$$M'_j = \sum_{i=1}^{t} F(t_i) m_{ij} \quad (10)$$

We believe that our second model ***M'*** would be able to describe the interests of bloggers more precisely as it adheres to nature of human beings compared with the simple strengthening strategy in ***M***.

4 Experiments and Results

To compare the performance of our ranking algorithm with others, we implement a prototype retrieval system based on the proposed algorithm. In the following sections, we'll describe the experiment strategy adopted in our work and then demonstrate the results.

4.1 Experiment Strategy

It's not easy to evaluate the performance of our ranking algorithm as there is no available standard corpus ready to use. Precision, recall or F1 measure, which is widely employed in evaluations of text retrieval and categorization, is no longer suitable. Therefore, in our experiment, we evaluate our algorithm through the efficiency in completing specific tasks instead.

Given several tasks, dozens of volunteers are invited to find out answers through searching. Firstly these volunteers are divided equally into two groups, one using our system and the other using Google blog search. All results are given out in our own format to ensure that volunteers would be unaware of which system they are using. Then they are asked to complete several tasks and their cost time is recorded. The average cost time of a group in finishing tasks is calculated and taken as the major criteria to evaluate the performance. Another two judgers make the decisions if the returned answers are appropriate ones.

As it is impractical for us to crawl as many blog pages as Google, we build our system based on the returned results by Google. Firstly, we set queries for each task in advance (volunteers can only use these queries) and save the results returned by Google for these queries as the initial corpus. Interest models are calculated for these bloggers based on all the posts in each one's blog. This strategy also ensures the comparison is made in same context. Another issue we have to concern is that volunteers might make mistakes in selecting answers. In that case, their cost time would be punished by adding in the maximum cost time in the same group.

The tasks selected in our experiments are shown as follows:

Task 1: *Find a blogger who is interested in sports.*
Task 2: *Find a blog post containing reviews on ipod.*
Task 3: *Find a blog post containing descriptions on ipod.*
Task 4: *Find the blog post containing the latest reviews on ipod.*

We distinguish between reviews and descriptions in that reviews are subjective personal comments while descriptions are objective introductions and we believe that users of blog search prefer the former.

4.2 Parameter Estimation and Model Selection

Two variables *alpha* and *beta* exist in our ranking algorithm. In our current work, we make the assumption that *alpha* plus *beta* takes one. Therefore, we only have to estimate one parameter indeed. A similar strategy as described above is adopted to evaluate performance when *alpha* varies from 0 to 1. Several volunteers are employed to complete the four tasks showed above using our system. We also compare the performance when different *interest models* are employed. Because of limited space, we only show the results of Task 1.

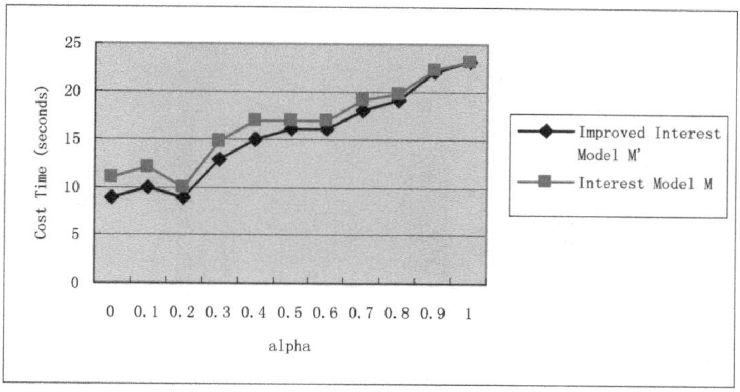

Fig. 1. Cost time in completing Task 1 using different values of parameters and interest models

One observation from the figure above is that the improved *interest model M'* outperforms the initial model *M*, which verifies our aforementioned assumptions. The two curves merge as *alpha* increases because the algorithm considers more on the document relevance rather than blogger interest as the weight of the blogger interest decreases. Another observation is that in both situations, the minimum cost time is obtained when *alpha* takes value of 0.2 which means that the coherence between query type and interest model to be the primary factor in ranking.

Results of other tasks also show the excellent performance of the improved *interest model M'*. However, they suggest that *alpha* should take different values in each task other than 0.2. The reason is that different tasks emphasize different features of the blog. For example, task 1 emphasizes more on the interest of the blogger while other tasks emphasize on the other factor. In order to unit different kinds of tasks into one single framework, in our current work, we just assign *alpha* with the average value of those in different tasks.

4.3 Results and Discussions

Figure below demonstrates the average cost time of the two groups in finishing each task. The results show that in tasks 1, 2, and 4, our system outperforms Google Blog search. The reason is that these tasks are all closely related to the features of blogs which Google has not taken into consideration. Specifically, in tasks 2 and 4, personal reviews of a product are more likely to exist in blogs of people who are really interested in that one or corresponding category. Therefore, our algorithm, that takes that feature into account, performs well in these two tasks. The performance of task 4 also shows the effectiveness of considering the document freshness. An exception is that in task 3 our algorithm performs a little worse than Google due to our naive relevance measurement. However, this kind of task only occupies a low percent in blog search and thus the poor performance would only affect the overall performance to a limited extent.

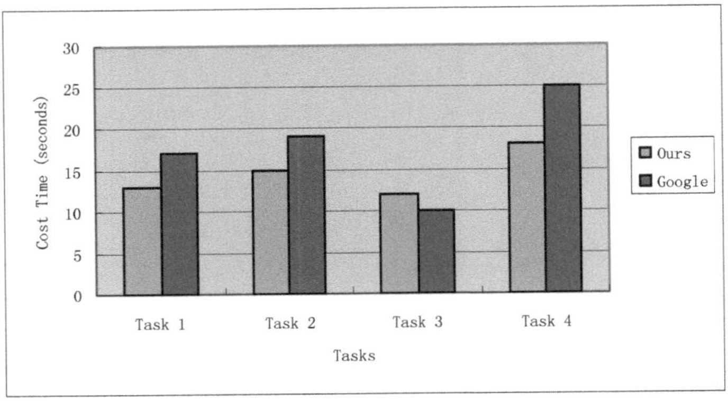

Fig. 2. Time cost in different tasks using our system and Google blog search

5 Conclusions and Future Work

With the flourish of blog, information seeking in this new media has become an emergent issue. Challenges exist in the ranking strategy of the blog posts as blogs possess of some unique features. In our work, we propose a novel algorithm to rank blog posts, combining multiple features linearly: coherence between the query type and interest of the blogger, document relevance and freshness. Specifically, we've put forward a user modeling method to describe interests of a blogger through the analysis of posts. In our experiments, we invite volunteers to complete several tasks through our system and Google and their cost time is taken as the primary criteria to evaluate the performance of our algorithm. The experiments show encouraging results.

In the future, we plan to investigate other combination methods to utilize different features other than the linear one. What's more, we also plan to implement a blog search system to provide services to users with a new style in result demonstration.

References

1. Page, L., Brin, S., Motwani, R., Winograd, T.: The PageRank Citation Ranking: Bringing Order to the Web. Stanford Digital Libraries Working Paper (1999), http://www-diglib.stanford.edu
2. Fujimura, K., Toda, H., Inoue, T., Hiroshima, N.: BLOGRANGER-A Multi-faceted Blog Search Engine. In: Proceedings of the WWW 2006 Workshop on the Weblogging Ecosystem: Aggregation, Analysis and Dynamics (2006)
3. Fujimura, K., Inoue, T., Sugizaki, M.: The EigenRumor Algorithm for Ranking Blogs. In: Proceedings of the WWW 2005 Workshop on the Weblogging Ecosystem: Aggregation, Analysis and Dynamics (2005)
4. Bloglines, http://www.bloglines.com
5. Blogpulse, http://www.blogpulse.com
6. Beeferman, D., Berger, A.: Agglomerative Clustering of a Search Engine Query Log. In: Proceedings of the sixth ACM SIGKDD international conference on Knowledge discovery and data mining, pp. 407–416 (2000)
7. Gravano, L., Hatzivassiloglou, V., Lichtenstein, R.: Categorizing Web Queries According to Geographical Locality. In: Proceedings of the twelfth international conference on Information and knowledge management, pp. 325–333 (2003)
8. Shen, D., Pan, R., Sun, J.-T., Pan, J.J., Wu, K., Yin, J., Yang, Q.: Q2C@UST: Our Winning Solution to Query Classification in KDDCUP 2005. In: ACM SIGKDD Explorations Newsletter, pp.100–110 (2005)
9. Beitzel, S.M., Jensen, E.C., Frieder, O., Grossman, D., Lewis, D.D., Chowdhury, A., Kolcz, A.: Automatic web query classification using labeled and unlabeled training data. In: Proceedings of the 28th annual international ACM SIGIR conference on Research and development in information retrieval, pp. 581–582 (2005)
10. Eirinaki, M., Vazirgiannis, M.: Web mining for web personalization. ACM Transaction on Internet Technology 3(1), 1–27 (2003)
11. Mulvenna, M.D, Anand, S.S., Buchner, A.G.: Personalization on the Net using Web mining: introduction. Communications of the ACM 43(8), 122–125 (2000)
12. Middleton, S.E., Shadbolt, N.R., De Roure, D.C.: Ontological User Profiling in Recommender Systems. ACM Transactions on Information Systems (TOIS) 22(1), 54–88 (2004)
13. Webb, G.I., Pazzani, M.J., Billsus, D.: Machine Learning for User Modeling. User Modeling and User-Adapted Interaction 11(1-2), 19–29 (2004)
14. Mishne, G.: Multiple Ranking Strategies for Opinion Retrieval in Blogs. In: TREC 2006. Proceedings of the fifteenth Text Retrieval Conference (2006)
15. Mishne, G., de Rijke, M.: A study of blog search. In: Proceedings of ECIR 2006, pp. 289–301 (2006)

Design and Analysis of a Watermarking System for Care Labels

Benjamin Ragan-Kelley and Nicholas Tran*

Department of Mathematics & Computer Science
Santa Clara University, Santa Clara, CA 95053-0290
{bragankelley, ntran}@scu.edu

Abstract. A watermarking system for embedding textile care labels directly onto fabric designs is proposed, and its stochastic properties are analyzed. Under the assumption that pixel values are independently and identically distributed with finite mean and variance, we derive i) the expected mean squared error between the original and watermarked images (transparency); and ii) an upper bound on the average absolute change to DCT coefficients of the watermarked image after one application of simulated fading (robustness). Experimental results demonstrate that the proposed scheme preserves image fidelity well and is very robust under simulated fading.

1 Introduction

We report on the design and analysis of a system for watermarking care labels directly onto textile designs (such as images on t-shirts). There are various reasons for doing away with the care labels: they sometimes get detached or damaged during the laundering process, and some consumers consider them unsightly or uncomfortable. It is plausible that in the near future fabric with embedded electronics would allow washers and dryers to automate the laundering process by extracting care information from the embedded watermark.

We are not aware of any previous work in this direction. Our system appears to be the first to apply watermarking in the context of textile materials; we envision it to be one of several parts of a comprehensive solution to this challenging problem.

Our objective is to devise a watermarking scheme that meets the unique requirements of the laundering process. In this setting, the requirements are: 1) the watermarked image must be visually indistinguishable from the original; 2) the embedded care information must be recoverable after numerous laundering cycles. The second requirement can be simplified to resistance to two main effects of laundering on clothes: fading and shrinking/wrinkling. The latter is a difficult problem to deal with satisfactorily, and hence we focus on studying the effect of fading for this project; our goal is to identify and study an application of

* Supported in part by NSF Grant IIS-0242435.

H.H.S. Ip et al. (Eds.): PCM 2007, LNCS 4810, pp. 724–733, 2007.

watermarking that is interesting, nontrivial, and yet the malefactors (washer & dryer) are more limited in their power so that theoretical results can be obtained.

Specifically, we use a spread-spectrum technique similar to the NEC algorithm described in [CKLS97] to embed care labels onto the fabric designs. The care label (a subset of the American Society for Testing and Materials standard D-3136-04) is first encoded using Reed-Solomon encoding to yield a watermark, which is then embedded onto randomly selected discrete-cosine transform coefficients of the image, so that each bit corresponds to $\mu_w \pm f\sigma_w$, where μ_w and σ_w are the mean and standard deviation of the DCT coefficients, and f is a multiplicative strength factor. To extract the embedded information, the DCT coefficients of the design's image are computed along with their mean μ'_w, and the selected locations are regenerated. A bit is interpreted to be a one iff its corresponding DCT coefficient is at least μ'_w. Note that the NEC algorithm, unlike ours, embeds a single bit onto the image.

We derive two results on the stochastic properties of the proposed scheme. Assuming that pixel values are independently and identically distributed with finite mean μ_o and variance σ_o^2, it is shown that the expected mean squared error between the $N \times M$ original image O and its watermarked counterpart W is

$$E[MSE(O,W)] \approx \frac{s}{NM}\left(\sigma_o^2 + f^2(\sigma_o^2 + \mu_o^2)\right),$$

where s is the length of the encoded care label and f is the multiplicative factor used in the embedding of the watermark ($\mu_w \pm f\sigma_w$); the exact formula is also obtained but is more complex. The mean squared error is a common (if somewhat simplistic) measure of image fidelity.

Second, it is shown the average absolute difference between DCT coefficients of the watermarked image before and after one application of simulated fading is bounded by

$$\frac{1}{NM}\sum_{u=0}^{N-1}\sum_{v=0}^{M-1}|C'(u,v) - C(u,v)| \in O\left(\frac{b \ln N \ln M}{\sqrt{NM}}\right).$$

Fading is simulated using the GIMP's hue-saturation tool to increase the image's lightness by b% and decrease the image's saturation by b%. For any reasonable image dimensions, the change is small enough to allow the watermark to survive fading applications the fabric undergoes in its lifetime.

We implemented the proposed scheme and tested it on a small set of images (consisting of landscape and portrait photos, text, drawing, and patterns) using different error-correcting and watermark strengths s and f. Experimental results demonstrate a smooth degradation of image fidelity as the error-correcting and watermark strengths increase, with the mean squared error much more sensitive to the f than s as predicted by the formula; they suggest that a five-fold Reed-Solomon redundancy and watermark strength of one standard deviation work well for most cases. Data also show that the watermarking scheme is quite robust with respect to simulated fading; in most cases the embedded information is still recoverable after 32 fading applications, even when the faded image appears completely white to us (we stopped at 32 applications due to time constraint).

The rest of this paper is organized as follows. Basic concepts are reviewed in Sec. 2 and the proposed watermarking embedding and extraction algorithms are described in Sec. 3. Stochastic analyses of transparency and robustness are presented in Secs. 4, 5 and 6. Experimental results appear in Sec. 7, followed by discussions in Sec. 8 and conclusions and directions for future work in Sec. 9.

2 Preliminaries

Rectangular $N \times M$ color images are coded in RGB format and represented as $N \times M$ rectangular matrices of triplets of integers between 0 and 255 inclusive; alternatively, color images coded in HLS format are represented as triplets of real numbers between 0.0 and 1.0 inclusive. We will assume that there is no dependence between the color components and treat all images as interleavings of three gray-level ones for the rest of this paper. Small differences between two $N \times M$ images I and I' are sometimes quantified using the *mean squared error* measure, defined as $MSE(I, I') = \sum_{i=0}^{N-1} \sum_{j=0}^{M-1} (I(i,j) - I'(i,j))^2$. The *Frobenius norm* of an $N \times M$ matrix A is defined as $\|A\| = \sum_{i=0}^{N-1} \sum_{j=0}^{M-1} (A(i,j))^2$. The *discrete cosine transform (DCT)* of an $N \times M$ matrix A is an $N \times M$ matrix C whose entries are given by the formula: $C(u,v) = c(u)d(v) \sum_{i=0}^{N-1} \sum_{j=0}^{M-1} A(i,j) \cos \frac{\pi u}{N}(i + \frac{1}{2}) \cos \frac{\pi v}{M}(j + \frac{1}{2})$, and the *inverse cosine transform* of A is an $N \times M$ matrix I whose entries are given by the formula: $I(i,j) = \sum_{u=0}^{N-1} \sum_{v=0}^{M-1} c(u)d(v)(A(u,v) \cos \frac{\pi u}{N}(i + \frac{1}{2}) \cos \frac{\pi v}{M}(j + \frac{1}{2})$. In the above formulae, $c(0) = \sqrt{1/N}$ and $c(k) = \sqrt{2/N}$ for $k \neq 0$, and where $d(0) = \sqrt{1/M}$ and $d(k) = \sqrt{2/M}$ for $k \neq 0$.

Expressed in matrix form, $C = PAQ$ and $A = P^T C Q^T$ for some orthogonal matrices P and Q. The following proposition summarizes some well-known properties of the DCT coefficients:

Proposition 1. *Let A be an $N \times M$ matrix and $C = PAQ$ be its DCT.*

1. $\|PAQ\| = \|A\|$;
2. $\sum_{i=0}^{N-1} \sum_{j=0}^{M-1} c(u)d(v) \cos \frac{\pi u}{N}(i+\frac{1}{2}) \cos \frac{\pi v}{M}(j+\frac{1}{2}) = \begin{cases} \sqrt{NM} & \text{if } u = v = 0 \\ 0 & \textit{otherwise} \end{cases}$;
3. $\sum_{i=0}^{N-1} \sum_{j=0}^{M-1} c^2(u)d^2(v) \cos^2 \frac{\pi u}{N}(i+\frac{1}{2}) \cos^2 \frac{\pi v}{M}(j+\frac{1}{2}) = 1$ *for all* $0 \leq u < N$, $0 \leq v < M$.

3 Watermarking and Extracting Care Labels

We assume care labels follow the American Society for Testing and Materials standard ASTM D-3136-04 [oTM], which enumerates exhaustively different options for laundering, drying, ironing, pressing, dry cleaning, and leather cleaning. Commonly used options are encoded in an 80-bit string l in a straightforward manner (a table of options has been omitted due to space constraint). Redundancy to allow error correction is then added to the bit string l using Reed-Solomon encoding to yield a "watermark" w of size s up to 1600 bits (20 times the original size).

The watermark is then embedded into the DCT coefficients of the design's image O (such as those on t-shirts) using a spread-spectrum technique similar to the NEC algorithm described in [CKLS97]. First, $s = |w|$ coefficients are selected randomly using a seed r; they are then set to $\mu_w \pm f * \sigma_w$ to represent a single bit, where μ_w is the mean of DCT coefficients for all three color channels, σ_w is their standard deviation, and f is a user-controlled strength factor. To prevent drastic changes to the image, coefficients in the first and last 32 rows or columns are excluded from the selection process. Note that the NEC algorithm, unlike ours, embeds a single bit onto the image.

The decoding algorithm first computes the DCT of the design's image C, calculates the mean μ'_w and standard deviation σ'_w of these coefficients and then extracts the embedded watermark w' by regenerating the random locations using the given seed r. A bit is interpreted as a 1 iff the corresponding coefficient is at least μ'_w.

4 Mean and Variance of DCT Coefficients

In this section we derive stochastic properties of the DCT coefficients to be used in our analyses of transparency and robustness of the proposed scheme in Secs. 5 and 6.

Let O be the original $N \times M$ (gray-level) image whose pixel values are independently and identically distributed with mean μ_o and variance σ_o^2. We are interested in the expected value and variance of each DCT coefficient of O as well as the expected value of their average and how each entry varies from this average.

Lemma 1. $\mu_c =^{\text{def}} E[C(u,v)] = \begin{cases} \mu_o\sqrt{NM} & \text{if } u = v = 0 \\ 0 & \textit{otherwise} \end{cases}, \quad 0 \le u < N, 0 \le v < M.$

Proof

$$\begin{aligned} E[C(u,v)] &= E[c(u)d(v)\sum_{i=0}^{N-1}\sum_{j=0}^{M-1} A(i,j)\cos\frac{\pi u}{N}(i+\frac{1}{2})\cos\frac{\pi v}{M}(j+\frac{1}{2})] \\ &= c(u)d(v)E[A(0,0)]\sum_{i=0}^{N-1}\sum_{j=0}^{M-1}\cos\frac{\pi u}{N}(i+\frac{1}{2})\cos\frac{\pi v}{M}(j+\frac{1}{2})] \\ &= \begin{cases} \mu_o\sqrt{NM} & \text{if } u = v = 0 \\ 0 & \text{otherwise} \end{cases}. \end{aligned}$$

Lemma 2. $\sigma_c^2 =^{\text{def}} Var[C(i,j)] = \sigma_o^2, \quad 0 \le u < N, 0 \le v < M.$

Proof

$$Var[C(u,v)] = Var[c(u)d(v)\sum_{i=0}^{N-1}\sum_{j=0}^{M-1} A(i,j)\cos\frac{\pi u}{N}(i+\frac{1}{2})\cos\frac{\pi v}{M}(j+\frac{1}{2})]$$

$$= Var[A(0,0)]\sum_{i=0}^{N-1}\sum_{j=0}^{M-1} c^2(u)d^2(v)\cos^2\frac{\pi u}{N}(i+\frac{1}{2})\cos^2\frac{\pi v}{M}(j+\frac{1}{2})] = \sigma_o^2.$$

Lemma 3.

$$\mu_w \stackrel{\text{def}}{=} E[\frac{1}{NM}\sum_{i=0}^{N-1}\sum_{j=0}^{M-1} C(i,j)] = \frac{\mu_o}{\sqrt{NM}}.$$

Proof

$$E[\frac{1}{NM}\sum_{i=0}^{N-1}\sum_{j=0}^{M-1} C(i,j)] = \frac{1}{NM}\sum_{i=0}^{N-1}\sum_{j=0}^{M-1} E[C(i,j)] = \frac{1}{NM}\mu_o\sqrt{NM} = \frac{\mu_o}{\sqrt{NM}}.$$

Lemma 4.

$$\sigma_w^2 \stackrel{\text{def}}{=} E[\frac{1}{NM}\sum_{i=0}^{N-1}\sum_{j=0}^{M-1} (C(i,j)-\mu_w)^2] = \sigma_o^2 + \frac{NM-1}{NM}\mu_o^2 \approx \sigma_o^2 + \mu_o^2.$$

Proof

$$\begin{aligned}
\sigma_w^2 &= E[\frac{1}{NM}\sum_{i=0}^{N-1}\sum_{j=0}^{M-1} (C(i,j)-\mu_w)^2] = \frac{1}{NM}\sum_{i=0}^{N-1}\sum_{j=0}^{M-1} E[(C(i,j)-\mu_w)^2] \\
&= \frac{1}{NM}\sum_{i=0}^{N-1}\sum_{j=0}^{M-1} Var[C(i,j)-\mu_w] + E^2[C(i,j)-\mu_w] \\
&= \frac{1}{NM}\sum_{i=0}^{N-1}\sum_{j=0}^{M-1} Var[C(i,j)-\mu_w] + \frac{1}{NM}\sum_{i=0}^{N-1}\sum_{j=0}^{M-1} E^2[C(i,j)-\mu_w] \\
&= \sigma_o^2 + \frac{1}{NM}(\mu_o\sqrt{NM}-\mu_w)^2 + \frac{NM-1}{NM}\mu_w^2 \\
&= \sigma_o^2 + \frac{NM-1}{NM}\mu_o^2 \approx \sigma_o^2 + \mu_o^2.
\end{aligned}$$

5 Transparency Analysis

The effect of embedding the care label into an image on its perceptual fidelity is considered in this section. We derive a formula for the expected value of the mean squared error between the original and the watermarked images.

Let O be the original $N \times M$ (gray-level) image whose pixel values are independently and identically distributed with mean μ_o and variance σ_o^2 and C be it DCT. Let W be the watermarked version of O using the scheme described in Sec. 3, and s be the size of the embedded bit string (i.e, the number of DCT coefficients modified). The embedded information can be represented as an $N \times M$ matrix X where

$$X(i,j) = \begin{cases} \mu_w \pm f\sigma_w - C(i,j) & \text{if } (i,j) \text{ is selected} \\ 0 & \text{otherwise} \end{cases},$$

and hence the watermarked image can be written as $W = P^T(C+X)Q^T = O + P^TXQ^T$.

Theorem 1

$$E[MSE(O,W)] = \frac{s}{NM}\left(\sigma_o^2 + (\mu_w \pm f\sigma_w)^2\right) \approx \frac{s}{NM}\left(\sigma_o^2 + f^2(\sigma_o^2 + \mu_o^2)\right).$$

Proof

$$\begin{aligned}
E[MSE(O,W)] &= E[MSE(O, O+P^TXQ^T)] = \frac{1}{NM}E[\|P^TXQ^T\|] = \frac{1}{NM}E[\|X\|] \\
&= \frac{1}{NM}E[\sum_{i=0}^{N_1}\sum_{j=0}^{M-1}X^2(i,j)] = \frac{1}{NM}\sum_{i=0}^{N-1}\sum_{j=0}^{M-1}E[X^2(i,j)] \\
&= \frac{1}{NM}\sum_{i=0}^{N-1}\sum_{j=0}^{M-1}Var[X(i,j)] + E^2[X(i,j)] \\
&= \frac{1}{NM}\sum_{k=1}^{s}Var[\mu_w \pm f\sigma_w - C(i_k,j_k)] + E^2[\mu_w \pm f\sigma_w - C(i_k,j_k)] \\
&= \frac{1}{NM}\sum_{k=1}^{s}Var[C(i_k,j_k)] + E^2[\mu_w \pm f\sigma_w] \\
&= \frac{s}{NM}\left(\sigma_o^2 + (\mu_w \pm f\sigma_w)^2\right).
\end{aligned}$$

We can take $E[C(i_k, j_k)]$ to be zero in the last expression since the embedding algorithm avoids choosing significant coefficients, including $C(0,0)$.

If μ_w is small, the expected mean squared error can be approximated by

$$E[MSE(O,W)] \approx \frac{s}{NM}\left(\sigma_o^2 + f^2(\sigma_o^2 + \mu_o^2)\right).$$

6 Robustness Analysis

The effect of one fading distortion application on the embedded information is considered in this section. We derive an upper bound on the average change to the watermarked image's DCT coefficients.

Recall that fading is modeled by calling the function `gimp-hue-saturation()` to increase the lightness by b and decrease the saturation by b each time, where $b = 16$. Since `gimp-hue-saturation()` works with the HLS color model (where each color is represented by a triple of real numbers between 0.0 and 1.0), for simplicity we assume that the original image matrix is in this format, and not the usual RGB format. (Formulae to convert colors in one format to the other exist.)

Let O be the original $N \times M$ image whose pixel values are independently and identically distributed with mean μ_o and variance σ_o^2. Let F be the $N \times M$ matrix whose entries repeat the pattern $0, b, -b, \ldots$; this matrix models one application of `gimp-hue-saturation()`. Let C be the DCT of O and C' be the DCT of $O + F$. We want to to bound the average of the entries of $|C' - C|$.

Lemma 5. *Let* $\alpha_i =^{\text{def}} (i + \frac{1}{2})\frac{\pi}{N}$, *and* $\beta_j =^{\text{def}} (j + \frac{1}{2})\frac{\pi}{M}$ *for* $0 \le i < N$ *and* $0 \le j < M$.

1. $\sum_{u=0}^{N-1} \cos \alpha_i u = \frac{1}{2}\left(1 + (-1)^i \cot \frac{\alpha_i}{2}\right) \leq \frac{1}{2} + \frac{1}{\alpha_i}$;
2. $\sum_{v=0}^{M-1} \cos \beta_j v = \frac{1}{2}\left(1 + (-1)^j \cot \frac{\beta_j}{2}\right) \leq \frac{1}{2} + \frac{1}{\beta_j}$.

Proof. We prove case 1 only; the proof for the other case is similar.

$$
\begin{aligned}
X &= \sum_{u=0}^{N-1} \cos \alpha_i u \\
2 \sin \frac{\alpha_i}{2} X &= \sum_{i=0}^{N-1} 2 \sin \frac{\alpha_i}{2} \cos \alpha_i u \\
&= \sum_{u=0}^{N-1} \sin(\alpha_i u + \frac{\alpha_i}{2}) - \sin(\alpha_i u - \frac{\alpha_i}{2}) \\
&= \sin(N\alpha_i - \frac{\alpha_i}{2}) + \sin \frac{\alpha_i}{2} & \text{(telescoping sum)} \\
&= \sin N\alpha_i \cos \frac{\alpha_i}{2} - \sin \frac{\alpha_i}{2} \cos N\alpha_i + \sin \frac{\alpha_i}{2} \\
&= (-1)^i \cos \frac{\alpha_i}{2} + \sin \frac{\alpha_i}{2} \\
X &= \frac{1}{2}\left((-1)^i \cot \frac{\alpha_i}{2} + 1\right) \\
&\leq \frac{1}{2}\left(\frac{2}{\alpha_i} + 1\right) & (\cot x \leq \frac{1}{x} \text{ for } 0 < x < \frac{\pi}{2}) \\
&= \frac{1}{2} + \frac{1}{\alpha_i}.
\end{aligned}
$$

Theorem 2. *Let b be the increase (decrease) of lightness (saturation) used in each invocation of* `gimp-hue-saturation()`.

$$
\frac{1}{NM} \sum_{u=0}^{N-1} \sum_{v=0}^{N-1} |C'(u,v) - C(u,v)| \in O\left(\frac{b \ln N \ln M}{\sqrt{NM}}\right).
$$

Proof. Let $\delta = \frac{1}{NM} \sum_{u=0}^{N-1} \sum_{v=0}^{N-1} |C'(u,v) - C(u,v)|$.

$$
\begin{aligned}
\delta &= \frac{2b}{NM} \sum_{i+j=1 \bmod 3} \sum_{u=0}^{N-1} \sum_{v=0}^{M-1} |C'(u,v) - C(u,v)| \\
&\leq \frac{2b}{NM} \frac{2}{\sqrt{NM}} \sum_{i+j=1 \bmod 3} \left((\frac{1}{2} + \frac{1}{\alpha_i})(\frac{1}{2} + \frac{1}{\beta_j}) \right) \\
&\leq \frac{4bNM}{NM\sqrt{NM}} \left(\frac{1}{12} + \frac{(\ln(2N-1) + \ln(2M-1))}{3\pi} + \frac{4 \ln(2N-1) \ln(3N-1)}{\pi^2} \right) \\
&\in O\left(\frac{b \ln N \ln M}{\sqrt{NM}}\right).
\end{aligned}
$$

7 Experimental Setup

Randomly generated care labels were embedded into a selection of color images, and the results were then subjected to repeated distortions simulating fading until the embedded information could no longer be extracted. Transparency (in terms of mean squared error) and robustness (in terms of number of fading applications required to render the embedded information unrecoverable) were measured and plotted in a graph against the redundancy of Reed-Solomon encoding and the strength factor f.

Nine images of various dimensions (most close to 640x480 pixels) typical of t-shirt designs were used in the experiments: one landscape photo, two portrait photos, one drawing, one text, three patterns, and one CAPTCHA (distorted text). They are shown in Fig. 1.

User-controlled parameters included Reed-Solomon redundancy (ranging from 4 to 20 times the original string size) and watermark strength factor (ranging from 0.5 to 2 times the standard deviation). Fading were modeled with the `gimp-hue-saturation` GIMP tool, increasing lightness and decreasing saturation in steps of 16. A graphical user interface, shown in Fig. 2, was implemented to facilitate the setting of these parameters.

The experiments were performed on a MacBook running Mac OS 10.4.9, 2 GHz Intel Core 2 Duo (Merom), 1 GB 667 MHz DDR2. Software used include Python 2.4.4, IPython 0.8.1 (for interactivity) , wxPython 2.8.0.1 (for graphical user interface), SciPy 0.5.3 (for `fft`), numpy 1.0.2 (for matrix operations), Reed-Solomon Python Extension Module, Python Image Library, and Gimp (image processing). Batch processing using Gimp were performed on a 64-bit Dell workstation running Red Hat Enterprise 4.

DCT was computed using the built-in `fft` function provided by scipy as follows: `dct(abcd)` = the first N elements of `dft(0a0b0c0d0a0b0c0d)`. Similarly, IDCT is computed using the scipy `ift` function: `idct(abcd)` = the first N elements (after scaling) of `ifft(abcd0dcbabcd0dcb)`.

8 Discussion

The transparency results (in terms of MSE) for all test images are plotted in Fig. 3. The charts, read from left to right, correspond the test images in the order given in Fig. 1. The color of a block in each chart indicates the mean squared error between the original and the watermarked version using a randomly generated care label and the corresponding error-correcting strength (y-axis) and watermark strength (x-axis). Black corresponds to the smallest value and white the largest. The result for the popular test image `lena` appears in Fig. 5.

These experimental results demonstrate a smooth degradation of image quality as the error-correcting and watermark strengths increase, except for `baboon`

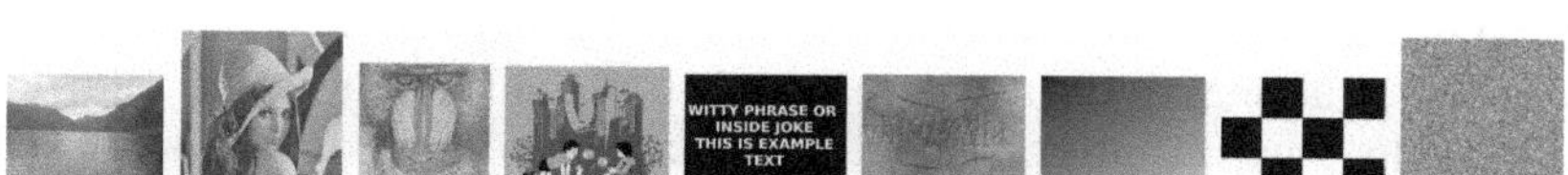

Fig. 1. `fjord`, `lena`, `baboon`, `drawing`, `text`, `captcha`, `gradient`, `grid`, `random`

Fig. 2. Graphical user interface allows setting of user-controlled parameters

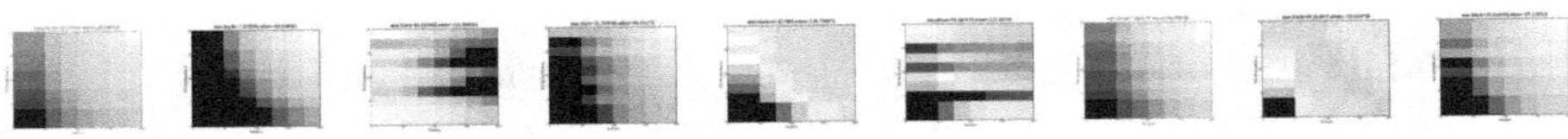

Fig. 3. MSE vs error-correcting strength and watermark strength for all test images (in listed order)

Fig. 4. Number of fading applications until failure vs error-correcting strength and watermark strength for all test images (in listed order)

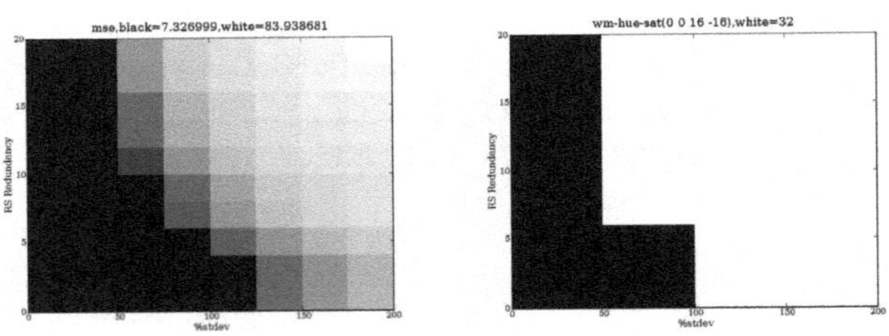

Fig. 5. *Left*: MSE for `lena`. *Right*: Number of fading applications until failure for `lena`

and `captcha`. They also agree with the theoretical result derived in Sec. 5, which shows that the mean squared error is much more sensitive to watermark strength f than error-correcting strength s. It appears from the charts that a five-fold Reed-Solomon redundancy and watermark strength of one standard deviation work well for most cases.

Similarly, the robustness results (in terms of number of fading applications until the embedded information can longer be recovered) are plotted in Fig. 4, in the same order as explained above. The color of a block in each chart indicates the number of fading applications required to make the embedded information unrecoverable; due to time constraint, this number is capped at 32 applications. The result for the popular test image `lena` appears in Fig. 5.

These experimental results suggest that the embedding method is quite robust with respect to fading; except for the drawing and gradient images, we were able to recover the embedded information for the other images after 32 fading applications, even when the faded image appears completely white to us.

9 Conclusions and Future Work

We proposed, implemented, and analyzed a watermarking system for embedding textile care labels directly onto fabric designs. Under the assumption that each pixel value is independently and identically distributed with finite mean and variance, we derived the expected mean squared error between the original and watermarked images; similarly we derived a bound on the absolute value of changes to DCT coefficients of the watermarked image after one fading application. Experimental and theoretical results indicated that the proposed system satisfies both stated goals of preserving image fidelity and robust resistance to fading. Future work includes extending the theoretical analyses of transparency and robustness to other probability distributions, modeling the effect of shrinking/wrinkling, and constructing a real-life prototype of our system.

References

[CKLS97] Cox, I., Kilian, J., Leighton, F., Shamoon, T.: Secure spread spectrum watermarking for multimedia. IEEE Transactions on Image Processing 6(12), 1673–1687 (1997)

[oTM] American Society of Testing and Materials. Standard terminology relating to care labeling for apparel, texttile, home furnishing, and leather products (D 3136 - 04)

Stroke Correspondence Based on Graph Matching for Detecting Stroke Production Errors in Chinese Character Handwriting

Zhihui Hu[1,2,3], Howard Leung[2,3], and Yun Xu[1,2]

[1] Department of Computer Science and Technology, University of Science & Technology of China, Hefei, China
[2] Joint Research Lab of Excellence, CityU-USTC Advanced Research Institute, Suzhou, China
[3] Department of Computer Science, City University of Hong Kong, Hong Kong, China
kittyhu@mail.ustc.edu.cn, howard@cityu.edu.hk, xuyun@ustc.edu.cn

Abstract. People may make mistakes in writing a Chinese character. In this paper, we apply error-tolerant graph matching to find the stroke production errors in people's handwriting of Chinese characters. A set of edit operations to transform one graph into another are defined for achieving this purpose. The matching procedure is denoted as a search problem of finding the minimum edit distance. The A^* algorithm is used to perform the searching. Experiments show that the proposed method outperforms existing algorithms in identifying stroke production errors. The proposed method can help in Chinese handwriting education by providing feedback to correct users who have stroke production errors in writing a Chinese character.

Keywords: Chinese handwriting education, stroke production error, graph matching, graph edit distance, moment function.

1 Introduction

Chinese characters have been part of the Chinese culture for several thousands of years. Chinese characters are ideograms instead of letters in an alphabetic system. Each Chinese character has its own structure formed by the strokes that should be written in the correct position, proportion and order. While people write the Chinese characters they may have some handwriting errors [1]. The major stroke production errors can be divided into four types (Fig. 1): (1) Missing stroke error; (2) Concatenated stroke error; (3) Extra stroke error; (4) Broken stroke error. Although there are other kinds of handwriting errors such as stroke order error or badly written strokes etc., in this paper we focus on detecting the stroke production errors.

In order to learn how to write a Chinese character properly, the student should be corrected if he/she makes handwriting errors. It is thus very important to know whether and where exactly the errors are. The nature of this Chinese character handwriting education problem makes it different from Chinese character recognition mentioned in [2]. The character recognition is focused on finding the similarity between the input character and a set of candidate characters, and then classifying the input into one of the

H.H.S. Ip et al. (Eds.): PCM 2007, LNCS 4810, pp. 734–743, 2007.

candidate character with the highest similarity. On the other hand, for the Chinese handwriting education system, it is necessary to find a detailed matching between the input character and a known template character in order to find out the exact difference.

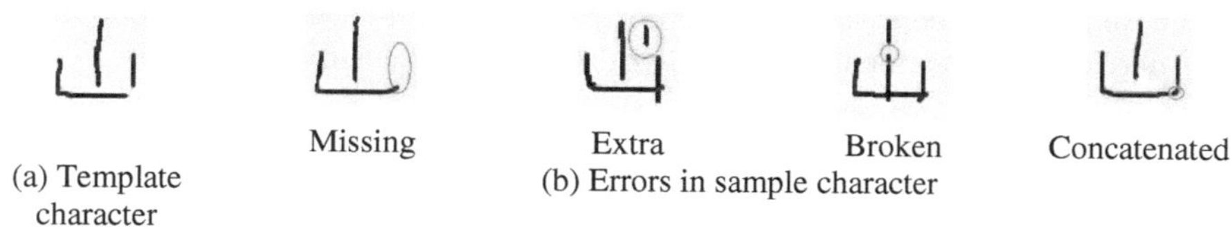

Fig. 1. Four types of production errors

There are three main types of Chinese handwriting education system. The first type is focused on teaching students how to write properly [3][4][5]. The second type helps students to write Chinese character in a beautiful way [6][8]. The last type involves a robotic arm to help students improve the writing skills including writing speed and direction of writing track [7]. There are some drawbacks in these existing systems. The system proposed in [3] restricts the way to practice handwriting. It only allows students to write in a certain way as in a copybook. The system proposed in [4] is read-only and user cannot practice handwriting through it. Tang and Leung [5] proposed a web-based education system which allows users to practice Chinese handwriting freely and check both the stroke production and sequence errors. However, it relies on the specific threshold used to distinguish between the problematic and non–problematic strokes. If the decision about a problematic/non-problematic stroke is wrong, then the actual handwriting error cannot be identified correctly. The system proposed in [6] could only show user a single kind of error even if the user has made multiple errors.

Due to the drawbacks of existing methods, we are motivated to propose a new way to help students to learn Chinese handwriting freely and more effectively. We will apply graph matching to achieve this goal, as it has been successfully used in many areas [9]. In our problem, a handwriting character is modeled as a graph with a node representing a stroke. Two graphs may be matched by first finding a mapping between corresponding nodes. The error–tolerant graph matching is used to handle the real data with possible noise and distortion. The basic solution to find the error–tolerant graph isomorphism between two graphs is to search for a pathway in the constructed state–space. We should find a sequence of edit operations that transform, with minimum cost, one of the given graphs into the other. In its most general form, a graph edit operation could either be deletion, insertion, or substitution [10][11]. We introduce two more graph edit operations, namely merging and splitting, for finding the graph isomorphism. A* algorithm is then used to get the optimal result. This provides information for identifying the stroke production errors of the input handwriting.

The remainder of this paper is organized as follows: In Section 2, the proposed graph matching method is described. Experiments and results are discussed in Section 3. Conclusions and future work are provided in Section 4.

2 Our Proposed Graph Matching Method

2.1 Representation of Chinese Character

A Chinese character consists of many strokes. We can use nodes in a graph to denote the strokes and edges to denote the relationship between the strokes (Fig. 2).

Fig. 2. Presentation of Chinese character

A graph $g = (V,E,\alpha,\beta)$ is composed of nodes and edges. V is the set of nodes and E is the set of edges in the graph g, i.e., $E = V\times V$. The size of a graph g is defined as the number of nodes of g and it is represented as $|V|$ and the number of edges as $|E|$. $\alpha : V \to L_V$ is the node labeling function. $\beta : E \to L_E$ is the edge labeling function. L_V and L_E are the finite set of labels for nodes and edges.

In our case, the set of nodes V correspond to the strokes of the Chinese character. The node labeling function $\alpha : V \to L_V$ returns the re-sampled dataset containing N data points for each stroke (node). In fact, each node stores the x and y coordinates of a stroke, i.e., the attributes of the node a is $a = (x_i, y_i)$, where $i = 1,2,...,N$. In this paper, we first focus on the node matching thus we do not consider the attributes for the edges. The edge labeling function of β is set to zero for the current work. The graph can then be simplified from $g = (V,E,\alpha,\beta)$ to $g = (V,\alpha)$.

2.2 Definition of Graph Edit Distances

Given an input character which is denoted by graph $g_1 = (V_1, \alpha_1)$ and a template character as $g_2 = (V_2, \alpha_2)$, an error–tolerant graph matching from g_1 to g_2 is a function $f : \hat{V}_1 \to \hat{V}_2$, where $\hat{V}_1 \subseteq V_1$ and $\hat{V}_2 \subseteq V_2$. The node $v_1 \in \hat{V}_1$ is substituted by the node $v_2 \in \hat{V}_2$ if $f(v_1) = v_2$. For our application, we apply a transformation, denoted by function f, from the input graph g_1 to the template graph g_2. This function f consists of many edit operations: 1) *substitution* implying that the input stroke is correct; 2) *merging* implying that the input strokes are broken strokes; 3) *splitting* implying that the input stroke is a concatenated stroke; 4) *deletion* implying that the input stroke is an extra one; 5) *insertion* implying that there is a missing stroke. It can be seen that these edit operations can identify the stroke production errors in the input handwriting. Each edit operation is described in more details as follows.

Substitution: The cost for substitution is the one-to-one stroke matching cost which is defined between a stroke in the sample character and a stroke in the template character. We use S to denote the set of sample strokes and T to denote the set of template strokes.

Assume that the data points of the sample stroke S_K are denoted by $S_K=(x_i^S,y_i^S)$ where $i=1,2,\ldots,N$, $K=1,2,\ldots,n_S$, and n_S is the number of the strokes in sample character. And the data points of the template stroke T_K are denoted by $T_K=(x_i^T,y_i^T)$, where $i=1,2,\ldots,N$, $K=1,2,\ldots,n_T$, and n_T is the number of the strokes in the template character. For the stroke matching cost, we consider the combined cost of the Euclidean distance ($C_{Dist}(S_K,T_K)$) and the direction difference ($C_{Dir}(S_K,T_K)$) between these data points [5] as shown in equation (1). The Euclidean distance C_{Dist} is the average Euclidean distance between data points on a sample-template stroke pair, whereas the direction difference C_{Dir} is the average sine values of the angle difference between stroke segments on a sample-template stroke pair.

$$C_{sub}=C(v_1\rightarrow v_2)=C_{Combined}(S_K,T_K)=w_{Dist}C_{Dist}(S_K,T_K)+w_{Dir}C_{Dir}(S_K,T_K) \quad (1)$$

where v_1 and v_2 are the nodes corresponding to the strokes S_K and T_K; w_{Dist} and w_{Dir} are determined based on the statistical analysis of the cost distributions for the matched strokes and non-matched strokes from the ground truth information about the stroke matching. It should be noted that the successful detection of the handwriting errors is not too sensitive to small changes of the weights w_{Dist} and w_{Dir}. On the other hand, for the method in [5], the correct classification of the problematic vs. non-problematic stroke using the threshold is a decisive factor for the accurate detection of handwriting errors.

The lower the substitution cost between the two nodes v_1 and v_2, the more similar the two strokes S_K and T_K are. For example, as shown in Fig.2, the graph matching is $f:1\rightarrow a,\ 2\rightarrow b,\ 3\rightarrow c$.

Merging: The cost for merging is obtained from the two-to-one stroke matching cost. This means that the data points of the stroke S_K in the sample character is formed by $S_K=S'_K+S''_K=\{(x_i^{S'},y_i^{S'}),(x_i^{S''},y_i^{S''})\}$ where $S',S''\in S$, $i=1,2,\ldots,N$, $K=1,2,\ldots,n_S$, and n_S is the number of the strokes in the sample character. The data points of the template stroke T_K are denoted by $T_K=(x_i^T,y_i^T)$, where $i=1,2,\ldots,N$, $K=1,2,\ldots,n_T$, and n_T is the number of the strokes in the template character. The cost for this merging edit operation is defined in equation (2):

$$C_{mer}=C(v_{1i},v_{1j}\rightarrow v_2)=C_{combined}(S_K,T_K) \quad (2)$$

where $v_{1i},v_{1j}\in V_1$. After merging the two nodes v_{1i},v_{1j} into a new node, we should get the matching cost between this new node and the template node v_2. If the two strokes S'_K and S''_K are real broken strokes, then the matching cost will be low.

Splitting: The cost for splitting is obtained from the one-to-two stroke matching cost. That means that the data points of the sample stroke S_K is formed by $S_K=(x_i^S,y_i^S)$, where $i=1,2,\ldots,N$, $K=1,2,\ldots,n_S$, and n_S is the number of the strokes in the sample character. The data points of the template stroke T_K are formed by $T_K = T'_K + T''_K = \{(x_i^{T'}, y_i^{T'}), (x_i^{T''}, y_i^{T''})\}$, where $T', T'' \in T$, and $i = 1,2,...,N$, $K = 1,2,...,n_T$, and n_T is the number of the strokes in the template character. This splitting operation focusing on the template stroke is similar to the merging operation that is focused on the sample stroke. The cost of this splitting edit operation is defined in equation (3):

$$C_{spl} = C(v_1 \rightarrow v_{2i}, v_{2j}) = C_{combined}(S_K, T_K) \quad (3)$$

where $v_{2i}, v_{2j} \in V_2$. A low cost means the stroke in the sample character S_K should be split into two strokes. It implies that this stroke in S_K is a concatenated stroke.

Deletion: After applying the substitution and merging operations, it can identify the well matched stroke pairs. The deletion operation should be applied to the remaining strokes in the sample character that are not matched to any template strokes. These remaining nodes in the sample graph g_1 undergoing the deletion operations imply that those strokes are extra ones.

Insertion: This operation is similar to the deletion operation. We should check the remaining nodes in the template graph g_2. Those remaining nodes undergoing the insertion operation imply that there are missing strokes.

Finally, we can finish the graph matching. Fig.3 gives an example.

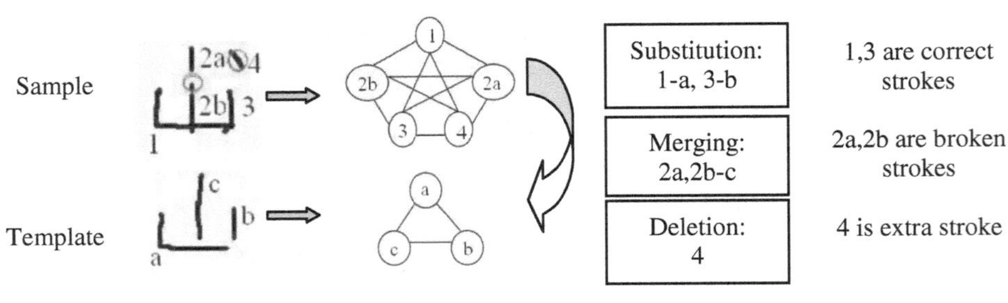

Fig. 3. Graph matching with edit operations

Ultimately let g_1 and g_2 be two graphs and f be an inexact matching, we could get the graph edit distance in equation (4):

$$Cost(f, g_1, g_2) = \sum C_{sub} + \sum C_{mer} + \sum C_{spl} + \sum C_{del} + \sum C_{ins} \quad (4)$$

where C_{sub}, C_{mer}, C_{spl}, C_{del}, C_{ins} are the costs of substitution, merging, splitting, deletion and insertion respectively.

2.3 Definitions of Matching Via State Space Search

The A^* algorithm is commonly used to search the state space tree to find the optimal graph matching. The whole actual matching cost is shown in equation (5):

$$h(n) = h_1(n) + h_2^*(n) \tag{5}$$

where $h_1(n)$ is the actual cost from the initial node to the current node n, and $h_2^*(n)$ is the actual cost from the node n to the goal node. The most important issue in the A^* algorithm is to identify a suitable evaluation function defined in equation (6):

$$h(n) = h_1(n) + h_2(n) \tag{6}$$

where $h_2(n)$ is an estimation for the cost from the node n to the goal node. If $h_2(n) \leq h_2^*(n)$ holds for any node n, then $h_2(n)$ is called a consistent lower bounded estimate of $h_2^*(n)$.

Let $g_1 = (V_1, \alpha_1)$ and $g_2 = (V_2, \alpha_2)$ be two graphs. A state in the state space tree denote a mapping between $g_1' = (V_1', \alpha_1')$ and $g_2' = (V_2', \alpha_2')$, where $g_1' \subseteq g_1, g_2' \subseteq g_2, V_1' \subseteq V_1, V_2' \subseteq V_2$. An error–tolerant graph matching from g_1' to g_2' is a function $f : V_1' \rightarrow V_2'$. The initial state is null without any mapping.

Definition of $h_1(n)$: in addition to the graph edit operation costs, we consider the holistic matching by using the Hu moments which have been widely used in two–dimensional pattern recognition applications [12][13]. The regular moments are defined in equation (7):

$$m_{pq} = \sum_x \sum_y x^p y^q \varphi(x, y) \tag{7}$$

where m_{pq} is the $(p+q)$th order moment. The value of $\varphi(x, y)$ is equal to one when (x, y) is a point on the stroke, otherwise it is equal to zero. The corresponding central moment is defined as $\mu_{pq} = \sum_x \sum_y \left(x - \bar{x}\right)^p \left(y - \bar{y}\right)^q \varphi(x, y)$ where the coordinates $\bar{x} = \frac{m_{1,0}}{m_{0,0}}, \bar{y} = \frac{m_{0,1}}{m_{0,0}}$ denote the centroids of $\varphi(x, y)$.

Hu [14] introduced seven moment functions that are invariant to scaling, rotation and translation. To simply the computation, we only choose four of these moment invariants shown as follows:

$$\begin{aligned}
\phi_1 &= \mu_{20} + \mu_{02} \\
\phi_2 &= \sqrt{(\mu_{20} - \mu_{02})^2 + 4\mu_{11}^2} \\
\phi_3 &= \sqrt{(\mu_{30} - 3\mu_{12})^2 + (3\mu_{21} - \mu_{03})^2} \\
\phi_4 &= \sqrt{(\mu_{30} + \mu_{12})^2 + (\mu_{21} + \mu_{03})^2}
\end{aligned} \tag{8}$$

The vector $(\phi_1,\phi_2,\phi_3,\phi_4)$ is used to capture the holistic information of the character. The matching cost between two sets of the Hu moment invariants is given in equation (9):

$$D_{S'T'} = \sqrt{\beta_1^2(\phi_{1S'}-\phi_{1T'})^2+\beta_2^2(\phi_{2S'}-\phi_{2T'})^2+\beta_3^2(\phi_{3S'}-\phi_{3T'})^2+\beta_4^2(\phi_{4S'}-\phi_{4T'})^2} \quad (9)$$

where S',T' denote the sample and template character; β_i is the regulatory factor used to normalize the different ranges of the Hu moment invariants.

Finally, we get the cost for $h_1(n)$ by combining the equations (4) and (9):

$$h_1(n) = Cost\ (f, g_1', g_2') + \sum_{i=1}^{n} D_{S'_{i-1}T'_{i-1}} \quad (10)$$

where $f: V_1'(n) \rightarrow V_2'(n)$ with $V_1'(n) \subseteq V_1$ and $V_2'(n) \subseteq V_2$ specifying the nodes that have been matched; S'_{i-1}, T'_{i-1} are used to denote the characters formed by the strokes whose mappings have not yet been found; *n* is the number of the edit operations.

Definition of $h_2(n)$:

$$h_2(n) = D_{S`_n T`_n} \quad (11)$$

where $S_n' = V_1 - V_1'(n)$, $T_n' = V_2 - V_2'(n)$. $h_2(n)$ denotes the similarity between the subgraphs formed by the remaining strokes whose mappings have not yet been found. From equation (10), it can be deduced that the actual cost $h_2^*(n)$ from the node *n* to the goal node is given by the sum of the cost of edit operations of remaining matched strokes and the expression $\sum_{i=n}^{goal} D_{S_i'T_i'}$. Obviously, $h_2(n)$ given in equation (11) is only part of the cost of $h_2^*(n)$ thus the condition $h_2(n) \leq h_2^*(n)$ is satisfied. An example of the matching cost of the characters in Fig.2 is shown in Fig.4.

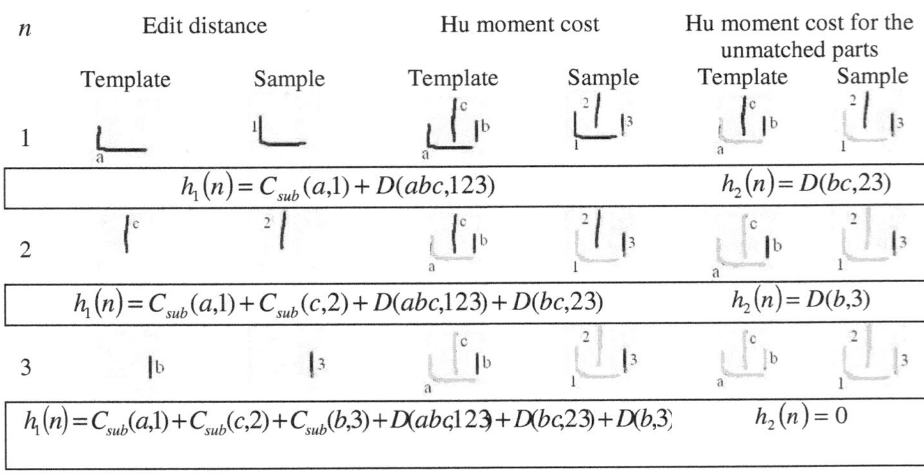

Fig. 4. Matching costs

3 Experiments and Results

In our experiment, we use 34 Chinese characters shown in Fig.5(a). These characters are written by different people and we get 917 various Chinese handwriting characters. Different people may write the same character in a different way. Sometimes there are some errors in the user's handwriting and we manually inspect those error types to obtain the ground truth information (Fig.5(b)). Then we apply our proposed algorithm for identifying those error cases. Afterwards we compare those errors identified by our algorithm with the ground truth errors to determine whether our result is correct. The accuracy of our proposed method can then be obtained.

丁上下火山王
卡出光乙水弓
廿中本甘牙四
凸田米企自門
式臣考革面啟
柳虐虛

(a) Characters used in the dataset

Types of Production Error	Count
Error free (correct handwriting)	486
Extra stroke error only	9
Missing stroke error only	28
Broken stroke error only	189
Concatenated stroke error only	163
More than two errors	42

(b) Types and count of handwriting errors

Fig. 5. The dataset

We have compared our proposed method with three existing methods: Tsay and Tsai 1993 [16], Tonouchi and Kawamura 1997 [17] and Tang and Leung 2006 [5]. The first two methods [16] and [17] have applied the string matching method to find the stroke correspondence. Although it works well sometimes, it always fails when the writing sequence of the sample and template strokes are not the same. Tang and Leung [5] proposed a system that allows users to practice handwriting freely, and it checks both the stroke sequence error and stroke production errors in the input handwriting simultaneously. There are two major steps in their approach. The first step is the identification of the problematic strokes with a matching cost larger than the threshold cost. In the second step, based on those problematic strokes, they try to get new character instances to identify the potential production error. The first step relies on the threshold and may not always work well. If the result from the first step is wrong then the final result would hardly be right.

The overall performance of our method compared with the other three existing methods is shown in Fig.6(a). It can be seen that our method yields a much lower error rate in identifying the stroke production errors. The computational time is illustrated in Fig.6(b). It can be seen that the time required for detecting stroke production errors for a character with 11 strokes is about 1.2 second showing that the feedback can be provided in a reasonable response time. Fig. 7 shows the performance comparison for specific error cases. Our proposed method works particularly well on finding the broken and concatenated stroke errors and even more complex errors containing more

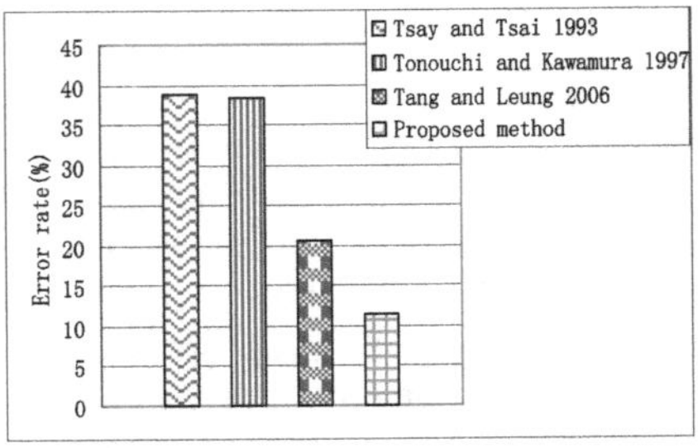

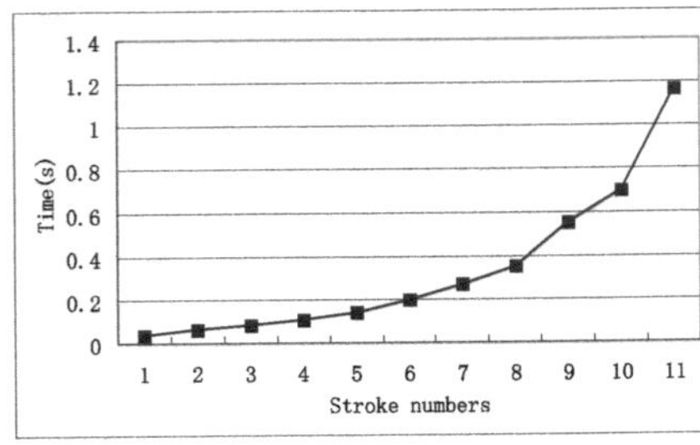

Fig. 6. (a) Overall performance comparison (b) Computational time

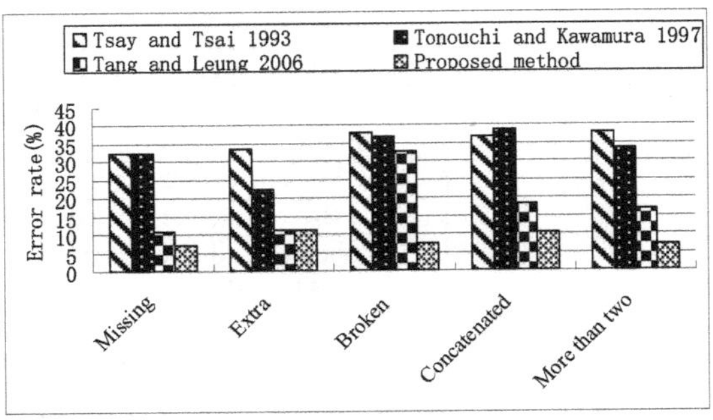

Fig. 7. Performance comparison for specific error cases

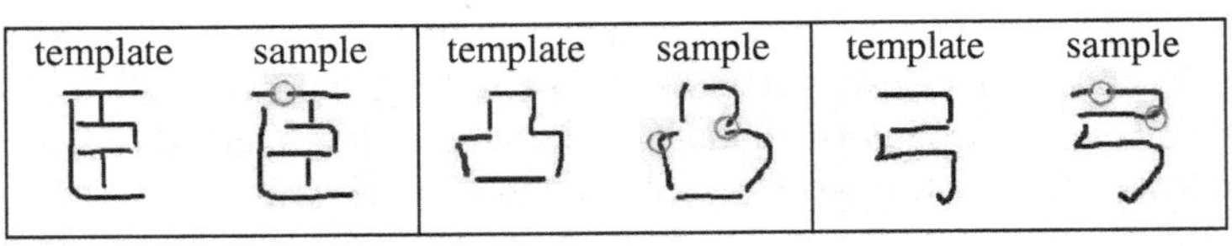

Fig. 8. Handwriting samples that can only be identified by our proposed method

than two stroke production errors. Fig. 8 shows some handwriting samples whose stroke production errors cannot be identified by the existing methods but our proposed method can handle these cases.

4 Conclusions and Future Work

In this paper we have applied the graph matching algorithm in finding the stroke correspondence between the input and template Chinese handwriting characters. The A* algorithm is used to search the state space tree to find the optimal graph matching. We have defined merging and splitting in addition to substitution, insertion and deletion as the edit operations for identifying stroke production errors. From the experiment, the performance of our proposed method is shown to be better than existing methods. As future work, we will add the edge labeling function to the graph which may bring much more structural information to help us to evaluate the elegance of the student's handwritings.

Acknowledgments. The work described in this paper was fully supported by a grant from City University of Hong Kong (Project No. 7001711).

References

1. Law, N., Ki, W.W., Chung, A.L.S., Ko, P.Y., Lam, H.C.: Children's stroke sequence errors in writing Chinese characters. Reading and Writing: An Interdisciplinary Journal, 267–292 (1998)
2. Tappert, C.C., Suen, C.Y., Wakahara, T.: The States of Art in One–Line Handwriting Recognition. IEEE Trans. Pattern Analysis and Machine Intelligence 12, 787–808 (1990)
3. Jianguo, L., Xiaozhen, Z.: The design and implementation of multimedia intelligent tutoring system for Chinese characters. In: IEEE Proc. of the 1st Intl. Conf. on Multi-Media Engineering Education, pp. 459–463 (1994)
4. Tzeng, C.-H., Hsu, L., Chen, C.-P., Uema, C.: A multimedia project in teaching Chinese and Japanese at Ball State University. In: IEEE Intl. Conf. on Multi Media Engineering Education, pp. 445–452 (1996)
5. Tang, K.–T., Leung, H.: A Web-based Chinese Handwriting Education System with Automatic Feedback and Analysis. In: ICWL. Intl. Conf. on Web-based Learning (2006)
6. Tan, C.K.: An algorithm for online strokes verification of Chinese characters using discrete features. In: 8th Intl. Workshop on Frontiers in Handwriting Recognition, pp. 339–344 (2002)
7. Teo, C.L., Burdet, E., Lim, H.P.: A robotic teacher of Chinese handwriting. HAPTICS, 335–341 (2002)
8. Coit, C.: Peer review in an online college writing course. In: IEEE Intl. Conf. on Advanced Learning Technologies, pp. 902–903 (2004)
9. Llados, J., Marti, E., Villanueva, J.J.: Symbol Recognition by Error–Tolerant Subgraph Matching between Region Adjacency Graphs. IEEE Trans. Pattern Analysis and Machine Intelligence 23, 1137–1143 (2001)
10. Bunke, H.: Error Correcting Graph Matching: On the Influence of the Underlying Cost Function. IEEE Trans. Pattern Analysis and Machine Intelligence 21, 917–922 (1999)
11. Messmer, B.T., Bunke, H.: A New Algorithm for Error–Tolerant Subgraph Isomorphism Detection. IEEE Trans. Pattern Analysis and Machine Intelligence 20, 493–504 (1998)
12. Liao, S.X., Lu, Q.: A Study of Moment Function and Its Use in Chinese Character Recognition. In: ICDAR. Fourth International Conference Document Analysis and Recognition, pp. 572–575 (1997)
13. Tzouveli, P.K., Ntalianis, K.S., Kollias, S.D.: Human Video Object Watermarking Based on HU Moments. Signal Processing Systems Design and Implementation, 104–109 (2005)
14. Hu, M.K.: Visual Pattern Recognition by moment invariants. IEEE Trans. Inform. Theory 8, 179–187 (1962)
15. Ambauen, R., Fischer, S., Bunke, H.: Graph Edit Distance with Node Splitting and Merging, and Its Application to Diatom Identification. In: IAPR Workshop (GbRPR), pp. 95–106 (2003)
16. Tsay, Y.T., Tsai, W.H.: Attributed String Matching by Split-and-Merge for On-line Chinese Character Recognition. IEEE Trans. PAMI 5, 180–185 (1993)
17. Tonouchi, Y., Kawamura, A.: An On-Line Japanese Character Recognition Method Using Length-Based Stroke Correspondence Algorithm. In: Proceedings of the Fourth Intl. Conf. on Analysis and Recognition, vol. 2, pp. 633–636 (1997)

Multi-modal Multi-label Semantic Indexing of Images Based on Hybrid Ensemble Learning

Wei Li[1], Maosong Sun[1], and Christopher Habel[2]

[1] State Key Lab of Intelligent Technology and Systems
Department of Computer Science and Technology, Tsinghua University
Beijing 100084, P.R. China
wei.lee04@gmail.com, sms@mail.tsinghua.edu.cn
[2] Fachbereich Informatik, Universität Hamburg
Hamburg, 22527, Germany
habel@informatik.uni-hamburg.de

Abstract. Automatic image annotation (AIA) refers to the association of words to whole images which is considered as a promising and effective approach to bridge the semantic gap between low-level visual features and high-level semantic concepts. In this paper, we formulate the task of image annotation as a multi-label multi class semantic image classification problem and propose a simple yet effective method: hybrid ensemble learning framework in which multi-label classifier based on uni-modal features and ensemble classifier based on bi-modal features are integrated into a joint classification model to perform multi-modal multi-label semantic image annotation. We conducted experiments on two commonly-used keyframe and image collections: MediaMill and Scene dataset including about 40,000 examples. The empirical studies demonstrated that the proposed hybrid ensemble learning method can enhance a given weak multi-label classifier to some extent, showing the effectiveness of our proposed method when limited number of multi-labeled training data is available.

1 Introduction

Automatic image annotation (AIA) refers to the association of semantic concepts to whole images which has become a hot research topic and increasingly required by many modern applications. For example, in the domain of semantic scene classification and medical image interpretation, multi-modal indexing through AIA enables each image or video clips to be associated with one or more descriptive concepts which allows for semantic browsing and retrieval of visual information via different keywords at different semantic levels when an ontology or concept hierarchy is available. Through the sustained efforts of experts and researchers, many approaches based on computer vision and machine learning theory have been proposed to attack this problem, which, in general, can be categorized into three major classes: generative models [1-4, 6-8, 13-18, 31]; discriminative approaches [5, 9-12,21, 27, 29-30] and search and mining-based annotation [25]. Some of these approaches have achieved the state-of-the-art performance and proved that automatic image annotation is an

H.H.S. Ip et al. (Eds.): PCM 2007, LNCS 4810, pp. 744–754, 2007.

effective solution to bridge the notorious semantic gap between low-level perceptual features and high-level semantic concepts. However, the key characteristic of automatic image annotation is that each image is usually assigned to multiple different semantic labels simultaneously instead of single label, because each image may contain multiple objects with different semantics. So multi-label classification model is more suitable than traditional single-label classifiers in that correlations between semantic labels can be incorporated rather than treating them as independent labels. In this case, label ambiguity or incompatibility can be avoided. For example, "*sky*" and "*ocean*" are more likely to co-occur than "*sky*" and "*computer*". Furthermore, multi-labeled training data is hard to obtain or create in large quantities which require large amount of human labeling effort, limited number of labeled training images can hardly represent the distribution of visual features for a concept of interest. Consequently, how to build accurate classification model using the limited multi-labeled image data to improve the annotation accuracy is becoming an important research issue.

The main contribution of this paper is three-fold: First, we formulate the task of image annotation as a multi-label, multi class semantic image classification problem under a joint classification framework called hybrid ensemble learning. Second, we review the multi-label learning approaches, and evaluate some of them on the image annotation task. Third, to enhance the annotation accuracy, single-label ensemble classifier based on bi-modal features is again fused to refine the classification results given by the multi-label classifier using the uni-modal features. To model the possible dependency between labels, correlations among labels obtained by using latent semantic indexing are incorporated into the bi-modal feature space. To the best of our knowledge, hybrid ensemble learning methods which integrate multi-label classifier based on uni-modal features and ensemble classifier based on bi-modal features into a joint classification model has not been carefully investigated in the domain of automatic image annotation.

This paper is organized as follows: Section 2 discusses related work. Section 3 first reviews the literature of multi-label learning and classification, and then describes the hybrid ensemble learning framework. Section 4 shows our experimental results and some theoretical analysis. Conclusions and future work are discussed in Section 5.

2 Related Work

Recently, many models using machine learning techniques have been proposed for automatic image annotation and retrieval. In general, these methods can be categorized into three classes: generative models, discriminative approaches as well as search and mining-based techniques.

Generative models:

$$P(l, v) = \sum_{s} P(l|s)P(v|s)P(s) \quad l \subseteq L, v \in V \tag{1}$$

where v dentoes the image data, l the subset of semantic concepts, s is the latent variable, L and V are concept lexicon and visual feature space respectively. By computing the joint distribution of visual features and associated concepts, the hidden correlation between this two modalities can be found and then is applied to annotate new images. Representative works are [1-4][6-8][13-18][31], especially R. Zhang et al[18] has achieved the state-of-the-art performance, G. Carneiro et al[31] proposed to use M-ary labeling and ignore the hidden variable which can reduce the model complexity.

Discriminative approaches:

$$P(w|v) \quad w \in L, v \in V \tag{2}$$

where w is a concept from L. Instead of joint modeling of semantic concepts and visual features, discriminative approaches treat each concept as a single class label and directly model the posterior probability of w given v. Some attractive works are [5][9-12][21][27]. Among them, K.Goh et al[10] and Cees G.M. Snoek[27] can provide better results. M. Bouttell et al[21] proposed the cross-training method to conduct multi-label scene classification and introduced some specific evaluation metrics.

In short, generative models can handle a large number of classes and class imbalance problem in some degree, but the model complexity is a major hurdle. While discriminative approaches are computationally efficient, however, they are unable to scale well to a large number of classes since it requires one model to be built for each class.

Search and Mining-based annotation:
Apart from annotation by learning, Wang et al. [25] proposed annotation by search and mining techniques which can not only makes use of web-scale images but also allows for unlimited vocabulary.

More recently, learning with unlabeled images has become an active research area due to fact that large amount of labeled training images is hard to obtain or create in large quantities while limited number of training images can hardly represent the visual distribution of target concepts and more information is contained in the large pool of unlabeled ones. Feng et al [30] and Song et al [29] introduced the use of co-training and combination of active learning together with semi-supervised ensembling to perform semantic annotation of images and video clips.

3 The Framework of Image Annotation Model

3.1 Formulation of Automatic Image Annotation

Given a training set of annotated images, where each image is associated with a number of semantic labels. We make an assumption that each image can be considered as a multi-modal document containing both the visual component and semantic component. Visual component provides the image representation in visual feature space using low-level perceptual features including color and texture, etc. While, semantic component captures the image semantics in semantic feature space based on textual annotations derived from a generic vocabulary, such as "*sky*", "*ocean*", etc. Automatic image annotation is the task of discovering the association model between visual and semantic component from such a labeled image database and then applying the association model to generate annotations for unlabeled images. More formally, let ID denote the training set of annotated images:

- $ID = \{I_1, I_2, \ldots, I_N\}$
- each image I_j in ID can be represented by the combination of visual features and semantic labels in a multi-modal feature space, i.e., $I_j = \{L_j; V_j\}$
- semantic component L_j is a bag of words described by a binary vector $L_j = \{l_{j,1}, l_{j,2}, \cdots, l_{j,m}\}$, where m is the size of generic vocabulary, $l_{j,i}$ is a binary variable indicating whether or not the i-th label l_i appears in I_j
- visual component V_j may be more complex due to a large variety of methods for visual representation, in general, it can also have the vector form $V_j = \{v_{j,1}, v_{j,2}, \ldots, v_{j,n}\}$, for patch-based image representation, i.e., image I_j is composed of a number of image segments or fixed-size blocks, each of them is described by a feature vector $v_{j,i}$, and n is the number of image components; for global image representation, $v_{j,i}$ only denotes a feature component and n is the dimension of selected feature space

For a given unseen image represented by v_u, the goal of automatic image annotation is to estimate:

$$l^* = \arg\max p(l|v_u), \quad l \subseteq L, v_u \in V \tag{3}$$

3.2 Underlying Theory of Multi-label Learning and Classification

In traditional classification problems, to reduce the model complexity, class labels are assumed to be mutually exclusive or independent from each other and each instance to be classified belongs to only one class. However, in the context of image annotation, it is natural that one image belongs to multiple classes simultaneously due to the richness of image content, causing the actual classes to overlap in the feature space. Furthermore, in most cases, it is quite hard and insufficient to describe the image content using only a keyword because image semantics is represented by both basic semantic entities in that image and the relationships between them. Consequently, multi-label learning is a more suitable and intuitive solution for automatic image annotation.

Multi-label learning refers to the problem where each example is associated with multiple different class labels simultaneously. It is now ubiquitous in real-world applications, e.g., text categorization [19][22][23], protein function prediction[26]. And in scene classification [21], if we treat every concept as a class label, each scene image may belong to several semantic classes, such as "*sky*" and "*clouds*". In all these cases, instances for training are each associated with a set of labels, and the task is to predict a candidate label set for the unseen instance.

An intuitive approach to solving multi-label problem is to decompose it into multiple independent binary classification problems (one per class). However, this kind of method suffers from many disadvantages. One is that it does not scale well to a large number of classes since a binary classifier has to be built for each class. Second, it does not consider the correlations between the different labels. Third, it may encounter imbalanced data problem when the minority classes are given only a few labeled training examples. Another group of approaches toward multi-label learning is label ranking which stems from preference learning. Instead of learning binary classifiers for each class, these approaches learn a ranking function from the labeled examples that order class labels for a given test example according to their relevance to the example. Compared to the binary classification approaches, the label ranking approaches are advantageous in dealing with large numbers of classes because only a single ranking function is learned.

3.3 Hybrid Ensemble Learning for Multi-modal Image Annotation

In this paper, we propose a two-stage joint classification framework called hybrid ensemble learning. The main idea is to train two classifiers, multi-class multi-label classifier at first stage and binary-class single-label ensemble classifier at second-stage using uni-modal and bi-modal features respectively. For a new, unseen image, the multi-label classifier is first used to predict the possible labels, and then the ensemble classifier is responsible for determining whether or not each predicted label is appropriate to describe the image semantics. To be more formal, let X be the image data, Y the finite set of predefined semantic labels and the size of Y is denoted by k. For multi-labeled classifier training, each training pair has the uni-modal form of (x, y), where $x \in \mathrm{X}$, $y \subseteq \mathrm{Y}$ While, for ensemble classifier, the training data is derived using a natural reduction of multi-labeled data to binary data. To be more specific, each example is mapped to a k binary-labeled bi-modal meta-examples of the form $((x, l, r), y[l])$ for all $l \in \mathrm{Y}$, where $y[l] = 1$ if $l \in y$ and -1 otherwise, r denotes the correlation between the label l and all the other labels. In this paper, the correlation among different labels is obtained by using latent semantic indexing. That is, the observation of each derived meta-example is (x, l, r) , and the associated binary label is $y[l] \in \{-1, 1\}$. For the classification of a new image, the multi-label classifier is initially applied and a label list containing candidate labels is output. Each candidate label is then appended to the feature vector of the new image to form the above-mentioned bi-modal meta-example; this meta-example is finally classified by the ensemble classifier to examine if each predicted label is relevant to the new, unseen image. In other words, the main task of the ensemble classifier is to conduct meta-example identification, to identify the positive and negative ones, then the appended label in the positive meta-example is considered as the correct label for the corresponding image and is kept in the predicted label list while the appended label in the negative one is removed from the predicted label list. Since in most multi-labeled image collections, the number of semantic labels for each image is rather small compared to the total number of predefined semantic labels, the produced bi-modal training data is extremely imbalanced in the sense that the number of negative meta-examples is much larger than that of positive meta-examples. To avoid the performance degradation of ensemble classifier due to the class imbalance problem, we propose to use the asymmetric bagging [24] to generate a classifier ensemble. The key idea behind asymmetric bagging is that keeping positive meta-examples the same for each base classifier and bootstrapping is only performed on the negative meta-examples to sample the same number as the positive meta-examples to construct a balanced training set. To build a desired ensemble classification model, maximizing the diversity of each base classifier while maintaining the consistency with the training data is known to be an important goal, so in our method, each sampled negative subset is different from each other to ensure the diversity of training data. Moreover, logistic regression is used as the base classifier which requires less training time and low storage for built models compared to support vector machines [20]. In addition, logistic regression classifier has achieved the state-of-the-art performance in image classification tasks [28]. To further guarantee the performance of ensemble classifier, we use boosting method, AdaBoost, to enhance each base classifier. The following figure 1 and figure 2 show the joint classification framework and the asymmetric bagging algorithm.

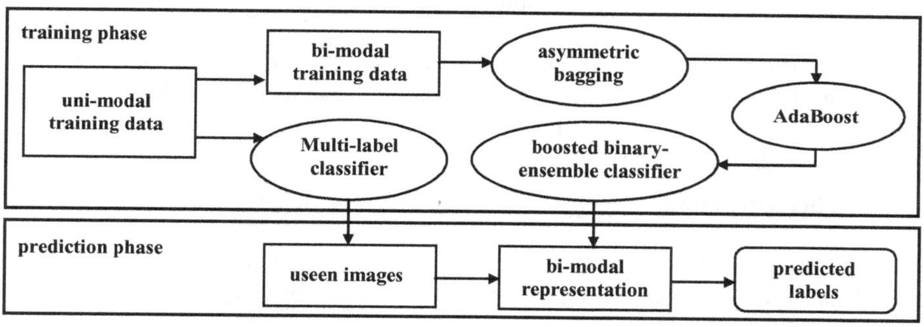

Fig. 1. Framework of Hybrid Ensemble Learning for Multi-Modal Image Annotation

---

Asymmetric Bagging Algorithm:
Input: positive meta-examples S^+, negative meta-examples S^-, base classifier I, number of base classifiers N, sampling factor α and the test meta-example t.
Output: final label l and classifier ensemble C
1. for i = 1 to N
2. S_i^- bootstrap samples from S^- using the criterion that $\alpha|S_i^-| = |S^+|$.
3. $I_i = I(S^+, S_i^-)$
4. $l = majority\_voting(I_i(x, S^+, S_i^-))$, $C = \{I_i\}$

Fig. 2. Algorithm of Asymmetric Bagging for Binary Classifier Training

4 Experimental Results

Data Set
Our experiments are carried out using two commonly-used keyframe and image datasets, MediaMill [27] and Scene [21] collection including about 42177 keyframes, 2407 images respectively. Table 1 shows the general information about the two data

collection. For the multi-label classifier, we use multi-label boosting [19] and multi-label C45[22] which have been successfully applied to text categorization tasks.

Mediamill: A number of color invariant texture features per pixel is firstly extracted. Based on these features, a set of predefined regions in a key frame image is labeled with similarity scores for a total of 15 low-level visual concepts. We vary the size of pre-defined regions to obtain a total of 8 concept occurrence histograms that characterize both global and local color-texture information. Finally, the histograms are concatenated to yield a 120-dimensional visual feature vector per keyframe image.

Scene: each image is divided into 49 blocks with the grid size of 7*7, then mean and variance of each block is computed in LUV color space, plus some computational inexpensive texture features, the resulting visual representation is 49 * 2 * 3 = 294 feature vector.

We here use the concepts of label cardinality and label density to describe the information of labels for each image. Let D be a multi-labeled image dataset including $|D|$ image pairs (x_i, y_i) and L the finite set of predefined semantic labels.

$$\textbf{label\_cardinality: } \frac{1}{|D|}\sum_{i=1}^{|D|}|y_i| \qquad \textbf{label\_density : } \frac{1}{|D|}\sum_{i=1}^{|D|}\frac{|y_i|}{|L|} \tag{4}$$

where label cardinality measures the average number of labels for each image and label density is the normalized representation of label cardinality.

Table 1. General Information of Two Datasets

Data Set	Examples		Feature Dimension	Labels	Label density	Label cardinality
	Training	Test				
MediaMill	29804	12373	120	101	0.0449	4.5369
Scene	1211	1196	294	6	0.1770	1.0619

Performance Metric

Multi-label Evaluation:

In contrast to traditional single-label classification, multi-label classification requires different evaluation metrics, here, we use the same metrics introduced in the literature. Let a multi-labeled image dataset denoted by D , which consists of $|D|$ image pairs (x_i, y_i) , L the lexicon of predefined semantic labels, y_i and z_i are the ground-truth and predicted label sequence respectively. In the following discussion, MLB and MLC45 refer to the multi-label boosting and multi-label C45 classifier. HMLB and HMLC45 with the suffix "H" refers to the boosted hybrid version of our method.

$$\textbf{Accuracy:} \frac{1}{|D|}\sum_{i=1}^{|D|}\frac{|Y_i \cap Z_i|}{|Y_i \cup Z_i|} \qquad \textbf{Precision:} \frac{1}{|D|}\sum_{i=1}^{|D|}\frac{|Y_i \cap Z_i|}{|Z_i|} \qquad \textbf{Recall:} \frac{1}{|D|}\sum_{i=1}^{|D|}\frac{|Y_i \cap Z_i|}{|Y_i|} \tag{5}$$

Table 2. Multi-label Evaluation of Two Datasets

DataSet	Mediamill				Scene			
Methods	MLB	HMLB	MLC45	HMLC45	MLB	HMLB	MLC45	HMLC45
Accuracy	0.3897	0.3902	0.3020	0.3092	0.5074	0.5103	0.5152	0.5171
Precision	0.4621	0.4695	0.3893	0.3917	0.5114	0.5156	0.5371	0.5401
Recall	0.7262	0.7379	0.6117	0.6316	0.9511	0.9543	0.6442	0.6463

Retrieval Evaluation:

We also use the precision to evaluate the performance of the proposed method, for a single query concept *w*, precision is defined as follows. Let I_j denotes the retrieved *j*-th image, t_j and a_j represent the ground-truth labels and predicted labels associated with the *j*-th image.

$$\textbf{precision}(w) = \frac{\left|\{I_j \middle| w \in t_j \wedge w \in a_j\}\right|}{\left|\{I_j \middle| w \in a_j\}\right|} \tag{6}$$

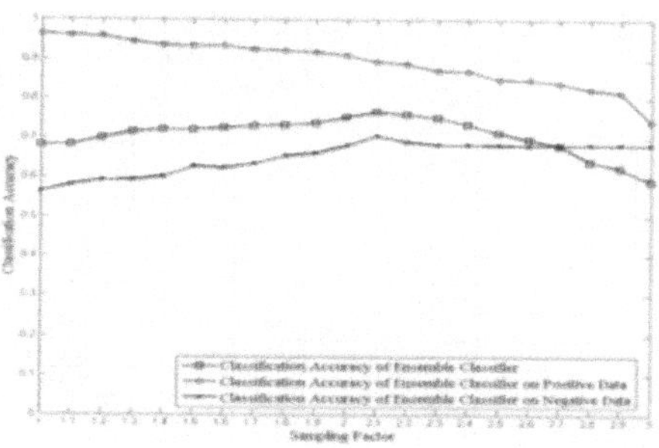

Fig. 3. Classification Accuracy vs Sampling Factor

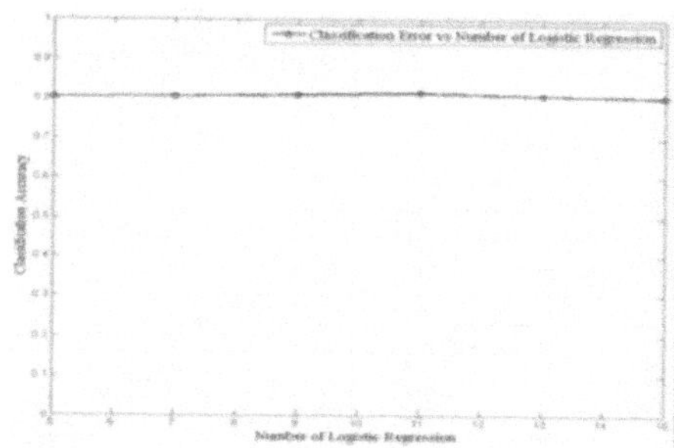

Fig. 4. Classification Accuracy vs Number of Logistic Regression

Figure 3 shows the classification accuracy of the ensemble classifier using different sampling factors in asymmetric bagging. We can see that using different sampling factor may lead to different classification accuracy. With the increasing of the sampling factor, classification accuracy of positive meta-examples may decreases while the classification accuracy of negative ones may increase, so we can find the best trade-off point to maximize the identification performance. In other words, maximizing the ability of discerning positive and negative meta-examples which ensures correctly predicted labels are kept in the candidate label list while the incorrectly predicted ones are removed.

Figure 4 illustrates the classification accuracy vs. number of logistic regression classifiers which verifies the fact that number of logistic regression has little effect on the classification accuracy of the ensemble classifier.

Table 3. Comparison of Precision using Different Methods

	concept	Training%	Test%	MLB	HMLB	MLC45	HMLC45		concept	Training%	Test%	MLB	HMLB	MLC45	HMLC45
1	aircraft	1.0267	0.986	0.1728	0.1868	0.0617	0.0617	56	maps	1.2012	1.2608	0.3333	0.3894	0.1131	0.125
2	allawi	0.218	0.0242	0	0	0	0	57	meeting	4.7141	5.0675	0.2446	0.2715	0.0898	0.073
3	anchor	5.2946	5.0594	0.3818	0.3962	0.3032	0.3197	58	military	4.3048	6.8698	0.2494	0.2501	0.1453	0.1567
4	animal	1.0368	0.9456	0.1304	0.1406	0.126	0.101	59	monologue	3.2278	2.4327	0.0902	0.129	0.0502	0.063
5	arrafat	0.6475	0.9133	0	0	0.0376	0.0264	60	motorbike	0.0537	0.1697	0	0	0	0
6	baseball	0.0134	0.4284	0	0	0	0	61	mountain	1.7045	1.0588	0.1029	0.134	0.0547	0.0612
7	basketball	0.7147	0.3556	0.1228	0.1344	0.0272	0.0317	62	natural_disaster	0.8388	0.9699	0.0781	0.0645	0.0501	0.0501
8	beach	0.0805	0.0647	0	0	0.0476	0	63	newspaper	0.3254	0.2829	0.3947	0.4148	0.1118	0.1208
9	bicycle	0.2113	0.0404	0	0	0.0149	0.0149	64	nightfire	0.1476	0.0566	0	0	0.0426	0.0589
10	bird	0.1879	0.2425	0.4118	0.4118	0.4286	0.4434	65	office	1.6273	1.8266	0.2727	0.2817	0.0418	0.0202
11	boat	0.812	0.5658	0.1014	0.1205	0.0512	0.0606	66	outdoor	33.989	40.006	0.5104	0.5363	0.5106	0.5364
12	building	7.1333	11.646	0.3198	0.3345	0.1924	0.2278	67	overlayed_text	37.784	35.796	0.4416	0.462	0.4463	0.4633
13	bus	0.4429	0.6708	0	0	0.0185	0.0185	68	people	80.764	79.189	0.8061	0.83	0.8375	0.8753
14	bush_jr	1.6743	0.5658	0.0811	0.0642	0.0136	0.0136	69	people_marching	2.0031	4.3078	0.3466	0.3324	0.1112	0.1268
15	bush_sr	0.208	0.0081	0	0	0	0	70	police_security	0.9596	0.8082	0	0	0.0223	0.0351
16	candle	0.0872	0.1051	0.1	0.1138	0	0	71	powell	0.047	0.493	0	0	0	0
17	car	5.0631	6.1909	0.2302	0.2529	0.1481	0.1667	72	prisoner	0.3456	0.2263	0	0	0.0056	0
18	cartoon	0.0872	0.2182	0.6	0.6328	0.2941	0.3024	73	racing	0.0906	0.1293	0	0	0	0
19	chair	0.6207	0.6062	0.2581	0.2789	0.1091	0.1258	74	religious_leader	0.2819	0.2344	0	0	0	0
20	charts	0.7851	0.5334	0.1597	0.171	0.0521	0.0332	75	river	0.1007	0.0889	0.1333	0.1501	0.0909	0.108
21	clinton	0.0503	0.2182	0	0	0.1333	0.1533	76	road	8.066	6.886	0.1974	0.2123	0.1326	0.1369
22	cloud	0.9059	1.6083	0.2576	0.2721	0.0709	0.0801	77	screen	1.5937	1.9801	0.08	0.061	0.049	0.0669
23	corporate_leader	2.6741	1.3578	0	0	0.0213	0.0213	78	sharon	0.0436	0.2021	0	0	0	0
24	court	0.2114	0.3152	0	0	0.0127	0.0127	79	sky	11.203	11.873	0.3547	0.3725	0.2564	0.2614
25	crowd	11.941	16.827	0.3856	0.3972	0.2726	0.3103	80	smoke	1.171	2.2387	0.3457	0.3526	0.1557	0.1709
26	cycling	0.1913	0.0323	0	0	0.0233	0.315	81	snow	0.4228	0.5496	0.0882	0.1081	0.0877	0.0935
27	desert	0.8388	1.5033	0.1887	0.1742	0.0402	0.0585	82	soccer	1.7347	0.3071	0.0577	0.0414	0.0641	0.0521
28	dog	0.1476	0.396	0.3	0.3218	0.0732	0.0607	83	splitscreen	0.8992	0.6223	0.25	0.28	0.0905	0.1072
29	drawing	0.0872	0.1778	0.5	0.4304	0	0	84	sports	3.9122	2.7237	0.105	0.1146	0.0716	0.0821
30	drawing_cartoon	0.1745	0.396	0.4167	0.4398	0.2083	0.2399	85	studio	14.206	14.823	0.4538	0.4628	0.4407	0.4525
31	duo_anchor	0.2751	0.1859	0.3077	0.3271	0.0441	0.0531	86	swimmingpool	0.0839	0.1051	0	0	0.0588	0.068
32	entertainment	20.427	13.101	0.1778	0.1935	0.1835	0.217	87	table	0.7751	0.5415	0.0543	0.0499	0.0341	0
33	explosion	0.5503	1.083	0.0962	0.0761	0.0562	0.0667	88	tank	0.0872	0.0808	0	0	0.0147	0
34	face	66.713	65.101	0.6983	0.7117	0.7365	0.7543	89	tennis	0.3523	0.5819	0.2143	0.2208	0.046	0.0557
35	female	4.5598	2.1983	0.1064	0.113	0.0402	0.0501	90	tony_blair	0.0503	0.2667	0	0	0	0
36	fireweapon	0.3624	0.5415	0.1429	0.1604	0.0332	0.0202	91	tower	0.7751	0.6547	0.0526	0.0433	0.0348	0.0412
37	fish	0.2785	0.1293	0.0741	0.0741	0.1389	0.1577	92	tree	0.8086	0.881	0.1032	0.1177	0.0747	0.0417
38	flag	1.3085	1.1719	0.2444	0.2628	0.0509	0.0625	93	truck	1.2112	1.0668	0.0543	0.0411	0.0383	0.0474
39	flag_usa	0.9563	0.9779	0.186	0.171	0.0539	0.0643	94	urban	12.25	9.1813	0.1969	0.1969	0.1374	0.1584
40	food	0.5234	0.8648	0.06	0.06	0.1908	0.2012	95	vegetation	4.0196	4.8412	0.1787	0.1911	0.1052	0.1241
41	football	0.2047	0.4041	0.1111	0.1264	0.0727	0.09	96	vehicle	7.9184	8.8984	0.2617	0.2751	0.1768	0.1974
42	golf	0.2617	0.3233	0	0	0.0577	0.0463	97	violence	8.3881	10.175	0.2899	0.3	0.197	0.2141
43	government_building	0.2852	0.194	0	0	0.0089	0	98	walking_running	14.156	17.571	0.2999	0.3114	0.2325	0.2431
44	government_leader	9.7269	8.2114	0.1956	0.2019	0.1132	0.1647	99	waterbody	2.4024	1.972	0.1344	0.1461	0.1335	0.1504
45	graphics	3.0097	3.6289	0.3162	0.3288	0.1631	0.1912	100	waterfall	0.0705	0.0808	0	0	0.1538	0.1752
46	grass	0.9361	0.6142	0.0494	0.0494	0.0379	0.041	101	weather	1.0301	1.3012	0.2917	0.3065	0.0878	0.0989
47	hassan_nasrallah	0.047	0.194	0	0	0	0								
48	horse	0.1711	0.0242	0	0	0	0								
49	horse_racing	0.1208	0.0242	0	0	0	0								
50	house	0.302	0.3799	0	0	0.0114	0.0157	1	beach	18.745	16.722	0.3848	0.3741	0.4605	0.4713
51	hu_jintao	0.0268	1.0749	0	0	0	0	2	fall foliage	13.625	16.639	0.6393	0.6508	0.7129	0.7483
52	indoor	20.376	22.129	0.4243	0.4485	0.415	0.4443	3	field	16.268	16.722	0.5246	0.5329	0.5481	0.5481
53	kerry	0.3053	0.0081	0	0	0	0	4	mountain	16.185	19.816	0.5158	0.5264	0.4821	0.5034
54	lahoud	0.312	0.1536	0.1429	0.1587	0.0676	0.0866	5	sunset	22.874	21.405	0.3377	0.3487	0.3558	0.3841
55	male	5.9388	2.4812	0.0924	0.1037	0.0607	0.0737	6	urban	18.497	17.308	0.3642	0.3714	0.4176	0.4299

Table 3 shows the precision results using different methods on Mediamill and Scene collection, which illustrates that our method can effectively remove the incorrectly predicted labels while keeping the correctly predicted ones. However, the performance of this method is dependent on the accuracy of the first-stage multi-label classifier; that is to say, we can not boost the zero-precision label outputted by the multi-label classifier. In addition, the precision value of concepts with sufficient training data is satisfactory in most cases, for example, "*people*", "*face*", etc. but, for the concept "*entertainment*" , its precision value is low, possible reasons are the large variation of visual feature distribution of this concept. So it is hard to learn the visual patterns for some concept of interest.

5 Conclusion and Future work

In this paper, we propose a general framework for automatic image annotation and retrieval based on hybrid ensemble learning in which multi-label classifier based on uni-modal features and single-label ensemble classifier based on bi-modal features are integrated into a unified joint classification framework. Empirical results indicate that the advantage of our proposed method is that it can enhance the accuracy of a given mutli-label classifiers in some cases when limited number of multi-labeled training data is available. While the disadvantage is that its accuracy is dependent on the performance of the multi-label classifier, for example, our method has no effect on the zero-precision label in the test set. In addition, we can also draw other conclusions: First, in some cases, applying a sampling ratio factor to asymmetric bagging can lead to improved performance when majority-minority ratio is large. Second, the number of logistic regression classifiers does not affect the model performance.

Acknowledgements

We would like to express our deepest gratitude to Marcel Worring and Jiebo Luo for making their datasets available. The research is supported by the National Natural Science Foundation of China under grant number 60573187 and 60321002 and 60520130299.

References

1. Barnard, K., Dyugulu, P., de Freitas, N., Forsyth, D., Blei, D., Jordan, M.I.: Matching words and pictures. Journal of Machine Learning Research 3, 1107–1135 (2003)
2. Barnard, K., Forsyth, D.A.: Learning the Semantics of Words and Pictures. In: Proceedings of International Conference on Computer Vision, pp. 408–415 (2001)
3. Duygulu, P., Barnard, K., de Freitas, N., Forsyth, D.: Ojbect recognition as machine translation: Learning a lexicon fro a fixed image vocabulary. In: Heyden, A., Sparr, G., Nielsen, M., Johansen, P. (eds.) ECCV 2002. LNCS, vol. 2350, pp. 97–112. Springer, Heidelberg (2002)
4. Jeon, J., Lavrenko, V., Manmatha, R.: Automatic image annotation and retrieval using cross-media relevance models. In: Proc. of SIGIR 2003, pp. 119–126 (2003)
5. Chang, E., Goh, K., Sychay, G., Wu, G.: CBSA: Content-based soft annotation for multimodal image retrieval using bayes point machines. IEEE Transactions on CSVT 13(1), 26–38 (2003)
6. Li, J., Wang, J.A.: Automatic linguistic indexing of pictures by a statistical modeling approach. IEEE Transactions on PAMI 25(10), 175–188 (2003)
7. Lavrenko, V., Manmatha, R., Jeon, J.: A model for learning the semantics of pictures. In: Proc. of the 16th Annual Conference on Neural Information Processing Systems (2004)
8. Blei, D., Jordan, M.I.: Modeling annotated data. In: Proceedings of the 26th intl. SIGIR Conf., pp. 127–134 (2003)

9. Li, B., Goh, K.: Confidence-based dynamic ensemble for image annotation and semantics discovery. In: Proc. of ACM MM 2003, pp. 195–206 (2003)
10. Goh, K., Li, B., Chang, E.: Semantics and feature discovery via confidence-based ensemble. ACM Transactions on Multimedia Computing, Communications, and Applications 1(2), 168–189 (2005)
11. Goh, K., Chang, E., Li, B.: Using on-class and two-class SVMs for multiclass image annotation. IEEE Trans. on Knowledge and Data Engineering 17(10), 1333–1346 (2005)
12. Fan, J., Gao, Y., Luo, H.: Multi-level annotation of natural scenes using dominant image components and semantic concepts. In: Proc. of ACM MM, pp. 540–547 (2004)
13. Feng, S.L., Lavrenko, V., Manmatha, R.: Multiple Bernoulli Relevance Models for Image and Video Annotation. In: Proc. of CVPR 2004 (2004)
14. Jin, R., Chai, J.Y., Si, L.: Effective Automatic image annotation via a coherent language model and active learning. In: Proc. of ACM MM 2004 (2004)
15. Kang, F., Jin, R., Chai, J.Y.: Regularizing Translation Models for Better Automatic Image Annotation. In: Proc. of CIKM 2004 (2004)
16. Monay, F., Gatica-Perez, D.: On image auto-annotation with latent space models. In: Proc. of ACM MM 2003. Conf. on Multimedia (2003)
17. Monay, F., Gatica-Perez, D.: PLSA-based image auto-annotation: Constraining the latent space. In: Proc. ACM Int. Conf. on Multimedia, New York (October 2004)
18. Zhang, R., Zhang, Z., Li, M., WY, M., Zhang, HJ.: A probabilistic semantic model for image annotation and multi-modal image retrieval. Multimedia Systems 12(1), 27–33 (2006)
19. Schapire, R., Singer, Y.: Boostexter: A boosting-based system for text categorization. Machine Learning 39, 135–168 (2000)
20. Wang, X.-R., Lin, C.-J.: LIBLR: a library for large regularized logistic regression (2007), Software available at http://www.csie.ntu.edu.tw/~cjlin/liblr/
21. Boutell, M., Luo, J., Shen, X., Luo, J.: Learning multi-label scene classification. Pattern Recognition 37(9), 1757–1771 (2004)
22. de Comite, F., Gilleron, R., Tommasi, M.: Learning multi-label alternating decision trees from texts and data. In: Proc. of MLDM 2003, pp. 35–49 (2003)
23. Gao, S., Wu, W., Lee, C.-H., Chua, T.-S.: A MFoM learning approach to robust multiclass multi-label text categorization. In: Proc. of ICML 2004, p. 42 (2004)
24. Tao, D., Xiaoou, T., Li, X., Wu, X.: Asymmetric Bagging and Random Subspace for Support Vector Machines-based Relevance Feedback in Image Retrieval. IEEE trans on PRMI 28(7), 1088–1099 (2006)
25. Wang, X., Zhang, L., Jing, F., Ma, W.-Y.: AnnoSearch: Image Auto-Annotation by Search. Proc. of CVPR (2006)
26. Chen, K., Lu, B.L., Kwok, J.T.: Effcient Classification of Multi-label and Imbalanced Data using Min-Max Modular Classifiers. In: Proc. of IJCNN 2006, pp. 1770–1775 (2006)
27. Snoek, C.G.M., Worring, M., van Gemert, J.C., Geusebroek, J.-M., Smeulders, A.W.M.: The challenge problem for automated detection of 101 semantic concepts in multimedia. In: Proc. Of ACM MM 2006, pp. 421–430 (2006)
28. Hoi, S.C., Jin, R., Lyu, M.: Batch Mode Active Learning and Its Application to Medical Image Classification. In: Proc. of ICML 2006, pp. 417–424 (2006)
29. Song, Y., Qi, G.-J., Hua, X.-S., Dai, L.-R., Wang, R.-H.: Video Annotation by Active Learning and Semi-Supervised Ensembling. In: Proc. of ICME 2006, pp. 933–936 (2006)
30. Feng, H., Chua, T.-S.: A bootstrapping approach to annotating large image collection. In: MIR 2003, pp. 55–62 (2003)
31. Carneiro, G., Chan, A.B., Moreno, P.J., Vasconcelos, N.: Supervised Learning of Semantic Classes for Image Annotation and Retrieval. IEEE trans on PAMI 29(3), 394–410 (2007)

Content Based Image Hashing Via Wavelet and Radon Transform

Xin C. Guo and Dimitrios Hatzinakos

Department of Electrical and Computer Engineering,
University of Toronto, Toronto, Canada
{cguo,dimitris}@comm.utoronto.ca

Abstract. Image hash function based on the image content has applications in watermarking, authentication and image retrieval. This paper presents an algorithm for generating an image hash that is robust against content-preserving modifications and at the same time, is capable of detecting malicious tampering. Robust features are first extracted from the discrete wavelet transform followed by the Radon transform. Probabilistic quantization is then used to map the feature values to a binary sequence. Results show that the proposed method can resist perceptually insignificant modifications such as compression, filtering, scaling and rotation. It is also able to successfully detect content changing attacks such as insertion of foreign objects.

Keywords: Image Hashing, Wavelet Transform, Radon Transform.

1 Introduction

Representing images with short binary sequences has widespread applications in watermarking, authentication and image indexing. Image hash algorithms based on image content have gained research interests in the past few years. Repeated use of the same watermark or signature gives the attackers the opportunities to guess and forge by observing for a long period of time. Recent techniques have been based on extracting features from the original image and use them to form a watermark or signature.

The most important step in both digital watermarking and signature generating schemes is to extract a set of features that resist content-preserving modifications. Because the original file might be subjected to lossy compression, noise, geometric distortion and filtering, it is essential for the content based watermarks and signatures to stay relatively constant. At the same time, malicious modifications such as object insertion and removal should cause major changes in the features and hence to preserve the integrity of the image content.

Fridrich *et al.* [1] proposed a method that projects the images onto a series of zero-mean, random smooth patterns. The idea was based on the observation that low-frequency components of the discrete cosine transform (DCT) are relatively the same if no visible changes are done to an image. Although this method

H.H.S. Ip et al. (Eds.): PCM 2007, LNCS 4810, pp. 755–764, 2007.

performed well under certain filtering operations, it is not robust against geometric distortions [2]. Venkatesan *et al.* [3] designed an image hash function based on the statistic information of the discrete wavelet transform (DWT). They observed that although the absolute values of the coefficients change after certain modifications, the statistical information such as the means and variances of the coefficients remain the same. However, Meixner and Uhl [4] have found that wavelet transform based methods are sensitive to local geometric distortions. Recently, Fourier-Mellin transform has been used by Swaminathan *et al.* [2] for image hashing applications. Using Fourier-Mellin transform's scale invariant property, the magnitudes of the Fourier transform coefficients were randomly weighted and summed. However, since Fourier transform did not offer localized frequency information, this method was not able to detect malicious local modifications. The Radon transform was first used by Lefevre [5] and further expanded by Seo *et al.* [6]. Affine invariant features could be extracted via Radon transform, followed by log mapping and then Fourier transform. The drawback of this method was similar to the previous one: local changes could be hard to detect. Another signature generation method was based on image features extracted from various edge detectors. Lu developed a different feature extraction method based on Gaussian kernel filtering [7]. Monga and Evans [8] used *end-stop* wavelets to detect corners in an image. This group of methods had very good localized feature detection capability; however, they would not work well for images that lack edges or discontinuities.

In this paper, an image hashing scheme based on the combination of discrete wavelet transform and the Radon transform is proposed. Taking the advantages of the frequency localization property of DWT and shift/rotation invariant property of the Radon transform, the algorithm can effectively detect malicious local changes, and at the same time, be robust against content-preserving modifications. The algorithm is particularly useful in image authentication applications such as photo journalism and photo forensics. Also, because two distinct images have distinct hashes, the proposed method could also be used in image searching and retrieval.

Section 2 formally introduces the properties of DWT, the Radon transform and the proposed image hashing scheme. Testing results are presented in Section 3, and concluding remarks and future directions are discussed in Section 4.

2 Image Hash Via Discrete Wavelet and Radon Transform

2.1 Discrete Wavelet Transform

The discrete wavelet transform and its variations have been used in many image hashing algorithms [3,9,8]. DWT not only captures the frequency content of an image, but also the spatial information by examining the output at different scales. This time-frequency localization property makes DWT more desirable than the discrete cosine or Fourier transform in tampering detection.

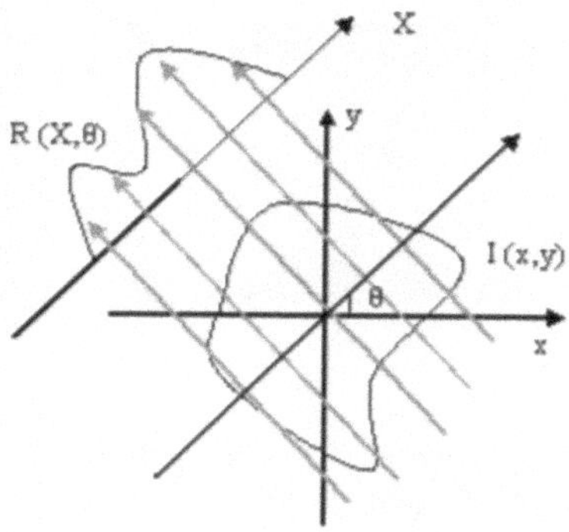

Fig. 1. Radon transform in θ direction

However, the main drawback of DWT is its variance to shifting. The features extracted based only on wavelet transform are generally sensitive to geometric distortions such as rotation and translation.

2.2 Radon Transform

Depicted in Fig.1, Radon transform is the projections of a two-dimensional (2D) function onto a set of lines. Formally, it can be written as

$$R(X,\theta) = \int_{-\infty}^{\infty}\int_{-\infty}^{\infty} I(x,y)\delta(x\cos\theta + y\sin\theta - X)dxdy \qquad (1)$$

where I(x,y) is a continues 2D function and $\theta \in [0,\pi]$ is the angle of the line with respect to the positive x-axis.

In image processing, the Radon transform has the following useful properties:

1. If an image is rotated by an angle ϕ, its Radon transform is shifted by the same amount,
$$I(x\cos\phi - y\sin\phi, x\sin\phi + y\cos\phi) \leftrightarrow R(X,\theta+\phi).$$
2. If an image is scaled by a factor ρ, its Radon transform is scaled by the same factor,
$$I(\rho x, \rho y) \leftrightarrow \frac{1}{\rho}R(\rho X,\theta).$$

The Radon transforms of the image Lena and rotated (10°), scaled (50%) Lena images are shown in Fig.2. Comparing to the original image, the Radon transform of the rotated image is shifted 10° to the right (Fig.2(b)). Fig.2(c) shows the Radon transform is scaled by a factor 0.5.

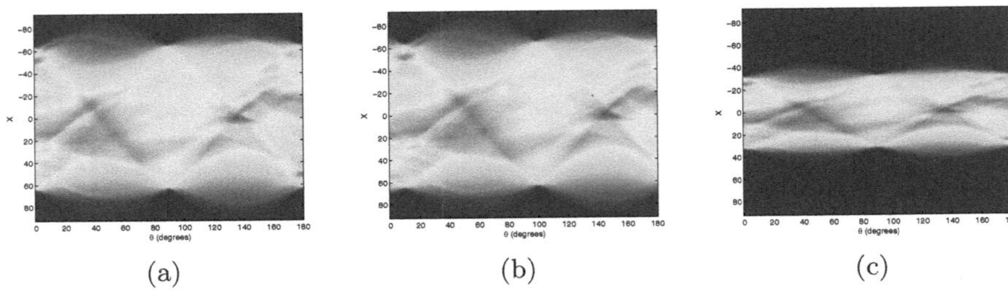

Fig. 2. Radon transforms of (a) original Lena image, (b) Lena image that is rotated by 10° and (c) Lena image that is scaled by 50%

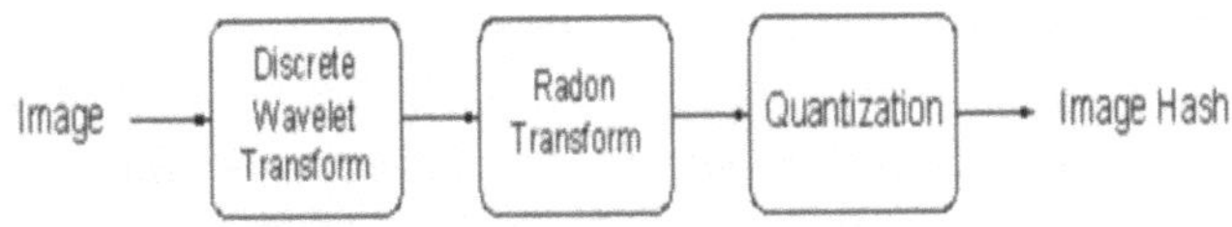

Fig. 3. The block diagram of the proposed system

2.3 Proposed Algorithm

A block diagram of the proposed algorithm is shown in Fig.3. The proposed algorithm consists of two main steps, preprocessing and quantization.

- *Preprocessing*: Wavelet transform is first applied to the images and then the Radon transform is performed on a chosen subband. The coefficients of the Radon transform at a predetermined angle, θ, forms the feature values for a particular image.
- *Quantization*: The feature values are quantized to get a binary representation. The probabilistic quantization method used in [8] is employed. The quantization bin boundary $[l_{i-1}, l_i)$ is defined as

$$\int_{l_{i-1}}^{l_i} p_f(k)dk = \frac{1}{L} \tag{2}$$

where $p_f(k)$ is the probability density function (pdf) of the features, L is the total number of quantization levels, and $1 \leq i \leq L$. The histogram of the features values is used as the pdf and the quantization value for each bin is i.

It is observed that although the absolute values of the Radon transform change if an image has undergone content-preserving modifications, the distribution of its coefficients remains consistent. On the other hand, if a malicious attack has occurred the distribution of the coefficients will change noticeably. As demonstrated in Fig.4, the original image and a noisy image have similar Radon transform coefficients distributions. However, a modified image has a different distribution between $X \in (50, 70)$.

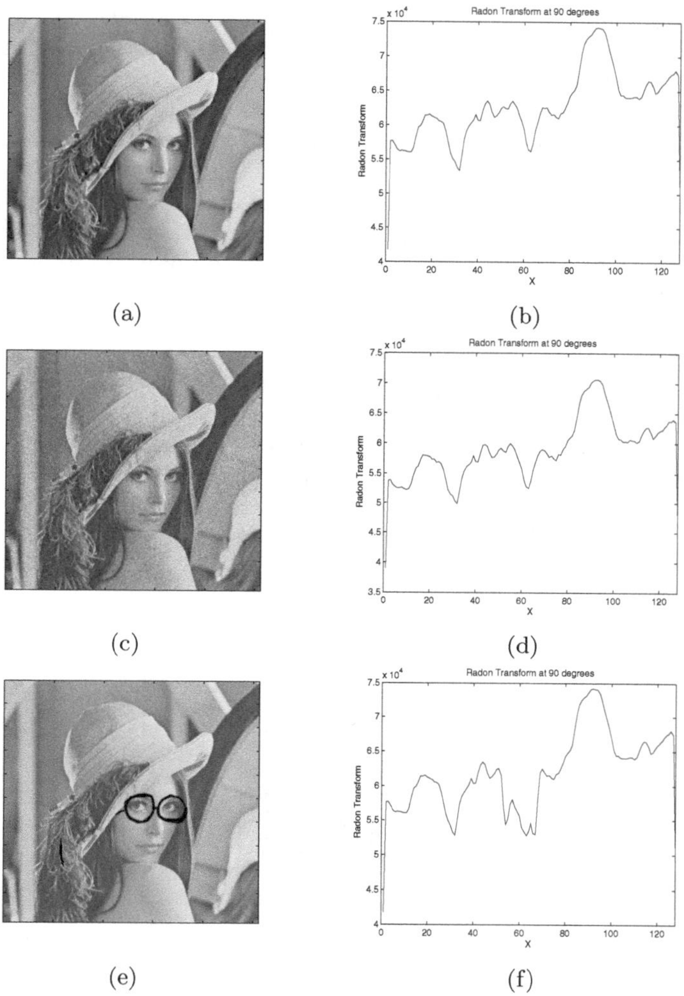

Fig. 4. A comparison of Radon transform coefficients. (a) Original Lena. (b) Radon transform of (a) at 90°. (c) Lena with uniform noise. (d) Radon transform of (c) at 90°. (e) Modified Lena. (f) Radon transform of (e) at 90°.

3 Results

Normalized Hamming distance is chosen as the measure of closeness between two hash values. Ideally, two perceptually similar image should have a distance of close to 0, whereas the separation between two different images should be around 0.5 [2,6].

A threshold, δ, is usually setup so that if

$$D_H(R, R^{'}) < \delta \tag{3}$$

where $D_H(\cdot)$ denotes the normalized Hamming distance and (R, R') denote hash values of two images, the two inputs are identical. Otherwise, they are distinct or tampering has occurred. δ is set to 0.1 in this paper.

The performance of the proposed algorithm is tested on a set of over 20 images including commonly used Lena, Baboon and Peppers. All images are first scaled to 512×512 using bicubic interpolation before applying the Cohen-Daubechies-Feauveau 9/7 wavelet transform. The LL subband image at scale 2 is then subjected to the Radon transform. It is observed that the other three subbands, LH, HL, and HH, are more sensitive to noise and filtering. The coefficients at $\theta = 90°$ are used as the feature values. 128 feature values of the highest magnitudes are quantized into $L = 16$ bins. The final hash consists of 512 bits.

3.1 Discriminative Capability

Fig.5 shows the histogram of the normalized Hamming distances of 50 different image hashes. The histogram shows that the algorithm performs fairly well in distinguishing different images with a mean separation of 0.496 and variance of 0.004.

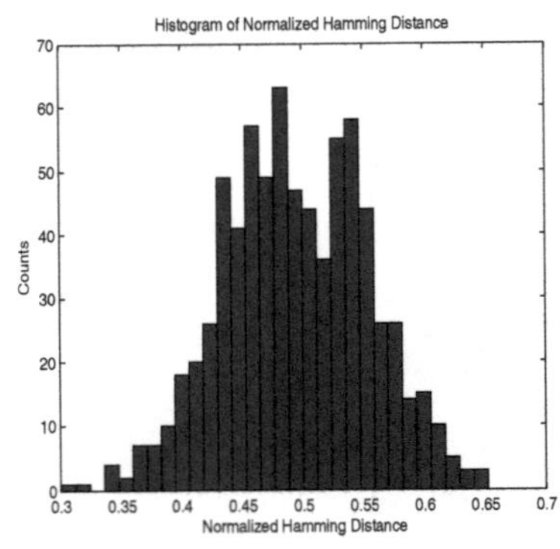

Fig. 5. Histogram of normalized Hamming distance between different images

3.2 Performance Evaluation Under Content Preserving Modifications

Venkatesan [3] and Seo's [6] methods are implemented for comparison purpose. These two particular algorithms are chosen because they are based on DWT and Radon transform respectively. Fig. 6 shows the normalized Hamming distance between the hash of the original image and that of a number of content-preserving modifications. The modified images are generated using the Stirmark software [10] and Adobe Photoshop CS.

In most cases, the Hamming distances are well below the threshold of 0.1 defined earlier for the proposed method. The use of wavelet transform to represent the image with its low-frequency components enables the algorithm to extract

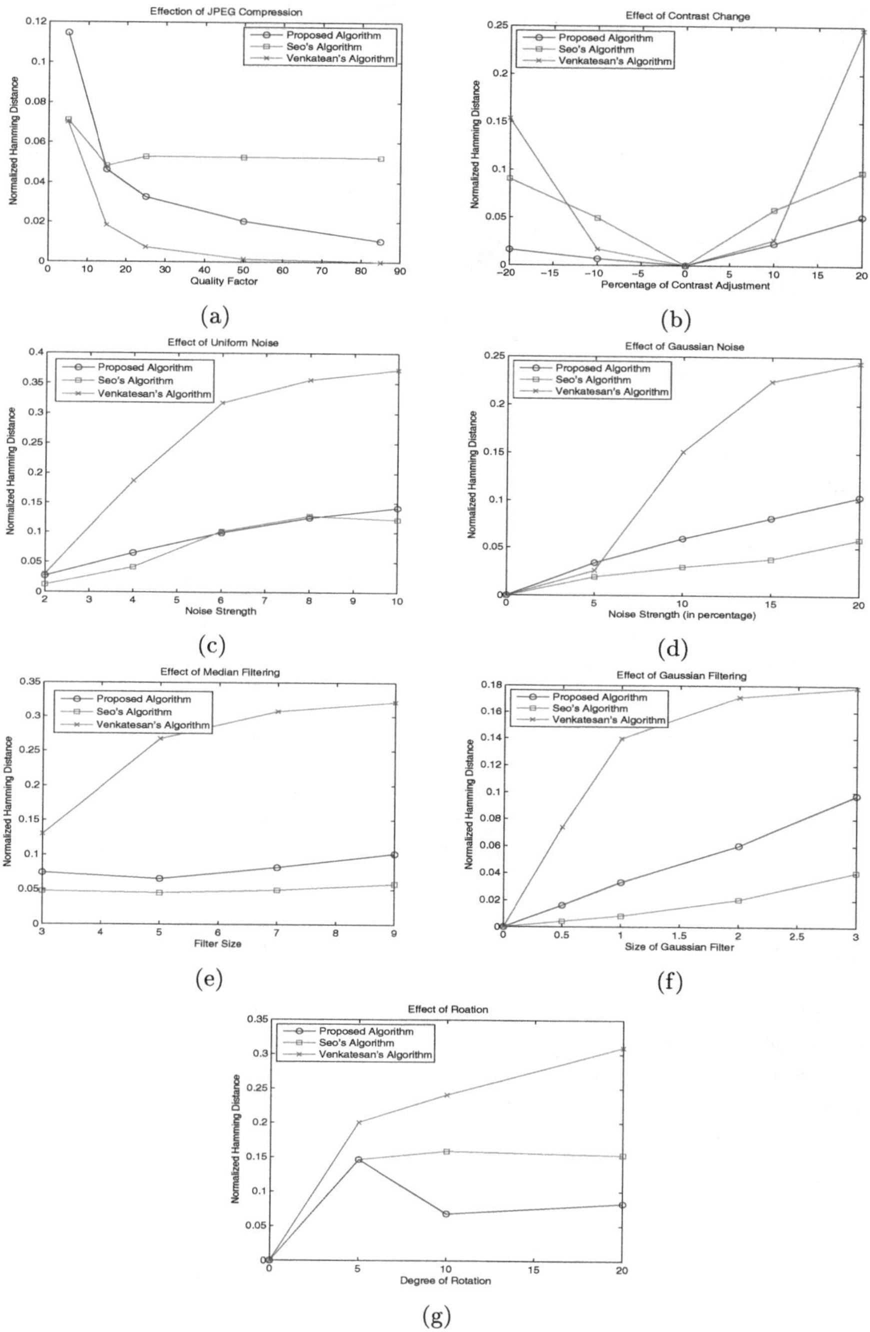

Fig. 6. Average Hamming distance between the original image and modified image in (a) JPEG compression, (b) contrast adjustments, (c) added uniform noise, (d) added Gaussian noise, (e) median filtering, (f) Gaussian filtering and (g) rotation

(a) (b) (c)

Fig. 7. Examples of tampered image (a) Lena, (b) Peppers, (c) Cars

invariant features from the image. As expected that although perceptually insignificant modifications might change the magnitudes of the Radon transform coefficients, the statistics remain the same.

Venkatesan's scheme, which based solely on DWT, performs the best under JPEG compression. However, it has relatively large Hamming distances in noise and filtering because DWT coefficients are sensitive to the changes. Seo's method has consistent results but the computation time is considerably higher than that of the other two algorithms.

3.3 Performance Evaluation Under Malicious Tampering

Another important advantage of the algorithm is its tampering detection capability. As shown in Section 2, the algorithm relies on the changes in the statistics of the Radon transform to detect malicious local changes. Fig. 7 shows the three images used in this test. The white boxes are added for illustration purpose only.

Table 1 shows that the proposed algorithm has considerably better results on average and all tampering can be detected with the threshold of $\delta = 0.1$.

To systematically test the algorithm, 1 to 10 icons of size 32x32 pixels are randomly inserted into over 20 test images. Fig. 8 shows examples of tampered Lena images. The total percentage of modified pixels is no larger than 4%.

The resulting Hamming distances between the original images and tampered images are presented in Fig. 9. The proposed algorithm shows the biggest sep-

Table 1. Comparison of normalized Hamming distance of the algorithms

Method	Lena	Peppers	Cars
Proposed	**0.1250**	0.1484	**0.3555**
Venkatesan	0.0063	0.0250	0.1000
Seo	0.0025	**0.3275**	0.2700

(a) (b) (c)

Fig. 8. Examples of Lena tampered with (a) two icons, (b) five icons, (c) eight icons

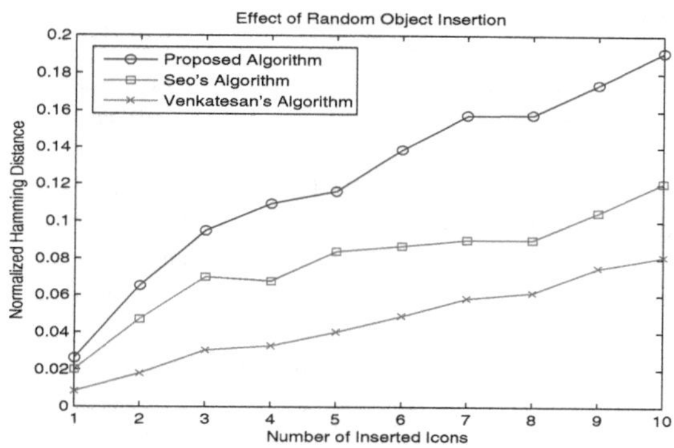

Fig. 9. Results for object insertion

aration in all cases. By setting the threshold at $\delta = 0.1$ insertion of 4 or more icons are detectable on average.

4 Conclusion

This paper proposes an image hash algorithm that is robust against perceptually insignificant changes and, at the same time, able to detect malicious content-changing modifications. The proposed scheme achieves good performance compared to Venkatesan [3] and Seo's [6] algorithms. In addition, results show that the algorithm can effectively detect local changes in an image. Therefore, the proposed algorithm is particularly powerful in authentication applications such as photo journalism and photo forensics. Furthermore, good discriminative capability with relatively small number of hash bits (512 bits for an image) suggests that the proposed method can be used in image searching and indexing applications. Future work includes developing and incorporating security techniques against estimation and forgery.

Acknowledgment

This work is supported by Bell Canada's University Laboratories R&D program.

References

1. Fridrich, J.: Visual hash for oblivious watermarking. In: Proc. IS&T/SPIE 12th Annu. Symp., Electronic Imaging, Security and Watermarking of Multimedia Content II, San Jose, CA, vol. 3971 (2000)
2. Swaminathan, A., Mao, Y., Wu, M.: Robust and secure image hashing. IEEE Transactions on Information Forensics and Security 1(2), 215–230 (2006)
3. Venkatesan, R., Koon, S.M., Jakubowski, M.H., Moulin, P.: Robust image hashing. In: International Conference on Image Processing, Vancouver, Canada, vol. 3, pp. 664–666 (2000)
4. Meixner, A., Uhl, A.: Analysis of a wavelet-based robust hash algorithm. In: Proc. IS&T/SPIE Security, Steganography Watermarking of Multimedia Contents VI, San Jose, CA, vol. 5306 (2004)
5. Lefebvre, F., Macq, B., Legat, J.D.: RASH: Radon soft hash algorithm. In: Proc. European Signal Processing Conference, Toulouse, France (2002)
6. Seo, J.S., Haitsma, J., Kalker, T., Yoo, C.D.: A robust image fingerprinting system using the rado transform. Signal Processing: Image Communication 19(4), 325–339 (2004)
7. Lu, C.S., Sun, S.W., Hsu, C.Y., Chang, P.C.: Media hash-depedent image watermarking resilient against both geometric attacks and estimation attacks based on false positive-oriented detection. IEEE Transactions on Multimedia 8(4), 668–685 (2006)
8. Monga, V., Evans, B.L.: Perceptual image hashing via feature points: Performance evaluation and tradeoffs. IEEE Transactions on Image Processing 15(11), 3453–3466 (2006)
9. Mihcak, M.K., Venkatesan, R.: New iterative geometric methods for robust perceptual image hashing. In: Proc. ACM Workshop Security and Privacy in Digital Rights Management, Philadelphia, PA (2001)
10. Petitcolas, F.A.P.: Watermarking schemes evaluation. IEEE Transactions on Signal Processing 17(5), 58–64 (2000)

Effective Corner Matching for Transformed Image Identification

Mohammad Awrangjeb and Guojun Lu

Gippsland School of Information Technology, Monash University,
Churchill Vic 3842, Australia
{Mohammad.Awrangjeb,Guojun.Lu}@infotech.monash.edu.au

Abstract. There are many applications, for example image copyright protection, where transformed images of a given test image need to be identified. The solution to the identification problem consists of two main stages. In stage one, certain representative features are detected for all images. In stage two, the representative features of the test image and the stored images are compared to identify the transformed images for the test image. We have reported the technique to extract robust representative features – corners – in our previous work [1]. This paper will focus on our stage-two work on effective corner matching technique for transformed image identification. Experimental results show that the proposed corner matching technique is very much effective in identifying the transformed images for a given test image.

Keywords: corner detection, corner matching, image matching, transformed image identification.

1 Introduction

In many applications, such as image copyright protection [2], one common problem is to identify images which may undergo unknown transformations. We can define this common problem as the *transformed image identification* (TII) where the goal is to identify both the geometric transformed and the signal processed images for a given test image. So the TII is different from the conventional *content-based image retrieval* (CBIR) [3], where all images having the same or similar semantic features, e.g., 'red car', 'rose', are considered relevant to each other.

The TII consists of two main stages. The first stage is *feature detection and representation* where a set of representative features are detected and represented for all images. We have reported the technique to detect robust representative features – corners – in our previous work [1]: the *affine-resilient curvature scale-space* (ARCSS) corner detector. It detects corners on planar curves and offers better performance in terms of both *average repeatability* and *localization error* than the existing CSS detectors [4, 5] under geometric transformations. Each corner is represented with information such as its position, absolute curvature value, corresponding curve number, and affine-lengths between this corner and other corners on the same curve.

H.H.S. Ip et al. (Eds.): PCM 2007, LNCS 4810, pp. 765–774, 2007.

The second stage, which is *feature matching*, is the focus of this paper. In this stage, the representative features of the test image and the stored images are compared to identify those database images which are geometric transformed and signal processed images of the same original image for a given test image. Feature matching solutions in the literature can be broadly categorized into two: those which use the local neighborhood of each feature for matching [7] and those which use feature information like its curvature but do not use neighbor intensity values for matching [16, 6, 8, 9, 12, 13, 10, 11]. The second category solutions can also be divided into two groups: model-based [12, 13, 10, 11] and model-free [16, 6, 8, 9] techniques. In model-based feature matching techniques, the correspondence between two point-sets is established with the help of some predefined (given) object models. In contrast, in model-free feature matching techniques, such predefined object models are absent and, therefore, the correspondence between the sets should be made directly without the help of the models. As a result, the model-free solutions are harder to design than their model-based counterparts. Moreover, the model-based techniques are application specific e.g., object recognition, while the model-free techniques are more general and can be used for copyright protection [2].

The proposed corner matching solution resides in the model-free group as it does not use any predefined object model to establish corner correspondences between two corner sets. The proposed matching technique is robust to both geometric transformations like rotation and scaling and signal processing like compression and noising. It can be used with any contour-based corner detector. Particularly, here we will use it with our previously proposed ARCSS corner detector [1], which makes necessary information, such as curvatures at the corner points and affine-lengths between corners, available to the matching algorithm.

We obtain the TII performance using the *precision-recall graph* and compare with the existing *gray-scale histogram* (GSH) matching technique [3]. In TII the database images which are originated (either geometric transformed or signal processed or both) from the same original image as the test image reside in the same group and are considered relevant to each other. Consequently, many existing CBIR techniques [3] may not be applicable to TII, since the goal of CBIR is different from that of TII. The GSH matching, which is a global feature (intensity frequency) based CBIR technique, is very much robust to geometric transformations [3] and, therefore, is chosen to compare with the proposed corner matching technique while both of them are applied to TII.

Note that the corner matching performance (how many repeated corners the matching technique can find) of the proposed corner matching technique was published in [17]. Experimental results showed that the proposed matching technique obtained maximum number of true corner correspondences. In this paper we have investigated its performance to identify the transformed images for a given test image. We have also proposed different strategies to reduce the search-space.

2 Proposed Matching Technique

Absolute curvatures of corners may change due to affine transformations; however, for many corners they either remain unaffected or change slightly. Moreover, the affine-length of a planar curve and the area of the triangle, consisting of three corners as vertices, are *relatively invariant* [15] to geometric transformations. In the proposed corner matching technique, for each corner we use its position, absolute curvature value, corresponding curve number, and affine-lengths between this corner and other corners on the same curve. The iterative matching procedure first finds three corner matches between a test image and a database image within a specific absolute curvature difference. If the three matching corners are non-collinear on each image and the ratio of areas of corresponding triangles in both the images is within a specific range, it obtains the geometric transformation parameters between these triangles. Then it transforms all corners in the database image using the estimated transformation matrix and matches with the test corner set. In rest of the paper, we will call the proposed matching technique as *affine-length and triangular area* (ALTA) matching technique.

2.1 Relative Invariants

We define the term *relative invariance* with respect to the *two-dimensional* (2D) space according to the classical geometric invariant theory from [15] as

Definition 1. *For a given 2D space Ω and a given transformation group χ active on Ω, the function $f(x,y)$ is relatively invariant to χ if and only if we have the transformed function $f_a(x,y) = g(f(x,y)) = h(\det(g)).f(x,y)$, $\forall\ (x,y) \in \Omega$ and $\forall g \in \chi$, where* $\det(g)$ *denotes the determinant of the transformation matrix for g and $h(\det(g))$ is some function of* $\det(g)$.

When $h(\det(g)) = 1$, the above relation becomes *absolutely invariant.* The affine-length between two points P_1 and P_2 of a planar curve $(x(t), y(t))$ is [1]

$$\tau = \int_{P_1}^{P_2} \sqrt[3]{\dot{x}(t)\ddot{y}(t) - \ddot{x}(t)\dot{y}(t)}dt, \tag{1}$$

where $\dot{x}(t)$ and $\dot{y}(t)$ are first and $\ddot{x}(t)$ and $\ddot{y}(t)$ are second order derivatives with respect to the arbitrary parameter t. We can show that the affine-length of a transformed curve is

$$\tau_a = (s_x s_y)^{1/3}.\tau. \tag{2}$$

where s_x and s_y are scaling factors along x and y axis. The relation in (2) shows that the affine-length is absolutely invariant to rotation and translation, but relatively invariant to scaling.

The area Δ of a triangle with vertices $v_1 = (x_1, y_1)$, $v_2 = (x_2, y_2)$, and $v_3 = (x_3, y_3)$, when v_1 is shifted to the origin, is

$$\Delta(v_1, v_2, v_3) = \frac{1}{2}|(x_2 - x_1)(y_3 - y_1) - (x_3 - x_1)(y_2 - y_1)|. \tag{3}$$

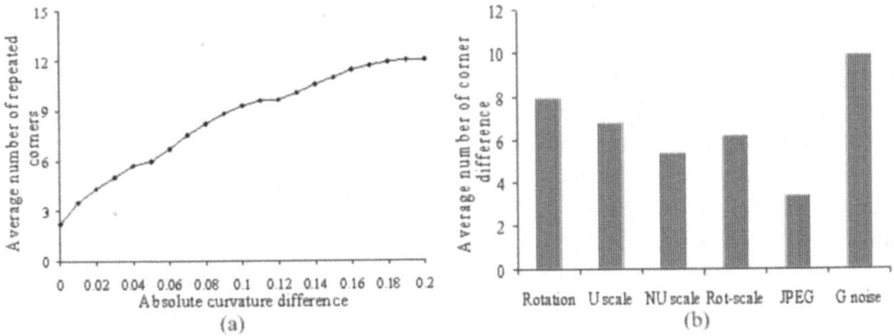

Fig. 1. Performance analysis of the ARCSS detector [1]: (a) average number of repeated corners and (b) average number of corner difference between original and test images

Similar to (2), we can derive the area of a transformed triangle as

$$\Delta_a(v_{1a}, v_{2a}, v_{3a}) = s_x s_y.\Delta(v_1, v_2, v_3), \tag{4}$$

which implies that the triangular area is also relatively invariant to scaling.

In the proposed matching technique, we use the affine-length between corners on the same curve to find corner matches and the triangular area to reduce the search-space. However, comparing (2) and (4), it is evident that the affine-length is less sensitive to geometric transformations than the triangular area, because in the former the power of $s_x s_y$ is $\frac{1}{3}$ but in the later it is 1. This means that in large scaling factors the search-space will not be reduced much. Therefore, we introduce other strategies to reduce the search-space (see Section 2.3).

2.2 Iterative Matching Procedure

A subset $\{I_p\}$ of the database images is selected (see Section 2.3a) as the set of possible transformed images for a given test image I_q. For each pair of images (I_p, I_q), the ALTA iterative corner matching procedure is as follows.

Algorithm 1. *ALTA corner matching algorithm.*

Input: *Two corner sets C_p and C_q of I_p and I_q respectively. Each corner is associated with its position, absolute curvature value, corresponding curve number, and the affine-length of its predecessor on the same curve.*
Output: *Information about image matches.*

1. *Set curvature difference threshold $T_{CD} = 0.2$, minimum corner matches $m = 3$, and output $O_{pq} = \varnothing$ where $\varnothing$ denotes the empty set.*
2. *Find the set of candidate corner matches C_c between C_p and C_q with curvature difference less than or equal to T_{CD}.*
3. *For each candidate match (c_p, c_q) in C_c, add new candidate match (c_{pn}, c_{qn}) to C_c if the affine-length ratio of corresponding curve segments $c_p \rightsquigarrow c_{pn}$ and $c_q \rightsquigarrow c_{qn}$ is within the range $[l, h]$.*

4. *For (next) three non-collinear candidate matches* (c_{p1}, c_{q1}), (c_{p2}, c_{q2}), *and* (c_{p3}, c_{q3}) *in* C_c, *if the ratio of areas of triangles* $\Delta_p(c_{p1}, c_{p2}, c_{p3})$ *and* $\Delta_q(c_{q1}, c_{q2}, c_{q3})$ *is within the range* $[l_a, h_a]$, *find* A_{RS} *and* T.
5. *Transform all corners in* C_p *using* A_{RS} *and* T*; i.e.,* $C_{pt} = A_{RS}.C_p + T$.
6. *Find the set of corner matches* C_m *between* C_{pt} *and* C_q.
7. *If* $(|C_m| > m)$, $O_{pq} = O_{pq} \cup [p, q, C_m, A_{RS}, T]$. *Go to step 4.*

Fig. 1(a) shows that the ARCSS detector [1] has on the average more than 12 repeated corners within curvature difference 0.2; however, we need only 3 of them to estimate the geometric transformation parameters. Therefore, in step 1 of Algorithm 1, T_{CD} is set to 0.2 experimentally, because for larger value the procedure becomes more expensive and for smaller value we may miss some relevant images. We also set m to 3 in step 1, because for any three non-collinear candidate matches there are already 3 matches. In step 2, we find the candidate corner matches within the curvature difference T_{CD}. In step 3, corners c_p and c_{pn} should have the same curve number in C_p and corners c_q and c_{qn} should have the same curve number in C_q. In this step, we add other possible candidate matches for each candidate match found in step 2. We only consider those curves which have more than 1 corners and at least 1 of them have already been selected as candidate matches in the previous step. For adding a new candidate match, we only consider affine-length ratio between this corner and an already added candidate corner on the same curve regardless of their curvature values. The ranges $[l, h]$ of the affine-length ratio in step 3 and $[l_a, h_a]$ of triangular area ratio in step 4 are set according to (2) and (4) respectively. While finding corner matches in step 6, we allow a maximum mean-square-error of 9, i.e., $RMSE \leq 3$ pixels.

2.3 Speeding Up the Identification

The loop of steps 4-7 may make the procedure computationally expensive. We apply the following measures to speed up.

a. Selecting the possible transformed images: Fig. 1(b) shows that the average difference in corner numbers between original and test images is maximum 11 (for Gaussian noise) by the ARCSS corner detector [1]. Therefore, a database image with 20 corners may not be a possible transformed image for a query image I_q with 80 corners, and vice versa. The subset $\{I_p\}$ of the database images are selected as possible transformed images of I_q such that $abs(|C_p| - |C_q|) \leq 25$. Consequently, for a given test image, we do not execute the corner matching procedure for all database images.

b. Pre-processing: Although more than 3 corners can be detected on each curve by the ARCSS detector, we need only 3 true corner matches to obtain the geometric transformation. Therefore, a pre-processing is carried out on the input corner sets C_p and C_q separately so that maximum 3 corners will have the same curve number in each input corner set, since we need only 2 more true matches along with a possible true match found in step 2. This pre-processing significantly reduces the number of false new candidate match additions in step 3 for each false candidate match found in step 2 and, hence, speeds up the iterative procedure by reducing the search-space.

c. Matching the triangular area: In step 4, the condition of the ratio of areas of two triangles to be in a specific range also reduces the number of tests in the loop with the false candidate corner-matches. However, (4) shows that the area of a triangle increases with the increase of scaling factors, i.e., when $s_x s_y > 1$. Because false triangular area matches will also increase when the upper-limit of the range $[l_a, h_a]$ increases with large scaling factors. Consequently, the search-space may not be reduced much in this situation using the triangular area matching.

d. Using the hash table: The procedure is further speeded up by using a simple *hash table* for storing the combinations of candidate corner matches already visited in step 4. Assuming that there will be maximum 99 (two digits) strong corners detected in each image, each key k stored in the hash table is 12 digits long (6 vertices of two triangles) where consecutive two digits denote a corner number (vertex). We use the division method [14] for mapping the key k into one of i slots in the hash table by taking the remainder of k divided by i. That means, the hash function is $h(k) = k \mod i$. The hash table can be effectively and efficiently implemented using the MATLAB cell data structure where each slot in the hash table is a variable-length one-dimensional array, initially set to zero size. We store all keys mapped to a particular slot in order of their arrival. In order to reduce the collisions, i.e., number of keys mapped to the same slot, the value of i is chosen to be a prime that is not too close to the exact power of 2. Again assuming maximum total 10,000 keys to store, the total number of slots i is chosen to be a prime number 3067, so that on average 3 keys are mapped in each slot, which makes the search very efficient. As an example of calculating the hash function, suppose corner numbers 12, 25, and 50 in the database image and 34, 65, and 84 in the query image are visited during an iteration of loop 4-7. Hence, the key $k = 122550346584$ is stored in the slot number $h(k) = k \mod 3067 = 942$ of the hash table.

e. Selecting the top corners: If all corners are considered, it may make the procedure still expensive depending on the number of corners in I_p and I_q. Fortunately, by selecting only top (say, 15) corners with higher curvature values, it not only speeds up the iteration but also offers better performance (see detail in Section 3).

3 Performance Study

For evaluating the identification performance, we applied ALTA and GSH matching [3] techniques for TII and compare them in the *precision-recall graph*. We used a large database of total 1700 images (including original and transformed).

Database. In the *identification database*, we had 100 different original 512 × 512 gray-scale images including 'Lena', 'Elaine', and 'Boat' [18] and their 1600 transformed images of five categories:

i) rotation at 4 different angles θ in [5° 20°] at 5° apart;
ii) uniform (U) scale factors $s_x = s_y$ in [0.85 1.15] at 0.05 apart, excluding 1.0;
iii) combined transformations (rot.-scale): $[\theta, s_x, s_y] = [5°, 0.8, 1.2]$ and $[10°, 0.7, 1.1]$;
iv) JPEG lossy compression at quality factors 20 and 25; and
v) zero mean white Gaussian (G) noise with noise-variances 0.005 and 0.01.

We had 5 queries for each original image: rotation 10°, uniform scale factor 1.05, combined transformation [5°, 0.8, 1.2], lossy JPEG compression with quality factor 20, and Gaussian noise with variance 0.005. Therefore, we had total 100 groups of images in this database, each group consists of 17 relevant images (16 transformed and 1 original) for a corresponding query, and in total 1700 images in the database. All images within each group are considered relevant to each other. We also cropped all rotated images so that the outer black parts were disappeared. This must diminish the bias of large black regions in rotated images for the GSH matching technique [3].

Evaluation Metrics. The database images which were originated from the same original image as the query image using some geometric transformations or signal processing are considered relevant to each other. We used *precision* and *recall* [3] collectively to measure the identification performance. *Recall* measures the system capacity to retrieve the relevant images from the database. It is defined as the ratio between number of retrieved relevant images r and total number of relevant images T (group size) in the database:

$$Recall = \frac{r}{T}. \tag{5}$$

Precision measures the retrieval accuracy. It is defined as the ratio between r and number of retrieved images R:

$$Precision = \frac{r}{R}. \tag{6}$$

In practice, the performance of an information retrieval system is presented using the *precision-recall graph*, where the higher the precision at a given recall value the better the performance of the retrieval system [3].

Results and Discussions. We have evaluated and compared the identification performance for both GSH matching and ALTA corner matching techniques. While the ALTA matching used the number of corner matches between the query and database images to rank the retrieved images, the histogram matching used the normalized L-1 distance [3]. In case of ALTA matching, we considered two cases – when all corners were considered and when only top 15 corners with the highest curvature values were considered. We selected top 15 corners based

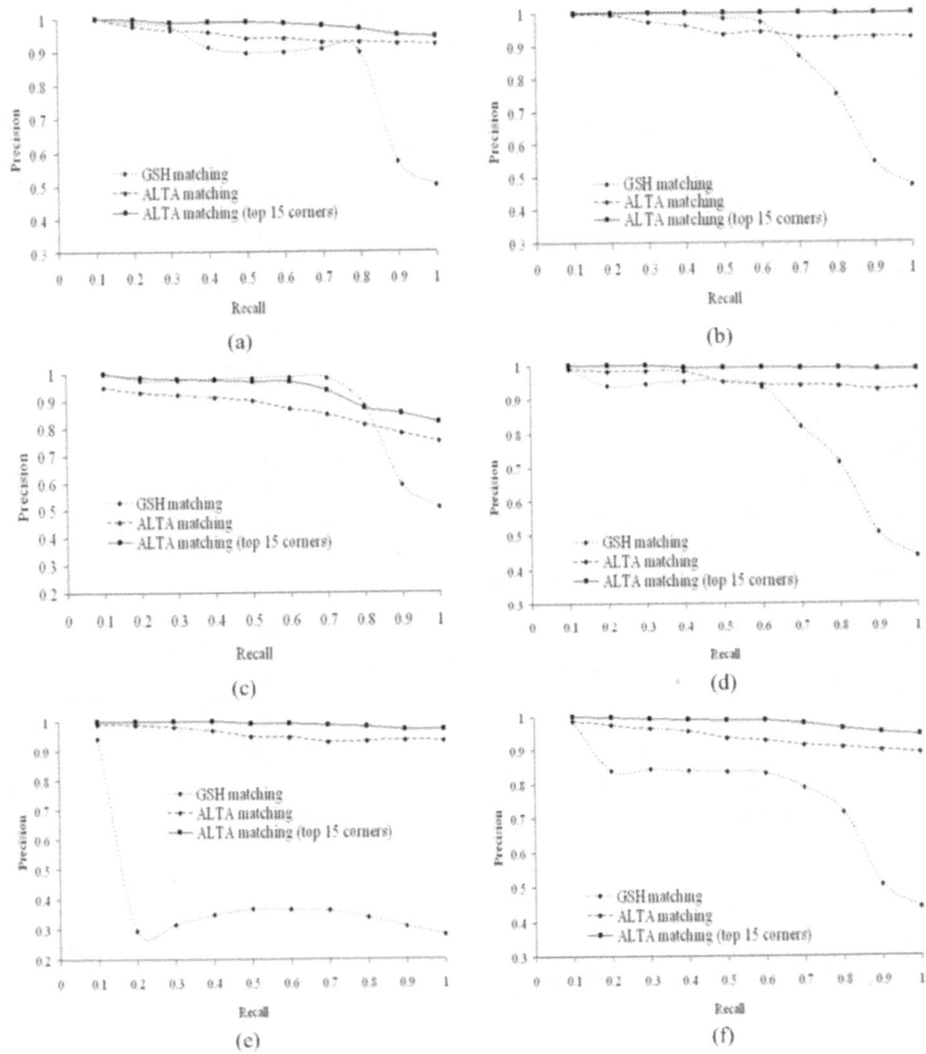

Fig. 2. The TII performance in (a) query 1: rotation ($\theta = 10°$), (b) query 2: uniform scale ($s_x = s_y = 1.05$), (c) query 3: rotation-scale ($\theta = 10°, s_x = 0.8, s_y = 1.2$), (d) query 4: JPEG (quality factor 20), (e) query 5: zero mean Gaussian noise (noise-variance = 0.005), and (f) average in all five queries (a)-(e).

on two observations. First, if more than 15, say 20 or more, were selected, the procedure became more expensive. Second, if less than 15, say 10 or less, were selected, almost the same number of corner matches were found for both relevant and irrelevant images in the database. Choosing top corners not only reduced the computational complexity but also improved the performance. Because if all the corners are used, there might be high number of corner correspondences between irrelevant images. By selecting top 15 corners based on the highest curvature values before establishing the corner correspondence decreased the probability of establishing such false corner correspondences.

Fig. 2(a)-(e) present the identification performance by the proposed ALTA matching and the existing GSH matching [3] techniques under five different queries on the identification database. The ALTA matching technique offered better performance than the GSH matching technique in most of the cases. Nonetheless, for lower recall values the GSH matching outperformed the ALTA matching, specially in queries comprising scaling (see Fig. 2(b)-(c)). However, for higher recall values while the precision of the ALTA matching decreased slightly, that of GSH matching dropped significantly in all queries. This might be due to two reasons. First, scaling may preserve the ratio of gray-scale intensities but in higher recall values different images may have the same histogram. Second, since ALTA matching considered all the detected corners, some irrelevant images may be retrieved.

Nevertheless, instead of considering all the detected corners, when we considered only top few corners from each image based on the highest curvature values, the TII performance in the precision-recall graph increased significantly. Moreover, the computational cost fell significantly as the number of corners decreased. Fig. 2(a)-(e) show that the ALTA matching with top 15 corners outperformed the GSH matching in most of the cases. The average performance in five queries is shown in Fig. 2((f). The precision of the ALTA matching procedure is above 90% which is almost the same in all recall values, but that of GSH matching dropped to 40% at 100% recall.

4 Conclusions

The proposed ALTA corner matching method can be used with any contour-based corner detector depending on the availability of the required information for establishing the corner correspondence. It takes the advantage of the affine-length invariance between corners on the same curve. It also uses the absolute curvature values which either remain unaltered or change slightly under geometric transformations. It follows different strategies to reduce the search-space.

While applying for TII, the ALTA matching technique offered much better retrieval performance in the *precision-recall graph* than the GSH matching technique [3]. The average precision (see Fig. 2(f)) by the ALTA matching is always above 90% under all recall values and, therefore, it is evident that the proposed matching technique could be successfully exploited in many computer vision applications including image copyright protection [2].

However, we observed that in spite of taking measures discussed in Section 2.3, the proposed ALTA matching technique required more time than the existing GSH technique when both were applied to TII. Future works include investigating the more time-efficient corner matching technique while maintaining at least the same performance.

References

1. Awrangjeb, M., Lu, G.: An Affine Resilient Curvature Scale-space Corner Detector. In: Proc. Int. Conf. on Acoustics, Speech, and Signal Proces, Hawaii, USA, vol. 1, pp. 1233–1236 (2007)
2. Awrangjeb, M., Murshed, M.: Robust Signature-based Geometric Invariant Copyright Protection. In: Proc. Int. Conf. on Image Proces, Atlanta, USA, pp. 1961–1964 (2006)
3. Lu, G.: Multimedia Database Management Systems. Artech House Inc., Norwood (1999)
4. Mokhtarian, F., Suomela, R.: Robust Image Corner Detection Through Curvature Scale Space. IEEE Trans. on Pat. Anal. and Mach. Intel. 20(12), 1376–1381 (1998)
5. Mokhtarian, F., Mohanna, F.: Enhancing the Curvature Scale Space Corner Detector. In: Proc. Scandinavian Conf. on Image Analysis, pp. 145–152 (2001)
6. Zhou, D., Li, G., Liu, Y.: Effective Corner Matching Based on Delaunay Triangulation. In: Proc. Int. Conf. on Robotics and Automation, pp. 2730–2733 (2004)
7. Matas, J., Chum, O., Urban, M., Pajdla, T.: Robust Wide Baseline Stereo From Maximally Stable External Regions. In: Proc. British Machine Vision Conference, pp. 384–393 (2002)
8. Jung, I., Lacroix, S.: A Robust Interest Points Matching Algorithm. In: Proc. Int. Conf. on Computer Vision, vol. 2, pp. 538–543 (2001)
9. You, J., Pissaloux, E., Cohen, H.: A Hierarchical Image Matching Scheme Based on the Dynamic Detection of Interesting Points. In: Proc. Int. Conf. on Acoustics, Speech, and Signal Processing, vol. 4, pp. 2467–2470 (1995)
10. Lee, K., Kim, Y., Myung, H., Kim, J., Bien, Z.: A Corner Matching Algorithm with Uncertainty Handling Capability. In: Proc. Int. Conf. on Fuzzy Systems, vol. 3, pp. 1469–1474 (1997)
11. Rutkowski, W.: Recognition of Occluded Shapes Using Relaxation. Comp. Graph. and Img. Process 19(2), 111–128 (1982)
12. Horaud, R., Skordas, T.: Stereo Correspondence Through Feature Grouping and Maximal Cliques. IEEE Trans. on Pat. Anal. and Mach. Intel. 11(11), 1168–1180 (1989)
13. Nasrabadi, N., Li, W.: Object Recognition by a Hopfield Neural Network. IEEE Trans. on Sys., Man and Cyb. 21(6), 1523–1535 (1991)
14. Cormen, T., Leiserson, C., Rivest, R.: Introduction to Algorithms. The MIT Press, London (1999)
15. Klein, F.: Elementary Mathematics From an Advanced Standpoint: Geometry. The Macmillan Company, New York (1939)
16. Hopcroft, J., Huttenlocher, D.: On Matching Planar Points Sets Under Affine Transformations. Technical Report TR. 89-986, Department of Computer Sceince, Cornell University, New York (1989)
17. Awrangjeb, M., Lu, G.: A Robust Corner Matching Technique. In: Proc. Int. Conf. on Multimedia and Expo., Beijing, China, pp. 1483–1486 (2007)
18. `http://personal.gscit.monash.edu.au/~awran/pcm.html` (2007)

Automatic Panel Extraction of Color Comic Images

Chung Ho Chan[1], Howard Leung[1], and Taku Komura[2]

[1] Department of Computer Science, City University of Hong Kong, 83 Tat Chee Avenue, Kowloon Tong, Hong Kong
{chchan, howard}@cityu.edu.hk
[2] Institute for Perception, Action and Behaviour, School of Informatics, University of Edinburgh, United Kingdom
tkomura@informatics.ed.ac.uk

Abstract. In this paper, an automatic approach for detecting and extracting panels in a color comic image is proposed. Panel extraction is challenging because the background color, the background pixel locations, the panel shapes and the panel layout are not known in advance. In our approach, uniform color stripes are first identified and used as separators to segment the color comic page image into sub-regions in a recursive manner. Panels are recognized as the sub-regions that cannot be further segmented. The structure of the panels is thus obtained in the extraction process and it contains the layout of the panels as well as the reading order. Panel extraction is useful because: 1) the extracted panels can be better fitted into a handheld device for viewing; and 2) the panels can then be further analyzed to extract features used for content based indexing and retrieval.

Keywords: Comic processing, panel extraction, image analysis, image segmentation.

1 Introduction

Reading comics is a kind of entertainment and there are varieties of comics for readers to choose from. Some comic stories are turned into animations or movies filmed with real actors. In recent years, some comic publishers start to digitize the traditional paper comics and provide the e-comic as an alternative format to enable people to enjoy reading them on a computer. Common forms of comics are comic strips and comic books and they can be in black and white or in color. A comic strip usually contains four panels and a comic book consists of many pages with several panels per page for conveying a story. In Hong Kong, tens of comic books are being published weekly and there is a growing demand to process such comics in digital format.

Several researches have been focused on comic representation and analysis. Shamir *et al.*'s system [1] can extract a sequence of important events from a continuous temporal story line and convert the events into a graphical representation automatically. Tanahashi *et al.* have proposed a comic emotional expression method using an abstract facial model [2]. Kawamura *et al.* have presented a method of

H.H.S. Ip et al. (Eds.): PCM 2007, LNCS 4810, pp. 775–784, 2007.

gradation approximation for vector based compression of comic images [3]. Furthermore, comics are utilized for education in language learning [4]. Comic actors can be used to represent software agents [5]. In [6], cartoon motion capture is performed from a sequence of frames. Cartoon character retrieval is studied in [7][8].

Handheld devices like personal digital assistant (PDA) have gained popularity in these recent years. However, the biggest constraint of handheld devices is the small screen display as mentioned in Qiu *et al*'s study about web interface on small display devices [9]. To solve the problem of Internet surfing in such devices, various researches have been conducted in the areas such as the adaptation of web content [10][11] and dynamic text presentation [12], etc. In this paper, we would like to adapt high-resolution comic images into a small display device.

This paper is focused on processing of color e-comic book consisted of many pages. On each page, panels are put together in a certain layout often with a uniform color background. Some examples of comic page images are shown in Fig. 1. A panel is a small sub-area in a color comic page and represents an instance of the storyline. We are targeting the panel extraction problem in which the panels should be extracted from each color comic page. Panel extraction is useful because: 1) the extracted panels can be better fitted into a handheld device such as PDA for viewing; and 2) the panels can then be further analyzed to extract features used for content based indexing and retrieval.

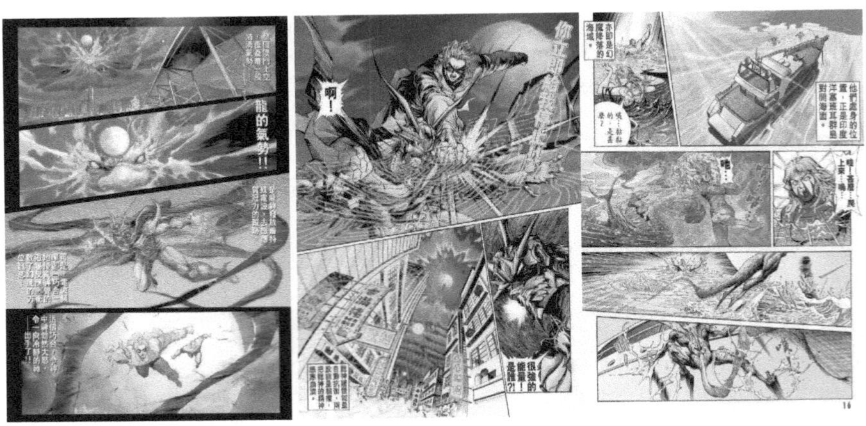

Fig. 1. Examples of comic page images

Existing software from ComicGURU [13] allows users to perform the panel extraction task and create the e-comic format suitable for viewing in handheld devices. However, these tools require users to specify each panel manually. We would like to develop an automatic approach for panel extraction to relieve the level of human intervention. It is a challenging task because the background color and the background pixel locations are not known in advance and they can vary among different comic pages as illustrated in Fig. 1. Moreover, the shapes of the panels are not always rectangular and the size of the panels can vary across a large range thus the panel layout is also a variable.

Panel extraction can be formulated as a problem in image segmentation [14]. Although Hough Transform [15] can be applied to detect the line segments on the background that can then be used to segment the panels, this method is not suitable for processing comics that can have numerous lines due to the nature of the comic content. Instead, we propose a pixel-based algorithm to handle this problem. In our approach, uniform color stripes are first identified and used as separators to segment the color comic page image into sub-regions in a recursive manner. Panels are recognized as the sub-regions that cannot be further segmented. The structure of the panels is thus obtained in the extraction process and it contains the layout of the panels as well as the reading order. Experiments show that it can provide good accuracy with acceptable speed.

This paper is organized as follows. The panel extraction algorithm is introduced in Section 2. The speed-up strategy is described in Section 3. Experiments and results are given in Section 4. Our implementation of a PDA comic viewer is presented in Section 5. The conclusions and future work are provided in Section 6.

2 Panel Extraction

Fig. 2 illustrates the flow of our panel extraction algorithm. Firstly, stripes formed by consecutive uniform color lines in a particular orientation are recognized. False stripes are removed in the next step. The image region is segmented accordingly to the recognized stripe. This process is repeated recursively until no more stripes are found. The final regions correspond to the extracted panels.

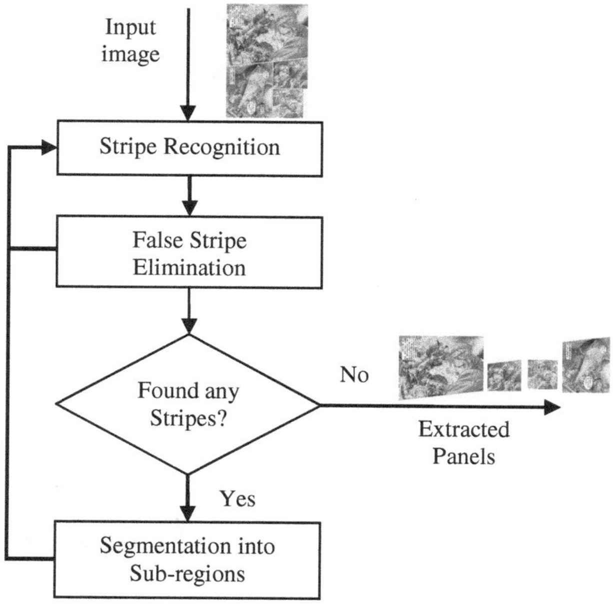

Fig. 2. Flowchart of panel extraction

2.1 Stripe Recognition

A stripe is a set of consecutive lines with uniform color and belongs to the background. The orientation can be horizontal, vertical or tilted as shown in Fig. 3. It can be used as a separator to divide a comic page image into panels.

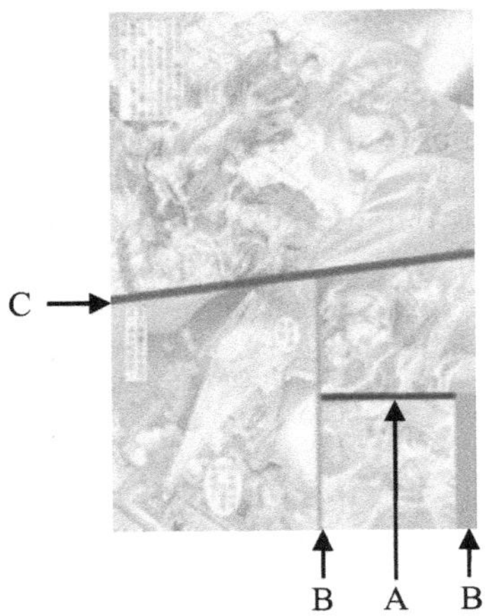

Fig. 3. Examples of stripes (A, B, C are horizontal, vertical and tilted stripes respectively)

Uniform color lines need to be first identified. This can be achieved by checking the intensity histogram of the pixels along each line. We scan each line on an image region according to the line equation $ax+by+c=0$ and compute the intensity histogram. Fig. 4 shows two horizontal lines, one from a stripe and one from a non-stripe, as well as the intensity histograms for each case.

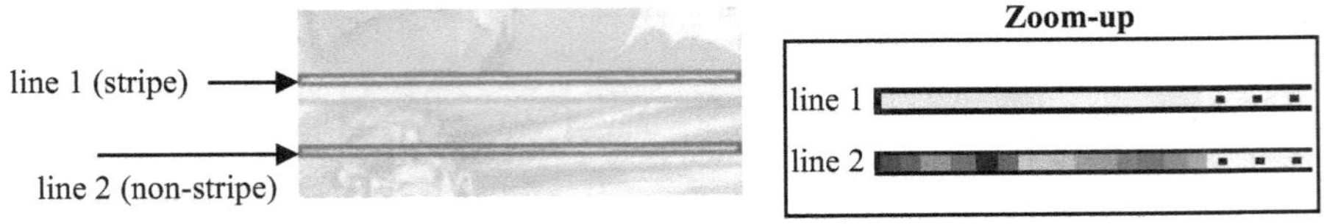

(a) line 1 (stripe) and line 2 (non-stripe)

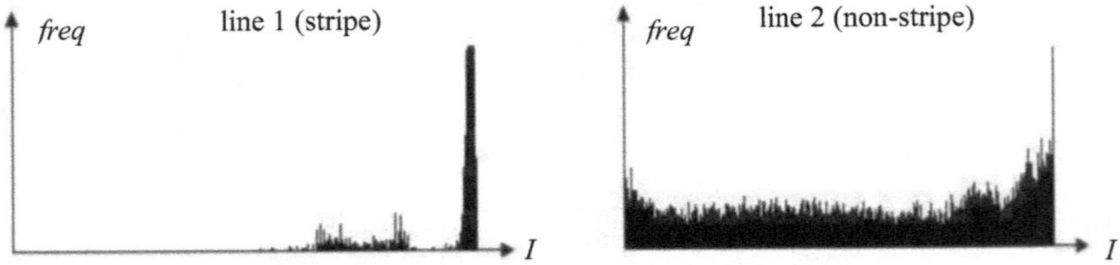

(b) Intensity histograms of line 1 (stripe) and line 2 (non-stripe)

Fig. 4. Intensity histograms of a stripe line and a non-stripe line

Fig. 4(b) shows that line 1 has uniform color whereas line 2 has larger variations across the intensity levels. Each line is checked to determine if it is a uniform color line by having more than 90% of pixels around the peak in the intensity histogram. Consecutive uniform color lines are then grouped together to form a stripe and this is how a stripe is recognized. The image region is first scanned horizontally, then vertically and then scanned in tilted lines with an angle in every degree. Whenever a stripe is found, it will be further checked if it is a false stripe. The final recognized stripe will be used to divide the image region into sub-regions.

2.2 False Stripe Elimination

It is possible that the stripe recognition is affected by the content of the comic image. As the input region is becoming smaller, the chance of recognizing wrong stripes is getting higher. Fig. 5 shows an example of a false stripe. In this example, a false stripe exists in the panel region that has uniform color. A true stripe should exist in the page background area that has uniform color.

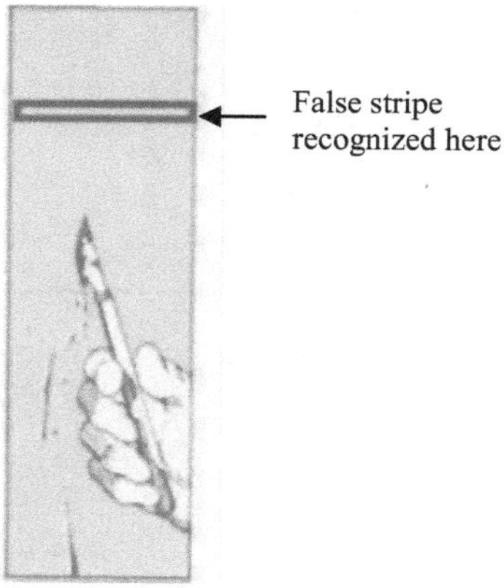

Fig. 5. Example of false stripe

A detected stripe is tested with the following two conditions to determine whether it is a false stripe.

1) False stripes often appear inside small panel regions. This means that at the beginning when the image region to be processed is large, a detected stripe consisted of uniform color lines is most likely a true one. The background color information can be recorded when the first stripe is recognized. The color of subsequent detected stripe can be checked with this background color. If the colors are not the same, then it is a false stripe.

2) A real stripe has a large contrast with the surrounding pixels. A false strip can thus be identified by checking its gradient along the boundary. We have found heuristically that if the percentage of pixels with similar color along the boundary is over 85%, then the detected stripe can be considered as a false stripe.

If a false stripe is identified, it is removed and the input region is further processed to recognize potential stripes. Otherwise, the detected stripe is used to segment the input region into sub-regions in the next step.

2.3 Segmentation into Sub-regions

The input region is divided into sub-regions using the recognized stripe as the separator. Each sub-region is processed recursively until no more stripes are found. The sub-regions can be represented in a tree structure. The reading order of the panels can be acquired by traversing the tree in preorder since the reading order of the comic is from top to bottom and from right to left for Chinese comics. For this paper, we focus on Chinese comics since there are already tens of thousands of Chinese e-comic volumes that are for sale online in Hong Kong.

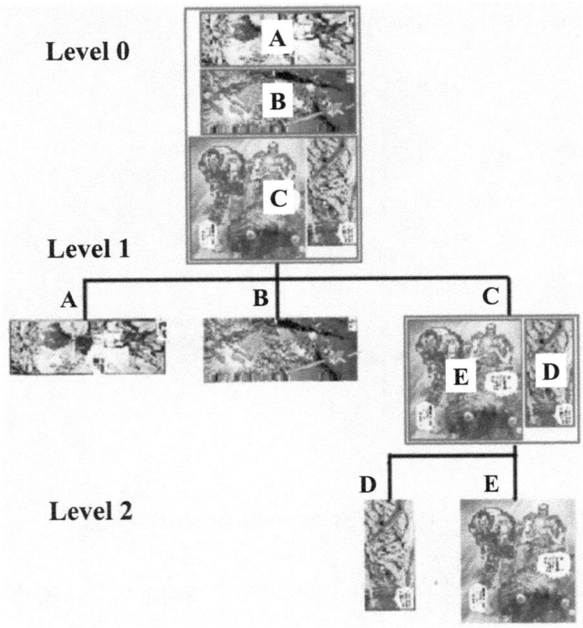

Fig. 6. Tree structure of sub-regions

Fig. 6 illustrates an example of the tree structure of sub-regions. The input comic page image is segmented into 3 sub-regions in level 1. As regions A and B do not contain any stripes, they are identified as panels. A stripe is found in region C thus it is further segmented into regions D and E in level 2. As regions D and E do not have any stripes, they are identified as panels. Furthermore, the reading order of the panels is found to be A, B, D, E using the preorder traversal along the tree.

3 Speed-Up Strategy

In our algorithm, most of the time is spent on checking all the pixels on each line to detect stripes. We present a strategy to accelerate our algorithm while preserving the accuracy of the system. It is observed that the beginning and ending pixels on a true stripe always have the same or similar color. As a result, before checking the histogram, these two pixels can be checked first. If they have different colors, then the line is a non-stripe line and no further checking is necessary. Experiments show that the speed-up strategy increased the speed by 70%. However, this strategy cannot be further applied to all other pixels along the line because there can be variations on the intensities for other pixels on a stripe line as indicated in Fig. 4(b).

4 Experiment and Results

In the experiment, we tested our approach on a comic image database containing 500 pages from 14 comic volumes offered by the Jade Dynasty Group Limited [16][17]. The comic volumes come from 4 different stories and authors. The resolution of each comic page image is around 700×1000 pixels. The experiment is carried out using a Pentium 4 PC with 1.7GHZ and 512M RAM.

The performance of our panel extraction algorithm is given in Table 1. There are altogether 2406 panels from the 500 comic page images. This information is obtained manually and used as the ground truth. On the other hand, we apply our algorithm to detect the panels automatically from these comic page images. As indicated in Table 1, our approach can correctly identify over 83% of panels with 2 seconds per page on average. The number of false panels is about 10%. The result shows that panel extraction can be performed correctly most of the time. Some human intervention may be required to correct the wrong results. With the accuracy of our algorithm, the required manual effort should be much less than if each panel has to be extracted manually.

Table 1. Performance of panel extraction

Total no. of true panels	2406
No. of panels correctly recognized	2016
Accuracy	83.8%
False detection rate	10%

Some examples of comic page images as well as the panel extraction results are shown in Fig. 7. The numbers in the extracted panels indicate the reading order. It can be seen that our algorithm is able to extract panels accurately under variations in panel sizes, shapes and layout.

Some panels cannot be identified mainly because the extended content from a panel causes the stripe recognition to fail so further panels cannot be detected. An example of such case is shown in Fig. 8(a). Sometimes a false stripe cannot be eliminated resulting in false detection. This is because the false stripe also has a large contrast along the boundary due to the panel color content as shown in Fig. 8(b).

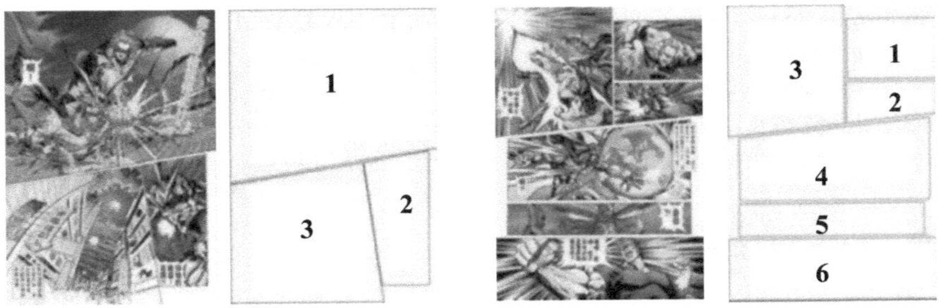

Fig. 7. Comic page images and the extracted panels with the reading order

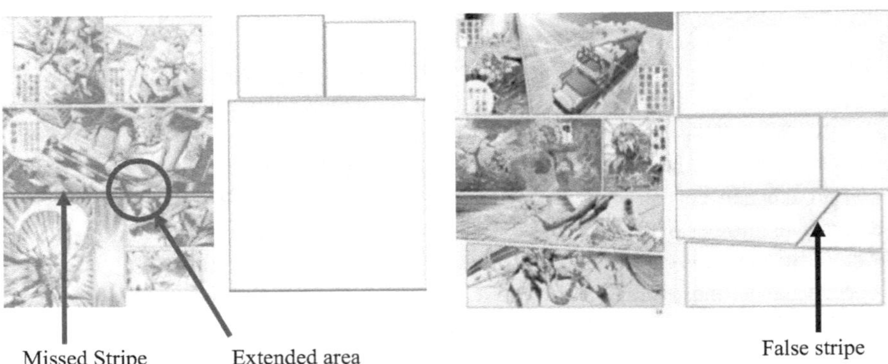

(a) (b)

Fig. 8. (a) Missed stripe due to the extended content; (b) False stripe due to the panel color content

5 PDA Comic Viewer

We have developed a PDA comic viewer to read the extracted panels as shown in Fig. 9. It provides a convenient and comfortable way to read comic on a PDA screen. It has common functions such as moving forward, backward or to a specific panel. The panel can be zoomed in different scales or viewed in full-screen mode. The auto-sliding function allows advancing to the next panel automatically after a fixed time interval.

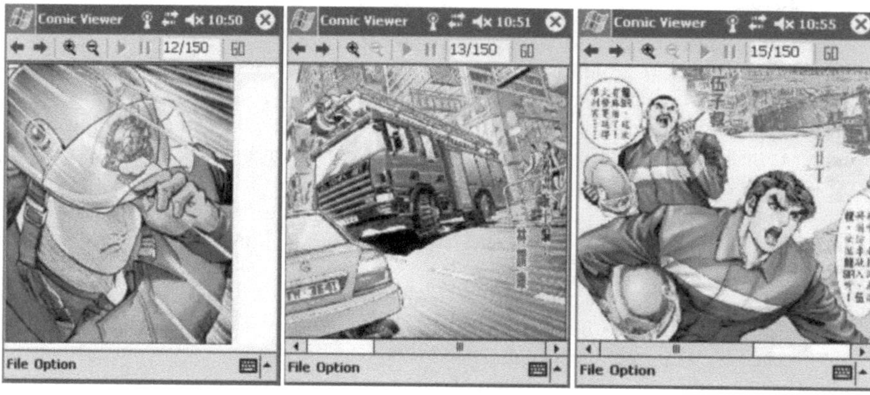

Fig. 9. PDA comic viewer

6 Conclusions and Future Work

This paper proposes an automatic approach for extracting panels in a color comic page image. Given an image region, the stripes are first recognized and false stripes are removed. A recognized stripe is used to divide the image region into sub-regions. This process is repated recursively until no more stripe is found. Experiments show that the panel detection high accuracy with reasonable speed.

As future work, we will detect the text boxes on the panel so that the graphics part and the text part in the panel can be viewed with different scales for better viewing on a small PDA screen. In addition, user behavior will be analyzed to customize parameters such as navigation, zooming and scrolling while reading comics.

Acknowledgments. We would like to thank the Jade Dynasty Group Limited for providing the comic images [16][17]. The work described in this paper was fully supported by a grant from City University of Hong Kong (Project No. 7001964).

References

1. Shamir, A., Rubinstein, M., Levinboim, T.: Generating comics from 3D interactive computer graphic. IEEE Computer Graphics and Applications 26(3), 53–61 (2006)
2. Tanahashi, S., Aoki, Y., Kim, S.-W.: A comic emotional expression method and its applications. In: TENCON 1999. Proc. of the IEEE Region 10 Conference, vol. 1, pp. 329–332 (1999)
3. Kawamura, K., Yamamoto, Y., Watanabe, H.: Gradation approximation for vector based compression of comic images. In: ICIP 2005. IEEE International Conference on Image Processing, vol. 3, pp. 489–492 (2005)
4. Lai, C.H., Bjornerud, P.M., Akahori, K., Hayashi, S.: The design and evaluation of language learning materials based on comic stories and comic strips. In: Proc. of International Conference on Computers in Education, vol. 1, pp. 677–678 (2002)

5. Manske, K., Rudisch, R.: Comic Actors representing software agents. In: MMM 1998. Proceedings of Multimedia Modeling, pp. 213–222 (1998)
6. Wang, H.B., Li, H.: Cartoon motion capture by shape matching. In: Proc. of 10th Pacific Conference on Computer Graphics and Applications, pp. 454–456 (2002)
7. Haseyama, M., Matsumura, A.: A cartoon character retrieval system including trainable scheme. In: ICIP 2003. Proc. of International Conference on Image Processing, vol. 3, pp. 37–40 (2003)
8. Haseyama, M., Matsumura, A.: A trainable retrieval system for cartoon character images. In: ICME 2003. Proc. of International Conference on Multimedia and Expo, vol. 2, pp. 393–396 (2003)
9. Qiu, M.K., Zhang, K., Huang, M.L.: An Empirical Study of Web Interface Design on Small Display Devices. In: WI 2004. Proceedings of IEEE/WIC/ACM International Conference on Web Intelligence, pp. 29–35 (2004)
10. González-Castaño, F.J., Anido-Rifón, L., Costa-Montenegro, E.: A New Transcoding Technique for PDA Browsers Based on Content Hierarchy. In: Paternó, F. (ed.) Mobile HCI 2002. LNCS, vol. 2411, Springer, Heidelberg (2002)
11. Henricksen, K., Indulska, J.: Adapting the Web Interface: An Adaptive Web Browser. In: Proc. of Australasian User Interface Conference 2001, Australian Computer Science Communications, vol. 23(5) (2001)
12. Öquist, G., Goldstein, M.: Toward an Improved Readability on Mobile Devices: Evaluating Adaptive Rapid Serial Visual Presentation. In: Paternó, F. (ed.) Mobile HCI 2002. LNCS, vol. 2411, pp. 240–255. Springer, Heidelberg (2002)
13. ComicGuru, a tool for converting comic strip images into Comic eBook for PDA [Accessed: April 16, 2007], [Online]. Available: http://www.comicguru.net/
14. Skarbek, W., Koschan, A.: Colour Image Segmentation - A Survey. Technical Report 94-32, Technical University of Berlin, Department of Computer Science, Germany (1994)
15. Illingworth, J., Kittler, J.: A survey of the Hough transform. Computer Vision, Graphics and Image Processing (CVGIP) 4, 87–116 (1988)
16. The Jade Dynasty Group Limited, Dragonman (in Chinese) ,vol. 2, pp.2–3, 6, 12, 20, 27; vol. 3, p.16, © JD Global IP rights Ltd. [Accessed: April 16, 2007], Available: http://www.kingcomics.com
17. The Jade Dynasty Group Limited, Firemen (in Chinese), vol. 1, p.18, 23, © JD Global IP rights Ltd. [Accessed: April 16, 2007], Available: http://www.kingcomics.com

Image Quality Assessment Based on Energy of Structural Distortion

Jianxin Pang, Rong Zhang, Lu Lu, and Zhengkai Liu

MOE-Microsoft Key Laboratory of Multimedia Computing and Communication,
Department of Electronic Engineering and Information Science,
University of Science and Technology of China, Hefei, Anhui P.R. China
waltonpang@ustc.edu, zrong@ustc.edu.cn, gemlu@mail.ustc.edu.cn,
zhengkai@ustc.edu.cn

Abstract. Objective image quality assessment (QA), which automatically evaluates the image quality consistently with human perception, is essentially important for numerous image and video processing applications. We propose a new objective QA method for full reference model based on the energy of structural distortion (ESD). Firstly, we collect the characteristics of the structural information by the normalization processing for the reference image. Secondly, the information of ESD is gained by projecting the image onto the characteristic signal of the structural information independently. Finally the objective quality score is obtained by computing the differences of ESD between the reference and distorted images. In this paper, we propose one implementation with simple parameters for our image QA. Experimental results show that the proposed method is well consistent with the subjective quality score.

Keywords: Image quality assessment, inner product, structural distortion, image structure.

1 Introduction

In the field of image processing, image quality assessment (QA) is a fundamental and challenging problem with many interests in a variety of applications, such as dynamic monitoring and adjusting image quality, optimizing algorithms and parameter settings of image processing systems, and benchmarking image processing system and algorithms [1]. Image QA can be classified as subjective and objective image QA [2]. The subjective QA is of more exactitude, however in practice, it is usually expensive, time-consuming, inconvenient, and environment-limited. Moreover this kind of method may be affected by various factors, for example the mood of the candidate, testing equipment, the individuality of the observers, and others. Therefore it is important to develop an objective image quality measure, which automatically and exactly evaluates the image quality. In this paper we focus on full-reference image QA, which means that the original image (we take it for granted that the original image is 'perfect' or of 'high quality') is completely known as the reference one.

H.H.S. Ip et al. (Eds.): PCM 2007, LNCS 4810, pp. 785–793, 2007.

In the past three decades, many objective image quality assessment methods have been put forward, which can be generally classified into the following three categories:

(1) Metrics based on the mathematical statistic of pixels, such as the mean square error (MSE), the root mean square error (RMSE), the signal to noise ratio (SNR), the peak signal to noise ratio (PSNR), and others. However, all of these mathematics-based means above cannot completely reveal the characteristic of human's perception [1] - [4], while they are still widely used in many situations since they are easy to calculate and independent to the test images.

(2) Metrics based on human visual systems (HVS). The idea based on HVS for image QA was put forward by Mannos and Sakrison [5] in 1974. Moreover Karunasekera and Kingsbury [6], Chou and Li [7], and Watson [8] also contribute much. Although the HVS-based metrics are mostly accepted, the complexity and the finitude of the cognizing of HVS keep this metric from going much further [1].

(3) Metrics based on structural distortion of images. This idea is first put forward by Wang *et al.* . [1]. On the assumption that "human visual perception is highly adaptive for extracting structural information from a scene", they propose the mean "Structural Similarity" metric (MSSIM) which compares the structural similarity between the reference and the distorted images. Shnayderman *et al.* [9] propose an idea of assessing the image based on the singular value decomposition (SVD) of the matrix of the images. This kind of metric is to work as an expansion for those mathematics-based metrics.

Generally, those mathematics-based metrics, simply using statistical variables such as variance and covariance, try to measure the error magnitude associating a scalar with every pair of pixels between the reference and distortion images. The metrics based on structural distortion such as MSSIM and SVD try to remove and measure the correlations between the image structures, and these methods try to overcome some drawback of those mathematics-based methods and agree with the human perception. In previous work [10], we have proposed a metric for image coding based on matching pursuit, and matching pursuit is introduced into extracting important image structures from the images and developing a set of structural characteristics for image QA. In this work we will try to develop a more universal image QA metric based on energy of structural distortion (ESD) without matching pursuit, and we also focus our attention to develop a new set of characteristics of structural information and structural distortion; moreover we hope that the proposed metric be of low computational complexity to replace the role of those mathematics-based metrics.

The paper is organized as follows: Section 2 introduces the proposed metric; In Section 3, we compare our experimental results with some other metrics. Section 4 concludes this paper.

2 The Proposed Metric

We develop a new set of characteristics of the structural information by the normalization processing for the reference image, and the information of ESD is gained by projecting the images onto the structural characteristic individually. The objective quality score is derived from computing the differences of ESD between the reference and the distorted images.

The reference image is firstly divided into **K** small blocks with the size $M \times L$, and the individual block is defined as one 2-D vector $\mathbf{b}_i$. $\mathbf{P}_i(x_i, y_i)$ is defined as one element of $\mathbf{b}_i$, and $\mathbf{S}_\mathrm{i}$ is the characterization 2-D vector of $\mathbf{b}_i$. Let E_i be the energy value of structural distortion of $\mathbf{b}_i$. $\mathbf{b'}_n$ and $\mathrm{E'}_n$ are defined similarly for the corresponding distorted image.

Let the energy of $\mathbf{S}_\mathrm{i}$ be 1 and $\mathbf{S}_\mathrm{i}$ is calculated as follows:

$$\mathbf{S}_\mathrm{i} = \frac{\mathbf{b}_i}{\sqrt{\sum_{x_i, y_i} \mathbf{P}_i(x_i, y_i)^2}} \tag{1}$$

Let "$\langle\ \rangle$" be the standard convolution operator (also called projecting or inner product). It is reasonable that in any given vector space a number of inner product can be defined. Here, we choose one simple method of inner product. Suppose **X**= {xij | i=1,…,M, j=1,…,L} and **Y**= { y_{ij} | i=1,2…M, j=1,2…L}, then

$$\langle \mathbf{X}, \mathbf{Y} \rangle = \langle \mathbf{Y}, \mathbf{X} \rangle = \sum_{i,j} x_{ij} * y_{ij}, i = 1, 2...\mathrm{M}, j = 1, 2...\mathrm{L} \tag{2}$$

So $\langle \mathbf{S}_i, \mathbf{S}_i \rangle = 1$. Here we normalize the signal to keep the the sum of the square of the pixels is 1. $\mathbf{S}_i$ is regarded as the structural characterization vector of the reference image.

We calculate E_i and $\mathrm{E'}_i$ by projecting the blocks onto $\mathbf{S}_\mathrm{i}$:

$$\mathrm{E}_i = \langle \mathbf{b}_i, \mathbf{S}_\mathrm{i} \rangle \tag{3}$$

$$\mathrm{E'}_i = \langle \mathbf{b'}_i, \mathbf{S}_\mathrm{i} \rangle \tag{4}$$

Define **SD** as the distortion intensity:

$$\mathbf{SD} = \sqrt{\sum_{i=1}^{\mathrm{K}} (\mathrm{E}_i - \mathrm{E'}_i)^2} \tag{5}$$

In our experiments, we observe that the subjective quality score is a logarithmic function of **SD**. In our simulations, it is interesting that PSNR shows quite satisfied performance on the valuation of WN(White Noise) distortion images quality (which is shown in Section IV), and in the paper [9], [11], [12], PSNR also shows good performance in the WN distortion valuation, while PSNR indicates that the relation between the WN intensity and the objective quality measurement is logarithmic. Therefore we carefully propose that our objective image quality intensity is a logarithmic function of the intensity of the energy of structural distortion which obeys the Weber-Fechner law [13] (a constant relative difference in the intensity corresponds to a constant absolute difference is in the logarithm of the intensity).

Finally, the predictive score of our measure based on ESD is defined as:

$$\mathbf{ESD} = \log(\mathbf{SD}) \ , \ \mathbf{SD}>0 \tag{6}$$

ESD models any distortion as the differences of ESD and measure the differences between the reference and distortion images by the projection processing. Here the structural characterization vector $\mathbf{S}_i$ is desired to describe the shape, edge, texture and others by itself. The energy values of structural distortion, which are gained by projecting the distorted images onto $\mathbf{S}_i$, are desired to represent the signal contribution along $\mathbf{S}_i$, and the variation of the images' degradation will be reflected by their energy values of structural distortion. Then we compare the differences of ESD values to measure the distortion magnitude. The typical ESD values range between 0 and 3. The actual value is meaningless, but the comparison between two values for different test images gives one measure of quality. The lower the predicted score of ESD is, the better the image quality is. When $\mathbf{b}_n = \mathbf{b}'_n$, the distortion and the reference images are identical, so **SD** =0.

Fig. 1 is the flow chart of our method.

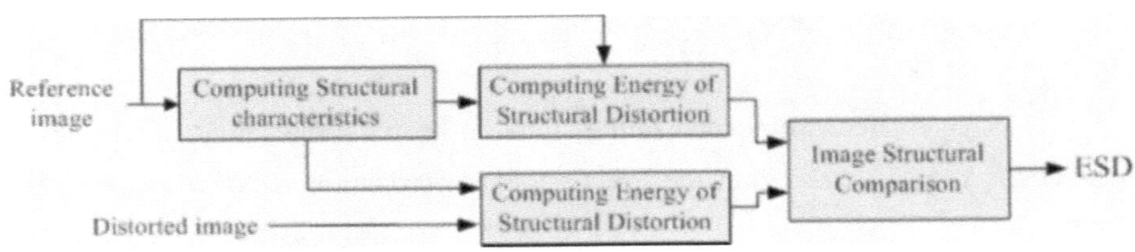

Fig. 1. The flow chart of the method of ESD

3 Experimental Results and Discussion

The database we use in our experiments is the known "LIVE Image Quality Assessment Database Release 2" [14], and the database consists of the color nature images. The subjective score of the images (DMOS, Difference Mean Opinion Score) comes from the newest database [12]. Some images in the database are randomly selected in Fig.2 as examples.

The database includes 29 reference color images, each of which contains 5 distortion types (total 799 images): Fast Fading Rayleigh (Fastfading, 145 images), Gaussian Blur (GBlur, 145 images), White Noise (WN, 145 images), JPEG (175 images), and JPEG2000 (169 images). The five distortion types will be introduced into the study, which could often happen in real practical applications. Fastfading is a simulation of transmission errors in compressed Jpeg2000 bit stream using a fast-fading rayleigh channel model. The RGB components are blurred using a circular-symmetric 2-D Gaussian kernel in GBlur distortion. WN distorts the images by adding white Gaussian noise to RGB components. JPEG and JPEG2000 compress the images at different bit rates, which could often happen in image and video processing applications. We evaluate the performances following the procedures in the Video Quality Experts Group (VQEG) Phase I FR-TV test [14]. We choose the most widely used metric: PSNR, and other two, namely MSSIM [1] and SVD [9] to compare with our metric.

Fig. 2. Some example images selected from the database

The chosen parameters are $M\times L = 8\times 8$ in Eq. (4). Here we choose $M\times L = 8\times 8$ just because it is a common size in many image processing applications and both SVD and MSSIM use this window size. The experiments work with the images' luminance which are separated from color information by converting color images into grayscale ones, and SVD and MSSIM also work with the luminance only.

3.1 Experimental Results

In Fig. 3 and Fig. 4, the X-axis is the objective score of each assessment metric and the Y-axis is DMOS. The lines in figures are non-linear fitting curves which are chosen for regression or fitting for each of those methods, and the logistic function is with five variables as follows:

$$\text{logistic}(x) = a_1 + \frac{a_4 - a_5}{1+\exp(\frac{x-a_3}{a_2})} \tag{7}$$

Fig. 3 is the results for all images, which shows the comparison of the performances in cross-type distortions; Fig. 4 is the results for JPEG and JPEG2000 which compare the performances for image coding.

Table 1 and Table 2 compare the correlation-coefficient (CC) between the four metrics and DMOS before and after fitting. Table 3 compares RMSE between the

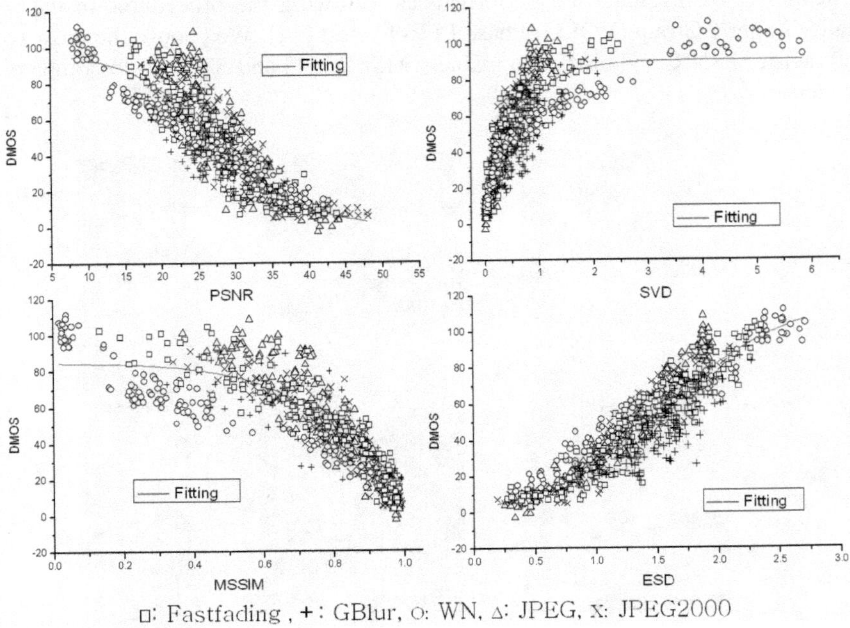

Fig. 3. Scatter plots for PSNR, SVD, MSSIM, and ESD for the 5 types of distortion

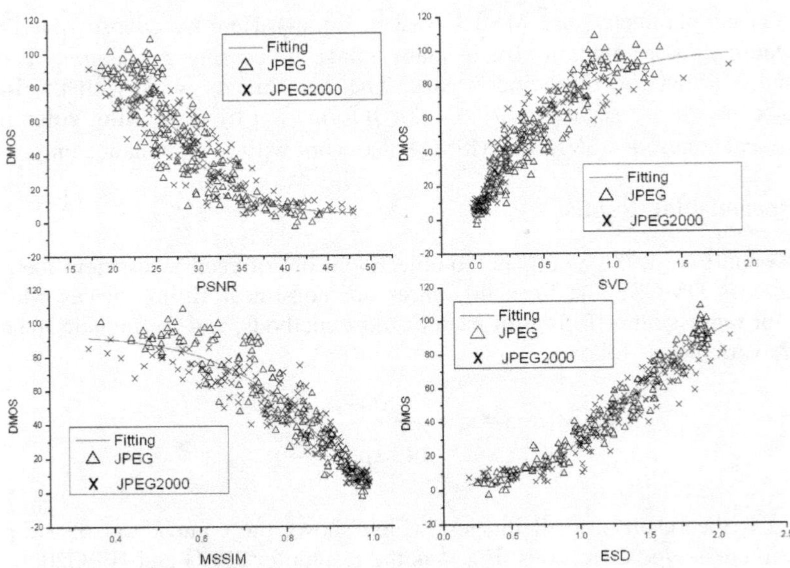

Fig. 4. Scatter plots for PSNR, SVD, MSSIM, and ESD for JPEG and JPEG2000

Table 1. CC-Based for PSNR, SVD, MSSIM and ESD before Non-linear Fitting

	PSNR	SVD	MSSIM	ESD
Fastfading	0.8781	0.8414	0.9010	0.9305
GBlur	0.7633	0.7159	0.8263	0.8387
WN	0.9779	0.9105	0.9652	0.9699
JPEG	0.8662	0.9412	0.9215	0.9681
JPEG2000	0.8738	0.8647	0.9049	0.9385
JPEG+JPEG2000	0.8608	0.9103	0.9089	0.9541
ALL	0.8579	0.6968	0.8237	0.9118

Table 2. CC-Based for PSNR, SVD, MSSIM and ESD after Non-linear Fitting

	PSNR	SVD	MSSIM	ESD
Fastfading	0.8936	0.8985	0.9422	0.9351
GBlur	0.7734	0.7220	0.8465	0.8536
WN	0.9844	0.9786	0.9699	0.9699
JPEG	0.8865	0.9589	0.9482	0.9796
JPEG2000	0.8980	0.9428	0.9407	0.9555
JPEG+JPEG2000	0.8863	0.9466	0.9377	0.9659
ALL	0.8693	0.8822	0.8984	0.9170

Table 3. RMSE-Based for PSNR, SVD, MSSIM and ESD after Non-linear Fitting

	PSNR	SVD	MSSIM	ESD
Fastfading	12.7859	12.5051	9.5481	9.9735
GBlur	11.7088	12.7795	9.8349	9.6224
WN	4.9192	5.7595	6.8167	6.8107
JPEG	14.7411	9.0365	10.1208	6.4021
JPEG2000	11.1016	8.4114	8.5588	7.4449
JPEG+JPEG2000	13.4290	9.3492	10.0742	7.5081
ALL	13.5029	12.8636	12.0018	10.8703

four metrics and DMOS the non-linear fitting. We compare the performance between the results before and after non-linear fitting to show the contribution of Eq. (6).

3.2 Discussion

From the figures and tables above we can draw the conclusion that PSNR is not adaptable well in almost all of the distortion types except WN. And it is reasonable that PSNR has good performance of all in WN, because the WN-distortion image is distorted and degraded only by WN, so PSNR can count quite accurately all these errors which are statistically independent. When the "errors" or characters which distort the images are not uncorrelated, PSNR cannot work well for these matters simply and accurately. The other three metrics try to overcome these systematic drawbacks of PSNR.

SVD and MSSIM have close performances, while SVD shows better in WN, JPEG and JPEG2000 but worse in Fastfading and GBlur than MSSIM. In individual distortion type, ESD outperforms the others in GBlur, JPEG and JPEG2000, and also have a good performance in Fastfading and WN. ESD has the best performance in cross-distortion types, especially in coding types. And all of the four metrics cannot deal with GBlur accurately and exactly. It is a task for future research to optimize the algorithm to adapt to more distortion types.

Although the performances of SVD and MSSIM have a distinct improvement after fitting, it is still inferior compared with ESD, whose performance increases little after fitting. That comparison between the results before and after fitting shows the contribution of Eq. (6) we propose. Our propose approach can be used as the role of PSNR.

There are some issues which are worth investigating. In Eq. (1), the normalization processing may be optimized for some special applications using some thresholds such as the brightness, contrast or energy distribution. All of the four metrics work only with the luminance of the images. However the subjective score DMOS is gained by the observers evaluating the color images. So when the distortion of color information which may not be detected in luminance channel happens, it is much difficult to assess those images exactly only using luminance information. In the database, Fastfading is the distortion which sometimes degrades the color information, so the plots of four metrics scatter in Fastfading. It will not be an easy job to study color distortion for QA. The sensitivity of ESD to slight distortions in rotation, shift and magnification is not satisfactory, which is to be taken into future study.

ESD has a less computational complexity compared with SVD and MSSIM. The implementation on a 768×512 image (bikes.bmp) on a Pentium IV, 3.0GHz laptop using the luminance information takes about 0.1 second.

4 Conclusion and Future Work

In this paper we propose an objective image assessment metric based on the energy of structural distortion. The proposed metric with simple parameters is of low computational complexity, which can be used to take the role of PSNR. And we also attempt to discuss the relationship between the structural distortion intensity and the subjective visual quality. The experimental results show that ESD has a better performance than PSNR, SVD, and MSSIM. This metric is not only well adaptable in individual distortion type, especially in image coding types, but also in cross-distortion types.

There are numerous distortion types for images in practice and this paper only deal with 5 types. Our future work is to explore into more aspects and investigate into the relationship between distortion of structural information and the subjective visual quality, and we will also focus on the research of the quality assessment for video using ESD.

References

1. Wang, Z., Bovik, A., Sheikh, H.R., Simoncelli, E.P.: Image Quality Assessment: From Error Visibility to Structural Similarity. IEEE Trans. Image Processing 13(4), 600–612 (2004)

2. Eskicioglu, A.M.: Quality measurement for monochrome compressed images in the past 25 years. In: Proc. IEEE Int. Conf. Acoustics, Speech, Signal Processing, Istanbul, Turkey, vol. 4, pp. 1907–1910 (June 2000)
3. Wang, Z., Bovik, A.C.: A universal image quality index. IEEE Signal Processing Letters 9, 81–84 (2002)
4. Wang, Z., Bovik, A.C., Lu, L.: Why is image quality assessment so difficult. In: Proc. IEEE Int. Conf. Acoust, Speech, and Signal Processing, Orlando, vol. 4, pp. 3313–3316 (May 2002)
5. Mannos, J.L., Sakrison, D.J.: The effects of a visual fidelity criterion on the encoding of images. IEEE Trans. Information Theory 20(4), 525–536 (1974)
6. Karunasekera, S.A., Kingsbury, N.G.: A distortion measure for blocking artifacts in images based on human visual sensitivity. IEEE Trans. Image Processing 4(6), 713–724 (1995)
7. Chou, C.H., Li, Y.C.: A perceptually tuned subband image coder based on the measure of Just-Noticeable-Distortion profile. IEEE Trans. Circuits and Systems for Video Technology 5(6), 467–476 (1995)
8. Watson, A.B.: DCT quantization matrices visually optimized for individual images. In: Presented at Human Vision, Visual Processing, and Digital Display IV, Bellingham, WA (1993)
9. Shnayderman, A., Gusev, A., Eskicioglu, A.M.: An SVD-based grayscale image quality measure for local and global assessment. IEEE Trans. Image Processing 15(2), 422–429 (2006)
10. Pang, J., Zhang, R., Lu, L., Liu, Z.: Quality assessment for image coding based on matching pursuit. In: Proc. IEEE International Conference on Multimedia & Expo, Beijing, China, pp. 296–299 (July 2007)
11. Sheikh, H.R., Bovik, A.C.: Image information and visual quality. IEEE Trans. Image Processing 15(2), 430–444 (2006)
12. Sheikh, H.R., Sabir, M.F., Bovik, A.C.: A statistical evaluation of recent full reference image quality assessment algorithms. IEEE Trans. Image Processing 15(11), 3441–3452 (2006)
13. Levine, M.W.: Fundamentals of sensation and perception, 3rd edn. Oxford University Press, New York (2000)
14. Sheikh, H.R., Wang, Z., Cormack, L., Bovik, A.C.(eds.): LIVE Image Quality Assessment Database Release, vol. 2 Available: http://live.ece.utexas.edu/research/quality
15. VQEG, Final report from the video quality experts group on the validation of objective models of video quality assessment (March 2000), Available http://www.vqeg.org/

SAR Speckle Mitigation by Fusing Statistical Information from Spatial and Wavelet Domains

Kart Lim[1], Nishan Canagarajah[2], and Alin Achim[2]

[1] Computer Vision and Image Understanding Department,
Institute for Infocomm Research, 21 Heng Mui Keng Terrace, Singapore 119613
kllim@i2r.a-star.edu.sg

2 Department of Electrical & Electronic Engineering, University of Bristol,
Merchant Venturers Building, Woodland Road, Bristol BS8 1UB, United Kingdom
{Nishan.Canagarajah, Alin.Achim}@bris.ac.uk

Abstract. We propose a novel algorithm for the de-speckling of SAR images which exploits a priori statistical information from both the spatial and wavelet domains. In the spatial domain, we apply the Method-of-Log-Cumulants (MoLC), which is based on Mellin transform, in order to locally estimate parameters corresponding to an assumed Generalized Gaussian Rayleigh (GGR) model for the image. We then compute classical cumulants for the image and speckle models and relate them into their wavelet domain counterparts. Using wavelet cumulants, we separately derive parameters corresponding to an assumed generalized Gaussian (GG) model for the image and noise wavelet coefficients. Finally, we feed the resulting parameters into a Bayesian maximum a priori (MAP) estimator, which is applied to the wavelet coefficients of the log-transformed SAR image. Our proposed method outperforms several recently proposed de-speckling techniques both visually and in terms of different objective measures.

Keywords: SAR Speckle, Method-of-Log-Cumulants, Wavelet Transform, Adaptive Filtering.

1 Introduction

A classical application of noise reduction techniques is in SAR imagery, where speckle noise occurs naturally during the image formation process. This specific type of noise constitutes a multiplicative contamination of the SAR data and has a granular appearance which severely degrades the visual quality of images. This makes data interpretation a difficult task in general. De-speckling is thus recognized as an important pre-processing operation before performing other SAR image analysis or interpretation tasks. Over the past few decades, SAR image de-speckling techniques have advanced considerably from early generic spatial filters such as the median and the Wiener filters, to filters which exploit statistical assumptions about the radar cross section (RCS). These include among others the well-known Lee and Gamma-Map filters. The introduction of wavelet transform in signal processing has also drawn the

H.H.S. Ip et al. (Eds.): PCM 2007, LNCS 4810, pp. 794–803, 2007.

interest of many researchers towards wavelet based algorithms [1]. In this context, some recent techniques are capable of employing prior information from both the spatial and wavelet domains [2, 3]. By fusing both the statistical information used in spatial filters with the statistical information exploited by wavelet filters, one should expect to achieve close to optimal de-speckling results.

A SAR system measures the in-phase (real part) and the quadrature channels (imaginary part) at the receiver, resulting in a complex image. If Gaussianity is assumed for the real and imaginary parts of the complex image, the image data can be shown to be Rayleigh distributed. Recently, several authors have suggested using more realistic assumptions about the image formation process [4, 5]. In [5], a GG distribution was assumed and it led to a new model for the amplitude RCS – the GGR density. On the other hand, appropriate statistical models should also be considered for modelling speckle noise. In [2, 3, 4], the authors modelled speckle with Gamma or Nakagami probability density functions (pdf) depending on whether the image is in amplitude or intensity format.

For the purpose of this paper we shall restrict our study to SAR images in amplitude format. Our work is conceptually similar to the de-speckling algorithms in [2, 3], whereby our novelty consists in modelling the RCS locally with the GGR pdf, whilst using a Nakagami model for speckle. In addition, we employ the Mellin transform for the parameter estimation of spatial models as documented in [4, 6]. A theoretical advantage of our proposed approach is that we work in a unified framework in which statistical assumptions about the actual data rely on the GG model in both the spatial and in the wavelet domains.

2 Parameter Estimation in the Spatial Domain

An observed SAR image represents a multiplicative mixture of signal and noise. Recently, "second kind statistics" [6] based on Mellin Transform has been proposed as an alternative to the classical MoM. Due to the usage of logarithmic scale in "second kind statistics", it can lend itself very well to the processing of stationary and multiplicative signals. Moreover, the author in [6] has shown that such estimation can yield a more accurate result than the MoM. Specifically, if we denote the observed SAR image, the RCS and the speckle terms as y, x and η respectively, it can be shown in [4, 6] that, if $P(y)$ is represented by the Mellin convolution between $P(x)$ and $P(\eta)$, then the n-order log-cumulants of $P(y)$ can be expressed as the sum between the n-order log-cumulants of $P(x)$ and $P(\eta)$ as given by [4, 6]:

$$\tilde{k}_{y(n)} = \tilde{k}_{x(n)} + \tilde{k}_{\eta(n)} \quad . \tag{1}$$

In order to solve (1), we need to estimate the first two log-cumulants of the observed SAR image [4, 6]:

$$\hat{\tilde{k}}_{y(1)} = \frac{1}{N}\sum_{k=1}^{N} \ln y_k \quad . \tag{2}$$

$$\hat{\tilde{k}}_{y(2)} = \frac{1}{N-1}\sum_{k=1}^{N}(\ln y_k - \hat{\tilde{k}}_{y(1)})^2 \ . \tag{3}$$

Notice that (2) and (3) are actually the "log-version" of the classical sample mean and variance estimator. Next, we model amplitude format SAR speckle under the assumption of being fully developed and uncorrelated with the L-looks Nakagami distribution. Its first two log-cumulants [4] as shown below can be easily computed based on the knowledge of L from a SAR image. The digamma and the v-order polygamma functions are denoted $\Psi(n)$ and $\Psi(v,n)$ respectively:

$$\tilde{k}_{\eta(1)} = \frac{\Psi(L) - \ln(L)}{2} \ . \tag{4}$$

$$\tilde{k}_{\eta(2)} = \frac{\Psi(1,L)}{4} \ . \tag{5}$$

In [5], the MoLC parameter estimation of the GGR distributed RCS is based on solving two sets of GGR log-cumulants equations. But, for the assumption of a GGR distributed RCS with a multiplicative L-looks Nakagami distributed speckle of an observed SAR amplitude image, we can still solve for the parameters of the GGR model by using (1), (3), (5) and (1), (2), (4) along with the GGR log-cumulants equations in [5] to obtain the following MoLC equations :

$$\hat{\lambda} = \left(\lambda^2 \cdot \Psi(1,2\lambda) + \lambda^2 \frac{G_2(\lambda)G_0(\lambda) - G_1(\lambda)^2}{G_0(\lambda)^2}\right) + \left(\frac{\Psi(1,L)}{4}\right) \ . \tag{6}$$
$$- \left(\frac{1}{N-1}\sum_{k=1}^{N}(\ln y_k - \frac{1}{N}\sum_{k=1}^{N}\ln y_k)^2\right)$$

$$\hat{\gamma} = \exp\left[\left(\lambda \cdot \Psi(2\lambda) - \lambda\frac{G_1(\lambda)}{G_0(\lambda)}\right) + \left(\frac{\Psi(L) - \ln(L)}{2}\right) - \left(\frac{1}{N}\sum_{k=1}^{N}\ln y_k\right)\right] \cdot \tag{7}$$

The functions, $G_v(\lambda)$ and $A(\theta,\lambda)$ are given by [5]:

$$G_v(\lambda) = \int_0^{\pi/2} \frac{\ln^v A(\theta,\lambda)}{A(\theta,\lambda)^{2\lambda}} d\theta, \ \mathrm{v} = 0,1,2,\ldots, \ \cdot \tag{8}$$

$$A(\theta,\lambda) = |\cos\theta|^{1/\lambda} + |\sin\theta|^{1/\lambda} \ . \tag{9}$$

We use a 9x9 size for the local window, since any smaller may lower the success rate of the MoLC estimation as a result of biasing in small samples while a larger window makes it less accurate when capturing local statistics. We first solve (6) for λ via a reliable root finding algorithm such as Brent's method before solving for γ in (7). Due to the involvement of the integral expression in (8), we also require a fast and fairly accurate 1D numerical integration method such as the adaptive Simpson quadrature or the composite Simpson rule. We run this procedure for all the pixels.

We also have to consider possible cases where the root finding method cannot yield any solution for (6). This is due to the nature of the GGR log-cumulant equation being lower bounded as mentioned in [5]. Specifically, if $\tilde{k}_{y(2)} < 0.296$, then (6) has no solution for λ. In this case, a possible solution would be to reduce the GGR to a one parameter model by pre-setting λ while solving normally for γ. We select and fix the smallest possible positive value for λ. Through experiments on several images, we found that setting λ=*0.1* gives the best compromise. We also compute the Equivalent-Number-of-Looks (*ENL*) of each window [1] as below for the MAP filtering process described later on:

$$ENL = (\frac{4}{\pi} - 1) \cdot \frac{mean^2}{variance} . \tag{10}$$

2.1 Derivation of Standard Cumulants

After solving for the parameters of the spatial models, we can compute their pdf expressions and consequently their n-order cumulants. But, in order to obtain an additive relationship for an observed SAR image, we must first perform log-transform to the image to derive the following:

$$Y = X + N . \tag{11}$$

As a result, we must also perform a change of variable to the pdf expression of the spatial models using the identity, $N = \ln \eta$, in order to derive their distributions logarithm. Thus, for a unit mean and variance of 1/*L*, we can obtain the pdf of the *L*-looks Nakagami distribution logarithm (log-Nakagami), which is used as a speckle model for $P(N)$ as follows [4, 6]:

$$P(N) = \frac{2L^L e^{2NL} e^{-Le^{2N}}}{\Gamma(L)} . \tag{12}$$

Similarly, by applying $X = \ln x$ to the GGR pdf in [5], we can obtain the pdf expression of the GGR distribution logarithm (log-GGR):

$$P(X) = \frac{\gamma^2 (1/\lambda)^2 e^{2X}}{\Gamma^2(\lambda)} \cdot \int_0^{\pi/2} \exp[-(\gamma \cdot e^X)^{1/\lambda} (|\cos\theta|^{1/\lambda} + |\sin\theta|^{1/\lambda})] d\theta . \tag{13}$$

Initially, we compute the raw moments of the distributions logarithm, before converting them into cumulants. In practice, it is easier to compute the n-order discrete raw moment which is given as:

$$\mu_n' = \sum_i X_i^n \cdot P(X_i) . \tag{14}$$

Then, we obtain the required n-order cumulants by using the identity between cumulants and raw moments as below:

$$
\begin{aligned}
k_1 &= \mu_1^{'} \\
k_2 &= -\mu_1^{'2} + \mu_2^{'} \\
k_3 &= 2\mu_1^{'3} - 3\mu_1^{'}\mu_2^{'} + \mu_3^{'} \\
k_4 &= -6\mu_1^{'4} + 12\mu_1^{'2}\mu_2^{'} - 3\mu_2^{'2} - 4\mu_1^{'}\mu_3^{'} + \mu_4^{'}
\end{aligned} \tag{15}
$$

3 MAP Estimation in the Wavelet Domain

After obtaining the spatial cumulants, we transfer this information into the wavelet domain through a relationship known to the spatial and wavelet cumulants. The authors in [3] assumed that the signal in the spatial domain is an "independent and random process". They exploit the Linear Time Invariant property of the Undecimated Wavelet Transform which is also known as the Stationary Wavelet Transform (SWT) [7] for establishing the relationship between spatial and wavelet cumulants. The m-order wavelet cumulants for a 1-D data is given as [3]:

$$
(K_{W_{X(n)}})^m = (K_{X(n)})^m * (h(n))^m . \tag{16}
$$

For a 2-D data e.g. an image, the matrices of the m-order wavelet cumulant are obtained by a series of successive row and column convolutions between the matrices of the m-order cumulant of the image in the spatial domain and the wavelet filters taken to the power of m. The scales and orientations of the wavelet cumulants are governed by the user defined numbers of row and column convolutions between the wavelet filters and the cumulants. Specifically, we require a pair of second and fourth order cumulants from each pixel modelled by log-GGR as well as a static pair from log-Nakagami since speckle is assumed stationary. After which, we relate the wavelet cumulants to their central moments using the following:

$$
\begin{aligned}
W_{m2} &= W_{k2} \\
W_{m4} &= W_{k4} + 3\cdot(W_{k2})^2
\end{aligned} \tag{17}
$$

After applying wavelet transform to the logarithm of a SAR image, due to linearity of the process, we retain the additive relationship in (11) for the wavelet coefficients of the image as follows:

$$
W_Y = W_X + W_N . \tag{18}
$$

In order to estimate the unknown noiseless wavelet coefficient, W_X, from the noisy wavelet coefficient, W_Y, given prior knowledge about their statistical distributions, we employ the MAP estimator for our proposed algorithm which is expressed as follows after applying Bayes' rule:

$$\hat{W}_X = \arg\max_{W_X}[\ln P(W_Y - W_X) + \ln P(W_X)] \cdot \quad (19)$$

In our case, both $P(W_X)$ and $P(W_Y - W_X)$ are represented by two GG prior models for signal and noise. The expression for the GG pdf is given by [8]:

$$P(W_X) \propto \exp(-\left|\frac{W_X}{S}\right|^P) \cdot \quad (20)$$

Analytically, the GG pdf can be expressed in terms of Gamma function for its variance and kurtosis, and we can obtain the two MoM equations as shown below [8]:

$$kurtosis = \Gamma(\frac{1}{P}) \cdot \Gamma(\frac{5}{P}) \Big/ \Gamma^2(\frac{3}{P}) \cdot \quad (21)$$

$$\text{var}iance = S^2 \cdot \Gamma(\frac{3}{P}) \Big/ \Gamma(\frac{1}{P}) \cdot \quad (22)$$

We can obtain parameters of the GG pdf for the modelling of signal and noise wavelet coefficients simply by applying (17) to (21) and (22).

From (19), by taking the derivative of the logarithm of (20) for both $P(W_X)$ and $P(W_Y - W_X)$ with respect to W_X, we can obtain the MAP expression below:

$$\hat{W}_X = \left[\frac{P_{W_N}}{S_{W_N}}\left|\frac{W_Y - W_X}{S_{W_N}}\right|^{P_{W_N}-1} \operatorname{sgn}\left(\frac{W_Y - W_X}{S_{W_N}}\right)\right] + \left[-\frac{P_{W_X}}{S_{W_X}}\left|\frac{W_X}{S_{W_X}}\right|^{P_{W_X}-1} \operatorname{sgn}\left(\frac{W_X}{S_{W_X}}\right)\right] \cdot \quad (23)$$

Since this expression is not analytical, we require a numerical root finding method such as Brent's method to solve for the unknown. In the low SNR scenario where $ENL \le L$, the local window sample which comprises mainly of speckle alone is not considered textured, thus, due to the dependency of the MAP estimator on the GGR parameters, it cannot perform as optimally as in the normal case. Therefore, we set $ENL \le L$ as a threshold value for indicating speckle dominated regions and consequently, we set to zero, wavelet coefficients of pixels which fall under this threshold. Likewise, we restrict the usage of the MAP estimator to cases where $ENL > L$.

Following the arguments in [1], a mean-bias problem occurs when log-transform is applied to the statistics of images and the error can be corrected by subtracting the mean value of the log-transformed speckle from the output of the inverse wavelet transform. In our proposed algorithm, we model the log-transformed speckle with the L-looks Nakagami distribution logarithm. We can numerically compute the speckle mean by applying (12) to (14) as given below:

$$\mu_1' = \sum_i N_i \cdot \frac{2L^L e^{2N_i L} e^{-Le^{2N_i}}}{\Gamma(L)} \cdot \quad (24)$$

Alternatively, we can also estimate the speckle mean from a randomly generated L-looks Nakagami distributed sample after applying log-transform to it.

We prefer to refer to our proposed algorithm as the GGRGGMAP since it relies on the GGR model to operate the GG prior MAP shrinkage function. A functional block diagram of the GGRGGMAP algorithm is shown below:

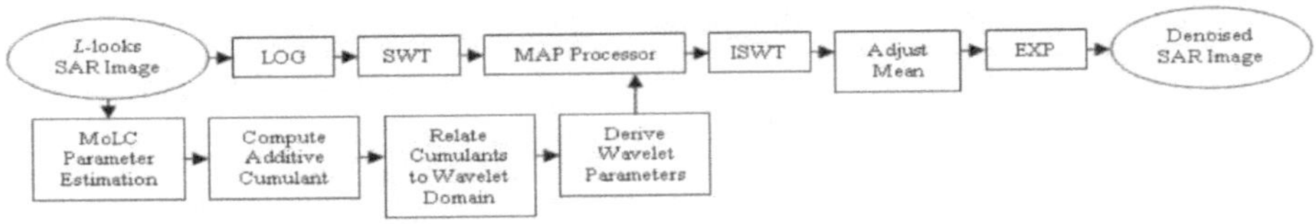

Fig. 1. Block diagram of our proposed GGRGGMAP algorithm for speckle suppression

4 Results and Comparison

We compare the performance of our proposed algorithm with the Lee filter as well as with other wavelet based algorithms including the classical Soft-thresholding, the recently proposed algorithm based on a Bivariate Cauchy model (Bi-Cauchy) [9] and also with our own implementation of Solbo's algorithm [2]. We keep the comparison fair by restricting to a 9x9 window size throughout for all local adaptive methods, and by using the Daubechies-2 wavelet (4 coefficients) for all wavelet methods. All the wavelet based methods are implemented using SWT with three decomposition levels. For soft-thresholding, we set the threshold to $t = 1.5\sigma_d$, which is computed from using the standard deviation of the noisy wavelet coefficients. The adjust mean step is further added to all except Solbo's algorithm and Lee filter. The log and exp-transform step are also implemented in the Bi-Cauchy since it was originally intended for denoising AWGN contaminated images. Our implementation of Solbo's algorithm is conceptually faithful to the original except for a few changes as follows: Instead of estimating the parameters of the Nakagami distribution (or Gamma in intensity format) using the EM-estimator, it is implemented with the MoLC. Also, due to computation complexity we prefer to perform Bayesian estimation using the MMSE estimator for the Normal Inverse Gaussian priors.

An ideal filter should exhibit good de-speckling capability while preserving fine details, especially for images showing crowded regions. We used the ratio image (mean and *ENL* of the de-speckled to original image ratio) which is also used in [4], the standard deviation to mean ratio (S/M), as well as the window *ENL* also used in [1] for quantifying the comparison. Both the ratio image quantities should be considered as an inseparable entity when comparing. Due to space limitation, we only show the de-speckling results for a monolook SAR image of an urban scene. Comparing the de-speckling results in Table.1, GGRGGMAP has the closest theoretical ratio image value for the mean and *ENL* (unity for both values). As for the S/M, although Lee filter has the best rating, it is evident visually in Fig. 2(b). that most of the fine details are oversmoothed, leading to it having the highest *ENL* values amongst all. Visually, Bi-Cauchy determines better edge preservation than all other methods. On the other hand, the performance of soft-thresholding is seen to be quite the opposite of Bi-Cauchy in the sense that although it achieves good speckle removal, it oversmoothen

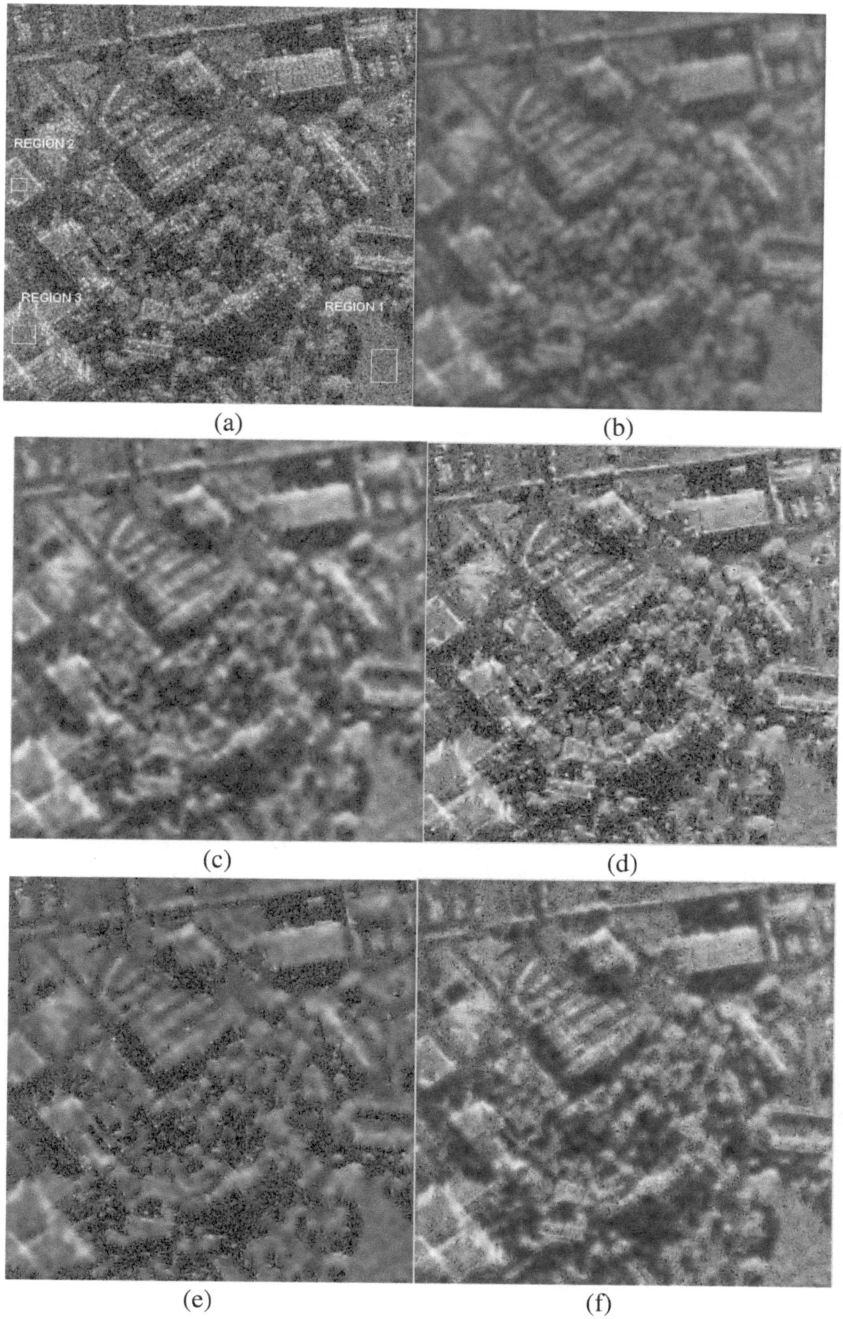

Fig. 2. Visual comparison of various de-speckling methods for a monolook SAR image of an urban scene (a) Original, (b) Lee filter, (c) Soft-thresholding, (d) Bi-Cauchy algorithm, (e) Solbo's algorithm, (f) our proposed GGRGGMAP algorithm

the fine details in the same way as Lee filter does. The de-speckled output of Solbo's algorithm is also seen to oversmoothen the image despite achieving better S/M and *ENL* values than soft-thresholding but performing poorly for the ratio image test. The overall performance of GGRGGMAP is pretty well balanced between that of soft-thresholding and Bi-Cauchy since it has shown to hold an optimal compromise between desirable de-speckling performance (as supported numerically by the ratio mean and visually) and strong edge preservation (as supported numerically by the ratio ENL as well as visually). Thus, we conclude that amongst all algorithms included in the comparison, our proposed algorithm achieve the best de-speckling result. We attribute this to the novel way in which our proposed algorithm fuses prior information from the two different domains.

Table 1. Comparison of various de-speckling results for the monolook urban scene SAR mage

Method	Ratio image		S/M	ENL		
	Mean	ENL		1	2	3
Noisy	-	-	0.58	2.28	2.16	1.79
Lee	1.0	1.18	0.36	56.38	13.81	32.01
Soft-Thres	0.91	1.19	0.50	10.29	10.25	8.74
Bi-Cauchy	0.81	1.75	0.54	4.41	5.37	3.58
Solbo	1.11	2.08	0.48	24.99	20.11	15.29
GGRGGMAP	0.93	0.96	0.53	6.87	6.68	5.17

5 Conclusions

In this paper, we have employed the recently proposed GGR distribution to solve a practical SAR de-speckling problem. We illustrated the versatility of the MoLC approach by solving a parameter estimation problem for SAR imagery for the case when the data is assumed to be GGR distributed. We also took a step further by coupling this result with the unique algorithm framework in [2, 3] such that we were able to enhance their assumption of a jointly Gamma distributed SAR image formation for the steering of a multiscale MAP filtering function in the wavelet domain. Moreover, our proposed algorithm is neatly setup in a unified framework of generalized Gaussanity for both the spatial and wavelet models. We also address the mean biasing problem for a log-transformed SAR image during the image reconstruction process. Our experimental results showed that our method achieves the best result, both visually and numerically, in comparison with several recently proposed de-speckling methods.

References

1. Xie, H., Pierce, L., Ulaby, F.: SAR speckle reduction using wavelet denoising and Markov random field modeling. IEEE Trans. Geosci. Remote Sensing 40, 2196–2212 (2002)
2. Solb ø, S., Eltoft, T.: Homomorphic Wavelet-Based Statistical De-speckling of SAR Images. IEEE Trans. on Geosci. and Remote Sensing 42(4) (April 2004)

3. Argenti, F., Rovai, N., Alparone, L.: De-speckling SAR Images In The Undecimated Wavelet Domin: A MAP Approach. In: IEEE International Conference on Acoustics, Speech, and Signal Processing, Proceedings, vol. 4, pp. 541–544 (March 2005)
4. Achim, A., Kuruoglu, E., Zerubia, J.: SAR image filtering based on the heavy-tailed Rayleigh model. IEEE Transactions on Image Processing 15(9), 2686–2693 (2006)
5. Moser, G., Zerubia, J., Serpico, S.B.: SAR amplitude probability density function estimation based on a Generalized Gaussian scattering model. Image Processing, IEEE Transactions on 15(6), 1429–1442 (2006)
6. Nicolas, J.M.: Introduction aux statistiques de deuxième espèce: applications des logmoments et des log-cumulants à l'analyse des lois d'images radar. Traitement du Signal 19, 139–167 (2002)
7. Nason, G.P., Silverman, B.W.: The stationary wavelet transform and some statistical applications, Univ. Bristol, Bristol, U.K., Tech. Rep. BS8 1Tw (1995)
8. Simoncelli, E., Adelson, E.: Noise removal via Bayesian wavelet coring. In: Third Int'l Conf on Image Proc, vol. I, pp. 379–382 (September 1996)
9. Achim, A., Kuruoglu, E.: Image denoising using bivariate α stable distributions in the complex wavelet domain. IEEE Signal Processing Letters 12(1) (January 2005)

Encoding Independent Sources in Spatially Squeezed Surround Audio Coding

Bin Cheng, Christian Ritz, and Ian Burnett

Whisper Laboratories, School of Electrical Computer and Telecommunications Engineering, University of Wollongong, Wollongong, Australia
bc362@uow.edu.au, chritz@elec.uow.edu.au, i.burnett@elec.uow.edu.au

Abstract. Spatially Squeezed Surround Audio Coding (S^{3}AC) was introduced as an approach to multi-channel audio compression which specifically aims to preserve original source localization information. In this paper, extensions to S^{3}AC that allow for the accurate coding of independent spatial sources overlapped in both frequency and time are described; these use compact side information. An evaluation of the coder applied to tone and band-pass spatial sources shows that S^{3}AC offers improved source localization performance while maintaining bit-rates, when compared with other state-of-the-art spatial audio coders.

Keywords: Audio Signal Processing, Multi-Channel Audio, Spatial Audio, Surround Sound.

1 Introduction

Existing approaches to spatial audio coding [1, 2, 3] have shown significant improvements in terms of bit rate efficiency and audio quality when compared with earlier techniques. However, these new approaches still have two significant drawbacks. Firstly, the successful recovery of accurate sound localization critically relies on the extra side information containing the inter-channel difference and coherence. Secondly, the actual surround sound field and source localization properties are not analyzed and taken into consideration during the coding process. *Spatially Squeezed Surround Audio Coding* (S^{3}AC) proposed by the authors recently [4, 5] offers a novel efficient solution to multi-channel spatial audio compression and addresses the problems of the existing approaches. Rather than being restricted to the usage of inter-channel spatial cues, S^{3}AC exploits the localization redundancy of the surround sound based on human psychoacoustic principles. The basic implementation approach of S^{3}AC was presented in [4], which also highlighted several advantages of S^{3}AC, including lower computational complexity. In addition, S^{3}AC shows significant advantages in preserving the source localization information compared with other spatial audio coding techniques [5] while not requiring additional side information representing spatial cues. For dynamically localized single sources, results in [5] show that S^{3}AC is subjectively indistinguishable to MPEG Surround 525

H.H.S. Ip et al. (Eds.): PCM 2007, LNCS 4810, pp. 804–813, 2007.

[3] with objective results showing an approximate 10 fold improvement in the localization accuracy of the rendered sources.

A significant challenge facing spatial audio coders is the ability to accurately code overlapping sound sources with coincident time and frequency components but being independent to each other and in discriminated locations. Existing research has proposed to overcome this problem by tracking the correlation between sources before determining Interaural Level Difference (ILD) and Interaural Time Difference (ITD) spatial cues [8]. However the correlation measures used require heavy computation. In addition, as stated in [8], "the superposition of sound emanating from several directions results in instantaneous ITD and ILD cues that most of the time do not correspond to any of the source directions". Hence, for wide band sources with narrow overlapping frequencies which have relatively low correlation, analyzing the spatial cues cannot easily distinguish the independent spatial separated sources. Hence, in this paper, we present a side information extension to S^3AC representing the spatial locations of each independent overlapping source as an alternative solution to this problem. According to psychoacoustical principles, this type of side information can be easily and efficiently quantized using techniques described in Section 3. However, for applications where side information transmission is not desired, standard S^3AC can be applied to decode the received downmix signals.

This paper is structured as follows. Section 2 presents the core frequency-azimuth analysis approach used in S^3AC while section 3 describes the use of side information for coding independent overlapping sources in S^3AC. Section 4 presents objective evaluation results for tonal and band-pass sound sources and conclusions are drawn in section 5.

2 Frequency-Azimuth Analysis in S^3AC

Sound sources and their localization properties are the most important points of interest in spatial audio coding. Most state-of-the-art spatial audio coders, such as BCC and MPEG Surround [1, 3], have no direct analysis of the sound field or the localization components with perceptual importance; as a result, some important sound localization properties could be lost during the channel mixing and quantization of cues. In contrast, the fundamental idea of S^3AC is to analyze the whole surround sound field and encode the sound localization information of a large sound field into a much smaller sound field. This process is aimed to be lossless in terms of 'perceptual localization'. Psychoacoustic research has shown that the human ear has a limited resolution in localizing a sound source [6], known as localization blur. Although different features may result from altering the frequency properties and the locations of the perceived sound objects, the localization blur does not drop below 0.5°. Since the numerical calculation during the stereo or surround audio mixing process can have a much higher resolution than the localization blur, a very small sound field for numerical analysis/synthesis purposes can contain enough sound localization information for perceptual listening purposes in a full surround field. Typically, a 60° stereo sound field can be used for compressing a standard ITU 5-channel [7] (Fig. 1) audio signal rendering a 360° surround sound, while backward compatibility to

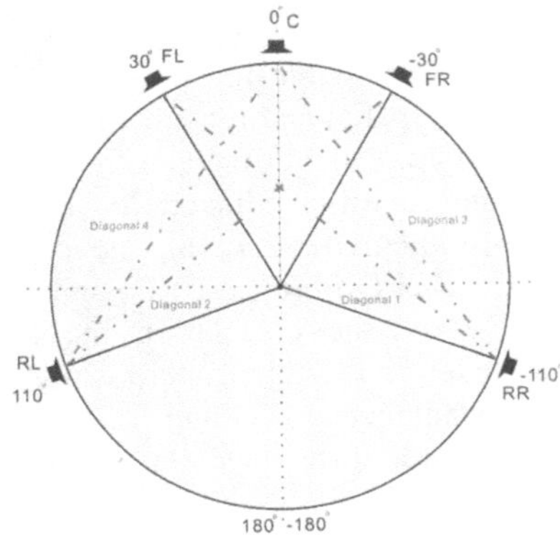

Fig. 1. 5-Channel Surround Speakers

conventional stereo systems is also maintained. The critical analysis of S^3AC is called frequency-azimuth analysis, aiming at working out every frequency domain source and its localization followed by an azimuth squeezing process. It is briefly described in the following.

Considering a speaker setup as shown in Fig.1, the five channels are abbreviated as: *Front Left* (FL), *Front Right* (FR), *Center* (C), *Rear Left* (RL) and *Rear Right* (RR) for simplicity purposes. Following the time-frequency transforming, for each frequency bin, every channel with non-negligible energy is analyzed and the channel pair with the maximum energy is chosen as the dominant channel pair rendering the dominant source in the sound field. Note that this process in fact assumes that each frequency bin possibly contains a *virtual sound source* if a dominant channel is found. The process can be expressed by:

$$\{A_a(k), A_b(k)\} = \max_{ij}\{[A_i(k), A_j(k)]\} \tag{1}$$

where $A_i(k)$ and $A_j(k)$ are the magnitudes of channel pair {i, j} as a function of frequency, k; $\{i, j\} \in \{FL, FR, C, RR, RL\}$ and $i \neq j$. The resulting dominant channel pair $A_a(k)$ and $A_b(k)$ is used in the inverse amplitude panning law to calculate the azimuth of the source, given by:

$$\theta_{ab} = \arctan\left[\frac{A_a(k) - A_b(k)}{A_a(k) + A_b(k)} \cdot \tan(\varphi_{ab})\right] \tag{2}$$

where φ_{ab} is the angular separation of the chosen channel pair a and b of Fig. 1 and θ_{ab} is the source azimuth in the 360° field. The resulting source is mapped to the 60° stereo sound field according to its azimuth based on a linear mapping criterion. The S^3AC downmix/upmix azimuth mapping has significant flexibility and can be manipulated to meet different requirement. An example is given in Table 1, where the 'fly-over' effect has a special interest; and it results in a stereo downmix sound field illustrated in Fig. 2. It has been shown in earlier S^3AC publications [4, 5] that S^3AC provides very constant coding performance between different mapping functions, especially in terms of the localization accuracy.

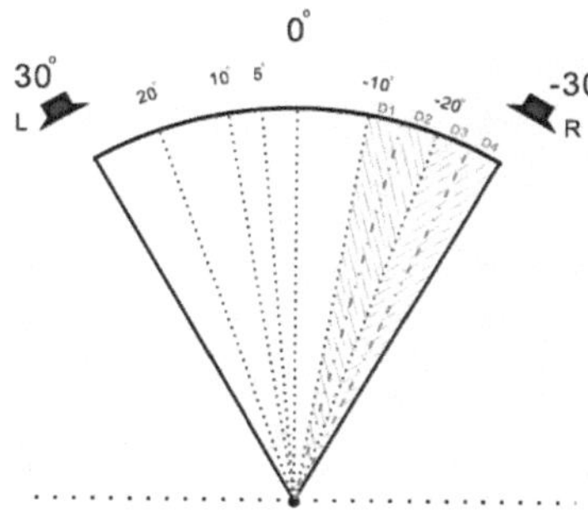

Fig. 2. S^3AC Stereo Downmix with the Squeezed Sound Field

The overall frequency-azimuth process described here is aiming at providing a complete analysis of the surround sound field in the frequency domain while maintaining all the source localization information in the final downmix sound field. During decoding, the S^3AC decoder applies a similar analysis on the downmix sound field to work out the frequency domain sound sources and their azimuth in the 60° sound field, followed by the inverse re-mapping of the sources to the 360° sound field. The full surround sound field is effectively recovered with all the source localization information preserved.

Table 1. S^3AC 360° to 60° azimuth mapping criterion

Linear Azimuth in 360°	Azimuth in 60°	Diagonal Azimuth in 360°	Azimuth in 60°
30°~ -30°	30°~ 20°	30°~ -110° (FL-RR)	-10°~ -15°
-30°~ -110°	20°~ 10°	110°~ -30° (FR-RL)	-15°~ -20°
-110°~ -180°	10°~ 5°	110°~ 0° (C-RL)	-20°~ -25°
180°~ 130°	5°~ 0°	0°~ -110° (C-RR)	-25°~ -30°
110°~ 30°	0°~ -10°		

3 Using Side Information for Coding of Independent, Overlapped Sources in S^3AC

3.1 Overlapping Spatial Sound Sources in the Frequency Domain

It is less likely that for a particular frequency bin or band, only one source ever occurs in each time-slot. Overlapping sound sources are defined here as the occasion that, for each frequency of a certain time slot, there are two or more sound sources rendered by different channel pairs concurrently. For example, for a frequency k, a primary source $S_{Pi}(k)$ is rendered by the FL-FR channel pair and a secondary source $S_{Se}(k)$ is rendered by RL-RR channel pair, as shown in Fig. 3(a). Although S^3AC provides a highly accurate recoverability of source localization, its performance will be affected if the

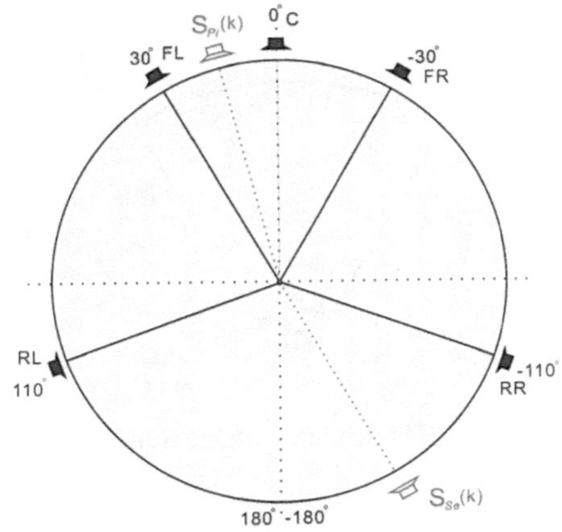

Fig. 3(a). Overlapping sound source in the 360° sound field

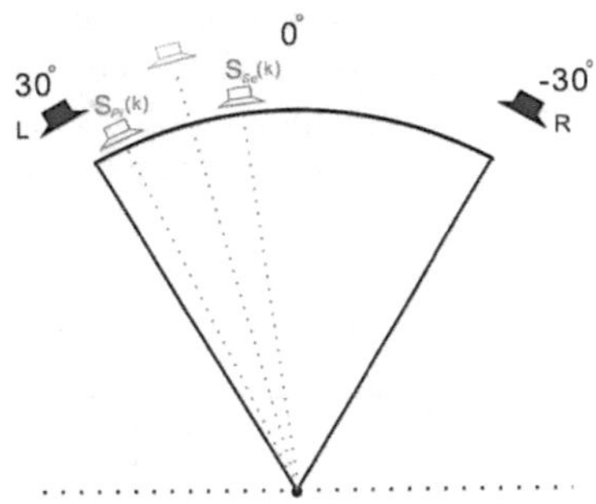

Fig. 3(b). Overlapping sound source and a phantom source (shown in red) in the 60° downmix sound field

sound field contains significant overlapping sound source components. In particular, when the two overlapping sources have energy close to each other, the two sound sources with the same frequency component in the downmix will result in one phantom source that has an azimuth between the two actual ones, as shown in Fig. 3(b). Similar problems exist for the inter-channel cue based spatial audio coding approaches, as the source overlapping makes it difficult to determine the transmitted cues; and the downmix process will mix the independent sources together without proper recoverability.

3.2 Side Information in S^{3}AC

To overcome the problem of overlapping sound sources described above, additional side information was introduced to S^{3}AC. As shown in Fig. 3(a), during sound field analysis, overlapping sound sources are discovered in the same frequency bin, while they are rendered by different channel pairs and have different spectral components and azimuths. This can be expressed by:

$$\{A_a(k), A_b(k)\} = \max_{ij}\{[A_i(k), A_j(k)]\}$$
$$\{i, j\} \in \{FL, FR, C, RR, RL\} \text{ and } i \neq j \tag{3a}$$

$$\{A_c(k), A_d(k)\} = \max_{mn}\{[A_m(k), A_n(k)]\}$$
$$\{m,n\} \in \{FL, FR, C, RR, RL\} \not\subset \{i, j\} \text{ and } m \neq n \tag{3b}$$

where $\{A_a(k), A_b(k)\}$ are the primary channel pair and $\{A_c(k), A_d(k)\}$ are the secondary channel pair. Note that this analysis contains two steps. The first step picks up the channel pair having the maximum spectral energy and results in the primary pair, which are removed from the candidates during the second step, i.e. only three channel candidates are used for selecting the secondary channel pair. The highest energy pair of these three channels is then identified as the secondary channel pair. This process can be repeated to identify further overlapping sources if required, especially during coding signal with more than 5 channels. The resulting two pairs are evaluated by inverse amplitude panning to determine the primary and secondary sound sources and their corresponding azimuths:

$$\theta_{Pi} = \arctan\left[\frac{A_a(k) - A_b(k)}{A_a(k) + A_b(k)} \cdot \tan(\varphi_{ab})\right]$$
$$S_{Pi}(k) = \sqrt{A_a^2(k) + A_b^2(k)} \tag{4a}$$

$$\theta_{Se} = \arctan\left[\frac{A_c(k) - A_d(k)}{A_c(k) + A_d(k)} \cdot \tan(\varphi_{cd})\right]$$
$$S_{Se}(k) = \sqrt{A_c^2(k) + A_d^2(k)} \tag{4b}$$

Subsequently, these two azimuths are mapped from 360° sound field to the 60° downmix field, and the stereo downmix signal is synthesized by:

$$\begin{aligned} L(k) &= S_{Pi}(k) \cdot \left[\tan(30^o) + \tan(\theta_{Pi}^{60})\right] + S_{Se}(k) \cdot \left[\tan(30^o) + \tan(\theta_{Se}^{60})\right] \\ R(k) &= S_{Pi}(k) \cdot \left[\tan(30^o) - \tan(\theta_{Pi}^{60})\right] + S_{Se}(k) \cdot \left[\tan(30^o) - \tan(\theta_{Se}^{60})\right] \end{aligned} \tag{5}$$

The two azimuths of the primary and secondary sources θ_{Pi}^{60} and θ_{Se}^{60} are saved as the supporting side information and transmitted with the stereo downmix to the decoder, so that, during decoding, the amplitudes of the two sources $S_{Pi}(k)$ and $S_{Se}(k)$ can be recovered by working out the two unknowns in Eq. (5), as:

$$S_{Pi}(k) = \frac{L(k) - \dfrac{L(k) + R(k)}{2 \cdot \tan(30^o)} \cdot \left[\tan(30^o) + \tan(\theta_{Se}^{60})\right]}{\tan(\theta_{pi}^{60}) - \tan(\theta_{Se}^{60})}$$
$$S_{Se}(k) = \frac{L(k) + R(k)}{2 \cdot \tan(30^o)} - S_{Pi}(k) \tag{6}$$

3.3 Quantization of the Side Information

Since the two azimuths θ_{Pi}^{60} and θ_{Se}^{60} saved in the side information can also be up-mapped (un-squeezed) to generate the original angles of the two sources in the 360° surround sound field, the primary and secondary sources can be re-panned to their original locations according to these results. According to the human localization blur properties, the precision for transmitting the S^{3}AC side information is relatively low. As the localization blur does not go under 0.5 °, any source azimuth can be rounded to an integer (the closest degree) without any loss in perceptual localization. In addition, as the human ear has much less sensitivity for localizing rear and side sources, compared with localizing frontal sound sources, a lower bit precision can be used for quantizing the azimuths of those sources away from the front, without perceptually losing any localization information. Typically, the localization resolution of human ear for the side and rear sound sources is between 5 ° and 10 ° [6], hence the bit rate for quantizing these source's azimuths can be reduced to 6bits per azimuth without perceptual loss.

Besides the location dependency, the localization blur is also frequency dependent. Considering a source in the front center direction, the most sensitive listening localization band for this source is between 0.5-1kHz, which has the localization blur of approximately 1°. However, for the band between 1kHz and 10kHz, the localization blur can go up to 3°. In addition, for frequencies lower than 300Hz and above 10kHz, the localization blur can even go far beyond 10 ° [6]. As a result, an efficient quantization of the side information can be easily achieved by adopting these psychoacoustical observations; however the implementation details are outside the scope of this paper.

4 Evaluation

S^{3}AC's ability to accurately recover overlapping sound sources and their locations, with the help of extra side information, is objectively evaluated in this section and compared with the MPEG Surround 525 coder [3]. Two test examples with overlapping sources were used:

1. Two moving signal sinusoidal tones, both at 1kHz: one rendered by the FL-FR channel pair and moving linearly from the FL to the FR; the other one rendered by the RL-RR channel pair and moving linearly from the RR to the RL. The energy of the front tone is 4.7dB higher than the rear tone, so that the front source has the dominant contribution to the overall sound scene.
2. Two moving bandpass noise sources. The front noise source has a pass band between 500Hz and 1.5kHz, rendered by FL-FR channel pair and moving from FL to FR. The rear noise source has a pass band between 1kHz and 2kHz, rendered by RL-RR channel pair and moving from RR to RL. The two narrow band noise sources thus have overlapping frequency bands between 1kHz and 1.5kHz. The energy of the front noise source is 3dB higher than the rear noise so that the front noise is the dominant source.

This evaluation aims to compare the front and rear source azimuth in the original sound field and the recovered sound field from S^{3}AC and MPEG Surround 525. The source azimuth is derived from inverse amplitude panning applied to the channel signal directly, as given in E.q. (2). The evaluation result of example 1 is shown in Fig. 4 (a) and (b). It can be identified easily that, while S^{3}AC provides near perfect recovery of both the front and rear original source azimuths, the MPEG Surround 525 has failed to recover the localization correctly. On the other hand, Fig. 5 illustrates the comparison between S^{3}AC and MPEG Surround 525 for example 2, where the x and y axes represent the frame number and FFT coefficients, respectively; and the z axis indicates azimuth on the 360° horizontal plan. The left column shows the original and the coded source in the front plane, while the right column shows the result for the rear source. To further analyze the results from Fig. 4 and 5, Table 2 shows the average azimuth error in degrees for the front and rear sources for both test examples. This error is calculated as the azimuth difference between the original source azimuths and the source azimuths in the two coded versions. It is shown that S^{3}AC offers a significant higher accuracy for reproducing the localization information of independent overlapping sound sources in comparison with MPEG Surround 525.

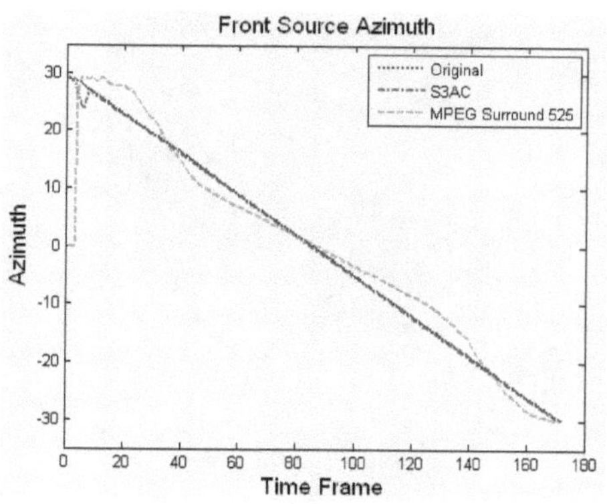

(a)

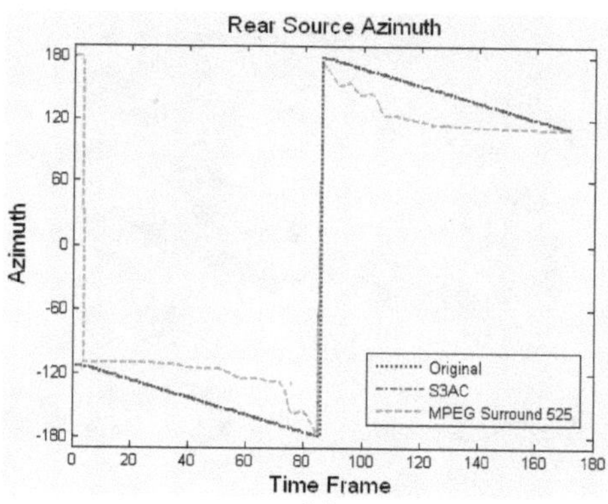

(b)

Fig. 4. **(a)**1kHz tone localization in the front plane, azimuth is between [-30 30]. **(b)**1kHz tone localization in the rear plane, azimuth is between [-180 -110] ∪ [110 180].

Table 2. Average azimuth error between the coded sound field from S^{3}AC and MPEG 525 and the original sound field, for example 1 and 2

	Example 1 (1kHz Tone)		**Example 2 (Band-Pass Noise)**	
	Front Source	**Rear Source**	**Front Source**	**Rear Source**
S^{3}AC	0.0657°	0.0084°	0.8929°	10.015°
MPEG Surround 525	2.4368°	25.8178°	2.9567°	45.415°

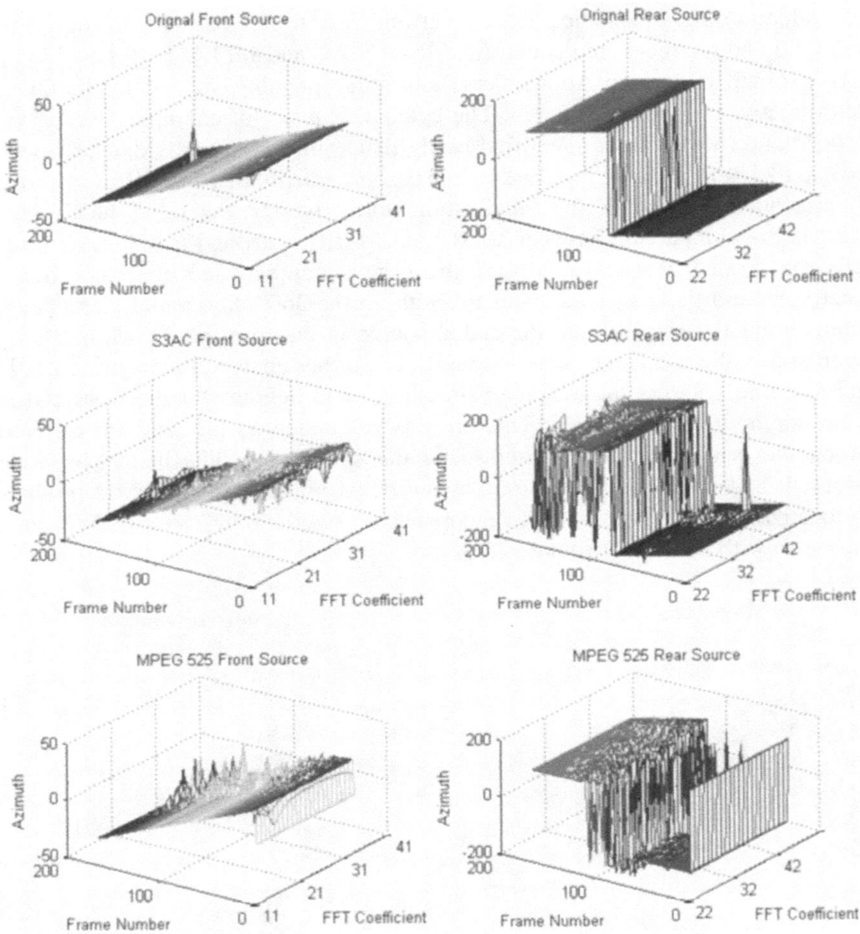

Fig. 5. The Original, S^3AC Coded and MPEG Surround 525 Coded localization for example 2. X and Y axes represent time frame number and FFT coefficients, Z axis represents source azimuth in degree in the 360° horizontal plane.

5 Conclusions and Further Work

The problem of coding overlapping sound sources with coincident time-frequency component in spatial audio has been discussed and an extension to the S^3AC spatial audio coder has been presented as a solution for this problem. The core frequency-azimuth sound field analysis of S^3AC is described. In addition, side information has been introduced to S^3AC to overcome the ambiguity when coding the overlapping sound sources. Earlier experiments have both objectively and subjectively proved that S^3AC offers high quality surround sound compression, in terms of both perceptual quality [4] and localization accuracy [5]. Further objective evaluation results presented here indicate that the extended S^3AC provides highly accurate localization recoverability for independent overlapping sources, and outperforms the state-of-the-art MPEG Surround in the test examples. Further work will focus on the extended analysis of more than two overlapping sources. Other future work will investigate the impact of mono masking models, as used in traditional audio coders, on spatial audio perception and coding.

References

1. Faller, C., Baumgarte, F.: Binaural Cue Coding – Part II: Schemes and Applications. IEEE Trans. on Speech and Audio Proc., 11(6) (November 2003)
2. Schuijers, E., Breebaart, J., Purnhagen, H., Engdegard, J.: Low Complexity Parametric Stereo Coding. In: Proc. 116th AES Convention, Berlin, Germany (2004)
3. Breebaart, J., Herre, J., Faller, C., Roden, J., Myburg, F., Disch, S., Purnhagen, H., Hotho, G., Neusinger, M., Kjorling, K., Oomen, W.: MPEG Spatial Audio Coding/MPEG Surround: Overview and Current Status. In: Proc. 119th AES Convention, New York, USA (2005)
4. Cheng, B., Ritz, C., Burnett, I.: Squeezing the Auditory Space: A New Approach to Multi-Channel Audio Coding. In: Zhuang, Y., Yang, S., Rui, Y., He, Q. (eds.) PCM 2006. LNCS, vol. 4261, pp. 572–581. Springer, Heidelberg (2006)
5. Cheng, B., Ritz, C., Burnett, I.: Principles and Analysis of the Squeezing Approach to Low Bit Rate Spatial Audio Coding. In: IEEE ICASSP 2007, Honolulu, USA (April 2007)
6. Blauert, J.: Spatial Hearing: the Psychophysics of Human Sound Localization. In: Revised Edition, MA, USA, MIT Press, Cambridge (1996)
7. ITU-R BS.775-1: Multichannel stereophonic sound system with and without accompanying picture (1994)
8. Faller, C., Merimaa, J.: Source Localization in Complex Listening Situation: Selection of Binaural Cues Based on Interaural Coherence. J. Acoust. Soc. Am. 116(5) (November 2004)

Efficient Storage and Progressive Rendering of Multi-resolution Mesh

Tong-zhu Fang and Zheng Tian

Northwestern Polytechnical University, Xi'an 710072, China
Fangtongzhu@163.com, zhtian@nwpu.edu.cn

Abstract. A multi-resolution model often costs more storage space, its communications from the CPU to the graphics system is the bottleneck of the visualization process. In this paper, a multi-resolution mesh and a primitive are proposed. The primitive is used both in the storage stage and in the rendering stage, decreasing the storage size of model and the transmission amount of vertices to the graphics system. The efficiency is measured by means of tests and results compared with the previous, obtaining better storage space cost and transmission cost.

1 Introduction

Mesh models are very popular in computer graphics. To represent the mesh surface concisely and efficiently, a few simple graphics primitives such as point primitive, line primitive and quadrilateral primitive, as well as the most common triangle primitive are proposed. Since the communications from the CPU to the GPU tend to be the most common bottleneck of the whole visualization process, complex primitive such as triangle strip (or triangle fan) is favored for avoiding storing much data and sending a larger amount of redundant information to the graphics system, for a triangle strip (or fan) is a set of connected triangle where a new vertex implicitly defines a new triangle. The main advantage of the strip representation over each separate triangle is that it makes it possible to reduce the number of vertices sent to the graphics system from 3n to n+2 in the best way.

The first multi-resolution model to take advantage of the triangle strip primitive in storage and rendering stage is Multi-resolution Triangle Strip (MTS) by Belmonte[1]. The model consists of a collection of multi-resolution strips, each of which represents a triangle strip at every LoD, only the strips that are modified between consecutive LoD extractions are updated before visualization. Some extended conclusions [2~4] based on MTS have been given.

Theoretically speaking, rendering one triangle strip of n triangles only need send $n+2$ vertices to the GPU in the best way. But in practical applications, the vertices of all levels of detail sent to GPU can be only reduced to nearly 55%, according to paper [4].

This paper proposes a graphics primitive, a multi-resolution representation and a simplification/refinement approach with this primitive, discusses the storage cost and

H.H.S. Ip et al. (Eds.): PCM 2007, LNCS 4810, pp. 814–821, 2007.

rendering efficiency of a multi-resolution mesh. Compared to the previous papers, ours has following benefits to offer:

Storage: a multi-resolution mesh can be stored in a form of proposed primitive, costing less storage space than its single-resolution mesh after storage optimization.
Rendering: a mesh can be progressively transmitted from the CPU to GPU in a form of proposed primitive, the transmission amount of all LoDs can be reduced to nearly a third of that using traditional triangle primitive.

In the following, some preliminary knowledge is given in section 2. Section 3 discusses a multi-resolution mesh and its construction approach with our primitive. In the remainder of paper, some experimental results and the conclusions are given.

2 Preliminaries

"Triangle contraction" operation contracts two vertices of a triangle into the third vertex, resulting in two vertices and four triangles collapse, none of new vertex or new triangle is generated, no storage space during the operation process is added.

2.1 Definition

As Figure 1 and Table 1(a) show, a triangle ΔBCA has three skirt triangles ΔBDC, ΔCEA and ΔAFB, they share three edges AB, BC and CA and three vertices B, C and A, these four triangles ΔBCA, ΔBDC, ΔCEA and ΔAFB are called a *star*, which can be represented compactly by (B C A D E F) as Table 1(b) shows, and triangle ΔBCA and its skirt triangles ΔBDC, ΔCEA and ΔAFB are called center triangle, middle triangle, right triangle and left triangle respectively.

In a star, the vertex A, vertices C and B are called substitution vertex, right vertex and left vertex respectively, and vertices D, E and F are called middle skirt vertex, right skirt vertex and left skirt vertex respectively.

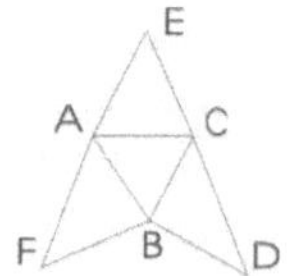

Fig. 1. A *star* in mesh

Table 1. A *star* in triangle list

(a)	(b)
B C A	
B D C	B C A D E F
C E A	
A F B	

2.2 The Simplification and Refinement Operations

A triangle mesh is stored in the form of triangle list and vertex list. If the mesh is simplified, it has a simplified triangle list, and if its triangle list is simplified, it has a simplified mesh. So the simplified mesh can be obtained through simplifying its triangle list. For example, Table 2(a) is the triangle list of Figure 2(a), if two indices 7 and 6 in the first triangle are substituted with the third one 5, then the first four triangles (a star) degenerate and several related triangles are updated, and Table 2(a) is simplified into 2(b), its mesh Figure 2(a) into 2(b) accordingly. In the same way, Table 2(b) can be simplified into 2(c), and its mesh Figure 2(b) into 2(c) accordingly.

For a triangle list (called "simplified triangle list") and an added star, an inverse operation called triangle split refinement can be performed as below.

Step1: Search all triangles sharing "substitution vertex" in the simplified triangle list.
Step2: Order those searched triangles into an ordered set *T* according to their neighboring relationship.
Step3: In the ordered set *T*, search three triangles respectively: the triangle with right skirt vertex (the *1st* triangle), the one with middle skirt vertex (the *2nd* triangle) and the one with the left skirt vertex (the *3rd* triangle), the subset of set *T* from the *1st* triangle to the *2nd* triangle and the one from the *2nd* triangle to the *3rd* triangle are called *T1* and *T2* respectively.
Step4: Replace the substitution vertices of triangles in subsets *T1* and *T2* by the right vertex and the left vertex respectively, then triangles in subsets are updated and the simplified triangle list is refined. E.g., after such an operation, the simplified triangle list Table 2(b) can be refined into 2(a).

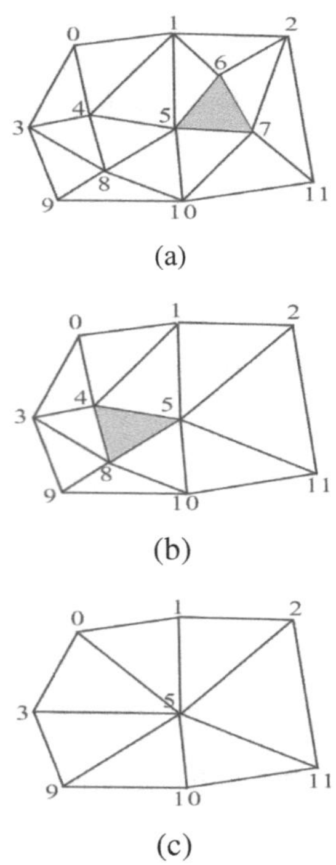

Fig. 2. Triangle contraction simplification in a mesh

Table 2. Triangle contraction simplification in a triangle list

(a)	(b)	(c)
7 6 5		
7 2 6		
6 1 5		
5 10 7		
4 8 5	4 8 5	
4 3 8	4 3 8	
8 10 5	8 10 5	
5 1 4	5 1 4	
4 1 0	4 1 0	5 1 0
3 4 0	3 4 0	5 0 3
3 9 8	3 9 8	5 3 9
8 9 10	8 9 10	5 9 10
7 10 11	5 10 11	5 10 11
7 11 2	5 11 2	5 11 2
2 1 6	2 1 5	5 2 1

3 The Multi-resolution Mesh

3.1 The Construction of Multi-resolution Mesh

An arbitrary manifold mesh can be simplified into a base mesh through a series of triangle contraction operations, then it can be constructed into a multi-resolution mesh as below.

1) Simplify a mesh M_n into a coarse base mesh M_0 through n times "triangle contraction" operations by certain simplification criterion, which yields a approximate model series M_n ,……, M_1, M_0.
2) Rearrange each triangle in the triangle list according to its collapse order. The one collapsed earlier is put in the front and the one collapsed later in the rear of the triangle list. Due to four triangles or a star collapsed simultaneously, they are put together and in an order of "center triangle", "middle triangle", "right triangle" and "left triangle". Then the triangle list is partitioned according to the stars, the *i*th star is the *i*th layer ($i=1,2,\ldots..n$) and the base mesh is the ($n+1$)th layer. E.g., after such a rearrangement, the triangle list Table 3(a) of mesh Figure 3(a) becomes Table 3(b), which is partitioned into 3 layers.
3) The indices of each star are rearranged respectively as below: left vertex, right vertex and substitution vertex for a "center triangle", left vertex, middle skirt vertex and right vertex for a "middle triangle", right vertex, right skirt vertex and substitution vertex for a "right triangle" and substitution vertex, left skirt vertex and left vertex for the "left triangle". So the three vertices of a center triangle are as the same as each first index of middle triangle, right triangle and left triangle, which features a star. And rearrange the triangles in base mesh so as not to feature a star. E.g., after such

Table 3. Rearrangements in triangle lists

0 4 1	5 7 6	7 6 5	0 1 5	0 1 5		
4 5 1	6 7 2	7 2 6	0 4 1	0 4 1	0 1 5 4 6 10	5 4 6 10
5 6 1	5 6 1	6 1 5	1 6 5	1 6 5		
6 2 1	5 10 7	5 10 7	5 10 0	5 10 0		
6 7 2	4 8 5	4 8 5	2 3 5	2 3 5		
5 7 6	3 8 4	4 3 8	2 8 3	2 8 3	2 3 5 8 10 6	5 8 10 6
7 11 2	5 8 10	8 10 5	3 10 5	3 10 5		
7 1011	4 5 1	5 1 4	5 6 2	5 6 2		
5 10 7	0 4 1	4 1 0	2 6 7	5 6 7	5 6 7	5 6 7
5 8 10	6 2 1	3 4 0	8 2 7	8 5 7	8 5 7	8 5 7
4 8 5	7 11 2	3 9 8	8 9 3	8 9 5	8 9 5	8 9 5
3 8 4	7 10 11	8 9 10	3 9 10	5 9 10	5 9 10	5 9 10
3 9 8	3 9 8	7 1011	0 10 11	5 10 11	5 10 11	5 10 11
8 9 10	8 9 10	7 11 2	0 11 4	5 11 4	5 11 4	5 11 4
0 3 4	0 3 4	2 1 6	4 6 1	4 6 5	4 6 5	4 6 5
(a)	(b)	(c)	(d)	(e)	(f)	(g)

rearrangement, the triangle list Table 3(b) becomes Table 3(c), in which 7, 6 and 5 are as the same as the first one of (7 2 6), (6 1 5) and (5 10 7).

4) Reorder vertices of the vertex list according to vertex collapse order, the one collapsed earlier put in the front and the one later in the rear of vertex list. So the vertex list is layered according to the collapse order, and all of indices in the triangle list are updated accordingly. E.g., after reordering vertex order in mesh Figure 3, its vertex list Table 4(a) becomes 4(b), and its triangle list Table 3(c) is updated and becomes 3(d).

After four rearrangement operations as above, both the triangle list and the vertex list of a mesh are partitioned into layers, in which all of multi-resolution information is implicit, the original triangle list is turned into a multi-resolution representation.

3.2 The Recovery of Levels of Detail

The multi-resolution representation above-mentioned is a triangle list, but it can be simplified progressively..Here it is called a simplification list and supposed it issimplified progressively from *SLn* to *SLn-1*, ……, *SL1* to *SL0*. After performed a transformation as follows, a simplification list *SLn* is turned into a refinement list which supports progressive recovery of LoDs or progressive rendering of a mesh.Judge whether the first layer of *SLi* is a star, if yes, assign the values of which to a temporary variable, and simplify this layer and update the remaining layers, *SLi* becomes *SLi-1* (*i* = *n,……,1*), if no, end the simplification. After such a transformation, a simplification list becomes a refinement list. So, a multi-resolution mesh can be stored in the refinement list. For being independent of refinement algorithm used, the refinement list can be used for mesh progressive rendering. E.g., after a transform as above, a simplified list Table 3(d) becomes a refinement one Table 3(e), from which 2 LoDs can be extracted.

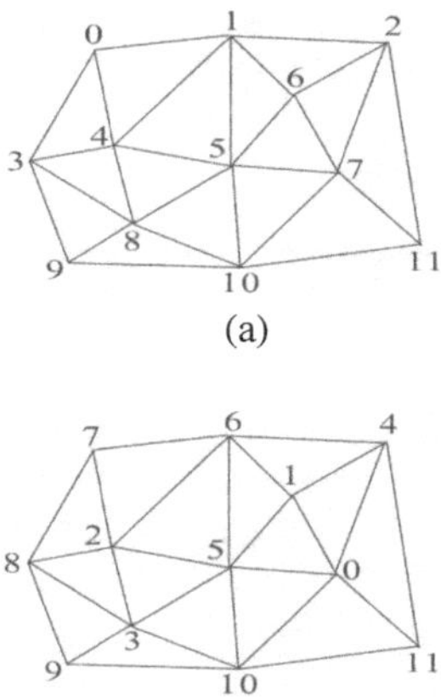

(a)

(b)

Fig. 3. Reorder of mesh vertex

Table 4. Rearrangement in vertex list

$x_0\ y_0\ z_0$	$x_7\ y_7\ z_7$
$x_1\ y_1\ z_1$	$x_6\ y_6\ z_6$
$x_2\ y_2\ z_2$	$x_4\ y_4\ z_4$
$x_3\ y_3\ z_3$	$x_8\ y_8\ z_8$
$x_4\ y_4\ z_4$	$x_2\ y_2\ z_2$
$x_5\ y_5\ z_5$	$x_5\ y_5\ z_5$
$x_6\ y_6\ z_6$	$x_1\ y_1\ z_1$
$x_7\ y_7\ z_7$	$x_0\ y_0\ z_0$
$x_8\ y_8\ z_8$	$x_3\ y_3\ z_3$
$x_9\ y_9\ z_9$	$x_9\ y_9\ z_9$
$x_{10}\ y_{10}\ z_{10}$	$x_{10}\ y_{10}\ z_{10}$
$x_{11}\ y_{11}\ z_{11}$	$x_{11}\ y_{11}\ z_{11}$
(a)	(b)

3.3 The Storage of Multi-resolution Mesh

Since a star can be compactly represented according to definition 2.1, the refinement list with stars also can be compactly represented, E.g., Table 3(e) can be compactly represented as 3(f). Due to the *i*th star in the *i*th row has two indices $(2i\text{-}2)$ and $(2i\text{-}1)$ which can be omitted, thus, the storage size of the refinement list can be reduced future, E.g., Table 3(f) can be represented as 3(g).

Thus each star can be represented by 4 indices, its representation cost is 4/3*4 = 0.333 if a star with 4 triangles, is 4/3*3 = 0.444.

The new refinement list can support the mesh progressive rendering as well: the base mesh M_0 is sent to graphics system and rendered first, then send the *n*th layer vertices and the *n*th compact represented star to graphics system, which recovers four triangles. And with this layer of vertices and triangles added, graphics system refines mesh M_0 into M_1 according to the refinement approach above-mentioned...... For a mesh M_k, send the $(n\text{-}k)$th layer vertices and the $(n\text{-}k)$th compact represented star to graphics system, which recovers a layer of triangles, and refine the mesh M_k into M_{k+1}....... till M_n is recovered and rendered.

In this way, the vertices transmission size of stars sent to graphics system is reduced to nearly a third of that of triangle primitive

4 Results

Models Dog, Buny, Cow, Fandisk, Pig, Horse and Happy are tested, their characteristics are in Table 5(b)(c). The experiments were carried out using a HP PC with a processor at 1Ghz and 562Mb RAM. Coding of the models was in C++.

After 452, 1213, 1395, 3152, 1754, 23987 and 24724 stars collapsed respectively and multi-resolution representations constructed, their multi-resolution meshes are generated. If the storage amount (in Kb) of original triangle lists (Tri. lists) are regarded as 100% (an integer with 4 bytes), our storage scheme costs nearly 35%, see Table 5(g), but the costs in [5] [6] are 110% and 69% respectively.

Table 5. The storage cost of ours scheme

Models	Triangles	Vertices	Base meshes	Tri. lists	Ours	Ratio (%)
Dog	1850	922	52	21.68	7.67	35.5
Bunny	5048	2540	202	59.156	21.832	36.9
Cow	5804	2903	228	68.016	22.596	33.2
Fandisk	12946	6475	347	151.7	53.1	35
Pig	7040	3522	43	82.5	27.9	33.8
Horse	96966	48485	1049	1136.3	409.1	36
Happy	100000	49794	1216	1171.9	398.4	34
(a)	(b)	(c)	(d)	(e)	(f)	(g)

The models can be progressively rendered through sending LoDs to the graphics system from the lower detail to the higher one. The number of vertices of all LoDs sent to the graphics system using our primitive can be measured and compared with those using triangle strips primitive such as [1][4]. If the model data using triangle primitive is 100%, the data using ours can be reduced to nearly 33%, whereas the one using Multi-resolution Triangle Strips (MTS) [1] reduced to nearly 61%, the one using Quality Strips (QS) [4] nearly 55% on average, see Table 6. Fig. 4 shows 9 levels of Bunny progressively rendered using our primitive.

Table 6. The storage cost of ours scheme

Models	Using MTS[1]	Using QS[4]	Using ours
Dog	62.3%	54.5%	32.5%
Bunny	61.1%	55.1%	33.4%
Cow	61.3%	54.8%	32.1%
Fandisk	61.6%	53.9%	33.4%
Pig	59.7%	54.3%	32.2%
Horse	60.9%	54.7%	33.9%
Happy	62.1%	53.1%	32.7%
(a)	(b)	(c)	(d)

Fig. 4. Levels of Bunny model progressively rendered using our primitive (from the low to the high: 202, 247, 315, 409, 670, 1309, 1929, 3019, 5048 faces)

5 Conclusions

This paper has proposed a simple multi-resolution representation and a primitive that can be used in the data structure and in the rendering stage, the main benefit of using this primitive is the decrease model storage size and vertices data transmission cost. Limited experimental results confirm that the model storage cost can be reduced to about 35% of its corresponding single resolution mesh, and the data transmission amount using our primitive is nearly a third of that using triangle primitive, less than those using multi-resolution triangle strip (MTS) [1] or quality strips (QS) [4]. Dislike the previous storage scheme that should be created before use each time, ours can be applied repeatedly for being independent of refinement algorithm used. The next work will focus on considering the extraction time and visualization time of a LoD, variable resolution rendering and improving the rendering quality or simplification criterion of multi-resolution mesh.

References

1. Belmonte, O., Remolar, I., Ribelles, J., Chove, M., Fernandez, M.: Efficiently using connectivity information between triangles in a mesh for real-time rendering. Future Generation Computer Systems. Elsevier 20(8), 1263–1273 (2004)
2. Ramos, F., Chover, M.: LoD Strips: level of detail strips. In: Bubak, M., van Albada, G.D., Sloot, P.M.A., Dongarra, J.J. (eds.) ICCS 2004. LNCS, vol. 3039, pp. 107–114. Springer, Heidelberg (2004)
3. Ramos, F., Chover, M.: Variable level of detail strips. In: Laganà, A., Gavrilova, M., Kumar, V., Mun, Y., Tan, C.J.K., Gervasi, O. (eds.) ICCSA 2004. LNCS, vol. 3044, pp. 622–630. Springer, Heidelberg (2004)
4. Ripollés, O., Chover, M., Ramos, J.: Quality Strips for Models with Level of Detail, Visualization, Imaging, and Image Processing 2005, pp. 268–273. ACTA Press (2005)
5. Bouvier, E., Gobbetti, E.: TOM: totally ordered mesh, a multi-resolution structure for time critical graphics application [J]. International Journal of Image and Graphics 1(1), 115–134 (2001)
6. Tongzhu, F.: Data Compression for Multi-resolution Mesh. Journal of System Simulation 17(3), 653–655 (2005)
7. Porcu, M., Sanna, B., Scateni, N.: Efficiently keeping an optimal stripification over a CLOD mesh. Journal of WSCG 13(1-3) (2005)
8. Ribelles, J., Lopez, A., Remolar, I., Belmonte, O., Chover, M.: Multi-resolution modeling of polygonal surface meshes using triangle fans. In: Nyström, I., Sanniti di Baja, G., Borgefors, G. (eds.) DGCI 2000. LNCS, vol. 1953, pp. 431–443. Springer, Heidelberg (2000)

An Improved Three-Step Hierarchical Motion Estimation Algorithm and Its Cost-Effective VLSI Architecture

Hai Bing Yin, Zhe Lei Xia, and Xi Zhong Lou

The information engineering department, China jiliang University,
Hangzhou, P.R. China
yinhb@cjlu.edu.cn, XIA663618@163.com, lou999@gmail.com

Abstract. This paper proposes a cost-effective VLSI architecture to improve the three-step search (TSS) algorithm for efficient motion estimation. A weighted SAD is defined as the new distortion measure instead of SAD for motion vector selection to remedy the fault of the TSS algorithm. The proposed TSS architecture is superior to conventional TSS architecture in terms of coding performance. Moreover, the additional hardware implementation cost of the proposed architecture is relatively negligible. The proposed architecture achieves best tradeoff in terms of speed and hardware cost.

Keywords: VLSI, Motion Estimation, TSS.

1 Introduction

Block matching is often performed for motion estimation (ME) in MPEG-x and H.26x video encoders. The full-search block-matching (FSBM) algorithm offers the optimal picture quality, whereas it is time-consuming and calculation-intensive. VLSI implementation for FSBM had attracted intensive attention [1] [2]. However, existing implementations of FSBM are computationally expensive and power hungry for its intrinsic property [3].

Faster methods are therefore developed to eliminate the disadvantages of the Full Search. Among them, the three-step search block matching algorithm (TSS BMA) is most widely used, although the coding performance is relatively inferior to the FSBM algorithm. In general, a typical VLSI implementation cost of TSS algorithm is reduced to only about one-tenth of that of this FSBM algorithm [3].

The TSS algorithm uses a hierarchical searching method to skip most of the candidate motion vectors to reduce the computation cost. Unlike full-search, the main problem of the TSS algorithm is its inability to locate the global minimum precisely. It is very easy to be trapped into local minima in the early steps as only nine points are considered. Multiple-candidate technology and overlapped search method are adopted and incorporated with TSS algorithm to overcome this drawback [3]. However, these measures suffer from increased hardware cost due to additional parallel TSS modules needed.

In this paper, we modify the matching criterion and propose a cost-effective VLSI architecture to improve the TSS motion estimator in video encoder. The following is

H.H.S. Ip et al. (Eds.): PCM 2007, LNCS 4810, pp. 822–830, 2007.

organized as follows: In Section 2, the TSS algorithm and its typical VLSI implementation architecture are reviewed, and the drawbacks of the TSS architecture are analyzed. The improved TSS algorithm and its modified architecture are proposed in Section 3. Simulation results are presented in Section 4. Finally, conclusions are drawn in Section 5.

2 Algorithm and Architecture

Block matching algorithm is performed according to the matching criterion sum of absolute difference (SAD), which is calculated for each candidate location (u,v) as:

$$SAD(u,v)=\sum_{i=0}^{N-1}\sum_{i=0}^{N-1}\left|f_t(x+i,y+j)-f_{t-1}(x+i+u,y+j+v)\right| \\ -W\leq u,v\leq W \quad (1)$$

Where f_t and f_{t-1} are two continuous frames, (x,y) is the position of the current block, N is the block size, and (u,v) is the candidate motion vector. The motion vector is determined by the least $SAD(u,v)$ for all possible (u,v) within the search window of $(2W+1)\times(2W+1)$.

In this paper, a search window of 31×31 is considered for relatively large size video applications to satisfy the increasing image quality of consumers. As a result, the TSS should be directly expanded to four steps to cover the doubled search range.

The TSS algorithm follows a coarse-to-fine search approach. In each step, nine candidate locations around the winner of the previous step are checked. The one with the least distortion is chosen as the center location for the next-step search. In the next step, the search is focused on the area centered at the selected point of the previous step, but the distance is shortened to one-half of that in the previous step. This procedure continues until the distance converges to one pixel, and the final motion vector is obtained.

A typical VLSI architecture of the TSS algorithm is shown in Fig.1 [4]. By employing nine parallel processing elements (PE), a dedicated TSS motion estimator chip[4] with a search range of 7x7 was developed. In this architecture, memory interleaving technique was introduced to enhance the structure regularity and reduce the memory size and bandwidth by utilizing cyclic-pipeline memory access. The complicated addressing problem was solved by the pseudoresidual permutation and realized with random logic.

The TSS algorithm limits checking points in the search area based on the assumption that the SAD distribution increase monotonically as the searched point moves away from the location of minimum distortion. However, this assumption is not always true for real-world sequences, and thus it makes the inappropriate choice in early steps. Especially when the TSS algorithm is expanded to four steps to support search range [-15, 15], the distance between checked points at early steps are enlarged exponentially. As a result, the probability of being trapped in local minimum significantly raise and the accuracy is thus dramatically reduced.

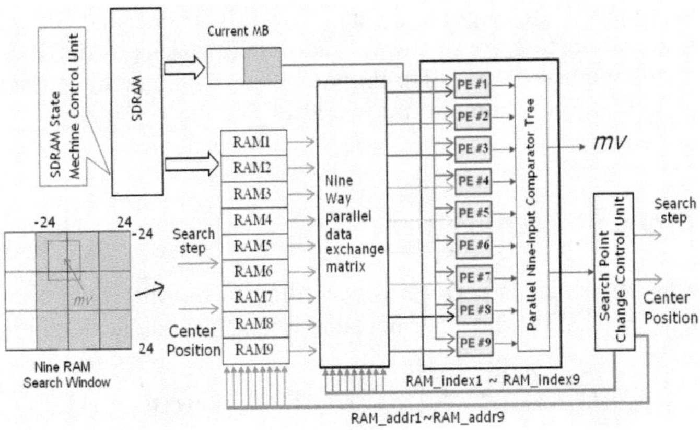

Fig. 1. A typical architecture for the TSS algorithm implementation

Jong et al. [3] proposed a scalable overlapping strategy which utilizes several independent TSS modules, each one with small search range, to cover the required large search ranges. Multiple-candidate technology was also adopted to overcome this drawback [3]. However, these measures suffer from increased hardware cost due to additional parallel TSS modules needed. Thus, efficient measure must be taken for TSS algorithm to avoid being trapped in local minimum to retain the matching accuracy, especially for large size search area.

An example in the case of "Mobile & Calendar" sequence is given in Fig.2 to illustrate the existence of multiple local minimum in the SAD distribution of all candidate motion vectors. It is the existence of multiple local minimum in the SAD distribution that prevents the TSS algorithm from precise motion vector selection.

The SAD distribution in Fig.2 is also shown as a gray image in Fig.3, in which the motion vector selection procedure of the TSS algorithm is illustrated. Obviously, the optimal integer motion vector should be (0,-6), which is marked as "R" in Fig.3. t8, t4, t2 and t1 are the selected point with the minimum SAD value in four step searches whose distance are 8, 4, 2 and 1 in conventional TSS algorithm, respectively. According to Fig.3, the selected point of the first step is (8,-8), which deviates from the true point (0, 8) markedly. Then, the TSS algorithm limits the search area within a window of 15×15 centered at t8. Orderly, the points t4, t2 are selected, and finally t1 is the matched motion vector, which differs from the true motion vector largely.

According to above analysis, it is the nonmonotonic property of the SAD distribution that results in wrong selection of the first step. In this example, the wrong selection occurs in the first step, certainly it may also occurs in the second, or the third steps. In general, the larger the distance of a step is, the larger the probability of being trapped in local minimum wrong selection is. In the TSS algorithm, the center position of a certain step is determined only according to the SAD value of nine adjacent points. As a result, the center position selected is usually incredible especially for large distance steps.

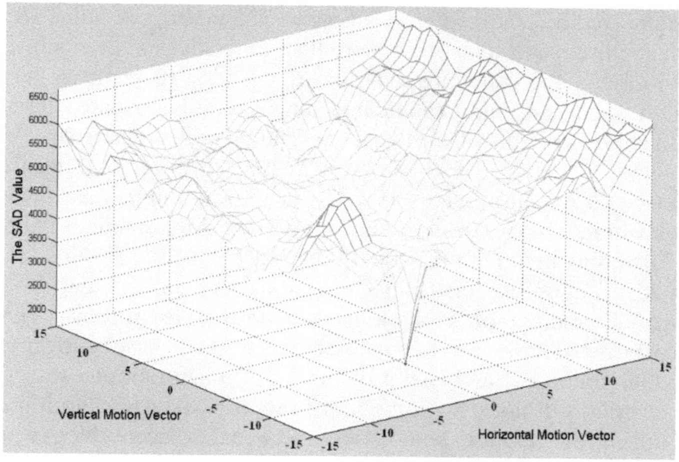

Fig. 2. An example of the SAD distribution

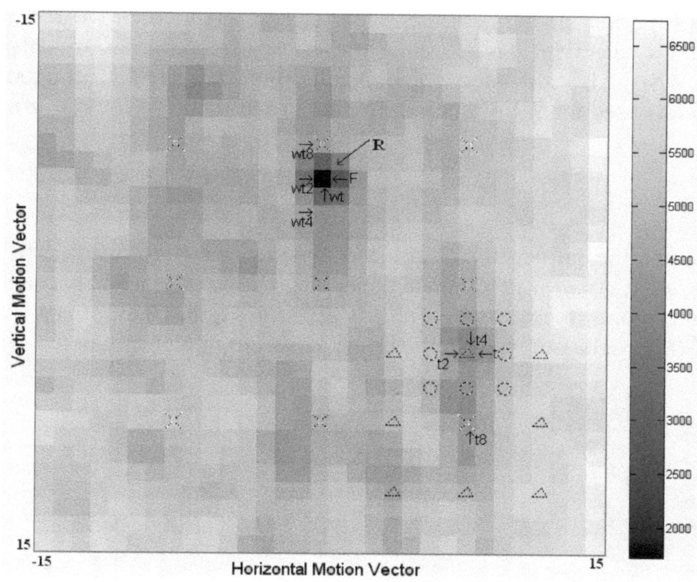

Fig. 3. The SAD image of the example in Fig.2 and the motion vector selection procedure of the conventional and the proposed TSS algorithm

3 The Improved TSS Algorithm and Its Architecture

According to the analysis in section 2, center position determined only depending on SAD comparison for next step search is ill-suited. One direct solution way is to determine the center position for the next step search by SAD comparison of more adjacent points, for example 18, 27 or 36 candidate points. The more candidate points used, the more credible the center position is. However, several TSS modules or higher frequency is desired to support more than nine adjacent points in each step. Is it possible to modify the matching criterion of selection to improve the accuracy of center position only using nine candidate points? Simultaneously, the advantage of the TSS architecture in terms of hardware cost and power is retained.

We have made in-depth investigation on motion vector smoothing for BMA ME algorithm before [5]. As our previous analysis, there is an implicit assumption in BMA that all pixels within a block undergo uniform motion. Motion edges existing within a block just violate this assumption. In addition, noise usually prevents the BMA from tracking the real motion especially in flat regions with insufficient spatial gradient. Sufficient spatial gradient of a block is also desired to improve the algorithm's robustness to noise. Thus, how to guarantee a block to have uniform motion and sufficient spatial gradient is a crucial problem for efficient motion estimation in BMA algorithms. Overlapped block motion compensation based ME algorithm is a typical method to utilize the motion smoothness between adjacent blocks to guarantee sufficient spatial gradient for efficient motion estimation.

Similar measure is adopted in this paper to define the so-called weighted SAD (WSAD) to replace conventional SAD for TSS algorithm optimization. Spatial gradient and motion smoothness are jointly employed to improve the accuracy of center position selection. To guarantee the motion smoothness of enlarged block where the WSAD is calculated on, only nine adjacent blocks centered about the current block is used for WSAD definition. In our work, the WSAD is defined as

$$WSAD(u,v) = \sum_{p=-1}^{1} \sum_{q=-1}^{1} \rho(p,q) SAD(u+p, v+q) \tag{2}$$

To minimize the influence of motion estimation accuracy resulted from motion edges, the weight $\rho(p,q)$ is determined depending on the distance between nine points and the center point in each step. $\rho(p,q)$ is given in Fig.4. Here, $\rho(p,q)$ is a value in terms of 2^{-t} (t is positive integer) to facilitate hardware implementation.

$\rho(p,q)$ / diatance	$\rho(-1,-1)$	$\rho(-1,0)$	$\rho(-1,1)$	$\rho(0,-1)$	$\rho(0,0)$	$\rho(0,1)$	$\rho(1,-1)$	$\rho(1,0)$	$\rho(1,1)$
8	1/16	1/8	1/16	1/8	1/4	1/8	1/16	1/8	1/16
4	0	1/8	0	1/8	1/2	1/8	0	1/8	0
2	0	1/8	0	1/8	1/2	1/8	0	1/8	0
1	0	0	0	0	1	0	0	0	0

Fig. 4. The relationship between ρ(p,q) and distance

Let's take the first step of the TSS search in Fig.3 for an example for analysis. The SAD differences of nine adjacent points of the first step marked as '×' are very small. Consequently, the search is easily strapped into local minima, the center point of the first step is wrongly determined as (8, 8), which is expected to be (0, -8). If the WSAD is employed as criterion for center position selection, relatively optimal trade-off between spatial gradient and motion smoothness is achieved. SAD(0,-7) is considerably smaller than SAD(0,-8), then WSAD(0,-8) is smaller than those of other eight candidate in the same step. As a result, the appropriate position (0,-8) is selected as the center for the next step search.

The four step search processes using SAD and WSAD are compared in Fig.3. wt8, wt4, wt2 and wt are the point with the minimum WSAD value in four step searches whose distance are 8, 4, 2 and 1 in the proposed TSS algorithm, respectively. According to the Fig.3, WSAD can avoid being trapped in local minima and track the motion vector correctly.

To implement the modified TSS algorithm using WSAD, it is necessary to modify the conventional TSS architecture in Fig.1. According to WSAD definition, the SADs of eight adjacent motion vectors should be calculated for each point. The PE structure of the conventional TSS architecture is shown in Fig.5. 256 pixels x255~x0 from the current MB are broadcasted to 9 PEs within 256 clocks in parallel. Nine way 256 pixels y255~y0 derived from nine RAM (RAM1~RAM9) are fed into nine PEs through a nine-way parallel data exchange matrix. The SAD value of a candidate position is calculated in a PE.

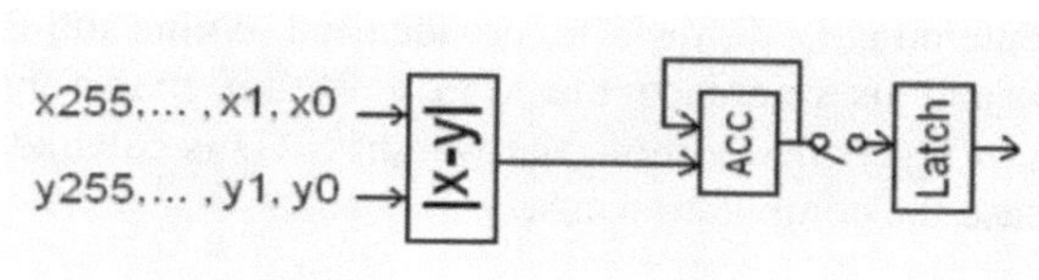

Fig. 5. The structure of PE in conventional TSS motion estimator

To obtain the WSAD of a candidate point at (u,v), we need to calculate the SAD of itself and those of its eight adjacent points at $(u+p,v+q)$ ($-1 \leq p, q \leq 1$). Thus, nine sub-PEs are needed to obtain SAD(u,v) and SAD$(u+p,v+q)$ to calculate the WSAD of the current point. The structure of the modified PE with nine sub-PEs is given in Fig.6. 256 pixels x255~x0 from the current MB are broadcasted to the center sub-PE

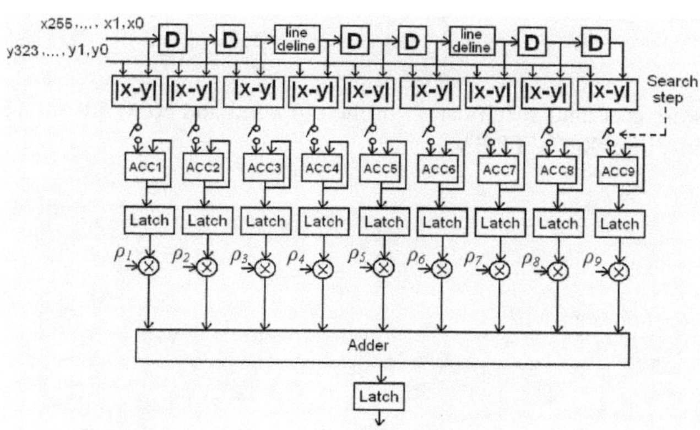

Fig. 6. The proposed structure of PE in the modified TSS motion estimator

Cycles	ACC1	ACC2	ACC3	ACC4	ACC5	ACC6	ACC7	ACC8	ACC9
1-18	x0~x15 y0~y15	x0~x15 y1~y16	x0~x15 y2~y17	Z	Z	Z	Z	Z	Z
19-36	x16~x31 y18~y33	x16~x31 y19~y34	x16~x31 y20~y35	x0~x15 y18~y33	x0~x15 y19~y34	x0~x15 y20~y35	Z	Z	Z
37-54	x32~x47 y36~y51	x32~x47 y37~y52	x32~x47 y38~y53	x16~x31 y36~y51	x16~x31 y37~y52	x16~x31 y38~y53	x0~x15 y36~y51	x0~x15 y37~y52	x0~x15 y38~y53
...	...	...	...	...	...	...	...	...	...
...	...	...	...	...	...	...	...	...	...
271-288	x240~x255 y270~y285	x240~x255 y271~y286	x240~x255 y272~y287	x224~x239 y270~y285	x224~x239 y271~y286	x226~x239 y272~y287	x208~x223 y270~y285	x208~x223 y271~y286	x208~x223 y272~y287
289-306	Z	Z	Z	x240~x255 y288~y303	x240~x255 y289~y304	x240~x255 y290~y305	x224~x239 y288~y303	x224~x239 y289~y304	x224~x239 y290~y305
307-324	Z	Z	Z	Z	Z	Z	x240~x255 y306~y321	x240~x255 y307~y322	x240~x255 y308~y323

Fig. 7. Data flow of a 16x16 block and its reference block in the proposed TSS architecture

(p=q=0), simultaneously fed into other eight sub-PEs after a delay of a certain clocks according to the offset (p,q). Correspondingly, 324 pixels y323~y0 within the reference frame centered at (x+8, y+8) are broadcasted to nine sub-PEs. The data flow of a 16x16 block and its reference block in a PE for the proposed TSS motion estimator is given in Fig.7. In addition, the weight SAD is calculated through binary right shift to decrease the computation cost.

Table 1. The Rate Distortion Performance of the Proposed TSS and Conventional TSS Architectures. (Rate: kbits/s, PSNR: dB) H.263 Encoder using TSS ME algorithm is used for test, P I frame ratio is 10 and fixed Quantizaition step 12 is used.

Sequence (CIF)		Bus	Football	Foreman	Mobile	News	Paris	Tempete	Akiyo	Children	Stefan	Susan
Full	Rate	894.68	893.10	365.53	1519.95	304.68	588.10	789.97	199.24	621.17	838.85	317.06
	PSNR	28.27	28.33	32.03	26.54	33.83	30.30	28.12	36.30	31.20	28.49	34.52
TSS	Rate	1031.28	997.10	376.04	1568.97	303.76	603.75	793.75	197.10	640.34	886.87	332.10
	PSNR	28.13	28.47	31.69	26.51	33.80	30.22	28.12	36.25	31.22	28.43	34.40
Proposed	Rate	987.32	944.51	363.66	1537.30	301.61	594.20	789.93	196.30	629.90	861.11	323.45
	PSNR	28.19	28.48	31.83	26.54	33.83	30.27	28.13	36.27	31.25	28.45	34.51

Table 2. Hardware cost amd specification of the proposed and conventional TSS architectures implemented ina Virtex XC2V FPGA

TSS Architecture	Conventional [10]	Proposed
Search Range	-7~7	-15~15
Resolution	up to 720x480	up to 4CIF
Frequency [MHz]	54	54
Percentage of CLBs	5%	7%
Percentage of LUTs	11%	12%
Percentage of Block RAMs	10%	12%

4 Simulation Results

The proposed TSS architecture and conventional TSS architecture are adopted to implement H.263 video encoder on Xilinx XC2V3000 FPGA for coding performance and hardware cost comparison. Eleven standard CIF format test sequences listed in Table 1 are stored in NAND flash memory and fed in the video encoder for comparison. The distance between two adjacent I frames is 10 frames, and fixed quantization step 12 is used for comparison. The rate distortion performances of the H.263 video encoders implemented with conventional and the proposed TSS MBA architectures are given in Table 1. For fair comparison, the same search [-15, 15] is also used in the proposed and conventional TSS algorithm. According to the results in Table 1, the modified TSS architecture using WSAD as selection criterion can achieve superior rate distortion performance compared with conventional TSS algorithm.

The synthesized results of the conventional and proposed TSS architectures are compared in Table 2. According to the results in Table 2, the increased hardware cost of the improved TSS architecture is acceptable and remarkably low compared with the measures adopted in [4]. In addition, only 68 additional clocks are needed in each step search in the modified TSS algorithm. Thus, the additional requirement of the system clock frequency is negligible.

5 Conclusions

In this paper, a cost-effective VLSI architecture is proposed to improve the three-step search (TSS) block matching algorithm. A weighted MAD is defined as the distortion measure instead of MAD for motion estimation to remedy the fault of the TSS algorithm. The effectiveness of the adopted weighted MAD is confirmed with simulation results. The rate distortion coding performance of the proposed architecture is considerably superior to that of the conventional TSS architectures. The additional hardware implementation cost of the proposed architecture is relatively negligible. The architecture achieves best tradeoff in terms of speed and hardware cost. This architecture is well suited for fixed and variable block size motion estimation in MPEG-x and H.26x video encoders.

References

1. Chen, T.-C., Chien, S.-Y., Huang, Y.-W., Tsai, C.-H., Chen, C.-Y., Chen, T.-W., Chen, L.-G.: Analysis and Architecture Design of an HDTV720p 30 Frames/s H.264/AVC Encoder. IEEE Trans. Circuits Syst. Video Technol., 166 (June 2006)
2. Tuan, J.-C., Chang, T.-S., Jen, C.-W.: On the Data Reuse and Memory Bandwidth Analysis for Full-Search Block-Matching VLSI Architecture. IEEE Trans. Circuits Syst. Video Technol., 121 (January 2002)
3. Jong, H.-M., Chen, L.-G., Chiueh, T.-D.: Accuracy improvement and cost reduction of 3-step search block-matching algorithm for video coding. IEEE Trans. Circuits Syst. Video Technol., 4(1), 88–90 (1994)

4. Chen, T.H.: A cost-effective three-step hierarchical search block-matching chip for motion estimation. IEEE Journal of Solid-State Circuits 338, 1253–1258 (1998)
5. Yin, H.B., Fang, X.Z., Yang, H., Yu, S.Y., Yang, X.K.: Motion Vector Smoothing for True Motion Estimation. In: IEEE Conference on Acoustics, Speech and Signal Processing 2006 p. II-241–II-244 (2006)

Author Index

Lecture Notes in Computer Science

Sublibrary 3: Information Systems and Application, incl. Internet/Web and HCI

For information about Vols. 1–4506
please contact your bookseller or Springer

Vol. 4877: C. Thanos, F. Borri, L. Candela (Eds.), Digital Libraries: Research and Development. XII, 350 pages. 2007.

Vol. 4872: D. Mery, L. Rueda (Eds.), Advances in Image and Video Technology. XXI, 961 pages. 2007.

Vol. 4871: M. Cavazza, S. Donikian (Eds.), Virtual Storytelling. XIII, 219 pages. 2007.

Vol. 4858: X. Deng, F.C. Graham (Eds.), Internet and Network Economics. XVI, 598 pages. 2007.

Vol. 4857: J.M. Ware, G.E. Taylor (Eds.), Web and Wireless Geographical Information Systems. XI, 293 pages. 2007.

Vol. 4853: F. Fonseca, M.A. Rodríguez, S. Levashkin (Eds.), GeoSpatial Semantics. X, 289 pages. 2007.

Vol. 4836: H. Ichikawa, W.-D. Cho, I. Satoh, H.Y. Youn (Eds.), Ubiquitous Computing Systems. XIII, 307 pages. 2007.

Vol. 4832: M. Weske, M.-S. Hacid, C. Godart (Eds.), Web Information Systems Engineering – WISE 2007 Workshops. XV, 518 pages. 2007.

Vol. 4831: B. Benatallah, F. Casati, D. Georgakopoulos, C. Bartolini, W. Sadiq, C. Godart (Eds.), Web Information Systems Engineering – WISE 2007. XVI, 675 pages. 2007.

Vol. 4825: K. Aberer, K.-S. Choi, N. Noy, D. Allemang, K.-I. Lee, L. Nixon, J. Golbeck, P. Mika, D. Maynard, R. Mizoguchi, G. Schreiber, P. Cudré-Mauroux (Eds.), The Semantic Web. XXVII, 973 pages. 2007.

Vol. 4822: D.H.-L. Goh, T.H. Cao, I.T. Sølvberg, E. Rasmussen (Eds.), Asian Digital Libraries. XVII, 519 pages. 2007.

Vol. 4816: B. Falcidieno, M. Spagnuolo, Y. Avrithis, I. Kompatsiaris, P. Buitelaar (Eds.), Semantic Multimedia. XII, 306 pages. 2007.

Vol. 4813: I. Oakley, S. Brewster (Eds.), Haptic and Audio Interaction Design. XIV, 145 pages. 2007.

Vol. 4810: H.H.-S. Ip, O.C. Au, H. Leung, M.-T. Sun, W.-Y. Ma, S.-M. Hu (Eds.), Advances in Multimedia Information Processing – PCM 2007. XXI, 834 pages. 2007.

Vol. 4809: M.K. Denko, C.-s. Shih, K.-C. Li, S.-L. Tsao, Q.-A. Zeng, S.H. Park, Y.-B. Ko, S.-H. Hung, J.H. Park (Eds.), Emerging Directions in Embedded and Ubiquitous Computing. XXXV, 823 pages. 2007.

Vol. 4808: T.-W. Kuo, E. Sha, M. Guo, L.T. Yang, Z. Shao (Eds.), Embedded and Ubiquitous Computing. XXI, 769 pages. 2007.

Vol. 4806: R. Meersman, Z. Tari, P. Herrero (Eds.), On the Move to Meaningful Internet Systems 2007: OTM 2007 Workshops, Part II. XXXIV, 611 pages. 2007.

Vol. 4805: R. Meersman, Z. Tari, P. Herrero (Eds.), On the Move to Meaningful Internet Systems 2007: OTM 2007 Workshops, Part I. XXXIV, 757 pages. 2007.

Vol. 4804: R. Meersman, Z. Tari (Eds.), On the Move to Meaningful Internet Systems 2007: CoopIS, DOA, ODBASE, GADA, and IS, Part II. XXIX, 683 pages. 2007.

Vol. 4803: R. Meersman, Z. Tari (Eds.), On the Move to Meaningful Internet Systems 2007: CoopIS, DOA, ODBASE, GADA, and IS, Part I. XXIX, 1173 pages. 2007.

Vol. 4802: J.-L. Hainaut, E.A. Rundensteiner, M. Kirchberg, M. Bertolotto, M. Brochhausen, Y.-P.P. Chen, S.S.-S. Cherfi, M. Doerr, H. Han, S. Hartmann, J. Parsons, G. Poels, C. Rolland, J. Trujillo, E. Yu, E. Zimányie (Eds.), Advances in Conceptual Modeling – Foundations and Applications. XIX, 420 pages. 2007.

Vol. 4801: C. Parent, K.-D. Schewe, V.C. Storey, B. Thalheim (Eds.), Conceptual Modeling - ER 2007. XVI, 616 pages. 2007.

Vol. 4797: M. Arenas, M.I. Schwartzbach (Eds.), Database Programming Languages. VIII, 261 pages. 2007.

Vol. 4796: M. Lew, N. Sebe, T.S. Huang, E.M. Bakker (Eds.), Human–Computer Interaction. X, 157 pages. 2007.

Vol. 4794: B. Schiele, A.K. Dey, H. Gellersen, B. de Ruyter, M. Tscheligi, R. Wichert, E. Aarts, A. Buchmann (Eds.), Ambient Intelligence. XV, 375 pages. 2007.

Vol. 4777: S. Bhalla (Ed.), Databases in Networked Information Systems. X, 329 pages. 2007.

Vol. 4761: R. Obermaisser, Y. Nah, P. Puschner, F.J. Rammig (Eds.), Software Technologies for Embedded and Ubiquitous Systems. XIV, 563 pages. 2007.

Vol. 4747: S. Džeroski, J. Struyf (Eds.), Knowledge Discovery in Inductive Databases. X, 301 pages. 2007.

Vol. 4744: Y. de Kort, W. IJsselsteijn, C. Midden, B. Eggen, B.J. Fogg (Eds.), Persuasive Technology. XIV, 316 pages. 2007.

Vol. 4740: L. Ma, M. Rauterberg, R. Nakatsu (Eds.), Entertainment Computing – ICEC 2007. XXX, 480 pages. 2007.

Vol. 4730: C. Peters, P. Clough, F.C. Gey, J. Karlgren, B. Magnini, D.W. Oard, M. de Rijke, M. Stempfhuber (Eds.), Evaluation of Multilingual and Multi-modal Information Retrieval. XXIV, 998 pages. 2007.

Vol. 4723: M. R. Berthold, J. Shawe-Taylor, N. Lavrač (Eds.), Advances in Intelligent Data Analysis VII. XIV, 380 pages. 2007.

Vol. 4721: W. Jonker, M. Petković (Eds.), Secure Data Management. X, 213 pages. 2007.

Vol. 4718: J. Hightower, B. Schiele, T. Strang (Eds.), Location- and Context-Awareness. X, 297 pages. 2007.

Vol. 4717: J. Krumm, G.D. Abowd, A. Seneviratne, T. Strang (Eds.), UbiComp 2007: Ubiquitous Computing. XIX, 520 pages. 2007.

Vol. 4715: J.M. Haake, S.F. Ochoa, A. Cechich (Eds.), Groupware: Design, Implementation, and Use. XIII, 355 pages. 2007.

Vol. 4714: G. Alonso, P. Dadam, M. Rosemann (Eds.), Business Process Management. XIII, 418 pages. 2007.

Vol. 4704: D. Barbosa, A. Bonifati, Z. Bellahsène, E. Hunt, R. Unland (Eds.), Database and XML Technologies. X, 141 pages. 2007.

Vol. 4690: Y. Ioannidis, B. Novikov, B. Rachev (Eds.), Advances in Databases and Information Systems. XIII, 377 pages. 2007.

Vol. 4675: L. Kovács, N. Fuhr, C. Meghini (Eds.), Research and Advanced Technology for Digital Libraries. XVII, 585 pages. 2007.

Vol. 4674: Y. Luo (Ed.), Cooperative Design, Visualization, and Engineering. XIII, 431 pages. 2007.

Vol. 4663: C. Baranauskas, P. Palanque, J. Abascal, S.D.J. Barbosa (Eds.), Human-Computer Interaction – INTERACT 2007, Part II. XXXIII, 735 pages. 2007.

Vol. 4662: C. Baranauskas, P. Palanque, J. Abascal, S.D.J. Barbosa (Eds.), Human-Computer Interaction – INTERACT 2007, Part I. XXXIII, 637 pages. 2007.

Vol. 4658: T. Enokido, L. Barolli, M. Takizawa (Eds.), Network-Based Information Systems. XIII, 544 pages. 2007.

Vol. 4656: M.A. Wimmer, J. Scholl, Å. Grönlund (Eds.), Electronic Government. XIV, 450 pages. 2007.

Vol. 4655: G. Psaila, R. Wagner (Eds.), E-Commerce and Web Technologies. VII, 229 pages. 2007.

Vol. 4654: I.-Y. Song, J. Eder, T.M. Nguyen (Eds.), Data Warehousing and Knowledge Discovery. XVI, 482 pages. 2007.

Vol. 4653: R. Wagner, N. Revell, G. Pernul (Eds.), Database and Expert Systems Applications. XXII, 907 pages. 2007.

Vol. 4636: G. Antoniou, U. Aßmann, C. Baroglio, S. Decker, N. Henze, P.-L. Patranjan, R. Tolksdorf (Eds.), Reasoning Web. IX, 345 pages. 2007.

Vol. 4611: J. Indulska, J. Ma, L.T. Yang, T. Ungerer, J. Cao (Eds.), Ubiquitous Intelligence and Computing. XXIII, 1257 pages. 2007.

Vol. 4607: L. Baresi, P. Fraternali, G.-J. Houben (Eds.), Web Engineering. XVI, 576 pages. 2007.

Vol. 4606: A. Pras, M. van Sinderen (Eds.), Dependable and Adaptable Networks and Services. XIV, 149 pages. 2007.

Vol. 4605: D. Papadias, D. Zhang, G. Kollios (Eds.), Advances in Spatial and Temporal Databases. X, 479 pages. 2007.

Vol. 4602: S. Barker, G.-J. Ahn (Eds.), Data and Applications Security XXI. X, 291 pages. 2007.

Vol. 4601: S. Spaccapietra, P. Atzeni, F. Fages, M.-S. Hacid, M. Kifer, J. Mylopoulos, B. Pernici, P. Shvaiko, J. Trujillo, I. Zaihrayeu (Eds.), Journal on Data Semantics IX. XV, 197 pages. 2007.

Vol. 4592: Z. Kedad, N. Lammari, E. Métais, F. Meziane, Y. Rezgui (Eds.), Natural Language Processing and Information Systems. XIV, 442 pages. 2007.

Vol. 4587: R. Cooper, J. Kennedy (Eds.), Data Management. XIII, 259 pages. 2007.

Vol. 4577: N. Sebe, Y. Liu, Y.-t. Zhuang, T.S. Huang (Eds.), Multimedia Content Analysis and Mining. XIII, 513 pages. 2007.

Vol. 4568: T. Ishida, S. R. Fussell, P. T. J. M. Vossen (Eds.), Intercultural Collaboration. XIII, 395 pages. 2007.

Vol. 4566: M.J. Dainoff (Ed.), Ergonomics and Health Aspects of Work with Computers. XVIII, 390 pages. 2007.

Vol. 4564: D. Schuler (Ed.), Online Communities and Social Computing. XVII, 520 pages. 2007.

Vol. 4563: R. Shumaker (Ed.), Virtual Reality. XXII, 762 pages. 2007.

Vol. 4561: V.G. Duffy (Ed.), Digital Human Modeling. XXIII, 1068 pages. 2007.

Vol. 4560: N. Aykin (Ed.), Usability and Internationalization, Part II. XVIII, 576 pages. 2007.

Vol. 4559: N. Aykin (Ed.), Usability and Internationalization, Part I. XVIII, 661 pages. 2007.

Vol. 4558: M.J. Smith, G. Salvendy (Eds.), Human Interface and the Management of Information, Part II. XXIII, 1162 pages. 2007.

Vol. 4557: M.J. Smith, G. Salvendy (Eds.), Human Interface and the Management of Information, Part I. XXII, 1030 pages. 2007.

Vol. 4541: T. Okadome, T. Yamazaki, M. Makhtari (Eds.), Pervasive Computing for Quality of Life Enhancement. IX, 248 pages. 2007.

Vol. 4537: K.C.-C. Chang, W. Wang, L. Chen, C.A. Ellis, C.-H. Hsu, A.C. Tsoi, H. Wang (Eds.), Advances in Web and Network Technologies, and Information Management. XXIII, 707 pages. 2007.

Vol. 4531: J. Indulska, K. Raymond (Eds.), Distributed Applications and Interoperable Systems. XI, 337 pages. 2007.

Vol. 4526: M. Malek, M. Reitenspieß, A. van Moorsel (Eds.), Service Availability. X, 155 pages. 2007.

Vol. 4524: M. Marchiori, J.Z. Pan, C.d.S. Marie (Eds.), Web Reasoning and Rule Systems. XI, 382 pages. 2007.

Vol. 4519: E. Franconi, M. Kifer, W. May (Eds.), The Semantic Web: Research and Applications. XVIII, 830 pages. 2007.

Vol. 4518: N. Fuhr, M. Lalmas, A. Trotman (Eds.), Comparative Evaluation of XML Information Retrieval Systems. XII, 554 pages. 2007.

Vol. 4508: M.-Y. Kao, X.-Y. Li (Eds.), Algorithmic Aspects in Information and Management. VIII, 428 pages. 2007.

SPRINGER NATURE

GPSR Compliance

The European Union's (EU) General Product Safety Regulation (GPSR) is a set of rules that requires consumer products to be safe and our obligations to ensure this.

If you have any concerns about our products, you can contact us on ProductSafety@springernature.com

In case Publisher is established outside the EU, the EU authorized representative is:

Springer Nature Customer Service Center GmbH
Europaplatz 3
69115 Heidelberg, Germany

Kolibri 360 GmbH
Ferdinand-Jühlke-Straße 7
99095 Erfurt, Deutschland
produktsicherheit@kolibri360.de